INTERNATIONAL ENCYCLOPEDIA OF TEACHING AND TEACHER EDUCATION

SECOND EDITION

Resources in Education

This is a new series of Pergamon one-volume Encyclopedias drawing upon articles in the acclaimed *International Encyclopedia of Education, Second Edition*, with revisions as well as new articles. Each volume in the series is thematically organized and aims to provide complete and up-to-date coverage on its subject. These Encyclopedias will serve as an invaluable reference source for researchers, faculty members, teacher educators, government officials, educational administrators, and policymakers.

The *International Encyclopedia of Teaching and Teacher Education, Second Edition*, contains 140 articles on teaching and teacher education. The purpose of the volume is to priovide classroom researchers, teacher educators, and teachers with a sound reasonable body of knowledge that can be used to guide their efforts to understand and improve the teaching–learning process.

While individual research studies may yield different results and recommendations, the compilation of such studies by experts in the field provides useful guidelines within which researchers, teacher educators, and teachers can operate. The entries in this Encyclopedia will provide a body of knowledge to inform, guide, and/or justify their teaching practice. A complete bibliography with further reading at the end of each article provides references for further research. Extensive name and subject indexes are also included.

Other titles in the series include:

POSTLETHWAITE (ed.)
International Encyclopedia of National Systems of Education, Second Edition

CARNOY (ed.)
International Encyclopedia of Economics of Education, Second Edition

TUIJNMAN (ed.)
International Encyclopedia of Adult and Continuing Education, Second Edition

PLOMP & ELY (eds)
International Encyclopedia of Educational Technology, Second Edition

DeCORTE & WEINERT (eds)
International Encyclopedia of Developmental and Instructional Psychology

KEEVES (ed.)
International Encyclopedia of Educational Research, Methodololgy, and Measurement, Second Edition

INTERNATIONAL ENCYCLOPEDIA OF TEACHING AND TEACHER EDUCATION

SECOND EDITION

Edited by

LORIN W. ANDERSON

University of South Carolina, Columbia, SC, USA

PERGAMON

UK   Elsevier Science Ltd, The Boulevard, Langford Lane, Kidlington, Oxford OX5 1GB, UK

USA   Elsevier Science Inc, 660 White Plains Road, Tarrytown, New York 10591-5153, USA

JAPAN   Elsevier Science Japan, Tsunashima Building Annex, 3-20-12 Yushima, Bunkyo-ku, Tokyo 113, Japan

Second edition 1995

Library of Congress Cataloging in Publication Data
International encyclopedia of teaching and teacher education / edited by Lorin W. Andeson. — 2nd ed.
    p.   cm.
    Rev ed. of: International encyclopedia of teaching and teacher education / edited by Michael J. Dunkin. 1987.
    Includes bibliographies and index.
    1. Teaching—Handbooks, manuals, etc.   2. Teachers—Handbooks, manuals, etc.   3. Teachers—Training of—Handbooks, manuals, etc.   I. Anderson, Lorin W.   II. International encyclopedia of teaching and teacher education.
LB1025.3.I58   1995
371.1'002'02—dc20   95-45385

British Library Cataloguing in Publication Data
A catalogue record for this book is available from the British Library.

ISBN 0–08–042304–3

Printed and bound in Great Britain by Cambridge University Press, Cambridge, UK.

Contents

Preface   XV

PART A: TEACHING   1

Section I: The Nature and Characteristics of Teachers   3

Introduction   3
L. W. ANDERSON

(a) Metaphors of Teachers   6

Teachers as Artists   6
S. DELAMONT

Teachers as Clinicians   9
J. CALDERHEAD

Teachers as Professionals   11
E. HOYLE

Teachers as Researchers   16
S. HOLLINGSWORTH

(b) A Psychological View of Teachers   20

Teachers' Knowledge   20
P. L. GROSSMAN

Teachers' Beliefs and Belief Systems   25
J. H. BLOCK AND K. HAZELIP

Teachers' Expectations   29
T. L. GOOD

Teacher Responsibility   35
F. K. OSER AND J.-L. PATRY

Teacher Development   41
A. GLATTHORN

Teacher Expertise   46
D. C. BERLINER

Teacher Stress and Burnout   52
R. L. SCHWAB

(c) A Sociopolitical View of Teachers 58

Social Status of Teaching 58
E. HOYLE

Teachers' Roles 61
B. J. BIDDLE

Political Work of Teachers 67
M. B. GINSBURG AND S. G. KAMAT

Supply of Teachers 72
R. J. MURNANE

Women and the Professionalization of Teaching 76
K. A. WEILER

Realities of Teaching 80
A. HARGREAVES

Section II: Theories and Models of Teaching 89

Introduction 89
L. W. ANDERSON

Paradigms for Research on Teaching 91
R. B. BURNS

Behavioristic Theories of Teaching 96
B. SULZER-AZAROFF

Cognitive Developmental Theories of Teaching 101
N. A. SPRINTHALL

Information Processing Theories of Teaching 107
P. H. WINNE

Social Psychological Theories of Teaching 112
D. W. JOHNSON AND R. T. JOHNSON

Linguistic and Sociolinguistic Theories of Teaching 117
R. YOUNG

Heuristic Models of Teaching 122
G. NUTHALL

Aptitude–Treatment Interaction Model of Teaching 127
R. E. SNOW

Implicit Theories of Teaching 131
P. W. MARLAND

Section III: Instructional Programs and Strategies   137

Introduction   137
L. W. ANDERSON

Cooperative Learning   139
R. E. SLAVIN

Direct Instruction   143
B. ROSENSHINE AND C. MEISTER

Discovery Learning and Teaching   149
P. TAMIR

Individualized Instruction   155
L. W. ANDERSON

Mastery Learning   161
T. R. GUSKEY

Open Education   167
G. THIBADEAU

Science Laboratory Instruction   171
E. HAZEL

Diagnostic–Prescriptive Teaching   174
A. HELMKE AND F.-W. SCHRADER

Reflective Teaching   178
L. M. VILLAR

Section IV: Teaching Skills and Techniques   185

Introduction   185
L. W. ANDERSON

(a) Planning the Classroom   188

Teacher Planning   188
R. J. YINGER AND M. S. HENDRICKS-LEE

Grouping Students in the Classroom   192
R. BARR

Seating Arrangements   196
N. M. LAMBERT

Instructional Alignment   200
S. A. COHEN

Time, Allocated and Instructional   204
L. W. ANDERSON

Lesson Structure   207
E. C. WRAGG

(b) Classroom Management   212

Instructional Pacing   212
L. W. ANDERSON AND P. TORREY

Classroom Rules and Routines   215
C. M. EVERTSON

Teacher Managerial Behaviors   219
E. T. EMMER

Reinforcement   224
I. E. SLADECZEK AND T. R. KRATOCHWILL

Analysis and Modification of Behavior   227
L. CAIRNS

(c) Teaching in the Classroom   232

Explaining   232
D. R. CRUICKSHANK AND K. K. METCALF

Demonstrating   238
L. C. COMBER AND J. P. KEEVES

Questioning   242
M. D. GALL AND M. T. ARTERO-BONAME

Feedback   249
R. E. MAYER

Discussion   251
J. T. DILLON

Teaching in Small Groups   255
S. SHARAN

Simulations and Games   260
A. L. CUDWORTH

Assignment and Supervision of Seatwork   264
L. M. ANDERSON

Homework   268
H. J. WALBERG AND R. A. PASCHAL

Tutoring   271
F. J. MEDWAY

Nonverbal Teacher Behavior   274
H. A. SMITH

(d) Assessing and Evaluating   279

Assessment in the Service of Learning   279
S. LANE AND R. GLASER

Evaluating   283
J. A. ZAHORIK

Diagnosing Students' Needs   286
A. HELMKE

Classroom Assessment   290
P. W. AIRASIAN

Individualized Testing in the Classroom   295
J. M. LINACRE

Grading and Evaluating Students   299
G. BORICH AND T. KUBISZYN

Section V: School and Classroom Factors   305

Introduction   305
L. W. ANDERSON

(a) Frame Factors   308

Frame Factors   308
U. TORPER

Class Size   310
J. D. FINN AND K. E. VOELKL

Age Grouping of Students   315
J. OAKES AND P. E. HECKMAN

Gender and Racial Differences Among Students   319
G. WEINER

Grade Repeating   324
L. A. SHEPARD

Student Diversity and Classroom Teaching   326
M. C. WANG

(b) Classroom Environments   332

School Culture and Peer Groups   332
J. HILL

Peer Relations and Learning   336
W. DAMON

Learning Environments   340
A. COLLINS, J. G. GREENO, AND L. B. RESNICK

Classroom Environments   344
B. J. FRASER

Contents

Goal Structures   349
D. W. JOHNSON AND R. T. JOHNSON

Group Dynamics   352
J. P. GALL AND M. D. GALL

(c) Paraprofessionals, Substitute Teachers, Parents, and Families   359

Technology and the Classroom Teacher   359
N. HATIVA

Availability and Use of Paraprofessionals   363
B. P. REYNOLDS

Substitute Teachers   367
L. W. ANDERSON AND C. GARDNER

School–Parent Relationships   370
M. A. PAYNE

Section VI: Students and the Teaching–Learning Process   375

Introduction   375
L. W. ANDERSON

(a) Student Entry Characteristics: Cognitive and Affective   378

Home Environment and School Learning   378
A. J. FULIGNI AND H. W. STEVENSON

Prior Knowledge and Learning   382
F. J. R. C. DOCHY

Cognitive Styles and Learning   387
S. MESSICK

Aspirations and Expectations of Students   391
L. J. SAHA

Motivation and Learning   395
W. LENS

Affect, Emotions, and Learning   402
M. BOEKAERTS

(b) Classroom Processes   408

Student Roles in Classrooms   408
S. J. MCCARTHEY AND P. L. PETERSON

Student Influences on Teaching   413
R. W. MARX AND R. M. B. COLLOPY

Student Perceptions of Classrooms   416
B. J. FRASER

Student Cognitive Processes 420
P. H. WINNE AND D. L. BUTLER

Attention in Learning 427
A. HARNISCHFEGER

Academic Learning Time 430
C. W. FISHER

Study Habits and Strategies 434
R. E. MAYER

Section VII: Teaching for Specific Objectives 437

Introduction 437
L. W. ANDERSON

Memory: Teaching and Assessing 439
M. PRESSLEY AND P. VAN METER

Comprehension: Teaching and Assessing 444
W. SCHNOTZ AND S.-P. BALLSTAEDT

Written Composition: Teaching and Assessing 450
S. W. FREEDMAN

Motor Skills: Learning and Instruction 454
J. M. M. VAN DER SANDEN

Concept Learning: Teaching and Assessing 457
R. D. TENNYSON

Problem-solving: Teaching and Assessing 463
R. E. MAYER

Critical Reading: Teaching and Assessing 467
A. LUKE AND C. WALTON

Learning Strategies: Teaching and Assessing 471
C. E. WEINSTEIN AND D. K. MEYER

Creativity: Teaching and Assessing 476
J. F. FELDHUSEN

Metacognitive Strategies: Teaching and Assessing 481
P. R.-J. SIMONS

Section VIII: The Study of Teaching 487

Introduction 487
L. W. ANDERSON

Teacher Evaluation 488
D. M. MEDLEY AND D. M. SHANNON

Student Evaluation of Teaching   493
H. W. MARSH

Classroom Observation   501
M. GALTON

Comparative and International Studies of Teaching and Teacher Education   506
M. J. DUNKIN

Synthesizing Research on Teaching   512
M. J. DUNKIN

Translating Research into Practice   517
F. E. WEINERT

PART B: TEACHER EDUCATION   523

Section I: Concepts and Issues in Teacher Education   525

Introduction   525
L. W. ANDERSON

(a) Students and Teachers   528

Characteristics of Prospective Teachers   528
J. NEURURER

Characteristics of Teacher Educators   531
E. R. DUCHARME

Adult Development and Teacher Education   535
S. N. OJA

(b) Organization and Curriculum   540

Planning Teacher Education   540
S. SHAH

Curriculum of Teacher Education Programs   543
M. BEN-PERETZ

Structure of Teacher Education Programs   548
M. J. GIMMESTAD AND G. E. HALL

Evaluation of Teacher Education Programs   552
G. R. GALLUZZO

Governance of Teacher Education   556
H. D. GIDEONSE

(c) Accreditation and Certification   561

Teacher Education Accreditation and Standards   561
J. RATHS

Teacher Certification and Standards   565
M. M. SCANNELL AND D. P. SCANNELL

Section II: Generic Initial Teacher Education   571

Introduction   571
L. W. ANDERSON

Microteaching in Teacher Education   573
G. MACLEOD

Laboratory Experiences in Teacher Education   578
K. K. METCALF

Case Methods in Teacher Education   583
A. R. MCANINCH

Student Teaching and Field Experiences   588
G. MORINE-DERSHIMER AND K. LEIGHFIELD

Supervision in Teacher Education   593
J. M. COOPER

Laboratory and Professional Development Schools   598
J. A. STALLINGS, S. L. KNIGHT, AND D. L. WISEMAN

Section III: Continuing Teacher Education   605

Introduction   605
L. W. ANDERSON

Teacher Placement and School Staffing   606
A. J. WATSON AND N. G. HATTON

Teacher Recruitment and Induction   612
R. BOLAM

Professional Socialization of Teachers   616
C. LACEY

Inservice Teacher Education   620
M. ERAUT

Onservice Teacher Education   628
R. GARDNER

List of Contributors   633

Name Index   639

Subject Index   655

Preface

Writing a preface to a second edition of any book is a difficult task. You want to incorporate into the Preface much of what was in the Preface of the first edition. After all, it is, in essence, the same book. At the same time, however, you want to make the reader aware of relevant and significant changes that have occurred between the two editions. That is, the reader needs to understand how the second edition differs from the first.

Writing a Preface to the second edition of an acclaimed, highly successful volume, which was edited by a respected colleague and friend, Dr Michael J. (Mick) Dunkin, is even more difficult. I began to prepare myself for writing this Preface by reading the Preface to the first edition. I found that many things had not changed. The purpose of the two editions was identical. In Mick's words, "this Encyclopedia is designed to enable readers to learn about key concepts from scholarly, comprehensive, and systematic expositions brought together within an organizing framework that facilitates integration and permits easy cross-referencing."

The quality of the authors responsible for writing the entries included in this Encyclopedia has not changed; it remains uniformly high. Furthermore, the authors continue to represent a wide variety of geographic and cultural perspectives. In the first edition, slightly more than 50 percent of the authors were from North America. In the second edition, this figure increased slightly (about four percent). However, the percentage of European and Asian authors also increased from about one-quarter to almost one-third from the first to the second edition. The major decrease occurred in the percentage of Australian and New Zealand authors (down from just under one-quarter in the first edition to about ten percent in the second edition). There is a practical explanation for this shift; when Mick could not find an author for an entry, he looked within Australia and when I could not, I looked within North America. The important point, however, is that a diversity of research agendas, ideas, and opinions are represented in both editions.

The intended audiences and the intended use of the Encyclopedia also have not changed. As I wrote in the prospectus for the second edition:

> Like the parent volume from which it is derived, the *International Encyclopedia of Teaching and Teacher Education, Second Edition* is intended for those who wish to obtain an overview of a specific area of education in a fairly short period of time. Members of this audience include graduate students, university professors working outside their areas of expertise, and elementary and secondary teachers searching for a body of knowledge to inform, guide and/or justify their teaching practices

The first edition was targeted to these same audiences.

With respect to the intended use of the Encyclopedia, I quote extensively from the Preface to the first edition:

> The reader might begin with the sections of the Preface concerned with the Conceptual Framework of the Encyclopedia and its Contents. Then the Table of Contents might be consulted in order to see the titles of individual articles and where they fit into the general framework. Next each section of the Encyclopedia begins with a figure illustrating which part of the conceptual framework is focused upon and an overview of the [entries] within it. These overviews include summaries of the [entries] and indicate associations between individual [entries] and others, both in the same section and in other sections. Again, readers will find helpful reference lists at the end of each article.
>
> Should the reader discover that there is no special [entry] on a particular topic, the Subject Index at the back of this volume should be consulted. Authors were asked to identify key words or phrases in their [entries] which constitute cornerstones in the structure of information they wished to convey. These terms formed the basis of the Subject Index. [Finally], the [Name] Index also provides a useful starting point

The intended use has not changed.

Conceptual Frameworks and Related Contents

The major differences between the two editions lie in their conceptual frameworks and the related contents. In the Preface to the 1985 volume, Mick wrote, "this Encyclopedia is an expression of the view of knowledge about teaching and teacher education in the 1980s." What was this view? It was influenced a great deal by the process–product paradigm which was generally accepted by researchers in education during most of the latter 1970s and early 1980s (e.g., Gage, 1989).

Within this paradigm there were believed to be observable teacher behaviors that influenced student achievement either directly, or indirectly through their influence on student behavior (the so-called "mediating process paradigm" (Doyle, 1987)). Consideration was given to the possibility that the nature and strength of the influence of teachers on learners depended to some extent on a variety of contextual factors (such as the availability of equipment and materials, the numbers of students in the classroom, and the social and ethnic background of the students in the classroom). However, the importance of contextual factors and the exact way in which these factors influenced the teaching–learning relationship was unclear; generally, these factors were conceptualized either as "extraneous variables" (within a rather traditional experimental psychological framework) or as "error variables" (within a rather traditional statistical framework).

The relationship of teacher education and teaching was believed to be almost as linear as that between teaching and learning. The role of teacher education was to provide teachers with a set of knowledge, behaviors, skills, and practices that were related to teacher effectiveness. Teacher educators influenced teachers who in turn influenced their students.

At the same time, however, there was a realization that an understanding of the relationship of teacher education, teaching, and learning, although primarily linear, required a great deal of thought and considerable research. As a consequence, Mick included in his conceptual framework categories labelled "Concepts and Models" (which allowed educators to "think about" teaching and learning) and "Methods and Paradigms for Research" (which permitted researchers to plan and conduct research on teaching and learning). His overarching conceptual framework is shown in Fig. 1.

Several significant changes have taken place since the entries for the first edition were written. Some of these changes are conceptual and theoretical; others are philosophical; still others are methodological. Conceptually, a fairly exclusionary psychological emphasis in research on teaching and learning has given way to a multidisciplinary point of view (which includes sociological and anthropological perspectives). Philosophically, the search for universal laws and truths has been replaced with a search for "conditional knowledge" (that is, the need to understand both the knowledge and the conditions within which this knowledge holds). Methodologically, structured observations and questionnaires have been complemented (and, unfortunately, sometimes

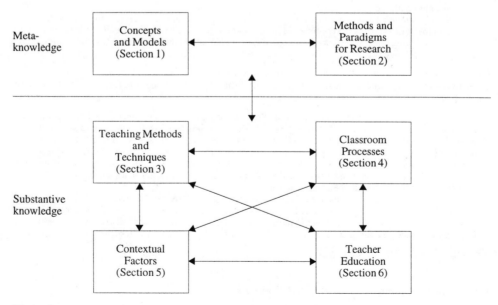

Figure 1
Schematic representation of the first edition of the Encyclopedia

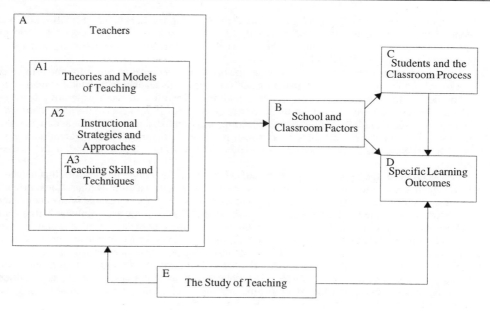

Figure 2
Schematic representation of the material in the second edition covering teaching and learning

completely replaced) by narratives or field notes and semistructured interviews. Calls for alternatives to traditional objective, paper-and-pencil measures of student ability and achievement also have been heard.

As a result of these changes, two new conceptual frameworks were developed for the second edition. The first, shown in Fig. 2, concerns teachers, schools, classrooms, students, teaching, and learning. The second, displayed in Fig. 3, indicates the relationships among the various components of teacher education.

The framework in Fig. 2 contains eight major concepts. Four of the concepts pertain to teachers and teaching. These four concepts are "nested" or embedded within one another. The outermost rectangle (Rectangle A) addresses teachers: their knowledge, beliefs, work, and development. As everyone knows, however, teachers teach. Thus, the next three rectangles (A1, A2, and A3) address three fundamental aspects of teaching: theories and models, strategies and approaches, and skills and techniques. Theories and models help us understand teaching. Strategies and

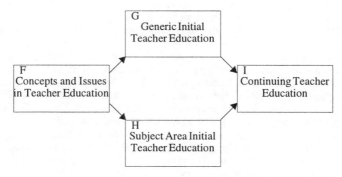

Figure 3
Schematic representation of the material in the second edition covering teacher education

approaches provide general guidelines for the ways in which teachers teach. Finally, skills and techniques enable teachers to operate within those general guidelines. Regardless of the strategy or approach used by a teacher, the teacher needs skills and techniques in planning, managing, teaching, assessing, and evaluating.

Suppose, for example, that a teacher accepts the fundamental precepts, concepts, and principles of a social psychological theory of teaching and learning. This teacher would likely endorse the instructional strategy known as cooperative learning. In order to use cooperative learning effectively, however, the teacher would need to acquire or develop a set of skills and techniques. Examples would include grouping students, leading classroom discussions, and teaching in small groups. The reader will find entries on "social psychology theories," "cooperative learning," "grouping of students," "classroom discussions," and "teaching in small groups" in the second edition.

The rectangle to the right of the teachers and teaching set (Rectangle B) indicates that teachers do not teach in a vacuum, nor do they typically teach one student at a time. Rather, teachers teach within social organizations called schools and classrooms. Factors associated with schools and classrooms may make teaching easier or more difficult. That is, some are "enablers"; others are "inhibitors." The culture of the school, the relationship of the school and the outside community, the method used to assign students to classrooms within the school, and the use of paraprofessionals and substitute teachers within the school—all of these influence our conception of teachers as well as the teachers' levels of success or effectiveness. Similarly, the number of students in the classroom, the differences among students in the classroom (in terms of their age, gender, abilities, interests, and the like), and the relationships among students in the classroom—all of these influence how teachers teach as well as how students learn.

In these schools and classrooms, teachers are not the only ones who influence what transpires. Students also influence classroom activities either indirectly by virtue of their presence or directly by their "actions, words, or deeds." Rectangle C includes entries related to the impact of students on the teaching–learning process. Examples include the home background of the students, their cognitive styles, their perceptions of the classroom, and the roles they are assigned or choose to play.

The entries in Rectangle D are based on the realization that teachers teach differently to achieve different learning outcomes. That is, teaching for the purpose of fostering memorization is quite different from teaching students how to solve problems. Thus, Rectangle D includes entries related to teaching and comprehension, concept learning, creativity, critical reading, learning strategies, memory, metacognitive strategies, motor skills, problem-solving, and written composition. Furthermore, the methods used to assess student learning in these specific areas are different. Thus, each entry includes a discussion of assessment as well as teaching.

Finally, the inclusion of Rectangle E in the conceptual framework recognizes the fact that the relationships among the other concepts (rectangles) are neither well established nor perfect. As a consequence, we need to continually study teachers and teaching and, based on the results of our study, suggest ways in which the teaching–learning process can be enhanced and improved. Entries in this section include "classroom observation," "teacher evaluation," and "translating research into practice."

As mentioned earlier, Fig. 3 contains the conceptual framework used to organize the entries on teacher education. Four concepts are included in this framework. The first (Rectangle F) consists of general issues and concerns that underline teacher education. These issues and concerns pertain to students and teachers; organization and curriculum; and accreditation, certification, and cost-effectiveness.

The other three concepts in Fig. 3 pertain to the timing of teacher education (e.g., preservice vs. "on the job") and the generality or specificity of teacher education (e.g., professional education vs. academic disciplines). Entries in Rectangle G examine teacher education from primarily a professional education perspective. These entries focus on the methods used in inservice teacher education, the relationship of teacher preparation institutions with elementary and secondary schools, and the relationship of formal course work with field experience.

Entries in Rectangle H address the subject-specific aspects of teacher education. These entries pertain to teacher education in reading, language arts, literature, mathematics, social studies, science, music, physical education, and the visual arts. Additional entries are concerned with preparing teachers to work with young children and children with special needs.

Finally, the entries in Rectangle I reflect the need to extend teacher education beyond initial certification and employment. Teachers do not emerge "full born" from teacher preparation institutions. The entries in this section include inducting teachers (that is, helping them make the transition from student to teacher or from one school to another), teachers' socialization, and providing teachers with opportunities for continued professional growth and development.

Acknowledgements

The development and production of any work of this magnitude requires the assistance of numerous people. I would like to mention several who have made my job as editor much easier. I would like to thank Mick Dunkin for asking me to take on this responsibility and providing me with the resources, information, and encouragement I needed to do so. Neville Postlethwaite and Torsten Husén, the Editors-in-Chief of the parent Encyclopedia, were simply wonderful to work with. Just knowing that Neville and Torsten were going to review my editing made me attend more carefully to it.

I would like to extend my appreciation to the other Section Editors of the parent Encyclopedia. Our relationships have been very cordial and our meetings have been rewarding both professionally and personally. To those Section Editors who contributed specific entries to this volume I owe special thanks.

I would like to thank all of the authors who contributed to this volume for their wealth of knowledge, their ability to communicate this knowledge, and their willingness to conform to page and time limits as well as some nontraditional stylistic requirements. As Mick wrote in the Preface to the first edition, "It is from them that those who use the Encyclopedia will learn."

Special thanks go to those at Elsevier Science Ltd who made this project a reality. In order of the length of time I have known them, I would like to acknowledge Barbara Barrett (with fond remembrances of the planning session in Marbella, Spain, and our subsequent trip to Grenada), Michèle Wheaton (with wonderment as to why she has continued to sit with me at those various luncheons and dinners), and Glenda Pringle (who obviously lost the coin toss and had to work with me despite what she had been told by her colleagues).

There are two very special people who deserve special commendation. I want my wife, Jo Anne, to know how much I appreciate her constant support as I flew around the world and spent countless hours in my office. Being a professional educator in her own right and helping to raise two teenage sons made this support even more amazing and important. Finally, my secretary, Cathy Schachner, was an absolute life saver. She did whatever was needed to produce quality manuscripts, meet deadlines, and, perhaps, most importantly, to shelter me from the demands of the outside world.

References

Anderson L W 1993 The International Encyclopedia of Teaching and Teacher Education, Second Edition: A Prospectus. Unpublished manuscript, Columbia, SC

Doyle W 1987 Paradigms for research. In: Dunkin M J (ed.) 1987 *The International Encyclopedia of Teaching and Teacher Education.* Pergamon, Oxford

Dunkin M J 1987 Preface. In: Dunkin M J (ed.) 1987 *The International Encyclopedia of Teaching and Teacher Education.* Pergamon, Oxford

PART A
Teaching

The Nature and Characteristics of Teachers

Introduction

L. W. Anderson

Teachers differ in numerous respects (e. g., age, sex, experience, expertise, educational background). Not surprisingly, much research has focused on these differences. At the same time, however, there are commonalities. Teachers in general progress through a fairly predictable series of stages as they move from novice to expert (Berliner). Teachers in general are members of a semi-profession (Weiler) which is held in fairly low status relative to other "true" professions, but which has higher status than other service providers and skilled manual and white-collar occupations (Hoyle). Teachers in general have lives outside schools and classrooms which impact on their professional commitment and their willingness to accept personal responsibility (Hargreaves, Oser and Patry).

The entries in this section address both similarities and differences among teachers, although the primary focus is on similarities. The first two entries discuss metaphors that are used to conceptualize teachers and teaching. They are "teachers as artists," "teachers as clinicians," "teachers as professionals," and "teachers as researchers." Not only do metaphors enable researchers to understand teachers and teaching, they also enable teachers to understand themselves (see Marland in Part A, Section II).

The current knowledge of teachers is derived primarily from research conducted within the context of two quite different traditions. The first can be termed "psychological." Researchers operating within this framework study teachers' knowledge, beliefs, expectations, responsibilities, development, expertise, stress, and burnout. The seven entries that form the second subsection contribute to the understanding of teachers when viewed from a psychological perspective.

The second tradition can be labeled "sociopolitical." Researchers operating within this framework examine teachers' social status and political work. They also study the roles assigned to or assumed by teachers, teacher supply and demand, the impact of the numbers of women on the professionalism of teachers, and the realities of teaching. The final six entries in this section provide a sociopolitical view of teachers.

1. Metaphors of Teachers

As was mentioned earlier, the metaphors used to describe teachers not only impact on how researchers and the public think about teachers, but on how teachers think about themselves. Based on these metaphors, teachers can be placed along a continuum. At one end are teachers who behave in accordance with specified rules and formulae (Delamont), who are more concerned with answers than with questions (Hollingsworth), and who possess a minimum of knowledge and skills and, hence, do what they are told (Hoyle). At the other end of the continuum lie teachers who, in addition to possessing knowledge and skills, realize that teaching requires creativity (Delamont), that informed decision-making is a vital aspect of teaching (Calderhead), and that a reasonable degree of autonomy is required for teachers to do their jobs well (Hoyle).

The differences in the metaphors we use to describe teachers are neither trivial nor merely semantic. They influence the social status of teachers (Hoyle) and the ways in which school administrators relate to them (Mitchell and Kerchner 1983). They may impact on the roles that teachers assume (Biddle) and on the perceptions that teachers have of themselves (Schwab).

One final comment about metaphors is important within the context of this volume. Metaphors typically do not lend themselves to empirical investigation (Delamont). This statement is not intended to downplay the importance of metaphors. Rather, it is intended to suggest that the choices made from among the available metaphors are more likely derived from beliefs and values (Block and Hazelip) than from research evidence.

2. A Psychological View of Teachers

What is known about teachers based on the research conducted within this tradition? Several generalizations can be offered.

First, teachers' knowledge and beliefs about teaching and learning are based primarily on their personal observations and experiences, rather than on what they hear or read (Grossman, Block and Hazelip). The inferences made from these personal observations and experiences influence, among other things, their beliefs about how students should be assigned to their classrooms (Block and Hazelip) and how students are likely to behave and achieve in the future (Good). Furthermore, because the inferences are made on the basis of *personal* observations and experiences, they are highly resistant to change (Block and Hazelip).

Second, teachers' knowledge and beliefs are quite complex, perhaps more complex than most people realize. Grossman identifies six domains of knowledge: content, learners and learning, general pedagogy, curriculum, context, and self. Several of these domains include subdomains (e.g., subject matter and pedagogical content knowledge lie within the domain of content knowledge). The complexity of this knowledge raises serious questions about both the *type* and *length* of teacher education needed to produce this knowledge in sufficient numbers of teachers. (See Part B, Sections II(a), (b), and (c).

Third, there is a clear relationship between teacher knowledge and teacher beliefs. Good, for example, suggests that teachers may establish lower expectations for students in those areas in which they, themselves, possess less knowledge. Conversely, teacher beliefs may inhibit the growth of teacher knowledge. For example, teachers continue to believe in the value of ability grouping of students despite the fact that there is little evidence that ability grouping benefits students; the practice may, in fact, harm them (Block and Hazelip).

Fourth, despite the fact that by their very nature teachers have moral obligations to their students (Hargreaves), teachers do not think about responsibilities and values very often (Oser and Patry). One possible reason for this state of affairs is that teachers tend to believe that "responsible action such as caring reduces their effectiveness with respect to . . . students' cognitive knowledge."

In other words, accountability for producing higher test scores may undermine teachers' acceptance of their moral responsibilities.

Finally, teachers progress through a series of stages from the beginning of their careers to the end. Berliner views this progression along a continuum from novice to expert. In between, teachers move through the stages of advance beginner, competency and proficiency. In contrast, Glatthorn postulates a movement from career entry through disengagement. After a period of stabilization which follows career entry, different teachers may move in different directions. Some may enter a period of experimentation and activism, while others may enter a phase of self-doubt and reassessment, "when disenchantment with the system leads many to consider changing occupations." This self-doubt and disenchantment in turn may lead to stress and burnout in increasing numbers of teachers (Schwab). Interestingly, those experiencing stress and burnout also move through a series of stages. The initial phase consists of chronic feelings of emotional exhaustion. Next, they remove themselves emotionally from the job and the setting. Finally, they yield to the belief that they are not accomplishing anything worthwhile. At this stage, burnout is complete.

3. A Sociopolitical View of Teachers

Those operating within the sociopolitical frame have also formed a set of generalizations. Three of the most notable are discussed below.

First, while many researchers and teachers endorse the ideal of a teaching profession, there are numerous barriers to making this ideal a reality. Among the most prevalent and frequently cited are the sheer number of teachers (Hoyle), the perception that teaching is "women's work" (Weiler), and the relatively low academic achievement of those entering teaching (Hoyle). Furthermore, Weiler questions that uncritical acceptance of the ideal of professionalism as promoted in the literature (Biddle), arguing instead for a "feministic professionalism" which would incorporate "familial and child-caring responsibilities into the structure of work; democratize the school as a workplace, emphasizing community rather than autonomy as the ideal for teachers; and insist on the value of children for the whole society."

Second, many attempts to restructure and reform education fail because they do not consider the realities of teaching (Hargreaves). Teachers have lives outside of their schools and classrooms. They encounter personal problems and have family responsibilities. They differ in their commitment to education. Some have what Hargreaves refers to as vocational commitment (or missionary zeal). Others possess professional commitment (that is, a commitment to knowledge, competence, and effectiveness). Still others are committed to teaching as a career. To them, security and extrinsic reward are of paramount importance. Reform and restructuring efforts are most likely to be effective with teachers with a professional commitment and least likely to be effective with those with a career commitment.

Finally, whether they like it or not, teachers are "political actors" (Ginsburg and Kamat). Part of the political aspect of teaching stems from the schools themselves. Rather than being objective and politically detached institutions, schools are "contested spheres that embody and express a struggle over what forms of authority, types of knowledge, forms of moral regulation, and versions of the past and future should be legitimated and transmitted to students" (Giroux, cited in Ginsburg and Kamat). In addition, teachers may belong to professional organizations that engage in political work (e.g., teacher unions) or may themselves be involved in the political work of the community (e.g., campaigning for candidates for elected offices).

4. Conclusion

The way in which teachers are thought about and the framework within which teachers are studied color much of what is known about them. As a consequence, each new study at best provides one more piece of the puzzle. Few single studies contribute to the overall understanding of teachers: who they are, what they do, and, perhaps, more importantly, why they do it.

By reading the entries in this section as a set, one can begin to understand teachers in a more holistic manner. This level of understanding is essential if progress is to be made toward improving the preparation and effectiveness of teachers, and ultimately the effectiveness and efficiency of the entire educational system.

Reference

Mitchell D E, Kerchner C T 1983 Labor relations and teacher policy. In: Shulman L S, Sykes G (eds.) 1983 *Handbook of Teaching and Policy*. Longman, New York

(a) Metaphors of Teachers

Teachers as Artists

S. Delamont

The idea of the teacher as artist is a metaphor. It is not an empirical research topic on which evidence can be amassed and evaluated. It is closely related to debates about appropriate styles of educational research, for if teaching is an art rather than a science, then teaching should be researched by aesthetic critics rather than scientific investigators. This entry examines the pervasiveness of the metaphor of teacher as artist, introduces the concept of indeterminacy, and explores the importance of the metaphor for researchers.

1. The Pervasive Metaphor

Most scholars start their discussion of the teacher as artist with James's *Talks to Teachers on Psychology* (1983), originally published in 1891. James wrote: "Psychology is a science, and teaching is an art: and sciences never generate arts directly out of themselves" (p. 15).

Writing on this topic in the 1980s and 1990s has not progressed beyond James's statement, in that little empirical evidence was gathered on teaching as an art, and little theoretical work was devoted to analyzing what "art" means in this widely used metaphor.

The lack of incisive theorizing and empirical material has not, however, prevented many authors from using the metaphor. For example, a British expert on teaching English as a second or foreign language, Morris (1954), called his book *The Art of Teaching English*, stating that a living language is "a source of aesthetic gratification" (p. 3), a perspective that should be conveyed by the teacher! Over a decade later Colman (1967) argued that all master teachers were also artists. His book sets out 20 different teaching methods, from the Socratic through the Jesuit and the Montessori to "Communist" methods, and ends with a chapter called "Be an Artist." Colman told his readers, who are believed to be teachers in training, that: "Variety remains the spice of life, and the teaching craftsman is never content until he develops a great repertoire of methods, techniques, and procedures for the production of his art" (p. 168).

In the 1970s Travers and Dillon (1975) produced a book centered on: "Teaching as a performing art, and in the performing arts, each player must give his own interpretation of that which he wishes to portray" (p. vii). Their model is Konstantin Stanislavski's approach to the training of actors and the production of plays, which he devised at the Moscow Art Theater to counteract artificial and overacted performances. Central to Stanislavski's ideal was the actor "becoming" the character, so that if cast as Hedda Gabler the actress must eat, sleep, walk, dress, and bathe as Hedda, not as herself. Travers and Dillon advocated that the student teacher should become as absorbed in the role of teacher as an actress cast as Hedda. Their book essentially presented a set of minidramas in classrooms which would allow students to rehearse their new roles as teachers.

In the 1980s Rubin (1985) again offered the metaphor. He wrote for "those teachers-in-training who believe teaching can be an art, and whose aim is to make themselves Artist Teachers" (p. iii). Early in this volume Rubin suggested there are two routes to being an artist teacher: "Some, blessed with natural gifts, rely principally on instinct. Others, less intuitive, cultivate equally impressive artistry through practice and effort" (p. 15).

All these books, from two continents, written over a 40-year period, invoked the metaphor of the teacher as an artist. None is particularly well-known or widely used. They all deployed the same metaphor, but not in a cumulative way, for none of the authors referred to the earlier volumes in the sequence. These were all prescriptive texts, not reports of research. Among researchers, the metaphor is rarely used.

2. The Metaphor and Research

In the 1990s the metaphor of the teacher as artist has been associated with Gage (1978) and Eisner (1977), both of whom paid tribute to the evocation of teaching produced by Jackson (1968). Gage's work was more concerned with establishing the scientific base on which the artist can build than with exploring what "artist" means. Eisner was more interested in artistry in educational research and evaluation than in artistry in teaching.

These two leading researchers have not been alone. Scholars doing empirical research on teachers and teaching have not made much use of the metaphor; nor have they tried to pin it down in their investigations. A content analysis of one of the leading journals in the field, *Teaching and Teacher Education*, revealed that in the 32 issues after its foundation in 1984–85, containing 288 articles written by authors based in 20 different countries from Australia to Thailand, only one paper used the metaphor of the teacher as artist (Trumbull 1986). (This paper drew on Rubin 1985.) Not a single paper in *Teaching and Teacher Education* has focused on Eisner's work on aesthetic criticism as an approach to the study of teaching.

Teaching and Teacher Education is a journal predominantly for researchers with a background in the psychology of education. The metaphor of the teacher as artist is equally rare in the sociological literature on teaching. Waller (1932) deployed several metaphors about teachers—especially the teacher as stranger—but not that of the teacher as artist. Similarly, the only time the British sociologist of teaching Hargreaves (1983) has used the phrase "The Art of Teaching" was when he was writing about the teaching of art and aesthetics. The Australian Connell (1985) also evoked many facets of teaching without the metaphor of artistry. One reason that researchers who gather data on teaching have not used the metaphor of teaching as artistry as often as those writing training manuals may be the vagueness of the idea. Moreover, few authors (except Travers and Dillon 1975) have examined the type of artist they are invoking.

3. The Unspecified Artist

The invocation of teaching as artistry is a vague one. Those who use the metaphor rarely specify what kind of artistic performer or creator they have in mind. Is the teacher an actor, a painter, a sculptor, a poet, a ballet dancer, a musician, a composer, a chef, a playwright, a novelist, a film-director, a choreographer, a quiltmaker, a fashion designer, or a singer? Is the teacher a performer of someone else's script, the creator of his or her own, or the director/conductor/choreographer of the children's performance? In general, no particular artistic role has been specified by educational writers. It is not clear whether the teacher should be emulating a reclusive novelist such as J D Salinger, a gregarious country and western star such as Dolly Parton, or a conductor such as Andrew Davies. Authors have left the idea of "artistry" unspecified and, apart from mentioning creativity, unexplored. Indeed the vagueness of the metaphor brings it perilously close to that other old warhorse: the

teacher as cultivator. Lacey (1970) was scathing about the "teacher as gardener" metaphor long ago:

> Educationalists and even sociologists frequently use gardening analogies when talking about the process of education, e.g. "cultivating" pupils. The metaphor is totally misleading. I have yet to hear of a gardener being reduced to a nervous wreck by errant plants, but I have not taught or done research in a school where at least one member of staff did not suffer chronic discipline problems. (p. 170)

At its unspecified and rhetorical worst, the metaphor of teacher as artist is just as misleading.

There is, however, a real issue behind the metaphor, and the work of Gage (1978) has addressed it. When Gage examined *The Scientific Basis of the Art of Teaching*, he was exploring the tension between rules and formulae on the technical side and creativity on the artistic. He wrote: "As a practical art, teaching must be recognised as a process that calls for intuition, creativity, improvisation, and expressiveness—a process that leaves room for departures from what is implied by rules, formulas and algorithms" (p. 15). This contrast has been written about extensively in the sociology of the professions: a literature ignored by authors on teachers and teaching. The contrast Gage made between "science" and "art" has elsewhere been described as a contrast between technicity and indeterminacy.

4. The Indeterminacy of Teaching

The French sociologists Jamous and Peloille (1970) made an attempt to reorganize sociological thinking about occupations by focusing on each job's location in a two-dimensional space of "indeterminacy" and "technicality." What writers on teaching such as Gage mean by "artist" is someone with what Jamous and Peloille called "indeterminate" skills.

Jamous and Pelolle argued that all occupations involve two contrasting types of skill and knowledge: technical and indeterminate. Technical skills and knowledge are the explicit, rule-governed, codified parts of the job. For example, a London taxi driver has to have a clean driving licence and pass a test on "the knowledge": a detailed examination of factual material on London streets, stations, hotels, taxi routes, and short cuts. A lawyer has to have a knowledge of legal codes and cases in the law books. A police officer has to know how to caution a suspect and what the local laws are. For Gage (1978) a teacher has to have subject-matter knowledge and a grasp of the research on teacher effectiveness—the scientific basis—and that is Jamous and Peloille's technicity.

Indeterminacy is the "hidden curriculum" of the job performance: all the tacit, implicit, unexamined facets of any job. All jobs involve rules of thumb and "judgment calls" that leave space for flair, genius, and unspecifiable virtuosities. For the taxi driver, dealing successfully with drunks, bewildered tourists, the police, other drivers, and hotel doormen involves such indeterminate skills and knowledge. For the lawyer it is dealing with judges, clients, and juries; for the police officer it is knowing when to caution and when to arrest, when to call for back-up and when to go in, how to cope with both criminals and victims and distinguish between them. (For further work on indeterminacy versus technicity see Atkinson et al. 1977, Atkinson 1983, Atkinson and Delamont 1985, Delamont and Atkinson 1994).

When educational writers say that teachers must be artists, what they actually mean is that the job of teaching has both technical and indeterminate aspects: educational research that loses sight of this is bound to fail. The lack of attention paid to the work of Jamous and Peloille in Anglo-American educational circles has been due to their French location and the fact that they have written about doctors. Educational researchers have been too narrowly focused on teachers to recognize research on other occupations as being central to their dilemmas.

5. The Lessons for Research on Teaching

There are two lessons for research on teaching. First, it is vital to do research that challenges the taken-for-granted boundaries of the "educator subculture" (Wolcott 1981). As Wolcott pointed out, it took a colleague from outside educational research "to jolt me into realising that the kinds of data teachers gather 'on' and 'for' each other so admiringly reflect the dominant society and its educator subculture" (p. 253).

Second, it is important to do research on the indeterminate aspects of teaching, not just the technical, even though the latter are easier to measure. Eisner (1985a, 1985b) pioneered the use of aesthetic criticism as a research style in educational inquiry. In the same vein, Lightfoot (1983) invoked the art of portraiture to describe her study of six outstanding American high schools. Both authors were attempting to capture indeterminate aspects of schooling and teaching. Good research on teachers will always have to capture the indeterminate as well as the technical.

See also: Teachers as Professionals; Teachers as Researchers; Teachers' Roles; Cognitive Development Theories of Teaching

References

Atkinson P 1983 The reproduction of professional community. In: Dingwall R, Lewis P (eds.) 1983 *Sociology of the Professions*, Macmillan, London

Atkinson P, Delamont S 1985 Socialisation into teaching: The research which lost its way. *Brit. J. Soc. Educ.* 6(3): 307–22

Atkinson P A, Reid M, Sheldrake P 1977 Medical mystique. *Sociology of Work and Occupations* 4(3): 243–80

Colman J E 1967 *The Master Teachers and the Art of Teaching*. Pitman, New York

Connell R W 1985 *Teachers' Work*. Allen and Unwin, Sydney

Delamont S, Atkinson P 1994 *Fighting Familiarity*. Hampton Press, Cresskiln, New Jersey

Eisner E 1977 On the uses of educational connoisseurship and educational criticism for evaluating classroom life. *Teach. Coll. Rec.* 78(3): 345–58

Eisner E 1985a *The Art of Educational Evaluation*: *A Personal View*. Falmer Press, London

Eisner E 1985b *The Educational Imagination*, 2nd edn. Macmillan Inc. New York

Gage N L 1978 *The Scientific Basis of the Art of Teaching*. Teachers College Press, New York

Hargreaves D H 1983 The teaching of art and the art of teaching. In: Hammersley M, Hargreaves A (eds.) 1983 *Curriculum Practice*. Falmer Press, Lewer

Jackson P W 1968 *Life in Classrooms*. Holt, Rinehart, and Winston, New York (2nd edn.) Teachers College Press, New York

James W 1983 (1st edn. 1891) *Talks to Teachers on Psychology*. Harvard University Press, Cambridge, Massachusetts

Jamous H, Peloille B 1970 Professions or self-perpetuating system. In: Jackson J A (ed.) 1970 *Professions and Professionalization*. Cambridge University Press, Cambridge

Lacey C 1970 *Hightown Grammar*, Manchester University Press, Manchester

Lightfoot S L 1983 *The Good High School*. Basic Books, New York

Morris I 1954 *The Art of Teaching English as a Living Language*. Macmillan, London

Rubin L J 1986 *Artistry in Teaching*. Random House, New York

Travers R M W, Dillon J 1975 *The Making of a Teacher*. Macmillan Inc., New York

Trumbull D J 1986 Teacher's envisioning, *Teaching and Teacher Education* 2(2): 139–44

Waller W 1932 *The Sociology of Teaching*. Wiley, New York

Wolcott H F 1981 Confessions of a "trained" observer. In: Popkewitz T S, Tabachnick B R (eds.) 1981 *The Study of Schooling*. Praeger, New York

Further Reading

Eisner E 1991 *The Enlightened Eye*, Macmillan Inc., New York

Gage N L 1989 The paradigm wars and their aftermath. *Teach. Coll. Rec.* 91(2): 135–50

Nespor J, Barber L 1991 The rhetorical construction of "the teacher". *Harv. Educ. Rev.* 61(4): 417–33

Wolcott H F 1990 On seeking—and rejecting—validity in qualitative research. In: Eisner E, Peshkin A (eds.) 1990 *Qualitative Inquiry in Education*. Teachers College Press, New York

Teachers as Clinicians

J. Calderhead

Teaching can be conceptualized as a form of problem-solving and decision-making which has many properties in common with the work of physicians. This conceptualization has led to a body of research which has investigated the decision-making of teachers, focusing in particular on the information about pupils that teachers use to make decisions and the way they tailor instruction to individual pupil needs. The resulting research has contributed to knowledge of teachers' planning and interactive thinking.

1. Historical Context

The metaphor of teaching as clinical decision-making initially arose in the 1970s, primarily as a result of three factors: a dissatisfaction with purely behaviorist conceptions of teaching; the development of interest in the cognitive aspects of teachers' work; and the growth of research in medical education concerning the nature and development of physician's decision-making. While much of the research on teaching at this time focused on the classroom behaviors of teachers, such as the types of questions teachers asked (e.g., Rosenshine 1971), it was recognized that an important aspect of effective teaching was the cognitive activity involved, for instance, in asking the appropriate question of the appropriate child at the appropriate time (Shavelson 1973). This recognition highlighted the importance of the decision-making of teachers, an area of enquiry that received particular support in the United States from the 1974 National Institute of Education conference on Studies in Teaching. One of the panels at this conference (panel 6) drew attention to the similarities between the teacher as diagnostician of children's learning and prescriber of fruitful learning activities, and the diagnostic and remediation functions of the physician (NIE 1975). Teachers, like physicians, the panel claimed, face the task of making sense of a diverse range of information, and bringing to bear a range of theories and evidence as well as personal beliefs and expectations on problem situations in order to form judgments and make decisions.

2. Research Focus and Methodology

This field of research has addressed questions concerning the nature of teachers' judgments and decisions, and the factors that influence them. The principal research methods employed have been policy-capturing and stimulated recall. In policy-capturing studies,

teachers have been given descriptions of problem situations and have been asked to make judgments or decisions. By systematically varying the nature of the information contained in the descriptions it becomes possible to trace back the factors influencing teachers' judgments. For example, Rohrkemper and Brophy (1983) provided a sample of 98 teachers with 24 vignettes describing problem students in uncooperative classroom situations, to which teachers were asked to say how they would respond. From these data, the researchers were able to identify factors associated with the children and with the classroom situations that influenced teachers' responses. These relationships were also tested for reliability against observational data.

In stimulated recall studies, a teacher's classroom interactions have been videoed, and the video replayed to the teacher shortly afterward with the request that the teacher recall what was going through his or her mind at the time. The resulting data have usually been classified into cognitive acts (whether teachers were making judgments or decisions, or simply expressing an awareness of a feature of classroom activity) and the content of the thinking (e.g., curriculum, children, teaching strategy). Morine-Dershimer (1989), for instance, in a study of 10 teachers, identified qualitatively different types of decision-making among teachers (e.g., reflective as opposed to "in-flight" decision-making) and the proportion of time in a lesson spent thinking of different content. In studies of the thinking and decision-making involved in the planning phase of teaching, teachers have frequently been asked to plan "out loud," verbalizing their normally covert thoughts which are then recorded (e.g., Yinger 1980).

The limitations of the methodology for research on teachers' thinking and decision-making have been discussed at great length in the literature. In particular, attention has been drawn to the importance of the inferences that teachers make in policy-capturing studies and the extent to which teachers' previous experience and existing knowledge is brought to bear in making judgments in problem situations. In the case of stimulated recall studies, researchers' concerns have focused mostly on the status of recalled thoughts, namely their incomplete nature and the extent to which they might represent post hoc rationalizations rather than actual thoughts at the time.

3. Major Findings

The findings emerging from this research have concerned the nature and content of teachers' thinking in both the planning and interactive phases of teaching.

They have led to new ways of conceptualizing the cognitive aspects of teachers' work with implications for teacher education and further research.

3.1 Teachers' Planning

Prescriptive models of teachers' planning have tended to depict the planning process as a linear deductive process, beginning with aims and objectives which are translated into content and procedures. Research on the thinking and decision-making of teachers, however, suggests first of all that planning occurs at various levels (yearly, termly, unit, daily, lesson). Furthermore, at the higher levels, its focus is on organization and content, whereas at the lower levels its focus is on the construction of activities and on what teachers and students will do. Rather than involving a linear deductive process, then, planning seems to involve a much more creative problem–finding and problem-solving process. In this process, teachers use their vast knowledge of children, the curriculum, teaching strategies, school facilities, and educational objectives to construct activities which will be manageable within the classroom context (Yinger 1980, McCutcheon 1980).

3.2 Interactive Teaching

Whereas the metaphor of teaching as clinical decision-making has initially presumed that teachers' classroom activity is characterized by diagnostic judgments and remediation decisions, research on teachers' thinking during interactive teaching suggests that teachers actually make few decisions in the classroom. Much of teachers' thinking focuses on the children and the instructional process and is concerned with implementing the planned activity or adjusting the activity to the children and context using well-established instructional routines.

During interactive teaching, teachers seem to be particularly attentive to cues that have strategic significance in indicating how the activity is progressing and whether children in general understand and are able to complete the activity. Lundgren (1972), for example, found that in whole class teaching in secondary science lessons, teachers took particular note of the progress of lower ability students and paced the lesson accordingly. Bromme (1987) also found that after teaching a lesson, secondary mathematics teachers were able to remember and comment on examples of children's understanding and misunderstanding. These examples represented significant moments in the lesson when the teacher found they had to explain, elaborate a point, or move on. However, teachers did not associate these incidents with the abilities or progress of individual children. Teachers, it seems, rarely act as diagnosticians and remediators of individual children's difficulties, but have developed ways of understanding and responding to difficulties which are more specifically adapted to the complex classroom context.

4. New Ways of Conceptualizing Teachers' Cognitions

Research on teaching as clinical decision-making has led researchers to develop further conceptualizations of teaching which recognize the complexity of teachers' knowledge and the interaction between teachers' preactive (i.e., planning) and interactive (i.e., in classroom) thinking. Putnam (1987) suggests that the diagnostic/remediation model does not fit well with the behavior of experienced teachers and suggests an alternative model based on the concepts of curriculum script and agenda. A curriculum script is viewed as an ordered set of goals and actions for teaching a particular topic. When teaching the topic, the script largely determines the teacher's agenda, a dynamic mental plan for the particular lesson. As the lesson is taught, the teacher notes various performance cues which are used to add to, revise, or update the agenda. Experienced teachers are seen as having a vast repertoire of curriculum scripts that provide the foundation for individual lesson agendas.

An alternative conceptualization is offered by Clark and Yinger (1987), who suggest that both planning and interactive teaching contain characteristics of a design process. They propose that Schon's (1983) notion of "reflection-in-action" captures well some of the creative aspects of teaching. When teachers encounter a novel situation, they draw upon their past experience to develop hypotheses about the nature of the problem and possible solutions to it. This reflection-in-action leads teachers to try out certain solution strategies, monitor their effects, and interpret the outcomes to determine future action.

5. Implications for Teacher Education

Research on the differences between experts and novices in the way they plan and think about their work, and research on the processes by which student teachers acquire knowledge related to the task of teaching have led to the consideration of alternative means of training teachers (see Clark 1988). In particular, research has highlighted the complexity of teachers' knowledge and the need to develop means by which the knowledge of the experienced teacher becomes more accessible to the novice (McAlpine et al. 1988). The importance of having opportunities for reflection and analysis in the training period has been emphasized (Clift et al. 1990). The value of case studies of classroom practice in offering opportunities for student teachers to explore how teachers' knowledge and particular contextual features have led to particular decisions and actions has also been acclaimed (Merseth 1991).

6. *Implications for Further Research*

Research into the thinking and decision-making of teachers has raised several questions about the knowledge that teachers and other professionals possess and use. Several enquiries into the qualitative differences in teachers' knowledge and the processes of knowledge growth have been made. The research has involved a move away from the earlier methods of stimulated recall and policy-capturing to much more fine-grained case studies involving detailed examination of the knowledge, knowledge use, and processes of knowledge growth of teachers (Beyerbach 1988, Calderhead and Robson 1991, John 1991, Clift 1991). It is expected that through such enquiry, clearer models will emerge of how student teachers learn to teach and how they learn to accommodate the individual differences among children in the context of the school curriculum and the complex classroom setting.

See also: Teacher Planning; Reflective Teaching

References

Beyerbach B A 1988 Developing a technical vocabulary on teacher planning: Preservice teachers' concept maps. *Teaching and Teacher Education* 4(4): 339–47
Bromme R 1987 Teachers' assessments of students' difficulties and progress in understanding in the classroom. In: Calderhead J (ed.) 1987
Calderhead J, Robson M 1991 Images of teaching: Student teachers' early conceptions of classroom practice. *Teaching and Teacher Education* 7(1): 108
Clark C M 1988 Asking the right questions about teacher preparation: Contributions of research on teacher thinking. *Educ. Researcher* 17(2): 5–12
Clark C M, Yinger R J 1987 Teacher planning. In: Calderhead J (ed.) 1987
Clift R T 1991 Learning to teach English – maybe: A study of knowledge development. *J. Teach. Educ.* 42(5): 357–72
Clift R T, Houston W R, Pugach M C 1989 *Encouraging Reflective Practice in Education: An Analysis of Issues and Programs.* Teachers' College Press, New York
John P D 1991 Course, curricular and classroom influences on the development of student teachers' lesson planning perspectives. *Teaching and Teacher Education* 7(4): 359–72
Lundgren U P 1972 *Frame Factors and the Teaching Process: A Contribution to Curriculum Theory and Theory on Teaching.* Almquist and Wiksell, Stockholm
McAlpine A, Brown S, McIntyre D, Hagger H 1988 *Student Teachers Learning from Experienced Teachers.* Scottish Council for Research in Education, Edinburgh
McCutcheon G 1980 How do elementary school teachers plan? The nature of planning and influences on it. *The Elementary School J.* 81(1): 4–23.
Merseth K K 1991 The early history of case-based instruction: Insights for teacher education today. *J. Teach. Educ.* 42(4): 243–49
Morine-Dershimer G 1989 Preservice teachers' conceptions of content and pedagogy: Measuring growth in reflective, pedagogical decision-making. *J. Teach. Educ.* 40(5): 46–52
Gage N (ed.) 1975 *Teaching as Clinical Information Processing: Report of Panel 6 National Conference on Studies in Teaching.* National Institute of Education, Washington, DC
Putnam R T 1987 Structuring and adjusting content for students: A study of live and simulated tutoring of addition. *Am. Educ. Res. J.* 24(1): 13–48
Rohrkemper M M, Brophy J E 1983 Teachers' thinking about problem students. In: Levine J M, Wang M C (eds.) 1983 *Teacher and Student Perceptions: Implications for Learning.* Lawrence Erlbaum Associates, Hillsdale, New Jersey
Rosenshine B 1971 *Teaching Behaviours and Student Achievement.* National Foundation for Educational Research, Slough
Schon D A 1983 *The Reflective Practitioner.* Basic Books, New York
Shavelson R J 1973 What is the basic teaching skill? *J. Teach. Educ.* 24(2): 144–51
Yinger R J 1980 A study of teacher planning: Description and a model of preactive decision-making. *Elem. Sch. J.* 80(3): 107–27

Further Reading

Calderhead J 1987 *Exploring Teachers' Thinking.* Cassell, London
Clark C M, Peterson P L 1986 Teachers' thought processes. In: Wittrock M C (ed.) 1986 *Handbook of Research on Teaching*, 3rd edn. Macmillan, New York
Kagan D M 1988 Teaching as clinical problem solving: A critical examination of the analogy and its implications. *Rev. Educ. Res.* 58(4): 482–505

Teachers as Professionals

E. Hoyle

The long-standing debate over whether teaching is or is not a profession has been unproductive. "The teaching profession" is a phrase in widespread usage not only among teachers themselves but among laypersons, politicians, and the media. However, the fact that teaching is widely referred to as a "profession" is only a starting point for the analysis of the nature of teaching as an occupation since the term "profession" is a potent metaphor and, at times, an ideological weapon. The debate about "teaching as a profession" and "teachers as professionals" is not primarily a matter of semantics, but raises a number of substantive issues which ultimately relate to the quality of education. The first section of this entry will discuss "profession" and related concepts. The second will outline major criticisms of the way in which the term has been deployed. The third will address a number of central issues, organized for heuristic purposes according to the main criteria attributed to the professions.

1. The Concept of a Profession

Systematic sociological analysis of the distinguishing criteria of professions began only in the early years of the twentieth century. A number of sociologists generated lists of putative criteria which were allegedly fully met by the undisputed professions, but met to a lesser degree by occupations termed "semi" or "quasi" professions. Thus, professions were placed along a hypothetical continuum, with teaching usually classified as a "semi-profession." "Emergent professions" were those in the process of meeting the criteria more fully and, hence, moving along the hypothetical continuum, a process usually referred to as "professionalization." The ideology which underpins an occupation's quest for professionalization tends to entail the assumption that, in meeting the criteria to an increased degree, the quality of service provided by the occupation will be enhanced. Although this may normally be the case, it cannot be taken as axiomatic. Thus, in the literature, the term "professionalism" is sometimes used to refer to the rhetorics and strategies used by occupations in their professionalization project, while the term "professionality" refers to the quality of skill and service provided.

A number of criteria have been designated by various writers, and it is often argued by critics that there is a lack of consensus among these lists. In fact, the opposite interpretation is possible and a high correlation has been demonstrated (Hickson and Thomas 1969). Rather than report any one of those lists, or attempt to conflate them, the major criteria can be presented according to the assumption implicit in the functionalist theory of the professions. This theory holds that the professions are those occupations whose members bring a high degree of knowledge and skill to those social functions which were most central to the well-being of society. Hoyle (1980) has summarized the theory and enumerated the criteria it generates:

(a) A profession is an occupation which performs a crucial social function.

(b) The exercise of this function requires a considerable degree of skill.

(c) This skill is exercised in situations which are not wholly routine, but in which new problems have to be handled.

(d) Thus, although knowledge gained through experience is important, this recipe-type knowledge is insufficient to meet professional demands and the practitioner has to draw on a body of systematic knowledge.

(e) The acquisition of this body of knowledge and the development of specific skills requires a lengthy period of higher education.

(f) This period of education and training also involves the process of socialization into professional values.

(g) These values tend to center on the pre-eminence of clients' interests, and to some degree they are made explicit in a code of ethics.

(h) Because knowledge-based skills are exercised in nonroutine situations, it is essential for the professionals to have the freedom to make their own judgments with regard to appropriate practice.

(i) Because professional practice is so specialized, the organized profession should have a strong voice in the shaping of relevant public policy, a large degree of control over the exercise of professional responsibilities, and a high degree of autonomy in relation to the state.

(j) Lengthy training, responsibility, and client-centeredness are necessarily rewarded by high prestige and a high level of remuneration.

Although variations occur between societies, teaching meets some of these criteria but usually not all. Furthermore, those criteria which teaching does meet are not always met in full. These criteria are not only the products of sociological theorizing, but also inform the rhetoric of professional elites as they negotiate with employers and governments on behalf of their members.

2. Criticisms of Traditional Approaches to the Professions

Several criticisms have been levelled at the traditional sociological approach to the professions. First, the debate about professions is an Anglo-Saxon phenomenon and has little relevance to, for example, the European context in which professionals are largely state employees. Moreover, professionalism as an ideology is to be viewed as relative to a particular historical period and can be seen as being in decline (Perkin 1989).

Second, the functionalist interpretation is held to be ahistorical. It thereby underestimates the degree to which the current high status of the leading professions can more appropriately be attributed to the acquisition of the power to control the market for its services than to the gratitude of the general public for services provided (Larson 1977). Third, the contention that only a relatively small proportion of the population has the potential to become professionals is an argument for closure and credentialism rather than an accurate portrayal of the pool of ability (Sykes 1987). Fourth, the criteria have been derived from an analysis of the structures of occupations which have already achieved status through controlling a market, and from the rationalizations of their elites rather than from an evaluation of professions at work. Thus, the criteria have only a limited relationship to reality. One example is that practitioner autonomy is, in fact, a form of protection against accountability (Bessant and Spaull 1972).

Finally, the term "profession" is almost invariably used in a rhetorical or ideological manner both by the professional elites and by governments (Ozga and Lawn 1981), and as a strategy of control at the school level (Shanker 1985).

The reification of the concept of "profession" has led to such frustration that it has been suggested that it be abandoned altogether. A less radical suggestion has been that sociologists should focus on what professionals actually do. There have been some excellent studies of professional practice using a variety of approaches which have remained unconstrained by the functionalist perspective. Nevertheless, because issues raised about autonomy, knowledge, responsiveness to client, and the like remain relevant, the concept of "profession" provides at least a heuristic perspective. However, it should be recognized that there are other approaches—notably the labour process view which takes its inspiration from the work of Braverman (1974).

3. Issues Relating to Teaching as a Profession

This section outlines some issues relating to the notion of teaching as a profession, organized around five key criteria of a profession: social function, knowledge, practitioner autonomy, collective autonomy, and professional values.

3.1 Social Function

Teaching undoubtedly performs a crucial social function since education is a key social process in both developing and developed societies. The functionalists would argue that teaching lacks the social status of medicine, law, dentistry, and other similar professions, because education is less central to the needs of society. This argument would be extremely difficult to substantiate. Differences in status are much more likely to be due to other factors (e.g., the size of the teaching profession, the characteristics of teachers, relationships with clients, and the work situation of teachers) than the importance of the social function.

The importance of education, and hence teaching, to the well-being of society as a whole is sufficiently self-evident.

The significance of education increases as the link with occupation (particularly in terms of credentials) tightens. However, there are a number of factors which militate against public perceptions of the importance of this function. One is related to timescale. The benefits of education accumulate over time and are the results of the efforts of many teachers. Individual contributions are difficult to identify. Moreover, the fact that children are taught in groups further militates against the identification of a single teacher with individual achievement.

Teaching also differs from the major professions in terms of the consequence of the service provided. Generally, this service is not, in the literal sense, vital. Much of the work of all professionals is routine and, in practice, they vary very little in this respect. However, there are occasions when judgments have profound consequences for the clients of doctors and lawyers in particular, but also those of accountants and architects. These moments rarely occur for teachers. Perhaps the importance of these moments has been overemphasized by the elites of the major professions and reinforced by the media. Nonetheless, the contribution of teaching to the well-being of society as a whole and to the well-being of individuals is difficult to evaluate.

3.2 Knowledge

The knowledge-base of teaching as a profession remains a highly contentious issue. That teachers need knowledge of the subject matter to be transmitted is not in dispute. However, there is considerably more skepticism among outsiders and teachers themselves about the knowledge which can be broadly termed "educational theory" (Jackson 1987). Teachers are thus confronted with a problem. If they criticize the theory to which they have been exposed in their training as irrelevant to practice, they are denying to themselves one of the traditional characteristics of a profession. If teaching is no more than an experience-based skill with a limited set of precepts, the occupation is indistinguishable from the crafts of, say, plumbing or motor mechanics.

However, the problem of the professional knowledge of teachers is complex. Necessary distinctions between different kinds of theoretical knowledge, between—to oversimplify—pedagogical, curricular, and socioeducational theory, are not always made, although they perform different functions. Another difficulty is that the venerable theory–practice debate has been largely conducted on the assumption that preexisting, systematic, codified knowledge is somehow applied to pupils. However, the pedagogic knowledge-base of "teacher" is being reconceptualized in a way in which it is more readily articulated with practice (Calderhead 1987).

The social dimension of practice, in the past a maligned element of educational theory, is being recognized in relation to medicine, law, architecture, and other professional areas. Teachers would appear to be moving from "restricted" to "extended" professionality (Hoyle 1974), particularly in those countries which have made a substantial commitment to the continuing professional development of teachers. However, there is a paradox here in that the forms which this development is taking are unlikely to enhance status. One must also note the argument that, at least in some systems, the opposite tendency is at work and that the closer control is resulting in the deskilling of teachers (Apple 1987).

3.3 Practitioner Autonomy

Practitioners greatly value their autonomy. However, no practitioner can expect complete autonomy. The debate about autonomy is somewhat complex in that its limits can function at different levels. Autonomy can be limited by the state (e.g., via a national curriculum, or prescribed textbooks), by administrators and principals, by the local community, and by peers. The patterns vary across systems. For example, French teachers have their autonomy limited by the state, but their attitude towards professionality is such that this is not experienced as a restriction. Within this framework, however, French teachers experience a high degree of autonomy in relation to administrators and colleagues. French teachers thus have a narrower view of their professional roles than the teachers in, say, the United Kingdom (Broadfoot and Osborn 1987).

An important issue concerns the limits to teacher autonomy imposed by administrators. A theoretical conflict between bureaucratic constraint and professional autonomy has a long history in sociology. This conflict between the constraints imposed by bureaucracy and the freedom of teachers to work is dependent upon a number of factors which vary over different systems (e.g., whether the role of the principal is seen as that of administrator or leading educational professional, the degree of hierarchy in the school, the nature of teacher evaluation, and the managerial style of the principal).

Although conflict between the principal's authority and the teacher's autonomy is an ever-present possibility and can become acute, in practice actual conflict is constrained partly by the structure of the school and partly by a widely accepted norm. Schools are loosely coupled in that the separate components—units and people—are relatively independent of the center. Teaching is not an activity which is amenable to close control. Thus, there tends to be a balance between control and autonomy underpinned by the acceptance that administrators and teachers have their proper spheres of influence which indeed overlap and generate the need for conflict resolution through negotiation and micropolitics, but which are generally in a state of mutual accommodation (Hanson 1979). However, as teaching becomes more stratified according to administrative roles, the conditions for differential status arise and the relationship between professionalism and bureaucracy becomes less clear. When this occurs, the managerial, rather than the teaching, element of professionalism comes to the fore.

Ironically, the threat to teacher autonomy is inherent not only in bureaucratic but also in collegial patterns of organization in which control by colleagues can be constraining. In many systems, there is a move towards a greater independence of teachers as they collaborate in curriculum development, staff development, organizational development, and schemes of peer appraisal. These may be inimical to individual autonomy and it may be the case that these elements in the conventional model of a profession will decline and a new form—collaborative professionality—might be emerging. It can be argued that some loss in individual autonomy may lead to an enhancement in the quality of provision (Anderson 1987).

3.4 Collective Autonomy

Teaching has been less successful than the major professions in achieving self-governing status and independence from the state. In perhaps the majority of countries, teachers are state employees expected to carry out the educational policies laid down by central government. The degree to which the organized profession is consulted in the shaping of these policies varies over countries and over time. In few systems have teachers succeeded in creating self-governing bodies responsible for admitting members and disciplining them, shaping policy, and determining the pattern of its implementation. Teachers are usually organized into unions rather than professional bodies, and this shapes their relationship with the state.

Nevertheless, teachers have, in some countries, enjoyed a great deal of influence over the practice of education which perhaps reached its apotheosis in some Western nations in the 1960s and early 1970s. In the 1990s this movement is being rolled back. This is the era of accountability and of a general backlash against the professional society. Thus, although teaching still aspires to the status of an independent profession, which it has nowhere achieved historically, contemporary social forces are strongly against this status. Indeed, the very professions which teaching has sought to emulate are themselves experiencing demands for greater accountability and attempts to reduce their autonomy.

3.5 Professional Values

Although professions are held to be distinguishable by a particular set of values, it is virtually impossible to make generalizations about this aspect in relation to professions in general or the teaching profession in particular. The field itself is inadequately mapped.

Perhaps the central professional value is that of "client centeredness," but there are those who claim that profit is as central to the professions as to business. Moreover, insofar as client centeredness exists, it is perhaps exhibited as much by craft workers and members of the service industry as by professionals.

Client centeredness among teachers is difficult to determine, not least because teachers have multiple clientele—including pupils, their parents, and the state—and the balance of sometimes conflicting interests is difficult to establish. In many societies, codes of ethics for teachers have been established, but their provenance varies (e.g., teacher unions, the state, independent commissions). Thus, there are differences in these codes, particularly in the extent to which priority is given to relationships between colleagues and relationships with clients. Despite the attention of a number of philosophers, the ethical basis of the teaching profession needs further development (Langford 1978).

4. Conclusion

By general usage, teaching is designated a profession. However, for a variety of reasons, its status is not as high as that of other professions owing to such factors as its size, the characteristics of its members, the nature of relationships with clients, and the teacher's work situation.

It is widely argued that there are likely to remain limits in the degree to which teachers can enhance their status (Bull 1990) and debates center on the quality of provision which teachers, as professionals, provide. Some writers, while retaining the concept of "profession," note that its inherent elitism distracts from the progressive strategy which would enhance service to clients (Burbules and Densmore 1991). On the other hand, there are those who continue to view the enhanced professionalization of teachers as a prerequisite to the enhancement of educational quality (Holmes Group 1986). Since the concept of "profession" remains contested, its usage in any debate must be clarified by the protagonists.

See also: Social Status of Teaching; Teachers as Researchers

References

Anderson L W 1987 The decline of teacher autonomy: Tears or cheers? *Int. Rev. Educ.* 33(3): 357–73
Apple M W 1988 *Teachers and Texts: A Political Economy of Class and Gender Relations in Education.* Routledge and Kegan Paul, New York
Bessant B, Spaull A D 1972 The myth of the teaching profession. In: Bessant B, Spaull A (eds.) 1972 *Teachers in Conflict.* Melbourne University Press, Carlton
Braverman H 1974 *Labor and Monopoly Capital.* Monthly Review Press, New York
Broadfoot P, Osborn M 1987 Teachers' conceptions of their professional responsibilities: Some international comparisons. *Comp. Educ.* 23(3): 287–301
Bull B 1990 The limits of teacher professionalization. In: Goodlad J I, Soder R, Sirotnik K P (ed.) 1990 *The Moral Dimensions of Teaching.* Jossey Bass, San Francisco, California
Burbules N L, Densmore K 1991 The limits of making teaching a profession. *Educational Policy* 5: 44–63
Calderhead T 1987 *Exploring Teachers' Thinking.* Cassell, London
Hanson E 1979 *Educational Administration and Organizational Behavior.* Allyn and Bacon, Boston, Massachusetts
Hickson D J, Thomas M W 1969 Professionalization in Britain: A preliminary measurement. *Sociology* 3(1): 37–53
Holmes Group 1986 *Tomorrow's Teachers: A Report of the Holmes Group.* Holmes Group Inc., East Lansing, Michigan
Hoyle E 1974 Professionality, professionalism and control in teaching. *London Educational Review* 3(2): 13–19
Hoyle E 1980 Professionalization and deprofessionalization in education. In: Hoyle E, Megarry J (eds.) 1980 *World Yearbook of Education, 1980: The Professional Development of Teachers.* Kegan Page, London
Jackson P 1987 Facing our ignorance. *Teach. Coll. Rec.* 88: 384–89
Langford G 1978 *Teaching as a profession.* Manchester University Press, Manchester.
Larson M S 1977 *The Rise of Professionalism: A Sociological Analysis.* University of California Press, Berkeley, California
Ozga J, Lawn M 1981 *Teachers, Professionalism and Class: A Study of Organized Teachers.* Falmer Press, Lewes.
Perkin H 1989 *The Rise of Professional Society: England Since 1880.* Routledge, London
Shanker A 1985 *The Making of a Profession.* American Federation of Teachers, Washington, DC
Sykes G 1987 Reckoning with the spectre. *Educ. Researcher* 16: 19–21.

Further Reading

Friedson E 1986 *Professional Powers.* University of Chicago Press, Chicago, Illinois
Halmos P (ed.) 1973 *Professionalization and Social Change: Sociological Review Monograph 20.* University of Keele, Keele
Leggatt T 1970 Teaching as a profession. In: Jackson J A (ed.) 1970 *Professions and Professionalization.* Cambridge University Press, Cambridge
Lortie D C 1977 *Schoolteacher: A Sociological Study.* University of Chicago Press, Chicago, Illinois

Teachers as Researchers

S. Hollingsworth

The international movement to recognize, prepare, and learn from teachers as researchers has come of age in the years since Elliott's entry on the topic (1985) in *The International Encyclopedia of Education 1st Edn*. This entry summarizes the breadth, diversity, and significance of the teacher-as-researcher movement across three interrelated areas: curriculum improvement, professional and structural critique, and societal reform. Since teacher researchers are concerned simultaneously with ways to (a) improve their practice, (b) change the situations in which they work, and (c) understand their practices within the larger society, the organization of this entry is not intended to be linear of hiearchical. The discussion, instead, is framed in terms of different organizing focuses.

1. Curriculum Improvement

Curriculum improvement research is a derivative of what was known as "action research" and which led to the conceptualization of teachers as researchers within a process model (Stenhouse 1983). The work in this area produced both immediate curriculum changes on the part of teachers (first-order research), and observations about teacher research from collaborating academics (second-order research).

1.1 Action Research

The use of experimental social science to investigate various programs of social action was popularized in the United States by social psychologist Kurt Lewin (1946). Corey (1953) adapted the concept to improve school practices. He and his faculty colleagues at Teachers College at Columbia University worked cooperatively with public-school personnel on curriculum projects in action. In the post-Sputnik climate of the late 1950s, however, primary funding went to curriculum projects which followed traditional research, development, and dissemination models. Action research, suspect as "unscientific" in such a climate, became "interactive R & D [research and development]," disseminating research results through inservice teacher training. Much of that federally funded work, however, supported regular seminars in which teachers were encouraged to investigate topics related to their practices. It was the curriculum reform movement in the United Kingdom, however, that first popularized teachers as researchers.

1.2 Teachers as Researchers

Stenhouse (1983) is credited with developing the concept of teachers as researchers at the University of East Anglia. As director of the Schools Council's Humanities Project, Stenhouse came to see teachers' authority and autonomy as a basis for curriculum improvement and innovation. Like Corey, Stenhouse used the scientific method of developing and testing curricular hypotheses, but felt that its use to develop replicable results across classrooms was limited. He also questioned the ethical stance of separating the performance from the performer. Stenhouse thus rejected the "objectives model" of curriculum adoption (Tyler 1949) and asked teachers to engage in a "process model" of curriculum innovation where professional and curricular development became part of the same enterprise.

1.3 Developing the Process Model

Three factors made action research in the process model a viable alternative in the late 1970s and 1980s: the difficulties of disseminating quantitative, experimental methodologies to local educational settings; (b) an increasing acceptance of the concept of curriculum as integrated with human deliberation (Schwab 1973); and (c) a professional and political reaction to post-Sputnik accountability as an approach for improving and changing curriculum. Elliott (1991), a colleague of Stenhouse, emphasized the interpretive-hermeneutic nature of inquiry. He saw action research as a pedagogical paradigm—a form of teaching. He argued that educational research should be modeled after action research: "a moral science paradigm to which teacher researchers would be the main contributors, rather than those in academic disciplines" (McKernan 1991, p. 23).

1.4 The Impact of First- and Second-order Research on Curriculum Improvement

First-order research examines changes in the curriculum made by teachers. Examples of such research are included in reports prepared by public-school teachers (Philadelphia Teachers Learning Collaborative 1984), descriptions of university-level teachers' research on their curricular practices (Lampert 1989), and summaries included in texts detailing the action of teacher researchers and academics (Clandinin et al. in press). Examples of second-order research (that is, discussions about teacher research) can be found in outlines of skills needed by teacher researchers (Hopkins 1985), in discussions of teacher researchers' cognitive development (Oja and Sumlyan 1989), in descriptions of teacher networks (Smith et al. 1991), and in understandings gained from teacher–university collectives (Carini 1988).

The cumulative effect of this work has changed the manner in which teachers are perceived as professional curriculum developers. It has also influenced collaborative research models and school restructuring plans which emphasize "teacher empowerment." One of the best examples of curriculum-based teacher research, one which improved practice and then led to theoretical, professional, and structural change, is the Bay Area Writing Project (BAWP). Reports from BAWP extensions across the United States range from first-order summaries (Fecho 1992) to second-order analyses of project participants' ideological differences (Schecter 1992).

2. Professional and Structural Critique

Emerging in the 1980s from the success of curriculum improvement research in the United Kingdom and the United States was an attempt to improve social environments and/or conditions of practice through structural and professional critique.

2.1 Structural Critique

Kemmis and his colleagues at Deakin University in Australia and elsewhere have articulated a model of a critical educational science. Their basic premise is that "new ideas are not enough to generate better education. Educational practices and patterns of school and classroom organization must also be changed to secure improvement" (Kemmis and McTaggert 1988, p. 34).

The critical stance of teachers as researchers, focusing on desired and possible changes in the educational structures, has also been noted within the United Kingdom and other countries. Simons (1992), of the University of Southampton, for example, has argued for collaborative partnerships in the teacher research movement, which take into account the practice-oriented views of the curriculum researcher and the structural views of the critical researcher. She points out that reforming schools from the outside cannot work—neither can simple calls for collaboration. Existing structures privilege privacy, hierarchy, and territory within the institution and across collaborative boundaries; thus, structural and professional relationships must change.

2.2 Critiques of Professionalism and Professionalization

Sockett (1989) has drawn educational scholars' attention to the need for professionalism in teaching as well as the professionalization or socialization process by which one becomes a professional. Teacher research is an important part of both processes. Posch (1992) in Austria also speaks of the importance of teacher research for the profession. He argues that teacher professionalism involves teacher research on student professionalism.

Preparing student teachers and experienced teachers to be critical professionals who challenge and change the workplace conditions (including curriculum) is an important part of a professional and structural critique. Feminists involved in teacher education help teachers to develop radical pedagogies or "styles of teaching which help make visible to pupils the structural social inequities which constrain their lives" (Middleton 1992 p. 18).

2.3 Impact on the Workplace and the Profession

Although the preparation of teachers as critical inquirers is not yet widespread, structural and professional changes influenced by this work have been widely noted in new policies for school and professional restructuring. In the United States, a California decision to retain and reshape the state-sponsored mentoring project followed teacher research investigations into its possibilities and limitations (see Ashton et al. 1990).

Many of the transformative results from the critical professional and structural stance, however, have been far less public and far more personal. The Boston Women's Teachers' Group (Freedman et al. 1983), for example, met for three years to cope with the isolated struggle of their daily work and to study how their work conditions affected them as teachers. Like other groups who have created similar structures, their professional work was critical rather than curricular. They focused on the creation of conditions under which participants could consider their own interests and develop curriculum innovations.

3. Societal Reform

The focus of teachers as researchers in the societal reform sense is on how schools and teaching are shaped in society and what epistemological views are needed for their transformation. In some countries, the societal focus resulted from an awareness of the increasing gap between the concept of democracy and the reality of domination and oppression. Fueled by the Civil Rights and Women's Movements in the United States, even popular teacher-promoted curricular projects challenging static views of knowledge and societal norms were not free from scrutiny (see, for example, Delpit's (1986) critique of the Bay Area Writing Project). Two broad areas of societal reform are epistemological critique and the problem of gender.

3.1 Epistemological Critique

This view of teachers as researchers developed simultaneously with philosophical critiques of societal positions based on privileged conceptions of knowledge. Bruner (1985), for example, questioned the power ascribed the paradigmatic or "rational" view of knowledge and discussed the power of its antitheses: a narrative view of knowledge. Harding (1991) questioned natural science's position on objectivity as too protective of the power-dominant, White, male society. Belenky et al. (1986) raised questions about alternative ways of knowing which could privilege some women over others. Culturally diverse ways of knowing and representing knowledge, such as those pointed out by Lourde (1984), also critiqued societally accepted knowledge. Finally, many critiques either implicitly or explicitly questioned the separation of hierarchically powered social structures and inquiry methods (Winter 1987).

3.2 The Problem of Gender

Zeichner (1990) challenged the problematic social and epistemological hierarchy by speaking of the importance of teachers as women in the second professional wave of educational reform. Zeichner stressed that "Teaching is not just work; it is gendered work" (p. 366). As he expressed hope for societal reform and emancipation in the press for teacher empowerment, he also offered caution. He pointed out the possibility of curricular reform missions being undermined unless teacher research is incorporated into, instead of added to, teachers' work.

For Hollingsworth (1992), the teacher-as- researcher movement takes on a perspective of feminist praxis. A consciousness of the teacher's personal position within society (i.e., most teachers throughout the world are women), an understanding of research, an appreciation of the teacher's ability to construct and critique knowledge, and the integration of those features in classroom teaching suggests that teaching itself is research. Thus, teachers are the researchers of educational and societal reform—a position Elliott (1991) had endorsed earlier from a curricular stance.

Weiner (1989) contrasts teacher research in the School Council Sex Differentiation Project with mainstream professional development or curricular teacher research. Rather than convince teachers of a need to change their practices, gender researchers in the United Kingdom wish to bring about improvements in the social and economic position of women. Similar research is being conducted in the United States (see McIntosh et al. 1992).

3.3 Impact of Societal Reform

Excellent examples of first-order research from the societal reform stance are currently available (Newman 1990). The publication of such work is indicative of the increasing involvement of teachers in emancipatory work. Further, not only are teacher researchers conducting their own professional meetings, but they are participating at national and international research conferences previously reserved for university researchers. For example, since 1989, the American Educational Research Association has registered a special interest group on teacher research. The National Research Center on Literature Teaching and Learning in the United States sponsored a Teacher

Research Institute in 1992. These are but a few examples of how the teacher-as-researcher movement is resulting in societal reform.

The concept of teacher-as-researcher is at the center of international attention to reform in all areas of the educational enterprise: research, teaching, the profession, its moral purpose, and its impact on societies. Some might worry that the political implications of teacher empowerment and societal reform might lead to a new and unknown world with unfamiliar epistemological and social norms. Others might be concerned that the growing popularity of teachers-as-researchers will ensure that it becomes yet another form of power and hierarchy inside schools. If so, the concept may be mandated, measured, and become meaningless to actual improvement of practice. Conversely, it may become a new process for reproducing existing school structures and societal outcomes. The trends found in the literature fail to resolve either of those worries. What is clear is that the movement is part of the larger evolution of society into the postinformation age—and that teachers-as-researchers are no longer marginally involved.

References

Ashton D et al. 1990 *Where Do We Go From Here in the California Mentor Teacher Program?: Recommendations by Seven Mentors.* Stanford/Schools Collaborative, Stanford University, Stanford, California

Belenky M F, Clinchy B M, Goldberger N R, Tarule J M 1986 *Women's Ways of Knowing: The Development of Self, Voice, and Mind.* Basic Books, New York

Bruner J S 1985 Narrative and paradigmatic modes of thought. In: Eisnes E (ed.) 1985 *Learning and Teaching the Ways of Knowing, 84th Yearbook of the National Society for the Study of Education.* University of Chicago Press, Chicago, Illinois

Carini P 1988 Prospect's documentary processes. Unpublished manuscript, Bennington, Vermont

Clandinin D J, Davies A, Hogan P, Kennard B in press *Learning to Teach: Teaching to Learn Stories of Collaboration in Teacher Education.* Teachers' College Press, New York

Corey S 1953 *Action Research to Improve School Practices.* Teachers College Press, New York

Delpit L 1986 Skills and other dilemmas of a progressive Black educator. *Harv. Educ. Rev.* 56(4): 379–85.

Elliott J 1991 *Action Research for Educational Change.* Open University Press, Milton Keynes

Fecho B 1992 The way they talk: An English teacher ponders his role. Paper presented at the Ethnography in Education Research Forum, University of Pennsylvania, Philadelphia

Freedman S, Jackson J, Boles K 1983 Teaching: An imperilled "profession." In: Shulman L S, Sykes G (eds.) 1983 *Handbook of Teaching and Policy.* Longman, New York

Harding S 1991 *Whose Science? Whose Knowledge? Thinking from Women's Lives.* Cornell University Press, Ithaca, New York

Hollingsworth S 1992 Learning to teach literacy through

collaborative conversation: A feminist approach. *Am. Educ. Res. J.* 29(2): 373–404.

Hopkins D 1985 *A Teacher's Guide to Classroom Research*. Taylor and Francis, London

Kemmis S, McTaggert R 1988 *The Action Research Planner*, 3rd edn. Deakin University Press, Geelong, Victoria

Lampert M 1989 Research into practice: Arithmetic as problem solving. *Arithmetic Teacher* 36(7): 34–36

Lourde A 1984 *Sister Outsider*. The Crossing Press, Freedom, California

Lewin K 1946 Action research and minority problems *J. Soc. Iss.* 2(4): 24–46.

McIntosh P, Style E, Tsugawa T 1992 *Teacher as Researcher*. National SEED Seeking Educational Equity and Diversity, Wellesley College Center for Research on Women, Wellesley, Massachusetts

McKernan J 1991 *Curriculum Action Research: A Handbook of Methods and Resources for the Reflective Practitioner*. St. Martin's Press, New York

Newman J D (ed.) 1990 *Finding our Own Way: Teachers Exploring their Assumptions*. Heinemann, Portsmouth, New Hampshire

Oja S N, Smulyan L (eds.) 1989 *Collaborative Action Research: A Developmental Process*. Falmer Press, London

Philadelphia Teachers' Learning Cooperative 1984 On becoming teacher experts: Buying time. *Lang. Arts* 61(7): 731–36

Posch P 1992 Teacher research and teacher professionalism. Paper presented at the Int. Conf. Teacher Research, Stanford University, Palo Alto, California

Schecter S R 1992 Ideological divergences in teacher research groups. Paper presented at the Ethnography in Education Research Forum, University of Pennsylvania, Philadelphia

Schwab J 1983 The practical 4: Something for curriculum professors to do. *Curric. Inq.* 13(3): 239–65.

Simons H 1992 Teacher research and teacher professionalism. Paper presented at the Int Conf Teacher Research, Stanford University, Palo Alto, California

Smith H, Wigginton E, Hocking K, Jones R E 1991 Foxfire teacher networks. In: Lieberman A, Miller L (eds.) 1991 *Staff Development for Education in the 1990's: New Demands, New Realities, New Perspectives*, 2nd edn. Teachers College Press, New York

Sockett H 1989 Practical professionalism. In: Cass W (ed.) 1989 *Quality in Teaching*. Falmer Press, New York

Stenhouse L 1983 Research as a basis for teaching. In: Stenhouse L (ed.) 1983 *Authority, Education and Emancipation*. Heinemann, Portsmouth, New Hampshire

Tyler R W 1949 *Basic Principles of Curriculum and Instruction*. University of Chicago Press, Chicago, Illinois

Weiner G 1989 Professional self-knowledge versus social justice: A critical analysis of the teacher- researcher movement. *Brit. Educ. Res. J.* 15(1): 41–51

Winter R 1987 *Action-research and the Nature of Social Inquiry: Professional Innovation and Educational Work*. Gower, Brookfield, Vermont

Zeichner K M 1990 Contradictions and tensions in the professionalization of teaching and the democratization of schools. *Teach. Col. Rec.* 92: 363–379

(b) A Psychological View of Teachers

Teachers' Knowledge

P. L. Grossman

While researchers have long been interested in issues related to teachers' knowledge, research in this area has proliferated in the decade from 1983 through 1992. As research on teaching moved from investigations of teacher behavior to considerations of the thinking and decision-making that accompany action, questions concerning the knowledge and beliefs that inform teachers' decision-making quickly arose. Issues related to what teachers know, how they acquire and store that knowledge, and how knowledge informs classroom practice are central to the work of all concerned with the initial preparation and continuing professional development of teachers.

The renewed interest in teachers' knowledge also parallels the movement within several countries to transform teaching into a recognized profession. Evidence of a specialized knowledge base necessary for the work of professionals is one hallmark of a profession. The interest in teacher knowledge since the early 1980s is motivated by practical, political, and academic concerns. Teachers' knowledge has been examined in terms of its domains, its forms or structures, and its relation to classroom practice. This entry will address these areas separately, although many of the issues are interrelated.

1. Domains of Teacher Knowledge

A number of researchers have proposed frameworks for domains of teacher knowledge (Carter 1990, Leinhardt and Smith 1985, Wilson et al. 1987). Although represented as discrete domains in these frameworks, the knowledge domains are usually regarded as interwoven in practice. One possible typology of teacher knowledge includes six domains: (a) knowledge of content, (b) knowledge of learners and learning, (c) knowledge of general pedagogy, (d) knowledge of curriculum, (e) knowledge of context, and (f) knowledge of self.

Content knowledge includes both subject matter knowledge and more explicitly pedagogical knowledge of the subject matter, termed "pedagogical content knowledge." Knowledge of learners and learning includes knowledge of learning theories; the physical, social, psychological, and cognitive development of students; motivational theory and practice; and ethnic, socioeconomic, and gender diversity among students. Knowledge of general pedagogy includes knowledge of classroom organization and management, and general methods of teaching. Curricular knowledge includes knowledge both of the processes of curriculum development and of the school curriculum within and across grade levels.

Knowledge of context includes knowledge of the multiple and embedded situations and settings within which teachers work, including the school, district, or area, and state or region. Knowledge of context also includes teachers' knowledge of their students and their families, as well as the local community. It can also include knowledge of the historical, philosophical, and cultural foundations of education within a particular country. Finally, knowledge of self includes teachers' knowledge of their personal values, dispositions, strengths, and weaknesses, and their educational philosophy, goals for students, and purposes for teaching.

While all of these domains are important to the work of teachers, research has concentrated on content knowledge, general pedagogical knowledge, and knowledge of self. For example, while much research within educational psychology has focused on topics related to learners and learning, relatively few studies have looked directly at what teachers know or believe in this area. For this reason, this entry will include discussions of the three domains in which the most research exists.

1.1 Knowledge of Content

While subject matter knowledge seems intuitively important for good teaching, early correlational research did not find a relationship between teachers' knowledge and student achievement. Later researchers critiqued the lack of conceptual frameworks to guide this early work and turned their attention to the relationships between teachers' subject matter knowledge and the processes of planning and instruction (Leinhardt and Smith 1985, Shulman 1987). This line of predominantly qualitative research suggests that teachers' knowledge of the content they teach affects both what teachers teach and how they teach it.

In developing curriculum for students, teachers are likely to emphasize those areas in which they are more knowledgeable and to avoid or de-emphasize the areas in which they have relatively less content knowledge (Carlsen 1991, Smith and Neale 1991). Teachers' content knowledge may also influence how they exploit the curriculum potential of a subject (Ben-Peretz 1975, Gudmundsdottir 1990, Wilson and Wineburg 1988). For example, studies of secondary-school social studies teachers have demonstrated how teachers' own disciplinary backgrounds affect how they adapt a given curriculum to match their own disciplinary knowledge (Wilson and Wineburg 1988).

Teachers' content knowledge also influences their interactive teaching. Teachers' knowledge of subject matter affects how they represent the nature of knowing within a content area to their students. Ball (1991), for example, demonstrated that teachers with relatively weak conceptual understanding of mathematics are likely to represent the nature of mathematical knowing as arbitrary and rule bound. Teachers' content knowledge also influences their ability to construct new explanations or activities for students (Leinhardt and Smith 1985, Smith and Neale 1991), as well as the kinds of questions they ask students (Carlsen 1991, Hashweh 1987). For example, in a study of beginning science teachers, Carlsen (1991) found that teachers were more likely to ask cognitively lower level questions in areas in which they were less knowledgeable and higher level questions in those areas where they felt themselves to be knowledgeable.

Studies of teachers' subject matter knowledge also revealed that teachers possess pedagogical knowledge of the content they teach, termed "pedagogical content knowledge" (Shulman 1987). Research on pedagogical content knowledge has examined teachers' beliefs and conceptions regarding purposes for teaching subject matter, their knowledge of students' understandings and misunderstandings of particular topics within a subject matter, and their curricular and instructional knowledge related to specific content. Research in this area suggests that teachers' pedagogical content knowledge is related to teachers' planning and to classroom instruction. Most researchers found a great deal of congruence between teachers' own conceptions of the purposes for teaching a subject and their instructional practice, especially in the case of experienced teachers. Work in mathematics also suggests a tentative link between teachers' pedagogical content knowledge and student learning (Peterson et al. 1991).

1.2 Knowledge of General Pedagogy

Knowledge of general pedagogy includes knowledge about classroom organization and management, general knowledge of lesson structure, and general methods of teaching. Researchers in the area of classroom knowledge have focused on teachers' efforts to establish and maintain order in the classroom during the process of instruction. Successful classroom managers are teachers who are more attuned to student signals and conscious of the overall flow and purpose of classroom activity (Carter 1990). In addition, effective teachers swiftly establish routines for classroom activities at the beginning of the school year (Leinhardt et al. 1987).

Related to work on teachers' routines is teachers' general knowledge of lesson structure, which includes the knowledge necessary to plan and teach lessons, to make smooth transitions between different components of a lesson, and to present clear explanations of content (Leinhardt and Smith 1985). While this kind of knowledge has been designated as general, it is possible that knowledge of lesson structure is implicitly tied to the content to be taught.

Finally, work on expertise in teaching suggests that experienced teachers process information about classrooms differently than do novices (Berliner 1986). For example, when shown slides of classroom activities, the experienced teachers were more likely to identify patterns and to make inferences about the activities they observed than were novices, who provided more literal and superficial descriptions of the activities.

Much of this work has focused more on what teachers do in classrooms and how they process information than what they know explicitly or implicitly about classroom organization and management. Some researchers have explored the relationship between classroom management and teachers' implicit metaphors regarding the role of the teacher. These researchers argue that changes in teachers' classroom management must begin with reconsiderations of these underlying metaphors.

Relatively little work has investigated teachers' knowledge of various instructional strategies or methods of teaching. One line of correlational research on teaching has attempted to isolate general teaching strategies used by effective teachers (Brophy and Good 1986). While this research has produced a set of generalizations about the correlations between particular teaching behaviors and student achievement, it did not investigate what teachers knew or believed that led them to adopt such strategies. Studies of teacher planning suggest that teachers organize their planning around the development of classroom activities (Clark and Peterson 1986), but little research has investigated how teachers think specifically about issues of method in teaching.

Some researchers have argued that teachers' knowledge of teaching methods is organized into curriculum scripts for particular topics (Putnam 1987); both the content and method of teaching are included in these scripts. The European tradition of *Didaktik* also emphasizes the integration of curriculum and method in teacher thinking (Hopmann 1992). Knowledge of teaching method may be filtered through teachers' understanding of the particular content to be taught and their own goals for teaching that content, suggesting an overlap between pedagogical content knowledge and this aspect of general pedagogical knowledge.

1.3 Knowledge of Self

In an early study of teacher knowledge, Elbaz (1983) identified knowledge of self as an important facet of teachers' practical knowledge. This knowledge of self includes teachers' awareness of their own values, goals, philosophies, styles, personal characteristics, strengths, and weaknesses as they relate to teaching. Some researchers have described how teachers draw upon and use this personal knowledge to negotiate classroom dilemmas and to reflect upon their practice (Lampert 1985). Others have documented how issues of self and identity are implicated in the process of learning to teach (Britzman 1986) and how teachers' personal values underlie other forms of knowledge such as pedagogical content knowledge (Gudmundsdottir 1990). Work on teachers' metaphors also stresses the importance of teachers' implicit beliefs in understanding how teachers view their own practice (Munby 1986).

Knowledge of self differs in important ways from the knowledge domains discussed above as it represents neither theoretical nor abstract knowledge, but a more personal and inevitably idiosyncratic domain. Work on many domains of teacher knowledge suggests that abstract or theoretical knowledge about teaching is filtered through teachers' own values, goals, and personal philosophies, leading some researchers to argue that all aspects of teacher knowledge are grounded in personal perspectives and experience (Clandinin and Connelly 1987). This line of research suggests the importance of individual biography in the process of teaching and learning to teach.

1.4 Integration of Knowledge Domains and the Creation of New Knowledge

While each knowledge domain has been addressed separately for analytic purposes, in actual use by teachers, these domains are not as clearly distinguishable. For example, lesson structure knowledge, categorized under general pedagogical knowledge, intersects with pedagogical content knowledge in determining particular content to be taught. Curricular knowledge, pedagogical content knowledge, and general pedagogical knowledge all play a role in creating curriculum scripts for particular topics. The need for teachers to draw from and integrate a number of knowledge domains under conditions of uncertainty has impor-

tant implications for teacher learning. Teaching these knowledge domains in isolation from one another may misrepresent the interconnected quality of knowledge use, posing difficulties for teachers who must integrate these various domains in practice.

Work on teacher knowledge also reveals its dynamic nature. Teachers' knowledge is not static. In the process of teaching and reflecting upon teaching, teachers develop new understandings of the content, of learners, and of themselves. While teachers can acquire knowledge from a wide variety of sources, they also create new knowledge within the crucible of the classroom. Because teaching has lacked a method for capturing and recording such knowledge, both researchers and practitioners have turned their attention to documenting the wisdom of practice of experienced teachers.

2. Forms of Teacher Knowledge and Relation to Classroom Practice

Researchers have argued about the various forms of teachers' knowledge; some researchers argue for the need for generalizable knowledge of principles of teaching and learning, while others contend that teachers' knowledge is inherently situational and personal, stored in the tacit forms of metaphors or images or the more explicit forms of stories or cases. In describing different potential forms for teachers' knowledge, this section uses Bruner's (1986) distinction between paradigmatic and narrative ways of knowing to describe at least two general forms of teacher knowledge.

Paradigmatic ways of knowing emphasize generalizable laws and principles applicable across a wide variety of contexts. Knowledge within the natural sciences has been described as paradigmatic knowledge. In contrast, narrative ways of knowing are more contextualized and situation-specific. Research on teaching has experienced a shift from the search for paradigmatic knowledge to an interest in narrative knowledge, a shift that has affected research on teacher knowledge.

2.1 Paradigmatic Forms of Knowledge

Some researchers on teaching have argued that teachers need to possess scientific principles regarding teaching, knowledge that has proved to be applicable across different contexts and settings (Gage 1978). These researchers stress the power of propositional knowledge about teaching and learning. Such principles might consist of propositions regarding the importance of "wait-time" for encouraging higher-order thinking, for example. These principles could be derived from large-scale research programs on effective teaching (e.g., Brophy and Good 1986) and taught directly to teachers.

Some researchers in this area have argued that research knowledge can directly affect practice by providing teachers with new principles or rules of practice to use in their own teaching. A number of experimental studies have attempted to teach experienced teachers such generalizable principles derived from correlational classroom research. While many of the studies were successful in the short run, there is little evidence that teachers continued to implement these principles of teaching over time.

Alternative ways in which paradigmatic knowledge can inform practice have also been suggested. Some researchers have argued that results of research on teaching can inform teachers' reasoning about classroom actions rather than dictate teachers' instructional practice (Fenstermacher 1986). Knowledge gained from research can influence classroom practice by influencing teachers' beliefs or by introducing new knowledge and beliefs into teachers' reasoning. Theoretical knowledge thus becomes one, but not the sole, source of knowledge that can guide teachers' curricular and instructional decision-making. A number of studies of knowledge use suggest that teachers sift generalizable principles through the filter of their own perspectives and situations; thus, this approach to using research knowledge may show promise for understanding the relationship between propositional knowledge and classroom practice.

2.2 Narrative Forms of Knowledge

Another line of work rejects the idea of generalizable knowledge and argues that teachers' knowledge is inherently personal and organized in terms of stories or narratives (Clandinin and Connelly 1987, Elbaz 1991). These researchers believe that teachers' knowledge can be best understood through their own stories of teaching, which preserve both the teachers' voice and perspective. Researchers in the area of personal practical knowledge argue that much of teachers' knowledge is inherently tacit, contained within the rituals, routines, and cycles that comprise teachers' work, and embedded within particular local contexts.

From this perspective, knowledge is embodied within classroom practice; distinctions between knowledge and classroom practice are not clear-cut. Others acknowledge a distinction between knowledge and practice, but argue that practice informs knowledge as much as knowledge influences practice. Studies of personal practical knowledge are not intended to inform as much as to illuminate classroom practice from teachers' perspectives. While narratives of personal practical knowledge offer a way of making sense of individual teachers' practice, readers can learn from these narratives through reflecting upon similar issues that arise in their own practice.

Another form of narrative knowledge might take the form of case knowledge, knowledge composed of experiences with a number of cases of particular pedagogical situations (Shulman 1991). Like personal practical knowledge, case knowledge is inherently situational and contextual. Researchers who study knowledge acquisition in ill-structured domains such as medicine or teaching believe that knowledge in these areas is organized into networks of concepts and cases. More general concepts are embedded within specific instances from actual practice. Practitioners within these ill-structured domains must integrate multiple knowledge domains in constantly shifting circumstances. From their experiences in classrooms, teachers construct a contextual understanding of classroom situations that allows them to recognize familiar features of new situations. The process of reasoning from case knowledge, then, is likely to be analogical.

Like personal practical knowledge, case knowledge has usually been represented in narrative form. However, most of these case narratives have explicitly pedagogical purposes. Advocates of case-based methods in teacher education stress the usefulness of cases in learning to teach. Cases can inform practice by offering precedents for handling particular pedagogical situations. The use of case methods can also develop pedagogical ways of reasoning, according to advocates. Most researchers in this area stress the importance of using multiple cases of a similar phenomenon to illustrate more accurately the complexity of practice.

3. The Future of Research on Teacher Knowledge

Research on teacher knowledge has clear implications for teacher education and continuing professional development. What teachers need to know and how they can best construct this knowledge are central questions facing policymakers and teacher educators alike. Considerations of the content, form, and sources of teacher knowledge are likely to become increasingly important as efforts to reform teacher education and to create a teaching profession gain momentum.

Future research will need to investigate further all of the domains of teacher knowledge, including the areas of curricular knowledge, knowledge of learners and learning, and knowledge of educational contexts. While work has been done in each of these areas, questions regarding issues such as what teachers know about motivating students, for example, remain unanswered. Documenting teachers' existing knowledge in all of the domains is essential, as teachers' prior knowledge and belief are likely to influence their future acquisition of knowledge.

Future research will also need to study the connections among teacher knowledge, school context, and student learning. Much of the research on teachers' subject matter knowledge, for example, has investigated the relationship between teachers' knowledge of the content and the processes of planning and instruction, but, with a few exceptions, has stopped short of looking for connections to student learning. As research provides increasingly sophisticated approaches to the assessment of student learning, the connection between teachers' and students' understandings may be studied more effectively.

Finally, research on teacher knowledge must continue to be informed by ongoing explorations into the nature of knowledge and cognition. Work in cognitive psychology and anthropology has demonstrated the contextual nature of cognition, a finding that has direct implications for investigations of teacher knowledge. Work on knowledge acquisition in ill-structured domains also holds implications for research on teacher knowledge. Theorists from both critical and feminist theory pose epistemological issues with which future research must grapple. Finally, work on the narrative aspects of cognition is likely to continue to inform research on teacher knowledge.

See also: Case Methods in Teacher Education; Teachers' Beliefs and Belief Systems

References

Ball D L 1991 Research on teaching mathematics: Making subject matter knowledge part of the equation. In: Brophy J. (ed.) 1991
Ben-Peretz M 1975 The concept of curriculum potential. *Curric. Theo.* 5: 151–59
Berliner D C 1986 In pursuit of the expert pedagogue. *Educ. Researcher* 15(7): 5–13
Britzman D P 1986 Cultural myths in the making of a teacher: Biography and social structure in teacher education. *Harv. Educ. Rev.* 56(4): 442–56
Brophy J E, Good T L 1986 Teacher behavior and student achievement. In: Wittrock M (ed.) 1986 *Handbook of Research on Teaching*, 3rd edn. Macmillan, New York
Bruner J 1986 *Actual Minds, Possible Worlds.* Harvard University Press, Cambridge, Massachusetts
Carlsen W S 1991 Subject matter knowledge and science teaching: A pragmatic perspective. In: Brophy J (ed.) 1991
Carter K 1990 Teachers' knowledge and learning to teach. In: Houston W R (ed.) 1990 *Handbook of Research on Teacher Education.* Macmillan, New York
Clandinin D J, Connelly M F 1987 Teachers' personal knowledge: What counts as personal in studies of the personal. *J. Curric. St.* 19(6): 487–500
Clark C M, Peterson P L 1986 Teachers' thought processes. In: Wittrock M (ed.) 1986 *Handbook of Research on Teaching*, 3rd edn. Macmillan, New York
Elbaz F 1983 *Teacher Thinking: A Study of Practical Knowledge.* Croom Helm, London
Elbaz F 1991 Research on teachers' knowledge: The evolution of a discourse. *J. Curric. St.* 23(1): 1–19
Fenstermacher G D 1986 Philosophy of research on teaching: Three aspects. In: Wittrock M (ed.) 1986 *Handbook of Research on Teaching*, 3rd edn. Macmillan, New York
Gage N L 1978 *The Scientific Basis of the Art of Teaching.*

Teachers College Press, New York
Gudmundsdottir S 1990 Values in pedagogical content knowledge. *J. Teach. Educ.* 41(3): 44–52
Hashweh M Z 1987 Effects of subject matter knowledge in the teaching of biology and physics. *Teach. Teach. Educ.* 3(2): 109–20
Hopmann S 1992 Starting a dialogue: Roots and issues of the beginning conversation between European didaktik and the American curriculum tradition. Paper presented at the annual meeting of the American Educational Research Association, San Francisco, California
Lampert M 1985 How do teachers manage to teach? Perspectives on problems in practice. *Harv. Educ. Rev.* 55(2): 178–94
Leinhardt G, Smith D A 1985 Expertise in mathematics instruction: Subject matter knowledge. *J. Educ. Psychol.* 77(3): 247–71
Leinhardt G, Weidman C, Hammond K M 1987 Introduction and integration of classroom routines by expert teachers. *Curric. Inq.* 17(2): 135–76
Munby H 1986 Metaphor in the thinking of teachers: An exploratory study. *J. Curric. St.* 18(2): 197–209
Peterson P L, Fennema E, Carpenter T P 1991 Teachers' knowledge of students' mathematics problem-solving knowledge. In: Brophy J (ed.) 1991
Putnam R T 1987 Structuring and adjusting content for students: A study of live and simulated tutoring of addition. *Am. Educ. Res. J.* 24(1): 13–48
Shulman L S 1987 Knowledge and teaching: Foundations of the new reform. *Harv. Educ. Rev.* 57(1): 1–22
Shulman L S 1991 Toward a pedagogy of cases. In: Shulman J (ed.) 1991 *Case Methods in Teacher Education.* Teachers College Press, New York
Smith D C, Neale D C 1991 The construction of subject-matter knowledge in primary science teaching. In: Brophy J. (ed.) 1991
Wilson S M, Shulman L S, Richert A E 1987 150 different ways of knowing: Representations of knowledge in teaching. In: Calderhead J (ed.) 1987 *Exploring Teachers' Thinking.* Cassell Education, London
Wilson S M, Wineburg S S 1988 Peering at history through different lenses: The role of disciplinary perspectives in teaching history. *Teach. Coll. Rec.* 89(4): 525–39

Further Reading

Britzman D P 1991 *Practice Makes Practice: A Critical Study of Learning to Teach.* SUNY Press, Albany, New York
Brophy J (ed.) 1991 *Advances in Research on Teaching, Volume 2: Teachers' Knowledge of Subject Matter as it Relates to their Teaching Practice.* JAI Press, Greenwich, Connecticut
Calderhead J (ed.) 1991 *Teachers' Professional Learning.* Falmer Press, London
Grossman P L 1990 *The Making of a Teacher: Teacher Knowledge and Teacher Education.* Teachers College Press, New York
Shulman J (ed.) 1991 *Case Methods in Teacher Education.* Teachers College Press, New York

Teachers' Beliefs and Belief Systems

J. H. Block and K. Hazelip

As developing and developed nations struggle with political, social, economic, and environmental problems, they typically call on their schools to provide solutions. During the late 1980s and early 1990s, these calls have taken the form of school reform or restructuring efforts which have sent educational researchers scurrying to find some magic reform/restructuring "pills."

Many researchers have responded by searching for ways of generating greater *skill* among teachers. A few veterans of past reform/restructuring efforts, though, have responded differently, turning their attention to the generation of greater "will" instead. These researchers (e.g., Sarason 1983) have especially focused their attention on teachers' beliefs and on how these beliefs shape school reform/restructuring attitudes, intentions, and actions.

1. The Nature of Beliefs

Beliefs convey ". . . the information that a person has regarding some attribute of an object . . . the object of a belief may be a person, a group of people, an institution, a behavior, a policy, and event, etc., and the associated attribute may be any object, trait, property, quality, characteristic, outcome or event" (Fishbein and Ajzen 1975 p. 12). In understanding the role of beliefs in the school reform/restructuring process, three things must be remembered. First, beliefs vary in strength depending on just how sure the person is that a particular object does indeed possess a certain attribute. Some teacher beliefs, especially about students and their learning, may be held so strongly that they are difficult, if not impossible, to change. Second, beliefs vary in kind: descriptive beliefs come from personal observation; inferential beliefs come from inferences about these observations; and informational beliefs come from outside sources. Descriptive beliefs, since they are rooted in teacher's school experience, are most resistant to change. Third, beliefs begin to cluster over time around related beliefs and form a system or network. Once such a belief system is formed, change in one teacher belief may be difficult or impossible without change in the system of which the belief is now a part.

2. Teacher's Beliefs

The best-known research on teachers' beliefs has focused largely on teachers' inferential beliefs about student success or failure in classroom achievement settings. Clark and Peterson (1986), for instance, have focused on teacher attributions for the causes of their students' achievement and teacher beliefs about their responsibility for students' success or failure. Considerations of student ability and effort, of the learning task, and of luck influence teacher attributions, and issues of teacher egos influence their responsibility beliefs. Some teachers—ego-servers—believe that they are responsible for their students' successes and not their failures. Other teachers—ego-protectors—believe the reverse.

Teacher beliefs about student ability and effort, and about serving or protecting thier own egos, are central not only to the literature on student achievement but on student motivation to achieve as well (see Stipek 1992). Many teachers apparently believe that ability should predominate over effort in school achievement settings. Indeed, they believe that children enter school with a childish conception of ability, where effort counts, that must be replaced with a more mature conception, where ability and effort have been separated and only ability reigns. Again, these teachers' beliefs about the primacy of ability allow teachers to ego-serve by demonstrating high ability themselves or to ego-protect by not demonstrating low ability (Ames and Ames 1984). In such ability-centered classrooms, teachers can brush aside low-ability students and concentrate on their more able peers.

Most of the literature on teacher beliefs and belief systems suffers from three basic problems. First, it is ethnocentric; much of it comes from Western, developed nations, especially the United States. Second, the literature rarely gets past teachers' inferential beliefs to their descriptive ones; too much of it, to use the language of ethnographers, is outsider or "etic" and not enough is insider or "emic". A third problem is that the literature tends to focus on teacher beliefs and belief systems about a small portion of their job; while issues of the management of student learning and classroom achievement are high on most teachers' daily planning list, issues of the management of learners and classroom discipline often are even higher.

Fortunately, work is beginning to appear that addresses each of these problems. On the ethnocentric front, writing has emerged that supplements the Western, industrialized belief literature. Thomas, for example, has companioned his volume on comparative theories of Western child development (Thomas 1992) with one on theories of eastern child development (Thomas 1988). Such supplementation seems especially important in light of cross-national work beginning to challenge the cross-cultural validity of findings from the central paradigm underlying Western teacher belief and belief systems research, namely, the paradigm of attribution theory. Apparently effort is much more highly valued by teachers in the East than by those in the West (Stevenson and Steigler 1992).

On the etic–emic front, culture of teaching scholars such as Feinman-Nemser and Floden (1986) have turned their attention to teachers' descriptive beliefs. The work of the Israeli scholar Freema Elbaz (1991) in giving voice to teachers' practical knowledge is illustrative. Elbaz has suggested, among other things, that teachers have various categories of practical knowledge involving self, milieu, subject matter, curriculum development, and instruction which they use to understand and structure their classrooms. This information is then organized in a hierarchy with general rules of practice (actions) at the bottom, practical principles (thoughts about actions) in the middle, and images (purposes for actions) at the top. Teachers' descriptive beliefs play a central role in shaping their images and, hence, their practical principles and rules.

Finally, on the job front, teacher education scholars (e.g., Lanier and Little 1986) and especially sociologists of teaching (e.g., Rosenholtz 1991) have begun to build a framework for understanding teacher beliefs more broadly. Working under the assumption that the nature of teacher's work shapes the nature of their beliefs, these scholars have focused on understanding the nature of teaching as an occupation. It is a complex and uncertain occupation, one given to the inculcation of beliefs that promote continuity and discourage change.

3. Sociology of Teaching and Teacher Beliefs

The picture that educational sociologists paint, at least of teachers in the United States, differs little in broad respects from that crafted by Waller (1932). Waller captured the basic work of teachers as involving the transmission of core cultural values to students whom the teachers believed were uncouth. Since students were believed inclined to resist these transmissions, the essence of teaching became a form of daily institutional dominance—convincing young wills to bend to older wisdom.

Building on the work of Dreeben (1970) and Lortie (1975), for instance, scholars have attempted to identify some of the core values transmitted by teachers in United States schools and some of the institutional constraints they face as they try to inculcate these values in their charges. Values such as achievement, individualism, universalism, and particularism still are transmitted in classrooms. Moreover, they still are transmitted in a climate where teachers feel internal pressure to get students to learn and external pressure to get them to be compliant (Cusick 1983). Maintain-

ing some semblance of balance between their internal hopes and their external reality generate ego issues of anxiety, self-doubt, and vulnerability (Doyle 1986).

Naturally, many teachers might turn to practices for transmitting these values that help them allay these ego issues. Classroom practices based on the belief that student ability should be the *sine qua non* of classroom life, practices such as competition and tracking (Oakes 1985), would certainly be appealing. High-ability students are believed to pose fewer behavioral and intellectual demands than students of lower ability (Cooper and Tom 1984), so by identifying students of high and low ability and by encouraging the initiations of the former and discouraging those of the latter, teachers could essentially create more ego-protective and, possibly, ego-serving classroom conditions. They also could gain some invulnerability with respect to the more problematic sociorelational aspects of their job, concentrate on its learning aspects, and lay claim to whatever psychic rewards that the learning of their more able students might provide.

Other sociologists have also begun to provide still larger frameworks for the study of teacher beliefs and belief systems. One especially relevant framework generalizes the analysis of scholars such as Lortie, who have compared teaching to other professions, by comparing it to other classes of occupations. In this framework, teachers are looked at as workers, broadly speaking, and scholars focus on the nature of their work and work-related beliefs. Some of these scholars are especially concerned with how teacher work and work-related beliefs shape the nature of their students' work and work-related beliefs. Since teachers are in some sense a student's first boss, the scholars in this framework want to know what kind of boss they are.

Anyon (1981), for instance, has examined the socialization of students by teachers in working-class schools where the majority of working parents were in unskilled and semi-skilled occupations; in middle-class schools where the parents were a mixture of highly skilled blue collar and white collar workers plus public school teachers, social workers, accountants, and middle managers; in an affluent professional school where most parents were highly paid doctors, television or advertising executives, and interior designers; and in an executive elite school where parents were at least vice presidents in multinational corporations or financial firms. Anyon found that students in each school type were socialized to appropriate social class conceptions of ownership of physical and cultural capital, of the structure of authority at work and in society, and of the content and process of one's own work activity. Such findings once again suggest that it makes sense for teachers to believe that their classroom work should be organized along ability lines. Higher-class occupations do seem to make greater demands on student's abilities than do lower-class ones. In emphasizing ability, therefore, the teacher is simply doing his or her cultural transmission job by reproducing the real world of work outside schools and bringing it inside.

Anyon's findings, however, add an important caveat to this sense-making process: the belief in ability alone may prepare students for at best middle-class work. Beliefs in other things—creativity and individualism or effort and social responsibility—are required to build students for professional and elite jobs respectively, so it makes sense to build classrooms on bases other than or in addition to ability.

4. Educational Researcher and Teachers' Beliefs

This entry has suggested that researchers are turning their attention to beliefs as one "magic pill" in the search for better school. Some of the frameworks they are using to study teacher beliefs and belief systems were mentioned. Thus far, these frameworks indicate that Western teachers, at least, believe and have reason to believe that their classrooms be organized primarily around student ability. Such classroom organization seems to serve or protect their egos.

Since serious research has begun comparatively recently, the picture drawn of teacher ability-oriented, ego-centered beliefs and belief systems is simplistic. Much remains to be studied regarding the what and why, not only of Western teachers' beliefs and belief systems but other teacher's beliefs and belief systems as well. Much remains to be studied especially from the perspective of the teachers themselves. In both respects, the work of scholars such as Elbaz (1991) who are striving to suggest ways to give teachers worldwide a "voice," especially a critical one, in describing what they do and why they do it in their schools, is welcomed.

It would be remiss, though, to leave researchers with the impression that the matter of better articulating teacher beliefs and belief systems lies solely in their skills at giving practitioners a voice. Researchers need a voice for talking to practitioners. The reason is simple. Teachers' beliefs and belief systems are grounded in their personal experiences and, hence, are highly resistant to change. Typically, though, these experiences are a byproduct of the school context in which they work. If school practitioners are not given outside information about this context that can help them be critical of their past experiences or about new contexts that portend some new experiences entirely, then the risk is that research will actually reify that context rather than reform or restructure it.

This reification-of-context process seems well underway in the early 1990s in the United States as mainstream scholars repeatedly report that teachers' belief systems remain closed especially around issues of student ability and control (Cusick 1983). Other scholars have repeatedly indicted such beliefs as not a solution for, but a cause of, the school reform/re-

structuring predicament. They have shown beliefs in ability to have constructive learning and motivational consequences for a few students and destructive ones for many. They also have suggested that beliefs in control assuage teachers' egos at the expense of most childrens' egos (Glasser 1990).

These latter scholars need to be heard. Part of a strategy in finding a voice for communicating with teachers must be rhetorical. It has long been known that the beliefs about student ability and control may be flawed. However researchers have avoided sharing that knowledge with teachers in ways that they can understand and appreciate. Floden (1985) has suggested some useful initial ideas for better shaping researchers' rhetoric so that their voices can and will be heard.

However, the larger part of a strategy in changing teacher beliefs and belief systems about student ability and control must be substantive. Rhetoric must be used to help conjure up alternative conceptions of schooling where factors other than ability, like effort, really count. Central to such conceptions will be systematic, informational belief work to examine and, where necessary, challenge teachers' descriptive and inferential beliefs about students and their learning and motivation to learn.

5. Conclusion

While Arthur Foshay (1973) was perhaps the first veteran United States school reformer to recognize that implicit beliefs and belief systems about the child and his or her learning power, it was his colleague, Benjamin Bloom (1976) who perhaps first reminded researchers that they have their implicit beliefs and belief systems about the child and his or her learning power.

Bloom summarized some of these beliefs and belief systems in the preface to his landmark volume *Human Characteristics and School Learning* as follows:

When I first entered the field of educational research and measurement, the prevailing construct was:

1. There are good learners and there are poor learners.

This was considered to be a relatively permanent attribute of the individual. It was also the prevailing view that individuals possessed it in different amounts and that a quantitative index of it could be made by the use of an appropriate intelligence, aptitude, or achievement test. Furthermore, it was believed that good learners could learn the more complex and abstract ideas, while poor learners could learn only the simplest and most concrete ideas. School systems throughout the world have been organized on the basis of this construct and the selection systems, grading systems, and even the curriculum has been built on the basis of it.

During the early 1960s, some of us became interested in

the Caroll Model of School Learning, which was built on the construct:

2. There are faster learners and there are slower learners.

While we were not entirely clear whether or not rate of learning was a permanent trait of individuals, we dedicated ourselves to finding ways by which the slower learners could be given the extra **time and help** they needed to attain some criterion of achievement. In this research, in both educational laboratories as well as classrooms in different nations, it became evident that a large proportion of slower learners may learn as well as faster learners. When the slower learners do succeed in attaining the same criterion of achievement as faster learners, they appear to be able to learn equally complex and abstract ideas, they can apply these ideas to new problems, and they can retain the ideas equally well—in spite of the fact that they learned with more time and help than was given to others. Furthermore, their interests and attitudes toward the school subjects in which they attain the achievement criterion are as positive as those of faster learners.

During the past decade, my students and I have done research which has led us to the view that:

3. Most students become very similar with regard to learning ability, rate of learning, and motivation for further learning—when provided with favorable learning conditions.

This research questions the first two constructs, especially about the permanence of good–poor learning ability or fast–slow learning characteristics. However, the research does demonstrate that when students are provided with unfavorable learning conditions, they become even more dissimilar with regard to learning ability, rate of learning, and motivation for further learning . . . It is this research which we believe has profound consequences for the prevailing views about human nature, human characteristics, and school learning. (Bloom 1976 pp. ix–x)

As Bloom's quote suggests, beliefs about students and their individual differences, especially their differences in ability, once dominated the thinking of educational researchers. In the early 1990s, beliefs about students and their individual sameness, especially their sameness in ability and in motivation to learn, are beginning to be recognized.

Education researchers can play a role in coaxing these beliefs from the sidelines of thinking about school reform and restructuring worldwide to center stage. After all, beliefs in the potential of virtually all students to learn as well as the best students do offers schooling possibilities for the many students that were once reserved for only the few. Attention to the many rather than the few makes moral sense.

See also: Mastery Learning; Evaluating

References

Anyon J 1981 Social class and school knowledge. *Curric. Inq.* 11: 1–42

Ames C, Ames R 1984 Systems of student and teacher motivation: Toward a qualitative definition. *J. Educ. Psychol.* 76(4): 535–56

Bloom B S 1976 *Human Characteristics and School Learning*. McGraw-Hill, New York

Clark C M, Peterson P L 1986 Teachers' thought processes. In: Wittrock M C (ed.) 1986 *Handbook of Research on Teaching*, 3rd edn. Macmillan, New York

Cooper H M, Tom D Y H 1984 Teacher expectation research: A review with implications for classroom instruction. *Elem. Sch. J.* 85: 77–104

Cusick P 1983 *The Egalitarian Ideal and the American High School. Studies of Three Schools.* Longman, New York

Doyle W 1986 Classroom organization and management. In: Wittrock M C (ed.) 1986 *Handbook of Research on Teaching*, 3rd edn. Macmillan, New York

Dreeben R 1970 *The Nature of Teaching, Schools and the Work of Teachers.* Scott-Foresman, Glenview, Illinois

Elbaz F 1991 Research on teachers' knowledge: The evolution of a discourse. *J. Curric. Stud.* 23: 1–19

Feinman-Nemser S, Floden R E 1986 The cultures of teaching. In: Wittrock M C (ed.) 1986 *Handbook of Research on Teaching*, 3rd edn. Macmillan, New York

Fishbein M, Ajzen I 1975 *Belief, Attitude, Intention, and Behavior.* Addison-Wesley, Reading, Massachusetts

Floden R E 1985 The role of rhetoric in changing teachers' beliefs. *Teaching and Teacher Education* 1: 19–32

Foshay A W 1973 Sources of school practice. In: Goodlad J I, Shane H G (eds.) 1973 *The Elementary School in the United States, The 72nd Yearbook of the National Society for the Study of Education.* University of Chicago Press, Chicago, Illinois

Glasser W 1990 *The Quality School. Managing Students Without Coercion.* Harper and Row, New York

Lanier J E, Little J W 1986 Research on teacher education. In: Wittrock M C (ed.) 1986 *Handbook of Research on Teaching*, 3rd edn. Macmillan, New York

Lortie D C 1975 *Schoolteacher. A Sociological Study.* University of Chicago Press, Chicago, Illinois

Oakes J 1985 *Keeping Track. How Schools Structure Inequality.* Yale University Press, New Haven, Connecticut

Rosenholtz S J 1991 *Teachers' Workplace.* Teachers College Press, New York

Sarason S B 1983 *Schooling in America: Scapegoat and Salvation.* Free Press, New York

Stevenson H, Steigler J 1992 *The Learning Gap.* Summit Books, New York

Stipek D 1992 *Motivation to Learn*, 2nd edn. Prentice-Hall, Englewood Cliffs, New Jersey

Thomas R M 1992 *Comparing Theories of Child Development*, 3rd edn. Wadsworth, Belmont, California

Thomas R M (ed.) 1988 *Oriental Theories of Human Development.* Peter Lang Publishers, New York

Waller W 1932 *The Sociology of Teaching.* John Wiley and Sons, New York

Teachers' Expectations

T. L. Good

In the 1960s, an experiment conducted in the United States by Rosenthal and Jacobson (1968) resulted in one of the most exciting and controversial reports in the history of educational research. These investigators presented data suggesting that teachers' experimentally induced expectations for student performance were associated with student performance. That is, students whom teachers expected to achieve at higher levels did in fact achieve at higher levels, even though there was no real basis for these expectations. The study was criticized on several methodological grounds. For example, no observations were conducted in the teachers' classrooms, so there was no basis on which to determine whether teachers interacted differently with the students based on their expectations.

This entry focuses on research on teachers' expectations that has been conducted since the publication of the Rosenthal and Jacobson study. It begins with a definition of teachers' expectations, discusses the major types of research on those expectations and the conceptual frameworks underlying this research, and examines ways in which different expectations are communicated to students, and the perceptions students have of these different teacher behaviors. The entry concludes with a discussion of possible directions for research on teachers' expectations.

1. Defining Teachers' Expectations

Teachers' expectations are inferences that teachers make about the future behavior or academic achievement of their students, based on what they currently know about these students. Teachers' expectations affect student outcomes because of actions that teachers take in response to their expectations. Expectations are an inescapable and important part of daily life (Jussim 1990a), influencing many social issues. Research on expectancies has examined such topics as gender role socialization, affirmative action, political person perception, and equality of educational opportunity. (For discussions of research on the role of expectancies in diverse social areas see Jussim 1990a, 1990b, Oyserman and Markus 1990.)

Cooper and Good (1983) noted that researchers have examined two types of teacher expectation effects. The first is the self-fulfilling prophecy effect, in which an originally erroneous expectation leads to behavior that causes the expectation to become true. The Rosenthal and Jacobson (1968) study deals with this type of expectation effect. In contrast, the sustaining expectation effect occurs when teachers expect students to

sustain previously developed behavior patterns to the point that teachers take these patterns for granted and fail to see and capitalize on changes in student potential. Self-fulfilling prophecy effects are more powerful than sustaining expectation effects because they introduce significant change in student behavior (and thinking) instead of merely sustaining established patterns. Self-fulfilling effects can be powerful when they occur, but the more subtle sustaining expectation effects occur more often.

2. Two Types of Research on Teachers' Expectations

To understand the research on teacher expectation effects, two types of studies must be distinguished. The first involves experimental attempts to induce teacher expectations by providing teachers with fictitious information about students. The second type of study uses the expectations that teachers form naturally on the basis of whatever information they have available (e.g., test scores).

Numerous studies have induced expectations in teachers and have explored the consequent effects on student learning (Good and Brophy 1990). Some studies did not produce changes in student outcomes, apparently because the teachers did not acquire the expectations the experimenters were trying to induce. Induced-expectation experiments have produced clear-cut positive results often enough, however, to demonstrate that teacher expectations can have self-fulfilling prophecy effects on student achievement. Such demonstrations are important, because studies of teachers' naturally formed expectations cannot establish cause-and-effect relationships. These experimental studies in classrooms have been enriched by laboratory research in social psychology that has focused on the formation, communication, and interpretation of expectancies (see Jones 1990, Jussim 1990b for reviews).

However, studies linking teachers' naturally formed expectations to their classroom interactions with students are also needed, because they provide information about how teachers' expectations can become self-fulfilling. As Good and Brophy (1990) noted, most studies of teachers' naturally formed expectations have related such expectations to teacher–student interaction rather than to student outcomes. These studies typically demonstrate that many teachers interact differently with students for whom they hold high expectations than they do with students for whom they hold low expectations. They also suggest the mechanisms that mediate sustaining expectation effects.

3. The Brophy–Good Model

In their early research on teacher expectation effects on individual students, Brophy and Good (1970) suggested the following model of the process by which teachers' expectations become self-fulfilling prophecies.

(a) Early in the year, the teacher forms differential expectations for student behavior and achievement.

(b) Consistent with these differential expectations, the teacher behaves differently toward various students.

(c) This treatment tells students how they are expected to behave in the classroom and to perform on academic tasks.

(d) If the teacher's treatment is consistent over time, and if students do not actively resist or change it, it will likely affect their self-concepts, achievement motivation, levels of aspiration, classroom conduct, and interactions with the teacher.

(e) These effects generally will compliment and reinforce the teacher's expectations, so that students will conform to these expectations more than they might otherwise have done.

(f) Ultimately this reciprocal process will affect student achievement and other outcomes. High-expectation students will achieve at or near their potential, but low-expectation students will not gain as much as they could have if taught differently.

The model begins with the assumption that teachers form differential achievement expectations for various students at the beginning of the school year. Teachers use many cues for forming expectations, including track or group placement, classroom conduct, physical appearance, race, socioeconomic status, ethnicity, gender, speech characteristics, and various diagnostic labels (e.g., see Baron et al. 1985, Jussim 1989).

Self-fulfilling prophecy effects of teacher expectations can occur only when all elements in the model are present (Good and Brophy 1990). Often, however, one or more elements is missing. The teacher may not have clear-cut expectations about every student, or those expectations may change continually. Even when expectations are consistent, the teacher may not necessarily communicate them through consistent behavior. Finally, students might prevent expectations

from becoming self-fulfilling by counteracting their effects or resisting them.

4. Communicating Differential Expectations

Given that teachers form differential expectations, how do they express those expectations to students in ways that might influence students' behavior? On the basis of several literature reviews, Good and Brophy (1990) suggested that the following behaviors sometimes indicate differential teacher treatment of high and low achievers: (a) waiting less time for "lows" to answer questions before giving the answer or calling on someone else; (b) giving lows answers or calling on someone else rather than trying to improve their responses by giving clues or repeating or rephrasing questions; (c) providing inappropriate reinforcement (e.g., rewarding inappropriate behavior or incorrect answers by lows); (d) criticizing lows more often for failure; (e) praising lows less often for success; (e) failing to give feedback to the public responses of lows; (f) paying less attention to lows or interacting with them less frequently; (g) calling on lows less often to respond to questions, or asking them only easier, nonanalytical questions; (h) seating lows further from the teacher; (i) demanding less from lows (e.g., teaching them less content; accepting lower quality or even incorrect responses from lows; providing excessive sympathy or unneeded help); (j) interacting with lows more privately than publicly, and monitoring and structuring their activities more closely; (k) grading tests or assignments differently (e.g., highs but not lows are given the benefit of the doubt in borderline cases), (l) engaging in less friendly interaction with lows, including less smiling and fewer other nonverbal indicators of support; (m) providing briefer and less informative feedback to questions of lows; (n) using less eye contact and other nonverbal communication of attention and responsiveness (forward lean, positive head nodding) in interactions with lows; (o) using less effective and time-consuming instructional methods with lows when time is limited; (p) accepting and using lows' ideas less often; and (q) exposing lows to an impoverished curriculum (e.g. limited and repetitive information, emphasis on factual recitation).

Three points should be noted when considering these forms of differential treatment. First, these teacher behaviors do not occur in all classrooms. Some teachers do not communicate low expectations; some provide appropriate expectations for all or most students. Second, some of the differences are due to students rather than to the teacher. For example, if lows volunteer less often, it is difficult for teachers to be sure that lows get as many response opportunities as highs. Third, some forms of differential treatment are necessary at times and may even represent appropriate individualizing of instruction rather than inappropriate projection of negative expectations. Low-achieving students in elementary schools appear to require more private structuring of their activities and closer monitoring of their work than do their peers.

When several of these differential communication patterns are observed in a classroom, however, and if the differentiation is significant, the teacher may be communicating inappropriately low expectations to some students. This is especially the case if the differential treatment directly affects students' opportunity to learn. For example, if lows receive less new information and feedback about their performance, they are almost certain to make less progress than highs, regardless of whether lows are aware of such differential treatment.

While research has focused on inappropriately low expectations, teachers can hold too high or too "narrow" expectations so that some students are pushed to do more but not allowed to take time to understand or enjoy academic work. The key is to challenge and guide students in appropriate ways to do more than they are at that time able to achieve (Vygotsky 1978).

5. The Importance of Teachers' Expectations

The effects of teachers' expectations on student learning have often been exaggerated. Indeed, in the popular press the effects have sometimes been touted as almost magical. For example, Good and Brophy (1977) lampooned an advertisement that appeared in *Reader's Digest*: "Just make a wish. Read about how it can come True." Although there is no clear way to predict with certainty the effects of teachers' expectancies on student learning, there is growing consensus among experts that expectancy effects are usually modest (e.g., Jussim 1990b estimates an average effect size of 0.2 to 0.3 standard deviations), but important (Brophy 1983). Even an effect size of 0.2 suggests that 10 percent of students who receive high expectations will show notable improvement, and that 10 percent of students exposed to low expectations will exhibit a significant decline in performance (Jussim 1990b).

There is no doubt that expectancies are common. Rosenthal and Rubin (1978) reported that some type of teacher expectancy effect occurred in about two-thirds of the 345 studies they reviewed. Although the potential importance of expectancies is shown by such reviews (and expectancy effects may compound over time), most students do not receive "average effects"; students are likely to be in classrooms where effects are very high, moderate, or nonexistent.

6. Students' Perceptions of Teachers' Differential Behavior

Unfortunately, many studies that have assessed the effects of teacher expectancies on student performance have not included process or interview data to de-termine students' perceptions of differential teacher behavior. In addition to expectation effects that occur directly through differences in exposure to content, indirect effects may occur as a result of teacher behavior that affects students' self-concepts, performance expectations, or motivation. Although numerous studies have examined students' achievement motivation and aspirations in classrooms, little of this research has studied these affective variables in relation to teacher behavior. Thus, little is known about how students interpret teacher behaviors and how those behaviors influence students' motivation and effort.

Studies that have been conducted suggest that students are aware of differences in teachers' patterns of interaction with students. Interview and questionnaire data indicate that elementary students see their teachers as projecting higher achievement expectations and offering increased opportunity and choice to high achievers, while structuring the activities of low achievers more closely and providing them with additional help and with more negative feedback about their academic work and classroom conduct (Cooper and Good 1983).

Furthermore, students are more aware of such differentiation in classes in which it occurs frequently (Weinstein et al. 1987). Brattesani et al. (1984) compared classrooms where the students described the teachers as differentiating considerably in their treatment of high and low achievers with classrooms in which students reported little such differentiation. They found that including teacher-expectation measures added from 9 to 18 percent to the variance in year-end achievement beyond what could have been predicted from prior achievement in the high-differentiation classes, but added only 1 to 5 percent in the low-differentiation classes.

7. Good's Passivity Model

Some students receive low expectations so consistently that they appear to internalize these expectations. Studies of expectations have increasingly emphasized how students internalize teachers' expectations, and models have been developed for exploring mediation effects (e.g., Cooper 1985). Good's (1981) passivity model suggested that certain forms of teacher treatment induce passivity in low-achieving students. Over time, differences in the ways teachers treat low achievers (e.g., in the third grade a student is praised or finds teacher acceptance for virtually any verbalization, but in the fourth grade the same student is seldom praised and is criticized frequently) may reduce the efforts of lows and contribute to a passive learning style. Other teacher behaviors may compound this problem. Low-achieving students who are called on frequently one year but infrequently the following year may find it confusing to adjust to different role definitions. Ironically, those students who have the least capacity to adapt may be asked to make the most adjustments as they move from classroom to classroom.

Greater variation among teachers in their interaction with low achievers may occur because teachers agree less about how to respond to students who do not learn readily. Teachers may treat lows inconsistently over the course of the school year as they try one approach after another in an attempt to find something that works.

When teachers provide fewer chances for lower achievers to participate in public discussion, wait less time for them to respond when they are called on (even though these students may need more time to think and form an answer), or criticize lows more per incorrect answer and praise them less per correct answer, the implications are similar. It seems that a good strategy for students who face such conditions would be not to volunteer or not to respond when called on. Students are discouraged from taking risks under such an instructional system (Good 1981). To the extent that students are motivated to reduce risk and ambiguity— and many argue that students are strongly motivated to do so (Doyle 1983)—students would likely become more passive in order to reduce the risk of critical teacher feedback.

Good et al. (1987) found that low achievers were just as likely to ask questions as other students in kindergarten classes, but that lows asked significantly fewer questions than their classmates in upper-elementary and secondary classes. Similarly, in a study involving grades two, four, and six, Newman and Goldin (1990) found that among sixth-graders, the lowest achievers had both the greatest perceived need for help and the greatest resistance to asking for help. Students' ambivalence about asking questions or getting help from teachers becomes especially acute during adolescence, when they are both more concerned about how they are perceived by peers and more sensitive to the costs as well as the benefits of seeking help.

8. Variation in Teachers' Expectations Over Time

Relatively little research has focused on students' classroom experiences over consecutive years, and no study examined students' reactions to differential teacher expectations over consecutive years prior to the work of Midgley et al. (1989). Midgley et al. conducted a longitudinal study in the United States of 1,329 elementary and junior high students, examining their self- and task-related beliefs in mathematics as a function of teachers' efficacy beliefs. They found that students who moved from high- to low-efficacy mathematics teachers during the transition from elementary to junior high school ended the junior high year with the lowest expectancies in perceived performance (even lower than students who had low-efficacy teachers both years) and the highest perceptions of

task difficulty. Furthermore, the differences in pre- and post-transitional teachers' views of their efficacy had more of an effect on low-achieving than on high-achieving students' beliefs about mathematics.

9. Increasing Expectations

There is growing evidence that when (a) low achievers are allowed to enroll in more challenging courses or (b) course content is altered to include more challenging material that is traditionally not available to low-performing students, student performance improves. The decision to allow students to engage in more challenging academic work (e.g., move to a higher reading group) is potentially a powerful strategy for increasing teacher and student performance expectations.

Mason et al. (1992) described a study in which 34 average-achieving eighth-grade mathematics students in an urban junior high were assigned to prealgebra classes rather than placed in traditional general mathematics classes. Results showed that students placed in prealgebra classes benefited from advanced placement in comparison to average-achieving eighth-graders from the previous year who took general mathematics (the cohort comparison group). Specifically, prealgebra students outperformed the comparison cohort group on a concepts subtest while maintaining equivalent performance on the problem-solving and computation subtests of the Comprehensive Assessment Program Achievement Series Test. Particularly important was that prealgebra students, in comparison with the cohort of general mathematics students, subsequently enrolled in more advanced mathematics classes during high school and obtained higher grades in these classes. Moreover, the presence of average achievers in prealgebra classes did not lower the performance of higher-achieving students in these classes.

Mason et al. qualified their findings. For example, the school in which the study took place was implementing a comprehensive school-improvement plan (higher expectations, active mathematics teaching). Hence, it was impossible to determine what instructional, curriculum, or peer effects were most influential in improving student performance. Further, the authors were aware of potential selection and history effects that can occur in a cross-sectional cohort design. Other investigators, however, have obtained similar results. Peterson (1989) found that remedial students who were placed in a prealgebra program for accelerated students achieved significantly higher results on all three mathematics subtests of the California Test of Basic Skills than did comparable students who were assigned to remedial and general mathematics classes. Such results strongly argue the need for educators to assess carefully the standards they use for assigning students to courses, since current standards may limit unnecessarily many students' access to mathematical knowledge, and potentially their access to future careers and advanced study.

Efforts to change low expectations for student performance can go beyond altering the practices of one teacher or a few teachers to include an entire school. For example, Weinstein et al. (1991) reported positive findings from a comprehensive intervention program designed to raise expectations for student achievement. This quasi-experimental field study involved collaboration between university researchers and teachers and administrators at an urban high school. The cooperating teachers attended university classes that focused on ways in which teachers can inadvertently maintain low expectations, and on the special motivational problems of low-achieving students. Teachers and researchers collaborated to develop a program for preventing and remediating low expectations.

The eight areas of the intervention program are: (a) task and curriculum (minimize tasks that heighten ability comparisons, give low achievers frequent opportunities to work on higher-order thinking and application of knowledge); (b) grouping (minimize ability grouping, make use of heterogeneous grouping and cooperative learning activities); (c) evaluation (emphasize qualitative evaluation, provide private feedback that stresses continuous progress achieved through a combination of ability and effort); (d) motivational climate (minimize competition, stress intrinsic rewards in addition to extrinsic rewards); (e) student role in learning (provide opportunities for students to make choices and to assume increasing responsibility for managing their own learning); (f) class relationships (develop a sense of community among the students that includes valuing diversity); (g) parent–teacher communication (emphasize students' positive attributes and progress rather than their deficiencies or problems); and (h) school-level supports (with cooperation from school administrators, establish increased and varied opportunities for low achievers to participate in school activities and get recognition for their achievements in and out of the classroom). The research procedures and organizational issues associated with this complex and innovative intervention cannot be presented here. However, both a rich description of the project (Weinstein et al. 1991) and an extensive analysis of the program (Weinstein 1991) are available.

The program has had some notable positive effects. For example, teachers were able to implement procedures designed to increase communication of positive expectations to low achievers. Project teachers' expectations for students, as well as their attitudes toward their colleagues, became more positive. Project teachers also expanded their roles and worked to change school tracking practices. Positive changes were also evident for the 158 project students. In contrast to 154 comparison students, project students had improved grades, fewer disciplinary referrals,

and increased retention in school one year later. Weinstein et al. (1991) noted, however, that progress was not uniform. Students' absences rose and their improved academic performance was not maintained over the 9-month period of the study. According to the researchers, the limited length and breadth of the intervention and evaluation (students' performance was evaluated only in English and history), although sufficient to retain students, may have been insufficient to affect students' attendance and performance. Moreover, some teachers left the project because of excessive time requirements and lack of administrative support.

10. Directions for Research

Expectations research can be expanded in many ways to enhance understanding of classroom teaching and learning. Two of the most promising research areas are teachers' decisions about content assignments and teachers' knowledge of subject matter.

10.1 Selection of Curriculum Content

Many educators have contended that textbooks define the curriculum, although some research challenges this simplistic view and suggests that teachers act as decision-makers, modifying the curriculum in relation to factors such as teachers' beliefs about students' aptitude, their instructional intentions, and their subject-matter knowledge. If teachers influence the curriculum, then their decisions about curriculum partially determine performance expectations for students, just as teacher behaviors and activity structures do.

According to Freeman and Porter (1989), teachers make many decisions that influence how much content students receive. For example, teachers decide how much time to spend on mathematics on a certain day, what topics should be taught, how much time should be allocated for each topic, whether all students are taught the same topics, and in what order topics should be presented. The time spent on instruction and the focus of instruction (e.g., concepts, skills, applications) seem prime ways in which expectations might be communicated. Subsequent research could profitably attempt to integrate teachers' decisions about how much and what type of content to present with teachers' expectations for students (e.g., how students are likely to learn).

10.2 Teachers' Subject-matter Knowledge

Teachers' subject-matter knowledge is likely an important factor affecting the performance expectations they communicate to students. Because some teachers know more about some subjects or concepts than others, teachers' beliefs about subject matter and how to present it to students would probably affect whether or not they set appropriate performance expectations for students. Carlsen (1991) documented the effects of four novice biology teachers' subject-matter knowledge on discourse in their classrooms as they taught eight science lessons. The findings imply that choice of instructional activity affects students' participation in classroom discussion. Teachers used lectures and laboratory activities, which are characterized by high rates of student questioning, with topics about which they were knowledgeable. They tended to use classroom activities that involved few student questions when they were unfamiliar with the subject matter.

Carlsen's results are especially intriguing in that they illustrate that, because all teachers, and especially novice teachers, have inadequate knowledge in some areas, teachers must develop strategies for teaching content that they are still learning themselves. These strategies might include using sources additional to the textbook, bringing in guest teachers who are more knowledgeable, telling students that this is an area about which they are still learning, and presenting to students the questions that the teachers are using to structure the unit (and their own learning).

Research that examines teachers' performance expectations for individual students along with teachers' subject-matter knowledge would be profitable. When teachers instruct students in topics about which teachers have little knowledge, they may exaggerate differential treatment (i.e., avoid unpredictable questions by low achievers; overly depend on students believed to be more capable). Furthermore, the accountability systems and task structures that teachers select may be a function of their subject-matter knowledge.

11. Conclusion

Research on teacher expectancies in the classroom was a rich and exciting area in the 1970s and 1980s and many useful constructs have been derived from this work. Although the importance of teacher expectation effects have sometimes been overstated, it is clear that they are important, especially when considered with other teaching abilities and other general variables (e.g., home–school correspondence). In the 1980s there has been growing interest in the active role that students play in interpreting, internalizing, or rejecting expectations that are conveyed through teacher behavior or classroom structures. In the 1990s and beyond researchers need to study teacher expectancies and student mediation simultaneously. Such work will be enriched if researchers are also willing to explore how curriculum content and teachers' and students' knowledge of content mediate both the communication and interpretation of performance expectations.

See also: Demonstrating; Synthesizing Research on Teaching

References

Baron R, Tom D, Cooper H 1985 Social class, race and teacher expectations. In: Dusek J (ed.) 1985 *Teacher Expectancies*. Erlbaum, Hillsdale, New Jersey

Brattesani K, Weinstein R, Marshall H 1984 Student perceptions of differential teacher treatment as moderators of teacher expectation effects. *J. Educ. Psychol.* 76(2): 236–47

Brophy J 1983 Research on the self-fulfilling prophecy and teacher expectations. *J. Educ. Psychol.* 75: 631–61

Brophy J, Good T 1970 The Brophy–Good System (dyadic teacher-child interaction). In: Simon A, Boyer E (eds.) 1970 *Mirrors for Behavior: An Anthology of Observation Instruments Continued, 1970 Supplement*, Vols. A and B. Research for Better Schools, Inc., Philadelphia, Pennsylvania

Carlsen W 1991 Subject-matter knowledge and science teaching: A pragmatic perspective. In: Brophy J (ed.) 1991 *Advances in Research on Teaching*, Vol. 2. JAI Press, Greenwich, Connecticut

Cooper H 1985 Models of teacher expectation communication. In: Dusek J (ed.) 1985 *Teacher Expectancies*. Erlbaum, Hillsdale, New Jersey

Cooper H, Good T 1983 *Pygmalion Grows Up: Studies in the Expectation Communication Process*. Longman, New York

Doyle W 1983 Academic work. *Rev. Educ. Res.* 53(2): 159–200

Freeman D, Porter A 1989 Do textbooks dictate the content of mathematics instruction in elementary schools? *Am. Educ. Res. J.* 26(3): 403–21

Good T 1981 Teacher expectations and student perceptions: A decade of research. *Educ. Leadership* 38(5): 415–23

Good T, Brophy J 1977 *Educational Psychology: A Realistic Approach*. Holt, New York

Good T, Brophy J 1990 *Looking in Classrooms*, 5th edn. Harper and Collins, New York

Good T, Slavings R, Harel K, Emerson H 1987 Student passivity: A study of student question-asking in K-12 classrooms. *Sociol. Educ.* 60(4): 181–99

Jones E 1990 *Interpersonal Perception*. Freeman, New York

Jussim L 1989 Teacher expectations: Self-fulfilling prophecies, perceptual biases, and accuracy. *J. Pers. Soc. Psychol.* 57(3): 469–80

Jussim L 1990a Expectancies and social issues: Introduction. *J. Soc. Issues* 46(2): 1–8

Jussim L 1990b Social reality and social problems: The role of expectancies. *J. Soc. Issues* 46(2): 9–34

Mason D, Schroeter D, Combs R, Washington K 1992 Assigning average-achieving eighth graders to advance mathematics classes in an urban junior high. *Elem. Sch. J.* 92(5): 587–99

Midgley C, Feldlaufer H, Eccles J 1989 Change in teacher efficacy and students' self- and task-related beliefs in mathematics during the transition to junior high school. *J. Educ. Psychol.* 81(2): 247–58

Newman R, Goldin L 1990 Children's reluctance to seek help with school work. *J. Educ. Psychol.* 82: 92–100

Oyserman D, Markus H 1990 Possible selves in balance: Implications for delinquency. *J. Soc. Issues* 46(2) 141–58

Peterson J 1989 Remediation is no remedy. *Educ. Leadership* 46(6): 24–25

Rosenthal R, Jacobson L 1968 *Pygmalion in the Classroom*:

Teacher Expectation and Pupil's Intellectual Development. Holt, Rinehart, and Winston, New York

Rosenthal R, Rubin D 1978 Interpersonal expectancy effects: The first 345 studies. *The Behavioral and Brain Sciences* 1(3): 377–86

Vygotsky L 1978 *Mind in Society: The Development of Higher Psychological Processes*. Harvard University Press, Cambridge, Massachusetts

Weinstein R 1991 Caught between paradigms: Obstacle or opportunity—a comment on the commentaries. *American Journal of Community Psychology* 19(3): 395–404

Weinstein R, Marshall H, Sharp L, Botkin M 1987 Pygmalion and the student: Age and classroom differ-

ences in children's awareness of teacher expectations. *Child Dev.* 58(4): 1079–93

Weinstein R et al. 1991 Expectations and high school change: Teacher–researcher collaboration to prevent school failure. *American Journal of Community Psychology* 19(3): 333–64

Further Reading

Blank P D 1993 *Interpersonal Expectations Theory, Research, and Applications*. Cambridge University Press, Cambridge

Teacher Responsibility

F. K. Oser and J.-L. Patry

Teacher responsibility deals with teachers' professional moral tasks. A procedural morality is suggested and discussed in this entry, with the aims of avoiding problems like relativism and enhancing student responsibility.

1. The Necessity of Professional Responsibility in Teaching

Control over the well-being, the interests, or the fate of someone includes, from an ethical point of view, certain obligations or a responsibility toward that person (Jonas 1987 p. 176). This responsibility can be defined legally. An authority (e.g., society, the parents) gives the teacher the responsibility to deal appropriately with the students, and the teacher's actions are judged (and possibly sanctioned) by these authorities. Responsibility can also be defined ethically as the individual obligation to act according to a set of moral or ethical principles to ensure the students' well-being and interests ("responsibleness"). According to both definitions, teachers have great responsibilities; however, the legal requirements placed upon teachers set only minimal standards (Strike 1990), they are often contradictory, and they vary from country to country. Further, they may be ethically questionable. The teachers' personal moral responsibility hence takes precedence over the legal one.

The traditional research on moral responsibility rests on the following basic premises:

(a) Research on responsibility is still dominated by "should's" (i.e. normative requirements demanded of teachers or sets of virtues that the teacher is expected to satisfy but which are, in reality, unattainable). Responsibility is often linked with the "character" or the "personality"

of a teacher, with the presupposition that a given person either has the corresponding virtues or does not. This means that responsibility cannot be learned.

(b) Most research on responsibility is based on a relativistic concept of morality (an example, Nash 1991, is discussed below). The point of view that moral values are evaluations of actions generally believed by the members of a given society to be either "right" or "wrong" (social relativism) is problematic for several reasons. For example, it seems unacceptable to regard it as morally right if a group of people believes it is entitled to harm or even kill another group, and acts accordingly (as happened in the Third Reich and still happens in many places).

(c) Researchers who study teacher responsibility tend to forget that a teacher is a person with a private life and extraprofessional responsibilities. The distinction between private life and schoolwork calls for a conception of professional morality where, as in private morality, any value (including extraprofessional values) can conflict with any other value.

These basic premises can account for serious deficits in the research on responsibility with, among others, the following consequences:

(a) There is almost no empirical research in the domain of responsible action in school.

(b) In teacher education, teachers usually do not learn to deal effectively with responsibility (Bergem 1992).

(c) Teachers do not think about responsibilities and values very often (Oser et al. 1991).

(d) Teachers often believe that responsible action such as caring for specific students reduces their effectiveness with respect to the students' knowledge acquisition (see, e.g., McLaughlin 1991). Thus, responsibility and effectiveness are dealt with separately in research.

There have been some attempts to remedy these deficiencies. Nash (1991), for example, has proposed three conceptions of applied ethics. First, a language of rules and principles is necessary to help teachers think in a formal and disciplined way about their daily ethical dilemmas. However, the "test of which ethical decision is 'right' is whether the justification is sufficiently convincing to impartial observers" (p. 165). This is a relativistic position.

Second, a deeper exploration of motives, intentions, ideals, and feelings on the part of the primary moral agent as well as the larger societal influences on one's ethical actions is called for. Again, this approach is relativistic since the basis of decision-making is the individual's intuitions about what is right and the norms of important reference groups, rather than a rational argument based on universal principles.

The third conception concerns "the private world of individual consciousness where each of us chooses our moral ideals, attempts to make sense of our deepest beliefs, and tries to ground the messages" (p. 169). If these beliefs are taken as moral rules, again, a relativistic viewpoint is defended: right is the moral rule of the individual.

Nash has pointed out that all three approaches must be seen together. However, all of them are relativistic (premise (b)). Further, while the first premise is taken care of to some degree, the third is not. Consequences (a) and (d) are not accounted for at all.

In contrast to the basic premises and to Nash (1991), a nonrelativistic moral responsibility is necessary. Ethical decisions must be based on principles which are universally valid. In Kohlberg's (1981) approach, the moral frame of reference is based on two principles: (a) "People are of unconditional value" and (b) "Every person has the right to an equal consideration of his or her claims in every situation, not just those codified into law" (p. 164). In research on the teachers' professional ethos, two additional principles turned out to be equally important (Oser et al. 1991): (c) "Any person in need has the right to be helped" (caring, see also Gilligan 1982) and (d) "In social situations, people have the obligation to be truthful in the sense of being authentic."

The three claims which are essential in teacher responsibility, namely justice (according to (b)), care (c), and truthfulness (d) are discussed below. Further, within a professional ethic, extraprofessional obligations should also be considered. A procedural approach can satisfy these requirements. Instead of a set of "should's" or of virtues, the focus is on

how problems can be solved without losing universal requirements (in contrast to Nash's approach).

2. What Does "Responsibility" Mean?

Responsibility deals with a person's choice. When a person doesn't have any choice (either because people do not influence the state of affairs, or because the particular person is denied choice or is not able to choose because of insufficient knowledge or for other reasons), he or she cannot have responsibility (Heid 1991). However, the freedom of choice is often underestimated. Many situations with apparently only one possibility contain other options as well, although most of them may have strong negative personal consequences. For instance, one has almost always the option of resistance against coercion. Whether the resistance can reasonably be expected, and if so, whether it is the most responsible solution, remains to be seen. It is clear that if the teacher is given sufficient autonomy, however, the teacher has more freedom to decide what solution is really the best; hence, autonomy is closely linked with responsibility (see Bull 1990).

The choice is always between two or more opposing values (i.e., between values that cannot be satisfied simultaneously). Dealing appropriately with such problems requires a clear distinction between descriptive statements and value judgments (including prescriptions) and the acknowledgment that each type of statement needs a different form of justification. This is not as easy as it seems. The two goals "tolerance" and "critical thinking," for instance, are so widely accepted that researchers (as well as teachers) often do not see them as values at all (Damon 1992).

3. Responsible Teaching

A teacher is in control of the classroom situation. The teacher, then, could decide how to operate within the classroom without consulting anyone. However, in most cases, a procedure-oriented approach with participation of all concerned people would seem to be more appropriate: the solutions are more likely to be justified (i.e., more in agreement with the universal principles), and the participants are more likely to be eager to put them into practice. Two kinds of situation can be differentiated: dilemma situations and situations where the students are supposed to acquire knowledge. In both, a procedural approach means that responsibility is delegated to the student.

3.1 Dilemma Situations

The first kind of situation is concerned with ethical dilemmas (i.e., with problems in which several values are at stake which cannot be satisfied simultaneously). In the procedural approach, instead of giving specific values or norms as to the outcomes of the decisions, some principles of the decision-making process are given which ensure that the interests and needs of all people involved in the particular situation are dealt with appropriately.

The steps of such a process are presented in Fig. 1. First, the teacher must decide for a given situation whether the problem is important enough to engage into a discourse process (1b) or whether other responsibility issues are more important (1a). If he or she decides that he or she is in charge, the central problem is how to coordinate three major moral criteria in cooperation with all concerned persons (the second level in Fig. 1). These criteria are justice (2a), care (2b), and truthfulness (2c). After balancing the three values, he or she must decide at the third level how much commitment he or she is willing to give to the solution (3b)—a commitment which might inhibit the realization of other needs, such as extraprofessional values (e.g., family life or stress reduction) (3a).

In a conflict situation, even if they feel they are treated justly (2a), students may not feel "cared for" (2b) or believe the teacher was not sufficiently truthful (2c). Perhaps the attempt to reconcile all these values

is too stressful for the teacher, so that after some time he or she has a nervous breakdown (3a vs. 3b). In this regard, Oser and his colleagues (Oser et al. 1991, Oser 1992) have found that teachers have a one-sided balancing behavior, that is, on level 2, they prefer care over the other two values (see also Dempsey's interviews reported in Rogers and Webb 1991).

When trying to coordinate the different issues five types of decision-making can be identified. First, there is avoiding behavior in which the teacher is aware that morality is at stake but doesn't deal with it: 1a is seen as more important than 1b. Second, the teacher is aware of his or her responsibility (1b) and acts accordingly, but decides that someone else (e.g., the principal, the school psychologist, or some other agency) can deal more appropriately with the problem. The decisions on level 2 are hence shifted to other people, and the third level can then be left out. Third, there is unilateral decision-making in which the teacher decides to act, but the responsibility (decisions on levels 2 and 3) rests only on his or her intuition and reflection. There is either no information about other people's claims, needs, and feelings, or the teacher alone decides which

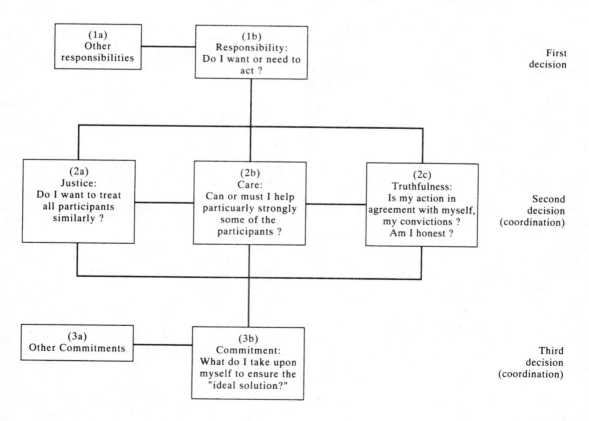

Figure 1
A model of the decision steps to solve a conflict situation

claims, needs, and feelings are valid and which are not. Fourth, the teacher can engage in "incomplete discourse." Here the teacher explains his or her reasons and listens to the concerned students and other participants, but does not include all people involved in the situation or does not allow full responsibility to all of them, believing that he or she must in the end assume the responsibility and thus try to coordinate.

Only the fifth type of decision making, "complete discourse," allows a full coordinated balancing among justice, care, and truthfulness. Here, the leader presupposes that the child can take responsibility and can participate in the decision-making even in very difficult situations. The important point is that the responsible teacher shifts responsibility to the participants (particularly to the child) without giving up all responsibility.

Four principles are crucial in this fifth type of decision-making (Oser 1992):

(a) The teacher must create the possibility for a discourse ("round table situation").

(b) The teacher must assume two compatible roles: as participant who defends his or her own needs, and as organizer who coordinates the different needs, demands, justifications, and explanations, and who ensures that the rules of discussion are kept.

(c) The teacher must presuppose that all participants (including the students) are able and willing to take responsibility, to search for the "truth," to decide autonomously, and to balance different requirements.

(d) Finally, the teacher must be convinced that whenever the first three principles are realized, solutions will be found which are in the interest of all and which have a morally legitimate character.

The model of decision-making, the five types of decision-making, and the four underlying principles of discourse were the topic of an extended empirical research project (Oser et al. 1991). Using both questionnaires and interviews, teachers were found to solve value conflicts in professional moral situations in different ways. Some practiced more discourse than others, and some practiced discourse in situations where others did not. Thus, the results showed there was a high person–situation interaction. However, Althof's (1993) analysis indicated that the higher the moral competence of teachers, in the sense of Kohlberg's (1984) model, the more consistent the teachers were across situations (either discursive in all situations or nondiscursive in all situations).

It is obvious that responsible action is not simply an application of general moral judgment competence to professional issues. For instance, in moral judgment competence one can say "the more (i.e., the higher the stage), the better." In conflict resolutions, one can only say "the more discursive decision making, the better," particularly if the conflict is a serious one. There are situations in which discursive problem solving would be inappropriate. However, qualitative analysis seems to suggest that moral judgment competence of a certain level (i.e., a stabilized stage 3 according to Kohlberg's stage theory) is important for an adequate understanding of and responsible dealing with interpersonal conflicts; beyond this level, contextual and biographical differences prevail (Althof 1993).

In an intervention study Oser et al. (1991) found that teachers can be trained to use the complete discourse model. Through training, they can develop an increased awareness of the difficult nature of ethical problems in general and the importance of consideration of people's needs and legitimate claims, yielding the recognition that there is not only one solution to the problem, but that there are several "truths." They can also increase their acknowledgment of the specific values of justice, care, and truthfulness, some of which had been neglected or not even recognized before the intervention.

3.2 Knowledge Acquisition Situations

The second type of situation concerns teaching in the narrow sense (i.e., situations in which the main aim is that the students learn content). Research has shown that very little is learned by someone who does not take the learning in his or her own hands (see, e.g., Salomon 1992). For optimal learning to occur, then, the students must be given responsibility for their own learning. The balance between teacher control and student control is a crucial issue in the discussion of responsibility and effectiveness. The teacher and the student both assume responsibility for learning, but they assume different aspects of the responsibility. The teacher sets the conditions of learning, tries not to hinder learning, and gives the necessary information (in what way this should be done is a question of effectiveness which cannot be dealt with here). The student is the active creator and controller of the learning process.

Salomon (1992) has called this teacher's role "exploration orchestration," which means that the teacher is the conductor of an orchestra but the musicians (children) play the instruments and often improvise (many examples are discussed in Oser et al. 1992). Among the many particularities of orchestration one is particularly important: grading. Learning that follows the principles of orchestration is more strongly based on a problem-solving approach than on memory learning. Thus, the trial-and-error phase is particularly important. In this phase children are not criticized for making errors rather they have the opportunity to check them out. If every action of or every product produced by children is graded, the students do not have the freedom to make errors. Grading, then, narrows the learning possibilities. It seems more appropriate to separate the phase of self-controlled learning and the phase of self-controlled grading, and to have the children well-informed about which phase is currently in action. Of course, grading then cannot be used as a motivator; however, it is not an appropriate means for motivating children anyway.

The point here is not that teachers give up control. Rather, control assumes another function. Furthermore, the amount of control may (and in fact should) vary from lesson to lesson (or even from situation to situation within a lesson; see Patry 1993). For instance, it is quite conceivable to lecture from time to time (high control, little orchestration) and then to have the children work on the information with a much higher degree of freedom.

4. Becoming a Responsible Teacher

As mentioned above the procedural-oriented approach can be learned. Student teachers, then, should acquire some competencies, develop their own value priorities, justify these priorities in the light of universals, and learn to act both in accordance with their convictions and in a discursive manner without becoming overwhelmed by the multitude of demands. To become a responsible teacher, however, additional qualities are necessary.

4.1 Moral Competence

A first necessary but not sufficient condition for responsible action is that the subject has a high moral competence (i.e., a high stage according to Kohlberg's stage theory). The higher the stage, the better; the minimal requirement seems to be stage 3 (Althof 1993).

A high moral competence does not guarantee analogous action. Moral competence deals with justice only, whereas responsibility involves other values (such as care and truthfulness) as well. In addition, behavior in general is not only determined by moral judgments, but also by situational conditions as well as other goals of the actor and other dispositions (Oser 1987). Further research is needed in this area, but at least a few conditions can be stated. The most important are concern for the child and awareness of values problems.

4.2 Concern for the Child

The discourse approach includes the teacher's presupposition of the child's competence and willingness to participate responsibly in the coordination process in order to balance justice, care, and truthfulness. In a more general way Fuller (1969) calls this "concern." Concern theory is part of responsibility theory. As Fuller (1969) and Janssen (1987) have shown, concern for the child has a very low priority for most teachers; on the other hand, there is some evidence that concern

for the child may enhance the children's achievements (e.g., Marsh and Penn 1987–88).

Concern for the child does not mean unconditional acceptance of all that a child does. This type of acceptance would be shifting over all of the responsibility to the child, instead of establishing a balance between the teacher's and the child's responsibility. It does, however, mean unconditional acceptance of the child as a person, as an autonomous individual. Like care (Rogers and Webb 1991), concern has two aspects: making sound decisions about students and their educational needs ("concern for the future") and helping to fulfill a child's basic need for security and attachment ("concern for the present").

Concern for the child, as described above, issues from a deliberate effort to be with the child, to understand the child, and to acknowledge that children are different from adults. This requires at least empathy (see Kurt-Schai 1991) and knowledge about the psychological development and the developmental stages of children; not only about the development of intelligence (Piaget 1963) but also of self-concept (Kegan 1982), moral judgment competence (Kohlberg 1984), social behavior (Selman 1980), developmental tasks (Havinghurst 1972), and crises (Erikson 1968).

Concern for the child means decision-making on behalf of the child, based on knowledge the child may not have. Implicitly, it contains all elements of the complete discourse approach mentioned above, including particularly the (possibly contrafactual) presupposition of the child's competence to decide and the use of "advocatory discourse" (Oser et al. 1991). Such decisions, then, will necessarily be those of orchestration and not of power imposition. Concern for the child can be learned.

4.3 Ability to Deal with Values

Several studies (Oser et al. 1991, Bergem 1992, Damon 1992) show that teachers do not think about their values. This could be remedied in teacher education. The problem of access to one's own values has been addressed in moral research studies using the method of "value clarification" (e.g., Simon et al. 1972). In this approach, strategies are used to prompt participants to present their values. A typical example is to ask them to decide which three objects they would take with them to a deserted island—the chosen objects are an indicator for their values or preferences.

It is important to note that value clarification in this context is only used as a means to enhance the teachers' awareness of the values they think are important (like Nash's three approaches discussed above). By no means does this imply that those values are appropriate or justified; this would be relativistic (Oser and Althof 1992) and hence inappropriate. Rather, once one has identified one's own value system, it is necessary to justify those values based on universal principles. If the values are not in accordance with these principles, teachers are required to restructure their value systems. This corrected value system then represents the system with respect to which the moral obligations are accepted by the individual (the reference system for responsibility in the sense of responsibleness).

5. Responsibility and Effectiveness

One of the oldest scientific superstitions of humans is the notion that morality inhibits effectiveness. Considering some of the complex problems that teachers must confront on a daily basis, there is a tendency to think that the most effective teachers are the tough, single-handed decision makers who manage the classroom without concerning themselves with matters of justice, truthfulness, and caring.

However, research on management has shown that success in fact depends on the so-called "lived value system" (Peters and Waterman 1982). Similarly in schools, a teacher who cares about students and about the learning taking place in the classroom is going to be more effective in the long run than one who does not (e.g., Solomon et al. 1992). In this sense, effectiveness and responsibility are complementary.

This complementarity, or "the new synthesis" (Oser et al. 1992), is not always obvious, neither in the research nor in the practical work of teachers. Although there are many examples of successful "syntheses," we still lack comprehensive research programs which address these issues in a systematic way. The theoretical framework is available (see Oser et al. 1992); it needs now to be criticized and specified.

References

Althof W 1993 Teachers' moral judgment and interpersonal problem solving in the classroom. In: Olechowski R, Svik G (eds.) 1993 *Experimental Research on Teaching and Learning*. Ludwig Boltzmann Institut, Vienna

Bergem T 1992 Teaching the art of living: Lessons learned from a study of teacher education. In: Oser F, Dick A, Patry J-L (eds.) 1992

Bull B L 1990 The limits of teacher professionalization. In: Goodlad J, Soder R, Sirotnik K A (eds.) 1990 *The Moral Dimensions of Teaching*. Jossey-Bass, San Francisco, California

Damon W 1992 Teaching as a moral craft and developmental expedition. In: Oser F, Dick A, Patry J-L (eds.) 1992

Erikson E 1968 *Identity, Youth and Crisis*. Faber and Faber, London

Fuller F F 1969 Concerns of teachers: A developmental conceptualization. *Am. Educ. Res. J.* 6(2):207–26

Gilligan C 1982 *In a Different Voice: Psychological Theory and Women's Development*. Harvard University Press, Cambridge, Massachusetts

Havinghurst R J 1972 *Developmental Tasks and Education*, 3rd edn. McKay, New York

Heid H 1991 Problematik einer Erziehung zur Verantwortungsbereitschaft. *N. Sammlung* 31:459–81

Janssen S 1987 What are beginning teachers concerned about? Paper presented at the first Joint Conference of the "Arbeitsgruppe für Empirische Pädagogische Forschung" and the "Onderzoeksthemagroep Onderwijsleerprocessen", Düsseldorf

Jonas H 1987 *Das Prinzip Verantwortung. Versuch einer Ethik für die technologische Zivilisation*, 7th edn. Insel, Frankfurt

Kegan R 1982 *The Evolving Self. Problems and Process in Human Development*. Harvard University Press, Cambridge, Massachusetts

Kohlberg L 1981 From *Is* to *Ought*: How to commit the naturalistic fallacy and get away with it in the study of moral development. In: Kohlberg L (ed.) 1981 *Essays on Moral Development. Vol. 1: The Philosophy of Moral Development. Moral Stages and the Idea of Justice*. Harper and Row, San Francisco, California

Kohlberg L 1984 *Essays on Moral Development. Vol. 2: The Psychology of Moral Development. The Nature and Validity of Moral Stages*. Harper and Row, San Francisco, California

Kurt-Schai R 1991 The peril and promise of childhood: Ethical implications for tomorrow's teachers. *J. Teach. Educ.* 42(3):196–204

Marsh D D, Penn D M 1987/1988 Engaging students in innovative instruction: An application of the stages of concern framework to studying student engagement. *Journal of Classroom Interaction* 23(1): 8–14

McLaughlin H J 1991 Reconciling care and control: Authority in classroom relationships, *J. Teach. Educ.* 42(3): 182–95

Nash R J 1991 Theme: The ethical responsibilities of teaching. *J. Teach. Educ.* 42(3): 163–72.

Oser F 1987 Das Wollen, das gegen den eigenen Willen gerichtet ist: Über das Verhältnis von Urteil und Handeln im Bereich der Moral. In: Heckhausen H, Gollwitzer P M, Weinert F E (eds.) 1987 *Jenseits des Rubikon. Der Wille in den Humanwissenschaften*. Springer, Berlin

Oser F 1992 Morality in professional action: A discourse approach for teaching. In: Oser F, Dick A, Patry J-L (eds.) 1992

Oser F et al. 1991 Der Prozess der Verantwortung. Berufsethische Entscheidungen von Lehrerinnen und Lehren. Bericht zum Forschungsprojekt 1.188–0.85 und 11.25470.88/2 des Schweizerischen Nationalfonds zur Förderung der wissenschaftlichen Forschung. Freiburg Pädagogisches Institut, Freiburg

Oser F, Althof W 1992 *Moralische Selbstbestimmung. Modelle der Entwicklung und Erziehung im Wertebereich. Ein Lehrbuch*. Klett-Cotta, Stuttgart

Oser F, Dick A, Patry J-L (eds.) 1992 *Effective and Responsible Teaching: The New Synthesis*. Jossey-Bass, San Francisco, California

Patry J-L 1993 Situation specificity in teaching. In: Olechowski R, Svik G (eds.) 1993 *Experimental Research on Teaching and Learning*. Ludwig Boltzmann Institut, Vienna

Peters T, Waterman R 1982 *In Search of Excellence—Lessons from America's Best-run Companies*. Harper and Row, New York

Piaget J 1963 *The Origins of Intelligence in Children*, Norton, New York

Rogers D, Webb J 1991 The ethic of caring in teacher education. *J. Teach. Educ.* 42 (3): 173–81

Salomon G 1992 The changing role of the teacher: From

information transmitter to orchestrator of learning. In: Oser F, Dick A, Patry J-L (eds.) 1992

Selman R L 1980 *The Growth of Interpersonal Understanding. Developmental and Clinical Analyses.* Academic Press, New York

Simon A B, Howe L W, Kirschenbaum H 1972 *Value Clarification. A Handbook of Practical Strategies for Teachers and Students.* Hart, New York

Solomon D, Watson M, Battistich V, Schaps E, Delucchi K 1992 Creating a caring community: Educational practices that promote children's prosocial development. In: Oser F, Dick A, Patry J-L (eds.) 1992

Strike K A 1990 The legal and moral responsibility of teachers. In: Goodlad J, Soder R, Sirotnik K A (eds.) 1990 *The Moral Dimensions of Teaching,* Jossey-Bass, San Francisco, California

Teacher Development

A. Glatthorn

Teacher development is the professional growth a teacher achieves as a result of gaining increased experience and examining his or her teaching systematically. This entry presents a conceptual model of teacher development, then the significant factors influencing teacher development are identified. The entry concludes by examining the effects of the processes intended to foster teacher growth.

1. The Concept and Related Terms

As Little (1992) notes, teacher development is marked by four types of growth—growth in knowledge, growth in skill, growth in judgment (all of which are classroom-related), and growth in the contributions teachers make to a professional community. Leithwood (1992) posits six increasingly complex levels of such development: (a) developing survival skills, (b) becoming competent in the basic skills of teaching, (c) expanding one's instructional flexibility, (d) acquiring instructional expertise, (e) contributing to the professional growth of colleagues, and (f) exercising leadership and participating in decision-making. Obviously there is a value judgment implicit in Leithwood's analysis, namely, that professional development finds its highest expression in the exercise of leadership. Not all teachers share that value, since many expert teachers seem satisfied to devote all their energies to teaching.

Teacher development can be differentiated from two closely related concepts, "career development" and "staff development." Career development is the growth that occurs as the teacher moves through the professional career cycle; this experiential growth is typically conceptualized as occurring in several clearly demarcated and sequential stages. Staff development is the provision of organized inservice programs designed to foster the growth of groups of teachers; it is only one of the systematic interventions that can be used for teacher development.

2. Factors Influencing Teacher Development

There are three groups of factors that seem to influence teacher development: those involving the teacher as a person, those relating to the context in which the teacher lives and works, and those involving specific interventions to foster teacher development. As shown in Fig. 1, these three factors interact in a complex manner, affecting each other and in turn influencing teacher development. The personal and contextual factors will be examined in this section; and the intervention processes designed to foster growth will be analyzed in the final section of this entry.

2.1 Personal Factors

Most researchers who have examined the personal factors factors influencing teacher development have taken a developmental perspective. Specifically, they have examined chronological age, ego development, moral development, interpersonal development, cognitive development, career development, and mo-

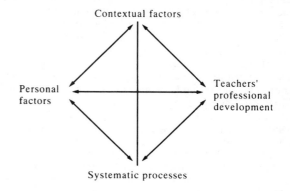

Figure 1
The stress cycle as it affects teachers

tivational development (see Burden 1990). Of these factors, the ones that seem to play the most significant role are the teacher's cognitive development, career development, and motivational development.

2.1.1 Cognitive development. The teacher's cognitive development is usually equated with the extent to which the teacher can reason conceptually. Building upon Hunt's work in conceptual development, Glickman (1981) posited three levels of abstract thinking—low, moderate, and high. Teachers at a low level think more concretely, differentiate fewer concepts, and tend to see problems simplistically; those at a high level can reason abstractly, see connections between disparate elements, and enjoy complexity.

Studies using conceptual level as the variable have concluded that teachers at the high level (as contrasted with those at the low level) are more adaptable and flexible in teaching style, are more empathetic, provide more varied learning environments, are more tolerant of stress, are more effective with students of diverse ethnic backgrounds, and prefer to learn through a discovery model. Although it would seem that cognitive level would be difficult to change, Sprinthall and Thies-Sprinthall (1983) provide evidence that cognitive development can be facilitated by placing persons in significant role-taking situations (such as mentoring), along with continuous guided reflection and ongoing support.

2.1.2 Career development. As noted above, "career development" denotes the growth experienced as teachers move through the stages of their professional careers. Several researchers have investigated the patterns of growth and stagnation that emerge as teachers remain in the profession, each using different terms to identify the stages. The conceptualization that seems to be the most rigorous in its formulation is that advanced by Huberman et al. (1989) (see also Huberman 1989 for a summary of the research).

Huberman's synthesis of the theory and research on career development posits five stages of the professional career, demarcated in terms of years of teaching experience. "Career entry," from the first to the third year, is a time of both survival and discovery. The survival theme is the one most often sounded in studies of beginning teachers; however, many beginning teachers report a sense of discovery as they work with their own pupils and become part of a collegial group. Teachers having from four to six years of teaching experience seem to move into a "stabilization" period when tenure is granted, a definitive commitment to the career of teaching is made, and a sense of instructional mastery is achieved.

Teachers having from 7 to 18 years of experience enter a divergent period. Some report this period as one of experimentation and activism, when they try out new approaches, develop their own courses, and confront institutional barriers. Others report this period as one of self-doubt and reassessment, when disenchantment with the system leads many to consider changing professions.

Divergence also occurs for teachers with 19 to 30 years of experience. For many, it is a time of relaxed self-acceptance and serenity, accompanied by a developing awareness of greater relational distance from their pupils. For others, this period is one of conservatism, with these teachers tending to complain a great deal, criticizing the administrators, their colleagues, and their students.

The final period, from 31 to 40 years of teaching experience, is a stage of disengagement, a gradual withdrawal as the end of the career looms. For some, it is a time of serenity; for others, a time of bitterness.

2.1.3 Motivational development. "Motivation" refers to the strength of the inner drive to achieve professional goals. Glatthorn (1990) has identified several factors that influence a teacher's motivational level. The first is a supportive environment consisting of five features: positive relationships with students and parents, the presence of effective leadership, adequate physical conditions, positive school climate, and a manageable teaching assignment. The second factor is meaningful work. The teacher has an appropriate degree of autonomy and believes in the significance of his or her work.

The third factor is the teacher's belief system. The following beliefs are essential for a high level of motivation. "I can perform successfully." "The actions I take will achieve the results I want." "The results I achieve will be recognized by rewards that I value." Rewards are particularly important. In the United States, teachers are more motivated by such intrinsic rewards as the satisfaction of improving student learning than they are by extrinsic ones such as merit pay (Dilworth 1991). However, a comparison of teachers in France and the United Kingdom concluded that inner-city French teachers are much less likely to perceive teaching as a means of giving meaning to life and are more likely to see it simply as a means of earning a living (Broadfoot and Osborn 1987).

The fourth factor is the teacher's goals. The teacher's level of motivation is more likely to be high when the teacher's goals are shared by peers, when the goal-setting process is a collaborative one, when the goals are specific, and when the goals are challenging but attainable.

The final factor in teacher motivation is the type and frequency of feedback. Several studies suggest that the teacher's level of motivation is more likely to increase when the teacher makes continuing assessments of student learning and uses positive results as reinforcement. Frequent and positive feedback from administrators and supervisors can also increase the level of teacher motivation.

2.2 Contextual Factors

Contextual factors include all those elements of the environment that impact upon teacher development. McLaughlin and Talbert (1990) have identified five embedded contextual layers. The most remote (but not necessarily the least influential) layer is the community and society. Increasing proximal layers are the school system or school district, the school, the teaching team or department, and the classroom.

2.2.1 Society and the community.

Although the societal and community contexts have not been given a great deal of attention in the literature on teacher development, there is evidence that they do play an influential role. The way in which society at large perceives teachers and teaching would likely affect the way teachers view their development. Louis (1990) discusses national differences in this regard.

In Denmark, the general perception is that teachers are collectively responsible for carrying out their job; their craft knowledge is highly valued. As a consequence, teachers are expected to be responsible for the design of improvement efforts. In France, on the other hand, teaching is seen as comprising highly analyzable skills, and teacher autonomy is protected by civil service and union regulations. Although the system is highly centralized, bureaucratic policies sharply limit what teachers can be expected to do relative to their professional development. Japan presents a third model. As Louis notes, cultural traditions there support a view of teachers as good technical experts, motivated by strong norms of collective professional behavior. It is not unusual for Japanese teachers to respond to a perceived problem by forming a voluntary Saturday morning study group.

2.2.2 The school system.

The school system, the next layer of influence, affects teacher development in several ways. Its policies on teacher supervision and evaluation might either constrain or facilitate the professional development of teachers. Its practices and procedures relative to staff development would similarly affect how teachers grow. During the 1980s, school systems in the United States, for example, based most of their staff development programs on a rather narrow conceptualization of the skills of direct instruction, an emphasis that in retrospect probably inhibited significant growth for many experienced teachers who had already internalized those basic skills.

2.2.3 The school.

The school level, the third layer of influence, has been studied more often than any other. The research suggests that, in general, two elements are most influential at the school level: the culture of the school (as manifested in its values and norms of behavior), and the nature of school leadership.

An analysis of the literature on school culture indicates that five beliefs play an instrumental role in teachers' professional development (Fullan 1990, Corcoran 1990, Rosenholtz 1989, Little 1990, Rutter 1987). First, the school is a cooperative community where people act with trust and collegiality. They value the cohesiveness that characterizes such a community. Hargreaves (1992), however, notes the dangers of what he terms "contrived collegiality"—superficial cooperation imposed by administrators in the guise of peer coaching.

Second, there is a belief in common goals. As Rosenholtz (1989) observes in her study of eight elementary schools, a strong consensus about goals leads the principal and the teachers toward a dynamic sense of community, in which professional growth is viewed as an essential part of professionalism. Third, school improvement can be achieved through a problem-solving orientation. Furthermore, professionals will spend the time necessary to solve important school-based problems. Fourth, all those in the school can achieve success; relatedly, people must hold high expectations for themselves and others. Finally, administrators and teachers believe that instruction is their highest priority. Thus, while professional development is essential, it is pursued as a means of improving instruction, not as an end unto itself.

The importance of school leadership in fostering teacher development has been noted in several publications; Leithwood (1992) presents perhaps the most fully developed conceptualization. Focusing upon teacher development as the most central function of instructional leadership, he offers four guidelines for discharging that function more effectively: (a) treat the teacher as a whole person, emphasizing psychological development along with the development of expertise; (b) establish a school culture based on norms of collaboration and professional inquiry; (c) diagnose the starting points for teacher development; and (d) recast routine administrative activities into powerful teacher development strategies.

2.2.4 The teaching team or department.

Teaching peers or colleagues can also influence teacher development. Peers influence each other in three crucial ways: they affect the decision-making of colleagues through informal exchanges in departmental offices, they influence each other in determining the predominant teaching style, and they establish and reinforce informal norms about peer interactions and professional development (Glatthorn 1990). Johnson (1990) underscores the strong influence exerted by department heads as they provide both internal leadership and external advocacy.

2.2.5 The classroom.

The final and most immediate layer is the classroom. A teacher who serves time with unmotivated students, lecturing and drilling, will see little need for professional growth. On the other hand, as Lieberman and Miller (1992) argue, teachers who engage students in problem-solving, who provide opportunities for students' primary research, who use students as teachers, and who connect school life with community life, are in reality growing by teaching. Such a learning-rich environment, they contend, will compel the teacher to grow in significantly new ways.

3. Fostering Teacher Development

Given the strength of those influential factors, what can school administrators, supervisors, and teachers do to foster teacher development? The answers to this question will be presented below from three perspectives: standard approaches to teacher development, alternative processes for teacher growth, and the likely future for teacher development.

3.1 Standard Approaches to Teacher Development

For several decades prior to the 1990s, school administrators and supervisors in most developed nations have relied upon clinical supervision and teacher evaluation as the primary means of fostering teacher development. While these approaches have achieved some success, the evidence tends to suggest that they might have outlived their usefulness for competent experienced teachers.

3.1.1 Clinical supervision. While clinical supervision takes many forms, almost all models include several common elements: a pre-observation conference, an observation of classroom performance, the analysis of observational data, and a post-observation debriefing conference. In a review of 25 studies from 1973 to 1983, Pavan (1983) concluded that the evidence on the effectiveness of clinical supervision was, at best, inconclusive. She also pointed out the pervasive methodological flaws in much of the research she reviewed. In contrast, in a review of studies conducted from 1978 to 1981, Adams and Glickman (1984) concluded that the clinical model has a positive effect on teacher attitude and teacher performance.

In addition to these somewhat mixed findings, clinical supervision has been questioned on other grounds. Glatthorn (1990) pointed out that clinical supervision suffers from several drawbacks: (a) an undue focus on the basic skills of teaching; (b) a failure to differentiate the needs of experienced teachers from those of novices; and, (c) a frequent superficiality in its application, since it is labor intensive. Similarly, Smyth (1989) observed that it has lost its original collaborative emphasis and has degenerated into a sophisticated mechanism of inspection and surveillance.

3.1.2 Teacher evaluation. By the early 1990s, the evaluation of teachers had received a great deal of attention, especially in the United States, where it has

developed as a somewhat predictable consequence of the concern for teacher accountability. In its standard form, a supervisor or an administrator takes to the classroom an observational "scorecard," which lists criteria loosely derived from the research on teacher effectiveness. The evaluator observes the class, completes the scorecard, and confers with the teacher in a conference that has been characterized as a "good news/bad news" session. Typically, the evaluator makes two or three such evaluative observations in the course of the school year and then arrives at a summative assessment that determines whether the teacher will be granted or denied tenure, dismissed or retained, promoted or not promoted.

The effect of these evaluations or inspections on teacher development has been almost totally negative, despite the claims by school systems that the evaluation process was designed to improve instruction (Glickman 1991). Stodolsky (1990) has identified several significant limitations of such observations. First, they do not yield insight into teachers' thinking. Second, they do not provide information on how teachers plan. Third, they give no data on how teachers work with colleagues, students, and parents.

In the light of such criticisms, experts in the field have proposed several alternatives. They are: (a) the use of self-assessment; (b) the development of a cumulative professional portfolio; (c) the administration of performance tests, in which teachers are expected to demonstrate skills and knowledge; and (d) the use of goal-based systems that focus on growth, not evaluation (Millman and Darling-Hammond 1990).

3.2 Alternative Approaches to Teacher Development

There are four alternative approaches to teacher development that seem to be gaining wide currency: self-directed development, cooperative or collegial development, change-oriented staff development, and new roles for teachers.

3.2.1 Self-directed development. In self-directed models of teacher development, the teacher typically identifies a significant goal related to his or her professional development. That goal may be derived from one or more of several sources: the school improvement plan, the advanced skills of teaching, or new knowledge about the subject or students for which the teacher is responsible. The teacher then identifies the means by which he or she will achieve that goal, the resources needed, and the way in which accomplishment will be assessed. In such a self-directed model, the principal or supervisor acts as a facilitator, clarifying goals and methods, providing resources, and sharing in the assessment process.

Clark (1992) has designed a set of seven guidelines for implementing self-directed development: "Write your own credo of teaching." "Start with your strengths." "Make a five-year plan." "Look in your own backyard (use your own classroom as the locus of growth." "Ask for support." "Go first class (pursue quality ventures)." "Finally, blow your own trumpet (let others know about your accomplishments)."

Self-directed models are reported to be effective by those advocating their use. One potential weakness is that growth requires objective feedback; some self-directed models do not provide for this.

3.2.2 Cooperative or collegial development.
"Cooperative professional development" is a term used by Glatthorn (1987) to describe his model of collegial development. In this model, small teams of teachers develop and implement their own approach to professional growth. They choose from several options: professional dialogues—structured discussions focusing on current educational issues that affect them directly; curriculum development—collaborative development of curriculum units and teaching materials; peer supervision—peer observations and debriefing sessions; peer coaching—the development of specific teaching skills through staff development and peer assistance; and action research—collaborative inquiry about a real problem.

The results of several pilot tests suggest that the cooperative model seems to be effective only when the following conditions are in place. First, it grows out of a collaborative organizational environment and is not the result of "contrived collegiality." Second, it has the strong support of administrators. Third, teachers are provided with sufficient time. Finally, teachers are given the training they need to implement the model successfully.

3.2.3 Change-oriented staff development.
Change-oriented staff development programs are recommended by several experts in the field. Rather than offering staff development programs that respond to some new fad, these experts argue that all staff development should be directly related to the school improvement process. Fullan (1990) is among those who have instituted such programs and reports initial success. In the Fullan model, the teacher-as-learner is seen as the central cog linking classroom improvement to school improvement. Throughout the three phases of the change process (initiation, implementation, and institutionalization), teachers work collaboratively to develop the skills and knowledge they need to effect significant and long-term school improvement.

3.2.4 New roles for teachers.
Expanding teachers' roles is seen as a means of both improving the school and facilitating teachers' growth. Typically, such "job-enhancement" strategies provide the teacher with expanded opportunities to make decisions which, in turn, lead to significant professional growth. Conley (1991) identifies four components of school management as possible focuses for increased teacher participation: direction (e.g., determining teaching assignments); organization (e.g., setting schedules for teachers and students); support (e.g., mentoring); and monitoring (e.g., evaluating performance). In all these components, she notes, the critical issue is not involvement, but influence. That is, do teachers have increased influence in the decision-making process?

3.3 Future Directions for Teacher Development
Extrapolating from trends in the larger society and the profession, several trends in teacher development are likely in the near 1990s. First, there will be increased coordination between the preservice and inservice education of teachers. The wide acceptance and early success of "Professional Development Schools" (schools that function as the site of much of the preservice training) should encourage teacher-training institutions to see professional development as an uninterrupted and well-coordinated sequence of experiences.

Second, the use of technology as the central means for delivering staff development programs will increase. The hardware is already available to enable teachers to interact with a distant expert, to participate in professional networks with teachers all across the country, to observe and critique their own teaching, to learn from electronic simulations, and to retrieve and synthesize information. Whether school systems have the resources, the will, or the know-how is uncertain.

Finally, there should be increased contact and collaboration with professionals from other human service organizations. Educators realize that the problems of poverty and ignorance do not stop at the classroom door. As a result, several school systems in the United States have taken a leadership role in using the local school as a one-stop center for families who need help. If services are to be coordinated, the next logical step is to engage teachers, social workers, therapists, and physicians in collaborative professional development.

See also: Inservice Teacher Education; Professional Socialization of Teachers; Teachers' Roles; Realities of Teaching

References

Adams A, Glickman C 1984 Does clinical supervision work? A review of research. *Tennessee Educational Leadership* 11: 28–40
Broadfoot P, Osborn M 1987 Teachers' conceptions of their professional responsibility: Some international comparisons. *Comp. Educ.* 23(3): 287–301
Burden P 1990 Teacher development. In: Houston W R (ed.) 1990 *Handbook of Research on Teacher Education.* Macmillan, New York
Clark C M 1992 Teachers as designers in self-directed professional development. In: Hargreaves A, Fullan M G (eds.) 1992 *Understanding Teacher Development.* Cassell, London
Conley S 1991 Review of research on teacher participation in school decision-making. In: Grant G (ed.) 1991 *Review of Research in Education*, Vol. 17. American Educational

Research Association, Washington, DC

Corcoran T B 1990 Schoolwork: Perspectives on workplace reform. In: McLaughlin M W, Talbert J E, Bascia N (eds.) 1990 *The Contexts of Teaching in Secondary Schools.* Teachers College Press, New York

Dilworth M E 1991 *Motivation, Rewards, and Incentives.* American Association of Colleges for Teacher Education, Washington, DC

Fullan M G 1990 Staff development, innovation, and institutional development. In: Fullan M G, Joyce B, Bruce B B 1990 *Changing School Culture through Staff Development.* Yearbook of the ASCD. Association for Supervision and Curriculum Development, Alexandria, Virginia

Glatthorn A A 1987 Cooperative professional development: Peer-centered options for teacher growth. *Educ. Leadership* 45(3): 31–35

Glatthorn A A 1990 *Supervisory Leadership.* Scott Foresman, Glenview, Illinois

Glickman C D 1981 *Developmental Supervision.* Association for Supervision and Curriculum Development, Alexandria, Virginia

Glickman C D 1991 Pretending not to know what we know. *Educ. Leadership* 48(8): 4–10

Hargreaves A 1992 Cultures of teaching: A focus for change. In: Hargreaves A, Fullan M G (eds.) 1992 *Understanding Teacher Development.* Cassell, London

Huberman M 1989 The professional life cycle of teachers. *Teach. Coll. Rec.* 91(1): 31–57

Huberman M et al. 1989 *La Vie des Enseignants.* Delachaux et Niestle, Lausanne

Johnson S M 1990 The primacy and potential of high school departments. In: McLaughlin M W, Talbert J E, Bascia N 1990 *The Contexts of Teaching in Secondary Schools.* Teachers College Press, New York

Leithwood K A 1992 The principal's role in teacher development. In: Fullan M, Hargreaves A (eds.) 1992 *Teacher Development and Educational Change.* Taylor and Francis, London

Lieberman A, Miller L 1992 Teacher development in professional practice schools. In: Levine M (ed.) 1992 *Professional Practice Schools.* Teachers College Press, New York

Little J W 1990 Conditions of professional development in secondary schools. In: McLaughlin M W, Talbert J E, Bascia N (eds.) 1990 *The Contexts of Teaching in Secondary Schools.* Teachers College Press, New York

Little J W 1992 Teacher development and educational policy. In: Fullan M, Hargreaves A (eds.) 1992 *Teacher Development and Educational Change.* Falmer Press, London

Louis K S 1990 School and community values and the quality of teachers' work life. In: McLaughlin M W, Talbert J E, Bascia N (eds.) 1990 *The Contexts of Teaching in Secondary Schools.* Teachers College Press, New York

McLaughlin M W, Talbert J E 1990 The contexts in question: The secondary school workplace. In: McLaughlin M W, Talbert J E, Bascia N (eds.) 1990 *The Contexts of Teaching in Secondary Schools.* Teachers College Press, New York

Millman J, Darling-Hammond L (eds.) 1990 *The New Handbook of Teacher Evaluation.* Sage, Newbury Park, California

Pavan B N 1983 Clinical supervision: Does it make a difference? Paper presented at annual meeting of the Council of Professors of Instructional Supervision, DeKalb, Illinois

Rosenholtz S J 1989 *Teachers' Workplace: The Social Organization of Schools.* Longman, New York

Rutter R A 1987 *Facilitating Teacher Engagement.* National Center on Effective Secondary Schools, Madison, Wisconsin

Smyth J 1989 Problematizing teaching through a "critical" perspective on clinical supervision. Paper presented at meeting of American Educational Research Association, San Francisco, California

Sprinthall N A, Thies-Sprinthall L 1983 The teacher as adult learner: A cognitive–developmental view. In: Griffin G (ed.) 1983 *Staff Development* (82nd yearbook of the National Society for the Study of Education). University of Chicago Press, Chicago, Illinois

Stodolsky S S 1990 Classroom observation. In: Millman J, Darling-Hammond L (eds.) 1990

Further Reading

Feiman S, Floden R E 1981 *A Consumer's Guide to Teacher Development.* Institute for Research on Teaching, East Lansing, Michigan

Hughes P (ed.) 1991 *Teachers' Professional Development.* Australian Council for Educational Research, Hawthorn, Victoria

Teacher Expertise

D. C. Berliner

The root word for experience and expertise is the same. At one time the two terms apparently signified the same thing. An experienced worker—for example, a brewer, a tanner, or a jewelry maker—had a form of knowledge that was beyond that possessed by ordinary individuals. Guilds and unions, through their apprenticeship systems, portrayed the senior members of their associations as experts. It was obvious, however, that some of those experienced individuals were superior to others and therefore not all who were experienced deserved to be called expert in their work. Thus the notion of expertise eventually became independent from the notion of experience, though the meanings of the terms are entangled and the latter is probably the most important prerequisite for the building of the former. Experts attain their status through experience of a special kind. In the domains in which they are acquiring their abilities, developing experts learn more from experience than do other people.

Although expertise is generally admired, it was not systematically studied by psychologists and others until comparatively recently. Certain areas in psychology were related to contemporary scholarship on expertise, however, such as research on idiot savants; training studies on the acquisition of complex skills, such as diagnosis in medicine or in electronic systems repair; and research on the acquisition of psychomotor skills. The training of telegraphers at the turn of the twentieth century by William Bryan and his student, Noble Harter (1899), was a remarkable example of the latter, revealing the importance of practice, organization, and automaticity in the development of expertise.

> The learner must come to do with one stroke of attention what now requires half a dozen, and presently in one still more inclusive stroke, what now requires 36. He must systematize the work to be done and must acquire a system of habits corresponding to the system of tasks. When he has done this he is master of the situation in his {professional field}. ... Automatization is not genius, but it is the hands and feet of genius. (Bryan and Harter p. 375)

1. The Development of Exemplary Performance

As experience is gained in teaching and other areas, such as computer programming, nursing, piloting an airplane, or playing chess, some individuals get better at what they do. Psychological theories of performance acquisition, corresponding to both common sense and empirical data, usually specify three levels or stages of development—a novice stage, where errors are frequent; an intermediate stage, where some consolidation of learning takes place and automaticity is developed; and, finally, for some who work hard at acquisition of their skills, there is a stage where high levels of performance occur (see Shuell 1990 for reviews of some of these models). The developmental model of Dreyfus and Dreyfus (1986) is a little more complex, but with adaptations, fits the data collected on the acquisition of pedagogical expertise. This heuristic model specifies five stages as an individual moves from novice to expert.

1.1 Stage 1: Novice Level

A teacher at this stage may be called a greenhorn, a raw recruit, or a novice. The commonplaces of the school and classroom environments must be discriminated, the elements of the tasks to be performed need to be labeled and learned, and a set of general (i.e., context-free) rules must be acquired. The novice teacher is taught the meaning of terms like "higher-order questions," "reinforcement," and "learning disabled." Novices are taught rules such as "give praise for right answer," "wait three seconds after asking a higher-order question," and "never criticize a student." This is a stage for learning the objective facts and features of situations and for gaining experience. It is the stage at which real-world experience appears to the learner to be far more important than verbal information. Student teachers and many first-year teachers may be considered novices.

1.2 Stage 2: Advanced Beginner Level

As experience is gained, the novice becomes an advanced beginner (see Bullough 1989 for a case study of a teacher in the transition from a novice to an advanced beginner). Many second- and third-year teachers are likely to be in this developmental stage. In this stage experience can become melded with verbal knowledge, where episodic and case knowledge is built up. Similarities across contexts are recognized. Without meaningful past episodes and cases to which experience of the present can be related, individuals are unsure of themselves; they do not know what to do or what not to do. In education advanced beginners might have difficulty knowing what to do when a child challenges the teacher's authority, neurotically seeks the teacher's attention, or boasts of their "A" performance. Strategic knowledge—when to ignore or break rules and when to follow them—is also developed in this stage as context begins to guide behavior. For example, teachers learn that praise does not always have the desired effect, as when a low-ability child interprets it as communicating low expectations. They also learn that criticism after a bad performance by a usually good student can be quite motivating. Experience is affecting behavior but the advanced beginner may still have no sense of what is important.

The novice and the advanced beginner, though intensely involved in the learning process, often fail to take full responsibility for their actions. This failure occurs because they are labeling and describing events, following rules, and recognizing and classifying contexts, but not yet actively determining through personal agency what is happening. The acceptance of full personal responsibility for classroom instruction occurs when one develops a sense of personal agency, willfully choosing what to do. This acceptance occurs in the next stage of development.

1.3 Stage 3: Competent Level

With further experience, and some motivation to succeed, most of the advanced beginners become competent teachers. Not all advanced beginners, however, are likely to reach this level. Evidence exists that some teachers remain "fixed" at a less than competent level of performance (Borko 1992, Eisenhart and Jones 1992). Nevertheless it is believed that many third- and fourth-year teachers, as well as most experienced teachers, reach a level of performance that is considered to be competent.

There are two distinguishing characteristics of competent performers of a skill. First, they make conscious choices about what they are going to do. They set priorities and decide on plans. They have rational goals and choose sensible means for reaching the ends they have in mind. Second, while enacting their skill, they can determine what is and what is not important. From their experience they know what to attend to and what to ignore. As a consequence, they also learn not to make timing and targeting errors. In this stage teachers learn to make curriculum and instruction decisions, such as when to stay with a topic and when to move on, based on a particular teaching context and a particular group of students.

Because they are more personally in control of the events around them, following their own plans and responding only to the information they choose, teachers at the competent stage tend to feel more responsibility for what happens. They are not detached and thus often feel emotional about success and failure in their area in a way that is different and more intense than do novices or advanced beginners. They also have more vivid memories of their successes and failures. Competent teachers are still not yet very fast, fluid, or flexible.

1.4 Stage 4: Proficient Level

Perhaps in about the fifth year, a modest number of teachers may move into the proficient stage of development, a stage at which intuition or know-how becomes prominent. To use an analogy, at some point in learning a dance step individuals no longer think about the kinds of adjustments needed; they stop counting their steps to keep time to the music, and develop a more "intuitive" sense of the situation.

Furthermore, out of the wealth of experience that the proficient individuals have accumulated comes a holistic way of viewing the situations they encounter. They recognize similarities among events that the novice fails to see. For example, the proficient teacher may notice, without conscious effort, that today's mathematics lesson is faltering for the same reason that last week's spelling lesson failed. At some higher level of pattern categorization, the similarities between disparate events are understood. This holistic recognition of patterns as similar allows the proficient individual to predict events more precisely, since they see more things as alike and as having been experienced before.

1.5 Stage 5: Expert Level

If the novice is deliberate, the advanced beginner insightful, the competent performer rational, and the proficient performer intuitive, the expert might be categorized as often arational. Experts have an intuitive grasp of the situation and seem to sense in nonanalytic and nondeliberative ways the appropriate response to be made. They show fluid performance, as most people do when they no longer have to choose their words when speaking, or think about where to place their feet when walking. People simply talk and walk in an apparently effortless manner.

Experts perform in a way that is qualitatively different from the novice or the competent performer. They are exemplified by a science teacher who reports that the lesson moved along so well today that she never really had to teach. Experts are not consciously choosing what to attend to and what to do. They are acting effortlessly and fluidly, and in a sense this is arational because it is not easily described as deductive or analytic behavior. Though beyond the usual meaning of rational, since neither calculation nor deliberative thought are involved, the behavior of the expert is certainly not irrational. Insight into the behavior of the expert can be obtained from the writings of Schon (1983), as he discusses knowledge-in-action, and from the work of Polya (1954), in his discussion of the role played by tacit knowledge in problem-solving.

Tasks carried out by experts usually work, and thus, when matters proceed without any trouble, experts are not solving problems or making decisions in the usual sense. When anomalies occur, when matters do not work out as planned or something atypical is noted, deliberate analytic processes are brought to bear upon the situation. When things are going smoothly, however, experts rarely appear to be reflective about their performance.

2. Descriptive Propositions about Teacher Expertise

The theory of the development of teacher expertise has heuristic value for thinking about educating and evaluating teachers. It is also reasonably well-supported by data collected since the late 1980s (Berliner 1987, Berliner et al. 1988). For example, Bents and Bents (1990) studied the transitions that occur between novice, advanced beginner, and expert teachers and verified the sensibility of these stages. They characterized the transition as moving from a teacher-centered or self-centered novice, to a more student-centered advanced beginner, to a stage in which the expert teacher was a much more integrated individual.

Almost all studies of pedagogical expertise have been small-scale and nonexperimental. However, there is some consistency across these studies, and there are a number of strong propositions about expertise in pedagogy. While some of these overlap with the general characteristics of experts, others are specific to the domain of teaching.

2.1 Proposition 1: Domain and Context

The first proposition is that experts excel mainly in their own domain and in particular contexts.

Chi et al. (1988) and Glaser (1987) note that experts excel primarily in a single domain because they have a great deal more experience in some domains than in others. In studies by Lesgold and his colleagues

(1988) expert radiologists were estimated to be looking at their 100,000th X-ray. Chess experts have spent 10,000–20,000 hours staring at chess positions (deGroot 1965, Newell and Simon 1972, Chase and Simon 1973). With the lengthy time commitments that are necessary to become expert in complex areas of human functioning, it is not surprising that individuals generally excel in only a single domain.

Time and experience play a similar role in the development of pedagogical expertise. Anecdotal reports suggest that teachers will not hit their peak performance until at least five years of on-the-job experience have been obtained. The expert teacher, say with 10 years experience, has spent a minimum of 10,000 hours in classrooms as a teacher, preceded by a least 15,000 hours in classrooms as a student, though it is unknown if the latter experience is of any value. Experience alone certainly will not make a teacher an expert, but it is likely that almost every expert pedagogue has had extensive classroom experience.

The domain-specific knowledge that is acquired through lengthy experience is quite contextualized. For example, expert teachers have reported that their expertise depends, in part, on knowing their students. They know the cognitive abilities of the students they teach regularly, giving them insight for determining the level at which to teach. They know their students personally, so that in their classrooms they do not need to rely on bureaucratic and formal mechanisms of control while teaching. Finally, their students knew about them and had certain expectations about what their teaching would be like. Expert teachers had students who expected to be well taught and to learn a great deal, even if they were pushed to their intellectual limits (Berliner et al. 1988).

2.2 Proposition 2: Automaticity

The second proposition is that experts often develop automaticity for the repetitive operations that are needed to accomplish their goals.

Glaser (1987) notes the efficient decoding skill of the expert comprehender in reading as an example of the way automaticity frees working memory to allow other more complex characteristics of the situation to be dealt with. The automaticity or routinization of some teaching functions among expert teachers serves the same purpose. For example, Leinhardt and Greeno (1986), in studying elementary school mathematics lessons, compared an expert's opening homework review with that of a novice. The expert teacher was found to be quite brief, taking about one-third less time than the novice. This expert was able to pick up information about attendance, about who did or did not do the homework, and was also able to identify who was going to need help later in the lesson. She elicited mostly correct answers throughout the activity and managed also to get all the homework corrected. Moreover, she did so at a brisk pace and never lost any control of the lesson.

In contrast, when the novice was enacting an opening homework review as part of a mathematics lesson, she was not able to get an understanding on who did and did not do the homework, she had problems with taking attendance, and she asked ambiguous questions that led to her misunderstanding of the difficulty of the homework. Of importance is that the novice showed a lack of familiarity with well-practiced routines. She seemed not to have habitual ways to act. Students, therefore, were unsure of their roles in the class. Additional research supportive of this proposition has been conducted by Brooks and Hawke (1985), Carter et al. (1987), Krabbe and Tullgren (1989), and Hawkins and Sharpe (in press).

2.3 Proposition 3: Task Demands and Social Situations

The third proposition is that experts are more sensitive to task demands and social situations when solving problems.

Housner and Griffey (1985), in a study of experienced and novice physical education teachers, provide evidence of the sensitivity of experienced teachers to task demands and social situations. They found that the number of requests for information made by experienced and novice teachers during the time they were planning instruction was about the same. Each group made reasonable requests for information about the number of students they would be teaching, their gender, their age, and so forth, but in two areas the experienced teachers made many more requests than did the novice teachers. They needed to know about the ability, experience, and background of the students they were to teach, and they needed to know about the facility in which they would be teaching. In fact, five of the eight experienced teachers in this study of planning and instruction demanded to see the facility in which they would teach before they could develop their plan. Novices made no such requests.

Experienced teachers were sensitive to the social and physical environment under which instruction was to take place. When actually teaching they implemented changes in their instruction more often than did novices, using social cues to guide their interactive instructional decision-making. They used their judgment about student performance as a cue to change instruction 24 percent more often than did novices. They used their judgments about student involvement as a cue 41 percent more often, student enjoyment of the activities as a cue 79 percent more frequently, and their interpretation of mood and student feelings 82 percent more often.

The novices used student verbal statements about the activity as their primary cue for instituting a change in their instructional activity. They responded to these cues 131 percent more often than did the experienced teachers. Clearly, the novice teachers changed what they were doing primarily when asked to; however, they seemed unable to decode the social cues emitted by students about the ways in which instruction was proceeding. The experienced teachers, on the other hand, were far more sensitive to the social cues emitted in the situation, and they used these social cues for adjusting their instruction. Other examples of this sensitivity to the task demands and social setting abound (Nelson 1988, Cushing et al. 1989, and Hawkins and Sharpe in press).

2.4 Proposition 4: Opportunism and Flexibility

The fourth proposition is that experts are more opportunistic and flexible in their teaching than are novices.

Glaser (1987) reports that experts are opportunistic in both their planning and their actions. They take advantage of new information, quickly bringing new interpretations and representations of the problem to light. Borko and Livingston (1988) use the term "improvizational performer" to characterize the opportunistic quality of the lessons of expert teachers. They see the expert teachers as having a well-thought-out general script to follow, but being very flexible in following it in order to be responsive to what students do.

Professor Richard Snow of Stanford University once described teaching using the metaphor of "the teacher as a Bayesian sheepdog." The image is that of the teacher or sheepdog letting the students or flock wander, to a certain extent, but bringing them back into line if they stray too far. The teacher can be flexible and opportunistic, but based on remembrances of past experiences (the Bayesian calculation of prior probabilities) the teacher also keeps the students on a course that has them conclude at an appropriate place.

2.5 Proposition 5: Approach to Problems

The fifth proposition is that experts represent problems in qualitatively different ways than do novices.

Chi et al. (1988) note that experts seem to understand problems at a deeper level than do novices. Experts apply concepts and principles that are more relevant to the problem to be solved. The understanding of novices seems to be at a more superficial level, with fewer instances shown of principled reasoning.

Nelson (1988) conducted a study in which expert and novice physical education teachers were the subjects. She concluded that experts displayed a greater variety of application of sound principles of teaching than did novices. The experts were also more creative and thorough in descriptions of ways to address teaching problems, and provided more solutions to each problem that they addressed. Similarly, Peterson and Comeaux (1987) found that the comments of experienced teachers reflected an underlying knowledge structure, while those of novices did not.

Expert teachers also differ in the inferences they make about the student cognitions used in answering an item. Experts seemed to have a fund of knowledge about the way students think and how those thoughts interact with the content of the specific mathematics or science items. In addition, the experts seemed able to think through the misalgorithms that students might apply. The experts had more experience dealing with student errors and therefore knew what types of errors students might make. Novices rarely discussed the issue of misalgorithms that students might apply to solve a problem.

2.6 Proposition 6: Interpreting Patterns

The sixth proposition is that experts have fast and accurate pattern-recognition capabilities. Novices cannot always make sense of what they experience.

The accurate interpretation of cues and the recognition of patterns reduces a person's cognitive processing load. Quick pattern recognition allows an expert chess player to spot areas of the board where difficulties might occur. Novices are not as good at recognizing such patterns, and when they do note them they are less likely to make proper inferences about the situation.

The ability of novices or other relatively inexperienced teachers to interpret classroom information in some reliable way is limited precisely because of their lack of experience. The information related to pedagogical events may be so rich and complex that novices and advanced beginners simply cannot agree on what is seen. In a study in which three television screens had to be monitored simultaneously, advanced beginners seemed to experience difficulty in making sense of their classroom observations and in providing plausible explanations about what was occurring within the classroom (Sabers et al. 1991). As a group, these first-year teachers seemed unable to make sense of what they saw. They experienced difficulty monitoring all three video screens at once. Thus, they often reported contradictory observations and appeared confused about what they were observing and about the meaning of their observations.

Carter et al. (1988) also found differences in the interpretive competency of experts and novices. In this study, novice, advanced beginner, and expert teachers were asked to watch a series of slides depicting science or mathematics instruction in a high school. The teachers held a remote control and were told to go through the 50 or so slides at their own pace, stopping to comment on any slides that they found interesting. The experts, more often than the subjects in the other groups, found the same slides worth commenting about, and made the same kinds of comments.

This reduction in variance by the experts is particularly noteworthy. It means they have learned to pay attention to some of the same things and to interpret visual stimuli in the same way. This similarity in what is attended to and how it is interpreted is what people hope for when they visit an expert ophthalmologist or automobile mechanic. Novices or advanced beginners—anyone in the early stages of skill acquisition—will not have acquired enough experience for that.

2.7 Proposition 7: Meaningfulness and Patterns

The seventh proposition is that experts perceive meaningful patterns in the domain in which they are experienced.

The superior perceptual skills of experts are readily apparent, but there is no reason to believe they are the result of any innate superior perceptual abilities (Chi et al. 1988). Rather, their superiority can be attributed to the way in which experience affects perception. After 100,000 X-rays, or the 10,000th hour of observing students, what is attended to and how that information is interpreted is likely to have changed for anyone motivated to learn from their experience. In this regard, Carter et al. (1988) asked expert, novice, and advanced beginners to view some slides of classrooms and describe what they saw. The slides were flashed on the screen for only a very brief time. The responses of the novices and advanced beginners to the slide were clearly descriptive, and usually quite accurate. In contrast to these literal descriptions typical of novices and advanced beginners, some of the expert teachers often responded with inferences about what they saw. For experts, the information that was often deemed important was information that had instructional significance, such as the age of the students or the teaching/learning activity in which they were engaged. They perceived more meaningful patterns than did novices.

In any field, the information that experts extract from the phenomenon with which they are confronted, stems, in part, from the concepts and principles that they use to impose meaning on phenomena in their domain of expertise. That is, experts in all domains appear to be top-down processors. They impose meaning on the stimuli in their domain of expertise.

2.8 Proposition 8: Problem-solving Characteristics

The final proposition is that, although experts may begin to solve problems slower, they bring richer and more personal sources of information to bear on the problem that they are trying to solve.

In Hanninen's (1985) study of expert and less expert teachers of gifted children, the mean time for a novice to read through a scenario and begin writing about ways to help solve the problems of a particular child was 2.6 minutes. The experienced teachers, who had no background in gifted education, took 3.0 minutes. The mean time for teachers with experience/expertise in teaching gifted children was 9.8 minutes. That is, from the start of reading their problem up to the start of presenting their solutions, it took the experts three or four times as long as the other two groups. When one knows a good deal more about teaching, or some other domain, more time seems to be needed to represent the problem and to access the relevant knowledge needed to address the problem. If one does not have much information in storage, one need not look too long for relevant information.

Experts, unlike novices, can bring to bear rich personal stores of knowledge when they begin to address the problems they face. Peterson and Comeaux (1987) found that their experienced teachers "often gave more elaborated answers to the questions and gave more justifications for their decisions or comments." Nelson (1988) found that experts "provide longer and more detailed analyses of situational data; were more creative and thorough in descriptions of ways to handle various teaching concerns; provided more solutions to problems; were more thoughtful to needs of individual students; displayed a greater variety of application of sound principles of teaching."

3. Conclusion

Capturing the uniqueness of expert teaching performance is difficult. All of the studies to date have been small, generally qualitative, and highly interpretive. Furthermore, they have tended to be descriptive rather than experimental. As a consequence, there are continuing problems in adequately identifying expert, proficient, and competent teachers, and these questions lead to problems with theory development.

On the other hand, the problem is not insurmountable for those in search of a heuristic rather than a scientifically adequate theory about the development of expertise. Theory, it should be remembered, is not to be judged on its truthfulness, but on its usefulness. The five-stage theory presented in this entry fits data well enough to allow educationalists and researchers to think sensibly about the development of knowledge and skill in teaching.

Generalizing from studies in this domain is not too difficult. The propositions offered by Glaser (1987) from studies of expertise across disparate fields are highly compatible with the ones derived from studies of teaching. Thus, teacher expertise provides an interesting case in which many imperfect studies, across many different fields, have yielded a coherent body of knowledge and a heuristic theory to think about the acquisition of expertise in teaching.

Individuals who excel at a task, whether it be physics, medical diagnosis, chess, or teaching are of great interest, and provide psychology with subjects that have unique perceptual, conceptual, and psychomotor skill. When people have reasons to master some domain, and the opportunity to do so, they can reach levels of competency, proficiency, and expertise not ordinarily achieved.

References

Bents M, Bents R 1990 Perceptions of good teaching among novice, advanced beginner, and expert teachers. Paper presented at the meeting of the American Educational Research Association, Boston, Massachusetts

Berliner D C 1987 In pursuit of the expert pedagogue. *Educ. Researcher* 15: 5–13

Berliner D C et al. 1988 Implications of research on pedagogical expertise and experience for mathematics teaching. In: Grouws D A, Cooney T J (eds.) 1988 *Perspectives on Research on Effective Mathematics Teaching*. National Council of Teachers of Mathematics, Reston, Virginia

Borko H 1992 Patterns across the profiles: A critical look at theories of learning to teach. Paper presented at the meeting of the American Educational Research Association, San Francisco, California

Borko H, Livingston C 1988 Expert and novice teachers' mathematics instruction: Planning, teaching, and post-lesson reflections. Paper presented at the meeting of the American Educational Research Association, New Orleans, Louisiana

Brooks D M, Hawke G 1985 Effective and ineffective session opening teacher activity and task structures. Paper presented at the meeting of the American Educational Research Association, Chicago, Illinois

Bryan W L, Harter N 1899 Studies of the telegraphic language: The acquisition of a hierarchy of habits. *Psychol. Rev.* 6: 345–75

Bullough R 1989 *First Year Teacher: A Case Study*. Teachers College Press, New York

Carter K, Cushing K, Sabers D, Stein P, Berliner D C 1988 Expert–novice differences in perceiving and processing visual information. *J. Teach. Educ.* 39 (3): 25–31

Carter K, Sabers D, Cushing K, Pinnegar P, Berliner D C 1987 Processing and using information about students: A study of expert, novice, and postulant teachers. *Teaching and Teacher Education* 3: 147–57

Chase W G, Simon H A 1973 Perception in chess. *Cognit. Psychol.* 4: 55–81

Chi M T H, Glaser R, Farr M 1988 *The Nature of Expertise*. Erlbaum, Hillsdale, New Jersey

Cushing K S, Sabers D, Berliner D C 1989 Expert–novice research studies: Implications for teacher empowerment. In: Kerrins J A (Ed.) 1989 *Empowering the Teaching Learning Process*, Proc. 6th Annual Conf. on Issues and Trends in Educational Leadership. Colorado Springs, Colorado

deGroot A D 1965 *Thought and Choice in Chess*. Mouton, The Hague

Dreyfus H L, Dreyfus S E 1986 *Mind over Machine*. Free Press, New York

Eisenhart M, Jones D 1992 Developing teacher expertise: Two theories and a study. Paper presented at the meeting of the American Educational Research Association, San Francisco, California

Glaser R 1987 Thoughts on expertise. In: Schooler C, Schaie W (Eds.), *Cognitive Functioning and Social Structure over the Life Course*. Ablex, Norwood, New Jersey

Hanninen G 1985 Do experts exist in gifted education? (Unpublished manuscript, University of Arizona, Tucson, Arizona)

Hawkins A, Sharpe T in press Field system analysis: In search of the expert pedagogue. *The Journal of Teaching in Physical Education*

Housner L D, Griffey D C 1985 Teacher cognition: Differences in planning and interactive decision-making between experienced and inexperienced teachers. *Research Quarterly for Exercise and Sport* 56: 44–53

Krabbe M A, Tullgren R 1989 A comparison of experienced and novice teachers' routines and procedures during set and discussion instructional activity segments. Paper presented at the meeting of the American Educational Research Association, San Francisco, California

Leinhardt G, Greeno J 1986 The cognitive skill of teaching. *J. Educ. Psychol.* 78: 75–95

Lesgold A et al. 1988 Expertise in a complex skill: Diagnosing X-ray pictures. In: Chi M T H, Glaser R, Farr M 1988

Nelson K R 1988 Thinking processes, management routines, and student perceptions of expert and novice physical education teachers. (Unpublished dissertation, Louisiana State University, Baton Rouge, Louisiana)

Newell A, Simon H A 1972 *Human Problem Solving*. Prentice-Hall, Englewood Cliffs, New Jersey

Peterson P L, Comeaux M A 1987 Teachers' schemata for classroom events: The mental scaffolding of teachers' thinking during classroom instruction. *Teaching and Teacher Education* 3: 319–31

Polya G 1954 *How to Solve It*. Princeton University Press, Princeton, New Jersey

Sabers D, Cushing K, Berliner D C 1991 Differences among teachers in a task characterized by simultaneity, multidimensionality, and immediacy. *Am. Educ. Res. J.* 28: 63–88

Schon D 1983 *The Reflective Practitioner*. Basic Books, New York

Shuell T 1990 Phases of meaningful learning. *Rev. Res. Educ.* 60: 531–48

Teacher Stress and Burnout

R. L. Schwab

The study of stress has captured the interest of both researchers and practitioners since the concept was first defined and explored by Seyle in the mid-1940s. According to Gmelch (1988), over 100,000 books, journals, and articles have focused on the phenomenon of stress. This entry focuses specifically on stress in the teaching profession. Common terms are defined, major sources of stress are identified, the effects of stress are described, ways in which teachers can cope with stress are suggested, and future directions for research are offered.

1. Defining Teacher Stress and Burnout

Seyle's (1946) early work defined stress as the nonspecific response of the body to any demand made upon it to adapt, whether that demand produces pleasure or pain. Since Seyle posited his initial definition, scholars have debated its validity and have tried to establish a common definition, of stress that incorporates current knowledge about the phenomenon. While contemporary scholars have not generated a common definition, they agree that stress is an integrated, multidimensional response that occurs when people perceive that the demands of a situation exceed their ability to meet or cope with those demands. This response includes the physiological, cognitive, and behavioral systems of the individual. (For a more complete explanation see Hiebert and Farber 1984.)

As in the case of stress, defining "burnout" has been a focus of debate among researchers. Freudenberger (1974) is credited with being the first to describe and define this phenomenon. He used the term to describe people in helping professions who experienced a state of exhaustion and fatigue brought on by working too long, too much, and too intensely with needy clients. Freudenberger's work was anecdotal and conjectural in nature rather than research-based. His work was important, however, because it laid the groundwork for subsequent empirical studies that focused on helping professionals.

Maslach was one of the first people systematically to study job burnout in the helping professions. Maslach and her colleagues at the University of California at Berkeley initiated a series of large-scale studies that included such human service professionals as social workers, counselors, day care workers, police officers, and public defense lawyers. According to Maslach (1982) burnout is the behavioral response of people who experience constant stress from working in occupations that require continual, intensive interactions with people. Those who cannot effectively cope with this work-related stress develop feelings of emotional exhaustion, negative attitudes toward their clients, and a sense that they are no longer accomplishing anything worthwhile in their job. These feelings are quite different from those experienced by helpers early in their career. A common one-liner by stress researchers is "you cannot burn out if you were never on fire to begin with."

Several large-scale international studies have extended Maslach's work to the field of teaching (e.g., Schwab and Iwanicki 1982a, Dewe 1986, Kremer-Hayon and Goldstein 1990, Friesen et al. 1988). While researchers may differ in their exact definition of teacher burnout, all indicate that it is a response of teachers who have trouble coping with the stress of the job. They also agree that the three types of behavioral reactions described in the following paragraphs are typical for teachers experiencing burnout.

One of the first symptoms of burnout is the development of chronic feelings of emotional exhaustion. Teachers in this stage express feelings of being tired, irritable, and emotionally drained. Affected individuals often express dread at having to get up in the morning to go to work. Emotionally exhausted teachers often develop negative, cynical attitudes toward their students. This change in attitude from "warm and caring" to emotionally removed is the second aspect of burnout and is often referred to as depersonalization. This stage is evidenced in various ways. A common way that teachers display depersonalized attitudes is by withdrawing from contact with students. For example, teachers who never stray from behind their desk may well be physically withdrawing from their students. Teachers may also psychologically withdraw from students by ignoring or refusing to acknowledge them. Treating students as impersonal objects, calling them derogatory names, or using labels to describe individual students are further indications of depersonalization.

A third aspect of burnout occurs when teachers begin to feel they are no longer accomplishing anything worthwhile in their work. Teachers enter the profession hoping to help students gain knowledge and to make a positive impact on society. When teachers feel they are no longer making a difference in students' lives they find that their profession offers few other rewards such as money or recognition. Low feelings of accomplishment combined with the effect of the other two aspects of burnout may reduce motivation to the point where failure becomes a way of life. Social psychologists refer to this as "learned helplessness."

There are many adverse consequences for both the individual and his or her organization as a result of teacher burnout. Those experiencing burnout are more likely to have a lower quality of personal life, be absent from work more often, exert less effort in teaching, and spend a considerable amount of time looking for a new line of work. In terms of health, the afflicted individual is more inclined to develop substance abuse problems and experience stress-related phenomena such as insomnia. Regardless of whether the consequences affect the individual or the organization, the teacher's students are the ultimate losers (Dworkin 1987).

2. Sources of Stress

The sources of stress for any individual teacher or school staff vary greatly. While research has identified several environmental and personal/background factors that are related to aspects of burnout, it has not been able to place these in any defensible order or hierarchy of importance. Figure 1 presents a framework for describing the stress cycle as it affects teachers.

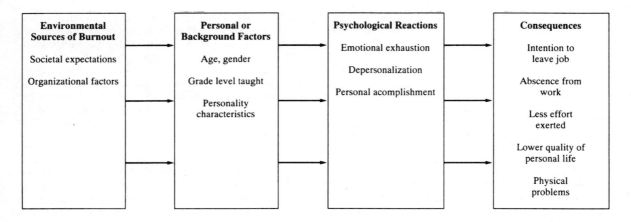

Environmental Sources of Burnout	**Personal or Background Factors**	**Psychological Reactions**	**Consequences**
Societal expectations	Age, gender	Emotional exhaustion	Intention to leave job
Organizational factors	Grade level taught	Depersonalization	Absence from work
	Personality characteristics	Personal acomplishment	Less effort exerted
			Lower quality of personal life
			Physical problems

Figure 1
The nature of teacher development

As indicated in Fig. 1, individuals react differently to environmental stress. How a person reacts to stress depends upon the nature of the stress encountered and his or her individuality. Noted stress researchers French and Caplan (1972) refer to this as "goodness of fit' between job demands and individual abilities. As illustrated in Fig 1, if the fit is one of incongruence, then the individual's psychological reaction could be burnout. Furthermore, when feelings of burnout persist, the person is more likely to develop behaviors that have negative consequences for the individual, the organization, and the students.

2.1 Societal Sources

Societal sources include those factors that are beyond the direct control of the individual or the organization in which he or she works. Most industrialized, as well as Third World countries, hold high expectations for their teaching force. While the historical context, organizational structure, and societal values may differ across cultures, some expectations are consistent. Teachers are expected to instill values, teach basic and higher order thinking skills, nurture the development of students to become independent learners, and encourage students to collaborate to achieve common goals. Further, educational institutions are seen as the key to economic growth and development which places an additional stress on teachers. While most societies have high expectations for what education can do, teachers perceive that the resources to accomplish this task are limited (Kremer-Hayon and Goldstein 1990).

An issue identified as a major stressor by teachers around the globe concerns the attitudes of students they are responsible for educating (Kyriacou 1987). Teachers indicate that the poor work attitude of students and their lack of motivation are among the most stressful issus faced on a daily basis.

For example, Friedman and Farber (1992) report that student misbehavior, lack of attentiveness, and low enthusiasm for learning material are significant contributors to burnout in Israeli educators. Similar findings have been reported in separate studies with teachers from New Zealand (Dewe 1986), Japan (Ninomiya and Okata 1990), the United Kingdom (Kyriacou 1987), the West Indies (Payne and Furnham 1987), Canada (Byrne 1992), and the United States (Goodlad 1984).

2.2 Organizational Sources

Organizational practices at the school and district level have been identified as major sources of stress for teachers. Two of the more frequently recognized organizational contributors to teacher burnout are role conflict and role ambiguity (Crane and Iwanicki 1986, Schwab and Iwanicki 1982a, Byrne 1992). Role conflict occurs when an individual is faced with two conflicting sets of inconsistent but expected role behaviors. Stress results from the individual's inability to reconcile the inconsistency. Role ambiguity is the lack of clear, consistent information regarding the rights, duties, and responsibilities of a person's occupation and how they can best be performed (Kahn et al. 1964). Stress results from this ambiguity.

Schwab et al. (1986) found that in addition to role conflict and role ambiguity other organizational factors contributed to higher stress levels. First, individuals with lower levels of burnout felt they had more freedom and autonomy in deciding what and how to teach. Second, teachers who believed they were able to participate in school-related decision-making processes also reported a lower incidence of stress. Third, teachers who felt their organization had a system for providing contingent rewards for good work and contingent punishments for sub-par efforts were less stressful.

The absence or presence of an effective collegial social support network in the work setting has been shown to be related to all aspects of burnout (Blase 1986, Jackson et al. 1986, Rodgers-Jenkinson and Chapman 1990). In this regard, it is important to note that social support from one's colleagues has been shown to be more important than administrator support. An effective support group includes people who provide emotional comfort, confront the individual in humane ways when the individual's behaviors are inappropriate, provide work-related support, present technical challenges that promote individual growth, serve as active listeners, and share similar values, beliefs, and perceptions of reality (Pines et al. 1981).

The majority of research studies that have examined the relationship of organizational variables to levels of teacher burnout have depended upon self-reported survey instruments. Samples of teachers have been primarily cross-sectional, while a few studies have used individual schools as the unit of analysis (Hubert et al. 1990). These studies have often used regression analysis or similar statistical procedures to identify stress factors having the highest relationship with burnout scores. Even the most complete and sophisticated studies explain only 20 to 40 percent of the variance in burnout. Thus, one might hypothesize that individual differences account for a great deal of variation in how stress is handled by teachers or that other environmental factors have not been identified.

2.3 Individual and Background Variables

Unfortunately, the science of personality inventories and tests is far from perfect, and comprehensive instruments are difficult, time-consuming and expensive to design and administer. Consequently, many studies have examined isolated personality characteristics and their relationship to teacher burnout, rather then holistically looking at personality differences and their contribution to burnout.

For example, McIntyre (1984) and Lutz and Maddirala (1990) found that teachers with an external locus of control were more likely to experience burnout than those with an internal locus. Teachers with an external locus of control are inclined to feel that their destiny is not in their own hands and their lives are controlled by others. They believe luck, fate, or powerful others are responsible for what happens to them. Individuals with an internal locus feel that events in one's life are within one's own control.

Anderson and Iwanicki (1984) and Malanowski and Wood (1984) found that when teachers felt that their higher order needs were addressed in their work they were less likely to experience job burnout. Higher order needs include self-actualization (i.e., need for success, achievement, achieving full potential) and self-esteem (i.e., self and others' respect for what one does).

In addition, several background factors are related to levels of burnout. Studies have shown that men are more likely to experience burnout than women, teaching at elementary school is less stressful than at the middle and secondary level, single people experience higher levels of stress than married individuals, and teachers in larger and urban schools experience more stress (Burke and Greenglass 1989, Farber 1991, Schwab and Iwanicki 1982b, Malonowski and Wood 1984).

3. Coping with and Alleviating Stress

Research on the effectiveness of intervention strategies to alleviate teacher stress is limited. The few studies that exist have focused on isolated aspects of managing stress. For example, Jenkins and Calhoun (1991) found teachers who received training in personal stress-reducing activities did engage in those activities more frequently after completing the workshops. They were not able to determine whether or not participating in those activities reduced stress levels. Only one study was found that examined an intervention on the organizational level and it had limited results. Schwab (1991) studied the effectiveness of different organizational approaches to establishing support groups for teaching interns. While his studies found some benefits when placing several teaching interns in the same school and holding regular support group meetings, he found little difference in stress levels of interns who participated in the alternative approaches.

4. Research Issues

The good news regarding the status of research on teacher stress and burnout is that a great deal more is known about the topic in the 1990s than was known 20 years before. The bad news is that much more needs to be known about the dynamic nature of how environmental factors interact with individual differences to cause burnout and what can be done about it. The following research activities should shed some light on these and other issues of importance.

First, there is a glaring need for longitudinal studies that focus on the complex interaction of personality type and environmental stressors. One-time, cross-sectional studies are fine for answering some questions but not for understanding the complexity that occurs within the dynamic interactions of personality and environment over time.

Second, valid and reliable inventories that accurately measure personality differences, levels of stress, and potential environmental factors that cause stress need to be refined and in some cases developed. Many valid and reliable instruments exist that look at pieces of the puzzle while comprehensive measures that could be useful in developing intervention strategies are limited.

Third, holistic intervention strategies that address organizational factors and individual coping strategies should be developed by interdisciplinary teams including psychologists, social psychologists, organizational behaviorists, medical researchers, educational administration researchers, and psychometricians. Studies that monitor the effectiveness of these intervention strategies must be longitudinally studied in order to determine if stress levels can be reduced and then sustained at these lower levels. Knowledge about the phenomenon is sufficient to begin such studies.

Finally, school reform and restructuring is occurring around the globe. As school restructuring efforts evolve, cross-cultural comparisons will present an exciting area of inquiry. For example, in the United States the move to site-based management, teacher involvement in decision-making, mainstreaming of all students into regular classrooms, outcome-based instruction, and numerous other advocated changes will have a direct effect on teachers. Will they reduce stress or create new pressures that lead to burnout?

5. Conclusion

The expectation that teachers can correct the ills of society, instill values, teach basic and higher order thinking skills, and prepare students for a globally competitive marketplace is unlikely to change in the future. There is little doubt that over the 1990s schools will be changing to address these multiple needs. Consequently, the subject of teacher stress will continue to be a major concern of those within and outside the profession.

See also: Teachers as Professionals; Teachers' Beliefs and Belief Systems; Teachers' Expectations; Teacher Evaluation; Motivation and Learning

References

Anderson M B, Iwanicki E F 1984 Teacher motivation and its relationship to teacher burnout. *Educational Administration Quarterly* 20(2): 94–132

Blase J 1986 A qualitative analysis of sources of teachers stress: Consequences for performance. *Am. Educ. Res. J.* 23: 13–40

Burke R J, Greenglass E R 1989 Psychological burnout among men and women in teaching: An examination of the Cherniss model. *Hum. Realt.* 42(3): 261–73

Byrne B M 1992 Investigating causal links to burnout for elementary, intermediate, and secondary teachers. Paper presented at the American Educational Research Association Annual Meeting, San Francisco, California

Crane S, Iwanicki E F 1986 Perceived role conflict, role ambiguity, and burnout among special education teachers. *Rem. Spec. Educ.* 7(2): 24–31

Dewe P 1986 Stress: Causes, consequences & coping strategies for teachers. ERIC Document Reproduction Service No. ED 280 807, Washington, DC

Dworkin A G 1987 *Teacher Burnout in the Public Schools: Structural Causes and Consequences for Children.* SUNY Press, Albany, New York

Farber B A 1991 *Crisis in Education: Stress and Burnout in the American Teacher.* Jossey Bass, San Francisco, California

French J R Jr., Caplan R D 1972 Organizational stress and individual strain. In: Marrow A J (ed.) 1972 *The Failure of Success.* Amacom, New York

Friedman I A, Farber B A 1992 Individual and socially reflected aspects of professional self-concept as predictors of teacher burnout. *Journal of Education Research* 38(2): 28–35

Friedman I A 1993 Burnout in teachers: The concept and its core meaning. *Ednc. Psychol. Meas.* 93(53): 1035–44

Freudenberger H J 1974 Staff burn-out. *J. Soc. Issues* 30: 159–65

Friesen D, Prokop C M, Sarros J C 1988 Why teachers burn out. *Educ. Res. Q.* 12(3): 9–19

Gmelch W 1988 Research perspectives on administrative stress: Causes, reactions, responses and consequences. *J. Educ. Adm.* 26(2): 134–40

Goodlad J I 1984 *A Place called School.* McGraw Hill, New York

Hiebert B, Farber I 1984 Teacher stress: A literature survey with a few surprises. *Can. J. Educ.* 9(1): 14–27

Hubert J A, Gable R K Iwanicki E F 1990 The relationship of teacher stress to school organizational health. In: Bacharach S B (ed.) 1990 *Advances in Research and Theories of School Management and Policy.* JAI Press, Greenwich, Connecticut

Jackson S E, Schwab R L, Schuler R A 1986 Toward an understanding of the burnout phenomenon. *J. Appl. Psychol.* 71(4): 630–40

Jenkins S, Calhoun J F 1991 Teacher stress: Issues and intervention. *Psychol. Sch.* 28(1): 60–70

Kahn R L, Wolfe D M, Quinn R P, Snoek J K, Rosenthal R A 1964 *Organizational Stress: Studies in Role Conflict and Ambiguity.* Wiley, New York

Kremer-Hayon L, Goldstein Z 1990 The inner world of Israeli secondary school teachers: Work centrality, job satisfaction and stress. *Comp. Educ.* 26(2–3): 285–98

Kyriacou C 1987 Teacher stress and burnout: An international review. *Educ. Res.* 29(2): 146–52

Lutz F W, Maddirala J 1990 Stress, burnout in Texas teachers and reform mandated accountability. *Educ. Res. Q.* 14(2): 10–21

Malanowski J, Wood P 1984 Burnout and self actualization in public school teachers. *Journal of Psychology* 117(1): 23–26

Maslach C 1982 Understanding burnout: Definitional issues in analyzing a complex phenomenon. In: Paine W S (Ed.) 1982 *Job Stress and Burnout: Research, Theory, and Intervention Perspectives.* Sage, Beverly Hills, California

McIntyre T 1984 The relationship between locus of control and teacher burnout. *Br. J. Educ. Psychol.* 54(2): 235–38

Ninomiya A, Okato T 1990 A critical analysis of job-satisfied teachers in Japan. *Comp. Educ.* 26(2–3): 249–57

Payne M A, Furnham A 1987 Dimensions of occupational

stress in West Indian secondary school teachers. *Br. J. Educ. Psychol.* 57(2): 141–150

Pines A, Aronson E, Kafry D 1981 *Burnout from Tedium to Personal Growth*. Free Press, New York

Rodgers-Jenkinson F, Chapman D W 1990 Job satisfaction of Jamaican elementary school teachers. *Int. Rev. Educ.* 36(3): 299–313

Schwab R L 1991 Stress and the intern teacher: An exploratory study. In: Conley S C, Cooper B S (eds.) 1991 *The School as a Work Environment: Implications for Reform*. Allyn and Bacon, Boston, Massachusetts

Schwab R L, Iwanicki E F 1982a Perceived role conflict, role ambiguity, and teacher burnout. *Educational Administration Quarterly* 18(1): 60–74

Schwab R L, Iwanicki E F 1982b Who are our burned out teachers? *Educ. Res. Q.* 7(2): 5–16

Schwab R L, Jackson S E, Schuler R A 1986 Educator burnout: Sources and consequences. *Educ. Res. Q.* 10(3): 14–30

Seyle H 1946 The general adaptation syndrome and diseases of adaptation. *Journal of Clinical Endocrinology* 6(2): 117–230

(c)   A Sociopolitical View of Teachers

Social Status of Teaching

E. Hoyle

Social status of teaching refers to the relative standing of teaching as an occupation in a hierarchy of all occupations. This entry begins with an exploration of the concepts of occupational status and prestige. Next, the place of teaching within the occupational hierarchies of different societies as indicated by studies of occupational prestige will be described. The final three sections will consider explanations which account for the relative prestige of teaching.

1. Concepts of Status and Prestige

The terms "status," "prestige," and "esteem" are used synonymously in everyday language and very often in the sociological literature. They are also given different connotations by individual sociologists. However, as there are inconsistencies in these various usages the connotations to be used in this entry can be briefly outlined.

The social status of an individual—the degree to which he or she is accorded deference—is determined by a number of factors including wealth, education, gender, ethnicity, and life-style. However, in most developed and developing societies the major determinant of status is held to be occupation. Although a number of personal factors may shape the esteem in which individuals are held in their community—including, for example, how well a teacher is regarded as doing his or her job in school and in making a wider contribution to the community—these factors are less significant than membership in an occupation.

Occupational status is the regard in which an occupation is held in comparison with other occupations. Thus, occupational status turns upon the image of an occupation held by other members of society. To establish the nature of an occupational image, and hence status, is difficult. One can analyse natural speech about an occupation, examine how it is represented in the media, or use a variety of other means. By far the most sophisticated study in methodological terms has been carried out by Coxon and Jones (1978, 1979).

The term "occupational prestige" is widely used to refer to the outcome of studies in which people are asked to rate sets of occupations according to some criterion of "higher" or "lower" and a rank order of occupations is produced. Well over a hundred such studies have been undertaken worldwide. The occupational lists have varied in size and content. The samples undertaking the ranking also have varied as have the instructions given to them.

"Schoolteaching" has appeared on virtually all the studies undertaken within this mode. Sometimes it has appeared as a single occupation, but other studies have subdivided it. One of the earliest studies of occupational prestige, undertaken specifically to determine the prestige of teaching, differentiated between primary and secondary teachers (Counts 1925). Most modern studies include hundreds of occupational titles in rank order—usually extrapolated from smaller samples of personal rankings—and differentiate not only between categories of teacher but also categories of principal. However, this entry, except where indicated, will focus on the general category of teacher.

2. The Occupational Prestige of Teaching

A number of studies have undertaken international comparisons of occupational prestige (e.g., Hodge et al. 1966) and have consistently demonstrated a high degree of correlation between occupational hierarchies despite variations in geographical location, stage of economic development, and point in time at which the study was undertaken. The most detailed analysis of these studies was carried out by Treiman (1977) who reviewed 85 studies carried out in 53 countries. The median correlation across studies was 0.81. Although the correlation is high, some studies show considerable variation by country, by region, and by characteristics of respondents.

He converted these findings into a single scale: the Standard International Occupational Prestige Score (SIOPS). Table 1 locates several teaching categories on the SIOPS continuum.

Data on the occupational prestige of teaching using

Table 1
Twenty selected occupations from the Standard International Occupational Prestige Scale

	Scale score	Rank order
Judge	78	1=
Physician	78	1=
University professor	78	1=
Architect	72	4
Dentist	70	5
Physiotherapist	67	6
Airline pilot	66	7=
Middle-rank civil servant	66	7=
Electrical engineer	65	9
High school teacher	64	10=
Pharmacist	64	10=
Minister of religion	60	12
Surveyor	58	13
Primary school teacher	57	14
Social worker	56	15
Nurse	54	16
Actor	52	17
Preprimary school teacher	49	18=
Real estate agent	49	18=
Police officer	40	20

Source: Derived from Treiman (1977)

SIOPS and other scales permit the following generalizations:

(a) Teaching is high in the range of all occupations.

(b) Teaching is relatively high within the group of public and personal service professions (e.g., nursing, social work, and police).

(c) Teaching is higher than that of skilled manual and white-collar occupations.

(d) Teaching is lower than that of the major professions, (e.g., medicine, law, and architecture).

Within the teaching profession as a whole:

(a) Principals are ranked more highly than classroom teachers.

(b) The rank order of teachers from high to low is: college, secondary school, elementary school, infant, and preschool (Bernbaum et al. 1969).

Variations in occupational prestige ratings require explanations in terms of cultural differences, whereas more general explanations are required in order to account for the relative consistency of the occupational prestige ratings over time and location. Three explanations are offered below, although they are not necessarily independent of one another.

3. The Social Functions of Teaching

The general form of this explanation is that occupational prestige is a reflection of the importance of the contribution to the well-being of society. This explanation is often termed the "functionalist" position. Treiman (1977), who uses the term "structuralist" for the same perspective, wrote that "the relative prestige of the social roles known as occupations is essentially invariant in all complex societies and that this must be so as a consequence of the inherent features of the division of labor as it exists in all societies" (p. 2). The implication is that those who fulfill key functions have knowledge, skill, power, privilege, and prestige.

There are, however, a number of arguments against this position. One alternative view is that the high prestige enjoyed by the professions owes more to their success in creating a market for a scarce resource and using the power thereby achieved to limit entry (Larson 1977) (See also *Teachers as Professionals*). Of course, the high correlations in prestige over time and location behove critics of the structural functionalist position to explain the consistency in the historical emergence of professional power.

The position of teaching below the major professions in the prestige hierarchy requires a critical look at the functionalist argument. There can be little doubt that education is a crucial social function in developed and developing societies. Teaching provides the transmission of the knowledge and skills required to sustain and enhance the quality of life in such societies. On this view, the functionalist argument appears less cogent than the argument that teaching has been unable to generate the power enjoyed by the major professions. There are two related reasons why this lack of power exists: the social characteristics of teachers, and the inherent nature of teaching as a professional activity.

4. The Social Characteristics of Teaching

A major barrier to enhanced status stems from the fact that teaching is by far the largest profession. Because the profession is so large, the total salary bill is high and thus individual salaries are depressed below those obtained in other professions. Moreover, because large numbers of teachers have constantly to be recruited, the status-bestowing characteristics of those recruited tend to be lower than those recruited to the major professions. The most important of these characteristics are social class background, gender, and academic achievement.

4.1 Social Class Background

The social class background of teachers is, on average, lower than that of entrants to the major professions and it is argued that this lower class background has a deleterious influence on status. However, apart from this broad generalization, reliable statements about the social class backgrounds of teachers are difficult to make, particularly as they have changed over time. Relatively few studies exist and they have mostly been undertaken in advanced societies. Moreover, relatively few studies (see Betz and Garland 1974 for an exception) take account of changes in the occupational structure over time. In industrialized societies, for example, there has been a shift from skilled craft occupations to technical service and quasiprofessional occupations.

As a very broad generalization relating to developed countries, one could say that teachers are recruited from the full range of social classes but with an underrepresentation from the highest and lowest social groups and with the modal background of all teachers increasing over time. Furthermore, women teachers come from a slightly higher social class background than men, and teachers in secondary schools come from a slightly higher social class background than those in elementary schools. These last two generalizations would at first seem to be incompatible since elementary schools tend to contain the highest proportion of women. Where detailed data exist, however, they show that the anomaly can be explained by the fact that the higher proportion of women in primary schools is offset by the considerably higher social class origins of both men and women in secondary schools.

Available data would indicate that there has been an increase in the social class background of teachers since the 1940s (Havighurst and Levine 1979, Bassett 1958, 1971). In Britain before the Second World War, for example, there were differences in social class backgrounds of teachers in the elementary schools and those in the highly selective secondary schools. However, in the postwar period, with the creation of secondary education for all, there was a degree of convergence between the social class background of teachers in the increasingly integrated system (Floud and Scott 1961). This trend has continued with the comprehensivization of secondary education.

4.2 Gender

The factor of gender functions relatively independently of social class background in the determination of the occupational prestige of teaching. There is a view that the relatively high proportion of women in teaching is detrimental to its social status because of the patriarchal attitudes which persist in many societies. However, whether or not this view is correct is difficult to demonstrate. One can only note that professions with a relatively low proportion of women (e.g., medicine and law) enjoy a higher occupational prestige than those with a relatively high proportion (e.g., teaching, nursing, and social work).

Because women tend to predominate in teaching in all societies one cannot deploy comparative data to test the proposition. One can note, however, that medicine enjoys a higher social status in the West than in the former Soviet Union where women predominate in the medical profession. As noted above, the prestige of primary school teachers, who are predominantly women, is lower than that for secondary school teachers, who are predominantly men. However, the relationship between gender and prestige is quite complex, involving both cultural and economic factors.

4.3 Academic Achievement

The academic achievements of teachers at all school levels is considerably higher than population averages. Nevertheless, the academic achievements of those who enter teaching is generally lower than those who enter the major professions. In the United Kingdom, for example, those entering Bachelor of Education (BEd) courses in colleges of education and polytechnics have lower school attainments than those entering BA and BS courses in universities. Furthermore, those who enter the one-year teacher training course in universities following their BA and BS degrees tend to have lower achievements (and come from slightly lower social class backgrounds) than those who enter other occupations (see Committee on Higher Education 1963).

5. The Nature of Teaching as an Activity

Class, gender, and academic achievement have been selected to indicate the characteristics of teachers which may help to determine their social status. However, although the data indicate social differences between those who enter teaching and those who enter other professions, these differences are not great and are perhaps diminishing. Moreover, as presented, the data imply a deficit model based on market forces and opportunity. Other determinants of teacher status are perhaps to be found in the nature of teaching as an occupational activity and the contexts in which teaching takes place.

Three factors inherent in teaching as an activity are related to the status of teaching. These factors are reviewed from the perspective of the lower standing of teaching vis-à-vis that of the major professions.

5.1 Knowledge and Skill

The knowledge and skills needed by teachers are regarded as being of a lower order than those required in the major professions. In this regard it is important to recognize that higher status generally is associated with specialization. This factor may account for the higher status of secondary school teachers relative to elementary and early childhood teachers. Furthermore, the uncertain relationship between educational and pedagogic theory, pedagogic practice, and learning outcomes detracts from its capacity to enhance its status.

5.2 Work Situation

The sustained relationship between teachers and pupils in an organized setting differs from the relatively infrequent contact which most professionals have with their clients in organizational settings or consultancy contexts. Thus, the work situation in which teachers find themselves may militate against the improved status of teaching.

5.3 Clients

Perhaps the most fundamental factor influencing the lower status of teaching vis-à-vis other professions is that teachers' immediate clients are children. In addition, virtually the entire adult population has had a sustained and direct experience of teachers at work. Thus, virtually everyone, to some extent, "accomplishes" schooling and leaves it behind as they leave behind their teachers. As Hoyle (1969) has noted, teachers are thus placed in an intermediate status on a number of dimensions: childhood–adulthood ("A man amongst boys and a boy amongst men"), school–work ("Those who can, do, those who can't, teach"), moral idealism–moral realism (The school as "a museum of virtue," Waller 1965), the dissemination of knowledge–the creation of knowledge (The teacher as one who "spreads other people's butter," Geer 1966).

The fact that all have had the experience of schooling robs teaching of any status-enhancing mystique. Moreover, all have seen teachers constantly seeking to maintain control, a problem which is exacerbated where older pupils are in compulsory and often reluctant attendance. This image is powerful and does not apply to other major professions or "semi-professions" where client control is rarely an issue.

6. Conclusion

The occupational prestige of teachers lies in the upper reaches of all scales. The social background of teachers tends to be clustered around the center, suggesting that teaching represents upward social mobility, to some degree, for many. Teachers' educational qualifications are in the upper reaches of the distribution, as is their remuneration. Insofar as teacher status is regarded as "low," this statement can be made only in comparison with the major professions. In this regard there would seem to be limits to the degree to which

teachers might enhance their status. These limits stem ultimately from the size of the profession and images of teachers and their work. Despite the high correlations between teachers' prestige ratings across countries, however, there are intercountry variations to indicate that the status of teaching is not wholly immutable.

See also: Political Work of Teachers

References

Bassett G W, 1958 The occupational background of teachers. *Australian Journal of Education.* 2: 79–90
Bassett G W 1971 The occupational background of teachers: Some recent data. *Australian Journal of Education.* 15: 211–14
Bernbaum G, Noble G, Whiteside T 1969 Intra occupational prestige differentiation in teaching. *Paedag. Eur.* 5: 1–59
Betz M, Garland J 1974 Intergenerational mobility rates of urban school teachers. *Soc. Educ.* 47: 511–22
Committee on Higher Education 1963 *Administrative, Financial and Economic Aspects of Higher Education* (Robbins Report), Appendix 2B. HMSO, London
Counts F A 1925 The social status of occupations. *Sch. Rev.* 33: 20–21
Coxon A P M, Jones C L 1978 *The Images of Occupational Prestige.* Macmillan, London
Coxon A P M, Jones C L 1979 *Class and Hierarchy: The Social Meaning of Occupations.* Macmillan, London
Floud J, Scott W 1961 Recruitment to teaching in England and Wales. In: Halsey A H, Floud J, Anderson C A (eds.) 1961 *Education, Economy and Society: A Reader in the Sociology of Education.* Free Press, New York
Geer B 1966 Occupational commitment and the teaching profession. *Sch. Rev.* 77(1): 31–47
Havighurst R J, Levine D U 1979 *Society and Education*, 5th edn. Allyn and Bacon, Boston, Massachusetts
Hodge R W, Treiman D J, Rossi P 1966 A comparative study of occupational prestige. In: Bendix R, Lipset S M (eds.) 1966 *Class, Status and Power: Social Stratification in Comparative Perspective*, 2nd edn. Free Press, New York
Hoyle E 1969 *The Role of the Teacher.* Routledge, London
Larson M 1977 *The Rise of Professionalism.* University of California Press, Berkeley, California
Treiman D J 1977 *Occupational Prestige in Comparative Perspective.* Academic Press, New York
Waller W 1965 *The Sociology of Teaching.* Wiley, New York

Teachers' Roles

B. J. Biddle

The phrase "teacher role" appears in hundreds of studies. In addition, chapters on teacher role may be found in both theoretical and hortative works concerned with teaching, its contexts, and its effects. Unfortunately,

use of this phrase is also vague, and several different concepts have been intended by authors who have written about teacher roles. Many who have used this phrase have seemed unaware that it has other uses than the one they intended; thus, the first task facing those reading about it is to distinguish among the major concepts to which the phrase has been applied. Three such concepts are distinguished in this entry. In addition, the use of the phrase "teacher role" declined during the 1980s, and alternative vocabularies have since been employed for teacher-role issues. As a consequence, this review stresses broad concerns rather than specific literature from the 1980s and 1990s that might also be interpreted as concerned with the roles of teachers.

1. Concepts of Teacher Role

Technical use of the social role concept appeared in the 1920s and reflected the influence of at least three seminal contributors: Ralph Linton, Jacob Moreno, and George Herbert Mead. These three men represented different disciplines in the social sciences and used the role concept somewhat differently. For simplicity, three separate concepts are distinguished here that may be designated by the phrase "teacher role" (see Biddle 1979).

1.1 Role as Behavior

Some authors use "teacher role" to refer to behaviors that are characteristic of teachers. Most who use "role" in this sense focus their interests on teacher behaviors in the work context (i.e., in the school or classroom). Nevertheless, teachers may also be found in nonwork contexts, and a few authors have discussed the role behaviors of teachers in their homes, the marketplace, or the political arena. Authors using "role" in this first sense presume that teacher behaviors are existential events that can be observed directly. Moreover, teacher roles may also be observed by other actors, hence are assumed to have the potential for affecting, and being affected by, the behaviors of pupils and other persons who interact with teachers.

1.2 Role as Social Position

Other authors use the phrase "teacher role" to refer to the identity or social position that is shared by teachers. In this usage the word "role" refers to the designating term ("teacher") and the set of persons who are designated by that occupational litle. This second usage focuses on static characteristics of teachers— on the recognition of teachers as a separate social position, the composition of the teacher population, the status of the teaching profession, or conditions for entry into or departure from the field. Authors who intend this second meaning often speak of teachers as "occupying" their roles.

1.3 Role as Expectation

A third group of authors use the phrase "teacher role" to refer to expectations that are held for teachers. Some

of these expectations are held by teachers themselves, whereas others are held by parents, school administrators, pupils, politicians, and members of the public. Some expectations are normative in mode, but others may represent beliefs, preferences, or other modes of thought. Some may be widely shared, while others may reflect divergent opinions and generate role conflicts for the teacher. Authors who follow this third usage tend to view teachers (and those with whom they interact) as persons capable of rational, reflective thought. Expectations are thought to be learned through experience and, once they are formed, will affect the behaviors of those who hold them in predictable ways.

None of these three concepts for teacher role precludes the others. Each represents a facet of the complexities that embed the teacher, and each is capable of generating information for educators and other social scientists. Each has also generated research literature. Nevertheless, the fact that such different concepts have all been designated by the same phrase poses problems for investigators and consumers alike. One must read each source carefully to establish the concept a given author intended by the phrase "teacher role," and one must be prepared to discount confusion that has been generated because some authors forgot their conceptual definition or misunderstood those of others.

2. The Behavioral Role of the Teacher

The behavioral role of the teacher may be defined as those behaviors that are characteristically performed by teachers. Like persons in other occupations and professions, teachers respond in characteristic ways. Most are regularly found in classrooms during the working day, and most spend much of that day supervising the instruction of pupils. When not in classrooms, teachers are likely to be found in the hallways or offices of the school building, or in the lunchroom or teachers' lounge. During the evening, teachers are likely to be grading papers, preparing lessons, or attending school-related functions. This does not mean that all teachers behave identically, but to learn that a person teaches for a living means that he or she is more likely to do certain things and less likely to do others, and it is the former that constitute the teacher's behavioral role.

Teachers characteristically do a great many things, so studies of the role of the teacher are normally limited in some fashion. Sometimes that limitation is contextual. For example, an investigator may examine the teacher's role in the classroom, the school, or in some other context in which membership of the teacher's social position is recognized and relevant. Sometimes, also, a sectoral limitation may be placed on the definition, in which case the investigator examines that portion of the teacher's role directed toward members of another social position, such as pupils. (Other sectors of the role are directed toward the school's principal, other teachers, or members of the public.) In contrast, if authors choose to discuss the teacher's role in noneducational contexts, usually that discussion focuses on behaviors that are presumed to be unique to teachers, that is, are not exhibited by other comparable actors.

Sometimes, also, functional limitations may be placed on the definition of the teacher's behavioral role. Like other professionals, teachers may accomplish a variety of things, and authors may single out one or more of those things for discussion. For example, many teachers are called upon to disseminate information to pupils, to serve as pupil counselors, and to grade pupils' performances on a regular basis. Each of these tasks requires somewhat different activities on the part of teachers, and simultaneous performance of these different activity sets may be difficult for the teacher to manage. The difficulty with functional analysis of the teacher's role is that no definitive set of functions is prescribed for most teachers, and behaviors characteristic of teachers may contribute to more than one identifiable function. As a result, many different lists of functions have been suggested for the teacher's role, and behavioral evidence concerning these functional distinctions is hard to find.

The issue of evidence raises another question concerning the behavioral role of the teacher. What is the best way to study such roles? Since behaviors are observable events, then surely the best way of studying them is to observe them directly. Up until about 1960 it was difficult to find studies of behavioral roles that were based on observation, but this has since changed (see Dunkin and Biddle 1974 and many subsequent reviews). Literally thousands of studies have appeared in which the classroom behaviors of teachers and pupils were observed, and these provide a wealth of data concerning the role of participants in that context.

It is more difficult to observe teacher behaviors elsewhere in the school, however, and more difficult still to study teacher activities in nonschool contexts. As a result, studies still appear in which the teacher's behavioral role is examined by asking teachers or others to discuss those activities in interviews and questionnaire responses. Technically, the latter forms of data are measures of what respondents think about the teacher's role and are more validly interpreted as measures of their expectations for teachers. To interpret them as measures of teacher role behavior assumes a simple relationship between role expectations and role behaviors, an assumption that is questioned below. Nevertheless, indirect evidence is better than no evidence, and much of what researchers presume to know about the teacher's behavioral role today is based on it.

3. The Social Position of the Teacher

A social position relates to a set of persons who share some characteristic and who are given a recognized label within the society. Teachers are those persons who regularly instruct pupils, thus the social position of the teacher may be defined as membership of the set of persons who regularly instruct pupils and are given such designations as "teacher," "instructor," "master," and the like. Occasionally the concept of teacher is also extended to include persons who teach students in postsecondary education. However, the teaching of adults involves activities quite different from those involved in the teaching of nonadult pupils, and those who teach adults are normally recruited and trained for their occupations in quite different ways than are teachers. Consequently, most persons who write about the social position of the teacher confine their attention to those who teach at the primary and secondary levels.

Several confusions surround the social position concept. As mentioned, some authors use the term "role" to refer to social position, so one may find articles in which "teacher role" is used to designate those who teach rather than the activities of teaching or expectations for the latter. Other authors use the term "status" to refer to social position, which is also confusing because the word "status" has another meaning concerned with the ranking of social positions vis-à-vis one another. (The status-ranking of teachers is discussed below.) Finally, some authors define the social position concept as a "location" or "niche" in a division of labor. Such definitions are confusing because they presume that all social positions are occupations. Whereas "teacher" is a recognized occupation in industrialized societies, teachers are not always paid for their services elsewhere but may still be recognized, even honored, for their activities.

3.1 The Status of Teachers

A number of characteristics of social positions have been studied over the years. One of these is status, which concerns the ranking of social positions in terms of characteristics deemed desirable. As a rule, three criteria for status ranking have dominated the literature: prestige, wealth, and authority. Members of social positions have prestige when they are able to attract deferential behavior from others who are not members of their social position. They have wealth when they are given or are allowed to control commodities. They have authority when they can get others to follow their dictates.

It is widely assumed that prestige, wealth, and authority go together and that social positions which have one of these qualities in abundance will also have the others. Although this is true on average, there are some social positions that are high on one or two of these criteria but not the others (e.g., church dignitaries, Mafiosi). Studies of the status of social positions may either focus on status as a presumed unitary concept or may involve separate investigations of prestige, wealth, and authority.

3.2 The Prestige of Teachers

Relatively few studies of the prestige of teachers have yet appeared, but these tend to place teachers toward the lower end of middle-class occupations and at the bottom of those occupations deemed to be professions. Moreover, this status ranking tends to hold throughout industrialized countries. A number of reasons have been suggested for the relatively low prestige of teachers: prevalence of women in the teaching profession, lack of specificity in the role expected of teachers, the fact that teachers work primarily with the young, devaluation of the knowledge deemed necessary to teach well, the large numbers of persons employed or available for employment as teachers, and so forth.

Lortie (1975) views teachers as having a "special but shadowed" prestige position. On the one hand, teachers' work is seen as having the aura of a "special mission," but on the other, teachers have largely lost whatever autonomy they once had to manage pedagogical theory and their classrooms because they have become functionaries in hierarchical organizations. Whatever may be the reason, teachers clearly do not attract as much deference as do the other, more secure professions: medicine, the law, the ministry. At the same time, however, teachers receive more deference than do most blue-collar occupations.

3.3 The Wealth of Teachers

Like all occupations, teachers are paid for their services. Most teachers in the West are the employees of organizations that receive public funds, so their salaries are a matter of public record. Not surprisingly then, many studies of the wealth of teachers have appeared and continue to appear on a regular basis. These studies suggest that teachers tend to be paid at about the scale appropriate to their prestige position—above the scale paid to blue-collar workers but below the scale paid to most professionnals. In fact, the wages paid to many teachers are probably sufficient to support a single person but insufficient to support a family. Since many married women do not work, this fact presumably explains why many male teachers find it necessary to work at a second job to supplement their teaching incomes.

The economic systems of most Western countries are capitalistic, and the relative wages paid to teachers tend to rise during periods of teacher shortage. Thus probably the major reason why teachers are not paid better wages is that they have never formed cartels to prevent entry of "unqualified" persons into the profession—as is done widely in medicine. Teachers have begun to unionize, however, and teacher wages have sometimes been improved through collective bargaining and industrial action.

3.4 The Authority of Teachers

Studies of the authority of teachers are quite rare, but as a rule that authority is confined to pupils, the school, and curricular matters. Like the hospital, prison, or university, the school is a people-processing organization, and most school systems feature a bureaucratic hierarchy in which the teachers are the "workers." Given this lowly authority-position, teachers must take orders from most of the rest of the personnel: department heads, subject specialists, principals and their assistants, superintendents, and school board members. Teachers have traditionally been assigned considerable power in the classroom, but this has recently been eroded through laws that constrain teacher conduct, administrative control over the curriculum, and pupil violence.

Despite these erosions, the teacher retains an authority in the classroom that is generated through custom, law, the teacher's expert knowledge, and the teacher's control over grades and promotions for pupils. Teachers also have some authority over parental conduct in matters relating to education, although teacher/parent relationships vary considerably among countries. (Within some countries, such as the United Kingdom, parents are often discouraged from "interfering" with the school, whereas in others, such as the United States, they are usually urged to involve themselves in the education of their children.)

4. The Expected Role of the Teacher

The expected role of the teacher may be defined as the set of expectations that are held for teacher behaviors by both teachers and other persons. Like persons in other social positions, teachers are subjected to a number of expectations for their conduct that reflect law, custom, habit, desires, and theories concerning their activities. These expectations form a context in which teacher conduct is interpreted, and role expectations for the teacher are presumably a major motivator for teacher conduct. On the one hand, those who hold expectations for teacher behavior are presumed likely to pressure teachers to conform to those expectations; on the other, teachers presumably want to follow their own expectations.

The concept of expected role is deceptively simple and hides several issues that should be exposed. First, expectations may be expressed in several different forms. Some expectations are expressed verbally, some are written down in news accounts or codes of conduct, and some are presumably held as covert thoughts by participants. Most authors who write about expectations for the teacher have the last form in mind, but covert expectations cannot be perceived directly. One learns about them by listening to respondents talk about teacher conduct or by asking questions about the topic. Consequently, studies of the expected role of the teacher are normally conducted by means of interviews or standardized questionnaires.

Second, at least three different modes of expectation appear in the literature on teacher role. Some investigators study norms for teacher conduct—statements that express what teachers ought to do. Others study preferences, that is, likes and dislikes, for teacher conduct. Still others study beliefs—statements that express subjective probability for the appearance of teacher behavior. Many investigators confuse these three modes or assume that they are interchangeable, but an expression of what teachers ought to do may not be what is preferred or what is thought likely, and evidence has appeared indicating that these three modes of expectation are not interchangeable (Bank et al. 1977).

Third, expectations for teachers may either be held by persons themselves or may be attributed by those persons to other actors. To illustrate, teachers normally hold expectations for their own conduct and attribute expectations for it to the principal of their school. The principal also holds expectations, of course, and usually he or she also attributes expectations to the teachers. These four different types of expectations are sometimes confused by researchers, or researchers may assume that by measuring one of them a good estimate is also obtained of another. Such assumptions are questionable.

Fourth and last, some authors assume that expectations for teachers are largely shared within the school or society, and teachers or other actors in the school may make similar assumptions. Such assumptions are unwise. Whereas some expectations are surely shared for teacher conduct, others are not. Moreover, teachers may be made quite uncomfortable when they are faced with contradictory expectations that are held by two or more persons who have authority over them. Such situations produce what is termed "role conflict" and have been widely studied for teachers and other employees of organizations.

4.1 Shared Expectations for Teachers

Teachers are employed to instruct pupils because of shared values concerning the importance of education and beliefs concerning the efficacy of schools for fulfilling those valued outcomes. Not surprisingly then, various authors have presumed that agreement also appears on functions or tasks that teachers are expected to perform. Several lists of such functions have been proposed, many of them drawn from the insights of Waller (1932) and Parsons (1959). An example of such a list appeared in Kelsall and Kelsall (1969) who argued that teachers are (consensually) expected to emancipate pupils from their home environments, encourage achievement among pupils, sort out and socialize "winners" and "losers" in the achievement game, inculcate societal norms in pupils, teach technical skills, instill interpersonal sensitivity and discipline, and aid pupils in making decisions and training for occupations.

The Kelsalls' list focused on tasks associated with pupils. Other authors have stressed functions generated by structural properties of the school as an organization or values in the wider society. Thus, it is presumed that teachers are also expected to maintain order in their classrooms, accept and promote a common curriculum, follow the orders of supervisors, maintain effective communication with parents, and exhibit "loyalty" for their schools.

Research has also appeared concerning shared expectations for the teacher. Some of this research concerned beliefs or stereotypes about classroom conduct. To illustrate, Mackie (1972) reported that Canadians believe teachers are sympathetic and supportive of pupils, but are also inclined to dominate the classroom. American studies summarized by Biddle (1969) found that teachers were presumed to be nonaggressive, acquiescent, and to sin largely by omission rather than by commission. Other United States studies uncovered shared preferences for fairness in grading, neatness, and willingness to help pupils (Wright and Alley 1977) and shared norms that teachers should not discriminate among pupils, should be thoughtful and friendly, and should maintain order and discipline in the classroom (Biddle et al. 1961). Such expectations may be fairly universal among Western countries, but the evidence so far available is insufficient to test this proposition. Unfortunately, most of these studies were conducted in the 1960s and 1970s, and research on role expectations for teachers seems to have declined since then.

4.2 Role Conflict, Strain, and Resolution

Not all expectations for teachers are shared, of course, and studies have also reported nonconsensual expectations for teachers. Most of these studies also appeared in the 1960s and 1970s, most focused on norms, and most authors interpreted their findings as indications of role conflict. Several forms of role conflict were suggested in this literature.

A common form of finding concerned evidence that persons in various social positions hold differing norms for teacher conduct. Such disparities were reported in both the United Kingdom and the United States among such social positions as teachers, school principals, parents, pupils, teacher trainees, teacher trainers, persons from differing social classes, and persons from rural and urban communities (see Kelsall and Kellsall 1969, Biddle 1979). Most of this research argued that these disparities pose problems for teachers because those who hold differing norms will presumably bring conflicting pressures to bear on teachers for conformity. However, it was not clear from most of these studies that others would actually produce such pressures, that teachers were aware of these disparate norms, or that teachers were actually made uncomfortable by their appearance.

Some teachers know when others hold disparate norms for their conduct, of course, and this awareness was also interpreted by other authors as role conflict. Studies reporting such awareness have appeared in various countries, and a major investigation appeared reporting equivalent findings from Australia, New

Zealand, and the United Kingdom, and the United States that were obtained from national samples of teachers (Adams 1970). This investigation found normative disparities in all four countries. Some findings were common in the countries studied; in particular, teachers everywhere were likely to view teachers as being at odds with principals and other school officials over such issues as willing acceptance of non professional duties, and with parents over curricular matters. Other findings were unique to specific countries. Presumed conflict between teachers and school officials was greatest in Australia, while conflicts involving parents were strongest in the United Kingdom.

The fact that teachers perceive normative disparities among differing groups of persons does not mean that these perceptions are accurate. Biddle et al. (1966) provided data indicating that teachers distort the actual views of principals, parents, and other actors concerned with schools in systematic ways. On the other hand, perceived normative disparities have been found associated with indicators of strain among both teachers and members of other occupations (see Biddle 1979).

Other expectational disparities are generated when a teacher also holds membership in alternative social positions whose tasks are at odds with those of teaching. Studies have appeared reporting role conflict between norms associated with teaching and coaching, teaching and counseling, and teaching and administrative responsibilities, but most of the research has concentrated on the conflicting demands of teaching and home making. Most studies of this latter topic have appeared in the United States, where the bulk of teachers are women, and interest in role conflicts involving women has blossomed. Such conflicts have also been found to be associated with strain.

What does the teacher do when confronted by situations of role conflict? When serious and persisting, such experiences may interfere with the teacher's performance or may cause the teacher to leave the profession. However, many teachers manage to resolve role conflicts in one way or another, by choosing to conform to one of the disparate norms in their behavior, or by compromising among the alternatives advocated.

A general theory of role conflict resolution was originally proposed by Gross et al. (1958) and has since been tested in many contexts. Dunkin (1972) examined reported role conflict resolution among Australian teachers and found that he could predict resolution strategies from personality characteristics. "Self-oriented" teachers appeared to be more likely to resolve conflicts in terms of their own needs whereas "other-oriented" teachers apparently paid more attention to the needs and authority of other persons to whom norms were attributed.

4.3 Role Expectations and Behaviors

Role expectations may be studied for themselves, as a major indicator of the subjective culture of persons who are members of social positions. However, most people who study role expectations do so because they presume that expectations predict behavior. Teachers are presumed to conform (or at least to "want" to conform) to expectations for their social position. Furthermore, others who hold expectations for teachers are thought to exert pressures on teachers for compliance.

The interesting thing about these "reasonable" propositions is that so little evidence is available to support them. Although many studies have been reported on both teacher role expectations and teacher role behavior, little of a systematic nature is known about relationships between these two realms of investigation. (See, however, 520025 and 520029).

A fundamental attraction of role theory for educators is that it presumes that persons are capable of thinking rationally about their own and others' conduct and that those rational thoughts will affect their behaviors in predictable ways. Unless there is a willingness to conduct more research on the relationships between role expectations and role behaviors, that attraction will remain based merely on speculation.

See also: Realities of Teaching; Student Influencies on Teaching; Teachers as Professionals; Teacher Development; Teacher Responsibility; Teachers as Artists; Teachers as Clinicians; Teachers as Researchers; Professional Socialization of Teachers

References

Adams R S (ed.) 1970 Symposium on teacher role in four English-speaking countries: Introduction. *Comp. Educ. Rev.* 14(1): 5–64

Bank B J, Biddle B J, Keats D M, Keats J A 1977 Normative, preferential, and belief modes in adolescent prejudice. *Sociol. Q.* 18: 574–88

Biddle B J 1969 Teacher roles In: Ebel R L (ed.) 1969 AERA Encyclopedia of Educational Research, 4th edn. Macmillan Inc., New York

Biddle B J 1979 *Role Theory: Expectations, Identities, and Behaviors.* Academic Press, New York

Biddle B J, Rosencranz H A, Rankin E F Jr. 1961 *Studies in the Role of the Public School Teacher.* University of Missouri Press, Columbia, Missouri

Biddle B J, Rosencranz H A, Tomich E, Twyman J P 1966 Shared inaccuracies in the role of the teacher. In: Biddle B J, Thomas E J (eds.) 1966 *Role Theory: Concepts and Research.* Wiley, New York

Dunkin M J 1972 The nature and resolution of role conflicts among male primary school teachers. *Sociol. Educ.* 45(2): 167–85

Dunkin J, Biddle B J 1974 *The Study of Teaching.* Holt, Rinehalt and Winston, New York

Gross N, Mason W S, McEachern A W 1958 *Explorations in Role Analysis: Studies of the School Superintendency Role.* Wiley, New York

Kelsall R K, Kelsall H M 1969 *The School Teacher in England and the United States: The findings of Empirical Research.* Pergamon Press, Oxford

Lortie D C 1975 *Schoolteacher: A Sociological Study.* University of Chicago Press, Chicago, Illinois

Mackie M 1972 School teachers: The popular image. *Alberta Journal Educational Research.* 18(4): 267–76

Parsons T 1959 The school class as a social system: Some of its functions in American society. *Harv. Educ. Rev.* 29(4): 297–318

Waller W 1932 *Sociology of Teaching.* Wiley, New York

Wright R, Alley R 1977 A profile of the ideal teacher. *Natl. Assoc. Sec. Sch. Princ. Bull.* 61(406): 60–64

Political Work of Teachers

M. B. Ginsburg and S. G. Kamat

Teachers work and live within unequal relations of power. Capitalism, patriarchy, racial, or ethnic group stratification; authoritarian, religious, or secular states, and/or imperialism, are embedded not only in local, national, and global communities but also in teachers' immediate work sites (classrooms and campuses) as well as in the educational system more generally. What teachers do in and outside their workplaces is dialectically related to the distribution of both: (a) the material and symbolic resources; and (b) the structural and ideological power used to control the means of producing, reproducing, consuming, and accumulating material and symbolic resources.

In these terms teachers can and should be considered as political actors (Carlson 1987). At its core politics consists of power relations. Politics "concerns the procedures by which scarce resources are allocated and distributed . . . between groups who uphold and those who challenge the status quo" (Dove 1986 p. 30). Teachers are engaged in political action in their pedagogical, curricular, and evaluative work with students in classrooms and corridors; in their interaction with parents, colleagues, and administrators in educational institutions; in their occupational group dealings with education system authorities and state elites; and in their role as citizens in local, national, and global communities.

It is sometimes believed that teachers can and should be "apolitical" (see Zeigler 1967). Such a belief rests partly on a distinction between professional or technical activity and political action. A related foundation for this belief is the contrast between personal and political matters or between activity in the public versus the private sphere (Weiler 1987). Teachers' work is thus characterized as professional or technical, involving personal relationships among individuals in the private sphere of the classroom or school. From this perspective, it is atypical or undesirable for "professional" teachers to venture into the public sphere, either in the educational system as members of organizations or in the community as members of political parties or social movements.

The alternate perspective on which this entry is based views teachers as political actors regardless of whether they are active or passive; autonomous or heteronomous vis-à-vis other political forces/groups; conservative or oriented toward change; seeking individual, occupational group, or larger collectivities' goals; and/or serving dominant or subordinate group interests. The literature reviewed in this entry sheds light on the various ways in which teachers can be understood as political actors in different historical periods in various societies. The discussion is organized around the following loci of action: classrooms, educational institutions, teacher organizations, and communities.

1. Political Work in the Classroom

Giroux (1988 p. 126) states: "Rather than being objective institutions removed from the dynamics of politics and power, schools actually are contested spheres that embody and express a struggle over what forms of authority, types of knowledge, forms of moral regulation and versions of the past and future should be legitimated and transmitted to students." Thus, teachers' curricular, pedagogical, and evaluation activities are viewed as forms of political action, in that they have consequences for power relations and the distribution of material and symbolic resources. Due to the constraints of space, the focus of this review is on curriculum choices, although similar issues could be developed in relation to pedagogy (e.g., Connell 1985, Lawn and Grace 1987) as well as evaluation activity (e.g., Dove 1986, Jansen 1990, Weiler 1988).

Curriculum content represents a selection of topics and a selection of ways of viewing these topics. Power relations are embedded in curriculum both in terms of who makes the decisions and whose interests are served by the topics and perspectives included or excluded. The content of the curriculum is emphasized here, but it should be remembered that the process of constructing the curriculum is a power struggle in which teachers play a more or less active role. While teachers generally do not have full autonomy to determine officially the curriculum, they do choose to accommodate themselves to, resist, or create alternatives to the curriculum determined by others (Apple 1988, Ozga 1988, Ginsburg 1988).

The knowledge included in or excluded from the curriculum may legitimate or challenge existing relations of power; curriculum is not neutral. A variety of studies in North America have shown how capitalist relations are preserved by promoting its "positive" features, ignoring or rationalizing as individuals' failings its "negative" features, or limiting what is known about groups who have struggled to create a more just and humane economic arrangement (see Zeigler 1967). In contrast, Sultana (1991) reports how some teachers in New Zealand, who were active in social movements, developed their curriculum in order to stress the "exploitation" of workers and indigenous groups under capitalism and the role of trades union activity and class and ethnic struggle in seeking to change or transform the system.

Studies in a range of societies have documented how unequal gender relations have been legitimated through the knowledge that teachers include in or exclude from the curriculum, portraying in an unproblematic manner males' paid labor and dominance in the economy and government and females' unpaid labor with respect to family care and house maintenance. Other teachers have been concerned to stress the problematic nature of gender relations, and have developed or used antisexist curricular materials, focused attention on how patriarchal relations limit females' (and males') lives, and encouraged students to consider alternatives to stereotyped gender roles in schools and society (Lawn and Grace 1987, Weiler 1988).

Teachers have developed or transmitted curricular knowledge that has either supported or undermined unequal racial or ethnic group relations. For example, in South Africa some teachers have promoted racist stereotypes and ideologies in their classrooms, while others have sought to "redefine curriculum content from its racist, sexist, and classist bias to the empancipatory goal of social relevance, political liberation, and social equality" (Jansen 1990 p. 67). Jarausch (1990) reports similar efforts by different groups of teachers in Nazi Germany to legitimate or criticize racial stereotypes and ideologies.

The knowledge and perspectives that teachers communicate to students may encourage support or critique of the governing elites and their actions. During the First World War, teachers who were affiliated to the revolutionary syndicalist movement in France challenged the authorities and sought to replace positive and romantic images of war with a view of it as barbaric, destructive, and futile for resolving disputes (Feeley 1989). There is also evidence that during the Second World War teachers waged "spiritual warfare for the fatherland" in Germany (Jarausch 1990 p. 29), carried out "ultranationalist indoctrination" for the military regime in Japan (Blum 1969), and in the United Kingdom, implemented curricular changes which were dictated by central government and were needed to support the war effort both materially and ideologically (Lawn and Grace 1987).

The concept of "cultural imperialism" seems useful in describing teachers' roles in legitimating colonial and neocolonial rule through their curriculum choices. Such political activity by teachers has occurred both before and after Independence in African countries (Bagunywa 1975). Moreover, many teachers in the Philippines, who were tightly controlled through training, curriculum guides, and inspection, acted as conduits of the technical and cultural knowledge and skills required by the colonial administration of the United States (Caniesco-Doronila 1987). There is also contrasting evidence of teachers' curricular work challenging imperialism. For example, rural teachers in Vietnam, despite efforts by French colonial authorities to impose a curriculum that met the needs of the colonizing power and denigrated Vietnamese culture, resisted and developed a curriculum which criticized French colonialism, celebrated Vietnamese culture, and stressed the capacity for self-rule (Kelly 1982).

2. Institutional Politics: The Politics of the Workplace

It is generally agreed that teachers are workers and educational institutions are workplaces (Connell 1985, Ozga 1988). Like those employed in other organizations, teachers, administrators, and others who work in schools are enmeshed in interpersonal or micropolitics, involving the tactical use of power to seek and maintain control of material and symbolic resources (Blase 1991). At the same time, because education and educational workers are part of a broader set of social relations, life in schools constitutes and is constituted by power relations on a micro as well as on a macro level.

In the United Kingdom different groups of teachers—namely, those whose careers are tied to academic subjects, as opposed to those identified with pastoral care or counseling responsibilities—have competed for material resources (salary levels and program funds), symbolic resources (status and recognition), and the power to shape the direction of their schools (Ozga 1988). Collegial relations among teachers in the United States are seen to involve strategies to acquire or protect symbolic resources, such as status and psychic rewards that come from feelings of success in working with students. Diplomatic friendliness, avoiding controversy and conflict, and mutual recognition of the sanctity of individual teachers' classrooms enable teachers to survive and obtain some level of satisfaction and control by retreating from the larger institutional setting that might otherwise be overtly fraught with struggles over material and symbolic resources (Blase 1991). However, although teachers' retreat into the security of the classroom is a creative strategy, it is one that likely allows miseducative and inequality-reinforcing aspects of the system to go unchallenged (Lawn and Grace 1987).

Research in Australia, the United Kingdom, and the United States has illuminated how administrative power over teachers has been constructed, accommodated, and resisted. Focusing on the context of Latin America, Oliveros (1975 p. 231) makes clear that these power struggles have implications for material resources, including employment, salary, and promotions, in that teachers "depend on the goodwill of their supervisors . . . to remain in the profession that goodwill in turn is paid for in loyalty and by 'not creating problems.'[2u]"

Power relations between teachers and administrators partially reflect the struggle over the educational labor process. Several studies in Canada, the United Kingdom, and the United States have focused on the sometimes contested developments through which many teachers have become "proletarianized" (i.e., their work has been deskilled and divested of power) and also on how some teachers have become "professionalized" (i.e., their work has been reskilled and they have been empowered again) (Ozga 1988, Ginsburg 1988). Seen from such a perspective, it becomes apparent that administrator–teacher relations reflect and have implications for class relations. Given the gender regime of schools where men often manage women, administrator–teacher relations also constitute a terrain on which patriarchy is reproduced and struggled over (see Apple 1988, Connell 1985).

3. Teacher Organizations and Political Work

Teachers all over the world have formed associations and unions, at least in part as a collective response to their shared experiences as employees involved in the politics of educational workplaces. In a variety of European, North American, and Third World societies teachers comprise the most highly organized category of workers (Dove 1986).

Teacher organizational activity is political in the sense that it involves relations with national and local states to shape the distribution of material resources (to teachers as opposed to other groups). Teachers have worked through their organizations to demand and/or obtain higher salaries, pensions, or other material benefits (Blum 1969, Feeley 1989, Lawn and Grace 1987, Oliveros 1975, Ozga 1988, Warren 1989). However, teacher organizations have sometimes accepted passively or even legitimated the decisions of state elites (Ginsburg 1991, Rosenthal 1969).

Part of the collective political activity of teachers has been concerned with winning the right to organize and engage in negotiations with the state, collective bargaining, strike, and other forms of "militant" action (Feeley 1989, Kelly 1982). At various times in many societies it has been illegal for teachers to withhold their labor. Historically, in Japan teacher unionism was repressed by the government before the Second World War, encouraged by the United States and allied occupying forces and the Japanese Socialist government from 1945–48, and then undermined when the Conservative Party assumed power in 1948 (Blum 1969).

Teacher organizations have also struggled with local and national state elites, educational administrators, parents, and other citizens as well as other teacher organizations over issues of power, control, and autonomy. Such struggles have concerned the capacity to determine working conditions, teachers' responsibilities, and management practices; pedagogy and curriculum, and examination systems; teacher appraisal systems; educational policy and salary determination mechanisms; and level of funding for education in general (Blum 1969, Ginsburg 1991, Lawn and Grace 1987, Oliveros 1975, Ozga 1988, Rosenthal 1969, Warren 1989).

Organized teachers have also engaged in political action in relation to the state to obtain symbolic resources, such as professional status associated with university-based preparation. Such status symbols have been seen to be valuable assets in teachers' (and other educated workers') professionalization projects, in which increased power or autonomy are also sought. While state action has sometimes functioned to reinforce teacher professionalization, teachers have also been the targets of deprofessionalizing or proletarianizing efforts by the state (Dove 1986, Ginsburg 1991, Jarausch 1990, Lawn and Grace 1987, Nwagwu 1977).

A major ideological weapon used both by teachers and by the state in such struggles, at least in the United Kingdom and former British colonies, is "professionalism." While there are multiple and contradictory meanings of the term "professionalism," both in social scientific literature and in everyday discourse, the notion of a hierarchical division of labor, legitimated by a meritocratic conception of educational attainment, is often a central element. In drawing on and reproducing this ideology, teachers help to legitimate a division of labor required by at least capitalist relations of production (Ginsburg 1988). This tendency is strengthened by the fact that some conceptions of professionalism distinguish professionals' organizational efforts from the "unionism" of members of the working class (Ozga 1988). This is part of the reason why in some societies the issue of teachers being affiliated to the broader labor movement stimulates such controversy, even though organized teachers have played a major leadership role in the labor movement in certain societies (Blum 1969, Feeley 1989, Ginsburg 1991).

Race relations have also affected and been shaped by the discourse and action of organized teachers. For instance, De Lyon and Migniuolo (1989) conclude that the interests of Black teachers in England and Wales were less well served by the various teacher unions and associations during the 1970s and 1980s, although the National Union of Teachers developed materials to be used by teachers in the classrooms to encourage multiculturalism and combat racism. Similarly, throughout the 1940s in the United States teachers' organizations were racially segregated, and many organized White teachers did not play a supportive role in Black teachers' organizations' struggles for equal pay (Warren 1989). The struggle by organized teachers in New York City in 1968 against Black community efforts to control their schools locally also indicates that teachers' desire for professional autonomy is related to the distribution of power among racial groups.

Teacher organizations' activity is also political as regards the perpetuation and challenging of gender relations. In Germany, the predominantly male secondary teacher organization sought to achieve and maintain professional status for their members by excluding and distancing themselves from corps of predominantly female primary teachers (Jarausch 1990). In the United Kingdom teacher organizations have tended to reflect male approaches to dealing with issues accorded more importance by male than female teachers, while ignoring concerns, such as childcare and domestic responsibilities, that affect women more than men (De Lyon and Migniuolo 1989). Historically in the United Kingdom, France, and the United States some teacher organizations have fought for equal pay for male and female teachers, while others have worked against it (Feeley 1989, De Lyon and Migniuolo 1989, Warren 1989). Moreover, while women have served in leadership roles in teacher organizations in some societies, females are often underrepresented in high positions in teacher organizations in even the same countries (De Lyon and Migniuolo 1989, Warren 1989, Weiler 1987, Zeigler 1967). This point, however, must be qualified insofar as male and female teachers may play different, yet active and essential, roles in organizing collective action such as strikes (Lawn and Grace 1987, Weiler 1987).

4. Political Work in the Community

Both individually and through their associations and unions, and due to either the dictates of political and economic elites or their own values and convictions, teachers have come to play an active political role in the community. It should be borne in mind that nonparticipation may also constitute a political act—a point well illustrated by the fact that governments have occasionally sought to restrict certain types of teachers' community-based political action (Blum 1969, Dove 1986, Jarausch 1990, Zeigler 1967).

In Africa, Asia, Europe, and Latin America teachers have played leading or active participatory roles in nationalist and independence movements, and in anticolonial or anti-imperial struggles (Blum 1969, Dove 1986, Kelly 1982, Lauglo 1982). Teachers have

also been prominent actors in revolutions, such as in China (White 1981), France (Feeley 1989), Mexico (Blum 1969), and Russia (Seregny 1989) during the early decades of the twentieth century, as well as in recent years in Cote d'Ivoire and Hungary (Ginsburg 1991). As Jansen (1990 p. 63) reports about his own and his colleagues' experiences in the revolutionary context of South Africa, at "moments of student–teacher–police confrontation made the transition from the technocratic teacher to political activist and, on occasion, to comrade in armed struggle."

More generally, teachers have served as community leaders, *animateurs*, and agents of social change (Dove 1986, Lauglo 1982). Sometimes they have challenged the political and cultural hegemony of dominant groups and at other times they have operated as agents of state and economic elites. Similarly, teachers have functioned as mediators between national state elites and the local citizenry, while trying to find room for autonomous action in the middle of a conflict between a secular state and the Church (Blum 1969, Meyers 1976). Dove (1986) concludes that teachers more often served in community leadership roles during the pre- and immediately post-Independence periods in "developing" countries than is the case in latter years , and Lauglo (1982) reports that historically, European and North American rural teachers have varied widely in the extent to which they performed such roles. In both cases the relative level of education of teachers compared to community members is seen as the key variable, with teachers being more active when they are more educated than community members.

In a variety of contexts heads of state, legislators, and other government officials have worked as teachers at one point of their lives (Berube 1988, Dove 1986, Jarausch 1990, Lawn and Grace 1987, Nwagwu 1977). Teachers have also been leaders of political parties as well as being overrepresented, compared to other occupational groups, as active party members (Ginsburg 1991). To varying degrees individual and organized teachers devote time to lobbying and candidate electoral work (Blum 1969, Warren 1989, Zeigler 1967).

Teachers' community-based political work has focused on a variety of issues. Teachers in the United States the United Kingdom have been active members in the feminist and civil rights movements fighting for universal suffrage, emancipation, racial desegregation, and tax reform (Lawn and Grace 1987, Warren 1989). In contrast to these more progressive actions, those secondary school teachers who had not been purged from their organization endorsed the Nazi regime in Germany in 1933. Jarausch (1990) also indicates that some teachers took a public stand against the Nazis' fascist and racist project, while others rationalized their duty to make at least minimal concessions to Hitler's demands.

During this same period teachers in Germany and

the United Kingdom contributed time and energy to community-based work to support their respective nations in the war effort (Jarausch 1990, Ozga 1988). Teachers have also become involved in antimilitarist peace movements, as in the case of Japanese teachers after the Second World War (Blum 1969) and French primary school teachers at the time of the First World War (Feeley 1989).

5. Conclusion

The actions that teachers engage in, or refrain from, in classrooms, educational institutions, teachers' organizations, and communities can be viewed as political. Although each has been discussed separately, these arenas in which teachers engage in political action should not be treated as discrete or unrelated. For example, teachers' involvement in community-based social movements may be reinforced or contradicted by how they select and organize curriculum knowledge. Their activity or inactivity in the community may be related to focusing students' attention on or ignoring inequalities, exploitation and oppression, and the role subordinate groups play in challenging such relations of power (Blum 1969, Connell 1985, Kelly 1982, Sultana 1991, Zeigler 1967).

In discussing the political work of teachers this entry has acknowledged that teachers are not a homogeneous group, and thus has endeavored to identify multiple means and ends of teachers' political work. Although some patterns and similarities obtain across a range of countries, over time, and among different groups of teachers in the same location and time period, there are also important differences internationally, historically, and intra-occupationally.

This entry has emphasized international comparisons, but historical comparisons are also instructive. For example, it has been noted that the relations between organized teachers and the state have varied according to historical period in the United Kingdom, Cote d'Ivoire, Germany, Hungary, Japan, Mexico, and the United States (see Berube 1988, Blum 1969, Ginsburg 1991, Jarausch 1990, Lawn and Grace 1987).

Divisions among teachers and their organizations also make general statements about their political work problematic. In a range of societies there are examples of teacher organizations fractioned by gender, race/ethnicity, social class-related differences in the level of the educational system in which their members work or were educated, subject matter taught, regional location, religious identification, political ideology or party affiliation, militancy and orientation to alliances with other groups of organized labor (Blum 1969, Feeley 1989, Ginsburg 1991, Lawn and Grace 1987, Jarausch 1990, De Lyon and Migniuolo 1989, Nwagwu 1977, Ozga 1988, Warren 1989, Zeigler 1967).

Thus, different groups of teachers at different times and places have engaged and continue to engage in a wide range of active and inactive forms of political work. The variation among teachers also means that the consequences of political work by different groups of teachers may sometimes reinforce and at other times challenge the existing distribution of material resources, symbolic resources, and power among various groups from the local to the global level. Moreover, because of the contradictions in power relations that are constitutive of and constituted by teachers' individual and collective action, it is often the case that a given teacher in a given time and place operates in a manner, for example, that partially serves the interests of both dominant and subordinate groups. The issue to be addressed, therefore, is not whether teachers should be political actors, but to what ends, by what means, and in whose interests teachers should engage in political activity.

See also: Comparative and International Studies of Teaching and Teacher Education

References

Apple M W 1988 *Teachers and Texts: A Political Economy of Class and Gender Relations in Education*. Routledge and Kegan Paul, New York
Bagunywa A 1975 The changing role of the teacher in African educational renewal. *Prospects* 5(2): 220–26
Berube M 1988 *Teacher Politics: The Influence of Unions*. Greenwood Press, New York
Blase J (ed.) 1991 *The Politics of Life in Schools: Power Conflict and Cooperation*. Sage, Newbury Park, California
Blum A (ed.) 1969 *Teacher Unions and Associations: A Comparative Study*. University of Illinois Press, Urbana, Illinois
Canieso-Doronila M L 1987 Teachers and national identify formation: A case study from the Philippines. *J. Educ. Equity and Leadership* 7(4): 278–300
Carlson D 1987 Teachers as political actors: From reproductive theory to the crisis of schooling. *Harv. Educ. Rev.* 57(3): 283–307
Connell R 1985 *Teachers' Work*. Allen and Unwin, Sydney
De Lyon H, Migniuolo F W (eds.) 1989 *Women Teachers: Issues and Experiences*. Open University Press, Milton Keynes
Dove L 1986 *Teachers and Teacher Education in Developing Countries*. Croom Helm, London
Feeley F M 1989 *Rebels With Causes: A Study Of Revolutionary Syndicalist Culture Among The French Primary School Teachers Between 1880 and 1919*. Peter Lang, New York
Ginsburg M 1988 *Contradictions In Teacher Education and Society: A Critical Analysis*. Falmer Press, New York
Ginsburg M (ed.) 1991 *Understanding Educational Reform In Global Context: Economy Ideology and the State*. Garland, New York
Giroux H 1988 *Teachers as Intellectuals: Toward a Critical Pedagogy of Learning*. Bergin and Garvey, Granby, Massachusetts

71

Jansen J 1990 In search of liberation pedagogy in South Africa. *J. Educ.* 172(2): 62–71

Jarausch K 1990 *The Unfree Professions: German Lawyers, Teachers and Engineers 1900–1950*. Oxford University Press, New York

Kelly G 1982 Teachers and the transmission of state knowledge: A case study of colonial Vietnam. In: Altbach P, Arnove R, Kelly G (eds.) 1982 *Comparative Education*. Macmillan, New York

Lauglo J 1982 Rural primary teachers as potential community leaders? Contrasting historical cases in Western countries. *Comp. Educ.* 18(3): 233–55

Lawn M, Grace G (eds.) 1987 *Teachers: The Culture and Politics Of Work*. Falmer Press, Lewes

Meyers P 1976 Professionalization and societal change: Rural teachers in nineteenth century France. *J. Soc. Hist.* 9(4): 542–58

Nwagwu N 1977 Problems of professional identity among African school teachers. *J. Educ. Admin. and Hist.* 9(2): 49–54

Oliveros A 1975 Change and the Latin American teacher: Potentialities and limitations. *Prospects* 5(2): 230–38

Ozga J (ed.) 1988 *Schoolwork: Approaches To The Labour Process Of Teaching*. Open University Press, Milton Keynes

Rosenthal A 1969 *Pedagogues and Power: Teacher Groups in School Politics*. Syracuse University Press, Syracuse, New York

Seregny S 1989 *Russian Teachers and The Peasant Revolution: The Politics Of Education In 1905*. Indiana University Press, Bloomington, Indiana

Sultana R 1991 Social movements and the transformation of teachers' work: Case studies from New Zealand. *Research Papers in Education* 6(2): 133–52

Warren D (ed.) 1989 *American Teachers: History of a Profession at Work*. Macmillan, New York

Weiler K 1988 *Women Teaching For Change: Gender Class and Power*. Bergin and Garvey, South Hadley, Massachusetts

White G 1981 *Party and Professionals: The Political Role of Teachers in Contemporary China*. M E Sharpe, New York

Zeigler H 1967 *The Political Life Of American Teachers*. Prentice-Hall, Englewood Cliffs, New Jersey

Supply of Teachers

R. J. Murnane

A recurring policy concern in many countries is whether there will be enough skilled teachers to educate all children. This entry describes economic factors that affect the supply of teachers, and summarizes evidence on how these factors impact on the career decisions of potential teachers, current teachers, and former teachers. It is these decisions that determine the supply of teachers.

1. Factors Affecting Teacher Supply

Key determinants of the supply of teachers in a particular country are salaries and working conditions for teachers relative to those in other occupations, and the cost of preparing to become a teacher relative to the cost of preparing for other occupations.

1.1 Salaries and Working Conditions for Teachers

At the center of the economics perspective on the determinants of teacher supply are salaries in teaching relative to salaries in other occupations. Barro and Suter (1988) have documented that the ratios of teachers' salaries to those in other occupations vary widely across countries, suggesting that the attractiveness of teaching as an occupation of choice also varies across countries. Table 1 presents Barro's estimates for ten industrialized countries of the average elementary school teacher salary and the average secondary school

teacher salary expressed as a percentage of per capita gross domestic product.

Two patterns are evident from the Table. First, the attractiveness of teaching salaries relative to a measure of per capita income level varies enormously across countries, ranging from relatively low levels in Sweden and the United States to quite high levels in South Korea. Second, while in some countries, such as the United States and Sweden, elementary and second-

Table 1

Average salaries of elementary and secondary school teachers relative to per capita gross domestic product, selected countries and years

Country	Year	Ratio (elementary)	Ratio (secondary)
Sweden	1984	1.15	1.37
United States	1984	1.37	1.44
Netherlands	1982	1.54	2.33
United Kingdom	1984	1.62	1.69
Denmark	1982	1.67	2.40
West Germany	1982	1.72	1.96
Japan	1984	1.84	2.03
Canada	1984	1.90	2.14
New Zealand	1986	2.02	2.54
South Korea	1984	3.32	3.32

Source: Barro and Suter 1988 Table 3

ary school teachers are paid approximately the same salaries, in other countries, such as the Netherlands and Denmark, secondary school teachers earn considerably more than elementary school teachers. As the next section documents, there is evidence that the supply of teachers is sensitive to relative salary levels.

The limited evidence from developing countries suggests the importance of living and working conditions in determining teacher supply. Ankhara-Dove (1982) and Klitgaard et al. (1985) point out that difficult living and working conditions in rural areas make it difficult to attract teachers to these areas, even when there is a surplus of teachers in cities.

In principle, working conditions should also influence the supply of teachers in industrialized countries. It has proven difficult, however, to collect meaningful data on working conditions because, as Johnson (1990) has explained, teachers care about difficult-to-measure variables such as the availability of materials, and the quality of administrative support. As a result, there is almost no solid evidence on the impact of working conditions on teacher supply in industrialized countries.

1.2 Opportunities in Other Occupations

In evaluating whether salaries and working conditions in teaching are sufficient to attract an adequate supply of skilled teachers, the critical concept is how well they stack up against the best alternatives available to potential teachers. In most countries, teachers are paid according to a uniform scale in which salaries depend on amount of formal education and years of teaching experience, and *not* on the field of subject specialization. Since college graduates trained in certain fields, such as chemistry and physics, can earn more in business and industry than graduates trained in the liberal arts, any single salary scale for teachers will appear more competitive for liberal arts graduates than for chemistry and physics graduates. For this reason, some countries, including the United States, have greater difficulty in staffing the schools with an adequate supply of chemistry and physics teachers than they do in finding a sufficient number of history teachers (Murnane et al. 1991). This illustrates the importance of identifying subject fields in analyzing teacher supply. Because of differences in opportunities in other occupations, the teaching profession is much more attractive to college graduates with certain subject specialties than to graduates with other specialties.

In some countries, the teaching profession has been able to attract relatively large numbers of women and minority group members because they have been denied access to occupations with better pay. Social changes resulting in improved access to other professions for women and minorities reduces the ability of the education sector to attract women and minority groups at relatively low salaries. One illustration of this phenomenon is the change in the occupational choices of Black female college graduates. Among

those graduating in the late 1960s and entering the full-time work force, seven in ten became teachers. By 1980, the comparable figure was one in four (Murnane et al. 1991). While the attraction of teaching also declined for other groups of college graduates during the 1970s, for no other group is the change so great. This illustrates the general point that the supply of teachers is influenced not only by salaries and working conditions in the teaching profession, but also by the quality of alternative career opportunities available to potential teachers. As a result, changes in opportunities in other fields are likely to have a significant impact on teacher supply.

1.3 Cost of Preparation

Many countries specify that potential teachers must satisfy certain conditions before obtaining a license permitting them to teach. Typically, these conditions include completion of a minimum number of years of formal education, and also frequently include completion of particular training programs, or achieving above a prespecified score on a test of subject matter knowledge or knowledge of pedagogy. The goal of these regulations is to assure that students are taught by competent teachers. However, they also restrict the number of people who choose to teach, by increasing the cost of entering the profession. The costs include not only tuition and fees for the formal education required for entry, but also forgone income during the training period. In addition, test score requirements reduce the supply of teachers by eliminating potential teachers who score below the cutoff score, and by deterring from teacher training potential teachers who fear that they may not pass the licensing test.

1.4 The Quality Dilemma

A major limitation in research on teacher supply is the difficulty in measuring quality. This is important because, in many countries, the primary adjustment mechanism when there is a shortage of "skilled" teachers is not that schools are closed; instead, the schools are staffed with teachers who lack the skills to teach effectively. A consequence of this adjustment mechanism is that research should focus on the supply of skilled teachers, recognizing that the need to staff schools with unskilled teachers may be almost as great a cost as denying schooling to children altogether. The difficulty in implementing this idea is that it has proven very difficult to identify variables that reliably distinguish skilled teachers from unskilled teachers. As Harbison and Hanushek (1992) explain, the number of years of formal education is not a strong predictor of teaching effectiveness, especially in industrialized countries where all teachers have completed at least 14 years of schooling. Teachers' scores on tests of cognitive skills are positively related to teaching effectiveness, as measured by students' test score gains. But even these variables explain only a small part of the variance in teachers effectiveness, as measured by the

73

test score gains of students. Consequently, available research evidence suggests that the criteria many nations use to license teachers do not reliably distinguish competent teachers from incompetent ones.

This inability to study the supply of skilled teachers is a major limitation of existing research. In particular, in interpreting research on teacher supply, one should be aware that almost no studies shed light on the impact of salaries and working conditions on the quality of the teaching force.

2. The Career Pipeline

The supply of teachers is determined by the career decisions of potential, current, and former teachers. This section summarizes the evidence on the roles which salaries, working conditions, and training costs play in influencing these career decisions.

2.1 Whether to Become a Teacher

Dolton (1990) has shown that the occupational decisions of college graduates in the United Kingdom are extremely sensitive to salaries. The more favorably teacher salaries compare to salaries in other occupations, the more likely graduates are to choose teaching.

Manski (1987) used information on college students in the United States in the 1970s to explore the role of salaries and test scores in the decision to become a teacher. He found that teaching salaries have marked effects on the size of the pool of college graduates who enter teaching: the higher the salaries, the larger the pool. He also found that salary levels did not have a marked impact on the ability distribution of the set of college graduates who enter teaching. The inference Manski drew from his analysis is that a strategy for upgrading the quality of new entrants to teaching must include salary increases and entry requirements that screen out weaker applicants. The difficulty in implementing Manski's strategy is identifying a variable that reliably distinguishes weaker candidates from stronger ones.

Murnane et al. (1991) have shown that the representation of Black college graduates in the pool of newly licensed teachers is extremely sensitive to test score requirements. They report that in the first four years after the state of North Carolina reinstituted a test score requirement for obtaining a teaching license, the proportion of Black graduates in the pool of new licensees fell from 20 percent to 10 percent. Smith (1987) has shown that even small changes in the minimum passing scores on written licensing tests have a large impact on the number of minority group applicants who obtain teaching licenses.

2.2 How Long to Stay in Teaching

The length of time teachers remain in teaching has a marked influence on the adequacy of the supply of teachers. For example, if two million teachers are needed to staff a nation's schools, and 20 percent of

the existing stock leaves the classroom each year, then 400,000 replacements are needed each year. If the attrition rate is 5 percent, only 100,000 replacements are needed.

As Grissmer and Kirby (1991) have explained, the average attrition rate for a stock of teachers is highly sensitive to the age and experience distribution. The reason is that the attrition rate is relatively high for novice teachers, especially young ones. The attrition rate is low for middle-aged, experienced teachers, and rises only as teachers approach retirement age. As a result, changes in the age and experience distribution of a stock of teachers affects the attrition rate even when there is no change in the attrition rate for teachers of a specific age with a specific amount of teaching experience.

Recent studies by Murnane et al. (1991) and Grissmer and Kirby (1991), based on data from the United States, have shown that the attrition rate of novice teachers is very sensitive to salaries and opportunities in other fields. Novice teachers who are relatively well-paid are less likely to leave teaching after only one or two years than are less well-paid novices. Novice chemistry and physics teachers, who tend to have well-paying alternative career options, are more likely to leave teaching than novice social studies and language arts teachers, who face less well-paying career alternatives. Novice teachers who score well on standardized tests, and who consequently are most likely to do well on the examinations required for entry to training programs for highly paid fields such as the legal profession, are more likely to leave teaching than are novices with lower test scores.

While the effects of salaries in teaching and in other occupations have strong effects on the decisions of novice teachers, they do not significantly affect the career decisions of teachers with more than seven or eight years of experience. As a result, the effect of salaries on the overall attrition rate is very sensitive to the proportion of novice teachers and very young teachers in the teaching stock: the larger the proportion of novices and young teachers, the larger the impact salary changes will have on the average attrition rate.

2.3 Where to Teach

A number of studies have shown that, as a result of geographical differences in salaries and working conditions, teacher surpluses and teacher shortages within a country can exist simultaneously. For example, Klitgaard (1985) reports the coexistence in Pakistan of an aggregate unemployment rate of more than 50 per cent for licensed teachers and a shortage of teachers in rural areas. Ankhara-Dove (1982) describes the conditions in rural areas of developing countries that make it difficult to attract skilled teachers and lead to extremely high teacher turnover rates.

Ferguson (1991) examined the role of salaries in attracting academically talented teachers in 900 local school districts in Texas, each of which sets its own salary scale. He documents that districts paying high salaries attract higher percentages of teachers who score well on standardized tests than do neighboring districts paying low salaries. Moreover, Ferguson shows that teachers' scores on this test predict student test scores. As a result, this study differs from almost all other studies of teacher supply in that it indicates that salaries affect teacher quality, as well as the number of college graduates who want to teach.

2.4 Whether to Return to Teaching

One of the surprising findings of recent studies on teacher supply in the United States is that the majority of newly hired teachers are not new college graduates making an initial career choice. Instead, they are older graduates either returning to teaching after a career interruption, or entering teaching after either raising children or working in another occupation (Kirby et al. 1991). This has led to significant interest in the concept of the "reserve pool," defined as individuals licensed to teach, but not currently teaching.

While the evidence on the reserve pool is restricted to the United States the lessons for teacher supply about the importance of demographic trends are generally applicable and significant. In the United States, the reserve pool is large for two related reasons. First, as a result of the baby boom of the 1950s and 1960s, the age cohorts currently in their late thirties and early forties are very large. Second, many college graduates in these age groups obtained teaching credentials in the late 1960s and early 1970s when jobs in teaching still seemed abundant, but were not able to find or retain teaching jobs in the late 1970s when the earlier baby boom was followed by a marked declined in the birthrate.

As the United States looks ahead to growing demand for teachers in the 1990s, a critical question is whether the reserve pool will continue to be the major source of supply that it was during the 1980s. It is unlikely that this will be the case because the large baby boom cohorts will be followed by smaller cohorts, reducing the size of the reserve pool, and also because the projected slow rate of labor force growth should create strong alternative career opportunities for college graduates, giving members of the reserve pool a variety of occupational choices.

3. Conclusion

The literature on teacher supply provides three basic lessons. The first is that incentives matter. Evidence from a variety of countries shows that the supply of teachers is sensitive to salaries and working conditions in teaching relative to those in other occupations. Second, demographics play a major role. Trends in birthrates and cohort sizes have long-term effects on the supply of teachers, both by influencing the number of potential teachers, and by influencing the likelihood that individuals who do prepare to teach will find teaching positions. Third, the important policy questions do not concern the generic issue of teacher supply, but rather the more detailed issues of: the supply of teachers of particular subjects, the quality of individuals entering and staying in the teaching profession, and the willingness of teachers to work in particular geographical areas.

Important questions concerning teacher supply about which little is known, and which are in critical need of study include: the effects that changes in licensing requirements have on the supply of teachers, factors influencing the timing of teachers' retirement decisions, the impact of working conditions on teacher supply, and the extent to which geographically specific pension plans inhibit teacher mobility.

References

Ankhara-Dove L 1982 The deployment and training of teachers for remote rural schools in less-developed countries. *Int. Rev. Educ.* 28(1): 3–27

Barro S M, Suter L 1988 *International Comparisons of Teachers' Salaries: An Exploratory Study.* National Center for Education Statistics, Washington, DC

Dolton P 1990 The economics of UK teacher supply: The graduate's decision. *Economic J.* 100(5): 91–104

Ferguson R F 1991 Paying for public education: New evidence on how and why money matters. *Harvard J. Legislation* 28(2): 465–98

Grissmer D W, Kirby S N 1991 *Patterns of Attrition Among Indiana Teachers, 1965–1987.* The Rand Corporation, Santa Monica, California

Harbison R W, Hanushek E A 1992 *Educational Performance of the Poor: Lessons from Rural Northeast Brazil.* Oxford University Press, New York

Johnson S M 1990 *Teachers at Work: Achieving Excellence in Our Schools.* Basic Books, New York

Kirby S N, Grissmer D W, Hudson L 1991 *New and Returning Teachers in Indiana: Sources of Supply.* The Rand Corporation, Santa Monica, California

Klitgaard R E 1985 The economics of teacher education in Pakistan. *Comp. Educ. Rev.* 29(1): 97–110

Manski C F 1987 Academic ability, earnings, and the decision to become a teacher: Evidence from the national longitudinal study of the high school class of 1972. In: Wise D A (ed.) 1987 *Public Sector Payrolls.* University of Chicago Press, Chicago, Illinois

Murnane R J, Singer J D, Willett J B, Kemple J J, Olsen R J 1991 *Who Will Teach: Policies That Matter.* Harvard University Press, Cambridge, Massachusetts

Smith G P 1987 *The Effects of Competency Testing on the Supply of Minority Teachers.* National Education Association and the Council of Chief State School Officers, Washington, DC

Further Reading

Bobbitt S A et al. 1991 Characteristics of stayers, movers, and leavers: Results from the teacher followup survey, 1988–89. National Center for Education Statistics, Washington, DC

Hafner A, Owings J 1991 Careers in teaching: Following members of the high school class of 1972 in and out of teaching. National Center for Education Statistics, Washington, DC

Kershaw J A, McKean R N 1962 *Teacher Shortages and Salary Schedules*. McGraw-Hill, New York

Murnane R J, Olsen R J 1989 Economics of the education industry: Will there be enough teachers? *American Economics Review Papers and Proceedings* 79(2): 242–46

Women and the Professionalization of Teaching

K. A. Weiler

Contemporary proposals for school reform frequently include the demand that teaching be made more of a profession. The call for "professionalization" includes a demand for greater respect for teachers, but it also follows a model taken from such male dominated professions as medicine and law. Implicit in these calls for the greater professionalization of teaching are conceptions of hierarchy, competition, and rationalization that have raised concerns among feminist educators.

1. Historical Development of Professionalism

The concept of the professional developed in the late nineteenth century with the founding of associations to oversee and set standards of competence for a variety of occupations, and with the passage of licensing laws by the state. Medicine, law, and dentistry, for example, all became regularized and organized by both the state and their own associations. This conception of professionalism as it developed in the late nineteenth and early twentieth century was of a rational, orderly body of knowledge mastered by the specialist, the professional, who could be trusted by clients and the society at large to make decisions and act in the best interests of clients. The professional was an expert and, as such, entitled to both interpret and control social relationships.

This early twentieth century view of professionalism as the rational employment of advanced knowledge for the common good continues to be accepted unproblematically in many discussions of professionalization. A more critical approach has emerged, however, that views professionalism as an ideology, and as a means to police and control populations and to justify power and privilege for professionals as a "new class" (Bledstein 1976, Larson 1977). Feminist analyses of professionalism have focused on the class, gender, and racial bias of the ideal of the professional. Liberal feminist studies of professionalism have focused on the attempts of women to enter the professions and on the discrimination women faced and continue to face, emphasizing the intersection of conceptions of gender and professional

ideas of "merit" and "competence" (Epstein 1970). As Glazer and Slater (1987) put it:

> In men, the drive for success was lauded as healthy ambition; in women, it was disdained as unfeminine . . . Certain men were seen as natural leaders; in women, leadership was always unnatural, especially if it meant supervising men. These attitudes were not easily compartmentalized. They permeated all areas of professional life and had a direct bearing on advancement, which itself depended on continual assessment and evaluation during training and beyond. (p.12)

The most developed feminist critique of the concept of professionalism has come from a number of sociologists and historians who have studied nursing. Melosh (1982 p. 5), in her study of the history of nursing, argues that the concept of professionalism obscures the realities of what she calls "occupational culture." She argues that it is this cultural knowledge, "constructed from workers' accumulated experiences and their understandings of the work place . . . that guides and interprets the tasks and social relations of work." A similar line of argument has been put forward in feminist analyses of teaching as women's work.

2. Teaching and Professionalization

While professionalization and the ideological nature of the concept of the professional have been explored by historians and sociologists, in educational studies and policy statements the ideal of professionalism has tended to be accepted uncritically. Both sociologists of education and educational policymakers have accepted a hierarchy of occupations, with professionals at the top, as "natural" in contemporary societies. This perspective derives from functionalist sociology and from the "common sense" view that the social world we observe is both natural and inevitable. The debate in education has concerned the location of teachers within an existing hierarchy of occupations, focusing on whether teachers are in fact professionals and whether they should strive for professional status. The articles in Etzioni's influential collection, *The Semi-Professions and Their Organization* (1969), for example, locate teaching with nursing and social work as "semi-professions," with less autonomy, privilege, and status than the established professions such as law or medicine. Etzioni points out that most of these occupations are filled by women, and therefore women's subordinate place in society is transferred to their jobs. This results in their never attaining the status of the "true" professions. Etzioni insists that he does not mean to be "prejudiced against a most attractive minority" but is simply reporting the facts (1969 p. viii). A similar line of analysis is found in the influential work of Lortie (1975). Both Lortie and Etzioni accept existing definitions of what it means to be a professional, and dispassionately note the ways in which teaching fails to meet these standards of elite knowledge and autonomy, in large part because most teachers are women.

The same uncritical acceptance of the concept of professionalism underlies the many education reports of the 1980s that emerged in industrialized countries such as the United States, the United Kingdom, Australia, and New Zealand. In the United States, both the Carnegie Report (1986) and the report of the Holmes Group (1987) have proposed the creation of more stringent certification requirements, merit pay, and a greater differentiation among teachers who have demonstrated "excellence." The Carnegie Report, for example, proposes that schools should be organized as hierarchies, with "lead teachers" who would achieve this position by sitting for a national examination and through seniority, and who would have greater pay and responsibility. A similar proposal has been put forward in Australia for the introduction of "advanced skill teachers." These reform proposals take for granted the desirability of following a model of professionalism taken from existing professional groups such as medicine or law.

The acceptance of professionalization as the most desirable model for teaching has not escaped criticism. Practicing teachers, while desirous of greater public recognition of the value of their work and certainly sympathetic to higher pay, have been suspicious of the schemes to create "lead teachers," "master teachers," or merit pay. Critics have noted the lack of clarity in what actually defines a "master teacher" and the emphasis on hierarchy and competition inherent in such schemes. They have also noted that schemes for the differentiation of teaching staffs and the creation of career ladders will in fact leave most teachers with even less autonomy and collective involvement in decisions about curriculum, pedagogy, and the organization of their workplace than they have in existing schools. At the same time that professionalization is trumpeted as necessary for the reform of education, the movement toward the de-skilling of teachers through the introduction of prepackaged "teacher-proof" curricula, the increased reliance on standardized tests, and the continued call for expert control over the work of classroom teachers has strengthened a view of teachers

as employees who require supervision and direction (Apple 1988, Densmore 1987).

3. "Professionalization" of Teaching: Feminist Critiques

Feminist scholars have expanded the critique of professionalism as ideology to consider what is implied when teaching is termed "women's work." While some liberal feminist educators have essentially accepted the idea of professionalization of teaching as desirable, and have argued that women teachers should be included in the professionalization of education, a growing number of feminist scholars in education have challenged the idea of professionalism itself.

3.1 Historical Genesis of Teaching as Women's Work

Teaching, particularly elementary school teaching, has been defined as "women's work" in most industrialized countries since the formation of state supported compulsory schooling in the late nineteenth and early twentieth centuries. The economic common sense behind hiring educated women, for whom there was virtually no other paid work available, was evident. Women teachers were cheap. An ideological defense of women teachers emerged at the same time, put forward in the mid-nineteenth century in the United States by such figures as Horace Mann and Catherine Beecher, which redefined teaching, in Beecher's famous phrase, as "women's true profession," because it called upon the virtues of compassion and nurturance that were the essence of womanly and motherly natures (Hoffman 1981). This use of the term "profession," of course, should be read with some caution, since both Beecher and Mann envisioned teaching as a brief period of an educated woman's life between her position as a daughter in her father's household and as wife in her future husband's household. This was hardly the concept of "professional" as applied to the male-dominated spheres of medicine and law.

By the end of the nineteenth century, with the rise of the first wave of feminism, an increasing number of women began to remain in teaching for much longer periods. With gains in women's higher education, more of these committed teachers rose to become principals and, in rural areas, county and even state superintendents of education. The numerical dominance of women teachers, along with the growing numbers of women teachers and administrators who made teaching a lifelong career, led to the "woman peril" panic of the early twentieth century, in which male educators argued that teaching was becoming "feminized," and that there was a desperate need to bring more men into teaching to make it more scientific and "professional." This vision of the educational professional emphasized scientific measurement and control; the nurturant and expressive work of women classroom teachers was ignored or rejected as unscientific. In the post-Second World War period, women were pushed out of most administrative positions in education and a model of schools staffed by women teachers and led by male administrators emerged, and in most cases continues to the present day.

3.2 Feminist Theories of Women's Psychology and Epistemology

One influential body of work with implications for a feminist critique of professionalism has emerged from developmental psychology, in particular the work of Gilligan (1982) and the jointly authored work of Belenky et al. (1986). These feminist psychologists claim to have identified a particular "women's way of knowing." In her studies of the moral development of young women, Gilligan has argued that girls and women hold different attitudes toward moral questions than do young men: boys and men base their statements on an abstract morality of rights, while girls and women make judgments from a contextual morality of responsibility and caring. Belenky et al. (1986) came to similar conclusions in their study of cognitive development. This approach applied to the work of women teachers can be seen in the work of Grumet (1988) and Pagano (1990) who have argued that teaching for women is similar to the emotional work of mothering.

A similar line of analysis can be found in the work of feminist philosophers like Noddings (1984) and Martin (1985). Martin, in her study of philosophies of women's education, argues that a fully developed conception of teaching should include the whole person, not just the abstract intellect, and that the traditionally "feminine" qualities of nurturance and caring are central. Noddings, a moral philosopher, proposes a feminist ethic based on caring. Like Grumet, she argues that nurturance and caring are essential to human relationships and to human society; these ideals should be acknowledged and celebrated as essential to relationships both in the family and public world. Her vision of teaching is modeled on the caring relationship of mother and child, not on the mastery and transmission of abstract knowledge. In this analysis, she defines professionalization as implying an elite knowledge and special language that separates teachers and administrators in schools from families and members of the community. It is an orientation "characterized by hierarchy, specialty, separation, objectification, and the loss of relation" (Noddings 1984 p. 200). Noddings (1984 p. 192) thus sees professionalization as a masculine project, "designed to detach the child from the world of relation and project him, as object, into a thoroughly objectified world". In place of the model of bureaucratic schools dominated by professionals, Noddings proposes an image of circles and chains, in which parents, teachers, and members of the community would share decision-making and create a caring world in which children could learn and grow.

These feminist critiques have presented powerful challenges to the ideology of professionalism. However, they have also raised criticisms from other feminist educators: first, that these approaches have tended to universalize women and thus have ignored differences among women such as race, ethnicity, language, class, sexuality, and so forth; second, that they tend toward essentialism, in that they seem to imply that women and men have different "natures." The danger here is in accepting the earlier male view that it is part of the essential and universal nature of men to be rational and of women to be emotional.

3.3 The Feminist Analysis of Teaching as Work

Another line of feminist critique of the concept of professionalism emerges from the materialist analysis of teaching as work. This approach, similar to Smith's (1987) sociological analysis of the invisible work that maintains "everyday" reality, examines the kinds of relationships and activities that actually shape the work of teachers in classrooms. These analyses note the dangers of a feminist essentialism that echoes nineteenth-century conceptions of women as natural nurturers. Laird (1988 p. 461), for example, in her analysis of the current education reform reports in the United States, argues for the intellectual validity and strengths of a feminist pedagogy that would build on the kind of caring work women have traditionally done in schools and elsewhere, while acknowledging the dangers of a "subordinate and domesticated maternalism." Thus Laird argues for the deconstruction of the ideology of "woman's true profession" while calling for a recognition of the significance of the kinds of affective and caring work teachers have always done.

A more specific analysis of the effects of the ideology of professionalism on women teachers can be found in Freedman (1990) and Biklen (1987). Freedman points to the historic exclusivity of the White male-dominated professions and in particular, the distance such professionals have sought to maintain between themselves and their clients. Echoing Noddings, Freedman asks what the effect of such a model of professionalism will mean for the relationship of parents (which, as she points out, means mothers) and teachers. And like Noddings, Grumet, Laird, and others, Freedman argues for the essential role of caring and nurturing in the work of teachers. But she makes explicit the historical and social construction of this emotional work as women's work:

> I want to emphasize here that in taking care giving seriously . . . I do not suggest that women are natural nurturers, that nurturing is more important than intellectual labor, or even that nurturing is, or should be, the mainstay of a teacher's work. I am arguing that care giving is *as* important as intellectual labor, and that ideally the two cannot be separated but are together the definition of good teaching. (Freedman 1990 p. 245)

Freedman argues that in place of the current model of the professional, teachers should demand changes in the organization of schools that would make the best teaching possible for all teachers, not just an elite. Biklen (1987) has argued that teaching should be restructured to provide more autonomy and better pay and working conditions, but rejects the conventional model of professionalism as the source for these changes. As she points out, the hierarchical nature of most proposals for the professionalization of teaching assume relationships of subordination and exclusion that will create a climate of competition and privilege antithetical to a society based on collectivity and caring.

4. Conclusion

Feminist critics have viewed professionalism as a historical and social construct shaped by male-defined conceptions of elite knowledge as quantifiable, objective, and abstract. They have highlighted the family ideology that underlies the ideology of professionalism; they point out that the "professional" is in fact an autonomous man, with no domestic or familial obligations, who can depend on the emotional, affective work of women at work as well as in his home. Such feminist critiques challenge, either directly or implicitly, the underlying assumptions about knowledge that underlie mainstream discussions of professionalism in education. They emphasize the significance of compassion and caring in teaching and point to the need for the consideration of questions of power and material privilege that underlie claims to the need for "expert" professional control of education. Feminist critics have argued for respect and support for a vision of teaching that acknowledges the nurturance and caring traditionally provided by women. Although they recognize the appeal of the idea of professionalism for women whose work has been defined as subordinate and "unscientific," they also emphasize the dangers of simply adopting a male model of professionalism. They have argued instead for a "feminist professionalism," which would incorporate familial and child-caring responsibilities into the structure of work; democratize the school as a workplace, emphasizing community rather than autonomy as the ideal for teachers; and insist on the value of children for the whole society and thus raise the status and pay for those who teach.

References

Apple M 1988 *Teachers and Texts: A Political Economy of Class and Gender Relations in Education.* Routledge, New York

Belenky M, Clinchy B, Goldberger N, Tarule J 1986 *Women's Ways of Knowing: The Development of Self, Voice and Mind.* Basic Books, New York

Biklen S K 1987 Schoolteaching, professionalism, and gender. *Teach. Educ. Q.* 14(2): 17–24

Bledstein B 1976 *The Culture of Professionalism: The Middle Class and the Development of Higher Education in America.* W W Norton, New York

Carnegie Task Force on Teaching as a Profession 1986 *A Nation Prepared: Teachers for the 21st Century.* The Carnegie Foundation, New York

Densmore K 1987 Professionalism, proletarianization and teacher work. In: Popkewitz T (ed.) *Critical Studies in Teacher Education: Its Folklore, Theory and Practice.* Falmer Press, London

Epstein C 1970 *Woman's Place: Options and Limits in Professional Careers.* University of California Press, Berkeley, California

Etzioni A 1969 *The Semi-Professions and their Organization: Teachers, Nurses, Social Workers.* Free Press, New York

Freedman S 1990 Weeding women out of 'woman's true profession': The effects of the reforms on teaching and teachers. In: Biklen S, Antler J (eds.) *Changing Education. Women and Radicals and Conservators.* State University of New York Press, Albany, New York

Gilligan C 1982 *In a Different Voice.* Harvard University Press, Cambridge, Massachusetts

Glazer M, Slater M 1987 *Unequal Colleagues: The Entrance of Women into the Professions, 1890–1940.* Rutgers University Press, New Brunswick, New Jersey

Grumet M 1988 *Bitter Milk: Women and Teaching.* University of Massachusetts Press, Amherst, Massachusetts

Hoffman N 1981 *Woman's 'True' Profession: Voices from the History of Teaching.* Feminist Press, Old Westbury, New York

Holmes Group 1987 *Tomorrow's Teachers.* Holmes Group, East Lansing, Michigan

Laird S 1988 Reforming 'Woman's true profession': A case for "feminist pedagogy in teacher education?" *Harv. Educ. Rev.* 58(4): 449–63

Larson M 1977 *The Rise of Professionalism: A Sociological Analysis.* University of California Press, Berkeley, California

Lortie D 1975 *Schoolteacher.* University of Chicago Press, Chicago, Illinois

Martin J 1985 *Reclaiming a Conversation: The Ideal of the Educated Woman.* Yale University Press, New Haven, Connecticut

Melosh B 1982 *The Physician's Hand: Work Culture and Conflict in American Nursing.* Temple University Press, Philadelphia, Pennsylvania

Noddings N 1984 *Caring: A Feminine Approach to Ethics and Moral Education.* University of California Press, Berkeley, California

Pagano J 1990 *Exiles and Communities: Teaching in the Patriarchal Wilderness.* State University of New York Press, Albany, New York

Smith D 1987 *The Everyday World as Problematic: A Feminist Sociology.* Northeastern University Press, Boston, Massachusetts

Further Reading

Arnot M, Weiler K 1993 *Feminism and Social Justice in Education.* Falmer Press, London

Connell R W 1985 *Teacher's Work.* Allen and Unwin, Sydney

Freedman S, Jackson J, Boles K 1988 The other end of the

corridor: The effect of teaching on teachers. In: Smythe J (ed.) 1988 *A "Critical Pedagogy" of Teacher Evaluation*. Deakin University Press, Deakin

Haskell T 1984 *The Authority of Experts*. Indiana University Press, Bloomington, Indiana

Kelly G 1989 *International Handbook of Women's Education*. Greenwood Press, New York

Lawn M 1987 *Servants of the State*. Falmer Press, London

Middleton S 1989 *Women and Education in Aotearoa*. Port Nicholson Press, Wellington

Noddings N 1992 *Challenge to Care in Schools: An Alternative Approach to Education*. Teachers College Press, New York

Realities of Teaching

A. Hargreaves

To speak of the realities of teaching is to address the nature and organization of teaching not in terms of ideals, fantasies, models, or rhetoric, but in terms of the complex actuality of the work, and the day-to-day shape it takes with real teachers, in real-classrooms, in real schools. To speak of the realities of teaching, therefore, is to speak of teaching-descriptively, not prescriptively: of how it is, more than how it should be. It is to see teaching holistically, as complex, interconnected sets of tasks, purposes, requirements, and constraints; rather than as fragmented domains of knowledge, skill, or motivation that can be addressed or improved in isolation. Understanding the realities of teaching and engaging with them effectively, therefore, entails understanding and engaging with what teachers actually do, rather than cajoling or exhorting them to do something better.

1. Change and Practicality

Educational reform and teacher reform in particular are often rather poor at recognizing the realities of teaching. Efforts to improve teaching quality have tended to focus on the characteristics of individuals—on knowledge, skill, and personal qualities—much more than on the patterns of work organization and leadership which limit or liberate teachers in their work. Poor teaching quality, it is commonly argued or assumed, tends to result from an absence of knowledge, skills, or qualities in individuals (for examples, see Department of Education and Science 1983). This implies a deficit model of teaching, where poor quality results from deficiencies in personality, gaps in learning, or weak matching of teachers' competencies to the tasks they are required to perform.

Teachers are not just technical learners, though; they are social learners too. As social learners, teachers actively interpret, make sense of, and adjust to the requirements their conditions of work place upon them. In this view, what some might judge to be "poor" teaching quality often results from reasoned and reasonable responses to occupational demands: from interpretive presences, not cognitive absences; from strategic strength, not personal weakness. "Poor" teaching quality, in this respect, often results from poor work environments. Similarly, enhanced work environments which are more collaborative and incorporate principles of recognition, reward, and risk-taking increase teachers' senses of efficacy (Ashton and Webb 1986) and the degree of positive influence they exert on student achievement (Rosenholtz 1989).

Recognizing that teachers are social learners draws attention not merely to their capacity for change, but also to their desires for change (and indeed for stability) (Louden 1991a). Political and administrative devices for bringing about educational change and improvement usually ignore, misunderstand, or override teachers' own desires. In this respect, the devices and desires of teacher development are often incongruent (Hargreaves 1993b). Change devices usually rely on principles of compulsion, constraint, or contrivance to get teachers to change. They presume that educational standards are low and young people are failing or dropping out because the practice of many teachers is deficient or misdirected. The remedy for these deficits and deficiencies, politicians and administrators believe, needs to be a drastic one, calling for decisive devices of intervention and control to make teachers more skilled, more knowledgeable, and more accountable.

At the heart of the realities of change for most teachers is the issue of whether it is practical. Judging changes by their practicality seems, on the surface, to amount to measuring abstract theories against the tough test of harsh reality, but there is more to it. In the ethic of practicality among teachers is a powerful sense of what works and what does not, not in the abstract, or even as a general rule, but for a particular teacher in a particular context. For teachers, the realities of teaching are the practicalities of teaching. To ask whether a new method is practical is therefore to ask much more than whether it works. It is also to ask whether it fits the context, whether it suits the person, whether it is tune with their purposes, and whether it helps or harms their interests.

2. Commitment and Purpose

Teaching is not just a technical business; it is also a moral one. There are two senses in which teaching is a moral enterprise. First, teachers are among the most important influences on the life and development of young children. They help create the generations of the future. Second, at the heart of teaching, as in many other kinds of professional action, is the making of discretionary judgments in situations of unavoidable uncertainty. Teaching is riddled with practical judgments that are also reflective ones, even if only in the most fleeting sense (Louden 1991b). For these decisions, there are few or no clear rules of thumb that can be applied in a systematic way from one situation to the next.

Because teaching is a moral craft, it has purpose for those who engage in it. There are things that teachers value, that they want to achieve through their teaching. There are also things they do not value, things they fear will not work or may actually do harm to the children in their charge. Teachers' purposes motivate what teachers do and explain why they often resist change which does not address those purposes. Stated somewhat differently, they are committed to these purposes. Nias (1989) describes three kinds of teacher commitment: vocational, professional, and career continuance. These forms of commitment do not describe three kinds of teacher; any one teacher may exhibit elements of each of the different forms. In many teachers, however, one of the forms is often dominant.

2.1 Vocational Commitment

This refers to the missionary character of teaching, to the care for and connectedness to young people which motivates many teachers in their work, especially at the primary or elementary level. What Gilligan (1982) calls the "ethic of care," where actions are motivated by concerns for care and nurturing of others and connectedness to others, is central among teachers of younger children. The primary teachers interviewed in Nias's (1989) study talked extensively about care, affection, and even love for their students. Book and Freeman (1986) note how purposes of care and nurturance are much more common as reasons for entering teaching among elementary than secondary school teachers. In Lortie's (1975) classic study of elementary teachers, the joys and satisfaction of caring for and working with young people were the prime psychic rewards of teaching.

Educational reform, however, is often propelled less by ethics of care than contrary (and arguably more stereotypically masculine) ones of responsibility, which stress professional obligations and improvements to planning and instruction. Ignoring the realities of teachers' purposes and vocational commitments is, in this regard, not only professionally disrespectful but also practically perverse. Neglect of teachers' purposes can lead to lowered teacher motivation and decreased effectiveness. Nias (1991) has described how the detailed demands of the National Curriculum in the United Kingdom have led to profound feelings of loss and bereavement among primary teachers, who no longer have time to care for and connect with their children's individual concerns in the ways they feel are important. Neufeld (1991) records similar responses among a group of Canadian elementary teachers pressed and stressed by the time demands of implementing a program of active learning to the exclusion of meeting their students' personal and emotional needs. Apple and Jungck (1992) in the United States describe how tendencies in teachers' work where teachers are becoming more subjected to the detailed, step-by-step requirements of prescribed programs, also erode their capacity to care for the young in the ways they would like.

Care is at the heart of the emotional and moral working life of many teachers. Reform efforts which do not recognize the centrality of care, fundamentally threaten or demean the emotional and moral character of teaching.

2.2 Professional Commitment

This describes the teacher's commitment to being knowledgeable, competent, and instructionally effective. Professional commitment is about doing a good job. As a source of satisfaction, professional commitment tends to strengthen once the earliest years of teaching have passed, and teachers begin to take pride in their own mastery, the breadth of their repertoires, and their capacity to improvise. Professional commitment as a prime commitment also tends to have more prominence among secondary school teachers than elementary school teachers. In secondary school teaching, professional commitment is mainly invested in subject mastery and subject expertise. Commitment to teaching a subject is the main reason why secondary teachers enter the profession (Book and Freeman 1986). Care for individuals is less important for them, a repeated difficulty that afflicts the capacity of many secondary schools to become more caring communities for their students (Hargreaves 1982).

In secondary school teachers' commitments to their academic subjects can be seen the intimate connection between the teacher's purpose and the teacher as a person. Subjects are not just intellectual communities. They are social and political communities as well. They bestow meaning and identity on those who teach in them. Secondary teachers are socialized into subject identities and commitments as school and university students. The subject department is often a more meaningful and visible community for them than that of the wider school. Subjects and their departments provide the major lines of career development and progression at the secondary school level.

Proposals for curriculum integration which challenge teachers' subjects are therefore construed as much more than rational attempts to reconstruct fields of knowledge and learning in tune with the needs and demands of contemporary times. They are also perceived and deeply experienced as threats to career, security, identity, and fundamental senses of competence. As Hargreaves (1980) points out, competence anxiety, the fear of appearing incompetent in front of one's colleagues, is perhaps the most basic anxiety of all in teaching. Proposals for curriculum integration therefore strike at fundamental and deep-seated realities of professional commitment, subject identities, and desires to retain competence among the teaching force.

2.3 Career-continuance Commitment

Career-continuance commitment is the commitment to remain in teaching for the security and extrinsic rewards it brings. Teachers can become committed *by* teaching, as well as *to* it. Teachers in later career who have put a lot of time and investment into their teaching, and have built up families, dependents, mortgages, and other life investments may feel obligated to stay in teaching even when innovation and change profoundly threaten their purposes and satisfactions.

Teachers who remain in teaching for these reasons are among those most prone to become disenchanted and resistant to change. However, the realities of teaching in mid-to-late career are more complex. Research undertaken by Huberman (1992), based on interviews with 160 secondary school teachers in Switzerland, indicated that most teachers in mid-to-late career were unlikely to embrace innovation with enthusiasm. Two groups, whom Huberman describes as "defensive focuses" and "disenchanted" were deeply cynical about change. They had (accurately) predicted the demise of past innovations, steered well clear of them then and continued to do so now, or they had invested a lot in them only to be "sold out" as resources were withdrawn, the innovation collapsed, and the innovators moved on.

Other teachers, whom Huberman calls "positive focusers," were less dismissive but still tempered in their reactions and enthusiasms. They were pragmatic about school-wide innovations, having seen several come and go before. Feelings of mortality were also becoming stronger, leading to greater wishes to balance work with life and tendencies to become more serene, a discovery and development experienced rather later by men than by women (Krupp 1989). These positive focusers were prepared to change, but in ways which built on, instead of overturning, their past expertise and efforts: adding to their repertoires in their own classes, rather than transforming everything they did. The reality of mid-to-late career teaching is a reality in which modest, gradual, and respectful change may be embraced with willingness, but where radical transformative change will almost certainly not be (Fullan and Stiegelbauer 1991).

3. Career and Life Cycle Influences on Teachers

The issues of midcareer teaching in particular point to more general career and life cycle influences that have important impacts on how all teachers teach. Teachers in early career, especially when this coincides with youth, are typically preoccupied with classroom management and establishing competence. They will devote endless hours to their work and, once initial competence has been established, embrace innovation with all the time, energy, and commitment they can muster. Consequently, they are receptive to innovation, but also prone to burnout (Knowles 1988). At the early stages of career entry, young teachers may also still be in relatively early stages of personal ego development in ways that affect their capacity to work successfully and confidently with others, since teachers with poorly developed ego boundaries or sense of self, fear "invasion" when working with others. Young teachers entering the profession can be especially vulnerable here, since they are entering a profession with complex responsibilities and interpersonal relationships, often long before their own personal growth has matured (Nias 1989).

However, age and experience do not necessarily bring greater wisdom: they may also bring fixed views, outmoded understandings, dogmatism, and bigotry. Stoddart (1991), for instance, in case studies of teachers entering teaching through patterns of alternate certification designed to bring people of greater maturity and experience into the profession, found that:

> These individuals brought to teaching strong commitments and personal attributes which could have formed the basis for the development of outstanding professionals. Unfortunately, these attributes were not enhanced by systematic professional education. Faced with teaching dilemmas, they had limited resources with which to develop flexible responses ... They developed a modal approach to practice which was shaped by the subject-specific curriculum and their own personal perspectives. They applied and misplaced these pedagogies with little opportunity to reflect on and critically analyze the consequences of their teaching actions. (p. 228)

Whatever the teacher's point in the life cycle, the need to reflect on and reconstruct experiences is demonstrable. This need is especially felt as teachers come to appreciate the profound and pervasive influences that their lives exert upon their work. Long-standing attachments to particular belief systems and ideologies can remain abiding influences on how teachers approach teaching and learning (Louden 1991b). Sometimes these commitments have important religious and spiritual dimensions which also influence their work, through, for instance, solicitous Catholicism (Woods 1981) or charismatic fundamentalism (Stoddart 1991). Ethnocultural attachments and identities can also affect teaching, most visibly where the teachers value more traditional, didactic approaches. Gender identity is also influential, though in varying and complex ways. Families and domestic obligations create an unwelcome triple or quadruple shift for many women (Acker 1990a), but for others they can be sources of strength, stability, support, and identity, personal anchors beyond the vocational vortex of work and career that help retain some sense of balance and perspective.

Intense and dramatic personal problems such as bereavement, divorce, family violence, or substance abuse are among the most obvious ways that teachers' lives intrude upon their work, sometimes impairing their performance. In schools where teachers are involved in collaborative working relationships of trust and support, the intermeshing of personal and professional lives is seen as normal and legitimate. In these schools, allowances are made for teachers who are sick, troubled, or stressed, and support is offered to them. Teachers here can show their vulnerabilities and share them with others.

If the research on teachers' lives has one flaw, it is its tendency to explain the relationship between teachers' lives and work in a one-sided way: with the life affecting the work but not vice versa. At its worst, this bias can lend (unintended) support to deficit-based explanations of teachers' problems which diagnose and treat them as personal and private problems when they may actually have their roots in the conditions and management of the workplace (Ashton and Webb 1986). It is important to remember also that problems in the workplace can have a profound impact on the quality of life outside it. This can happen positively as well as negatively. Indeed an important priority for future research on teachers' lives might well be to identify which patterns of schooling and teachers' work enrich rather than enervate the lives of teachers. In particular, there is a case for forging a bond between research on school improvement on the one hand and teachers' lives on the other; to see whether, in the long term, successful and innovative schools drain their teachers dry until nothing of their personal lives and selves is left, or whether they enrich and energize those lives through the ways they generate personal enjoyment and fulfillment.

4. Coping Strategies

Teaching is at least in part a matter of strategy. Teachers are products of their present and previous work environments. They are creatures of circumstance. The ways they teach evolve as strategies to pursue purposes that are important to them. These strategies develop as ways of adjusting to the particular pressures, contingencies, and expectations of their environment. Where these pressures are extreme, teachers' strategies can become desperate, a matter of sheer survival. Even in the most favorable circumstances, all teaching is in part a constructive trade-off (sometimes calculated, sometimes routine and taken for granted) between ideal purposes and practical realities. These constructive trade-offs, or coping strategies, are a key aspect of teaching.

Coping strategies connect the purpose and the person of teachers to the context in which they work. The connection of strategy to context is complex, for teachers' strategies are mediated by all kinds of other factors, such as the teacher's personal biography, career stage, educational purpose, and the ethos or institutional bias of the school. These complexities explain why attempts to "test" coping strategies theory by trying to establish a clean and clear one-to-one match between teaching strategies and the contexts in which they take place, have not been particularly successful. However, in connection with the other realities of teaching, the context of teachers' work remains extremely important in influencing teachers' actions and helping shape the coping strategies which characterize their work.

5. Context

Three forms of work context help frame the realities of teaching: continuing contexts, changing or contemporary contexts, and contexts of variability or diversity.

5.1 Continuing Contexts

The continuing contexts of teaching are to be seen in what Sarason (1990) calls the fundamental regularities of teaching: the apparently fixed, pervasive, and intractable features of the work that define how it is done and that defy attempts to change it. These seemingly fixed regularities, however, have quite specific and deep historical roots (Cuban 1984). Modern school systems, as educational historians have noted, emerged as factory-like systems of mass education designed to meet the needs of manufacturing and heavy industry. They processed pupils in batches, segregated them into age-graded cohorts called "classes" or "standards," taught them in a standardized course or curriculum, and used teacher-centered methods of lecturing, recitation, question-and-answer, and seatwork. These systems of mass education for an increasingly massified society with large laboring classes were supplemented by more selective systems of state and private secondary education for commercial and social elites, rooted in academic and aristocratic traditions of contemplative study, disengaged from utilitarian concerns, and grounded in defined domains known as subjects that conferred cultural capital on those who successfully acquired them. These social and historical conditions have set the parameters and assumptions within which much of teachers' work takes place and which have come to define "real school" for many people. Punctuated lesson periods, age-segregated classes, the subject-based academic curriculum, and paper-and-pencil testing are therefore highly specific sociohistorical products, yet they have come to define a paradigm of teaching and teachers' work that is hard to break or reconstruct, even as the emerging educational needs of the postindustrial age seems to call for new patterns of teaching and teachers' work organization to meet them (Hargreaves 1993b).

5.2 Contemporary Contexts

Notwithstanding the realities and regularities of the continuing context of teachers' work by the accumulation and expansion of new tasks and responsibilities, this work is also changing in quite fundamental respects as the world outside schools also changes. Based on interviews with elementary teachers, Fullan and Hargreaves (1991) recorded teachers' perceptions of how their work is changing in terms of more "social work" responsibilities; the challenge of dealing with an increased range of abilities and behaviors in their classes (particularly since the move toward integration of special-needs students into ordinary classes); greater cultural and ethnic diversity and the demands this places on more diverse and sensitive programming; increased accountability and form-filling; and escalating amounts of time required to work, communicate, and meet with parents, principals, and other colleagues to meet the increasingly complex and pressing demands with which schools are having to deal. Two of the main explanations for this changing contemporary context are those of professionalization and intensification.

Arguments organized around the principle of professionalization emphasize the struggle for, and in some cases the realization of, greater teacher professionalism through extension of the teacher's role. Teachers, especially those in elementary schools, are portrayed as having more experience of whole-school curriculum development, involvement in collaborative cultures of mutual support and professional growth, experience of teacher leadership, commitment to continuous improvement, and engagement with processes of extensive school-wide change. In these accounts, teaching is becoming more complex and more skilled. What Hoyle (1975) calls "extended teacher professionalism" and Nias (1989) more cautiously terms "bounded professionality" is, in this perspective, both an emerging reality and a point of aspiration.

A second line of argument is broadly derived from Marxist theories of the labor process that look at teaching less as a profession or craft, and more as a kind of work with its own distinctive and changing labor process. This approach highlights major trends towards deprofessionalization in teachers' work. Teachers' work is portrayed as becoming more routinized and deskilled, more and more like the degraded work of manual workers, and less and less like that of autonomous professionals. Teachers are depicted as being increasingly controlled by prescribed programs, mandated curricula, and step-by-step methods of instruction.

In addition, drawing on Larson's (1980) broader analysis of the labor process among professionals or semiprofessionals, it is claimed that teacher's work is becoming increasingly intensified, with teachers expected to respond to greater pressures and comply with multiplying innovations under conditions that are at best stable and at worst deteriorating. Intensification, it is argued, leads to reduced time for relaxation and relief of stress, lack of time to upgrade one's skills, insufficient opportunities to collaborate with one's co-workers, chronic and persistent overload with resulting dependency on outside experts and materials, cutting of corners and reductions in quality, and spreading oneself too thinly. Under this view, extended professionalism is a rhetorical ruse, a strategy for getting teachers to collaborate willingly in their own exploitation as more and more effort is extracted from them in the name of shared leadership and the like.

Hargreaves' (1992) investigation of 28 Canadian elementary teachers and their interpretations of and responses to additional preparation time which had been won by their teacher federations raises some critical questions about the intensification thesis and suggests important modifications to it. First, some teachers resisted additional time because it took them away from their own classes and the care they could offer them (it undermined their purposes). Second, preparation time opportunities for teacher collaboration and enhanced professionalism often became administratively contrived and controlled in ways that undermined that professionalism. Third, shortages of specialist expertise among teachers required to cover classes during preparation time perversely led to program dependency, deskilling, and reduction of quality in some of these classes (reproducing the effects of intensification in a context meant to combat it). Acker's (1990b) study of English primary school teachers and their work raises similar questions about being too ready to interpret the changes in teachers' work as ones that amount to deskilling.

The contemporary changes in teachers' work can neither be encompassed by heroic proclamations of increased professionalism, nor by critical theories of intensification and deskilling derived from neo-Marxist theories of the labor process. Unintended consequences, bureaucratic complexities, and the expanded expectations for teaching that follow in an increasingly postmodern society which is pluralistic, culturally diverse, informationally dense, suffused with uncertainty, and intensely influenced by accelerated change and the compressed character of time and space, all help to shape the contemporary context of teachers' work (Hargreaves 1993a).

6. Contexts of Diversity

As well as the continuing and contemporary contexts of teaching that affect most teachers and frame the realities of their work, there are also contexts of difference and diversity that lead to variations in the realities of teaching according to the settings in which it is performed. In a major study of secondary school work contexts, McLaughlin (1993) has conceptually and empirically delineated a range of such contexts and their impact on teachers' work, including the contexts of the students, the subject department, the school, the community, and the system.

Metz (1990) points out that teachers are in many respects defined by their students: successful, high status students reflect and reinforce the perceptions of status that attach to their teachers; and teachers will sometimes, as a result, seek to avoid contact with students who threaten to undermine these perceptions. This reality of teaching is one reason why many teachers avoid assignments to low-track classes if they can; it also provides a justification for detracking or destreaming to counter such inequities (Oakes 1985).

As mentioned earlier, the secondary school subject department provides a more immediate and meaningful context for many secondary teachers than their overall school. Departments vary in the strength of their culture, leadership, and support in ways that impact on the quality of teaching and on willingness to innovate.

They also vary in terms of their shared beliefs about and practices in the areas of pedagogy, subject matter, assessment, and student grouping. Common innovations like curriculum integration or destreaming have a very different reality depending on the departments in which they are experienced.

The same can be said for the differences between communities in which schools are located. McLaughlin's (1993) study, for instance, indicates that teacher collaboration can take on very different meanings depending on the socioeconomic status of the community in which the school is embedded. In middle-class schools, collaboration tends to focus on program and academics. In working-class schools it is more oriented to dealing with the needs and demands of students.

7. Culture

Teachers' commitments, identities, and strategies are not established alone. They are built up and defined through interaction with others who are significant for them. Among these significant others are their colleagues. Teachers' relations with their colleagues comprise what have come to be called "cultures of teaching."

Hargreaves (1993a) distinguishes between two aspects of the teacher cultures: content and form. The content of teacher cultures consists of the substantive attitudes, values, beliefs, habits, assumptions, and ways of doing things that are shared within a particular teaching group or among the wider teaching community. Many different kinds of teacher cultures can be and have been differentiated by their content (e.g., academic elementary and developmental cultures; subject cultures).

The form of teacher cultures consists of the patterns of relationship among members of these cultures. It is through the forms of the teacher culture that the contents of these cultures are realized, reproduced, and redefined. Changes in beliefs, values, and attitudes among the teaching force, may, in this respect, be contingent upon prior or parallel changes in teachers' relations with their colleagues. Hargreaves identifies four forms of the teacher culture: individualism, balkanization, collaborative culture, and contrived collegiality.

7.1 Individualism

Individualism (also known as isolation or privatism), is characterized by situations in which teachers teach mainly alone in their insulated classroom "boxes," giving and receiving little help, advice, support, or feedback, and engaging in little joint planning or reflective dialogue about practice (Fullan and Stiegelbauer 1991). Individualism continues to be the dominant cultural form for most teachers. Although individualism is sometimes celebrated and justified as professional autonomy, history has created it, architecture and school timetables have reinforced it, and teachers have themselves actively and strategically retained it as a way of fending off the overwhelming constraints of bureaucracy. In addition, some teachers also actively elect to work individualistically to maintain care and contact with their own students and to experience the comfort and creativity of personal solitude against the pressures and cultural restraints of groupthink (Hargreaves 1992). While solitude at certain times for certain individuals seems educationally beneficial, widespread cultures of individualism appear to lead to personal insecurity, lowered levels of risk, and reduced levels of teaching quality (Rosenholtz 1989).

7.2 Balkanization

Balkanization is characterized by the fragmentation of teachers into separate and competing subgroups (such as subject departments) pursuing different self-interests in an environment where common purposes, joint understandings, and multiple group memberships are rare. Hargreaves and Macmillan (1992) argue that balkanization makes it difficult for teachers to establish common school goals, leads to inconsistency and redundancy in program and pedagogy, reinforces invidious political and status differences between different kinds of subjects and different forms of knowledge, and reduces teachers' opportunities to learn from one another across territorial boundaries. In balkanized cultures, the organizational whole is less than the sum of its parts.

7.3 Collaborative Cultures

Collaborative cultures among teachers are those where collegial relationships express principles of help, support, advice, planning, reflection, and feedback as joint enterprises. Little (1990) has identified four kinds of collegial relations among teachers which form a continuum from scanning and storytelling, to help and assistance, sharing and joint work. Only the latter, she argues, expressed in activities like team teaching, peer coaching, and action research, constitutes a strong form of collaboration. With Rosenholtz (1989), Little recognizes that these stronger forms reduce uncertainty, increase risk-taking, foster commitment to continuous improvement, and thereby raise teachers' senses of efficacy and, with that, the successes they have with their students (Ashton and Webb 1986). While advocacy for collaborative school cultures is increasing, they remain a relatively rare cultural reality of teaching.

7.4 Contrived Collegiality

This describes forms of collaboration that are administratively forced more than facilitated (Grimmett and Crehan 1992). While it can help provide structured frameworks to get collaboration going, more often it captures, contains, and constrains it, subordinating teachers' purposes to those of administrators and engaging teachers in efforts that are superficial, wasteful, or divisive. Contrived collegiality is evidenced in such measures as mandatory peer coaching, compulsory collaborative planning, and scheduled meetings with special education teachers. It is a form of collaboration that does not so much create empowerment, as entrapment, enticement, or enslavement.

8. Conclusion

The rhetorics of teaching quality and teacher development are often dominated by discourses of knowledge, skill, and competence. The realities of teaching quality and teacher development are more ones of commitment, context, culture, and career. Reform efforts are at last beginning to address some of these realities but it would be unrealistic not to acknowledge that there still remains a long way to go.

References

Acker S 1990a Creating careers; Women teachers at work. *Curric. Inq.* 22(2): 141–63

Acker S 1990b Teachers' culture in an English primary school: Continuity and change. *Br. J. Sociol. Educ.*, 11(3): 257–73

Apple M, Jungck S 1992 You don't have to be a teacher to teach in this unit: Teaching, technology, and control in the classroom. In: Hargreaves A, Fullan M (eds.) 1992 *Understanding Teacher Development*. Cassell, London

Ashton P, Webb R 1986 *Making a Difference: Teacher's Sense of Efficacy and Student Achievement*. Longman, New York

Book C, Freeman D 1986 Differences in entry characteristics of elementary and secondary teacher candidates. *J. Teach. Educ.*, 37(2): 47–51

Cuban L 1984 *How Teachers Taught: Constancy and Change in American Classrooms (1890–1980)*. Longman, New York

Department of Education and Science 1983 *Teaching Quality*, Cmnd 8836. HMSO, London

Fullan M, Hargreaves A 1991 *What's Worth Fighting for in Your School?* Open University, Milton Keynes

Fullan M, Stiegelbauer S 1991 *The New Meaning of Educational Change*, 2nd edn. Cassell, London

Gilligan C 1982 *In a Different Voice: Psychological Theory and Women's Development*. Harvard University Press, Cambridge, Massachusetts

Grimmett P, Crehan E 1992 The nature of collegiality in teacher development: The case of clinical supervision. In: Fullan M, Hargreaves A (eds.) 1992 *Teacher Development and Educational Change*. Falmer Press, London

Hargreaves A 1992 Cultures of teaching: A focus on change. In: Hargreaves A, Fullan M (eds.) 1992 *Understanding Teacher Development*. Cassell, London

Hargreaves A 1993a *Changing Teachers; Changing Times: Teachers' Work and Culture in the Postmodern age*. Cassell, London

Hargreaves A 1993b Individualism and individuality: Reinterpreting the teacher culture. *Int. J. Educ. Res.* 19(3): 227–45

Hargreaves A, Macmillan R 1992 Balkanized secondary schools and the malaise of modernity. Paper presented at the annual meeting of the American Educational Research Association, San Francisco, California

Hargreaves D 1980 The occupational culture of teaching. In: Woods P (ed.) 1980 *Teacher Strategies*. Croom Helm, London

Hargreaves D 1982 *The Challenge for the Comprehensive School: Culture, Curriculum and Community*. Routledge and Kegan Paul, London

Hoyle E 1975 The study of schools as organizations. In: Machugh R, Morgan C (eds.) 1975 *Management in Education*. Ward Lock, London

Huberman M 1992 *The Lives of Teachers*. Cassell, London

Knowles J 1988 The failure of a student teacher: Becoming educated about teachers, teaching and self. Paper presented at the annual meeting of the American Educational Research Association, New Orleans, Louisiana

Krupp J 1989 Staff development and the individual. In: Caldwell S (ed.) 1989 *Staff Development: A Handbook of Effective Practices*. National Staff Development Council, Oxford, Ohio

Larson S 1980 Proletarianization and educated labour. *Theory and Society* 9: 131–75

Little J W 1990 The persistence of privacy: Autonomy and initiative in teachers' professional relations. *Teach. Coll. Rec.* 91(4): 509–36

Lortie D 1975 *Schoolteacher*. University of Chicago Press, Chicago, Illinois

Louden W 1991a Collegiality, curriculum and educational change. *Curriculum Journal* 2(3): 361–73

Louden W 1991b *Understanding Teaching*. Cassell, London

McLaughlin M 1993 What matters most in teachers' workplace context? In: Little J W, McLaughlin M (eds.) 1993 *Cultures and Contexts of Teaching*. Teachers College Press, New York

Metz M 1990 How social class differences shape teachers' work. In: McLaughlin M, Talbert J, Basia N (eds.) 1990 *The Contexts of Teaching in Secondary Schools: Teachers' realities*. Teachers College Press, New York

Neufeld J 1991 Curriculum reform and the time of care. *Curriculum Journal* 2(3): 283–300

Nias J 1989 *Primary Teachers Talking*. Routledge and Kegan Paul, London

Nias J 1991 Changing times, changing identities: Grieving for a lost self. In Burgess R (ed.) 1991 *Educational Research and Evaluation: For Policy and Practice?* Falmer Press, London

Oakes J 1985 *Keeping Track: How Schools Structure Inequality*. Yale University Press, New Haven, Connecticut

Rosenholtz S 1989 *Teachers' Workplace: The Social Organization of Schools*. Longman, New York

Sarason S 1990 *The Predictable Failure of School Reform*. Jossey-Bass, San Francisco, California

Stoddart T 1991 Learning to teach English and mathematics in an alternative route to certification. *Curriculum Journal* 2(3): 259–81

Woods P 1981 Strategies, commitment and identity: Making and breaking the teacher role. In: Barton L, Walker S (eds.) 1981 *Schools, Teachers, and Teaching*. Falmer Press, London

SECTION II
Theories and Models of Teaching

Introduction

L. W. Anderson

Most experienced teachers practice their craft within the context of some theory or conceptual framework. Some theories and frameworks are formulated by educational theorists and researchers. Others are derived by the teachers themselves as they engage in the practice of teaching.

This section begins with an overview of theories and models within the rubric of paradigms (Burns) and ends with a discussion of teacher's implicit theories and their role in teaching practice (Marland). The remaining entries in this section describe seven theories and models that have been used by educators and researchers in their attempts to understand and explain the teaching-learning process as it occurs in classrooms throughout the world. These theories and models range from behavioral through social psychological to heuristic.

The theories and models differ in several respects. Four primary differences are described briefly in this introduction. They are the primary aim or purpose, the underlying assumptions, the guiding principles, and the main thrust of inquiry. In combination, the entries in this section are intended to provide the reader with a rudimentary understanding of the available theories and models of teaching as well as an appreciation for the role of theories and models in the practice of teaching.

1. Paradigms, Models, and Theories

Paradigms define the ways in which groups of scholars, scientists, and researchers view their world and operate within it. As such, paradigms include shared values, theories, and models. They also help to define legitimate problems and questions, as well as appropriate means by which problems are solved and questions are answered.

Models specify the major concepts that we use to understand our worlds along with the relationships among these concepts. As a consequence, they are often referred to as conceptual frameworks. Examples

of such concepts appropriate for understanding teaching and learning include "teacher pedagogical content knowledge," "student prior knowledge," "teacher behavior," "classroom interactions," "student cognitive processing," "student achievement," and "student social skills." Within a model containing these concepts, we might hypothesize that teacher pedagogical content knowledge influences teacher behavior, or that student prior knowledge and classroom interactions influence student cognitive processing which, in turn, effects student achievement. These hypotheses define the relationships among the concepts included in the model.

Models permit researchers to describe and predict. In contrast, theories allow them to explain. Stated somewhat differently, models enable researchers to answer questions about "Who?" "How?" "What?" and "When?". Only theories permit them to address the question "Why?"

Understanding the paradigm within which researchers or educators are operating enables us to understand both the *content* of their study and the *orientation* of their inquiry. Within the field of classroom research, Burns has identified three content and two orientation categories. The three content categories are setting, instruction, and teaching, while the two orientation categories are external and internal.

Instruction refers to a well-defined program or strategy, while teaching refers to the interactive processes or behaviors of individual teachers. An external orientation focuses on factors which can be observed (e.g., teacher behavior). In contrast, an internal orientation emphasizes factors that are unobservable (e.g., student cognitive processing).

2. Aims and Purposes

Theories and models differ in their primary aims and purposes. For example, Nuthall suggests that the aim of heuristic models is to "make students independent thinkers and learners who take responsibility for creating their own understanding and knowledge".

Similarly, the major purpose of linguistic and socio-linguistic theories is to "understand what is happening in the classroom . . . [by examining] the language being used and [studying] speech interaction" (Young). Finally, the ultimate goal of the application of cognitive developmental theories is the "production of an informed citizen reading to guide the process of democratic governance" (Sprinthall).

An understanding of its aim or purpose is central to understanding a particular model or theory. The aim or purpose defines the parameters within which the model or theory is expected to operate. It also specifies the limits within which research findings and subsequent explanations are likely to be valid.

3. Underlying Assumptions

Theories and models also differ in their underlying assumptions. For example, behavioral theories assume that "human behavior is shaped by contextually relevant consequences of behavior" (Sulzer-Azaroff). Information process theories, on the other hand, assume that "students are active inquiring agents who seek to guide their information processing based on instructional cues" (Winne). Social psychological theories rest on the assumption that "education is fundamentally an interpersonal process involving teachers and students, aimed at transmitting knowledge, skills, and culture from one generation to the next" (Johnson and Johnson). Finally, the aptitude-treatment interaction model is based on the assumption that "characteristics of persons moderate the effects of instructional conditions on those persons" (Snow). As a consequence, no educational treatment is likely to be equally beneficial for all students.

In order to understand theories and models, it is critical that the assumptions made by their developers and proponents are understood. Just as different aims lead to different theories and models, so do different assumptions.

4. Guiding Principles

Virtually every theory or model comes complete with a set of guiding principles. Some sets of principles are explicit, while others are implicit. Perhaps because behavioral theories are among the oldest, the principles are explicit, finite, and well-defined. They include the principles of reinforcement, chaining, shaping, and stimulus control (Sulzer-Azaroff). Principles of social psychological theories include interpersonal expectations, social interdependence, and distributive justice (Johnson and Johnson). Finally, principles of cognitive developmental theories are derived from concepts such as developmental stages, developmental appropriateness, assimilation, accommodation, and equilibrium (Sprinthall).

In many respects, principles define a theory just as concepts define a model. The relationships postulated in principles often provide theories with the explanatory power they need. Without principles, theories are likely to remain untested and untestable.

5. Main Thrust of Inquiry

Neither theories nor models are cast in stone. Rather, they change as new information is obtained and considered. Both theories and models, then, must be considered tentative and, as a consequence, must constantly suggest directions for new research. The theories and models described in this section differ in the kinds of questions that would be asked by researchers working within these frameworks.

Questions raised by those conducting research on linguistic or sociolinguistic theories might include "How do the linguistic resources of teachers and learners affect teaching effectiveness?" and "How do interactive speech processes facilitate or inhibit teaching effectiveness?" (Young). Similarly, questions raised by those conducting research within the context of information-processing theories might include "How do students acquire, remember, and apply knowledge?" or "How can teachers guide students to engage in tasks that call for particular forms of cognitive processing?" or "Once cognitive processing is underway, how can teachers support students' information processing at successive stages of learning?" (Winne). Finally, studies conducted by those working within the behavioral framework may center around the question, "How are particular antecedents and consequences related to observed educational performances?" (Sulzer-Azaroff).

The questions raised by those working within particular theories or models are important if we are to understand both what is known and what remains to be known. Theories and models that have more answers than questions should be viewed with some suspicion.

6. Conclusion

Contrary to popular opinion, theories are not the exclusive property of theorists. All teachers need theories if they are to negotiate the demands of teaching and be effective in their classrooms on a daily basis. This point is made most clearly by Marland. In his words:

> The classroom actions of teachers are guided by internal frames of reference which are deeply rooted in personal experiences, especially in-school ones, and are based on interpretations of those experiences. . . . These frames . . . can be said to constitute a type of theory, a theory which shapes action in the classroom and is constructed from interpretation of past actions.

In essence, theories and models enable teachers to

make sense of and to respond rationally to classroom events. Unfortunately, teacher-unique theories require that each teacher must discover the realities of classroom for himself or herself. The entries in this section may provide teachers with starting points for theory development and/or refinement. In addition, they may enable teachers to develop common frameworks for thinking about teaching and a shared language for talking about teaching that allow them to discuss and ultimately to solve difficult teaching problems.

Paradigms for Research on Teaching

R. B. Burns

Thousands of studies have been conducted in an effort to understand teaching and learning in classrooms. The concept of paradigm has played an important role in identifying groups of researchers sharing similar approaches to the study of teaching and learning. Paradigms have come to represent ways of differentiating the diversity of inquiry and substantive focus of these studies. Furthermore, several educators and researchers have used the concept to organize the research literature. This entry examines the concept of paradigm and its treatment in the literature on research on teaching.

1. The Concept of Paradigm

Prior to the publication of Kuhn's *The Structure of Scientific Revolutions* (1962), paradigm was used in psychology to refer to any well-used experimental situation or procedure, drawing upon its natural language sense of a recurring pattern, example, or model. With Kuhn's influential work, the concept took on a more significant meaning.

Briefly, Kuhn's thesis was that "normal science" is periodically marked by crises that change the way scientists conceptualize the world. Unexplained observations lead to these crises, a new theory is constructed to explain them, and a new paradigm replaces the older one. The new paradigm gains acceptance by explaining what the earlier paradigm explained plus the anomalous observations. Thus, the concept of paradigm is central to Kuhn's view on scientific progress.

A Kuhnian paradigm is typically characterized as a shared commitment within a scientific community to the nature of the legitimate problems and theories used to study a particular discipline or field. While this characterization captures some of what Kuhn meant by paradigm, it is incomplete and, in some ways, misleading. Kuhn used the concept of paradigm in two fundamental senses—one sociological, what he called "disciplinary matrix," and the other psychological, what he called "shared exemplars." After Kuhn (1974), the two senses will be labeled paradigm 1 and paradigm 2, respectively.

Paradigm 1, the sociological sense of paradigm, is the one typically implied when the concept of paradigm is used. Kuhn outlined four components of this disciplinary matrix: (a) symbolic generalizations (agreed-upon laws or formal expressions of theoretical relationships); (b) commitments to particular models (models, according to Kuhn, provide permissible analogies and metaphors that help determine acceptable explanations); (c) values about the way to practice science and judge theories; and (d) exemplars, the accepted solutions to the problems that prospective scientists are exposed to in laboratories and textbooks, primarily during their graduate training. This fourth component is identical to the more limited psychological sense of paradigm.

Paradigm 2, shared exemplars, is a psychological concept about how scientists acquire their discipline's knowledge during their training. Kuhn asked a basic question about the education of scientists: How is it that novice scientists learn to apply their knowledge of the theories and laws of a discipline to new situations? His answer was that a student discovers (either unaided or with instruction) "a way to see his problem as *like* a problem he has already encountered" (Kuhn 1970 p. 189). This ability to see new situations as similar to earlier ones is the result of doing exemplary problems; it is this learning process that helps a novice scientist come to see the world in a "time-tested and group-licensed way of seeing" (Kuhn 1970 p. 189).

This conception of paradigm as problem solution suggests that paradigm 2 is first and foremost a learning theory, a theory of how prospective scientists learn to think like scientists. What is learned are the "paradigmatic" achievements and beliefs of the discipline: the theories, models, and values shared by practicing scientists. In learning these achievements and beliefs, novice scientists come to see the world in a particular way, the way those who write textbooks and direct laboratories see the world. Having acquired the current theories and models of the discipline, new scientists use them to order their thinking and observations. Paradigm 2, the individual learning theory, offers an explanation for how paradigm 1, an inherently sociological concept, comes about.

The concept of paradigm was also used by Kuhn to

Gage (1963)	Doyle (1978)	Gage (1978)	Gage (1985)	Shulman (1986)	This Entry
1. Criterion of effectiveness	1. Process–product	1. Process–product	1. Process–product	1. Process–product	Process–product
2. Teaching process	2. Mediating response	2. Extended process–product	2. Extended process–product	2. Time and learning 3. Pupil cognition 4. Teacher cognition and decision–making	Extended process–product
	3. Classroom ecology 3a. Ethnographic 3b. Ecological psychology		3. Ethnographic/ sociolinguistic	5. Classroom ecology	Ethnographic Ecological psychology
			4. Intact teaching style		Teaching methods; aptitude–treatment interaction
3. Machine			5. Behaviour modification 6. Interactive educational technology 7. Instructional design	(Psychology of instruction)	Instructional psychology

Figure 1
A chronology of paradigms

characterize the development of disciplinary science. Kuhn described the initial early transformation for a discipline from a "preparadigmatic" period of science to a paradigmatic one. The preparadigmatic period is characterized by competing schools of thought vying for dominance. If and when a school achieves some major achievement, Kuhn suggested that the remaining schools of thought are eliminated, and the achieving school becomes dominant, setting the stage for a more "mature" and paradigmatic approach to disciplinary science. Kuhn later modified this position and stated that schools of thought also possess paradigms and that it was not the acquisition of a paradigm but the elimination of all but one paradigm that defined a mature science (see Kuhn 1970 pp. 178–79, 1974 pp. 460–61).

This part of Kuhn's theory has generated considerable debate among social scientists since it implies that disciplines without a single dominant paradigm are less advanced and do not practice paradigmatic science. Social scientists have responded in at least two basic ways. One response has been to accept Kuhn and attempt to justify the existence of a paradigm or paradigms within their discipline, arguing that if such paradigms can be shown to exist, then by definition their discipline is "paradigmatic." A second response has been to reject Kuhn, arguing that Kuhn's account

of scientific progress does not apply to the social sciences. Shulman (1986), for example, argues that multiple, competing paradigms not only characterize the social sciences, but that such plurality is to be preferred over the hegemony of a single paradigm.

2. Paradigms for Research on Teaching

Kuhn's work has drawn an extraordinary amount of attention. In the field of research on teaching, the concept of paradigm has been used to organize the large and diverse body of research making up this field. In this section, five well-referenced discussions of paradigms are reviewed. Because the number of paradigms varies across discussions, and there are some inconsistencies in labels and research literatures defining the paradigms, Fig. 1 provides a chronological map of the paradigms through the five discussions.

2.1 Gage (1963)

In 1963 Gage was unaware of Kuhn's work, using the concept of paradigm in the natural language sense of recurring pattern or model. Paradigms, according to Gage, were general ways of considering a phenomenon, where the variables of the phenomenon and their relationships were often represented in schematic form. He used the word "commitment" to characterize a researcher's orientation to a research problem once a paradigm was chosen, the paradigm acting as an implicit "framework" or "sense of the whole" for the more specific study. Gage identified three paradigms for research on teaching: (a) criterion of effectiveness, (b) teaching process, and (c) machine.

The criterion of effectiveness paradigm characterized much of the early, pre-1960 research on teaching. The paradigm is simple: a criterion of teacher effectiveness is defined and possible predictors of this criterion are sought. Hundreds of studies correlated measures from these two classes of variables. To help organize this literature, Barr et al. (1952) conceptualized criteria as falling along an "ultimate–proximate" continuum, where the effects of teachers (e.g., pupil success in life, pupil achievement) were classified as ultimate criteria, and teacher characteristics (e.g., teacher knowledge of subject matter, teacher intelligence) were classified as proximate criteria. Mitzel (1960) expanded this continuum to three classes of criterion variables, distinguished temporally: presage (teacher characteristics), process (teacher and student behavior), and product (pupil change). In an unpublished 1957 paper (discussed extensively in Gage 1963), Mitzel added a fourth class of variables, contingency factors (now called context variables), and conceptually related the four classes of variables in one of the first pictorial "models" of teaching.

Gage's second paradigm, the teaching process paradigm, summarized a number of models that described or conceptualized teaching behavior but whose primary concern was not establishing empirical predictor–criterion relationships. Gage characterized these models according to four sequential classes of variables: (a) teacher perceptual and cognitive processes, (b) teacher action, (c) pupil perceptual and cognitive processes, and (d) pupil action. These classes of variables foreshadow a number of future paradigms, including the "mediating process" paradigm of Doyle (1978), the "extended process–product" paradigm of Gage (1978), and the teacher cognition and decision-making paradigm of Shulman (1986).

The machine paradigm, Gage's third and final paradim, used the teaching machine as an analogue for teaching behavior. Although the analogy is dated, his depiction of the "human equivalent" flow diagram (p. 131) and his suggestion that "the programs teachers carry around 'in their heads' need analysis" (p. 132) reflect early information-processing language now popular in instructional psychology and cognitive approaches to instruction.

2.2 Doyle (1978)

The second major paper on paradigms was written by Doyle (1978). Doyle explicitly acknowledges Kuhn and defines a paradigm as an "implicit framework that defines legitimate problems, methods, and solutions for a research community," (p. 164) and as a "shared perception of adequacy" (p. 164) for judging and interpreting research and its findings. Three paradigms were identified by Doyle: (a) process–product, (b) mediating process, and (c) classroom ecology.

The process–product paradigm has been the most dominant paradigm for research on teaching to date. The full model of Dunkin and Biddle (1974) specifies temporal relationships between 13 classes of variables organized into the four categories: presage, context, process, and product. Most attention has been given to relationships between measures of teacher behavior (process) and measures of student learning (product), and consequently, the shorter process–product label has been used.

Dunkin and Biddle described the process–product model as a heuristic to "organize the findings of research on teaching," (p. 36), and captioned their pictorial representation "A Model for the Study of Classroom Teaching" (p. 38). They considered "not what teaching is about theoretically" but looked at "teaching from the viewpoint of those who have studied the actual behaviors of teachers and students" (p. 31). The Dunkin and Biddle model was the logical and formal extension of the criterion of effectiveness paradigm, an atheoretical schematic relating four clusters of variables, the relationships being determined primarily by their self-evident temporality.

Doyle's second paradigm was the mediating process paradigm. Noting the exclusive focus on observable teacher and student behavior in the process–product paradigm, Doyle described a paradigm characterized by attention to student's cognitive processes (mediation) that intervene between teaching behavior and learning outcomes. Doyle presents a diverse body of literature under this paradigm, ranging across research on programmed instruction, audiovisual media, special education, prose learning, paired-associate learning, process–process studies, time and learning, and attentional processes. Rather than representing a Kuhnian community of researchers, then, these literatures share an interest in variables intervening between the stimulus conditions of teaching and the responses of students.

Noting the laboratory nature of these literatures and their lack of representativeness to real classroom settings, Doyle described a third paradigm, the classroom ecology paradigm. This paradigm focuses on the demands of the classroom environment and the cognitive strategies students might employ to meet those demands. Doyle framed the paradigm as one where the classroom was viewed as a complex environment with multiple and competing stimuli and one where students are required to develop perceptual and cognitive strategies to negotiate its complexities. Doyle suggested that the classroom ecology paradigm is in an early stage of development, and he characterized the paradigm as consisting "primarily of a set of tentative propositions derived from a two-stage process: identifying environmental demands, and speculating about the mediational strategies necessary to meet those demands successfully" (p. 176). Doyle reviewed two literatures under this paradigm, ecological psychology and ethnographic studies of classrooms. These two literatures represent two very different groups of researchers.

Ecological psychology developed during the early 1950s with the work of Barker and Wright who discovered that some behavior was more predictable by knowing the setting inhabited than knowing the individual person. The concept of "behavior setting" was invented and the methodology for describing such settings was developed (see Barker 1968). Gump has applied the concept to classrooms as a way of characterizing the action programs of different instructional segments (see Gump 1987).

In sharp contrast to ecological psychology is ethnographic research, the second literature considered by Doyle under the classroom ecology paradigm. Borrowing from anthropology, sociology, and sociolinguistics, ethnographic research on teaching is diverse and eclectic, making it elusive to characterize succinctly. Moreover, because it is often defined methodologically rather than substantively, ascertaining its boundary conditions is often difficult.

A limited sense of this paradigm can be obtained from considering a paper by Bolster (1983). In essence, Bolster argues that research on teaching will have little impact on educational practice until it follows a more effective "model" of research, that is, ethnography. The reason why past research on teaching has not been effective, Bolster contends, is because practitioners and researchers conceptualize teaching in fundamentally different ways and therefore the knowledge constructed by researchers has little to offer to the knowledge teachers develop and use to teach in classrooms.

2.3 Gage (1978)

Gage (1978) provides a third discussion of paradigms for research on teaching. He characterizes paradigms as "overarching approaches and theoretical formulations that determine the major purposes, problems, variables, and methods of research workers" (p. 69).

Gage responds to Doyle's (1978) criticism of the process–product paradigm by suggesting an alternative paradigm, the extended process–product paradigm. As the name implies, Gage's second paradigm is not so much an alternative to the process–product paradigm as it is a way of incorporating the mediating response and classroom ecology paradigms of Doyle within a larger process–product framework. Gage argues that the two additional paradigms of Doyle have not "undermined" the process–product paradigm so much as they have "strengthened it" (p. 69). Conceptually, however, it is important to distinguish the boundary conditions between the two.

Gage does not disagree with the largely perceptual point of view of the classroom ecology paradigm (complex classroom environments present a variety of cues that are differentially responded to by students) nor the cognitive point of view of the mediating response paradigm (there are individual differences in how students process information). Rather, he merely sees the emphasis on classroom environmental cues and student mediation of those cues as intervening between teaching behaviors and student product variables.

2.4 Gage (1985)

Gage (1985) now defines paradigms as an "integrated cluster of *substantive* concepts, variables, and problems attacked with corresponding *methodological* approaches and tools" (p. 42). A paradigm, according to Gage, "gathers unto itself a community of investigators" (p. 42) who owe allegiance to the paradigm, citing each others' work more frequently, attending conferences with each other, and publishing in the same journals with each other.

Later in his discussion of paradigms, there is a hint of the discord that surfaced during the 1980s with respect to "paradigm wars" (Gage 1989). For example, Gage asks " . . . are there strongholds of concepts and methods inside which huddle together mutually supportive groups of investigators who have something less than unbound admiration for outsiders, the adherents of other paradigms?" (p. 44). He answers in the affirmative, and outlines seven paradigms for research on teaching: (a) process–product, (b) extended process–product, (c) ethnographic/ sociolinguistic, (d) intact teaching styles, (e) behavior modification, (f) interactive educational technology, and (g) instructional design.

The first three paradigms have already been discussed. The fourth paradigm, what Gage calls "intact teaching styles," has traditionally been labeled "teaching methods" research. The search for the best teaching method has a history nearly as long as that of the teacher-effectiveness literature. Despite what would appear to be closely related subject matter, the two literatures overlap very little. The reason is the way teachers and teaching are conceptualized.

In teacher effectiveness research, individual teachers are the focus of study, where differences in individual teacher behavior are related to variation in student performance. In teaching methods research, interest is on the pattern of teaching prescribed by the teaching method, not single teacher behaviors, and individual teachers are important only insofar as they faithfully implement the teaching method.

Two developments during the 1960s changed the nature of teaching methods research. First, researchers became interested in entire systems of individualized instruction encompassing both teacher behavior and teaching method. Second, largely as a result of the work of Cronbach (1957), the question of what teaching method is most effective was reframed as what teaching method is best for what kind of students. This more refined question led to the systematic search for aptitude–treatment interactions and Cronbach and Snow's (1977) classic examination of the teaching-methods literature.

The final three paradigms identified by Gage—behavior modification, interactive educational technology, and instructional design—are grouped together in Fig. 1. Although each of these fields has made important contributions to educational psychology in general as well as instructional psychology, they have been peripheral to mainstream research on teaching. Much of the work in these three fields has led to the development of technologies that work in specialized settings but have yet to demonstrate widespread applicability to problems of classroom teaching.

2.5 Shulman (1986)

Shulman (1986) has also written on paradigms, defining a paradigm as an "implicit, unvoiced, and pervasive commitment by a community of scholars to a conceptual framework" (p. 4). As mentioned in Sect. 1, he disagrees with Kuhn's characterization of the social sciences as "developmentally disabled" and stuck in "a state of preparadigmatic retardation" (Shulman's phrases) because they possess competing "schools of thought" rather than single dominant paradigms. On the contrary, Shulman sees different schools of thought as legitimate and healthy, and suggests the concept of "research program" (Lakatos 1970) may better characterize the social sciences. Shulman outlines five paradigms (research programs) for research on teaching: (a) process–product, (b) time and learning, (c) pupil cognition and the mediation of teaching, (d) classroom ecology, and (e) teacher cognition and decision-making.

His wide-ranging and complex presentation of paradigms connects research literatures on different levels, but his basic structure of five paradigms closely overlaps the previous four discussions. Shulman explicitly recognizes the close similarities between the first three paradigms, remarking that the "time and learning" and "pupil cognition" paradigms share a "fundamental family membership in the process–product tradition" (p. 18). Indeed, both time and learning and pupil cognition focus on student-intervening variables and thus fit the extended process–product paradigm of Gage (1978). The classroom ecology paradigm of Shulman is similar to that of Doyle (1978) except that Shulman restricts this paradigm to the ethnographic approach.

Shulman's fifth and final paradigm, teacher cognition and decision-making, is a logical addition to the extended process–product paradigm. The subject matter of this paradigm covers teachers' beliefs about students and teaching, their thought processes and decisions while planning instruction, and the kinds of decisions they make during teaching (Clark and Peterson 1986). This paradigm focuses on one of the

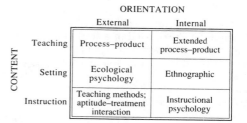

Figure 2
Paradigms for research on teaching

four classes of variables identified by Gage (1963). By adding this class of variables to the extended process–product paradigm, similar to what Winne and Marx (1977) suggest, then the causal sequence is as follows: teacher cognition→teacher behavior→student cue resources and interpretation→student mediating responses→student behavior.

2.6 Summary of Paradigms for Research on Teaching

Figure 2 organizes the paradigms reviewed into six categories, generated by crossing three content areas (teaching, setting, and instruction) with two orientations (internal and external). The paradigms reviewed vary in terms of their primary content focus: teachers and students (teaching), environment (setting), and method variables (instruction). They also vary in terms of their orientation. Paradigms with an internal orientation focus primarily on the cognitive processes of the participants and the meaning attributed to properties of the immediate environment. In contrast, paradigms with an external orientation focus primarily on the properties of the immediate environment and the behavior of the participants in that environment.

These six paradigms are the same as those indicated on the right side of Fig. 1. Together, the two figures represent the evolutionary history and a current conceptual organization of substantive approaches to research on teaching.

The external and internal orientations reflect two fundamental ways with which to view humans: by their actions or by their thoughts. These two orientations might also be loosely described as behavioral and cognitive orientations. It is interesting to note that these two competing points of view are consistent with Kuhn's (1970) observation about paradigm 2 in the social sciences. In contrast to the textbook knowledge learned by students in the natural sciences, Kuhn noted that the student in the social sciences: "is constantly made aware of the immense variety of problems that the members of his future group have, in the course of time, attempted to solve. Even more important, he has constantly before him a number of competing and incommensurable solutions to these problems, solutions that he must ultimately evaluate for himself" (p. 165).

3. Conclusion

In much of the social science literature, the concept of paradigm has been used in a fairly casual manner, inviting confusion. Paradigm 1 and paradigm 2 have not been distinguished, the applicability of the concept to the social sciences has not been well justified, and substantive and methodological issues have become intertwined in discussions of paradigms.

It has become popular, for example, to use the concept of paradigm to distinguish methodological approaches to educational research, the "paradigm wars" described by Gage (1989) being a case in point. Yet there is little in Kuhn to suggest methodology as a basic characteristic for paradigms. Indeed, Kuhn characterized paradigms as theories, models, values, and exemplars, all substantive characteristics, and his examples of paradigm shifts during periods of revolutionary science were all examples of change in theory, not method. Whatever the virtues of distinguishing methodological approaches to research, those who make such distinctions should probably not ground them in Kuhnian paradigms.

In light of what has been said, it might also be prudent to ask whether the concept of paradigm is even appropriate for organizing the field of research on teaching. It may be that the concept provides a convenient but inherently difficult concept to apply that leads to unnecessary polarization among researchers studying teaching. If Kuhn is correct in recognizing that the social sciences are characterized more by points of view than paradigmatic consensus, then it may be time to recognize the insights of each points of view in the attempt to understand teacher and student behavior and cognition in classrooms.

References

Barker R 1968 *Ecological Psychology: Concepts and Methods for Studying the Environment of Human Behavior.* Stanford University Press, Stanford, California

Barr A et al. 1952 Report of the committee on the criteria of teacher effectiveness. *Rev. Educ. Res.* 22(3): 238–63

Bolster A 1983 Toward a more effective model of research on teaching. *Harv. Educ. Rev.* 53(3): 294–308

Clark C, Peterson P 1986 Teachers' thought processes. In: Wittrock M (ed.) 1986 *Handbook of Research on Teaching*, 3rd edn. Macmillan, New York

Cronbach L 1957 The two disciplines of scientific psychology. *Am. Psychol.* 12: 671–84

Cronbach L, Snow R 1977 *Aptitudes and Instructional Methods: A Handbook for Research on Interactions.* Irvington, New York

Doyle W 1978 Paradigms for research on teacher effectiveness. *Rev. Res. Educ.* 5: 163–98

Dunkin M, Biddle B 1974 *The Study of Teaching.* Holt, Rinehart and Winston, New York

Gage N 1963 Paradigms for research on teaching. In: Gage N (ed.) 1963 *Handbook of Research on Teaching.* Rand McNally, Chicago, Illinois

Gage N 1978 *The Scientific Basis of the Art of Teaching.* Teachers College Press, New York

Gage N 1985 *Hard Gains in the Soft Sciences: The Case of Pedagogy.* Phi Delta Kappa, Bloomington, Indiana

Gage N 1989 The paradigm wars and their aftermath: A "historical" sketch of research on teaching since 1989. *Educ. Res.* 18(7): 4–10

Gump P 1987 School and classroom environments. In: Stokols D, Altman I (eds.) 1987 *Handbook of Environmental Psychology*, Vol. 1. Wiley, New York

Kuhn T 1962 *The Structure of Scientific Revolutions.* The University of Chicago Press, Chicago, Illinois

Kuhn T 1970 *The Structure of Scientific Revolutions*, 2nd edn. The University of Chicago Press, Chicago, Illinois

Kuhn T 1974 Second thoughts on paradigms. In: Suppe F (ed.) 1974 *The Structure of Scientific Theories.* The University of Illinois Press, Urbana, Illinois

Lakatos I 1970 Falsification and the methodology of scientific research programmes. In: Lakatos I, Musgrave A (eds.) 1970 *Criticism and the Growth of Knowledge.* Cambridge University Press, Cambridge

Mitzel H 1960 Teacher effectiveness. In: Harris C (ed.) 1960 *Encyclopedia of Educational Research*, 3rd edn. Macmillan, New York

Shulman L 1986 Paradigms and research programs in the study of teaching: A contemporary perspective. In: Wittrock M (ed.) 1986 *Handbook of Research on Teaching* 3rd edn. Macmillan, New York

Winne P, Marx R 1977 Reconceptualizing research on teaching. *J. Educ. Psychol.* 69(6): 668–78

Behavioristic Theories of Teaching

B. Sulzer-Azaroff

Behavioral theories of teaching assume that human behavior is shaped by contextually relevant consequences of behavior. The discipline therefore applies principles derived from experimental analyses of behavior to the enhancement of educational performance. The accomplishment of specific motivational, management, and learning objectives are viewed in relation to their contingent consequences, antecedents, and other contextual factors.

Often preceded by supportive events, behavior followed virtually immediately by sufficient reinforcing consequences is more likely to be repeated. The omission of reinforcers, the substitution of aversive consequences, and/or the presence of unfavorable antecedent events decreases the likelihood that the behavior will be repeated.

An extensive literature documents the effectiveness of the application of behavioral principles in classroom teaching. Proper application of these principles can result in increased levels of academic, motor, social, and professional performance.

1. Behavioral Teaching Theories

Behavioral teaching theories rest on the natural science notion that, like the survival of species through natural selection, a behavioral repertoire evolves within an individual's lifetime as a function of selection by consequences (Catania 1992, Skinner 1981). Influenced by each individual's physical makeup, status, and learning history, behaviors are actions—what people do and say—that impact the environment.

The main thrust of inquiry in behavioral theory is studying how particular antecedents and/or consequential stimuli relate to observable educational performances. These stimuli can differ in their form, timing, scheduling, and quantity. Observable educational performances include students' and staffs' rates of acquiring, sustaining or transferring particular skills or knowledge.

2. Behavioral Principles Especially Applicable to Teaching

Scientific analyses, conducted by examining and/or modifying the relations between behavior (B), its consequences (C), and its antecedents (A), as set in particular contexts, have yielded many important principles. The application of those principles toward enhancing student and staff performance is the essence of behavioral teaching (see Sulzer-Azaroff and Mayer, 1991, 1994). Consequences, antecedents, and other features of the environment may be presented, withheld, removed, or altered in form, intensity, frequency, and in additional ways found to be optimally effective.

Literally thousands of experimentally controlled behavioral studies have been conducted to produce an extensive array of findings especially promising for education. Simultaneously, over several decades, strategies for incorporating these principles into educational research and practice have been evolving into an effective and efficient technology of behavioral teaching and program evaluation.

A subset of fundamental principles of behavior that have been found to be especially relevant to education follows.

2.1 The Reinforcement Principle

The probability that a behavior will strengthen is increased through reinforcement; that is, when consequences are reinforcing for the individual under the current circumstances and a sufficient amount of reinforcing consequences are very frequently received immediately following the behavior. For example, if students who like to solve problems correctly (that is, those for whom being correct is reinforcing) check their answers immediately and find them to be right, they are more likely to solve those and similar problems correctly in the future. Similar results can be achieved when students for whom grades, praise alone, or solving a problem correctly, have no reinforcing value. Instead, along with praise and a good grade, check marks are given that can be exchanged along with other check marks for access to a special activity they do find reinforcing.

2.2 The Chaining Principle

The probability that a behavior will be learned is increased when new behaviors can be constituted from behaviors the individual has already learned. These pre-established behaviors are linked by reinforcing combinations of those components in a process called "chaining." Take, for example, the case of a student who can add, subtract, multiply, and do short division. To then teach long division, reinforcement is delivered as the student connects each element properly to the adjacent sequence.

2.3 The Shaping Principle

The probability that a behavior will be learned is increased when a behavior resembling the learning objective is reinforced. As variation in responding more closely resembling the learning objective occurs, this successive approximation produces reinforcement instead. This *shaping* process continues until the learning objective is reached. A case is a situation where members of a debating team are trying to learn a specific set of effective debating strategies. Each time improvement is shown, the debater is praised by the coach. Performance continues to improve.

2.4 The Stimulus Control Principle

The probability that a behavior will be learned is increased when a behavior that the person can produce consistently needs to occur sometimes but not at other times (that is, it must be brought under *stimulus control*). When the student detects the circumstances under which the behavior is and is not to occur and acts accordingly, reinforcement follows in a process called "differential reinforcement." Prompting helps to set the occasion for, or evoke, those behaviors already in the repertoire but not yet reliably produced on cue. However, supplemental prompts need to be *faded* if the behavior is or is not to occur under circumstances when prompts are normally absent.

For example, running and shouting in the playground is reinforced; in the library it is not. In the playground, reticent children who are prompted with "It's all right to run and shout here," and are praised when they do, increase their running and shouting there. In a different instance, a trainee who correctly detects all defective parts coming off the assembly line for a week is graduated to a regular job as inspector.

2.5 *Principles of Diminishing Behavior*

The probability that an unwanted behavior will diminish is increased when: (a) a behavior with which it cannot co-exist is strengthened; (b) it is no longer followed by reinforcement; (c) it is followed immediately and consistently by an event unpleasant or aversive to the student; and (d) preliminary activities impede or help the individual to avoid unwanted responses. Consider the following examples:

(a) rushing through an assignment and missing some critical aspects is found by the student to lead to the teacher requiring that it be re-done, while completing assignments to standards of acceptability consistently produces the immediate recognition and high grades the student loves. The student learns to work more slowly and carefully and errors diminish.

(b) Answers that are shouted out are ignored by the teacher. Raising one's hand and waiting, however, usually leads to being called upon to speak, so students stop shouting out.

(c) When the teacher orally reviews the story and its pictures in advance, children make fewer subsequent trial reading errors (Singh and Singh 1984).

2.6 *Transfer of Behavior Principles*

The probability that a behavior will transfer (or generalize) to other appropriate situations is increased when (a) reinforcement has been positive rather than aversive; (b) elements common to those new situations are detected and the generalized response is reinforced; (c) the same behavior is learned under many varying conditions; and (d) natural circumstances reinforce and perhaps cue the behavior intermittently (not every time) when and wherever it is to occur. (See Comunidad Los Horcones 1992 for a discussion of this topic.) For example, students receive reinforcement in the form of teacher approval and by seeing evidence of their improved performance when they regularly write down their assignments in each of their classes. Writing down assignments becomes part of their regular routine.

2.7 *Principles Pertaining to the Maintenance of Behavior*

The probability that a behavior will be maintained over time is increased when: (a) the behavior is fully mastered and expressed fluently, or at a high and steady rate under appropriate but not under inappropriate circumstances; (b) positive reinforcing consequences natural to the setting gradually diminish but continue at low levels; and, (c) any artificial prompts are gradually removed or faded. For example, fewer and fewer prompts are supplied and more and more check marks required of students' for correct problem solutions in order for them to gain access to an enjoyable activity. Over time, checks and special activities are eliminated while praise and immediate good grades continue, but at a diminishing rate.

3. *A Technology of Teaching Based on Behavioral Theories*

A technology of teaching has evolved because several requirements must be met if behavioral principles are to be applied properly and effectively. The most important requirements are discussed in this section. Instructional objectives must be very clearly specified so that educators know and can arrange to provide specific behaviors or behavioral combinations with appropriate consequences under particular conditions. (Mager 1990). Ongoing behavioral change related to these objectives is assessed by delineating and applying valid, objective measures repeatedly within and across sessions at individual and programmatic levels.

The influence of the application of behavioral principles on accuracy, rate, durability, generality, and other aspects of change is analyzed by using experimental methods designed to eliminate competing explanations for the results (see Johnston and Pennypacker 1993). Such evaluation of performance permits educators to make data-based decisions, rather than choosing methods arbitrarily or on the basis of dogma. In this regard the PLA-check technique (Risley and Cataldo 1973), the repeated probing of the number of students actively engaged in assigned activities within a time block, is a popular way of estimating the proportion of students "on-task" under given circumstances (e.g., Wilczenski et al. 1987). Similarly, practitioners of *precision teaching* count the frequency per time unit of skills performed to criteria in a range from basic to higher order subject matters.

Students' repertoires of responding relevant to objectives are thoroughly assessed to identify each person's well-established behaviors, the combination of circumstances and events that reliably function as reinforcers, and what stimuli evoke what responses under what conditions. Thus, educators are able to select curriculum materials, instructional styles, social arrangements, and consequences for current and future use and to avoid using ineffective, unnecessary, or intrusive prompts or reinforcers.

The student's physical and social environment in and out of school should be assessed with respect to performances essential to the learning objectives. Such an *ecobehavioral assessment* permits the identification and perhaps adjustment of supports and impediments to change.

One approach to ecobehavioral assessment involves students, teachers, supervisors, parents, and/or community members in the specification of particular objectives, measures, materials, methods of intervening, and/or consequences, recording progress, and the delivery of consequences. Implementation of these specifications often occurs within a formally negotiated *behavioral contract* (Brooks 1974, see also Sulzer-Azaroff and Reese 1982). One frequently used method is the daily report card (Schumaker et al. 1977) on which teachers check how well the student performs each day or period according to preset standards, such as attending punctually, and parents provide reinforcing consequences based on the report cards.

4. Programs of Behavioral Instruction

About the time that Skinner (1958) wrote the paper in which he elaborated the concept of the teaching machine, behavior principles began to be systematically applied towards educational improvement. Often this application has involved the rearrangement of single or multiple antecedents or consequences, while at other times principles have been combined into instructional, motivational, or management programs or *procedural packages*. Regardless of the particular form of application, all categories of behavioral education emphasize active student engagement and regularly attained, appropriate consequences. The most demonstrably successful and widely applied models and programs are discussed in this section.

4.1 Token Economies

In token economies neutral symbolic reinforcers, such as objects or check marks, are presented immediately following the desired behavior, behavioral combination, or behavioral approximation. Later, at a more convenient time, those "tokens" are exchanged for items or events of demonstrated reinforcing value for the student. In one such instance (Sulzer et al. 1971), fifth-grade students worked at their own paces in reading and spelling workbooks. On completion of a section, the number of correct answers was tallied and the student was awarded points exchangeable for trinkets or preferred activities in the future. Misbehavior diminished and daily performance increased strikingly, while standardized achievement test scores doubled or tripled in contrast with previous years.

4.2 Peer Proctoring or Tutoring

Properly trained and supervised, peers have been found to serve effectively as tutors of their classmates and they themselves benefit from the experience academically and socially. Peers increase the amount of time in which students engage constructively in aca-

demic activities and the reinforcement and feedback the students receive. Peer tutors have increased opportunities for reinforced practice and fluency training while tutoring can also lend social status to the tutor (an immediate, natural reinforcer).

At Juniper Gardens, an extensive educational intervention program for families living in poverty in Kansas City, Kansas, a class-wide peer tutoring program has been formalized and tested to teach a variety of basic tool subjects. The highly successful system has also been replicated for tutoring in spelling across schools, students, teachers, and school years (Greenwood et al. 1987). Peers have also been effectively involved in promoting social effectiveness, play skills, affection, and numerous other skills by demonstrating or modeling the desired behavior and/or reinforcing it when it occurs.

4.3 Group Management Methods

When members of small groups with similar skill levels receive reinforcement for working together or toward a common goal, as in *cooperative learning* (Johnson and Johnson 1983), they tend to assist one another and benefit academically and socially (see *Cooperative Learning*). Similarly, a group management system, the "Good Behavior Game," in which teams disrupting less or behaving appropriately more often receive access to rewarding activities, has demonstrated its ability to improve student conduct very rapidly (Saigh and Umar 1983; Fishbein and Wasik 1981). These systems work especially well because, beyond providing arranged reinforcement, positive social events (such as attention, recognition, and encouragement) are brought naturally into play when peers are acting suitably.

4.4 Social Skills Training

Expressing appreciation, requesting help, refusing or disagreeing inoffensively, entering and participating in play or conversational groups, and other alternatives to socially objectionable behavior have been enhanced through social skills training programs. Specific skills are selected on the basis of observations of the students' deficits and excesses as well as an examination of the environment. Training consists of discussing rationales for the change, cuing, demonstrating, and practicing the skill under simulated or natural conditions, and providing ongoing feedback and reinforcement for progress (see Sulzer-Azaroff and Mayer 1994).

4.5 Programmed Instruction

In programmed instruction, critical information is presented through the media of teaching machines, computers, or workbooks. Students monitor and respond sequentially to small steps of instruction called "frames." Their responses are followed immediately with positive or corrective feedback and sometimes other events such as detailed praise. Depending on the extent to which sufficiently challenging instructional objectives are matched to students' behavioral repertoires, responding accurately and fluently is optimally reinforced. Prompts are precisely selected, applied, and faded to enable correct, fluent responses to be sustained. In this way learning can be rapid, durable, and satisfying.

Programmed instructional programs permit students to progress at varied paces and are capable of widespread use across student populations and subject areas. They mitigate the requirement that teachers be expert in all areas of instructional content and style. Whether the instruction is presented through a machine or a text, however, it is only as effective as the fidelity with which it adheres to fundamental principles of behavior. Insufficiently challenging or interesting material contained in steps too large or small for the student, low success rates, inadequate or inappropriate feedback and reinforcement, too many or too few prompts faded too rapidly or slowly will attenuate the value of any given program within a particular student population. Given the growing sophistication of computer technology, making the necessary adjustments in instructional programs is becoming increasingly feasible.

4.6 Personalized System of Instruction

Primarily applied in higher education to teach a broad spectrum of subjects, the "Personalized System of Instruction" (PSI) (Keller 1968) closely resembles programmed instruction, but with a few fundamental exceptions. In PSI, the size of the steps tends to be larger (paragraphs or pages in length rather than a few sentences) and feedback is provided by a "proctor" (usually a peer who has already mastered the unit of instruction). Prompts are supplied in the form of study questions that students answer in advance; mastery of the material is assessed via a unit quiz.

Immediately after the quiz the proctor gives the student feedback as to the correctness of the items and, if necessary, details how the student needs to prepare further to display mastery on a different form of the quiz that covers the same content. Once students demonstrate mastery of the material by scoring above a given level (usually 90 percent), they may proceed to the next unit. According to a meta-analysis of over 350 reports (Kulik et al. 1979), PSI has succeeded in significantly enhancing academic performance.

4.7 Precision Teaching

Precision teaching emphasizes fluency building by augmenting the student's rate of response. First, students master a simple or complex fact or skill (for example, correctly spelling a word, applying a mathematical algorithm, giving a list of episodes preceding a historical event, changing a spark plug). This mastery is often accomplished with the assistance of the

teacher, programmed material, or formalized, scripted, small group, interactive instruction such as "direct instruction" (Becker and Carnine 1981) (see *Direct Instruction*).

Students continue practicing their skills until they achieve consistently high rates and levels of precision (i.e., fluency) (Bell et al. 1991; Hofmeister et al. 1989)

Often, students monitor their own rates by charting them on logarithmic charts. Used with advanced and delayed learners as well as both children and adults with learning disabilities and economic disadvantages, precision teaching, alone or in combination with direct instruction, peer tutoring, and/or supplementary reinforcement, has been found to multiply academic progress rates many times over. By analyzing the component elements of tool subjects and teaching and building these skills to fluency, Johnson and Layng (1992) have helped children gain two years of academic growth in one year and adults two grades per month. Precision teaching also enhances maintenance and generalization or transfer of learning to other, often more advanced, subject matters and settings.

5. Emerging Trends, Issues, and Future Research

Numerous controlled studies have supported the conclusion that behavioral teaching methods are capable of producing high levels of achievements among students and educators. Although systematically applied and analyzed for over 40 years, the approach is only beginning to be adopted more broadly. Work organizations are starting to use these techniques to teach literacy, numeracy, and job skills. Ecological research on the supports and impediments to the transfer of this technology to school systems is ongoing and will undoubtedly increase. The impact of involving school principals, pupil personnel specialists, school board members and other public servants in the design, implementation and/or assessment of the programs, is also being studied.

Concurrently, new computer technology is stimulating a resurgence of research and development in programmed instruction. Studies of curriculum content, optimal sequencing, prompting and fading strategies, supplemental graphic aids, varied response modes, alternative ways of supplying feedback and reinforcement, and many other aspects of computer-aided instruction are proliferating. Relevant findings from behavioral research on cognitive activity are likely to be increasingly incorporated into instructional design.

Finally, ideal combinations of motivational, management, and instructional packages need to be identified for given individuals and populations. At the same time, the advanced levels of personnel training and labor intensiveness inherent in practical, cost-effective curriculum construction need to be addressed. In these ways, the contributions of behavioral theories of teaching to educational effectiveness should increase.

See also: Cognitive Developmental Theories of Teaching; Linguistic and Sociolinguistic Theories of Teaching; Heuristic Models of Teaching

References

Becker W C, Carnine D W 1981 Direct instruction: A behavior theory model of comprehensive educational intervention with the disadvantaged. In: Bijou S W, Ruiz R (eds.) 1981 *Behavior Modification: Contributions to Education.* Erlbaum, Hillsdale, New Jersey

Bell K E, Young R, Salzberg C L, West R P 1991 High school driver education using peer tutors, direct instruction, and precision teaching. *J. Appl. Behav. Anal.* 24(1): 45–51

Brooks B D 1974 Contingency contracts with truants. *Pers. Guid. J.* 52(5): 316–20

Catania A C 1992 *Learning.* 3rd edn. Prentice Hall, Englewood Cliffs, New Jersey

Comunidad Los Horcones 1991 Natural reinforcement: A way to improve education. *J. Appl. Behav. Anal.* 25(1): 71–5

Fishbein J E, Wasik B H 1981 Effect of the good behavior game on disruptive library behavior. *J. Appl. Behav. Anal.* 14(1): 89–93

Greenwood C R et al. 1987 Field replication of classwide peer tutoring. *J. Appl. Behav. Anal.* 20(2): 151–60

Hofmeister A, Engelmann S, Carnine D 1989 Developing and validating science education videodiscs. *J. Res. Sci. Teach.* 26(8): 665–77

Johnson D W, Johnson R T 1983 Effects of cooperative, competitive, and individualistic learning experience on social development. *Excep. Child.* 49: 323–29

Johnson K R, Layng T V J 1992 Breaking the structuralist barrier: Literacy and numeracy with fluency. *Am. Psychol.* 47: 1475–90

Johnston J M, Pennypacker H 1993 *Strategies and Tactics of Human Behavioral Research.* 2nd edn. Erlbaum, Hillsdale, New Jersey

Keller F S 1968 Goodbye, teacher . . . *J. Appl. Behav. Anal.* 1(1): 79–89

Kulik J A, Kulik C-L C, Cohen P A 1979 A meta-analysis of outcome studies of Keller's personalized system of instruction. *Am. Psychol.* 34: 307–18

Mager R F 1990 *Preparing Instructional Objectives.* Kogan Page, London

Risley T R, Cataldo M F 1973 *Planned Activity Check: Materials for Training Observers.* Center for Applied Behavior Analysis, Lawrence, Kansas

Saigh P A, Umar A M 1983 The effects of a good behavior game on the disruptive behavior of Sudanese elementary school students. *J. Appl. Behav. Anal.* 16(3): 339–44

Schumaker J B, Hovell M F, Sherman J A 1977 An analysis of daily report cards and parent managed privileges in the improvement of adolescents' classroom performance. *J. Appl. Behav. Anal.* 10(3): 449–64

Singh N N, Singh J 1984 Antecedent control of oral reading errors and self-corrections by mentally retarded children. *J. Appl. Behav. Anal.* 17(1): 111–19

Skinner B F 1958 Teaching machines. *Science* 128: 969–77

Skinner B F 1981 Selection by consequences. *Science* 213: 501–4

Sulzer B, Hunt S, Ashby E, Koniarski C, Krams M 1971 Increasing rate and percentage correct in reading and spelling in a 5th grade public school class of slow readers by means of a token system. In: Ramp E A, Hopkins B L (eds.) 1971 *A New Direction for Education.* University of Kansas Follow Through Program, Lawrence, Kansas

Sulzer-Azaroff B, Reese E P 1982 *Applying Behavior Analysis: A Program for Developing Competence.* Holt, Rinehart and Winston, New York

Sulzer-Azaroff B, Mayer G R 1991 *Behavior Analysis for Lasting Change.* Harcourt Brace, Fort Worth, Texas

Sulzer-Azaroff B, Mayer G R 1994 *Achieving Educational Excellence Using Behavioral Strategies.* Western Image, San Marcos, California

Wilczenski F L, Sulzer-Azaroff B, Feldman R S, Fajardo D E 1987 Feedback to teachers on student engagement as a consultation tool. *Professional School Psychology* 2: 261–72

Further Reading

Alberto P A, Troutman A C 1990 *Applied Behavior Analysis for Teachers,* 3rd Edn. Merrill Publishing Company. Columbus, Ohio

Jenson W R, Sloane H N, Young K R 1988 *Applied Behavior Analysis in Education.* Prentice Hall. Englewood Cliffs, New Jersey

Johnson D W, Johnson R T 1975 *Learning Together and Alone: Cooperative, Competitive and Individualistic Learning.* Prentice Hall, Englewood Cliffs, New Jersey

Kazdin A E 1989 *Behavior Modification in Applied Settings,* 4th Edn. Brooks Cole, Pacific Grove, California

Maher C A, Forman S G (eds.) 1987 *A Behavioral Approach to Education of Children and Youth.* Erlbaum, Hillsdale, New Jersey

Markle S 1991 *Designs for Instructional Designers.* Stipes Publishing. Champaign, Illinois

Skinner B F 1968 *Technology of Teaching.* Prentice Hall, Englewood Cliffs, New Jersey

Cognitive Developmental Theories of Teaching

N. A. Sprinthall

One of the most perplexing issues in education is the question of how to enhance student learning. On the surface the answer seems simple; present the information the pupil is required to learn in a straightforward manner using a variety of methods, and positive results will follow. The real answer, however, is more problematic.

The United States first recognized psychologist,

William James, provides an apt metaphorical account by comparing teaching to warfare.

> In war, all you have to do is work your enemy into a position in which natural obstacles prevent him from escaping . . . then fall on him in numbers superior to his own . . . Just so in teaching; you must simply work your pupil into such a state-of-interest with every other object of attention banished from his mind; then reveal it to him so impressively that he will remember it to his dying day; and finally, fill him with a devouring curiosity to know what the next steps are. (James 1958 p. 106).

The difficulty, as James goes on to say, is that the student, like the opposing general, may be working just as keenly and avidly for a different set of goals. Just what the students think and want may be as difficult for the teacher to discern as the enemy commander.

The cognitive–developmental framework attempts to resolve these difficulties by focusing on both the teacher and the learner. Both contribute to the learning process. Thus, when either is out of phase, learning is reduced.

The rationale for a cognitive–developmental approach to teaching can be found in the original theories of Dewey (1966) and Freire (1981), and in the research of Piaget (1974), Kohlberg (1984), and Vygotsky (1978). Essentially, in this view, teaching is interactive, a dialectic or dialogic between teacher and learner. The student is viewed as an active participant in the process. The teacher's role is to promote the intellectual, interpersonal, and social development of the child. As Dewey noted, "The cause of education . . . is one of development focusing indeed in the growth of students, but to be conceived even in the connection as part of the larger development of society" (1966 p. 69).

Freire (1981), echoing these views, indicated that the aim of education should be fostering critical consciousness, awareness of the political, social, and economic causes of injustice on the part of democratic citizenship: "I was convinced that the Brazilian people could learn social and political responsibility only by experiencing that responsibility through intervention in the destiny of their children's schools (and other agencies) . . . They could be helped to learn democracy through the exercise of democracy" (1981 p. 36).

Simply stated, the educational goals in the cognitive–developmental view of teaching and learning include not only such traditional ideas as literacy broadly defined, but also requisite experiences which will produce an informed citizen ready to guide the process of democratic governance.

1. Traditional Views of Teaching and Learning

The Dewey and Freire views are at odds with teaching practices in most of the world in the 1990s. Reviews of classroom instruction both in the United States and throughout the world reveal a consistent and enduring pattern of rote learning via classroom recitation.

Students reciting the fact-based content across the curriculum was first documented in the early part of the twentieth century. Bellack et al. (1966) reported that in the early 1900s students recited rote answers to teachers' questions at the rate of four per minute. Some 70 years later the rate was three per minute. As Goodlad (1984) noted: "In over half the classrooms, the worksheet, recitation rote memory routines were the only method practiced—no films, slides, videos, simulation tapes, teaching machines, or field visits" (p. 241).

Freire (1981) has argued that such a traditional method which he refers to as "banking education," the memorization of bits and pieces of disconnected facts, reinforces all the wrong goals. Students are viewed as inert, empty vessels, to be filled with prescribed knowledge.

Piaget (1974) has noted that to know by heart is not to know. Dewey called this the phonograph method with the teachers inscribing information upon empty phonograph disks, to be replayed later. Vygotsky (1978) referred to this as "ossification." Thus the world over, traditional teaching methods remain entrenched and seemingly resistant to revitalization. The world's classrooms can be summed up in the French phrase, "Plus ça change, plus c'est la même chose"—the more things change, the more they remain the same.

In the United States, there is major concern as a result of national assessments of educational attainment, and with good cause. The results, particularly at the secondary school level, represent an indictment of traditional teaching methods. Of course, such indexes have been available for some time, yet not on such a comprehensive level.

The basic results indicate that elementary age pupils are learning fundamentals, or the three "R's." At the secondary school level, however, comprehension has decreased. This means, for example, that young students learn to break the reading code, add, subtract, and know the capitals of South American countries. By high school, they have less of a grasp of the meaning of what they read, have great difficulty with so-called "word problems" in mathematics (Jones 1988), and exhibit major ignorance of fundamental principles of democratic government (Nickerson 1988).

It is indeed difficult to imagine the traditional method of teaching producing different results. In a classic study Tyler (1933) found a lack of comprehension almost endemic to all of education. The results of Flanagan's (1973) massive study Project TALENT resulted in the same conclusion, as did the more recent study by Goodlad (1984) which was already noted. These studies are summarized in Sprinthall and Sprinthall (1990).

2. Cognitive–Developmental Learning

In cognitive–developmental learning, teaching is to start with the students, particularly, with the understanding that they are not midget-sized adults, empty vessels, or blank phonograph disks. It was Piaget's (1974) pioneering work starting in the 1920s that began to outline the methods of learning that students actually employ when confronted with educational problems to solve. He was able to outline a sequence of stages of conceptual growth: sensory–motor, intuitive, concrete, and formal operational. Each stage represents a qualitatively distinct method of cognitive processing.

Piaget's work, first limited to Europe and then replicated in many other countries, has become the basis for what is called the Attribute Treatment Interaction (ATI) (See *Aptitude–Treatment Interaction Model of Teaching*). According to this conceptual framework, learning is determined by the attributes of the students, including their cognitive stage, interacting with the teaching strategies and content. This reflects the truism that teaching must start where the learner is currently functioning.

The cognitive–developmental view provides a detailed and comprehensive picture of where the learners are. Although the Piaget framework has been continually challenged and modified, the overall framework of stage characteristics and sequence remains intact (Ginsberg and Opper 1988).

A second developmental domain, especially for democratic societies, has been Dewey's notion of educational aims vis-à-vis values and ethics for citizenship. In this regard, the work of Kohlberg (1984) has resulted in a scheme of stages which parallels Piaget's. In the Kohlberg scheme, moral judgment and ethical reasoning proceeds through a sequence from self-centered physical dominance/submission (Stage 1), materialistic hedonism (Stage 2), social conformity (Stage 3), and legal sanctions (Stage 4), to democratic principled thought (either utilitarian consequentialism or deontological universalism). There is also a clear similarity between Kohlberg's stages and nearly all of Freire's stages of consciousness (i.e., Freire's intransitive, semi-intransitive, and naive transitive are the same as Kohlberg's Stages, 1, 2, and 3, and critical consciousness is the same as principled reasoning, Stages 5 and 6). Kohlberg's research began in the United States, and has been expanded to over 50 countries with significant empirical evidence to support both the cross-cultural validity of his work and the gender-neutral component of the sequence of stages. The latter point has been challenged, but meta-analyses by Rest (1986) with 6,000 subjects and by Walker (1986) with 10,000 subjects, find no evidence to support any gender bias.

3. Cognitive–Developmental Teaching: The Student

Piaget and Kohlberg both originally assumed that applying these theories to practice was premature, and

in fact something that Piaget had warned against (his scathing comments about educational acceleration being "An American Question"). Nonetheless, there have been numerous applications which actually support the Dewey–Freire goals, Vygotsky's aims, and Piaget's and Kohlberg's stages.

Walberg (1986) has shown that the student's Piagetian stage makes a significant contribution to his or her comprehension of intended learning outcomes, particularly in the field of science. For example, if teachers ignore the developmental stage of the student in scientific thought, the students do not understand what they are supposed to learn. Similarly, a series of studies by Renner et al. (1976) has shown the deleterious effects of science teaching that assumes rather than promotes Piagetian development. The work of Feuerstein (1980) with Israeli immigrants also has shown the positive effects of relating pupil developmental stage to instructional methods. Most importantly, his work has shown the applicability of his instructional program across a wide range of academic aptitude.

The research of Barrett (1975), however, has shown the futility of attempting to accelerate development. His work in England demonstrated that trying to teach the meaning of abstract concepts prior to the onset of formal reasoning resulted in no gain in comprehension. While the older students could quickly grasp the concepts after a short review, younger students were unable to grasp them at all. Thus, the teacher who spends a great amount of classroom time trying to teach abstract concepts to concrete learners is destined to be frustrated.

Duckworth (1987) best captures the essence of developmental teaching and learning with her aphorism, "Either we're too late, or they know it already" (p. 31). The implications are two-fold. First, the framework requires an understanding of the current preferred mode of problem-solving, that is, the cognitive–developmental stage of the student. Second, and equally important, is the cognitive–developmental stage of the teacher.

4. Cognitive–Developmental Teaching: The Teacher

One of the major changes in the cognitive–developmental framework has been a massive revision in theory. Until the 1970s, the general assumption had been that stages of growth ended somewhere in late adolescence or early adulthood. However, the cognitive–developmental researchers all made the fortuitous mistake of conducting longitudinal research and found a continuation of stage growth during adulthood itself. While Piaget concentrated on early childhood and adolescence, he raised the issue of continuing development in one of his later works

(Piaget 1972). Kohlberg (1984) had to revise his earlier views after reviewing his follow-up studies, conducted at five-year intervals. Similar developmental changes have been found in other stage domains (e.g., ego and conceptual development). As a consequence, teachers are now conceptualized as adult learners in a stage and sequence model. What was true for students is now true for teachers.

A major researcher in this area has been Hunt (1974), first in the United States and then later in Canada at the Ontario Institute for Studies in Education. Hunt found that the teacher's ability to understand student cognitive strategies (that is, to start where the learner is), and to modify the curriculum materials and teaching strategies accordingly, depended upon the stage of conceptual development of the teacher. He used the phrase "read and flex" to denote this higher order of ability of teachers (related concepts would include cognitive flexibility and cognitive adaptability).

Hunt was able to show that effective "reading and flexing" produces an effective learning environment, through the use of concrete examples (the rule–example–rule method) for low conceptual stage students and the opposite method (the inductive examples-only model) for higher stage students. Positive outcomes result from effective matching, while negative outcomes follow from employing an inappropriate strategy.

Whether the teacher is capable of appropriate "reading and flexing" is a question of the cognitive complexity of the teacher. In fact, Hunt has used the same system to measure the concept learning capability of both students and teachers. Teachers with higher levels of concept learning capability adapt innovation; view students as teacher–learners (in Freires terms); are comfortable providing detailed highly structured materials for some, and just as comfortable with low-structure inductive teaching for others; and do not follow a single prescriptive approach. In contrast, teachers at lower levels of concept learning capability resist innovation; employ "tried and true" direct methods for all; and are confused by flexible team teaching, learning centers, and cooperative methods. In this regard, Joyce and McKibbin (1980) found that the low developmental stage teachers who attended workshops and were presented with some 100 innovative teaching methods over the course of an entire year used almost none of those methods one year later, while the opposite was true for the higher stage teachers.

A meta-analysis by Miller (1981) of over 200 studies supported the validity of teacher concept learning capability as a predictor of effective teaching. This single finding may explain why so many national attempts to infuse the schools with new and exciting curriculum guides in language, social studies, mathematics, and science have failed so completely. The truism from these multiple failures has been that there is no such thing as a teacher-proof curriculum. The best material

in the world will fail unless the teachers themselves are at least at a moderate to a moderately high stage of conceptual development.

A major problem, of course, is that teacher education programs, as presently organized, are themselves no more competent at promoting stage growth than are the schools. Both operate with a seemingly blind eye to the developmental stage of the learner, whether the learner is a student at school or a teacher in training. A review of teacher education programs by a Dutch educator (Veenman 1984) found the framework promising, yet hardly in place. In fact, Hunt (1974) has always claimed that the missing link in teacher education has been the need to view the teacher as a learner within a conceptual stage framework.

In the case of school programs designed to promote moral and ethical reasoning, the same results hold. For example, Oser (1984) in Switzerland and Berkowitz (1985) in the United States have found the effective use of the Socratic approach to moral dilemma discussions to be dependent upon the stage of development of the teachers. Managing student dialogue on controversial dilemmas requires a higher order teaching ability; namely, the ability to clarify and extend student ideas on one hand and to challenge student thinking on the other. In fact, Berkowitz has found that if the teacher is unable to do both, student cognitive growth does not occur.

5. Goals of Both Teachers and Students: Conceptional and Moral Development

In a sense, the same teaching and learning rules apply whether this goal is the achievement of conceptual complexity in any of the requisite school disciplines or the promotion of ethical and moral reasoning. The cognitive–developmental model is based on the dialectic of the equilibrium and disequilibrium; of the learner's need to assimilate and accommodate. When the current system of problem-solving is challenged effectively, the equilibrium between "old" learning and "new" learning is upset. Furth (1981) has aptly described this disequilibrium as the dissonance created by a mismatch between current stage process and a knowledge perturbation. Furthermore, Furth asserts that this problem cannot be solved in the current educational system.

Growth depends upon the slow taking-in (accommodation) of new and more complex cognitive processes. In this regard, Furth provides an example of a German youth, a concrete thinker, experiencing the dissonance of seeing a church without a steeple during a Sunday bicycle ride. Whether growth occurs in this example depends upon the dialogue that ensues. Vygotsky (1978) suggests that the learner needs time to gradually give up the old method of perceiving and solving problems for the new. This gradual development of more complex cognitive structures which allow the learner to become more efficient and more effective in the process of critical thinking is referred to as a structuralist approach to learning.

6. The Cost of Growth

In the context of the cognitive–developmental framework, the learner (whether student or teacher) must part with the old "tried and true" method of problem-solving. In Piagetian terms, for example, the learner may give up concrete thought for formal operational thought. In Kohlbergian terms the learner would reject social conformity (Stage 3) in ethical decision-making for legal sanctions (Stage 4).

The psychological resistance to such growth has been understated. Most developmental theorists have embraced some version of the "plus one" idea. The learner is attracted to the higher stage because it is a better organization (ensemble or schema) for thought in either the conceptual or the moral domain (Rest 1986). A number of more clinically oriented theorists have suggested that the learner experiences substantial psychological dissonance during the transition phase (Kegan 1982). The learner actually feels less competent and sometimes angry or depressed as the old method reveals itself as inadequate to the problem-solving perturbation at hand. The learner might not in fact excitedly demand to know the next steps in the higher order sequence of problem solving. In James's metaphor of teaching and war, this explains why the student may be working so hard to subvert the teacher.

Kegan suggests exactly this point. New learning creates a period of wary antagonism and initial rejection of the new requirements, as the old method is comfortable to the learner and has produced successful outcomes. These new insights can help to expand the instructional methods particularly during transitions from stage-to-stage (vertical *décalage*) as well as growth within a stage (horizontal *décalage*).

7. Method Characteristics

For students, the most common developmental methods of instruction are aligned with the Dewey and Freire requirements of active learning combined with guided reflection. Ironically, given the continued reliance on banking education through the memorized transmission of culture, there was a major eight-year longitudinal study in the 1930s which provided empirical support for the superiority of the project method (called the activity-based curriculum) over the lectures methods. In this study, teachers used small groups, cooperative learning, research projects, field trips, and role-plays from an interdisciplinary standpoint. The experimental and control samples were large (almost 3,000 pupils participated) and the results on some 18 outcome measures favored the activity approach (Aiken 1942).

A similar, more recent, cross-sectional study of experiential, social role-taking programs (e.g., peer counseling, teaching, and community internships for students) produced similar findings; such programs produce not only an increase in conceptual growth, but also an increase in ethical reasoning (Sprinthall and Collins 1988). Role taking as opposed to role playing requires that students set aside their own self-preoccupations and learn an "iron discipline" of listening. Social perspective taking develops, as does empathy, and both these induce greater moral sensitivity. At the same time the requirement to reflect, read, and analyze such experiences ("praxis" in Freire's terms) promotes cognitive structural growth. Standard or conventional academic courses do not have similar effects (Rest 1986, Hunt 1974).

For teachers, the same framework holds. Teachers usually function at low to modest levels of conceptual and ethical development. Regular academic training during initial student teaching and for inservice programs produces little in the way of development in these domains. The effect of such training on pupils is indirect, yet nevertheless discouraging. Boring routines and passivity among students are common.

Of even greater concern is the impact of these experienced teachers on the student teachers they supervise. One study showed the negative effect of a developmental mismatch: student teachers at higher conceptual and ethical stages than their supervisors (Thies-Sprinthall 1980). The study also demonstrated that higher stage supervising teachers were more effective with a wide range of student teachers.

In general, higher stage teachers tend to be more flexible with their students (Oser 1984). The same holds true for supervisors and indeed for other school personnel such as counselors, principals, and other professionals (Sprinthall and Thies-Sprinthall 1983).

8. Conclusion

The cognitive–developmental framework represents a major shift in thinking about teaching and learning. The basic concepts were developed by Dewey and Freire. In combination, these concepts indicate the importance of viewing the processes of teaching and learning as interactive.

For democratic societies this framework asserts that a direct aim of education is both conceptual and ethical development in order to promote active citizenship throughout the life span. In this regard, Piaget and Kohlberg provide a detailed sequence of stages that can be used to understand the learner's preferred methods of problem-solving.

The dialectic approach implied by the framework involves varying content and method in accord with the learner's stage characteristics. The continuing failure of traditional teaching methods attests to the need for such a change.

The cognitive–developmental framework, however, is not singularly focused on students, but on the teacher as well. There are a number of model programs which demonstrate how the framework can be applied to both learner and teacher.

See also: Implicit Theories of Teaching; Linguistic and Sociolinguistic Theories of Teaching; Heuristic Models of Teaching; Social Psychological Theories of Teaching

References

Aiken W M 1942 *The Story of the Eight Year Study.* Harper and Row, New York

Barrett B 1975 Training and transfer is combinational problem-solving: The development of formal reasoning during early adolescence. *Dev. Psychol.* 11(8): 700–4

Berkowitz M W 1985 The role of discussion in moral education. In: Berkowitz M W, Oser F (eds.) 1985 *Moral Education: Theory and Application.* Erlbaum, Hillsdale, New Jersey

Bellack A, Kliebard H, Hyman R, Smith F 1966 *Language of the Classroom.* Teachers College Press, New York

Dewey J 1966 *Democracy and Education. An Introduction to the Philosophy of Education.* The Free Press, New York

Duckworth E 1987 *The Having of Wonderful Ideas and Other Essays on Teaching and Learning.* Teachers College Press, New York

Feuerstein R 1980 *Instrumental Enrichment: An intervention Program for Cognitive Modifiability.* University Park Press, Baltimore, Maryland

Flanagan J C 1973 Education: How and for what. *Am. Psychol.* 28: 551–56

Freire P 1981 *Education for Critical Consciousness.* Continuum, New York

Furth H 1981 *Piaget and Knowledge. Theoretical Foundations.* University of Chicago Press, Chicago, Illinois

Goodlad J 1984 *A Place called School.* McGraw-Hill, New York

Ginsberg H, Opper S 1988 *Piaget's Theory of Intellectual Development,* 3rd edn. Prentice Hall, Englewood Cliffs, New Jersey

Hunt D 1974 *Matching Models in Education.* Ontario Institute for Studies in Education, Toronto

James W 1958 *Talks to Teachers.* W. W. Norton, New York

Jones L V 1988 School achievement trends in mathematics and science, and what can be done to improve them. In: Rothkopf E Z (ed.) 1988 *Review of Research in Education,* Vol. 15. American Educational Research Association, Washington, DC

Joyce B, McKibbin M 1980 Psychological states and staff development. *Theory Pract.* 16(4): 248–55

Kegan R 1982 *The Evolving Self: Problems and Process in Human Development.* Harvard University Press, Cambridge, Massachusetts

Kohlberg L 1984 *The Psychology of Moral Development.* Harper and Row, San Francisco

Miller A 1981 Conceptual matching models and interactional research in education. *Rev. Educ. Res.* 51(1): 33–84

Nickerson R S 1988 On improving thinking through instruction. In: Rothkopf E Z (ed.) 1988 *Review of Research in Education,* Vol. 15. American Educational Research Association, Washington. DC

Oser F 1984 Cognitive stages of interaction in moral discourse. In: Kurtines W M, Gewirtz G L (eds.) 1984 *Morality, Moral Behavior, and Moral Development.* Wiley, New York

Piaget J 1972 Intellectual evolution from adolescence to adulthood. *Hum. Dev.* 15: 1–12

Piaget J 1974 *Adaptation vitale et psychologie de l'intelligence.* Hermann, Paris

Renner J et al 1976 *Research, Teaching, and Learning with the Piaget Model.* University of Oklahoma Press, Norman, Oklahoma

Rest J 1986 *Moral Development: Advances in Research and Theory.* Praeger, New York

Sprinthall N A, Collins W A 1988 *Adolescent Psychology: A Developmental View.* McGraw-Hill, New York

Sprinthall N A, Thies-Sprinthall L T 1983 The teacher as an adult learner. In: Griffin G (ed.) 1983 NSSE *Staff Development (82nd Yearbook).* NSSE, Chicago, Illinois

Sprinthall N A, Sprinthall R C 1990 *Educational Psychology: A Developmental Approach,* 5th edn. McGraw-Hill, New York

Thies-Sprinthall L 1980 Supervision: An educative or miseducative process. *J. Teach. Educ.* 31(4): 17–20

Tyler R W 1933 Permanence of learning. *J. Higher Educ.* 4: 203–06

Veenman S A M 1984 *Onderzack van het onderwijzen en do cognitief-structurele ontiockkelmgsbenadering.* Instituit Voor Onderwijskunde, Nijmegen

Vygotsky L 1978 *Mind in Society: The Development of Higher Psychological Processes.* Harvard University Press, Cambridge, Massachusetts

Walberg H 1986 Synthesis of research on teaching. In: Wittrock M C (ed.) 1986 *Handbook of Research on Teaching,* 3rd edn. Macmillan, New York

Walker L 1986 Sex differences in the development of moral reasoning: A rejoinder to Baumrind. *Child Dev.* 57(2): 522–26

Information Processing Theories of Teaching

P. H. Winne

In simple terms, information processing theories of teaching characterize instruction as a series of repeating cycles. Each cycle involves two phases. First, the teacher selects and arranges elements in the instructional environment so that, as students participate in instruction, they are guided to process particular information cognitively. Second, by performing these cognitive processes, students generate their own cognitive representations of subject matter, as well as cognitive representations of other information about learning strategies, self concept, and the formats and norms for participating in various instructional activities. In judging whether instruction has been effective, information processing theories of teaching consider three kinds of achievements: (a) when students' mental representations of information are accurate, appropriate, and complete; (b) when, if a future task calls for that information, they can remember it; and (c) when students are motivated to use that information in performing tasks that correspond to objectives set by the teacher and the students.

Considered in these terms, a thorough information processing theory of teaching must address two main issues. The first is how students acquire, remember, and apply knowledge. The second is how instruction can guide students to engage in tasks that call for particular forms of cognitive processing, and, once these cognitive processes are underway, how teaching can support students' information processing at successive stages of those tasks.

This entry focuses on research-based theories and models that describe teaching in classrooms, and teaching as conveyed by texts and computer software that students study on their own. It highlights how teachers and their surrogates (e.g., textbooks, computer systems) engage and guide students' cognitive processing of information in order to promote achievements. Detailed illustrations of these approaches are presented in Joyce et al. (1992) and Reigeluth (1987).

1. The Cognitive Mediational Paradigm

Students bring prior knowledge to any instructional setting. Prior knowledge is an aptitude (Snow 1992) that mediates how students perceive the setting, how they are inclined to participate in the instructional activities therein, and what they are able to learn by their participation (Winne 1985).

Information processing theories of teaching catalog types of knowledge—both prior knowledge and knowledge that is to be achieved by participating in instruction. Two principal categories are conceptual knowledge and metacognitive knowledge (see *Student Cognitive Processes*). Conceptual knowledge is information that comprises academic subject matter—facts, principles and rules, frameworks and schemata, and basic skills. Metacognitive knowledge includes: (a) information about methods for learning (cognitive strategies) and for directing one's efforts to learn (self-regulation) within the instructional situation(s) that the teacher (or surrogate) has created; (b) information about self-preferences and attitudes, strengths and weaknesses, motivation, feelings, and so on; (c) information about tasks, how they are structured, and how they unfold; and (d) information about goals the student holds and plans for reaching those goals. Students' prior knowledge can aid or interfere with information processing and, thus, facilitate or inhibit achievement.

During instruction, the teacher (or surrogate) presents subject-matter information that students are to learn (in explicit models) or makes this information available implicitly in materials and within tasks that students pursue to inquire about a topic (inquiry models). The teacher (or surrogate) also provides information that is intended to cue or guide students' information processing of conceptual and metacognitive information. For example, the title given to an activity or to a textbook chapter reveals something what the instructional session is about. This is subject-matter information. The teacher may also intend the title to engage the student in predicting, a particular cognitive routine that jointly manipulates prior knowledge and information that will arise as the activity progresses. For example, the teacher may expect the title to signal to the student that he or she should predict the main idea of a text and then take notes that confirm, deny, or modify that prediction.

Students interpret the subject matter information that the teacher (or a surrogate) presents to construct a personal representation of it. Students also interpret and choose whether and how to use guidance for cognitively processing information that becomes available as the instructional activity unfolds. Therefore, links between instructional events that the teacher structures and achievements that students gain by participating in instruction are mediated by each student's prior knowledge (Winne and Marx 1987, Snow 1992). Information processing theories of teaching address how students' mediations of instruction can strengthen, weaken, or distort effects predicted by theory (Winne 1987).

In information processing theories of teaching, it is usually assumed that students are attentive and motivated to learn, and that they follow rules for the activity structures that typify the lesson. To the extent that these conditions are not satisfied, the explanatory strength of information processing theories is diminished.

2. Explicit Teaching in Classrooms

Explicit teaching is one of the most long-standing and fundamental models of teaching. In this form of teaching, the major objective is for students to elaborate (i.e., supplement or refine) prior knowledge of subject matter by adding to it facts, concepts, principles, basic skills, and other forms of conceptual knowledge (Alexander et al. 1991, Rosenshine 1987, Gagné et al. 1992). Winne (1985) describes this model as consisting of the following key elements.

A lesson or study session begins with the instructor or surrogate identifying goals to be achieved by students. This goal identification provides information students can use to: (a) monitor their progress during the lesson and (b) guide their information processing by applying means–ends analysis during learning (Frederiksen 1984). There then follows a short review of prerequisite knowledge that is intended to activate the prior knowledge the student will use in assembling more elaborate structures of subject-matter information. These structures fuse prior knowledge with new content presented in the lesson. The review also invites the student to recall learning and self-regulatory strategies for cognitively processing forthcoming information.

New subject matter is then presented in relatively small steps to avoid overloading the limited capacity of the student's working memory. Details, clear explanations, and demonstrations of rules are provided to enrich the student's elaborations of new information by assembling it with prior knowledge. During the presentation, students are invited to respond to questions or work out small exercises. Typically, these are organized so that those questions which call for direct retrieval or straightforward application of information outnumber questions that involve processing information or solving a problem to generate an answer by a factor of about 3:7. The aim of these activities is to engage the student in rehearsing information, assembling it into larger, more meaningful structures termed schemata, and translating newly developed structures of information into analogous representations, images, and personally meaningful metaphors (Winne 1985).

Following the presentation, students work alone or in small groups on exercises that involve retrieving and applying the newly presented information. At first, tasks repeat and straightforwardly extend those presented in the lesson. The teacher or a peer provides guidance and, as necessary, directly assists the student when the student cannot complete the task independently. This support, called "scaffolding," becomes more prominent as tasks are gradually extended into the student's zone of proximal development, that is,

the region of performance where a student has the potential to achieve but needs some assistance. Systematic feedback to correct errors in students' work is provided as required. As students assemble schemata (e.g., typical forms for persuasive compositions, classes of algebra word problems) and develop automaticity in applying rules of the subject matter (e.g., monitoring for invalid logic in developing an argument, simplifying algebraic expressions), the teacher and scaffolding are withdrawn. Through further practice, the student's retrieval and use of subject-matter rules and cognitive strategies becomes skilled and self-regulated, and transfer of the lesson's information to different and more complex tasks is approached.

2.1 Sequencing

In explicit teaching, the teacher determines the subject-matter information presented within each lesson and across lessons that comprise larger units of study. In both situations, considerations about sequencing information need to be addressed. Van Patten et al. (1986) distinguished microsequencing, namely concern for sequencing information about an individual concept or rule within a lesson, from macrosequencing, a concern about sequencing multiple units of information both across ideas within a lesson and across lessons.

Regarding microsequencing, generalizable definitions are distinguished from instances (examples or nonexamples) of the generalized form. When the objective of a lesson is that students apply the generalized form of information in tasks that are not very different from those encountered in the lesson—that is, tasks that call for near transfer—research suggests that the teacher should first present the generalized form followed by a series of instances of it. When the objective of instruction is that the student transfer the generalized form to tasks that are considerably different from those studied in the lesson—that is, a situation involving far transfer—the more effective sequence is an inductive one in which multiple instances precede presentation of the generalized form. In both cases, successive instances should be ordered from simple to complex, and the instances should be as different from one another as possible (Van Patten et al. 1986).

Research which investigates macrosequencing in classrooms is uncommon probably because of difficulties of valid implementation of complex instructional treatments in the dynamic social setting of a classroom. Macrosequencing, however, has been examined when information processing theories of teaching have been operationalized in text presentations, and thus will be reviewed in Section 5 below.

3. Reciprocal Teaching

In reciprocal teaching (Palincsar and Brown 1984), the teacher or a surrogate (e.g., a more competent peer, or a computer system) engages the student in a dialogue about learning. The dialogue is designed to reveal essential information about subject matter and to illustrate how to self-regulate information processing that constructs achievements. Although reciprocal teaching was developed to teach young children how to understand narratives, the theory can be extended to most subject areas and to other ages.

Reciprocal teaching begins with the teacher modeling the elements of tasks and showing how information can be used to construct achievements from these tasks. At each stage, the teacher explicitly describes the nature of information processing that builds knowledge. After students have been introduced to information processing tasks, they and the teacher (or they and their peers) alternate between the roles of instructor and learner. In the role of learner, students perform the task, monitor how the instructor's comments guide learning in the task, and elaborate on how they are constructing achievements. In the instructor's role, the student leads and monitors a dialogue that addresses four principal kinds of cognitive engagements with information. These engagements create focused opportunities for students to elaborate their routines for processing information. They are as follows:

(a) Learners generate questions about subject-matter information intrinsic to the task and about means for learning it. By generating questions, they are cognitively engaged in monitoring the instructor's activities to discover the essentials of the subject matter and how participating in the task contributes to learning. They are also alerted and aided in monitoring their comprehension as the task proceeds.

(b) Learners are encouraged to clarify difficulties they have in understanding the subject matter, and problems they encounter in carrying out and regulating their cognitive tactics. Clarifying highlights features of the work where the learner might increase attention or reconfigure information processing. It also helps to prevent an accumulation of cognitive and motivational deficits that might overwhelm the student and lead to disengagement.

(c) At the seams between steps of a task or between exercises, learners predict the next stage. To make such predictions, they must stimulate prior knowledge and assemble with it the relevant information about the subject matter and the task that has developed so far. Not only does prediction increase the likelihood that the next steps toward achievement will have meaning for the learner, but making predictions also activates prior knowledge that might otherwise remain inert. Finally, the learner can use prior knowledge to monitor his or her level of understanding as the next stages in the task unfold.

(d) Also at the seams of a task and between exercises,

the learner summarizes what has developed so far. Summarizing involves two main activities. The first is monitoring the subject matter to identify its main ideas, a repetition and refinement of monitoring that has already taken place. The other is assembling relations among these key elements or main ideas to construct a high-level representation of the subject matter. This activity increases the student's power to generalize beyond the particulars of the specific tasks so far encountered. Summaries of the information processing that was used to perform tasks also can be prepared.

4. Inquiry-oriented Instruction

The defining feature of inquiry-oriented instruction is that students are not told explicitly the conceptual or metacognitive information that comprises objectives for instruction. Rather, the teacher creates an intellectual and social environment within which students explore to discover both the essentials of subject matter and the cognitive strategies that are useful in those explorations. The principle underlying this orientation is that, by personally constructing plans to identify and acquire knowledge, the subject matter will be inherently comprehensible, tasks will be intrinsically motivating, and metacognitive knowledge will develop naturally. Through the same process of exploration, students also gain a view of aptitude and knowledge as malleable, and they come to interpret processes for learning as developmental, successively building on and refining earlier methods for learning.

Probably the most well-known approach to inquiry-oriented instruction has been developed by Suchman (see Joyce et al. 1992). The model, although initially developed to teach science, applies to all subjects in which data can be organized according to principles. Instruction begins with the teacher presenting a puzzling situation to students. Optimum puzzles are those that challenge students' views of the world, creating a discrepancy between what they observe in the puzzle and their prior understandings of how the world "really" works. Such puzzles are believed to be intrinsically motivating, drawing students to investigate the discrepancy for its own sake, as opposed to merely carrying out an investigation in order to complete a task set by the teacher.

Following presentation of the puzzle, the teacher explains that students, working individually or in groups, should frame hypotheses and seek data with which to test those hypotheses. Their objective is progressively to develop an overarching principle or theory that can account for the initial discrepancy without contradicting other established facts. Upon concluding the investigative period, which may span a considerable time, the teacher and students jointly re-examine the information processing involved in striving to develop, test, and justify the principle(s) that the students generated. This phase of the model addresses cognitive strategies that are applied in problem-solving and self-regulative processes that guide investigations. Thus, as they move through all the stages of inquiry, students engage in the same kinds of information processing activities as in explicit and reciprocal teaching.

5. Teaching by Text

Because experiments using texts to teach are relatively easier to conduct than studies in classrooms, text-based studies of instruction have often been spawning-grounds for information processing models of classroom instruction. Moreover, because adolescent and adult students engage in reading to learn, as often as, if not more frequently than, they participate in classroom lessons, theories of learning from text are an essential complement to those that address students' information processing in classrooms. In practice, almost all educational settings make extensive use of both modes for teaching.

Authors preparing instructional texts for students to study strive to guide students' information processing in two ways. First, they carefully select conceptual knowledge for the text to ease students' assembly of new information with prior knowledge. Second, through supplements to the text such as headings, graphical adjuncts, and rhetorical devices, authors invite students to engage in information processing during and after reading. In principle, an author's planning parallels that which teachers conduct in preparing for classroom lessons. In both cases, theories of students' information processing guide the instructor in creating an effective setting for students to develop knowledge. A common feature of current research on teaching by text is that students are first taught cognitive tactics that match cognitive processing to cues the author includes in the text. When students learn how to identify cues for cognitively processing textual information and how to apply the cognitive routines that the cues signal, and when they are motivated to spend the cognitive effort required to apply these techniques, achievement improves (Pearson and Fielding 1991).

A central task the student faces in comprehending a text is determining which information is important, that is, the gist, topic, macrostructure, or theme of the text (Dole et al. 1992). Research clearly and repeatedly documents that the students who can identify important information are those who comprehend and learn more of the subject matter. Features of the text, such as italics and headings, can be used to cue students to locate these key ideas.

A second main task in learning thoroughly from a text is to summarize its content and so construct a new, substantively equivalent synthesis of the text's macrostructure. Three distinct operations are involved in summarizing: discriminating important ideas from less central ones, condensing information

by introducing superordinate knowledge that subsumes individual ideas, and integrating information to create a coherent structure (Hidi and Anderson 1986). Authors can guide students' construction of summaries by presenting summaries directly (Reder 1985) and/or providing readers with an advance organizer, that is, subject-matter information that is at a higher level of generality or abstraction than information in the body of the text. To involve students in generating summaries, supplemental activities such as making concept maps, preparing to instruct a peer about the information in the text, and, of course, writing summaries, have proven effective (Pearson and Fielding 1991). Figures can also cue students to important information and provide an alternative medium for representing summarized material (Mayer 1989). More effective figures are labeled with important information about the text's topic.

Every text invites the reader to draw inferences, a third central task in textual comprehension (McNamara et al. 1991). In framing inferences, students use prior knowledge to develop and elaborate mental models with which they extend the information that is presented explicitly in the text. One means of inviting inferences is to insert, preferably at the beginning of a text, objectives or questions that explicitly guide students toward making inferences (Hamaker 1986).

Finally, in learning from text, readers need to be actively involved in processing information deeply and monitoring the results of these activities (Pearson and Fielding 1991). Deep processing includes the three preceding activities—identifying key ideas, summarizing, and inferencing—as well as cognitive activities such as generating analogies for information the text presents and analyzing new information in terms of known schemata. Readers' self-questioning and their monitoring of their own comprehension creates a platform for assembling new structures of information and helps to prevent an accumulation of gaps in comprehension that undermine learning (see e.g., Walczyk and Hall 1989).

6. Instruction by Computer Systems

Computer systems are, in one sense, merely another medium for instructing. However, because they can receive information from students and process it in order to adapt instruction to the student, computer systems are importantly different from teaching with static texts. Information processing theories of instruction adapted to computer systems blend elements from all the preceding orientations. Two issues within these hybrid theories are active areas of current research: balancing instructional guidance with learner control, and using a model of the student's information processing as a basis for adapting instruction during a lesson.

6.1 Learner Control

Instructional computing systems can be programmed to offer the student varying degrees of control over access to information and to instructional guidance. For example, in many systems, students can exit instruction when they judge their achievement to be adequate. Other systems offer students menus of topics and of media, including text, graphics, dynamic animations, video, voice and aural information (e.g., music), simulations of systems, and actions performed by machines and robots.

Research on self-regulation (or learner control) is investigating students' adeptness in making such choices. To date, it appears more effective to guide the learner, based on research-based principles coded in the computing system, than to give control over to the student. This finding is reminiscent of research which shows that learners have considerable difficulty developing conceptual knowledge of a new subject and simultaneously guiding their own learning metacognitively (Dole et al. 1992).

6.2 Student Models

A vital professional skill in teaching is knowing what to attend to and what to ignore in planning instruction and then adapting that plan as the student participates in a lesson. This human talent is a major challenge for instructional computing systems. Their model of a student begins as an incomplete theoretical representation of the student's prior knowledge complemented by an organized set of principles for guiding instruction. As a tutorial unfolds, every interaction a student has with the system is a potential datum that might be used to revise the system's model of the student's cognitive participation in instruction and thereby adapt instruction to the student's progress. This immense quantity of data easily overwhelms theoretical models of students' information processing.

Self (1990) offers several suggestions for addressing this surfeit of data. First, rather than straining the system to infer unobserved qualities of the student's information processing, Self suggests that the system rather be designed to elicit metacognitive knowledge directly from the student. In this way, the student can guide the system by constraining the alternatives it considers about guiding instruction. Second, the computing system should not attempt to guide instruction if theory does not address how to do that. Moreover, rather than adopting a reactive stance based on diagnosing students' mistakes, the system should gather descriptive data that researchers can examine to improve the theoretical models for its use in the future. Finally, to stimulate the student's metacognition and deep processing, the system might display its representations of the student's knowledge and invite the student to analyze these. Together, these principles involve students in self-directed learning,

implement some elements of reciprocal teaching models (though over a longer time span than in classroom teaching), and directly reflect issues raised in the cognitive mediational model of learning from instruction (Winne 1992).

7. Conclusion

Students are active inquiring agents who seek to guide their information processing based on instructional cues. Two central factors that guide a student's cognitive participation in instruction are prior knowledge (both conceptual and metacognitive) and elements in the instructional environment. If students lack prior knowledge or if cues about useful forms of information processing are vague or absent, the student will apply metacognitive knowledge to improvise, sometimes ineffectively. Information processing theories of teaching seek to understand how to coordinate the knowledge students are to learn with their prior knowledge, and how to guide students' interactions with knowledge so that the desired results are achieved. While successes based on this research are increasing, there is much knowledge still to be gained.

See also: Student Cognitive Process; Tutoring; Direct Instruction; Discovery Learning and Teaching

References

Alexander P A, Schallert D L, Hare V C 1991 Coming to terms: How researchers in learning and literacy talk about knowledge. *Rev. Educ. Res.* 61: 315–43
Dole J A, Duffy G G, Roehler L R, Pearson P D 1992 Moving from the old to the new: Research on reading comprehension instruction. *Rev. Educ. Res.* 61: 239–64
Gagné R M, Briggs L J, Wager W W 1992 *Principles of Instructional Design.* Harcourt Brace Jovanovich, Orlando, Florida
Frederiksen N 1984 Implications of cognitive theory for instruction in problem solving. *Rev. Educ. Res.* 54: 363–407
Hamaker C 1986 The effects of adjunct questions on prose learning. *Rev. Educ. Res.* 56: 212–42
Hidi S, Anderson V 1986 Producing written summaries: Task demands, cognitive operations, and implications for instruction. *Rev. Educ. Res.* 56: 473–93
Joyce B R, Weil M, Showers B 1992 *Models of Teaching,* 4th edn. Prentice-Hall, Englewood Cliffs, New Jersey
Mayer R E 1989 Systematic thinking fostered by illustrations in scientific text. *J. Educ. Psychol.* 81(2): 240–46
McNamara T P, Miller D L, Bransford J D 1991 Mental models and reading comprehension. In: Barr R, Kamil M L, Mosenthal P B, Pearson P D (eds.) 1991 *Handbook of Reading Research,* Vol. 2. Longman, New York
Palincsar A S, Brown A L 1984 Reciprocal teaching of comprehension-fostering and comprehension-monitoring activities. *Cognition and Instruction* 1: 117–75
Pearson P D, Fielding L 1991 Comprehension instruction. In:

Barr R, Kamil M L, Mosenthal P B, Pearson P D (eds.) 1991 *Handbook of Reading Research*, Vol. 2. Longman, New York

Reder L M 1985 Techniques available to author, teacher, and reader to improve retention of main ideas of a chapter. In: Chipman S F, Segal J W, Glaser R (eds.) 1985 *Thinking and Learning Skills. Vol. 2: Research and Open Questions*. Erlbaum, Hillsdale, New Jersey

Reigeluth C M (ed.) 1987 *Instructional Theories in Action: Lessons Illustrating Selected Theories and Models*. Erlbaum, Hillsdale, New Jersey

Rosenshine B V 1987 Explicit teaching. In: Berliner D C, Rosenshine B V (eds.) 1987 *Talks to Teachers: A Festschrift for N. L. Gage*. Random House, New York

Self J A 1990 Bypassing the intractable problem of student modeling. In: Frasson C, Gauthier G (eds.) 1990 *Intelligent Tutoring Systems: At the Crossroads of Artificial Intelligence and Education*. Ablex, Norwood, New Jersey

Snow R E 1992 Aptitude theory: Yesterday, today, and tomorrow. *Educ. Psychol.* 27: 5–32

Van Patten J, Chao C-I, Reigeluth C M 1986 A review of strategies for sequencing and synthesizing instruction. *Rev. Educ. Res.* 56: 437–71

Walczyk J J, Hall V C 1989 Effects of examples and embedded questions on the accuracy of comprehension self-assessments. *J. Educ. Psychol.* 81: 435–37

Winne P H 1985 Steps toward promoting cognitive achievements. *Elem. Sch. J.* 85: 673–93

Winne P H 1987 Why process–product research can not explain process–product findings and a proposed remedy: The cognitive mediational paradigm. *Teaching Teach. Educ.* 3: 333–56

Winne P H 1992 State-of-the-art instructional computing systems that afford instruction and bootstrap research. In: Jones M, Winne P (eds.) 1992 *Foundations and Frontiers of Adaptive Learning Environments*. Springer-Verlag, Berlin

Winne P H, Marx R W 1987 The best tools teachers have: Their students' thinking. In: Berliner D C, Rosenshine B V (eds.) 1987 *Talks to Teachers: A Festschrift for N L Gage*. Random House, New York

Social Psychological Theories of Teaching

D. W. Johnson and R. T. Johnson

Education is fundamentally an interpersonal process involving teachers and students, aimed at transmitting knowledge, skills, and culture from one generation to the next. Thus social psychology (the study of interpersonal, small-group, and organizational dynamics) is perhaps the most relevant social science for educators. The social nature of education is the first issue described in this article. The application of social psychological knowledge to educational practice is then discussed. The theories and research findings included in this article were chosen on the basis of their relevance to educational practice.

1. The Social Nature of Education

A defining characteristic of the human species is the transference of knowledge and tradition from one generation to the next. The process of transferring accumulated knowledge, skills, and cultures across generations is fundamentally a social process, requiring communication and interaction among people who exchange ideas, skills, attitudes, and feelings. Schools have been developed and have evolved to enhance and systematize this transfer. The transfer is conducted not by computers, teaching machines, textbooks, laboratory equipment, and videotapes; rather it is the direct result of interaction between human beings—between teachers and students, and students themselves. Teachers in the middle grades, for example, typically engage in about 200 interpersonal interchanges per hour (Jackson 1968). How much students learn and how successful teachers are depends on the nature and the quality of these classroom interactions.

2. Educational Social Organizations and Role Theory

The transfer of culture from one generation to the next is organized within schools. Schools are social organizations—a planned set of interpersonal relationships structured to achieve certain goals. The better teachers understand how the school works as a social organization, the more effectively they can teach. All social organizations are based on cooperation among members to achieve goals, maintain effective working relationships, and adapt to change. The success of the school depends on cooperative relationships among its members. Relationships are structured through the assignment of roles and the establishment of norms.

The school, like all social organizations, contains a variety of positions, such as teacher, student, and administrator. For each position there is a "role"—a set of prescribed behaviors that anyone who occupies that position should perform. The roles define how adults, children, and adolescents are to relate to one another in repeated and reliable ways so that the school's goals are achieved. The roles are interdependent and complementary. Roles contain both obligations, which individuals in complementary roles expect from a person, and rights, which individuals in complementary roles will do for a person. A teacher, for example, is obligated to structure instructional situations so that students learn; students in turn have the right to expect the teacher to do so.

People in certain roles are expected to behave in certain ways, both by themselves and by those in other roles. When a person holds positions in two different groups that make contradictory demands, there is "interrole conflict." If a student, for example, is in a science class that requires a major report to be written tonight and is also on the football team and is expected to go to rest for tomorrow's game, then there is a conflict between the roles of student and football player. "Intrarole conflict" occurs when other roles hold incompatible expectations of a particular role. If the history teacher, for example, expects students to complete three hours of homework tonight and the science teacher expects the same students to complete a major report, then students have a role conflict.

"Norms" define general expectations for everyone in the school. "No running in the halls" is an example of a school norm. Norms make explicit what behavior is appropriate or inappropriate within the school, and they have a specific "ought" or "must" quality. Roles and norms influence educators' actions so that a coordinated division of labor results within schools.

Because schools are organizations, all the social psychological knowledge contained within the fields of organizational psychology and group dynamics is relevant to educational practice. The continual effectiveness of schools, furthermore, depends on their ability to change and develop over time. Social psychologists have applied organizational development and change theory to schools (Miles 1964). Based on the research, schools are being encouraged to change to team-based cooperative organizational structures (Johnson and Johnson 1989b).

Organizational and role theories help educators understand a wide variety of dynamics within schools. By redesigning roles the effectiveness of schools may be increased. By identifying and reducing role conflicts the productivity of individual members may be increased. Teachers, for example, may coordinate when tests are given and reports are due so that students are not faced with competing assignments on any one night. By changing individuals' roles their perspectives, attitudes, and behavior can change. When students are given the responsibility of teaching other students, for example, their attitudes toward homework may change.

3. Interpersonal Expectations and Performance

Closely related to role theory is expectancy theory. Students have a tendency to live up (or down) to teacher expectations. Expectancy theory predicts that what

teachers and classmates expect from students tends to influence how much students actually learn (Rosenthal and Jacobson 1968). A number of studies have confirmed this prediction. In addition, there is evidence that people will believe and do what prestigeful others suggest. In order to maximize achievement, both the teacher and classmates should expect students to achieve realistic but challenging learning goals.

4. Social Interdependence Theory

Perhaps the most influential social psychological theory for educational practice is social interdependence theory. For each lesson, teachers must decide whether to structure the learning goals cooperatively, competitively, or individualistically. The first experimental studies on social interdependence were conducted in the 1890s in England, Germany, and the United States. The basic theory, based on Kurt Lewin's (1935) field theory, was formulated by Morton Deutsch (1949). Social interdependence exists when each individual's outcomes are affected by the actions of others. Within any social situation, individuals may join together to achieve mutual goals, compete to see who is best, or act independently on their own.

There are two types of social interdependence: cooperative and competitive. The absence of social interdependence results in individualistic efforts. Cooperation exists when one perceives that one is linked with others in a way so that one cannot succeed unless others succeed (and vice versa), and/or one's work benefits others and others' work benefits one. Competition exists when one perceives that one cannot succeed unless others fail (and vice versa) and/or one's work decreases others' chances for success and others' work decreases one's chances for success. Individualistic efforts exist when one perceives that one's success is unrelated to the success or failure of others.

Over 550 experimental and 100 correlational studies have been conducted on this theory (Johnson and Johnson 1989a). These studies demonstrate that working cooperatively, compared with competitive and individualistic efforts, will result in higher student achievement, more positive relationships among students (including between White and minority students, and nonhandicapped and handicapped students), and greater psychological adjustment, social competencies, and self-esteem. Cooperative learning has such consistent, powerful, and numerous effects on educational outcomes that it should probably be used the majority of the school day. A number of social psychologists have worked with schools in implementing cooperative learning within the classroom and cooperative teaching teams within the school (see Johnson et al 1990). Teachers at all grade levels need to be trained in how to structure lessons cooperatively (See also *Goal Structures*).

5. Distributive Justice

Closely related to social interdependence theory are theories of distributive justice (Deutsch 1985). Distributive justice deals with how benefits such as grades are granted to group or organizational members. The equity (or merit or competitive) view is that a person's rewards should be in proportion to his or her contributions to the group's effort. The equality (or cooperative) view is that all group members should benefit equally. The need view is that group members should be rewarded in proportion to their need. Whether teachers utilize an equity, equality, or need system, students have to perceive the system as "just." When rewards are distributed unjustly, the group may be characterized by low morale, high conflict, and low productivity. The evidence indicates that before a task is performed the equity reward system is perceived to be fairest, while after a task is performed the equality system is perceived to be most just. Before starting a project, members of a learning group may wish to be ranked from best to worst and given grades accordingly. After the project is completed, students will wish to have all members receive the same grade, believing that the diverse contributions cannot be "justly" ranked from most to least valuable. With increased experience, students tend to achieve higher under the equality system. When a groupmate suffers a life crisis (such as parents getting a divorce), furthermore, students usually wish to have the teacher take "need" into consideration. In terms of giving grades to students and rewarding educators, an equality system or some combination of the three would probably be most effective.

6. Conflict Theory

For instructional effectiveness and classroom order, teachers both create intellectual conflict to improve instruction and teach students how to negotiate and mediate in order to reduce discipline problems and improve the quality of life within schools. Controversy exists when one person's ideas, information, conclusions, theories, or opinions are incompatible with those of another, and the two seek to reach an agreement. When academic controversies are structured in the classroom, students are required to conduct research and prepare a position; rehearse orally the relevant information; advocate a position; teach their knowledge to peers; analyze, critically evaluate, and rebut information; reason both deductively and inductively; and synthesize and integrate information into factual and judgmental conclusions with which all sides can agree (Johnson and Johnson 1989a). Controversy theory is based on developmental theories of Piaget (1950), Berlyne (1965), Hunt (1964), and others, who posit that cognitive and social development as well as learning depend on creating cognitive disequilibrium, conceptual conflict, cognitive uncertainty, and epistemic curiosity. Controversy (compared with individualistic and competitive learning, debate, and concurrence-seeking) creates higher achievement, problem-solving, critical thinking, creativity, motivation to learn, and task involvement. Instead of suppressing intellectual conflict among students by lecturing, competition, and individualistic work, according to this theory teachers should structure and encourage it to promote learning.

There are times when the wants and goals of students conflict and procedures for negotiating integrative agreements are needed (Johnson and Johnson 1991). Social psychology has provided a long history of theorizing and research on negotiating integrative agreements (Deutsch 1973). The traditional family, neighborhood, and community procedures for teaching children how to manage conflicts have broken down. Students come to school with diverse ideas about how conflicts should be managed. Teachers need to teach all students to use the same set of procedures and skills in negotiating wise resolutions to their conflicts. Such training programs consist of two steps: (a) teaching all students a negotiation procedure, and (b) involving students in a peer mediation program where they help their classmates negotiate wise agreements to their conflicts (Johnson and Johnson 1991). Students need to be taught to state what they want and how they feel, provide the reasons underlying their wants, accurately take their opponent's perspective, propose at least three options for an agreement, and reach a mutually satisfying agreement. Teaching students how to resolve their conflicts constructively reduces discipline problems and empowers students to regulate their own behavior rather than rely on adult authorities to do so.

7. Achievement Motivation Theory

The instructional methods teachers use affect how motivated students are to achieve. Motivation to achieve is the degree to which individuals commit effort to achieve goals they perceive as meaningful and worthwhile. While humans may be born with a motivation to increase their competencies, how meaningful goals appear to be and how much effort individuals decide to exert are basically determined by internalized past relationships, present relationships, or current interaction patterns within the learning situation (Johnson and Johnson 1989a). The two most important theories of achievement motivation were formulated by Atkinson and Feather (1965) and David McClelland (1965). Atkinson states that achievement motivation is a balance between the tendency to achieve success and the tendency to avoid failure. The tendency to achieve success is assumed to be a function of the general motive to achieve success, the subjective probability of success, and the incentive to succeed. McClelland has demonstrated that, with training, the achievement motivation of adults can be increased. Together, their work provides a basis for educators to ensure that students develop a high level of achievement motivation.

One application of achievement motivation to education is Richard DeCharms' (1976) work with personal causation. Students can see their behavior as originating in themselves (they are an origin) or as being the result of external pressure (they are a pawn). Students treated as origins tend to like school tasks, work hard at them, and be more involved in them than are students treated as pawns. Students, furthermore, want to be the origin of their behavior and constantly struggle against the constraint of external causes. The more students believe they are studying because they freely choose to do so, operate under their own control, and are personally committed to learn, the greater their task motivation.

8. Attribution Theory

Causal attributions answer "why" questions, such as "Why did I fail this exam?" "Why" questions are asked more frequently after negative, unexpected, or atypical outcomes. The reasons to which students attribute their failures influence how hard they work on subsequent tasks. Attribution theory is concerned with people's explanations of the causes of (a) their own and other's behavior and (b) events (Graham 1991; Heider 1958). Growing out of the social psychological theories on social perception, attribution theory focuses on whether people attribute the causes of behavior to the situation or the individual, ways in which responsibility for success or failure is determined, and how attributional decisions affect subsequent behavior. Causes can be dispositional (within people) or situational (within environment). Students can claim their success is due to their ability or the amount of effort they exerted (dispositional causes) or because the task was easy or they were lucky (situational causes). In most cases, students should be trained to attribute their success to themselves and their failures to situational causes.

Generally, there are three dispositional causal dimensions: locus, stability, and controllability (Weiner 1986). The locus dimension defines the location of a cause as internal or external to the individual. The stability dimension designates causes as constant or varying over time. The controllability dimension refers to whether a cause is subject to one's own volitional influence. Ability is an internal, stable, and uncontrollable cause. Effort is internal, unstable, and controllable.

Teachers should ensure that students think through why they succeeded or failed, while guiding them toward the conclusion that their failure is caused by a lack of effort or using the wrong strategy. What emotions teachers express toward students seems to affect the attributions students make about the causes of their success or failure. Teacher sympathy for failure tends to be interpreted as indicating low ability, while teacher anger towards failure seems to be interpreted as indicating low effort.

9. Self-esteem Theory

Students who are confused as to who they are or who lack confidence in themselves hesitate to attempt difficult and challenging learning tasks. Teachers make their jobs easier in many ways by helping students gain a clear and positive sense of identity and self-esteem. Every student needs to acquire a positive self-identity, a sense of self that remains the same over time no matter what else has changed in one's life and environment (Erikson 1968). A person is not born with a sense of self. It is during the first two or three years that a kind of crude self-awareness develops, such as being able to make distinctions between what is part of his or her body and what is part of something else. It takes many years of maturation before full adult self-awareness comes into being. As people develop self-awareness, they formulate a self-conception and develop processes through which they derive conclusions about their self-worth. Self-esteem and self-identity develop primarily from relationships with other people, including working with others to achieve challenging goals; being known, liked, and respected by others; and knowing others well enough to identify similarities and differences. The more teachers involve students in joint projects that allow personal and supportive relationships to develop, the more positive will be students' self-identity and self-esteem.

Self-esteem may also be approached from a social-learning perspective that emphasizes students' perceived competence and self-efficacy, which influence students' choices of tasks, willingness to invest effort in task accomplishment, and persistence in the face of subsequent failure (Bandura 1986). Perceived competence is heavily influenced by initial encounters with novel tasks or new subjects. Individuals who experience initial success or failure in some new undertaking tend to infer that they possess relatively high or low aptitude/competence in that area. Once formed, these beliefs in one's competence are resistant to change. The implication for teaching is that at the beginning of each new class, students should be given success experiences in ways that lead them to believe they have an aptitude for the subject area.

10. School Culture

There is considerable evidence that the work environment can affect the meaning of work to the worker. Schools are no exception. The way the school is managed and the policies it espouses tend to affect staff and student motivation. Within each school a culture has to be built based on shared perceptions of (a) desired goals worth striving to achieve and (b) how these goals may be attained. Differences in school culture help explain why some schools are better than others. School culture comprises four interdependent dimensions (Maehr and Braskamp 1986): (a) goal structures (for both students and staff, cooperative efforts are more productive than are competitive or individualistic efforts), (b) roles and power relationships (students and staff should see themselves as autonomous and self-reliant individuals who are the "origin" of their efforts to achieve, rather than as passive pawns who are controlled), (c) evaluation and feedback systems (internal, student-centered evaluation creates greater task orientation and intrinsic motivation to achieve than does external, teacher-dominated evaluation), and (d) symbols of identity and purpose (effective schools stand for something—goals, values, and expectations for student behavior are expressed through slogans, posters, songs, and role models). A clear and strong school culture is especially important when students are culturally diverse.

11. Social Psychology of Education

Almost all social psychological knowledge could contribute to educational practice. In order to help teachers, social psychologists have (a) specifically operationalized social psychological knowledge into teaching and managing practices and (b) implemented organizational change procedures to ensure innovations are adopted by schools.

Education takes place through interpersonal interactions structured through roles and norms to achieve the school's goals. Understanding the nature of social organizations and role theory helps teachers clarify the rights and obligations of themselves and their students. The expectations teachers hold for students not only help define their role but also influence how much students learn. The school by its very organizational nature is a cooperative enterprise, but within any lesson teachers may structure students' learning goals cooperatively, competitively, or individualistically. Related to social interdependence theory are theories of distributive justice that help teachers give rewards in ways that are perceived to be "just," and conflict theory which has relevance for improving instruction (especially higher level reasoning) and decreasing discipline problems within the school. Social psychology has developed several theories of achievement motivation that influence how curriculum is designed and how teaching is conducted. Like all organizations, schools develop cultures around the goals they consider worth achieving and how the goals are to be attained.

Social psychology has much to offer teachers. Both preservice and inservice teacher education should emphasize social psychological knowledge. Social scientists interested in education should both advance social

psychological theories through systematic research programs and operationalize their findings into more effective teaching procedures. Each of the theories discussed requires considerably more research to maximize its value to teachers. Key studies are especially needed on the ways a cooperative structure provides the context in which the impact of the other theories is maximized. The major problems facing education, furthermore, are inherently social psychological and provide a fertile field for new social psychological research. Ensuring that diversity among students results in mutual understanding, respect, creativity, and sophistication is an inherently social psychological problem. Reducing destructive antisocial behaviors such as drug abuse, suicide, criminality, sexual promiscuity, and so forth requires the application of social psychological knowledge. Motivating at-risk students, lowering dropout rates, and ensuring that women and minorities become interested in mathematics and science require social psychological interventions. Both in its basic nature and in its need to solve major problems, education relies heavily on social psychological knowledge.

See also: Behavioristic Theories of Teaching

References

Atkinson J, Feather N (eds.) 1966 *A Theory of Achievement Motivation*. Wiley, New York

Bandura A 1986 *Social Foundations of Thought and Action*. Prentice-Hall, Englewood Cliffs, New Jersey

Berlyne D 1965 Curiosity and education. In: Krumboltz J (ed.) 1965 *Learning and the Educational Process*. Rand-McNally, Chicago, Illinois

DeCharms R 1976 *Enhancing Motivation*. Irvington, New York

Deutsch M 1949 A theory of cooperation and competition. *Human Relations* 2(2): 129–52

Deutsch M 1973 *The Resolution of Conflict*. Yale University Press, New Haven, Connecticut

Deutsch M 1985 *Distributive Justice*. Yale University Press, New Haven, Connecticut

Erikson E 1968 *Identity: Youth and Crisis*. Norton, New York

Graham S 1991 A review of attribution theory in achievement contexts. *Educational Psychology Review* 3(1): 5–39

Heider F 1958 *The Psychology of Interpersonal Relations*. Wiley, New York

Hunt J 1964 Introduction: Revisiting Montessori. In: Montessori M (ed.) 1964 *The Montessori Method*. Schocken Books, New York

Jackson P W 1968 *Life in Classrooms*. Holt, Rinehart and Winston, New York

Johnson D W, Johnson R 1989a *Cooperation and Competition: Theory and Research*. Interaction Book Company, Edina, Minnesota

Johnson D W, Johnson R 1989b *Leading the Cooperative School*. Interaction Book Company, Edina, Minnesota

Johnson D W, Johnson R 1991 *Teaching Students to*

be Peacemakers. Interaction Book Company, Edina, Minnesota

Johnson D W, Johnson R, Holubec E 1993 *Circles of Learning*. Interaction Book Company, Edina, Minnesota

Lewin K 1935 *A Dynamic Theory of Personality*. McGraw-Hill, New York

Maehr M, Braskamp L 1986 *The Motivation Factor: A Theory of Personal Investment*. Lexington Press, Lexington, Massachusetts

McClelland D 1965 Toward a Theory of Motive Acquisition. *Am. Psychol.* 20(5): 321–33

Miles M 1964 *Innovation in Education*. Teachers College Press, New York

Piaget J 1950 *The Psychology of Intelligence*. Harcourt, New York

Rosenthal R, Jacobson L 1968 *Pygmalion in the Classroom*. Holt, Rinehart, and Winston, New York

Weiner B 1986 *An Attributional Theory of Motivation and Emotion*. Springer-Verlag, New York

Further Reading

Bar-Tal D, Saxe L (eds.) 1978 *Social Psychology of Education*. Hemisphere, Washington, DC

Feldman R 1986 *The Social Psychology of Education*. Cambridge University Press, Cambridge, Massachusetts

Johnson D W 1970 *The Social Psychology of Education*. Holt, Rinehart and Winston, New York

Linguistic and Sociolinguistic Theories of Teaching

R. Young

When teaching is observed, what is actually seen is talking, writing, and other forms of communication that occur between teachers and learners. If one wants to understand what is happening in the classroom, then, it seems reasonable to examine the language being used and to study speech interaction (that is, the social process of language use). Whereas linguistic theories of teaching examine the way in which the linguistic resources of teachers and learners affect the success of teaching, sociolinguistic theories examine the way that interactive speech processes facilitate or inhibit teaching effectiveness.

1. Relationships with Other Theories of Teaching and Learning

Most researchers engaged in the study of language and teaching take the view that linguistic or sociolinguistic theories of teaching are alternatives to behavioral and cognitive theories. Some, however, see all of these theories as complementary. In the complementary view, there is a division among the various theories, as follows:

(a) behavorial theories explain why learning has or has not taken place;

(b) cognitive theories explain the role of logic and the learner's cognitive structure in learning; and

(c) language-based theories explain the role of communication in teaching and learning, as well as the impact of the linguistic encoding of information on the form of what is learned.

When linguistic theories are regarded as alternatives to cognitive theories, explanations in terms of conceptual cognitive structures are replaced by analyses of semantic cognitive structures (Vygotsky 1978). Similarly, behavioral theories of learning as reward-inducing or need-reducing stimulus–response associations are seen as explaining an underlying mechanism of learning, rather than specifying in particular instances what is learned or permitting specification in advance of the causes of learning.

Some behavioral theories define rewarding features of an organism's environment as reinforcers of behavior. This definition has a circular character, because whatever has induced learning tends to be defined as a reinforcer, and it is sometimes difficult to specify reinforcers in advance. In principle, sociolinguistic theories can identify culturally valued aspects of relationships as well as instances of the communicative assignment and recognition of these valued meanings. Sociolinguistic theories, then, explain both why any learning at all will occur and why a certain type of learning will take place. Whatever the final outcome of this theory rivalry, and regardless of whether or not an "alternative" theoretical approach is adopted, it is fairly clear that language-based theories can provide useful information about the nature and antecedents of "higher order" or complex learning.

In any case, the reader of language-based analyses of teaching will be struck by the almost complete absence of reference to, or connection with, classical conditioning theory, operant conditioning theory, or social learning theory. Only cognitive-development or socioconstructivist theories of learning appear in the background of language-based research, and, as stated above, there is a tendency to restate cognitive theories in terms of semantic processing rather than to retain their original language of "conceptual schemata" and "logical structure." The picture is further complicated by the fact that one of the most important forms of learning is language itself, and by the fact that language is the medium for other forms of learning.

2. Overview of Major Language-based Theories of Teaching

The field covered in this entry is quite diverse. Some theories contain well-developed principles of the role of language in learning (Vygotsky 1978), others say very little about either what is going on inside the learner, or in the interaction process between teacher and learner (Bernstein 1975), and still others focus on that interaction process (Edwards and Mercer 1987, Cazden 1988), with or without an auxiliary psycholinguistic theory. The first cluster of theories will be called "psycholinguistic," because despite giving much weight to the social character of language, they lack detailed analysis of the social structures of teacher–learner interaction. The second cluster will be called "structuralist," because they rely mainly on the identification and association of language codes and structures, while not saying a lot about processes. The third cluster will be called "interactionist," because they centre on process-through-time descriptions of communicative interaction, while also containing some reference to both language structures and psychological dimensions of learning. A fourth cluster of theories can also be identified. Characterized by a certain eclecticism, they permit an open approach, in which a diversity of analyses of a single classroom event is brought together. Finally, while it is possible in all of these approaches to inject an evaluative or "critical" dimension, there is also a "critical" approach to the study of language.

3. Psycholinguistic Theories

Piaget's pioneering cognitive-evolutionary or genetic theory of learning contained a sceptical view of the efficacy of teaching as a means of promoting cognitive development. Although Piaget identified a form of learning-related speech in children, which he called "egoistic speech," he saw children's development as a general product of innate tendencies and interaction with the material environment rather than with any deliberate process of teaching. Teachers could facilitate this interaction with the environment, but could not otherwise affect it. Where teachers could have an impact was in the less important form of learning which involved adding routine information and skills at a given level of development (Kohlberg 1971, Piaget 1972).

The Russian educator and psychologist, Vygotsky,

had a different view. He thought that the internalization by the learner of teacher speech was a key part of the learning process. The process of problem-solving in learning, which Vygotsky saw as a developmental process in a manner only broadly similar to Piaget, is something that at first is directed by adults, such as teachers, and gradually internalized by the learner. The adult's model of reasoning is adopted and imitated by the child. At first this imitation shows in the private speech of preschool children, as they "give instructions" and "reasons" to themselves, *sotto voce*. At approximately 7 years of age, this speech becomes silent, "inner speech." The same sequence is repeated in later life when new material has to be mastered (Vygotsky 1978).

The social role of the teacher is to press the child into the zone where the problem to be solved requires the child to develop a higher level of functioning in order to succeed; the "zone of proximal development." The teacher's task is to provide sufficient cognitive demand to stretch children but sufficient support (called "scaffolding") for them to succeed. However, the details of the linguistic interaction involved in promoting development are not well-developed by this group of theorists. Clearly, these theories provide an account of the link between speech and cognitive change (through internalization). However, the task of analyzing the connection between this process and actual problems of classroom speech remains to be carried out.

4. Structuralist Theories

The emphasis in structuralist theories of language and learning is on the degree to which students from different class or cultural backgrounds are equipped to benefit from the linguistic environment of the classroom, or to express themselves in linguistically approved ways in language performances, such as written examinations, in which learner's knowledge of both language and other subject matter is assessed. Perhaps the best known of these theories is that of Bernstein .

Although it is commonly believed that Bernstein argued that "working class" children suffered from a "linguistic deficit," this is not the case. He argued that working class children's facility in a language code not much valued in schools was greater than their facility in the code which schools did value. By "code," Bernstein meant the way the resources of words and structures of a language are used, particularly the degree to which they are dependent or independent of shared contextual knowledge. Bernstein's theory is complex, and the significance of his views is in dispute, but the area of language differences among minorities, social classes, and special groups is still a lively focus of research. Bernstein argued that schools are the site of a set of communicative practices which encode "ideology" in society by privileging certain ways of using language and marginalizing others (Bernstein 1975).

Poststructuralist analyses have returned to themes of the connection between communication practices and ideology. It is argued by some poststructuralists, influenced by the French philosopher Foucault, that schooling is a part of a process of symbolic control in which teachers exercise "pastoral power" in the creation of the kind of identity or "subjectivity" societies demand. Education systems are an important part of the regimes of power and knowledge on which modern societies are based. Classrooms are a site where the form of control characteristic of modern societies is reproduced and only some process of "critical pedagogy" might offer the hope of overcoming this control (Aronowitz and Giroux 1991).

5. Interactionist Theories

Interactionist theories of language in teaching and learning are as diverse as theories of language in general. Nevertheless, there are common features. First, there is general agreement about the dominant pattern of classroom speech. Second, there is widespread agreement that speech is best analyzed "from the top down", that is, from the perspective of larger segments of interaction, such as "relationships" through "episodes," to "sequences" and finally, to "utterances," "sentences," "clauses," and "words." All of the above terms appear in quotation marks because each theory tends to have its own, often equivalent, terminology. The point, though, is that words or utterances only make interactive sense, and "learning sense," if they are located in wider structures such as relationships, academic subjects, the teaching year or semester, and lessons or lesson sequences.

Third, there is a common dualism in the analyses, one which is most explicit in Green's distinction between the social text (the social roles and the process of cooperative task completion) and the academic text (the structure of the subject matter as academic content) (see Green et al. 1988). Earlier analyses identified this duality as a problem rather than an opportunity, because the teacher's problem of control (basically, getting cooperation in the playing of the social roles of teacher and learner) tended to lead teachers to favor a form of social text which permitted only a "second best" kind of academic text (called above "the dominant pattern").

Fourth, there has been considerable educational common ground among interactionists. Whether guided by a view of learning in which the child's active construction and reconstruction of schemata is central, or politically informed liberal or democratic educational values in which learner autonomy and capacity for independent critical thought are given prominence, interactionists have agreed on the educational inadequacy of the traditional pattern where classroom speech is not only orchestrated, but functionally dominated by the teacher.

5.1 The Dominant Pattern

The dominant pattern of classroom speech is one in which the teacher speaks before and after each learner speaks, the teacher speaks around 70 percent of the words spoken in "official" classroom speech, and the speaking role of the teacher involves either exclusive or dominant rights to many important speech functions such as asking questions, evaluating the speech of others, making long statements (including explanations), giving orders, criticizing previous statements, changing or setting the topic, controlling who will speak at any juncture, and interrupting all other speakers. This pattern has been observed in all its essentials as early as 1912 (Hoetker and Ahlbrand 1969). When it is not found in classrooms, as often as not the reason is that students are doing "seatwork" in which the same communicative relationships between teacher and learner are embodied in the written materials. Only the emergence in the 1980s and 1990s of group work, particularly in elementary school classrooms, has substantially broken down this pattern by permitting a great deal of functionally flexible learner–learner speech. However, even in classrooms where group work is the norm, it is common for the part of official or "on task" talk which is teacher–learner speech to be patterned on the dominant pattern.

5.2 Top-down Analysis

A top-down view of this pattern suggests that what is at stake educationally is the way learners relate to authority when they deal with problems or with new information. The relationship between learner and teacher is a dependent, possibly disabling one, since it does not seem to be predicated on helping learners to acquire the skills, dispositions, and knowledge necessary to solve problems for themselves. The dependency of the relationships shows up in the way the task of individual lessons is conceived and in the way the teacher and the learner interact in the subtask structure of lessons.

The smallest interactional unit in the social/academic text is the IRE: initiation, response, evaluation. The initiator is usually the teacher and the initiation is often a question. The responder is usually the learner, while the evaluator is also the teacher. A typical (constructed) example is:

T: (initiation) What is the GNP? (pause)
John? (indicating John who has his hand up)
J: (response) The value of the things produced in a country.
T:(evaluation) Good. The value of all the goods and services produced by a national economy.

From a top-down point of view, the nature of the teacher–learner relationship, the nature of the subject

119

of economics as taught by this teacher, and the general character of the lesson, can all be seen in microcosm in this short exchange. (It should be noted, though, that while this example typifies the dominant pattern it would be hazardous to infer the existence of that pattern from a single instance of an IRE of this type. That would be a bottom-up analysis and to be safe would require a large sample of speech. Top-down analysis requires the correlation of ethnographic background information with particular instances of speech so that the communicative character of particular segments can be reliably identified).

5.3 The Academic–Social Dualism

In the academic text of the dominant pattern, the learner is not required to sustain a line of inquiry, since the teacher asks the questions. In a string of such exchanges, which is the most common form in which IREs appear, it is the teacher who follows a line of questioning in them. The learner is not required to evaluate individual statements made in answer to questions (which form the building blocks of any accumulation of knowledge across the course of a sequence of such exchanges), or to evaluate the accumulation of previously accepted statements to see if they form a complete argument.

The social text, the speaking roles, does not permit the learner to employ all the functions of speaking necessary to full participation in common inquiry: criticizing, judging, approving, agreeing, doubting, rejecting, accepting, and explaining. If the learner is an active acquirer of a schemata or theory about the subject matter, there is little opportunity for him or her to meet the needs which arise in assimilating new data or in adapting schemata when the problems faced require more than piecemeal development. The linguistically passive role appears better suited to incremental growth of existing schemata but ill-adapted to stage-transcending learning situations.

5.4 Educational Inadequacy of the Dominant Pattern

The reasons why many teachers still display the dominant pattern despite almost a century of negative comment from researchers are still unknown. It is speculated quite persuasively that it is because it permits teachers a certain economy of effort while achieving a relatively high level of control and at least minimal levels of student achievement. Alternative task structures, which involve a wider variety of modes of learner participation, involve more teacher preparation (a textbook is not enough) and pose problems of surveillance and control as lessons move out of the "whole class" instruction pattern into group work and related complex communication patterns. It may also be difficult for learners to know what is required of them in newer patterns, or to provide a productive task structure for themselves, leading to more frustration and "off task" behavior. However, teachers who are willing to try lesson patterns in which learners' speaking roles are more open may find teaching less stressful and more interesting, providing the task structure for learners is made clear (Green et al. 1988).

In an effort to gain a broader understanding of what is at stake in different participation structures, Green et al. (1988) examined a pair of lessons from several standpoints. The propositional structure of knowledge, the way narrative is constructed, the structure of question sequences, and participation structures are analyzed in relation to one another, revealing something of the enormous complexity of what happens in classrooms. When placed alongside traditional psychological approaches, these perspectives from anthropology, sociology, linguistics, computer science, and philosophy are clearly enriching, with profound consequences for interdisciplinary study and for awareness of the complexity of what is at stake in classroom research. The too easy assumption that multivariate behavioral models would provide a scientifically grounded technology of teaching is rapidly losing its credibility as possibilities of collaborative inquiry open up new understandings of the way societal structure, culture, organizational structure, interactional structure, speech, inner speech, and cognition are interlinked in educational processes.

6. Critical Theories

Critical theories of teaching and learning are both linguistic and sociolinguistic. The theory commonly labelled "critical pedagogy" brings a particular value agenda to the analysis of language and learning. However, its proponents argue that this agenda is neither an afterthought nor an addition to some objective analysis. In general, these theorists argue that both the process of teaching and learning and its study are inherently evaluative in character. As a consequence, the description of such processes in intersubjectively acceptable (objective) ways is only a step in a wider critical process. This assertion marks a paradigm split in the study of pedagogy.

Themes of emancipation from the constraints of social institutions and structures, particularly institutions which are regarded as repressing the existential interests of whole classes of people, are key themes of most critical approaches. Oppression is actualized or realized through structured expectations about the interactional roles of different categories of participants such as men and women. Blacks and Whites, adults and children, authority figures and subordinates. All these come into play within the knowledgeable–ignorant relationships of teachers and learners. In addition, existing languages, dialects, and subcultural codes, as well as the terminology and labels of particular professions, embody sedimentations of past subordination or superordination.

Critical theories could be considered within the

framework of any of the other theories mentioned earlier, since each theory could and has been employed in conjunction with certain educational values to examine topics where issues of social justice are at stake. For instance, behavioral sociolinguistic studies of the communicative participation of women and girls have shown both quantitative and qualitative disadvantage in the typical patterns of their participation in teaching/learning talk (Cazden 1988).

Some critical linguists, however, (see, e.g. Young 1992) argue that language is inherently evaluative not only because speech expresses participants' values or interests directly or indirectly, but because languages both as systems of words and rules and as structured communicative expectations, represent the concrete operationalization or realization of those values. Furthermore, the interests and values realized are not the personal interests and values of individuals, which others can readily accept or reject, but are constitutive of a social world in which other people's roles as subordinate and the self's role as superordinate are part of the way meaning itself is constructed.

A variety of adaptations of other, noncritical approaches to language have been employed by critical analysts. Critical theorists have sharply divided into two camps which are nevertheless uneasily seeking a rapprochement: the traditional critical theorists and the postmodern or poststructural theorists (mainly feminists). The traditional critical theorists are to some extent rationalists. The possibility is held out that problems of injustice can be resolved through awareness, reflection, and argumentation, leading to reforms of the offending patterns of interaction.

The poststructural position is less optimistic. While the "deconstruction" of existing discourses can uncover oppression, grounds for optimism concerning the possibility of discourses that are less oppressive are few and far between. Thus, perhaps a reconciliation will not be possible. Poststructuralist analyses of critical theories have attempted to identify latent oppression in them and the question of whether it is possible in some sense to have "ideology-free" or even relatively ideology-free interaction remains unresolved.

7. Conclusion

Linguistic and sociolinguistic theories of teaching will be recognized, even if for no other reason, for their contribution in making an understanding of the complexity of classrooms come closer to reality. In turn, the demands of this complexity are fostering new modes of interdisciplinary inquiry and are forcing theoretical and methodological innovations which are moving educational research away from models of simple linear relationships among a few variables of somewhat doubtful relevance to teaching and learning. Critical appraisal of the educational value of the patterns observed has now begun to move toward the exploration of the conditions under which new, more adequate patterns can be realized. A constructive interplay among openly ideological critical pedagogy, poststructuralist, and feminist approaches, and more traditional scientific modes of inquiry is resulting in a crossfertilization in which empirical researchers are allowing questions of value to guide their choice of topics and analyses of data. Similarly, more radical theorists are alerted to the requirements of empirical demonstration of the practical implications of their theories. If discussion were to be opened up with behavioral, social, and cognitive learning theories, an even more fruitful critical dialogue could ensue, leading to an understanding of teaching in a rounded way for the first time.

See also: Implicit Theories of Teaching; Behavioristic Theories of Teaching; Cognitive Development Theories of Teaching

References

Aronowitz S, Giroux H 1991 *Postmodern Education: Politics, Culture and Social Criticism.* University of Minnesota Press, Minneapolis, Minnesota
Bernstein B 1975 *Class, Codes and Control,* Vol. 3. Routledge and Kegan Paul, London
Cazden C 1988 *Classroom Discourse: The Language of Teaching and Learning.* Heinemann Educational Books, Portsmouth, New Hampshire
Edwards A D, Mercer N 1987 *Common Knowledge: The Development of Understanding in the Classroom.* Methuen, London
Green J L, Weade R, Graham K 1988 Lesson construction and student participation: A sociolinguistic analysis. In: Green J L, Harker J O (eds.) 1988 *Multiple Perspective Analyses of Classroom Discourse.* Ablex, Norwood, New Jersey
Hoetker J, Ahlbrand W 1969 The persistence of the recitation. *Am. Educ. Research J.* 6: 145–67
Kohlberg L 1971 The concept of developmental psychology is the central guide to education. *Proceedings of the conference in Psychology and the Process of Schooling in the Next Decade: Alternative Conceptions.* University of Minnesota, Minneapolis, Minnesota
Piaget J 1972 Development and learning. In: Lavatelli C S, Stendler F (eds.) 1972 *Readings in Child Behavior and Development.* Harcourt Price, New York
Vygotsky L 1978 *Mind in Society: the Development of Higher Psychological Processes.* Harvard University Press, Cambridge, Massachusetts
Young R E 1992 *Critical Theory and Classroom Talk.* Taylor and Francis, London

Further Reading

Atkinson P 1986 *Language, Structure and Reproduction: An Introduction to the Language of Basil Bernstein.* Methuen, London

Green J L, Wallat C (eds.) 1980 *Ethnography and Language in Educational Settings*. Ablex, Norwood, New Jersey

Lemke J L 1986 *Using Language in the Classroom*. Deakin University Press, Geelong

Masschelein J 1991 *Kommunikatives Handeln und paedagogisches Handeln*. Deutscher Studien Verlag, Weinheim

Perrott C 1988 *Classroom Talk and Pupil Learning: Guidelines for Educators*. Harcourt Brace Jovanovitch, Sydney

Heuristic Models of Teaching

G. Nuthall

Heuristic models of teaching are those models of teaching in which the primary aim is to provide students with strategies or heuristics for solving problems, thinking effectively, or learning for themselves. The aim of these models is to make students independent thinkers and learners who take responsibility for creating their own understanding and knowledge. Proponents of heuristic models of teaching have argued that in a complex and constantly changing society, in which knowledge and technology are quickly outdated, it is more important for students to learn how to think and create new knowledge and solutions to problems for themselves than it is for them to acquire existing knowledge.

1. Historical Development

Heuristic models of teaching have been proposed within European culture for many centuries. Wittrock (1985) traced their origins to Plato's dialogues, especially Plato's account of Socrates teaching the Pythagorean theorem to a young slave. Plato's dialogues exemplify a style of teaching in which the teacher and student engage in a process of rational argument and careful consideration of the validity of evidence. For Plato, true knowledge lies hidden behind the appearance of things and can be discovered through logical analysis and debate about the evidence obtained through the senses.

In later Roman and early medieval European times, rhetoric or the art of public speaking and persuasion had a central place in the education of the ruling classes. As in other societies in which valued knowledge was not widely available in written or printed form, considerable emphasis was placed on accurate memorization of information. In preliterate societies, survival depended on the ability of selected individuals to memorize the society's store of natural and supernatural wisdom. In these and early European societies, methods of memorization had a central place in education. They employed mnemonic heuristics, which involved the use of imagery, rhythmical and musical chanting, and techniques (such as the method of locuses) to link new information to familiar events or places (Metge 1986).

The rise of publicly funded universal education in European societies in the nineteenth century and other societies in the twentieth century resulted in an emphasis on receptive methods of teaching and a decline of interest in heuristic methods. Teaching children to think for themselves became less important than teaching them to become effective workers and morally decent citizens. However, with the extension of democracy there followed the belief that society depends on a more broadly educated population whose members can make informed decisions for themselves. Thus, there has been a renewed interest in heuristic models of teaching. In the United States, for example, Dewey (1933) argued that the skills of reflective thinking must be the prime concern of education for a democracy. Students, he claimed, must develop the habits of mind of skeptical rationalism.

The models of heuristic teaching that emerged in the late twentieth century owed much to the development of cognitive science and to growing dissatisfaction with behavioral models of teaching. The extensive research of Piaget and Bruner served to focus attention on the active nature of the child's mind. The child's intelligence came to be seen as the product of the ways in which the child comprehended and acted upon the physical and social world. Consequently training the child to interpret and think about reality more effectively could increase the development of intelligence.

Also important were studies of the ways in which experts perceive, think about, and solve problems in their area of expertise. Traditional methods of teaching were seen as paying little attention to the heuristics that experts within each discipline use. It has been argued that students in areas such as science and mathematics will not become proficient in these disciplines unless they are given explicit instruction in the heuristics used by expert scientists and mathematicians (Brown and Campione 1990).

There is now evidence that many students who graduate from high school and even college still hold serious misconceptions about basic scientific and social principles and concepts. Gil-Perez and Carrascosa (1990) argued that a major reason for the persistence of these misconceptions is that they reflect historically primitive ways of understanding the world. Receptive methods of teaching may be good at imparting knowledge, but they fail to teach the important attitude of skepticism and the skills of enquiry that underlie modern scientific thinking.

2. Modern Models of Heuristic Teaching

There has been a proliferation of models of teaching whose major purpose is to provide students with heuristics for thinking, problem-solving, understanding, and self-regulated learning. Underlying the design of these models are conceptions of how students' minds work; these have determined both the heuristics that should be taught and the methods of teaching that should be used. To be flexible and effective the teacher also needs to have an understanding of the student's mind. For example, the teacher needs to understand that the student needs to know many different learning and thinking strategies and how and when to use these strategies. The student needs to be reflective and planful, to be free from the fear of failure, and to believe in the efficacy of personal effort. In addition, the student should have a wide background of relevant knowledge and to have experienced reward and support for acting as an effective self-regulated learner and thinker (Borkowski and Muthukrishna 1992, White 1992).

The modern models of heuristic teaching tend to fall into five general types. Each of these will be described below, along with one or two examples of each type.

3. The Reciprocal and Transactional Strategy Instruction Models

There is a family of heuristic models of teaching that see the student as engaged in a kind of "cognitive apprenticeship" (Collins et al. 1989). In these models, cognitive processes characteristic of an effective or expert thinker or learner are demonstrated to the student, who is helped to imitate and achieve mastery of the processes through guided practice. The most difficult task for the teacher is to make visible and explicit for the student cognitive processes that normally take place in the head of the expert (Brown and Campione 1990).

Perhaps the best-known of these models is the "reciprocal teaching" model developed by Palincsar and Brown (1984). In this model the teacher demonstrates or models a cognitive process (such as predicting what is going to happen next while reading a narrative text), explaining at the same time what he or she is doing and why he or she is doing it. The students are required to try to imitate the model. As the students try out the process and develop their skill in using it, the teacher ceases to provide the model and takes on the role of

coach, providing cues, hints, corrective feedback, and encouragement. Students are then helped to take over control of the process for themselves and to engage in self-evaluation of their performance (Palincsar 1986).

The teacher's role is described as providing "scaffolding," within which the student does as much as he or she can and the teacher does the rest (Cazden 1988). By being sensitive to the level of the student's understanding and progress, the teacher is working within the student's "zone of proximal development" (Vygotsky, 1978). If the teacher's guidance is too far in advance of the student's skill, the instruction is less likely to be effective.

Although this model was initially developed as a way of teaching comprehension skills to poor readers, it has been extended to cover the teaching of mathematics and science. Brown and Campione (1990) described the use of the reciprocal teaching model in mathematics education. Their procedures involved the use of a "reflection board" on which a group of students record their progress toward the solution of a mathematical problem. The students recorded what they knew about the problem (their background knowledge), how they planned to solve the problem, their progress through the solution steps, and their checking of the accuracy and the plausibility of the solution they reached. The important role of the "reflection board" was to provide the students with a record they could use to think about and reflect on their problem-solving processes. They identified the procedures that succeeded or failed and learned to think heuristically about solving mathematics problems.

The model of "transactional strategy instruction" described by Pressley et al. (1992) is similar in many respects to the reciprocal teaching model, but it was developed to teach a wider range of thinking, learning, and comprehending skills in a more open-ended and flexible manner. According to Borkowski and Muthukrishna (1992), the model encourages habitual reflecting and planning by students. Teachers using the model "foster an environment in which such reflection is valued more than the completion of assignments or the production of right answers" (p. 479). Teachers have to be sensitive to the needs of the students and encourage them to "evaluate and manage their own learning" (p. 490).

In their analysis of the most successful transactional strategy instruction programs, Pressley et al. (1992) identified the following characteristics. The teachers introduced one strategy at a time. They took extended time to teach each strategy and engaged in a great deal of direct explanation of each strategy. The teachers modeled each strategy themselves, describing what they were doing, and explaining why the strategy worked and when it should be used. The teachers provided the students with consistent and frequent feedback as they practiced and applied the strategy, and provided further description and explanation whenever any difficulties occurred. Throughout the process the teachers kept the students' motivation high, and encouraged the students to plan their use of the strategy carefully and to reflect constantly on how the strategy was working.

4. Direct Strategy Instruction

The transactional strategy instruction model has been contrasted with another family of heuristic models of teaching described as "direct strategy instruction." Although these two models have many features in common, direct strategy instruction is carefully structured and depends on the teacher following a closely prescribed pattern of behaviors. Kline et al. (1992) described eight steps for teaching a cognitive strategy. In the first stage, the students are pretested and a contract is set up between the teacher and the students in which the students make a commitment to learn and use the strategy. In the second and third stages the teacher describes the strategy, models it for the students, and encourages the students to try using it. During the fourth and fifth stages, the students learn to use the strategy, to name and explain the steps involved, and to practice it on increasingly difficult material. In the sixth stage, the students practice the strategy on real problems in and out of school, following an individualized program of work, until they reach mastery. In the seventh stage the students are given a posttest. The teacher and students then review progress, celebrate the students' achievements, and make a commitment to continue using the strategy. In the final stage, the teachers guide the students in practicing the strategy in a variety of situations.

5. Self-instructional Strategy Training

A different approach to providing students with the heuristics they need to become self-sufficient learners has been described by Miller and Brewster (1992). Self-sufficient learners are described as those students who know about the parameters that affect their cognition, know how to control their own cognitive endeavors, and believe that cognitive effort results in academic success. Self-instructional strategy training involves training students to talk to themselves as they engage in learning and problem-solving processes. There are five types of cognitive processes for which self-verbalizations are taught: (a) analyzing the task and the goals to be achieved ("What do I have to do?"); (b) formulating a plan of action ("How should I do it?"); (c) evaluating the effectiveness of each of the steps in the plan ("How am I doing?"); (d) giving positive feedback for succeeding with each step ("That's good work."); and (e) dealing with obstacles, employing corrective actions ("That's not quite right." "Keep cool." "I will try again.").

When teaching students to carry out these verbalizations, teachers are encouraged to model and display the steps and the verbalizations, to use real learning situations, and to provide students with information about why the verbalizations are necessary and how effectively they work. Self-verbalization training needs to be undertaken in conjunction with training in self-motivation and self-attribution to ensure that students believe in their ability to take control of their own lives and succeed.

6. Generative and Interactive Teaching Models

A different type of heuristic teaching model has been variously described as "generative" and "interactive" teaching. This type of model is based on the premise that all significant learning is a generative or constructive process. While it is true that students can memorize and reproduce the information presented to them by teachers or textbooks, for that information to become part of their thinking and guide the way in which they understand and interact with the world, they have to construct or reconstruct it for themselves. All lasting knowledge is the product of the way in which the student's background knowledge and beliefs interact with new experiences (Wittrock 1991, White 1992).

It follows from this premise that students need to learn how to guide their own knowledge construction processes. They need to be taught to take responsibility for the ways in which they understand and question their own beliefs, the new experiences they encounter, and the match or mismatch that may occur between them.

6.1 Generative Teaching Models

Wittrock based his description of the generative teaching model on an analysis of the way in which the mind comprehends new experience and information. Understanding is a process of identifying and building relations between prior knowledge and new knowledge, and between the component parts of the new knowledge. For example, when reading a text, the student must identify how the content of the text relates to the student's prior knowledge and beliefs, and also identify the relations that exist between words, sentences, phrases, and topics within the text.

The teacher who uses the generative model of teaching must begin by identifying the preconceptions, beliefs, and experiences that the student brings to the learning situation. The teacher must then organize classroom experiences so that the student connects the new information to his or her prior knowledge and constructs a new understanding or model of the phenomenon. The teacher must help the student see his or her role as one of generating understanding by relating concepts presented in class to real-world experience.

The student must take "control and responsibility for being active in learning, for generating meaning from teaching and attributing success to this active effortful learning" (Wittrock 1991 p. 175). Thus, students must be taught the metacognitive and self-control strategies they need to direct their own cognitive and affective thought processes. The students need to be taught that success in school begins with belief in themselves, their abilities, and their effort.

6.2 Interactive Teaching Models

Closely related to the generative teaching model is the heuristic teaching model described as "interactive teaching" by Biddulph and Osbourne (1984). As with the generative teaching model, the concern is with students taking responsibility for the extent and the validity of their knowledge. This model has been developed in the context of science education and involves five sequential components.

During the first stage a topic for investigation is selected by the teacher. This may be related to the students' current concerns, interests, or problems. The topic should be relevant to the way the students make sense of everyday events and can be related by the students to things that have practical and social significance in their lives. It should also be an area in which it is possible for students to carry out simple practical investigations. During the second stage the teacher encourages the students to think and talk about the topic. The students may engage in exploratory activities, observing, recording, and finding relevant print materials. During this stage the teacher should make it clear that the students' ideas and beliefs are interesting and important. During the third stage the teacher identifies the questions that the students would like answered about the topic. These questions are developed and clarified so that they can form the basis for serious investigation. The teacher must make sure that the questions are important to the students. During the fourth stage, the students develop their plans for carrying out investigations and gathering information to answer their questions. The teacher guides the students, helping them to reflect on their plans and to consider alternative ways of carrying out their investigations. In the fifth and final stage the teacher and students reflect together on the results of the investigations and on the whole process. The teacher helps them to consider alternative explanations of their results and to plan further investigations. It is important that students come to feel both that their ideas are valued and that they are responsible for developing them.

7. Logical Argument Models

Models of teaching have been proposed that focus on thinking as "logical argument." In these models the skills and forms of argument and analysis that are used to argue a case or to defend a proposition against counterclaims are taught. For example, Kuhn (1992) studied the forms of argument and reasons and evidence that people use when they discuss and defend their views on significant social issues. She suggested that an effective heuristic teaching program needs to engage students in guided practice in using reason and evidence. Argument about significant social issues offers the teacher a way to externalize, discuss, and modify the internal and usually unobserved thinking strategies that students use in their everyday lives. However, as Kuhn noted, teachers are wary of introducing genuine debate about controversial issues into the classroom and consequently students are rarely given the chance to have their beliefs challenged or to experience genuine debate.

Ziedler and Lederman (1992) were also concerned with teaching students the use of reason and evidence. They argued that learning critical thinking skills involves learning how to evaluate evidence and reasons and how to identify and avoid common logical fallacies. For example, students need to learn how to distinguish verifiable facts from value claims, how to determine the credibility of a source of information, how to distinguish relevant from irrelevant information, and so on. They should also be taught to identify common fallacies such as begging the question, *ad hominem* or *ad feminam* argument, and the fallacies that arise from ambiguity of terms and normative reasoning. They suggested that this learning should take place in the context of classroom discussion and debate focused on scientific and social issues of relevance to the students' lives.

8. Major Characteristics of Heuristic Teaching Models

The models described in this entry are very diverse but they have some common characteristics. Most involve the teacher in modeling or making visible the thinking or learning processes that the students are required to learn and use. This may involve using visible or verbal aids, such as flowcharts, diagrams, or checklists of procedures. It may also involve naming strategies and developing and using a language for talking about how, when, and where they are used. Most are concerned with avoiding superficial processing of information or rote memorization of procedures. There is an underlying cognitive model of the student as an active, planful, and reflective learner or thinker. Most are concerned with making the student an independent thinker or learner who has the skills, the motivation, and the beliefs required to take responsibility for his or her own achievement and personal development.

The role of the teacher is usually portrayed as flexible and sensitive to the students' skills and background knowledge and experiences. The teacher's role changes during the course of the program as the students' needs change from providing direct descriptive instruction about strategies, through being an "expert"

125

model, to becoming a supportive colleague or coach, encouraging, guiding, and helping. Students report that they learn to think better when they are stimulated by real cognitive challenges, already have considerable relevant background knowledge, are provided with positive models of the strategies they need, and are working in a classroom environment that offers and encourages autonomy (Collins 1992).

The learning process implied by most of the models is one of "internalization." Students are shown a model that is an externalization of cognitive processes that are normally internal and covert. They are expected, through guided practice, to internalize the model and make it a normal part of their internal cognitive processing. This is what is meant by "cognitive apprenticeship" (Collins et al. 1989).

9. Problems of Training Teachers and Assessing Outcomes

Several writers have noted that it takes considerable time and dedication to train teachers to use heuristic models of teaching effectively. Teachers must become committed to a model and incorporate it into their own philosophy of teaching (El-Dinary et al. 1992). They need strong informal peer support and commitment from the administration to support them during the process of change that is required (Kline et al. 1992). The process of training may take several years and the training should itself be structured according to a heuristic model of teaching.

Heuristic models of teaching are primarily concerned with the ability of students to think and learn independently, and are only secondarily concerned with traditional student achievement. As a consequence, they pose considerable challenges for developing appropriate methods of assessing their effectiveness. As Ziedler et al. (1992) have suggested, the problem is to find effective ways of obtaining and evaluating "performances of thought." Although tests of critical thinking have been available for some time, more general methods of assessing how students use their minds are still in the early stages of development and validation (Wolf et al. 1992).

See also: Behavioristic Theories of Teaching; Metacognitive Strategies: Teaching and Assessing; Information Processing Theories of Teaching

References

Biddulph F, Osbourne R 1984 *Making Sense of Our World: An Interactive Teaching Approach.* University of Waikato Science Education Research Unit, Hamilton

Borkowski J G, Muthukrishna N 1992 Moving metacognition into the classroom: "Working models" and effective strategy teaching. In: Pressley M, Harris K R, Guthrie J T (eds.) 1992

Brown A L, Campione J C 1990 Interactive learning environments and the teaching of science and mathematics. In:

Gardner M et al. (eds.) 1990 *Toward a Scientific Practice of Science Education.* Erlbaum, Hillsdale, New Jersey

Cazden C 1988 *Classroom Discourse: The Language of Teaching and Learning.* Heinemann Educational, Portsmouth, New Hampshire

Collins C 1992 Improving reading and thinking: From teaching or not teaching skills to interactive interventions. In: Pressley M, Harris K R, Guthrie J T (eds.) 1992

Collins A, Brown J S, Newman S E 1989 Cognitive apprenticeship: Teaching the craft of reading, writing and mathematics. In: Resnick L (ed.) 1989 *Cognition and Instruction: Issues and Agendas.* Erlbaum, Hillsdale, New Jersey

Dewey J 1933 *How We Think: A Restatement of the Relation of Reflective Thinking to the Educative Process.* Heath, Boston, Massachusetts.

El-Dinary P B, Pressley M, Schuder T 1992 Teachers' first year teaching strategies: Case studies in the Students Achieving Independent Learning (SAIL) strategies instruction program. Paper presented to the American Educational Research Association Conference, San Francisco, California

Gil-Perez D, Carrascosa J 1990 What to do about science "misconceptions". *Sci. Educ.* 74(5): 531–40

Kline F M, Deshler D D, Schumaker J B 1992 Implementing learning strategy instruction in class settings: A research perspective. In: Pressley M, Harris K R, Guthrie J T (eds.) 1992

Kuhn D 1992 Thinking as argument. *Harv. Educ. Rev.* 62(6): 155–78

Metge J 1986 *Learning and Teaching: He Tikanga Maori.* Ministry of Education, Wellington

Miller G E, Brewster M E 1992 Developing self-sufficient learners in reading and mathematics through self-instructional training. In: Pressley M, Harris K R, Guthrie J T (eds.) 1992

Palincsar A S 1986 The role of dialogue in providing scaffolded instruction. *Educ. Psychol.* 21(1–2): 73–98

Palincsar A S, Brown A L 1984 Reciprocal teaching of comprehension-fostering and comprehension-monitoring activities. *Cognition and Instruction,* 1(2): 117–75

Pressley M et al. 1992 Beyond direct explanation: Transactional instruction of reading comprehension strategies. *Elem. Sch. J.* 92(5): 513–55

Vygotsky L S 1978 *Mind in Society: The Development of Higher Psychological Processes.* Harvard University Press, Cambridge, Massachusetts

White R T 1992 Implications of recent research on learning for curriculum and assessment. *J. Curric. St.* 24(2): 153–64

Wittrock M C 1985 Heuristic models of teaching. In: Husén T, Postlethwaite T N (eds.) 1985 *The International Encyclopedia of Education, 1st edn.* Pergamon Press, Oxford

Wittrock M C 1991 Generative teaching of comprehension. *Elem. Sch. J.* 92(2): 169–84

Wolf D, Bixby J, Glenn J, Gardner H 1992 To use their minds well: Investigating new forms of student assessment. In: Grant G (ed.) 1992 *Review of Research Education,* . Vol 17. American Educational Research Association, Washington, DC

Ziedler D L, Lederman N G, Taylor S C 1992 Fallacies and student discourse: Conceptualizing the role of critical thinking in science education. *Sci. Educ.* 76(4): 437–50

Further Reading

Fleer M 1992 Identifying teacher–child interaction which scaffolds scientific thinking in young children. *Sci. Educ.* 76(4): 373–97

Gardner M et al. (eds.) 1990 *Toward a Scientific Practice of Science Education.* Erlbaum, Hillsdale, New Jersey

Pressley M, Harris K R, Guthrie J T 1992 *Promoting Academic Competence and Literacy in School.* Academic Press, San Diego, California

Aptitude–Treatment Interaction Model of Teaching

R. E. Snow

An aptitude–treatment interaction (ATI) occurs when the characteristics of persons moderate the effects of instructional conditions on those persons. Conversely, ATI implies that the importance of personal characteristics in relation to valued educational outcomes depends on what instructional conditions are administered. The study of aptitude–treatment interactions in education aims at understanding when, how, and why different kinds of persons benefit from different kinds of instruction, so that educational conditions for individual learners can be improved. An adaptive instructional system with respect to individual differences among persons is the goal (see *Individualized Instruction*).

Aptitude–treatment interaction research is a special case of the scientific study of person–environment interaction. The possibility of interactions has long been routinely acknowledged in the physical scientist's qualifier "other things being equal ... " and in the social scientist's question "Can we generalize to other groups (communities, cultures, etc.)?" Evolutionary biology is basically interactionist. Interactions have been put to practical use in medicine; for example, the physician's choice of antibiotic depends on the patient's answer to the test question: "Have you ever had an allergic reaction to penicillin?"

Cronbach (1957, 1975), recognized that person–environment interaction was both a fundamental concept and a fundamental problem for psychology. Interactional research has accumulated in a variety of fields of psychology (Dance and Neufeld 1988, Endler and Magnusson 1976, Magnusson and Allen 1983, Pervin and Lewis 1978, Snow 1991). Although interactional thinking has been evident in educational philosophies since ancient times, the full implications of aptitude–treatment interaction for education have been systematically addressed only since the 1970s (Cronbach and Snow 1977, Snow 1989).

1. Substantive Definition and Implications for Education

In education, many kinds of individual differences among learners can be observed and measured. When such measures predict individual differences in learning from instruction, they are interpreted as indicators of aptitude, that is, readiness to profit from instruction. When aptitude measures provide differential predictions for learning under different instructional conditions, a conclusion of aptitude–treatment interaction is justified.

Many kinds of aptitude differences among students have been studied, including general and special cognitive abilities, personality and motivational attributes, and cognitive styles. Many kinds of instructional treatments have also been compared. Since ATI findings often occur, there is no doubt that ATI exists in education (Cronbach and Snow 1977). Theoretical and practical understanding of ATI is not, in the early 1990s, sufficient to allow routine use of ATI in educational planning or instructional design.

It is clear, however, that routine use of ATI is both possible and necessary in educational evaluation. Aptitude–treatment interaction methodology is a requisite part of any evaluation study aimed at comparing alternative teaching methods or environments because the evaluation question is never simply which treatment is best on average? It is always which treatment is best for each of the individual learners to be served?

Aptitude–treatment interactions are of interest theoretically because they demonstrate construct validity for aptitude and learning measures in a new way: they show how aptitude–learning relations can be experimentally manipulated and thus understood in a causal rather than only a correlational framework. Neither aptitude constructs nor educational learning processes can be fully understood without reference to one another. Therefore, it is possible that common psychological processes underlie both aptitude and learning differences.

Furthermore, as interactions have appeared ubiquitous in education, they show the need to understand not only persons and situations, but their interface. Learning and aptitude come to be seen as operating in the person–situation union, not just in the heads of persons, thus posing a new theoretical and philosophical problem (Snow 1992).

Practical interest stems from the possibility that ATI

can be used to adapt instruction to fit different learners optimally. Many attempts at individualizing instruction have failed to eliminate individual differences in learning outcome because they adapted only to limited aspects of individual performance; for example, by allowing differences in pace. The hope is that research on ATI can provide decision rules that indicate how to vary instructional conditions in ways that mesh with particular learner strengths while avoiding particular learner weaknesses. A related hope is that such research will indicate how best to develop aptitudes directly for persons with different initial aptitude profiles.

Again, the general question for research, and for evaluation studies, is which of the available or conceivable teaching methods, media, or environments is most likely to provide equality of educational opportunity to each individual learner, for his or her aptitude development and educational achievement. The commitment to optimal diversity of educational opportunity (e.g., truly to provide adaptive education as defined by Glaser 1977), demands that educational environments be chosen or invented and evaluated within an ATI perspective (Corno and Snow 1986).

At the same time, however, ATI research has shown that interactions are complex. No simple or general principles for matching students and teachers, teaching methods, or school environments have emerged. Part of the problem stems from the difficulty of conducting ATI research and a widespread lack of understanding of appropriate methods, but part also can be attributed to the multidimensional, dynamic, and often local and even transient character of the person–environment interface. Results to date suggest that work toward instructional theories that seek to optimize instruction for individuals in real school settings will need to be built up from continuous local diagnosis, description, and evaluation activities; local instructional models rather than general educational theory seem to be the more realizable goal (Snow 1991).

2. Statistical Definition and Methodology

Normally, ATI is defined as a statistical interaction: the multiplicative combination of at least one person variable and one treatment variable in affecting one dependent or instructional outcome variable. The interaction exists whenever the regression of an instructional outcome from one treatment upon some personal characteristic of learners differs in slope from the regression of that outcome from another treatment on the same characteristic.

Figure 1 gives the basic patterns of possible relationships. Each graph assumes that student aptitude scores taken before instruction and student outcome scores taken after instruction have been plotted, on the abscissa and ordinate respectively, to form a bivariate

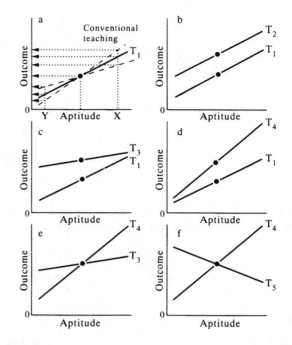

Figure 1
Possible effects of alternative instructional treatments (T) on outcome averages and outcome-on-aptitude regressions

distribution for each treatment under investigation. Linear regression slopes have been fitted to each distribution and treatment average effects have been identified (the heavy centered dots). In Fig. 1(a), labeled "conventional teaching," the solid slope (T_1) depicts an aptitude– outcome relationship corresponding to a correlation coefficient of 0.50; the dashed slopes depict variation in this relationship between coefficients of 0.30 and 0.70. These data approximate what has often been found in United States public schools, using general intelligence or prior achievement tests as aptitude measures and cognitive achievement measures to reflect instructional outcomes. Note that a student with aptitude score at X is predicted (dotted arrows) to obtain outcome scores above the mean while a student with aptitude score at Y is predicted to obtain outcome scores below the mean.

An important aim of educational research is to improve upon this state of affairs by finding or devising instructional treatments such as T_2 in Fig. 1(b) that raise the average outcome for everyone over that expected from T_1. When such regression slopes are parallel, as shown here, there is no ATI; T_2 is the better treatment for all students regardless of aptitude. Unfortunately, many educational studies have looked only for such average treatment differences, assuming that aptitude slopes were parallel without investigating them.

The pattern in Fig. 1(c) schematizes the goal of special education and of much research on individualized instruction, where it is hoped that a treatment T_3 can be found to improve achievement of lower aptitude students while maintaining the high achievements of higher aptitude students. However, in searching for generally improved treatments the result shown in Fig. 1(d) can also be obtained; treatments such as T_4 turn out to be most beneficial for the higher aptitude students rather than for the lower aptitude students. One can think of T_4 as the goal of special programs for the gifted.

The T_3 result has at times been obtained for programmed instruction in comparison to conventional instruction T_1, while the T_4 result has sometimes been obtained in studies of discovery or inductive teaching. This leads to the possibility of combined results such as those in Fig. 1(e). Here, alternative treatments produce improvements for different kinds of students; it is apparent that T_4 should be given to high aptitude students, while T_3 should be given to low aptitude students. In the extreme, if optimal instructional treatments could be found or devised for students like X and Y, the result depicted in Fig. 1(f) might be expected. Negative slopes approximating T_5 do occur at times using cognitive measures, but are more likely when personality or attitudinal characteristics rather than cognitive abilities are used as aptitudes.

Research on ATI seeks to detect nonparallel regression slopes of the sorts shown in Fig. 1 and to understand how instructional treatments can be designed to produce such effects. To the extent that stable interactions like those of Fig. 1(e) and 1(f) can be established, they can be used as suggested above to form decision rules for the assignment of students to optimally different treatments. The regression slopes cross to define the point on the aptitude continuum where persons should be divided to achieve optimal outcome in different instructional treatments. The same regression slope expectations apply to compensatory education programs or to other attempts to develop aptitude directly. The same patterns can be used to interpret evaluation results not aimed at adapting instruction to individual differences. For example, an evaluation that obtained a pattern like that of Fig 1(e) might suggest a revision of T_4 that would improve it specifically for learners below the aptitude mean.

Beyond the simplest cases shown in Fig. 1, there are many technical complications involved in particular study designs and data analyses. Aptitude, treatment, and outcome variables can be multiple; regressions can be nonlinear. Special problems in ATI research attach to the disattenuation of measurements, the evaluation of power of statistical inferences, and the disentangling of regression effects at different levels of aggregation (e.g., individual student, classroom, and school). Since an adaptive instructional system based on ATI would presumably involve periodic aptitude monitoring and reclassification of students, there are also technical issues involved in the sequential assessment of aptitudes and outcomes, and the evaluation of utilities in placement decisions. On these and related topics, see Cronbach and Snow (1977) and Cronbach (1982, 1991).

3. Examples of Instructional Systems

An adaptive instructional system such as that envisioned by Glaser (1977, see also Corno and Snow 1986) could be based on ATI. It would contain at least two alternative instructional routes to successful attainment of some criterion achievement level. The route or treatment taken by each learner would depend on an initial diagnosis of aptitude for learning in each available treatment. Also available in such a system would be at least one form of compensatory, direct training of aptitude for learners diagnosed as unready for any of the available instructional treatments.

A variety of alternative instructional treatments have been evaluated using measures of prior ability and generalized achievement as aptitudes. From a summary of that research (Snow 1989), it appears that instructional treatments differ in the information-processing burdens they place on, or remove from, the responsibility of the learner, and the regressions of achievement outcome on scholastic ability become steeper or shallower, respectively, as a result. As learners are required to puzzle things out for themselves, organize their own study, and build their own comprehension, more able learners do well—they can capitalize on their strengths profitably—while less able learners do poorly. However, as instructional treatments relieve learners from difficult reading and inferencing or analyzing of complex concepts on their own, the more such treatments seem to compensate for or circumvent less able learners' weaknesses. Unfortunately, the structured and simplified treatments that seem to help less able learners are suboptimal for able learners, relative to the more burdensome treatments where they excel. The ATI results from a variety of studies of this hypothesis often approximate the pattern shown in Fig. 1(e), and occasionally that in Fig. 1(f).

For some courses of instruction, then, alternative treatment T_4 might be designed to provide relatively unstructured and minimal guidance and to encourage learner self-direction in a discovery-oriented approach. The teacher might guide the inductive process, but instruction would clearly be student centered. In contrast, T_3 might be designed to break down the learning task to give clear step-by-step guidance, feedback, and correction through a series of small units, with frequent summary and review, and simplified demonstrations of the concepts to be learned. Students would be assigned to either T_3 or T_4 on the basis of prior scholastic ability scores taken at the start of instruction. Periodic aptitude and achievement assessments would show the degree to which outcome criterion levels were being achieved for each learner in the particular treatment assigned.

For those students who might not be expected to profit from either alternative, compensatory aptitude training would be assigned. This training might consist of directed work on academic learning or reading skills, study habits, self-management skills, and so on. The aim of this training would be to develop readiness for entry into treatment T₃ as soon as possible.

Student anxiety might also be considered as an aptitude in this adaptive instructional system. It has often been found that more anxious students do relatively poorly under unstructured or student-centered forms of instruction, as compared to teacher-structured conditions. In contrast, less anxious students often appear not to need teacher structure. Furthermore, ability and anxiety appear to combine in higher order interaction in relation to this treatment contrast.

The initial placement decision in the instructional system would thus depend on both prior ability and anxiety indices. Able learners showing little anxiety would be assigned to treatment T₄. The more anxious, able learners and the less able, less anxious learners would receive treatment T₃. The least able and the most anxious students might be given compensatory training adapted to their particular needs: cognitive skills training focused on ability deficits and therapeutic interventions designed to alleviate the effects of anxiety. Periodic monitoring would need to be designed to indicate when particular learners should be switched to alternative treatment assignments.

While these examples provide a hypothetical demonstration, no such system can be properly designed in the abstract. Local conditions must be considered, aptitude measures and alternative treatment designs must be adjusted to these conditions, and periodic evaluation must be relied upon to realize an effective system.

4. Prospects for Research and Development

It is noteworthy that much research in instructional psychology contrasts two treatments without evaluating ATI. Voluminous research on teaching has compared direct teacher-centered instruction with guided discovery. Now research on new instructional technology considers essentially the same contrast in arguments about mastery-oriented computerized tutoring versus discovery learning in computerized microworlds (Glaser and Bassok 1989), again without evaluating ATI. Also, a large number of learning style hypotheses have been developed for use by teachers in adapting classroom instruction to student differences; each such style construct produces an ATI hypothesis, though none have been evaluated as such. Thus, one important prospect for further work is to conduct evaluative research on these developments from an ATI perspective (Cronbach 1982)

A second important line for further research aims at improved analysis of the many different kinds of aptitude constructs and measures that have been used in ATI work (Gustafsson 1989). Several lines of cognitive information processing research have provided analyses of cognitive ability constructs, identifying the underlying component processes and strategies on which individuals may differ (Lohman 1989, Snow 1989, Sternberg 1985a, 1985b).

Another approach has been to examine the differences in learning strategies students engage in during instruction that appear to mediate aptitude–outcome relations. Task analyses of instructional conditions also suggest mediational differences among alternative treatments that may control aptitude–outcome relations. Important new work is investigating prior knowledge differences in relation to cognitive and affective aptitudes for instruction (Schneider and Weinert 1989). There are also important advances in research on cognitive and affective aptitudes (Heckhausen et al. 1985, Kuhl and Kraska 1989).

Finally, more intensive analysis on outcome measures may help diagnose in detail the particular kinds of cognitive effects that derive from particular aptitude–treatment combinations (Snow and Lohman 1984, 1989). Future research on all these fronts in instructional psychology can be brought together within the ATI framework (Snow and Swanson 1992).

See also: Paradigms for Research on Teaching; Individualized Instruction

References

Corno L, Snow R E 1986 Adapting teaching to individual differences among learners. In: Wittrock M C (ed.) 1986 *Handbook of Research on Teaching*, 3rd edn. Macmillan, New York

Cronbach L J 1957 The two disciplines of scientific psychology. *Am. Psychol.* 12(11): 671–84

Cronbach L J 1975 Beyond the two disciplines of scientific psychology. *Am. Psychol.* 30(2): 116–27

Cronbach L J 1982 *Designing Evaluations of Educational and Social Programs*. Jossey-Bass, San Francisco, California

Cronbach L J 1991 Emerging views on methodology. In: Wachs T D, Plomin R (eds.) 1991 *Conceptualization and Measurement of Organism–Environment Interaction*. American Psychological Association, Washington, DC

Cronbach L J, Snow R E 1977 *Aptitudes and Instructional Methods: A Handbook for Research on Interactions.* Irvington, New York

Dance K A, Neufeld R W J 1988 Aptitude–treatment interaction research in the clinical setting: A review of attempts to dispel the "patient uniformity" myth. *Psych. Bull.* 104(2): 192–213

Endler N S, Magnusson D (eds.) 1976 *Interactional Psychology and Personality*. Hemisphere, Washington, DC

Glaser R 1977 *Adaptive Education: Individual Diversity and Learning*. Holt, Rinehart, and Winston, New York

Glaser R, Bassok M 1989 Learning theory and the study of instruction. *Ann. Rev. Psychol.* 40: 631–66

Gustafsson J E 1989 Broad and narrow abilities in research on learning and instruction. In: Kanfer R, Ackerman P L, Cudeck R (eds.) 1989 *Abilities, Motivation, and Methodology*. Erlbaum, Hillsdale, New Jersey

Heckhausen H, Schmalt H D, Schneider K 1985 *Achievement Motivation in Perspective*. Academic Press, Orlando, Florida

Kuhl J, Kraska K 1989 Self-regulation and metamotivation: Computational mechanisms development and assessment. In: Kanfer R, Ackerman P L, Cudeck R (eds.) 1989 *Abilities, Motivation, and Methodology: The Minnesota Symposium on Learning and Individual Differences*. Erlbaum, Hillsdale, New Jersey

Lohman D F 1989 Human intelligence: An introduction to advances in theory and research. *Rev. Educ. Res.* 59(4): 333–73

Magnusson D, Allen V L (eds.) 1983 *Human Development: An Interactional Perspective*. Academic Press, New York

Pervin L A, Lewis M (eds.) 1978 *Perspectives in Interactional Psychology*. Plenum Press, New York

Schneider W, Weinert F E (eds.) 1989 *Interactions Among Aptitudes, Strategies, and Knowledge in Cognitive Performance*. Springer-Verlag, New York

Snow R E 1989 Aptitude-treatment interaction as a framework for research on individual differences in learning. In: Ackerman P L, Sternberg R J, Glaser R (eds.) 1989 *Learning and Individual Differences*. Freeman, New York

Snow R E 1991 The concept of aptitude. In: Snow R E, Wiley D E (eds.) 1991 *Improving Inquiry in Social Science*. Erlbaum, Hillsdale, New Jersey

Snow R E 1992 Aptitude theory: Yesterday, today, and tomorrow. *Educ. Psychol.* 27(1): 5–32

Snow R E, Lohman D F 1984 Toward a theory of cognitive aptitude for learning from instruction. *J. Educ. Psychol.* 76(3): 347–76

Snow R E, Lohman D F 1989 Implications of cognitive psychology for educational measurement. In: Linn R L (ed.) 1989 *Educational Measurement*, 3rd edn. Macmillan, New York

Snow R E, Swanson J 1992 Instructional psychology: Aptitude, adaptation, and assessment. *Annu. Rev. Psychol.* 43: 583–626

Sternberg R J 1985a *Beyond IQ: A Triarchic Theory of Human Intelligence*. Cambridge University Press, Cambridge

Sternberg R J 1985b (ed.) *Human Abilities: An Information Processing Approach*. Freeman, New York

Further Reading

Snow R E 1982 Education and intelligence. In: Sternberg R J (ed.) 1982 *Handbook of Human Intelligence*. Cambridge University Press, New York

Implicit Theories of Teaching

P. W. Marland

The explanations given by teachers for what they do are typically not derived from what they were taught in teacher education programs. Though study in such fields as educational foundations, academic disciplines, and curriculum theory is expected to give rise to knowledge relevant to teaching, such knowledge rarely features in the explanations and justifications offered by teachers for their classroom behaviors. Rather, the classroom actions of teachers are guided by internal frames of reference which are deeply rooted in personal experiences, especially in-school ones, and are based on interpretations of those experiences.

These frames of reference include beliefs about educational goals, learners, and learning; images of good and bad teaching; and conceptions of the roles of teachers and students. They are applied daily by teachers to make sense of, and respond rationally to, classroom events; to identify appropriate courses of action; and to realize worthwhile goals. Collectively, these frames of reference allow teachers to identify important variables in teaching and the interrelationships among these variables. They also endow teachers with some capacity to predict what will work and thus produce desired outcomes. These frames therefore can be said to constitute a type of theory, a theory which shapes action in the classroom and is constructed from interpretations of past actions. For this reason, these frames of reference have been referred to as theories for action or practical theories.

Parts of these theories, however, are tacitly held and cannot be readily articulated. For this reason, practical theories are also referred to as implicit theories. The implicit nature of practical theories is usually attributed to: (a) the roots of teaching behaviors being so deeply embedded in the life histories of teachers that they are simply unaware of them, and (b) reasons for what they do in the classroom being forgotten, as patterns of thoughtful action become routinized. Moreover, teachers have had little need to make their practical knowledge explicit and are provided with few opportunities and little encouragement to be introspective. Teachers' implicit theories of teaching are thus the products of teachers' efforts to make sense of their experiences and to generate a basis for effective action in the classroom.

Implicit theories cannot be regarded as scientific

theories because, as Sanders and McCutcheon (1986) point out, "theories that count as 'scientific' theories are expected generally to be conceptually precise, specifically explicated, and able to withstand rigorous logical tests. They also are expected to be subject to public disconfirmation" (p. 57). These are characteristics which teachers' implicit theories mostly lack. Implicit theories are at best rough estimates of what will work because the contexts in which they are applied are so variable, indeterminate, unpredictable and capricious; furthermore, because the contexts are not reproducable, the theories cannot be subjected to rigorous tests.

Implicit theories of teaching do not rate as scientific theories on two other counts. In contrast to scientific theories which are universal and impersonal, implicit theories are both context-specific and intensely personal. Each implicit theory has been individually crafted and reflects the unique personal history of an individual and the interpretations of those experiences by that individual. Though teachers' implicit theories may have some elements in common, each teacher's implicit theory is unique. Moreover, a teacher's implicit theory has been abstracted from experiences in a very restricted set of sites and from the perceptions of one person about events in those sites. Accordingly, there is no expectation that an individual's implicit theory will have generalizability.

There is also a general awareness among teachers that what works in one classroom context will probably not be effective in another. Even where a single class is involved, teachers know well that differences in time of day for a lesson, class moods, and the focuses of preceding lessons can render some approaches inappropriate and ineffective. The implicit theory held by one teacher cannot be used in all the contexts in which that teacher works, but has to be adapted to suit the special circumstances of each context.

1. Importance of Recognizing Teachers' Implicit Theories

Interest in the implicit theories of teachers has sparked reforms in research, teaching, and teacher education, many of which are only beginning to gain momentum in the 1990s. Recognition of the existence of such theories and their influence on classroom practice, learning to teach, and the fate of educational innovations reflect a new appreciation of the value of practical knowledge and the importance of experience in, and reflection on, practice. The new status accorded practical knowledge and implicit theories, a status previously denied them, has resulted in shifts in the focus and conduct of research on teaching. The agenda in research on teaching is no longer dominated by a search for causal links between teaching processes and student outcomes ("process–product" or "black box"

research), but by attempts to see into the minds of teachers, to document their thinking and knowledge ("glass box" research). The impact of this shift generally has been to elevate the teacher from a position of potential user of research knowledge to one of source and creator of such knowledge. This shift has required a redefinition of the teacher's role in research from being simply an object of research to being a collaborator or partner. The case for recognizing teaching as a profession could not fail to be strengthened by these developments.

The role of teachers in their own professional development has also undergone some marked changes. Professional development is no longer seen as something done to teachers but as something teachers do to themselves. Hence teachers are now viewed as principal agents in promoting their own professional growth. Consequently, the climate is now more favorable for teachers to take the initiative in professional development matters. A much higher priority is given to teachers sharing knowledge with colleagues, reflecting on practice, and articulating their personal philosophies. Where such activities have occurred, teachers have become aware of their belief systems and how their frames of reference affect their teaching roles. By understanding their own implicit theories, teachers are in a better position to improve the quality of their professional actions.

Another worthwhile development has involved teachers exploring their personal metaphors for teaching. Researchers who sponsored this work have reported teacher disclosure of aspects of their practical knowledge of which they were previously not aware (Munby and Russell 1989). Others (e.g., Tobin 1990) have reported that, by constructing new metaphors to reconceptualize their teaching roles, teachers have been able to effect significant changes in instructional practices and improvements in classroom learning environments. The account of the teacher who developed the metaphor of "self as travel agent" to explore and implement constructivist approaches in a science classroom is an example of this (Ritchie and Russell 1991).

Recognition of the implicit theories of student teachers has significant implications for preservice teacher education as well. Assisting student teachers to become aware of their attitudes and beliefs, and the images they have of themselves as teachers, will help to reveal to them the basis for their actions in the classroom and enable them to identify more readily what is inappropriate or problematic in their implicit theories. Teacher educators also need to have knowledge of how their student teachers think. Insights into the implicit theories of student teachers provide a basis for teacher educators to plan more effective specific and generic teaching strategies to help them learn to teach and to effect changes in their beliefs. Attending to the language that student teachers use to talk about their classroom roles might also provide helpful clues about the causes of problems they face in the classroom.

2. Factors Influencing Development of Teachers' Implicit Theories

Implicit theories of teaching are not held only by those who teach. They are products of the culture and life experiences of individuals and form part of the intellectual property of every person. They probably begin to take shape in infancy during informal learning experiences in family settings, but are then molded by 13 or more years of formal schooling. This long exposure to teachers and school life inevitably informs students about the work of teachers, the classroom roles of teachers and students, the nature of knowledge, and culturally endorsed values, beliefs, and behavior norms—all important elements of implicit theories of teaching. Accounts by student teachers of information gained during this extended "apprenticeship" include frequent references to, on the one hand, model teachers and powerful illuminating learning experiences, and on the other, to deficiencies in schooling and gross insensitivity on the part of teachers to the needs of learners.

Experiences in schools and contacts with teachers have been powerful factors in shaping the implicit theories and classroom practices of those just embarking on a teaching career (Calderhead 1988). The critical role of prior beliefs in learning to teach is widely acknowledged (Hollingsworth 1989). These early perspectives or conceptions of teaching are very durable and resistant to change, so much so that they can neutralize the best efforts of preservice teacher educators to change them. In fact, the irrelevance of preservice teacher education to professional development has long been alleged by teachers.

However, the trend in the literature to be dismissive of the effects of preservice programs on implicit theories has been challenged in research from the late 1980s. Preservice teacher education programs can effect changes in beliefs, help transform subject matter knowledge into a pedagogically relevant form, and provide schemata for critically analyzing and improving schooling (Hollingsworth 1989). Another important factor in the development and refinement by teachers of their implicit theories is possession of metacognitive skills. Changes in implicit theories are more likely to occur if teachers are aware of limitations of their implicit theories and can exercise executive control over cognitive processes to extend and refine them (Calderhead 1988, Hollingsworth 1989).

Whereas opinion is divided as to the impact of on-campus components of preservice programs on implicit theories, there is no such ambivalence about the effects of classroom experience. It is widely asserted that most of a teacher's implicit theory is developed through on-the-job experience (Sanders and McCutcheon 1986). How teachers learn from experience is still somewhat unclear; however, cognitive dissonance, or discomfiture with what is, and a commitment and ability to conduct and learn from "practice-centred inquiry" are cited as key components of experiential learning (Sanders and McCutcheon 1986). The earlier view that learning to teach was simply a matter of learning and applying theory is now largely discredited.

3. Methods of Studying Implicit Theories

Implicit theories cannot be studied until they are first made explicit. Disclosure of implicit theories, however, is not easily achieved. Teachers' minds cannot simply be unzipped to allow close inspection of the contents. What compounds the problem of making the implicit explicit is that the substance and structure of implicit theories are not known completely even to the teachers themselves. Hence, asking teachers to articulate their implicit theories inevitably involves them in a process of discovery—a process in which there are few clues for determining when explanations of implicit theories are complete, accurate, and valid. Finding appropriate and valid ways of making implicit theories explicit is therefore a major methodological challenge.

Research undertaken so far has proceeded on the assumption that implicit theories can be discovered in teachers' discourse about teaching, and in their actions, since actions are overt expressions of implicit theories. Accordingly, techniques have been used which call on teachers to generate self-reports of their knowledge and beliefs about teaching. Teachers have been interviewed using approaches labeled as "clinical", "structured", "unstructured", and "ethnographic", to name but a few. Interview procedures involving the use of records of task performance to stimulate recall of in-task thinking have also been used. Teachers have been invited to keep journals or write biographical sketches and stories about themselves and their thinking, and to react to video records of teaching and written accounts of teaching incidents. Teachers have been asked to allow observers and those who wish to adopt a participant–observer role into their classrooms. The data and insights gleaned by these visitors are then used to infer features of the theories implicitly held by teachers. The repertory grid technique, based on personal construct theory and the view of humans as theory builders, has also been used to study teachers' implicit theories. In most studies, some combination of the methods outlined above has been employed.

The next step involves interpreting the data generated by the above methods and assembling models or representations of teachers' tacitly held theories in symbolic or semantic form. In this process, close collaboration between teachers and those wishing to study their implicit theories is essential to ensure that representations of implicit theories ring true. One threat to the validity of these models is the uncritical use of constructs from codified knowledge. The search for frameworks and constructs which accurately represent the ways implicit theories are held has only just begun.

4. Research in Teachers' Implicit Theories

One of the first indications of research interest in the implicit theories of teachers was given by Gage (1978), who observed that the topic might well become " . . . an additional substantive direction for research on teaching" (p. 80). Almost a decade later, the study of implicit theories of teaching was still being described as "nascent" (Clark and Peterson 1986). Over the intervening years there has been a considerable upsurge of interest in research in this field; however, while implicit theories of tertiary teachers have come under some scrutiny (see, e.g., Hughes 1990), most attention has been focused on the theories of elementary and secondary teachers and the contrasts between theories held by experienced or expert teachers and those held by novices.

In their 1986 review of this inchoate research, Clark and Peterson noted that a variety of terms was being used in studies of implicit theories: "personal perspective," "conceptual system," "principles," "practical knowledge," and "beliefs." Some of these terms have lost currency. Terms which have come into favor include "metaphor," "image," and "pedagogical content knowledge." These have not been adopted on the basis of a whim. On the contrary, their emergence reflects important advances in understanding the nonpropositional nature of teachers' knowledge and ways of conceptualizing the form and substance of teachers' implicit theories.

4.1 Metaphors for Teaching

It has been pointed out that when teachers talk about their work, their discourse is replete with metaphorical language. This, it is argued, is because " . . . the human conceptual system is defined and structured metaphorically, . . . human thought processes are largely metaphorical" (Munby and Russell 1989 p. 3). Hence, internal representations of reality are also constructed in metaphorical terms. Researchers have argued that the metaphorical language used by teachers in talking about their teaching will reveal how they have made sense of classroom realities and how they see the roles of learners and teachers. In short, analysis of the metaphors in teacher talk will disclose much about their implicit theories of teaching.

An amazing number of metaphors used by teachers to explain their approaches to teaching have been documented. The list includes teacher as cook, entertainer, counselor, timekeeper, engineer, preacher, conductor,

mother figure, horticulturalist, actor, and ship's captain. Frequently, the language of any one teacher about teaching contains references to a number of metaphors. Teachers tend to live by such metaphors—that is, the metaphors used by teachers to conceptualize their role in the classroom are manifest in and consistent with their behaviors (Tobin 1990).

This consistency can be a blessing or a blight. It is a blight when the metaphor is inappropriate or overused. Research indicates that the transmission metaphor, which represents teaching as a mechanical process of knowledge transfer, might well be in this category. Work with metaphors has gone well beyond the identification stage whereby a teacher's language is analyzed to pinpoint the metaphors that inform their teaching and thinking about teaching. Metaphors have also been used as a heuristic device to assist teachers to generate alternative metaphors to redefine their roles in the classroom and to change and improve their teaching (Tobin 1990).

4.2 Images

The notion of images has emerged as another useful way of representing components of teachers' implicit theories. Clandinin (1986), who has broken new ground in her work with this concept, views an image not just as a snapshot stored in memory of some person or event but as a mental coalescence of private and professional experiences. These coalescences or summaries of experience become an important part of a person's life force and "modus operandi." They may find expression verbally, for example as a metaphor, or practically, in a person's private and professional life. Because life experiences are rich in effect and perceived as good or bad, harmful or helpful, so too do images possess emotional and moral dimensions.

Clandinin's study of the implicit theories of two teachers provides compelling evidence of how images link the present with the past and how images constructed from past experiences can provide explanations for what teachers do in the classroom. Images isolated from the professional discourse of Stephanie, an experienced Grade 1/2 teacher in the Clandinin study, included "classroom as home," "herself as a maker," "teaching as teaching children to be makers," "the high school math experience," and "the policeman." The first of these, "classroom as home," was shown to have its origins in Stephanie's private life, namely in her view of herself as an atypical child and the contrasts she made between her home life experiences, characterized by cooperation and extensive interaction, and those she had in schools and during teacher training. In her formal education, the emphasis was on conformity and compliance.

The "classroom as home" image reflected her judgment that the kind of educational packaging she endured at school was harmful and should not have happened. This judgment gave her image a moral dimension. At the same time, the emotional dimension of her image was conveyed in her talk about the quality of relationships in families and her reactions to the depersonalizing effects of formal educational processes. The view that the classroom environment for lower elementary children should be like a home was firmly held and found expression in a range of activities—cooking, growing seeds, celebrations, displays, and farewells—as well as strenuous efforts to establish a convivial atmosphere in which students would feel comfortable and cared for.

4.3 Pedagogical Content Knowledge

A vigorous new program of research has emerged, based on the proposition that teachers' beliefs about, and understandings of, subject matter have a powerful influence on the instruction they provide. It is also proposed that teachers, through learning how to make subject matter teachable, acquire new understandings of content, how to teach it, and how students learn it. This new form of knowledge, referred to as pedagogical content knowledge, cannot be equated either with the special content knowledge of the academic expert or with the knowledge of generic principles of pedagogy. Rather, pedagogical content knowledge is regarded as a unique blend of teacher brands of subject-matter knowledge, topic-specific pedagogy, and psychology of learners and learning. Though there are cross-study variations in how pedagogical content knowledge is construed, it is generally thought to include " . . . overarching conceptions of what it means to teach a particular subject, knowledge of curriculum materials and curriculum in a particular field, knowledge of students' understanding and potential misunderstandings of a subject area, and knowledge of instructional strategies and representations for teaching particular topics" (Grossman 1989 p. 32).

Studies of the pedagogical content knowledge of experienced teachers confirm that their conceptions of subject matter are different from those held by scholars in the field (Gudmonsdottir 1990, Gudmonsdottir and Shulman 1987). Conceptions of content, however, do not stand alone within pedagogical content knowledge. Instead they are amalgamated with pedagogy to form models which are unique and personal to each teacher and undergird the teaching approach adopted by that teacher. Illustrative of these models is one from Naomi, a secondary teacher of English, who describes her model as a "layered onion" with English literature as the inner core: "Surrounding the core are layers that she (Naomi) peeled off in classroom discussions as she examined the text. The first layer involved understanding the text; the second involved probing for deeper significance and the third focused on multiple orientations" (Gudmonsdottir 1990 p. 47).

Gaps in the pedagogical content knowledge of some teachers have also been identified, as well as substantial disparities between the pedagogical content knowledge of expert and novice teachers in terms of extent, richness, complexity, and flexibility of use (Gudmonsdottir and Shulman 1987). A start has also been made on examining the contribution of specific curriculum studies to the development of pedagogical content knowledge in student teachers, but much more work still needs to be done. What is clear is that pedagogical content knowledge is central to the work of teaching and constitutes an essential part of the professional knowledge base of teachers.

4.4 Other Research

Research into teachers' implicit theories has been proceeding on several other fronts. Studies have investigated the knowledge structures or schemata that teachers use to process the plethora of stimuli that classrooms present. Experienced teachers have been shown to have schemata which enable them, by comparison with novice teachers, to screen out irrelevant classroom data more effectively, to better conserve their information-processing capacities, and to interpret classroom events in more instructionally relevant ways. The greater facility of experienced teachers in anticipating, avoiding, and handling in-class problems (behavioral or conceptual) has been attributed to their possessing better developed schemata.

The beliefs and belief systems of teachers have continued to attract the interest of researchers. The pervasive and critical influence of teacher beliefs in shaping, for example, their task performance, how they learn from experience, the environments they create, and their acceptance or rejection of new curricula has been acknowledged in numerous studies. Progress in this field has been slow, however, impeded by the deep-seated implicitness of beliefs and the intractable problems of articulating, classifying, and assessing them. The development of a theoretically based model of belief systems to facilitate systematic and comparative studies in this area is still some way off.

There have also been attempts to map teachers' implicit theories in their entirety rather than focussing on one element such as beliefs or principles. Representations of teachers' conceptualizations of teaching have included elements such as goals, beliefs, student states which teachers sought to create, strategies and conditions affecting teaching, and the relationships among these elements (Brown and McIntyre 1988, Marland and Osborne 1990). Still other research has focused on the implicit theories teachers hold about student learning, evaluation, and planning. These studies have exposed substantial differences between the theories of practitioners and textbook theories.

5. Conclusion

Though study of implicit theories of teaching is still in its infancy, it has demonstrated the crucial importance of practical knowledge and practical ways of knowing.

Some progress in revealing the substance, form, and origins of implicit theories has been made. The vital contributions of this research to delineating the professional knowledge base of teaching and to reforming the content and delivery of preservice and inservice teacher education have been recognized.

See also: Realities of Teaching; Behavioristic Theories of Teaching; Social Psychological Theories of Teaching

References

Brown S, McIntyre D 1988 The professional craft knowledge of teachers. *Scottish Educ. Rev.* Special issue: 39–47

Calderhead J 1988 The development of knowledge structures in learning to teach. In: Calderhead J (ed.) 1988 *Teachers' Professional Learning*. Falmer Press, Lewes

Clandinin D J 1986 *Classroom Practice. Teacher Images in Action*. Falmer Press, Lewes

Clark C M, Peterson P L 1986 Teachers' thought processes. In: Wittrock M C (ed.) 1986 *Handbook of Research on Teaching*, 3rd edn. Macmillan, New York

Gage N L 1978 *The Scientific Basis of the Art of Teaching*. Teachers College Press, Columbia University, New York

Grossman P L 1989 Learning to teach without teacher education. *Teach. Coll. Rec.* 91(2): 191–208

Gudmonsdottir S 1990 Values in pedagogical content knowledge. *J. Teach. Educ.* 31(3): 44–52

Gudmonsdottir S, Shulman L S 1987 Pedagogical content knowledge in social studies. *Scand. J. Educ. Res.* 31(2): 59–70

Hollingworth S 1989 Prior beliefs and cognitive change in learning to teach. *Am. Educ. Res. J.* 26(2): 160–89

Hughes J A 1990 The teaching theories of community college faculty. Paper presented at the annual meeting of the Association for the Study of Higher Education, Portland, Oregon

Marland P, Osborne A 1990 Classroom theory, thinking and action. *Teaching and Teacher Education* 6(1): 93–109

Munby H, Russell T 1989 Metaphor in the study of teachers' professional knowledge. Paper presented at the annual AERA meeting, San Francisco, California

Ritchie S M, Russell B 1991 The construction and use of a metaphor for science teaching. Paper presented at the annual AARE conference, Surfers' Paradise,

Sanders D P, McCutcheon G 1986 The development of practical theories of teaching. *Journal of Curriculum and Supervision* 2(1): 50–67

Tobin K 1990 Changing metaphors and beliefs: A master switch for teaching. *Theory Pract.* 29(2): 122–27

Further Reading

Batten M, Mailand P, Khamis M 1992 *Knowing How to Teach Well. Teachers Reflect on Their Classroom Practice*. Research Monograph No 44, ACER, Mellbourne

Calderhead J, Robson M 1991 Images of teaching: Student teachers' early conceptions of classroom practice. *Teaching and Teacher Education*. 7(1): 1–8

Grimmett P P, Mackinnon A M 1992 Craft knowledge and the education of teachers. *Rev. Res. Educ.* 18

Johnson S 1990 Understanding curriculum decision-making through teacher images. *J. Curric. St.* 22(5): 463–71

Johnson S 1992 Images: A way of understanding the practical knowledge of students. *Teaching and Teacher Education* 8(2): 123–36

Kagan D M 1990 Ways of evaluating teacher cognition: Inferences concerning the goldilocks principle. *Rev. Educ. Res.* 60(3): 419–69

Leinhardt G 1990 Capturing craft knowledge in teaching. *Educ. Researcher* 19(2): 18–25

Marshall H H 1990 Metaphor as an instructional tool in encouraging student teacher reflection. *Theory Pract.* 29: 128–32

Pinnegar S, Carter K 1989 Comparing theories from textbooks and practising teachers. *J. Teach. Educ.* 40(1): 20–27

Provenzo E F, McCloskey O S A, Kottkamp R B, Cohn M M 1989 Metaphor and meaning in the language of teachers. *Teach. Coll. Rec.* 90: 551–73

Tamir P 1991 Professional and personal knowledge of teachers and teacher educators. *Teaching and Teacher Education* 7(3): 263–68

SECTION III

Instructional Programs and Strategies

Introduction

L. W. Anderson

Instructional programs and strategies enable educators to translate theories and models into practice. Specifically, instructional programs and strategies are the "master plans" for these translations. Once a decision has been made as to the appropriate master plan, teaching skills and techniques are used to operationalize them (see Part A, Section IV).

In this section, six instructional programs and three strategies are identified and discussed. Some of these programs and strategies are unique to specific academic disciplines (e.g., science laboratory instruction, simulations and games), but most are appropriate to all disciplines (e.g., direct instruction, open education, reflective teaching).

The programs and strategies described in this section differ on a number of dimensions. Three are discussed in this introduction. They are: (a) the amount of teacher direction, (b) the size and composition of the learning group, and (c) the impact of the program or strategy on teachers.

1. Teacher Direction

Teacher direction can be conceptualized as a continuum ranging from direct to indirect. Alternatively, the poles of this continuum can be termed formal and informal (Thibadeau).

The direct or formal end of the continuum is exemplified by the entry on direct instruction. When using direct instructional strategies teachers explain, demonstrate, model, guide, provide practice, and give feedback. They are "in charge." Like all instructional programs, the intended outcomes of direct instruction can vary from the acquisition of basic skills to the ability to develop and use cognitive strategies effectively (Rosenshine and Meister).

Open education (Thibadeau) and many forms of individualized instruction (Anderson) define the other end of the continuum. Thibadeau offers the following features of open education: learning by doing, informal styles of teaching, student choice of activity, and

richness of learning materials to encourage student exploration. These features also tend to be common to Individually Guided Education (IGE), the Personalized System of Instruction (PSI), and the Adaptive Learning Environments Model (ALEM) (Anderson).

There is increasing realization and evidence that some midpoint on the continuum is, in fact, most effective. Teachers need to provide structure and guidance for students; the question is how much of each should be provided (Tamir, Thibadeau, Slavin). Too much structure and guidance deny students the responsibility for their own learning; too little grants students license to learn (or not learn) as or what they wish.

2. Size and Composition of the Learning Group

What is the optimal group size for teaching students? The authors of these entries differ in their answer to this question. Some would advocate that, initially, teachers should instruct the entire class (Rosenshine and Meister, Guskey). Others would promote the formation of small groups (e.g., two of five students) (Slavin, Hegarty-Hazel). Still others would suggest that the most effective instruction occurs between a single teacher and a single student (Helmke and Schrader, Anderson).

Similar disagreements exist with regard to the composition of the learning groups, regardless of their size. Thibadeau recommends the formation of multiage groups (that is, students of different ages in the same group). Slavin supports the formation of multiachievement groups (that is, groups composed of students who differ in their prior achievement). In contrast, Guskey supports the formation of "mastery" and "nonmastery" groups based on their initial achievement during each instructional unit.

The vast majority of the authors of the entries in this section agree that both the size and composition of the learning groups depends on the purpose or goal of learning. In addition, because purposes change, a

137

variety of grouping practices is likely to be needed if overall teaching effectiveness is to be achieved.

3. *Programs as Prescriptions versus Guidelines*

While some teachers see instructional programs as *prescriptions* (Anderson, Villar-Angulo), the authors of most of these entries see them as providing *guidelines* for teachers. In this regard, Helmke and Schrader remind us that even the so-called "prescriptions" in the diagnostic-prescriptive strategy are, in fact, "tentative hypotheses."

Because these instructional programs provide guidelines, teachers cannot simply assume the programs will "work" (or in the case of more skeptical teachers, will not "work"). Rather teachers must be cognizant of their and their students' successes and failures, seek reasons for them, and look for alternatives that will increase the probability of success (Villar-Angulo, Helmke and Schrader). In this regard, Villar-Angulo suggests a three-stage process: (a) technical rationality (in which teachers plan their actions based on what they know); (b) practical action (in which they engage in these actions); and (c) critical reflection (in which teachers monitor the effectiveness of their teaching and make adjustments accordingly).

In his entry, Villar-Angulo contrasts reflective teaching with two alternatives. The first is the "mindless following of learning theories [or instructional programs based on these theories]." The second is the use of "unexamined teaching practices." It is this second alternative that has led to the barriers to change described below.

4. *Barriers to Programmatic Change*

For generations of educators, the norm has been whole-class, teacher-directed instruction (Cuban 1984) with teachers "doing their own thing." The authors of the entries in this section have clearly made the claim that changes must be made if educational effectiveness is to be increased dramatically. At the same time, however, these authors realize that such change will not be easy. In this regard, they have identified some of the major barriers that must be removed if change efforts are to be successful. Among the most frequently cited barriers are time and effort, classroom control, and external pressures.

The majority of the instructional programs described in this section require an increased workload on the part of teachers (Thibadeau). Workload may be increased by having to locate and provide alternative instructional materials and resources (Thibadeau, Anderson) or by virtue of spending time with students who need more time to learn (Guskey).

The majority of these programs also require teachers to confront the problem of classroom control.

The question, as posed by Thibadeau, is how to maintain order without being authoritarian. Many teachers maintain order by virtue of their status in the classroom. Alternatives must be found if order is to be maintained when "teacher as knowledge-giver" is replaced by "teacher as facilitator-of-learning" (Thibadeau).

Teachers experience severe external pressures which may lead to their acceptance of traditional practices and the status quo. In some countries, one of the most severe pressures stems from the need to cover a certain amount of content in a specific period of time (Guskey, Tamir). Teachers must confront the fact that requiring students to achieve mastery (Guskey) or helping them induce concepts (Tamir) takes more time than simply presenting material to students for their consideration and use.

In addition, teachers may find themselves having to produce students who not only learn but are able to demonstrate their learning on some type of external examination or assessment. The evidence of the effectiveness of many of these programs included in this section is fairly strong in terms of problem-solving, critical thinking, curiosity, conflict resolution, and self-esteem (Slavin, Tamir, Thibadeau). On the other hand, there is little evidence of superior performance of the students in these programs on standardized achievement tests. Moreover, when economic factors are considered, the evidence of effectiveness that does exist is typically overwhelmed by the costs involved in their design and implementation (Anderson).

5. *Conclusion*

Teachers have a wide variety of instructional programs and strategies at their discretion. These programs and strategies differ in terms of the amount of teacher direction, the number and type of students being taught at any given time, and the way that the programs and strategies impact on teachers. Teachers must select from among these programs and strategies based on their purpose in teaching, their understanding of the teaching-learning process, and considerations of cost effectiveness. Furthermore when a selection is made, teachers must be willing to confront and overcome the barriers to change that typically exist in educational systems throughout the world. If proper choices are made and barriers are overcome, then the claim that Thibadeau makes for open education can be made for virtually every educational program and strategy. "Open classrooms, *carefully organized and operated by well-trained teachers*, have much to offer teachers [and their students]."

Reference

Cuban L 1984 *How Teachers Taught*. Longman, New York

Cooperative Learning

R. E. Slavin

Organizing students to work together in small groups is an ancient practice in education throughout the world. While practice varies widely within the various countries, there is a sharp distinction between the approaches to cooperative learning prevalent in the United States and those prevalent in Europe, Israel, and the British Commonwealth. In the United States cooperative learning most frequently takes the form of relatively structured programs focused on mastery of skills, concepts, and information. These programs are likely to involve four-member, heterogeneous learning groups which remain together over a period of several weeks or more. In most cases, the groups receive recognition or occasionally grades based on their learning or performance as a group. In contrast, cooperative learning outside of the Unites States is more likely to focus either on relatively unstructured discussions or on group projects. Group membership is more likely to change from discussion to discussion and project to project. Furthermore, the purpose of the activity is at least as much socialization and general higher-order thinking or problem-solving skills as it is the learning of specific subject matter content.

Research on these different approaches to cooperative learning also differs sharply. Research on approaches developed in the United States (including that conducted in other countries) emphasizes experiments comparing cooperative and traditional methods, with a primary focus on academic achievement as the outcome of interest. Group Investigation, a structured technique based on Dewey's project method that was developed in Israel, has also been studied in experiments of this kind (e.g., Sharan and Shachar 1988). In contrast, there is far less research done on more informal cooperative learning approaches, and that which does exist tends to provide rich descriptions of the cooperative activities rather than any assessment of the outcome of those activities (e.g., Barnes and Britton 1969).

This entry presents a review of research on cooperative learning involving comparisons of cooperative and traditional approaches. With the exception of Group Investigation, all of these programs were developed in the United States. However, research on these and other closely related programs has also been conducted in Canada, Israel, Germany, the Netherlands, and Nigeria.

1. Cooperative Learning Methods

While social psychological research on cooperative learning dates back to the 1920s (see Slavin in press),

research on specific applications of cooperative learning to the classroom did not begin until the early 1970s. At that time, three independent groups of researchers in the United States and one in Israel began to develop and research the use of cooperative learning methods in classroom settings. In the early 1990s, there are researchers all over the world studying practical applications of cooperative learning principles, and there are many cooperative learning methods in use. The most widely researched are described in the following sections.

1.1 Student Team Learning

Student team learning methods are cooperative learning techniques developed and studied at Johns Hopkins University. More than half of all experimental studies of practical cooperative learning methods involve student team learning methods.

All cooperative learning methods share the idea that students work together to learn and are responsible for one another's learning as well as their own. In addition to the idea of cooperative work, student team learning methods emphasize the use of team goals and team success which can only be achieved if all members of the team learn the objectives being taught. In student team learning, therefore, the students' tasks are not to do something as a team but to learn something as a team.

Three concepts are central to all student team learning methods: "team rewards," "individual accountability," and "equal opportunity for success." In these techniques, teams may earn certificates or other team rewards if they achieve at or above a designated standard. The teams are not in competition to earn elusive rewards; all (or none) of the teams may achieve the standard in a given week. Individual accountability means that the team's success depends on the individual learning of all team members. Thus, the activity of the team members is focused on tutoring one another and making sure that everyone on the team is ready for a quiz or other assessment which students will be expected to complete without teammate help. Equal opportunity for success means that students contribute to their teams by improving over their own past performance. This ensures that high, average, and low achievers are equally challenged to do their best, and the contributions of all team members will be valued.

Research on cooperative learning methods has indicated that team rewards and individual accountability are essential elements for producing basic skills achievement (Slavin 1983a, 1983b, in press). It is not enough simply to tell students to work together. They must have a reason to take one another's achievement seriously. Further, research indicates that if students are rewarded for doing better than they have in the past, they will be more motivated to achieve than if they are rewarded based on their performance in comparison to others, because rewards for improvement make success neither too difficult nor too easy for students to achieve (Slavin 1980).

There are four principal student team learning methods that have been extensively developed and researched. Of these, two are general cooperative learning methods adaptable to most subjects and grade levels: Student Teams–Achievement Divisions (STAD) and Teams–Games–Tournament (TGT). The remaining two are comprehensive curricula designed for use in particular subjects at particular grade levels: Team Assisted Individualization (TAI) for mathematics in grades 3–6, and Cooperative Integrated Reading and Composition (CIRC) for reading and writing instruction in grades 3–5.

1.1.1 Student Teams–Achievement Divisions (STAD). In STAD (Slavin 1986), students are assigned to four-member learning teams that are mixed in performance level, sex, and ethnicity. The teacher presents a lesson, and then students work within their teams to make sure that all team members have mastered the lesson. Finally, all students take individual quizzes on the material, at which time they may not help one another.

Students' quiz scores are compared to their own past averages, and points are awarded based on the degree to which students can meet or exceed their own earlier performance. These points are then summed to form team scores, and teams which achieve certain standards may earn certificates or other rewards. The whole cycle of activities, from teacher presentation to team practice to quiz, usually takes from three to five class periods.

This method has been used in a wide variety of subjects, from mathematics to language arts to social studies, from Grade 2 through college. It is most appropriate for teaching well-defined objectives with single right answers, such as mathematical computations and applications, language usage and mechanics, geography and map skills, and science facts and concepts.

1.1.2 Teams–Games–Tournament (TGT). Teams–Games–Tournament (DeVries and Slavin 1978, Slavin 1986) was the first of the Johns Hopkins cooperative learning methods. It uses the same teacher presentations and teamwork as in STAD, but replaces the quizzes with weekly tournaments in which students compete with members of other teams to contribute points to their team scores. Students compete at three-person "tournament tables" against others with similar past records in mathematics. A "bumping" procedure keeps the competition fair. The winner at each tournament table brings the same number of points to his or her team, regardless of which table it is. Thus, low achievers (competing with other low achievers) and

high achievers (competing with other high achievers) have equal opportunities for success. As in STAD, high-performing teams earn certificates or other forms of team rewards.

1.1.3 Team Assisted Individualization (TAI). Team Assisted Individualization (TAI) (Slavin et al. 1986) shares with STAD and TGT the use of four-member mixed ability learning teams and certificates for high-performing teams, but where STAD and TGT use a single pace of instruction for the class, TAI combines cooperative learning with individualized instruction. Also, where STAD and TGT apply to most subjects and grade levels, TAI is specifically designed to teach mathematics to students in Grades 3–6 (or older students not ready for a full algebra course).

In TAI, students enter an individualized sequence according to a placement test and then proceed at their own rates. In general, team members work on different units. Teammates check each others' work against answer sheets and help one another with any problems. Final unit tests are taken without teammate help and are scored by student monitors. Each week, teachers total the number of units completed by all team members and give certificates or other team rewards to teams which exceed a criterion score based on the number of final tests passed, with extra points given for perfect papers and completed homework.

Because students take responsibility for checking each others' work and managing the flow of materials, the teacher can spend most of the class time presenting lessons to small groups of students drawn from the various teams who are working at the same point in the mathematics sequence. For example, the teacher might call up a decimals group, present a lesson on decimals, and then send the students back to their teams to work on decimal problems. The teacher might next call the fractions group, and so on.

1.1.4 Cooperative Integrated Reading and Composition (CIRC). The newest of the student team learning methods is a comprehensive program for teaching reading and writing in the upper elementary grades called Cooperative Integrated Reading and Composition, or CIRC (Stevens et al. 1987). In CIRC, teachers use basal readers and reading groups, much as in traditional reading programs in the United States. However, students are assigned to teams composed of pairs of students from two different reading groups. While the teacher is working with one reading group, students in the other groups are working in their pairs on a series of cognitively engaging activities including reading to one another; making predictions about how narrative stories will come out; summarizing stories to one another; writing responses to stories; and practicing spelling, decoding, and vocabulary. If the reading class is not divided into homogeneous reading groups, all students in the teams work with one another. Students work as a total team to master main idea and other comprehension skills. During language arts periods, students engage in writing drafts, revising and editing one another's work, and preparing for publication of team books.

In most CIRC activities, students follow a sequence of teacher instruction, team practice, team pre-assessments, and quiz. That is, students do not take the quiz until their teammates have determined that they are ready. Certificates are given to teams based on the average performance of all team members on all reading and writing activities.

1.2 Jigsaw

Jigsaw was designed by Elliot Aronson and his colleagues (Aronson et al. 1978). In the original Jigsaw method, students are assigned to six-member teams to work on academic material which has been broken down into sections. For example, a biography might be divided into early life, first accomplishments, major accomplishments, major setbacks, later life, and impact on history. Each team member reads his or her section. Next, members of different teams who have studied the same sections meet in "expert groups" to discuss their sections. Then the students return to their teams and take turns teaching their teammates about their sections. Since the only way students can learn sections other than their own is to listen carefully to their teammates, they are motivated to support and show interest in one another's work.

Slavin (1986) developed a modification of Jigsaw at Johns Hopkins University and then incorporated it in the Student Team Learning program. In this method, called Jigsaw II, students work in four- or five-member teams as in *TGT and STAD*. Instead of each student being assigned a unique section, all students read a common narrative, such as a book chapter, a short story, or a biography. However, each student receives a topic on which to become an expert. Students with the same topics meet in expert groups to discuss them, after which they return to their teams to teach what they have learned to their teammates. Then students take individual quizzes, which result in team scores based on the improvement score system of *STAD*. Teams which meet preset standards may earn certificates.

1.3 Learning Together

Researchers at the University of Minnesota developed the Learning Together model of cooperative learning (Johnson and Johnson 1987). The methods they have developed and studied involve students working in four- or five-member heterogeneous groups on assignments. The groups complete a single assignment and receive praise and rewards based on the group product. Their methods emphasize team building activities before students begin working together and regular discussions within groups about how well they are working together.

1.4 Group Investigation

Group Investigation, developed by Shlomo Sharan at the University of Tel-Aviv (Sharan and Sharan 1992), is a general classroom organization plan in which students work in small groups using cooperative inquiry, group discussion, and cooperative planning and projects. In this method, students form their own two- to six-member groups. After choosing subtopics from a unit being studied by the entire class, the groups further break their subtopics into individual tasks and carry out the activities necessary to prepare group reports. Each group then makes a presentation or display to communicate its findings to the entire class.

2. Research on Cooperative Learning

More than 90 high-quality studies have evaluated various cooperative learning approaches over periods of at least four weeks in regular elementary and secondary schools; 96 of these have measured effects on student achievement. These studies all compared effects of cooperative learning to those of traditionally taught control groups on measures of the same objectives pursued in all classes. Teachers and classes were either randomly assigned to cooperative or control conditions, or they were matched on pretest achievement and other factors.

2.1 Academic Achievement

Of the 96 studies of the achievement effects of cooperative learning, 60 (63%) have found significantly greater achievement in cooperative than in control classes; 31 (32%) found no differences; and in five studies did control groups outperform the experimental groups. However, the effects of cooperative learning vary considerably according to the particular methods used.

As noted earlier, two elements must be present if cooperative learning is to be effective: group goals and individual accountability (Slavin 1983a, 1983b, in press). That is, groups must be working to achieve some common goal and the success of the group must depend on the individual learning of every group member. In studies of approaches which include these elements, effects on achievement have been consistently positive; 47 out of 61 such studies (77%) found significantly positive achievement effects. In contrast, only 13 out of 35 studies (37%) lacking group goals and individual accountability found positive effects on student achievement (Slavin in press).

Cooperative learning generally works equally well for all types of students. While occasional studies find particular advantages for high or low achievers, boys or girls, and so on, the great majority find equal benefits for all types of students. Sometimes a concern is expressed that cooperative learning will hold back high achievers. The research provides absolutely no support for this claim; high achievers gain from cooperative learning (relative to high achievers in traditional classes) just as much as do low and average achievers (Slavin in press).

2.2 Intergroup Relations

Social scientists have long advocated interethnic co-operation as a means of ensuring positive intergroup relations in desegregated settings. Contact theory (Allport 1954), the dominant theory of intergroup relations in the United States, predicts that positive inter-group relations will arise from school desegregation if, and only if, students are involved in cooperative, equal-status interaction sanctioned by the school. Research on cooperative learning methods has borne out these predictions. Specifically, students were asked to list their best friends at the beginning of the study and again at the end. The number of friendship choices students made outside their own ethnic groups was the measure of intergroup relations. Positive effects on intergroup relations have been found for STAD, TGT, TAI, Jigsaw, Learning Together, and Group Investigation models (Slavin 1985, in press).

Two of these studies, one on STAD (Slavin 1979) and one on Jigsaw II (Ziegler 1981), included followups of intergroup friendships several months after the end of the studies. Both found that students who had been in cooperative learning classes still named significantly more friends outside their own ethnic groups than did students who had been in control classes. Two studies of Group Investigation (Sharan et al. 1984, Sharan and Shachar 1988) found that students' improved attitudes and behaviors toward classmates of different ethnic backgrounds extended to classmates who had never been in the same groups. Similarly a study of TAI (Oishi 1983) found positive effects of this method on cross-ethnic interactions outside as well as in class.

The United States studies of cooperative learning and intergroup relations involved Black, White, and (in a few cases) Mexican–American students. A study of Jigsaw II by Ziegler (1981) took place in Toronto, where the major ethnic groups were Anglo-Canadians and children of recent European immigrants. The Sharan (Sharan et al. 1984, Sharan and Shachar 1988) studies of Group Investigation took place in Israel and involved friendships between Jews of European and Middle Eastern backgrounds.

2.3 Mainstreaming and Integration

Although ethnicity is a major barrier to friendship, it is not so large as the one between physically or men-tally handicapped children and their normal-progress peers. The movement called "mainstreaming" in North America and "integration" in Europe seeks to place as many children as possible in regular classrooms. This movement has created an unprecedented opportunity for handicapped children to take their place in the mainstream of society. It has also created enormous practical problems for classroom teachers, however, and thus often leads to social rejection of handi-capped children. Cooperative learning has been used to increase the social acceptance of the mainstreamed student.

The research on cooperative learning and main-streaming has focused on the academically handi-capped child. In one study, STAD was used to attempt to integrate students performing two years or more below the level of their peers into the social struc-ture of the classroom. The use of STAD significantly reduced the degree to which the normal-progress students rejected their mainstreamed classmates, and increased the academic achievement and self-esteem of all students, mainstreamed as well as normal-progress (Madden and Slavin 1983). Other research using cooperative teams has also shown significant improvements in relationships between mainstreamed academically handicapped students and their normal-progress peers (Cooper et al. 1980, Slavin et al. 1984, Slavin in press).

2.4 Self-esteem

Students in cooperative learning classes have been found to have more positive feelings about themselves than do students in traditional classes. These improve-ments in self-esteem have been found for TGT and STAD (Slavin 1983a), for Jigsaw (Blaney et al. 1977), and for the three programs combined (Slavin and Karweit 1981). Improvements in student self-concepts have also been found for TAI (Slavin et al. 1984).

2.5 Other Outcomes

In addition to effects on achievement, positive inter-group relations, greater acceptance of mainstreamed students, and self-esteem, effects of cooperative learn-ing have been found on a variety of other important educational outcomes. These include liking of school, development of peer norms in favor of doing well academically, feelings of individual control over the student's own fate in school, cooperativeness, and al-truism (see Slavin in press). In addition, TGT (DeVries and Slavin 1978) and STAD (Janke 1978) have been found to have positive effects on students' time on-task. Finally, a remarkable study in the Kansas City (Missouri) schools found that lower socioeconomic-status students at risk of becoming delinquent who worked in cooperative groups in sixth grade had better attendance, fewer contacts with the police, and higher behavioral ratings by teachers in seventh through elev-enth grades than did control students (Hartley 1976).

3. Conclusion

Research on cooperative learning supports its useful-ness for improving such diverse outcomes as student achievement at a variety of grade levels and in many subjects, intergroup relations, relationships between mainstreamed and normal-progress students, and student self-esteem. The widespread and growing use of cooperative learning demonstrates that, in addition to its effectiveness, cooperative learning is practical and attractive to teachers.

See also: Group Dynamics

References

Allport G 1954 *The Nature of Prejudice.* Addison-Wesley, Cambridge, Massachusetts

Aronson E, Blaney N T, Stephan C, Sikes J, Snapp M (eds.) 1978 *The Jigsaw Classroom.* Sage, Beverly Hills, California

Barnes D, Britton J 1969 *Language, the Learner, and the School.* Penguin, Harmondsworth

Blaney N T, Stephan S, Rosenfeld D, Aronson E, Sikes J 1977 Interdependence in the classroom: A field study. *J. Educ. Psychol.* 69(2): 121–28

Cooper L, Johnson D W, Johnson R, Wilderson F 1980 Effects of cooperative, competitive and individualistic experiences on interpersonal attraction among heterogeneous peers. *J. Soc. Psychol.* 111: 243–52

DeVries D L, Slavin R E 1978 Teams–Games–Tournament (TGT): Review of ten classroom experiments. *J. Res. Dev. Educ.* 12: 28–38

Hartley W 1976 Preventive outcomes of small group education with school children: An epidemiologic follow up of the Kansas City School Behavior Project. Education Report. National Institute of Mental Health, Rockville, Maryland

Janke R 1978 The Teams–Games–Tournament (TGT) method and the behavioral adjustment and academic achievement of emotionally impaired adolescents. Paper presented at the annual convention of the American Educational Research Association, Toronto, April

Johnson D W, Johnson R T 1987 *Learning Together and Alone,* 2nd edn. Prentice-Hall, Englewood Cliffs, New Jersey

Madden N A, Slavin R E 1983 Cooperative learning and social acceptance of mainstream academically handicapped students. *J. Spec. Educ.* 17: 171–82

Oishi S 1983 Effects of team assisted individualization in mathematics on cross-race interactions of elementary school children. Doctoral dissertation, University of Maryland, College Park, Maryland

Sharan S et al. 1984 *Cooperative Learning in the Classroom: Research in Desegregated Schools.* Erlbaum, Hillsdale, New Jersey

Sharan S, Shachar C 1988 *Language and Learning in the Cooperative Classroom.* Springer-Verlag, New York

Sharan Y, Sharan S 1992 *Expanding Cooperative Learning Through Group Investigation.* Teacher's College Press, New York

Slavin R E 1979 Effects of biracial learning teams on cross-racial friendships. *J. Educ. Psychol.* 71(3): 381–87

Slavin R E 1980 Effects of individual learning expectations on student achievement. *J. of Educational Psychology* 72: 520–24

Slavin R E 1983a *Cooperative Learning.* Longman, New York

Slavin R E 1983b When does cooperative learning increase student achievement? *Psych. Bull.* 94(3): 429–45

Slavin R E 1985 Cooperative learning: Applying contact theory in desegregated schools. *J. Soc. Issues* 41(3): 45–62

Slavin R E 1986 *Using Student Team Learning,* 3rd edn. Center for Research on Elementary and Middle Schools, Johns Hopkins University, Baltimore, Maryland

Slavin R E in press *Cooperative Learning: Theory, Research, and Practice,* 2nd edn. Allyn and Bacon, Boston

Slavin R E, Karweit N 1981 Cognitive and affective outcomes of an intensive student team learning-experience. *J. Exp. Educ.* 50:29–35

Slavin R E, Leavey M B, Madden N A 1984 Combining cooperative learning and individualized isntruction: Effects on student mathematics achievement attitudes and behaviors. *Elem. Sch. J.* 84:408–22

Slavin R E, Leavey M B, Madden N A 1986 *Team Accelerated Instruction—Mathematics.* Mastery Education Corporation, Watertown, Massachusetts

Stevens R J, Madden N A, Slavin R E, Farnish A M 1987 Cooperative integrated reading and composition: Two field experiments. *Read. Res. Q.* 22(4): 433–54

Ziegler S 1981 The effectiveness of cooperative learning teams for increasing cross-ethnic friendship: Additional evidence. *Human Organization* 40:264–68

Direct Instruction

B. Rosenshine and C. Meister

"Direct instruction" is a general term that has acquired a number of different meanings, with each meaning referring to somewhat different instructional practices. The purpose of this entry is to examine five different meanings of direct instruction, comment upon their origins, and explore the differences among them. Each meaning is explained briefly and is given a label that can be used to differentiate it from the others. First, "direct instruction" has been used in a general sense to refer to instruction led by the teacher, as in "the teacher provided direct instruction in solving these problems" (the teacher-led meaning). The term "direct instruction" has also been used to refer to three types of specific instructional procedures: (a) procedures that emerged from the teacher effectiveness research (the teacher effectiveness meaning), (b) procedures used by teachers and researchers when they teach cognitive strategies to students (the cognitive strategy meaning), and (c) procedures associated with the DISTAR program (the DISTAR meaning). Finally, some authors have used the term "direct instruction" to refer to teaching behaviors that they believe should be avoided (the undesirable teaching meaning).

1. The Teacher-led Meaning

The teacher-led meaning of direct instruction is the most general of the meanings and refers to academic instruction led by the teacher, without reference to how the instruction was done. This use of direct instruction appeared as early as 1893 in Rice's book, *The Public School System of the United States*. Rice complained that "in many of the grades the children received direct instruction for no more than two or two and a half of the five hours spent in school, the pupils being engaged in busy-work more than half the time" (pp. 153–54). Thus, for Rice, "direct instruction" was a general term, one which referred to all instruction led by the teacher.

This general term has appeared in many articles since then and remains in use in the 1990s. "In direct instruction the teacher, in a face-to-face reasonable formal manner, tells, shows, models, demonstrates, teaches the skill to be learned. The key word here is teacher, for it is the teacher who is in command of the learning situation and leads the lesson, as opposed to having the lesson 'directed' by a worksheet, kit, learning center, or workbook" (Baumann 1984 p. 287). This meaning can also be found in a description of a reading program that noted: "A child spends part of each hour receiving direct instruction from a teacher in skills development and spends the remainder of the hour in reinforcement activities under the supervision of an aide" (Broward County Schools 1974). The general teacher-led meaning of direct instruction actually encompasses the entire range of different meanings; the remaining four meanings are subsets of this meaning.

2. The Teacher Effectiveness Meaning

Another meaning of direct instruction refers to a specific pattern of instruction used by more effective teachers—effectiveness being determined by their students' scores on achievement tests. This literature is referred to as the "teacher effectiveness," "teacher effects," or "process–product" research.

The research in the process–product tradition begins by locating 20 to 30 teachers, all of whom are teaching the same grade level. All the classrooms are then administered pretests in reading or mathematics or the subject of interest. Next, observers visit the teachers' classrooms and record the frequency of oc-currence of a large number of different instructional behaviors. Such behaviors include the number and type of questions that are asked, the frequency of feedback provided by the teacher, the amount of time spent in presentation and in guided practice, and how the teacher prepares students for independent practice. At the end of these observations, all the students take a posttest, and the pretest and posttest scores are statistically analyzed to determine which teacher's classrooms made the largest and smallest gains, after adjusting for differences in the initial abilities of the students. The final step consists of comparing the instructional behaviors of those teachers whose classes made the largest gains with the instructional behaviors of those teachers whose classes made the smallest gains. These naturalistic studies and subsequent experimental studies in mathematics and reading have yielded a wealth of information on the instructional behaviors of successful teachers (see Brophy and Good 1986).

McDonald and Elias (1976) and Rosenshine and Stevens (1986) believe that the results in these studies fit a pattern they called "direct instruction." Rosenshine and Stevens concluded that, across a number of studies, when teachers taught well-structured topics (e.g., arithmetic computation, map skills), the effective teachers used the following pattern:

(a) begin a lesson with a short review of previous learning;

(b) begin a lesson with a short statement of goals;

(c) present new material in small steps, providing for student practice after each step;

(d) give clear and detailed instructions and explanations;

(e) provide a high level of active practice for all students;

(f) ask a large number of questions, check for student understanding, and obtain responses from all students;

(g) guide students during initial practice;

(h) provide systematic feedback and corrections;

(i) provide explicit instruction and practice for seatwork exercises and, where necessary, monitor students during seatwork.

Rosenshine and Stevens further grouped these instructional procedures under six teaching "functions," as shown in Table 1.

Although Hunter (1982) does not refer to her work as direct instruction, there is a good deal of similarity between the instructional procedures in her six-step lesson plan and the instructional procedures that emerged from the teacher effects research. Her work,

Table 1
Teaching functions for direct instruction based on the teacher effectiveness research

Review
    Review homework
    Review previous learning
    Review prerequisite skills and knowledge
Presentation
    State lesson goals
    Provide clear and detailed instructions and explanations
Guided practice
    Ask a large number of questions
    Check for student understanding
    Obtain responses from all students
    Guide students during initial practice
    Obtain a high success rate
Feedback and corrections
    Provide systematic feedback and corrections
Independent practice
    Provide explicit instruction and practice for seatwork exercises
    Monitor and assist students during seatwork
Weekly and monthly reviews

then, is another example of the teacher effectiveness meaning of direct instruction.

3. The Cognitive Strategies Meaning

As early as 1968 (and perhaps much earlier), researchers used "direct instruction" as a summary term for the instructional procedures used to teach higher-level cognitive tasks. For example, in summarizing the results of the 27 projects involving 20,000 students in the First-Grade Reading Studies, Dykstra (1968), one of the coordinators of the project, asserted that direct instruction in comprehension was essential. Other researchers referred to direct instruction in combining sentences (Hart 1971), in "process skills" (Deane 1972), in test-taking strategies (Woodley 1975), and in reflective thinking (Readence and Bean 1977).

Beginning around 1980, a number of investigators attempted to teach tasks such as reading comprehension by giving students instruction in higher-order cognitive strategies such as summarization and question generation. Many of these investigators used the term "direct instruction" to describe the instructional procedures that the investigator or teacher used to teach the cognitive strategies. Thus, Dermody (1988) referred to her work as "direct instruction of the specific comprehension strategies of predicting, clarifying, question-generating, and summarizing" (p. 57). Likewise, Grajia (1988) referred to her work as "direct instruction of a summarization strategy" (p. 89). Similar uses of "direct instruction" appeared in the descriptions of a number of additional studies in reading comprehension (Palincsar and Brown 1989), in scientific reasoning (Linn 1977), and in solving physics problems (Larkin and Reif 1976).

Experimental studies in which students were taught cognitive strategies in reading, writing, and mathematics have been reviewed by Pressley et al. (1990) and by Collins et al. (1990). By and large, in these studies, students who received direct instruction in cognitive strategies significantly outperformed students in the control group in comprehension as assessed by experimenter-developed short answer tests, summarization tests, and recall tests.

Some investigators have abstracted the instructional procedures that appeared in these studies with significant results to provide suggestions for using direct instruction in the learning of cognitive strategies (Collins et al. 1990, Rosenshine and Edmonds 1990). The predominant instructional procedures for teaching a cognitive strategy involve providing students with "scaffolds," or temporary supports, on which they can rely during initial learning. Some of these instructional procedures or scaffolds are:

(a) modeling of the strategy by the teacher;

(b) thinking aloud by the teacher as choices were made;

(c) providing cue cards of specific prompts to help students carry out the strategy;

(d) dividing the task into smaller components and teaching each component separately, gradually combining the components into a whole process;

(e) anticipating student errors;

(f) encouraging student thinking-aloud during strategy use;

(g) providing for reciprocal teaching by teacher and students;

(h) providing check lists;

(i) providing models of completed work.

The scaffolds are diminished as students learn the strategy and become independent.

4. The DISTAR Meaning

Another use of direct instruction is in reference to the DISTAR programs and to the specific instructional procedures that accompany those curriculum packages (Becker 1977). The acronym originally stood for Direct Instruction Systems in Arithmetic and Reading, although it is now known simply as DISTAR. The DISTAR instructional procedures overlap with the earlier meanings in that it is teacher-led and includes many of the instructional procedures also used in the teacher effectiveness meaning. However, it should be noted that instructional procedures in the teacher effectiveness meaning and those in DISTAR were developed independently.

The DISTAR procedures, developed by Englemann and his associates in the 1960s, are connected to the specific instructional materials that are part of the DISTAR package. The DISTAR procedures were never developed into general procedures for teachers as was the case with the teacher effectiveness results.

Researchers (Gersten et al. 1987) in the DISTAR tradition write that their meaning of "direct instruction" has six critical features:

(a) an explicit step-by-step strategy;

(b) development of mastery at each step in the process;

(c) specific strategy corrections for student errors;

(d) gradual fading from teacher directed activities toward independent work;

(e) use of adequate and systematic practice through a range of examples of the task;

(f) cumulative review of newly learned concepts (p. 49).

Many of the DISTAR programs have been quite successful in promoting student achievement for "at risk" students. For a review comparing the effectiveness of DISTAR and other programs for at-risk students, see Kennedy (1978). Thus, there have been experimental studies using each of the three instructional meanings in which students in the experimental groups obtained achievement results that were significantly higher than those obtained by the students in the control group.

Regardless of the success, instructional procedures in DISTAR programs, such as asking for student choral responses after very short teacher presentations, have been sharply criticized by many educators for being overly directed and rigid.

5. The Undesirable Teaching Meaning

In some of the literature, "direct instruction" is used in a pejorative sense, referring to different types of undesirable teaching. The undesirable teaching meaning is most often a statement of criticism toward various forms of teaching, which include teacher-led teaching, the teacher effectiveness pattern, and DISTAR.

Examples of this undesirable teaching meaning include descriptions of direct instruction as "authoritarian" (McKeen et al. 1972), regimented (Borko and Wildman 1986), "fact accumulation at the expense of thinking skill development" (Edwards 1981), and focusing upon tests (Nicholls 1989). Direct instruction has also been portrayed as a "passive" mode of teaching (Becker 1980), and in terms of a metaphor of pouring information from one container (the teacher's head) to another container (the student's head) (Brown and Campione †1990 p. 112).

6. The Nature of Direct Instruction

In summary, there are five overlapping uses of the term "direct instruction":

(a) all classroom settings in which instruction was led by the teacher (teacher-led meaning);

(b) instructional procedures used by effective teachers in the teacher effectiveness studies (teacher effects meaning);

(c) instructional procedures used by teachers when they taught cognitive strategies to students (cognitive strategy meaning);

(d) instructional procedures used by Direct Instruction Systems in Arithmetic and Reading (DISTAR meaning);

(e) many classroom settings in which instruction was led by the teacher, particularly settings where the teacher lectures and the students sit passively (undesirable teaching meaning).

This problem of different meaning in use for the same term occurs for other terms in education. For example, the term "Montessori" originally referred to the structured procedures used by Maria Montessori in her school, but in the 1990s "Montessori Schools" range in practice from highly structured to highly unstructured.

In educational psychology, the term "reinforcement" refers to the events that follow a behavior; but in classrooms, the term also refers to additional practice that teachers provide to reinforce the learning. The meanings of terms frequently shift as people use them, and "direct instruction" is an example of this shift during use.

6.1 Distinctiveness and Overlap

These five meanings attributed to the term "direct instruction" do not have distinct boundaries that can separate them. It is impossible to present neatly organized tables or Venn diagrams showing where and how the meanings overlap. Nor is there the luxury of modifying meanings to remove this messiness.

The first meaning, the general teacher-led meaning, is the broadest. It is so broad that it covers the entire range, and each of the remaining meanings are a subset of it. The three instructional meanings overlap a good deal. Instructional procedures such as guided practice, active student participation, and fading of teacher-directed activities appear in all three meanings, as do scaffolds such as modeling by the teacher and coaching of students. As noted, the cognitive strategy meaning was derived from research on the teaching of "less structured" tasks such as reading comprehension and scientific reasoning, and the teacher effectiveness meaning was derived from research on the teaching of "well-structured" tasks such as arithmetic computation. Nonetheless, despite these differences in origins, there are many common instructional elements in the two meanings. These common elements include the following:

(a) presenting new material in small steps;

(b) modeling of the procedure by the teacher;

(c) thinking aloud by the teacher;

(d) regulating the difficulty of the task during guided practice;

(e) guiding initial student practice;

(f) providing students with cue cards;

(g) providing systematic corrections and feedback;

(h) providing students with fix-up strategies;

(i) providing expert models of the completed task;

(j) providing for extensive student independent practice.

The undesirable teaching meaning contains a variety of criticisms of direct instruction, some of them directed at all direct instruction and some directed only at the teacher effectiveness or DISTAR meanings. For some critics, all teacher-led instruction is criticized as teacher-dominated, militaristic, and authoritarian.

Unfortunately, by criticizing all teacher-led instruction as "teacher dominated," one extends this negative label to those instructional procedures used in many of the studies cited in the cognitive strategies meaning, studies that were quite successful in teaching students cognitive strategies that promote student independence.

Within the undesirable meaning there is reference to a specific, undesirable pattern of instruction, one in which the teacher lectures and there is little or no guided practice and student participation. There is a need for a term to describe this pattern, but none is available; however, "direct instruction" is not the term that should be used to label ineffective teaching. Rather direct instruction in both the cognitive strategy or teacher effectiveness traditions is legitimate and quite useful.

6.2 Direct Instruction of Cognitive Strategies

A search of the ERIC (Educational Resources Information Center) database was made for examples of the use of the term "direct instruction." There were a surprising number of studies in which investigators used the term "direct instruction" to refer to the instructional procedures used to teach tasks such as reading comprehension, writing, and study skills. Resnick (1987) also described some 15 studies in which attempts were made to teach students general thinking skills, and she referred to the instructional procedures as "direct strategy training" (p. 25).

Further, an examination of the specific instructional procedures used in these studies—modeling by the teacher, use of cue cards and checklist, beginning with simplified material, and teaching the components of the task separately—would lead one to wonder why critics would refer to such procedures as "autocratic," "teacher dominated," and "focused on the test". Furthermore, these studies make it difficult to reconcile the critics' statements that direct instruction is only useful for teaching lower-order skills. All of these studies obtained significant results using direct instruction to teach cognitive strategies that led to improved reading comprehension, writing, and study skills.

7. Suggestions for the Future

Despite the castigations that come from supporters of the undesirable teaching meaning, the term "direct instruction" has been used consistently since the early 1960s to refer to quite legitimate educational activities, not only for the teaching of well-structured activities, but also as a summary term for instructional procedures that teach students cognitive strategies that enable them to become independent learners. The term "direct instruction" has been used consistently to describe instruction that has helped students acquire and apply cognitive strategies that in turn help them complete higher-level academic tasks. Although some authors have written that direct instruction cannot be used to teach students higher-level cognitive skills, the term "direct instruction" has been used, as part of the cognitive strategy meaning, to refer to precisely such activities.

In the future, when direct instruction is criticized, writers should refer to the specific meaning and specific practices that are being criticized. Distortions will still take place. In 1989 Nicholls wrote that the teacher effectiveness meaning stands for "tests all the time and scrub the teaching methods." But at least readers would know what direct instruction meaning and accompanying practices are being criticized.

Studies using each of the three instructional meanings have shown the validity of the direct instructional procedures. It is to be hoped that the educational community will begin to recognize the validity of each of the instructional meanings so that teachers who use the instructional procedures in cognitive strategy direct instruction, teacher effectiveness direct instruction, or DISTAR direct instruction can be proud of their contributions to student learning.

See also: Implicit Theories of Teaching; Behavioristic Theories of Teaching

References

Baumann J F 1984 The effectiveness of a direct instruction paradigm for teaching main idea comprehension. *Read. Res. Q.* 20(1): 93–115

Becker R M 1980 Teacher behaviors related to the mathematical achievement of young children. *J. Educ. Res.* 73(6): 336-40

Becker W C 1977 Teaching reading and language to the disadvantaged: What we have learned from the field research. *Harv. Educ. Rev.* 47: 518–43

Borko H, Wildman T 1986 *Recent Research on Instruction.* Beginning Teacher Assistance Program, Department of Education, Commonwealth of Virginia, Richmond, Virginia

Brophy J, Good T 1986 Teacher behavior and student achievement. In: Wittrock M (ed.) 1986 *Handbook of Research on Teaching,* 3rd edn. Macmillan, New York

Broward County Schools 1974 *Exemplary Reading Programs.* Title I Reading Center Program, Fort Lauderdale, Florida (ERIC Document Reproduction Service No. ED 108 148)

Brown A L, Campione J C 1990 Interactive learning environments and the teaching of science and mathematics. In: Gardner M et al. (eds.) 1990 *Toward a Scientific Practice of Science Education.* Erlbaum, Hillsdale, New Jersey

Collins A, Brown J S, Newman S E 1989 Cognitive apprenticeship: Teaching the crafts of reading, writing, and mathematics. In: Resnick L (ed.) 1989 *Knowing, Learning, and Instruction: Essays in Honor of Robert Glaser.* Erlbaum, Hillsdale, New Jersey

Deane E M 1972 Generalizing of process skills developed in elementary science, by fourth graders, to objectives of Florida history with implications for curriculum development. Doctoral dissertation, Florida State University, Tallahassee, Florida

Dermody M 1988 Metacognitive strategies for development of reading comprehension for younger children. Paper presented at the annual meeting of the American Association of Colleges for Teacher Education, New Orleans, Louisiana (ERIC Document Reproduction Service No. ED 292 070)

Dykstra R 1968 Classroom implications of the first-grade reading studies. Paper presented at the College Reading Association Conference, Knoxville, Tennessee (ERIC Document Reproduction Service No. ED 022 626)

Edwards C H 1981 A second look at direct instruction. *High School J.* 64: 166–69

Gersten R, Carnine D, Woodward J 1987 Direct instruction research: The third decade. *Rem. Spec. Educ.* 8: 48–56

Grajia M L 1988 Direct instruction of a summarization strategy: Effect on text comprehension and recall in learning disabled students. Doctoral dissertation, Pennsylvania State University, University Park, Pennsylvania

Hart M M S 1971 An assessment of the ability to manipulate syntactic structures as described by transformational grammar theory. Doctoral dissertation, University of Oregon, Eugene, Oregon

Hunter M 1982 *Mastery Teaching.* TIP Publications, El Segunda, California

Kennedy M 1978 Findings from follow-through planned variation study. *Educ. Researcher* 7(6): 3–11

Larkin J H, Reif F 1976 Analysis and teaching of a general skill for studying scientific text. *J. Educ. Psychol.* 72: 348–50

Linn M C 1977 Free choice experiences: How do they help children learn? Advancing education through science-oriented programs. Report PSC-20. Lawrence Hall of Science, University of California, Berkeley, California (ERIC Document Reproduction Service No. ED 139 613)

McDonald F J, Elias P 1976 *Executive Summary Report,* DHEW *Beginning Teacher Evaluation Study, Phase II, 1973–74.* National Institute of Education, US Department of Health, Education, and Welfare, Washington, DC

McKeen et al. 1972 *Peer Interaction Rate, Classroom Activity, and Teaching Style.* Center at Oregon for Research in the Behavioral Education of the Handicapped, University of Oregon, Eugene, Oregon (ERIC Document Reproduction Service No. ED 070 210).

Nicholls J G 1989 *The Competitive Ethos and Democratic Education.* Harvard University Press, Cambridge, Massachusetts

Palincsar A S, Brown A L 1989 Instruction for self-regulated learning. In: Resnick L, Klopfer L E (eds.) 1989 *Toward the Thinking Curriculum: Current Cognitive Research.* Association for Supervision and Curriculum, Arlington, Virginia

Pressley M et al. 1990 *Cognitive Strategy Instruction That Really Improves Children's Academic Performances.* Brookline Books, Cambridge, Massachusetts

Readence J E, Bean T W 1977 *Modification of the Impulsive-cognitive Style: A Review.* College of Education, Kansas State University, Topeka, Kansas (ERIC Document Reproduction Service No. ED 147 773)

Resnick L B 1987 *Education and Learning to Think.* National Academic Press, Washington, DC

Rice J M 1893 *The Public School System of the United States.* The Century Company, New York

Rosenshine B, Edmonds J 1990 New sources for improving instruction: The implicit skills studies. *Journal of Personnel Evaluation in Education* 4: 59–73

Rosenshine B, Stevens R 1986 Teaching functions. In: Wittrock M C (ed.) 1986 *Handbook of Research on Teaching*, 3rd edn. Macmillan, New York

Woodley K K 1975 Test-wiseness: A cognitive function? Paper presented at the annual meeting of the National Council on Measurement in Education, Washington, DC

Discovery Learning and Teaching

P. Tamir

"Let him not be taught science; let him discover it" (Rousseau 1773). As can be seen in Rousseau's citation the concept of discovery learning is not new. Discovery learning was a major focus of research and development during the curriculum reform movement of the 1960s. Its central role in this educational reform may be traced to the Woods Hole conference convened by the National Academy of Science in the United States, chaired by Jerome Bruner of Harvard. The discovery approach, as conceived in Woods Hole, was succinctly summarized in *The Process of Education* (Bruner 1960). Twenty to thirty years later the virtues and limitations of discovery learning are still debated in educational journals (Harris and Taylor 1983, Wellington 1981). Discovery learning has also been mentioned in association with the constructivist approach to learning (Driver 1989). In this entry the nature of discovery learning will be described, various interpretations of the role of the teacher and the student in discovery learning will be examined, findings of selected relevant research will be reported, the relationship between the discovery, inquiry, and constructivist approaches will be explored, and the future of discovery learning and teaching will be considered.

1. The Meanings of Discovery Learning and Teaching

A major problem with the concept of discovery has been its use in different contexts to describe different attributes. With regard to the process of learning it refers to the unique individual experience by which concepts evolve in the mind of the learner rather than being transmitted ready made. "Discovery applies so long as a specific rule or generalization is not mentioned by a teacher. It is usually confined to hierarchically arranged subject matter in which the learner has considerable background. With instructions he has a fairly high probability of deriving by himself correct answers and generalizations" (Wittrock 1966 p. 44). Discovery learning is the opposite of "reception" or "being told" or "being passive" (Shulman and Tamir 1973 p. 1111).

Discovery learning is commonly equated with inductive learning when the subject proceeds from the specific to the general. It is just as plausible, however, to assume that the learner begins with a high-order generalization from which he or she derives more specific conclusions and thus discovers answers and even generalizations (Wittrock 1966 p. 42). "Discovery is something that the student does beyond merely sitting in his seat and paying attention . . . Discovery is a process of search and selection . . . What is sought for and selected varies with the kind of learning that is taking place" (Gagné 1966 pp. 149–50). As far as teaching is concerned "the discovery method of teaching is a frequent description of modes of instruction that are contrasted with other forms of instruction called 'traditional', 'expository', 'guided', 'didactic', 'teacher centered', 'deductive' or 'dogmatic'" (Shulman and Tamir 1973 p. 1111).

2. Presumed Advantages of the Discovery Method

Four major advantages have been attributed by Bruner (1960) and others to the method of discovery:

(a) Discovery learning is more meaningful and hence results in better retention. "To be amenable to learning by discovery what is taught can never be meaningless, useless, or arbitrary. Instead, it must be somehow rational and structured" (Wittrock 1966 p. 29). "Instead of mechanically memorizing isolated bits of information, the student discovers the very principles which connect them" (Tamir and Goldminz 1974 p. 25).

(b) Discovery learning enhances motivation, interest, and satisfaction. Satisfaction is associated with intrinsic motivation which is derived from a drive towards competence.

(c) Discovery learning enhances the development of intellectual capacities, information, and problem-solving skills. Students learn how to discover, how to learn, and how to organize what they have learned.

(d) A generalized heuristics of discovery which has

been developed enables the students to solve problems in new contexts, thus increasing transfer of learning.

3. Presumed Disadvantages of Discovery Learning

Discovery learning has not gained easy access in most schools. Several reasons may have accounted for reservations and reluctance on the part of many teachers to adopt it (Harris and Taylor 1983, Wellington 1981). These include:

(a) unfamiliarity and lack of experience on the part of teachers;

(b) time pressure to cover the mandated curriculum;

(c) difficulties encountered by students, especially by slow learners;

(d) failure of teachers to recognize and exercise flexibility in dimensions such as guidance, sequence, and source of direction;

(e) many of the expected benefits from discovery learning do not show up in regular achievement tests;

(f) discovery learning can arouse feelings of uncertainty in both students and teachers, shaking the self-confidence of both;

(g) the image of science often conveyed through students' activities in class is mechanistic, distorted, and false;

(h) the challenge of discovery learning, especially in physics when many concepts, laws, and theories are counterintuitive, may be too high and lead to failure and dissatisfaction.

4. Dimensions of Discovery Learning

In the mid-1960s it was said about discovery learning that there was "precious little substantiated knowledge about the advantages it offers and under what conditions these advantages accrue" (Cronbach 1966 p. 77). Stated somewhat differently, "many claims for learning by discovery are made in educational psychology but almost none of these claims has been substantiated or even clearly tested in an experiment" (Wittrock 1966 p. 33). In the 1990s there are much more data to support certain positions, even though these positions may remain controversial. Major progress in this respect has become possible as people realize that discovery learning is not an "all or none" phenomenon, and that reception and discovery should be looked upon as opposites on a continuum.

Three dimensions have been frequently used to distinguish discovery from nondiscovery learning, each

Table 1
Levels of openness in the teaching of inquiry

	Problem	Ways/means	Answers
Level 0	given	given	given
Level 1	given	given	open
Level 2	given	open	open
Level 3	open	open	open

of which constitutes an independent continuum. These dimensions will be described following Shulman and Tamir (1973 pp. 1111–16).

4.1 Guidance

A useful framework for viewing the question of guidance has been suggested by Schwab (1962). In describing the use of an enquiring laboratory for the teaching of biology, Schwab first distinguishes among three components of the learning situation:(a) problems, (b) ways and means for discovering relations, and (c) answers. As can be seen in Table 1, there are a number of possible ways to permute these components to arrive at different levels of guidance or "openness and permissiveness" in Schwab's terms.

"The manual can pose problems and describe ways and means by which the student can discover relations he does not already know from his books. At a second level, problems are posed by the manual but methods as well as answers are left open. At a third level, problem, as well as answer and method, are left open: the student is confronted with the raw phenomenon . . ." (Schwab 1962 p. 55). Herron (as reported by Shulman and Tamir 1973) added the most highly guided dimension where all three levels are given and designated it as Level O, namely, discovery is missing altogether. Herron analyzed the proposed laboratory exercises in the manuals of two secondary science programs, Physical Science Study Curriculum (PSSC) and Biological Science Curriculum Study (BSCS), using the framework proposed by Schwab. He reports that of the 52 PSSC laboratory activities, 39 (nearly 80 percent) are at the zero level of total guidance. Eleven are at Level 1, two at Level 2, and none at Level 3. The data for BSCS are hardly more impressive. The BSCS Blue version laboratory materials show 45 out of 62 laboratory exercises at the zero level, thirteen at Level 1, four at Level 2 and, once again, none at Level 3. Thus, although reading the theoretical literature would surely lead to an anticipation that the new curricula would be filled with discovery teaching, Herron's analysis finds that there is a massive difference between philosophy and practice, despite the claim that the laboratory had changed from a verification-demonstration

Table 2
Variations of guidance and sequence in science instruction

	Inductive	Deductive
Guided	Examples of different organisms are given before names of phyla and principles of classifications are given (example-rule sequence).	Names of phyla and principles of classification are given. Subsequently, specific organisms are given as illustrations (rule-example sequence).
Unguided	Examples of organisms are left to students to characterize and then classify. After students have done their own classifications they may be given conventional phyla.	Principles of classification are given. Students are then confronted with an array of organisms which they must classify.

activity under traditional programs to an inquiry activity under new programs.

4.2 Sequence of Instruction

Although degree of guidance or openness in instruction is the most intuitively sensible meaning for discovery, it is by no means the most widely employed in studies of discovery teaching. Most often the more easily manipulated experimental dimension of "instructional sequence" serves as independent variable. An "inductive sequence," wherein examples or observations precede generalizations, is inevitably dubbed the discovery treatment, while a "deductive sequence," in which generalizations are provided first to be followed by illustrations, is labeled the expository or nondiscovery treatment. The facile manner in which inductive sequencing is identified with discovery reflects a prevalent misunderstanding of how science is conducted. It reflects the pervasive influence of a tradition usually attributed to Bacon and Mill with a little help from generations of science textbook writers who managed to compound the problem by badly misinterpreting Dewey on scientific method. It should be noted that contemporary philosophy and history of science has rejected characterizing science as an objective inductive process. The analyses of scientific thought by Popper, Schwab, Kuhn, Medawar, and others have amply demonstrated the hypothetico-deductive character of modern science. This implicit allegiance to the Baconian inductive myth may reflect how far from current thinking about science are many of those who conduct empirical studies of teaching and learning science.

Table 2 illustrates the interdependence of the guidance and sequence versions of discovery as independent variable. A guided sequence can be inductive or deductive. An inductive presentation can be highly guided or very open. The research on the effects of sequence has not been very productive. One of the reasons for this may be the limited way in which it has been experimentally manipulated. There are at least four different levels at which one can look at the educational consequences of instructional sequence:

(a) the order in which the elements of instruction are presented within a single lesson;

(b) the order in which lessons are sequenced within an instructional unit;

(c) the order in which units are sequenced within an instructional term (may be of several months, half-year, full academic year, or even several years' duration);

(d) the order in which instructional programs are sequenced and/or correlated across a multiyear curriculum.

In the early 1970s, the experimental studies of sequence in science learning, and school learning generally, were almost exclusively of the first type—manipulations of within-lesson sequence. The remaining three levels remained relatively free of empirical trammeling albeit extremely important for educational planning and curriculum development.

Since the 1970s the place of the laboratory in the sequence has received considerable attention. Thus in an inquiry-oriented course the laboratory should lead and take place prior to the theoretical study of the topic in class, or to the presentation of its findings in the textbook (Schwab 1962). Certain particular sequences have been employed and found to be particularly effective. A good example is the "learning cycle," which has been described in detail and its effectiveness confirmed experimentally (Lawson et al. 1989).

4.3 Source and Direction of Classroom Transactions

A different quality often attributed to the inquiring classroom or the discovery method of teaching is the active and initiatory role of the learner. Though this role may be influenced by the degree of guidance, it can be more readily indexed by identifying who initiates and controls the transactions in a learning situation—the teacher or the student.

An example of a student-controlled transaction is the inquiry-training approach to the teaching of science developed by Suchman around 1960. After being shown a brief film clip of an intrinsically anomalous event, the students must conduct the ensuing inquiry through interrogation of the teacher in a format much like "Twenty Questions." This is quite different from what is classically called the "Socratic Method." In Socratic teaching, students are encouraged to formulate principles to account for some phenomenon or to resolve an apparent problem. The teacher then takes control through a series of skillful questions to confront the student with contradictions or internal inconsistencies in the student's position. The teacher usually makes use of a variety of examples, analogies, or metaphors in Socratic teaching. The control of the transaction is clearly in the hands of the teacher.

Ironically, although the control and direction of communications are exactly opposite in the two examples, both are usually classified toward the discovery/inquiry end of the pedagogical continuum. This is probably because both methods employ a great deal of discussion and this characteristic is usually associated with the inquiring classroom. Schwab has always made a great deal of the role of discussion as an instructional technique, both in his earlier "Eros and education" (Schwab 1954) and in his later work on science teaching (Schwab 1962). The lecture, characterized by high levels of guidance (problems, ways and means, and answers all given), typically deductive sequencing, and teacher control of transactions with little or no pupil participation, stands firmly as the epitomization of traditional teaching method. Its diametric opposite would be minimum guidance (problems, methods, and answers all left to student invention or discovery) and undetermined sequences left to student control. Examples of such minimum guidance and a great deal of students' interdependence are the exploration phase in the "learning cycle" (Lawson et al. 1989), the BSCS Second Course *Interaction Between Ideas and Experiments*, and individual research projects carried out by students, usually after school hours.

It should be emphasized that between the two extremes of method just delineated lie an impressive variety of pedagogical procedures. Even though more research on discovery learning is available in the 1990s than in the 1970s, it is still difficult to make sense of the data and apply them in teaching, since few researchers bothered to define their instruction in terms of the dimensions described above. It is hoped that future research will fare better in this respect.

5. Discovery and Inquiry

Learning by discovery is often considered to be identical to learning by inquiry. Indeed there are many similarities between inquiry and discovery, yet they are different. Bruner's conception of the structure of the disciplines implies that any learner, if guided properly, can discover that structure. Schwab's conception of structure is fundamentally different. For Schwab structure such as that of science is not an existing entity to be discovered, but rather a framework imposed by the scientist on the subject matter. Hence,

one can talk about inquiry as a property of science or as an instructional method which is similar to discovery. As already observed by Shulman and Tamir (1973 p. 1104) Schwab's distinction between "science as enquiry" and "teaching–learning as enquiry" is an important one. The first defines the substantive focus of the classroom—what is taught and learned. The second refers to the syntax of the classroom and its consequences, the nature of the transactions that will be conducted, the enquiry skills that will be mastered, and the attitudinal "metalessons" that will be learned. In this definition of teaching–learning as enquiry, the activity in which the student participates is not scientific enquiry per se but the critical analysis, interpretation, and evaluation of reports of scientific enquiry. Although this simulates many of the processes in which the scientist engages reflectively during enquiry, it does not require the student to conduct original enquiries in a laboratory.

Schwab (1962) proceeds to contrast the "dogmatic classroom" and the "enquiring classroom" in terms of the ends they seek and the means they employ to achieve those ends. The aim of the enquiring classroom "is not only the clarification and inculcation of a body of knowledge but the encouragement and guidance of a process of discovery on the part of the student" (p. 66). After Schwab (1962) characterizes the full range of activities and purposes of the enquiring classroom, he observes that it is "by no means the only version nor necessarily the most desirable version in all schools for all students. Of the two components—science as enquiry and the activity of enquiring—it is the former which should be given first priority as the objective of science teaching in the secondary school" (p. 71). Criticism and reservations have usually alluded to inquiry as a teaching method, namely discovery learning. The desirability of the conception of "science as inquiry" rather than "rhetoric of conclusions" has reached a high level of consensus among science educators.

6. Discovery and Constructivism

There is now extensive research that shows that "what pupils learn from lesson activities, whether these involve talk, written text, or practical work, depends not only on the nature of the tasks set but on the knowledge schemes that pupils bring to these tasks . . .Learning involves progressive development and restructuring of learners' knowledge schemes" (Driver 1989 p. 84). Since it is assumed that knowledge schemes are constructed by the student, this process of learning has been broadly termed constructivist.

Since knowledge construction is an active process of the learner, the learning process appears to be very similar to discovery learning. However, whereas discovery learning refers to construction done by individual students based on their direct experiences, the constructivist approach realizes that the socially and culturally constructed ideas, principles, theories, and models "cannot all be discovered by individuals through their empirical enquiry . . . Learning involves being initiated into the culture of science . . . Learners need to be given access not only to physical experiences but also to the concepts and models of conventional science" (Driver 1989 p. 85). Thus the construction process involves all kinds of input including discovery and reception inputs, and the role of the teacher is to help pupils process the inputs and construct their knowledge as well as appreciate and apply it.

7. Research Findings

Shulman and Tamir (1973) concluded their review by cautiously stating that "although it has repeatedly been noted that no firm evidence in support of the superiority of discovery learning exists, there are enough suggestive studies and strong advocates, such as Schwab, to maintain the seriousness of the hypothesis that under certain conditions, such as those in which highly transferable problem-solving proficiencies and attitudes toward inquiry in science are the objectives of instruction, those sorts of activities advocated by Bruner or Schwab are more likely to be fruitful than those so strongly supported by Gagné or Ausubel" (p. 1118). The following review of 20 years of subsequent research supports that conclusion. Unfortunately, empirical research carried out since the early 1970s on discovery learning has been scarce. The studies described in the following sections represent a variety of methodologies and were carried out in different countries.

7.1 Meta-analysis

A special issue of the *Journal of Research in Science Teaching* (1983) reports results of several meta-analyses which reflect findings of about 20 years of research. Three of these analyses are relevant to this entry's topic. Shymansky et al. found that the performance of the average student exposed to the discovery-oriented curricula of the 1960s exceeded the performance of 65 percent of the students who studied traditional curricula (pp. 387–404). Wise and Okey found that the average effect size for cognitive achievement was 0.41, whereas the effect size for other outcomes was only 0.15—both in favor of discovery learning (pp. 405–17). Finally, Lott found no difference (effect size 0.06) between inductive or deductive instruction in terms of student achievement.

7.2 Theoretical Analysis and Synthesis of Research Findings

Chi (1991) discusses the relationship between the process of making scientific discoveries and the process

of learning science. She notes that the comparisons which are often made between scientific thinking and scientific discovery lead to the metaphor of the lay adult or the child as an intuitive scientist. Since it seems to be impossible to capture the actual process of discovery, she suggests that research should focus on the structure of the mental representation at the time that such discovery was made. Hence research on the first two steps in the discovery process, sensing anomalies and formulating a problem, appear to be more profitable than the common focus on the final steps, formulating and testing the hypotheses. Since the first two steps depend on and stem from a conceptual change, teaching for conceptual change is an essential component of scientific discovery and consequently of learning by discovery as well. "The processes of discovery by medieval students and the processes of learning by naive students must be similar because they both require this radical conceptual shift" (Chi 1991 p. 10). An important implication of this statement for teaching is that "to have students find out themselves would be . . .too difficult for students to undertake" (Chi 1991 p. 14). Instead, it is preferred to teach the correct scientific theory as a prerequisite for discovery. Finally, it is not necessary to "refute students' naive conceptions, since there is evidence that naive and scientific theories can and do co-exist in the minds of expert physicists . . . People are capable of maintaining two separate domains of knowledge analogous to two microworlds" (Chi 1991 p. 2).

7.3 Retrospection

In *The Process of Education*, Bruner (1960) hypothesized the existence of four major advantages to discovery learning (see Sect. 2 above). Tamir and Goldminz (1974) attempted to test these hypotheses empirically by asking science student teachers in Israel to recall from their student days one occasion of learning by discovery and to describe it in as much detail as they could. This description would serve as empirical evidence about the extent of retention. In addition they were requested to indicate their present judgment as to the effect of this learning experience regarding the presumed advantages. The following findings were made:

(a) Retention: 55 percent of the experiences described related to the college level, 45 percent to the high school and 5 percent to the elementary school. In all the cases the subjects described clearly the problem, the technical details, the process of inquiry, and the conclusions. Thus, these data serve as direct evidence for the high rate of retention obtained as a result of discovery learning. Further support for the high level of retention was given by the explicit reference of the subjects to this effect.

(b) Motivation, interest, and satisfaction: most students reported the contribution of discovery learning to be an increase in motivation, curiosity, and interest.

(c) Intellectual capabilities, information, and problem-solving skills: most students mentioned two cognitive outcomes, acquisition of new knowledge and getting insight to new relationships. Very few mentioned either application, correcting misconceptions, or developing reasoning skills.

(d) Heuristic of discovery: few students mentioned learning how to discover.

A replication of the study in a subsequent year supported the previous results and reconfirmed that for close to half of the students the major contribution of discovery learning had been a higher level of understanding and retention.

7.4 Comparative Studies Using Discovery and Non-discovery Instruction

Selim and Shrigley (1983) compared the effectiveness of discovery and expository instruction on science achievement and attitudes of fifth-grade pupils in Egypt. The results indicated that pupils taught by discovery scored higher in science achievement, both recall and application, and had a more positive attitude toward science than their counterparts who were taught by expository instruction. This was equally true for male and female pupils. Discovery learning included the following components: role playing, improvisation, conformity, discrepancy, and satisfaction. In addition to experiencing firsthand the processes of science, the pupils also played the role of inanimate objects or science concepts. For example, seven students wearing different colors of the spectrum were expected to order themselves into the sequence of the rainbow colors. It seems unclear which components of the treatment can be accounted for the results. Perhaps experiential learning in small groups is a better description of the independent variable than discovery learning.

Mulopo and Fowler (1987) compared the outcomes of Grade 11 students in Zambia learning chemistry by discovery and their counterparts taught by a traditional approach. The discovery approach resulted in higher scores of formal reasoners in understanding the nature of science and all the students in attitudes. The traditional approach resulted in higher achievement scores. Overall formal reasoners scored higher than the concrete reasoners.

8. A Look Toward the Future

Several reviews juxtaposing advantages and possible weaknesses of the discovery approach have been published (Harris and Taylor 1983, Wellington 1981).

These reviews usually base their criticism of the discovery approach on arguments associated with doubts about the purported similarity between scientific discovery and teaching by discovery. These critics make no attempt to find what happens in science classrooms and how undesirable are the common alternatives which may be characterized as "rhetoric of conclusions." Tamir's observation of many science classes indicates that in spite of their limitations the discovery–inquiry modes of instruction generally bring about better outcomes, both cognitive and affective. There exist various sources which provide circumstantial support to this conclusion. For example, as may be seen in a special issue of *The Gifted Child Today* (1989) many science museums, like that of Ann Arbor, Michigan, "encourage the natural curiosity of young people to explore, participate, and get involved in exhibits, demonstrations and activities." Similarly, "goals of the Children's Museum in Boston are to encourage curiosity, skepticism, and realism while providing opportunities for discoveries and new insights."

It has been posited that the social shift from rural to urban life has created a youth population richer in information than in experience. The implication is that the school has to provide more opportunities to learn from experience. Discovery learning has an important role in this respect. It is not suggested that discovery learning should dominate school learning. However, it is recommended that a substantial portion of learning will employ discovery approaches, provided that the necessary adjustments are made in guidance, sequence, and source of direction.

References

Bruner J S 1960 *The Process of Education*. Harvard University Press, Cambridge, Massachusetts
Chi M T M 1991 Conceptual change within and across ontological categories: Examples from learning and discovery in science. In: Giere R (ed.) 1991 *Cognitive Models of Science—Minnesota Studies in the Philosophy of Science*. University of Minnesota Press, Minneapolis, Minnesota
Cronbach L 1966 The logic of experiments on discovery. In: Shulman L S, Kieslar E R (eds.) 1966 *Learning by Discovery: A Critical Appraisal*. Rand McNally, Chicago, Illinois
Driver R 1989 The construction of scientific knowledge in school classrooms. In: Millar R (ed.) 1989 *Doing Science: Images of Science in Science Education*. Falmer Press, Lewes
Gagné R M 1966 Varieties of learning and the concept of discovery. In: Shulman L S, Kieslar E R (eds.) 1966 *Learning by Discovery: A Critical Appraisal*. Rand McNally, Chicago, Illinois
Gifted Child Today 1989 (special issue)
Harris D, Taylor M 1983 Discovery learning in school science: The myth and the reality. *J. Curric. St.* 15(3): 277–89

Journal of Research in Science Teaching 1983 20(5): 379–509 (special issue)

Lawson A, Renner J, Abraham H 1989 *The Learning Cycle.* NARST Special Publication, No. 1

Mulopo M M, Fowler H S 1987 Effects of traditional and discovery instructional approaches on learning outcomes for learners of different intellectual development: A study of chemistry students in Zambia. *J. Res. Sci. Teach.* 24(3): 217–27

Schwab J J 1954 Eros and education. *Journal of General Education* 8: 54–71

Schwab J J 1962 The teaching of science as enquiry. In: Schwab J J, Brandwein P (eds.) 1962 *The Teaching of Science.* Harvard University Press, Cambridge, Massachusetts

Selim M A, Shrigley R L 1983 The group dynamics approach: A sociopsychological approach for testing the effect of discovery and expository teaching on the science achievement and attitudes of young Egyptian students. *J. Res. Sci. Teach.* 20(3): 213–24

Shulman L S, Tamir P 1973 Research on teaching in the natural sciences. In: Travers R M W (ed.) 1973 *Second*

Handbook of Research on Teaching. Rand McNally, Chicago, Illinois

Tamir P, Goldminz E 1974 Discovery learning as viewed in retrospect by the learners. *Journal of College Science Teaching* 1: 23–26

Wellington J J 1981 "What is supposed to happen, Sir?" Some problems with discovery learning. *School Science Review* 63(222): 167–73

Wittrock M C 1966 The learning by discovery hypothesis. In: Shulman L S, Kieslar E R (eds.) 1966 *Learning by Discovery: A Critical Appraisal.* Rand McNally, Chicago, Illinois

Further Reading

Ausubel D P 1968 *Educational Psychology: A Cognitive View.* Holt, Reinhart and Winston, New York

Henson K T 1980 Discovery learning. *Contemporary Education* 51(2): 101–03

Shulman L S, Kieslar E R (eds.) 1966 *Learning by Discovery: A Critical Appraisal.* Rand McNally, Chicago, Illinois

Individualized Instruction

L. W. Anderson

Individualized instruction can be defined as an attempt on the part of teachers and/or school administrators to adapt instruction to individual differences among students so that their personal, social, and academic growth is enhanced beyond that possible with traditional, nonindividualized instruction (Washburne and Marland 1963). The relationship between individualized instruction and student learning is quite clear, since, as Hunt (1981) has pointed out, "Teachers' adaptation to students is the heart of the learning process" (p. 59). During the 1980s, the terms "individualized instruction" and "adaptive education" came to be used interchangeably. However, with the exception of a brief discussion of the Adaptive Learning Environments Model, the term "individualized instruction" will be used throughout this entry.

1. A Brief History of Individualized Instruction

The importance of adapting to individual differences has been recognized as a key component of instruction since at least the fourth century BC (Corno and Snow 1986). In more modern times attempts to individualize instruction can be traced fairly directly to the work of Frederic Burk of the San Francisco State Normal School at the beginning of the twentieth century (Kulik 1982). In the 1920s, Carleton Washburne, Burk's student, brought both the concept and application of

individualized instruction to international attention with his Winnetka plan (Washburne and Marland 1963). Several other individualized instructional plans were developed during the 1920s, including the Dalton plan in the United States (Lawry 1985) and the Decroly method in Belgium (Dubreucq-Choprix 1985). The twenty-fourth yearbook of the National Society for the Study of Education, published in 1925, was devoted entirely to individualized instruction (Whipple 1925).

This attention to individualized instruction, however, was short-lived. By the end of that decade, "meaningful experimentation on individualized instruction virtually stopped, and individualized systems began to fade from view" (Kulik 1985 p. 2799). Almost no discussion or use of individualized instruction took place during the late 1930s, the 1940s, or the 1950s.

The mid-1960s and early 1970s brought renewed interest in individualized instruction. Programs developed around the philosophy and principles of individualized instruction began to proliferate. Among the most popular of these programs were Individually Guided Education (IGE), Individually Prescribed Instruction (IPI), Mastery Learning, Personalized System of Instruction (PSI), and Program Learning in Accordance with Needs (PLAN) (Kulik 1982, Corno and Snow 1986, Fletcher 1992).

By the late 1970s, however, individualized instruction was on the decline (Rothrock 1982). By the

Table 1
The relationship between individual differences and instructional adaptations

Nature of Individual Differences	Primary Instructional Adaption
Ability	Ability grouping, tracking, or streaming; assigning tasks of appropriate complexity and difficulty
Learner characteristics and learning styles	Different methods or modes of presentation (e.g., highly structured, visual displays)
Desire to learn	Teacher enthusiasm; high level of student success and/or interest
Rate of learning	Student pacing

late 1980s, it was rarely seen in any schools worldwide. For example, in a large-scale international study involving 429 classrooms located in 275 schools in eight countries representing five continents, teachers were asked how often they individualized instruction (Anderson et al. 1989). Their response options were "very frequently," "often," "sometimes," and "rarely, never." Across all countries, an average of one-fifth of the teachers reported that they rarely if ever used individualized instruction. In contrast, only 1 in 20 teachers reported that they used individualized instruction very frequently. Observational data collected in the classrooms confirmed the accuracy of these self-reports.

2. The Nature of Individual Differences Among Students

Before instruction can be adapted to differences among students, the nature of these differences must be understood. Students can differ in terms of their ability (i.e., what they are capable of learning), their characteristics and learning styles (i.e., how they learn), their desire to learn (i.e., how much they want to learn), or their learning rates (i.e., how fast they learn). Unfortunately, many individualized instructional programs attempt to adapt to as many of these differences as possible, thus making it difficult either to determine or explain their success or failure.

Furthermore, differences among students can be viewed as permanent or temporary. As shall be seen, most individualized instructional programs assume that differences among students are permanent (i.e., students will always differ in terms of their abilities, learning styles, motivation, and/or rate of learning). As shall also be seen, mastery learning is a noteworthy exception to this assumption. The relationship between the nature of individual differences and the

accommodations made in the instructional program is summarized in Table 1.

2.1 Adapting to Differences in Student Ability

As shown in Table 1, one method of adapting instruction to individual differences in student ability is to place students in different curricula or different courses within a curriculum. This practice, called ability grouping, streaming, or tracking, is common throughout the world, particularly at the secondary level. Within these curricula or courses, careful attention is often given to the sequencing of content and objectives so that success in earlier units enhances the likelihood of success in later units.

Researchers have questioned the extent to which students, particularly those in the lower groups or tracks, benefit from this attempt to individualize instruction (Slavin 1987a). Specifically, students in lower track courses tend to receive exposure to less demanding topics and skills, cover less material, be taught by the weaker teachers, and engage in more drill and practice activities. At the same time, however, students in upper track courses who receive more complex and accelerated curricula or content do benefit more than their peers of similar ability who are placed in heterogeneous classrooms (Kulik and Kulik 1984). As a consequence, this approach to individualized instruction results in increasing academic differences between students in higher and lower tracks over time (Oakes 1992).

A second way of adapting to individual differences in ability is to assign students tasks at appropriate levels of difficulty. There is substantial empirical support for a correlation between assigning appropriate tasks and higher levels of student achievement (Fisher et al. 1980, Mortimore et al. 1988). Tasks of appropriate difficulty are likely to foster or ensure students' success, a factor which is related to student motivation and is therefore, addressed below in Sect. 2.3.

Many teachers advocate ability grouping because it is easier to assign tasks that are of appropriate difficulty for large numbers of students. It should be pointed out, however, that ability grouping is not the only way to ensure that tasks of appropriate difficulty are assigned to students. It is both possible and desirable to assign different tasks to different students in the same classroom. With the exception of primary-school reading classes, however, this practice is seldom used.

2.2 Adapting to Differences in Student Aptitudes or Learning Styles

Differences in student learning may be attributed to differences in student personality, specific learning abilities, and cognitive styles (Snow 1985). In combination, these differences are included under the general rubric of aptitude (Corno and Snow 1986).

Adaptations to these differences may take one of two forms. First, students can be placed in a setting or an environment which matches their aptitudes broadly defined (Hunt and Sullivan 1974). Highly anxious students, for example, can be placed in a more structured learning environment, whereas less anxious students can be placed in a less structured learning environment (Corno and Snow 1986). Similarly, students who prefer to learn visually can be taught using visual representations of the subject matter, while those who prefer to learn auditorily can be given a tape recording of the same material (Dunn and Dunn 1979). In this form of adaptation, the decision to place students in appropriate learning environments rests with the teacher.

Second, alternative instructional routes to successful learning can be provided to students, who then select the one or ones most appropriate for them. For example, the same information can be included in a textbook or on audiotape, with or without accompanying visual representations. In this example, four instructional routes are available to students (textbook with visuals, textbook without visuals, audiotape with visuals, and audiotape without visuals). Unlike the first form of adaptation to differences in student aptitudes, the choice of instructional route in this form of adaptation rests with the students.

The success of this method of individualizing instruction depends primarily on two factors: (a) the accurate assessment of the student's strengths or styles, and (b) the proper match of instructional demands with the student's strengths. When both of these issues are addressed satisfactorily, there is evidence that individualized instruction based on this framework is successful (Corno and Snow 1986).

At the same time, however, there is little evidence that simply providing a variety of instructional materials or teaching methods results in substantial increases in learning. In fact, giving students license to choose what they want to learn and/or how they want to learn is, apparently, unwise. As Mortimore et al. (1988) concluded:

the progress of pupils benefited when they were not given unlimited responsibility for planning their own daily programme of work, or for choosing work activities, but were guided into areas of study or exploration and taught the skills necessary for independently managing that work. (p. 252)

2.3 Adapting to Differences in the Learner's Desire to Learn

Many individualized instructional programs have attempted to adapt to learner differences in their motivation and/or interests. The Decroly method (Dubreaucq-Choprix 1985), for example, emphasizes the importance of adapting instruction to student life experiences and interests. Similarly, the Dalton plan (Lawry 1985) makes use of contracts between teachers and students to increase student motivation to complete tasks and units. Furthermore, teacher enthusiasm is seen as a motivating tool within the Personalized System of Instruction (Kulik 1985).

The Adaptive Learning Environments Model (ALEM) (Wang et. al. 1985) includes student choice as a key component. Within the framework of ALEM, student choice is believed to increase both motivation to learn and responsibility for learning. In addition, students who are more successful in their prior learning efforts are more likely to spend more time and effort in subsequent attempts (Fisher et al. 1980).

2.4 Adapting to Differences in Learning Rates

The vast majority of individualized instructional programs developed during the 1920s and 1930s focused on differences in the rate of student learning. In fact, Snow (1985) attributed the failure of many of these programs to their exclusive focus on differences in learning rates. Nonetheless, virtually all of the instructional programs developed during the 1960s permitted students to proceed through the programs "at their own rate." For example, Individually Prescribed Instruction (IPI) encouraged students to progress at their own pace through a series of individualized learning packets (Shimron 1976).

In support of Snow's (1985) contention, existing data question whether allowing students to pace their learning is likely to lead to higher student achievement. There is ample evidence, for example, that student pacing is negatively related to the amount of classroom time that students spend on-task (Burns 1984). Similarly, Shimron (1976) found that student pacing permits students with greater aptitude and perseverance to complete more learning units, while those with less aptitude and perseverance are able to complete fewer units. Thus, the data on the effectiveness of self-paced instruction are generally quite negative.

3. Descriptions of Selected Individualized Instructional Programs

Despite the conflicting results of research on each of

these factors or components of individualized instruction, several composite individualized instructional programs have been implemented on a large scale, have attained international recognition and acclaim, and have been used in schools and classrooms over an extended period of time. Four of these programs are briefly summarized in this section.

3.1 Individually Guided Education (IGE)

Individually Guided Education is a school-wide project which seeks not only to change the instructional program but also the basic assumptions and traditions underlying the program (Wiersma 1986). The initial step in the teaching–learning process is to determine appropriate learning objectives for students based on their achievement and motivational profiles. Once appropriate learning objectives have been determined, a variety of instructional experiences are provided to the students to enable them to achieve the objectives. The instructional program consists of a combination of teacher guidance, interaction with other students, interaction with a variety of instructional media, and a combination of small and large group activities. Student progress is assessed periodically and modifications in the students' instructional programs are made as necessary.

The expertise of the teacher is central to the success of IGE since, as Corno and Snow (1986) point out, IGE (as its name implies) is a guide for teachers, not a prescription for them. Nonetheless, Popkewitz et al. (1982) documented several inflexible and rigid applications of IGE.

3.2 Personalized System of Instruction (PSI)

Five factors differentiate PSI courses from traditional ones. Personalized System of Instruction courses are:

(a)   mastery oriented;

(b)   individually paced;

(c)   use few lectures (primarily to stimulate and motivate students);

(d)   provide printed study guides; and

(e)   administer frequent quizzes, with student proctors used to evaluate performance on those quizzes (Kulik 1985).

Personalized System of Instruction courses are organized into a series of instructional units. Each unit contains an introduction, explicit objectives, recommended instructional resources, and study questions to help students prepare for the unit tests.

Personalized System of Instruction places the primary responsibility for learning on the students themselves. In this regard, the title of Keller's article "Goodbye, teacher . . ." is quite appropriate. The role of the teacher in PSI is to establish direction for the course, design assessments of student progress, and provide resources to aid students in their learning.

3.3 Adaptive Learning Environments Model (ALEM)

The overall goal of ALEM is to "establish and maintain school environments that ensure optimal opportunities for learning success for most, if not all, students" (Wang et al. 1985 p. 191). In order to accomplish this goal ALEM combines prescriptive instruction (taken from its forebear Individually Prescribed Instruction) with independent inquiry and social cooperation (taken from open education).

Teachers employing ALEM are taught to include 12 critical dimensions in their instructional program. They are:

(a)   arranging space and facilities;

(b)   creating and maintaining instructional materials;

(c)   establishing and communicating rules and procedures;

(d)   managing aides;

(e)   diagnostic testing;

(f)   record keeping;

(g)   monitoring and diagnosing;

(h)   prescribing;

(i)   interactive teaching;

(j)   instructing;

(k)   motivating; and

(l)   developing student self-responsibility (Wang et al. 1985).

3.4 Mastery Learning

Like ALEM, mastery learning is based on the philosophy that all students can and will learn what they should or must learn in order to be successful in the later stages of schooling and life. Anderson (1985) has identified six essential features of mastery learning. These features are:

(a)   clearly specified learning objectives;

(b)   short, highly valid assessment procedures;

(c) preset mastery performance standards;

(d) a sequence of learning units, each comprised of an integrated set of facts, concepts, principles, and skills;

(e) provision of feedback of learning progress to students; and

(f) provision of additional time and help to correct specified errors and misunderstandings of students who are failing to achieve the preset mastery learning standards (p. 257).

Guskey (1987) added a seventh essential feature, namely, that there is a need for consistency among all of the previous six features. That is, assessment procedures should be consistent with the desired learning objectives. Similarly, the provision of feedback should be consistent with the learning problems identified by the assessment procedures using the mastery performance standards.

Mastery learning differs from most other attempts to individualize instruction in that its overall goal is to produce students who are themselves able to adapt to different situations, settings, and demands. Stated somewhat differently, the primary purpose of adaptation within mastery learning is to enable students to adapt. Thus, individual differences among students are believed to be alterable, not stable (Bloom 1981).

The concept of individual differences and individualized instruction underlying mastery learning, then, is quite similar to the definition of adaptive teaching offered by Corno and Snow (1986):

> Adaptive teaching is teaching that arranges environmental conditions to fit . . . individual differences. As learners gain in aptitude through experience with respect to the instructional goals at hand, such teaching adapts by being less intrusive. Less intrusion, less teacher or instructional mediation, increases the learner's information processing and/or behavioral burdens, and with this the need for more learner self-regulation. (p. 621)

4. Research on the Effectiveness of Individualized Instructional Programs

Substantial research has been conducted on the effectiveness of various individualized instructional programs. Unfortunately, summaries of this research are inconsistent. This inconsistency can in part be explained by the motive of the reviewer of the research. Proponents of a particular program tend to find quite positive results. Skeptics, critics, or cynics, on the other hand, look for and thus tend to find the program they are studying has only marginal effects. Two examples serve to illustrate this point.

Initial research on the effectiveness of mastery learning suggested that mastery learning was quite effective (Block and Burns 1976). Slavin (1987b), however, reviewed a series of studies that, from his point of view, questioned the effectiveness of mastery learning. A number of responses to Slavin pointed out a series of flaws in his analysis and suggested once again that mastery learning was very effective (e.g., Kulik et al. 1990).

Similarly, initial research on the effectiveness of the Adaptive Learning Environments Model (ALEM) attested to the effectiveness of the model (Wang et al. 1985). Simply stated, the model was taught to teachers and was properly implemented by them, the overall effect being an increase in student achievement. Fuchs and Fuchs (1988), on the other hand, argued that the available data were insufficient to suggest that ALEM was a "successful, large-scale, full-time mainstreaming program" (p. 115).

5. The Future of Individualized Instruction

In the future, individualized instruction is not likely to be widely endorsed nor widely used in schools as they are currently structured. There are at least four reasons for this prediction: tradition, effectiveness, cost effectiveness, and findings from research on teaching.

5.1 Tradition

Cuban (1984) has documented the stability of teacher-centered classrooms over the second half of the twentieth century in the United States. At the very minimum, individualized instruction requires a student-centered approach to teaching. Thus, tradition must be overcome before attempts to individualize instruction are likely to be successfully sustained.

5.2 Effectiveness

Tomic and Van Der Sidje (1989) summarize their view of the effectiveness of individualized instruction and its consequent bleak future as follows:

> The most common form of instruction, a teacher teaching a group of about 25 students, appears unlikely to change in the near future. This form is popular in part because there is little convincing evidence that other forms are more efficient. . . . Attempts to replace this form of classroom teaching by individual instruction with the assistance of such media as programmed and computer-assisted instruction did not appear to show results that justify the "abolition" of classroom teaching. (pp. 41–42)

5.3 Cost Effectiveness

In addition to the problem of tradition and the lack of consistently demonstrated effectiveness, individualized instruction suffers from a third problem. Fletcher (1992) summarizes it succinctly:

> The problem does not seem to be with individualization by itself but with the costs and increased workload that systems of individualization may require. . . . Computer

technology may help. As computing becomes more established in homes and more routinely used as a tool by students, instructors, and administrators in schools, its support of individualized instructional systems may contribute substantially to their acceptance, integration, and use. (p. 618)

5.4 Findings from Research on Teaching

Research on teaching has identified a set of variables that are quite beneficial for virtually all students. For example, virtually all students benefit from structure in their learning environment although highly anxious students tend to benefit more. Interactive teaching (i.e., teachers working directly with groups of students or individual students) has consistently been found to be associated with higher levels of student achievement for all types and levels of students. Classrooms that are work centered and purposeful result in positive student achievement as well as attitude. Finally, the provision of feedback to students and intervention and assistance at an early stage for those having difficulty learning is, once again, positively related to student learning for virtually all students.

These assertions do not mean that some students do not gain greater benefit than others from certain types of instruction. Highly anxious students may benefit more from structured instruction than do students with lower levels of anxiety. At the same time, however, both highly anxious and less anxious students may benefit somewhat from structured instruction. This point is made by Corno and Snow (1986) in their summary of the effects of cooperative learning:

> These results favor cooperative learning as a form of instruction for circumventing student inaptitude; lower ability students performed better in the small-group approach. It is noteworthy, however, that higher achievers also benefited from this form of instruction. (p. 622)

6. Conclusion

Individualized instruction is a primary example of an educational idea which has not become reality. As a concept, individualized instruction is sound. In practice, however, individualized instruction has struggled to succeed. The inertia of tradition, the questions of effectiveness and cost effectiveness, and the findings derived from research on teaching call into question both the need for and value of completely individualized instruction in schools.

See also: Mastery Learning

References

Anderson L W 1985 A retrospective and prospective view of Bloom's "Learning for Mastery." In Wang M C, Walberg H J (eds.) 1985 *Adapting Instruction to Individual Differences*. Wadsworth Publishing, Berkeley, California
Anderson L W, Ryan D W, Shapiro B J (eds.) 1989 *The IEA Classroom Environment Study*. Pergamon Press, Oxford
Block J H, Burns R B 1976 Mastery learning. In: *Shulman L S* (ed.) *Review of Research in Education* Vol. 4. Peacock, Itasca, Illinois
Bloom B S 1981 *All Our Children Learning*. McGraw-Hill, New York
Burns R B 1984 How time is used in elementary schools: The activity structure of classrooms. In: Anderson L W (ed.) 1984 *Time and School Learning*. Croom Helm, Beckenham
Corno L, Snow R E 1986 Adapting teaching to individual differences among learners. In: Wittrock M C (ed.) 1986 *Handbook of Research on Teaching* 3rd edn. Macmillan, New York
Cuban L 1984 *How Teachers Taught. Constancy and Change in American Classroom, 1890–1980*. Longmans, New York
Dubreucq-Choprix F L 1985 Decroly method. In: Husén T, Postlethwaite T N (eds.) 1985 *The International Encyclopedia of Education*, 1st edn. Pergamon Press, Oxford
Dunn R S, Dunn K J 1979 Learning styles/teaching styles: Should they . . . can they . . . be matched? *Educ. Leadership* 36(4): 238–244
Fisher C W et al. 1980 Teaching behaviors, academic learning time, and student achievement: An overview. In: Denham C, Lieberman A (eds.) 1980 *Time to Learn*. National Institute of Education, Washington, DC
Fletcher J D 1992 Individualized systems of instruction. In: Alkin M C (ed.) 1992 *Encyclopedia of Educational Research*, 6th edn. Macmillan, New York
Fuchs D, Fuchs L S 1988 Evaluation of the Adaptive Learning Environments Model. *Excep. Child.* 55(2): 115–27
Guskey T R 1987a The essential elements of mastery learning. *Journal of Classroom Interaction* 22(2): 19–22
Hunt D E 1981 Teachers' adaptation: "Reading" and "flexing" to students. In: Joyce B R, Brown C C, Peck L (eds.) 1981 *Flexibility in Teaching*. Longman, New York
Hunt D E, Sullivan E V 1974 *Between Psychology and Education*. Dryden, Hinsdale, Illinois
Kulik C E, Kulik J A, Bangert-Downs R L 1990 Effectiveness of mastery learning programs: A meta-analysis. *Rev. Educ. Res.* 60(2): 265–99
Kulik J A 1982 Individualized systems of instruction. In: Mitzel H E (ed.) 1982 *Encyclopedia of Educational Research*, 5th edn. Macmillan, New York
Kulik J A 1985 Keller plan: A personalized system of instruction. In: Husén T, Postlethwaite T N (eds.) 1985 *The International Encyclopedia of Education*. Pergamon Press, Oxford
Kulik J A, Kulik C C 1984 Synthesis of research on effects of accelerated instruction. *Educ. Leadership* 42(2): 84–89
Lawry J R 1985 Dalton plan. In: Husén T, Postlethwaite T N (eds.) 1985 *The International Encyclopedia of Education*. Pergamon Press, Oxford
Mortimore P, Sammons P, Stoll L, Lewis D, Ecob R 1988 *School Matters. The Junior Years*. Open Books, Wells
Oakes J 1992 Grouping students for instruction. In: Alkin M C (ed.) 1992 *Encyclopedia of Educational Research*, 6th edn. Macmillan, New York
Popkewitz T L, Tabachnick B R, Wehlage G 1982 *The Myth of Educational Reform. A Study of School Responses to a Program of Change*. University of Wisconsin Press, Madison Wisconsin
Rothrock D 1982 The rise and decline of individualized instruction. *Educ. Leadership*. 39 (7): 528–30
Shimron J S 1976 Learning activities in Individually Prescribed Instruction. *Instr. Sci.* 5 (4): 391–401

Slavin R E 1987a Grouping for instruction: Equity and effectiveness. *Equity and Excellence* 23 (1–2): 31–36

Slavin R E 1987b Mastery learning considered. *Rev. Educ. Res.* 57 (2): 175–213

Snow R E 1985 Aptitude-treatment interaction models. In: Husén T, Postlethwaite T N (eds.) 1985 *The International Encyclopedia of Education*. Pergamon Press, Oxford

Tomic W, Van Der Sijde P C 1989 *Changing Teaching for Better Learning*. Swets and Zeitlinger, Amsterdam

Wang M C, Gennari P, Waxman H C 1985 The Adaptive Learning Environments Model: Design, implementation, and effects. In: Wang M C, Walberg H J (eds.) 1985 *Adapting Instruction to Individual Differences*. Wadsworth Publishing, Berkeley, California

Washburne C W, Marland S P 1963 *Winnetka: The History and Significance of an Educational Experiment*. Prentice-Hall, Englewood Cliffs, New Jersey

Wiersma W 1986 Individually guided education. *Education*. 107: 85–97

Whipple G M (ed.) 1925 *Adapting the Schools to Individual Differences* (24th Yearbook of the National Society for the Study of Education, Part 2). Public School Publishing, Bloomington, Illinois

Mastery Learning

T. R. Guskey

Programs based on the ideas of "mastery learning" have excited educators since the early 1970s. In addition, few strategies have been implemented as broadly or evaluated as thoroughly. Mastery learning programs operate in nations around the world at every level of education, from preschool to graduate and professional schools. More importantly, evaluations of these programs show that students in mastery learning classes consistently learn better, reach higher levels of achievement, and develop greater confidence in their ability to learn and in themselves as learners (Guskey and Pigott 1988, Kulik et al. 1990a).

Accompanying the excitement about mastery learning, however, has been confusion and misinterpretation (Guskey 1994). Questions are frequently raised about the essential elements of mastery learning, how those elements are applied, and the extent of change mastery learning requires of teachers interested in implementing the process. This entry will shed light on these and other related issues.

1. The Development of Mastery Learning

Although the basic tenets of mastery learning can be traced to such early educators as Comenius, Pestalozzi, and Herbart (Bloom 1974), most modern applications stem from the writings and research of Benjamin S Bloom of the University of Chicago. In the mid-1960s, Bloom began a series of investigations on how the most powerful aspects of tutoring and individualized instruction might be adapted to improve student learning in group-based classes. He observed that while students learn at different rates, virtually all learn well when provided with the necessary time and appropriate learning conditions. Under these more appropriate conditions, Bloom believed nearly all students could reach the same high level of achievement that usually is attained by only a few, top students under more traditional forms of instruction.

To determine how this result might be practically achieved, Bloom first considered how teaching and learning take place in typical group-based classroom settings. He observed that most teachers begin their teaching by dividing the material they want students to learn into smaller learning units. These units often are sequentially ordered and correspond, in many cases, to chapters in the textbook used in teaching. Following instruction on the unit, a quiz or test is administered to students covering the unit material. To the teacher, this test is an evaluation device, used to determine who learned the material well and who did not. Then, based on the results from this test, students are sorted into categories and assigned grades. To the students, however, this test signifies the end of instruction on the unit and the end of the time they need to spend working on the material. It also represents their one and only chance to demonstrate what they learned. After the test is administered and scored, marks are recorded in the grade book, and instruction begins on the next unit where the process is repeated.

When teaching and learning proceed in this manner, only a small number of students usually learn well and receive the highest marks. Bloom found only about 20 percent of the students in a class generally learn excellently what the teacher set out to teach. Under these conditions, the distribution of achievement among students at the end of the instructional sequence looks much like a normal or bell-shaped curve.

Seeking a strategy that would produce better results, Bloom drew upon two sources of information. The first was knowledge of the ideal teaching and learning situation where an excellent tutor is paired with an individual student. In other words, Bloom tried to determine what critical elements in one-to-one tutoring might be transferred to group-based instructional settings. The second source from which he drew was descriptions of the learning strategies employed by academically successful students. Here Bloom sought to identify the activities of high achieving students in group-based learning environments that distinguish them from their less successful counterparts.

Bloom saw dividing the material to be learned into units and checking on students' learning with a quiz or test at the end of each unit as useful instructional techniques. He believed, however, that the tests used by most teachers did little more than show for whom the initial instruction was or was not appropriate. If, alternatively, these checks on learning were accompanied by a "feedback and corrective" procedure, they could serve as valuable learning tools. That is, instead of using these checks solely as evaluation devices marking the end of each unit, Bloom recommended they be used to diagnose individual learning difficulties (feedback) and to prescribe specific remediation procedures (correctives).

This type of feedback and corrective procedure is precisely what takes place when a student works with an excellent tutor. If the student makes an error, the tutor first points out the error (feedback), and then follows up with further explanation and clarification (corrective). Similarly, academically successful students typically follow up the mistakes they make on quizzes and tests, seeking further information and greater understanding so that their errors are not repeated.

With this in mind, Bloom outlined a specific instructional strategy to make use of this feedback and corrective procedure. He labeled the strategy "Learning for Mastery" (Bloom 1968), and later shortened it to simply "Mastery Learning" (Bloom 1971). In this strategy, the concepts and material students are to learn are first organized into instructional units. For most teachers, a unit is composed of the concepts presented in about a week or two of instructional time. Following initial instruction on the unit, a quiz or assessment is administered to students. Instead of signifying the end of the unit, this assessment is used primarily to give students information, or feedback, on their learning. In fact, to emphasize its new purpose Bloom suggested it be called a "formative assessment," meaning "to inform or provide information." A formative assessment identifies for students precisely what they have learned well to that point, and what they need to learn better.

Also included with the formative assessment are explicit suggestions to students as to what they might do to correct the learning difficulties identified on the assessment. Because these suggested corrective activities are specific to each item or set of prompts within the assessment, students need to work on only those concepts not yet mastered. In other words, the correctives are "individualized." They may point out additional sources of information on a particular topic, such as the page numbers in the course textbook or workbook where the topic is discussed. They may identify alternative learning resources such as different textbooks, alternative materials, learning center activities, or computerized instructional lessons, or they may simply suggest sources of additional practice, such as study guides, independent practice, or guided practice activities. With the feedback and corrective information gained from a formative assessment, each student has a detailed prescription of what more needs to be done to master the concepts or desired learning outcomes from the unit.

When students complete their corrective activities, usually after a class period or two, they are administered a second, parallel formative assessment. There are two major reasons for this second assessment. First, it is necessary to check on the effectiveness of the correctives in helping students overcome their individual learning difficulties. Second, and more important, a second formative assessment offers students a second chance at success. Hence, it serves as a very powerful motivational device.

Through this process of formative assessment, combined with the systematic correction of individual learning difficulties, Bloom believed all students could be provided with a more appropriate quality of instruction than is possible under more traditional approaches to teaching. He recognized that with careful planning, a teacher's initial approach to teaching is likely to be appropriate for many, and perhaps even most, of the students in the class. Because of the individual differences among students, however, that approach is also likely to be inappropriate for some. Corrective procedures make other, hopefully more appropriate, approaches available to those students so that a much larger portion of students learn well and reach high levels of achievement. Bloom believed that by providing students with these more favorable learning conditions, nearly *all* could learn excellently and truly master the subject (Bloom 1971).

2. The Essential Elements of Mastery Learning

Since Bloom first set forth his ideas, much has been written about the theory of mastery learning and its accompanying instructional strategies (e.g., Block and Anderson 1975, Levine et al. 1985). Still, programs labeled "mastery learning" are known to vary greatly from setting to setting (Burns 1987). As a result, educators interested in applying mastery learning often have found it difficult to get a clear and concise description of the essential elements of the process and the specific changes required for successful implementation.

Two elements have been defined as essential to the implementation of mastery learning (Guskey 1987a). Although the actual appearance or format of these elements may vary, they serve a very specific purpose in a mastery learning classroom and most clearly differentiate mastery learning from other instructional approaches. These two essential elements are the "feedback, corrective, and enrichment process"; and "congruence among instructional components."

2.1 Feedback, Correctives, and Enrichment

To use mastery learning, a teacher must offer students regular and specific information on their learning progress. Furthermore, that information must be both diagnostic and prescriptive. That is, the information or "feedback" students regularly receive should: (a) reinforce precisely what was most important to learn in each unit of instruction, (b) recognize what was learned well, and (c) identify to what students need to devote more time. This feedback also must be appropriate for students' level of learning if it is to be effective.

By itself, however, feedback will not help students greatly improve their learning. For significant improvement to occur, the feedback they receive must be paired with specific corrective activities. These "correctives" offer students explicit guidance and direction on how they can correct their learning errors and remedy their learning problems. Most important, the correctives must be different from the initial instruction. Simply having students go back and repeat a process that has already proven unsuccessful is unlikely to yield any better results the second time. Therefore, corrective activities must offer students an instructional alternative. Specifically, they must *present* the material differently and *involve* students differently than did the initial teaching. This means the correctives should incorporate different learning styles or learning modalities. In addition, corrective activities should be effective in improving performance. A new or alternative approach that does not help students overcome their learning difficulties is inappropriate as a corrective and ought to be avoided.

In most group-based applications of mastery learning, correctives are accompanied by "enrichment" or "extension" activities for students who attain mastery from the initial teaching. Enrichment activities provide these students with exciting opportunities to broaden and expand their learning. To be effective these enrichments must be both rewarding and challenging. In general they are related to the subject area being studied, but need not be tied directly to the content of a particular unit. Hence, enrichments offer an excellent means of involving students in challenging, higher level activities such as those designed for gifted and talented students.

This feedback, corrective, and enrichment process can be implemented in a variety of ways. In many mastery learning classes, teachers use short, paper-and-pencil quizzes as formative assessments to give students feedback on their learning progress. However, a formative assessment can be any device teachers use to gain evidence on the learning progress of their students. Thus, essays, compositions,

projects, reports, performance tasks, skill demonstrations, and oral presentations can all serve as formative assessments.

Following a formative assessment, some teachers divide the class into separate corrective and enrichment groups. While the teacher directs the activities of students engaged in correctives, enrichment students work on self-selected, independent learning activities that provide opportunities for them to extend and broaden their learning. Other teachers team with colleagues in order to exchange students, so that while one oversees corrective activities the other monitors the enrichment activities. Still other teachers engage students in cooperative learning activities in which corrective and enrichment students work together in teams to ensure all reach the mastery level. If all attain mastery on the second formative assessment, the entire team receives special awards or credit (Guskey 1990a).

Feedback, corrective, and enrichment procedures are crucial to the mastery learning process, for it is through these procedures that mastery learning "individualizes" instruction. In every unit taught, students who need extended time and opportunity to remedy learning problems are offered these through correctives. Furthermore, students who learn quickly and for whom the initial instruction was highly appropriate are provided with an opportunity to extend their learning through enrichments. As a result, all students are provided with favorable learning conditions and more appropriate, higher quality instruction.

2.2 Congruence Among Instructional Components

While feedback, correctives, and enrichment are extremely important, they alone do not constitute mastery learning. To be truly effective, they must be combined with the second essential element of the mastery learning process: congruence among instructional components.

The teaching and learning process generally is perceived as having three major components. To begin one must have some idea of what students are to learn, or the "learning outcomes." This is followed by "instruction" that is intended to result in "competent learners"—students who have learned well and whose competence can be assessed through some form of "evaluation." Mastery learning adds an additional component, the "feedback and corrective" component, that allows teachers to determine for whom the initial instruction was appropriate and for whom an alternative must be planned.

Although essentially neutral with regard to what is taught, how it is taught, and how resultant learning is evaluated, mastery learning does demand there be consistency and alignment among these instructional components. For example, if students are expected to learn higher level skills such as those involved in application or analysis, mastery learning stipulates that instructional activities be planned to give students

163

opportunities to engage actively in those skills. It also requires that students be given specific feedback on their learning of those skills, coupled with directions on how to correct any learning errors. Finally, procedures for evaluating students' learning should reflect those skills as well.

While congruence among instructional components is essential for mastery learning, it is an essential component of effective teaching and learning in general. Suppose, for example, a language arts teacher offered students feedback on their learning through short, multiple-choice quizzes on grammar and punctuation, but then evaluated their learning in terms of the clarity and precision with which they organized ideas in written compositions. In this case, although students received regular feedback, that feedback clearly was not congruent with the procedures used to evaluate their learning. Students may know the rules of grammar and punctuation, but be unable to apply those rules in their writing. Or, they may prepare a composition with perfect grammar and punctuation, but receive a low grade because of inadequate content or poor organization.

In a mastery learning class, the feedback students receive should always be congruent with the specified learning outcomes and the procedures used to evaluate their learning. If students' writing skill, their organization of ideas, and the content of their writing are the criteria by which their learning is to be evaluated, they should receive diagnostic feedback based on those criteria, and prescriptive guidance to correct whatever learning difficulties they may be experiencing.

This element of congruence among instructional components has led some to criticize mastery learning as simply "teaching to the test." The important issue in this regard, however, is what forms the basis for teaching. If a test is the basis of teaching, and if what is taught is determined primarily by that test then, indeed, one is "teaching to the test." Under these conditions, the content and format of the test dictate not only what is taught but also how it is taught. With mastery learning, it is the desired learning outcomes that are the basis of teaching and these, generally, are determined by the teacher. In using mastery learning, teachers simply ensure their instructional activities and the procedures they use to evaluate students' learning match what they have determined to be important for students to learn. Thus, instead of "teaching to the test," mastery learning teachers are more accurately "testing what they teach."

Admittedly, identifying the desired learning outcomes requires teachers to make some crucial decisions. They must decide, for example, what concepts or skills are most important for students to learn and most central to students' understanding of the subject. It is also important, however, for all teachers to recognize that they are already making these decisions. Every time a test is administered, a paper is graded, or any evaluation of learning is made, teachers communicate to their students what they consider to be most important. The use of mastery learning simply compels teachers to confront these decisions more thoughtfully and to make them more intentionally than is often done.

3. Misinterpretations of Mastery Learning

Some early attempts to implement mastery learning were based on very narrow and, in a few instances, inaccurate interpretations of Bloom's ideas. These programs attempted to break learning down into extremely small segments and insisted students "master" each segment before being permitted to move on. Many focused exclusively on lower level cognitive skills and were based on strict adherence to a rigid "scope and sequence" of learning objectives. Teachers were regarded in these programs as little more than managers of materials and record-keepers of student progress.

Unfortunately, similar misinterpretations of mastery learning still exist in the 1990s. The narrowness and rigidity of these early programs were never Bloom's intent, however. Nowhere in his writings can even the suggestion of such be found. Bloom always considered thoughtful and reflective teachers to be essential to the successful implementation of mastery learning. In fact, in his earliest descriptions of mastery learning, Bloom stressed flexibility in the process:

> There are many alternative strategies for mastery learning. Each strategy must find some way of dealing with individual differences in learners through some means of relating the instruction to the needs and characteristics of the learners . . . . The nongraded school . . . is one attempt to provide an organizational structure that permits and encourages mastery learning. (Bloom 1968 pp. 7–8)

Bloom also emphasized the need to focus instruction in mastery learning classrooms on higher level learning outcomes, not simply basic skills. He noted:

> I find great emphasis on problem solving, applications of principles, analytical skills, and creativity. Such higher mental processes are emphasized because this type of learning enables the individual to relate his or her learning to the many problems he or she encounters in day-to-day living. These abilities are stressed because they are retained and utilized long after the individual has forgotten the detailed specifics of the subject matter taught in the schools. These abilities are regarded as one set of essential characteristics needed to continue learning and to cope with a rapidly changing world. (Bloom 1978 p. 578)

Research studies show that mastery learning is highly effective when instruction focuses on high-level outcomes such as problem-solving, drawing inferences, deductive reasoning, and creative expression (Arredondo and Block 1990, Mevarech 1985, Soled 1987).

Although Bloom considered mastery learning to be neutral with regard to curricular focus and teaching methodology, he believed it could be a powerful supplement to any teacher's instructional procedures. Mastery learning was designed to give teachers a practical and efficient tool better to meet the needs of individual students within the demanding environment of a group-based classroom. As such, it also presents teachers with a means to provide their students with the kinds of experiences educators now recognize as essential to the development of thinking skills and other complex cognitive processes.

4. Implications and Research Results

Several important implications stem from this description of mastery learning. The first is that mastery learning is quite flexible in its application. It is possible, for example, for two teachers to implement mastery learning successfully in identical courses or grade levels using very different approaches. Both would employ the same essential elements of the mastery learning process, but the way they conduct their initial teaching, the type of formative assessments they use, the kind of corrective activities and enrichments in which their students engage, all could be different. In other words, there is no one best way to implement mastery learning. Successful applications depend, to a large extent, on teachers' ability to adapt the essential elements of mastery learning to the particular context in which they teach and the unique characteristics of their students.

A second implication is that mastery learning is broadly applicable. It is apparent to most how mastery learning might be used to teach subjects that are structured and hierarchical, such as mathematics, but the mastery learning process is equally effective when applied to instruction in less structured subjects such as language arts and social studies.

In teaching creative writing, for example, the first thing the teacher must be able to do is describe, in some detail, the differences between a composition that is creative and one that is not; for if these differences cannot be described, what is the teacher to teach? Describing these differences is an essential prerequisite to teaching the higher level skills associated with creative writing. As soon as these differences are described, however, a basis is established for offering students feedback on their writing, as well as guidance in correcting their errors and making revisions, so a composition that is not creative becomes more like one that is.

In a writing class, students' compositions serve as the formative assessments. They are submitted to the teacher and evaluated in terms of criteria the teacher has taught and discussed with students. In some cases, fellow students may offer evaluative feedback, with directions for doing so provided by the teacher. Compositions are then returned to their writers with suggestions for revision based upon the specified criteria. Corrective activities would involve helping students to make their revisions, using different techniques from those employed in the initial teaching. Once completed, revised compositions are submitted to the teacher again as the second formative assessment.

A third implication of the essential elements of mastery learning is that most teachers need not drastically alter what they are doing to use the process. Unlike many new ideas and strategies that are designed to replace teachers' current teaching methods, mastery learning builds upon those techniques. Rather than having to abandon the practices they have developed and refined over the years, mastery learning provides teachers with a means for improving those practices. It empowers teachers to make the best use of the skills they already have. Most excellent teachers are undoubtedly using some form of mastery learning already. Others are likely to find the mastery learning process blends well with many of their present teaching strategies. Given the demanding nature of teaching and the difficulties generally associated with approaches that require major changes or extensive revisions in teaching procedures, this is an exciting prospect.

Finally, although implementing the essential elements of mastery learning does not require drastic change, extensive research evidence shows the use of these elements can have very positive effects on student learning (Guskey and Pigott 1988, Kulik et al. 1990a). Providing feedback, correctives, and enrichments, and ensuring congruence among instructional components can be accomplished by most teachers with relatively little time or effort, especially if tasks are shared among teaching colleagues. Furthermore, evidence gathered in the United States (Walberg 1984), Asia (Kim et al. 1969), Australia (Chan 1981), Europe (Dyke 1988, Langeheine 1992, Mevarech 1985), and South America (Cabezon 1984) shows that the careful and systematic use of these elements can lead to significant improvements in student learning.

Equally important is the fact that the positive effects of mastery learning are not restricted only to measures of student achievement. The process also has been shown to yield improvements in students' school attendance rates, their involvement in class lessons, and their attitudes toward learning (Guskey and Pigott 1988). This multidimensional impact has been referred to as the "multiplier effect" of mastery learning (Guskey et al. 1982), and makes it one of the most cost-effective means of educational improvement in the 1990s.

One review of the research on mastery learning, contrary to all previous reviews, indicated that the process had essentially no effect on student achievement (Slavin 1987). This finding surprised not only scholars familiar with the vast research literature on mastery learning, showing it to yield very positive results, but also large numbers of practitioners who had experienced its positive impact first hand. A close inspection of this review shows, however, that it was conducted using techniques of questionable validity (Hiebert 1987), employed capricious selection criteria (Kulik et al. 1990b), reported results in a biased manner (Walberg 1988), and drew conclusions not substantiated by the evidence presented (Guskey 1987b). Most importantly, two much more extensive and methodologically sound reviews published since (Guskey and Pigott 1988, Kulik et al. 1990a) have verified mastery learning's consistently positive impact on a broad range of student learning outcomes and, in one case (i.e., Kulik et al. 1990b), showed clearly the distorted nature of this earlier report.

5. Conclusion

The future for mastery learning looks particularly bright from the perspective of both educational practitioners and researchers. Although strikingly different from their personal educational experiences, many classroom teachers in the 1990s recognize the value of the essential elements of mastery learning. Increasing numbers are coming to see the importance of using assessments as learning tools, rather than simply as devices to categorize students and assign grades. Many are also offering corrective activities to students who may need a little more time or another instructional approach to learn well. They are providing enrichment activities for fast learners who can benefit from the opportunity to extend and broaden their learning. Many, too, are working hard to ensure their instructional methods, feedback and corrective procedures, and assessment strategies are congruent with the learning outcomes they most value. For these teachers, mastery learning offers the tools they need to have a more powerful influence on the learning of their students. It empowers them to be more effective and, as a result, makes teaching more rewarding and enjoyable (Guskey 1986).

Researchers have also come to recognize the value of the essential elements of mastery learning and the importance of these elements in effective teaching at any level. As a result, fewer studies are being conducted on the mastery learning process per se. Instead, researchers are looking for ways to enhance results further, adding to the mastery learning process additional elements that positively contribute to student learning in hopes of attaining even more impressive gains. Work on the integration of mastery learning with other innovative strategies appears especially promising (Arredondo and Block 1990; Guskey 1990a, 1990b).

Mastery learning is not an educational panacea and will not solve all the complex problems facing educators at the end of the twentieth century. It also does not reach the limits of what is possible in terms of the potential for teaching and learning. Exciting work is continuing on new ideas designed to attain results far more positive than those typically derived through the use of mastery learning (Bloom 1988). Careful attention to the essential elements of mastery learning will, however, allow educators at all levels to make great strides toward the goal of all children learning excellently.

See also: Instructional Alignment; Individualized Instruction

References

Arredondo D E, Block J H 1990 Recognizing the connections between thinking skills and mastery learning. *Educ. Leadership* 47(5): 4–10
Block J H, Anderson L W 1975 *Mastery Learning and Classroom Instruction*. MacMillan, New York
Bloom B S 1968 Learning for mastery. Instruction and Curriculum. *Evaluation Comment* 1(2): 1–12
Bloom B S 1971 Mastery learning. In: Block J H (ed.) 1971 *Mastery Learning: Theory and Practice*. Holt, Rinehart and Winston, New York
Bloom B S 1974 An introduction to mastery learning theory. In: Block J H (ed.) 1974 *Schools, Society and Mastery Learning*. Holt, Rinehart and Winston, New York
Bloom B S 1978 New views of the learner: Implications for instruction and curriculum. *Educ. Leadership* 35(7): 563–76
Bloom B S 1988 Helping all children learn well in elementary school—and beyond. *Principal* 67(4): 12–17
Burns R B 1987 *Models of Instructional Organization: A Casebook on Mastery Learning and Outcome-based Education*. Far West Laboratory for Educational Research and Development, San Francisco, California
Cabezon E 1984. The effects of marked changes in student achievement patterns on the students, their teachers, and their parents: The Chilean case. Doctoral dissertation, University of Chicago, Chicago, Illinois
Chan K S 1981 The interaction of aptitude with mastery versus non-mastery instruction: Effects on reading comprehension of grade three students. Doctoral dissertation, University of Western Australia, Perth
Dyke W E 1988 The immediate effect of a mastery learning program on the belief systems of high school teachers. Paper presented at the annual meeting of the American Educational Research Association, New Orleans, Louisiana
Guskey T R 1986 Staff development and the process of teacher change. *Educ. Researcher* 15(5): 5–12
Guskey T R 1987a The essential elements of mastery learning. *J. Classroom Interaction* 22(2): 19–22
Guskey T R 1987b Rethinking mastery learning reconsidered. *Rev. Educ. Res.* 57(2): 225–29
Guskey T R 1990a Cooperative mastery learning strategies. *Elem. Sch. J.* 91(1): 33–42
Guskey T R 1990b Integrating innovations. *Educ. Leadership* 47(5): 11–15
Guskey T R 1994 Bloom's "Learning for Mastery" revisited: Modern perspectives and misinterpretations. *Outcomes* 13(1): 16–39

Guskey T R, Barshis D, Easton J Q 1982 The multiplier effect: Exploring new directions in community college research. *Community and Junior College Journal* 52(8): 22–25

Guskey T R, Pigott T D 1988 Research on group-based mastery learning programs: A meta-analysis. *J. Educ. Res.* 81(4): 197–216

Heibert E H 1987 The context of instruction and student learning: An examination of Slavin's assumptions. *Rev. Educ. Res.* 57(3): 337–40

Kim H et al. 1969 *A Study of the Bloom Strategies for Mastery Learning.* Korean Institute for Research in the Behavioral Sciences, Seoul

Kulik C C, Kulik J A, Bangert-Drowns R L 1990a Effectiveness of mastery learning programs: A meta-analysis. *Rev. Educ. Res.* 60(2): 265–99

Kulik J A, Kulik C C, Bangert-Drowns R L 1990b Is there better evidence on mastery learning? A response to Slavin. *Rev. Educ. Res.* 60(2): 303–07

Langeheine R 1992 State mastery learning: Dynamic models for longitudinal data. Paper presented at the annual meeting of the American Educational Research Association, San Francisco, California

Levine D U et al. 1985 *Improving Student Achievement through Mastery Learning Programs.* Jossey-Bass, San Francisco, California

Mevarech Z R 1985 The effects of cooperative mastery learning strategies on mathematical achievement. *J. Educ. Res.* 78(6): 372–77

Slavin R E 1987 Mastery learning reconsidered. *Rev. Educ. Res.* 57(2): 175–213

Soled S W 1987 Teaching processes to improve both higher and lower mental process achievement. Paper presented at the annual meeting of the American Educational Research Association, Washington, DC

Walberg H J 1984 Improving the productivity of America's schools. *Educ. Leadership* 41(8): 19–27

Walberg H J 1988 Response to Slavin: What's the best evidence? *Educ. Leadership* 46(2): 28

Open Education

G. Thibadeau

Open education is a form of education, the goal of which is to respond to children on the basis of their individual behaviors, needs, and characteristics. Its intellectual roots draw on Froebel's directive to bring out, develop, and use each child's unique skills. Open educators employ Dewey's "learning by doing" method because they believe that young children need very concrete situations in order to think. Other intellectual theorists, such as Pestalozzi and Rousseau, contributed to the development of the open classroom.

According to Thibadeau (1992) open education began in the sixteenth century with Comenius's acknowledgment of the differentiation in the growth rate of children. Its scientific roots can be found in the works of Piaget, who was frequently mentioned in the well-publicized report published in the United Kingdom titled *Children and Their Primary Schools (United Kingdom Department of Education and Science 1967)*. This report, commonly known as the Plowden Report, recognized and authenticated the informal styles of teaching and learning that had gradually been developed in English primary schools during the previous 40 years.

During the late 1960s 50 percent of all schools built in the United States were of open design. A similar percentage of such schools were also built in Canada, New Zealand, Australia, and the United Kingdom (Bennett et al. 1980). While early advocates of open education made claims that have not been substantiated by researchers, the principles and practices of open education have continued to influence teachers in such diverse countries as Japan, Norway, Thailand, and Israel.

1. Primary Features of Open Education

The concept of classroom openness has been a difficult one to operationalize. Although numerous studies designed to define the concept of open education have been conducted (Barth and Rathbone 1969, Walberg and Thomas 1972, Marshall 1981), an exact definition of open education remains problematic. Because open education settings have varied widely in practice, no single model, set pattern, or perceived arrangement can be identified. While Horwitz (1979) grouped the outcome variables, he ignored differences in definitions of openness as well as differences in sample size, design, and analysis. He defined open education as "a style of teaching involving flexibility of space, student choice of activity, richness of learning materials, integration of curriculum areas, and more individual or small-group than large-group instruction" (pp. 72–73). However, as Marshall (1981) argued, open classrooms have varied in the degree to which they implement various features of open education. He suggested "that research on what has been termed Open Education be restructured so as to consider the separate component dimensions of open classrooms as important interventions in themselves rather than continuing to struggle with widely varying definitions of the global concept of classroom openness" (p. 181).

Giaconia and Hedges's (1982) synthesis of research identified seven primary features common to most open education programs: emphasis on the active role of children in guiding their own learning; use of a diverse set of materials and resources to stimulate exploration; multiage grouping; individualized instruction; team teaching; diagnostic evaluation; and flexible use of space and furnishings. They observed that studies of open-education programs that defined open education as featuring only open space, multiage grouping, and team teaching were more likely to be found in the United States than in the United Kingdom.

Harrison and Glaubman (1990) noted that open education in Israel, where it is known as activity education, has differed somewhat from its counterparts in the United Kingdom and the United States. Their research suggested that the degree of similarity between definitions of open education has been, to a certain degree, overestimated. In previous research Harrison and Glaubman (1982) had compared the conceptions of open education in the United States, United Kingdom, and Israel by analyzing 51 documents from the three countries and additional studies describing the development of open education in each country. Because of the scarcity of studies on the concept of open education in Israel, 18 Israeli educators recognized as authorities were interviewed. The assembled data revealed that educators in all three countries had common attitudes about how children learn and emphasized five assumptions in their definitions of open education: children learn through active interaction with their environment; children can make decisions about their own learning; development is diverse and individual; the emphasis in school should be on learning not teaching; and education is both child-centered and teacher-centered.

Bennett et al. (1980), in a major study in the United Kingdom, concluded that the existence of an open architectural design does not guarantee the existence of open education, although there is a relationship between openness in design and openness in the teaching organization. That is, the majority of teachers observed were teaching independently (defined as operating on their own with no, or minimal, cooperation with other teachers in the unit), irrespective of the age of children taught. However, when the design of teaching space was taken into account, more teachers were teaching cooperatively where shared teaching space was available. Consequently, an open classroom is the result of an educator's philosophy, not the result of spatial manipulation.

Some teachers found it difficult to take advantage of the opportunities for flexible use of space and attempted to retain their own territory. In a Canadian study (Traub et al. 1976), observers noted that teachers teaching within open designs used a variety of means to establish their territories, the most common being the positioning of blackboards and bookshelves. In fact, many teachers who have used open methods have prefered the self-contained classroom because it provides the security of familiar structure, privacy, and quiet.

Schubert and Baxter (1982) maintained that because of the inherent advantages of the self-contained classroom, it is a viable, if not superior, environment in which to practice open education in the elementary grades. They defined open education in terms of the range of students' independence in the learning process rather than from the mere physical or architectural style of the building. The notion that architecture can modify the environment and yet not impact the activities taking place in the environment has made educators aware of the crucial role of the teacher.

2. The Role of the Teacher in Open Education

The teacher in an open classroom holds a demanding instructional role with broad, creative responsibilities. When the open classroom is divided into learning centers, an individual approach to learning is promoted and opportunities for teacher–child interaction are enhanced. Rogers (1971) and Barth (1972), early advocates of this movement in the United States, characterized the open-classroom teacher as one possessing the attitudes and skills of a facilitator of learning (a term that continues to appear in the literature). They further maintained that the traditional function of teaching and the function of the teacher as a facilitator of learning defined two distinct models of teaching. As a facilitator of learning, the teacher utilizes combinations of instructional materials to meet the individual student's learning needs and works with students as a stimulator, advisor, consultant, and resource, rather than as a giver of knowledge. The teacher divides the time into small, concentrated periods, working with individual children or small groups, rather than addressing the whole class as one group all day. Common to all facilitators is an enormous trust in learners and the ability to relinquish large amounts of control. Facilitators are more effective if they themselves are involved in learning and challenge their own beliefs and practices when confronted by students (Herman 1982). Because, generally speaking, there is no standard curriculum imposed upon the students, three teacher functions have been identified as critical roles of the open-classroom teacher: individualizer of instruction, resource person and counselor, and provider of suitable materials and activities (Traub et al. 1972). As teachers in the United Kingdom have frequently pointed out, the teacher's primary responsibility is to create an environment that stimulates learning and to alter and expand the environment as the needs of each student change. Doyle (1986) characterized the open-classroom teacher as an effective manager who ensures that students are concentrating on appropriate work in an environment where they have a high degree of choice.

The redefinition of the teacher's role as that of a facilitator also encourages short-term decisions directed toward individual students and increases cooperation among staff members (McLaughlin 1976). Because intrinsic rewards (i.e., to play a significant role in students' lives) are important for open teachers and because the classroom is the major arena for the receipt of these rewards (Sederberg and Clark 1990), teachers in open schools show no significant inclination to move back into the self-contained classroom. However, a large number of studies report adverse teacher comments, reporting increased workload and insufficient preparation time, as teaching in an open classroom requires continuous innovation, monitoring of students' performance, and well-developed skills in maintaining order without being authoritarian. New Zealand teachers (Gill 1977) stated that increased workload was their major problem and that demands on them were very high, citing the necessity for continuous student evaluation and careful curriculum planning.

3. Open Education Practices

A study of a systematic random sample of 42 Israeli elementary schools, of which 17 had been implementing open education practices for at least 3 years, found that teachers in open-education schools were significantly younger and less experienced than teachers in conventional schools (Harrison and Glaubman 1990). Teachers in the open schools reported having more frequent discussions of school goals with administrators and more frequent meetings and discussions for the purpose of problem-solving. They used more resources for curriculum development and had more exchanges of ideas with supervisors, parents, and inspectors. Teachers in schools adopting open education reported a larger number of hours of school-based, inservice training and a more decentralized school decision-making structure than did teachers in more conventional schools.

A second study in Israel evaluated educational programs in five elementary schools in Jerusalem that were recognized by the Ministry of Education as "open" schools and five schools using traditional methods of teaching (Klein and Eshel 1980). A total of 46 classrooms—23 "open" and 23 traditional, from the first, second, and third grades in these schools—provided data for a cross-cultural perspective on open education in the United States, United Kingdom, and Israel. Certain dimensions were common to all three countries; namely pupils in open classrooms received greater amounts of positive rewards, were allowed to move more freely about the classroom, were more encouraged to seek information independently, participated more actively in class, were more involved in learning tasks, and were less inattentive. The more flexible schedule and less uniform learning environment of the open classroom (as compared with the traditional classroom) appeared to influence teacher behavior because they entertained more unexpected answers from students and functioned in an environment in which silence was not mandatory.

4. Open Education and Student Outcomes

As might be expected, there has been a close relationship between teachers' attitudes toward open education and noncognitive student outcomes. Teachers have almost uniformly rated themselves as more open than they are and the difference is especially pronounced in the traditional classroom (Schubert and Baxter 1982). When open and traditional classrooms are compared, students in an open-space school or a closed-space school where teachers have favorable attitudes toward open education principles, consistently scored higher with regard to level of curiosity and self-esteem than students of teachers with unfavorable attitudes toward open education.

Elias and Elias (1978) conducted as study of 297 third-and fourth-grade students of which 121 were in a traditional school and 176 attended an open-space or open-concept school. Both the open and traditional schools were located in the same school district and the students came from predominantly middle- to upper-middle-class families. Students in an open school (open group) were compared with students in traditional classrooms where teachers demonstrated highly favorable attitudes toward open education (favorable group) and with students of teachers who reacted unfavorably toward open education (unfavorable group). Comparisons were made between the students in the open school and those in the traditional school and also between the favorable and unfavorable groups within the traditional school. Their results indicated that the attitude of the teacher toward open education may play an important role in affecting certain personality characteristics. When students in the open and traditional schools were compared without regard to teacher attitudes, the results were inconclusive.

Giaconia and Hedges (1982) conducted a meta-analysis of over 150 studies of open education. They concluded that four features (role of the child, diagnostic evaluation, materials to manipulate, and individualized instruction) were associated with higher nonachievement outcomes (self concept, creativity, favorable attitude toward school). Three additional features (multiage grouping, team teaching, open space) failed to distinguish effective from ineffective open education programs. They concluded that open education had worthwhile effects on creativity, independence, cooperation, attitudes toward teachers and schools, psychological adjustment, and curiosity. The effects on achievement were minimal, with programs having positive effects on attitude, creativity, and self-concept actually being associated with lower achievement scores on standardized tests.

Harrison et al. (1981), in a study designed to consider the trends of findings from English-speaking countries, explored the impact of open and traditional classes in Israel on the achievement and creativity of elementary pupils in the first, third, and fifth grades. They found no appreciable differences with regard to pupil achievement. However, first-grade pupils in open education attained significantly higher scores in both figural and verbal creativity while the third and fifth grades showed enhanced figural creativity—higher than verbal creativity.

In summary, numerous studies have confirmed that students' attitudes toward their school experience and learning in general will be more positive in informal than in formal classrooms; furthermore, students in open classrooms are more likely to take their school experiences into the home and the community. There does, however, appear to be a danger in open schools that pupils might display less involvement in their tasks and, consequently, learn less. A survey undertaken by the schools inspectorate in the United Kingdom observed vivid examples of time-wasting and concluded that students in open schools spend more time in transitional activities. Similarly, New Zealand elementary students who were taught at tables rather than seated in rows had increased peer interaction and transition time between activities (Gill 1977).

5. Conclusion

The large number of research findings indicating that achievement levels were not significantly different in open classrooms from those in traditional classrooms hastened the decline of open education and by the end of the 1970s, the movement in the United States was clearly in retreat. The reasons for the decline have not been fully documented. As one researcher noted, "my search of the literature for explanations of the demise of open classrooms proved frustrating" (Rothenberg 1989 p. 84). The failure to achieve the exaggerated claims of its supporters hastened the decline of the movement. Its critics (and some supporters) misunderstood the fundamental principles of the open classroom. As a consequence, there was a failure to obtain community participation and support, inadequate teacher training, and unsuccessful implementation procedures. In addition, several widely reported studies that found students in open classrooms had significantly lower academic achievement than students in traditional classrooms (later shown to be erroneous) seriously eroded support for the movement.

It should be pointed out, however, that open classrooms, carefully organized and operated by well-trained teachers, have much to offer students. Many schools have continued to offer students the option of being in open classrooms. Furthermore, periodic descriptions of effective open programs have continued to appear in the literature. Because widespread research has indicated that students in open classrooms are more independent, less conforming, act more cooperatively, and display more creativity than students in traditional classrooms (Rothenberg 1989), openclassroom strategies have been implemented in many classrooms that are not labeled as such. The view that open education is not a well-defined educational method and that studies on open education should focus on the relationship between a specific feature of open education and its impact on program effectiveness is widely accepted. It will probably shape the direction of future evaluative studies.

References

Barth R S 1972 *Open Education and the American School.* Agathon, New York
Barth R S, Rathbone C J 1969 The open school: A way of thinking about children, learning and knowledge. *The Center Forum* 3:7
Bennett N, Andrae J, Hegarty P, Wade B 1980 *Open Plan Schools: Teaching, Curriculum, Design.* National Foundation for Educational Research, Windsor
Doyle W 1986 Classroom organization and management. In: Wittrock M C (ed.) 1986 *Handbook of Research on Teaching,* 3rd edn. Macmillan, New York
Elias S F, Elias J W 1978 Open education and teacher attitudes towards openness: The impact on students. *Education* 99(2): 208–14
Giaconia R M, Hedges L V 1982 Identifying features of effective open education. *Rev. Educ. Res.* 52(4): 579–602
Gill W M 1977 A look at the change to open-plan schools in New Zealand. NZ *J. Educ. Stud.* 12: 3–16
Harrison J, Glaubman R 1982 Open education in three societies. *Comp. Educ. Rev.* 26: 352–73
Harrison J, Glaubman R 1990 Innovations and school improvements. *J. Res. Dev. Educ.* 24(1): 21–33
Harrison J, Strauss H, Glaubman R 1981 The impact of open and traditional classrooms on achievement and creativity: The Israeli case. *Elem. Sch. J.* 82(1): 27–35
Herman R (ed.) 1982 *The Design of Self-directed Learning: A Handbook for Teachers and Administrators.* Rev. edn. Department of Adult Education, Ontario Institute for Studies in Education, Toronto
Horwitz R A 1979 Psychological effects of the "Open Classroom." *Rev. Educ. Res.* 49(1): 71–85
Klein Z, Eshel Y 1980 The open classroom in cross cultural perspective: A research note. *Socio. Educ.* 53(2): 114–21
Marshall H H 1981 Open classrooms: Has the term outlived its usefulness? *Rev. Educ. Res.* 51(2): 181–92
McLaughlin M W 1976 Implementation as mutual adaptation: Change in classroom organization. *Teach. Coll. Rec.* 77(3): 339–51
Rogers C R 1971 Forget you are a teacher. In: Thibadeau C (ed.) 1971 *Opening up Education in Theory and Practice.* Kendall/Hunt, Dubuque, Iowa
Rothenberg J 1989 The open classroom reconsidered. *Elem. Sch. J.* 90(1): 69–86
Schubert N A, Baxter M B 1982 The self-contained open classroom as a viable learning environment. *J. Educ.* 102(4): 411–15

Sederberg C H, Clark S M 1990 Motivation and organizational incentives for high vitality teachers: A qualitative perspective. *J. Res. Dev. Educ.* 24(1): 6–13

Thibadeau G 1992 The influence of Comenius on American teacher education reforms. *Proceedings of the Second International Conference on Comenius*, Charles University, Prague

Traub R, Weiss J, Fisher C 1976 *Openness in schools: An evaluation study. Research in Education* Series 5. Ontario Institute for Studies in Education, Toronto

Traub R, Weiss J, Fisher C W, Musella D 1972 Closure on openness: Describing and quantifying open education. *Interchange* 3(2–3): 69–74

United Kingdom Department of Education and Science 1967 *Children and Their Primary Schools*, Vol. 1. HMSO, London

Walberg H J, Thomas S C 1972 Open education: classroom validation in Great Britain and the United States. *Am. Educ. Res. J.* 9: 197–208

Further Reading

Silberman C E (ed.) 1973 *The Open Classroom Reader.* Vintage Books, New York

Weber L 1971 *The English Infant School and Informal Education.* Prentice-Hall, Englewood Cliffs, New Jersey

Science Laboratory Instruction

E. Hazel

Laboratory work conducted by students has long been considered the hallmark, the unique feature, of science education. The reason for this tradition is that most of the physical and biological sciences are essentially empirical in nature: research is conducted, knowledge is produced, and progress is made in the professional laboratories of scientists. It has seemed logical to science educators that the features of student science should reflect those of professional science; thus, science students should be taught for at least part of the time in laboratory classes. Issues to be addressed in this entry are the different types of laboratory classes, the educational goals pursued, and the types of classroom life which eventuate for students and teachers in laboratories (Boud et al. 1989, Hegarty-Hazel 1990).

1. Types of Laboratory Classes

Within a science course, the term "practical work" may be taken to include any activity involving students in real situations using genuine materials and properly working equipment. In many of the physical and biological sciences, practical work takes place in a laboratory and thus is often known as laboratory work. Field work in animal behavior would be an example of practical work which does not take place in a laboratory. Laboratory teaching is now an umbrella term which covers controlled exercises, laboratory kits and packages, enquiries, problems and projects, case study approach, audiotutorial/laboratory method, simulations, and computer-assisted laboratory instruction (Boud et al. 1989).

Despite the variety of approaches available, much of the thinking is influenced by what Ogborn (1977) called the great tradition of university laboratory work. Such laboratory work contains a number of experiments, many of them ingenious and elegant, each in some way a microcosm of the art of experimentation, though the emphasis may be laid more on one aspect than another. Each is more or less equivalent to the others in the thinking it demands, the time it takes, and the difficulties it presents. In the physical sciences and engineering, there is often no special order in which students do the experiments, while in the biological sciences, there has been more of a trend toward integrated and developmental approaches. However, this tradition has often been questioned and challenged. For example, tracing the history of laboratory teaching from Liebig's chemistry laboratories at Giessen in the 1830s to the 1990s, Layton (1990) found that his analysis brought him into agreement with the common criticism that much student laboratory work is aimless, trivial, and badly planned. He claimed that from the standpoint of philosophy of science, there is an urgent need for critical reappraisal of the function of student science laboratory work.

2. Goals of Laboratory Instruction

Goals for laboratory instruction have been identified in all of the major categories described by Klopfer (1971): knowledge and comprehension (including conceptual development, conceptual change, metacognition); technical skills; processes of scientific enquiry; appreciation of the ways in which scientists work; scientific attitudes and interests; and application of scientific knowledge and methods. Key issues for science students are socialization into the discipline and acquisition of professional skills. For other students, the issues are more of scientific literacy and understanding the ways in which scientists work. Which of these goals is laboratory teaching best suited to achieve? From reviews of comparative learning research (Bates 1978, Hegarty-Hazel 1989), some generalizations emerge.

Student laboratory work is the method of choice for teaching technical skills and increasing understanding of the apparatus involved. It is valuable in giving practice in processes of scientific enquiry and problem-solving skills, developing appreciation of ways in which scientists work, developing scientific attitudes and attitudes to science, developing laboratory resourcefulness, and providing for individual differences among learners. Student laboratory work also can be effective in teaching applications of scientific knowledge and methods. However, lectures, discussions, and demonstrations can be superior for the presentation of complex material and more efficient for the presentation of large amounts of factual information and concepts.

2.1 Technical Skills

From a synthesis of the literature, Hegarty-Hazel (1990) concluded that technical skills can be well learned in suitably designed laboratory classes. Examples of such skills include techniques such as diluting, titrating, preparing chemical solutions, dissecting, preparing and staining smears and sections of animal and plant tissues, together with the use of equipment such as balances, microscopes, and spectrophotometers. When mastery of laboratory skills is required, teacher demonstrations, film, television, computers, and simulations cannot substitute for individual laboratory work. However, they can complement it in many effective ways including methods overviews, showing fine details of technical manoeuvres and providing introductions to equipment which is especially complex, fragile, or expensive.

Studies with adult learners have shown that effective learning of technical skills requires practice as well as feedback on the success of attempts. In addition, the experimenter must have an overview of the method (the order and purpose of the steps in the method). Examples from chemistry show how the conditions for effective learning can be met. Students used techniques-kits to obtain practice in weighing, titrating, preparing standard solutions, and using a spectrophotometer. The success of this practice was examined by having the students complete exercises which required precise execution of the technique and measuring the errors. This practice and feedback reduced average student errors by five-to ten-fold.

2.2 Process of Scientific Inquiry

From 1960 onward, secondary school students were encouraged to act as scientific enquirers. Klopfer (1990) described the role of teaching in the laboratory for development of students' enquiry skills in especially attuned contexts. Studies using questioning on goals and learning environment inventories have shown that high school students in the United Kingdom, the United States, Australia, and Israel were aware of the enquiry orientation and the experience of investigating scientific problems although they had not necessarily become more scientifically curious as a result (Edwards and Power 1990, Friedler and Tamir 1990). By comparison, studies of university students in the same countries and content analysis of their laboratory exercises have shown significantly less awareness of scientific enquiry (Hegarty 1978, Hegarty-Hazel 1990).

The conclusion of a major United States national report, *Case Studies in Science Education* (Stake and Easley 1978), was that the inquiry-oriented science curricula had failed in practice to materialize due to a variety of contextual factors. In response, Welch et al. (1981) proffered a reassessment, whereby they suggested that enquiry objectives would only be achieved when they were consistent with a student's psychological needs and personal goals and in a school and community environment which is conducive to enquiry Fensham (1990) has offered a further reassessment of the implications for student laboratory work of "Science for All".

At universities, the use of short or long projects in science laboratory teaching is a time-honored way of providing some experience in scientific enquiry (Ogborn 1977, Dowdeswell and Harris 1979, Boud et al. 1989, Bliss 1990). Criticisms of projects on grounds other than cost-effectiveness include the uncontrolled nature and variability of experience of scientific enquiry skills. There are many occasions in which learning-challenge sequences (Hegarty 1982) could provide experience with a similar range of enquiry skills with fewer organizational uncertainties.

2.3 Knowledge and Comprehension

Laboratory teaching is not very efficient for the presentation of factual information. Reception of knowledge via texts or lectures is superior in this regard. It is ironic, then, that so many laboratory exercises are devoted to the illustration of well-known concepts.

When new concepts are introduced, laboratory teaching can provide concrete experience which gives meaning to these concepts. In this way laboratory teaching seems especially suited to the promotion of meaningful learning as distinct from rote learning (memorization without understanding). It has been suggested that one role of laboratory work may be to provide vivid memory episodes which aid the linking of theory and practice, but Atkinson (1990) reported that the matter is far from simple. Some laboratory work may work well, other potential episodes may prove useless to a student in bridging theory and practice. Much depends on the student's conceptual development.

2.4 Conceptual Development, Conceptual Change, and Metacognition

Laboratory teaching is being explored in research and action projects as a setting for helping students construct knowledge for creating cognitive conflict, confronting students' misconceptions, and encouraging students to accommodate a new conception of the subject matter. If experience has taught students misconceptions, then it is unlikely that formal instruction will overcome them. A laboratory setting could provide the link with prior experience. It is likely that peer-group discussion and specific teacher challenges would be required for a student to clarify the difference between his or her notion of a science concept and the expert or desired notion (Gunstone and Champagne 1990).

Baird (1990) has reported on the associations of teacher questioning techniques in the laboratory with students' cognitive and metacognitive outcomes. In developing their answers, Baird suggests that students could be encouraged to use various techniques including laboratory experiments and the concept-mapping and V-mapping techniques recommended by Novak (1990). Baird claims that for laboratory work to play its role well in metacognition training, it must provide a challenging range of contexts which give students freedom to pursue productive enquiry. Students must have adequate levels of control, involvement, and interaction, and the work must build on students' existing conceptions, intellectual skills, and metacognitive competencies. Much more explicit attention needs to be given to the processes as well as the content of science.

3. Life in Laboratory Classes

Life in laboratory classes is a constantly changing balance between encounters whereby students learn from teachers or other students, and private engagements of students with phenomena. Possible teacher roles can vary correspondingly from provider of information to facilitator, manager, and supplier of materials, and from demonstrator of techniques to questioner, challenger, and promoter of enquiry. Most observational studies suggest the former roles are most favored but seem to be at odds with fostering student openness to scientific enquiry. These studies also show busy teachers who do a great deal of telling and demonstrating, who may have little or no technical assistance, and who spend a disproportionately large amount of time on laboratory management activities (Stake and Easley 1978).

At university level, the report of the Higher Education Learning Project in England (Ogborn 1977) gives an overwhelming impression of laboratory classes considered by science students and staff alike as valuable places of learning, but not especially enjoyable or stimulating. Teachers tend to play shepherding roles, caring for their students and making certain that equipment is safe and functioning smoothly. Indeed, university teachers seem to regard ensuring smooth functioning of all aspects of students' laboratory work as perhaps their major role.

Quantitative data on behavior of students and teachers in science laboratories at high school and university levels has been reviewed (Power 1977, Hegarty 1982, Friedler and Tamir 1990, Hegarty-Hazel 1990). Teachers talk for much of the time; their dominant concerns are the development of substantive content, supervision of laboratory activities, and organization of laboratory materials and procedures. There is little emphasis on any aspect of scientific enquiry. Even lower level enquiry processes such as data interpretation, prediction, and formulation of conclusions are uncommon in discussion. Teachers seldom ask students for new approaches to a problem or the design of an experiment to help solve a problem.

A comparison was made in Israel of behaviors in laboratory classes at a university with those at a high school using an explicitly enquiry-oriented curriculum (Tamir 1977). At the university level, verification dominated enquiry behavior, while at high school level, the emphasis on enquiry was associated with the use of "postlab" discussion concerning the analysis of data and interpretation of results. Postlab discussions were uniformly nonexistent in the university laboratories observed.

Hegarty (1978) reported on changes in laboratory behaviors within a biological science course at an Australian university when laboratory work changed in enquiry emphasis from low to high. For students, talk on scientific processes increased some 30-fold between set exercises and controlled enquiry exercises and 10-fold for a change to more open enquiry exercises. Most of this change was accounted for by peer group interaction. There was no increase in teachers' talk on scientific processes. University teachers took a dominant role in the development of substantive content and knowledge of procedures, but took on the role of resource person or manager when dealing with students' bench work.

4. Conclusion

The literature suggests that science laboratory instruction follows many traditional paths, not all of them well-founded. Research would be valuable on the philosophical underpinnings of the traditional methods and on teacher coping strategies. Likewise, detailed studies of successful innovations would be valuable.

A traditional area where science laboratory instruction often does not work well is in engagement of students in scientific inquiry or in understanding the processes of inquiry, yet it is deemed one of the most important purposes of laboratory instruction for science students. Research reviewed in this section suggests that enquiry-oriented behavior of students and teachers (such as questioning, challenging, encouraging hypothesis formation, design of experiments) was expected by investigators but seldom found. Research should address the question of whether this situation would change if there were much more explicit debate and explanations and experience for teachers and students with the philosophical underpinnings of inquiry-oriented programs (Layton 1990), and if teacher programs were more supportive to a new teacher role.

A more recent area of research shifts the focus from the teacher to the student; the development of students' metacognition and their learning to learn ability in the science laboratory (Baird 1990, Novak 1990). Research indicates that these are very powerful concepts but that such programs are not readily introduced successfully in isolation. Further research should be discipline specific and should seek to document the conditions for sustained effect.

See also: Demonstrating

References

Atkinson E P 1990 Learning scientific knowledge in the student laboratory. In: Hegarty-Hazel E (ed.) 1990
Baird J R 1990 Metacognition, purposeful enquiry and conceptual change. In: Hegarty-Hazel E (ed.) 1990
Bates G C 1978 The role of the laboratory in secondary school science programs. In: Rowe M B (ed.) 1978 *What Research Says to the Science Teacher*, Vol. 1. National Science Teachers Association, Washington, DC
Bliss J 1990 Students' reactions to undergraduate science: Laboratory and project work. In: Hegarty-Hazel E (ed.) 1990
Boud D J, Dunn J G, Hegarty-Hazel E 1989 *Teaching in Laboratories*, rev. edn., Open University/Society for Research in Higher Education and Nelson, London
Dowdeswell W H, Harris N D C 1979 Project work in university science. In: International Council of Scientific Unions Committee on the Teaching of Science, McNally D (eds.) 1979 *Learning Strategies in University Science*. University College, Cardiff
Edwards J, Power C 1990 Role of laboratory work in a national junior secondary science project: Australian Science Education Project (ASEP). In: Hegarty-Hazel E (ed.) 1990
Fensham P 1990 Practical work and the laboratory in science for all. In: Hegarty-Hazel E (ed.) 1990
Friedler Y, Tamir P 1990 Life in science laboratory classrooms at secondary level. In: Hegarty-Hazel E (ed.) 1990
Gunstone R F, Champagne A B 1990 Promoting conceptual change in the laboratory. In: Hegarty-Hazel E (ed.) 1990
Hegarty E H 1978 Levels of scientific enquiry in university science laboratory classes: Implications for curriculum deliberations. *Res. Dev. Higher Educ.* 2: 133–42
Hegarty E H 1982 The role of laboratory work in science courses: Implications for college and high school levels. In: Rowe M B (ed.) 1982 *Education in the 80s: Science*. National Education Association, Washington, DC
Hegarty-Hazel E 1989 Research on laboratory work. In: Boud D J, Dunn J G, Hegarty-Hazel E 1989
Hegarty-Hazel E (ed.) 1990 *The Student Laboratory and the Science Curriculum*. Routledge, London
Klopfer L E 1971 Evaluation of learning in science. In: Bloom B S, Hastings J T, Madaus G F (eds.) 1971 *Handbook on Formative and Summative Evaluation of Student Learning*. McGraw-Hill, New York
Klopfer L E 1990 Learning scientific enquiry in the student laboratory. In: Hegarty-Hazel E (ed.) 1990
Layton D 1990 Student laboratory practice and the history and philosophy of science. In: Hegarty-Hazel E (ed.) 1990
Novak J D 1990 The interplay of theory and methodology. In: Hegarty-Hazel E (ed.) 1990
Ogborn J M (ed.) 1977 *Practical Work in Undergraduate Science*. Heinemann, London
Power C N 1977 A critical review of science classroom interaction studies. *Stud. Sci. Educ.* 4: 1–30
Stake R E, Easley J A 1978 *Case Studies in Science Education*. Center for Instructional Research and Curriculum Evaluation, University of Illinois, Urbana-Champaign, Illinois
Tamir P 1977 How are the laboratories used? *J. Res. Sci. Teach.* 14(4): 311–16
Welch W W, Klopfer L E, Aikenhead G S, Robinson J T 1981 The role of inquiry in science education: Analysis and recommendations. *Sci. Educ.* 65(1): 33–50

Diagnostic–Prescriptive Teaching

A. Helmke and F.-W. Schrader

The term "diagnostic–prescriptive teaching" (DPT) is used in both a broad and a narrow sense (Colarusso 1987). In a broad sense, it is a general label for instruction based on assessment and diagnostic data (i.e., adapting instruction to the different needs of students). In a narrow sense, the term refers to specific models used in special education for remediating learning difficulties. The first part of this entry focuses on the traditional concept of DPT and some of its basic assumptions. The remainder deals with the relationship between assessment (diagnosis) and instruction (prescription) in a broader context.

1. General Features of Diagnostic–Prescriptive Teaching

Most descriptions of DPT refer to two basic features: (a) an initial assessment or diagnosis with respect to variables related to academic learning or achievement; and (b) the use of these diagnostic data to specify prescriptions about effective instruction or intervention (see, e.g., Arter and Jenkins 1979, Ysseldyke and Salvia 1974).

Assessment in DPT has two main general functions (see Lloyd 1984). The first is determining what to teach (i.e., identifying targets for instruction). These can be learning goals that have not yet been attained as well as deficits in basic abilities that are supposed to cause learning problems. The second function is specifying how to teach. The latter function depends on students' learning styles and how they interact with instructional methods. One possibility in making decisions about how to teach is to observe how students react to instructional methods applied in a preliminary way. Sometimes this is called trial-teaching. It can be regarded as a further characteristic feature of DPT.

1.1 DPT in General Education

In general education, DPT mainly refers to strategies of individualizing instruction. Often it is considered as a general approach that forms the basis of various models of individualization. Examples of models include Individually Prescribed Instruction (IPI), Program for Learning in Accordance with Needs (PLAN), and Individually Guided Education (IGE). These models follow a diagnostic–prescriptive teaching cycle where the teacher's activities consist of: (a) finding out what the pupil knows; (b) providing learning materials that are appropriate for the pupil; (c) assigning learning materials for individual student work and monitoring student work; (d) assessing progress and mastery; and (e) offering additional work in case of a student's failure to reach mastery (Kulik 1982).

Sometimes DPT is considered as a specific method of individualization. Establishing objectives, especially behavioral objectives, is usually a first step. Diagnosis then aims at ascertaining which objectives the student has or has not already reached. Prescription is the process of assigning activities for student learning that are supposed to lead to the objectives. Finally, criterion measurement is used to determine whether the student, after completing prescribed activities, has attained the goals (Charles 1980).

1.2 DPT in Special Education

In special education, DPT refers to the setting up of an Individual Educational Program (IEP) for students who are handicapped or have learning difficulties. In special education, DPT is based on the traditional "medical" or "disease" model, which regards learning or behavioral problems as symptoms of some underlying "defect." According to the medical model, diagnosis aims at a classification based on a particular nosological system which in many cases also suggests proven means of treatment. For academic problems, however, diagnosis based on the medical model does not necessarily lead to effective treatment. As a rule, learning problems cannot be accounted for by a single underlying defect to a satisfactory degree; usually many additional factors are involved. Furthermore, empirically supported relations between specific deficits and effective interventions are lacking. Thus, the link between diagnosis and treatment is usually rather weak (Shapiro 1989). Another problem with classification in special education is that it often leads to the labeling of students which may lead to unfavorable psychosocial consequences.

In special education, DPT has often been equated with the so-called ability training model which considers basic abilities or processes (perceptual, attentional, memory, psycholinguistic) as causes of learning problems. It tries to remedy these causes directly or to circumvent them by special treatment. Empirical support for this model, however, is insufficient. As an alternative, a skill-development model has been proposed, which does not focus on general abilities or processes, but more directly on skills underlying academic competence (Arter and Jenkins 1979, Ysseldyke and Salvia 1974).

2. Assumptions of Diagnostic–Prescriptive Teaching

Basic to DPT is the assumption that diagnosis prescribes instruction (i.e., that initial assessment and diagnosis can be used to specify effective instruction and intervention). The validity of this argument rests on a series of related assumptions. These assumptions can be summarized in a single sentence: learners differ with respect to many characteristics which can be assessed in a reliable and valid manner, and which either (a) are directly related to academic learning and achievement, or (b) interact with instructional methods. Reviews on the ability training model in special education (Arter and Jenkins 1979, Ysseldyke and Salvia 1974) have shown that the validity of these assumptions may be questionable, for several reasons. First, reliability has often proven to be insufficient for individual diagnosis, and validity has been questionable. Second, direct remediation of abilities has often turned out to be unsuccessful and/or improvement of the abilities did not lead to higher achievement. Third, empirical support for stable interactions between abilities and instructional treatments has been weak.

Research on aptitude–treatment interaction (ATI) (Cronbach and Snow 1981) can be considered as the most important conceptual and empirical basis for DPT. Aptitudes comprise general and specific intellectual abilities as well as motivational characteristics and cognitive styles (Corno and Snow 1986). Interactions with instructional treatments are found when achievement is differentially related to aptitudes under different instructional conditions. For example, students with low abilities benefit more from highly structured instruction, while the reverse is true for high-ability students (see Cronbach and Snow 1981).

Although only few ATIs have been confirmed in a strict manner (Cronbach and Snow 1981), some general recommendations seem possible. Research on ATIs suggests that instructional treatments differ with respect to the information-processing and/or behavioral control demands that are placed on learners (Corno and Snow 1986). Teachers can try to adapt instructional methods according to the different information-processing capabilities and/or behavioral control capabilities of learners, thus reducing processing and control burdens for weak learners and placing higher demands on good learners.

Although ATI research represents the conceptual and empirical basis for adaptive instruction, its implications for teaching practice are limited. One reason is that in an actual instructional situation numerous individual factors (such as teacher and student personality), teaching style, and classroom context factors may interact with instructional methods in an unpredictable manner (Christenson and Ysseldyke 1989). In other words, conclusions based on ATI group data may not always be applicable to individual students (Shapiro 1989).

Two approaches to assessing student characteristics have emerged: direct assessment, and an idiographic orientation. As its name implies, direct assessment is focused directly on what is taught and typically includes the assessment of learning behaviors and skills in their natural environment (Shapiro 1989). This approach is in accordance with principles of behavioral assessment, where situational and environmental factors, in addition to personal factors, are taken into account.

An idiographic orientation essentially entails focusing on individual performance, tailoring instructional interventions to the individual case, and examining individual change relative to previous performance instead of making interindividual comparisons (Fuchs and Fuchs 1986). As there are many idiosyncratic factors which may interact in an unpredictable way, interventions based on diagnosis should be conceived as tentative and treated as empirically testable hypotheses. That is, interventions should be monitored and, if necessary, modified. In principle, this is a shift from a diagnostic–prescriptive to a formative approach (Deno 1986).

3. Integration of Assessment and Instruction

The key to the success of diagnostic–prescriptive teaching is the integration of assessment and instruction. Both formal and informal assessment are useful in this regard.

3.1 General Considerations

The integration of assessment and instruction is a topic that has received new interest in the 1980s and 1990s (Fuchs and Fuchs 1986). A major topic of discussion has been the knowledge base of teachers and how that knowledge base is activated and used for planning, preparing, and realizing instruction (Clark and Peterson 1986). There is now a broad consensus that informal diagnosis, mainly teacher judgment based on classroom observation, plays a crucial role. Formal assessment methods, especially tests, are also important because they yield information that can be directly relevant for instructional decisions.

According to Nitko (1989), four decisions can be distinguished when teachers attempt to adapt instruction to students' characteristics. *Placement* decisions are made at the beginning of a course or a longer instructional sequence. The purpose of these decisions is to place students, according to their prior knowledge or other learning prerequisites, into a sequence of instructional units at an appropriate level. *Diagnostic* decisions determine the objectives that are attained and not attained by the students. Furthermore, they are based on what the reasons for success or failure might be and, as a consequence, represent the basis for remedial work. *Monitoring* decisions are based on data concerning whether instructional activities are efficient, meet plans and goals, pose unexpected difficulties, or should be altered (formative evaluation). Finally, *attainment* decisions relate to a final evaluation of achievement and learning at the end of an instructional period (summative evaluation).

In the case of placement decisions, the usefulness of assessment of students' achievement and prior knowledge has been questioned (Nitko 1989). Formal testing for placement decisions is useful if (a) only little information about students' prior knowledge is available, and (b) the instructional system is indeed capable of adapting teaching to students based on this information.

In contrast to placement tests, diagnostic testing usually takes place after instruction has taken place for some time. Diagnostic testing has two major functions: (a) identifying instructional objectives not yet attained, and (b) discovering possible causes for the failure to attain these objectives. Methods of diagnostic testing include analysis of achievement or trait profiles, learning prerequisites, mastery of behavioral objectives, and identification of errors.

Monitoring decisions refer to students' activities and learning processes during instruction. Students' engagement and time-on-task are important indicators in this context. Monitoring as well as diagnostic testing serve a feedback function (i.e., they can be used for modification of learning and teaching). In regular classroom teaching, monitoring decisions are mostly based on informal teacher observations and judgments.

3.2 Formal Assessment

Formal assessment refers to the use of methods (especially tests) which are constructed and applied according to scientific standards. These tests differ with respect to their usefulness for instructional decisions.

Commercial *norm-referenced* tests, which sample a broad range of academic skills within a content area, have often been criticized with respect to their role in instructional decision-making and intervention planning (Shapiro 1989). One reason is that there may be little overlap between the curriculum and the test which may lead to incorrect decisions. Specifically, student failure may be attributed to personal ineptitude rather than to insufficient instruction. Another reason is that broad norm-referenced tests are insensitive to instruction and subtle changes in student achievement.

Criterion-referenced tests examine students' mastery of specific skills; ideally, they are based on objectives derived from the curriculum. Individual achievement is not compared with the distribution of results in a reference group, but with an objective standard. Assessment of students' profiles of strengths and weaknesses with respect to curricular objectives informs the teacher about targets for instruction.

Diagnostic tests, which focus on learning prerequisites and errors, are likely to provide even more specific information for instruction (see Nitko 1989). Standardized and easy-to-apply methods for the analysis of these knowledge structures were unavailable in the early 1990s but have considerable potential, especially if computer-based assessment methods can be used.

3.3 Informal Assessment

Informal teacher judgments are crucial for instructional decision-making. Often, preactive and interactive decisions are distinguished. *Preactive* decisions refer to the planning and preparation of instruction and usually occur outside the actual teaching situation. In contrast, *interactive* decisions occur during teaching. Whereas informal judgments in the preinstructional phases can be seen as analogous to placement tests, teacher judgments during interactive teaching phases serve a monitoring function (Shavelson and Stern 1981). Informal judgments may also serve a diagnostic function, in that observations and questions are used to obtain information about students' actual cognitive processing and learning difficulties.

Empirical support for the role of informal teacher diagnosis for instruction and teaching effectiveness comes from a study by Helmke and Schrader (1987). Teachers' accuracy in judging their students' achievement was considered as an indicator of diagnostic competence. Interestingly, diagnostic competence was not related to growth of achievement. However, there were significant interactions of diagnostic competence with two teaching variables, namely the frequency of teachers' structuring cues and teachers' supervision of individual students during seatwork. Classroom achievement gain was particularly high when both teachers' diagnostic competence and either of the two teaching variables were above average. Thus, it is likely that certain teaching methods are only successful when they are applied by a competent educational diagnostician who can then adapt his or her teaching methods to students' actual achievement levels. Of course, further research is needed to clarify the role of teacher judgment and diagnosis for adaptive teaching.

4. Diagnostic Assessment as Based on a Model of Effectiveness of Instruction

Traditional methods of assessment have almost exclusively focused on stable, trait-like learner characteristics. Furthermore, problems of learning were believed to be located primarily within the learner. In contrast, Christenson and Ysseldyke (1989) presented a comprehensive model in which student performance is influenced by three major groups of factors: student characteristics, school factors, and home factors. Student learning results from an interaction of these three classes of factors. School factors include teaching resources, academic focus, and interstaff collaboration. Home factors refer to variables such as participation, expectations, monitoring, and homework involvement.

This is in accordance with recent models of school learning and of educational productivity that emphasizes the existence of multiple determinants of learning and academic achievement. Advocates of these models believe that models that consider only one group of causes (individual, home, school, peer, media) are necessarily incomplete and biased (Walberg 1990). Both school and home factors influence classroom teaching which, in turn, affects instructional outcomes (see Brophy and Good 1986). The interplay and causal structure of these groups of variables is nicely demonstrated in the IEA *Classroom Environment Study* (Anderson et al. 1989).

From a diagnostic–prescriptive perspective, then, student assessment consists of gathering information as to whether instruction has been appropriate or effective for each individual student. Assessment of the educational environment (e.g., by teacher interview and/or classroom observation) is supplemented by assessing family and home background factors. Intervention aims at altering those variables that are supposed to impact on student learning. When intervention is unsuccessful alterations are made. Within this framework, then, the function of diagnosis is not to find prescriptions that are expected to work automatically, but to yield hypotheses about successful intervention which have to be empirically confirmed during subsequent instruction.

5. Conclusion

The traditional DPT model, with its emphasis on initial diagnosis of stable learner characteristics as a basis of effective instruction and intervention, is questionable.

There are serious doubts about whether such initial diagnosis is appropriate for prescribing instruction. Several researchers have attempted to link assessment with instruction. In general, they have arrived at the following conclusions.

First, assessment should directly focus on what is taught, and should include environmental factors as well as student characteristics. Selection of the factors and characteristics to be assessed should depend on their empirically demonstrated relations with student achievement.

Second, further research is needed to establish a stable knowledge base about the relationship between instructional and family factors, on the one hand, and achievement and academic problems, on the other, which can be used for practical work. Research on aptitude-treatment interactions should be part of this endeavor.

Third, educational practice seems to require, in addition to a well-established research base, an idiographic orientation. That is, educators must consider individual achievement profiles, intraindividual comparisons, and individually tailored interventions.

Finally, prescriptions derived from assessment data should be considered as tentative hypotheses. Accordingly, instructional interventions should be monitored in order to examine whether they were as effective as expected. Modifications should be made, when necessary.

See also: Heuristic Models of Teaching; Reflective Teaching

References

Anderson L W, Ryan D, Shapiro B J 1989 *The IEA Classroom Environment Study*. Pergamon Press, Oxford

Arter J A, Jenkins J R 1979 Differential diagnosis–prescriptive teaching: A critical appraisal. *Rev. Educ. Res.* 49(4): 517–55

Brophy J, Good T L 1986 Teacher behavior and student achievement. In: Wittrock M C (ed.) 1986 *Handbook of Research on Teaching*, 3rd edn. Macmillan Inc., New York

Charles C M 1980 *Individualizing Instruction*, 2nd edn. Mosby, St Louis, Missouri

Christenson S L, Ysseldyke J E 1989 Assessing student performance: An important change is needed. *Journal of School Psychology* 27(4): 409–25

Clark C M, Peterson P L 1986 Teachers' thought processes. In: Wittrock M C (ed.) 1986 *Handbook of Research on Teaching*, 3rd edn. Macmillan Inc., New York

Colarusso R P 1987 Diagnostic–prescriptive teaching. In: Wang M C, Reynolds M C, Walberg H J (eds.) 1987 *Handbook of Special Education. Research and Practice. Vol. 1: Learner Characteristics and Adaptive Education*. Pergamon Press, Oxford

Corno L, Snow R E 1986 Adapting teaching to individual differences among learners. In: Wittrock M C (ed.) 1986 *Handbook of Research on Teaching*, 3rd edn. Macmillan Inc., New York

Cronbach R J, Snow R E 1981 *Aptitudes and Instructional Methods: A Handbook for Research on Interactions*. Irvington, New York

Deno S L 1986 Formative evaluation of individual student programs: A new role for school psychologists. *School Psychol. Rev.* 15(3): 358–74

Fuchs L S, Fuchs D 1986 Linking assessment to instructional intervention: An overview. *School Psych. Rev.* 15(3): 318–23

Helmke A, Schrader F-W 1987 Interactional effects of instructional quality and teacher judgement accuracy on achievement. *Teaching and Teacher Educ.* 3(2): 91–98

Kulik J A 1982 Individualized systems of instruction. In: Mitzel H E (ed.) 1982 *Encyclopedia of Educational Research*, Vol. 2, 5th edn. Macmillan, New York

Lloyd J W 1984 How shall we individualize instruction—or should we? *Rem. Spec. Educ.* 5(1): 7–15

Nitko A J 1989 Designing tests that are integrated with instruction. In: Linn R L (ed.) 1989 *Educational Measurement*, 3rd edn. Macmillan Inc., New York

Shapiro E S 1989 *Academic Skills Problems: Direct Assessment and Intervention*. Guilford Press, New York

Shavelson R J, Stern P 1981 Research on teachers' pedagogical thoughts, judgments, decisions, and behavior. *Rev. Educ. Res.* 51(4): 455–98

Walberg H J 1990 A theory of educational productivity: Fundamental substance and method. In: Vedder P (ed.) 1990 *Fundamental Studies in Educational Research*. Taylor and Francis, London

Ysseldyke J E, Salvia J 1974 Diagnostic–prescriptive teaching: Two models. *Excep. Child.* 41(3): 181–85

Reflective Teaching

L. M. Villar

Reflective teaching refers to a process of critical analysis whereby teachers develop logical reasoning skills, thoughtful judgment, and attitudes supportive of reflection. Thus, reflective teaching has both cognitive and affective components. In a larger framework, reflective teaching may be thought of as a construct that emphasizes the need for understanding and resolution of contradictions in order for teachers to develop professionally. A teacher is prompted to engage in reflective teaching when trying to determine the rationality and justification of ideas and actions in order to develop new understanding and appreciation of phenomena.

This entry describes the main characteristics of reflective teaching; interprets the potential value of reflective teaching for teachers; specifies attitudes that are necessary for being reflective; summarizes a process for making teaching reflective; and describes the potential role of reflective teaching for teacher education. The entry closes with a discussion of tactics that can be used to promote reflective teaching. The discussion is limited to teaching which occurs in school classrooms or institutions of teacher education.

1. The Nature of Reflective Teaching

An inquiry into the nature of reflective teaching suggests a degree of commonality in the researchers who conceptualize it. One of the most important writers on reflective teaching, Dewey suggests that reflection is the "active, persistent and careful consideration of any belief or supposed form of knowledge in light of the grounds that support it and further conclusions to which it tends" (1933 p. 9). Thus, reflection moves from a stage of uncertainty, doubt, and perplexity, to a goal of mastering the problematic situation or gaining satisfaction when one finds material that will resolve the dilemma.

Dewey (1933) suggested that the development of reflective teaching implied learned predispositions to respond positively to certain situations or persons. Among the most important of these dispositions were open-mindedness, responsibility, and wholeheartedness.

Open-mindedness is a cognitive component that suggests the predisposition to seek out and construct alternative structures in an educational field of study. Open-minded teachers welcome risk-taking and would not automatically accept or reject a teaching hypothesis or the predefined educational and organizational orthodoxy of a school or classroom. Rather, these teachers would examine it in the light of their experience and compare their ideas with those of students, parents, researchers, and the community. They prefer to view problems as having plural, contextual solutions.

Responsibility is a performance component which engages teachers in the consideration of long-term as well as short-term consequences of action. Responsible teachers take an essentially moral stance, emphasizing a conception of teaching and learning in which attention is paid to the social, political, and economic context of educational decisions. Furthermore, responsible teachers inquire about their actions in the light of ethical considerations.

Wholeheartedness is an effective component. It implies that attitudes are not confined to particular teaching situations or disciplines, but permeate the whole of the teacher's instructional and political life.

In support of Dewey, studies conducted by Schön (1987) have shown that teachers, regardless of their age and the academic discipline they teach, make judgments regarding the adequacy of their responses to situations and problems for which no overt rationale has been declared. According to Schön, reflective teaching involves the development of strategies and techniques to deal with the complex, uncertain, unstable, and unique situations of the teaching practice. Acknowledging the complex characteristics of educational settings is the process that Schön calls "reflection-in-action." Thus, teaching is not a technical, fixed, and planned series of activities, but an artistic process. Also, it is an intuitive, creative, and improvisational action and a moral enterprise which requires critical thinking in order to develop contextually theories of good teaching practice. The opposite of reflective teaching is the mindless following of learning theories or unexamined teaching practices.

Reflective teaching entails knowledge of teachers' critical thinking, self-direction, problem-solving strategies, and creative thinking. It implies personal knowledge, self-awareness, and the awareness of the classroom context (Elliott 1991). Reflective teachers seek reasons, are well-informed, use and cite valid sources, look for alternatives, and consider others' points of view.

2. The Evaluation of Reflective Teaching

Reflective teaching evaluation has mirrored the contemporary debates surrounding research methodology in education. The state of reflective teaching evaluation in the early 1990s can be reasonably characterized as lying somewhere on a continuum of research methodology between positivism and naturalism, nomothetic and idiographic, and empirical–analytic and "illuminative." Much of the past research on reflective teaching has fallen at the positivist, nomothetic, and empirical–analytic end of the continuum. Psychometric interests dominated this research in which the aim was to generate technical and rational knowledge, usually in the form of causal explanations. Reflection was defined in terms of a measurable set of phenomena within the teaching–learning process; the criteria for evaluating reflection were reduced to observable dimensions of the interactive teaching act.

The major purpose, according to this view of reflective teaching, was to develop teachers who were capable of executing technical skills of teaching to achieve prespecified goals. This approach, which was dominant in the behavioristic paradigm of teacher education, included operationally stated objectives, criterion tasks, gradually increasing difficulty, active student participation, and feedback as important components of effective teaching.

More recently, the methodological emphasis has been on qualitative, ethnographic, or interpretative studies. This change in methodology has been due in part to the complexities of reflective teaching. Varying subject-matter knowledge, complex political and ethical principles underlying teaching, and problematic education institutions do not readily generate plausible and discrete hypotheses to test. Reflective teaching cannot be evaluated using a fixed set of procedures. Typically, the first data on reflective teaching are collected by observing teachers at work gathering data on site and describing the teachers' practical reasoning through extended interviews. In these interviews, teachers are asked to ascribe meaning and values to specific things (e.g., students behavior, parents' educational roles, or their own classroom performance). Finally, there is the problem of determining the merit of reflective teaching: what constitutes good or bad reflection? (Kagan 1990).

3. Processes of Reflective Teaching

Drawing on the theory of Habermas, Van Manen (1977) has suggested that reflection occurs at three different stages. These stages correspond to three forms of knowledge and the associated cognitive interests: technical rationality, practical action, and critical reflection.

Technical rationality. At this empirical–analytic level, reflectivity is concerned with the application of knowledge to the pursuit of some desired goal or end point. The dominant concern of the teacher is efficient and effective application of pedagogical knowledge. This level of reflectivity is central in the tradition of pragmatic modes of thinking.

Practical action. At the hermeneutic–phenomenological level, reflectivity focuses on understanding the interaction of individuals. The teacher becomes concerned with clarifying the predispositions underlying competing educational aims and with evaluating the educational consequences toward which a teaching action leads.

Critical reflection. At the critical–theoretical level, reflectivity employs an emancipatory theory of truth. The teacher incorporates moral and ethical criteria into the discourse about practical actions, and reflects upon the underlying assumptions that constrain or shape the practice.

4. Reflective Teaching and the Curriculum of Teacher Education

There are several important features of reflective teaching in the preservice teacher education curriculum. Some of the most important are outlined briefly below.

Critical approaches. The curriculum will emphasize critical approaches to field experiences, seminars, methods courses, and social foundations courses. Programs should strive to prepare students critically to analyze ethical and value-based educational practices and to examine knowledge in the following dimensions: teaching-learning process, disciplines, political and ethical assumptions underlying school and university teaching, and, most broadly, the nature of school and university institutions and society itself.

Skills and attitudes. The curriculum will seek to combine certain skills which are involved in classroom inquiry, practical action, and classroom competence, and attitudes of open-mindedness, responsibility, and wholeheartedness. The interests, ideologies, values, dispositions, role functions, and differentiated responsibilities form the dynamic and tacit course context in which preservice teacher education curriculum decisions will be made.

Process model. The curriculum will stress a process model in which teachers will develop "self-monitoring and self-inquiring" habits and be able to evaluate and revise their own practice reflectively. This cyclical or spiralling process provides the fundamental dynamic of teachers' practical theories; the teacher is viewed as a producer of knowledge. Thus, action research can be used as a powerful vehicle for encouraging teachers to tell their own stories, and it also relates to the more socially progressive strands of the teacher-as-researcher movement.

Curriculum integration. Courses will approach an integration of the curriculum. Educators argue that an interdisciplinary curriculum increases student teachers' motivation, enables the learners to confront problems that are ignored by separate disciplines, and relates educational curriculum and research to the student teacher's own insights, reflections, and judgments. Curriculum integration is developed as an interpersonal process among educators and student teachers. This curriculum approach implies the need for a collaborative and cooperative enterprise.

5. Field Experiences for the Preparation of Reflective Teachers

Field experience is essential to the reflective process, since it will either reinforce or modify what schooling and curriculum mean to student teachers. The aims of critical reflection can be accomplished through a defined set of field experiences and concomitant workshops which occur in three phases.

In the first phase, the field experiences and workshops are intended to enable teachers to problematize (i.e., problem posing rather than problem solving) the settings in which they work. Through conversation among themselves working as a group, teachers can problematize dilemmas and issues they want to work on in their own practice.

In the second phase, field experiences and workshops provide an opportunity to observe others teach and to discuss their observations with one another. The sharing of experiences inherent in reflective teaching potentially has three positive outcomes. First, student teachers may come to value their personal and craft knowledge (Grimmett and MacKinnon 1992) instead of viewing it as inferior to the pedagogical knowledge produced by expert teachers. Second, shared experiences may lead to strong collegiality. Third, peer collaboration allows meaning to be constructed jointly by student teachers through the process of collegial dialogue and postobservational supervisory conferences. Questions raised during the peer coaching conversation focus student teachers' attention on their initial problematic thoughts and attitudes during teaching, redefine the contextual interpretations of teaching dilemmas, generate the advantages and disadvantages of various solutions within the particular teaching practice context, and permit the consideration of various approaches to evaluating the results.

In the third phase—exploratory experimentation—student teachers are encouraged to consider issues from different perspectives, to reframe the problematic situation in light of its characteristics, to view all solutions of problems as possible, and to act deliberately to produce an end, monitoring the effects of any solution attempted.

Teacher educators need to develop strategies which will actively encourage student teachers' reflection upon practice. In this regard, teacher educators should:

(a) recognize that it is their responsibility to train student teachers to reflect upon their teaching practice;

(b) expose student teachers to the social context and the real and conflicting world of the classroom;

(c) set valid standards by which students' reflection can be measured and judged; and,

(d) create field experiences that require student teachers to function as conscious moral agents in order to create a just society.

6. Professional Development of Reflective Practitioners

The image of teacher research is undergoing reevaluation. Teachers' language and judgments have become the medium of school social life as well as the focus of interpretative inquiry. The interpretation of teachers' thoughts, speech, and actions occurs within a social and educational context. The questions teachers ask, the ways they write, and the schemata they use to frame classroom practices can be powerful in heightening teachers' awareness of their own professional reasoning. Within this framework teachers are neither uninformed participants nor merely collaborative resources. Rather, they are simultaneously researchers, instructors, and ana-

lysts. Teachers are guided to reveal and examine their craft knowledge and improvisational performance by engaging in four types of analysis: "analysis of self as a practitioner; analysis of the meaning of one's professional actions; analysis of underlying assumptions; and reconsideration of teaching practices in light of the fruits of analysis" (Lalik et al. 1989).

According to Smyth (1989), teachers should engage in four forms of actions in order to change ideologies and the working conditions that constrain them. These actions are describing, informing, confronting, and reconstructing.

Describing is a stage where a teacher answers the question: "What do I do?" As teachers reflect about their actions, they describe the knowledge, beliefs, and principles that characterize their practice. Teaching is viewed as a text written in the language of teachers; the use of journals or diaries comprises the events and dilemmas that form teachers' tacit knowledge.

Informing is a stage initiated by the guiding question: "What does this mean?" Teachers uncover their short-range, explanatory, or local theories that inform their teaching action. As teachers describe, analyze, and make inferences about classroom events, they are creating their own pedagogical principles. These subjective theories help them make sense of what is going on in the school and society and guide further action.

Confronting is a stage at which the teacher responds to the question: "How did I come to be like this?" Teachers seek out the constructions of their assumptions, ideas, values, and beliefs, and how social and institutional forces have influenced them. They see knowledge as constructed symbolically by the mind through social interaction with others.

Reconstructing is the stage at which teachers answer the question: "How might I do things differently?" The intention of this form of action for teachers is to critique and uncover the tensions that exist between particular teaching practices and the larger cultural and social contexts in which they are embedded. The primary characteristic of this social reconstructionist conception is its commitment to reflection as a communal activity where teachers can support each other's knowledge (Zeichner and Tabachnick 1991).

Despite the efforts to promote reflective teaching courses, this approach remains insufficiently widespread. Sykes (1986) gives five broad explanations for the relative absence of reflection-in-action. They are:

(a) The limitations of human information processing. The assumption is that teachers use basic and limited cognitive processes in their daily school lives.

(b) The nature of teaching as work. Teaching is viewed as an unstable and confused activity which does not warrant systematic reflectivity.

(c) The socialization and training of teachers. Prospective teachers have followed a conventional and traditional curriculum of teacher education based on the technocratic tradition.

(d) The organizational context of teaching. School work does not favor inquiry.

(e) The modal characteristics of teachers. This controversial speculation points out that teachers are selected with certain academic characteristics.

7. Strategies for Promoting Reflection

Some authors have restricted the focus of reflection to an examination of means, rather than ends. From this perspective, reflective teaching consists of controlled and thoughtfully designed teacher experiences (Gore 1987). Central to this approach is the need to acquire technical teaching skills, such as systematic classroom observation of others, self-assessment of student teaching, journal writing, and simulated teaching (Freiber and Waxman 1990). Schön (1987) portrays the way in which sensitive dialogue, modeling, and the establishment of challenging practical experiences can produce professional artistry or reflective competence in teaching. In addition, Kottkamp (1990) has developed a catalogue of means or tactics to facilitate reflection among teachers and other professionals. Included in this catalogue are the following items:

(a) writing—writing is used to capture teachers' thought processes and yield a product that can be evaluated and reformulated.

(b) journals—data provided in daily records may be used to search for patterns of meaning;

(c) case records—writing a case record is a structured activity that expands the number of teaching alternatives;

(d) contrived situations—these include simulated teaching situations, like role plays, case studies, simulations, and microteaching;

(e) instrument feedback—scales and inventories can be used to provide teachers with data useful for reflection on their actions;

(f) electronic feedback—videotaping teachers' actions provides records of events, issues, and feelings for reflection-on-action;

(g) metaphors—metaphors can be used to clarify the personal meaning teachers attach to their particular teaching's action:

(h) platforms—these are, according to Schön (1987), teachers' espoused theories, their stated intentions. Writing a platform engages teachers in a reflective process on the congruity or incongruity between espoused theory and theory-in-use.

8. Future Trends

In the early 1990s there appears to be a major shift in the way teaching and teacher education are conceptualized. There is a greater interest in teacher cognitions and reflective thinking. Research on reflective teaching is under way at major universities in several countries (Korthagen 1985, Carr and Kemmis 1986, Pollard and Tann 1987). The emerging preservice teacher education curriculum points to the emergence and development of the reflective teaching paradigm. There is a growing need for descriptions of existing models of reflective teaching, each specifying its own problems as well as successful solutions. At the same time, however, knowledge about reflective teaching has increased substantially since the late 1980s.

See also: Teachers as Researchers; Paradigms for Research on Teaching

References

Carr W, Kemmis S 1986 *Becoming Critical: Education, Knowledge and Action Research.* Falmer Press, London
Dewey J 1933 *How We Think.* Heath, Boston, Massachusetts
Elliott J 1991 *Action Research for Educational Change.* Open University Press, Milton Keynes
Freiber H J, Waxman H C 1990 Reflection and the acquisition of technical teaching skills. In: Clift R T, Houston W R, Pugach M C (eds.) 1990 *Encouraging Reflective Practice in Education: An Analysis of Issues and Programs.* Teacher College Press, New York
Gore J M 1987 Reflecting on reflective teaching. *J. Teach Educ.* 38(2): 33–9
Grimmett P P, MacKinnon A M 1992 Craft knowledge and the education of teachers. In: Grant G(ed.) 1992 *Review of Research in Education,* Vol. 18. American Educational Research Association, Washington, DC
Kagan D M 1990 Ways of evaluating teacher cognition: Inferences concerning the Goldilocks principle. *Rev. Educ. Res.* 60(3): 419–69
Korthagen F 1985 Reflective teaching and preservice teacher education in the Netherlands. *J. Teach. Educ.* 36(5): 11–15
Kottkamp R B 1990 Means for facilitating reflection. *Educ. Urban Soc.* 22(2): 182–203
Lalik R V, Niles J A, Murphy S B 1989 Using your head and your heart: A study of a process for promoting reflection among student teachers. Paper presented at the American Educational Research Association, San Francisco, California
Pollard A, Tann S 1987 *Reflective Teaching in the Primary School. A Handbook for the Classroom.* Cassell, London
Schön D A 1987 *Educating the Reflective Practitioner. Toward a New Design for Teaching and Learning in the Professions.* Jossey-Bass, San Francisco, California
Smyth J 1989 Developing and sustaining critical reflection in teacher education. *J. Teach. Educ.* 40(2): 2–9
Sykes G 1986 Teaching as reflective practice. In: Sirotnik K A, Oakes J (eds.) 1986 *Critical Perspectives on the Organization and Improvement of Schooling.* Kluwer, Nijhoff, Boston, Massachusetts

Van Manen M 1977 Linking ways of knowing with ways of being practical. *Curric. Inq.* 6(3): 205–28

Zeichner K M, Tabachnick B R 1991 Reflections on reflective teaching. In: Tabachnick B R, Zeicher K M (eds.) 1991 *Issues and Practices in Inquiry-Oriented Teacher Education.* Falmer Press, London

Further Reading

Gore J M, Zeichner K M 1991 Action research and reflective teaching. *Teaching Teach. Educ.* 7(2): 119–36

Habermas J 1971 *Knowledge and Human Interests.* Beacon Press, Boston, Massachusetts

Smith D 1991 Educating the reflective practitioner in curriculum. *Curric.* 12(2): 115–24

Villar L M 1991 *El profesor como profesional reflexivo: Formacion y desarrollo personal.* ICE y Servicio de Publicaciones de la Universidad, Granada

Zeichner K M, Liston D P 1987 Teaching student teachers to reflect. *Harvard Educ. Rev.* 57(1): 23–48

SECTION IV

Teaching Skills and Techniques

Introduction

L. W. Anderson

A variety of teaching skills and techniques is needed to implement successfully every one of the instructional programs or strategies included in Part A, Section III. Stated somewhat differently, instructional programs and strategies represent the "master plans" of teachers. In contrast, teaching skills and techniques enable them to operate within these plans on an hourly, daily, and weekly basis. Metaphorically speaking, these skills and techniques give life and meaning to the instructional programs and strategies in which they are embedded.

The 28 entries in this section are divided into subsections which represent four of the primary teaching functions (Rosenshine and Stevens 1986). They are: planning, classroom management, teaching, and assessing and evaluating. Teachers must perform each of these functions regardless of the instructional program or strategy within which they choose to operate. Exactly *how* they perform these functions (that is, which of the specific skills and techniques they choose to use), however, depends on the instructional program or strategy being implemented as well as on the background and characteristics of the teachers themselves.

1. Planning

The eight entries in the subsection on planning all deal with teacher planning. Yinger and Hendricks-Lee's entry provides an overview of planning. In their words, "Often, the best that planning can accomplish is to prepare teachers to participate thoughtfully and effectively in classroom interaction. Planning produces frames for action: preparation produces a frame of mind."

The remaining entries in this subsection are concerned with elements of the classroom for which teachers must plan. In today's classrooms, for example, teachers must plan for the use of technology (Hativa). Hativa contends that one of the major barriers to the use of technology in classrooms is the extra burden it

places on the time and effort needed for planning and preparation.

Teachers must decide in advance how they will seat the students in their classrooms (Lambert). These seating arrangements are based primarily on the purpose of the lesson and the type of interactions needed to accomplish that purpose. If group discussions or cooperative working arrangements are necessary, the seating arrangements must be conducive to these activities (Barr).

As part of their planning, teachers must ensure that what students are being taught is consistent with objectives contained in the curriculum and, perhaps more importantly in some countries, the objectives embedded in formal tests and assessments (Cohen). In addition, teachers must ensure that sufficient time is allowed for the desired learning to occur (Anderson and Torrey). In this regard, teachers would be wise to remember the simple axiom that learning takes time.

All of these planning decisions are made within the context of a variety of temporal units: years, terms, marking periods, and lessons (Yinger and Hendricks-Lee). Wragg's entry focuses on one of the smaller units, lesson planning. Interestingly, the same matters that must be confronted by teachers on annual and monthly bases also must be addressed within each lesson.

2. Classroom Management

There is an easy way to differentiate classroom management from teaching. Classroom management focuses on the management of *learners*, while teaching emphasizes the management of *learning* (Anderson and Block 1977). Similarly, Evertson reminds us of the distinction between problems of order (classroom management) and problems of learning (teaching). The five entries in the second subsection pertain to classroom management; those in the third, to teaching.

Classroom management involves the use of both preventive and reactive strategies (Emmer). Two of

185

the entries in this subsection focus almost exclusively on preventive strategies: instructional pacing, and classroom rules and routines.

Anderson argues that the pace of instruction is critical to both order and learning. Too slow a pace permits misbehavior to occur and can impact negatively on student learning (e.g., too much redundancy). With respect to pacing, then, order and learning are clearly interrelated.

Classroom rules and routines establish the parameters within which behaviors and learning are expected to occur (Evertson). Rules are "general norms for expected behavior. They govern the moral and ethical life of the classroom" (Evertson). In contrast, routines are the "'how to's' for day-to-day functioning within the value system provided by the rules" (Evertson).

The remaining three entries in this subsection address both preventive and reactive matters. In his entry, Emmer emphasizes the role of the teacher in classroom management. Three aspects of this role are particularly important: the way in which teachers begin the school year, how they maintain the flow of activity in the classroom and thus preventive misbehavior, and what teachers do when misbehavior occurs.

Sladeczek and Kratochwill describe the concept of reinforcement while Cairns discusses the larger matter of behavioral analysis and modification. The authors of both entries argue that teachers have three primary options with respect to modifying student behavior. First, they can reward those behaviors they wish to promote or encourage (positive reinforcement). Second, they may withhold expected rewards when students exhibit behaviors teachers wish to extinguish or discourage (negative reinforcement). Third, teachers may punish students that exhibit improper behaviors (punishment or aversive stimuli). The advantages and disadvantages of these options along with means by which they can be implemented in classrooms are examined in these entries.

3. Classroom Teaching

Teachers have a variety of tools available to them as they attempt to teach their students well. The 11 entries in the subsection on teaching in the classroom discuss many of these available tools. The first four entries address tools that teachers use primarily when they engage in direct instruction, although these tools can be used with a variety of instructional strategies. They are: explaining (Cruickshank and Metcalf), demonstrating (Comber and Keeves), questioning (Gall and Artero-Boname), and providing feedback (Mayer).

The next five entries include tools that teachers frequently make use of as they move from direct to indirect instruction (or from formal to informal teaching). Some of these tools involve a collaborative relationship between teachers and students: discussion (Dillon), and small group teaching (Sharan). Others give primary responsibility for learning to students: simulations and games (Cudworth), seatwork (Anderson), and homework (Walberg and Paschat).

The final two entries concern tools that teachers tend to use infrequently or delegate to others (tutoring) or may use without even knowing they are doing so (nonverbal behavior). As Medway suggests "Tutoring most often supplements traditional classroom instruction . . . for those students who require remedial help or those who have difficulty learning by conventional methods." Furthermore, tutoring often "refers to instruction not provided by a student's regular teacher."

Finally, Smith details the complexity of nonverbal classroom behavior. Nonverbal classroom behavior includes such diverse elements as proxemics (that is, the use of a teacher or student's social and personal space in the classroom), haptics (that is, touching behavior), kinesics (that is, observable gestures, body movements, postures, and eye and facial behaviors), silence, and chronemics (that is, the use of time). Smith also discusses paralanguage (that is, voice pitch, volume, tempo, and intensity) which lies somewhere between verbal and nonverbal behavior.

4. Assessing and Evaluating

Once teachers have planned, managed, and taught, they find themselves having to assess and evaluate. Assessment is a concept that is broader than testing. The purpose of assessment is to gather information that teachers can use to make and defend decisions about students and their instruction. Tests are certainly one means by which teachers can make such decisions. However, teachers can also use observations of classroom behaviors and student performances, student performance on daily and weekly assignments, and long-term student projects (e.g., term papers).

In contrast to assessing, evaluating implies making judgments about the information gathered. These judgments may pertain to placing students into appropriate learning settings and situations, monitoring the present level of learning and achievement of students, diagnosing the probable causes for students' learning difficulties and problems, and determining the level of student attainment so that grades or marks can be assigned (Helmke).

All but one of the six entries in this subsection focus on the importance of assessment and evaluation in facilitating student learning. Lane and Glaser make this point most clearly. Zahorik discusses the ways in which teachers continually evaluate their classrooms and their students, while Helmke focuses on the use of information to identify students needs. Airasian describes both informal and formal (or official) assessments made by teachers, while Linacre argues that if testing is to provide the information that teachers need to make instructional and learning decisions, the focus must be on the individual student rather than groups of students. The final entry, by Borich and Kubiszyn raises a number of issues pertaining to grading or marking students based on the information available to teachers.

5. Conclusion

If teachers are to be effective in their classrooms, they must be able to perform consistently four primary functions: planning, classroom management, teaching, and assessment and evaluation. Furthermore, in order for teachers to perform these functions, they must (a) acquire and possess a variety of skills and techniques, (b) use these skills and techniques as the need arises, and (c) make adjustments as needed.

The best way to conceptualize the entries in this section, then, is to visualize a toolbox within which teachers place the individual skills and techniques they acquire and possess. Each of the entries represents one tool (e.g., seating arrangements = screwdriver; classroom rules and routines = hammer; questioning = wrench). Like a carpenter, then, teachers must not only have the necessary tools, but also must be able to use them well and appropriately.

References

Anderson L W, Block J H 1977 Mastery learning. In: Treffinger D, Davis J K, Ripple R (eds.) 1977 *Handbook on Teaching Educational Psychology*. McGraw-Hill, New York

Rosenshine B V, Stevens R 1986 Teaching functions. In: Wittrock M C (ed.) 1986 *Handbook of Research on Teaching*, 3rd edn. Macmillan, New York

(a) Planning the Classroom

Teacher Planning

R. J. Yinger and M. S. Hendricks-Lee

Planning is an essential component of teaching. Teachers are responsible daily and over the course of the year for selecting and designing subject matter-based learning experiences reflecting a school curriculum and community learning goals. A teacher must also be ready to respond to student needs and interests and be ready to make the most of unanticipated learning opportunities arising in instructional interactions. Doing this successfully requires preparation.

1. Conceptions of Planning

Planning and preparation have been the object of educational theory and research since the early 1950s. Since then, there have been major shifts in philosophy, disciplinary theory, and research methods. Dominant conceptions of teaching have moved from scientific, to managerial, to professional. Likewise, research on teaching has shifted from being dominated by psychological conceptions to incorporating concepts from sociology, anthropology, linguistics, and philosophy.

Within psychology, orientations have changed from entirely behavioral to cognitive and sociocultural. Research methods have expanded during these years from almost exclusively laboratory-based and experimental to embrace naturalistic, field-based approaches. The findings of research on teacher planning and the emerging conceptions about planning's role in teaching are best understood in the context of this dynamic research environment. Research on teacher planning can be characterized as a shift from technical to psychological to ecological conceptions of planning and instruction.

1.1 Technical Conceptions

Prior to 1970 the study of teacher planning was largely confined to theoretical prescriptions focusing on the form that good plans should take. These models, similar to rational decision making models defining rational practice in other fields, recommended four basic planning steps: (a) specify objectives, (b) select learning activities, (c) organize learning activities,

and (d) specify evaluation procedures (Tyler 1950, Popham and Baker 1970). Underlying this model was the dominant assumption that student learning is under the control of the teacher and that careful design and management of small units of instruction is the major determinant of student success. This assumption undergirded scientific and technical models dominating teaching in the 1950s and 1960s. It expressed itself in the almost exclusive focus on precise (usually behavioral) specification of learning objectives and instructional tasks (Mager 1962).

1.2 Psychological Conceptions

In 1970 educational researchers began to study the actual planning processes of classroom teachers. One factor leading to this interest was the observation that the linear, objective-driven planning procedures that dominated teacher education were rarely found useful by experienced and successful classroom teachers. Were teachers abandoning rationality for expediency or was there another form of reasonableness in their practice? In effect, this question framed research on teacher planning from 1970 to the mid-1980s.

Early empirical studies in the 1970s confirmed the hypothesis that teachers' instructional planning did not tend to follow the prescribed planning models. Taylor's (1970) study of course planning strategies reported by teachers in British secondary schools found that the needs, abilities, and interests of pupils rather than predetermined objectives dominated syllabus planning. Zahorik (1975) found similar results in his examination of the reported use of behavioral objectives and the "separate ends–means" model in comparison to the "integrated ends–means" model proposed by Eisner (1967) that viewed objectives as implicit in learning activities. Planning decisions most frequently listed by teachers in his study related to pupil activities, and just over half of the teachers said they began their planning by making decisions about lesson content.

Studies observing teacher decision-making during simulated or controlled classroom planning sessions in the mid-1970s yielded findings similar to those above.

Peterson et al. (1978) examined teachers' plans as they prepared to teach an unfamiliar group of students in a laboratory situation. They found teachers spent the largest proportion of their planning time on the content to be taught, the next largest amount on strategies and activities (instructional processes), and the smallest portion on objectives.

Morine-Dershimer and Vallance's (1976) study of written plans collected for experimenter-prescribed lessons found teachers paid little explicit attention to behavioral objectives, diagnosis of pupils' needs, evaluation procedures, and alternate courses of action in their written plans. However, the teachers reported that writing plans for researcher-prescribed lessons was not typical of their planning, and observations of their classroom teaching revealed that much of what the teachers had planned was not reflected in their written outlines (Morine-Dershimer 1979).

The growing influence of cognitive psychology on research on teaching in the 1970s led to research questions and studies focusing on describing the mental processes involved in teacher planning. Laboratory studies of teachers' decisions and judgments during planning (Clark and Yinger 1979, Shavelson and Borko 1979) confirmed the self-reports from earlier studies that content and student concerns rather than well-specified objectives were the focus of planning deliberations for most teachers. These studies also suggested that the instructional activity was an important organizing framework for teacher thought and behavior.

An extended classroom case study of teacher planning by Yinger (1980) combined process-tracing methods from cognitive psychology with ethnographic methods from anthropology to create a broad description of planning processes over the course of a school year. The most significant finding of this study was the complex ways in which planning deliberations were embedded in a particular teaching context. Lesson planning was found to be situated in and dependent upon a complex network of yearly plans, term plans, unit plans, and weekly and daily plans. The teacher's knowledge and experience with the particular students and subject matter materials from one day to the next contributed to a highly responsive and recursive mode of planning and teaching.

These observations and a review of research on planning in other professional fields led Yinger (1980) to propose a cyclical process model describing planning as a progressive elaboration of both goals and activities over time, based on a teacher's knowledge of past successes and failures and the ability to fine-tune instruction in response to anticipated student needs and abilities. Though this model was focused on describing teachers' mental planning processes, it clearly revealed the degree to which teacher thought and action is situated in complex social, cultural, and historical contexts.

This grounding of teacher thinking was dramatically revealed in a later study by Yinger and Clark (1982) when they asked teachers to judge the quality of plans for language arts instructional activities. A process tracing analysis of these teachers' judgments revealed that they were unwilling and unable to judge quality or usefulness without mentally projecting and visualizing the plans as they played out in their own classrooms with their current set of students. Smith and Sandelbach (1979) found similar mental projections in the unit planning of sixth grade teachers' science instruction.

1.3 Ecological Conceptions

Research since 1980 has moved from examining planning as an individual psychological process and has begun investigating the connections between planning and classroom interaction, the ways planning and teaching respond to subject matter content, and the give and take that occurs in classrooms. Carnahan (1980) studied the planning and subsequent instructional behavior of nine fifth-grade teachers teaching the same mathematics unit. He found that the main relationship between written plans and instructional interaction was organizational and structural rather than predicting and specifying particular verbal behavior. These findings are similar to those in Clark and Yinger's (1979) survey of the planning of 78 teachers who reported that written plans rarely serve the purpose of providing detailed lesson scripts to be implemented by the teacher in class. Instead, the teachers' written responses to why they plan fell into three clusters:

(a) planning to meet immediate personal needs (e.g., to reduce uncertainty and anxiety, to find a sense of direction, confidence, and security);

(b) planning as a means to the end of instruction (e.g., to learn the material, to collect and organize materials, to organize time and activity flow); and

(c) direct use of plans during instruction (e.g., to organize students, to get an activity started, to aid memory, to provide a framework for instruction and evaluation).

McLeod's (1981) study based on stimulated recall interviews with 17 kindergarten teachers found that on the average an equal amount of intended learning outcomes are formulated during classroom interaction as during planning. These, as well as other studies examining planning and interaction (Acosta 1986, Broeckmans 1985, Peterson et al. 1978, Zahorik 1970) taken together, suggest that teacher planning does influence opportunity to learn, content coverage, grouping for instruction, and the general focus of classroom processes. They also highlight that the finer details of classroom interaction are unpredictable and, therefore, are not planned. Planning frames the broad outlines of what is possible or likely to occur while teaching (Creemers and Westerhof 1982), but once interaction begins, planning moves to the background and instructional improvisation becomes more important (Yinger 1987).

The trend in research on teaching has been to study teaching and classroom practices from a more holistic perspective. Fewer studies have focused on planning as a separate teaching component. Rather, planning is being described and analyzed as it is connected to classroom practices and teacher knowledge. For example, Leinhardt and her colleagues have sought to understand how teachers use subject matter knowledge in planning lesson frameworks ("agendas") and during interactive instruction (Leinhardt et al. 1987). In her study comparing expert and novice mathematics instruction (Leinhardt 1989) she found mathematics lessons composed by expert teachers incorporating rich agendas, consistent but flexible lesson structures, and clear, understandable explanations.

Borko and Livingston (1989), in their study of beginning and experienced teachers of mathematics, also found that much of the success of experienced teachers lay with their abilities to think more broadly and long-term about intended outcomes, to draw upon a richer representational repertoire for lesson content and structure, and to be more responsive to incorporating students' questions and interests into lessons. These and other classroom studies of teaching practice (e.g., Dillard 1992, Lampert 1986) indicate that both planning and classroom interaction are responsive, compositional, and situated (i.e., contextualized).

2. Classroom Interaction and Teacher Planning

Studies of language and social interaction in classrooms describe the social and cultural nature of lessons (Cazden 1986). Though teachers enter classrooms with purposes and plans, these studies detail how both teaching and learning are jointly constructed, socially negotiated, and embedded in an interactional history (Mehan 1979). Not only are memories, understandings, and actions present on an individual basis, but studies of sustained interaction in learning communities indicate that memory and meaning are created and shared synergistically and often are known only in the actions of the group (Wertsch 1987).

A number of studies of teacher interaction suggest that improvisation rather than implementation or decision-making is a more powerful way of describing the performance skills of many teachers (Borko and Livingston 1989, Buswinka 1990, Haley-Oliphant 1990, Yinger 1987). The ability to respond to the give-and-take of learners and situations is largely based on a sophisticated repertoire of subject matter appropriate knowledge and activity frameworks. Skillful teaching, these studies suggest, is deeply situated (contextualized) both within the subject matter and the place of the classroom, school, and community.

Portraying the interactive components of teaching as responsive, compositional, and situated helps explain the findings of much of the research on teacher planning. Getting ready for interaction as dynamic as that which occurs during instructional lessons seems to be less a matter of prediction and control and more a matter of preparation and responsiveness. In this framework, planning that produces more general, flexible, and activity-based plans will be more useful than narrowly specified, objective-oriented plans. Also, plans become more useful if they are not designed to be implemented as a means of controlling interaction, but rather as a framing device that provides a starting point of instructional interaction.

Rather than seeing planning and classroom interaction as separate activities or processes, then, research findings highlight their connectedness and similarity.

Planning	Interaction
Intention (individual)	Intention (individual and jointly constructed)
Knowledge (individual)	Knowledge (individual and shared)
Interaction (individual: mental and physical)	Interaction (social and mutual)
Place (deliberate: known and envisioned)	Place (interactive: experienced and created)
To create	To create
↓	↓
Frames for action (plans) Frames of mind (preparation)	Activity, understanding, and relationship

Figure 1
Differences between planning and interaction

Goals, purpose, and intention are a part of both planning and interaction. Both processes are highly interactive and sensitive to context and place.

3. Differences Between Planning and Interaction

As Fig. 1 outlines, the major difference between planning and interaction is that intention, knowledge, and interaction in planning are limited by the individual's knowledge and experience and the inability to control, predict, or even comprehensively understand what is to come in the future. Planning seeks to anticipate activities, conversations, questions, responses, and relationships in classrooms. Often, the best that planning can accomplish is to prepare teachers to participate thoughtfully and effectively in classroom interaction. Planning produces frames for action; preparation produces a frame of mind.

Once instruction begins, intention, knowledge, and interaction must respond to a created context and to multiple participants. Intentions become negotiated, knowledge shared, and interactions mutual. A well prepared teacher can harness this dynamic energy to achieve the understanding and relationships important to student learning. Exactly how this gets accomplished in a particular situation becomes part of a teacher's repertoire of knowledge and experience and thus a potential contributor to future planning and preparation.

See also: Teachers' Roles; Frame Factors

References

Acosta J M 1986 Pensamiento del Profesor y la Planificación de la Enseñanza. Paper presented at the 1st International Congress on Teacher Thinking and Decision Making, La Rabida

Borko H, Livingston C 1989 Cognition and improvisation: Differences in mathematics instruction by expert and novice teachers. *Am. Educ. Res. J.* 26: 473–98

Broeckmans J 1985 Developments in student-teachers' preactive teaching. Paper presented at International Study Association on Teacher Thinking conference, Tilburg University, Tilburg

Buswinka H F 1990 A Change in practice: A case study of teacher thinking-in-action. Doctoral dissertation, University of Cincinnati, Cincinnati, Ohio

Carnahan R S 1980 *The Effects of Teacher Planning on Classroom Processes.* Wisconsin R & D Center for Individualized Schooling, Madison, Wisconsin

Cazden C 1986 Classroom discourse. In: Wittrock M C (ed.) 1986 *Handbook of Research on Teaching*, 3rd edn. Macmillan, New York

Clark C M, Yinger R J 1979 Three studies of teacher planning. Paper presented at American Educational Research Association, San Francisco, California

Creemers B P M, Westerhof K 1982 *Routinization of Instructive and Management Behaviors of Teachers.* Educational Research Institute, North Haren

Dillard J A 1992 Voice in the conversation of practice: A case study of teacher thinking-in-action. Doctoral dissertation, University of Cincinnati, Cincinnati, Ohio

Eisner E W 1967 Educational objects: Help or hindrance *Sch. Rev.* 75: 250–60

Haley-Oliphant A 1990 Classroom ecology in a science class: A description of interaction patterns in the margins of lessons. Doctoral dissertation, University of Cincinnati, Cincinnati, Ohio

Lampert M 1986 Knowing, doing and teaching multiplication. *Cognition and Instruction* 3(4): 305–42

Leinhardt G 1989 Math lessons: A contrast of novice and expert competence. *J. Res. Math. Educ.* 20(1): 52–75

Leinhardt G, Wideman C, Hammond K M 1987 Introduction and integration of classroom routines by expert teachers. *Curric. Inq.* 17(2): 135–76

Mager R F 1962 *Preparing Instructional Objectives.* Fearon Publishers, Belmont, California

McLeod M A 1981 The identification of intended learning outcomes by early childhood teachers: An exploratory study. Doctoral dissertation, University of Alberta, Edmonton

Mehan H 1979 *Learning Lessons: Social Organization in the Classroom.* Harvard University Press, Cambridge, Massachusetts

Morine-Dershimer G 1979 *Teacher Plan and Classroom Reality: The South Bay Study.* Institute for Research on Teaching, East Lansing, Michigan

Morine-Dershimer G, Vallance E 1976 *Teacher Planning.* Far West Laboratory, San Francisco, California

Peterson P L, Marx R W, Clark C M 1978 Teacher planning, teacher behavior, and student achievement. *Am. Educ. Res. J.* 15: 417–32

Popham J W, Baker E L 1970 *Systematic Instruction.* Prentice-Hall, Englewood Cliffs New Jersey

Shavelson R J, Borko H 1979 Research on teachers' decisions in planning instruction. *Educational Horizons* 57(4): 183–89

Smith E L, Sandelbach N B 1979 Teacher intentions for science instruction and their antecedents in program materials. Paper presented at the American Educational Research Association, San Francisco, California

Taylor P H 1970 *How Teachers Plan Their Courses.* National Foundation for Educational Research, Windsor

Tyler R W 1950 *Basic Principles of Curriculum and Instruction.* University of Chicago Press, Chicago, Illinois

Wertsch J 1987 Collective memory: Issues from a sociohistorical perspective. *Quarterly Newsletter of the Laboratory of Comparative Human Cognition* 9(1): 19–22

Yinger R J 1980 A study of teacher planning. *Elem. Sch. J.* 80(3): 107–27

Yinger R J 1987 By the seat of your pants: An inquiry into improvisation and teaching. Paper presented at the American Educational Research Association, Washington, DC

Yinger R J, Clark C M 1982 *Understanding Teachers' Judgments about Instruction: The Task, the Method, and the Meaning.* Institute for Research on Teaching, East Lansing, Michigan

Zahorik J A 1970 Effects of planning on teaching. *Elem. Sch. J.* 71: 143–51

Zahorik J A 1975 Teachers' planning models. *Educ. Leadership* 33(2): 134–39

Further Reading

Borko H 1970 An examination of some factors contributing to teacher preinstructional classroom organization and management decisions. Paper presented at the American

Educational Research Association, Toronto, Ontario

Mintz S L 1970 Teacher planning: Simulation study. Paper presented at the American Educational Research Association, San Francisco, California

Grouping Students in the Classroom

R. Barr

The issue of how students can best be organized for instruction in classrooms has stimulated much theoretical and ideological debate. This entry addresses cross-national differences in the social organization of schools and classrooms; briefly describes the trends in the historical literature; examines the findings from the more recent case study and survey literatures pertaining to elementary, middle, and secondary schooling; and speculates about future patterns of social organization.

1. Cross-national Differences

Because of national differences in historical experiences, schools in different countries serve such varied functions as education for the masses, entrance into the labor force, formation of governing and social elites, and inculcation of moral values. Consequently, different kinds of schools have developed in different nations, with different boundary lines drawn between levels of schooling. There also are differences within levels in how aggregates of students are grouped for instruction.

Educational systems in all societies deal with issues of how students can best be grouped together to profit from instruction and arrive at varying solutions to this problem depending on social and historical circumstances. "Streaming" in the lower schools in the United Kingdom, for example, represents an approach similar to some forms of ability grouping in schools in the United States. In both countries, teachers tend to group students within classes on the basis of ability (Jackson 1964). However, private schools attended by the socially elite provide a form of stratification that is more prominent in the United Kingdom than in the United States. Differentiation in the United Kingdom as well as in continental Europe occurs as well through the development of different types of schools, particularly at the secondary level (Hamilton 1987, Kerckhoff 1986, Stevenson and Stigler 1992).

Japan represents a major exception in this pervasive tendency to group elementary school students on the basis of ability for instruction (Cummings 1980). Japanese schools do, however, confront the problems

of diversity by different means such as a slow instructional pace, out-of-school tutoring, and parental involvement through home instruction (Mason et al. 1989, Stevenson and Stigler 1992). This early whole-class instruction in elementary schools is, however, followed by instruction in differentiated secondary schools (Kariya and Rosenbaum 1987).

In general, where secondary schools are distinguished by type and ability (as in Japan, the United Kingdom, and the European continent), the curriculum is not highly differentiated within schools. In contrast, where high schools are of the comprehensive type serving highly diverse student populations (as in the United States and, to a lesser extent, in the United Kingdom), tracking and curriculum differentiation prevail (Oakes et al. 1992). Trends similar to those in the United Kingdom are reported for Israel (Shavit and Williams 1985).

2. Traditional Studies Assessing the Effectiveness of Ability Grouping

An assumption underlying an ability grouping strategy is that the content of instruction needs to be matched to the prior knowledge of students for them to realize optimal learning. The validity of this assumption has been questioned. Traditionally, researchers have been concerned mainly with two questions: (a) Are more homogeneous groups of learners created through grouping? and (b) Do students grouped by ability learn more than comparable students in more heterogeneous groups?

The literature contains two major waves of reviews, one in the early 1930s and another in the 1960s. With respect to group homogeneity, educational researchers in the 1930s found that student performance in one area was not highly related to that in another, and that classes formed to be high and low in achievement were, in fact, highly overlapping in distribution. More recent appraisals continue to reveal significant overlap among groups, with less overlap among ability groups for reading instruction at the primary level than in intermediate grades (Barr and Dreeben 1991).

The reviewers of both periods criticize the adequacy

of the quasi-experimental studies that had been undertaken and emphasize the equivocal and inconsistent results from study to study. Yet these two groups of reviewers differ in their conclusions even though they are based, for the most part, on the same evidence. A substantial number of the early reviewers concluded, for example, that ability grouping benefited "slow" students. Many from the second wave, in contrast, discerned a tendency for high achievers in homogeneous groups to learn more than comparable students in heterogeneous groups, but for low achievers to do less well in homogeneous than heterogeneous groups (Barr and Dreeben 1991).

The findings from this quasi-experimental literature have been summarized using approaches such as meta-analysis (see, e.g., Slavin 1990). Still the main point in thinking about the traditional literature on grouping is its inconclusiveness. Ability grouping has not been shown to be clearly advantageous. Moreover, why one should expect more than inconsistent results is interesting. A social arrangement, of itself, does not lead directly to learning outcomes; rather, it is the instructional activities that students experience that influence what they learn and how they feel about it.

3. Descriptions of How Ability Grouping Schemes Work

Research in the 1980s and 1990s examines grouping in more broadly conceived ways, focusing on the instruction that students in different ability groups receive. It has become clear that membership in an ability group or track does not mean the same thing in different schools or even in the same school. The educational experiences of students vary markedly across tracks or groups, depending on the level and quality of the curricular materials used, the capabilities of teachers, and the aggregate characteristics of students from class to class. Reviews of this literature focus mainly on the results from case studies and surveys (Barr and Dreeben 1991, Oakes et al. 1992).

Concern with equality spawned several lines of inquiry, some going beyond narrow ideological concerns and leading to conceptualizations of ability grouping as part of the social systems of schools and classrooms. Some of the more interesting research of the 1970s and 1980s stems from concern with the mechanisms, such as curriculum differentiation and instructional quality, through which social background might influence education and life changes (Alexander and Cook 1982). Barr et al. (1983), for example, argue that the rate of curricular presentation is responsive to group ability, and it, in turn, influences the learning of students (for similar formulations, see Rowan and Miracle 1983, Sørenson and Hallinan 1986).

Along somewhat different lines, Cohen (1986) considers how individualized versus more traditional forms of teaching influence classroom authority, friendship among students, the attribution of status, and collaboration among teachers. She and her associates argue that traditional forms of instruction (restricted curricular tasks, ability grouping, and comparative grading) serve as the occasion for attributing low status to low achievers, thereby depressing their interaction and learning (see also Bossert 1979).

Explanations based on case studies of classrooms and schools tend to focus on the quality of instructional interaction, the perceptions and attitudes of participants, and their interpretations of events. Rather than positing linear models of events, these researchers describe the intentions of participants and the constellations of factors that characterize the instructional experiences of low and high achieving groups and classes (Rist 1970, Schwartz 1981).

Survey studies which explore the mechanism intervening between group structure and learning and rich case study descriptions of classroom events, in combination, yield evidence on how ability grouping works (Gamoran and Berends 1987). Some of the main issues addressed include the nature of organization patterns, placement of students in groups or tracks, stability of grouping schemes, curriculum differentiation, instructional interaction in groups and classes, and student outcomes.

3.1 Organizational Patterns

Although grouping in elementary schools is often described in terms of the types of ability grouping within and between classes, the experiences of students typically involve a mixture of total class, ability group, and individual experiences. Ability groups are frequently organized for reading instruction, sometimes for mathematics instruction, and rarely for social studies and science instruction. Although the percentage of time students spend in heterogeneous groups (cooperative groups, partnerships, writing workshops) has been minimal, the United States case study literature suggests an increase.

United States secondary schools vary in the extent to which they are tracked internally—some with most students enrolled in a single level, others with a fairly rigid three-track system, and still others with a more flexible system of levels. Schools seem to be moving away from more rigid forms of tracking toward systems of enrollment based on student course selection. Yet, even then, various mechanisms preserve the reality of tracks, as indicated by the high overlap among students taking honors courses and those taking remedial classes (Oakes et al. 1992).

3.2 Placement of Students in Ability Groups

Elementary students are sometimes placed into classes on the basis of ability; they are often also grouped within classes. Placing students in classes and tracks is typically an administrative matter, whereas forming groups in classes represents an interactive decision in which teachers derive a grouping pattern in response to the characteristics of students. Several investigators have examined how teachers form ability groups. Barr et al. (1983) found, for example, that the number of low-ability children in a class influenced the number and relative size of the reading groups formed. It has been argued that teachers assign students to groups using such characteristics as their cleanliness and nonagressiveness (Rist 1970), but others have found teachers to be less strongly influenced by social class or racial characteristics than achievement-related considerations (Haller 1985, Sørensen and Hallinan 1984).

While placement in high-school courses is responsive to student preferences, other criteria such as test scores, prior placement, and advisor recommendations have a bearing (Oakes et al. 1992). In particular, studies of high-school tracking show that middle-school choices by students in such areas as foreign language or algebra or their ability group placement may determine future track or school placements (Rosenbaum 1976).

Case studies of secondary students in the United States suggest that those of lower social status and those speaking English as a second language are given placement information biased toward lower track placements. Although it is difficult to assess the extent to which background experiences confound ability measures, the weight of the evidence from survey studies supports the view that the direct effects of student ability and prior achievement are more important than those of social status (Gamoran and Berends 1987).

3.3 Stability of Groups and Track Assignments

The assertion is repeatedly made that ability groups, once established, are highly stable. Observational evidence, however, suggests some mobility between ability groups within classes, in the range from 20 to 35 percent in Grades 1 to 3, and from 10 to 25 percent in Grades 4 to 7. Teachers show different patterns of group changes; more effective teachers tend to move more students up than down (Barr et al. 1983).

There has been relatively little documentation of the stability of ability group membership from year to year. Gamoran (1989) reports a high degree of stability from first to second grade, particularly in schools where second grade placement was based on first grade basal placement; in some schools, however, groups were reformed on the basis of standardized test results. Similarly, researchers in the United Kingdom report little change in stream membership during the primary years (Barker-Lunn 1970).

Stability of track placement in secondary schools appears to be higher when track systems are more rigidly adhered to than when students have greater discretion in course selection. Further, the stability of track membership is influenced by the extent to which middle school course choices determine future course placements (Oakes et al. 1992).

3.4 Curriculum Differentiation

Case studies in elementary and high schools have examined the academic task characteristics of low and high groups. With respect to the curriculum, low group members typically cover less material, complete simpler assignments, and perform more drill and skill work than students in higher achieving groups (Allington 1983, Barr and Dreeben 1991). While content differences have been emphasized, these differences may be of minor significance in relation to the similarities in curriculum that characterize elementary school instruction in the United States. Most children in a school use the same reading and mathematics textbooks and workbook materials, and although groups may proceed at somewhat different paces through the materials, the curricular tasks are essentially the same (Barr 1992).

At the secondary level, students in the United States are allowed considerable choice, with a balance between elective courses and those required for graduation. Courses, however, vary considerably in their demand. Typically, lower level courses have different syllabuses and easier textbooks, with fewer, less demanding topics and more concrete illustrations than higher level courses. Emphasis on basic skills and more superficial treatment of course concepts characterize lower level courses in contrast to more engaging and authentic assignments in higher level courses. Less of the text is covered in lower level classes. Moreover, lower level students have fewer academic course choices, particularly in the areas of mathematics and science (Gamoran and Berends 1987).

3.5 Instructional Interaction

Case studies have also revealed the nature of the interaction during instruction. In elementary schools, low reading group members tend to experience a greater number of intrusions and less time-on-task than do students in higher achieving groups. Lower group members read orally more often, focus on smaller units of print and have decoding rather than meaning emphasized, are asked more questions that require recall of information rather than reasoning, receive different prompts from teachers, and are provided with more structure through the provision of advanced organizers for lessons than their higher group peers. While some instructional researchers also claim that low group members receive less instructional time, others have not found differential time allocations (Allington 1983, Barr and Dreeben 1991).

Findings are similar in middle and high school classes. Low-level class members experience less problem-solving and answer more questions with prespecified answers, and they have less influence on the nature of their assignments than their peers in higher level courses. There is a greater emphasis on control and management issues, and students in lower level classes are less involved in discussion and initiate fewer questions than those in higher level classes (Oakes et al. 1992).

Interpretive studies at the secondary level link the instructional treatment of students to teacher assumptions about the potential learning of their students. Because they are perceived as being unwilling or incapable of completing academic work, they are given simplified tasks and they learn correspondingly little. Similarly, it is typically concluded on the basis of the elementary school evidence that low-ability group members are being treated unfairly and that their instruction is causing them to achieve poorly (Allington 1983). It is assumed that low group members would learn more if they participated in more challenging instruction. But before it can be concluded that this assumption is valid, low groups and classes need to receive and respond positively to the same kind of instruction that their higher achieving peers receive.

3.6 Student Outcomes

Friendship choices and attitudes toward school are also associated with group and track placement. Group membership increasingly determines friendship choices as the year progresses in elementary, middle, and secondary schools (Hallinan and Sørenson 1985). Students in high groups or tracks have more favorable attitudes toward school than do their peers in lower groups or tracks (Rosenbaum 1976, Schwartz 1981).

Results from elementary school studies show differences in learning related to ability group placement. This research, however, goes beyond earlier studies by linking these differences to curricular coverage and instructional time (Barr and Dreeben 1991, Oakes et al. 1992). At the secondary level, track location influences achievement (basic cognitive skills and subject matter knowledge), though the evidence is mixed. However, as evidence accumulates and research designs become more sophisticated, there is increasing reason to believe that patterns of course-taking related to track location contribute to academic achievement. Further, the evidence generally indicates that track location influences aspiration for education beyond high school as well as the actual attainment of it (Alexander and Cook 1982).

4. Changing Existing Patterns

Changes in established grouping practices seem to be less influenced by the empirical literature than by prevailing views. Important among these is concern with equality, and the *de facto* segregation that may result from ability grouping. In the United States, well-articulated ideological positions identify tracking as a practice that violates the principle of equal educational opportunity (Oakes 1985, Rosenbaum 1976). Also important, a shift has occurred from behavioristic perspectives on learning to those emphasizing its social constructive nature. These perspectives challenge the basic assumption of ability groups by asserting that what is to be learned cannot be easily fractured into hierarchically ordered pieces that correspond to measures of student ability. These changes in perspective have led to a greater variety of grouping procedures, and researchers have begun to describe these alternatives and their effectiveness.

Studies of alternatives to traditional ability grouping include classroom studies of cooperative group work, heterogeneous grouping, and total class instruction. Elementary students instructed in heterogeneously composed small groups have been shown to learn as well as those in ability groups in primary reading and intermediate level mathematics (Barr and Dreeben 1991). Generally, in studies where cooperative peer groupwork takes the place of seatwork, student achievement is often enhanced; it is usually not negatively affected by diverse grouping arrangements (Slavin 1989).

Total class instruction has long been a favored method in intermediate grades and secondary schools when students are grouped into classes on the basis of ability. Studies have suggested the effectiveness of primary and intermediate total class instruction with heterogeneous groups. With the total class instruction, small group work may be needed to support the learning of children making slow progress (Barr and Dreeben 1991).

Further research can be expected to provide additional evidence on the advantages and limitations of alternative grouping arrangements. While most existing studies involve individual classroom cases, researchers are also beginning to examine the consequences of school, district, and statewide change in grouping arrangements. This emerging literature reveals the political volatility of the change process and the number of related curricular, instructional, and professional development issues that must be considered (see, e.g., Anderson and Barr 1990).

See also: Student Diversity and Classroom Teaching

References

Alexander K L, Cook M A 1982 Curricula and coursework: A surprise ending to a familiar story. *Am. Soc. Rev.* 47: 626–40
Allington R 1983 The reading instruction provided readers of differing reading abilities. *Elem. Sch. J.* 83: 548–59
Anderson C, Barr R 1990 Modifying values and behaviors about tracking: A case study. In: Page R, Valli L (eds.) 1990 *Curriculum Differentiation: Interpretive Studies in US Secondary Schools.* State University of New York Press, Albany, New York
Barker-Lunn J C 1970 *Streaming in the Primary Schools.* National Foundation for Educational Research in England and Wales, London

Barr R 1992 Teachers, materials, and group composition in literacy instruction. In: Dreher M J, Slater W H (eds.) 1992 *Elementary School Literacy: Critical Issues*. Christopher-Gordon, Norwood, Massachusetts

Barr R, Dreeben R 1991 Grouping students for reading instruction. In: Barr R, Kamil M, Mosenthal P, Pearson P D (eds.) 1991 *Handbook of Reading Research*, Vol. 2. Longman, New York

Barr R, Dreeben R, Wiratchai N 1983 *How Schools Work*. University of Chicago Press, Chicago, Illinois

Bossert S T 1979 *Tasks and Social Relationships in Classrooms*. Cambridge University Press, New York

Cohen E G 1986 On the sociology of the classroom. In: Hannaway J, Lockhead M E (eds.) 1986 *The Contribution of the Social Sciences to Educational Policy and Practice 1965–1985. McCutchan, Berkeley, California*

Cummings W K 1980 *Education and Equality in Japan*. Princeton University Press, Princeton, New Jersey

Gamoran A 1989 Rank, performance, and mobility in elementary school grouping. *Soc. Q.* 30(1): 109–23

Gamoran A, Berends M 1987 The effects of stratification in secondary schools: Synthesis of survey and ethnographic research. *Rev. Educ. Res.* 57: 415–35

Haller E J 1985 Pupil race and elementary school ability grouping: Are teachers biased against black children? *Am. Educ. Res. J.* 22(4): 465–83

Hallinan M T, Sørensen A B 1985 Ability grouping and student friendships. *Am. Educ. Res. J.* 22(4): 485–99

Hamilton S F 1987 Apprenticeship as a transition to adulthood in West Germany. *Am. J. Educ.* 95(2): 314–45

Jackson B 1964 *Streaming*. Routledge and Kegan Paul, London

Kariya T, Rosenbaum J E 1987 Self-selection in Japanese junior high schools: A longitudinal study of students' educational plans. *Sociol. Educ.* 60(3): 168–80

Kerckhoff A C 1986 Effects of ability grouping in British secondary schools. *Am. Soc. Rev.* 51(6): 842–58

Mason J M et al. 1989 Learning to read in Japan. *J. Curric. Stud.* 21(5): 389–407

Oakes J 1985 *Keeping Track: How Schools Structure Inequality*. Yale University Press, New Haven, Connecticut

Oakes J, Gamoran A, Page R N 1992 Curriculum differentiation: Opportunities, outcomes, and meanings. In: Jackson P W (ed.) 1992 *Handbook of Research on Curriculum*. Macmillan, New York

Rist R 1970 Student social class and teacher expectations: The self-fulfilling prophecy in ghetto education. *Harv. Educ. Rev.* 40(3): 411–51

Rosenbaum J E 1976 *Making Inequality: The Hidden Curriculum of High School Tracking*. Wiley, New York

Rowan B, Miracle A W 1983 Systems of ability grouping and the stratification of achievement in elementary schools. *Sociol. Educ.* 56(3): 133–44

Schwartz F 1981 Supporting or subverting learning: Peer patterns in four tracked schools. *Anthropol. Educ. Q.* 12(2): 99–120

Shavit Y, Williams R 1985 Ability grouping and contextual determinants of educational expectations in Israel. *Am. Soc. Rev.* 50(1): 62–73

Slavin R E 1989 *Cooperative Learning: Theory, Research, and Practice*. Prentice-Hall, Englewood Cliffs, New Jersey

Slavin R E 1990 Achievement effects in ability grouping in secondary schools: A best evidence synthesis. *Rev. Educ. Res.* 60(3): 471–99

Sørenson A B, Hallinan M 1984 Effects of race on assignment to ability groups. In: Peterson P L, Wilkinson C, Hallinan M (eds.) 1984 *The Social Context of Instruction*. Academic Press, San Diego

Sørenson A B, Hallinan M T 1986 Effects of ability grouping on growth in academic achievement. *Am. Educ. Res. J.* 23(4): 519–42

Stevenson H W, Stigler J E 1992 *The Learning Gap*. Summit Books, New York

Further Reading

Svensson N E 1962 *Ability Grouping and Scholastic Achievement*. Almqvist and Wiksell, Stockholm

Yates A (ed.) 1966 *Grouping in Education*. Almqvist and Wiksell, Stokholm

Seating Arrangements

N. M. Lambert

This entry explores the research literature on the nature of students who select different seats in the classroom, the evidence that changing environments improves student learning and interactions, and the use of teacher-determined seating arrangements to fulfill various classroom objectives. Relationships of seating arrangements with on-task behavior and interactions between teachers and students, and among students, are discussed.

Even a casual observer in a classroom might conclude that where a student sits in a classroom affects his or her experiences in the classroom. Seating location results in more or less teacher attention and interaction. Conversely, students in some seats are more likely to pay attention to the teacher and to class assignments, and in turn, receive higher grades. The classroom observer also might notice that teachers use physical resources such as movable classroom seats and desks to facilitate interaction among students, to improve opportunities for teacher–student interaction in discussion sessions, or to improve a student's learning.

In general, the research supports these observations. Weinstein (1979), for example, stated that the arrangement of the teachers, students, furniture, and equipment in the classroom affected both student and teacher behavior. She also noted that the interest in school architecture and seating arrangements since the 1960s was enhanced by the changes in building design from single classrooms to multipurpose spaces where two or more classes of students might share the same large area.

The philosophy underlying the design of these new school buildings emphasized the importance to children's learning of environments in which children were more able to explore actively—classrooms furnished with a variety of learning materials, and in which children were more able to interact with their teachers and classmates. In flexibly furnished classrooms children could work alone or in groups, and those promoting these new designs argued that children's attitudes toward school, themselves as learners, and their cognitive and social development would be enhanced. As variations in seating arrangements and other features of the classroom physical environment were explored, researchers began to contribute evidence on the effects of these environmental manipulations on teacher and student behavior.

1. Classroom Seating Location and Teacher Interactions and Judgment

Where children sit in a classroom affects the type and extent of teacher interaction with them. Moore and Glynn (1984) manipulated the seating position of second- and third-grade students in an international urban primary school. By moving children around the classroom and making observations of their behavior and teacher interactions in different seating arrangements, they found that location of the seat had an effect on the frequency with which teachers addressed questions to the children, regardless of variations in the students' classroom behavior. The research cited here suggests that seating position has the potential for affecting teacher judgment about students as well as the extent of interaction with them, irrespective of children's individual characteristics.

When teachers were asked to make judgments about students when given information only about gender and the location of their seat on a chart of a fictional classroom, Daly and Suite (1981–82) reported that teachers judged children seated in the front of the classroom more positively than those at the rear, but boys sitting in the rear and girls sitting forward were given more favorable ranks. Presumably teachers had implicit theories about characteristics of students who selected different seating locations in the room. Teacher attributes seemed also to effect the kinds of judgments they made; teachers who were more anxious about communicating with their students were more likely to differentiate among students on the basis of the seat they had in the class.

2. Seating Arrangements and Effects on Social Interactions among Students

Several studies have centered attention on the relationship between seating position in the classroom and its potential effect on friendships as well as social interactions among children from different language and cultural backgrounds. Schmidt et al. (1987), for example, concluded that teachers can achieve the goal of greater social interaction and acceptance among children by using integrated patterns of seating in the classroom. Specifically, class member acceptance of minority children improved in classroom interactions in these classrooms and this effect appeared to generalize to other activities at school.

These findings can be understood in the context of the Thirkell and Worrall (1989) research using Bengali children. Children were given pictures of seating arrangements of White and Bengali boys and girls and then asked what choices of seats they would make. Although the children made in-group choices, when asked why they made the choices, the children offered a variety of reasons such as friendly versus angry faces, being good students, and other pragmatic explanations. The children evidently were using factors other than cultural background and gender when they made their selections.

Elbing and Ellgring (1977) studied the effects of seat location on the reduction of anxiety among children in fifth to eighth grade. Their results supported the conclusion that the anxiety levels of highly anxious students were reduced when they were seated with children with lower anxiety levels.

Where children sit in a classroom when they are given a choice reflects their personal views of preferred classmates (Kaufman 1974) and personality factors such as self-concept (Dykman and Reis 1979). Seating location has been related to the strategies children use to recall the names of their classmates. Approximately one-half of the children in Bjorklund and Zeman's (1983) study appeared to use the social organization of the class to guide their recollection of the names of their classmates. When the children were asked the basis for their remembering some children and not others, seating arrangement and gender, as well as social grouping, operated as bases for recall, leading to the conclusion that seating location in the classroom can be employed by teachers to promote the development of social relationships and friendships among the students.

Seating location has also been reported to facilitate language interactions among children from foreign language backgrounds. Adger (1985) found that the language interactions and social relationships among first graders increased when children of foreign language backgrounds were seated throughout the year with English-speaking children. Similarly, but with older subjects, Garza (1984) arranged seats in a semicircle without tables or desks to help class members become acquainted and to be less self-conscious in learning a new language.

3. Seating Location, Student Behavior, and Student Outcomes

The focus of some early studies of classroom environments centered attention on the interaction patterns of students who self-selected their seats in the classroom. Becker et al. (1973) for example, reported that rates of participation and earned grades were higher for students sitting in the front rows and center of a classroom in which the location of the seats was fixed. The questions raised by these studies was whether the location of the seat and the nature of the environment students experienced in those seats was the determining factor (the environmental hypothesis), or whether particular types of students selected this area of the classroom (the self-selection hypothesis).

Adams (1969) had noted that most of the verbal interaction in fixed seat classrooms took place in the front row and center seats of other rows. They termed this phenomenon the "action zone." Not all investigators replicated these findings, however. Saur et al. (1984) concluded from their studies that action zones were not present in all classes, and that factors other than placing of the student's seat were more important in determining the nature of the teacher–student interactions.

Knowles (1982), reviewing Griffith's (1921) seminal work on classroom performance and seating location, pointed out that the most clear-cut test of the effects of a particular location of a seat in the classroom on grades resulted only from those studies in which students were randomly or alphabetically assigned seats rather than permitted to select their seating location. In this regard, Levine et al. (1980) compared the performance of students who initially selected their seats with their performance when the seats were randomly assigned to them. Test scores were higher when the students were seated in the "action zone" or "target zone" than at the sides in both the self-selected and randomly assigned conditions. Stires (1982) countered that since the students knew that they were participants in a research study, self-selection factors (ability, achievement level, self-concept) were possibly as powerful as the location of their seats in producing the results they reported. However, when Aggarwal and Singh (1974) studied the self concepts and motivational orientation of "front benchers" and "back benchers," students who selected seats at the back of the room had lower self-concepts and were oriented toward external motivating factors while those in the front benches had high self-concepts and were more intrinsically motivated.

Grades, self-concepts, and motivation orientation are not the only outcome measures employed in research on the "action zone" or the "target" location in the classroom. Jones (1990) studied the relationship between target students (those getting the most teacher attention) and their seating location, and found that seating location made no difference in the amount of teacher interaction, and that there was no area in the classroom in which children were seated where they were likely to receive more attention. Sommer (1989) examined seating location and student social orientation, and reported that students in the back of the classroom knew more names of students than those in the front, while students in the front of the classroom were more academically oriented, lending support to Wulf's (1977) conclusion that it is not the physical environment per se, but individual difference factors such as high achievers, frequent responders, and interest in the class content that accounted for the differences reported and observed.

4. Use of Seating Arrangement to Facilitate On-task Behavior and Reduce Disruptive Behavior

As described in the above sections, the characteristics of pupils affect the places in class that they choose to sit, their social interactions and friendships among classmates, and the quality of teacher interactions. A complete picture of the impact of the seating environment on behavior requires a further examination of student behavior when students are assigned particular seats in the classroom. If the goal of the teacher is to assure that students are paying attention to lessons and working independently, then assignment of class members to seats or tables in rows rather than in other types of more informal arrangements such as groups of seats, or clusters of them, increases the likelihood of accomplishing this goal.

Several investigators have designed studies to determine whether or not assigning children to seats in rows affects the extent to which they pay attention to the lesson material. In these studies the investigators have moved pupils from rows to tables (Wheldall and Lam 1987), and from rows to groups (Bennett and Blundell 1983), have used same sex and opposite sex children seated in rows at tables (Wheldall and Olds 1987), and have made observations of on-task and disruptive behavior of the students when they were in rows in contrast to other seating arrangements. The results generally show that teachers can improve the quantity of work performed when children are sitting in rows, and that the performance level improves when children of opposite sex are seated in rows at two-person tables. The amount of disruptive behavior also was reduced when children sat in rows, and in opposite sex arrangements at tables. For some classroom purposes the seating arrangement per se, and not individual differences among students, may be the more powerful variable in determining on-task behavior.

Other studies indicate that seating arrangement is only one factor in student behavior or learning. Gill (1977) compared a traditional classroom to those in an open-plan school. The desks were arranged in rows and columns, in a horseshoe pattern, and in clusters. When student characteristics were matched for each seating pattern, there were no statistically significant differences in observations of student behavior or learning.

5. Teacher Orchestration of Classroom Seating Arrangement: Moving Toward the Future

The literature cited in this entry indicates that student selection of seats in a classroom is related to a variety of individual difference factors such as ability, achievement level, self-concept, and motivational orientation. Teachers can also promote particular student behaviors such as paying attention to seat work, and reduce classroom disruption by assigning students to particular seating arrangements. Teachers can also facilitate social interactions among boys and girls, and among children from different language and cultural backgrounds by selecting students to sit in specified locations.

How to arrange the seating in the classroom and for what purposes, then, will depend on teachers' goals, the conditions they wish to set for the learning activities, and their objectives for classroom control. Getzels (1974) observed that different desk arrangements reflect differences among teachers in the ways that they view students. A rectangular arrangement of fixed desks and the teacher at the front implies an empty learner to be filled with knowledge; a square arrangement with the teacher's desk at the side assumes active learners; a circular arrangement assumes a social learner; and an open classroom with flexible seating arrangements supports the stimulus-seeking learner. The emphasis in many classrooms of the 1990s is on promoting student development by providing for many opportunities for teacher–student and student–student interactions. Obviously such an instructional goal will not be promoted by fixed seating arrangements; flexibility will be a necessary prerequisite for the interactive classroom.

Rosenfield et al. (1985) provided evidence that seats in circles and clusters, rather than rows, promoted the kinds of interaction and classroom participation among students that would be necessary for facilitating cognitive and social development. Furthermore, the extent of disruptive behavior evidenced among the students was not excessive. In combination, these findings suggest that a teacher can alter the physical environment with different seating arrangements without having to cope with an unacceptable extent of disruptive behavior problems.

Ultimately teachers may want to determine the preferences of their students for different seating arrangements for the different activities in the classroom. Teachers and students from 50 Israeli classrooms (Raviv et al. 1990) were asked to report on the organizational characteristics of their real and ideal classrooms. Classrooms with group arrangements of seats, as compared to those in rows, were characterized by being more innovative and having more teacher support for students. Likewise, students perceived significantly more innovation and affiliation in group seating rather than row seating. Ultimately, the ways that teachers choose to arrange the seats in the classroom depends on their instructional objectives. The research evidence supports the conclusion that classroom physical environments permitting seats to be arranged in a variety of ways will be more supportive of a range of instructional goals than a classroom with all the seats arranged in rows.

See also: Attention in Learning; Classroom Environments; Student Roles in Classrooms; Group Dynamics

References

Adams R W 1969 Location as a feature of instructional interaction. *Merrill-Palmer Q.* 15 (4). 309–22

Adger C R 1985 Improving conversational engagement in the culturally diverse classroom. Paper presented at the Annual Ethnography in Education Research Forum, Philadelphia, Pennsylvania

Aggarwal Y P, Singh M 1974 A study of locus of control and self-concept of front-benchers and back-benchers. *Manas* 21 (2): 1–7

Becker F D, Sommer R, Bee J, Oxley B 1973 College classroom ecology. *Sociometry* 36 (4): 514–25

Bennett S N, Blundell D 1983 Quantity and quality of work in rows and classroom groups. *Educ. Psychol.* 3 (2): 93–105

Bjorklund D F, Zeman B R 1983 The development of organizational strategies in children's recall of familiar information: Using social organization to recall the names of classmates. *International Journal of Behavioral Development* 6 (3): 341–53

Daly J A, Suite A 1981–82 Classroom seating choice and teacher perceptions of students. *J. Exp. Educ.* 50 (2): 64–69

Dykman B J, Reis H T 1979 Personality correlates of classroom seating position. *J. Educ. Psychol.* 71 (3): 346–54

Elbing E, Ellgring J H 1977 Reduction of test anxiety by modeling in the classroom. *Pscychologie in Erzichung und Unterricht* 24 (1): 1–10

Garza T J 1984 Beyond Lozanoz: Practical Applications of the Intensive Method in Foreign Language Teaching. Paper presented at the Annual Meeting of the Teachers of English to Speaker of Other Languages, Houston, Texas

Getzels J W 1974 Images of the classroom and visions of the learner. *Sch. Rev.* 82 (4): 527–40.

Gill W M 1977 Classroom architecture and classroom behaviours: A look at the change to open-plan schools in New Zealand. *N. Z. J. Educ. Stud.* 12 (1): 3–16

Griffith C R 1921 A comment upon the psychology of the audience. *Psychol. Monogr.* 30: 36–47

Jones M G 1990 Action zone theory, target students, and

science classroom interactions. *J. Res. Sci. Teach.* 27 (7): 651–60

Kaufmann I 1974 Preferred classmates: Report on partial results of a pilot study (1968–70). *Praxis Kinderpsychologic und Kinderpsychiatric* 23 (6): 220–26

Knowles E S 1982 A comment on the study of classroom ecology: A lament for the good old days. *Pers. Soc. Psychol. Bull.* 8 (2): 357–61

Levine D W, O'Neal E C, Garwood S F, McDonald P J 1980 Classroom ecology: The effects of seating position on grades and participation. *Pers. Soc. Psychol. Bull.* 6 (3): 409–12

Moore D W, Glynn A 1984 Variation in question rate as a function of position in the classroom. *Educ. Psychol.* 4 (3): 233–48

Raviv A, Raviv A, Reisel E 1990 Teachers and students: Two different perspectives? Measuring social climate in the classroom. *Am. Educ. Res. J.* 27 (1): 141–57

Rosenfield P, Lambert N M, Black A 1985 Desk arrangement effects on pupil classroom behavior. *J. Educ. Psychol.* 77 (1): 101–8

Saur R, Popp M, Isaacs M 1984 Action zone theory and the hearing-impaired student in the mainstreamed classroom. *J. Classroom Interact.* 19: 21–25

Schmidt R E, Stewart J P, McLaughlin T F 1987 Effects of two classroom seating arrangements on classroom participation and academic responding with Native American junior high school students. *Techniques* 3 (3): 172–80

Sommer R 1989 Classroom ecology and acquaintanceship. *Educ. Psychol.* 9 (1): 63–66

Stires L K 1982 Classroom seating location, order effects, and reactivity. *Pers. Soc. Psychol. Bull.* 8 (2): 362–64

Thirkell B, Worrall N 1989 Differential ethnic bias in Bengali and White children. *Educ. Res.* 31 (3): 181–88

Weistein C S 1979 The physical environment of the school: A review of the research. *Rev. Educ. Res.* 49 (4): 577–610

Wheldall K, Lam Y Y 1987 Rows versus tables: II The effects of two classroom seating arrangements on classroom disruption rate, on-task behaviour and teacher behaviour in three special school classes. *Educ. Psychol.* 7 (4): 303–12

Wheldall K, Olds D 1987 Of sex and seating: The effects of mixed and same-sex seating arrangements in junior classrooms. *N. Z. J. Educ. Stud.* 22 (1): 71–85

Wulf K M 1977 Relationship of assigned classroom seating area to achievement variables. *Educ. Res. Q.* 12 (2): 56–62

Further Reading

Conners D A 1983 The school environment: A link to understanding stress. *Theory Pract.* 22 (1): 15–20

Rivlin L G, Weinstein C S 1984 Educational issues, school settings, and environmental psychology. *Journal of Environmental Psychology* 4 (4): 347–64

Instructional Alignment

S. A. Cohen

"Instructional alignment" refers to how precisely two or more activities match. The term is most often applied to the match between instructional activities and assessment activities. The more precisely these two activities align, the higher the probability that learners will be competent, assuming, of course, those assessment activities represent the intended competency.

To achieve alignment, instructional designers transform teaching outcomes into criterion assessment indicators, most often test items. Teachers then design instruction by moving backwards from these indicators in the following manner. They begin by creating instructional activities nearly identical to these indicators. Then, lessons are planned to shape the prerequisite components of each activity. Each lesson is designed by first structuring that lesson's assessment indicators recreating the "moving backwards" paradigm at this subordinate level. Alignment thus becomes the fundamental principle underlying instructional design.

The effect of alignment on test scores rivals the effect of academic aptitude. Aptitude, however, changes slowly; some argue almost never. In contrast, alignment is a malleable feature of instructional design, and therefore, produces immediate and very marked effects.

1. Origins of Instructional Alignment

The term "instructional alignment" comes from two constructs: stimulus control, which underlies experimental research in learning theory (Ferster and Skinner 1957); and curriculum alignment, a popular term among outcome-based theorists (Neidermeyer 1979).

1.1 Stimulus Control

Any performance, such as reading, writing, saying, or doing something, involves human actions and two types of related events. One type is the reinforcing event. When stimuluses called "discriminative events" are present in the environment, human actions elicit reinforcers from the environment. Reinforcers link an action to discriminative events present when the action occurs. That linkage is called "learning."

When children learn to read the word "dog," for example, reinforcers link their "comprehending" actions (saying the word and associating appropriate thoughts and feelings) to the letters d-o-g, the discriminative events. Reinforcers may be such events as teacher approval or "self satisfaction." Learning occurs when these reinforcers cause comprehending actions to come under control of the letters, d-o-g. These letters are said to be the discriminative events' critical features.

Certain actions must already exist in learners' repertoires before they can learn something new. For example, before learning to read the word "dog," students need to know what a dog is, recognize the word when they hear it, and say it when they see one. Thus, students do not really learn new actions. Instead, they learn new linkages. Reinforcers link existing actions to discriminative events.

Typically, experimental learning researchers ask two questions: (a) Which events are the reinforcers that link actions to discriminative events? and (b) Which events are (or should be) the discriminative ones to which these actions are linked? Instructional alignment researchers ask two analogous questions: (a) How efficiently can formal instruction reinforce an appropriate action when specified discriminative events occur? and (b) Which discriminative events define the outcomes that are sought?

When discriminative events vary among activities, they are said to "misalign." The most common misalignments occur between assessment events and instructional events. The less misalignment between these two events, the higher the probability of observing the intended instructional outcome. "Misalignment," then, is the instructional designer's term for what experimental researchers call "stimulus control problems."

In summary, learning occurs when reinforcing events link pre-existing actions to discriminative events. It is not the actions per se, but the linkage, which defines a learned behavior or performance. The same action (e.g., saying dog) is a different behavior when discriminative events of time one differ at time two. Behaviors are aligned when the discriminative events are the same or most nearly the same. They are misaligned when variations occur in those events.

1.2 Curriculum Alignment

Instructional alignment is a more precise application of Neidermeyer's curriculum alignment construct popularized in the late 1970s (Neidermeyer 1979). According to Neidermeyer, a curriculum includes objectives, instruction, and assessment. When all three align, then schooling effects are "impressive." He called that match "curriculum alignment."

In one study, Neidermeyer and Yelon (1981) trained teachers to align instructional materials, activities, and "essential skills" expressed as behavioral objectives, producing what was referred to as "outcome-based

instruction." The results were patchy. Nevertheless, the curriculum alignment construct became popular among United States educators associated with outcome-based instruction (Burns and Squires 1987).

Cohen and Hyman (1982) speculated that Neidermeyer's patchy results were caused by two problems. First, behavioral objectives cannot specify discriminative events precisely enough to insure a close match because they are expressed in ordinary language. Second, the match should have included not only the discriminative events characterizing the materials, instruction, and intended outcome (stated objective), but the commercially published standardized tests used to assess Neidermeyer's curriculum efforts. Cohen and Hyman proposed using the term "instructional alignment" instead of "curriculum alignment" to emphasize the precise matching of reinforcers and discriminative events needed to ensure stimulus control.

Cohen (1984) pointed out that assessment items' critical features are the discriminative events to which learners' actions must link appropriately. Therefore, he proposed that instruction and assessment will be more precisely aligned when assessment items rather than behavioral objectives are used as outcomes. This precision underlies Cohen's affirmation that "teaching to the test" is the most efficient way to deliver instruction.

1.3 Opportunity to Learn

This affirmation was further supported by various International Association for the Evaluation of Educational Achievement (IEA) studies across 20 to 24 different countries (Postlethwaite and Lewy 1979). From IEA's first international mathematics study (referred to as "FIMS"), Purves and Levine (1975) summarized 17 correlations between school-related factors and mathematics achievement scores. Such factors as age of school entry, attitudes toward mathematics, and teachers' degrees of freedom to teach showed low to negative correlations with the criterion. Amount of mathematics instruction hours also had a surprisingly small correlation with mathematics achievement scores. However, OTL (opportunity to learn) the mathematics concept tested in specific items explained very large amounts of mathematics test score variance.

For example, in the original FIMS study, Husén (1967) grouped the data into four subpopulations and discovered that OTL explained 16, 41, 53, and 64 percents of the variance in mathematics achievement scores. When IEA researchers designed the second international mathematics survey (SIMS), they took special note of this OTL predictor. According to Phillipps (1986), SIMS planners wanted to analyze achievement effects of instructional factors such as course syllabuses and texts. They suspected, however, that what teachers choose to teach from these resources is, in the final analysis, what students have the opportunity to learn. So, they developed more sophisticated survey items to investigate this OTL phenomenon in 21 countries.

Visual inspection of Phillipps's tables (Phillipps 1986 pp. 103–09) clearly shows the enormous OTL effect on mathematics achievement scores observed in the SIMS data. In addition, results of IEA's second science study across 24 countries revealed that OTL explained more variance in science achievement test scores than did scores on mathematics, word knowledge, and science process laboratory tests (Jacobson and Doran 1988).

Thus, the original alignment construct, a microinstructional factor, emerged from instructional research based on operant theory. However, simultaneous to this research, IEA's macro-educational surveys generated the same conclusion: Achievement score variance is a direct effect of the degree to which the assessment item's specific features match those of instruction.

2. Research on Instructional Alignment

By 1981, alignment research had demonstrated instructional effects three to four times greater than what most experiments on "effective instruction" have reported. For example, a full year's growth on a fourth grade, norm-referenced, standardized reading achievement test represents an instructional effect equal to about 0.67 of a standard deviation (or a 0.67 sigma effect). A well-taught lesson by an average classroom teacher generates about a 0.37 sigma effect (Walberg 1990). In contrast, proven instructional factors generate an average effect of 0.96 sigma (Lysakowski and Walberg 1982).

A review of 34 effect sizes in instructional alignment experiments report an average magnitude of 1.76 sigma (Cohen et al. 1989). These 34 effect sizes ranged from a low of 0.82 sigma to a high of 3.58 sigma with 27 values exceeding a full sigma and 16 values exceeding 1.7 sigma. In several studies, alignment eliminated aptitude effects. Some of these studies are summarized in Section 2.1 below.

Many of these experiments compared effects of three alignment levels: precise, less precise, and control. "Control" represented what usually occurs in the typical "well-taught" classroom lesson. "Less precise" involved "mild" misalignments but, nevertheless, better aligned than the control treatments.

That large effects result from matching stimulus events of instruction and tests is intuitively logical. Critics, however, argue that schooling's effect should extend beyond tomorrow's test to the varying stimuluses of everyday life (Mehrens and Kaminsky 1989). In other words, the larger purpose of schooling is for misalignment, or what previous theorists called "transfer of learning" (Ellis 1965, Gick and Holyoak 1987). Section 2.2 below describes recent experiments in which controlled misalignment was systematically manipulated to shape learners' abilities to transfer what they learned in school.

2.1 Instructional Alignment Studies

To estimate alignment's effect, Cohen and Stover (1981) taught sixth graders three different mathematics word problem-solving techniques, randomly assigning one technique per student. All three groups received the same posttest items, a third of which were best solved using one technique, another third the second technique, and so on. Thus, only one third of the posttest items' discriminative events were aligned with the practice items used to teach each student. By comparing each subject's scores on each group of items, each subject was his or her own control, and each control was also an experimental subject for one of the other two techniques.

The study's purpose was not to test the obvious: that is, students tend to learn precisely what they are taught. Instead, the purpose was to assess the magnitude of effect of instructional alignment. In two out of the three groups, those students who scored at the 50th percentile under aligned conditions performed as well as or better than 99 percent of students receiving instruction that was less aligned with the posttest. In the other group, students in the aligned condition performed better, but the difference was less dramatic (effect size = 1.44 sigma).

Koczor (1984) taught high achieving fourth graders six different typical fourth grade lessons. Each lesson covered a different content or skill area such as vocabulary, science, and arithmetic. For example, high achievers were taught to write Arabic numerals for Roman numerals. On the posttest, all got the same items, except half had to write Roman for Arabic (slight misalignment with instruction), while the other half had to do the reverse, Arabic for Roman, just as the instruction taught (aligned). That slight misalignment caused effects ranging from 1.10 to 2.74 sigma, even with these high achievers.

Fahey (1986) provided corroborating evidence that selecting the best statement of a main idea is easier than choosing the best title, and that both are easier than writing a main idea statement after reading a selection. All three represent varying discriminative events for what many teachers think of as the same "main idea skill." Fahey demonstrated that when taught how to spot main ideas under what he called "positive misalignment conditions," these lower aptitude community college students performed as well as higher aptitude students taught under more "tradiional" conditions. "Positive misalignment" is when the instructional task is more difficult than the assessment task, but has discriminative stimuluses that guarantee the latter is able to be performed. This term is analogous to the more popular expression, "overlearning."

Wishnick (1989) designed a formal alignment measure which she validated by measuring alignment between a school district's competency tests and item clusters from commercially published norm-referenced tests (NRTs). She discovered that 60 percent of the variance could be explained by her alignment score. Wishnick's study culminated a decade of alignment research because it formally defined alignment's components. This set the stage for a new use of alignment—as a tool to teach transfer of learning.

2.2 Alignment and Transfer of Learning

As early as 1982, Cohen called misalignments between instruction and application, or between instruction and assessment, "transfer demand" (Cohen 1982). A decade later, two of his doctoral students systematically taught elementary and high school students to tolerate increasingly misaligned conditions. Nolen (1991) called this "tolerance for cognitive stretching." He gave community college students a set for transfer by teaching them to analyze misalignments in chemistry mathematics problems. During instruction, each problem's stimulus events became increasingly varied from the previous problem's events. Successful problem solving required both the correct analysis of the misalignment as well as the correct answer to the problem. Nolen reported transfer effects greater than one sigma.

Boris(1991) also used controlled misalignment to teach sixth graders to transfer their mathematics learning. She reported effects of just under one sigma and just over one sigma for low achievers. In addition, Boris observed some evidence of transfer effect across content areas, as for example, from mathematics to vocabulary, or from economics to mathematics.

3. Implications for Testing

The alignment model is often criticized by those identified with norm referenced tests (NRTs). For example, Mehrens and Kaminsky (1989) disapprove of aligning instruction and assessment because it reduces test score variance. They advocate using test items that misalign with instruction causing sufficient variance to produce normally distributed scores. Traditional psychometrics requires that variance to produce test reliability coefficients.

In contrast, instruction is intended to produce competency which reduces test score variance, especially when competency is defined as a quality rather than more or less of a phenomenon. Cohen and Hyman (1991) argue that schools should not be using test items to induce variance, but to monitor how well instruction produces excellent performance. Excellent performance is defined by assessment indicators that generate scores of mastery or nonmastery rather than more or less mastery. Thus, the criterion for designing test items should not be how well they discriminate, but how well they align with instruction and with intended outcomes. When items align with effective instruction, variance among students' test scores decreases as everyone approaches mastery. Instruction thereby eliminates the random distribution of academic performance, replacing variance with universal mastery.

Mehrens and Kaminski (1989) also argue that when assessment and instruction align with too much precision, learned performance is observed rather than "true" academic abilities. Alignment theory makes no distinction between performance and ability; it assumes that academic ability is a hypothetical construct inferred from performance, and that it is learned rather than inherited. From an instructional alignment perspective: (a) ability is competency, (b) competency is learned performance,(c) individuals vary in the rate at which they learn specific performances, and (d) that rate is a function of the instruction's quality which shapes the individual's repertoire of prerequisite components needed to learn new performances (Bloom 1976).

4. Philosophic Implications

Fundamental philosophic differences underly this debate. Each side has a different vision of instructional effect. One side expects it to be random. That expectation has generated psychometric principles that cause assessment score variance displayed as the bell-shaped, normal distribution. It has also generated schooling and testing practices that guarantee such variance.

The other side views this random distribution as an effect of instructional ineptitude. That ineptitude is maintained by: (a) a belief that school effect's random distribution is statistically inevitable, and (b) a practice of misaligning what is taught and what is assessed.

Alignment theorists expect academic instruction to eliminate such variance. That vision has transformed into the use of assessment indicators as instructional outcomes and of directly instructing to those indicators. Schools will have profoundly different effects on society when one or the other of these fundamental visions is embraced.

See also: Affect, Emotions, and Learning

References

Bloom B S 1976 *Human Characteristics and School Learning*. McGraw-Hill, New York
Boris R B 1991 Using controlled degrees of misalignment to teach cognitive stretching: A set for transfer of learning mathematics and vocabulary misalignment. Doctoral dissertation, University of San Francisco, San Francisco, California

Burns R, Squires D 1987 Curriculum organization in outcome-based education. *Outcomes* 3:1–9

Cohen S A 1982 Components of effective instruction. Paper presented at the Annual Meeting of the American Educational Research Association, New York

Cohen S A 1984 Implications of instructional psychological research on mastery learning. *Outcomes* 2:18–25

Cohen S A, Stover G 1981 Effects of teaching sixth grade students to modify format variables of math word problems. *Read. Res. Q.* 16(2): 175–200

Cohen S A, Hyman J S 1982 Components of effective instruction. Paper presented at the Annual Meeting of the American Educational Research Association, New York City

Cohen S A, Hyman J S, Ashcroft L, Loveless D 1989 Comparing effects of metacognition, learning styles, and human attributes with alignment. Paper presented at the Annual Meeting of the American Educational Research Association, San Francisco, California

Cohen S A, Hyman J S 1991 Can fantasies become facts? *Educational Measurement: Issues and Practices* 10(1):20–23

Ellis H C 1965 *The Transfer of Learning*. Macmillan, New York

Fahey P A 1986 Learning transfer in main ideas instruction: Effects of instructional alignment and aptitude on student scores on main idea test scores. Doctoral dissertation, University of San Francisco, San Francisco, California

Ferster C B, Skinner B F 1957 *Schedules of Reinforcement*. Appleton–Century–Crofts, New York

Gick M L, Holyoak K J 1987 The cognitive basis for knowledge transfer. In: Cormier S M, Hagman J D (eds.) 1987 *Transfer of Learning*. Academic Press, New York

Husén T (ed.) 1967 *International Study of Achievement in Mathematics, A Comparison of Twelve Countries*, Vol. 2. Almqvist and Wiksell, Stockholm

Jacobson W J, Doran R L 1988 *Science Achievement in the United States and Sixteen Countries: A Report to the Public*. International Association for the Evaluation of Educational Achievement (IEA), New York

Koczor M L 1984 Effects of varying degrees of instructional alignment in posttreatment tests on mastery-learning tasks of fourth grade children. Doctoral dissertation, University of San Francisco, San Francisco, California

Lysakowski R, Walberg H 1982 Instructional effects of cues, participation, and corrective feedback: A quantitative synthesis. *Am. Educ. Res. J.* 19(4): 559–78

Mehrens W, Kaminsky J 1989 Methods for improving standardized test scores: Fruitful, fruitless or fraudulent? *Educational Measurement: Issues and Practices* 8:14–22

Neidermeyer F C 1979 Curriculum alignment—A way to make schooling more understandable. SWRL Professional Paper No. 41. Southwest Regional Educational Laboratory Educational Research and Development, Los Almitos, California

Neidermeyer F C, Yelon S 1981 Los Angeles aligns instruction with essential skills. *Educ. Leadership* 38:618–20

Nolen L L 1991 Cognitive stretching—Using instructional alignment theory to teach community college chemistry students how to transfer learning. Doctoral dissertation, University of San Francisco, San Francisco, California

Phillipps R W 1986 Cross national research in mathematics education. In: Postlethwaite T N (ed.) Pergamon Press, Oxford 1986 *International Educational Research: Papers in Honor of Torsten Husén*. Pergamon Press Oxford

Postlethwaite T N, Lewy A 1979 *Annotated Bibliography of IEA Publications (1962–1978)*. IEA, University of Stockholm, Stockholm

Purves A, Levine D (eds.) 1975 *Educational Policy and International Assessment*. McCutchan, London

Walberg H 1990 Productive teaching and instruction: Assessing the knowledge base. *Phi Del. Kap.* 71(6): 470–78

Wishnick T K 1989 Relative effects on achievement scores of SES, gender, teacher effect and instructional alignment: A study of alignment's power in mastery learning. Doctoral dissertation, University of San Francisco, San Francisco, California

Further Reading

Cohen S A 1987 Instructional alignment: Searching for a magic bullet. *Educ. Researcher* 16(8): 16–20

Crowell R, Tissot P 1986 *Curriculum Alignment*. US Office of Educational Research and Improvement, Washington, DC

Time, Allocated and Instructional

L. W. Anderson

Among the many resources that impact on the quality of education provided to students, time is among the most important. At the most general level, the way in which time is allocated and used in schools informs students of what educators believe to be important. Furthermore, the allocation and use of time has been found to be consistently related to the type and amount of student learning that occurs in schools.

1. Allocated Time

Allocated time refers to the amount of time devoted to schooling or to particular aspects of schooling (e.g., reading, mathematics, art, physical education). Allocated time can be enhanced by including the amount of time that students spend on school-related academic matters outside of school (e.g., homework).

For the most part, allocated time can be determined by looking at schedules, calendars, and policies. School may be scheduled to begin at 9:00 a.m. and end at 3:00 p.m. In this case, six hours would be allocated to the school day. In the northern hemisphere, the school calendar may indicate that school begins in early September and ends in late May or early June.

When vacations and holidays are taken into consideration, approximately 180 days might be allocated to the school year. Federal, regional or state, or local policies may dictate that students attend school from the age of six until the age of 16. Students also may be required to complete three years of high school mathematics. Therefore, a minimum of 11 years would be allocated to the school career, with a minimum of three years allocated to high school mathematics for those receiving a high school diploma.

1.1 Descriptive Studies of Allocated Time

Countries differ in the number of days per year that students attend school, the number of hours per day and number of years devoted to the study of specific subject areas, and the total number of hours per year devoted to specific topics or goals within a subject area. The average student in the average country is in school for 192 days per year. The apparent range is from 125 days per year in Ghana (World Bank 1990) to 240 days per year in Japan (Walberg and Fredrick 1991).

There are also between-country differences in the number of hours per day that students are in school. Japanese students are in school for just over nine hours per day, while United States students are in school for slightly more than seven hours per day (Stigler and Stevenson 1991). German students may be in school for as little as five hours per day (Flood 1991). Large within-country differences in the number of hours students spend in school also have been noted (Mortimore et al. 1988).

When in school, the World Bank (1990) estimates that in developing countries twice as much time is spent on literacy as numeracy. In primary schools in Western countries, this difference may be even greater (Anderson 1994). In this regard, Anderson et al. (1989) found that the time spent per day on mathematics instruction across countries was quite small, ranging from 20 minutes to 50 minutes.

Finally, within specific subject matters different amounts of time are devoted to different goals, objectives, and/or topics. Porter (1989), for example, found that three-fourths of the time that United States' students were studying mathematics, the instruction focused on the teaching of mathematical operations involving addition, subtraction, multiplication, and division. Relatively little time was allocated to understanding mathematical concepts or solving mathematical problems. Similarly, based on her research, Durkin (1978–79) concluded that little time in the teaching of reading was spent on comprehension; rather, most of the time was spent on phonics, word recognition skills, and so on.

1.2 Increasing Allocated Time Through Homework

As mentioned above, allocated time may or may not include homework. There is little doubt that homework can increase the amount of time that students spend on school-related, academic matters. The question remains as to how much homework does increase allocated time.

Leone and Richards (1989) estimated that upper elementary and lower secondary students spent, on average, about 6.4 hours per week on homework. Walberg and Fredrick (1991) reported that the average upper secondary student in the United States spent slightly less than five hours per week on homework. Anderson et al. (1989) found that few teachers, typically fewer than 40 percent across eight countries, assigned homework four or five times per week.

Based on these estimates, it seems reasonable to conclude that students spend no more than seven hours per week on homework. This figure represents somewhat less than 20 percent of the total time that students spend in school. That is, for every five hours students spend in school, they devote approximately one hour to homework. From a slightly different perspective, this figure is approximately one-fifth of the time that United States students spend watching television (Walberg and Fredrick 1991).

1.3 Allocated Time and Student Achievement

While the relationship between allocated time and student achievement is consistently positive, the magnitude of this relationship tends to depend on the measure of allocated time used in the study. Summarizing a series of studies conducted under the auspices of the International Association for the Evaluation of Educational Achievement (IEA), Anderson and Postlethwaite (1989) found that the relationship between the number of years spent studying a specific subject matter and achievement in that subject matter was positive. In contrast, the relationship between the number of days per year spent on a subject matter and achievement in that subject matter was essentially zero.

While the former statement has received corroboration (Welsh et al. 1982), the latter has been contradicted by some other reviews. Walberg and Fredrick (1991), for example, found that adding to the length of the school year was positively correlated with student achievement in 10 of 11 studies summarized, with a mean correlation between allocated time and achievement of 0.22. Similarly, Smythe (1985) summarized 26 studies and found that adding to the length of the school day or school week was positively related to student achievement in 23 of the studies, with a mean correlation between allocated time and achievement of 0.40.

The results of using homework to increase the amount of time allocated to schooling and academics have been uniformly positive (see *Homework*). In 12 of 14 studies conducted in eight developing countries, Fuller (1987) found the relationship of homework and student achievement to be positive. Similarly, Smythe (1987) found the relationship between homework and achievement to be positive in 88 percent of 43 studies, with a mean correlation of 0.23. Finally, Cooper (1989) found that positive relationships between homework and student achievement existed in 14 of 20 studies, with the results being more pronounced at the secondary school level.

2. Instructional Time

Instructional time is a composite of that portion of the school day during which students receive instruction and that portion of classroom time during which the teacher is teaching. With respect to the school day, lunch, recess, and movement from classroom to classroom are not counted as instructional time. In terms of the classroom, taking attendance, disciplining students, cleaning up and putting away materials, and movement from activity to activity (referred to as "transitions") detract from instructional time.

2.1 Descriptive Studies of Instructional Time

A report issued by the World Bank (1990) illustrates how easily allocated time can slip away in many developing countries. "The school day often began late, teachers frequently were absent on Tuesday and Friday (market days), and 48 public holidays were celebrated" (p. 19). Industrialized countries have the same problem. In the United States, approximately one-fourth of the allocated time in elementary schools is spent on recess, lunch, and similar activities (Walberg and Fredrick 1991). In the United Kingdom, the estimate of the percentage of allocated time that is instructional time is virtually identical (Mortimore et al. 1988).

In the classroom, between 7 and 27 percent of the time is spent on noninstructional matters. Figures less than 10 percent appear to be found only in Asian countries (Anderson et al. 1989, Stigler and Stevenson 1991). Figures above 15 percent occur in Australia, Canada, and the United States (Anderson et al. 1989, Sanford and Evertson 1983).

2.2 Attendance and the Loss of Instructional Time

Both teachers and students are in school and in their classrooms more than 90 percent of the time (Anderson et al. 1989). Nonetheless, variations in attendance consistently are related to variations in student achievement. Fogelman (1978) found a significant relationship between student attendance and student achievement after controlling for the socioeconomic status of the students. Monk and Ibrahim (1984) concluded that student absences accounted for from 32 to 48 percent of the variation in mathematics achievement. Finally, Reynolds and Walberg (1991) found that multiple correlations of attendance and homework (see section above) with science achievement averaged 0.53, which was higher than all other factors included in their predictive model.

2.3 Instructional Time and Student Achievement

The relationship between instructional time and achievement is generally stronger than that between allocated time and achievement (Walberg and Fredrick 1991). For example, Fredrick (1980) found that in high-achieving schools the difference between allocated and instructional time was 25 percent, while in low-achieving schools the difference was almost 50 percent.

3. Conclusions and Recommendations

The way in which time is allocated and used in schools and classrooms communicates to students what educators value and influences what and how much they learn. The way in which time is allocated to various subjects and activities should be carefully examined. Is literacy twice as important as numeracy? Are the fine arts and physical education really "second class citizens" in curricula throughout the world?

Once decisions concerning allocated time have been made, attention must be turned to using as much of that allocated time for instructional purposes as is possible. Most of the suggestions for improvement in this regard are relatively straightforward and easy to implement. They perhaps can be best summed up by a set of recommendations offered by the World Bank (1990).

> Maintaining instructional time requires administrative and/or parental interventions to ensure that (a) schools are open during official hours and children are in attendance, (b) teachers are present and teaching during the official instructional periods, (c) temporary distractions, such as administrative or visitor interruptions, are avoided, and (d) appropriate arrangements are made for continuing instruction under routine inclement weather conditions. (p. 20)

References

Anderson L W 1994 What time tells us. In: Anderson L W, Walberg H J (eds.) 1994 *Time Piece: Extending and Enhancing Learning Time*. National Association of Secondary School Principals, Reston, Virginia

Anderson L W, Postlethwaite T N 1989 What IEA studies say about teachers and teaching. In: Purves A C (ed.) 1989 *International Comparisons and Educational Reform*. Association for Supervision and Curriculum Development, Reston, Virginia

Anderson L W, Ryan D W, Shapiro B J 1989 *The IEA Classroom Environment Study*. Pergamon Press, Oxford

Cooper H 1989 Synthesis of research on homework. *Educ. Leadership* 47(3): 85–91

Durkin D 1978–79 What classroom observations reveal about reading comprehension instruction. *Reading Res. Q.* 14(4): 481–533

Flood R 1991 Are you being served? *The Economist* 320 (7722): 8

Fogelman K 1978 School attendance, attainment, and behaviour. *Br. J. Educ. Psychol.* 48: 148–58

Fredrick W C 1980 Instructional time. *Eval. Educ.* 4: 117–18

Fuller B 1987 What factors raise achievement in the third world? *Rev. Educ. Res.* 57: 255–92

Leone C M, Richards M H 1989 Classwork and homework in early adolescence: The ecology of achievement. *J. Youth Adolescence* 18(6): 531–48

Monk D H, Ibrahim M A 1984 Patterns of absence and pupil achievement. *Am. Educ. Res. J.* 21: 295–310

Mortimore P, Sammons P, Stoll L, Lewis D, Ecob R 1988 *School Matters. The Junior Years.* Open Books, Wells

Porter A 1989 A curriculum out of balance: The case of elementary school mathematics. *Educ. Researcher* 18(5): 9–15

Reynolds A J, Walberg H J 1991 A structural model of science achievement. *J. Educ. Psychol.* 83(1): 97–107

Sanford J P, Evertson C M 1983 Time use and activities in junior high classes. *J. Educ. Res.* 76(3): 140–47

Smythe W J 1987 Time. In: Dunkin M J (ed.) 1987 *The International Encyclopedia of Teaching and Teacher Education.* Pergamon Press, Oxford

Stigler J W, Stevenson H W 1991 How Asian teachers polish each lesson to perfection. *American Educator* 15(1): 12–20, 43–47

Walberg H J, Fredrick W C 1991 *Extending Learning Time.* United States Department of Education Office of Educational Research and Improvement, Washington, DC

Welsh W W, Anderson R E, Harris L J 1982 The effects of schooling on mathematics achievement. *Am. Educ. Res. J.* 19: 145–53

World Bank 1990 *Primary Education.* The International Bank for Reconstruction and Development, Washington, DC

Further Reading

Ben-Peretz M, Bromme R (eds.) 1990 *The Nature of Time in Schools. Theoretical Concepts, Practitioner Perceptions.* Teachers College Press, New York

Fisher C W, Berliner D C (eds.) 1985 *Perspectives on Instructional Time.* Longman, New York

Lesson Structure

E. C. Wragg

The structure of a lesson can vary considerably, depending on the subject matter, the age and ability of the learners, the policies of the school, the beliefs, preferred teaching styles, and strategies of the teacher, the time, space, and material resources available, and any requirements laid down by local or national government. This entry discusses the ways in which lessons may be structured and the factors influencing their shape and direction.

1. What is a Lesson?

Originally, a lesson was a piece of reading, from the Latin *lectio*. Today, however, reading is but one of a multitude of possible lesson components. The contemporary concept of a lesson is very elastic. It can embrace exactly 40 minutes of time, devoted exclusively to the teaching of chemistry to 14-year olds in a laboratory, signaled by the sounding of a bell at the beginning and end. It might equally be a 1½-hour session between the start of the school day and morning break, during which 7-year olds engage in a variety of activities in an open-plan school, with no formal indication, other than a signal from the teacher, as to when it should begin or end.

Where students are on individual programs, the concept of a lesson is stretched even further. The development of educational technology, such as the microcomputer and interactive videodisk, and the availability of videos, sound cassettes, books, and other print and nonprint materials in a school's library or resource center, mean that one group may be completing a traditional textbook exercise in the classroom, another may be working with the teacher, and the remaining groups or individuals may be researching topics or studying alone in the resource center. All, in theory, would be taking part in the same lesson. For the purposes of this entry the assumption is that most or all the students are in the same classroom, or part of the school, with a single teacher for the duration of the lesson.

2. Factors Influencing Lesson Structure

Teachers are not always free to determine the structure of their lessons. They are first of all subject to macroinfluences, such as government policy, which may determine the nature of the curriculum to be studied, the textbooks approved for use in schools, and even teaching strategies. In some countries, for example, there are nationally prescribed lists of textbooks; furthermore, teachers of a foreign language may be required to conduct their lessons entirely or substantially in the foreign language. In other countries localism prevails and teachers are given considerable freedom to determine what takes place in the classroom. The United States is an example of a country that does not have a centrally prescribed curriculum, whereas

England and Wales are examples of countries that, following the 1988 Education Act, moved from a locally to a centrally determined curriculum.

Alongside these macroinfluences are numerous microinfluences, such as school policy, which may encourage or discourage formality, systematic instruction, topic and project work, or collaborative teaching. The nature of the environment in which learning takes place, for example, whether the building or classroom is spacious and well-equipped, permitting free movement and practical work, or narrow and cramped, constraining teachers into a limited range of possible activities, can also partly determine how a lesson is structured. This entry concentrates on the microinfluences, rather than the macro ones, even though the latter are of considerable importance.

2.1 Planning and Preparation

The preactive phase of a lesson (i.e., its planning and preparation) can have a considerable influence on lesson structure. Some lessons may be constructed around the showing of a video, a technology project, or even a single key question, like "Is a bird an insect?" or "What do you understand by the word 'prejudice'?"

However, the common assumption that lessons consist of carefully selected objectives, predetermined teaching strategies, and systematic evaluation does not always stand up to careful scrutiny. In an intensive study of six experienced Finnish teachers, Kansanen (1981) found that they tended to have a mental outline of what they intended to do, rather than a written plan, and that none of the six mentioned specific objectives. Written notes and log books may be more in evidence with trainee teachers or others required to meet demands for accountability. Left to their own preferences, many experienced teachers appear to opt for minimal formal preparation, and structure their lessons more intuitively and spontaneously.

2.2 Academic Focus

Different traditions have evolved in different subjects and Wragg (1973), in a study of 578 lessons given by 104 student teachers, found that foreign language lessons usually commenced with a period of rapid-fire questions and answers in the foreign language (often to review previous learning), followed by new material. Science lessons frequently were assigned longer periods of time, so that an initial exposition could be followed by practical work and a recapitulation of what had been discovered. Similarly, Leinhardt (1985) contrasted studies of mathematics lessons, in which a short presentation phase was followed by a production or practice phase, with reading lessons, where much of the work was done in small groups, and lasting from 60 to 90 minutes, some children working with the teacher, others on their own.

A different pattern would be observed in many United Kingdom primary schools. In a study of 32 teachers, each covering topics in science and English

with their pupils, Wragg (1993) found that in science lessons teachers were much more likely to give or elicit examples and summaries, engage in eye contact, and ask closed questions, than in English lessons, though they were much less likely to involve the imagination or give verbal cues.

2.3 Grouping

The use of small groups within a class varies according to the age of pupils, the activity in which students are engaged, and the country. In a study of 60 United Kingdom primary-school teachers, Wragg (1993) found that one-third of lesson time was spent on whole class teaching, either using teacher recitation or teacher–pupil interaction, whereas two-thirds was spent on individual and group work. In contrast, in a study of German secondary schools, Roeder (1990) found that out of 389 observed lessons only 20 contained any group work at all.

The evidence regarding the effectiveness of group work is mixed, for it is possible for teachers to establish different sizes and types of group for different purposes. Some teachers establish ability groups within the class; others deliberately arrange groups so that they are of mixed ability. When whole classes of mixed ability pupils are taught, there is some evidence, not only in the United Kingdom and the United States, but also in Sweden (Lundgren 1977) that teachers may aim their teaching at a "steering" or "target" group of pupils just below halfway down the ability range. Bridges (1979) concluded that the incorporation of small-group work within the lesson structure can result in higher participant satisfaction, more spoken contributions from participants, and, when the group is cohesive, a high degree of commitment to it. The evidence relative to achievement, however, is mixed. Quite clearly, matters of taste and value are involved, as teachers may decide that the ability to engage in teamwork and collaborate with others is in itself a worthwhile goal.

The Teacher Education Project (Wragg 1984) studied 40 United Kingdom secondary schools over a three-year period and found that teachers admitted greatest difficulty in their lessons with more able and less able pupils. More able pupils were perceived to be especially difficult to accommodate because they frequently finished work early and complained about boredom. A common response from teachers was to set them more exercises of the same kind, rather than extension work.

2.4 Teacher and Student Roles

Though some aspects of lesson structure may be predetermined by the teacher's planning and preparation, the roles that pupils play soon override initial intentions. A physical education teacher may decide that the first 5 minutes of the lesson will be devoted to warming-up exercises, and the next 20 minutes to gymnastics. Once a lesson has begun, however, most teachers will adjust their initial intentions in the light of events. Misbehavior by pupils, miscalculation by the teacher about how much time might be needed for an activity, or overestimation or underestimation of the ability of the class to cope with subject matter can all lead to a spontaneous change of plan. Indeed, remaining sensitive to feedback about the extent to which pupils are engaged in the task is a professional skill of some importance.

There is considerable debate in many countries about the roles that pupils and teachers should play in decisions about the nature of classroom activities. This debate is often stereotyped or labeled as "traditional" versus "progressive," "informal" versus "formal," or "authoritarian" versus "permissive." Bennett (1976), for example, used cluster analysis to group teachers according to their questionnaire responses on items about whether freedom of movement was permitted, whether there was regular testing of pupil learning, and the extent to which teachers taught single separate subjects, or cross-curricular topics and projects. He categorized teachers as "formal," "informal," or "mixed" and found slight learning gains for "formal" groups, though in a later analysis he revised this conclusion and found little significant difference (Aitkin et al. 1981).

Irrespective of research findings, however, the professional debate about the extent to which pupils should be encouraged to make choices for themselves continues. Traditionalists like Bantock (1965) argue that teachers are legally in charge, older than their pupils, psychologically different, and should determine the content and structure of lessons. Power, he contends, is an inescapable element of adult life and should not be concealed from the young. In contrast, lessons influenced by the writings of Dewey, Froebel, Montessori, and others on what is often called the "child-centered" view of teaching are based on the proposition that for learning to be effective, learners must themselves be party to decision-making. Furthermore, choosing is also an inescapable element of adult life.

Thus, in a classroom in which the teacher practices "child-centered" education there should be a considerable element of input from the pupils. Many United Kingdom primary teachers, particularly in infant schools for 5 to 7-year olds, make "choosing" an important part of lessons. Some design their day on what has sometimes been called the "drills and frills" principle, with more formal activities, such as language and number work in the morning, and pupil choice of topic or project in the afternoon.

2.5 Activities

Observation of primary and secondary classrooms reveals a very wide range of activities, sometimes even within the same lesson. Children may read, write, listen to the teacher, speak to others, engage in practical work, move around the classroom or school, watch a video, listen to a cassette, study a multimedia pack, make something, conduct a science experiment, play a competitive sport, paint, sing, or perform a role play. Teachers often need to structure their lessons in such a way that these activities can take place in the appropriate space, with any suitable equipment or materials to hand. In classrooms where one group of children are reading quietly and others are painting, these two activities could interfere with each other if the teacher's classroom management and planning skills are inadequate. Teaching mixed ability classes in particular puts a premium on the teacher's competence at managing pupil behavior and learning.

Activities are different not only in their nature, but also in their quality. Some teachers structure their lessons in such a way that a high level of pupil work is achieved, with considerable application to the task; others are less successful. Kerry (1984) analyzed 1,638 classroom transactions between teachers and pupils in secondary classrooms and found that in 54 percent of cases emphasis was on management, in 42 percent of instances instruction was being given, but in only 4 percent was there stimulation of pupil thinking at a higher level than data recall.

2.6 Pacing

The matter of pacing a lesson is very much related to the other issues included in this section. If the class is being taught as a whole, then the teacher can take direct control over the speed at which material is covered, though there is no guarantee that speed is related to learning, and the opposite can sometimes apply. When individuals and groups are working separately, the determination of pace is to some extent in the hands of the children themselves, and the teacher's role changes. Many teachers use what Kounin (1970) called "group alerting," a public summary of progress, often conducted center stage, to let the class know that the teacher is taking stock of progress, expecting certain activities to have been completed before long, or is concerned about lack of progress.

Some teachers give regular time messages, signaling how much longer pupils can have to finish their assignment. This signaling is sometimes used to clear space for revision or recapitulation at the end of the lesson. In a study of teachers' explaining science topics to 8- and 9-year olds, Wragg (1993) found that teachers were likely, in about half the lesson segments analyzed, to make time to summarize what had been learned at the end of the explanation. Eliciting an explanation from pupils was much less frequent.

3. Lesson Structure and Context

There are considerable differences in practice according to the context in which learning takes place. Theories of learning or personal preferences that are appropriate in one environment may be completely irrelevant in another. Compare, for example, two groups of pupils, one learning to throw the discus in a physical education lesson, another practicing the past tense in a foreign language lesson. An issue faced by teachers at the planning and implementation stages of both lessons is the matter of practice. Specifically, the issue is whether practice should be massed or distributed, that is, whether the learner should engage in several repetitions in a short burst, or spread these over a longer period.

In the physical education lesson such factors as fatigue and possible injury to the arm and shoulder rule out too many repetitions. In the foreign language lesson, however, there is no risk of physical injury, although the teacher will need to consider the question of fatigue. However, both teachers need to consider the issue of transfer, that is, the extent to which a skill learned in one context can be applied in another. Throwing a discus is a repeated action of the same set of movements, whereas learning the past tense of one verb does not ensure that the student will be able to use it in all contexts, or have a grasp of other past tense forms.

4. Methods of Analysis

The methods employed by investigators of lesson structure are similar to those used in classroom interaction analysis generally. Indeed, some of the well-known interaction analysis schedules have often been applied to various sections of lessons, such as the introduction, development, revision, and summary phases, in an attempt to contrast teaching styles in terms of different phases of the lesson.

4.1 Teacher–Pupil Interaction

There are numerous published schedules and category systems; some are based on pioneering work of classroom researchers like Flanders (1970), while others are specially assembled to study mathematics lessons, science classes, or kindergarten groups. Typically a time unit is determined, perhaps in 1-minute or 2-minute blocks, and the observer either notes the categories of teacher–pupil interaction which occur in that period or makes freehand notes.

In the case of systems like that of Flanders, a much smaller time unit, three seconds, is employed, and the observer records whatever category best represents what is happening, noting not only interactions, but also the nature of activities observed. Alongside this positivist approach there is a well-established alternative, based on social anthropological perspectives, which involves the observer making freehand notes about events during each lesson phase, and then interviewing participants (i.e., teachers and/or students) to elicit their perceptions of what transpired.

4.2 The Pupil Perspective

Studies of teacher–pupil interaction have often been criticized for concentrating too much on the teacher and paying insufficient attention to the learner. A method of rectifying this problem is for the investigator to study lesson structure from the pupil's vantage point. One approach is to conduct a "pupil pursuit," that is, to select a child and concentrate entirely on him or her, noting down what happens and the extent to which the child is involved. There may be a close match between the teacher's stated objectives and what the pupil under study actually does in the lesson, but there can also be considerable dissonance between intention and reality.

A variation of the pupil pursuit is to select a group of "target pupils" and study these in the same way as the pupil pursuit, to elicit what the lesson structure is in reality for different pupils. Usually six pupils are selected, one boy and one girl each of high, medium, and low ability, to give a representative cross section of the whole class.

5. Future Research

One of the problems in classroom research is that carrying out experiments according to classical experimental design, which would reveal whether different lesson structures have different effects, is extremely difficult. Most research takes place in naturalistic settings, in schools themselves, and researchers are in the hands of teachers and administrators. It is not easy to persuade teachers to teach what are virtually scripted lessons, and the children themselves react in a spontaneous manner and can soon unscramble the most carefully conceived design by their natural energy, enthusiasm, and response to events.

Nonetheless, teachers can experiment with different lesson structures in their own classrooms. Unfortunately, many adopt favored formats without reevaluating them periodically. Wragg (1973), for example, found, in a study of 104 trainee teachers, that even some beginners had fallen into a predictable routine.

Implementation studies are greatly needed. These studies inquire as to the extent to which teachers carry out their initial plan for the lesson. If they change it, why do they do so? Experiments in which teachers vary their common or preferred lesson structures to explore and evaluate alternatives are also needed, as are studies of the pupil perspective. Finally, investigations of the constraints on teachers (i.e., factors preventing teachers and pupils from embarking on lesson structures they would like to try were conditions favorable) are necessary.

See also: Realities of Teaching

References

Aitkin M, Bennett S N, Hesketh J 1981 Teaching styles and pupil progress: A re-analysis. *Br. J. Educ. Psychol.* 51:170–86

Bantock G H 1965 *Freedom and Authority in Education.* Faber, London

Bennett S N 1976 *Teaching Styles and Pupil Progress.* Open Books, London

Bridges D 1979 *Education, Democracy and Discussion.* National Foundation for Educational Research, Windsor

Flanders N A 1970 *Analyzing Teaching Behaviour.* Addison-Wesley, London

Kansanen P 1981 The way thinking is: How do teachers think and decide? In: Komulainen E, Kansen P (eds.) 1981 *Classroom Analysis: Concepts, Findings, Applications.* Institute of Education, University of Helsinki, Helsinki

Kerry T 1984 Analysing the cognitive demand made by classroom tasks in mixed-ability classes. In: Wragg E C (ed.) 1984

Kounin J S 1970 *Discipline and Group Management in Classrooms.* Holt, Rinehart and Winston, London

Leinhardt G 1985 Lessons, types of content in. In: Husén T, Postlethwaite T N (eds.) 1985 *The International Encyclopedia of Education.* Pergamon Press, Oxford

Lundgren U P 1977 *Model Analysis of Pedagogical Processes.* Stockholm Institute of Education, Stockholm

Roeder M 1990 *On Coping with Individual Differences in the Classroom.* Max Planck Institut, Berlin

Wragg E C 1973 A study of student teachers in the classroom. In: Chanan G (ed.) 1973 *Towards a Science of Teaching.* National Foundation for Educational Research, Windsor

Wragg E C (ed.) 1984 *Classroom Teaching Skills.* Croom Helm, London

Wragg E C 1993 *Primary Teaching Skills.* Routledge, London

(b)   Classroom Management

Instructional Pacing

L. W. Anderson and P. Torrey

Classroom teachers have great discretion in establishing the pace at which their students move through instructional programs and curriculum materials. In fact, pacing is one decision that is made almost exclusively at the classroom level. Teachers can make the decision themselves (teacher-paced instruction), can turn the decision over to their students (student-paced instruction), or can rely on mechanical means to pace students (e.g., computers, videotapes). If teachers make the decision, the same pace can be set for all students in the classroom or different paces can be established for different groups or individual students.

The pacing of instruction, then, involves two separate issues. First, who (or increasingly what) will set the pace? Second, how rapidly will the pace be set? The issues are critical because, in most schools, there is a great deal of content to cover and students learn this content at different rates.

1. The Control of Pacing

Research on this issue has focused on the relative merits of teacher, student, or mechanical control of the speed at which students are moved through the curriculum or individual lessons within the curriculum (Stodolsky 1988). Studies have been conducted in such diverse fields as algebra, automechanics, human physiology, and military training.

In most traditional elementary and secondary school classrooms, pacing is controlled by the teacher. In 1989, the extent of this control was summarized quite succinctly: "The vast majority of teachers preferred . . . to retain almost complete control over the amount of time spent on the work, and the way in which the work was undertaken, except in areas that the teacher considered peripheral" (Mortimore et al. 1989 p. 83). "Peripheral considerations" may in part explain Stodolsky's (1988) finding that teacher control of pacing was more frequent in elementary school mathematics than in elementary school social studies.

Despite the prevalence of teacher pacing, various forms of student pacing have appeared periodically on the educational landscape. Student pacing, termed self-pacing, was a hallmark of many of the individualized instructional programs developed during the 1960s and early 1970s (Lindvall and Bolvin 1967, Flanagan et al. 1975, Klausmeier 1976). In the 1980s and 1990s, the issue of student pacing has been discussed within the frameworks of computer-based instruction (Milheim 1990) and distance education (Fenwick 1985). Within these frameworks, pacing is generally thought to be one of a constellation of variables associated with learner control. Other variables in this cluster include the control of content, sequence, method, assessment, location, and schedule.

1.1 The Basis for Teacher Control Decisions

As mentioned above, teachers may pace the entire class of students, small groups of students, or individual students. Regardless of the unit of pacing (i.e., whole class, small group, individual), there is evidence that teachers adjust the pace of their instruction to the achievement levels of their students (Cooley and Leinhardt 1980).

When pacing an entire class of students, teachers tend to rely on the reactions and achievements of a small group of students referred to either as the steering group (Lundgren 1985) or criterion group (Arlin 1984). Typically, this group consists of students who are performing slightly or somewhat below average. Obviously, whole-class pacing decisions based on small-group data are not optimal for all students. The pace tends to be too slow for many faster, brighter students and too fast for the slowest and least bright (Arlin 1984).

Decisions concerning the pacing of small groups and individual students also appear to be based on student reactions and achievements. However, because the unit of decision-making (e.g., small groups, individual students) is generally the same as the unit on which the data are collected, the consequences of the decisions are likely to be quite different. One example is an approach known as flexible pacing (Daniel and Cox 1988).

Flexible pacing allows individual students to move

forward in the curriculum as they master content and skills. Daniel and Cox (1988) believe that with flexible pacing, all students can progress through school at a pace that provides a steady challenge without crippling frustration or unreasonable pressure. Methods of flexible pacing include continuous progress, compacted courses, advanced level courses, grade skipping, early entrance, concurrent or dual enrollment, and credit by examination.

1.2 Control of Pacing and Student Learning

The relationship between the control of pacing and student learning appears to be quite complex. The majority of studies suggest that teacher pacing is preferable to student pacing in terms of student learning (see, e.g., Crawford 1981, Filby and Cahen 1985, Higginbotham–Wheat 1990). Other studies, however, suggest the opposite (see, e.g., Thompson 1985, Stodolsky 1988).

One possible explanation for this ambiguity is that student pacing is beneficial for certain students (who are bright, highly motivated, and have some familiarity with the content) and detrimental to others (who are likely to procrastinate or have difficulty understanding on their own). This explanation is consistent with data presented by Shimron (1976) and Higginbotham–Wheat (1990).

2. Pacing as Rate

The rate issue in pacing can be reduced to the amount of content (i.e., knowledge and skills) that is presented to students within a given period of time. In this regard, pacing can be estimated by the number of pages covered (Barr et al. 1988), the number of items on a criterion test which included content on which students had received instruction (Anderson et al. 1989), or the number of student lessons that are devoted to the learning of new content (rather than the review of previously taught and learned content (Anderson et al. 1989). In general, the greater the number or percentage of text pages, test items, or new lessons, the more rapid the pace of instruction.

2.1 The Pace of Instruction

The pace at which instruction is presented to students worldwide is quite varied and generally quite slow. Exceptions to this generalization have been reported in South Korea (Anderson et al. 1989) and Japan (Stigler and Stevenson 1991).

With respect to variation, Barr and Dreeben (1983) found large differences in the pace of first grade reading instruction. In their study, one group of first graders was exposed to fewer than 50 words in a year, while another group was exposed to more than 400 words in the same year.

Anderson et al. (1989) reported equally large variation across classrooms in several countries in the percentage of items on a criterion test which included content that students had been taught prior to their being tested. In Australia, for example, this percentage ranged from 8 to 100, while in Thailand, it ranged from 0 to 100.

With respect to the actual pace at which new content and material is presented to students, Anderson et al. (1989) documented the percentage of lessons devoted to the review of previously taught content in six countries. These percentages ranged from less than 5 in South Korea to more than 60 in Nigeria. Across all countries, approximately three-fifths of the lessons were devoted primarily to the teaching of new knowledge and skills.

2.2 Content Coverage and Student Learning

As in the case of pacing as control, the relationship of pacing as rate of content coverage and student learning is complex. In general, the more rapid or brisk a pace, the greater the achievement of the students (Zahn 1966, Good et al. 1978, Barr and Dreeben 1983, Gastright 1985).

Again, however, several factors contribute to the strength of this relationship. Karweit (1985), for example, argues that subject matter is one such factor. Specifically, in those subject matters which are hierarchically or cumulatively structured, the relationship between pacing and student learning may be diminished. Leinhardt (1985) suggests that the achievement level of the students being taught may be another factor. Because teachers tend to adapt their pacing of instruction to the achievement levels of their students, the relationship between pacing and student learning in more complex models of teaching and learning may be essentially zero.

3. Pacing and the Dilemma of Classroom Teachers

Pacing decisions are difficult for many classroom teachers for at least two reasons. First, teachers constantly feel the tension between coverage and mastery. Shaunnessey (1982) states this dilemma quite succinctly:

> Many teachers feel torn, at times, between the desire to have their students learn as much and as quickly as possible and the knowledge that superficial treatment of a great deal of material leaves their students with nothing they can really use. (p. 30)

The issue for teachers to resolve, then, before they can make defensible pacing decisions is what is important for students to learn and how well they are expected to learn it.

Second, while teachers understand the need for students to be responsible for the amount and quality of their own learning, many are confronted daily with classrooms of irresponsible and undisciplined students. Rather than allow such students to control their own destinies, they tend to rely on calendars and deadlines to control students.

4. The Future of Instructional Pacing

While pacing is, on the surface, a rather simple concept, making decisions about pacing is quite complex. Pacing decisions (e.g., who should make the decisions? how rapidly should instruction be paced?) are influenced by numerous factors. Furthermore, while some form of external pacing (e.g., teacher, mechanical) is generally more effective than internal pacing (e.g., student) and while more rapid pacing is generally more effective than slow, leisurely pacing, there are important exceptions to each of these generalizations.

The most obvious implication of what is known about pacing is the need to imbed pacing within larger conceptual frameworks if the role of pacing in effective teaching and learning is to be properly understood. In this regard, the conditions under which pacing is and is not an important educational variable should be identified, and the range within which increased pacing is beneficial (and outside of which it is not) should be established.

In the meantime, teachers would do well to attempt to resolve the dilemmas concerning pacing mentioned earlier. External pacing at a fairly rapid rate appears to be a reasonable place to start. At the same time, however, teachers will need to monitor the effectiveness of this "starting point" and make changes as necessitated by different situations and individual students.

See also: Individualized Instruction; Grouping Students in the Classroom; Frame Factors

References

Anderson L W, Ryan D W, Shapiro B J (eds.) 1989 *The* IEA *Classroom Environment Study*. Pergamon Press, Oxford

Arlin M 1984 Time, equity, and mastery learning. *Rev. Educ. Res.* 54(1): 65–86

Barr R, Dreeben R, Wivatchai N 1988 *How Schools Work*. University of Chicago Press, Chicago, Illinois

Cooley W W, Leinhardt G 1980 The instructional dimensions study. *Educ. Eval. Policy Anal.* 2: 7–25

Crawford G 1981 Student completion rates during three different pacing conditions. Paper presented at the Annual Meeting of the American Educational Research Association, Los Angeles, California (ERIC Document Reproduction Service No. 259 221)

Daniel N, Cox J 1988 Flexible pacing for able learners. ERIC Digest. (ERIC Document Reproduction Service No. ED 314 916)

Fenwick J E 1985 *Individualized Learning*. Distance Education Service, Lincoln College, Canterbury (ERIC Document Reproduction Service No. ED 266 698)

Filby N N, Cahen L S 1985 Teacher accessibility and student attention. In: Fisher C W, Berliner D C (eds.) 1985 *Perspectives on Instructional Time*. Longman, New York

Flanagan J C, Shanner W M, Brudner H J, Market R W 1975 An individualized instructional system: Program learning in accordance with needs. In: Talmage H (ed.) 1975 *Systems of Individualized Education*. McCutchan, Berkeley, California

Gastright J F 1985 Time on any task?: The relationship between instructional pacing and standardized achievement test gains. Paper presented at the Annual Meeting of the American Educational Research Association, Chicago, Illinois (ERIC Document Reproduction Service No. 258 983)

Good T L, Grouws D A, Beckerman T M 1978 Curriculum pacing: Some empirical data in mathematics. *Curriculum Studies* 10(1): 75–81

Higginbotham–Wheat N 1990 Learner control: When does it work? In: Association for Educational Communications and Technology (ed.) 1990 *Proceedings of Selected Paper Presentations at the Convention of the Association for Educational Communications and Technology*. AECT, Washington, DC (ERIC Document Reproduction Service No. 323 930)

Karweit N 1985 Time scales, learning events, and productive instruction. In: Fisher C W, Berliner D C (eds.) 1985 *Perspective on Instructional Time*. Longman, New York

Klausmeier H J 1976 Individual guided education. *J. Teach. Educ.* 27: 199–207

Leinhardt G 1985 Instructional time: A winged chariot? In: Fisher C W, Berliner D C (eds.) 1985 *Perspectives on Instructional Time*. Longman, New York

Lindvall C M, Bolvin J O 1967 Programmed instruction in the schools: An application of programming principles in "Individually Prescribed Instruction." In: Lange P C (ed.) 1967 *Programmed Instruction*. Sixty-sixth Yearbook of the National Society for the Study of Education. National Society for the Study of Education. Chicago, Illinois

Lundgren U P 1985 Frame factors. In: Dunkin M J (ed.) 1985 *International Encyclopedia of Teaching and Teacher Education*. Pergamon Press, Oxford

Milheim W D 1990 The effects of pacing and sequence control in an interactive video lesson. *Educ. Train. Tech. Int.* 27: 7–19

Mortimore P, Sammons P, Stoll L, Lewis D, Ecob R 1988 *School Matters*. University of California Press, Berkeley, California

Shaunnessey M 1982 Less is more: Pacing in the ESL class. In Boyd J R, Haskell J F (eds.) 1982 *Selected Papers from the Illinois* TESOL/BE *Annual Conference*. Chicago, Illinois (ERIC Document Reproduction Service No. 224 349)

Shimron J 1976 Learning activities in Individually Prescribed Instruction. *Instr. Sci.* 5: 391–401

Stigler J W, Stevenson H W 1991 How Asian teachers polish each lesson to perfection. *Am. Educ.* 15: 12–20, 43–47

Stodolsky S S 1988 *The Subject Matters*. University of Chicago, Chicago, Illinois

Thompson J 1985 *Individualized Learning Systems of Instruction at* TAFE *colleges*. TAFE National Centre for Research and Development, Payneham (ERIC Document Reproduction Service No. 275 872)

Zahn K G 1966 Use of class time in eighth grade arithmetic. *Arithmetic Teacher* 13: 113–20

Classroom Rules and Routines

C. M. Evertson

Some of the most fundamental decisions for classroom teachers are concerned with organizing and managing academic tasks and activities and controlling student behavior. Solving the problem of order in classrooms (Doyle 1986) has much to do with developing a workable set of rules and routines and teaching these to students (Emmer et al. 1980, Evertson and Emmer 1982). Rules and routines function to support and frame learning in classroom settings in much the same way that laws and directions guide behavior in the larger society. "Both policy-directed and descriptive studies indicate that life in classrooms begins with the creation of a work system and the setting of rules and procedures to hold the system in place, and that a considerable amount of energy is devoted to this process" (Doyle 1986 p. 413). While this process may seem common sense to most educators, research from different perspectives on how rules and routines function in classrooms has revealed considerable complexity.

This entry will examine research perspectives on this crucial aspect of classroom life, beginning by establishing what is meant by the terms "rules" and "routines." It will discuss briefly how rules and routines function to support or constrain learning in classrooms from three research perspectives: process-product/behaviorals, ethnographic/interpretive, and systems communication. How rules and routines are established, and how they function in classrooms will be examined.

An additional key issue has to do with consequences for noncompliance with established rules and routines and how these relate to various behavioral intervention strategies designed to regain compliance. While this issue is at the heart of many school discipline programs, it is beyond the scope of this entry. However, Emmer and Aussiker (1990) have written a critical review of research related to the effectiveness of several commonly used disciplinary intervention systems.

1. What Are Rules and Routines?

The first step in understanding rules and routines is to define them. While in the literature the two terms are often used interchangeably, it is useful for both researchers and practitioners to distinguish between them. A third term, "procedures," is frequently used synonymously with "routines." The distinction between the two terms is subtle, and for the purposes of this entry, "routines" will be assumed to include procedures.

Rules and routines can be distinguished from each other by content and scope. For example, in a grocery store, it is a stated rule that one must pay for all goods which leave the store. It is a stated routine, or procedure, that to pay for goods, the purchaser stands in a particular line. Similar layers of rules and routines are apparent in classrooms, although the universality of a rule such as paying for goods is rare in classrooms, where even such widespread standards as "Raise your hand before speaking" have frequent exceptions.

Simply stated, rules are general norms for expected behavior. Thus, they govern the moral and ethical life of the classroom, and tend to be stated in global terms: "Show respect for yourself and others," or "Come to class prepared to learn." Rules are the class values underpinning all classroom activity. Routines, in contrast, are procedures for accomplishing particular classroom tasks; they are the "how-to's" for day-to-day functioning within the value system provided by the rules. Routines govern physical relationships, space, and materials, and tend to be very specific: "If you need help, raise your hand." "Use the pencil sharpener only before the bell rings." Rules can be distilled down into a few guiding principles for the classroom, while routines are much more numerous.

Clearly there is overlap between rules and routines as they have been defined here. While rules may sound universally applicable, ethnographic studies such as that of Hargreaves et al. (1975) indicate that, in practice, the rules "in play" at various points in a lesson may differ greatly, making them much more situational, and hence more like routines. The notion that only rules carry the values of the classroom is also overly simplistic; clearly the routines which are enacted and enforced communicate who or what is important at any one time. This point will be further elaborated in the section on ethnographic studies below.

The importance of routines to the effective functioning of classrooms has been discussed from a cognitive psychology perspective by Leinhardt (1987), building on the findings of Evertson and Emmer (1982, see also Emmer et al. 1980). Leinhardt et al. contrast rules with routines by defining rules as limits to behavior, while routines are systems of exchanges that are set up to accomplish tasks and allow instruction to take place. The "small cooperative scripts of behavior" (p. 135) which are routines serve to reduce unnecessary cognitive demands on teachers and students by developing certain frequent tasks into schemata, thus making them automatic. Teacher planning and instruction are facilitated by these schemata: "The instruction to 'pass your papers in' results in all actors understanding the expected actions and executing them in a routine way" (p. 138).

Leinhardt et al. describe three types of routines: management routines, support routines, and exchange routines. Management routines include housekeeping, discipline, maintenance, and people-moving tasks. One example of a management routine is "how to line up for lunch." Support routines define and specify the behaviors and actions necessary for a learning–teaching exchange to take place, for example, "how to pass in papers." Exchange routines specify the interactive behaviors that permit the teaching–learning exchange to occur. They govern the language contacts between teachers and students—for example, routines for choral responses.

Rules and routines are not always stated or taught explicitly by teachers. In their study of deviance in classrooms, Hargreaves et al. (1975) identified rules and routines in order to document deviance from them. They found identification to be a complex task because teachers and students could not consistently verbalize the rules and routines of the classroom, even though most participants seemed to be functionally fluent in their applications and to share an understanding of why sanctions were applied in certain situations. Thus, generally speaking, rules and routines were public knowledge. Observations of classrooms and interviews with teachers and students revealed a complex set of norms and expectations which were highly context-dependent and which shifted not only from setting to setting, but from activity to activity within each setting.

Using the term "rules" as an umbrella encompassing both rules and routines, Hargreaves et al. identified three levels of rules which operate in a school. The first category, institutional rules, govern behavior in public places, such as hallways, cafeteria, and playground. When asked about "the school rules," these are the rules teachers and students were likely to recite. The second category, "situational rules," apply only in particular locations, such as in assembly or in classrooms. Situational rules supplement institutional rules in some settings. The last category was "personal rules," which are rules unique to a single teacher. One teacher in this study, for example, required students to stand when a visitor entered the classroom. Under a previous headmaster, this had been an institutional rule, but it had since fallen into disuse by everyone except the one teacher, becoming one of her personal rules. Students who moved from classroom to classroom thus had the task of interpreting and acting on different teachers' personal rules as well as the academic demands of the classroom.

Hargreaves et al. (1975) grouped classroom rules, which are situational and personal, under five themes. Generally, rules govern areas of teacher and student talk, movement, time, teacher–student relationships, and student–student relationships. The five themes

overlap heavily in practice, with most rules covering more than one area and the placement of rules into categories dependent on the context in which the rule is invoked. For example, a teacher issuing a reprimand to two students talking could be interpreted as a "student–student relationship" rule if the issue is one student disrupting another's work, or as a "talk" rule, indicating that talk is prohibited during this part of the lesson.

Rules and routines may be formal (stated, taught, and practiced), or informal (unstated, but expected and understood by participants). The two types of rules and routines have typically been studied through the lenses of different research perspectives (Everton and Smylie 1987). Research in the behavioral psychological tradition has examined the planning, teaching, and effectiveness of formal, stated rules. Many rules and routines, however, are part of students' and teachers' tacit knowledge of classrooms (e.g., "Must I raise my hand in this particular discussion?" "Need I head my rough draft in the same way as my final draft?"). Ethnographic/interpretive research is more likely to address the evolution of such rules and routines. Informal rules and routines are highly context-dependent and their identification frequently requires prolonged observation of the classroom culture and microlevel analysis of classroom activity and communication.

2. Rules and Routines from a Behavioral Psychological Perspective

The focus of process–product/behavioral research on rules and routines has been on rules constructed *a priori* and implemented to structure the learning environment, manage resources, and control student attention and behavior. Of primary concern has been the form of rules and routines. Using research which demonstrates that productive use of class time correlates with higher student achievement as their rationale, process–product researchers have examined how effective use of rules and routines contributes to effective use of class time. "The opportunities for teachers to devote significant portions of class time in productive ways is determined in large part by the rules and routines teachers implement to structure and maintain their classroom environment" (Evertson and Smylie 1987 p. 358). Smooth and efficient routines for transitions, paperwork, and similar classroom events provide more time for academic work in the classroom.

More effective classroom managers devote significant amounts of time to teaching rules and routines at the beginning of the year, particularly in elementary classrooms but also in secondary classrooms (Emmer et al. 1980, Evertson and Emmer 1982, Leinhardt et al. 1987). Successful managers spent much of the first days of school actively teaching routines which would be used throughout the coming year. Content lessons during these first two days served as vehicles for conveying appropriate routines.

3. Rules and Routines from an Ethnographic/Interpretive Perspective

Process–product/behavioral research provides essential information about what practices for rules and routines are associated with student task engagement and achievement. Ethnographic/interpretive research on classroom communication, which focuses on much smaller samples (often only one classroom) in much greater detail, provides information about how rules and routines function in particular classrooms. While process–product research asks questions such as, "What rules and routines are associated with success?," ethnographic/interpretive research asks questions such as, "How do rules and routines function in this classroom? For whom, and for what purposes?"

Classroom communication researchers conceive of all classroom interaction as rule-governed (Green 1983). The focus of the research is on the functional rules and expectations that govern communicative interaction in the classroom. These rules are mutually constructed by teachers and students and constantly evolve during interactions, shifting and changing according to task or lesson phase. The rules, however, do not strictly limit classroom communication; instead, they provide a framework within which teachers and students improvise (Erickson 1982).

Studies about classroom communication—verbal and nonverbal ways that norms, rules, and expectations are signaled—show how both students and teachers actively mediate and construct the learning environment (see Erickson 1986 and Green and Smith 1983 for reviews). Studies identify what students need to understand in order to participate in lessons and how teachers orchestrate that participation. Some ritualistic activities, such as passing out papers, require little understanding. However, nonritualistic activities require students to "read" the requirements correctly or risk negative evaluations of their behavior and abilities (Green and Harker 1982). A close look at how class activities evolve reveals the need for a system of rules and routines that is visible, established, monitored, modified, refined, and reestablished.

Rules and routines thus take on broader meanings from the ethnographic/interpretive perspective. In this body of work, their definitions are extended to include spoken and unspoken norms for participation, often at a micro level of classroom interaction. For example, the routines of a classroom are assumed to include not only the expectation that students will raise their hands to request assistance, but also the subtle shifts in teacher and student behavior that signal when hand-

raising is appropriate, whose hands will be recognized, and when calling out is the actual expected behavior.

Hargreaves et al. (1975) identified rules and routines as context-dependent within an individual class period or lesson. In the classes they observed, different rules were in play during each of five phases of a class session: entry, settling down/preparation, the lesson proper, cleaning up, and exit. For example, students were allowed to chat during the entry and settling down phases, but not during the lesson proper. Such differences have been consistently found by researchers; ecological studies, in fact, use such shifts in "rules of appropriateness" (Erickson and Shultz 1981) to divide a lesson chronicle into segments (Doyle 1986). These differences were not explicitly stated by the teacher in the classrooms Hargreaves et al. observed; rather, they were unspoken norms which seemed to be an expectation of classroom life shared by teachers and students. By identifying unspoken expectations, such research points out how misunderstandings and miscommunications can occur, and helps to explain the process–product finding that time spent at the beginning of the year making classroom rules and routines explicit is crucial to effective management.

Numerous studies of classroom communication have examined the rules in play in particular classroom activity settings, with the emphasis on demands for social participation. For example, Wallat and Green (1979) have examined group interactions in a kindergarten class, including the cues which signal participation structures. As an example, Wallat and Green describe the norms for participation in "sharing time." The stated rule is that only one person may speak at a time. However, through nonverbal communication with the teacher (such as eye contact) and through verbal gestures (such as staying on-topic), a child could successfully negotiate an out-of-turn comment. Thus, the rules in play at any time are dependent on context, and are constructed in an ongoing process of interaction between teacher and students. Furthermore, Wallat and Green emphasize the importance of unspoken rules and routines, noting that, to an outsider, it may appear that a teacher is not making his or her expectations clear, when in fact both teacher and students may understand the verbal and nonverbal signals being given.

Ethnographic/interpretive research also provides information about why it is important to look beneath the surface of student behavior to determine how the rules in play are functioning. An overemphasis on following rules and routines can mask how they support or constrain what students are learning. Students may follow rules without taking the further step of engaging in substantive content. Their behavior is mere "procedural display" or "mock participation" (Bloome et al. 1989). In such cases, the "doing" of the routine replaces making sense of the content as a definition of learning.

4. Systems Communication, Rules, and Routines

Wubbels et al. (1988) describe a third approach which can be applied to an understanding of rules and routines: the systems communication approach to classroom interaction. They distinguish systems communication from other studies of classroom communication because of the former's emphasis on the long-term development of routine and ritual rather than on the generally short interaction units addressed by sociolinguists. From the systems communication perspective, routines develop over time as a part of the process by which teachers and students try to define what kind of relationship they have. Routines or rituals are thus the stabilized interaction patterns which develop in a classroom over time.

In a further explication of the same body of work, Creton et al. (1989) describe the circular effects of teacher and student behavior. As each participant acts, his or her behavior informs the action of the other participant, which in turn informs the behavior of the first participant. Thus, as routines develop and progress, it is impossible to distinguish cause and effect, and events which could appear isolated are actually shown to be connected. Dysfunctional routines develop as well as functional ones, and the issue for teachers, rather than assigning blame, is to acknowledge and act on their own contributions to dysfunctional routines. For example, the teacher in Creton et al.'s study had severe behavior problems in her classroom. Early in the year, she blamed the inappropriate behavior on students, and responded with punitive measures which seemed unfair to students and further contributed to their misbehavior, which they blamed on the teacher. As long as teacher and students continued to blame each other, they were locked into a dysfunctional system of routines which led to ongoing escalations in misbehavior and punishment. When given information about the routine which had developed, the teacher was able to break her part of the system, in this case by seeking positive student accomplishments rather than negative ones. Over time, as actions within this new system reinforced each other, more functional routines developed. Leinhardt et al. (1987) also documented dysfunctional routines which developed in two of the elementary school classrooms they observed.

5. Conclusion

While studies from both the ethnographic/interpretive and the process-product/behavioral traditions point to the importance of understanding rules and routines as a guide to understanding classroom functioning, they also point to the danger of focusing on rules and routines to the exclusion of the substance of the lesson. A focus on the doing rather than the meaning allows observers, teachers, and students to see procedural display as a desirable outcome, when in fact little or no actual learning may be taking place. Rules and routines can support instruction, but it is an error to focus solely on them rather than looking at the kinds of teaching and learning that they support. As Doyle (1986) has pointed out, there is a gap in the literature between research on the problem of order in classrooms, including the roles of rules and routines, and research on the problem of learning. This is a gap which must be bridged in order for either body of work to be meaningful.

See also: Teacher Managerial Behaviors

References

Bloome D, Puro P, Theodorou E 1989 Procedural display and classroom lessons. *Curric. Inq.* 19(3): 265–91
Creton H A, Wubbels T, Hooymayers H P 1989 Escalated disorderly situations in the classroom and the improvement of these situations. *Teaching and Teachers Education* 5(3): 205–15
Doyle W 1986 Classroom organization and management. In: Wittrock M C (ed.) 1986 *Handbook of Research on Teaching*. Macmillan, New York
Emmer E T, Aussiker A 1990 School and classroom discipline programs: How well do they work? In: Moles O C (ed.) 1990 *Student Discipline Strategies*. State University of New York Press, Albany, New York
Emmer E T, Evertson C M, Anderson L M 1980 Effective classroom management at the beginning of the school year. *Elem. Sch. J.* 80(5): 219–31
Erickson F 1982 Classroom discourse as improvisation: Relationships between academic task structure and social participation structure in lessons. In: Wilkinson L C (ed.) 1982 *Communicating in the classroom*. Academic Press, New York
Erickson F 1986 Qualitative methods in research on teaching. In: Wittrock M C (ed.) 1986 *Handbook of Research on Teaching*. Macmillan, New York
Erickson F, Shultz J 1981 When is a context? Some issues and methods in the analysis of social competence. In: Green J L, Wallat C (eds.) 1981 *Ethnography and Language in Educational Settings*. Ablex, Norwood, New Jersey
Evertson C M, Emmer E T 1982 Effective management at the beginning of the school year in junior high classes. *J. Educ. Psychol.* 74(4): 485–98
Evertson C M, Smylie M A 1987 Research on teaching and classroom processes: Views from two perspectives. In: Glover J A, Ronning R R (eds.) 1987 *Historical Foundations of Educational Psychology*. Plenum Press, New York
Green J L 1983 Research on teaching as a linguistic process: A state of the art. In: Gordon E W (ed.) 1983 *Review of Research in Education*, Vol. 10. American Educational Research Association, Washington DC 151–252
Green J L, Harker J O 1982 Gaining access to learning: Conversational, social, and cognitive demands of group participation. In: Wilkinson L C (ed.) 1982 *Communicating in The Classrooms*. Academic Press, New York
Green J L, Smith D 1983 Teaching and learning: A linguistic perspective. *Elem. Sch. J.* 83(4): 353–91

Hargreaves D H, Hester S K, Mellor F J 1975 *Deviance in Classrooms*. Routledge and Kegan Paul, London
Leinhardt G, Weidman C, Hammond K M 1987 Introduction and integration of classroom routines by expert teachers. *Curric. Inq.* 17(2): 135–76
Wallat C, Green J L 1979 Social rules and communicative contexts in kindergarten. *Theory Pract.* 18(4): 275–84
Wubbels T, Creton H A, Holvast A 1988 Undesirable classroom situations: A systems communication perspective. *Interchange* 19(2): 25–40

Further Reading

Bossert S T 1979 *Tasks and Social Relationships in Classrooms*. Cambridge University Press, Cambridge
Emmer E T, Evertson C M, Clements B S, Worsham M E 1994 *Classroom Management for Secondary Teachers*, 3rd edn. Allyn and Bacon, Boston, Massachusetts
Evertson C M, Emmer E T, Clements B S, Worsham M E 1994 *Classroom Management for Elementary Teachers*, 3rd edn. Allyn and Bacon, Boston, Massachusetts

Teacher Managerial Behaviors

E. T. Emmer

The classroom setting, including the myriad demands placed on the teacher's attention by large numbers of pupils, is a complex context. Order and cooperation are necessary in such a setting to conduct activities in which learning can occur. Teacher managerial behaviors organize the setting, establish appropriate behavior, prevent problems, and deal with disruptions. These actions can be viewed as a process starting with planning and preparation at the beginning of the school year or term and continuing with maintenance of the behavior setting over time.

1. The Classroom Context

Classrooms are busy places, full of children or adolescents, not all of whom are present by choice. Securing cooperation so that learning can take place is a necessary goal of the classroom teacher. Thus, providing instruction and managing behavior are complementary aspects of the teacher's classroom role.

To appreciate the complexity of the teacher's managerial task, it is instructive to consider a few cross-sectional glimpses of classroom life—a teacher providing instruction using a small group format, for example. In this activity, the teacher instructs a small group of students while the remainder of the class works independently. To prepare for the activity, the teacher needs to attend to the following issues: where to meet with the small group, how to move students to and from the small group location, what activities are suitable for the students not in the small group, what materials to use in the small group and with the students working independently, what routines to use for monitoring and providing assistance, and what procedures to establish governing student talk and movement. Even as seemingly straightforward an activity as presenting a lesson in a whole class format needs sound management. The physical setting must be arranged, appropriate materials prepared and kept at hand, and expectations for student participation made clear.

In addition to these planned, preactive aspects of management, other more reactive managerial behaviors continue throughout the conduct of the activities. The teacher monitors student behavior, captures and recaptures student attention, fends off interruptions and intrusions, and, when necessary, deals with disruptions to the activity. The on-going management of students during instruction is complicated by the rapidity with which behaviors occur, calling for split-second, seemingly reflexive decisions. Time for reflective contemplation of potential actions and for a careful balancing of long- and short-range outcomes is in very short supply during the active phases of teaching.

Other features of classroom teaching that are significant for teacher management are the "groupness" of instruction, the teacher's isolation from other teachers during much of the workday, and the social and organizational structure of schools and teaching. In most schools, teachers instruct students in groups for most of the day. Consequently, many managerial decisions must be made and carried out in full view of all students in the group, even if they involve only one student or a small number of students. Thus, the impact of a behavior or strategy on the total class must be considered, and the teacher is usually constrained by the necessity of monitoring the whole class while reacting to individual problems. The absence of other adults in the classroom, except for occasional evaluation visits, limits the amount of external feedback the teacher receives.

Standardized data on pupil progress comes only once a year, if that, so changes in the teacher's managerial behaviors are affected mainly by students' immediate reactions. Teachers generally feel some pressure to cover the grade-level curriculum, especially at the elementary level in basic skills subjects and at the secondary level in subjects that are prerequisite to further work. Instructional and managerial problems arise as individual differences in student interests, temperament, abilities, and achievement intersect the rigidity of the curriculum and available time.

2. Critical Concepts

Establishing and maintaining classroom order has long been accepted as one of the teacher's major roles. Although some assistance from school administrators is expected by most teachers, chiefly in the form of dealing with insubordinate students, most teachers accept the responsibility for managing behavior in their own classrooms.

2.1 Teacher Control of Students

By implication, accepting responsibility for establishing order becomes a duty to control students. As Denscombe (1985) notes, teachers lack technological and material resources to control students (although some special education settings may provide exceptions), so must rely on personalized authority and personal commitments. Denscombe places control strategies into one of three general categories: domination, cooptation, and classwork management.

"Domination" strategies autocratically impose the teacher's ideas of order on the students through restricted activities, consequences, and insistence on obedience. "Cooptation" seeks to win over the students' cooperation by involving the students in governance, emphasizing choices and logical consequences rather than punishments, and developing more involving curricula. "Classwork management" strategies focus on creating lessons that keep students on-task, so that cooperation with the lesson structure prevents misbehavior. In effect, the teacher controls the students indirectly, via the requirements of the activities; control is accomplished through maintaining a smooth activity flow, limiting diversions from the primary "vector of action," and preventing competing secondary vectors of action from becoming established (Doyle 1986). While the three strategies are conceptually distinct, most teachers' practices are a mixture, with the degree of utilization of each strategy a matter of values, training, and personal experiences.

2.2 Classroom Activities

Activity structures (Berliner 1983) are unique features of classrooms that influence teacher managerial behaviors. An "activity" can be defined as a predictable pattern of teacher and student behaviors occurring for a segment of time. Transitions between activities are marked by significant shifts in the teacher's and the students' behaviors. Some of the more common activities in classrooms are whole class, teacher-led, presentations, recitations, and discussions; small group instruction and small group projects; individ-

ual seatwork; and tests. Some subjects have unique activities (e.g., the science laboratory or the choir performance), but most activity types cross content boundaries. The teacher must arrange a sequence of activities so that proper instruction can take place within the constraints imposed by the available time. Activities are thus building blocks for instruction. Because different activities, by definition, require different behaviors, the teacher needs to understand the behavioral requirements of each and be prepared to teach these to the students, to monitor compliance, and to redirect behavior when necessary.

2.3 Routines and Procedures

Efficient routines and procedures, characteristic of the classrooms of expert teachers, are important aids to management because they provide recurrent, predictable patterns of behavior that simplify the students' and teacher's task of making their way through the complexities of the behavioral environment (Berliner 1988). A "procedure" is a simple behavior designed to accomplish something specific; a "routine" is usually a combination of several procedures. Once students have learned the routines and procedures that are used in a class, the teacher's management task is simplified.

If, however, routines are not available or practiced for commonly used activities, then the lack of structure can result in lost instructional time and difficulty in group management. If a secondary teacher fails to establish a routine for the beginning of the class period, students might wander about the room, talk excessively, and delay the start of instruction, while at the same time the teacher might have difficulty taking attendance, enforcing school rules for tardiness, managing previously absent students, and beginning the day's content development activity.

2.4 Preventive and Reactive Strategies

Conceptualizations of teacher managerial behaviors frequently distinguish between "prevention" and "reaction." Preventive strategies include arrangement of the physical setting, establishing general rules and routines to guide student behavior, establishing predictable consequences, developing an efficient work system, and conducting lessons in ways that maintain student involvement (Emmer et al. 1989). The goal of preventive strategies is to set up an environment that has strong cues for appropriate behavior and that encourages student engagement in class activities. Reactive strategies occur in response to a lack of cooperation; for example, to student behaviors that interfere with the flow of appropriate behavior in an activity, to noncompliance with school or classroom rules, and to aggressive or disruptive behaviors.

Reactive strategies (Kerr and Nelson 1983, Stoner et al. 1991) vary in complexity. Those requiring little time or teacher effort include eye contact or other signals and verbal desists. Somewhat more time-consuming or involving strategies are brief removal of the student from the activity, using an established consequence, or changing the task requirements for the student. Still more complex and time-consuming are strategies such as arranging a contract for appropriate behavior, holding a conference with the student or parents, or developing a contingency management program to reduce inappropriate behavior and to establish desirable behavior. When choosing to react, key considerations for the teacher are the amount of time available for intervention, the seriousness of the problem (will it spread or become more intense?), and whether the problem can be dealt with in the classroom and during the on-going activity.

2.5 Academic Tasks

The concept of the "academic task" (Doyle and Carter 1984) helps bridge the domains of managerial behaviors, the curriculum, and instructional behaviors. An academic task is defined in terms of the products or outcomes produced by the student, such as a writing sample, a completed set of problems, or an oral performance, and the resources available to help the student achieve the outcome. Classroom resources include curricular materials, the teacher, other students, and available time. Teacher managerial behaviors thus support student achievement to the extent that they facilitate or make available the resources needed by students.

Similarly, curricular planning and instruction influence management, according to the degree to which the academic task structure engages students and promotes success. Discipline problems occur most frequently in classrooms in which there are large numbers of students with a poor match between the academic task structure and their interests and prior academic achievements. Dealing with the situation as purely a managerial or disciplinary problem will address only one side of the equation; curricular and grouping/tracking practices must be altered in order to achieve a better solution (Slavin 1989, Jones 1989).

3. Integrative Analysis: A Comprehensive Perspective of Teacher Managerial Behaviors

Research on the managerial behaviors of teachers has been extensive and multidisciplinary. It has included detailed ethnographic analyses of (usually) one or a few classes and teachers; other forms of naturalistic inquiry, such as observational studies in the tradition of ecological psychology and of sociolinguistics; large-scale process–product studies; and applied behavior analysis. Other research has been a hybridization of methodologies, reflecting crossfertilization in the field of research on teaching. This research has yielded a substantial amount of knowledge.

3.1 Classroom Management and the Beginning of the School Year

Although much of the research in classrooms takes a cross-sectional view of events, some longitudinal studies have included observations of the first few days and weeks of school, as well as interviews with teachers about their management strategies at the beginning of the year (Everston and Emmer 1982). These studies indicate that teachers who have well-managed classrooms later in the year have a well-developed conception of what student behaviors are desirable and undesirable. In addition, they have a good idea of the procedures and routines that will be needed in their classrooms. In other words, classroom management begins before students arrive.

In a sense, all prior experiences of teachers contribute to their cognitive and behavioral maps of the classroom, and planning for management is comingled with thinking about the curriculum and instruction. Yet it is clear that teachers develop a distinct system of management that includes arranging the physical setting (to facilitate monitoring and accessibility; to limit distractability), identifying specific procedures and routines in many areas (e.g., talk and movement in particular activities, out-of-room policies, handling previously absent students, use of materials, communicating assignments), planning general or specific rules or guidelines (some teachers make this a cooperative effort with students), deciding what consequences (rewards and penalties) will be used, and planning initial activities to use during the first week or so of school. These areas of management are worked out before students arrive; if not, then there is a higher risk of students learning inappropriate behaviors at the beginning of the year, and greater demands being placed on the teacher's ability to monitor student behavior and react to problems as the year progresses.

3.2 Initial Meetings with Students

Teacher managerial behaviors at the start of school can be viewed broadly as directed at socializing students into the classroom setting and putting into place the procedures and routines that define the management system. In effect, students need to learn what behaviors are appropriate in the various activities. Students are made aware of norms directly when the teacher states expectations about particular behaviors, explains procedures, and directs students' activities. Often a set of rules or guidelines for behavior are presented to (or developed cooperatively with) students.

Students also learn about appropriate behavior as the result of feedback from the teacher and consequences of their behavior. In addition, students learn about expectations indirectly by observing other students' behaviors and the consequences that occur or do not occur. Classroom norms become established over time, in the context of the activity structure used by the teacher, rather than as some unique task divorced from instruction. In the early grades, the socialization process occurs over many weeks or even months; in later grades, the process takes place more rapidly, as teachers and students draw upon prior experience in familiar activities.

3.3 On-going Teacher Management: Maintaining Activity Flow

The establishment and maintenance of appropriate behavior and the prevention of inappropriate behavior depend substantially on the teacher keeping students productively engaged in academic activities. In a well-respected set of naturalistic studies, Kounin (1970) and his colleagues identified a rich set of concepts to describe group management strategies.

During whole class activities, teachers can foster student involvement and keep activities free of disruption by nipping incipient misbehavior in the bud ("withitness") before it spreads or becomes more intense. "Overlapping," that is, handling simultaneously two or more events or situations, also helps keep order in the busy classroom. Activities that are conducted smoothly (minimal teacher-induced interruptions and irrelevances) and with good momentum (briskly paced) are the goals. Teachers also can use alerting or focusing strategies (signals or statements that capture whole class attention), accountability (communicating that student work or performance will be checked or observed), and activity formats that require more than just passive sitting and listening.

Management of independent seatwork activities is aided by greater task and format variety and by teacher comments which engender interest in and motivation for the activities. Transitions between activities can be the source of behavior problems, both during transitions and spilling over into the subsequent academic activity; however, such problems can be reduced by teacher structuring and monitoring of student behavior during the transition (Arlin 1979).

3.4 Teacher Management of Problem Behaviors

In addition to preventive management and to the on-going management of student behaviors via maintenance of activity flow during instruction, teachers must deal with disruptive and other problem student behaviors. Although much research in different countries (e.g., Wheldall and Glynn 1989, Doyle 1986) indicates that the predominant forms of misbehavior are individually not very threatening or destructive (e.g., talking out of turn, wasting time, wandering around the classroom), their presence in large amounts can be very detrimental to the maintenance of order and to the conduct of academic activities. Furthermore, some forms of misbehavior such as aggressive acting out, interference with the activities of the teacher or other students, abusive language, or frequent refusal to follow reasonable classroom rules

and routines, are encountered to some degree by most teachers.

Many of the recommended strategies for teachers were developed initially for special populations, such as behavior-disordered students. Generally, the strategies draw heavily from the field of applied behavior analysis, although they may also include components from psychotherapeutic and psychoeducational perspectives (Gallagher 1988, Maurer 1988). Examples of specific strategies that have some research base in the applied behavior analysis literature include time-out, partial exclusion, self-recording of behaviors, charting behaviors, individual concrete rewards, token reward systems, group activity rewards, goal setting, withholding rewards or privileges systematically, response cost systems, providing differential feedback and attention, and reducing distracting cues.

Applied behavior analysis strategies begin with a careful assessment of the classroom environment (and possibly external settings) to determine cues for the problem behavior and its consequences. A similar analysis is often done for desirable behaviors that can substitute for the problem behaviors. Then an intervention, which typically has goals of reducing the problem behavior and substituting more desirable ones, is implemented. Intervention usually requires altering the environment (e.g., teacher's behavior, materials, other students' behaviors, seating arrangements, assignments) to eliminate cues for the inappropriate behavior and to establish signals for the desirable alternative. The intervention usually will include changes in the consequences for the behaviors. Typically, reinforcers for the undesirable behavior will be eliminated and rewards for the desirable behavior will be added or strengthened. Since generalization of the acquired behaviors is often a problem, fading of extrinsic reinforcement is needed in order to have the best chance of producing a lasting change in behavior.

Therapeutic interventions generally attempt to alter the students' cognitions as well as behaviors. Although many such interventions are designed for long-term use by professionals outside the classroom, some have been specifically developed for teachers. A widely applied approach has been Glasser's "reality therapy."

A teacher following this intervention model initially meets with the student. After the nature of the problem behavior is clarified, the teacher works with the student to evaluate whether the behavior is helpful or harmful and to obtain a commitment to change the behavior. A plan for change is agreed upon and tried out. Failure to follow the plan results in another conference or in agreed-upon consequences. The assumption in working with the student is that behavior is a matter of choice, and that acceptance of responsibility for behavior and understanding its consequences go hand in hand. Evaluations of this approach to dealing with problem behaviors indicate support for its effectiveness in reducing a variety of disruptive behaviors (Emmer and Aussiker 1990).

4. Emergent Trends and Issues

Greater attention has been given in research to the role of teacher and student cognition in the management process. Cognitive processes such as teacher and student attributions about causes for behaviors, efficacy beliefs, and evaluations influence teacher decision-making about management strategies. Furthermore, research has begun to focus more attention on students' views of teacher managerial behaviors (Allen 1986), providing a more balanced view of effects. As more of the research on teacher and student cognition moves from analog and questionnaire formats to naturalistic studies in classrooms, a clearer picture should appear of the relationships between these cognitive factors and managerial behaviors and outcomes.

Although the education of children and adolescents occurs in a variety of contexts, most research on teacher management has been done in traditional classrooms. Examination of teacher managerial behaviors in such settings as cooperative learning groups, computer-dense classrooms, and alternative schools would be very useful, as more and more communities experiment with varied forms of schooling. Some of the findings from initial looks at management in nontraditional contexts suggest that new conceptions may be needed. For example, Cohen (1991) reports on the negative effects of teacher direction in group instruction formats focused on higher order thinking objectives. Thus, some of the emphasis on structuring activities and tasks may be inappropriate for management in this setting.

Research on teacher managerial behaviors generally does not take into account the complex interplay of teacher emotion and behavior, nor has the field taken advantage of advances in knowledge from behavioral science research. Yet, the enormous range of emotions surrounding teaching and, especially, discipline would seem to make this a fertile field for inquiry. For example, Cambone (1990), in a year-long study of a teacher's struggle to manage and teach a group of seriously disturbed children, makes a strong case for love as a core category to explain the teacher's motivation and behavior. Thus, knowledge about teacher managerial behaviors is building upon a strong behavioral research base, while moving toward a broadened view of relevant settings, teacher and student characteristics, and underlying processes.

See also: Classroom Rules and Routines; Teacher Planning

References

Allen J D 1986 Classroom management: Students' perspectives, goals, and strategies. *Am. Educ. Res. J.* 23(3): 437–59

Arlin M 1979 Teacher transitions can disrupt time flow in classrooms. *Am. Educ. Res. J.* 16(1): 42–56

Berliner D C 1983 Developing conceptions of classroom environments. *Educ. Psychol.* 18(1): 1–13

Berliner D C 1988 *The Development of Expertise in Pedagogy.* American Association of Colleges for Teacher Education, Washington, DC

Cambone J 1990 Teachers and teaching. Tipping the balance. *Harv. Educ. Rev.* 60(2): 217–36

Cohen E G 1991 Classroom management and complex instruction. Paper presented at the annual meeting of the American Educational Research Association, Chicago, Illinois

Denscombe M 1985 *Classroom Control: A Sociological Perspective.* Unwin-Hyman, London

Doyle W 1986 Classroom organization and management. In: Wittrock M (ed.) 1986 *Third Handbook of Research on Teaching.* Macmillan, New York

Doyle W, Carter K 1984 Academic tasks in classrooms. *Curric. Inq.* 14(2): 29–49

Emmer E T, Aussiker A 1990 School and classroom discipline programs: How well do they work? In: Moles O C (ed.) 1990 *Student Discipline Strategies: Research and Practice.* State University of New York Press, Albany, New York

Emmer E T, Evertson C M, Sanford J, Clements B, Worsham M 1989 *Classroom Management for Secondary Teachers*, 2nd edn. Prentice-Hall, Englewood Cliffs, New Jersey

Everston C M, Emmer E T 1982 Effective management at the beginning of the year in junior high classes. *J. Educ. Psychol.* 74(4): 485–98

Gallagher P A 1988 *Teaching Students with Behavior Disorders.* Love, Denver, Colorado

Jones N (ed.) 1989 *School Management and Pupil Behavior.* Falmer Press, London

Kerr M M, Nelson C M 1983 *Strategies for Managing Behavior Problems in the Classroom.* Merrill, Columbus, Ohio

Kounin J S 1970 *Discipline and Group Management in Classrooms.* Holt, Rinehart and Winston, New York

Maurer R E 1988 *Special Educators Discipline Handbook.* Center for Applied Research in Education, West Nyack, New York

Slavin R E (ed.) 1989 *School and Classroom Organization.* Lawrence Erlbaum, Hillsdale, New Jersey

Stoner G, Shinn M R, Walker H M (eds.) 1991 *Interventions for Achievement and Behavior Problems.* National Association of School Psychologists, Silver Spring, Maryland

Wheldall K, Glynn T 1989 *Effective Classroom Learning: A Behavioral Interactionist Approach to Teaching.* Basil Blackwell, Oxford

Further Reading

Bowers C A, Flinders D J 1990 *Responsive Teaching: An Ecological Approach to Classroom Patterns of Language, Culture, and Thought.* Teachers College Press, New York

Good T L, Brophy J E 1987 *Looking in Classrooms*, 4th edn. Harper and Row, New York

Jones V F, Jones L S 1989 *Comprehensive Classroom Management*, 3rd edn. Allyn and Bacon, Boston, Massachusetts

Pitcher G D, Poland S 1992 *Crisis Intervention in the Schools.* Guilford Press, New York

Reinforcement

I. E. Sladeczek and T. R. Kratochwill

Reinforcement represents a rational relationship between the incidence of behavior, the occurrence of a consequence, and the increased or decreased likelihood of that behavior occurring in the future. As such, the notion of reinforcement was initially advanced by the prominent behavioral psychologist Skinner (1938) who reported that causes of behavior (both in animals and humans) could be explained by studying the environment in which behavior occurs and, more specifically, by examining the interaction between behavior and environment. Both the concept of reinforcement and the application of the concept play a major role in helping to explain human behavior. More specifically, positive reinforcement is a procedure whereby a response is strengthened by the onset of an event which follows the response in time. This event, termed a positive reinforcer, typically produces an increase in the probability of the behavior occurring again in the future. Thus, when a child who has been working diligently on a book report hands it in and the teacher says "Good for you!", the praise "good for you!" may act as a positive reinforcer in that a child is likely to turn in book reports in the future. If the child does so, the positive statement by the teacher is functioning as a positive reinforcer. It is important that the positive reinforcer be presented immediately after the desired response to ensure that the behavior occurs again.

Negative reinforcement, on the other hand, is a procedure whereby a response is followed by the cessation or reduction of an event. The cessation or reduction of an event is referred to as a negative reinforcer. For example, if an adult wants to increase a young child's napkin usage, he or she can briefly remove the child's bib when the child is eating, and increase napkin usage. It is important, however, not to confuse negative reinforcement with punishment, since punishment produces a weakening of behavior. Like reinforcement, however, punishment is defined completely within the context of its functional influence on behavior.

1. Types of Reinforcers

Primary (unlearned) reinforcers are stimuli that are necessary for life or for the satisfaction of physiological needs (Kratochwill 1985). For example, milk, for a thirsty infant, has a type of inborn capacity to strengthen behavior. In other words, primary reinforcers are reinforcing in and of themselves; they need no history to explain their reinforcing properties. Food, water, sexual release, rest and sleep, and the opportunity to breathe are all examples of primary reinforcers. Secondary (learned) reinforcers, on the other hand, are initially neutral. However, when they are linked to a primary reinforcer they acquire reinforcing properties. There are several different types of secondary reinforcers. A tangible reinforcer is an object (e.g., a toy, pin, or marbles) or an activity (e.g., helping the teacher, playing a game) that increases the likelihood of a particular behavior occurring in the future when that reinforcer is presented after the behavior (Heron 1987). The use of social reinforcers was investigated in a classic study by Hall et al. (1968). In this study, a teacher was cued as to when students were engaging in study or nonstudy behavior. When students engaged in the former, the teacher would respond in one of three ways: (a) pat them on the back; (b) approach their desk; or (c) use social praise. Non study behavior was ignored. Findings indicated that the use of social reinforcers significantly increased the time students spent in appropriate study behavior, and when this reinforcement condition was reversed (i.e., no reinforcement was given for either behavior) study behavior significantly decreased.

Finally, a generalized reinforcer "is a type of conditioned reinforcer the effectiveness of which does not depend upon a single kind of deprivation" (Ferster and Culbertson 1982 p. 371). In other words, these types of reinforcer are effective since they can act as primary or secondary reinforcers. Money and tokens are examples of generalized reinforcers.

2. Schedules of Reinforcement

Schedules of reinforcement specify when behaviors will be reinforced. If every instance of behavior is reinforced, a continuous reinforcement schedule is in place. If, however, as occurs in everyday living, reinforcement occurs now and then, an intermittent reinforcement schedule is present. Intermittent reinforcement schedules are, however, not haphazard occurrences; rather, the time when reinforcement is to occur is planned. In this regard, reinforcement is on a ratio schedule if reinforcement takes place after a specific number of behaviors have been emitted. Similarly, reinforcement is on an interval schedule if a specific amount of time must have elapsed before receiving the reinforcer (Deitz 1985). Finally, extinction occurs when no behavior is reinforced. A fairly complete set of reinforcement schedules is presented in Table 1.

Table 1
Reinforcement schedules

Type of reinforcement schedule	Definition
Fixed ratio	When a given number of responses must be emitted prior to reinforcement (e.g., every sixth correct response is reinforced).
Variable ratio	When the number of responses prior to reinforcement varies (e.g., on an average every 13th response is reinforced).
Fixed interval	Reinforcement occurs after a designated amount of time (e.g., the first correct response following the passage of 5 minutes is reinforced).
Variable interval	Reinforcement occurs after a correct response, but intervals between reinforcement are random (e.g., reinforcement of a correct response may occur after 1 minute, 5 minutes, 10 minutes).
Concurrent schedule	Reinforcement occurs when two or more intermittent schedules are operating independently or at the same time for two or more behaviors.
Multiple schedule	Two or more schedules of reinforcement are presented in a random sequence.
Chained schedule	Cues for reinforcement are presented in a given order (e.g., reinforcement of responding to the first component leads to the presentation of the second component).
Mixed schedule	Same as the multiple schedule except that the mixed schedule has no discriminative stimulus associated with the schedule in effect.
Tandem schedule	Same as the chained schedule except that no discriminative stimulus or cues are associated with components in the chain.
Alternative schedule	Reinforcement follows the completion of either a ratio schedule or an interval schedule requirement.
Conjunctive schedule	Reinforcement follows the completion of a ratio schedule and an interval schedule requirement.

3. Use of Reinforcers in the Classroom

Principles of reinforcement have been used extensively in schools and other educational environments to address a variety of problems: (a) school-based aggression (e.g., Shapiro and Derr 1987); (b) improvement of the school climate (e.g., Coppedge and Exendine 1987); (c) improvement of learning-disabled students' mathematical skills (e.g., Ross and Braden 1991); (d) antisocial behavior (e.g., Bernagozzi 1991); and (e) contextual control of problem behavior in students with severe disabilities (e.g., Haring and Kennedy 1990). These represent only a few of the different types of issues that can be addressed with reinforcement procedures.

Four studies will be discussed in more detail for illustrative purposes. For example, in the United States, Davies and McLaughlin (1989) issued a daily report card rating of three male students' disruptive behavior. The parents were asked to praise positive reports (i.e., reinforcement) and ignore negative reports (i.e., extinction). Findings indicated that the intervention was effective in reducing inappropriate behaviors, while at the same time increasing assignment completion. Ratings by parents, teachers, peers, and subjects supported the effectiveness of the interventions.

In the United Kingdom, Randall and Gibb (1987) compared the effectiveness of two interventions (behavior management techniques, including positive reinforcers versus developmental stimulation) with a three-year-old female experiencing autism. Findings indicated marked improvement in tantrum control, expressive language, and reduced obsessional behaviors with the use of behavior management techniques. However, developmental stimulation (i.e., play and positive adult contact) produced no significant changes.

Rosemberg et al. (1990) utilized positive reinforcement to teach educators in Venezuela to use assertive behavioral procedures to maintain discipline. Four types of reinforcers were used: symbolic reinforcers (i.e., stamps, diplomas); social reinforcers (i.e., recreational activities); sign stimuli to remind students of new rules; and a time-out procedure (i.e., removing the student from the classroom). Finally, in Australia, Craven et al. (1991) used positive verbal feedback (e.g., "Sally, you have a lot of strengths in mathematics. You can add sums, multiply numbers, and solve problems") to enhance children's academic self-concept. The results of numerous studies conducted around the world suggest that the use of reinforcement techniques in the classroom and school setting is highly effective in dealing with student behaviors.

4. Possible Research Directions

In this entry a few applications of reinforcement and its major contributions to education have been noted. In fact, a tremendous amount of research on the use of reinforcement principles with instructional implications has occurred in psychology and education. Unfortunately, one of the major issues confronting the field is the dissemination of already existing effective technologies from behavior analysis research. This issue is not a new theme. Kazdin (1981) noted:

> Within the scientific and technological discipline, several questions remain to be investigated to increase the overall understanding of existing practices and to extend their effectiveness. However, even at this point in time, remarkable advances have been achieved in identifying techniques and applications that improve student and teacher behaviors. A major limitation in applying behavior modification in education pertains to dissemination and extension of the existing techniques to a large number of settings likely to profit from their use. The dissemination and implementation problems pertain to the social and political action that is required following development of an effective technology. As yet, behavioral techniques have not been implemented on a large scale outside of the context of research programs, even though applications have strongly attested to their efficacy. . . . Hence, although major questions remain within the field of behavior modification, perhaps even larger questions exist for society at large regarding the failure to act on existing advances. (p. 52)

Unfortunately, this situation changed little after 1981 and this concern was the focus of a special issue of the *Journal of Applied Behavior Analysis* in 1991 wherein numerous authors lamented the failure of the large-scale dissemination of behavior analysis techniques (see Geller 1991).

Several issues are important in terms of research directions on reinforcement and the dissemination of behavior analysis interventions. First, since the problem continues to be one of dissemination of behavioral treatments, a behavior analysis of the variables inhibiting effective dissemination needs to occur. In many ways this activity may necessitate broader theoretical and technological frameworks than have been developed in the field. In fact, the lack of wide-scale dissemination of behavioral techniques provides documentation of the need for development of strategies to facilitate this dissemination. It could even be argued that the lack of dissemination reflects a problem in both theoretical and technological research applications of the principles.

Second, one possible direction for the study of reinforcement and other principles within behavior analysis pertains to developing integrative knowledge of how reinforcement works in applied settings to solve particular problems. Specifically, the solution to problems of dissemination may not necessarily be one of doing more research to demonstrate that reinforcement works, but rather to provide reviews of the existing literature to document its effective applications and the conditions under which it is successful or unsuccessful. Indeed, documentation of unsuccessful applications may prompt new theoretical and technological solutions to deal not only with the dissemination problem but the implementation of reinforcement techniques with socially significant behaviors.

In this regard, it is also important for future researchers to specify in greater detail the conditions of their research so as to increase the knowledge of what makes implementation of reinforcement and other behavioral principles effective in practice. Such a focus may necessitate more attention to describing the independent variable in more detail than has been true of past research (see Geller 1991 for a review of this point).

Another important area for future research is the functional analysis of behavior. Research in this area is designed to answer the question related to what type of assessment provides information about the functions of behavior and how such assessment improves treatment selection and design (Neef and Iwata 1994).

Finally, behavior analysts might consider a broader consideration of other theoretical perspectives that have been offered to psychologists and educators in practice. For example, a variety of cognitive theories have been advanced to explain learning, memory, and a variety of other instructional issues prominent in the educational field. It would be very useful for behavioral analysts to review other theoretical approaches and describe how various operant techniques, such as reinforcement, might be useful in explaining the results of research driven by these other theoretical persuasions. Such an analysis might enrich the conceptual, theoretical, and technological base of behavior analysis in consideration of a broader range of research issues.

See also: Motivation and Learning; Behavioristic Theories of Teaching

References

Bernagozzi T 1991 The whole class hated Anthony. *Learning* 20(1): 61–63
Coppedge F L, Exendine L 1987 Improving school climate by expanding dimensions of reinforcement. *NASSP Bulletin* 71(497): 102–10
Craven R G, Marsh H W, Debus R L 1991 Effects of internally focused feedback and attributional feedback on enhancement of academic self-concept. *J. Educ. Psychol.* 83(1): 17–27
Davies D E, McLaughlin T F 1989 Effects of a daily report card on disruptive behavior in primary students. *J. Spec. Educ.* 13(2): 173–81
Deitz S M 1985 Schedules of reinforcement. In: Bellack A S, Hersen M (eds.) 1985 *Dictionary of Behavior Therapy Techniques.* Pergamon Press, New York

rFerster C B, Culbertson S A 1982 *Behavior Principles*, 3rd edn. Prentice-Hall, Englewood Cliffs, New Jersey

Geller E S (1991). Is applied behavior analysis technological to a fault? *J. Appl. Behav. Anal.* 24: 401–06

Hall R V, Lund D, Jackson D 1968 Effects of teacher attention on study behavior. *J. Appl. Behav. Anal.* 1(1): 1–12

Haring T G, Kennedy C H 1990 Contextual control of problem behavior in students with severe disabilities. *J. Appl. Behav. Anal.* 23(2): 235–43

Heron T E 1987 Operant reinforcement. In:. Cooper J O, Heron T E, Heward W L (eds.) 1987 *Applied Behavior Analysis*. Merrill, Columbus, Ohio

Kazdin A E 1981 Behavior modification in education: Contributions and limitations. *Dev. Rev.* 1: 34–57

Kratochwill T R 1985 Primary reinforcement. In: Bellack A S, Hersen M (eds.) 1985 *Dictionary of Behavior Therapy Techniques*. Pergamon Press, Oxford

Neef N A, Iwata B 1994 Current research on functional analysis methodologies: An introduction. *J. Appl. Behav. Anal.* 27(2): 211–14

Randall P E, Gibb C 1987 Structured management and autism. *Br. J. Special Educ.* 14(2): 68–70

Rosemberg F K, Lapco A, Llorens M 1990 The teacher's role in the application of an assertive discipline program for students in a Venezuelan primary school. *School Psychology International* 11(2): 143–46

Ross P A, Braden J 1991 The effects of token reinforcement versus cognitive behavior modification on learning-disabled students' math skills. *Psychology in the Schools* 28(3): 247–56

Shapiro E S, Derr T F 1987 School interventions for aggression. *Special Services in the Schools* 3(3–4): 5–19

Skinner B F 1938 *The Behavior of Organisms: An Experimental Analysis*. Appleton-Century-Crofts, New York

Further Reading

Kazdin A E 1989 *Behavior Modification in Applied Settings*, 4th edn. Brooks/Cole, Pacific Grove, California

Kratochwill T R, Bijou S W 1987 The impact of behaviorism on educational psychology. In: Glover J A, Ronning R R (eds.) 1987 *Historical Foundations of Educational Psychology*. Plenum, New York

Analysis and Modification of Behavior

L. Cairns

In the field of teaching few issues arouse such strong teacher emotions and as much discussion as classroom management and control. Much of the discussion falls under the broad term of "discipline," a term which may refer to (a) the methods used by teachers to control their students, (b) a state of effective pupil work and behavior, or (c) the consequences that teachers use to maintain order and appropriate work levels. There are many different views of appropriate ways to approach classroom management and control. These range from the more humanistic, personalized approaches often rooted in post-Freudian (Dreikurs et al. 1982) or other psychological theories (Glasser 1985, 1990), through the more social-psychological approaches based on group emphasis and the study of classrooms as social systems (Kounin 1970, Johnson and Bany 1970), to more behavioristic approaches based on the operant psychology of Skinner (1976). Furthermore, more recent approaches have adopted various elements of a number of the older systems in differing degrees of eclecticism (Canter and Canter 1976, 1992).

1. The Operant Model in Education

The application of operant psychology to classroom practice has occurred since 1940. This work has been both influential and, at times, controversial. In specific application to classroom behavior, this approach is most frequently described by the general term, "behavior modification." Both the basic theory and its history are firmly rooted in the behaviorist, operant model (Skinner 1976). The model, as applied to education, has four basic principles:

(a) The emphasis is on the behavior to be learned (i.e., there is no concern with innate or internal causes).

(b) The consequences of behavior affect the likely repetition and learning of the behavior.

(c) These consequences can be altered, which in turn affects learned behavior.

(d) Careful examination of behavior and its consequences enables teachers to modify the behavior of their students.

Many research studies and school programs consistent with these principles were prominent in the late 1960s and 1970s, particularly in the United States, mostly within the special education context. Since that time the methodology and the basic concepts have settled more into the mainstream of education, largely as one of the many and varied sets of approaches, theoretical positions, and applied therapies which psychologists and teachers see as part of their professional tools of trade. Some members of these professions view behaviorism as an area of theory and practice which they have difficulty implementing. Others reject it as too overtly manipulative.

2. Behavior Modification in the Classroom

The basis of the application of behavior modification in the classroom is for the teacher to have a clear understanding of the principles mentioned above. With these in mind, the approach, within the context of classroom management, rests on two aims. Teachers are motivated to increase productive and work-oriented behavior while at the same time decreasing the incidence of disruptive and inappropriate behavior. From time to time teachers may emphasize different levels and proportions of these two simple aims, but they remain their major emphases. Indeed, the rise to prominence of the approach known as "Assertive discipline" during the 1980s has shown how many teachers are ever conscious of "being in charge" and of avoiding or handling what they see as disruptive behavior in their classrooms.

It is important to note that theorists other than operant or behavior modification advocates discuss classroom behavior and its treatment with very different views as to cause and effects. The question of what psychological stresses, disabilities, or disturbances might underlie a pupil's aberrant behavior in the classroom are not the concern of those advocating the behavior modification approach. The observed overt behavior exhibited by the pupil, not the "inner workings," forms the treatable content.

In applying the behavior modification approach in the classroom the teacher needs first to focus on the context within which the program is to be introduced (i.e., the school, classroom, home). Next, the teacher must observe pupil behaviors to document those to be modified. Finally, the teacher must identify appropriate consequences which will be utilized in an effort to change pupil behaviors. While these steps appear easy, careful attention must be paid to each one prior to implementation.

2.1 Examining the Context

The first step for the classroom teacher is to examine the context. The policies and practices the local school board or educational authorities have in place need to be clearly assessed. Any proposed program needs to be consistent with local adopted policy. Second, the teacher should discuss the proposed program with parents, giving them as much information about the approach and the consequences which will be utilized as possible. Last but not least, the child whose behavior is to be modified should be fully involved and briefed about the approach. In those situations in which a child with severe behavioral problems is involved, the family, the psychologist, and the classroom teacher work together with a plan and a set of consistent consequences, all with the knowledge and understanding of the child concerned.

2.2 Observing Children

The purpose of observing children is to identify the behaviors to be modified and appropriate consequences which reinforce the behavior. The key points to note in the initial observation of pupil behavior are that the teacher notes, counts, records, and checks.

"Notes" refers to the actual observation and pinpointing of the behaviors the teacher wishes to increase or, more likely, those the teacher finds disruptive and wishes to decrease. "Counts" refers to the systematic tallying of the incidence of the behavior as observed by the teacher. Some operant psychology and behavior modification programs recommend that counting should also take account of the rate of the behavior (i.e., the frequency per time segment, such as 20 times per minute).

"Records" refers to making a written record of the observation. This may take the form of graphical presentation of the behavior rate over a period of a week or days, or the data may be presented in simple charts or other forms. The purpose of such records is to monitor the change or modification once the program commences. To monitor change some baseline data are needed. The baseline level is that rate or incidence of the behavior which is observed to be the "normal" level prior to the implementation of any program aimed at change.

Finally, "checks" refers to the need to verify the initial observations to establish the genuine levels of the baseline and to lay the groundwork for the habit of frequently checking and monitoring the program and its progress. It is not uncommon, for example, for the act of systematic observation of a problem behavior by the teacher to actually act as a deterrent during the initial baseline observation phase to the point of negating the necessity for the full program to be implemented.

2.3 Selecting the Behaviors and Consequences

A behavior modification program in the classroom may attempt to increase desired pupil behaviors, decrease undesired pupil behaviors, or change some elements of both aspects. The teacher needs to select and, in the case of specific individualized modification programs, ensure the cooperation of the pupil and the parents to determine which behaviors are to be "treated" or scheduled for actions aimed at some modification. In general terms, it is often the case that teachers and parents will focus on pupil behaviors which they wish to see reduced or eradicated. Severe maladaptive, dangerous, or antisocial behaviors are usually the subject of programs aimed at total eradication or modification. Most classroom applications are aimed at reducing disruptive or disturbing behaviors and increasing the behaviors which are seen as more appropriate to regular classroom functioning. Some of the undesirable behaviors include fighting, swearing, and continued interruption of others.

Whether the teacher wishes to implement a program

to enhance desirable behaviors or reduce undesirable behaviors he or she will need to make use of a range of consequences. As shown in Fig. 1, these consequences vary along two dimensions: contingency application or removal, and positive or aversive stimulus.

2.3.1 Positive reinforcement. The contingent application of a positive stimulus is termed positive reinforcement. The term "positive reinforcement" is defined as a stimulus which, when contingently presented following a behavior, will increase the likelihood of that behavior being repeated. There are many different types of positive reinforcers which may be utilized in the classroom.

Nonverbal reinforcement includes gestures or facial expressions from the smile to the waving of a finger. Usually, they are accompanied by some verbal comment and occur in a socially defined situation. Verbal reinforcement refers to deliberate, contingent use of terms of praise and encouragement. Not all teacher praise is actually reinforcement; much is simply indiscriminate or noncontingent. Therefore, praise of this type does not qualify in terms of this definition.

Both nonverbal and verbal reinforcement are manifestations of social reinforcement. The term "social reinforcement" means that the value of the reinforcer has been learned or acquired. This fact does not make the reinforcement any less efficacious. Most social reinforcers become the most frequently used in modern society. (As a consequence, they are often criticized as subtle manipulations of everyday life.)

Token reinforcement refers to the use of some symbol (such as a gold star, a simple check mark, or a cross on a page) as a contingently linked reinforcer. Such reinforcers must have some value for the student. The value might be as a redeemable token (ten stars entitles the pupil to some more tangible reward) or some activity or socially significant role in the classroom or school setting. Activity reinforcers refers to the use made in the classroom of activities which the pupil would like to complete being made contingent upon certain prescribed behaviors. Token reinforcement can be built into a total token economy system whereby the whole class or school system has a range of tokens and values which function similarly to the economy of nations.

2.3.2 Negative reinforcement. The term "negative reinforcement" is frequently misused by teachers and others as synonymous with the term "punishment." However, it has quite a different meaning. Negative reinforcement refers to the contingent removal of a stimulus which is regarded as an aversive or unpleasant stimulus. For example, a person removes a shoe which is pinching his or her foot (an aversive stimulus) and gains some relief. This action reinforces the learning that when a shoe hurts, one takes it off. Negative reinforcement is not a common aspect of classroom management.

2.3.3 Time out and response cost. Time out refers to the actual removal of the pupil from the classroom for a time. In terms of Fig. 1, time out results in the contingent removal of a positive stimulus. Time out is one method of coping and responding to some classroom management behaviors where both the student and the teacher can benefit from a "break" in the pattern. The pupil is sent to an area, office, or other teacher for a specified time out of the regular classroom.

Response cost is similar to time out in that it refers to the removal of reinforcement contingent upon behavior; however, it relates to the removal of particular amounts of positive stimulus rather than time away from the positive stimulus. Examples of a response cost in the classroom would be the removal of some stars or points gained as a result of positive reinforcement being applied. In society at large one of the major examples of a response cost approach is the use of fines for speeding on the roads. The fine (removal of money) is contingent upon the act of speeding; therefore, the behavior has led to a cost or the contingent removal of a positive stimulus.

2.3.4 Punishment. Within the behavior modification approach, the term "punishment" means the contingent presentation or application of an aversive stimulus. Whatever the moral or personal views on the use of punishment in homes and schools, it is an aspect which has had a long history of application and some research. Most modern educators argue strongly that punishment is not an appropriate pathway to pursue and therefore should be avoided.

3. Implementation

Once the teacher has analyzed the pupil behavior, recorded the baseline levels of behavior, and determined appropriate consequences, he or she is ready to embark upon implementation. There are a number of aspects of implementation about which the teacher should be aware. These include the schedules to be adopted, and the monitoring and evaluation of the program.

	Contingent application	Contingent removal
Positive stimulus	Positive reinforcement	Time out and response cost
Aversive stimulus	Punishment	Negative reinforcement

Figure 1
Two dimensions of behavioral consequences

3.1 Schedules of Reinforcement

"Schedules of reinforcement" is a descriptor which refers to the behaviors to be reinforced and frequency of reinforcement, and involves consideration of the appropriateness of different types of schedules depending on whether the teacher is planning to increase, decrease, or extinguish a single behavior or set of behaviors. Based on these factors, different schedules of reinforcement are likely to be necessary. For example, pupils at a young age respond positively to tokens and some verbal and activity reinforcement, whereas older teenaged pupils will demonstrate a greater level of sophistication in responding to various reinforcers.

Teachers have at least three strategies at their disposal in choosing appropriate schedules of reinforcement. "Rules, praise, and ignoring" suggests that teachers need to establish the class and individual rules first, make these explicit by classroom display, and then proceed systematically to praise pupils who conform to these rules while ignoring those who deviate. This strategy is based on the early work of Madsen et al. (1968) and is still advocated as a basic approach (Charles and Barr 1992). A variation of this strategy is the RRP or "rules, reward, and punishment" strategy. This variation offers the same clear initial specification of rules and the use of praise or rewards but does not ignore the deviations. The punishment, neither physical nor severe, is the application of immediate aversive stimuluses following inappropriate behavior. The punishments are frequently specified by and negotiated with the pupils before this strategy is implemented. This strategy is usually applied with older pupils.

Two other strategies, both quite extensively utilized in schools in the 1970s and 1980s, are self-management and contracting. Self-management means that pupils administer various types of reinforcements according to agreed schedules. Contracting is a strategy which lends an air of pseudo legal responsibility to the reinforcement process. The teacher and pupils complete a specific document which sets out the behavior to be executed by the child, the frequency or levels of the behavior, and the consequences or reinforcement to follow.

3.2 Evaluating the Program

It is important that the initial observation and record-keeping processes are maintained and utilized in evaluating the success of the behavior modification program. In this evaluation process the teacher should consider careful and systematic use of the data gathered and the use of simple experimental designs. Procedures such as establishing a baseline for the targeted behavior, introducing the modification techniques, removing the techniques (referred to as "return to baseline"), and then reimplementing the modification technique may be useful at some stages of the process. However, the decision to stop and start may lead to more problems than the evidence of change is worth. Any evaluation should also be cognizant of the opinions and feelings of the pupils and their parents regarding the success of the program.

4. Contrasts with Other Approaches

The behavior modification approach to classroom management and control has a long, well-researched, and popular history among teachers, academics, and parents. As mentioned above, there are also a number of criticisms of and reactions to the approach. Some of the questioning frequently revolves around philosophical differences among educators. Other perceived problems relate to the implementation process which is seen as overly mechanistic and systematized. These criticisms can be neither simplistically rejected nor dismissed since there are many scholarly as well as practical educators engaged in alternative approaches who argue vehemently against behavior modification.

Alternative approaches to classroom management and control are many and varied. In fact, this aspect of teaching has generated a large body of writing, research, and suggested practice. A discursive examination of some of the more successful models (in terms of implementation of the models in schools) has been conducted by Charles and Barr (1992). While this publication does not aim to be exhaustive in its treatment, it offers succinct and useful summaries of eight models in common use (including one based on behavior modification).

The analysis and modification of children's behavior in classrooms in the interests of effective classroom management is an area in which research and development are needed. Pupil involvement in identifying the processes and determining the strategies which bridge the school and the home is needed. That the school as an institution in modern societies is in a state of constant change and in need of adaptation should be paramount in further research. Additionally, the questions of the relative rights of teachers and pupils is a feature of the philosophical questioning that underpins much of the criticism of behavioral methods and strategies. Research which clarifies values and the relevance of behavior modification within the context of these values will be most beneficial.

See also: Behavioristic Theories of Teaching; Paradigms for Research on Teaching; Teacher Managerial Behaviors; Classroom Rules and Routines

References

Canter L, Canter M 1992 *Assertive Discipline: Positive Behavior Management for Today's Classroom.* Lee Canter and Associates, Santa Monica, California

Charles C M, Barr K B 1992 *Building Classroom Discipline*, 4th edn. Longman, London

Dreikurs R, Grunwald B, Pepper F 1982 *Maintaining Sanity in the Classroom*. Harper and Row, New York

Glasser W 1985 *Control Theory in the Classroom*. Perennial Library, New York

Glasser W 1990 The Quality School: *Managing Students Without Coercion*. Perennial Library, New York

Johnson L V, Bany M A 1970 *Classroom Management: Theory and Skill Training*. Macmillan, New York

Kounin J S 1970 *Discipline and Group Management in Classrooms*. Holt, Rinehart and Winston, New York

Madsen C H, Becker W C, Thomas D R 1968 Rules, praise, and ignoring: Elements of elementary classroom control.
J. Appl. Behav. Anal. 1(2): 139–50.

Skinner B F 1976 *About Behaviorism*. Vintage Books, New York

Further Reading

Craighead W E, Kazadin A E, Mahoney M J 1981 *Behavior Modification: Principles, Issues and Applications*, 2nd edn. Houghton Mifflin, Boston, Massachusetts

Sulzer B, Mayer G R 1972 *Behavior Modification Procedures for School Personnel*. Dryden Press, Hinsdale, Illinois

(c) Teaching in the Classroom

Explaining

D. R. Cruickshank and K. K. Metcalf

Explanation has been explored as a concept, subjected to measurement and studied as a teacher and student competency. Among other things, it is clear that: (a) the term has a variety of usages, (b) scholars have identified different types of explanations, (c) criteria for judging whether an explanation is satisfactory have been formulated, (d) explanations are significant classroom occurrences during receptive learning and productive thinking, (e) explanations are a component of the larger construct "clarity" which is related to pupil learning, (f) teacher explanation is the subject of empirical study, and (g) instruments exist for its measurement.

1. Explanation as a Concept

Explanation means different things to different people. As a concept, explanation can be best understood by considering its functions and types.

1.1 Functions

The literature on explanation can be confusing unless it is understood that the term serves different semantic purposes in everyday language. In one instance, its meaning is to make some concept, procedure, or rule plain and comprehensible. Thus, a teacher might "explain" a concept (global warming), a procedure (how to subtract), or a rule (we raise our hands to be recognized). In this instance, explanation is synonymous with specification. However, such explanations do not account (that is, give reasons) for any of these things.

In a second instance, explanation is used to account for the occurrence of things. In this instance, explanation requires the teacher to present the "why" of global warming, tell students why subtraction is performed in a specified manner, and explain why pupils must raise their hands. Here explanation is synonymous with giving reasons.

Explanations are generally thought of as provided by teachers and directed toward students. However, students often are called upon to explain their observations, learning, answers, or values. In addition to verbal explanations, explanations can be provided in written form (e.g., textbooks, student essays) or through recordings (e.g., films, videotapes).

1.2 Types

Within these two general functions, academics have identified numerous types of explanations. Hudgins (1974), for example, listed four types: causal (e.g., "Objects fall to the ground because of gravity"), normative (e.g., "They no longer prohibit the sale of alcohol in the United States because of the 21st Amendment to the Constitution"), process (e.g., "This is how matters get to the United Nation's Security Council"), and teleological (e.g., "Certain specialized behaviors observed among animals prior to copulation serve to attract the opposite sex").

Similarly, Fairhurst (1981) identified four types of explanation used by teachers in primary schools: descriptive, prescriptive, aesthetic, and analytic. Descriptive explanations are concerned with what is the case. They include word explanations (definitions), interpretive explanations (e.g., the meaning of a proverb or fable), causal explanations (e.g., the freezing point of water), reason-giving explanations (e.g., discussing a generalization that falls short of a causal explanation), structural explanations (e.g., pointing out the structure of the Union Jack), classificatory explanations or making comparisons (e.g., "this is a tree"), teleological explanations (pointing to a purpose or goal), and sequent explanations or telling a sequence of events.

As the name implies, prescriptive explanations are concerned with prescriptions for action. They include social explanations (e.g., pointing out social rules), ethical explanations (e.g., pointing out a principle of conduct, and procedural explanations (i.e., how to do something to achieve some goal).

Aesthetic explanations include value-giving explanations (e.g., the criteria for grading) and aesthetic interpretive explanations (e.g., interpreting a poem). Finally, analytic explanations pertain to procedures and propositions that inform and clarify concepts and rules (e.g., how to solve a mathematical equation).

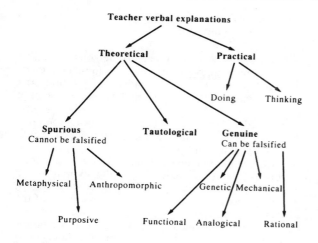

Figure 1
Dagher's Descriptive Framework
Source: The nature of verbal teacher explanations in junior high science classrooms 1989 (Doctoral dissertation, The University of Iowa)

Dagher (1989) examined teacher explanation in the context of junior high school science teaching. Based on the results of her study, Dagher formed 10 classifications of science teachers' explanations: "how to," metaphysical, purposive/intentional, anthropomorphic, functional, genetic, mechanical, analogical, rational, and tautological. Because of the number and complexity of her types of explanations, Dagher interrelated them as shown in Fig. 1.

MacDonald (1991), drawing on Ennis (1969), suggests three types of explanation: interpretive (which provides the meaning of concepts or terms), descriptive (which specifies a procedure to be followed), and reason-giving (which clarifies why something is done the way it is or why some event has occurred or is occurring).

Clearly, there are many schools of thought with regard to the meaning of the term "explanation." Based on the results of her study, Dagher (1989) noted that there is little consensus on the functions and forms of explanations. She reiterates Garfinkel's (1981) admonition that an account of the "algebra of explanations" is needed that would serve as a kind of consumer's guide to the use and study of explanation. Table 1

Table 1
Types of explanation

Hudgins (1974)	Fairhurst (1981)	Dagher (1989)	MacDonald (1991)
	Aesthetic Value giving, interpretive		
Process Descriptive, illuminating a process	*Prescriptive* Prescribe action	*How to* Prescribe action	*Descriptive* Specifies a procedure
Normative Providing accepted fact	*Descriptive* Describe what is the case	*Anthropomorphic* Attributes human characteristics to non-humans	*Interpretive* Provides meaning of concepts of terms
		Genetic Relates an antecedent sequence of events (not why)	
		Analogical Makes use of analogy	
	Analytic Procedures and propositions that inform and clarify	*Rational* Evidence is provided for a statement	
		Tautological Restatement of a how or why statement without additional information	
Causal Reason giving		*Metaphysical* A supernatural agent is the cause	*Reason Giving* Why, causal
		Functional Cause that is a function is identified	
		Mechanical Causal relationships that are physical in nature	
Teleological Cause points to some subsequent purpose or goal		*Purpose/Intentional* Cause points to some subsequent purpose or goal	

is an initial attempt to integrate the various types of explanations identified by various scholars.

2. Criteria for Judging Explanations

A number of persons speak to the need to identify criteria of a good explanation. Social studies educators seem to be among the most interested. Metcalf (1963) notes the general failure of historians to validate adequately the explanations they make for theses they promote (e.g., Turner's frontier thesis). He also admonishes them for not validating reasons they give for current or past events (e.g., causes of the Gulf War). Since historians fail in this regard, Metcalf argues that pupils should learn how to gauge the logical correctness of historical explanations they receive. "This procedure, highly effective as it is, could not help but make history clearer even to the slowest student, and would reveal in a given case precisely whether an historian knew what he was talking about" (p. 953). Additionally, Metcalf faults social studies textbook writers for confronting pupils with other persons' explanations without providing detail with regard to how or whether they were reached in some valid way.

Swift (1959) suggests that explanations be subjected to analysis using the following criteria: presence of law-like statements, testability of such statements, their truth, and their internal validity, that is, whether the statement describing or naming the event to be explained follows logically from the reasons stated in the major and minor premises.

Swift identified different types of student explanations and categorized them further according to their logical rigor. "Nonrelational explanations" are descriptions or interpretations. For example, the teacher may ask students to explain the separation of powers in government. Students often respond with nonrelational explanations or specifications of what separation of powers is. Rational explanations, on the other hand, are those that explain a phenomenon in terms of some other affair, condition, or situation (Swift 1959 p. 124). Metcalf (1963) concludes that Swift's approach to the analysis of explanation should be made known to preservice and inservice teachers so that, in turn, they may use it to teach students about the importance of valid explanation (p. 961).

Armbruster and Anderson (1984) have been interested in psychological explanations of historical events. A proper textbook explanation in this case should meet each of the following conditions or "frames":

(a) What was the goal of the protagonist(s)? What were the human motives?

(b) What was the plan for attaining the goal?

(c) What action was taken in response to the plan?

(d) What was the outcome(s) of the action taken with respect to the goal?

Additionally, Armbruster and Anderson require that social science textbook responses to the above questions be appropriate for the readers (i.e., within their realm of meaning and understanding, and complete); coherent (i.e., the ideas flow clearly, easily, and in a logical order); and unified (i.e., the information presented is relevant and the amount of text devoted to each question is about right).

Fairhurst (1981) operationally defines an explanation as requiring something to be explained; an explainer or other communication source such as print material; and an explainee who is the recipient of the explanation. She points out that an explanation might be considered satisfactory according to three points of view. From the explainer's point of view, it must meet the conditions of "clarity, orderly presentation and intention to explain." From the explainees' view, the explanation must be a "gap-filler, i.e., it satisfies curiosity or removes a puzzlement expressed in terms which are intelligible . . . and related to . . . previous experience" (pp. 206–07). From the detached observer's point of view, the explanation must be a distinct attempt to clarify a point or situation. Additionally, to the observer it must be true, testable, appropriate, adequate, and not circular. Finally, Fairhurst notes that some types of explanation are better in that they meet additional criteria: truth, testability, appropriateness, and noncircularity (pp. 208–12).

MacDonald (1991) prescribes two main requirements of a good explanation. The explanation should be appropriate to the situation and it should be thorough, accurate, and understandable. He provides the following guidelines for presenting logically sound explanations:

(a) Have a clear conception of the purpose of the explanation. Is it to be interpretive, descriptive, reason-giving, or some combination of the three?

(b) Recognize the potential ambiguity of the word "explain" when a student makes an unclear request for information. Does he or she require an interpretive, descriptive, or reason-giving explanation?

(c) When giving an interpretive explanation make sure it is operationally stated, for example a subtrahend is a quantity or number that is subtracted or taken away from another quantity called a minuend. Use of synonyms and examples may be further helpful but should not be substituted for careful analysis of meaning of the term.

(d) Avoid circularity when giving interpretive or reason-giving explanations. Do not define a term using a synonym unless the synonym is understood or it, in turn, is carefully analyzed. Do not use circularity when providing reason-giving explanations, for example, "Communism has failed because it didn't work."

(e) When descriptive explanations are called for, break the procedure to be explained into parts and present the parts in some carefully chosen order. Thus, break down the process of subtraction and present it step-by-step.

(f) Make sure reason-giving explanations are complete or whole (pp. 140–41).

MacDonald (1991) also argues that in addition to explanations being logically sound they must be psychologically appropriate. Among other things, this is accomplished by centering on the learner's frame of reference, providing only enough information that can be assimilated, and using techniques to enhance clarity and emphasis. To center on the learner's frame of reference means to help student rearrange and extend what they already know.

Fairhurst (1981) points out that when giving a proper explanation a primary teacher might use more than one type. She notes: "In explaining the structure of the Union Jack, a teacher would be giving a structural definition, but he might also be showing the class how to draw the flag (a procedural explanation), and whilst he was drawing it he might tell the children how this union of flags came about (a sequent explanation)" (p. 208).

Perceptive teachers recognize that they must be prepared to offer multiple explanations, particularly when teaching mathematical problem-solving and when teaching pupils with divergent learning styles. Relatedly, mathematicians and computer scientists are developing intelligent tutoring systems, for example to teach algebra, "that provide multiple explanations for dynamically generated algebraic word problems" (Schulze 1989–90 p. 236). These systems take into account what individual students know, their current misconceptions, terminology with which they are familiar, and the most effective forms of explanation for them.

3. Explanation in Receptive Learning and Productive Thinking

As one consequence of the United States, effort to develop and promote Smith et al.'s (1969) notion of protocol materials, a catalog of significant pedagogical concepts was written by Hudgins (1974). The concepts Hudgins chose for inclusion fell within the framework of "interactive teaching" defined as "including all the events and transactions that occur in the classroom during the time the teacher and pupils are mutually engaged in implementing the educational program" (p. 8). Explanation appears as a significant pedagogical

concept twice, under reception learning (pp. 33–36) and under productive thinking (pp. 45–48).

Reception learning refers to activities whereby pupils receive information (knowledge) and are asked to recall it. Hudgins uses the term "explanation" in the context of reception learning to denote "a pupil statement which provides an account of specified events or conditions in terms of processes, procedures, or cause and effect relationships. The statement represents what the student recalls of an explanation which has been considered previously" (p. 33). Thus, pupils might be asked to recall when the colonization of Australia took place or to recall a teacher or a textbook explanation of why colonization began at that time. "Indicators" of explanation in reception learning, according to Hudgins, are threefold:

(a) Such explanations result from an effort to clarify. However, in this case, the explanation provided by the student is not his or her own but one recalled from another source.

(b) Recalled student-given explanations are often partial and require supplementation by teachers.

(c) Explanations, according to Hudgins (and described earlier), are of four types: (i) causal, (ii) normative, (iii) process, and (iv) teleological.

In the context of productive thinking, Hudgins uses the term explanation to denote "the set of cognitive operations and outcomes by which pupil formulate own account of something or apply knowledge of an explanation to a particular instance in which that explanation applies" (p. 45).

"Indicators" here are:

(a) students engaged in clarifying something which they have not explained before;

(b) an explanation which is arrived at independently, although it may not be novel; or

(c) the cognitive process in which the pupils engage, and which is more complex than recounting.

Causal, normative, and process explanations are appropriate for productive thinking.

4. Explanation As a Teacher Competency

That teachers should be competent in explanation seems to be unquestionable. According to Slavin (1991), effective teachers use many explanations and explanatory words (e.g., "because," "in order to," "consequently"). They also frequently use a rule–example–rule pattern when explaining new concepts. This pattern requires that a rule be stated, "Matter may change form but it is never destroyed." An example of the rule is given, "A paper when burned merely combines with oxygen and changes to a gas, mostly carbon dioxide." The rule is then restated, "The matter did not disappear but merely changed form" (p. 273).

There is also strong empirical justification for use of explanation from research on teacher clarity. Students have reported that a teacher's ability to provide thorough, understandable explanations is important in helping them learn the content (Cruickshank and Kennedy 1986, Metcalf and Cruickshank 1991). To be judged clear in this case, teachers must use examples, work examples and explain them, explain unfamiliar words, show similarities and differences between or among things, and explain something and pause to allow students to think.

Scholars in the field of reading and mathematics have studied how effectively teachers explain. Faculty at Michigan State University have looked at the phenomenon of teacher explanation in the context of the teaching of reading. Specifically, they have examined the effects of "explicitness of teacher explanations" on student reading achievement and student reports of what was taught (Duffy et al. 1985). Across studies, Duffy and his colleagues have found that explicit teacher explanations are associated with high pupil awareness of lesson content. However, they are only minimally associated with student achievement (Duffy et al. 1986).

Although mathematicians and mathematics educators believe K-12 pupils should be mostly skilled in problem solving, they are not. This finding seems partly to be the case because K-12 teachers allocate more instructional time to the teaching of computational skill. One possible reason for such time allocation is that "most teachers do not know how to explain cognitive reasoning processes associated with strategies used by successful problem solvers" (Herrmann 1989 p. 1).

5. Methods Used in the Study of Explanation

Instruments have been developed which have been used to study explanation. As a consequence of interest in utilizing logic in the analysis of teaching, two major instruments were developed for use in coding teacher–student linguistic activity. Among other things, both attend to explanation.

5.1 The Illinois Instrument

The Illinois Instrument was developed under the leadership of B O Smith. Smith and Meux (1970) noted two broad types or classes of classroom linguistic activities, "monologues" and "episodes." Monologues follow the common definition, that is, one occurs whenever a single speaker talks for an extended time. Episode is use to describe exchanges between or among speakers.

According to Smith and Meux, episodes typically are initiated by a teacher question, for example, "What causes an eclipse?" Each such question or "entry" has an ideal or more appropriate logical response which would answer the question in the sense it was proposed. The eclipse question above would seem to best call for an explanation. Besides explanation, there are a dozen other concepts used to categorize entries (Dunkin and Biddle 1982 p. 281).

Entries calling for an explanation require that some general rule or set of conditions be given to explain a result or consequence thereof. Explanation is divided into six categories: (a) mechanical (e.g., "How do crickets make sounds?"); (b) causal (e.g., "What makes people lethargic?"); (c) sequential (e.g., "What events led to the Gulf War?"); (d) procedural (e.g., "How do you tack when sailing?"); (e) teleological (e.g., "Why did you teach the lesson as you did?"); or (f) normative (e.g., "Why was South Africa the target of international sanction?"). The Illinois Instrument has been used in studies conducted by Nuthall and Lawrence (1965), Smith and Meux (1970), and Tisher (1970).

Dunkin and Biddle (1982) report that regardless of the subject matter taught and the geographic (national) location of the study, approximately one-fourth of the episodes fall into the "describing" category. "Designating" and "explaining" are also popular. Where teachers ask for explanations that are either of a sequential or procedural kind, students handle them. However, in general, when teachers ask for explanations of a causal, teleological, or normative type, pupils do not generate congruent or logical responses (Nuthall and Lawrence 1965, Tisher 1970). Teachers often responded to student inability to answer the question by attempting to clarify it. Dunkin and Biddle ask, "Could it be that when teachers ask higher level questions, vagueness often enters in and interferes with the communication to pupils?" (p. 293). In this regard, Tisher found that one-fifth of the explanations teachers did accept were logically inappropriate given the question asked.

5.2 The Columbia University Instrument

A second instrument emerged from the work of Bellack et al. (1966) who worked toward identifying and analyzing instruction from a logical perspective. They studied the instructional process and felt it could be described by a series of "moves" or verbal behaviors of teachers and students: structuring, soliciting, responding, and reacting. Thus, whereas the Illinois Instrument categorized only how pupils logically should respond to episode opening entries, mainly questions or solicitations, the Bellack et al. or Columbia University Instrument is capable of classifying everything teachers do, including their monologues or lectures. The Bellack et al. categories are nine in number and not unrelated to Smith and Meux's. Explaining is one category. It is used to refer to: (a) statements of relations between or among objects, events, principles; (b) conditional inference; (c) cause–effect; (d) explicit comparison contrast; and (e) statements of principles, theories, or laws. The other categories are defining–general, defining–denotative, defining–connotative, interpreting, fact stating, opining, justifying, and "logical process not clear." The Columbia University Instrument has been used in studies conducted by Furst (1967), Lundgren (1972), and Power (1971).

With regard to "solicitations," Bellack et al. (1966) found about 80 percent of them were concerned with empirical processes and slightly more of these with "explaining" than with "fact finding." Unlike the findings of investigators using the Illinois Instrument, Columbia University Instrument users found pupil responses to teacher questions to be congruent 85 percent of the time.

While researchers using the Illinois and Columbia University Instruments observed the general use of logic and linguistics during classroom discourse, investigators at Stanford, under the direction of N L Gage, concentrated on the single phenomenon of teachers' ability to explain. Relatedly, Rosenshine (1968) studied lecturing. He found that effective lectures contained more explaining links, that is, "propositions and conjunctions which indicate the cause, result, means, or purpose of an event or idea" (p. 8). Examples include "because," "in order to," "if . . . then," "therefore," and "consequently."

Hiller et al. (1969) also studied lectures using the same data as did Rosenshine. They found in general that vagueness was negatively associated with student achievement. Vagueness is defined as when "a performer . . . does not sufficiently command the facts or the understanding required for maximally effective communication" (p. 670). In other words, what is not known well cannot be explained clearly.

5.3 The Rating Teacher Explanation Instrument

The Rating Teacher Explanation Instrument (Duffy et al. 1985) contains two parts. Part I focuses on the information the teacher presents about the cognitive processes students should follow to do a reading task, and asks observers to rate such information in terms of its clarity, consistency, and explicitness. Part 2 focuses on the means by which the teacher makes clear the information presented. It asks observers to record how the teacher (a) modelled how to do the required cognitive processing, (b) directed attention if students became confused, (c) provided students with independent or guided practice using cognitive processing in a contrived sample (workbook page, ditto sheet, etc.), and (d) helped students apply the cognitive processing when reading basal text stories or in other connected situations.

Mathematics educators have also studied cognitive processing or how students learn. They, too, are interested in how well K-12 teachers communicate successful student learning strategies to their own pupils. Consequently, Herrmann (1989) has used a modification of the Rating Teacher Explanation Instrument to rate teacher explanations given during mathematics instruction in problem-solving.

5.4 Herrmann's Pupil Awareness Rating Form

Herrmann's Pupil Awareness Rating Form (Herrmann 1989) is used to rate pupil responses to three questions asked during a post-teaching interview. The questions are: "What was taught?" "When and how *would* what was taught be used?" and "When and how *could* what was taught be used?". Two other related instruments are presented (Herrmann 1989 pp. 15–17) as well as a sociolinguistic mapping procedure she followed to identify characteristics of more and less explicit units of teacher talk.

6. Need for Further Scholarship and Research

Persons working to understand explanation seem not to be organized. Relatedly, there seems to be no guru or individual who, over time, has engaged in significant related inquiry.

Should the aggregate of researchers in the field be formed into a true group it might argue for scholarship and research such as the following:

(a) a compilation of concepts, definitions, facts, and conditional propositions or "if then" statements that would shed light on precisely what is known about explaining;

(b) the collection and analysis of instruments used for the study of explaining and related concepts;

(c) discussion of perspectives on explaining, its observation and measurement; and

(d) projections of further studies that might include gaining concurrence and consensus of what explaining is, devising further descriptive or qualitative study of it, looking for characteristics of good explainers, determining relationships between explaining and pupil learning and satisfaction, and determining whether teachers can be trained in explanation and the effect of training on student outcomes.

References

Armbruster B B, Anderson T H 1984 Structures of explanations in history textbooks, or so what if Governor Stanford missed the spike and hit the rail? *Curriculum Studies* 16(2): 181–94

Bellack A A, Kliebard H M, Hyman R T, Smith F L 1966 *The Language of the Classroom*. Teachers College, Columbia University, New York

Cruickshank D, Kennedy J 1986 Teacher clarity. *Teaching and Teacher Education* 2(1): 43–67

Dagher Z R 1989 The nature of verbal teacher explanations in junior high science classrooms. (Doctoral dissertation, University of Iowa)

Duffy G G, Roehler L R, Wesselman R 1985 Disentangling the complexities of instructional effectiveness: A line of research in classroom reading instruction. In: Niles J, Lakil R (eds.) 1985 *Issues in Literacy: A Research Perspective. Thirty-fourth Yearbook of the National Reading Conference.* National Reading Conference, Rochester, New York

Duffy G G, Roehler L R, Rackliffe G 1986 How teachers' instructional talk influences students' understanding of lesson content. *Elem. Sch. J.* 87(1): 3–16

Dunkin M, Biddle J 1982 *The Study of Teaching.* University Press of America, Washington, DC

Ennis R H 1969 *Logic in Teaching.* Prentice-Hall, Englewood Cliffs, New Jersey

Fairhurst M A 1981 Satisfactory explanations in the primary school. *J. Phil. Educ.* 15(2): 205–14

Furst N F 1967 The multiple languages of the classroom. (Doctoral dissertation, Temple University)

Garfinkel A 1981 *Forms of Explanations: Rethinking the Questions in Social Theory.* Yale University Press, New Haven, Connecticut

Herrmann B A 1989 Characteristics of explicit and less explicit explanations of mathematical problem solving strategies. *Reading Research and Instruction* 28(3): 1–17

Hiller J, Fisher G, Kaess W 1969 A computer investigation of verbal characteristics of effective classroom lecturing. *Am. Educ. Res. J.* 6(4): 661–75

Hudgins B B 1974 *A Catalogue of Concepts in the Pedagogical Domain of Teacher Education.* Graduate Institute of Education, Washington University, St. Louis, Missouri

Lundgren U P 1972 *Frame Factors and the Teaching Process: A Contribution to Curriculum Theory and Theory on Teaching.* Almqvist and Wiksell, Stockholm

MacDonald R E 1991 *A Handbook of Basic Skills and Strategies for Beginning Teachers.* Longman, White Plains, New York

Metcalf K K, Cruickshank D R 1991 Can teachers be trained to be more clear? *J. Educ. Res.* 85(2): 107–16

Metcalf L E 1963 Research on teaching the social studies. In: Gage N L (ed.) 1963 *Handbook of Research on Teaching.* Rand McNally, Chicago, Illinois

Nuthall G A, Lawrence P J 1965 *Thinking in the Classroom: The Development of a Method of Analysis.* New Zealand Council for Educational Research, Wellington

Power C N 1971 The effects of communication patterns on student sociometric status, attitudes, and achievement in science. (Doctoral dissertation, The University of Queensland)

Rosenshine B 1968 Objectively measured behavioral predictors of effectiveness in explaining. Paper presented at the annual meeting of the American Educational Research Association, Chicago, Illinois

Schulze K G 1989–90 The use of multiple explanations in an open-ended intelligent tutoring system. *Journal of Educational Technology Systems* 18(3): 221–25

Slavin R E 1991 *Educational Psychology. Theory into Practice.* 3rd edn. Prentice-Hall, Englewood Cliffs, New Jersey

Smith B O, Cohen S B, Pearl A 1969 *Teachers for the Real World.* American Association of Colleges for Teacher Education, Washington, DC

Smith B O, Meux M O 1970 *A Study of the Logic of Teaching.* University of Illinois Press, Urbana, Illinois

Swift L F 1959 Explanation as an aspect of critical thinking in secondary school social studies. (Doctoral dissertation, The University of Illinois)

Tisher R P 1970 The nature of verbal discourse in classrooms and association between verbal discourse and pupil understanding in science. In: Campbell W J (ed.) 1970 *Scholars in Context: The Effects of Environment on Learning.* Wiley, Sydney

Demonstrating

L. C. Comber and J. P. Keeves

Demonstration methods of teaching are perhaps the oldest and most common of all teaching methods, not only in the school, but also in the home, at play, and in the workplace. Demonstration is employed to teach a variety of skills ranging from tying shoelaces to neurosurgical operations. In these cases, demonstration is used because it is too complicated to provide a verbal description of the skills. However, demonstrations are not limited to the teaching of specific skills; they also are employed to teach analytical processes. As a method of teaching, demonstration is largely ignored by researchers and teacher educators (with the possible exception of the field of physical education).

1. Understanding Demonstration

Demonstration, which may be defined as "teaching by showing," has the advantage of communicating with learners visually and orally at the same time. Through visual presentation, language barriers can be overcome, communication can be enhanced, and rapport between the teacher and the learner can be established. Through oral presentation what is seen by the learners can be introduced, explained, and summarized by the teacher. In many ways demonstration is the "natural" method of teaching. It provides the imitative behavior so important in learning in early childhood before language is sufficiently developed.

Throughout human history, teaching by demonstration has been the primary method of preparation for living and for passing on the cultural heritage. With the development of trades and crafts, demonstration provided the foundation for apprenticeship training in the medieval guilds and was firmly related to the teaching of practical skills. It was not, however, restricted to the teaching of such skills. Art and music, for example, were two areas in which demonstration by the master to the pupil was particularly productive. Similarly, the demonstration of experimental processes has had a central role in science. The successes in these subject areas raise the question of the extent to which demonstrations can be employed in other subjects.

2. Effects of Technology

The rapid development of educational technology has widened the scope for demonstration methods in education and training. Additionally, technology has greatly increased the instructional effectiveness of demonstration. Initially, films were used to great advantage. With the development of television and videorecording, however, new possibilities have emerged. The smallest details can now be seen by all who observe a demonstration or witness a replay of it from a videorecording. Perhaps the most remarkable developments have occurred in surgery, where not only can the surgeon see more clearly the progress of the operation, but all in the operating theater can now see what is taking place. Moreover, the development of the overhead projector to present computer output on a screen and the distribution of televised programs by satellite have the potential to advance teaching by demonstration, because they have the capacity to increase the clarity of what is presented to increasingly large numbers of students.

3. Art of Demonstration

An important element in many learning situations is the relationship between the demonstration given by the teacher and the practice given to the student. The most effective balance between the two depends upon the learning task, the situation provided for practice, and the quality of communication achieved by the teacher. It is necessary, however, to recognize that human learning through demonstration extends beyond imitative behavior to a wide range of intellectual activities. The art of demonstration is to show the process to be learned in such a way that understanding and the building of internalized links are established. Learning to drive a motorcar, or to fly supersonic jet fighter aircraft, involves more than the development of a certain level of manual dexterity. It requires understanding and analytical skills that will enable appropriate actions to be taken in the case of an emergency or unexpected happenings. Thus, although imitation plays its part in such learning, the simultaneous building of understanding and analytical skills, while the manual operations and procedures are being learned to the degree that they become largely automatic, is also required. The art of teaching by demonstration involves the establishment of competence and complete mastery in all envisaged circumstances through the development of the intellectual basis of action.

From this perspective it is possible to specify seven steps which are involved in teaching by demonstration.

(a) The initial step involves the thorough analysis of the skills and competencies involved in the demonstrated operation. The prerequisite skills and competencies, including knowledge and understanding, must first be identified. There is little point demonstrating how to undertake long division to students who cannot add and subtract. These prerequisite skills and competencies must be placed in a logical or temporal sequence for the purposes of instruction.

(b) The second step involves choosing an appropriate situation within which to present the demonstration. The ideal may not be accessible and, therefore, the choice of the best available situation may need to be made. Sometimes a film or a videorecording is more effective than a direct demonstration.

(c) Since demonstration involves both visual and oral presentation (or in some cases visual and written instruction), it is necessary to plan the manner in which the visual and the oral presentations are to be linked in an ordered sequence. It is at this third step that the analysis of the skills and competencies carried out in the first step is used. The emphasis, however, must always be on understanding, and the nature and sequence of presentation should be directed toward this end.

(d) Since emphasis is on understanding, the learner should always be allowed opportunity to ask questions in order to ensure that understanding is developing. However, it must be recognized that understanding is rarely complete at an early stage, since, like performance skills and competencies, it develops over time. Thus, it is important to recognize that the development of understanding also continues through practice.

(e) In the fifth step the learner is provided with the opportunity to repeat the entire operation (or a section of it) under guidance and in circumstances in which questions can be asked of the instructor both to avoid errors and to advance understanding. In addition, the instructor should prompt, check for understanding, correct, and repeat when necessary.

(f) In the sixth step, the learner is permitted to repeat the operation until mastery is achieved. In this case, mastery means achieving a degree of understanding that will permit appropriate action in a novel situation. This step also includes the development of speed and accuracy of performance.

(g) The final step involves evaluation and, when necessary, repeated practice until perfection or near-perfection is achieved.

4. Demonstration in Specific Subject Areas

The art of demonstration, illustrated in the seven steps outlined above, has been applied in several subjects. Its application in physical education, mathematics, and science is discussed in this section.

4.1 Demonstration in Physical Education

Physical education involves teaching a large number of psychomotor skills. Consequently, visual demonstration is one of the most effective ways of fostering such development. Learners must identify with the demonstrator if they are to duplicate the demonstrator's actions. At the same time, while observing an expert often has an entertaining effect, it does not necessarily have an educating effect. If learners feel that they are comparable in age, experience, and physical characteristics to the demonstrator, they are more likely to acquire the demonstrator's skill and facility. Nevertheless, the actions of the demonstrator must be of reasonable quality and provide an appropriate model for duplication (Karlin and Mortimer 1963).

A film or a videorecording can provide an effective form of presentation if practice follows soon after the viewing (Zuckerman 1950). In addition, verbal instruction must be appropriately placed with respect to action in the film. Both film and videorecording have the advantage that they can be slowed down, stopped, or reversed and rerun to show clearly the detail involved in performing the skill. Moreover, the use of videotaping has the further advantage that it can be used to record the practice of the learners, who can then examine objectively their performance with respect to that shown in the demonstration, a most effective form of feedback.

4.2 Demonstration in the Teaching of Mathematics

A substantial portion of elementary mathematics involves learning specific algorithmic procedures. Although electronic calculators have reduced the extent to which some algorithms need to be mastered with speed and accuracy, the understanding of mathematical operations in general is built upon the demonstration of proofs, problem solving procedures, relationships and identities, and the solving of equations. The most common approach to instruction in mathematics is for the teacher to demonstrate the steps to be followed and then ask questions of students and monitor their answers to check for understanding. After a satisfactory level of understanding has been achieved, teachers provide a series of problems or exercises and help students as they work through them by providing prompts and corrections. As students attain a level of proficiency they move to independent practice which is commonly undertaken as homework.

A major part of the instructional process is the initial demonstration during which the students see what to do and listen to the teacher-led discussion of *why* the prescribed steps are followed. Sometimes the teacher reverts to demonstration during guided practice to clarify a step, so that, while practice and formative evaluation are important and necessary, demonstration is clearly the key instruction.

Rosenshine and Stevens (1986), from a review of research, state that from Grades 4 to 8, more effective teachers spend more time on demonstration in mathematics classes than do less effective teachers. More effective teachers give on average 23 minutes of a 50-minute daily period to presentation, that is, to demonstration and discussion, while less effective teachers give 11 minutes, less than half that time. In addition, Rosenshine and Stevens specify four important aspects of good presentation in mathematics classrooms: (a) clarity of goals and main points; (b) step-by-step presentation; (c) specific and concrete procedures; and (d) checking for students' understanding. However, they note that there is little conclusive research on such issues as: (a) how should new material be organized so that it can be learned most effectively? (b) what are the characteristics of an effective demonstration? (c) how many examples and of what kind should a teacher use? (d) is there an effective way for sequencing examples? and (e) how much information should be presented in the instructional steps?

4.3 Demonstration in Science Teaching

Science is based on evidence obtained through the senses from the natural world. In learning science, observation and experimentation are essential ingredients, and demonstration can contribute to both. Thus, a necessary requirement of demonstration in science classrooms is that every step be clearly seen by every member of the class. With this in mind, some schools have science classrooms with a serviced demonstration bench and tiered seating. However, demonstration experiments and observation can be carried out by students working alone or more commonly in small groups. Under these circumstances a laboratory with flexible furniture is more useful, and a preferred setting for science teaching. Nevertheless, much of the science teaching carried out in a laboratory is essentially in the form of a demonstration rather than an investigation, so that the principles of demonstration teaching apply. Teacher demonstration as opposed to student demonstration as a mode of teaching in science is selected for one or more of the following reasons: (a) to show certain manipulative skills and procedures; (b) because the processes involved are costly, dangerous, difficult, or time consuming; and (c) because the force of a logical argument might be lost if the students' attention is concentrated on performing the practical tasks involved.

Particular attention has to be given in demonstrations in science teaching to employing apparatus, such as scales and meters of sufficient size, so that all members of the group can see for themselves. Where this is not possible, authenticity is achieved by using members of the class as assistants to make the observations and relay them to the class. This approach has the further advantage that it frees the teacher to ask questions of the students that will augment understanding, as opposed to focusing on the set lecture with illustrative material.

The teacher should conduct a trial run of a more complex procedure to ensure that the equipment is in good working order. Demonstrations that do not work, while perhaps not uncharacteristic of scientific investigation, disappoint and disillusion science classes, because students have a high level of expectation and interest when being shown a scientific demonstration. Thus an effective demonstration requires attention to the smallest detail and meticulous rehearsal. Judgment must be exercised and decisions made concerning every step (for example, whether anything is lost if reagents are measured out beforehand, or the electrical connections made so that all that is necessary is to turn on a switch). Fumbling to connect wires or groping for a box of matches can be a distraction.

In general, a demonstration should set a high standard in preparation and manipulation. However, above all, attention should be given to logical presentation and the structure of the scientific argument, since science involves not only the learning of content, but also the development of the processes of investigation and inquiry through observation and experimentation. Toward this end, questioning of the students serves to emphasize investigation and can be used for induction, deduction, and the making of general statements to summarize and recapitulate the findings.

5. Collaborative Demonstration

Collaborative demonstration is concerned more with teaching the processes of investigation and inquiry than with the presentation of specific content. In the learning of science and many other subjects, such as problem solving in mathematics, there is need to engage in more open-ended and heuristic activity so that the skills of inquiry may be appreciated and developed. However, this form of demonstration teaching is much less of a set piece and demands a high level of teaching skill for its success. The demonstrator outlines the problem and then invites the class to advance ideas on how to proceed, what questions to ask, how to obtain answers to these questions, how to assess the value of the evidence, and how to draw conclusions. The method demands skill on the part of the teacher in eliminating suggestions that are going to be unproductive, while accepting those that can lead in a profitable direction or that can be submitted to a thorough discussion, without inhibiting responses from the group.

Much of the value of the demonstration lies in the following of false trails, but pursuing every trail is both time consuming and unrewarding, especially as some students and the teacher may have foreknowledge of the result. Therefore, instead of a rehearsed flow of clearly defined stages along a predetermined path, the demonstration consists of a series of improvisations skillfully managed to achieve the double objectives of extending the students' understanding while at the same time developing their powers of investigation. Preparation for such teaching lies in thinking out what kinds of materials and resources might be required and having them readily available, but out of sight, so that the students are not predisposed to follow routes predetermined by the teacher. The demonstration therefore follows a course which is generally in the desired direction, but to which the students' suggestions have substantially contributed after discussion, refinement, and acceptance by the class as a whole.

New opportunities have arisen for this open-ended type of demonstration teaching with the advent of the desktop computer that may be programed for a simulation study in all fields of learning where evidence is available and where hypotheses or models may be postulated and checked against evidence. The value of such a demonstration lies in learning to work as a group, learning the inquiry approach, learning how to confirm or reject, and above all learning that there may not be a single right answer to every question. While a group is not essential for such demonstration teaching, if groups are used they should be of sufficient size to generate ideas, but not so large as to exclude some members from participating. The critical operation comes at a late stage when ideas are submitted to the test, although the results may frequently lead to starting again along another path or set of paths.

Torrence (1986) reports that such methods of teaching are being used with gifted students, but the approach employed in collaborative demonstration methods of teaching is of such importance that studies using this method with ordinary students are clearly required. In this type of demonstration, the emphasis is on process rather than content. The students themselves, their thoughts, and the procedures they advance are the focus of attention, not the task being undertaken.

6. Conclusion

Demonstration methods of teaching have a long tradition and have proved to be very productive. They have dominated science teaching in some countries in continental Europe at the expense of student-based laboratory work. They have led to the building of special theaters, for example at the University of Uppsala centuries ago, for the teaching of medicine. They have a new role to play as television, video recordings, and other technological advances contribute to the advancement of teaching. However, research in this field would appear to be seriously deficient—almost nonexistent. The reasons for the failure to research this field are difficult to identify, and a cost is borne by all, through the use of less effective and less efficient methods of teaching and learning.

See also: Explaining; Discussion; Tutoring

References

Karlin L, Mortimer R G 1963 Effect of verbal, visual and auditory augmentary cues on learning a complex motor skill. *J. Exp. Psychol.* 65: 75–79
Rosenshine B, Stevens R 1986 Teaching functions. In: Wittrock M C 1986 *Handbook of Research on Teaching*, 3rd edn. Macmillan, New York
Torrence E P 1986 Teaching creative and gifted learners. In: Wittrock M C 1986 *Handbook of Research on Teaching*, 3rd edn. Macmillan, New York
Zuckerman J V 1950 Effects of variations in commentary upon the learning of perceptual-motor tasks from sound motion pictures. *Am. Psychol.* 5: 363–64

Questioning

M. D. Gall and M. T. Artero-Boname

Interest in teachers' questioning strategies is strong. A search of the Educational Resources Information (Center) ERIC database using the descriptor "questioning techniques" will yield well over 100 research reports and professional papers annually for the decade from 1982. In addition, manuals for teachers on questioning strategies continue to appear including Morgan and Saxton 1991.

This extensive literature reflects the central role of questions in the instructional process. Teachers' oral questions have been found to consume from 6 to 16 percent of classroom time, depending upon subject and grade level (Doneau 1985), and students spend much additional time answering written questions in seatwork, homework, and quizzes.

Prior to the early 1980s, most researchers used quantitative methods to describe teachers' questioning behaviors and to identify which of those behaviors facilitate students' academic achievement. Since then, qualitative researchers have contributed many studies of the context and meaning of the questions teachers ask in their classrooms. An international, collaborative investigation of classroom questioning by philosophers, sociolinguists, cognitive and social psychologists, and traditional quantitative researchers (Dillon 1988) illustrates the range of studies. Sociolinguistic research (Carlsen 1991) has been a particularly rich source of new knowledge about teachers' questioning practices. The discussion that follows synthesizes the findings of both quantitative and qualitative research, and emphasizes studies published since the review by Doneau (1985).

1. Types of Question

1.1 Lower and Higher Cognitive Questions

In one of the largest studies of instruction ever, Sirotnik and colleagues (Sirotnik 1983) observed lessons in more than 1,000 United States classrooms (kindergarten through high school). They found that teachers' questions were "almost invariably closed and factual" (p.29). A large-scale study of Florida classrooms (Micceri et al. 1990) and classroom research in Czechoslovakia, Germany, and India (reviewed by Klinzing and Klinzing-Eurich 1987) yielded similar findings, as have other studies spanning most of the twentieth century.

Educators have reacted to these findings by exhorting teachers to ask more higher cognitive questions, the assumption being that this change in practice would improve student learning. Research testing this assumption has been the subject of several meta-analytic reviews, most recently by Samson et al. (1987). They concluded that teacher emphasis on higher cognitive questions generally has a modest positive effect on student achievement.

Carlsen (1991) and Gall and Rhody (1987) have identified six major problems with the studies on which Samson et al. as well as other reviewers have based their conclusions about the effectiveness of higher cognitive questions.

First, some students do not give higher cognitive answers to the teachers' higher cognitive question (Dantonio and Paradise 1988). As a consequence, if teachers increase their emphasis on higher cognitive questions, this change alone probably would be insufficient to improve these students' learning. Teachers also may need to use techniques such as extended wait time and corrective feedback to help students process the questions and generate acceptable responses.

Second, because teachers ask so many factual questions in instruction, it probably is easy for them to emphasize such questions when asked to do so under experimental conditions. Teachers who are asked to emphasize higher cognitive questions in an experiment, however, must make much greater adjustments in their teaching behavior. Consequently, they may not be able to implement this experimental condition effectively.

Third, researchers have classified the cognitive level of teachers' questions independently of the instructional context. Thus, their basis for classification primarily has been the form and content of the question. For example, questions beginning with "Why" typically are classified as higher cognitive. However, some students might answer such questions by simply recalling previously learned information. If so, the researcher's classification is invalid.

Fourth, higher cognitive questions vary in difficulty. Thus an easy higher cognitive question possibly might have less effect on student learning than a challenging lower cognitive question (e.g., one that solicits recall and integration of several related facts). Also, a higher cognitive question might be so difficult that it does not engage student effort, and therefore no learning occurs. This aspect of higher cognitive questioning has not been addressed adequately in past research.

Fifth, many achievement tests used in past research were designed to reflect the school curriculum, which traditionally has emphasized knowledge and skill acquisition. These tests would be inappropriate to assess the effects of higher cognitive questions in instruction because, while such questions may promote knowledge and skill acquisition, they are intended primarily to improve students' thinking. Tests of thinking skills developed comparatively recently (e.g., Clark 1992) appear more likely to reveal the intended effects of teacher emphasis on higher cognitive questioning.

Finally, much of the research to date has classified teachers' questions as lower cognitive or higher cognitive based on the taxonomy developed by Bloom and his colleagues (1956). This taxonomy, however, is not grounded in a theory of instruction and learning. Thus it does not provide a sound basis for deciding which questions can be answered by lower cognitive processes and which by higher cognitive processes.

These six problems may explain why research has shown only a modest positive effect for higher cognitive questions. Solutions to these problems in future research might reveal stronger positive effects. In the meantime, the existing research findings do warrant a recommendation that teachers increase their frequency

of use of higher cognitive questions beyond the current low level.

1.2 Recitation and Discussion Questions

Sociolinguists have furthered understanding of teachers' questions by studying the context in which they occur. Context, for them, has two meanings: the situation as the question-asker or question-responder finds it when he or she begins speaking; and the situation that the speaker creates in the process of asking or answering questions. An important contextual feature of classroom instruction is participant structure, that is, the arrangement of speakers and listeners and their rules for discourse (Carlsen 1991).

The dominant participant structure in classrooms continues to be recitation (Gall and Rhody 1987, Sirotnik 1983), which is characterized by the teacher asking frequent questions, often in rapid-fire fashion, to test students' mastery of information contained in an authoritative source, typically a textbook. Teachers have nearly total control of recitation. They can ask questions, while the students cannot. Thus, teachers are free to determine the content of questions, the students who will answer them, and their reaction to the answers. The student's role is constrained to answering questions when called on by the teacher and to listen to other teacher–student interchanges.

Researchers (e.g., Eddinger 1985) have found that recitation promotes better student learning than alternative instructional methods that do not involve teacher questioning. Also, asking many questions during a recitation is more effective than asking few questions (Rosenshine 1987).

Researchers are investigating classroom participant structures that involve very different discourse patterns than recitation. For example, Nystrand and Gamoran (1991) studied occurrences of "substantively engaging" conversation in eighth- and ninth-grade English classes. This type of participant structure is characterized by teachers asking authentic questions (which are questions that invite students to express their own ideas), responding to students' ideas by building on them, and asking new questions based on what students have said.

Other researchers have studied similar conversational patterns in elementary school science lessons in Brazil (Kleiman 1990), and literature lessons in United States junior high schools (Rogers 1987) and high schools (Alpert 1991). In the high school study, the researcher identified an atypical teacher who made room for students' personal knowledge and feelings in his questions, for example, by asking: "Do you feel sorry for any of the characters?"; "Do you want Eliza to marry Freddy?"; "Did you see his way as somewhat less worthwhile than hers?" (p.359). Also, discourse in this teacher's classroom was characterized by use of informal, everyday language.

Programs of research have been undertaken to develop and test teaching methods that emphasize these discourse patterns as an alternative to recitation. For example, Wood et al. (1991) reported a case study in which they trained an elementary school teacher for an entire school year in a method of "collaborative dialogue," which is based on constructivist theories of learning. Using this participant structure, the teacher engaged in various instructional activities, including asking students questions to help her understand the thinking processes that the students used to solve mathematics problems. When a child's understanding was incorrect or incomplete, the teacher would "negotiate" a better understanding by asking further questions and providing information, but always within a frame of reference that was meaningful to the child.

Collaborative dialogue in this study contrasts with the traditional recitation pattern in mathematics lessons, where the teacher's intent is to ask questions that elicit the answer to a mathematical problem rather than the thinking process behind the answer. Also, in recitation the teacher typically reacts to an incorrect answer by providing corrective feedback or calling on another student to provide the answer, rather than by asking follow-up questions of the same student to understand his or her thinking processes.

Little is known about the effectiveness of these alternative questioning processes in promoting learning. However, their goals and participant structures resemble critical features of the discussion method. For this reason the label "discussion questions" is used here to characterize teachers' questions in these discourse patterns.

Research on the discussion method has demonstrated its effectiveness for various instructional objectives, especially higher cognitive learning (Gall and Gall 1990). These positive findings for the discussion method suggest that similar techniques—substantively engaging conversation, authentic questions, collaborative dialogue—will be similarly effective.

The different participant structures involved in recitation and discussion may explain the finding by Dillon (1985) that teachers' questions tend to produce simple, terse responses by students, whereas teacher statements produce lengthy, complex responses. The teachers' statements were meant to elicit discussion, while their questions apparently followed a recitation discourse pattern. If so, the teachers' questions understandably would elicit brief student responses. More effective would be a few thought-provoking questions to initiate talk among students. Occasional teacher comments and other techniques suggested by Dillon (1991) would stimulate further student talk without risking loss of the student-centered discourse pattern characteristic of the discussion method.

1.3 Test-relevant Questions

Teachers periodically give tests to assess students' learning. If an item on the test was rehearsed by a teacher question during instruction, researchers classify it as intentional. By contrast, an incidental item asks students to recall information or ideas that were not the subject of prior teacher questioning.

Research has found that students do better on intentional test items than on incidental test items when prior instruction involves recitation (Wixson 1983) or questions inserted in reading passages (Hamaker 1986). This finding supports the common notion that if teachers want their students to do well on a test, they should "teach to the test." In practice, this means conducting recitations and assigning worksheets in which students are asked test-relevant questions, that is, questions similar to those that will appear on the test.

2. Contextual Factors in Questioning

Until the early 1980s, researchers and practitioners had not considered systematically the context of teachers' questioning behaviors. This situation is changing. There is, in the early 1990s, a growing literature that explains how various contextual factors influence the purpose, content, and effectiveness of questioning.

2.1 Student Characteristics

Researchers have discovered that teachers' questioning patterns vary depending upon whether they are interacting with high-achieving or low-achieving students. In a review of this research, Good and Brophy (1987) found that teachers call on low-achieving students less often to answer questions, wait a shorter time for them to answer questions, and give them less feedback and less opportunity to improve their answers.

Teachers' questioning behavior also is affected by student gender. Barba and Cadinale (1991) found that high school science teachers called on female students much less often than on male students and asked them fewer higher cognitive questions. Whereas female students were much more likely to give task-relevant answers and to attract the teacher's attention appropriately by raising their hand, they were much less likely to be a "target" student (someone who had four or more interactions with the teacher during one class period.) Barba and Cadinale suggested that this gender-biased questioning process may dissuade female students from taking science courses.

McCarty et al. (1991) reviewed research demonstrating that Native American students respond poorly to recitation questioning. They set out to solve this problem by developing an inquiry-based social studies curriculum that emphasized open-ended teacher questions, student inductive-analytic reasoning, and student problem-solving. Their research found that students' responses to the teachers' questions improved dramatically. McCarty and colleagues attributed the improvement to the close match between

Native American children's learning style in natural situations outside the classroom and the learning style encouraged by the new curriculum and teacher questioning process.

Au and Mason (1983) found that recitation was similarly ineffective with native Hawaiian students. Their academic performance improved when the teacher asked questions and then allowed the children to use native Hawaiian speech patterns, such as concurrent speech (children are free to speak when they wish, even if they overlap another child's talk).

2.2 Teacher Characteristics

Carlsen (1992) found that science teachers' knowledge about their subject matter affects their questioning practices. Less knowledgeable science teachers tend to rely more heavily on the textbook, emphasize lower cognitive questions, and discourage student questions. More knowledgeable teachers include subject matter not in the textbook and emphasize questions that require students to synthesize information.

In their review of questioning research in Germany, Klinzing and Klinzing Eurich (1987) concluded that teacher gender has no relationship to frequency of question use, but teacher experience does. More experienced teachers ask a greater number of lower cognitive questions and questions directed to the whole class. More and less experienced teachers do not differ in their frequency of higher cognitive questions, however.

2.3 Participant Structures

Participant structures are an important contextual factor in classroom instruction because they define the role of teacher and students and the rules governing their interaction. As explained above, the participant structure of recitation places central authority for question-asking on the teacher. Other participant structures provide more opportunity for student question-asking and talk, as in the discussion methods described earlier. The reciprocal teaching method (Palincsar et al. 1989) differs dramatically from these two methods, because its participant structure puts students in the central role of questioner. In reciprocal teaching, students process reading selections in small groups, and take turns as the "teacher." When it is a student's turn to be the teacher, she or he asks the other students a set of generic questions about a passage in the reading selection. A variation on this method is for students individually to generate questions and answer them on their own. Wong (1985) reviewed 27 studies of student question-generating and found positive effects on student reading comprehension in the majority of them.

A participant structure can be highly individualized, as in the case of one-to-one tutoring or a student at a computer terminal responding to questions posed by an instructional software program. Several studies of the latter type of participant structure have been conducted, including an experiment with college students by Shiang and McDaniel (1991). The students interacted individually with a computer screen that presented text interspersed with either lower cognitive questions, higher cognitive questions, or prompts to generate their own questions. Students in the three experimental conditions did not differ significantly on a test of critical thinking about the text subject matter. Thus, while computers are being used increasingly in instruction, the results of Shiang and McDaniel's experiment raise questions about the effectiveness of participant structures that isolate students from each other and the teacher. Other participant structures, such as having students form dyads to answer questions on a computer screen, may be more effective.

2.4 Instructional Sequences

Elementary and secondary school instruction typically is organized into units lasting from two to five weeks. Little is known about whether the purpose and content of teachers' questions change, or should change, as a unit of instruction progresses. An exception is research on teachers' use of questions to review previously taught content (Rosenshine 1987). This research has found that teachers' periodic use of review questions for previously taught content both within and across units improves students' academic achievement. Questions in the form of periodic quizzes also perform a review function, and they too are effective (McKenzie 1973).

Gall and Rhody (1987) reviewed research on effective types of questions within different phases of a classroom lesson. The findings suggest that teachers should ask questions that cause students to activate relevant mental schemas prior to instruction. They should also ask questions that check whether students are acquiring the desired knowledge and skills during instruction. Finally, they should provide seatwork and homework questions that elicit practice after instruction.

2.5 Subject and Grade Level

Little is known about whether teachers' questioning practices vary across subjects and grade levels, and whether questioning practices that are effective for one subject or grade level are effective for other subjects and grade levels. A national study of United States classrooms reported by Sirotnik (1983) revealed relatively little variation in teachers' emphasis on lower cognitive questions at the junior high and high school levels in five academic subjects (mathematics, English, social studies, science, and foreign language). The percentage of class time spent on such questions varied between five and nine percent in all the subject and grade level combinations. Greater variation was found in the percentage of class time spent on discussion, which presumably includes more use of higher cognitive questions. At the high school level, the percentage of class time spent on discussion was lowest for mathematics (2%) and highest for social studies (10%).

Extensive research has been done to identify effective questioning techniques for the basic skill areas of reading and mathematics (Rosenshine 1987). Much less research has been conducted on other subjects taught in school. A review of research on second-language learning by Chaudron (1986) suggests that this type of research is needed because many aspects of questioning in second-language instruction are not considered in the general literature on questioning.

3. Helping Students Answer Questions

Even though a teacher asks instructionally relevant questions, this does not mean that students will be able to answer and learn from them. Teachers' phrasing of questions, methods for calling on students to answer them, and reactions to students' answers all affect whether the questions aid students' learning.

3.1 Asking Clear Questions

The clarity of a teacher's questions obviously affects students' ability to answer them. Questions that have a complex grammatical structure or that contain abstract language are likely to be unclear for some students. Asking multiple questions (i.e., several questions in succession before calling on a student to respond) is another impediment to clarity, because it is difficult for students to sort out the core question from the verbiage. Borg et al. (1970) observed a high incidence of this behavior among elementary teachers: an average of 14 multiple questions in a 20-minute lesson. This behavior is also prevalent among German teachers (Klinzing and Klinzing-Eurich 1987). Wright and Nuthall (1970) found that the higher the incidence of multiple questions, the less well students learned the content of an instructional unit.

3.2 Wait Time

After asking a question, the teacher must decide how long to pause before calling on a student to respond. Teachers typically wait less than a second before calling on a student, but researchers have demonstrated that it is more effective to wait at least three seconds. In a review of this research, Tobin (1987) found that extending wait time increases the number and length of student responses in a lesson. In addition, the complexity and cognitive level of students' responses show improvement. Better student test performance also was found in several of the investigations.

Tobin suggested that extended wait time has these positive effects because it provides students the opportunity to think. Another explanation is that extended

wait time creates a relaxed atmosphere that in turn promotes thinking. By contrast, the typical wait time of less than a second can raise some students' anxiety level, which in turn causes a learning decrement.

3.3 Calling on Students to Respond

In the participant structure of recitation, the teacher typically calls on a single student to respond to each question. Thus students' opportunities to give oral responses are very limited. Other participant structures give more students the opportunity to respond to teachers' questions. Elementary school teachers who called on individual students to respond to questions were compared with teachers who asked all students to respond to each question with a nonverbal gesture (e.g., "If you think it would rain here, raise your hand") (McKenzie 1979). Calling on all students to respond resulted in more on-task behavior, less test anxiety, and better academic achievement than calling on individual students.

Maheady et al. (1991) evaluated a cooperative learning method called Heads Together, which gives all students the opportunity to respond to questions prepared by the teacher. In this method students are assigned to four-member teams that are heterogeneous in ability.

Each student in each group is assigned a number from 1 to 4. During the questioning period of a lesson, students are instructed to "put their heads together" to create their best answer, and to make sure that everyone in the team knows the answer. The teacher then selects a number and calls on each student in each team with that number to answer. This process is repeated with each teacher question. Compared with the recitation method of a teacher calling on individual students, the Heads Together method resulted in more student on-task behavior, better test performance, and greater satisfaction with instruction.

3.4 Reacting to Students' Answers

A typical teacher reaction to a student answer is simply to repeat the answer. Borg and his colleagues (1970) found that elementary teachers repeated student answers an average of 31 times in a 20-minute lesson. A more effective method may be for the teacher to react to a student's answer by acknowledging and building on it. Brophy and Good (1986) reviewed research on this technique and concluded that it generally has positive effects on student academic achievement and attitudes.

Another effective teacher reaction to a student's answer is praise. However, Brophy (1981) concluded from his review of research that praise is effective only if it is specific and credible. Also, he found that praise is not equally effective for all students. It has most effect for students who are insecure or who come from families of low socioeconomic status.

Additional effective techniques for reacting to student answers were identified by Rosenshine (1987) in his review of research on basic skills instruction and the teaching of well-defined concepts and procedures. If the student's answer is correct but hesitant, it is effective for the teacher to affirm the answer's correctness and to explain why it is correct. If the student's answer is incorrect, the teacher can react effectively by providing corrective feedback, which can take the form of asking simpler questions (sometimes called "probing questions"), providing hints, or reteaching the information.

3.5 Training Students in Question-answering Techniques

Teaching techniques such as wait time, praise, and corrective feedback may be insufficient to enable some students to participate satisfactorily in the complex process of classroom questioning. These students may require explicit instruction in answering questions. Raphael and Wonnacott (1985) developed and tested a procedure for this purpose. Elementary students were trained to answer three types of reading comprehension questions by recognizing how each type of question related to textbook content and the student's personal knowledge. Raphael and Wonnacott found that the training procedure improved students' ability to answer questions.

4. Training Teachers in Questioning Skills

Gliessman et al. (1988) did a meta-analytic review of 26 studies in which teachers were trained to increase the frequency with which they asked various types of questions (primarily higher-cognitive and probing questions). The studies yielded convincing evidence that training is effective for this purpose. A surprising finding, however, is that it is not necessary to provide practice in order to increase teachers' use of questioning skills. Having teachers view, identify, categorize, or construct examples of questions is sufficient. Other findings of their review were that training is equally effective for experienced and inexperienced teachers, and for elementary and secondary teachers.

Klinzing (1990) reviewed an extensive set of training studies conducted in West Germany since the early 1970s. Many of these studies involved laboratory settings in which teachers were trained in teaching skills that included asking higher cognitive questions and probing questions, and emphasizing indirect teaching (which includes acknowledgement and use of students' ideas). The training procedures included theory presentation, self-analysis, demonstrations by models, discrimination training, and controlled practice with feedback. Klinzing concluded from his review that teachers improved their questioning skills as a result of training and that they viewed the training favorably.

A limitation of the studies reviewed by Klinzing and by Gliessman et al. is that they only evaluated the immediate or short-term effects of training teachers in questioning skills. Little is known about the long-term effects of this type of training, other than the three-year follow-up study done by Borg (1972). He found good long-term retention of most of the questioning skills in which inservice teachers were trained by a program based on microteaching techniques.

5. Implications for Practice

Researchers are continuing to shed new light on teachers' questioning strategies. Their findings have not yielded a definitive set of guidelines for practice, but they do suggest what teachers should think about in planning and conducting lessons: how much emphasis to place on lower cognitive and higher cognitive questions; whether to use a recitation or discussion participant structure; how to frame questions clearly; how much wait time to allow before eliciting a response; whether to elicit an individual or group response; how to react to students' answers; and how to adjust one's questioning strategy to a particular instructional context. As described above, manuals and training methods have been developed to help teachers improve their skill in making and carrying out these complex decisions.

See also: Student Influences on Teaching; Student Roles in Classrooms; Characteristics of Teacher Educators

References

Alpert B 1991 Students' resistance in the classroom. *Anthropo. Educ. Q.* 22(4): 350–66
Au K H, Mason J M 1983 Cultural congruence in classroom participation structures: Achieving a balance of rights. *Discourse Processes* 6(2): 145–67
Barba R, Cadinale L 1991 Are females invisible students? An investigation of teacher–student questioning interactions. *School Science and Mathematics* 91(7): 306–10
Bloom B S (ed.) 1956 *Taxonomy of Educational Objectives, Handbook 1: Cognitive Domain.* David McKay, New York
Borg W R 1972 The minicourse as a vehicle for changing teacher behavior: A three year follow-up. *J. Educ. Psychol.* 63(6): 572–79
Borg W R, Kelley M L, Langer P, Gall M 1970 *The Minicourse: A Microteaching Approach to Teacher Education.* Macmillan, New York
Brophy J E 1981 Teacher praise: A functional analysis. *Rev. Educ. Res.* 51(1): 5–32
Brophy J E, Good T L 1986 Teacher behavior and student achievement. In: Wittrock M C (ed.) 1986 *Handbook of Research on Teaching*, 3rd edn. Macmillan, New York
Carlsen W S 1991 Questioning in classrooms: A sociolinguistic perspective. *Rev. Educ. Res.* 61(2): 157–78

Carlsen W S 1992 Subject-matter knowledge and science teaching: A pragmatic perspective. In: Brophy J E (ed.) 1992 *Advances in Teaching. Vol. 2: Teacher's Subject Matter Knowledge and Classroom Instruction*. JAI Press, Greenwich, Connecticut

Chaudron C 1986 The interaction of quantitative and qualitative approaches to research: A view of the second language classroom. TESOL *Quarterly* 20(4): 709–17

Clark J L 1992 The Toronto Board of Education's benchmarks in mathematics. *Arithmetic Teacher* 39(6): 51–55

Dantonio M, Paradise L V 1988 Teacher question-answer strategy and the cognitive correspondence between teacher questions and learner responses. *J. Res. Dev. Educ.* 21(3): 71–75

Dillon J T 1985 Using questions to foil discussion. *Teaching and Teacher Education* 1(2): 109–21

Dillon J T (ed.) 1988 *Questioning and Discussion: A Multidisciplinary Study*. Ablex, Norwood, New Jersey

Dillon J T 1991 Conducting discussions by alternatives to questioning. In: Wilen W W (ed.) 1991 *Teaching and Learning through Discussion*. Charles C Thomas, Springfield, Illinois

Doneau S J 1985 Soliciting in the classroom. In: Husén T, Postlethwaite T N (eds.) 1985 *The International Encyclopedia of Education: Research and Studies*. Pergamon Press, Oxford

Eddinger S S 1985 The effect of different question sequences on achievement in high school social studies. *Journal of Social Studies Research* 9(1): 17–29

Gall J P, Gall M D 1990 Outcomes of the discussion method. In: Wilen W W (ed.) 1990 *Teaching and Learning through Discussion*. Charles C Thomas, Springfield, Illinois

Gall M D, Rhody T 1987 Review of research on questioning techniques. In: Wilen W W (ed.) 1987 *Questions, Questioning Techniques, and Effective Teaching*. National Education Association, Washington DC

Gliessman D H, Pugh R C, Dowden D E, Hutchins T T 1988 Variables influencing the acquisition of a generic teaching skill. *Rev. Educ. Res.* 58(1): 25–46

Good T, Brophy J 1987 *Looking in Classrooms*, 4th edn. Harper and Row, New York

Hamaker C 1986 The effects of adjunct questions on prose learning. *Rev. Educ. Res.* 56(2): 212–42

Kleiman A B 1990 Cooperation and control in teaching: The evidence of classroom questions. ERIC Document Reproduction Services No. ED 329 121, Washington, DC

Klinzing H G 1990 Research on teacher education in West Germany. In: Tisher R P, Wideen M (eds.) 1990 *Research on Teacher Education: International Perspectives*. Palmer Press, London

Klinzing H G, Klinzing-Eurich G 1987 Teacher questioning. *Questioning Exchange* 3: 1–16

Maheady L, Mallette B, Harper G F, Sacca K 1991 Heads together: A peer-mediated option for improving the academic achievement of heterogeneous learning groups. *Rem. Spec. Educ.* 12(2): 25–33

McCarty T L, Lynch R H, Wallace S, Benally A 1991 Classroom inquiry and Navaho learning styles: A call for reassessment. *Anthropol. Educ. Q.* 22(1): 42–59

McKenzie G R 1973 Quizzes: Tools or tyrants. *Instructional Science* 2(3): 281–93

McKenzie G R 1979 Effects of questions and test-like events on achievement and on-task behavior in a classroom concept learning presentation. *J. Educ. Res.* 72(6): 348–51

Micceri T et al. 1990 Consistent patterns in observed teacher performance: Results from a large-sample multi-year study. ERIC Document Reproduction Services No. ED 317 600, Washington, DC

Morgan N, Saxton J 1991 *Teaching Questioning and Learning*. Routledge, London

Nystrand M, Gamoran A 1991 Instructional discourse, student engagement, and literature achievement. *Research in the Teaching of English* 25(3): 261–90

Palincsar A S, Ransom K, Derber S 1989 Collaborative research and development of reciprocal teaching. *Educ. Leadership* 46(4): 37–40

Raphael T E, Wonnacott C A 1985 Heightening fourth-grade students' sensitivity to sources of information for answering comprehension questions. *Read. Res. Q.* 20(3): 282–96

Rogers T 1987 Exploring a socio-cognitive perspective on the interpretive processes of junior high school students. *English Quarterly* 20(3): 218–30

Rosenshine B V 1987 Explicit teaching. In: Berliner D C, Rosenshine B V (eds.) 1987 *Talks to Teachers*. McGraw Hill, New York

Samson G E, Strykowski B, Weinstein T, Walberg H J 1987 The effects of teacher questioning levels on student achievement: A quantitative synthesis. *J. Educ. Res.* 80(5): 290–95

Shiang C P, McDaniel E 1991 Examining the effects of questioning on thinking processes with a computer-based exercise. *J. Educational Computing Research* 7(2): 203–17

Sirotnik K A 1983 What you see is what you get—consistency, persistency, and mediocrity in classrooms. *Harv. Educ. Rev.* 53(1): 16–31

Tobin K G 1987 The role of wait time in higher cognitive level learning. *Rev. Educ. Res.* 57(1): 69–95

Wixson K K 1983 Questions about a text: What you ask about is what children learn. *Read. Teach.* 37(3): 287–93

Wong B Y L 1985 Self-questioning instructional research: A review. *Rev. Educ. Res.* 55(2): 227–68

Wood T, Cobb P, Yackel E 1991 Change in teaching mathematics: A case study. *Am. Educ. Res. J.* 28(3): 587–616

Wright C J, Nuthall G 1970 Relationships between teacher behaviors and pupil achievement in three experimental elementary science lessons. *Am. Educ. Res. J.* 7(4): 477–91

Feedback

R. E. Mayer

Feedback is information provided to a learner concerning the correctness, appropriateness, or accuracy of the learner's actions (Mayer 1982). This definition has three components: (a) feedback occurs after a learner exhibits behavior of some kind, (b) feedback is observable by the learner, and (c) feedback describes the effects of the learner's behavior. In short, feedback is information about a learner's performance.

1. Educational Uses of Feedback

Feedback is pervasive in education. In academic learning tasks, feedback refers to information concerning the correctness of a student's performance, such as praising a student for giving the correct answer to a teacher's question during classroom discussion, giving a grade on a student's test, or having a smiling face appear on a computer screen whenever a student selects the right answer in a computerized drill-and-practice program. In behavior management tasks, feedback provides information concerning the appropriateness of a student's behavior, such as scolding a student for disruptive classroom behavior or giving a student a prize for engaging in constructive classroom behavior. In skill learning tasks, feedback provides information concerning the accuracy of a student's behavior, such as allowing a student to throw a ball and see whether or not it lands on a target.

2. Behaviorist and Cognitive Views of Feedback in Learning

The behaviorist and cognitive approaches to educational psychology offer alternative interpretations of the role of feedback in learning (Mayer 1987). Behaviorists view feedback as reward or punishment that automatically strengthens or weakens, respectively, the tendency to give a particular response. According to Thorndike's (1913) classic law of effect, a response that leads to satisfaction is more likely to recur in the same situation and a response that leads to discomfort is less likely to recur in the same situation. In Skinner's (1968) reinforcement theory, a reinforcer that is contingent on a learner's response increases the frequency of that response in the future whereas a punishment administered after a learner's response decreases the frequency of responding. In both versions of behaviorist theory, the rewards and punishments

operate automatically on the learner's specific responses, that is, without the need for conscious interpretation by the learner. Feedback that reinforces a response automatically increases or strengthens the tendency to repeat that response, whereas feedback that punishes a response automatically decreases or weakens the tendency to repeat the response. However, behaviorist theory has been revised to emphasize the use of reinforcement as a more effective method of changing behavior than punishment. According to the behaviorist view, feedback is a central mechanism in learning; learning cannot occur without feedback and the effects of feedback are automatic and specific.

In contrast, cognitive psychologists view feedback as information that the learner interprets and uses to alter his or her knowledge (Mayer 1987). Feedback provides learners with knowledge of results that guides their construction of knowledge; this newly constructed knowledge can generate more successful behavior in the future. Thus, feedback does not automatically change behavior; instead, learners' interpretation of feedback is used to change their knowledge, which in turn can affect their behavior. As in behaviorist theories of learning, feedback is viewed as a central mechanism in learning; however, in contrast to behaviorist theories, the impact of feedback depends on the way that the learner interprets the feedback.

In summary, the behaviorist and cognitive interpretations of feedback differ with respect to what is learned (change in specific behavior versus change in knowledge) and how it is learned (passive and automatic versus active and effortful).

3. Behaviorist and Cognitive Views of Feedback in Instruction

The two views also suggest different instructional prescriptions, as can be seen within the context of three traditional uses of feedback: programmed instruction in academic learning tasks, contingency contracting for classroom management tasks, and drill-and-practice in skill learning tasks.

First, behaviorist and cognitive views of feedback suggest conflicting prescriptions for the design of programmed instruction for academic learning. For example, the behaviorist view holds that programmed instruction should be designed to elicit frequent simple responses that are followed immediately by feedback and are usually correct (Skinner 1968). According to this view, instruction should allow many opportunities for the learner to produce specific responses that are rewarded. On the other hand, cognitive theory holds that students need detailed feedback that will help in the construction of new knowledge and that they learn from receiving negative feedback after an incorrect or incomplete response. In contrast to the prescriptions of behaviorist theory, studies of concept learning demonstrate that making errors is indispensable for learning, concepts are often learned in all-or-none manner rather than gradually, and students actively test hypotheses (Bruner et al. 1956, Trabasso and Bower 1968). For example, the cognitive approach provides the basis for cognitive process instruction, in which beginning students describe their learning and thinking processes for a given task and then receive feedback in the form of descriptions of the corresponding strategies used by successful learners (Lochhead and Clement 1979, Pressley 1990)

Second, behaviorists and cognitivists hold conflicting views of how feedback serves to decrease unwanted behaviors or increase desired behaviors in a classroom management task. For example, in contingency contracting the teacher and student make a formal agreement that if a student engages in a certain specific behavior there will be a specific consequence. According to behaviorist theory, the rate of responding should change gradually when the contingency is put into effect; for example, a disruptive behavior should gradually decrease if it is punished each time it occurs. This prediction conflicts with the finding that when the teacher simply tells a student that the contingency contract is effect, the student's behavior changes immediately, a result that is consistent with the cognitive view of the learner as an active interpreter of information (Sulzbacher and Houser 1968).

Similarly, there is conflict between the behaviorist and cognitive views of how rewards such as verbal praise or awards serve to increase certain desired classroom behaviors. For example, Lepper et al. (1973) rewarded some preschoolers for drawing a picture during their free time; some students (expected reward group) were told they would receive an award if they drew a picture whereas other students were not told in advance that they would receive the award (unexpected reward group). According to behaviorist theory, both groups should increase their rate of drawing activity on subsequent days because both were rewarded. In contrast, the expected reward group showed a decrease in drawing behavior as compared to a control group, whereas the unexpected reward group showed an increase. This pattern is consistent with cognitive theory: the expected reward children could mentally justify their drawing in terms of the reward they expected, whereas the unexpected reward children could only justify their drawing behavior in terms of their enjoyment. The potentially negative effects of rewarding students for doing something they already like to do has been called "the hidden costs of reward" (Lepper and Greene 1978).

Finally, the two views offer different prescriptions concerning the use of feedback for drill-and-practice in skill learning tasks. In conflict with behaviorist theory, presenting detailed feedback about a person's performance—such as how many inches away from a target the learner's response was—results in faster learning than presenting simple feedback about whether or not the response was successful (Trowbridge and Cason 1932, Adams 1968). This pattern is consistent with the cognitive view that the learner uses feedback as information that can be interpreted, so better quality feedback allows for more efficient changes in the learner's knowledge (Mayer 1987). In order to explore the role of feedback within cognitive theory, Brown and Burton (1978) developed a test that can diagnose the incorrect procedure that a student may be using for multicolumn subtraction. For example, one common bug in an otherwise correct subtraction procedure is always to subtract the smaller number from the larger number in each column, such as:

$$\begin{array}{r} 463 \\ -398 \\ \hline 135 \end{array}$$

Feedback concerning the specific bug(s) in a student's procedure can form the basis for individualized computer tutoring systems. For example, a student who makes errors on subtraction problems because of this bug could receive feedback specifying the need to subtract the bottom from the top number rather than the smaller from the larger number in each column.

4. Conclusion

In summary, feedback is a critical component in effective instruction, and its use in education is changing as behaviorist theory gives way to cognitive theory. Educational practice through the 1950s was dominated by the behaviorist view of feedback as a reinforcer that automatically stamps in responses. The result was an emphasis on drill-and-practice in which a teacher asks a question, a student gives an answer (usually one word), and the teacher indicates whether or not the answer was correct. For example, in some high school classrooms teachers asked questions at the rate of two to four or per minute over the course of a 45-minute class period (Cuban 1984).

In contrast, as cognitive theory has dominated psychology since the 1960s, educational practice has begun to reflect new ways of using feedback. When learners are viewed as active processors of information who construct knowledge rather than as response acquisition machines, educators provide feedback about the learner's cognitive processes used to arrive at an answer rather than feedback solely about the answer produced by the learner. In these classrooms, for example, students describe their thought processes for solving a problem, listen to the thought process described by an expert, and then compare what they did to what the expert did. In short, a continuing shift in the educational use of feedback involves emphasizing feedback about process rather than product.

References

Adams J A 1968 Response feedback and learning. *Psych. Bull.* 70:486–504

Brown J S, Burton R R 1978 Diagnostic models for procedural bugs in basic mathematical skills. *Cognit. Sci.* 2(2):155–92

Bruner J S, Goodnow J J, Austin G A 1956 *A Study of Thinking*. Krieger, Huntington, New York

Cuban L 1984 *How Teachers Taught: Constancy and Change in American Classrooms 1890–1980*. Longman, New York

Lepper M R, Greene D 1978 *The Hidden Costs of Reward*. Erlbaum, Hillsdale, New Jersey

Lepper M R, Greene D, Nisbett R E 1973 Undermining children's intrinsic interest with external rewards: A test of the overjustification hypothesis. *J. Pers. Soc. Psychol.* 28:129–37

Lochhead J, Clement (eds.) 1979 *Cognitive Process Instruction: Research on Teaching Thinking Skills*. Franklin Institute Press, Philadelphia

Mayer R E 1982 Learning. In: Mitzel H E (ed.) 1982 *Encyclopedia of Educational Research*, 5th edn. Free Press, New York

Mayer R E 1987 *Educational Psychology: A Cognitive Approach*. Scott, Foresman and Co., New York

Pressley M 1990 *Cognitive Strategy Instruction that Really Improves Children's Academic Performance*. Brookline Books, Cambridge, Massachusetts

Skinner B F 1968 *The Technology of Teaching*. Prentice-Hall, Englewood Cliffs, New Jersey

Sulzbacher S I, Houser J E 1968 A tactic to eliminate disruptive behaviors in the classroom: Group contingent consequences. *American Journal of Mental Deficiency* 73:88–90

Thorndike E L 1913 *Educational Psychology*. Columbia University Press, New York

Trabasso T R, Bower G H 1968 *Attention in Learning: Theory and Research*. Wiley, New York

Trowbridge M H, Cason H 1932 An experimental study of Thorndike's theory of learning. *J. Gen. Psychol.* 7:245–58

Discussion

J. T. Dillon

Through discussion, people join with others to form answers to their questions about what to think and how to act. Discussion is also used to educate children. While discussion is an ancient and essential educative activity, it is rarely practiced in schools. The principal things to learn about discussion are its nature, conduct, and rationale. What is it? How does one do it? Why use it?

1. Nature of Discussion

Discussion is a particular kind of back-and-forth talk wherein group members examine and resolve together some question at issue for them; something they need to understand, appreciate, or decide. It is free and open communal address with mutual exchange and response, as discussants join in thinking and forming together their own ideas, sentiments, and solutions. This is not a common form of discourse in society or in schools. Other contrary forms of discourse are much preferred socially and much more practiced scholastically.

1.1 Terminology

Educators, like most people, use the term discussion in two ways: as a rubric covering all manner of back-and-forth talk or interaction; and as a designator of one distinct form of back-and-forth talk. As a rubric, "discussion" covers talk which is also termed "conversation," "bull session," "debate," "argument," or "recitation." The term is stretched to include interview, negotiation, and even lecture ("I will now discuss ..."). Each of these varieties of talk is denominated by a specific term in addition to the umbrella term of discussion. The second usage of "discussion," is to designate a particular kind of back-and-forth talk. Thus, for example, in the first case talk that is called conversation can also be called discussion. In the second case, there is talk that is called only discussion, there being no other term available by which to call it.

This entry treats discussion in the second usage, a specified form of back-and-forth talk that has no other name and which, accordingly, must be understood from the start not to include recitation, debate, bull session, and the rest. These terms are commonly confused in education and there is no point in trying to define them away by stipulation. The point is to keep clear the thing to which reference is being made. On that score it is easy to distinguish discussion from other forms of interaction in terms of the particular characteristics of talk in discussion, the preconditions of its use, and the intentions of the participants (detailed in Dillon 1988a, c, 1994b). On a loftier plane, the concept of discussion can be finely delineated (Bridges 1979,

Paterson 1970), but less readily seen, touched, or felt. In practice, observers and participants such as students can readily tell when they are in a discussion or when the interaction is something else.

Discussion can be characterized as a form of group interaction wherein members join together in answering a question of common concern, exchanging and examining different views to enhance their understanding, appreciation, or judgment of the matter at issue. Since it is their question and they need a good answer, they want to hear divergent views and are willing to change their view for a better one if it stands up to group scrutiny. These and like sentiments inform the distinctive talk in discussion and make it plainly different from the talk in right-answer recitation, opinion-venting bull sessions, position-defending and victory-seeking debates and arguments, and the aimless wandering and insouciant chatter of conversation. These, rather than discussion, are the predominant forms of interactive talk in classrooms.

1.2 Usage

Discussion is hardly ever heard in classrooms. Teachers may well say that they use discussion a lot, but their self-reports are demonstrably unreliable.

Whereas a high-school English teacher reported discussion to be her most preferred method of teaching, used at least three or four times a week—with recitation specifically her next preference—observation revealed that she used discussion 5 percent of the time and recitation 45 percent (Conner and Chalmers-Neubauer 1989). Although two dozen middle school teachers of various subjects reported using discussion, moreover defining it by contrast to related forms of talk, only seven of them could be observed using discussion; the others used recitation and lecture with question–answer (Alvermann et al. 1990).

Extensive observations of 1,000 elementary and secondary classrooms across the United States have revealed that discussion (i.e., undifferentiated back-and-forth talk) could probably be seen only 4 to 7 percent of the time (Goodlad 1984). Intensive observations of three dozen fifth-grade mathematics and social science classrooms in a United States city have revealed discussion—by specific contrast to recitation, also observed—being used in no more than 3 percent of the instructional episodes (Stodolsky et al. 1981).

1.3 Tradition

No one knows the history of discussion. The tradition is fragile and impossible to trace in any direct or developmental line. Its greatest sources can be savored, however, for they are invoked to sustain modern efforts at discussion.

These earliest sources of discussion start with Socrates in fifth-century BC Greece, in his dialogues as recounted by Plato and Xenophon, as well as the deliberations by Athenians of Socrates' time, recounted in the histories of Thucydides and Xenophon, and in the orations of Demosthenes. Later sources are found in first-century AD Rome and the *Discourses* of Musonius Rufus, and in twelfth-century Paris with the dialectician Peter Abelard in his *Sic et Non*.

The rest of the tradition comes in the main through England and liberal political theory. Francis Bacon in the sixteenth century is significant, less for his famous writings on scientific method than for his quiet practices of deliberation in nascent parliamentary committees. Even more important are John Stuart Mill's manifesto *On Liberty* in 1859, and John Dewey's corpus of writing on group participation in democratic society, as in *Democracy and Education* in 1916.

In the 1930s courses and textbooks on discussion and its practice throughout entire curricula appeared in select United States universities. The Second World War era in the United States and Anglo-Saxon countries saw a vast and intensified aspiration toward discussion as a means of democratic decision-making, or at least involvement, poignantly revealed in books such as *Democracy through Discussion* (Lasker 1949), in innumerable discussion groups, in radio and television panels, in all manner of citizen and community organizations, in book clubs, unions, industry, religion, police, and social work, psychotherapy, and adult education.

Nothing much is known to have happened regarding discussion in schools. However, the intellectual and moral tradition of discussion has been given contemporary impulse by Bridges (1979) in his *Education, Democracy and Discussion*. The background to Bridges' argument takes in the whole of English liberal political democracy, and Dewey as well, with epistemological grounds stretching clearly all the way back to Socrates. Haroutunian-Gordon's (1991) study, *Turning the Soul*, makes a connection between today's United States inner-city schools and Plato, if not Socrates, via teenage discussion of a play by Shakespeare. The field of education continues in this tradition through group efforts to spread discussion among Scottish schools (Francis 1986); through multidisciplinary efforts by United States, Canadian, United Kingdom, and German scholars to understand discussion together (Dillon 1988b); through efforts by Dutch, French, English, Australian, and United States colleagues to understand group deliberation (Dillon 1994a); through anthologies of theory, research, and practice of discussion (Wilen 1990); and through teacher manuals or textbooks on discussion in classrooms (Dillon 1994b).

2. Conduct of Discussion

For a group to engage in discussion, the members must have some topic at issue and they must be disposed to discuss it. Given these two elemental conditions, students of any age can discuss any subject matter in school. They need only a willing teacher to help them do it.

2.1 Subject Matters

The requirement of an issue, or a topic in question, is widely mistaken to exempt from discussion "hard" subject matters like mathematics and science, together with facts in all subjects, including "soft" ones like literature and social studies. However, there are controversial issues in the hard as in the soft subjects, and issues other than controversial ones in all subjects. Moreover, any topic at all can come to issue, including a matter of fact.

In education, one of the grounds for discussing facts and other matters in any subject is that students need to learn and to use them. Students have to identify them, assess, know, and understand them, apply, modify, articulate and communicate them. Students also need to learn the processes surrounding these matters; discerning the fruitful problem formulation, the relevant principle, the apt method, the pertinent data, the alternative solution, the sound conclusion, and the suitable application, not to mention the moral, ethical, and social concerns respecting these. All of these considerations apply not just to the familiar areas such as social studies, but also to the supposedly undiscussable subjects of mathematics (Hoyles 1985), biology (Dreyfus and Lieberman 1981), chemistry (Fasching and Erickson 1985), and genetics (Hendrix et al. 1983).

2.2 Dispositions

Once having a topic at issue the group must further be disposed to discuss it. This disposition comes down to little more than a basic willingness to discuss: a willingness to talk the issue over with others, to listen to other views, to change one's own view, and to form together a better understanding, judgment, or decision in response to the question at hand. Such willingness embraces as a matter of course a number of sentiments including open-mindedness, reasonableness, truthfulness, and respect for other persons (detailed in Bridges 1979). People do not need virtues and excellences in order to discuss, however; all they need is the basic willingness to discuss. Without this basic disposition people cannot engage in discussion; to the extent that they enjoy this disposition, they will engage in discussion.

Skills are also evident in discussion (particularly communication and social skills) as are intelligence, experience, knowledge, and wisdom. Well-developed skills and high accomplishments are required for a highly developed discussion, but they are not essential requirements for discussion. The youngest children in school can talk and listen to one another, can wonder, think, and work together. Far from being a prerequisite

for discussion, skills and accomplishments can be developed through discussion.

2.3 Pedagogy

It is the students who discuss. Accordingly, the teacher's actions must be those that help the students to discuss. The pedagogy of discussion is distinct in behavior and spirit from that of other types of lessons such as recitation.

To lead a classroom discussion the teacher needs to possess fundamental dispositions—intellectual, moral, and democratic sentiments if not commitments—which appear to be unusual and even contrary to predominant pedagogical practices. At very least the teacher has to show a basic willingness to have the class discuss and an aspiration to help it discuss. The teacher's approach in discussion is far less didactic, directive, controlling, and instructional than in the normal teaching situation. It is more suited to a moderator, facilitator, and exemplifier of discussion, who is able to discourage efforts and tendencies that work against discussion.

A teacher's role as discussion leader involves an additional service: helping the students to learn how to discuss at the same time as helping them to discuss the topic in question. It is a hard task, and achieving it is one of the accomplishments of teaching. Yet no teacher is required to be an excellent discussion leader. Willing teachers are only being asked to conduct discussion: to join with students in the basic activity, to do it as well as they can, and to try to do a bit better next time. The discussion they hold may be elementary, but elementary discussions are no less discussion than the most sophisticated ones.

So disposed, the teacher's first act is to prepare the question for discussion. The teacher conceives and carefully formulates the question. He or she then outlines the related and subsidiary questions likely to arise in the course of discussing this question. In the classroom the teacher's first act is to present the question, writing it on the board, and telling the class essential points about it, such as why it is a question for this class now and what its terms mean. Presentation of the question takes two minutes, and it is the sole question the teacher will pose during the class hour. Having posed it, the teacher falls silent to allow the students to begin addressing the question.

As students speak, the teacher acts to maintain and to model discussion, by attentively listening and responding to contributions. Rather than asking questions, the teacher uses a range of nonquestion moves: various statements, signals, silences, and student questions (detailed in Dillon 1988c, 1994b). These prove to enhance discussion processes, whereas teacher questions foil discussion and turn it into some other group talk (Dillon 1985, 1990).

Toward the end of the lesson, or at suitable midpoints, the teacher helps by summarizing the discussion and stating the question that now seems to face the class. As the students gain experience with discussion the teacher helps them to work out the summaries and questions. A new question may then serve for subsequent class activity, the next reading or presentation, or continuing discussion. In that way the question for discussion arises out of the students' previous engagement with the subject matter and gives force and sense to both the ongoing and upcoming engagement.

3. Rationale

Only a conviction of its goodness and centrality as an educative activity would encourage the use of discussion, while powerful pragmatic forces frustrate the move and sometimes even the very idea of its attempt. Of the many things that discourage the use of discussion, only a very few attach to discussion itself. The majority reflect on other matters such as the incapacity of teachers and the antipathy of systemic conditions.

3.1 Reasons Against the Use of Discussion

Discussion has to be learned and both students and teachers must take a long time to learn it. It is time-consuming, uncertain of outcome, and difficult to conduct. Furthermore, critics of discussion claim that it does not cover subject matter content or convey information, it is neither efficient nor effective in producing results, and it is not a step-by-step procedure that can be trained, implemented, and evaluated by checklist.

The incapacity of teachers to engage in discussions consists of a lack of experience and know-how, but above all a lack of disposition to hold discussions in their classes. Teachers might not have a strong sentiment of inquiry, interest in student thinking, trust of group process, nor indeed democratic attitudes generally and in particular toward knowledge and authority. They may be worried about the waste of time in discussion (of "not getting anywhere"), the curriculum material not being covered, the topic not being closed, the immaturity and incorrectness of student opinion, the rise of conflict and emotion, the loss of authority and control over the whole process. They may be left with the debilitating sense that they do not even seem to be teaching when using discussion. These are powerful reasons against using discussion.

Even more powerful are systemic conditions in school and society, in which not much discussion can be seen nor much room where it might fit in. Predominant features of schooling offer no support of efforts to discuss, and moreover they actively support practices contrary to discussion. Social norms and practices make discussion foreign to everyday life and experience as well as to education. These norms and practices emphasize individual over group, privacy of thought and pursuit over public participation, authority instead of inquiry, and policy over community as source of knowledge and decision. The pattern of discourse is chatter, conversation, assertion, persuasion, and deception, by contrast to disciplined concert of reason, analysis, and evidence. An entire mind-set regards the essence of things to be their effectiveness or payoff in results, products, and outcomes. In face of systemic antipathies all around, discussion understandably keeps a low profile.

3.2 Reasons for the Use of Discussion

Through discussion things are learned and processes enhanced. Students acquire the subject matter in question, gain greater knowledge and understanding, and are able to make judgments regarding it. Through discussion, students also learn how to discuss. Above all they learn democratic attitudes and behaviors, such as befit group deliberation in a democratic polity and intellectual inquiry in a free society of thought and action. Thus, the considerations in favor of discussion count not just products but also processes, and not just intellectual processes but also attitudinal and behavioral ones. Discussion enhances cognitive, affective, and communicative processes as well as the group's collaborative, constructive, and deliberative powers.

Yet none of these considerations is primary. All of them might be construed to refer to discussion in its instrumentality, as if it were a technique competing with others in the gimmickry of efficient production of outcomes. Discussion is a fundamental educative activity in itself. People discuss for community and inquiry in the lived moment as well as for participation with others in communal reflection, discovery, and decision. This is the ancient usage of discussion, which inspires people to discover together through discussion what is right and true and then to act on it.

4. Conclusion

Rather than demonstrate or vindicate discussion by its outcomes or effectiveness, researchers might better describe and promote its good use. Studies might describe not just the processes of discussion, but also the conditions of its use and success. Knowledge is needed of what discussion looks like when it is going well in a classroom and when it is not. Thoughtful writings that exhort, persuade, and provide motivation to action, to the right use of discussion, and to perseverance in its practice are also needed.

For willing practitioners, the one recommendation is to practice discussion. Through study, observation, participation, and reflection practitioners can learn much about discussion. Thereafter, it is a matter of long and faithful trying.

See also: Group Dynamics

References

Alvermann D E, O'Brien D G, Dillon D R 1990 What teachers do when they say they're having discussions of content area reading assignments. *Read. Res. Q.* 25: 296–322

Bridges D 1979 *Education, Democracy and Discussion.* NFER, Slough

Conner J, Chalmers-Neubauer I 1989 Mrs Schuster adopts discussion. *English Education* 21: 30–38

Dillon J T 1985 Using questions to foil discussion. *Teaching and Teacher Education* 1: 109–21

Dillon J T 1988a Discussion vs. recitation. *Tennessee Educational Leadership* 15: 52–64

Dillon J T (ed.) 1988b *Questioning and Discussion: A Multidisciplinary Study.* Ablex, Norwood, New Jersey

Dillon J T 1988c *Questioning and Teaching: A Manual of Practice.* Croom Helm, London

Dillon J T 1990 *The Practice of Questioning.* Routledge, London

Dillon J T (ed.) 1994a *Deliberation in Education and Society.* Ablex, Norwood, New Jersey

Dillon J T 1994b *Using Discussion in Classrooms.* Open University Press, Buckingham

Dreyfus A, Lieberman R 1981 Perceptions, expectations and interactions: The essential ingredients for a genuine classroom discussion. *Journal of Biological Education* 15(2): 153–57

Fasching J, Erickson B 1985 Group discussions in the chemistry classroom and the problem-solving skills of students. *Journal of Chemical Education* 62(10): 842–46

Francis E 1986 *Learning to Discuss.* Scottish Curriculum Development Service, Edinburgh

Goodlad J T 1984 *A Place Called School.* McGraw-Hill, New York

Haroutunian-Gordon S 1991 *Turning the Soul: Teaching Through Conversation in the High School.* University of Chicago, Chicago, Illinois

Hendrix J, Mertens T, Smith J 1983 Facilitating effective small group discussions of controversial issues. *Journal of College Science Teaching* 13: 21–25

Hoyles C 1985 What is the point of group discussion in mathematics? *Educ. Stud. Math.* 16(2): 205–14

Lasker B 1949 *Democracy through Discussion.* Wilson, New York

Paterson R K 1970 The concept of discussion: A philosophical approach. *Stud. Adult Educ.* 2(1): 28–50

Stodolsky S, Ferguson T, Wimpelberg K 1981 The recitation persists, but what does it look like? *J Curric. Stud.* 13(2): 121–30

Wilen W (ed.) 1990 *Teaching and Learning through Discussion: The Theory, Research and Practice of the Discussion Method.* Thomas, Springfield, Illinois

Teaching in Small Groups

S. Sharan

When the classroom is subdivided into a number of small groups that serve as the social units in which learning is pursued, the role of the teacher differs considerably from that typical of the traditional classroom. While various cooperative small-group learning methods make somewhat different demands on teachers, the fact that students' attention in all of these methods is to be focused on their group mates with whom they interact and not on the teacher, results in a host of consequences for teachers' instructional behavior. Furthermore, introduction into a classroom of an alternative instructional method that diverges from the teaching patterns generally practiced by most other teachers has many school-wide implications for teachers' instructional behavior: decisions about curriculum, the nature of their relationship with colleagues, and the school's policy and administration (Sarason 1982, 1990, Sharan and Sharan 1991). These changes in instructional behavior and teachers' relationships with colleagues may not be identical for all small-group teaching methods. Nevertheless, the differences in teachers' behavior required by the different group-learning methods are probably more a matter of degree than of essence.

For purposes of discussion, the teacher's role in the Group Investigation method (Sharan and Sharan 1992) will be explored as an example of what teachers must consider when implementing cooperative learning in small groups. A short description of the Group Investigation method precedes the discussion of the teacher's role.

1.1 The Group Investigation Method

Small-group instructional methods most often seek to embody a set of theoretical principles derived from a basic philosophical, psychological, or sociological orientation toward the educational process. They are not merely collections of practical procedures. Group Investigation embodies the principles of Dewey's (1938) view of school learning as an investigatory process conducted in collaboration with one's peers. Students plan together what they will study about problems they have identified that invite genuine inquiry (Miel 1952, Thelen 1954, 1981).

The Group Investigation method can be conceived as a sequence of six stages. First, after the teacher presents a general problem for investigation, the class determines subtopics for study and organizes into research groups. Students probe a variety of sources, propose questions, and sort them into categories that serve as topics of investigation for study groups.

Second, groups plan their investigations cooperatively in terms of what they will study, how they will proceed, where they will seek information, and how they will divide the work among themselves.

In the third stage, groups carry out their inves-

Table 1
Five dimensions of classroom instruction

Dimension	Whole-Class	Group Investigation
Behavior of teachers	Sole determiner of study materials, tasks, pace of instruction, criteria for evaluation	Guide students, respond to their initiatives, involve them in planning and decision-making.
Tasks	Uniform for entire class. Products are predetermined	Students choose subtopics and learning activities. Final products unspecified. Tasks foster cooperation among members of small groups.
Behavior of students	Obey instructions, play passive role in determining study tasks and methods	Ask questions, plan, initiate activities. High involvement in learning. Make decisions about various aspects of classroom life.
Physical setting	Permanent, appropriate for one teaching method only	Flexible structure that changes with the nature of the tasks, methods, students' needs.
Communication	Unilateral or bilateral, subject to teacher's mediation	Multilateral among members of groups or between groups.

tigations. They organize and analyze their findings, exchange and clarify ideas through discussion, reach conclusions, and integrate their work into a group product.

Fourth, groups plan their presentations, avoiding lengthy lectures, and seeking interactive methods of presentation such as exhibitions, role-plays, simulations, experiments, learning stations, dramatizations, and demonstrations. A group's presentation must be coordinated with those of other groups in the classroom.

At the fifth stage, groups make their presentations. The audience not only participates but also evaluates presentations.

Finally, group products and individual learning are evaluated. Evaluations can involve students as well as teachers.

2. Five Dimensions of Classroom Teaching: Whole-class and Cooperative-learning Classes Compared

With the emphasis clearly on groups of students and students as both teachers and learners, a key question emerges: What is the role of the teacher in the successful implementation of the Group Investigation method?

One approach to examining the role of the teacher is by viewing classroom instruction as consisting of five dimensions to which teachers must attend in order to implement instruction effectively. These five dimensions and their implications for the behavior of teachers and students in the traditional whole-class and small-group classrooms appear in Table 1. As shown in Table 1, the teacher's behavior in the cooperative small-group classroom conducted with the Group In-

vestigation method differs in many ways from what teachers do in the traditional classroom.

2.1 The Teacher's Control Function

First and foremost, in the Group Investigation method the small groups become the center of learning activity through peer interaction, verbal and nonverbal. The teacher must relinquish center stage and transfer some degree of control to the small groups. This control refers to the interpersonal interaction that occurs in the group (i.e., the discussion and exchange of plans, ideas, suggestions, and observations), as well as the management of the group's work through such techniques as role differentiation within the group (e.g., chairperson, recorder, and resource person) or various forms of division of labor relevant to the content of the group's task. Teacher-centered control is not compatible with free exchange of ideas among students, as is well-known from studies of human organization in general. Indeed, teachers who implement cooperative learning in small groups become less concerned with their control function than those who prefer the traditional whole-class form of instruction (Sharan and Hertz-Lazarowitz 1982).

Furthermore, teachers take their cues, in terms of the pace of learning as well as the identification of specific learning tasks, from the progress of the groups. Teachers counsel the groups and help them overcome problems that crop up during the course of their work, both in respect to the study materials as well as in respect to the students' relationships within the groups. Teachers try to encourage students to pursue avenues of study of which students become aware as they pursue their work, thereby taking advantage of the students' initiative and self-motivation. This role differs markedly from the lock-step pace of instruction typical of whole-class teaching.

2.2 Teachers and Students as Curricular Decision-makers: The Design of the Learning Task

Students must be convinced that the teacher has in fact empowered them to make a wide range of decisions regarding the selection of learning tasks and the nature of the process of investigation. Since teachers are typically the sole determiners of such decisions, students are unlikely to engage in these activities freely until they have tested the teacher and discovered that they have the legitimate right to make and carry out their decisions.

When students are given a genuine role in determining some aspects of the content of learning tasks, a much wider range of possible topics for study is likely to emerge. Moreover, student choice in selecting or identifying desirable topics of study can evoke a wider range of abilities and talents than might be called upon by learning activities set exclusively by the teacher, even when the teacher determines the general domain of the students' investigation on the basis of the school's curriculum. When student choice is permitted or encouraged, the teacher must plan carefully, particularly in terms of the variety of resources that should be made available to the students (Cohen 1986, Sharan and Sharan 1992).

The curricular and behavioral diversity supported by the small-group approaches to classroom learning implies a distinct departure from the uniformity in curricular content and learning activities inherent in traditional instruction. The expectation that all students in the class must study the same material at the same pace and that they should all reach the same educational outcomes is one of the bedrock assumptions of public education in general and of secondary school education in particular. It is precisely this concern for uniformity that is a major impediment to effective instruction in culturally and ethnically heterogeneous classrooms.

Finally, teachers in the small-group classroom must design the learning task to facilitate cooperation and mutual assistance among members of small groups so they have a common goal and purpose for working together. The task must also invite a variety of perspectives or approaches, and not demand simple informational solutions which are easily available in the textbook. Multifaceted and open-ended tasks of this nature encourage participation by many students who can contribute their unique resources to their group's project. Teachers are asked to become aware of these task-design features that are a necessary prerequisite for group-centered learning (Cohen 1986, Sharan and Sharan 1992). If the task does not enable students to cooperate with one another and to perceive their group as a productive arena for achieving academic goals, the group is likely to disintegrate into a collection of individuals working toward uncoordinated goals.

2.3 Students' Role in Seeking Information

Another fundamental feature of the teacher's role in the small-group classroom is the orientation of students toward an investigatory approach to learning rather than the ingestive mode that prevails in most schooling. Such an orientation can be as foreign to the students as it is to teachers. Seeking information to generate ideas and knowledge is a distinctly different form of learning than being told the information, performing various exercises with the information, and then being tested on it. It cannot be assumed that students will know how to participate effectively in the work of a small group. Teachers are advised to provide students with some experience with interactive skills before asking them to function in task-oriented groups (Cohen, 1986, Graves and Graves 1985, Schmuck and Schmuck 1992).

In traditional instruction, the teacher most often asks the questions that students are expected to answer. In small-group instruction, the students' work is directed by the questions they themselves have asked about the subject in hand. The teacher's role is to encourage students to ask questions that can direct their study, to help groups plan and carry out projects that involve the search for and use of information about academic topics. Thus, the change in the teacher's role can be realized only if a parallel change occurs in the manner in which students are expected to behave during the pursuit of learning.

In sum, then, successful learning in small groups entails basic changes in classroom behavioral norms. Students must come to understand that they are expected to help one another in achieving group and individual goals, and realize that teachers value high-quality group products.

2.4 Classroom Organization to Support Student Interaction

Classroom organization must be adapted to the specific needs of the learning tasks and afford opportunities for effective interaction among students. Therefore, classroom organization may undergo changes even during the course of a single lesson as a function of changes in the students' stage of learning activity. Small-group instruction requires flexibility in organizing seating patterns, setting aside corners of the classroom for holding meetings, and preparing other spaces in or out of the classroom where various activities can be conducted by small groups of students engaged in group investigation projects. In small-group instruction, the teacher assumes the role of classroom organizational manager, a role he or she may not be called upon to perform in the traditional classroom where the structure of the classroom remains uniform throughout the year (Sharan 1994).

2.5 The Teacher as Manager of Classroom Communication

Finally, teachers must alter their patterns of communication with students if the small groups are to function effectively. Teachers may have to unlearn many skills and habits they acquired as part of their experience with traditional instruction in terms of how they address the class (Hertz-Lazarowitz and Shachar 1990). The verbal expository mode of information transfer and questioning which involves mainly unilateral or bilateral channels of speech must be replaced by group-centered multilateral patterns of communication. When this change is made, students can engage in productive talk and not be inhibited or intimidated by the teacher's dominant role (Shachar and Sharan 1994).

Another salient aspect of classroom communication that needs to be revised to fit the needs of small-group instruction is the asking of questions. Stimulating students to ask questions about what and how to study subject matter instead of subjecting them to perpetual interrogation is an important feature of small-group instruction, yet doing so may run counter to much of what teachers are taught during their professional education. Indeed, texts on teaching focus on teachers' questions as one of the primary instruments of instruction. These texts fail to deal extensively with ways in which teachers can stimulate and encourage students to ask most of the questions. This omission is tragic, since it is the students' curiosity that must be engaged if they are truly to learn.

3. Teachers as Observers

Most authors of books on small-group instruction urge teachers to stand aside on occasion and observe how the groups in their classroom are functioning. Several texts provide extensive lists of categories teachers can use to direct their observations in order to note if students in fact are cooperating and interacting in a constructive fashion (Cohen 1986, Johnson and Johnson 1987).

Teachers can employ the five-category system presented in Table 1 as an observation schedule to ascertain the extent to which group learning with the Group Investigation method is being implemented appropriately in their classrooms. Do the procedures now in use approximate the descriptions in the "Whole Class" column or the "Group Investigation" column? If they are more similar to the "Whole Class", the probability is that a large number of students find themselves excluded from the process of learning. If the procedures in use are more similar to those appearing in the "Group Investigation" column, the likelihood is that students are interacting with one another in positive ways and are actively involved in the process of learning.

It should be noted that the effective implementation of small-group methods in general and the Group Investigation method in particular requires that all five components set forth in Table 1 be implemented in a coordinated fashion. If one component is omitted

or implemented as if the class was being taught with the whole-class approach, the net result will be faulty implementation that can disrupt the learning process and result in frustration for both students and teachers. To be effective, teachers must plan for the appropriate use of all five dimensions simultaneously.

In many classrooms one can observe that the teacher has organized students into small groups sitting around tables, but the lesson is delivered in the typical presentation–recitation format. Similarly, teachers provide small groups with learning tasks directed at individual students that require individual work. The groups have no collective task at all, or the task is so routine that no real group effort is required, such as seeking answers to questions of simple fact (who, what, where, when, and how?). The net result is that the students sitting around the table do not really form a group since there is no constructive interaction between them.

4. The Teacher, the School, and the Classroom

Discussions of the teacher's role as a classroom instructor should treat the issue of the teacher's relationship with the school administration and with colleagues on the teaching staff of the school as a whole. The school as an organization, with its instructional policy (explicit or implicit) and its expected patterns of relationships among teachers and administrators, exerts considerable, sometimes decisive, influence on teachers' instructional roles as they are carried out in practice, or portrayed in various public pronouncements. The effects of school-wide factors on individual teacher's classroom instruction is often made particularly palpable when teachers seek to implement alternative teaching methods such as small-group instruction or cooperative learning. Since small-group instruction diverges from traditional patterns of instruction, its implementation requires a multitude of adjustments by teachers both in attitude and instructional practices that may conflict with the normative practices of the school as a whole (Sharan 1994).

Cooperative small-group instruction often diverges from the school's standard instructional policy, from fundamental attitudes held by teachers, or both. Topics on which cooperative small-group instruction typically diverges from the norms accepted in traditionally organized schools include the following:

(a) All students in the class are expected to master all of the material in given units of study. These expectations relate to uniformity in the pace and scope of learning.

(b) The pace and scope of instruction is often monitored in various ways by school authorities, usually through testing programs to evaluate achievement levels. The tests are standardized and not criterion referenced (that is, not based on what students have studied in specific classrooms).

(c) Implementation of group projects on occasion may entail the extension of class time. Such extensions require coordination of class schedules with other teachers. These projects may also entail students' visits to sites outside the school for purposes of direct observation, conducting interviews with various experts, and the like. Schoolwide scheduling exerts powerful constraints on a teacher's ability to employ alternative instructional methods in the classroom.

(d) If many teachers in a school continue to employ traditional whole-class forms of instruction, teachers seeking to use cooperative small-group approaches may experience some conflict with colleagues. Teachers become concerned with students' expectations and patterns of behavior as they move through the grades in a given school when the students are exposed to distinctly different instructional methods. In such cases, it becomes necessary to negotiate with colleagues and to determine school policy on the subject of instructional methods across the grades.

Given the fact that learning tasks appropriate for small-group instruction must be designed differently from the kinds of tasks generally provided by the curriculum, teachers interested in implementing cooperative small-group methods are often called upon to prepare portions of the curriculum on their own. Often, teacher preparation time in school is very limited. Also, teachers need the collaboration and assistance of colleagues to generate group-centered curricula that challenge groups of students and arouse their genuine curiosity and interest. Thus, preparation of suitable study materials for small-group teaching must become the concern of the school's administration, and cannot be left to the initiative or responsibility of the individual teacher.

Finally, to effect the successful implementation of significant innovation in instruction, teachers must participate in an ongoing process of problem-solving, negotiation, and decision-making on topics relevant to classroom teaching in all of its manifestations, not just in terms of its immediate implications for a given classroom or subject. Teachers may not be prepared by their professional education and experience to assume responsibility for organizational decision-making. Moreover, this role may not even be perceived as a legitimate component of the teacher's professional duties. There is a growing awareness on the part of educators that a significant change in teachers' professional role is a prerequisite for affecting the practice of instruction in the classroom (Darling-Hammond 1988, Murphy 1991, Sarason 1990).

See also: Cooperative Learning; Social Psychological Theories of Teaching; Grouping Students in the Classroom

References

Cohen E 1986 *Designing Groupwork*. Teachers College Press, New York
Darling-Hammond L 1988 Policy and professionalism. In: Lieberman A (ed.) *Building a Professional Culture in Schools*. Teachers College Press, New York
Dewey J 1938 *Experience and Education*. Macmillan, New York
Graves N, Graves T 1985 Creating a cooperative learning environment: An ecological approach. In: Slavin S et al. (eds.) 1985 *Learning to Cooperate, Cooperating to Learn*. Plenum Press, New York
Hertz-Lazarowitz R, Shachar H 1990 Teachers' verbal behavior in cooperative and whole class instruction. In: Sharan S (ed.) 1990 *Cooperative Learning: Theory and Research*. Praeger, New York
Johnson D, Johnson R 1987 *Learning Together and Alone*, 2nd edn. Prentice-Hall, Englewood Cliffs, New Jersey
Miel A 1952 *Cooperative Procedures in Learning*. Teachers College Press, New York
Murphy J 1991 *Restructuring Schools*. Teachers College Press, New York
Sarason S 1982 *The Culture of the School and the Problem of Change*, 2nd edn. Allyn and Bacon, Boston, Massachusetts
Sarason S 1990 *The Predictable Failure of Educational Reform*. Jossey-Bass, San Francisco, California
Shachar H, Sharan S 1994 Talking, relating and achieving: Effects of cooperative learning and whole class instruction. *Cognition and Instruction* 12(4)
Sharan S (ed.) 1994 *Handbook of Cooperative Learning Methods*. Greenwood Press, Westport, Connecticut
Schmuck R, Schmuck P 1992 *Group Processes in the Classroom*, 6th edn. Brown, Dubuque, Iowa
Sharan S, Hertz-Lazarowitz R 1982 Effects of an instructional change project on teachers' behavior, attitudes and perceptions. *Journal of Applied Behavioral Science* 18: 185–201
Sharan S, Sharan Y 1991 Changing instructional methods and the culture of the school. In: Wyner N (ed.) 1991 *Current Perspectives on School Culture*. Brookline Books, Cambridge, Massachusetts
Sharan Y, Sharan S 1992 *Expanding Cooperative Learning Through Group Investigation*. Teachers College Press, New York
Thelen H 1954 *Dynamics of Groups at Work*. University of Chicago Press, Chicago, Illinois
Thelen H 1981 *The Classroom Society*. Croom-Helm, London

Simulations and Games

A. L. Cudworth

In 1894 the British playwright and novelist Oscar Wilde wrote:

Education is an admirable thing
But it is well to remember
That nothing that is worth knowing
can be taught.

The view expressed here is one shared by many who use games and simulations in their learning programs. Often the most forceful learning situation is real-life experience, particularly when someone makes a wrong decision and is left to pay the consequences. Experiential learning is all about providing opportunities for participants to make decisions (good and bad) and allowing them to experience the results of those decisions in a protected environment. Games and simulations contribute enormously to this philosophy and often provide the vehicle by which the experience can be gained.

Games and simulations have long been used and many authors have contributed to the body of knowledge that is now available. While it is impossible in this entry to identify all of those authors, the works of Elgood (1981), Greenblat (1990), and Jones (1985, 1988, 1989) should be consulted by those beginning their study of the field.

1. Definition of Simulations

Although defining simulations and games is not easy, several definitions exist. Jones's (1980) definition contrasts simulations with case studies: "In case studies participants are on the outside examining the documents and forming conclusions whilst in the simulation they are taking part and making decisions." This participation element of simulations is supported by Adams (1973), who asserts that "simulation games are an action-oriented, participant centered educational alternative to aid learning in an atmosphere of openness" (p. 1). He further suggests that "in making decisions and taking actions himself, even if only in a game, the student has to recall the ideas and relationships that are part of the simulation structure and previous experience."

According to Boocock and Schild (1968), the major difference between simulation games and other educational innovations such as programmed learning is that the latter "refer to individual relationships between student and subject and there is no interaction between the participants." The authors above all suggest that in gaming and simulation there must be an element

of participation by the student, but only in Schild's definition do the words "interaction between" appear. This is an important point, for in real-life situations it is rare for decisions not to affect other parties—professional work is rarely conducted in isolation.

An abstract definition of a simulation is given by Barton (1970): "The dynamic execution or manipulation of a model of an object system for some purpose." This definition is echoed by Livingston and Stoll (1973): "A simulation is a working model of an object situation whilst games are activities with goals and rules." Finally, Gibbs (1974) suggested that "a simulation is a dynamic representation which employs substitute elements to replace real or hypothetical components."

Perhaps the nature of a simulation exercise is best explained by Tansey (1971). Tansey suggested that

simulation takes those who take part out of the role of spectator and moves them into the role of players. It need not be concerned with here and now, but can transport the participant to the past or future. It can make time fly so that the action which, in a simulation, takes an hour, can represent a week, a month, a year in real time. It can make time slow down or pass normally. It can change a player from what he is to what he might be. It can make him examine his attitudes and those of others. It transforms the concept of learning because this learning takes place because it is necessary *at the time*.

2. Nature of Educational Simulations

Jones (1980) suggested that a simulation should have three parts: briefing, action, and debriefing. The briefing enables the tutor to distribute all the basic information that students require and which is essential for the simulation (including any reports, maps, plans, legal documents, administrative procedures or instructions). During the briefing session the tutor should explain clearly the aims and objectives of the exercise together with the roles, duties, and responsibilities of those taking part. It is vital that all those taking part understand why they are doing the exercise and what they are expected to do. The tutor must also explain all the procedures of the exercise, the time limits, and what resources are available for the participants to use.

During the action the tutor observes the behavior and the communication between the participants (or between those playing different roles) and notes important points for later feedback sessions. In some instances students may be used as observers, reporting back later to tutors.

Debriefing often requires a change of role for the

tutor. Specifically, the tutor often plays a far more active role, asking questions, discussing decisions, and assessing participants' affective skills. This form of debriefing is called "formative assessment" and tends to concentrate on the practical skills of the participants rather than theoretical matters. It is not suggested here that the cognitive skills are totally ignored, but in undertaking simulation techniques the real value lies in carrying out certain tasks rather than answering theoretical questions. The importance of feedback and debriefing sessions cannot be overemphasized and is summed up by Taylor and Walford (1978): "The experience gained during the simulation, game, or simulation/game, needs to be capitalized upon the focussed into consciousness or else time spent on the experience will have been largely wasted."

3. Advantages and Disadvantages of Simulations

A simulation is self-motivating. In many cases students work as part of a team, learning from each other and practicing cooperative skills. It has been suggested that simulations enable the less successful student to learn from the more successful (Livingston and Stoll 1973). Abt (1968), on the other hand, warned of the effect that simulations may have in discouraging the slow learner; the effect of "dramatizing student inequalities whilst feeding the conceit of the skillful."

A simulation places students in a certain situation in which there are many alternative courses of action open to them. The use of role-playing techniques not only places the participant in a certain situation, but also identifies their obligations and responsibilities. Simulations provide participants with opportunities to reflect upon the consequences of their actions without the responsibility they would carry in the real world. Many of the consequences of these actions can be discussed during the debriefing or feedback sessions. During these sessions, students are made aware not only of the consequences of their courses of action, but also of the consequences of other courses of action that were open to them. The effect of their decisions on other students in the simulation and on any third parties can also be made clear to them during discussions.

A further advantage is evident when group work is involved. The opportunity to interact with other students who are perhaps playing other roles helps to develop and practice better communication.

4. Definition of Games and Gaming

Gibbs (1974) suggested that a game "is an activity which is carried out by cooperating or competing decision makers seeking to achieve their objectives within a framework of rules." Likewise, Short (1977) defined games as "procedures in which participants play for

payoffs in ways which are permitted by the rules." Livingston and Stoll (1973) suggested that a game is an activity with rules. They further contended that a simulation/game is one that is intended to represent some other situation; whereas an instructional game is intended for teaching a subject or skill. A management game is "an exercise in which the management situation is simulated, usually by means of a mathematical model. The situation is one demanding decision-making on the part of the players. . . . The management game tries to eliminate the risks associated with past decisions and considerably reduce the delay between taking a decision, implementing it and realizing the effects in practice" (Speed and Harris 1977).

From the many definitions of games available there appears to be a number of similar components which are important for those definitions. First, the game must be designed for a particular purpose and must seek to achieve definite objectives, such as teamwork, practice in professional procedures, developing improved communications, or specific management objectives. In many cases it is advisable to inform the students of the objectives. This information may avoid further confusion at a later date.

Second, there must be a clear set of rules. The more basic rules and the fewer rules there are, the better.

Third, gaming is "ongoing" in that students have to make decisions and abide by the rules. In return they receive "payoffs," valued according to their success at making the correct decisions. The students influence the course of events by their decisions and in so doing may affect the success not only of their own involvement in the particular exercise but also of the other players. Without active participants there would be no game.

For a game to be a success there is a need to reward sound judgment and penalize poor judgment. It is also necessary for students to see successes and failures in order to stimulate their concentration. Games should be played in a competitive atmosphere; there usually is a need to provide a winner. Payoffs can be in the form of money, points, sales, or promotions.

Not all successful payoffs are related to sound judgment. In many games payoffs are made in relation to a chance element, such as the throw of a dice or by choosing a card. Chance is a perfectly acceptable component in gaming and it is often easier to make payoffs related to it rather than sound judgment.

5. Nature of Educational Games

Abt (1968) suggested that educational games can be classified according to whether they emphasize skill, reality, or fantasy as well as according to whether they are strategic or "showdown" games. There is a danger in game design that too much emphasis will be placed upon the chance element, resulting in Adams's (1973) contention that "if the game only requires people to throw dice and move tokens—then that is all they will learn."

Short (1977) argued that games can serve a variety of purposes:

Traditional games, even without external reference of their content, appear to exercise perceptual and motor skills, plan making, decision making, respect for constraints imposed both by rules and by decisions of others, appreciation of complex or changing situations, and realistic self assessment. All of these would appear to be desirable in the education of most professional students. In most educational games the designer also imports into the world of the game real world subject matter and problems which allow the reinforcement of specific knowledge, attitudes and skills. A case will be advanced that games also permit a distinctively more rich structuring of learned material in which learners can be stimulated to reason not only forwards from cause to effects, but also back from effects to probable causes. This is of special interest in early undergraduate medical training.

The effect of gaming on participants seems to vary according to a person's sensitivity and personal involvement. In this regard, Radley (1978) said that "some students not enjoy gaming and disturbed by it whilst others that participating in a game their knowledge . . . improved and they had a greater understanding of group behavior through learning how to analyze and act upon the receipt of informative data." Thus the tutor needs to choose a strategy that seems to be the best for a particular situation. It should be pointed out, however, that participants may prefer other techniques or strategies and may not understand or fully benefit from the tutor's choice of technique. There is therefore a need to carry out research and experiment with new or alternative teaching strategies.

One particular reservation is "whether games should entertain as well as educate." Abt (1968) argued for the educational value of educational games. Livingston and Stoll (1973), however, attested to the entertainment value of educational games: "the key characteristics of games for learning is their ability to motivate students—games are fun partly because they have an element of surprise and partly because they give rise to joking and banter among the players." Holt (1970), in a critical analysis of traditional teaching methods, highlighted the importance of encouraging freedom of mind in children to explore alternative solutions. This freedom in an atmosphere of excitement and the unknown often adds to the quality of the work undertaken.

6. Assessment of Experimental Learning Techniques

The assessment of simulations and games can take a number of forms. A measure of success can be seen from the total payoffs received, such as profit, sales, promotion, or an alternative "game currency." These payoffs, however, constitute only a small part of what needs to be assessed.

The methods used to assess other objectives are similar to the observations suggested for evaluating simulations. Whatever methods are used, it is important to assess the contribution made by "chance" to a particular exercise and for the players to be made aware of that contribution. Feedback and discussion sessions, either on a group or individual basis, are vital to the success of any game or simulation.

The contribution of games and simulations to the general intellectual development of the student must also be observed and recorded. Many students believe that important issues in reality are clear cut, easily identified, and can be seen as "black and white." In practice, this is not the case. Thus, normal student development entails a move from this position to a more relativistic position as described by Perry (1970):

the student after a period recognizes some kinds of knowledge as *Contextual*. That is, the answers depend on so many circumstances that individual judgements have to be made in each context . . . *Later on* the student discovers that more and more of the knowledge he previously considered to be Absolute is in fact Contextual. The student then comes to recognize that the personality; attitudes and skills appropriate in a relativistic world are different from those sustained by a simple belief in certainty.

7. Future Developments in Gaming and Simulation

Three key issues are likely to dominate future developments in gaming and simulation. They are cross-cultural games and simulations, computer games and simulations, and real-time games.

7.1 Cross-cultural Games and Simulations

A great deal of interest has been shown in the area of cross-cultural games and simulations and exercises in cross-cultural communication. For example, Project IDEALS aims to provide American International students in United States universities with opportunities for developing cross-cultural communication skills and international understanding.

7.2 Computer Games and Simulations

The use of computers in gaming and simulation is now vast. The computer has provided a new dimension to gaming and simulation and these activities are becoming more and more complex. There is a danger in any computer simulation that the participants may only become adept at pressing the keyboard rather than experiencing an increase in technical knowledge and understanding. One innovative simulation/game is "Ghosts in the Machine" by British designers Alan Coote and Clive Loveluck.

The simulation concentrates on the design of computer simulations and is a departure from traditional formats. Conference papers from societies such as the Association of Business Simulations and Experiential Learning (ABSEL), International Simulation and Gaming Association (ISAGA), and the Society for Computer

Simulations provide useful information on the topic of computer games and simulations.

7.3 Real-time Games

It is a distinguishing characteristic of "real time" as an endogenous variable in the structure of games involving decision-making that game time is continuously elapsing in a constant ratio to real time. The determination of that ratio is the responsibility of the game designer/administrator and is, therefore, an exogenous variable. Only under this condition does the timing of decisions become a genuine option in the decision maker's range of alternatives, and games become models of dynamics rather than comparative statics.

One attempt at producing a "real-time" game is Project Proteus, developed at the Manchester Business School (Gunz 1988). Proteus operates in simulated real time. As in real life, the "managers" of the simulated company can implement decisions by doing something or by leaving things alone: either way, the organization carries on.

Another example is that of FLEXIGAME (Loveluck 1988). In this game, decisions are made on price, advertising, and sales promotion at the start of the game. Time then runs continuously at a controllable rate and participants need make no decisions until they wish to. All results—and market shares—are displayed graphically on a continuous basis. Again, allowing the participant to choose when to make decisions—as well as which decisions—fulfills a characteristic of endogenous time: timing becomes a decision in its own right.

One thing is clear: the optimum method of introducing time "consumption" as a strategic variable in games will involve the development of games designed to be played in "real time." As currently developed, games use time in the sense of comparative statics, rather than as a genuine dynamic variable. Thus, time is used in an exogenous way (a variable controlled by the game designer or administrator) rather than as an endogenous variable (a variable that extends the decision maker's options in implementing strategy). To reflect contemporary management practice, time must be introduced into game construction as an endogenous variable. "Real-time" games (which will involve the formulation of multiuser computer models) must be developed into which time compression and consumption are made specific decision alternatives.

See also: Learning Environments

References

Abt C C 1968 *Games for learning*. In: Boocock S S, Schild E O (eds.) 1968 *Simulation and Games in Learning*. Sage, London

Adams D M 1973 *Simulation Games—An Approach to Learning*. Jones Publications, Washington, Ohio

Barton R F 1970 *A Primer on Simulations and Gaming*. Prentice-Hall, Englewood Cliffs, New Jersey

Boocock S S, Schild E O 1968 *Simulation and Games in Learning*. Sage, London

Elgood C 1981 *Handbook of Management Games*. Gower, Aldershot

Gibbs G I 1974 *Handbook of Game and Simulation Exercises*. Spon, London

Greenblat C 1988 *Designing Games and Simulations*. Sage, London.

Gunz H 1988 PROTEUS. *Perspectives on Gaming Simulation 13*. Sagset, Loughborough

Holt J 1970 *How Children Learn*. Penguin, Harmondsworth

Jones K 1980 *Simulation: A Handbook for Teachers*. Kogan Page, London

Jones K 1985 *Designing your own Simulations*. Methuen, London

Jones K 1988 *Interactive Learning Events: A Guide for Facilitators*. Kogan Page, London

Jones K 1989 *A Sourcebook of Management Simulations*. Kogan Page, London

Livingston S A, Stoll C S 1975 *Simulation Games: An Introduction for the Social Studies Teacher*. Free Press, London

Loveluck C 1988 FLEXIGAME. Mitre International Training Consultants, Bryndu, Sennybridge, Powys

Perry W G 1970 *Forms of Intellectual and Ethical Development in the College Years*. Holt, Rinehart, and Winston, New York

Radley G W 1978 The dynamics of groups in gaming. In: Megarry J (ed.) 1978 *Perspectives on Academic Gaming and Simulations*. Kagan Page, London

Boocock S, Schild E O (eds.) 1968 *Simulation Games in Learning*. Sage Publications, Beverley Hills, California

Short A H 1977 *Learning by Games*. Pamphlet MUPCET, Nottingham

Speed T J, Harris F C 1977 *Management Games for Use in the Construction Industry*. Occasional Paper 15, The Institute of Building, Ascot

Tansey P J 1971 *Educational Aspects of Simulation*. McGraw-Hill, Maidenhead

Taylor J L, Walford R 1978 *Learning and the Simulation Game*. Oxford University Press, Milton Keynes

Further Reading

Association for Business Simulation and Experiential Learning 1990 (ed. Gentry J) *Absel Guide to Business Gaming and Experiential Learning* Nichols, East Brunswick, New Jersey

Gibbs G I 1975 *Academic Gaming and Simulation in Education and Training*. Kogan Page, London

Gibbs G I 1982 *Twenty Terrible Reasons for Lecturing*. Standing Committee on Educational Development Services in Polytechnics (SCEDSIP)

Kolb D A 1984 *Experiential Learning Experience as the Source of Learning and Development*. Prentice-Hall, Englewood Cliffs, New Jersey

Loveluck C 1964 *Notes on The Construction, Operation, and Evaluation of Management Games*. Management Games Ltd, London

Loveluck C 1975 *Management and Training Handbook*. McGraw-Hill, London

Mitre 1991 MATREX—*Management Training Examples* (quarterly journal). Mitre International Training Consultants, Chellaston

Peter L J, Hull R 1969 *The Peter Principle*. Souvenir Press,

London

Thatcher D C, Robinson J 1987 *An Introduction to Simulation and Games in Education*. Solent Simulations, Portsmouth

Assignment and Supervision of Seatwork

L. M. Anderson

Seatwork has traditionally been defined as pupil schoolwork, usually written, performed independently at school, often while the teacher is instructing other pupils. In this entry, seatwork is considered to be only one of several possible forms of academic assignments completed by students while in school. Understanding seatwork and how it can best be conducted requires a broader understanding of the purposes and outcomes of academic work in any form. Developments in research on teaching and learning are presented to demonstrate why this broader view is necessary in order to understand seatwork. Three issues regarding academic assignments are addressed and recommendations for future research are offered.

1. Changing Perspectives on Seatwork and Other Forms of Academic Assignments Since 1980

Studies of classrooms in the 1970s and early 1980s often identified "seatwork" as a common lesson format (Dunkin 1987). Early research on teaching identified several seatwork principles associated with higher engagement rates and achievement test scores. Teachers should give assignments that can be completed successfully with reasonable effort; teachers should provide clear directions and lead students through practice examples before students are released to work independently; teachers should circulate in the room to monitor progress and provide help, but they should keep helping interactions brief to allow contact with all students (Brophy and Alleman 1991). The research on which such principles were based did not attend in depth to students' cognitive processing of the assignments, nor did it concern itself with the nature of what was learned from the assignments.

During the 1980s, research on teaching shifted emphases toward such concerns. For example, Bennett et al. (1984), in a study of United Kingdom elementary classrooms, found that assignments were often poorly matched to the pupils' capabilities. Similarly, Anderson et al. (1985), studying United States classrooms, found that few pupils understood the content-related purposes of their assignments, and that lower achievers adopted maladaptive strategies

for completing their work so that they would not be penalized for lack of effort.

Other researchers who analyzed seatwork assignments also criticized prevailing practices. For example, Osborn (1984) examined workbooks that accompanied basal readers, the source of many assignments in United States elementary reading instruction. She found that "a good proportion of workbook tasks are at best imperfect and not very efficient and at worst misleading and confusing" (p. 54). Similarly, Mergendoller et al. (1988) examined assignments in secondary United States science classrooms and concluded that the tasks presented minimal cognitive demands, usually requiring reproduction of information as presented in texts or lectures, seldom requiring pupils to generate ideas or demonstrate understanding.

Such empirical studies contributed to growing dissatisfaction with the nature of academic work done in schools. At the same time, conceptual work by several scholars provided new ways to think about school assignments. Doyle (1983, 1986) was particularly influential in stimulating discussions about the role of academic tasks in the ecology of classrooms. He stressed relationships among mental processes required to complete a task and what the pupil actually learns, describing ways that many school tasks foster learning only at low cognitive levels. Blumenfeld et al. (1987) built on Doyle's work by highlighting ways that tasks socialize not only what is learned about academic content but also attitudes about school work, self-perceptions, and motivation. They concluded: "Given the types of tasks prevalent in many classrooms, we may be creating workers desirous of doing the least possible in an individualist fashion" (p. 145).

Such criticisms of typical school assignments coincided with (and built upon) evolving thinking about learning and instruction. The 1980s saw a resurgence in concern about the quality of learning in schools, especially in the United States, where assessments revealed low levels of skills for solving complex problems. By the end of the 1980s, prevailing views of learning highlighted the constructive nature of meaningful learning (as opposed to rote learning that characterized much schooling), the situatedness of learning in social and cultural settings (which called into question the arbitrariness of much school learning), and the importance of social mediation of children's learning by other people (emphasizing the role that could be played by true teacher–student or student–student dialogue in schools instead of so much independent silent work like the traditional seatwork format) (Collins et al. 1989, Glaser 1991). As part of this concern with the nature of learning in schools, some scholars turned their attention to subject matter itself, and the ways in which disciplinary knowledge was represented to pupils through instruction and assignments (McDiarmid et al. 1989).

2. Issues about Academic Assignments

Taken together, the empirical and conceptual work of the 1980s suggests that it no longer makes sense to describe school assignments on the basis of superficial characteristics such as the activity form (independent vs. small group vs. teacher-led discussions) or location (in-class assignments vs. homework). Instead, three more fundamental issues have arisen as critical to understanding of whether and how academic assignments contribute to pupils' learning.

2.1 How Academic Assignments Contribute to Pupils' Construction of Flexible Understanding

McDiarmid et al. (1989) characterized flexible understanding as the ability to see relationships among ideas within a subject as well as across disciplinary fields and to the world outside of school. Flexible understanding of subject matter would also involve a sense of how disciplinary knowledge is created, and how one can increase one's own understanding through active manipulation of ideas. For example, flexible understanding of mathematics enables a pupil to see how fractions and division are related conceptually, and to identify occasions when this knowledge is useful. A pupil without flexible understanding may have learned only to calculate fraction problems, using memorized algorithms, but would not be able to summon that knowledge in a situation outside of school, or even in school when the problem was presented in an unfamiliar form.

The nature of the pupils' engagement with subject matter determines whether flexible understanding, as opposed to rote learning, is acquired. Pupils must manipulate ideas, building on prior understanding and using subject matter knowledge to solve complex and ill-structured problems (Collins et al. 1989). As noted above, several empirical studies of schoolwork suggest that pupils often do not engage with content in ways that promote flexible understanding. One explanation is that the nature and form of academic tasks determine the form of engagement that is provoked.

Selmes (1986), for example, studied United Kingdom secondary school pupils' approaches to studying.

He found instances of both a "deep" approach (characterized by more active manipulation of ideas and likely to lead to flexible understanding) and a "surface" approach (characterized by attention to procedural elements of the task and memorization, less likely to lead to flexible understanding). Selmes determined that, while some differences in approaches were related to individual pupil dispositions, other differences were related to the tasks themselves and their instructional contexts. When the tasks called for more open-ended responses (e.g., relating ideas to each other and to personal experiences), "deep" approaches were more likely to be used by the pupils. When tasks called for more memorization and were assessed by a strict criterion, then "surface" approaches were more likely. Doyle (1986) offered additional United States examples of how task features influenced the ways in which pupils engaged with ideas represented in academic tasks. Blumenfeld et al. (1987) also offered an analysis of how the forms in which assignments are presented influence what is learned from the assignments.

In a comparative international study, Stigler and Stevenson (1991) examined elementary classes in the United States, Japan, and Taiwan, in an effort to understand why United States mathematics achievement scores were lower than in other countries. In contrast to the United States, where mathematics assignments often consisted of multiple calculation problems with which pupils practiced applying algorithms, in the Asian classes a single complex problem was often the focus of the pupils' assignment for a given lesson; the problem engaged them in thinking about conceptual relationships, not just procedural applications. One implication is that the differences between the United States and Asian pupils' mathematics learning might be accounted for by the differences in the forms of engagement created through their schoolwork.

Lampert (1990) also highlighted the importance of the problems selected as the basis of lessons, saying that "The most important criterion in picking a problem was that it be the sort of problem that would have the capacity to engage all of the students in the class in making and testing mathematical hypotheses" (p. 39). In her study, as pupils discussed their hypotheses about the problem, they engaged in construction of flexible understanding about the mathematics, not just practice of calculation algorithms. Brophy and Alleman (1991) also emphasized the importance of considering curriculum goals for meaningful learning, and offered several guiding principles for evaluating academic activities for the likelihood that they will engage pupils with significant ideas in ways that will build flexible understanding.

2.2 Social Contexts Within which Academic Assignments are Completed

While the design of suitable school assignments is a necessary condition for the construction of flexible understanding, it is not sufficient in and of itself. The larger social context within which assignments are carried out also determines what is learned from them. Two aspects of the social context are especially critical: the accountability system, and the role of public discussion among pupils about their schoolwork.

Within classrooms, pupils are held accountable for cooperating and participating in certain ways. There are both behavioral and academic accountability systems in place, sometimes formal and explicit, sometimes implicit. Doyle (1983, 1986) pointed out the many ways that tasks, and the cognitive processes they provoke in pupils, are inextricably bound up with the accountability systems of the classroom and managerial moves of the teacher. Many forces in classrooms push both pupils and teachers toward creation of tasks that are unambiguous and low in risk, which simplify both the pupils' ability to work within the accountability system and the teachers' ability to manage the classroom. Unfortunately, moves that reduce ambiguity in classroom tasks usually change the cognitive demands, resulting in engagement that is not as likely to promote flexible understanding.

A second aspect of the social context within which academic assignments are completed is whether and how pupils' thinking about their work is shared with each other in ways that prompt further learning. Typically, seatwork has been considered to be completely independent work, viewed only by the teacher. However, developments in theories of learning and instruction have called into question the reliance on such individual, private work, and highlighted the importance of public expression of ideas to which others can respond. Glaser (1991) emphasized ways that public expression of thinking can contribute to pupils' self-regulatory skills in a way that individual work cannot. He wrote:

> A social context for learning elevates thinking to an observable status. As students participate, the details of various problem-solving procedures, strategies of reasoning, and techniques for accomplishing goals become apparent . . . Thus, school instruction might well consider how teaching practice can make apparent the forms of students' thinking, in ways that can be observed, transmitted, discussed, reflected upon, and moved toward more competent performance and dispositions for reasoning. (pp. 134–35)

Public discourse can only have such positive effects, however, when the pupils have indeed engaged in thinking that they can talk about, and that will only occur when the academic assignment provoked what Selmes (1986) called "deep" rather than "surface" approaches to the task. A worthwhile assignment may have limited value if it is not extended to such public discussion, where each pupil has the opportunity to further revise and clarify new understandings. Thus, whether and how pupils learn from a given assignment is a joint function of the nature of the task and the opportunities for dialogue about that task. Examples

of this interdependence are evident in the studies described above by Stigler and Stevenson (1991) and Lampert (1990).

2.3 Support of Pupils' Thinking as they Complete Academic Assignments

When academic assignments are thought of as seatwork, to be carried out independently while the teacher is busy with instruction of other pupils, it is considered virtuous if the assignment can be completed successfully by the pupil without assistance from the teacher. Indeed, the first empirical research that called the worthiness of much seatwork into question did so on the grounds that many pupils were not succeeding easily with their work (Anderson et al. 1985, Bennett et al. 1984). However, conceptualizations of learning have called into question the assumption that errorless performance is desirable. Instead, scholars now argue that the most important learning (i.e., most likely to lead to flexible understanding) occurs when learners are supported and guided as they reason through complex problems that would be too difficult to solve independently, but which are solvable with some assistance (Collins et al. 1989, Glaser 1991).

This situation is created in classrooms when teachers create tasks that pose challenges (in that responses or answers are not immediately evident to pupils) and then create circumstances in which pupils' thinking through tasks is supported. One form of support has already been described: public expression of individuals' ideas as they attempt to solve a problem. Hearing the ideas of peers can suggest ways of improving one's own thinking about a task. Two other forms of support are teacher–pupil dialogue around academic assignments, and assistance that is built into assignments that pupils do on their own.

In many classrooms (especially in the United States), teacher–student interactions around content are limited to known-answer questions, which elicit particular answers that may be judged for correctness. When tied to an academic assignment, this form of discourse maintains attention on the correct answer, not the reasoning processes used to arrive at the answer. In contrast, teacher–pupil dialogue that focuses on how a pupil is reasoning about a question or problem, suggesting cues and prompting thinking, is more likely to contribute to flexible understanding. Collins et al. (1989) characterized such dialogue as a gradual process of skillful modeling, coaching, and fading by the teacher as pupils' attempts to reason like experts are gradually shaped and refined. Stigler and Stevenson (1991), in their depiction of Japanese and Taiwanese classrooms, and Lampert (1990), in her depiction of a United States classroom, provide illustrations of such dialogues. In both cases, the teacher–pupil dialogue is interwoven with pupil–pupil dialogue about an academic assignment, so that public expression of ideas provides many occasions for the teacher to enter the dialogue with modeling and coaching of pupils' thinking.

Sometimes, however, it is appropriate for students to work alone or in small groups without the teacher's immediate assistance. In such circumstances, it is still possible to build into assignments assistance that cues pupils to reflect on their thinking and to ask themselves questions that will further their thinking. Glaser (1991) suggested some ways this might be accomplished in task design. Other teacher-created examples were offered by Scheu et al. (1988). Technology offers much promise in this regard. For example, Zellermayer et al. (1991) described an Israeli effort to aid high school students in their independent writing. They created a computer program that prompted pupils to be metacognitive about their writing. Pupils who completed their assignments with the aid of the computer program not only produced better essays, but also appeared to internalize the guidance offered by the program and to perform better in later writing tasks when the computer was not available.

Thus, the form of the assignment can provide assistance to pupils with regard to the kind of thinking they do, enabling them to take on challenging assignments even when working alone. Such an approach to the design of assignments stands in contrast to the conclusions of research before 1980 that teachers should assign work that could be done easily without any assistance. It seems reasonable to conclude that most assignments which have potential to contribute to a pupils' flexible understanding will of necessity be too difficult to complete quickly and easily, and teachers and curriculum developers must consider ways to provide assistance as pupils reason through the assignments.

3. Future Directions for Research and Practice

The work of the 1980s has both clarified and complicated the picture of when and how academic assignments contribute to pupils' learning. Two sets of questions for future work seem most pertinent in the 1990s. First, what must teachers know and understand in order to choose or create academic assignments and then to use them in ways that promote flexible understandings by pupils? Gone are the days when anyone would expect that teachers can or should simply follow prepackaged curriculum guides and assignments. What is involved for teachers when they consider the issues raised here and attend to the nature of the task, its social context, and the support made available to learners? Managing all this in a busy classroom is certainly no small feat, and more attention is needed on issues of teacher learning about academic assignments.

Second, pupils' perspectives on academic assignments cannot be ignored. Although the issues raised here have been derived from the views of educators intent on improving schools, they will not seem so sensible to pupils who hold very different presumptions about what is supposed to happen in school. Many attempts to change the form and conduct of academic assignments are likely to meet with resistance from students, especially if they feel at risk because of perceived ambiguity about what will count as successful performance. More knowledge is needed about how to help pupils move from traditional notions of academic assignments to forms of schoolwork more likely to help them develop flexible understanding.

See also: Metacognitive Strategies: Teaching and Assessing; Student Roles in Classrooms

References

Anderson L M, Brubaker N L, Alleman-Brooks J, Duffy G G 1985 A qualitative study of seatwork in first grade classrooms. *Elem. Sch. J.* 86(2): 123–40

Bennett N, Desforges C, Cockburn A, Wilkinson B 1984 *The Quality of Pupil Learning Experiences*. Erlbaum, London

Blumenfeld P C, Mergendoller J, Swarthout D 1987 Task as a heuristic for understanding student learning and motivation. *J. Curric. St.* 19(2): 135–8

Brophy J, Alleman J 1991 Activities as instructional tools: A framework for analysis and evaluation. *Educ. Researcher*, 20(4): 9–23

Collins A, Brown J S, Newman S E 1989 Cognitive apprenticeship: Teaching the craft of reading, writing, and mathematics. In: Resnick L B (ed.) 1989 *Knowing, Learning, and Instruction: Essays in Honor of Robert Glaser*. Erlbaum, Hillsdale, New Jersey

Doyle W 1983 Academic work. *Rev. Educ. Res.* 53(2): 159–99

Doyle W 1986 Content representation in teachers' definitions of academic work. *J. Curric. St.* 18(4): 365–79

Dunkin M 1987 Lesson formats. In: Dunkin M (ed.) 1987 *The International Encyclopedia of Teaching and Teacher Education*. Pergamon Press, Oxford

Glaser R 1991 The maturing of the relationship between the science of learning and cognition and educational practice. *Learning and Instruction* 1(2): 129–44

Lampert M 1990 When the problem is not the question and the solution is not the answer: Mathematical knowing and teaching. *Amer. Educ. Res. J.* 27(1): 29–63

McDiarmid G W, Ball D L, Anderson C W 1989 Why staying one chapter ahead doesn't really work: Subject-specific pedagogy. In: Reynolds M C (ed.) *Knowledge Base for the Beginning Teacher*. Pergamon Press, Oxford

Mergendoller J R, Marchman V A, Mitman A L, Packer M J 1988 Task demands and accountability in middle-grade science classes. *Elem. Sch. J.* 88(3): 251–65

Osborn J 1984 The purposes, uses and contents of workbooks and some guidelines for publishers. In: Anderson R C, Osborn J, Tierney R J (eds.) 1984 *Learning to read in American Schools: Basal Readers and Content Texts*. Erlbaum, Hillsdale, New Jersey

Scheu J A, Tanner D K, Au K H 1988 Integrating seatwork with the basal lesson. In: Winograd P, Lipson M, Wixson K (eds.) *Using Basal Readers to Teach Reading*. Teachers College Press, New York

Selmes I P 1986 Approaches to normal learning tasks adopted by senior secondary school pupils. *Br. Educ. Res. J.* 12(1): 15–27

Stigler J W, Stevenson H W 1991 How Asian teachers polish each lesson to perfection. *American Educator* 15(1): 12–20, 43–7

Zellermayer M, Salomon G, Globerson T, Givon H 1991 Enhancing writing-related metacognitions through a computerized writing partner. *Am. Educ. Res. J.* 28(2): 373–91

Further Reading

Brophy J E 1992 *Advances in Research on Teaching Vol. 3: Planning and Managing Learning Tasks and Activities.* JAI Press, London

Mergendoller J R (ed.) 1988 Special issue on schoolwork and academic tasks. *Elem. Sch. J.* 88(3)

Homework

H. J. Walberg and R. A. Paschal

The word "homework" is defined inconsistently. Derived originally from the term referring to industrial work done outside factories, the customary meaning is used in this entry—the study of school subjects outside of regular school classes. The first syllable of the word "homework" implies study done at home, but the word commonly also refers to study done during free periods in the school day, during transportation, in museums and workplaces, and in other times and places. In fact, some work assigned to be completed at home is done during regular school classes. While scholars, parents, and students themselves have debated the advantages and disadvantages of homework, small-scale experiments and large-scale surveys show fairly consistent positive effects on learning. Surveys also reveal large variations in the amount of homework done by students within and among countries. These variations partly explain the amount learned, by students in these countries.

world, such as the Australian "outback" and the less densely populated areas of Africa and South America, receive instruction at home by satellite transmission. Comparative studies suggest that they can learn as well as comparable children who study in regular schools in their countries (Walberg 1991). Some technical visionaries believe that expansion of such programs in both industrialized and developing countries would efficiently increase learning and the range of choices available to families. The Open University in the United Kingdom, which has greatly enlarged educational opportunities for many "stay-at-homes," has set an interesting and useful precedent in this area.

Notwithstanding the wide range of beliefs and practices, this entry concerns the more usual case when homework is considered useful supplementary study outside regular classrooms. The issues considered are the amount of homework done, its effect on learning, and worthwhile homework practices.

1. Opinions about Homework

Educators' opinions about the effects and merits of homework have varied widely (Paschal et al. 1984). At one extreme is the recommendation that all academic work should be done in school under the direct supervision of teachers. Some educational egalitarians, for example, believe that homework might give the children of better educated families an advantage. If this recommendation were to be followed, moreover, teachers would presumably detect and remedy errors before they become bad habits.

Among educators who advocate homework are those who believe students should assume more responsibility for their own learning (especially in the "real" world outside school). Another group, "home schoolers," often religiously devout, make sacrifices to educate their children at home.

Some children who live in remote areas of the

2. Homework: How Much is Done?

Contrary to the extreme positions advocated, most children go to school and do some homework. Often assigned by teachers, it may also be encouraged or imposed by parents, tutors, or the students themselves, but how much homework is actually assigned and completed? An international team conducted a large survey of students around the world to find out about this and other questions (Postlethwaite and Wiley 1992). The results are summarized in Fig. 1. The horizontal axis of the figure shows that the country averages range from about 4.5 to 9 hours of homework per week by 14-year olds. Of course, the range of homework within a given country for individual students varies much more widely.

Students in Hungary, Japan, the Netherlands, Poland, Israel, and Italy averaged nearly twice as much homework as Sweden. Students in the highest achieving countries—Hungary, Japan, and the Netherlands—

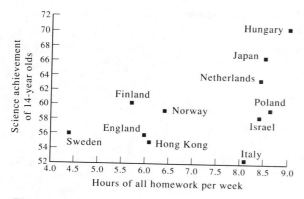

Figure 1
Homework and achievement

did more homework than those in low-achieving countries such as Sweden, Finland, England, Hong Kong, and Norway. Students in Poland, Israel, and Italy, in contrast, had relatively low levels of achievement in light of the amount of time spent on homework.

3. Total Study Time

The amounts of educative time within and outside school are powerful determinants of learning (Frederick and Walberg 1980). Extramural time is by far the largest segment of the student's life—about 87 percent of the waking hours of American students in the first 18 years of life. Thus, extramural time constitutes a potentially powerful influence on learning, both directly and indirectly as it increases the efficiency of school learning time. If, for example, students add 3 hours of homework to the 30 hours per week they attend school, homework would increase their study time by 10 percent; 20 hours would constitute a 67 percent increase—a big advantage.

Comparative studies of students' amounts of total

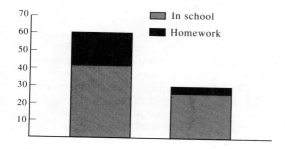

Figure 2
Study hours per week among high school students in Japan and the United States

study time and other uses of time are rare. Indeed, Juster and Stafford (1991) were able to find only one set of comparable data, which happened to be obtained on American and Japanese students. These students consistently rank among the lowest and highest groups, respectively, in international achievement surveys. Fig. 2 shows that Japanese senior high school students averaged 60.5 hours per week on total study time, while the United States students spent only 30.0 hours per week on average.

Both primary and secondary school students in Japan spent almost twice as much time in school on average than did American students. Furthermore, Japanese students exceeded United States students by a factor of 4 to 5 in studying outside school. United States students spent substantially more time at nonschool work, sleeping, and socializing.

Various research methods for obtaining estimates of total study time can yield different results. Leone and Richards (1989), for example, monitored the activities of 400 American fifth- to ninth-graders over a period of several weeks using beepers and response sheets that students completed whenever the beeper went off (on a random schedule within two-hour time blocks from 7:30 am to 9:30 pm). Only 15.5 hours per week were spent paying attention to classwork, and only 6.4 hours were spent doing homework. This method yielded an estimate of 21.9 hours of total study time per week, 27 percent lower than the Juster and Stafford (1991) estimate of 30 hours per week for American students.

4. Effect of Homework on Learning

Pashcal et al. (1984) searched Canadian and United States literature for published and unpublished estimates of the effect of homework on learning among primary and secondary school students. In the 15 studies found, the average effect size of homework was 0.36 of a standard deviation. An effect size of this magnitude means that the achievement of the typical student (50th percentile) doing no homework would increase to the 65th percentile if the average amount of homework was done. Furthermore, among 81 comparisons of groups of students with varying amounts and standards of homework, 69 (or 85%) favored groups with more homework. Thus, both the magnitude and the consistency of the homework effect appears to be substantial.

The synthesis of Pashcal et al. (1984) yielded an interesting finding relevant to educational policy and the practice of teaching. As shown in Fig. 3, homework that was merely assigned without feedback from teachers appeared to raise the typical student learning moderately on average. In contrast, homework that was marked, graded, or commented upon yielded a more substantial effect on learning. Indeed, the graded homework effect is among the larger effects found by educational researchers (Walberg 1984).

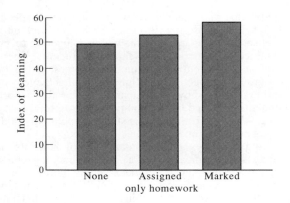

Figure 3
Effect of homework on learning

More recent studies continue to show positive effects of homework on learning. Leone and Richards's (1989) careful and extensive observational study, for example, showed that increased time on homework among fourth to ninth grade students was positively related to achievement. High achievers averaged 64 percent more time doing homework than did low achievers. The differences were more marked at the higher grades, and homework was more effective if parents were active in supervising it.

5. Student Attitudes Toward Homework

If homework helps, why is it that some students do so little? The main reason is apparently is that some students find studying unsatisfying. As a group, for example, American adolescents like class work, studying, and thinking less than all other major activities except work (Csikszentmihalyi and Larson 1984). They strongly prefer being alone or with family and friends over spending time with classmates. Furthermore, they rank time with strangers as only slightly less preferable than that with classmates. Similarly, Leone and Richards (1989) found that the mood of students while doing homework was less positive than for most other activities in which they engaged.

The slackening of academic effort including homework may be a manifestation of "the Matthew Effect" (Walberg 1984), a phrase taken from the "rich-getting-richer" and the "poor-getting-poorer" phenomenon mentioned in the Book of Matthew in the Bible. Students who fall behind academically find their classroom work and homework more difficult and, as a result, less satisfying. As a consequence, they may put forth less effort and therefore find the work still more difficult and dissatisfying. This vicious circle leads to gradually deepening failure and eventual resignation.

6. How Much Homework Should Be Done?

Studies of highly accomplished youth and adults in various fields show that they have almost always put in many hours of high-quality practice and effort. Mastery of academic subjects is no different. It is, nonetheless, impossible to state exact requirements of excellent performance aside from the generalization that more is usually better, though obviously not to the point of exhaustion.

Although time and effort hardly seem causes of undue stress, too much external pressure, of course, can produce anxiety. If students feel driven by parents and teachers, if they fall far behind their peers and have little hope of catching up or blame themselves for failure to attain perfection, or if they lose a sense of control and autonomy, they can become depressed and feel helpless. Encouragement, the setting of realistic goals, support and recognition for accomplishment, and learning for its own sake seem the treatments of choice.

7. Promoting Homework

What kind of homework policies work best? Little research is informative on this question, but some general principles of learning are suggestive (Walberg 1984). Homework that is stimulating, related to classroom work, carefully designed, and suitable to student abilities is likely to produce the best effects. Frequent assignments of moderate amounts of work are likely to yield more learning and longer retention than larger but fewer assignments, even though the total amounts of time may be equal. Rapid, detailed, and individualized feedback is likely to be appreciated and to yield larger effects than delayed, general, and group feedback. Finally, other things being equal, larger amounts of study time, including homework, can generally be expected to result in more learning.

It may be easier to recommend more homework than it is to grade homework once more is assigned. Learning to write, for example, requires writing, criticism, and rewriting; practice and coaching make for better performance. However, teachers with 5 classes of 25 students per day may not be able to annotate and grade, say, a weekly two-page essay for each student.

One solution to the problem of grading homework is to employ aides, possibly part-time workers, and even underemployed homemakers. They can be paid considerably less than teachers and do grading as well as coaching during or after regular school hours under teacher supervision. In many countries, strict labor laws and unions, however, often prevent this efficient practice.

Japan offers another solution. Small within-class work groups, called *han*, are given considerable autonomy by the teacher. They assist each other in planning, conducting, and evaluating group and individual work.

They can evaluate one anothers' work done in class or at home. They not only learn academic subjects better under this arrangement, but they also learn skills prized for industrial work and the emerging information society—cooperation and mutual aid.

See also: Home Environment and School Learning

References

Csikszentmihalyi M, Larson R 1984 *Being Adolescent: Conflict and Growth in the Teenage Years.* Basic Books, New York
Frederick W C, Walberg H J 1980 Learning as a function of time. *J. Educ. Res.* 73 (4): 183–94
Juster F T, Stafford F P 1991 The allocation of time: Empirical findings, behavioral models, and problems of measurement. *J. Econ. Lit.* 29 (2): 471–522
Leone C M, Richards M H 1989 Classwork and homework in early adolescence: The ecology of achievement. *Journal of Youth and Adolescence* 18 (6): 531–48
Postlethwaite T N, Wiley D E (eds.) 1992 *The IEA Study of Science 2: Science Achievement in 23 Countries.* Pergamon Press, Oxford
Paschal R, Weinstein T, Walberg H J 1984 Effects of homework: A quantitative synthesis. *J. Educ. Res.* 78 (2): 97–104
Walberg H J 1984 Improving the productivity of America's schools. *Educ. Leadership* 41 (8): 19–27
Walberg H J 1991 Improving school science in advanced and developing countries. *Rev. Educ. Res.* 61: 25–699

Further Reading

Cooper H M 1989 *Homework.* Longman, White Plains, New York
Keith T Z 1986 *Homework.* Kappa Delta Pi, West Lafayette, Indiana
Kellaghan T, Sloan K, Alvarez B, Bloom B S 1993 *Home Environments and School Learning.* Jossey-Bass, San Francisco, California

Tutoring

F. J. Medway

Tutoring is a method of teaching in which one student (or a small group of students) receives personalized and individualized instruction. This entry provides both a historical perspective on tutoring and a contemporary framework for understanding and investigating tutoring.

Methods for tutoring are examined with particular attention paid to programs in which students teach one another. Research on the effectiveness of tutoring for both those who tutor and those who learn is presented, as is research on variables which facilitate successful tutoring. Finally, guidelines and resources for effective tutoring are presented.

In tutoring, the person doing the teaching is called a tutor, while the student is called a tutee. Tutoring most often supplements traditional classroom instruction which is typically conducted in large groups for those students who require remedial help and those who have difficulty learning by conventional methods. Tutoring also is used for students with special needs or life circumstances who are unable to participate in a regular instructional program.

Tutoring is widely used with learners of all ages. It most often is used with learners in primary and elementary school settings; however, tutoring also is practiced in secondary education, higher education, adult education, and vocational education settings.

In most cases tutoring refers to instruction not provided by a student's regular teacher. The tutor may be a paid private instructor, a volunteer, a school aide, a parent or guardian, another student, or a computer or other teaching machine. The tutor may or may not be similar to the learner in age, ability, background, or personal characteristics. The tutor may or may not be trained as an instructor; he or she may focus on one or several subject matter areas; and, like a large group instructor, the tutor may or may not reinforce, encourage, and counsel the student. Another usage of the word tutor is a college or university official who advises undergraduates, maintains discipline standards, and has teaching assignments (for example, at many colleges and universities in the United Kingdom and Australia, and at some United States colleges).

1. Tutoring of Children and Early-age Adolescents

Tutoring of school-age children is widespread and most tutors are adults. In the home, parents and siblings help other family members with lessons and assignments. In the school, parents and retired persons commonly serve as tutors of children in need of assistance. In the United States programs such as Head Start employ nonprofessionals who teach infants and toddlers basic skills in order to reduce their risk of future learning problems. Further, in several communities high school students provide tutoring to elementary school students as part of community service and research programs (Medway and Elkin 1975, Sprinthall and Scott 1989).

Since the early 1970s many reports and studies have described programs in which students tutor other students (Allen 1976, Greenwood et al. 1988). This practice is known as "peer tutoring" when students and tutors are similar in age. The term "cross-age tutoring" is used when students and tutors differ in age.

Paolitto (1976) traced the historical roots of cross-age tutoring back to the first century AD when Quintilian noted the practice of having younger students taught by older ones in his *Institutio Oratoria*. Cross-age tutoring was used on a limited basis in Germany and Spain in the sixteenth century.

Organized and widespread use of cross-age tutoring is generally credited to Andrew Bell, a Scotsman, who in the late eighteenth century established a school for orphans of British soldiers and Indian mothers in Madras, India. Bell modified the ancient Hindu tutoring system and in 1797 reported on the successful application of individual and group tutoring for instruction and discipline.

Bell's methods were adopted by the English educator Joseph Lancaster. In what came to be called the Bell–Lancaster system, professional teachers instructed older students who in turn instructed younger students, with younger students teaching still younger ones. Although variations of this system spread throughout Europe in the early 1800s its popularity was short-lived due to the growing recognition of teaching as requiring special talents and professional training. Nevertheless, in the United States, peer and cross-age tutoring were practiced in one room schoolhouses of the colonial period and in rural schools throughout much of the nineteenth century.

Renewed interest in peer tutoring in the United States began in the early 1960s because of shortages of teaching personnel and the belief that some children might show more interest in learning if given the opportunity to work with another student rather than an adult. Among the advantages attributed to peer teachers are the tutor's similarity in culture and language to the tutee, the tutor's motivation, and the tutor's empathy for the learner's situation.

One of the first and most extensive cross-age tutoring programs was the High School Homework Helpers Program started in 1962–63 in New York City. In this program approximately 1,000 16 to 18 year-old students served as paid tutors to approximately 6,000 14 to 16 year-old students from disadvantaged backgrounds with reading problems.

A second major project designed to improve the reading skills of children from impoverished, inner-city homes was the Youth Tutoring Youth Program. This project was originated by Mary Kohler who operated an independent agency in New York City called the National Commission on Resources for Youth. Youth Tutoring Youth programs were started in several large cities including Washington, DC and Chicago, and more than 3,500 people were trained in tutoring techniques (Gartner et al. 1971).

A third noteworthy program was the cross-age tutoring project developed by Lippitt and Lippitt in Michigan and California which was designed to improve the achievement and self-esteem of elementary school students. Each of these projects is described by Allen (1976).

Although tutoring practices vary widely across settings, much research evidence supports the effectiveness of peer and cross-age tutoring as teaching methods. One of the first studies was the 1967 evaluation of the Homework Helpers Program. Students who received reading tutoring for four hours a week for five months gained more in reading comprehension than did a group of nontutored children. The study also found that tutors improved in reading even more than did tutored students. This was one of the first studies to show the benefits of tutoring for the tutor.

During the 1970s tutoring programs were instituted in schools around the world, including Great Britain, Australia, Hong Kong, Germany, and Israel (Quicke 1986, Sharpley et al. 1983). For example, in just one year, more than 6,000 children participated in Israel's Perach Project, a cross-age tutoring program in which college students tutor disadvantaged children (Eisenberg et al. 1983).

Several research reviews, such as one by Cohen et al. (1982), have found many benefits for tutors and tutees across a wide variety of academic and social measures. Tutoring improves school achievement, self-concept, and attitudes toward school, and students gain more by being tutored than they do through lectures and large group discussion. Studies have also documented the advantages of tutoring for preschool children as well as children with learning and behavior problems.

During the 1970s and 1980s researchers became interested in the factors that serve to increase the likelihood that tutoring will be effective (Medway 1991). Most research evidence suggests that cross-age tutoring is superior to peer tutoring. An excellent study by DePaulo et al. (1989) showed that the benefits of tutoring are particularly impressive when tutors are older than tutees, when tutors and tutees work in a cooperative context, and when both tutors and tutees are high achievers. This last finding clearly shows the advantages of tutoring for competent students as well as those who require more than large group instruction can provide.

2. Tutoring of Late Adolescents and Young Adults

Tutoring is used widely with young adults in need of academic and/or vocational instruction. Tutoring is provided by high schools, colleges, and universities for underprepared students and those who do not learn well with traditional instructional methods. Bloom (1984) reported that the average tutored high school and college students mastered more material than 98 percent of comparable students taught using conventional large group lecture methods.

There are at least three basic varieties of high school and college tutoring: course tutoring, emergency tutoring, and structured tutoring. In course tutoring a tutor provides a tutee with additional assistance and explanation of material that is covered by the teacher or professor. This type of tutoring is a key component of Keller's (1968) Personalized System of Instruction (PSI). In the PSI method students are provided with lessons or units of instruction and progress through them at their own pace. Each student must attain a certain level of proficiency (commonly 90% mastery) before being allowed to proceed to a more advanced unit. Tutors of PSI, known as proctors, grade students' tests, review course material, encourage and support students, and provide administrative help to the professor. Another example of course tutoring is reciprocal tutoring in which students take turns teaching one another course material.

Emergency tutoring is provided to students who need help quickly because of an impending examination, test anxiety, or personal crisis. Finally, in structured tutoring the tutor makes use of computer–generated material. The tutor teaches the tutee how to learn to use a computer lesson. Since the mid-1980s there have been major advances in computer-based instruction, many of which have been published in journals such as the *Journal of Computer-based Instruction, Electronic Learning, Teaching and Computers,* and *Classroom Computer Learning.* A new field has emerged known as Intelligent Tutoring Systems (Frasson and Gauthier 1990) which makes use of advances in artificial intelligence, cognitive psychology, and interactive video.

3. Tutoring Guidelines and Resources

The effectiveness of tutoring either children or adults greatly depends upon the quality of the tutorial relationship, the training of the tutor, and the way the tutoring is organized and structured. This is true regardless of the age of the tutor. Medway (1991) concluded, based on research studies, that the more tutors plan ahead, provide learning tips, employ question-asking strategies, use reinforcement, and have high expectations for tutee success, the greater the benefits of tutoring. Several resources are available which address selecting participants, pairing tutors and students, and choosing the most appropriate instructional approach (e.g., Koskinen and Wilson 1982).

The tutor's attitude toward tutoring and the tutee is very important. The tutor should be encouraging, accepting, and reassuring. Tutor and tutee should have a good interpersonal relationship and feel good working together. They should cooperate with one another and each should respect the efforts of the other. The tutor should attempt to emulate the behaviors of a good

counselor and a good teacher. This entails proper use of question-asking and feedback techniques.

Generally it is best to select tutors who are at least 10 or 11 years of age. Such tutors, and especially adults, are more likely than younger children to use reinforcement and are more able than younger children to learn how to teach general problem-solving strategies. Tutors should be supervised if they are not professional educators.

Tutoring episodes must be limited to a reasonable amount of time given the needs of the student so as to prevent restlessness and frustration. Finally, the success of tutoring programs in schools and other organizations depends on administrative support and should be appropriately evaluated in terms of benefits relative to costs. Excellent descriptions of practical tutoring techniques and ways to set up and structure peer tutoring programs are provided by Allen (1976), Koskinen and Wilson (1982), and Miller and Peterson (1987).

4. Future Directions

Additional research is needed to determine the types of tutor and tutee behavior which facilitate learning. Only a few studies have been conducted examining the dynamics of tutor–tutee communication, the effects of personality styles, and the contexts (e.g., cooperative versus competitive) in which learning occurs.

Little is known about the most appropriate ways for tutors to present information and the most beneficial questioning strategies. Also, little is known about the relative effectiveness of adolescents and older adults as tutors. Further, tutoring has yet to be systematically compared with other forms of learning such as computer-assisted instruction, and experiential learning.

Finally, given the benefits of tutoring, there is little information on factors which might cause educators to use or not use tutorial programs in schools. Studies are needed on tutoring's acceptability by educators along the lines of Witt's research on behavioral interventions (e.g., Witt 1986). Witt's research suggests that tutoring programs are most likely to be instituted in schools when the proposed programs require minimal staff time, require few additional trained staff, intrude little into the ongoing activities of the classroom, and have little or no effect on those not involved in the tutoring program.

See also: Individualized Instruction

References

Allen V L (ed.) 1976 *Children as Teachers: Theory and Research on Tutoring.* Academic Press, New York
Bloom B J 1984 The search for methods of group instruction as effective as one-to-one tutoring. *Educ. Leadership* 41(8): 4–17

Cohen P A, Kulik J A, Kulik C C 1982 Educational outcomes of tutoring: A meta-analysis of findings. *Am. Educ. Res. J.* 19(2): 237–48

DePaulo B M et al. 1989 Age differences in reactions to help in a peer tutoring content. *Child Dev.* 60(2): 423–39

Eisenberg T, Fresko B, Carmeli M 1983 A follow-up study of disadvantaged children two years after being tutored. *J. Educ. Res.* 76(5): 302–6

Frasson C, Gauthier G (eds.) 1990 *Intelligent Tutoring Systems: At the Crossroad of Artificial Intelligence and Education.* Ablex, Norwood, New Jersey

Gartner A, Kohler M C, Reissman F 1971 *Children Teach Children: Learning by Teaching.* Harper and Row, New York

Greenwood C R, Carta J J, Hall R V 1988 The use of peer tutoring strategies in classroom management and educational instruction. *Sch. Psychol. Rev.* 17(2): 258–75

Keller F S 1968 "Good-bye teacher …" *J. Appl. Behav. Anal.* 1(1): 79–89

Koskinen P S, Wilson R M 1982 *Developing a Successful Tutoring Program.* Teachers College Press, New York

Medway F J 1991 A social psychological analysis of peer tutoring. *J. Dev. Educ.* 15(1): 20–26, 32

Medway F J, Elkin V B 1975 Psychologist–teacher collaboration in developing and team-teaching high school psychology courses. *Psychol Sch.* 12(1): 107–12

Miller J A, Peterson D W 1987 Peer-influenced academic interventions. In: Maher C A, Zins J E (eds.) 1987 *Psychoeducational Interventions in the Schools.* Pergamon Press, New York

Paolitto D P 1976 The effect of cross-age tutoring on adolescence: An inquiry into theoretical assumptions. *Rev. Educ. Res.* 46(2): 215–37, 239

Quicke J C 1986 Pupil culture, peer tutoring and special educational needs. *Disabil. Handicap, Soc.* 1(2): 147–64

Sharpley A M, Irvine J W, Sharpley C F 1983 An examination of the effectiveness of a cross-age tutoring program in mathematics for elementary school children. *Am. Educ. Res. J.* 20(1): 103–11

Sprinthall N A, Scott J R 1989 Promoting psychological development, math achievement, and success attribution of female students through deliberate psychological education. *J. Couns. Psych.* 36(4): 440–46

Witt J C 1986 Teachers' resistance to the use of school-based interventions. *J. Sch. Psychol.* 24(1): 37–44

Further Reading

Ehly S W, Larsen S C 1980 *Peer Tutoring for Individualized Instruction.* Allyn and Bacon, Boston, Massachusetts

Nonverbal Teacher Behavior

H. A. Smith

Nonverbal classroom behavior of teachers and students is an important, though infrequently studied, aspect of classroom life. This entry examines the use of nonverbal behavior in elementary and secondary school classrooms. A brief historical overview is given and a summary of selected research on six major categories of nonverbal behavior (proxemics, haptics, kinesics, paralanguage, silence, and chronemics) is presented. The entry concludes with implications for future research.

1. A Brief History of the Study of Nonverbal Behavior

The study of nonverbal behavior has continued unabated since the beginning of recorded history. Early studies examined the dances and rituals of the ancient Aztecs; gestures, mimes, and dances of the Romans and Greeks; the sign language of the Australian Aborigines; the gestures and postures of Chinese theater; and the courtesy books of Renaissance Italy (Davis 1972, Key 1977).

The publication in 1872 of Charles Darwin's *The Expression of the Emotions in Man and Animals* initiated serious interest in the nonverbal domain as a viable research area and yielded research questions and findings that are still valid in the 1990s. Some of the research topics generated by Darwin have been characterized by both active and dormant periods of activity. For example, research on human facial expression was active during the 1920s and 1930s, languished during the 1940s, and began with renewed vigor during the 1950s. In the early 1990s, facial expression is featured prominently in any discussion of nonverbal behavior and is often associated with the work of Ekman and his associates (see, e.g., Feldman and Rimé 1991).

Darwin's seminal work led to parallel streams of inquiry by others in areas such as cross-cultural comparisons, developmental patterns, emotional expression, and the psychodiagnosis of personality. Relevant problems are pursued by researchers in overlapping academic disciplines that include ethology, communications, sociology, anthropology, psychology, education, and semiotics. In particular, interest in semiotics, the study of signs, has exploded since the mid-1960s with nonverbal behavior as one of its prime areas of concern. Academic interest in nonverbal behavior has been accompanied by a spate of publications aimed at consumption by the popular market. Some of these latter works have been supported by ample research findings; some have not.

In education, thoughtful practitioners and researchers have long been aware of the importance of nonverbal behavior for understanding various classroom phenomena. However, in the teaching profession before 1960, only minor attention was paid to the nonverbal domain as a subject for formal research. Relevant suggestions at that time usually involved teachers' use of their eyes and physical proximity to control students' behavior. The focused study of classroom nonverbal behavior began in the early 1960s and blossomed in the 1970s.

Representative surveys of educational research on nonverbal behavior have been prepared by Smith (1979), Woolfolk and Brooks (1983), and Neill (1991). Before discussing these summaries, it is worth noting that one topic involving major nonverbal elements with potentially important educational implications remains unsettled after 25 years of investigation—the self-fulfilling prophecy (see Wineburg 1987 and the accompanying responses by Rosenthal and Rist for a debate on this issue).

2. Nonverbal Behavior in Classrooms

Because of its inherent complexity, nonverbal behavior has often been subdivided by investigators into varying numbers and types of categories. To simplify discussion, the major research concepts and findings will be discussed under four main headings. However, it is important to note that, in practice, nonverbal behavior seldom lends itself to simple fragmentation.

2.1 Proxemics and Haptics

Proxemics refers to the use of one's social and personal space in situations that typically involve other persons. When teachers and students are in whole-class situations, the closer teachers are to students, the greater the amount of student participation in class activities. In classrooms where teachers teach mainly from the front, decreasing amounts of student participation occur from the front to back rows both in crowded seminar rooms and in laboratories with lines of workbenches. Should the teacher remain at the front center of the traditional classroom with its rows of desks, a triangle of participation can often be seen extending across the front row of seats and including the front two-thirds of the center column of student desks. These data suggest that teachers should make concerted efforts to move away from the front in order to involve students in all parts of their classrooms.

When teachers must conduct their lessons from the front, students consider themselves to be more included in class activities when the teachers make a habit of standing before the desk rather than behind it. Results have shown that teacher placement behind the front desk is related negatively to perceived teacher affection for and inclusion of the students. In general,

teachers are judged to be less warm as the distance from students increases; conversely, teacher proximity is seen to indicate liking, approval, and friendliness toward the students. However, the reverse is also true: students choosing to sit closer to teachers are seen to be more attentive, likable, and responsive than students who select seats in more remote regions of the classroom.

Cultural differences are reflected in the interpersonal distances adopted by interacting persons. For example, northern European teachers placed in southern European classrooms may be perceived by the students as cool, distant, and not liking them. In contrast, southern European teachers may cause initial discomfort in northern European students by standing uncommonly close to them and by making physical contact with them, such as by placing a hand on the student's shoulder.

Touching behavior, or haptics, is a natural part of the human condition but the where and when of its manifestation bears strong cultural overtones. Some cultures, such as the Japanese, use little touch after childhood (Ishii 1987). However, in high contact cultures such as the southern Italian, where touch is used regularly and frequently in interaction, the total absence of touch in teaching situations may trigger negative reactions toward both speaker and situation. In strict Islamic communities, there should be no touching of females in public, especially by males outside the family.

Further, in most teaching situations, touch carries connotations of power and authority: teachers may touch students, but students may not touch teachers. From an instructional perspective, it appears that some students may be more responsive to touch than to verbal or visual communications. In general, touch should emerge as a natural part of the classroom situation and should be employed only by teachers who feel comfortable using it.

2.2 Kinesics

The term kinesics refers to observable gestures, body movements, postures, and eye and facial behaviors manifested by an individual. Of the categories considered here, kinesics is the one which has received the most research attention during recent years. For example, Neill (1991) has produced a comprehensive review of research on kinesics that is especially relevant for United Kingdom classrooms.

One important component of kinesics involves the use of gestures. In teaching, the more frequent use of gestures has been associated with a more affiliative classroom style that elicits liking and cooperation from others. Although gestures are influenced by personality style and cultural background, they also reflect the amounts of involvement that teachers bring to a task. In most cultures, some moderate level of gestural activity (between the extremes of lethargic and hyperkinetic activity) is associated with the hard-to-define concept of "enthusiasm," which in turn has been related to teaching effectiveness.

The display and comprehension of gestures and associated body movements are particularly important for cultural groups, such as native North Americans, that are more visually than verbally oriented when compared to the surrounding majority cultures (Philips 1983). Because particular gestures can vary widely in meaning from culture to culture, it is important that teachers working in cultural settings other than their own become especially familiar with common face, hand, and finger movements of their hosts. Although it may be unrealistic to expect teachers to change their own basic behavioral patterns and cultural assumptions, they should have a working knowledge of the kinesic differences represented in their students and an empathy for children from dissimilar cultural backgrounds.

Teacher posture constitutes another relevant nonverbal factor. Teachers who have better control of their classes and who are more accessible to their students tend to manifest a relaxed and open bearing toward their students. Such teachers display fewer signs of defensiveness and anxiety (e.g., hands on hips, clenched fists, and tightly crossed arms). Teachers who tend to lean forwards are seen as accepting the students, involved with them, and liking them.

Similarly, the gestures, postures, and other body movements displayed by students can have important effects on teachers. In North American schools, students who appear interested and involved in the ongoing lessons are viewed in positive terms by the teachers. In addition to sitting near the teacher, such appearances typically include upright posture, forward leaning, alert demeanor, sufficient eye contact with the teacher, and active behavioral displays (such as hand waving and audible verbal emissions such as "Me . . . me") to gain the teacher's consent to respond. Students who behave otherwise are judged to be uninterested, uncomprehending, or unsupportive of class activities.

In many cultures, however, students interested in class activities follow other behavioral scripts. For example, to show respect Vietnamese students typically sit quietly and listen attentively to their teachers; these behaviors are often misinterpreted by these same teachers as representing passive and nonresponsive attitudes (Dinh Te 1989). Native North American students compete less than non-Natives for teachers' attention and show a more even distribution of talk among class members than is the case for non-Native students (Philips 1983). Again, this constellation of behaviors can be misinterpreted by teachers accustomed to the norms of European-American culture.

Use of the eyes, or gaze, has been implicated repeatedly in considerations regarding effective teacher behavior in North American classrooms. In these settings, increased numbers of disruptions are observed whenever the average amount of teacher eye contact with the class declines. In order to restore classroom order most teachers are aware of the effectiveness of a cold stare directed at offending individuals. For instructional purposes, looking at the students promotes their attentiveness, involvement, and positive regard for the teacher. These elements are particularly important when the teacher is working with a single student. In addition, students are expected to look directly at the teacher when speaking or when being spoken to. Otherwise, students may be perceived by teachers as being inattentive, uncooperative, or despondent.

However, eye contact is a behavior that is particularly sensitive to cultural standards. In many cultures, the direct eye contact that is valued so highly by the majority of North American teachers is considered an invasion of privacy, an act of defiance, an expression of deep passion, or a demonstration of lack of trust. For Muslims, direct gaze is aggressive, intrusive, and in violation of traditional Islamic norms. Vietnamese students avoid eye contact when talking to someone who is not an equal or of the same sex. Japanese culture is so highly non-gaze that even teachers frequently refrain from eye contact with their listeners. Even within North America, African-American and Native American students often avoid eye contact with their teachers with no intent to disrupt the ongoing instructional agendas.

Gaze can affect other students as well. For example, some highly anxious students find eye contact with their teachers extremely anxiety provoking. These students will seek to avert their gazes or to avoid direct eye contact altogether. Sensitive teachers should either reduce their amounts of gaze or ask the students if eye contact is distressing.

One facial behavior with important classroom implications is smiling. Although most beginning teachers are advised not to smile until December to promote classroom control, the more pertinent directive may be that teachers should not smile while discussing classroom rules and associated disciplinary measures. In fact, in many classrooms, the presence of teacher smiles seems to play an important role in classroom life. More than one study has found that teachers who smile are associated with thoughtful and responsive students over a variety of performance measures. Smiling has also been related to warmth and to the fostering of supportive and nonthreatening classroom climates that promote the development of positive student attitudes and achievement. However, the nature and context of the smile is important, since smiling can also be interpreted as a sign of weakness.

In turn, teachers tend to favor students who smile although once again cultural norms must be considered. For example, Vietnamese students may smile to apologize for minor offences (such as being late to class), to express embarrassment, to substitute for verbal expressions such as "I'm sorry" or "Thank you," to respond to a compliment, or to show no ill toward someone scolding them for mistakes made. But, for many teachers, students who smile while being reprimanded are displaying high levels of disrespect and scorn.

2.3 Paralanguage, Silence, and Chronemics

Paralanguage constitutes nonverbal characteristics of speech such as voice pitch, volume, tempo and intensity, intruding sounds, and silent pauses. In general, it appears that teachers who use lower voice volume and pitch are perceived to be in better control of their classes than teachers who shout constantly at a higher voice pitch. In addition, sarcasm, wherein the intended meaning of a message is transmitted by paralinguistic elements, is often not understood by children in elementary school. Finally, backchannel signals (such as "hmmm" or "right"), that are often used by Anglo listeners and that are interpreted by teachers as paying attention, are not universal among cultures. For example, Finnish students often display low levels of backchannel behavior. Also, native North American students can listen quietly to the teacher without displaying overt signs of attention and while looking at their peers.

Depending on when and where it occurs in an interaction, silence can communicate the full range of emotional expression from scorn and dislike to indifference to sympathy and love. In many cultures around the world, such as the Japanese, silence does not mean emptiness but instead is an effective and powerful means of communication. Unfortunately, many teachers tend to perceive student silence as passivity and indifference rather than as respect and attention.

Chronemics refers to the use of time. Most classroom instruction is very time oriented, and teachers are expected to complete all of their assigned tasks within firm time limits. Most skilled teachers have developed a sense of rhythm or pacing which allows sufficient time for the performance of necessary actions as well as for smooth transitions from one instructional activity to the next. Unskilled teachers with deficient rhythms tend to produce uneven transitions with increased probabilities of student confusion and misbehavior.

To promote most teachers' positive impressions, students must produce correct answers in the right forms at appropriate times. They must also know when to address questions to teachers and must respond quickly to teacher requests. They must know additional rules of the classroom culture, such as when to look at the teacher and for how long. These students will also know when and how to misbehave to avoid teacher sanctions (Brooks and Woolfolk 1987).

Of course, students coming to the classroom with different cultural expectations will operate at a disadvantage in all of these respects. One example concerns

response time. It has been noted that Finnish students take longer to respond than Swedish students and display little backchannel behavior to the teacher. Native North American students do not feel compelled to respond immediately to requests made of them. Finally, in English language classrooms, students who speak English as a second language take longer than usual to respond to teacher directives.

2.4 Other Factors

This section includes factors which do not constitute nonverbal behaviors in themselves but which influence the nonverbal behaviors emitted by human actors. The relevant variables to be mentioned briefly here are environmental factors and physical characteristics.

Environmental factors concern the effects of the physical attributes of settings on behavior. Although teacher plans can override the design features of architects (for instance, in open plan schools, teachers have often continued to teach in the traditional way), the type and arrangement of furniture in classrooms can promote or deny various activities.

When physical elements are arranged to allow orderly flow patterns and sufficient room to move, students exhibit more productive and fewer disruptive behaviors. Various studies have shown that an abundance of color, flexible lighting, comfortable seats, and the incorporation of student ideas and materials can substantially influence pupil attitudes and behavior even when effects on academic performance cannot be observed.

Physical characteristics refer to the influence of sex, varying human physiques, degrees of attractiveness, body odors, and hair or skin color on behavior. Each culture places different values on various combinations of these features which for the most part cannot be altered significantly by the individual. Students who display features valued by society tend to be considered attractive by others from that society. Children rated as more attractive are also more popular with their peers and possess better self-images than children rated as less attractive.

In the classroom, teachers make attractiveness judgments about students and tend to consider the more attractive ones as more intelligent, enthusiastic, and academically successful than less attractive students. Clearly, before entering the classroom, teachers should become aware of their own biases concerning what they consider as attractive or unattractive in students.

It may be worth mentioning one topic not considered in this entry: the use of nonverbal behaviors to comprehend and to reach students with a variety of personal and interpersonal difficulties (Heimlich and Mark 1990). Relevant groups include students who are abused, mentally retarded, autistic, and hyperactive. Increasingly, however, teachers are encountering these students in their classrooms and so should be prepared to respond to them in positive and helpful ways.

3. Implications for Future Research

As the foregoing sections indicate, much is now known about causes and effects of different forms of classroom nonverbal behavior but much still remains to be investigated. For example, the majority of the published research involves the traditional North American classroom. Whether these findings are maintained in different classroom or instructional configurations based in various cultural settings remains to be explored.

One important area of endeavor involves the methods used to prepare beginning teachers in the use of, and sensitization to, the nonverbal elements of classroom life. Acquaintance with classroom and other situational rules and familiarity with student behaviors that do not conform to local cultural norms are worthy of attention in preservice programs. These programs pay little attention to the nonverbal domain. Finally, research is needed to determine the most effective ways to instruct teachers so that their behavioral changes endure for substantial periods of time.

See also: Classroom Observation

References

Brooks D M, Woolfolk A E 1987 The effects of students' nonverbal behavior on teachers. *Elem. Sch. J.* 88: 52–63

Davis M 1972 *Understanding Body Movement: An Annotated Bibliography*. Arno Press, New York

Dinh Te H 1989 Introduction to Vietnamese culture. In: Chhim S-H, Luangpraseut K, Dinh Te H (eds.) 1989 *Introduction to Cambodian Culture-Laos Culturally Speaking-Introduction to Vietnamese Culture*. San Diego State University, San Diego, California

Feldman R S, Rimé B (eds.) 1991 *Fundamentals of Nonverbal Behavior*. Cambridge University Press, Cambridge

Heimlich E P, Mark A J 1990 *Paraverbal Communication with Children: Not Through Words Alone*. Plenum, New York

Ishii S 1987 *Nonverbal Communication in Japan*. The Japan Foundation, Tokyo

Key M R 1977 *Nonverbal Communication: A Research Guide and Bibliography*. Scarecrow, Metuchen, New Jersey

Neill S 1991 *Classroom Nonverbal Communication*. Routledge, London

Philips S 1983 *The Invisible Culture: Communication in Classroom and Community on the Warm Springs Indian Reservation*. Longman, New York

Smith H A 1979 Nonverbal communication in teaching. *Rev. Educ. Res.* 49(4): 631–72

Wineburg S S 1987 The self-fulfillment of the self-fulfilling prophecy. *Educ. Res.* 16(9): 28–37

Woolfolk A E, Brooks D M 1983 Nonverbal communication in teaching. *Rev. Res. Educ.* 10: 103–49

Further Reading

Axtell R E 1991 *Gestures: The Do's and Taboos of Body Language Around the World*. Wiley, New York

Hall E T 1966 *The Hidden Dimension*. Doubleday, New York

Kleinfeld J 1972 *Effective Teachers of Indian and Eskimo High School Students*. University of Alaska, Fairbanks, Alaska

Sebeok T A 1981 *The Play of Musement*. Indiana University Press, Bloomington, Indiana

Theory into Practice 1971 10(4), 1977 16(3), 1985 24(1)

Wolfgang A (ed.) 1984 *Nonverbal Behavior: Perspectives, Applications, Intercultural Insights*. Hogrefe and Huber Lewiston, New York

(d) Assessing and Evaluating

Assessment in the Service of Learning

S. Lane and R. Glaser

Educators, cognitive psychologists, and psychmetricians are reaffirming that the intent of instruction is to promote students' abilities as thinkers, problem-solvers, and inquirers. Underlying this goal is the view that meaningful understanding is based in the active construction of knowledge and often involves shared learning. Assessments, if they are to be aligned with current views on instruction and human learning, must more closely resemble meaningful learning tasks and assess the acquisition of high-level thinking and reasoning abilities as integral to subject-matter knowledge. New conceptual frameworks for the design of assessments require new psychometric theories that reflect current advances in research on cognition and human learning.

1. Traditional Tests and Test Theories

The psychological theory implicit in the design of traditional achievement assessments measuring long-term educational outcomes and growth in the United States has been derived primarily from behavioral theories of the 1960s. These generated behavioral objectives but could not adequately describe complex processes of thought, reasoning, and problem-solving. Tests were generally designed to be administered following instruction, rather than to be integrated with learning. For achievement assessments to inform instruction, analysis of the knowledge and cognitive processes that comprise competency within a subject-matter domain is required, so that assessments reflect the cognitive structures and processes that underlie the complexities of performance.

Techniques for measuring academic achievement have relied on the psychometric technology that emerged in the context of selection and placement testing. Standard test theory characterizes performance in terms of the difficulty level of response–choice items and focuses primarily on measuring the amount of declarative knowledge that students have acquired. This view of performance is at odds with current theories of cognition, which emphasize the meaningful learning that entails reasoning and problem-solving and involves the active construction of knowledge. Assessments that are integral to instruction and allow students to display the thinking, reasoning, and strategic processes that underlie their competencies can ensure more valid inferences regarding the nature and level of students' understanding.

2. Implications of Cognitive Psychology for Assessment

In conjunction with prevailing views on the acquisition of knowledge and competence, some cognitive psychologists now employ a cognitive-process-oriented assessment approach (Snow and Lohman 1989). Analysis of the structures of knowledge and cognitive processes that reveal degrees of subject-matter competence and descriptions of the differences between expert and novice performance can provide useful information for designing assessments. For example, expert–novice studies indicate that new learners often construct loosely connected knowledge structures that reflect partial understanding of the subject matter. As learning takes place, they broaden, integrate, and restructure their knowledge to accommodate new, qualitatively different information and connections, thus deepening their level of understanding within the subject-matter domain (Glaser and Chi 1988). Assessments should be capable of determining the nature and depth of students' understanding by reflecting the organization and coherence of their knowledge structures.

To promote students' acquisition of coherent knowledge structures, instruction and assessment should emphasize knowledge construction and possibilities for learning in collaborative settings. In classrooms, meaningful knowledge is often constructed through collaborative efforts in the attempt to reach common goals, for instance in discussions reflecting differences in perspective, which in turn lead to self-reflection. Changes in students' knowledge structures are more likely to occur when they are required to explain, elaborate, or justify their position to others, as well as to themselves (Brown and Palincsar 1989). Such classroom interactions allow for the display of various levels of student understanding and provide a rich environment for assessments of achievement and growth that are integral to learning and teaching.

Assessments should be constructed or selected to ensure their alignment with instructional activities and the results of assessment should be available for formative planning and change. Those that reflect the classroom learning situation can provide valuable information for instructional decision-making before, during, and after instruction. In order to provide an appropriate foundation for instruction, teachers can assess students' prior knowledge and understandings so that instruction can be shaped to meet their needs and abilities. By embedding them within instructional activities that display students' thinking and knowledge, assessments can provide useful information for diagnosing the needs of individual students and for monitoring the success of instructional activities. When administered at the end of instruction, assessments can indicate whether students have acquired subject-matter competencies. Hands-on performance assessments, open-ended tasks, journals, computer simulations of meaningful tasks, and portfolio assessments can all provide valuable information for instructional decision-making and for students' self-evaluation.

3. Considerations for Assessments and Measurement

The changing view of instruction and learning requires new criteria to ensure reliable and valid assessments (Glaser 1990, Frederiksen and Collins 1989, Linn et al. 1991). These criteria should guide the design of both classroom assessments and achievement assessments that measure more long-term educational outcomes and growth.

3.1 Assessments as Access to Educational Opportunities

As Linn (1989) has indicated, the most important challenge for educational assessment and measurement is "to make measurement do a better job of facilitating learning for all individuals" (p. 9). Assessments should be designed to uncover and display ways in which students represent and solve problems so they provide information to facilitate student learning. Underlying the interpretation of scores derived from many traditional tests is the assumption that students have had equivalent or similar educational opportunities. However, students with the same scores on a traditional test may have different understandings of the subject matter and may have employed different strategic processes. Delineating these differences can inform instruction.

Dynamic assessment, for example, a process-oriented approach that can provide information about the nature and depth of a student's understanding, is also possible. A common feature across differing forms of dynamic assessment is the emphasis on surveying the cognitive processes involved in individual student learning and observing change in the presence of instructional guidance. Dynamic assessment has its roots in Vygotsky's (1978) "zone of proximal development" namely, the level of performance a student can achieve by working initially with other students or with adults. By assessing learning in the zone of proximal development, information can be obtained about the level at which new knowledge and strategies can best be developed.

As a measure of learning potential, dynamic assessment can provide information about the processes and strategies that a student uses to solve problems, the degree to which these enable a student to respond to opportunities to acquire new strategies and knowledge, and the effectiveness of instructional procedures for strengthening the student's strategies (Campione and Brown 1990). In dynamic assessment, the assessment setting is modified in order to evaluate how easily students can improve on their performance level (Campione and Brown 1990). Modification may involve altering task formats, providing feedback, encouraging the use of self-monitoring skills, or providing instruction in domain-specific or general problem-solving strategies. Of importance is students' efficiency in acquiring and implementing these strategies and the resulting improvement in their acquisition of subject-matter knowledge. Dynamic assessment has the potential to identify students who may not have had the opportunity to acquire the knowledge or strategies being assessed, but who would be able to master them if given the opportunity. Therefore, dynamic assessment is particularly important when assessing students with differing educational and experiential backgrounds.

If students understand the criteria for evaluating performance, they can be encouraged to internalize the criteria, to aid each other in attaining them, and to assess their own performances more effectively (Frederikson and Collins 1989). The integration of assessment with instruction in a group environment affords students numerous sources of reflection on their own knowledge and performance. Such enriched self-assessment can help substantially in facilitating students' achievement of specific subject-matter competencies.

In collaborative settings, students and teachers can assess not only students' growing ability to reason and learn but also their facility in adapting to help and guidance. When students' performances are measured so that thought and reasoning processes are apparent, their zone of proximal development becomes clear. As they perform within an appropriate range of competence, teachers or peers can assist with the realization of higher levels of performance.

Assessments that are more representative of meaningful learning may require an entire period or a number of days and may take the form of a task to be undertaken outside the classroom setting. As an example, an extended task in science may require students to plan and conduct a study. Students would need to formulate research questions, to gather data to answer the research questions, to analyze this data, and to develop a report describing their findings. Such an extended task allows for both individual and collaborative work and promotes the display of student thinking.

3.2 Criteria for Valid and Reliable Assessments

Judgments regarding the cognitive significance of an assessment begin with an analysis of the cognitive requirements of the tasks as well as the ways in which students attempt to solve them (Glaser 1990). Although performance assessments may appear to be valid forms of assessment, in that they resemble meaningful learning tasks, these measures may be no more valid than scores derived from response–choice items (Linn et al. 1991). Evidence is needed to assure that assessments require the high-level thought and reasoning processes that they were intended to evoke (e.g., Magone et al. 1994).

Validation involves the examination of the actual and potential consequences of test use and score interpretation, as well as of more traditional empirical evidence (Messick 1989). To validate assessments in terms of their consequential basis, an analysis of the intended and unintended effects of assessments is needed. For example, the type of assessment administered may have direct consequences for instruction. Sole dependence on tests consisting of response–choice items may lead to instruction that emphasizes recall of facts and application of memorized routines and procedures. However, if the assessment requires synthesis of information, divergent thinking, and evaluation, instruction is more likely to include activities that promote these skills.

In line with Messick's conceptualization of consequential validity, Frederiksen and Collins (1989) proposed that assessments have "systemic validity" if they encourage behaviors on the part of teachers and students that promote the learning of valuable skills and knowledge, and allow for issues of transparency and openness, that is access to the criteria for evaluating performance. The collection of evidence on teachers' and students' (and administrators' and policymakers') interpretations of assessment results, as well as on the actions they take as a consequence, should thus be a feature of assessments that are designed for this kind of validity. Changes in instructional and curriculum goals and allocation of time to various instructional activities that enforce desired skills would constitute evidence for validating an assessment.

In interpreting the results of a particular assessment

procedure or instrument for various groups of students, an examination of its differential validity is necessary. For example, group differences in prior knowledge and experiences should be considered when developing assessments. As Messick (1989) has pointed out, to help ensure that one group is not at a disadvantage requires that the assessment fully represents the construct domain being measured and that it does not measure irrelevant constructs (such as reading ability or the context of the problem situation in a mathematics assessment). Differential item functioning (DIF) procedures can be applied to performance assessments, which in turn provide evidence for their fairness. DIF procedures are used to examine whether tasks are functioning the same way for students at the same ability level (as defined by performance on the test or some other criterion) but from different gender/ethnic/racial groups. To apply these procedures, a relatively large number of tasks need to be administered. As was indicated by Linn et al. (1991), the logical examination of the actual assessment tasks and procedures by a panel of professionals, as well as an extensive analysis of the ways in which students from various groups respond to the tasks, are crucial in establishing the fairness of assessments.

The degree to which there can be generalization from performance on an assessment to the larger construct domain is dependent on the breadth of the content represented in the assessment. Performance assessments allow for an extended and rich description of the nature and level of students' understanding of subject-matter knowledge. However, because performance assessments require more time on each task, the breadth of the content covered may be jeopardized. For classroom assessment, using a variety of assessment tasks and procedures that are aligned with instruction will help ensure valid inferences and generalizations regarding students' understanding in subject-matter domains. For achievement assessments at the school level that measure more long-term educational outcomes and growth, a matrix sampling approach (i.e., one in which each student receives a subset of the assessment tasks) will help ensure valid inferences and generalizations regarding school-level outcomes in the subject-matter domain (e.g., Lane et al. 1994).

4. Implications for Test Theory

To provide information useful for instructional decision-making, theories of cognition and performance are being called upon in the design of assessments. Consequently, cognitive models and psychometric technology should be integrated. Despite numerous changes in measurement since the 1970s, models and measurement procedures that capture students' thinking and reasoning and that provide useful information to teachers are at an early stage of development (Linn 1989).

The general principles that led to the development of

item response theory (IRT) can provide the foundations of an improved test theory that better reflects the goals of instruction and assessment (Mislevy 1989). IRT models for graded scoring of direct writing assessments have proven to be an effective means of constructing scales from evaluations of open-ended responses (Harris et al. 1988). Using these models, students' abilities can be characterized by parameters that express the probability of scoring at one of a number of continuous levels or discrete states of proficiency. This relationship enables performances on each task to be used to estimate students' ability on the construct being measured.

Harris et al. (1988) have applied partial credit analysis to student responses to a set of narrative writing tasks. Their goals were to identify component skills and knowledge that comprise writing competency and to use a description of these components as the basis of an assessment scheme. In contrast to holistic scoring, which provides a global score, this approach provides information for individual student diagnosis and instructional decision-making. In their study, the students' written stories received a score on each of eight scales (e.g., characterization development and coherence and story structure). Each scale provides a continuum of developing proficiency; a student is assigned to a region on the continuum based on the student's ability estimate. The level of proficiency is the same for students within a region on the continuum. For example, the lowest of the nine score levels of the scale for coherence and story structure indicates that the student's story most probably had "few connections, isolated ideas; reader must make large leaps" (p. 338), whereas the highest level of this scale indicates that there was most probably a "balanced integration of subplots contributing to the story" (p. 338). A student's pattern of scores on the eight scales identifies individual needs and strengths. Further studies of this kind, presenting procedures that successfully integrate cognitive theory and psychometric technology, are needed.

5. Conclusion

The educational goal of enabling students to be effective thinkers and problem-solvers requires a reconceptualization of both instruction and assessment. Traditional didactic instruction and traditional assessments of achievement are not suited to modern educational demands. Instruction that emphasizes student-constructed knowledge and the interactive nature of learning will provide an environment conducive to the acquisition and use of high-level thinking and reasoning abilities in the context of acquiring subject-matter knowledge. Achievement assessments must be an integral part of instruction, in that they should reflect, shape, and improve student learning. This will require that they simulate meaningful learning tasks and be aligned to modern conceptions of cognition and learning. The merger of cognitive theory and quantitative psychometric models is necessary in the design of performance assessments that reflect meaningful learning tasks.

See also: Indiviualized Testing in the Classroom; Prior Knowledge and Learning

References

Brown A L, Palincsar A S 1989 Guided, cooperative learning and individual knowledge acquisition. In: Resnick L (ed.) 1989 *Knowing, Learning, and Instruction: Essays in Honor of Robert Glaser*. Erlbaum, Hillsdale, New Jersey

Campione J C, Brown A L 1990 Guided learning and transfer: Implications for approaches to assessment. In: Frederiksen N, Glaser R, Lesgold A, Shafto M G (eds.) 1990 *Diagnostic Monitoring of Skill and Knowledge Acquisition*. Erlbaum, Hillsdale, New Jersey

Frederiksen J R, Collins A 1989 A system approach to educational testing. *Educ. Researcher* 18(9): 27–32

Glaser R 1990 Testing and assessment: O Tempora! O Mores! Horace Mann Lecture, University of Pittsburgh, LRDC, Pittsburgh, Pennsylvania

Glaser R, Chi M T H 1988 Overview. In: Chi M T H, Glaser R, Farr M J (eds.) 1988 *The Nature of Expertise* Erlbaum, Hillsdale, New Jersey

Harris J, Laan S, Mossenson L 1988 Applying partial credit analysis to the construction of narrative writing tests. *Appl. Measurement in Educ.* 1(4): 335–46

Lane S, Stone C, Ankenmann R, Liu M 1994 Empirical evidence for the reliability and validity of performance assessments. *Int. J. Educ. Res.* 21(3): 247–66

Linn R L 1989 Current perspectives and future directions. In: Linn R L (ed.) 1989 *Educational Measurement*, 3rd edn. Macmillan Inc., New York

Linn R L, Baker E L, Dunbar S B 1991 Complex performance-based assessment: Expectations and validation criteria. *Educ. Researcher* 20(8): 15–21

Magone M, Cai J, Silver E, Wang N 1994 Validity evidence for cognitive complexity of performance assessments: An analysis of selected QUASAR tasks. *Int. J. Educ. Res.* 21(3): 317–40

Messick S 1989 Validity. In: Linn R L (ed.) 1989 *Educational Measurement*, 3rd edn. Macmillan Inc., New York

Mislevy R J 1989 *Foundations of a New Test Theory*, Research Report No. 89–52-ONR. Educational Testing Service, Princeton, New Jersey

Snow R E, Lohman D F 1989 Implications of cognitive psychology for educational measurement. In: Linn R L (ed.) 1989 *Educational Measurement*, 3rd edn. Macmillan Inc., New York

Vygotsky L S 1978 *Mind in Society: The Development of Higher Psychological Processes*. Harvard University Press, Cambridge, Massachusetts

Further Reading

Bennett R E, Ward W C (eds.) 1993 *Construction versus Choice in Cognitive Measurement: Issues in Constructed Response, Performance Testing and Portfolio Assessment*. Erlbanm, Hillsdale, New Jersey

Evaluating

J. A. Zahorik

Teacher evaluating behavior refers to the feedback teachers provide for their students during classroom instruction regarding the progress that students are making towards identified goals. Teacher evaluating behavior in relation to two major learning tasks will be examined, followed by a discussion of emerging issues related to teacher evaluating behaviors.

1. Introduction

Examining classroom life is a complex problem. If one stands close to the classroom and focuses on micro aspects of teaching, such as types of questions or wait time, the larger activity in which these behaviors are embedded may be obscured. If one stands far from the classroom and focuses on macro aspects of teaching, such as the instructional leadership provided by the principal or the impact of achievement tests on teaching and learning, teaching itself will not be illuminated. The vantage point that has come to be seen as a productive middle distance between micro verbal and nonverbal actions of teachers and macro school level variables is the instructional task.

A task, according to Doyle (1983), is the work in which students engage in the classroom. A task consists of a product students are to develop, the procedures they are to follow in developing the product, and the resources they are to use. Doyle asserts that four types of tasks can be found in schools: (a) memory tasks, in which students are to reproduce information; (b) procedural tasks, in which students are to apply a formula; (c) comprehension tasks, in which students are to transform information, solve problems, and make predictions; and (d) opinion tasks, in which students are to reveal preferences. A similar list of tasks developed by Bennett and Desforges (1988) consists of incremental tasks, restructuring tasks, enrichment tasks, and practice tasks.

These tasks are compressed into two by Rosenshine and Meister (1992): well-structured tasks and less structured tasks. Well-structured or knowledge acquisition tasks are those that students can achieve directly by following a fixed sequence of steps (e.g., following the subtraction algorithm). The task product is invariable; that is, there is a single product that can be evaluated with a single criterion or set of criteria. Less structured or higher-order thinking tasks are those for which there exists no fixed sequence of steps for the student to follow. For these tasks (e.g., reading comprehension, science problem-solving), the teacher can provide a temporary heuristic as a model of the process to be followed or product to be developed, but the

student must interpret, transform, and modify this instructional aid to accomplish the task. In higher-order thinking tasks the teacher can influence the student's thinking, but the teacher cannot lead the student to the acceptable completion of the task because the routes to completion as well as the product that is produced by the student are personal and variable.

Although there undoubtedly are generic teaching behaviors that are appropriate for any instructional task, it seems reasonable to assume that since different tasks focus on different products, procedures, and materials, different teaching techniques are required. Thus, while many teacher evaluating behaviors fit any task structure, some are especially appropriate for knowledge-acquisition tasks, while others are required for higher-order thinking tasks.

2. Knowledge-acquisition Tasks and Teacher Evaluating Behavior

In knowledge-acquisition tasks the teacher's purpose is to enable students to learn some predetermined concept or skill. To ensure success, teachers should provide appropriate learning activities and materials and engage in appropriate verbal interactions with students. The behaviors that the teacher uses following student acts are referred to as teacher evaluating behaviors. These behaviors are critical because they inform students of the appropriateness of their actions in terms of the goal. If students have no knowledge of the results of their actions, learning progress is halted. Successes need to be confirmed; errors need to be identified and eliminated.

The process–product researchers of the 1970s and early 1980s did not explicitly set out to study teaching related to knowledge-acquisition tasks. Since, however, this research focused primarily on the teaching and learning of reading and mathematics at the elementary school level and used standardized achievement test scores as a measure of teaching effectiveness, the knowledge acquisition basis for the research was evident. Summaries of this research reveal the types of teacher evaluating behavior that are related to student achievement on knowledge acquisition tasks (Brophy and Good 1986).

Having examined scores of studies, Brophy and Good conclude that effective teacher evaluating behavior varies with the quality of students' responses. For correct responses the teacher should publicly indicate that the answer is correct with some overt oral behavior (e.g., "Right!") or nonverbal behavior (e.g., nod affirmatively). The purpose of the acknowledgement is to confirm that the answer was correct.

Effusive praise is not needed, and may actually detract from learning. For partly correct responses, the teacher should indicate the correct part and rephrase the question, give students clues, or actually provide the correct response regarding the incorrect part. Finally, for incorrect responses the teacher should first indicate that the answer is incorrect by using simple negative feedback rather than personal criticism. Next, the teacher should rephrase the question and/or provide clues that allow the student to attempt a correct response. The correct answer plus an explanation of why the answer is correct can also follow the negation. Brophy and Good further suggest that teachers encourage students to answer every question asked, even if only to say that they do not know the answer. Rephrasing, clueing, or providing the correct answer should then follow.

Rosenshine's (1983) review of process–product research yields similar suggestions regarding teacher evaluating behavior. Correct, quick, and firm student responses should be followed by another question or a short acknowledgement statement that does not interrupt the flow of the lesson. If the response is correct but the student is hesitant the teacher should provide short statements of acknowledgement and feedback concerning why the answer is correct. Incorrect but careless answers should be followed by a teacher correction and then movement to the next question. For incorrect answers caused by knowledge deficiency the teacher should provide clues or ask simpler questions or, when the student error is substantial, the teacher should reteach the material. Rosenshine emphasizes that the important point, according to research, is that "errors should not go uncorrected" (p. 343) because uncorrected errors result in subsequent learning problems.

A review of nearly 8,000 process–product studies at both the elementary and secondary school level conducted by Fraser et al. (1987), a team of Australian and United States researchers, found that teacher reacting behavior in the form of cues, reinforcement, and correctives (i.e., suggestions for making corrections) is a critical element in learning. Examining teacher reacting behavior in general, rather than in relation to the quality of students' responses, Walberg (1991) found that cuing can take a variety of forms: advance organizers or brief overviews, adjunct or key questions, goal setting, sequenced learning, and pretests. Reinforcement in the form of praise, Walberg found, has a small positive effect, but may be less effective than token rewards for younger students and grades or personal standards for more mature students. Corrective feedback or reteaching to eliminate error was found to have a moderate effect on student learning.

3. Higher-order Thinking Tasks and Teacher Evaluating Behavior

In contrast to teaching associated with knowledge-acquisition tasks, which is based largely on a behavioral conception of learning, teaching associated with higher-order thinking tasks is based on a constructivist view of learning. In terms of the latter tasks, teacher evaluating behavior serves not to strengthen associations between stimuli and responses, but to help students to build and enrich their internal knowledge structures. From the constructivist perspective, learning is a matter of establishing or constructing a network of relationships by connecting new knowledge to existing knowledge. Growth in knowledge, according to Resnick (1985), is a "result of learners' self-modification of their own thought processes and knowledge structures" (p. 2579).

The types of teacher evaluating behavior that facilitate student construction of the personal knowledge that higher-order thinking tasks require consist of supporting, linking, challenging, and modeling. These types of teacher evaluating behavior increase student self-evaluation and promote critical thinking.

3.1 Supporting

Supporting, or what Nystrom and Gamoran (1991) refer to as high-level evaluation, is behavior that occurs naturally in conversation and signals to the speaker that his or her thoughts are being taken seriously by the listener. It serves to maintain engagement with substantive ideas. Comments such as "That's an intriguing point" build on what students say, encourage students' thinking, and maintain classroom discourse at a high level. Through meaningful discussion, in contrast to more typical question–answer–evaluation recitation, students can construct their own meanings.

3.2 Linking

Linking refers to tying main ideas together, to providing a structure of ideas that students can use to build their own knowledge structures. The teacher who uses linking evaluating behavior points out the relationship of new knowledge to other new knowledge or to prior knowledge. Ausubel's (1978) advance organizers, when made in reaction to a student comment, can be viewed as linking acts. They provide an organization of major concepts into which supporting facts and details can be inserted.

Likewise, Shulman's (1986) content transformation is a form of linking. When teachers use analogies, examples, and illustrations to portray content, they are relating unknown content to known content. In response to students' real or anticipated misunderstandings, teachers can relate new content to previously taught content, to students' out-of-school experiences, and to content embedded in hypothetical situations (Zahorik 1992).

3.3 Challenging

Sigel (1984) suggests that to generate thinking and to cause students to integrate ideas and refine their knowledge structures, teachers should, "draw a child's attention to a discrepancy, contradiction, or inconsistency" (p. 21). The value of creating puzzlement is also supported by Gallagher and Wansart (1991). Coming to see gaps in understanding can result from teacher evaluating behavior, but it can also be a product of individual or group work on various projects.

3.4 Modeling

Modeling refers to giving students a model, heuristic, or guide that they can use to get started on an activity and to which they can refer to judge the adequacy of their actions or the progress of their thinking. The model can be given to students as products (that is, what is to be accomplished) or processes (that is, how the student is to accomplish what is expected). Examples of modeling include the provision and demonstration of guide questions (King 1989), process sequences (Taylor 1985), plan sheets (Englert et al. 1991), and cue cards (Billingsley and Wildman 1984). Each of these types of assistance provides students with a set of suggested ideas to be used in attempting to write a paragraph, summarize a story, or perform some other higher-level thinking task.

Another type of modeling is what Palinscar and Brown (1984) refer to as reciprocal teaching. The teacher and students take turns being the teacher. The teacher models the process for students. When students "teach" the process, they use the teacher's model as a guide and their progress is revealed to the teacher.

Building on the work of Vygotsky (1978), Rosenshine and Meister (1992) and others suggest that scaffolding be used when providing models. Scaffolding is a form of temporary guidance in which the model is presented but then gradually withdrawn as students become more independent and self-reliant in their actions. The effectiveness of providing models through scaffolding has been well documented by Collins et al. (1989).

Although all of the teacher evaluating behavior associated with higher-order thinking tasks seeks to make students their own evaluators as they construct knowledge, modeling differs somewhat from the other techniques in that it provides the means to determine adequacy in advance.

4. Emerging Issues

In regard to teacher evaluating behavior and knowledge acquisition tasks, there seems to be little controversy. Praise, reinforcement, and knowledge of results from the teacher can facilitate the learning of simple skills and basic content by students. In regard to teacher evaluating behavior and higher-order thinking tasks, however, a number of issues are emerging. The main issue is the amount of help or direction that students should be given as they attempt to understand ideas and reform existing cognitive structures through problem-solving and related activities. In this regard, one could look at supporting, linking, challenging, and modeling as existing in a hierarchy, with linking and modeling being used early in a learning sequence when students are unclear about task demands, and supporting and challenging being used later after students have formed meaningful connections and have gained confidence in their structures.

In contrast, one could see these two pairs of evaluating behavior as conflicting and incompatible acts. Some might question whether the links and models provided by the teacher stimulate or stymie students' development of their own knowledge structures, because the teacher link or model could be perceived by the student as a firm structure rather than a heuristic device. It could be argued that if one is serious about helping students develop personal knowledge structures, the less directive techniques of support and challenge would encourage students to be more self-monitoring. This argument is particularly compelling if these acts are used in conjunction with learning activities and problems that are highly meaningful to students. It is to be hoped that future research will deal with the comparative nature of various types of teacher evaluating behavior used with higher-order thinking tasks.

See also: Classroom Environments; Questioning; Synthesizing Research on Teaching

References

Ausubel D 1978 In defense of advance organizers: A reply to the critics. *Rev. Educ. Res.* 48(2): 251–57
Bennett N, Desforges C 1988 Matching classroom tasks to students' attainments. *Elem. Sch. J.* 88(3): 221–34
Billingsley B, Wildman T 1984 The effects of pre-reading activities on the comprehension monitoring of learning disabled adolescents. *Learning Disability Research* 4(1): 36–44
Brophy J, Good T 1986 Teacher behavior and student achievement. In: Wittrock M (ed.) 1986 *Handbook of Research on Teaching*, 3rd edn. Macmillan, New York
Collins A, Brown J, Newman S 1989 Cognitive apprenticeship: Teaching the crafts of reading, writing, and mathematics. In: Resnick L (ed.) 1989 *Knowing, Learning, and Instruction: Essays in Honor of Robert Glaser.* Erlbaum, Hillsdale, New Jersey
Doyle W 1983 Academic work. *Rev. Educ. Res.* 53(2): 159–99
Englert C, Raphael T, Anderson L, Anthony H, Stevens D 1991 Making strategies and self-talk visible: Writing instruction and special education classrooms. *Am. Educ. Res. J.* 28(2): 337–72
Fraser B, Walberg H, Welch W, Hattie J 1987 Syntheses of educational productivity research. *Int. J. Educ. Res.* 11(2): 73–145
Gallagher J, Wansart W 1991 An assimilative base model of strategy–knowledge interactions. *Rem. Spec. Educ.* 12(3): 31–41

King A 1989 Effects of a metacognitive strategy on high school students' comprehension of lectures. Paper presented at the annual meeting of the American Educational Research Association, San Francisco, California

Nystrom M, Gamoran A 1991 Student engagement: When recitation becomes conversation. In: Waxman H, Walberg H (eds.) 1991 *Effective Teaching: Current Research*. McCutchan, Berkeley, California

Palincsar A, Brown A 1984 Reciprocal teaching of comprehension-fostering and comprehension-monitoring activities. *Cognition and Instruction* 1(2): 117–75

Resnick L 1985 Instructional psychology. In: Husén T, Postlethwaite T N (eds.) 1985 *International Encyclopedia of Education*, 1st edn. Pergamon Press, Oxford

Rosenshine B 1983 Teaching functions in instructional programs. *Elem. Sch. J.* 83(4): 335–51

Rosenshine B, Meister C 1992 The use of scaffolds for teaching higher-order cognitive strategies. *Educ. Leadership* 49: 26–33

Shulman L 1986 Those who understand: Knowledge growth in teaching. *Educ. Researcher* 15(2): 4–14

Sigel I 1984 A constructivist perspective for teaching thinking. *Educ. Leadership* 42(3): 18–21

Taylor B 1985 Improving middle-grade students' reading and writing of expository text. *J. Educ. Res.* 79(2): 119–25

Vygotsky L 1978 *Mind in Society: The Development of Higher Psychological Processes*. Harvard University Press, Cambridge, Massachusetts

Walberg H 1991 Productive teaching and instruction: Assessing the knowledge base. In: Waxman H, Walberg H (eds.) 1991 *Effective Teaching: Current Research*. McCutchan, Berkeley, California

Zahorik J 1992 Connection making in teaching. Paper presented at the annual meeting of the American Educational Research Association, San Francisco

Further Reading

Caine R, Caine G 1991 *Making Connections: Teaching and the Human Brain*. Association for Supervision and Curriculum Development, Alexandria, Virginia

Marzano R 1992 *A Different Kind of Classroom: Teaching with Dimensions of Learning*. Association for Supervision and Curriculum Development, Alexandria, Virginia

Newmann F, Wehlage G 1993 Five standards of authentic instruction. *Educ. Leadership* 17: 8–12

Perkinson H 1993 *Teachers without Goals, Students without Purposes*. McGraw-Hill, New York

Prawat R 1993 The value of ideas: Problems versus possibilities in learning. *Educ. Researcher* 22: 5–16

Diagnosing Students' Needs

A. Helmke

Optimizing student learning requires an assessment of those student aptitudes which are relevant for learning. There are several ways for the teacher to collect such diagnostic information, ranging from standardized tests to informal observations; each serves a different purpose. This entry focuses on the strengths and weaknesses of various diagnostic tools, with special emphasis on teacher diagnoses of students' learning needs.

1. The Relevance of Diagnosing Students' Needs

Students' needs occur are related to the attainment of basic educational goals, especially the goal of cognitive growth. Differences among students in the attainment of such goals are caused in part by differences in their cognitive characteristics (such as intelligence and prior knowledge) and their motivational characteristics (such as need to achieve, self-concept of ability, and test anxiety). To optimally foster students' cognitive and affective growth, the teacher must be able to diagnose interindividual differences in those learning characteristics. Furthermore, teachers should be sensitive to intra-individual changes over time. From this perspective, diagnosis of students' needs

is not restricted to pupils with problems, deficits, or handicaps; rather, it includes the diagnosis of specific strengths and favorable prerequisites as well.

The proper diagnosis of learning-related student characteristics before, during, and after instruction is important for a variety of decisions. The scope of these decisions ranges from the planning and preparation of a single lesson to the design, presentation, and evaluation of the course of instruction. In the preactive phase of teaching, teacher decisions about the planning of instruction, the selection of appropriate materials, or the formation of instructional groups require judgments about each student's strengths and weaknesses as well as the distribution of these strengths and weaknesses in the classroom. During the interactive phase of instruction, several teacher activities are influenced by judgments about student aptitudes (e.g., posing questions or assigning tasks to students). The concept of the "steering group" is illustrative of interactive decision-making (see, for example, Clark and Peterson 1986). Many teachers determine the pacing of instruction by their perceptions of the reactions of a steering group (i.e., a reference group consisting of, for example, the students in the bottom one-fifth of the ability distribution). A major requirement for optimizing student learning is a satisfactory match between those teacher decisions and the actual needs of students.

Some teaching strategies (see *Diagnostic–Prescriptive Teaching; Individualized Instruction*) are explicitly based on the systematic relation between the results of differential diagnoses and teachers' instructional and didactical activities. Also, in research on teacher expertise, diagnostic competence of the teacher is regarded as a core component of teacher expertise (Weinert et al. 1990). Finally, teachers' judgments about the students are central to models of teaching as decision-making. According to the influential model of Shavelson and Stern (1981), teaching is regarded as consisting of a multistep process, which includes a variety of pedagogical decisions. These decisions depend on three sets of variables: (a) individual characteristics of the teachers themselves, (b) their use of judgment heuristics, and (c) the nature of the task. These constructs, however, do not affect pedagogical decisions directly, but are mediated by teachers' judgments about the students and the content being taught.

2. Methods of Diagnosing Students' Needs

There is a large variety of methods for assessing students' needs which can be classified with respect to at least the following five dimensions.

2.1 Data Source

There are three main kinds of data sources underlying teacher diagnoses: tests (or questionnaires), direct observation of student behavior, and student work. Data from these sources must be integrated by the teacher to make judgments about the student.

2.2 Goal

Summative evaluation focuses on the final product; examples would include minimum competency tests and final course examinations. The goal is grading or classifying students. In contrast, formative evaluation focuses on the process, not the final product. The goal is the continuous assessment of students' present knowledge, and the monitoring of their learning progress.

2.3 Degree of Formality

Examples of formal diagnoses are standardized tests, as they are frequently administered in the evaluation of schools or in educational research. In contrast, informal diagnoses comprise teacher-made tests or other procedures that elicit student work, as well as implicit teacher judgments that occur many times during classroom instruction.

2.4 Standard of evaluation

Three types of evaluative standards are typically used in teacher decision-making. Social standards involve the comparison of student achievement with the distribution of a given reference group, typically the classroom. Criterial standards involve the comparison of student achievement with a previously defined "mastery standard," which, as a rule, is derived from the respective curriculum. Finally, individual standards focus not on the absolute level, but on the intra-individual change over time (i.e., the extent to which the achievement of the student has improved or deteriorated).

2.5 Consideration of Dynamics

Traditional diagnosis of student aptitude (in particular, of intelligence) has focused on the students' competencies at a given point in time. Since it is based on the actual status of achievement, this diagnosis is static in nature. In contrast, the prototype of a dynamic procedure is the "learning potential" or "dynamic assessment" approach (Feuerstein 1980, Guthke 1992). This procedure, derived from Vygotsky's concept of the "zone of proximal development", assesses how much the competency profile of a given student can be improved by means of training and systematic support, utilizing a test–train–retest design. Competence is conceptualized as the capability to benefit from training. Although this procedure has been applied primarily to the diagnosis and remedying of deficiencies of poor learners, the principles could also be applied to domain-specific aptitudes of students in general.

3. The Use of Tests for Diagnosing Students' Achievement

Traditionally, standardized tests have been used to diagnose students. Since the 1980s, however, several alternative testing procedures have been used.

3.1 Standardized Achievement Tests

A widespread method for diagnosing student achievement is the standardized test. The major advantages of standardized tests are obvious: high objectivity and reliability. Furthermore, their use is very economic. There are, however, several problems associated with the use of standardized tests.

The first problem concerns the curricular validity of the test. It is well-known that there are considerable differences in the official curriculum both between and within different states or regions. Even within the same school, teachers can often select learning materials and determine the sequence of content covered. These differences among states, regions, or teachers themselves all contribute to the problem of the curricular validity of tests. Specifically, the smaller the overlap of instructional content which was actually taught with the content of the test, the lower the curricular validity of that test.

A second problem with standardized tests concerns the effects of achievement tests on teaching and learning. The increasing use of such tests (especially, but not only, in US schools) may contribute to a strong bias in education (Frederiksen 1984) because such standardized multiple-choice tests assess predominantly basic skills and factual knowledge. This emphasis may discourage teachers' efforts to teach to other equally important cognitive goals (e.g., understanding, problem-solving, application, evaluation, and creativity).

3.2 Alternative Approaches

Most standardized tests have been developed and are administered for summative evaluation purposes and are often less appropriate for formative evaluation and remediation. Therefore, and to overcome some of the critiques mentioned earlier, there is an increasing trend toward replacing or at least complementing traditional standardized tests with informal and diagnostic tests.

Teacher-developed informal tests are a widespread tool for determining students' actual achievement profiles. Their main advantages are sensitivity to the actual content of instruction and the possibility of diagnosing errors. Informal tests usually use open-ended questions rather than the multiple-choice format. As a consequence, they are often problematic with respect to objectivity and reliability.

A second alternative is diagnostic tests, which have been developed specifically for diagnostic purposes, in particular in mathematics and reading (Nitko 1989). One major category of these tests focuses on the detection of students' errors. Ideally, such a test would provide a one-to-one relationship between a specific wrong solution (an error) and a corresponding misconception. Obviously, this kind of diagnostic test is very useful for instruction because it facilitates a detailed analysis of erroneously learned rules, missing skills, and misconceptions. In other words, the teacher can learn why certain tasks or routines are not solved, and draw implications for his or her instruction (e.g., the selection of learning materials).

4. Teacher Judgments of Student Characteristics

Teachers' diagnoses of students' learning needs are based on a variety of sources: tests, school records, past grades, casual observation of students' behavior, information provided by the parents, and the anecdotical reports of other teachers. It is obvious that successful teaching requires that these assessments be valid. As Corno and Snow (1986) point out: "If differential treatment of learners is based on invalid assessments, the teaching system may become maladaptive, even discriminatory in the extreme" (p. 607). Also, teachers' perceptions of their students' ability form the basis for their expectations, which in turn influence students' self-concepts of their ability (Stipek and Tannatt 1984). Hence, the validity of teacher judgments has become an important issue in recent research.

The starting point of this research tradition, usually labeled the "judgment accuracy approach", is that accuracy requires an objective standard against which the teacher diagnosis can be measured. Thus, accuracy of judgments is determined by comparing respective teachers' judgments with some external criterion, mostly tests or other objective instruments. This approach, however, is characterized by several methodological problems, especially when accuracy is determined by computing difference scores between judgments and objective measures. This computation leads to a confusion of widely disparate judgmental biases and errors. Although suggestions have been made as to how to overcome these methodological problems, these problems are a major reason for research in this field being nearly abandoned. Only recently has there been a renaissance of the judgment-accuracy approach in education (Funder 1987).

Teachers are typically faced with the task of diagnosing several characteristics (e.g., various learning prerequisites) of several target persons (e.g., all students in the classroom). Under these circumstances, teacher judgment can be analyzed with respect to several statistically and logically independent components (Cook 1979): level (general underestimation or overestimation of mean competence), differentiation (underestimation or overestimation of within-class variance), and rank (correlations between teacher judgments and actual competencies). Most of the research on teacher judgment accuracy has dealt with the last component. (For psychometric properties of teacher judgments in general, see Hoge 1983.)

4.1 Teachers as Diagnosticians of Their Students' Achievement and Understanding

Hoge and Coladarci (1989) reviewed 16 studies dealing with the question of how accurately teachers judge their students' achievement. In these studies correlations of teachers' ratings of their students' academic achievement with achievement test scores were explored. The data support the validity of teachers' judgments of their students' achievement. The median judgment criterion correlation was 0.62 for teacher ratings of student achievement and 0.69 for teachers' prediction of students' test scores. Interestingly, large differences among teachers in their judgment accuracy were found (see also Helmke and Schrader 1987). Future research should investigate the contextual factors and teacher characteristics that account for this variability.

Research based on a cognitively oriented paradigm has begun to investigate what teachers know about their students' intuitive knowledge, their ways of thinking, and their understanding. A series of studies conducted in the area of mathematics instruction in the elementary school (e.g., Peterson et al. 1989) has shown that teachers were, on average, rather successful in judging the relative difficulties of various types of mathematical tasks. Furthermore, most of the teachers, when faced with videotapes of first-grade children solving various word problems, were also able to judge which strategies children of that age would generally use. However, when the task was to predict which of six selected students of their own classroom would apply certain strategies and whether they would solve those problems, teachers were only moderately knowledgeable. In other words, teachers were successful in judging the general developmental level of their students, but were less successful in differential diagnosis of individual students.

4.2. Teachers' Perceptions of their Students' Affective and Emotional Characteristics

Although researchers and teachers agree that fostering learning must take into account factors other than cognitive student characteristics, the salience of affective, motivational, volitional, and emotional determinants of learning is still underestimated. A major reason for this state of affairs may be the predominant cognitive orientation in today's mainstream psychology. Empirical studies on determinants of achievement often include the whole range of cognitive determinants (such as intelligence and prior knowledge) but typically only a very small (and often unreliably measured) subsample of noncognitive variables. However, as Helmke (1992) has demonstrated, if one uses a broad range of noncognitive variables, their predictive power for later achievement test performance is as high as the combined impact of intelligence plus prior knowledge, and is even higher for the prediction of grades.

4.2.1 Data sources for teacher judgments of non-cognitive variables.
Information about noncognitive student characteristics is typically gathered by formal instruments, such as questionnaires given to students, and teachers' judgments. The use of personality questionnaires in a nonanonymous setting with possibly crucial consequences for the tested person is questionable, and will probably not yield valid results. Therefore, teachers and school psychologists should be cautious in using the results of such questionnaires for individual diagnoses.

Teacher judgments are a more promising way of getting information about noncognitive student characteristics. However, it might be very helpful for the teacher to administer questionnaires on achievement-related attitudes and subjective ratings of the difficulty of instruction on an anonymous basis to get information about salient learning issues that exist within a classroom of students.

For implicit teacher judgments about their students' noncognitive characteristics the concept of accuracy is not applicable, since the standards against which teacher diagnoses are compared may be "soft" or ambiguous. The empirical evidence about teachers as diagnosticians of noncognitive student characteristics should be interpreted within these restrictions.

4.2.2 Judgment of motivational variables: Empirical research.
Most of the research concerning teacher judgments of noncognitive student variables has been conducted for achievement-related attitudes, attributions, self-concepts, emotions, and motives (Helmke and Fend 1982, Carr and Kurtz 1991). These, and most of the other studies, have shown that correlations between students' self-reports and the correspondent teacher ratings of these same variables are generally very low, ranging from about −0.10 to 0.35.

One reason for the low covariations is certainly the low psychometric quality of instruments tapping motivational variables, as compared with those measuring achievement and intelligence. There may in fact be no valid empirical indicators for the noncognitive constructs under consideration. For example, some test-anxious students may be able to hide their subjective emotional experience and to control their motor behavior. Similarly, the construct may be difficult to judge because its indicators are ambiguous. For example (as in the case of test anxiety again), there may be considerable interindividual differences with regard to its manifestation. Some students express anxiety in the form of heightened motoric, gestic, postural, and mimic activity, whereas others appear to be paralyzed. Finally, teachers may be more or less able and/or motivated to actually use existing behavioral cues for their judgments.

5. Conclusion

Although there is a considerable body of research on various methods and tools of teachers' diagnoses of students' needs, at least three areas are underrepresented in research on this topic.

First, attempts to analyze students' understanding and their content-specific knowledge structures, including the analysis of errors and misconceptions, are a necessary counterweight against the widespread use of standardized multiple-choice achievement tests. The growing use of computerized testing in diagnosis (Bunderson et al. 1989, Jäger 1991) appears to be very promising and is likely to facilitate and accelerate the appropriate and efficient use of diagnostic methods. Second, although there is now agreement about the importance of noncognitive student characteristics for learning, the focus of research on teacher diagnosis is strongly biased toward cognitive characteristics. Future teacher training should focus more on affective growth as an important educational outcome, and teachers should become more sensitive to observable manifestations of motivational aspects of learning. Third, this entry has concentrated on teachers' diagnoses of their students' needs. Although there is as yet little empirical research, it should not be overlooked that diagnosis by parents of their children may be important as well (Helmke and Schräder 1990).

See also: Diagnostic–Prescriptive Teaching; Aptitude-Treatment Interaction Model of Teaching; Individualized Instruction; Classroom Assessment

References

Bunderson C V, Inouye D K, Olsen J B 1989 The four generations of computerized educational measurement. In: Linn R L (ed.) 1989 *Educational Measurement*, 3rd edn. Macmillan, New York

Carr M, Kurtz B E 1991 Teachers' perceptions of their students' metacognition, attributions, and self-concept. *Br. J. Educ. Psychol.* 61(2): 197–206

Clark C M, Peterson P L 1986 Teachers' thought processes. In: Wittrock M C (ed.) 1986 *Handbook of Research on Teaching*, 3rd edn. Macmillan, New York

Cook M 1979 *Perceiving Others: The Psychology of Interpersonal Perception*. Methuen, London

Corno L, Snow R E 1986 Adapting teaching to individual differences among learners. In: Wittrock M C (ed.) 1986 *Handbook of Research on Teaching*, 3rd edn. Macmillan, New York

Feuerstein R 1980 *Instrumental Enrichment: An Intervention Program for Cognitive Modifiability*. University Park Press, Baltimore, Maryland

Frederiksen N 1984 The real test bias: Influences of testing on teaching and learning. *Am. Psychol.* 39: 193–202

Funder D C 1987 Errors and mistakes: Evaluating the accuracy of social judgment. *Psych. Bull.* 101: 75–90

Guthke J 1992 Learning tests—the concept, main research findings, problems and trends. *Learning and Individual Differences* 4(2): 137–51

Helmke A 1992 *Selbstvertrauen und schulische Leistungen*. Hogrefe, Göttingen

Helmke A, Fend H 1982 Diagnostic sensitivity of teachers and parents with respect to the test anxiety of students. In: Schwarzer R, van der Ploeg H M, Spielberger C D (eds.) 1982 *Advances in Test Anxiety Research*, Vol. 1. Erlbaum, Hillsdale, New Jersey

Helmke A, Schrader F W 1987 Interactional effects of instructional quality and teacher judgement accuracy on achievement. *Teaching and Teacher Education* 3(2): 91–98

Helmke A, Schrader F W 1990 Are mothers good diagnosticians of their children? Analyses of components and determinants of judgment accuracy. *The German Journal of Psychology* 14: 221–22

Hoge R D 1983 Psychometric properties of teacher-judgment measures of pupil aptitudes, classroom behaviors, and achievement levels. *J. Spec. Educ.* 17(4): 401–29

Hoge R D, Coladarci T 1989 Teacher-based judgments of academic achievement: A review of literature. *Rev. Educ. Res.* 59(3): 297–313

Jäger R S 1991 Computer diagnostics—survey of practical applications of computerized assessment—theoretical principles and perspectives. *Rev. Psy. App.* 41: 247–68

Nitko A J 1989 Designing tests that are integrated with instruction. In: Linn R L (ed.) 1989 *Educational Measurement*, 3rd edn. Macmillan, New York

Peterson P L, Carpenter T C, Fennema E 1989 Teachers' knowledge of students' knowledge in mathematics problem solving: Correlational and case analyses. *J. Educ. Psychol.* 81(4): 558–69

Shavelson R J, Stern P 1981 Research on teachers' pedagogical thoughts, judgments, decisions, and behavior. *Rev. Educ. Res.* 51(4): 455–98

Stipek D J, Tannatt L M 1984 Childrens' judgements of their own and their peer academic competence. *J. Educ. Psychol.* 76(1): 75–84

Weinert F E, Schrader F W, Helmke A 1990 Educational expertise: Closing the gap between educational research and classroom practice. *School Psychology International* 11(3): 163–80

Classroom Assessment

P. W. Airasian

Classroom assessment is the process teachers use when they collect, synthesize, and interpret information to aid them in decision-making. When classroom assessment is viewed from teachers' decision-making perspectives, rather than as the application of particular evidence-gathering techniques, its dimensions are greatly broadened. Both the number of viable assessment purposes and useful information-gathering techniques expand considerably.

The genesis of the teacher-centered view of classroom assessment can be traced over years of close examination of teachers' classroom responsibilities and the decisions needed to carry them out. Teachers' classroom lives have been reported on by Jackson

(1990), Lortie (1975), and Bullough (1989). Teachers' thought processes have been studied and described by Calderhead (1987), Clark and Peterson (1986), Elbaz (1991), Feiman-Nemser and Floden (1986), and Schon (1983). General collections on teachers and teaching are also available (Anderson 1989, Wittrock 1986).

A synthesis of this body of research leads to four generalizations that provide a useful perspective for considering the nature and dimensions of classroom assessment. First, classrooms are both social and academic environments. To survive and succeed in classrooms, teachers must know their pupils' social, personal, and emotional characteristics as well as their academic ones. Second, the classroom is an ad hoc, informal, experiential, person-centered environment which calls for constant teacher decision-making. Third, most of the decisions that confront teachers are immediate, practical ones that involve particular students and contexts. Classroom decision-making must invariably take into account the unique qualities of the students and situations involved, thereby requiring teachers to rely on their tacit, practical knowledge of students and the classroom context. Fourth, teachers are both assessors and participants in the classroom society, which has implications for their objectivity in collecting and interpreting assessment information.

Although the general, overriding purpose of classroom assessment is to help teachers make decisions, there are many different decisions and decision contexts that define the nature of classroom assessment. General categorizations of teachers' classroom decisions have been identified. One such organizational schema is based on social/personal, instructional, and bureaucratic teacher decisions (Airasian 1994), while another classifies decisions in terms of whether they occur before, during, or after instruction (American Federation of Teachers National Council on Measurement in Education National Education Association 1990). While there is a great deal of overlap between these two schemata, the categorization based on assessments made before, during, and after instruction will be used in this review.

1. Assessment Before Instruction

Before instruction can begin, teachers must address two assessment needs: (a) learning about their pupils' characteristics, needs, and abilities, and (b) planning their instruction.

1.1 Learning Pupil Characteristics

Before teachers can organize their pupils into classroom societies that are characterized by communication, order, and common goals, they must learn about their pupils' unique strengths, weaknesses, and personalities. This process of "sizing up" others, which occurs in all social settings, is used to form perceptions and expectations that can be used to establish rapport and guide future interactions. Because classrooms are interactive social and academic settings, they require teachers to assess and make decisions about their students' personal, social, and academic characteristics. These decisions produce the perceptions, expectations, interaction patterns, and practical knowledge which teachers rely upon when interacting with, managing, planning for, or instructing students (Feiman-Nemser and Floden 1986, Elbaz 1991).

Many kinds of information are used to inform these "sizing up" decisions, including formal academic pretests in the subject matter, hearsay evidence, students' modes of dress, their friends, and siblings' past performance. Teachers collect this information primarily through naturalistic observation. By the end of a week or two, most classroom teachers can provide detailed descriptions of each student's personal, social, and academic strengths and weaknesses. These initial, tacit perceptions, which remain quite stable over the school year, guide teachers' future academic and social interactions with students.

In spite of their inevitability and the trust teachers place in them, these initial perceptions and expectations often have limited validity and reliability (Airasian 1994). Much of the evidence that teachers use to inform these decisions at the beginning of the year is based upon spontaneous, informal observations which are rarely uniform across either pupils or occurrences. Moreover, the judgments teachers make about students often have little to do with the evidence they observed as, for example, when teachers commonly rely on observations of students' mode of dress, peer group membership, in-class posture, or homework neatness to judge their abilities or motivation. Finally, these initial decisions about pupils' characteristics are, of necessity, made quickly and often on the basis of small samples of behavior, leading to concern about the reliability of the assessment evidence. This concern is especially warranted since the first few days of school often elicit atypical student behavior.

1.2 Planning Instruction

The processes of planning and delivering instruction are important for classroom teachers, partly because they occupy a great deal of their time but mainly because they provide teachers with their chief source of professional satisfaction (Lortie 1975). When teachers plan instruction, they consider information both about student characteristics (such as ability levels, work habits, and readiness) and instructional resources (such as materials, time, space, equipment, and prior teaching experience in the subject area). A synthesis of this information results in a plan which outlines the nature of the instructional activities and goals that will be implemented with students. The primary motive for planning is to help teachers gain control over the instructional process by reducing their uncertainty and anxiety about teaching, reviewing the material to be presented, and identifying ways to get instruction started (Clark and Peterson 1986).

Among the materials teachers consider when planning instruction, none is more important than the textbook, or, more appropriately, the instructional package that is used in a subject area. In most classrooms at most grade levels, the traditional textbook has been replaced by an instructional package, which supplements the textbook with additional instructional and assessment resources such as educational objectives, daily lesson plans, chapter and unit reviews, chapter tests, practice worksheets, motivational activities, follow-up exercises, and so on. The instructional package could conceivably provide all the resources teachers need to plan, carry out, and assess instruction, and studies have shown that a large portion of the elementary school student's learning time and the teacher's instructional time, up to 75 percent, is focused on textbook use (Stodolsky 1988). This heavy reliance on packaged instructional plans and activities is understandable when one considers that many teachers must prepare many daily lesson plans.

Although the instructional package provides virtually all the resources needed to prepare, conduct, and assess a lesson, teachers should determine the appropriateness of these materials for their own particular settings and groups of pupils. Textbooks or instructional packages are intended to have applicability across a range of schools, teachers, and classes. They are not tailored to meet the unique needs and readiness of every group of users. It is, therefore, the responsibility of classroom teachers to assess the appropriateness of the instructional package for their own students and classroom contexts, using criteria such as clarity, comprehensiveness, pertinence, and pupil readiness (Airasian 1994, Brophy and Alleman 1991). Regardless of whether teachers develop lesson plans from scratch or select them from an instructional package, they have a responsibility to collect and examine assessment information both about students' needs, abilities, and work habits and the instructional materials in order to decide which instructional plan is most appropriate.

Thus, even before instruction begins, teachers must carry out considerable assessment and decision-making. They must learn enough about their students' academic and personal characteristics to feel sufficiently familiar with them to create a classroom social setting that encourages communication, order, and learning. Once the classroom society is organized, teachers begin the task of planning their instruction, a task they will repeat daily throughout the school year. In carrying out their planning, teachers consider and meld information about their students and instructional resources into an appropriate plan for instruction.

2. Assessment During Instruction

During instruction, teachers perform two activities. They implement the instructional plans developed or selected during the planning period, and they assess and make decisions about the success of the plan's implementation. As might be expected given the dynamic nature of instruction, teachers rely heavily upon informal observations and questions to collect evidence for their decisions. They focus on pupils' facial expressions, posture, participation, eye contact, deportment, and questions asked or answered to indicate how a lesson is going. They refer to the necessity of "reading" their audience to help them make decisions while

teaching (Clark and Peterson 1986, Jackson 1990).

The information teachers collect is used to make decisions about the curriculum, student learning, and class management. Curriculum decisions involve the appropriateness of materials, educational objectives, and activities, as well as the adequacy of their presentation to students. Learning decisions concern whether students understand or follow the main points of instruction. Management decisions monitor whether the students are paying attention or whether they need to be refocused on the lesson.

Assessments during instruction are formative. Their purpose is to monitor and, if necessary, remediate the instructional process. This largely informal approach to assessment during instruction creates two potential problems for the resulting decisions (Airasian 1994). First, classroom teachers may lack objectivity when assessing the adequacy of their teaching and its effects on student learning. Because teachers derive their main professional satisfactions from their instructional successes, it may be hard for them to observe and judge objectively. Every time a favorable judgment about instruction or learning is made, teachers are, in part, rewarding themselves.

Second, the incompleteness of the indicators teachers use in making assessments during instruction also creates a problem. Because instruction is an activity-based, interactive process, it is logical for teachers to focus their assessments on the process itself and students' immediate reactions to it. Such a focus, however, ignores the results of the process on student learning. The fact that students are responsive, attentive, or involved does not necessarily mean that they are learning, although this is a conclusion many teachers make. To increase the validity of assessments made during instruction, information should be collected not only about student reactions to the process, but also about their learning from it. Oral questioning and written assignments (including homework) are the most feasible techniques to utilize in these assessments.

3. Assessment After Instruction

Assessment carried out after the completion of instruction is usually designed to inform decisions about grading, placing, or promoting pupils. Postinstructional assessments focus on summative, bureaucratic decisions that teachers are required to make by virtue of their official positions within the school organization. The preponderance of these decisions are related to assessing students' attainment of the content, skills, and behaviors they were taught during instruction.

Postinstructional assessments lead to decisions that are both public and important. They are recorded in school files, sent home in periodic school reports, and discussed by students, parents, and teachers. They reflect important summative judgments about pupils that can affect their immediate opportunities, future educational placements, and, in some cases, life chances. For these reasons, assessment procedures used to gather evidence about pupil achievement after instruction is completed rely heavily on formal techniques that produce "hard," usually numerical, evidence of performance. This emphasis differs from the reliance on less formal, non-recorded, often impressionistic evidence for most assessments conducted before and during instruction.

Two features of assessments made after the completion of instruction are noteworthy. First, such postinstructional assessments often become the basis for subsequent planning decisions. There is, then, a cycle that unites assessment decisions made before, during, and after instruction. Second, the usefulness of postinstructional, summative assessments of achievement is dependent upon many of the assessments teachers make before and during instruction. To insure valid interpretations and decisions about pupil achievement after instruction, it is necessary that before and during instruction teachers know their students' status and needs, plan instructional activities and outcomes appropriate to these, provide effective instruction, construct or select assessment procedures that assess what their students have been taught, score performance objectively, and assign grades or marks fairly. If there are gaps or inadequacies in one or more of these prerequisite steps, the validity of postinstruction assessments and decisions will likely be diminished.

The primary goal in assessing learning after the completion of instruction is to insure that students are given a fair opportunity to demonstrate how much they have learned from the instruction they were given. A range of formal assessment techniques can be used to attain this goal. These techniques, which are the primary focus of traditional courses and textbooks in educational measurement (Airasian 1991), include teacher-made or textbook-supplied paper-and-pencil tests, performance assessments, and standardized tests. General discussions of assessment topics such as writing test items, observing and rating performance, test scoring, grading and marking, and test administration can be found in many textbooks. It is known that very few classroom teachers have had formal training in these or the other assessment areas described here (Schafer and Lissitz 1987).

The most commonly used postinstructional assessment technique is the teacher-made or textbook-supplied paper-and-pencil achievement test administered at the end of instruction on a unit or chapter of text. Most teacher-made and textbook-supplied tests tend to focus assessment on lower level rote learning, primarily because these are the kinds of behaviors for which it is easiest to construct test items. Although the ready availability of textbook-supplied tests makes them a convenient source of assessment material, these tests should be examined in terms of their appropriateness to teachers' particular classroom objectives and instructional emphases. In general, the more teachers deviate from the textbook during instruction, the less valid a textbook-supplied test is likely to be.

Many classroom achievements are not suitably assessed by paper-and-pencil tests. For example, such methods are not useful for assessing performances such as using a microscope, oral reading or speaking, cutting with scissors, bouncing a ball, or cooperating in group activities. These behaviors are best assessed by formally observing and rating students as they perform them (Burstall 1986). Although much of the assessment that teachers carry out before and during instruction also gathers evidence through teachers' observations of students' performance, these observations are primarily informal, unplanned, and spontaneous, in contrast to the formal, planned observations used to assess achievement after instruction. The use of formal performance assessments is being encouraged to replace perceived overreliance on paper-and-pencil tests in assessing students' learning (National Commission on Testing and Public Policy 1990).

Standardized tests are the third type of formal assessment used to inform postinstructional decisions about students. A standardized test is one which is designed to be used in many different locations and to be administered, scored, and interpreted in the same way no matter when or where it is administered. Most standardized tests provide information about how a given pupil achieved in comparison to his or her peers nationwide. Although the results of these tests are not very influential in teachers' overall assessment repertoires or decision-making, parents, students, and school administrators do take them seriously.

In sum, there are three general domains of assessment: those that occur before, during, and after instruction. Assessments in these domains differ in terms of timing, purpose, evidence-gathering techniques, formality, and record-keeping. All have consequences for student learning and classroom interaction. Taken together, they reflect the richness, complexity, and importance of teachers' classroom assessment activities.

4. Interpreting Classroom Assessments

Before assessment evidence of any kind can be used in decision-making, teachers must interpret it. Interpretation is a subjective process calling for teachers' judgments, and in classrooms, interpretations are heavily influenced by both the sizing-up decisions teachers make of their pupils and teachers' personal theories about children, schools, and learning. Within this framework, a few guidelines can be stated to improve teachers' interpretations and decision-making (Airasian 1994). First, assessment information describes students' learned behaviors and present status. Teachers should not interpret assessment information as representing the fixed "potential" or "capacity" of their students or the way the students necessarily will perform in the future.

Second, all assessment evidence contains some error or imprecision and thus should be interpreted as providing an estimate, not an exact indication, of pupil characteristics or learning. Some assessment error is random and uncontrollable, while other error is related to factors such as teacher bias or inadequate sampling of students' behaviors. Rarely should small differences in students' assessed performance be interpreted as representing significant or meaningful differences.

Third, a single assessment is a poor basis for making important decisions such as grading or promotion. Multiple sources of evidence provide a more valid and reliable indication than single assessments, especially when the decision to be made has significant import for the student. Corroboration of any single source of assessment information is desirable.

Fourth, assessments describe performance; they do not explain it. Assessment that identifies how a student did on a mathematics test or how a learning activity was received by students cannot itself explain why the student and class reacted as they did. To explain assessment results generally requires the collection of additional evidence.

These guidelines suggest the following teacher behaviors in interpreting assessment information: base interpretations on multiple sources of evidence; recognize the range of cultural and educational factors that can influence a student's performance; consider contextual factors which might provide alternative explanations for students' performance; and recognize that any single assessment provides an estimate of performance that can alter with changes in the student or classroom environment.

5. Ethical Aspects of Classroom Assessment

Teaching is both a practical and moral undertaking. Classroom teachers are professionals who have great autonomy in their classrooms, who possess knowledge their students do not, and who are permitted to make decisions that affect their students' lives. As a consequence, teachers, like other professionals, have ethical responsibilities to their students (Fenstermacher 1990). In the areas of assessment and decision-making, teachers' ethical responsibilities include both the collection and appropriate use of assessment information. Consequently, teachers are responsible for demonstrating behaviors such as re-

spect for student diversity, fairness in grading and judging students, collecting the best evidence possible on which to base decisions, interpreting evidence correctly, and respecting students' privacy.

See also: Teacher Planning; Student Evaluation of Teaching

References

Airasian P W 1991 Perspectives on measurement instruction. Educ. Meas.: *Issues Pract.* 10(1): 13–16
Airasian P W 1994 *Classroom Assessment.* McGraw-Hill, New York
American Federation of Teachers National Council on Measurement in Education National Education Association 1990 Standards for teacher competence in educational assessment of students. *Educ. Meas.: Issues Pract.* 9(4): 30–32
Anderson L W 1989 *The Effective Teacher.* McGraw Hill, New York
Brophy J E, Alleman J 1991 Activities as instructional tools: A framework for analysis and evaluation. *Educ. Res.* 20(4): 9–23
Bullough R 1989 *First-Year Teacher. A Case Study.* Teachers College Press, New York
Burstall C 1986 Innovative forms of assessment: A United Kingdom Perspective. *Educ. Meas.: Issues Pract.* 5(1): 17–22
Calderhead J (ed.) 1987 *Exploring Teachers' Thinking.* Cassel, London
Clark C M, Peterson P L 1986 Teachers' thought processes. In: Wittrock M C (ed.) 1986
Elbaz F 1991 Research on teachers' knowledge: The evolution of discourse. *J. Curric. Stud.* 23(1): 1–19
Feiman-Nemser S, Floden R E 1986 The cultures of teaching. In: Wittrock M C (ed.) 1986
Fenstermacher G D 1990 Some moral considerations in teaching as a profession. In: Goodlad J L, Soder R, and Sirotnik K A (eds.) 1990 *The Moral Dimensions of Teaching.* Jossey-Bass, San Francisco, California
Jackson P W 1990 *Life in Classrooms*, 2nd edn. Teachers College Press, New York
Lortie D C 1975 *Schoolteacher. A Sociological Study.* University of Chicago Press, Chicago, Illinois
National Commission on Testing and Public Policy 1990 *From Gatekeeper to Gateway: Transforming Testing in America.* Boston College, Chestnut Hill, Massachusetts
Schafer W D, Lissitz R W 1987 Measurement training for school personnel: Recommendations and reality. *J. Teach. Educ.* 38(3): 57–63
Schon D A 1983 *The Reflective Practitioner. How Professionals Think in Action.* Basic Books, New York
Stodolsky S S 1988 *The Subject Matters. Classroom Activity in Math and Social Studies.* University of Chicago Press, Chicago, Illinois
Wittrock M C (ed.) 1986 *Handbook of Research on Teaching.* Macmillan, New York

Individualized Testing in the Classroom

J. M. Linacre

Individualized testing can be quickly and easily instituted in the classroom by means of computer-adaptive testing. Computers in the classroom give teachers flexibility in the way that instruction is presented and tests are scored. Useful achievement measurements and performance diagnostic information can be obtained from even the first test administration with a small teacher-constructed item bank. The teacher can then continue to develop the item bank and administer subsequent related tests to the students. Each student's progress can be tracked and particular learning difficulties identified in a far more immediate and informative manner than with conventional paper-and-pencil testing. The algorithms underlying the test procedures can be based on Rasch measurement concepts and are simple to program and use. The data management requirements are not complex.

1. Computer-adaptive Testing (CAT) Redefined for the Classroom

The theory required for the management of testing where different tests are administered to individual students based on their observed or expected performances is well-known. It was initially developed in the context of the availability of a large number of test items, a large number of students to test, and an expensive testing environment. The prime design consideration was that the tests administered be as short and efficient as possible. The goal was to obtain for each student one number representing that student's performance level.

In the classroom, however, the design considerations are quite different. There are fewer test items and fewer students, but detailed indications of students' strengths and weaknesses are often more important than overall performance level summaries. Timely reporting is essential, as information even a few days old may no longer be relevant to the classroom instruction currently under way. Compared to paper-and-pencil tests, individualized test administration by computer can streamline testing, reporting, and record-keeping, and, after the initial set-up phase, lessen the clerical effort.

The theory generally applied to CAT is that each content area can be expressed in terms of an operationally defined variable representing a latent trait. Each item has a certain difficulty level and each student a certain ability in the content area. The probability of a student succeeding on a particular item can be modeled in a number of ways. The Rasch model, however, not only has the most desirable measurement characteristics,

but also the most satisfactory estimation characteristics for small samples.

2. Testing Individuals in the Classroom

The teacher begins with the area of curriculum or chapter in a text-book that is to be tested, and constructs test questions or "items" that follow from and probe this material. These items can be in multiple-choice format, but computer administration also facilitates free-form responses and automatic scoring of arithmetic problems and cloze questions.

To begin with, item writing can be time-consuming and require extra effort on the part of the teacher, but software aids, such as HyperCard (™Apple Corp.), can lessen the burden. The art of writing items to probe the material that has just been taught is easily mastered and professionally satisfying. In CAT, useful information is obtained even when the initial set of teacher's items, now called an item bank, is only the test that would have been administered in a conventional classroom paper-and-pencil test. Items can then be added to or deleted from this bank as desired, clarifying the focus of the testing, and also developing and enlarging the teacher's testing resources.

Initially the specific difficulties of the items may not be well-known, but even stratifying the items by hypothesized difficulty is productive. The range of values of item difficulties is often set so that the middle difficulty items are given difficulty calibrations around 0 logits (log-odds units). Assigning initial calibrations of -1 logits (log-odds units) to the easy items, 0 logits to the medium items and +1 logits to the hard items is helpful both from the viewpoint of selecting items suitable for each examinee and for diagnosing unexpected behavior (Yao 1991).

To administer these items to a student, a computer program is needed. Though there are elaborate published programs, for example, MicroCAT (Vale and Weiss 1987), CALL (Eurocentres Learning Service 1991) and intricate descriptions of professionally developed systems (Reckase 1974, Nitko and Hsu 1984), the actual computer programming required is simple, straight-forward and within the capabilities of any school's computer science department. Locally developed software is easier to tailor to local needs, and often much less expensive than professionally developed systems.

Administration of each test begins with the assignment of any reasonable initial ability estimate to the student. A starting ability estimate can be in the lower central part of the range of item difficulties, for example 0 to −1 logit, or else can be derived from the student's previous performances, for example, previously able students could start at +1 logit.

The CAT program then selects an item to present to the student. For statistical efficiency, this is of about the same difficulty as the student is thought to be able to deal with. There are situations, however, when it is desirable to give the student a feeling of having "succeeded" on the test in order to lessen test anxiety and other negative feelings (Gershon 1992). Accordingly, the CAT program can deliberately select items that are slightly easy for the particular student. This does not affect the validity of the test, but can mean that a few more items must be administered in order to obtain a given level of measurement precision.

As each further item is administered, a better estimate of the student's ability is obtained. If the student succeeds on the first item, the ability estimate is increased slightly. Failure decreases the ability estimate slightly. An item appropriate to the revised ability estimate is selected and administered and the process repeated. As the number of items administered increases, the precision with which the ability is estimated also increases so that the standard error of the ability estimate decreases. The test can end when the standard error becomes less than some preset amount, or when the student has been administered the maximum number of questions considered relevant, or when there are no more relevant questions in the item bank, or when a time-limit is reached, or just when the student becomes tired.

As the CAT system develops in use, refinements are easily added. Further item selection and stopping rules can be introduced to investigate unusual response patterns and to insure balanced use of the items in the bank. Students can be allowed to review and change previous answers or even to skip questions (Lunz et al. 1992). In particular, control over testing by the teacher permits variations in item format and presentation that are not feasible with standard CAT software or published tests.

Unless there is some test-coverage requirement which forces the administration of very easy or very hard questions, administering items on which there is less than 10 percent chance of failure or success, that is, more than 2.2 logits distant from the student's estimated ability, tends to provoke guessing or carelessness. Such off-target items do not expedite the measurement process. Indeed, it is the elimination of such inappropriate questions which is one of the main aims of CAT. Targeting item selection not only shortens the test but also reduces the provocation of irregular behavior and of the negative feelings so often associated with a test experience.

On completion of the test, the student can be informed immediately of the level of success by reporting an ability estimate rescaled from logits into some more familiar range of numbers, and also whatever diagnostic feedback the teacher deems useful.

Reported to the teacher is the ability estimate and diagnostic information concerning which easier items the student unexpectedly failed and which harder items the student unexpectedly answered correctly. This gives the teacher a performance profile of each student's strengths and weaknesses relative to that student's overall performance level, thus enabling the teacher to give special, appropriate instruction to each student and to groups of students with similar profiles. Using graphical aids in these reports permits teachers with little numerical background to make immediate and accurate use of this information (Masters et al. 1990).

As the items are administered, better information accumulates about their difficulty and validity. Poorly specified items can be revised or deleted. Item difficulties can be recalibrated to correspond to how difficult the students actually found the items. Then the next time these items are used, the measures they produce will have greater validity. New items can be added to the bank corresponding to each newly taught content area. The next test administered by the CAT program can thus include both new items and older items. This enables the relative difficulty of new and previous items to be compared, and, even more usefully, the progress of each student to be tracked in terms of increasing logit ability estimates. The use of previous items also reinforces student recall of earlier material.

The CAT item selection algorithm is used to prevent the administration of unproductively easy or hard items. Since the item bank can be entirely under the teacher's control, there is never the need to use an undesired item just because it happened to be in a published test or was used last year.

3. Adaptive-testing Algorithms

The Rasch algorithms used in classroom CAT have as good or better theoretical measurement properties than the large-scale adaptive testing algorithms. They are simple to implement as computer programs on classroom-level computer equipment.

Estimation of the student measures can be done by applying maximum likelihood methods directly (Wright and Stone 1979 pp. 15–20). A CAT program using such a method requires only a few pages of BASIC computer code (Halkitis 1993). For classroom use, however, results which are identical for all practical purposes can be produced by even simpler approximations (Wright 1988).

3.1 Testing to Determine Ability

Using the PROX algorithm (Cohen 1979), a useful current estimate of student ability at any point during the testing process is given by accumulating the following information:

(a)   The number of items administered so far = L.

(b) The number of right answers = R
(if there are no right answers yet, then let R = 0.5).

(c) The number of wrong answers = W
(if there are no wrong answers yet, then let W = 0.5).

(d) The sum of the item difficulties administered = SUMCAL.

(e) The sum of squares of those item difficulties = SUMSQCAL.

(f) Calculate the mean item difficulty administered, MEANCAL = SUMCAL/L.

(g) A dispersion factor for the spread of the item difficulties is
DF = $\sqrt{(1 + (\text{SUMSQCAL}/L - \text{MEANCAL}*\text{MEANCAL})/2.89)}$.

(h) The ability estimate, B, in logits is
B = MEANCAL + DF * LOG(R/W).

(i) The precision of estimate, B, is the standard error of measurement, SE,
SE = DF * $\sqrt{(L/(R*W))}$.

(j) The student's ability is estimated to be in the range B ± SE.

(k) Stop test, if stopping criteria are satisfied.

(l) Select the next item to administer randomly from the difficulty range, B±1, or, for an easier test, (B−1)±1.

The range of items, from which the best next one to administer is selected at random, can be defined by a range or window of item difficulties. Random selection of the next item administered from a relevant range of items promotes balanced use of the items and ensures that students of similar difficulties experience different tests, so reducing the possibility of earlier test-takers coaching later ones. If the target success rate by each student on the items is to be 50 percent, then the next item to be administered could have a difficulty level within about ±1 logit of B.

When it is desired to give the student a positive experience in an examination so that the student leaves the test with a general feeling of success, suitable, slightly easy items are those on which the student has an overall 70 percent (say) chance of success. Such items are those in the difficulty range centered about 1 logit less than B, the student's estimated ability. The item selection window is the range of difficulties B-2 to B, that is, (B-1)±1 logits.

3.2 Speeding up Item Presentation

Though computers can generally present items far faster than students can respond, very able students may become frustrated if their almost instantaneous responses to simple recall items cause them to wait for the computer to display each subsequent item.

Speedier item presentation occurs when the computer selects the next item while the student is still answering the current one. Since the difficulty of the selected items only changes slowly, this has little effect on the statistical efficiency of the test.

To obtain speedier item administration:

(a) Select two items initially.

(b) Display one of the selected items on the screen.

(c) Capture the student's response.

(d) Immediately display another selected item.

(e) While the student reads the displayed item, perform steps (a)-(1) of 3.1, based on the earlier item and the student's response in (c). Step (1) of 3.1 selects the next item.

(f) Loop back to (c), unless the test is to stop.

(g) If test is to stop, capture student's response to last displayed item, and calculate student's final ability estimate from steps (a)-(j) of 3.1.

3.3 Test Anxiety

For various reasons, students may exhibit uncharacteristically low performance levels on the first few items of a CAT test. The computer can make note of the ability level estimated after, say, the first four items. If later ability estimates are significantly higher, then test anxiety or other factors may have degraded initial performance. A simple correction is to drop the first four items from ability estimation, recomputing the student's ability as though the test started at the fifth item.

3.4 Testing to Determine Mastery

When the purpose of the test is not to estimate a student's ability, but simply to decide whether that ability is above or below a certain criterion level, a simple adjustment to the CAT algorithm suffices.

Start by administering an item close to the criterion level, C. Continue by administering items corresponding to the student's current ability estimate, using steps (a)-(1) of 3.1. Stop testing when the ability estimate is significantly distant from the criterion level, C. This occurs when the ability estimate, B, is at least one standard error (or, at most, two) from C. For a student with ability 1 logit from the criterion level, this would require a test of 15–20 questions.

There will be occasions when a student's ability level is too close to the criterion level to reach a pass/fail decision promptly. The test stops after some maximum number of items is administered. The decision relative to the criterion then depends on the purpose of the test. The student has neither clearly exceeded nor clearly fallen short of the criterion level. If the purpose is to verify mastery, then the student must clearly exceed the criterion level. If the purpose is to verify failure, then the student must clearly fall short of the criterion level.

3.5 Using CAT Tests for Diagnosis

From the teacher's viewpoint, diagnostic information about a student's performance is usually more valuable than a single, holistic measure of ability. Several types of information can be obtained from one test.

First, the content area can be divided into different strands or objectives. The student's ability on each strand can be estimated independently and thus a profile of the student's performance obtained which identifies strengths and weaknesses among strands. To facilitate this, the item administration process can be designed to select items from all strands in an even pattern.

Second, deficiencies or special strengths in the student's performance profile can be detected. In the course of the test administration, each student is likely to meet, or can be arranged to meet, a few questions that are somewhat hard and a few that are somewhat easy. If any of these off-target items provoke unexpected responses, the misfitting responses can be investigated for their diagnostic implications. Excessively hard items however, provoke wild guessing. Excessively easy items provoke specious answers to student-perceived "trick" questions.

Third, test items can be designed such that even incorrect answers provide useful diagnostic information about the student's performance (Adams 1988). Partially correct answers can also focus item selection and assist in estimating student ability.

3.6 Calibrating the Item Bank

Item banks developed and maintained in the classroom have the advantage that test items can be added or deleted at any time. All estimates of item difficulty are, of course, only approximate. Even well-established items require periodic checks to insure they continue to perform as intended. The deliberate inclusion, among the items used in each test session, of items in the same content area from other test sessions enables the entire item bank to be regarded as one comprehensive test, of which any particular student is administered a small section at any one time. Recalibration of the item bank enables the relative difficulties of all items in a content area to be obtained and maintained.

In order to validate or recalibrate the item difficulties, the responses made to the items by each student, along with that student's final ability estimates, are saved in an archive file after the test is completed. These archive files form a database used to obtain revised item difficulty estimates via standard Rasch estimation algorithms and computer programs or by using an algorithm equivalent to the one used for obtaining ability estimates.

Thus, for each item:

(a) The number of students who administered the item = N.

(b) The number of right answers by them to the item = R (if there are no right answers yet, then R = 0.5).

(c) The number of wrong answers by them to the item = W (if there are no wrong answers yet, then W = 0.5).

(d) The sum of abilities of those answering the item = SUMMES.

(e) The sum of squares of those student abilities = SUMSQMES.

(f) Calculate the mean student ability for the item, MEANMES = SUMMES/N.

(g) A dispersion factor for the spread of the student abilities is
DF = $\sqrt{(1 + (\text{SUMSQMES}/N - \text{MEANMES}*\text{MEANMES})/2.89)}$.

(h) The item difficulty estimate, D, in logits is
D = MEANMES – DF * LOG(R/W)

(i) The precision of estimate, D, is the standard error of measurement, SE,
SE = DF * $\sqrt{(N/(R*W))}$.

Diagnostic information equivalent to that for the students can also be obtained for items. This indicates whether each item is functioning as intended.

4. Item Bank and the Curriculum

The item bank contains items written to represent a content area. After bank recalibration, the difficulty estimate of each item is an indication of how difficult the students found that item. Consequently, the difficulty ordering of the items is an empirical representation of the acquisition ordering of the content area (Wright and Bell 1984). In general, a teacher presents the easiest material first, advancing to more complex material. The empirical ordering of items in the bank informs the teacher as to whether the teacher's organization of the material coincides with the student's experience. This can give the teacher greater confidence in the presentation sequence in use, or lead the teacher to alter the degree of emphasis or sequence of presentation of the material in order to expedite student learning.

5. Tracking Student Progress

Because the difficulty of each test is positioned in the metric frame of reference of the curriculum content area item bank, the ability of each student is also positioned within that frame of reference. During each subsequent testing session a further ability estimate for that student is obtained on the same metric. These ability estimates are directly comparable with items having numerically equivalent difficulty calibrations. Thus these items give a criterion meaning to that ability measure.

Over time, quantitative ability estimates for each student describe a developmental sequence and can be used to track student progress. This progress can be reported not only in terms of position relative to the rest of the class, but more substantively in terms of the particular items in the bank which have been mastered, and consequently in terms of the material in the curriculum which corresponds to the student's ability at any given time. The need for and type of special instruction thus becomes clear, and, when undertaken, its effect can be clearly observed by tracking the progress of the student's further ability estimates.

References

Adams R J 1988 Applying the partial credit model to educational diagnosis. *Applied Measurement in Education* 1(4): 347–61
Cohen L 1979 Approximate expressions for parameter estimates in the Rasch model. *Br. J. Math. S.* 32(1): 113–20
Eurocentres Learning Service 1991 CALL Computer Assisted Language Learning Authoring Program. Author, Zurich Switzerland
Gershon R C 1992 Test Anxiety and Item Order: New Concerns for Item Response Theory. In: Wilson M (ed.) *Objective Measurement: Theory into Practice*. Vol. 1. Ablex, Norwood, New Jersey
Halkitis P N 1993 Computer-adaptive testing algorithms. *Rasch Measurement* 6(4): 254–55
Lunz M E, Bergstrom B A, Wright B D 1992 The effect of review on student ability and test efficiency for computerized adaptive tests. *Appl. Psychol. Meas.* 16(1): 33–40
Masters G et al. 1990 *Profiles of Learning: The Basic Skills Testing Program in NSW. Australian Council for Educational Research, Hawthorn*
Nitko A J, Hsu T-C 1984 A comprehensive microcomputer system for classroom testing. *J. Educ. Meas.* 21(4): 377–90
Reckase M D 1974 An interactive computer program for tailored testing based on the one-parameter logistic model. *Behavior Research Methods and Instrumentation* 6(2): 208–12
Vale C D, Weiss D J 1987 *MicroCAT Testing System*. Assessment Systems Corporation, St Paul, Minnesota
Wright B D 1988 Practical adaptive testing. *Rasch Measurement* 2(2): 21
Wright B D, Stone M H 1979 *Best Test Design*. MESA Press, Chicago, Illinois
Wright B D, Bell S R 1984 Item banks: What, why, how. *J. Educ. Meas.* 21(4): 331–45
Yao T 1991 CAT with a poorly calibrated item bank. *Rasch Measurement* 5(2): 141

Further Reading

Alderson J C, North B (eds.) 1991 *Language Testing in the 1990s: The Communicative Legacy*. MacMillan, London
Baker F B 1986 Item banking in computer-based instructional systems. *Appl. Psychol. Meas.* 10(4): 405–14
Schoonman W 1989 *An Applied Study on Computerized Adaptive Testing*. Swets and Zeitlinger, Rockland, Massachusetts

Grading and Evaluating Students

G. Borich and T. Kubiszyn

In the United States the type of system teachers use to assign grades (or marks) to students is often determined at the district or school level. Most teachers have little choice of whether an "A through F," "Excellent–Good–Satisfactory–Unsatisfactory," or numerical (e.g., 0–100 points) system is used. However, teachers do have considerable flexibility in deciding how the grades are assigned to students within the system.

1. Types of Comparison used in Grading Students

Assigning a grade to a student typically involves some type of comparison. A student's classroom performance can be compared with the performance of other students (norm-referenced grading), established standards of excellence, mastery, or minimal competency (criterion-referenced grading), the student's aptitudes, the student's effort, or the student's improvement in his or her performance. Each of these types of comparison has advantages and disadvantages.

1.1 Comparisons with Other Students

This approach to grading is often referred to as "grading on the curve." Grading on the curve means that the grade assigned to a student is based on the performance of other students in the class. Certain percentages of the class are assigned A's, B's, C's, D's, and F's, depending upon how they performed relative to others, regardless of their absolute level of performance. A student who answers 50 percent of the items on a test correctly might get an A, F, or any grade in between, depending on how his or her score of 50 percent compares with the scores of other students in the class. A school may encourage grading on the

Table 1
Distribution of Students based on standard deviations

Standard deviations from the mean	Letter grade	Approximate percentage of students
+1.50	A	7
+.75 to +1.49	B	16
mean ±.74	C	54
−.75 to −1.49	D	16
−1.50	F	7

curve by suggesting the approximate percentages of students who should be assigned various marks. For example, 10 percent may be assigned A's and F's, 20 percent may be assigned B's and D's, with the remaining 40 percent assigned C's.

The main advantage of such a system is that it simplifies grading decisions. There is no apparent need for deliberation over what scores constitute cut-offs for the various grades since these cut-offs can be provided by reference to the distribution of scores (e.g., the top 10 percent of the students receive A's). Assuming the distribution of scores follows the normal or bell-shaped distribution, standard deviation units from the mean can be used to determine divisions between the marks. For example, Table 1 shows the percentages of students that may be assigned to each of five grade categories for a normally distributed set of scores.

Statistical techniques (see Kubiszyn and Borich in press) may be used in selecting and revising test items to assure the required normal or bell-shaped distribution. In practice, however, grading on the curve is often used with non-normal distributions by selecting asymmetrical cut-off scores around the mean with which desired percentages can be obtained.

There are several disadvantages with grading on the curve. First, this approach fails to consider differences due to the overall ability level of the class. Imagine the disappointment that would result if such a system were imposed on a class of intellectually gifted students, none of whom had ever earned less than a B. Suddenly, 77 percent would be transformed into C through F students. Regardless of their achievement, in such a system some students will always get A's, some will always get F's.

Another disadvantage involves specifying percentages: why have 5 percent A's, not 15 percent A's? These percentages, or the standard deviations from the mean from which they are derived, are often arbitrarily set. Furthermore, the meaning of an A may not be clear: Has the "A" student mastered all course content? Or, was the student graded with a class of less able learners? Such a system fails to indicate *absolute* achievement, which makes comparisons across grades and schools difficult.

1.2 Comparison with Established Standards

In this approach it is possible for all students or no students to get A's or F's or any grade in between. The performance of the rest of the students in the class is irrelevant to a student's grade. All that is relevant is whether a student attains a defined standard of achievement or performance. This approach is sometimes labeled "criterion referenced." In a criterion-referenced system, letter grades may be assigned based on the percentage of test items answered correctly. Answering correctly 85 percent of the items or more may earn an A, while answering between 75 and 84 percent correctly might earn a B. Decreasing percentages can be used to differentiate grades of C, D, and F. Thus, a student who answers 79 percent of the test items correctly earns a B, regardless of whether the rest of the class did better, worse, or about the same. The successful use of this approach requires some prior knowledge of what level of achievement or performance it is reasonable to expect from students given the difficulty of the test.

There are several advantages to such a system. First, it is possible, in theory, for all students to obtain high grades if they show sufficient effort (assuming the percentage cut-offs are not unreasonably high). Second, the assignment of grades is simplified. A student either has answered 75 percent of the items correctly or has not. As with comparison with other students, there is no apparent need to deliberate over assigning grades, once the desired percentages are selected. Finally, assuming that ability levels of incoming students remain fairly constant and that tests remain comparable in validity and difficulty, teachers who work to improve their teaching effectiveness should see improvement in grades with the passage of time.

Such a system also has some disadvantages. Establishing standards may be difficult. What it is reasonable to expect for an "A" may vary from school to school, across time, across students, across communities, and across curricula. For example, should the same standards be maintained for a gifted or a less able class as for a class of average learners? Another limitation is that some parents and administrators may have difficulty accepting a grading system that potentially allows everyone to make an "A."

1.3 Comparisons with Aptitude

Aptitude is another name for potential or ability. In an approach based on aptitude, students are compared neither to other students nor to established standards. Instead, they are compared to themselves. That is, grades are assigned according to how close their achievement is to their potential. Thus students with high aptitudes who are achieving at high levels would get high grades, since they would be achieving at their potential. Those with high aptitude and average achievement would get lower grades, since they would be achieving below their potential. Students

Table 2
Relationships between aptitude, achievement, and marks in marking systems based on comparisons of achievement with aptitude

Aptitude level	Achievement level	Marks
High	High Average Low	High Average Low
Average	High Average Low	High High Average
Low	High Average Low	High High High

with average aptitude and average achievement would also get high grades, since they would be considered to be achieving at their potential. Although such a system appears attractive, several problems exist, as illustrated in Table 2.

Table 2 illustrates that the concept of assigning grades based on the congruence of a student's achievement with the student's aptitude may be reasonable for high-aptitude students but not for low-aptitude students. If a student's aptitude is very low, it would be unlikely the student would achieve below his or her potential. Thus, the student would always be achieving at or above the expected level. Thus, this approach might not be fair to students of moderate and high ability. Perhaps more importantly, this approach greatly complicates interpreting grades. For example, a C for a high-aptitude student might indicate 70 percent mastery, while for an average-aptitude student it might indicate 60 percent, and perhaps 50 percent mastery for the low-aptitude student. The same grade may mean very different things in terms of absolute achievement.

Another drawback is the tendency for the achievement scores of lower aptitude students to increase and the achievement scores of higher aptitude students to decrease on repeated testing. This phenomenon is called the "regression toward the mean" effect; the more extreme an achievement score, the further it can be expected to "regress" or fall back toward the average or mean of all students at another testing. Finally, this approach requires more complex record-keeping than the first two approaches discussed.

1.4 Comparison of Achievement with Effort

Approaches that compare achievement with effort are similar to those that compare achievement with aptitude. Students who obtain average test scores but have to work hard to get them are given high marks.

Students who get average scores but do not have to work hard are given lower marks.

Several problems exist with approaches to grading based on effort. First, there may be no known acceptable measures of effort. Unlike aptitude, for which reliable and valid measures exist, effort is at best estimated by informal procedures. Second, some students may be punished for excelling quickly, while others are rewarded for taking a longer time to master concepts. Third, there is once again the problem that the grades themselves may not represent academic achievement. Effort may not coincide with academic attainment, making grades all the more difficult to interpret. Finally, record-keeping is once again complicated.

The advantage cited for grading based on effort is that it serves to motivate the slower or poorly motivated students. However, it may also serve to discourage the brighter students who would quickly see such a system as unfair. Whatever the case, the primary function of grading—to provide feedback about academic achievement—is less likely to be achieved by teachers who use this approach.

1.5 Equating Achievement with Improvement

In this approach, the amount of improvement between the beginning and end of instruction is used to assign grades. Through a system of pretesting and posttesting, students who show the most progress are awarded the highest grades. However, a problem occurs for students who do well on the pretest. Improvement for such students is likely to be less overall than for students who do poorly on the pretest. More proficient learners sometimes have been known to "underperform" on pretests on purpose when this approach is used. Other shortcomings include the statistical problems mentioned with regard to regression toward the mean and the added burden of constructing and administering pretests.

1.6 Selecting the Best Approach

Since each approach has advantages as well as limitations, many schools and districts have adopted multiple marking systems, such as assigning separate grades for achievement and effort or for achievement, effort, and improvement. As long as the achievement portion of the grade reflects *only* achievement, such systems are defensible. Two disadvantages of such systems are worth noting, however. First, they increase the number of grades to be assigned and interpreted, leading to an increase in record-keeping and in the time needed to report the grades to others. Second, unless the purpose of each grade is explained clearly on the report card, multiple marking systems are often difficult for parents to decipher. When feedback about academic achievement is the primary goal, comparison with established standards is the method of choice.

2 Types of Symbols

Within grading systems, a variety of symbols has been used. The more common types are letter grades, numerical grades, pass–fail grades, and checklists.

2.1 Letter Grades

The use of letter grades is the most common kind of grading. Over 75 percent of the high schools in America use the letters A–F to report marks (Kubiszyn and Borich in press). Sometimes, plus and minus signs are used to indicate finer distinctions between the letter grades, providing as many as 15 separate symbols. This system along with its variation (Excellent, Good, Satisfactory, Unsatisfactory) has several advantages that have led to its widespread adoption and popularity.

First, the letter system is widely understood. Students, teachers, parents, administrators, and employers understand, at least in a general sense, that grades of A represent excellent or exceptional performance and grades of D to F represent marginal or poor performance. Second, such a system is compact, requiring only one or two spaces to report a summary mark of the work for a grading period. Third, such a system has about the optimal number of levels that can be easily distinguished without the use of interpretative aids.

Limitations of this system can also be noted. First, the specific meaning of letter grades varies from class to class and from school to school. Different schools and districts tend to use different grading systems and also tend to combine and weight the components of a grade differently. Consequently, a grade of A in one school or school district may represent performance similar to a grade of B or even C in another. Second, letter grades fail to indicate clearly the student's actual level of mastery. There is often a considerable difference between the achievement of a "low B" student and that of a "high B" student. Finally, averaging letter grades often results in a loss of information or misinterpretation of the student's actual achievement. When averaging letter grades, it is necessary to go back to the actual numerical grades to obtain the "correct" average.

2.2 Numerical Grades

Such a system usually employs 100 as the highest mark, and report cards often carry letter grade equivalents for the range of numerical grades. For example: A (90–100), B (80–89), C (70–79), D (60–69), and F (below 60).

Numerical grades have three main advantages. First, like letter grades, they provide a convenient summary mark for a term's or year's work. Second, unlike letter grades, numerical grades are easily averaged to obtain the "correct" final marks. Third, they are widely understood—most pupils and parents understand that there are substantial differences between a mark of 95 and one of 75.

There are also disadvantages to such a system. First, the number of possible discriminations may be greater than an untrained user can make reliably. For example, few individuals could make the 40 distinctions required between the grades of 61 and 100 reliably. In other words, it may not be possible to determine the real difference between a grade of 67 and a grade of 68 or between a grade of 95 and a grade of 96. Second, as with letter grades, it may not be possible to know what a grade means, since standards may vary considerably from school to school.

2.3 Pass–Fail Grades

Pass–Fail (P–F) is another grading symbol system. Few schools, however, employ this approach today because of its many shortcomings. The major weakness is that such symbols do not provide sufficient information. "P" could mean the student exhibited anywhere from exceptional to marginal performance in the class. This makes it difficult for employers and admissions officers to evaluate applicants. Students themselves often complain about the same lack of information; that is, they do not know how well they actually did or how much they must improve. Finally, students tend to do the minimum necessary to earn a "P" under such systems.

2.4 Checklists

A common adjunct to a letter or numerical symbol system is a checklist. Since both letter and numerical symbol systems fail to define just what a student can or cannot do, many report cards include skill checklists (specifying, e.g., independence, thoroughness, effort) to accompany their grade symbols for each subject. Checklists are also used to provide information about nonacademic aspects of the learner. For example, checklists are often used to identify problems in the areas of conduct, social skills, responsibility, and organization. Properly utilized checklists represent useful supplements to letter or numerical grades and can convey more detailed information about the student without contaminating or confusing the interpretation of a student's overall achievement level. More detail on this and the other systems and symbols for grading may be found in Kubiszyn and Borich (in press).

3. New Trends in Grading

A recent trend in grading and testing has been the "performance assessment of learning." Following the work of Resnick and Resnick (1989), performance assessment of learning calls for the evaluation of student work in the form of oral reports, extended projects, portfolios of work, scientific investigations, creative scores and scripts, and physical models. These and other similar overt signs are attempts to determine whether acquired "bits" of knowledge have been successfully converted into an "integrated performance" in a context different from that in which they were learned. Performance assessments typically take place over a period of hours or days in which students work at their own pace. Based on guidelines provided by the teacher, students select the tasks and projects with which to demonstrate their competence against a set of published criteria.

The goal of performance assessment is to reduce the importance of artificial knowledge that may be unintentionally promoted by the exclusive or heavy reliance on true–false, multiple choice, and some types of essay tests, and to increase the importance of verbal explanations and justifications, critical thinking, and problem-solving related to authentic professional and social responsibilities pertaining to adult life. A secondary goal is to diminish the implicit weight generally accorded to traditional test-taking skills in grading students, especially for those for whom such skills are determined to be weak.

The performance assessment of learning involves the use of checklists, scales, or numerically equivalent codes in the form of ratings and awards which indicate the success of a learner in meeting established standards for the specific production to be evaluated. For example, a typical "production" might require the learner to complete a scientific investigation, scale model, or literary script on his or her own that would include essential features of adequacy (for example, theoretical understanding, planning, design, use of procedures and equipment, and possible alternative solutions). The product would be compared with established guidelines or an existing model, rated, and given a particular code of achievement.

The performance assessment of learning is not so much a new method of grading as it is an increase in emphasis upon higher order cognitive processes which include decision-making, problem-solving, independent judgment, and creativity. For this reason it shares much in common with the comparison with established standards approach of grading and the checklist method of reporting. A distinctive feature of the performance assessment of learning lies with the fact that the codes of achievement obtained are reported separately on the grade report rather than as part of a letter grade.

References

Kubiszyn T, Borich G in press *Educational Testing and Measurement: Classroom Application and Practice*, 5th edn. Harper Collins, New York

Resnick L, Resnick D 1989 *Assessing the Thinking Curriculum: New Tools for Educational Reform*. University of Pittsburgh, Learning Research and Development Center, Pittsburgh, Pennsylvania

Further Reading

Mitchell R 1992 *Testing for Learning: How New Approaches to Evaluation an Improve American Schools*. The Free Press, New York

Popham W J 1994 *Classroom Assessment: What Teachers Need to Know*. Allyn and Bacon, Boston, Massachusetts

School and Classroom Factors

Introduction

L. W. Anderson

Teachers face several constraints as they attempt to create inviting, active, and productive classrooms. In the vernacular teachers many times find themselves having to "play the hand they are dealt." The entries in this section all pertain to what may be termed the "givens" of teaching.

This section is divided into three subsections. The first six entries describe factors that are typically imposed on teachers by virtue of laws, regulations, or policies. In his entry, Torper refers to these as "frame factors." Laws, regulations, or policies govern, among other things, how students are assigned to classrooms (e.g., by age, ability, or prior achievement), how many students are assigned to a single classroom (i.e., class size), the curriculum used to teach specific subjects (including the language that is incorporated in both the curriculum and the teaching), and whether students should be retained at certain grade levels if they fail to achieve certain standards for promotion.

The next six entries discuss limitations that teachers often create for themselves by virtue of the ways in which they design and operate within their classrooms. These limitations are caused both by what teachers know and do not know as well as what they do and do not do. For example, peer groups and peer relations are particularly important to adolescents in many countries. By prohibiting student–student interaction in classrooms, teachers may be unwittingly denying their students a potentially valuable source of productive learning.

Similarly, teachers may structure their lessons competitively (where student goal attainment comes at the expense of other students), cooperatively (where students must work together to achieve a goal), or individualistically (where goal attainment is independent of the other students in the classroom). These lesson or goal structures have quite different impacts on students. If teachers are unaware of these impacts, they may find themselves unduly constrained.

The final four entries pertain to factors that may or may not impact on the classroom environment.

Technology may or may not be in place in classrooms and, if in place, may or may not be used or be used well or poorly. Similar statements can be made for paraprofessionals (i.e., teacher aides), substitute teachers, and parents and other family members. The presence, absence and use of all of these factors have been found to impact the teaching-learning process.

1. Frame Factors

Frame factors are those that "limit, but do not determine, educational and classroom processes" (Torper). Furthermore, they cannot be manipulated by teachers. The entries in the first subsection are concerned with two major frame factors: class size (Finn and Voelkl) and classroom composition (Oakes and Heckman, Weiner, and Shepard). The final entry (Wang) discusses the impact of student diversity on classroom teaching.

One of the major points agreed upon by the authors of these entries is that frame factors (or what Wang refers to as "distal variables") do not *directly* effect student achievement. Consider class size, for example. The results of studies examining the relationship between class size and student achievement are typically mixed. If class size is to exert an influence on student achievement, teachers must adapt their instruction to smaller class settings (Finn and Voelkl). When such adaptations are made, class size has an *indirect* effect on student achievement by virtue of its direct effect on the teaching–learning process that occurs within smaller classes.

A second point on which most authors agree is that frame factors have different effects on different types or categories of students. Boys, girls, white, and minority children experience schooling quite differently. Weiner argues that the curricula of many subjects emphasize white males and the language used to teach the curriculum subordinates women and ethnic minorities. The benefits of smaller class size tend to be greater for younger children and those from racial or ethnic minority groups (Finn and Voelkl).

At the same time, however, there are some frame factors that appear to impact negatively large numbers of students. There is, for example, substantial evidence that requiring students to repeat grade level "decreases achievement and increases the likelihood of dropping out of school" (Shepard). Nonetheless, policies requiring grade repeating continue to persist in many countries.

2. Classroom Environments

Classrooms can be models of cohesiveness or exemplars of friction; prototypes of goal direction or paragons of disorganization (Fraser). Similarly, classrooms can be structured competitively, cooperatively, or individualistically (Johnson and Johnson). In addition, classrooms can be organized so as to facilitate or inhibit communication between and among students (Gall and Gall).

Finally, within classrooms, teachers can choose to transmit pre-existing knowledge to students or to enable students to construct knowledge for themselves (Collins, Greeno, and Resnick). In this context, peer groups can be seen as "threats to intergenerational continuity" (Hill) (and, hence, teacher authority), or as aids to help students cope with life's demands and uncertainties.

Decisions on each of these issues can produce quite different classroom environments, both as perceived by detached, "objective" observers and, perhaps more importantly, by the students themselves (Fraser). These differences, in turn, can have a substantial impact on both what occurs within classrooms and what students learn as a result.

One common theme that emerges from the six entries in this subsection is that students not only have a major role to play in their own learning (see also the entries in Part A, Section VI), but they also have a substantial role to play in their classmates' learning. In this regard, there are several advantages of using peer groups to enhance student achievement.

First, the very nature of adult-child relationships leads many children to an "uncritical acceptance of the adult world and an overreliance on imitation" (Damon). Child–child relationships, on the other hand, permit the "trying out of new ideas in a relatively supportive and uncritical environment" (Damon). Peer collaboration in learning, then, fosters both social and academic development.

Second, classrooms in which peers routinely interact with one another are typically seen by students as more cohesive and less divisive. Cohesiveness, along with perceived goal-direction, has been found consistently to be related to student achievement (Fraser).

Third, if peer groups are not involved positively in children's development, they are quite likely to be involved negatively. In this regard, Hill reminds us that the goals of some peer groups may influence students away from the official educational goals of the school. As a consequence, Hill advises that teachers would be wise to "harness" the energy of peer groups.

3. Paraprofessionals, Substitute Teachers, Parents, and Families

The introduction of paraprofessionals and substitute teachers into the classroom environment poses many challenges for teachers and students alike. In fact, much of what is known about paraprofessionals and substitute teachers is primarily negative.

Paraprofessionals (that is, non-certified adults who help teachers) tend to possess minimal qualifications (e.g., high school graduates) and have little, if any, formal training in teaching, tutoring, or working with students. At the same time, however, there has been a gradual shift over the years for paraprofessionals to be more involved in instructional responsibilities and less involved in clerical duties (Reynolds). Unfortunately, there is little evidence that paraprofessionals make a difference in terms of student achievement even though their presence obviously decreases the adult-student ratio in classrooms (Finn and Voelkl).

Substitute teachers have reported a litany of problems they encounter on a regular basis. They receive little information about classroom rules and regulations or about the students for whom they will be responsible. They either receive no lesson plans or the plans they receive are very sketchy. Finally, they often find themselves teaching out of their areas of expertise. The most frequently observed results of having substitute teachers in classrooms, then, are quite predictable: idleness, passivity, and boredom (Anderson and Gardner).

In the light of the consistent relationship between home environment and student achievement, moves toward increased parent involvement in children's education and schooling are unsurprising. This does not mean, however, that these moves are always welcomed by teachers. Teachers often take a patronizing attitude toward parents; meaningful dialogue about issues and problems is too frequently replaced by one-way communication (teacher-to-parent). In this regard, Payne has suggested that if parent involvement is to be successful and productive, "school-family partnerships" should be established, inservice training for administrators and teachers should be provided, home-school liaisons should be appointed, and convenient and comfortable physical locations for meetings and discussions should be made available.

4. Summary

While learning is an individual matter, classroom teaching typically involves groups of potential learners. So major tasks for teachers include organizing classrooms in ways that comply with legislative and administrative regulations and policies; are comfortable, productive learning environments for students; and make effective use of other adults who may enter them.

It is perhaps useful to restate Torper's definition of frame factors at this time. They are factors that limit, *but do not determine*, educational and classroom processes (emphasis mine). In order to organize classrooms that do all these things, teachers must be more flexible and adaptable than they are (Wang) and rely more on peers and families (Hill, Payne) than many currently do.

(a) Frame Factors

Frame Factors

U. Torper

The purpose of this entry is to examine factors that limit, but do not determine, educational and classroom processes (so-called "frame factors"). Curriculum, school laws, and administrative regulations as frame factors are considered. Frame factors are examined within the context of a larger theoretical framework, which is contrasted with another one. Speculations on the future of research on frame factors are offered.

1. Frame Factor Theory: Scope and Limits

The fundamental problems addressed within frame factor theory concern the reproduction of culture in modern society and the role of state-controlled schools in this process. The frame factor theory originated in the 1960s when Dahllöf (1971a, 1971b) proposed a model for evaluating educational processes. His main argument was that it is not possible to compare educational outcomes in a meaningful way without taking into consideration the teaching and learning processes producing these results and the factors affecting those processes. Dahllöf identified frame factors as influencing teaching and learning processes; these were factors that teachers and students could not manipulate but which put limits upon their behavior. Frame factors were of an organizational nature (e.g., school, streams, pupil selection, class size, and teacher supply). Dahllöf pointed out that the relationship between frames and educational outcomes was not one of simple cause–effect, thus breaking with the dominant tradition in educational research that tried to relate organizational factors and teacher and pupil characteristics to outcomes within a simple behavioristic cause–effect model. Educational phenomena must be studied simultaneously on a structural level and on the level of social action.

In the late 1960s and early 1970s interest in the sociology of education soared. Marx, Durkheim, and Weber were once again used as theoretical underpinnings of educational research. Frame factor theory was influenced by these ideas. A structuralist view is clear in Lundgren's (1972) discussion of the relation between the frames and the teaching process. In the

same way as a society is governed by certain rules for interpersonal relations and by social perceptions, teaching is governed by frames and perceptions that functionally form the rules for the participants. The teaching process can be systematically studied and stable patterns of behavior discovered. These patterns are seen as realizations of underlying rules that steer and shape the process. Ideas from Bellack et al. (1966)—who saw the educational process as a pedagogical game played according to specified rules—were incorporated; ideas originally developed by Wittgenstein (1958) in his study of language. Lundgren (1984) concluded: "the frames are seen as realizations of fundamental structural conditions. As a consequence the frame factor theory is part of a perspective that opens up questions not only concerning how these frames come about and restrict possible pedagogical acts but also how they can be transcended" (p.74).

Several attempts have been made to broaden the frame factor concept. Three types of pedagogical frames were identified: physical and administrative frames, legislative frames, and curricular frames (Lundgren 1977). Physical and administrative frames were seen as constraining the process. Legislative frames (i.e., the marking system, the examination system) were seen as regulating the process. Finally, curricular frames (expressed in the syllabus, the textbooks, and the teaching materials) were seen as governing the content of the process.

2. Frame Factors and the Teaching Process

In the original model Dahllöf (1971b) postulated that under a certain combination of frames the teachers use a teaching strategy called the the steering group strategy. In basic units of teaching, a small group of pupils (in percentiles 10–25 in general ability) served as a reference point for the teacher in deciding when to leave one teaching unit and go on to the next. The steering group was seen as a product of the dynamic interplay between the time allotted to the unit, the amount to be learned, the time needed for the pupils in the class to master it, and the teacher's interpretation of these factors. These propositions were largely substantiated in a study by Lundgren (1972). There was a differentiation within the class, mainly in quantitative terms, so that the pupils in the steering group were more involved in the communication when a transition was made from one unit of teaching to the next. These patterns of communication were surprisingly stable across subjects, grades, and countries (see also Gustafsson 1977; Pedro 1981).

Gustafsson (1977) analyzed if other groups of pupils played important pedagogical roles in the class. Her conclusion was that teachers and pupils interact in the same way irrespective of the pupils' characteristics, but some pupils participate more than others. Other researchers have demonstrated that structural variables such as sex and social background influence the patterns of interaction in the classroom (Pedro 1981; Pettersson and Åsén 1989).

One of the best known results coming out of this research tradition is the phenomenon of "piloting." In a number of studies of mathematics it was found that the teacher, in dealing with the class collectively or in interaction with individual students, framed his or her questions in such a way that students could answer them without really having the prerequisite knowledge to understand the subject matter (Lundgren 1977). Piloting was not restricted to mathematics, but was also found in physics, civics, and art education. The phenomena of piloting is created by frames, and the tighter the frames the more frequent piloting becomes. Thus, a number of things are learned by the pupils in addition to mastering (or not mastering) the subject matter. They learn whether they lack (or do not lack) the ability to understand instruction; they also learn the rules of the "teaching game."

3. Frame Factors and Curriculum Theory

Different researchers have taken different structuralist theories as a basis for their research. Most researchers within the tradition have been fundamentally influenced by Bordieu (Callewaert and Nilsson 1980, Broady 1990) and Bernstein (Kallós 1978, Bernstein and Lundgren 1983, Dahlberg 1985). Much of the empirical work concerned with the relation between society and the frames has centered around studies of the curriculum in an attempt to develop a curriculum theory. In fact, Lundgren (1979) used a very broad definition of curriculum encompassing all the experience the learner has under the guidance of the school. Within this broad definition, all research done within the frame factor tradition could be seen as part of an effort to develop a curriculum theory. Criticizing traditional curriculum theory for being normative, Lundgren (1981) states that curriculum theory should strive to build knowledge of how the goals, content, and methods of educational processes are formed in a specific society and a specific culture. Curriculum studies consistent with Lundgren's contention

have been done at the preschool level (Kallós 1978, Selander 1984) and at the compulsory school level (Kallós and Lundgren 1979, Lundgren 1981, Torper 1982, Englund 1986).

4. Future Research

Summing up the research done within the frame factor theory Lundgren (1984) concluded that tradition could serve as an alternative explanation to the existing rules of the teaching game. Traditional conceptions about what to teach and how to teach it could shape the teaching process. Efforts have been made to disentangle the complex relationship between traditions and frames (e.g., Selander 1984, Arfwedson 1985, Du Rietz et al. 1987, Pettersson and Åsén 1989).

Many European countries are in a process of changing their educational systems to be more market oriented. As a consequence, the factors governing, steering, and controlling teaching processes are likely to change. Frame factor theory, with its wide theoretical scope and its ambition to encompass the deep structures of society, is well suited to the task of analysing these processes. An understanding of the societal changes needed to transform the educational system from centralized to decentralized is important. How do government steering and control mechanisms develop, and what social forces shape them? Are the rules of the teaching game changing and, if so, what are the consequences for teaching and learning? What will happen when the frames of teaching change? Will tradition change and, if so, how? These and related questions require answers.

References

Arfwedson G 1985 *School Code and Teachers' Work. Three studies on Teacher Work Contexts*. Liber förlag, Malmö

Bellack A A, Kliebard H M, Hyman R T, Smith F L 1966 *The Language of the Classroom*. Teachers College Press, Columbia University, New York

Bernstein B, Lundgren U P 1983 *Makt, kontroll och pedagogik*. Liber, Lund

Broady D 1990 *Sociologi och epistemologi. Lektionsanalyses*. HLS förlag, Stockholm

Callewaert S, Nilsson B 1980 *Skolklassen som socialt system*. Lunds bok och tidskrifts, Lund

Dahlberg G 1985 *Context and the Child's Orientation to Meaning*. Liber förlag, Lund

Dahllöf U 1971a Relevance and fitness analysis in comparative education. *Scand. J. Educ. Res.* 15(3): 101–21

Dahllöf U 1971b *Ability Grouping, Content Validity and Curriculum Process Analysis*. Teachers College Press, Columbia University, New York

Du Rietz L, Lundgren U P, Wennås O 1987 *Ansvarsfördelning och styrning på skolområdet*. DsU 1987:1 Utbildningsdepartementet, Allmänna förlaget, Stockholm,

Englund T 1986 *Curriculum as a Political Problem Changing Educational Conceptions, with Special Reference to*

Citizenship Education. Acta Universitatis Upsaliensis. Uppsala Studies in Education 25, Studentlitteratur, Uppsala

Gustafsson C 1977 *Classroom Interaction*. Studies in Education and Psychology no 1. Liber, Lund

Kallós D 1978 *Den nya pedagogiken*. Wahlström & Wistrand, Stockholm

Kallós D, Lundgren U P 1979 *Curriculum as a Pedagogical Problem*. Liber läromedel, Gleerup, Lund

Lundgren U P 1972 *Frame Factors and the Teaching Process*. Almqvist & Wiksell, Stockholm

Lundgren U P 1977 *Model Analysis of Pedagogical Processes*. Liber läromedel, Gleerup, Lund

Lundgren U P 1979 Background, the conceptual framework. In: Lundgren U P, Pettersson S (eds.) 1979 *Code, Context and Curriculum Processes*. Liber läromedel, Gleerup, Lund

Lundgren U P 1981 *Att organisera omvärlden*. Liber förlag, Stockholm

Lundgren U P 1984 "Ramfaktorteorins" historia. *Skeptron no 1. Symposions förlag, Stockholm*

Pedro E 1981 *Social Stratification and Classroom Discourse*. Liber läromedel, Gleerup, Lund

Pettersson S, Åsén G 1989 *Bildundervisningen och det pedagogiska rummet*. HLS förlag, Stockholm

Selander S 1984 *Textum institutionis*. Liber förlag, Malmö,

Torper U 1982 *Tidsramar, tidsanvändning och kunskapsutveckling i den svenska grundskolan*. Liber läromedel, Gleerup, Lund

Wittgenstein I 1958 *Philosophical Investigations*. Basil Blackwell, Oxford

Further Reading

Callewaert S, Lundgren U P 1976 Undervisningsforskning och Social Reproduktion. In: Lundberg S, Selander S, Öhlund U (eds.) 1976 *Jamlikhetsmyt och Klassherravälde*. Bo Cavefors Bokförlag AB, Lund

Dahllöf U 1970/71 Curriculum process analysis and comparative evaluation of school systems. *Paedag. Eur.* 6: 21–36

Granheim M, Lundgren U P 1991 Steering by goals and evaluation in the Norwegian education system. *J. Curric. St.* 23(6): 481–505

Kallós D 1973 *On Educational Scientific Research*. Report from the Institute of Education No. 36, University of Lund, Lund

Kallós D 1974 Educational Phenomena and Educational Research. In: Dockrell B, Hamilton D (eds.) 1974 *Rethinking Educational Research*. Hodder and Stoughton, London

Kallós D 1976 *The Study of Educational Processes*. Report from the Institute of Education No. 3, University of Lund, Lund

Kallós D, Lundgren U P 1977 Lessons from a Comprehensive School System for Curriculum Theory and Research. *J. Curric. St.* 9: 3–20

Class Size

J. D. Finn and K. E. Voelkl

The question "Are smaller classes better than larger classes?" continues to be debated among teachers and administrators, and in the research community. In the years since the first edition of the *International Encyclopedia of Education* (Husén and Postlethwaite 1985) was published, a great deal of writing and some excellent research on the topic has appeared. Proponents of small classes argue that both teacher morale and the amount of attention to individual pupils are increased. The ultimate result—and the ultimate criterion by which small classes would be evaluated—is improved achievement on the part of all students or of particular subgroups. When research does indicate the superiority of smaller classes, however, cost considerations and tradition often stand as barriers to any meaningful change in practice. Thus it is clear that the issue of optimal class size does not stand by itself but is enmeshed in a complex of additional issues.

Unfortunately, the empirical research is confounded by lack of agreement about how the basic construct—class size—should be measured. Some analyses use measures such as student–teacher ratio or student–professional staff ratio for a school or larger unit

(e.g., country). These measures are less than useful for understanding interactions between teachers and students in a classroom (see Odden 1990). They do not indicate the actual number of students in any given class setting and may mask tremendous variation from one class to another or one school subject to another. Even the number of students on a class roster may not represent the number actually present on a given day or the number engaged in learning activities. Thus, while in-class measures are better than student–staff ratios for understanding educational process, a refined understanding of the connotations of "class size" is still needed.

1. The Glass–Smith Meta-analysis and its Aftermath

Almost without exception, studies of the relationship of class size to academic and behavioral outcomes cite the classic *Meta-analysis of Research on the Relationship of Class Size and Achievement* (Glass and Smith 1978). The authors collected and summarized nearly 80 studies of the relationship of class size and academic performance that yielded over 700 class-size comparisons on data from nearly 900,000 pupils. The two primary conclusions to be drawn from their massive review were: "That reduced class size can be expected to produce increased academic achievement" (p. iv), and "The major benefits from reduced class-size are obtained as size is reduced below 20 pupils" (p. v).

Other summaries of the research have followed, most notably the extensive work by Robinson and Wittebols (1986). Their conclusions partially contradict and clearly qualify the earlier findings of Glass and Smith:

> Existing research findings do not support the contention that smaller classes will of themselves result in greater academic achievement . . . There is research evidence that small classes are important to increased pupil achievement in reading and mathematics in the early primary grades . . . There is evidence that pupils with lower academic abilities tend to benefit more from smaller classes than do pupils with average ability. (pp. 18–19)

Robinson and Wittebols emphasize that small classes may not benefit all groups of students equally, an important consideration in all class size research. Unfortunately, their review failed to distinguish the best designed studies from those using the poorest methodology, and thus their conclusions must be viewed with a degree of skepticism.

2. Approaches to the Study of Class Size

Research on class size has been conducted at different grade levels, in numerous school subjects, and employing a variety of analytic techniques. Unfortunately, there are almost as many disparate findings as there are individual studies. Three general approaches to the study of class size—the ecological approach, the cost-related approach, and the classroom-focus approach—are described below.

2.1 Ecological Approach

The ecological approach involves the study of class size in historical or geopolitical perspective. For example, Tomlinson (1988) tabulated the median number of pupils per class in the United States from 1960 to 1984. The numbers decreased regularly during this period from 30 to 24 in the elementary grades and from 27 to 22 in secondary schools. Tomlinson also summarized research showing that there was a decline during the same period "on virtually all standardized tests of academic aptitude and achievement, in all grades, among many different strata of students, in many subjects, and in every region" (p. 23). Student–teacher ratios decreased between 1965 and 1985 in other countries as well, declining by approximately

11 percent in "low" and "lower middle" income countries and by about 19 percent in "upper middle" income countries (Lockheed and Verspoor 1991). Test data were not available to document an association with student performance, however.

The implication that might be drawn from the trend in the United States is that large classes are superior or that, at least, small classes are not. Other explanations for declining performance are equally plausible, however. Among them, the 1960s and 1970s saw dramatic changes in the nature of the school-aged population. Specifically the proportion of minorities entering United States schools increased substantially. It is equally if not more likely that this factor as well as a multitude of institutional and cultural changes that occurred during these decades are responsible for the decline in test scores.

The studies reported by the International Association for the Evaluation of Educational Achievement (IEA) also permit ecological comparisons, but among countries rather than over time. The Second International Study of Achievement in Mathematics (McKnight et al. 1987) found great variation in the average size of mathematics classes in the 13-year-old population among 18 countries, from 19 to 20 students in Belgium, Sweden, and Luxembourg, to 41 to 44 in Japan, Hong Kong, Thailand, and Swaziland. At the same time, Belgium, Japan, and Hong Kong were among the top half of the countries in mean mathematics achievement, while Sweden, Luxembourg, and Swaziland were in the lower half. In general, there is no clear association of average class size with mathematics performance at the national level, a finding that is repeated for each age group studied and on most subtests.

The same conclusion can be drawn from the Second International Study of Achievement in Science (Postlethwaite and Wiley 1991). At the 10-year-old level, Hong Kong, Japan, the Philippines, and South Korea had the largest average class sizes, while Finland and Hungary were among countries with the smallest. However, Japan, Finland, Hungary, and South Korea were found to have achievement scores that were high in the cross-national rankings at this age level while the Philippines was among the lowest.

The ecological approach to studying class size leaves many questions unresolved. When units of measurement as large as countries are characterized by a single average, a plethora of other important effects is camouflaged. National differences in such factors as educational expenditures, educational goals, teacher preparation practices, and student characteristics, may contribute both to the average class size in a country and to the average achievement level. Further, class size often varies substantially within a country. At the extreme, the IEA Classroom Environment Study (Anderson et al. 1989) indicated that Thailand had class sizes from 17 to 57 pupils. Even a relatively homogeneous region, Canada (Quebec), ranged in class size from 24 to 33 pupils. Large achievement differences within countries are also the rule rather than the exception. For example, in the Second IEA Science Study, Japan scored well on subtests in biology and physics, and relatively poor on the chemistry subtest at the 10-year-old level. Thus, associations across countries obscure the true impact of class size on the individuals within a school.

2.2 Cost-related Approach

Cost-effectiveness analysis examines both costs and consequences in considering alternatives for decision-making. In educational applications, outcomes are typically assessed in terms of school attainment. Cost-effectiveness ratios are characteristically based upon the average effect and cost per student.

Levin (1988) reviewed the comparison of costs and effects among four strategies for educational improvement: cross-age tutoring, computer-assisted instruction, lengthening the school day, and reducing class size. Data on class size were taken from 14 evaluations collected in previous research. Costs were estimated using the "ingredients approach" which involved the identification of ingredients of each intervention and their respective values, and determination of the overall cost of implementation. For example, the ingredients needed to reduce class size include personnel, facilities, and equipment. While the projected annual cost per student of reducing class size by five students was not found to be as great as either lengthening the school day or use of computer-assisted instruction, larger reductions in class size become quite expensive. The estimated annual costs per student, per subject in school were US$45, US$63, US$94, and US$201, respectively, for reductions in class size from 35 to 30 students, 30 to 25 students, 25 to 20 students, and 35 to 20 students. From a cost-effectiveness perspective, reducing class size was found to be especially inefficient for increasing reading achievement. Peer tutoring, in contrast, was more cost-effective.

A second cost-related perspective on class size research is the production function approach. Relying heavily on multiple regression analysis, this quantitative approach directly relates a series of inputs, or cost factors, to an output. As applied to the analysis of class size, the output of the educational process is assumed to be student achievement. The selected inputs include indicators of instructional expenditures such as teacher experience, teacher education, and class size or student–teacher ratio. These instructional expenditures, in turn, make up approximately two-thirds of total school expenditures. Holding constant family background and other inputs, partial regression coefficients are considered to be estimates of the effects of the inputs on achievement.

Hanushek (1986) reviewed 147 studies that used the educational production function approach to examine these three expenditure parameters (i.e., inputs). Of the 147 studies reviewed, 112 provided information on the relationship between student–teacher ratio and student achievement. Only nine showed a significant relationship in the expected positive direction. Hanushek (1986) concluded, "There is little apparent merit for schools to pursue their ubiquitous quest for lowered class sizes" (p. 1167). Teacher experience and education failed to have the expected positive effect on student achievement as well, leading to the conclusion that there is no strong or systematic relationship between school expenditures and student achievement. In particular, reducing class size does not appear to be an economically efficient strategy for increasing school performance.

2.3 Classroom-focus Research

Classroom-focus investigations include both experimental and nonexperimental studies directed toward answering the primary questions: Are small classes superior to large classes in terms of academic and/or affective outcomes? If small classes are better, do they benefit particular groups of students identified by characteristics such as ability, age, race, or enrollment in specific courses? And finally, what aspects of classroom process are affected when regular-sized classes are reduced to smaller numbers of students?

A careful evaluation of research on class size was conducted by Slavin (1989). Rather than undertake a comprehensive integration of studies, Slavin reviewed only those that met three important criteria, as follows: (a) The studies were of nontrivial duration, that is, lasted a minimum of one year. Unfortunately, much research has been of limited duration (e.g., 30 minutes) and cannot reveal the impact of policy decisions to reduce class size for an entire school year, even if it is only at one grade or for one subject area. (b) Only substantial reductions in class size were examined, so that larger classes were compared to classes that were at least 30 percent smaller and had 20 students or fewer. This limited the selection of studies to those that are typical of public school classes in the United States and that involve a "real" reduction in the number of students in the classroom. (c) The studies involved random assignment of youngsters to class sizes or, as an alternative, "matching" to assure that the class groups were equivalent initially. Thus the studies had high internal validity.

Of all the research summarized by Glass and Smith (1978) as well as more recent work, Slavin identified only eight studies that met these criteria. From these studies, Slavin concluded that substantial reductions in class size have a positive effect on student achievement, but that the effect is small; the median effect size for the eight studies was approximately one-eighth of a standard deviation. In addition, the effect was not cumulative and even disappeared in later years. Finally, while teachers may change their behaviors in small classes, the changes are so slight that they are unlikely to make important differences in student achievement.

Slavin's conclusions are consistent with those of Glass and Smith (1978) and with the concept of a class-size threshold. Small reductions in class size are accompanied by little or no academic improvement. Larger reductions, however, result in modest achievement gains in the early school years. The Project STAR results described in Sect. 3 below add further support to this finding.

In contrast, research on the secondary school years is very mixed. Robinson and Wittebols (1986) reviewed 22 studies in the United States that related class size to student achievement in Grades 9 to 12. Ten of the 22 studies involved classes with more than 45 students, and only five studies involved classes of fewer than 22 students. Very few studies favored either smaller or larger classes, and many showed no significant differences in achievement between small and large classes. The diversity of the evidence about class size at the secondary level does not yield any generalizable findings.

The classroom processes that distinguish small from large classes have proven to be remarkably elusive. Finn and Achilles (1990) proposed three process dimensions that may be affected: (a) With fewer students in the class, teachers may be more enthusiastic, which may in turn impact on students' motivation to learn. (b) Fewer students per teacher could result in increased student–teacher interaction and more individualized instruction. (c) Students in smaller classes may be more compelled to attend to, and participate in, learning activities.

A well-designed study that focused on processes such as these was conducted in Toronto (Shapson et al. 1980). Teachers and students in 62 Grade four classes were randomly assigned to four class sizes: 16, 23, 30, or 37. Measures were taken during and at the end of the school year. In Grade five, the students and teachers were again assigned at random and were followed for a second year. In addition to achievement measures, repeated ratings of the classrooms were made by trained observers. The rating scales included measures of teacher–student interaction, student participation, student satisfaction, method of instruction, subject emphasis, physical conditions, use of educational aids, classroom atmosphere, and four indicators of the quality of classroom activity. Additional questionnaires were administered to the students and to the teachers.

The analysis of the data was exemplary, but the findings were mixed with most being negative. Teachers initially expected smaller classes to facilitate more individualized programs and stated later that their expectations were confirmed. They generally had more positive attitudes in the smaller classes and were pleased with the ease of managing and teaching in the small class setting. However:

> The observation of classroom process variables revealed very few effects of class size. Class size did not affect the amount of time teachers spent talking about course content or classroom routines. Nor did it affect the choice of audi-

ence for teachers' verbal interactions; that is, when they changed class sizes, teachers did not alter the proportion of their time spent interacting with the whole class, with groups, or with individual pupils, (Shapson et al. 1980 pp. 149–50)

Further, no differences were found in pupil satisfaction or affective measures, and no differences were found for most teacher activities, subject emphasis, classroom atmosphere, or the quality measures. Shapson et al. (1980) also found only minor differences in academic achievement, but this might be expected given the lack of process effects. This study is a clear illustration of the difficulty encountered in trying to understand how classes as distinct as those with 16 and 37 pupils differ operationally.

3. A Major Classroom-focus Study: Project STAR

Project STAR (Student–Teacher Achievement Ratio), the largest controlled study of the effects of reduced class size, was conducted in 76 elementary schools in the state of Tennessee from 1985 to 1989. Within each school, children entering kindergarten were assigned at random to one of three class sizes: small, with an enrollment range of 13–17 pupils; regular, with an enrollment of 22–25 pupils; or regular, with a teacher aide. Teachers were also assigned at random to the class groups. The within-school design was particularly effective in controlling for differences among school settings including, but not limited to, the socioeconomic status of the student body, per-student expenditures, and the manner in which schools are administered.

Every class remained the same type—small, regular, or regular with an aide—for four years, until the students were in Grade three. A new teacher was assigned at random to the class each year. Standardized achievement tests were administered to all participating students at the end of each school year. Also, curriculum-based tests reflecting the State's instructional objectives in reading and mathematics were administered at the end of Grades one, two, and three. In all, over 6,000 youngsters in more than 300 classrooms participated in the four-year longitudinal study. The results of the study are reported in Finn and Achilles (1990) and Word et al. (1990), and are summarized in the Fall 1989 issue of *The Peabody Journal of Education*.

Cross-sectional analysis at each grade level found statistically significant advantages for youngsters in the small classes on every achievement scale each year. When the means on the standardized tests were converted to percentiles, the small-class advantage ranged from 6.2 to 10.3 percentile points in reading and from 4.9 to 11.3 percentile points in mathematics; these correspond to average "effect sizes" of 0.23σ in reading and 0.21σ in mathematics. Mastery rates on the curriculum-based tests were between 7.2 percent and 11.5 percent higher in small classes in reading, and between 6.3 and 6.7 percent higher in mathematics.

It is noteworthy that these effects were realized on a large scale for four years without any special training or policy changes to assist teachers in the small-class setting. They provide the most definitive evidence to date of the benefits of small classes in the elementary grades. The effects of a full-time teacher aide, in contrast, were mostly nonsignificant.

Other findings from Project STAR are also informative. First, each year, some of the "interactions" of class size with race were statistically significant. In each instance, minorities—whose overall achievement levels are below those of nonminority students—benefitted significantly more from small classes than their nonminority peers. The small-class advantage for minorities was greater than that for nonminority students in 18 of 20 comparisons. There is a strong suggestion that smaller classes are helpful especially for students who would otherwise be expected to perform most poorly.

Second, a longitudinal analysis of the Project STAR data indicated that the initial benefit to small classes occurred in the first year of the study (kindergarten). The small class advantage increased significantly in Grade one but only in reading. After that, small classes maintained a constant performance advantage over regular sized classes that neither increased nor decreased significantly for the duration of the study.

A follow-up component to the study was conducted in Grade four, once all students were returned to regular sized classes. Students who had attended small classes during the preceding years continued to score significantly above their classmates on all achievement tests. The effect sizes were not as great as they had been during the experimental years, however, indicating that the benefit may be diminishing. Grade four teachers also rated a sample of students on a 29-item "student participation questionnaire." Students who had been in small classes during the preceding years displayed significantly more effort to learn in the classroom, took more initiative in learning activities, and exhibited less nonparticipatory or disruptive behavior than their peers.

Other large-scale demonstration projects have been undertaken including Indiana's Project PRIME TIME (Center for School Assessment 1986). To date, however, Tennessee's Project STAR remains the only large-scale study that employed a full set of sound scientific principles.

4. Alternatives and Conclusion

While some gains are associated with reducing class size, small classes are not without their costs and practical difficulties, and many regard them as inefficient and counterproductive. A policy of having small classes may encourage schools to hire less qualified teachers, and result in increased expenditures and only trivial benefits for student achievement (Tomlinson 1989). Not counting the expense of additional classrooms, Tomlinson (1988) estimated that the cost of reducing average class size in the United States in 1986 from 24 to 23 students would require approximately 73,000 additional teachers and US$5 billion. To reduce to 15 students, the "optimum" number, would cost almost US$69 billion and require an additional one million teachers. In an effort to save US$26.2 million, one state actually proposed increasing class size from 24 to 25 students in Grades one to four, and from 27 to 29 students in Grades five to twelve.

Odden (1990) explored whether the effect of reducing class size on student achievement could be achieved with other lower-cost policy alternatives, or whether larger effects could be produced through other interventions at the same cost. After reviewing a number of alternatives, he concluded that particular uses of small classes are worthwhile, especially in kindergarten to Grade three. He recommends reducing class size in classes with students achieving below grade level to allow for individual or small-group tutoring, and combining individual tutoring with classes reduced to 15 students for language arts/reading instruction.

Odden (1990) proposed further that these two strategies for implementing small classes be coupled with a "larger, comprehensive set of strategies, with class size reduction used sparingly and strategically" (p. 223). These include interventions shown to be especially effective for low-income, ethnic, and language minority students; that is, early childhood education for three- and four-year-olds, extended day kindergarten, computer-assisted instruction, cooperative learning, and peer or volunteer tutoring. Most of these have been shown to improve student achievement by at least 0.5σ. Systematic comparisons of these strategies for affecting learning outcomes have been made by Levin (1988) and Slavin (1989).

It is remarkable that, after all the years of research and debate over the issue of class size, more questions remain unanswered than resolved. Within the limited domain of classroom-focus studies, the effects of small classes in the upper grades or particular school subjects have not been explored systematically, and the processes that distinguish small classes in elementary grades are not clear. The potential for substantial gains if teachers are encouraged or trained to adapt instruction to a small-class setting has not been examined at all.

In the broader perspective, the question "are small classes worth the investment?" remains unclear, primarily because educators are unable to attach a value to a given increment in learning in one subject area or many. The worth of improved teacher attitudes and morale is all the more difficult to assess. Given these limitations, the extreme view advanced by Hanushek (1986) is understandable: "Stop requiring and paying for things that do not matter" (p. 1167). On the other hand, strong sentiment and some solid evidence indicates that benefits can be effected in reduced-size classes. That these will not be realized if the status quo is maintained is indisputable.

See also: Teacher Managerial Behaviors; Seating Arrangements; Grouping Students in the Classroom

References

Anderson L W, Ryan D W, Shapiro B J (eds.) 1989 *The IEA Classroom Environment Study*. Pergamon Press, Oxford

Center for School Assessment 1986 *The Relationship Between Class Size and Achievement for First Grade Students in Indiana (PRIME TIME Report)*. Indiana Department of Education, Indianapolis, Indiana

Finn J D, Achilles C M 1990 Answers and questions about class size: A statewide experiment. *Am. Educ. Res. J.* 27 (3): 557–77

Glass G V, Smith M L 1978 *Meta-Analysis of Research on the Relationship of Class Size and Achievement*. Far West Laboratory for Educational Research and Development, San Francisco, California

Hanushek E A 1986 The economics of schooling: Production and efficiency in public schools. *J. Econ. Lit.* 24 (3): 1141–77

Husén T, Postlethwaite T N (eds.) 1985 *The International Encyclopedia of Education*, 1st edn. Pergamon Press, Oxford

Levin H M 1988 Cost-effectiveness and educational policy. *Educ. Eval. Policy Anal.* 10: 51–69

Lockheed M E, Verspoor A M 1991 *Improving Primary Education in Developing Countries*. Oxford University Press, Oxford

McKnight C C et al. 1987 *The Underachieving Curriculum: Assessing U.S. School Mathematics From an International Perspective*. Stipes, Champaign, Illinois

Odden A 1990 Class size and student achievement: Research based policy alternatives. *Educ. Eval. Policy Anal.* 12 (2): 213–27

Peabody Journal of Education 1989 Vol. 6, Fall (entire issue)

Postlethwaite T N, Wiley D E 1991 *Science Achievement in Twenty-Three Countries*. Pergamon Press, Oxford

Robinson G E, Wittebols J H 1986 *Class Size Research: A Related Cluster Analysis for Decision Making*. Educational Research Service, Arlington, Virginia

Shapson S M, Wright E N, Eason G, Fitzgerald J 1980 An experimental study of the effects of class size. *Am. Educ. Res. J.* 17 (2): 141–52

Slavin R E 1989 Achievement effects of substantial reduction in class size. In: Slavin R E (ed.) 1989 *School and Classroom Organization*. Erlbaum, Hillsdale, New Jersey

Tomlinson T M 1988 *Class Size and Public Policy: Politics and Panaceas*. US Department of Education, Washington, DC

Tomlinson T M 1989 Class size and public policy: Politics and panaceas. *Educ. Policy* 3: 261–73

Word E et al. 1990 *Student/Teacher Achievement Ratio (STAR): Tennessee's K-3 Class Size Study*. Final summary report 1985–90. Tennessee Department of Education, Nashville, Tennessee

Age Grouping of Students

J. Oakes and P. E. Heckman

Since the mid-nineteenth century, most schools have placed students into groups with the objective of reducing student variability, thereby easing the teaching task. While most choose to place children of the same age together into grades, multigraded and nongraded school structures are alternatives that yield at least comparable achievement outcomes and nearly always enhance social growth. Many of these alternative ways of grouping students attempt to pursue simultaneously the goals of reduced variability and of increased individualization. New knowledge about learning, however, combined with the increased diversity of school populations, has prompted educators to reconsider these goals as well as the practices they have spawned.

1. The Age-graded School

Age-graded schooling practices first emerged in Europe and the United States during the late seven-

teenth and early eighteenth centuries, replacing a less formalized arrangement whereby children and young adults learned together with a single schoolmaster over several years (Aries 1962). Over time, the practice of separating students into age-specific classrooms, each with its prescribed and standardized curriculum, brought a specialized and hierarchical structure into schools. Each grade level's work was a building block necessary to construct an educated adult. By the late nineteenth century, age-graded schools mimicked practices in newly bureaucratized factories, where manufacturing was being made more "scientific" and efficient by being broken down into discrete steps to ensure the uniform production of parts that could be assembled into a whole product (Pratt 1983).

Educators hoped that age-specific groups would decrease the variability of both students and the curriculum and provide a better match between the two. Curriculum guides suggested topics, knowledge and skills, and activities appropriate for each grade, which, in turn, generated textbooks, workbooks, and supplemental materials with grade level designations. Standardized achievement test scores were transformed into grade equivalency scores, so that any child's performance can be interpreted in light of the graded school structure.

Some children of the same age still inevitably learned more quickly than others. In order to reduce this inefficient variability, educators have commonly employed a tracking strategy. Children of the same age and grade are assigned to homogeneous subgroups based on ability, achievement, and/or interest. Children who failed to keep pace with even the slowest groups typically are not promoted to the next grade. The next year, these retained children repeat the curriculum with younger children. Sometimes slower children repeat several grades. Educators have supported these practices in the belief that each curricular building block must be mastered before a new layer of learning can be added; these practices continue to dominate schools.

2. Alternatives to Age Grouping

Goodlad and Anderson (1959) note that educators have questioned these grouping practices and have sought alternatives to the graded school structure since shortly after its formation. The alternatives have included multigrade classrooms, cross-grade regrouping, individualized instruction, and nongraded schools. Like traditional graded structures, these alternatives seek to cope with the variability in achievement, ability, motivation, and interest among learners. Early experimenters—including John Dewey in the United States, Peter Petersen in Germany, Maria Montessori in Switzerland, and the founders of the British infant and primary schools—sought alternatives that mitigate the problems associated with variability by promoting students' social, personal, and cognitive development.

2.1 Multigrade/Combination Classes

In many nations, schools place children from two or three grade levels together in "combination" classes, most often to keep classes at roughly the same size. Similarly, small schools with few students at each grade level combine classes, especially in sparsely populated rural areas of the United States, Canada, and many developing nations. Most multigrade classes depart only slightly from traditional age-grading, since teachers usually teach students as distinct subgroups and work with them on "grade-level" material.

2.2 Nongraded Schooling

With the publication of *The Nongraded Elementary School* in 1959, Goodlad and Anderson created a comprehensive model for elementary education in the United States that drew upon prior American and

European attempts to overcome problems in the graded school design. Essentially, Goodlad and Anderson sought a school structure that would "implement a theory of continuous pupil progress: since the differences among children are great and since these differences cannot be substantially modified, school structure must facilitate the continuous educational progress of each pupil. Some pupils, therefore, will require a longer period of time than others for achieving certain learnings and attaining certain developmental levels" (p. 52). These ideas spawned an elementary school structure with fewer major divisions—for example, primary, intermediate, and upper elementary—with classes in each division comprised of students spanning a three- to four-year age range. Here, children of different ages would progress continuously as individuals through a curriculum unbound by grade-level distinctions. Initially, teachers were assigned one class of multiage students and stayed with them for three or more years; later, team teaching enhanced the model. Concurrent with this activity in the United States, similar conceptions of continuous progress and individual development advocated by Peter Petersen and the German Progressive School movement formed the basis of the Dutch *Jenaplan* nongraded schools, of which there were more than 200 by 1990 (Anderson 1992).

Not suprisingly, given the preoccupation with student variability as an instructional obstacle, most nongraded schools attempted to "reduce the range of abilities with which the teacher must cope" (Goodlad and Anderson 1959 p. 65). For example, many educators assumed that language arts and mathematics were sequential and skill-based subjects that demanded homogeneous groups of learners, even in nongraded settings. Others, however, disagreed with any form of homogeneous grouping and advocated the random assignment of children to multiage groups. Still others considered personality, interests, and other factors in making assignments.

2.3 Cross-grade Regrouping

One nongraded variant was to regroup students across grade levels for instruction in reading and language arts. Many traditional schools adopted plans (usually referred to as "Joplin plans," owing to their origin in Joplin, Missouri) wherein students who spent most of their day in single-grade classrooms were regrouped by reading skills into multigrade groups. Thereby, schools reduced the variability in students' reading skills and provided students with more direct instruction than was permitted by traditional within-class reading groups. In nongraded schools, Joplin plans eased the logistical difficulties of moving away from graded materials and practices in reading and language arts, and called attention to students' abilities and rates of learning, rather than age or grade (Floyd 1954). Subsequently, educators approached mathematics and other curriculum areas by delineating skills, allowing for various rates of learning, and then grouping according to the skills and the rate of learning without regard to age (Provus 1960).

2.4 Mixed-age Groupings

Katz et al. (1990) distinguish between nongrading and mixed-age grouping: "The former is primarily intended to homogenize groups for instruction by ability or developmental level rather than by age; the latter is intended to optimize what can be learned when children of different—as well as the same—ages and abilities have opportunity to interact (p. 1)." Thus, mixed-age grouping challenges nongrading's focus on continuous progress and sequential, predetermined curricula.

Katz et al. also advocate promoting rather than narrowing differences among individuals in a group because children's construction of knowledge is enhanced as they interact and share meanings through talk and activity. Mixed-age grouping permits children to draw on a wide range of expertise from peers and adults.

2.5 Individualized Instruction

Given the emphasis on individual learners (rather than on the group as a whole) in nongraded schools, it is not surprising that individualized instruction gained popularity during the early years of nongrading. Individually Guided Education (IGE) is perhaps the most highly technological attempt to provide individualized instruction in nongraded school structures (Klausmeier et al. 1977). One of many individualized programs that required students to use self-paced materials, study guides, and pre- and posttests (Bangert et al. 1983), IGE specified that nongraded units of 100 students work with a team of four teachers, a unit leader, teaching aides and clerks, and appropriate curriculum materials. Its proponents considered the nongraded structure well-matched to a complex technology for identifying objectives, estimating how many objectives students could attain, and diagnosing students' levels of achievement relative to these objectives, their motivation, and learning styles.

2.6 Open Schools

Far less technological than individualized instruction plans, open schools also sought to accommodate variation among children's learning rates and styles, the curriculum, and individual goals (Pavan 1973). Teachers in open-space schools ". . . work with individuals or small groups, allow more peer interaction, have less need to direct pupil behavior, use more supplementary materials, and respond to individuals more frequently" (Pavan 1973 p. 340).

3. Effects of Alternatives to Age Grouping

In spite of the limited implementation of alternatives to age-grouping, research permits some conclusions about their effects. Effects on both achievement and noncognitive outcomes have been studied.

3.1 Effects on Achievement

Researchers draw conflicting conclusions about the effects of alternatives to age-grouping on student achievement. For example, Pavan's (1977) review of studies comparing traditional and multigrade structures concludes, "There is definitive research evidence to confirm the theories underlying nongradedness" (p. 340). In contrast, after reviewing the research on multiage grouping before 1981 (including those studies examined by Pavan), Pratt (1983) reported that multiage grouping showed no consistent relationship with academic achievement.

Gutierrez and Slavin (1992) have completed a "best evidence" review. Sorting nongraded plans into different types, they report positive effects for nongraded, one-subject programs (i.e., Joplin plans) and for more comprehensive nongraded plans that are regrouped by skill levels. In contrast, nongraded schemes incorporating individualized instruction, including IGE, yielded no achievement advantages over age-grading.

Gutierrez and Slavin conclude that nongrading enhances achievement because it allows teachers to reduce the number of within-class groups in reading and mathematics, thereby increasing the amount of direct instruction students receive. Other research suggests that mixed-age grouping may enhance learning because such settings increase the variability of knowledge and skills on which members of the group can draw (Rogoff and Lave 1984).

3.2 Noncognitive Outcomes

Research on social and emotional effects shows clearer patterns of benefits for nongraded settings. For example, Pavan (1973) reviewed 16 studies that included measures of noncognitive outcomes and reported that only three studies favored traditional settings. More recently, Katz et al. (1989) concluded from their review of 17 studies that mixed-age group interactions promote helping, sharing, and taking turns; they provide older children with important leadership opportunities and younger children with more complex play opportunities than they experience in age-homogeneous settings. Other studies reveal that, outside of school, many societies—including the United States (Barker and Wright 1955), the United Kingdom (Sluckin 1981), and other non-Western cultures (Whiting and Whiting 1975)—socialize children and encourage them to develop friendships in age groups wider than traditional age-graded schools permit.

4. Issues for Theory, Research, and Practice

New scholarship about how children learn, the impact of increased student diversity in contemporary schools, and demands on schools to prepare students for a postindustrial world all call into question schools' efforts to create groupings that reduce learner variability and support standardized, sequential curricula. For example, developments in cognitive science suggest the importance of social interaction between experts and novices as a way of acquiring knowledge (Katz et al. 1990, Rogoff and Lave 1984, Newman et al. 1989). Hence, interactions among individuals with a range of experience and expertise allow greater opportunities to acquire important elements of the culture. This work suggests that the goal of limiting variability is not only illusive, but unproductive.

In most highly industrialized Western countries, for example, poverty has increased dramatically, and immigrants have infused once homogeneous societies with new languages and cultures. Whether this increased variability among students promotes or interferes with learning seems to depend upon the characteristics of the schools that children attend. School practices grounded in new conceptions of learning may prove more powerful in educating diverse school populations. For example, Rosenholtz and Simpson (1984) distinguish between unidimensional and multidimensional classrooms, providing evidence that the latter more effectively accommodated variability among learners. Yet, both traditional age-graded and many nongraded schools tend toward the unidimensional—narrow definitions of academic ability, hierarchical arrangement of the curriculum, and homogeneous ability or achievement groups that result in the tacit or overt stratification of students into high and low status groups.

In contrast, Katz et al.'s mixed-age grouping model more closely approximates multidimensionality with its promotion of a broad conception of ability, achievement, and intelligence; multiple performance criteria and diverse methods for achievement, and a high degree of student autonomy and peer interaction resulting in less pressure to perform (Rosenholtz and Simpson 1984).

Finally, school structures that attempt to reduce variability among individuals and standardize learning run counter to the demands of a postindustrial age. For example, cooperation and group problem-finding and problem-solving in nonroutine circumstances with people of diverse backgrounds and abilities are essential skills if organizations are to flourish in turbulent economic, political, and social systems. Taken together, these trends suggest that school structures that mimic or attempt to improve upon assembly-line models of production require further scrutiny by educators and researchers.

See also: Open Education; Individualized Instruction

References

Anderson R H 1992 The nongraded elementary school: Lessons from history. Paper presented at the Annual Meeting of the American Educational Research Association, San Francisco, California

Aries P 1962 *Centuries of Childhood*, Vintage, New York

Bangert-Drowns R L, Kulik J, Kulik C C 1983 Individualized systems of instruction in secondary schools. *Rev. Educ. Res.* 53: 143–58

Barker R G, Wright H F 1955 *Midwest and Its Children: The Psychological Ecology of an American Town*. Row, Peterson, Evanston, Illinois

Floyd C 1954 Meeting children's reading needs in the middle grades. A preliminary report *Elem. Sch. J.* 55: 99–103

Goodlad J I, Anderson R H 1959 *The Nongraded Elementary School*. Teachers College Press, New York

Gutierrez R, Slavin R E 1992 Achievement effects of the nongraded elementary school: A retrospective and prospective review. *Rev. Educ. Res.*

Katz L G, Evangelou D, Hartman, J A 1990 *The Case for Mixed-Age Grouping in Early Childhood Education Programs*. ERIC Clearinghouse on Elementary and Early Childhood Education, Urbana-Champaign, Illinois

Katz L G, Evangelou D, Hartman, J A 1990 *The Case for Mixed-Age Grouping in Early Childhood Education*. National Association for the Education of Young Children, Washington, DC

Klausmeier H J, Rossmiller R A, Saily M (eds.) 1977 *Individually Guided Education*. Academic Press, New York

Newman D, Griffin P, Cole M 1989 *The Construction Zone Working for Cognitive Change in School*. Cambridge University Press, New York

Pavan B N 1973 Good news: Research on the nongraded elementary school. *Elem. Sch. J.* 73: 333–42

Pavan B N 1977 The nongraded elementary school: Research on academic and mental health. *Texas Tech Journal of Education* 4: 91–107.

Pratt D 1983 Age segregation in the schools. Paper presented at the Annual Meeting of the American Educational Research Association, Montreal, Canada

Provus M M 1960 Ability grouping in arithmetic. *Elem. Sch. J.* 60: 391–98

Rogoff B, Lave J (eds.) 1984 *Everyday Cognition: Its Development in Social Context*. Harvard University Press, Cambridge, Massachusetts

Rosenholtz S, Simpson C 1984 Classroom organization and student stratification. *Elem. Sch. J.* 85: 21–37.

Sluckin A 1981 *Growing up in the Playground: The Social Development of Children*. Routledge and Kegan Paul, London

Whiting B B, Whiting J W M 1975 *Children of Six Cultures: A Psycho-Cultural Analysis*. Harvard University Press, Cambridge, Massachusetts

Gender and Racial Differences Among Students

G. Weiner

The concept of "differences" in education is problematic. The term can be used, among other things, to celebrate diversity, to denote injustice, or to ascribe inferiority and powerlessness. It is also a concept used more by educational psychologists than sociologists or teachers. The latter two groups are more likely to conceptualize the problem of educational difference in terms of the manifestation of unequal power relations in schools or in addressing educational equality and inequality. In contrast, psychologists have tended to focus on gender and race at psychological and interpersonal levels rather than infusing their studies with an understanding of how a social order maintains dominance or how school relations perpetuate existing unequal social relations. Moreover, exploration of educational differences has a higher profile in studies of gender compared with those of race, possibly because racial differences are far more complex and politically sensitive than the relatively clear male/female dualism.

1. Historical Perspective

It is important to see theories of difference as they have emerged historically. Biological attributions of gender and racial inferiority held in the nineteenth and early twentieth centuries have lost ground in the second half of the twentieth century as societal and educational factors emerged as more important, reliable, and acceptable. There has also been some debate about the nature and extent of gender and racial differences. For example, in their extensive survey of sex differences, Maccoby and Jacklin (1974) found relatively little overall difference between the performance of females and males. Further, the educational effects of sociological factors such as low income and the relative heterogeneity of different cultural groups have rendered the identification of racial differences problematic.

Moreover, the possibility that identifying difference will lead to an increase in educational equality within a fundamentally unequal society has been challenged. Sarup (1986) poses the following question: "If society is differentiated on the basis of power, wealth, and education, how can children coming into the educational system from various parts of that differentiated society ever, as it were, line up equally?" (p. 3). Nevertheless, researchers have explored and identified patterns of educational inequality, mostly focusing on gender but with some consideration of race. These are now provided in some detail.

2. Language

Language has been identified as one means by which male, White dominance of power relationships is sustained and recreated. Spender (1980) criticized the ways in which language, both in the classroom and more generally, is used both to subordinate girls and women and to define them sexually. The dominant male experience is both reflected and constructed through language so that women are defined principally in sexual or domestic servicing roles.

Language has also proved problematic for Black and ethnic minority students. For example, the dialects used by Black American and British African-Caribbean students were originally thought of as simply mispronounced and poorly spoken Standard English: hence, the emergence of linguistic deficit hypotheses which accord little respect to dialects. However, in the 1960s, this position was reconsidered by social scientists who began to see Black English as a valid dialect of Standard English. However, problems arising from linguistic differences still continue, as emphasis on Standard English is increasingly being promoted, for example, in the British National Curriculum. A strategy to overcome these differences suggested by Cooper and Stewart (1987), is to point out differences without critizing student speech, thus highlighting linguistic difference rather than linguistic deficit.

Further, gender differences in writing style and reading choice are also evident. Female students are likely to read more widely and gain greater enjoyment from reading fiction than their male counterparts who tend to focus their reading on informational, nonfictional texts (Gorman et al. 1988). It is argued that these reading patterns have an effect on writing styles, resulting in female students' preference for essay-type narratives in contrast to male students' preference for factual, briefer forms of communication (Stobart et al. 1992).

3. Student Self-concept

How students feel about themselves has been perceived as crucial to their school performance: thus, studies of differences in student self-concept have been of much interest. However, research evidence is inconclusive: findings range from little evidence of difference in self-perception between male and female students (Chapman and Boersma 1983) to males having far higher self-images (Connell et al. 1975).

The similar claim that Black children come to see themselves as failures and are nonachievers because of their negative self-concept and low esteem has also been challenged. Milner (1983), for example, suggests that Black people who are ashamed of their color feel this way because White society has forced them to accept its own appraisal of them. In contrast, Stone (1981) found the British research on Black self-concept and self-esteem to be inconclusive and contradictory. In her view, there is no basis for the belief that Black children have poor self-esteem and negative self-concept; rather the negative self-concept hypothesis serves to obscure the real issues which are of power, class, and racial oppression.

4. Socialization

Socialization into masculinity and femininity, and/or being Black or White, it is argued, begins within the family from the moment a child is born. Milner (1983) maintains that the socialization process is the most important determinant of prejudice. Similarly, Nash (1979) argues that children learn to apply stereotypes, whether in relation to gender or to racial differences before they start school. Cultural factors such as language, literature, and art also contribute to stereotypical and prejudicial thinking by conventionally using whiteness as a metaphor for all things good and pure, and blackness to denote badness and evil. Schools condone rather than challenge these stereotypes. Thus, just as parents give more attention to their sons and are more likely to reprimand them, the same patterns of differential treatment of the sexes is apparent at school.

5. Teachers' Perceptions of Students

Teachers are more likely to chastise male students and pay them more attention, while at the same time creating greater dependency in their treatment of female students (Fagot 1977). Hence, both male and female teachers encourage in their female students stereotyped traits of obedience and passivity yet prefer their male students to adopt the more male-identified characteristics of aggression and independence (Etaugh and Hughes 1975).

Research has also shown that teachers have lower expectations of female students (as do parents and students themselves), are more intellectually encouraging and demanding of male students, and are more likely to reward female students for good behavior and tidy presentation. Teachers also direct male and female students into conventional subjects and careers and believe female careers to be less important than male ones (Arnot and Weiner 1987). Further, they are likely to be sexist in their allocation of tasks within school; for example, at elementary level, choosing girls to help keep the classroom clean and tidy and the often physically smaller boys to move furniture or equipment (Clift 1978).

Similarly, Black and ethnic minority children are perceived as problems rather than potentially enriching to school life. Teachers also have lower expectations of these children's abilities and potential achievements. For example, Proctor (1984) found that low expectations of students are associated with minority group membership, nonconforming personality, and nonstandard speech. There is a tendency to encourage Black students' sporting and musical abilities to the detriment of their academic studies. Further, teachers are apparently more severe in disciplining Black students, blaming "bad" behavior on what teachers see as the inadequacies of Black family life (Brah and Minhas 1985; Phoenix 1987).

Whether teachers are male or female has been found to be important in terms of their interactions with students in the classroom. In a study of sixth and eleventh grade classes, Griffin (1972) found that male teachers were generally more direct and authoritarian, and female teachers warmer and less direct. However, there is little evidence to indicate that male and female teachers differ in their generally traditional and stereotypical treatment of male and female students.

6. Curriculum

Attention has focused on both the formal and hidden (implicit) school curriculum. In terms of the formal curriculum, syllabuses and content tend to exclude the experiences of girls and women whether Black or White; textbooks and reading schemes generally portray a traditional view of middle-class family life (Deliyanni-Kouimtzi 1992). Where choice is available, female students opt for the humanities, languages, and social sciences while male students select mathematical, scientific, and technological subjects despite various initiatives to counter this trend (Elkjaer 1992). Furthermore, the hidden curriculum exerts enormous pressure on students (and teachers) to conform in sex-specific ways.

At the institutional level there are gender-specific regulations on clothing (especially in the United Kingdom with its increasing adoption of school uniform) and discipline. Similarly, sexual harassment and verbal abuse have been found to be common features of school life (Lees 1987).

Black and ethnic minority experience is also underrepresented in the content of school syllabuses and texts; racist institutional practices inhibit the progress of Black students in climbing the educational ladder. For example, there is evidence to show that irrespective of their actual ability, Black students are assigned to lower ability groups than their White counterparts. These students are consequently restricted in the level of school qualifications open to them (Wright 1987), and future channels into higher education, and the labor market (Brennan and McGeevor 1990).

7. Student Performance and Achievement

Attempts to establish differences in intelligence between various social groups have proved less than successful. In fact, Pidgeon (quoted in Goldstein 1987) argues that any differences emerging from tests are manufactured rather than "natural." Similarly, contemporary cultural assumptions and expectations influence test construction resulting in relatively poor performances from lower status groups (Gould 1981). According to Pidgeon, differences, say, between male and female students' test performances are likely to be due to differences in the balance of items favoring one sex or the other. Thus, it is possible for "fair" tests to be constructed where appropriate selection of items will yield tests without gender or cultural bias.

It has also been found that forms of testing are likely to affect the relative performance of male and female students, with male students achieving better on multiple choice examinations and female students on essay-type questions (Stobart et al. 1992). There is little research on the different test responses of different ethnic groups. Ethical decisions now confront test constructors as to whether it is legitimate, as is currently the case, to formulate a theoretical description of achievement which is sexually and culturally biased (Goldstein 1987), or should test constructors be working toward a more gender and culturally fair mode of assessment, as Stobart et al. (1992) suggest?

The appearance of differences between social groups in subject areas has been less controversial. Female students tend to perform better in reading, spelling, and verbal skills while male students, in the later school years, tend to excel in mathematics and problem solving (Maccoby and Jacklin 1974). Further, girls tend to be academically ahead in the elementary school phase. One perceived reason for this is that the elementary atmosphere is more "feminine" and thus more comfortable for girls. Another is that girls are relatively more mature than boys, though the concept of maturity in relation to academic achievement has been heavily criticized by Goldstein (1987).

As female students progress through the school, however, their achievement levels slip, particularly in mathematics and science (Becker 1981). A variety of reasons have been given for this finding. For example, female students favor serialistic learning (proceeding from certainty to certainty, learning, remembering, recapitulating) whereas male students are likely to take a holistic approach (more exploratory, working

towards an explanatory framework). Scott-Hodgetts (1986) suggests that male students are likely to be more successful learners, say in mathematics, because they are more versatile and capable of switching learning strategies where necessary.

Other studies have found that female students are more likely than their male counterparts to display "learned helplessness" (Licht and Dweck 1983). Whereas male students are more likely to attribute success to their ability and failure to a lack of effort, female students tend to relate success to effort and failure to lack of ability. Female students show a stronger tendency to view their successes as due to factors such as "luck," which implies some uncertainty about their ability to succeed in the future (Nicholls 1979).

8. Classroom Context

Mixed-classroom studies have repeatedly found that male students receive more teacher attention than do female students (e.g. Galton et al. 1980). Teachers tend to place more importance on male learning and give male students more teacher time. Yet, it is often male students themselves who demand attention by asking questions or by making heavier demands on the teacher in other ways. Teacher attention need not necessarily be thought of as positive. In her ethnographic study of a comprehensive school in Birmingham, England, Wright (1987) found that African-Caribbean students, both male and female, received more attention than their White counterparts, but that this attention was demoralizing and prejudicial in achievement terms.

A study by Sikes (1971) of seventh and eighth grade classrooms found that the many more contacts that male students had with teachers related not only to misbehavior (negative attention) but to academic contexts, both teacher and student initiated (positive attention). This study also found that male students were asked a higher percentage of abstract (rather than factual) questions and showed a greater willingness to guess when unsure of the answer. Female students had a higher percentage of positive contacts with their teachers, but they were more likely to remain silent in classroom discussion. While these patterns of classroom interaction have been found at all levels of education, there are some specific age-related factors.

8.1 Elementary or Primary Classrooms

A review of British primary schools by Brophy and Good (1974) found that, although boys are criticized more often than girls, they are praised as often and sometimes more often. Teachers not only check on boys' work more but also tend to question them more during the lesson. Further, boys are more likely to call out answers and thus, proactively, make greater demands on the teacher. A study by French and French

(1984) similarly revealed that boys are far more able to make their comments heard and to be addressed by the teacher. In addition, certain boys in the class develop strategies which increase their chances of being asked a question by their teachers and which ensure, during the lesson, that they become the focus of attention for the whole class.

On average, elementary boys appear to misbehave much more often and more intensively than girls, thus eliciting more frequent criticism and punishment for misbehavior. However, this praise and criticism is not distributed equally among all boys in the classroom. Brophy and Good (1974) found that a large proportion, sometimes even the majority of the criticism, may be directed to a small group of boys who are perceived as likely to misbehave and who are often low achievers. In Britain, this group typically includes an overrepresentation of Black and ethnic minority students. Meanwhile, a high proportion of praise (for academic accomplishment) goes to another small group of generally White boys who are high achievers.

Overall, then, the data suggest that differences between elementary boys and girls in patterns of interactions with their teachers are as likely to be due to differences in the behavior of the students themselves as due to the tendency of teachers to treat the two sexes differently.

8.2 High-school or Secondary Classrooms

As has been discussed, the advantage in achievement held by girls at the elementary school level is not sustained as they move to the secondary school. Moreover, it is claimed that this slippage is due to the prevention of older, female students from achieving their academic potential because of inappropriate teacher expectations and other aspects of institutionalized sexism in the school system (Becker 1981).

Significantly, early high school studies found striking differences in the teachers' treatment of males and females, invariably favoring the male students. Jones (1971), for example, found that all kinds of interactions favored male students. Particularly significant were the number of direct questions, open questions, student-initiated contacts, teacher-initiated work contacts, and positive teacher–student contacts. In addition, male students received more behavioral warnings and criticisms than did their female counterparts.

As male students get older and move toward college and university, the conflict that once seemed to have existed between the student role and the male sex role disappears. The converse happens to female students as their perceived future domestic role as wife and mother narrows their career aspirations. Since achievement in school is perceived as a stepping stone toward later performance as either the family "breadwinner" or the family "carer" occupation becomes a basic part of student expectations. At the same time, familiar patterns of interaction between teachers and students continue. Stanworth (1983) found that British female secondary students found it more difficult to engage successfully in conversation with the teachers and that they were more "invisible." Hence, many of the teachers in Stanworth's study found difficulty in recalling girls' names and admitted to the fact that they could not, in some cases, distinguish one female student from another.

9. Social Relationships within the School

Many student experiences in the school context are shaped by the way they are perceived by their peer group. Evidence is now emerging that students are profoundly affected by these experiences. Two British studies illustrate this concern; the first regarding the subjective world of adolescent girls (Lees 1987), and the second the impact of racism on children's lives (Troyna and Hatcher 1992).

Lees' study aimed to explore the system of social relations in the school, Specifically how boys treat girls and how girls respond in the classroom. What emerged was that, regardless of social class or ethnic group, adolescent girls are concerned and anxious about their sexual reputation; that is, whether they are "slags" (girls who sleep around) or "drags" ("nice" girls who do not and who are considered by boys as marriageable rather than "easy lays"). Lees commented on the sheer volume of denigratory terms for women and the tight control exercised over female students' autonomy with the intent of protecting their sexual reputations.

Offensive labeling also plays a part in Black children's lives. In their study of predominantly White primary schools, Troyna and Hatcher (1992) found, first, that race and racism are significant features of school life, and that racist name-calling is by far the most common expression of racism.

> There is a wide variation in black children's experiences of racist name-calling. For some it may almost be an everyday happening. For others it is less frequent, with occurences remembered as significant events whose reoccurrence remains a possibility in every new social situation. For all, it is in general the most hurtful form of verbal aggression from other children. (p. 195)

Significantly, differences between the experiences of children in different schools were accounted for in terms of the effectiveness of the stance of staff and particularly the head (principal) in dealing with racist incidents. Again, as in the Lees (1987) study, verbal harassment was found to induce fear and construct systems of control over Black students.

10. Conclusion

Males and females, and students of different races, experience schooling quite differently. They are perceived and treated differently by their teachers and their classmates (particulary those of the opposite sex or from different races). They are assigned or select different curriculums. They achieve at different levels, partly because of the type and form of tests administered. They develop different interests and preferences, and they may come to perceive themselves and their abilities quite differently.

The importance of research on gender and racial differences is that findings derived from such research can raise consciousness about current inequalities in the schooling system and thus enable changes to be made. At the same time, however, raising consciousness does not guarantee that the necessary improvements will be made (see Weiner 1994). Substantial improvement will probably require fundamental changes in the economic and social structures within which schools currently operate.

References

Arnot M, Weiner G (eds.) 1987 *Gender and the Politics of Schooling*. Hutchinson, London

Becker J 1981 Differential teacher treatment of males and females in mathematics classes. *J. Res. Math. Educ.* 12(1): 40–53

Brah A, Minhas R 1985 Structural racism or cultural difference. In: Weiner G (ed.) 1985 *Just a Bunch of Girls*. Open University Press, Milton Keynes

Brennan J, McGeevor P 1990 *Ethnic Minority and the Graduate Labour Market*, Commission for Racial Equality, London

Brophy J, Good T 1974 *Teacher–Student Relationships: Causes and Consequences*. Holt, Rinehart and Winston, New York

Chapman J W, Boersma F J 1983 A cross-national study of academic self-concept using the Student's Perception of Ability Scale. *N. Z. J. Educ. Stud.* 18(1): 69–75

Clift P 1978 And all things nice.... Unpublished paper, Open University, Milton Keynes

Connell W F, Stroobant R E, Sinclair K E, Connell R W, Rogers K W 1975 *Twenty to Twenty*. Hicks Smith, Sydney

Cooper P, Stewart L 1987 *Language Skills in the Classroom: What Research Say to the Teacher* National Educational Association, Washington, DC

Deliyanni-Kouimtzi K 1992 "Father is out shopping because mother is at work": Greek primary school reading texts as an example of educational policy for gender equality. *Gender and Education* 4(1–2): 67–79

Elkjaer B 1992 Girls and information technology in Denmark—An account of a socially constructed problem. *Gender and Education* 4(1–2): 25–40

Etaugh C, Hughes V 1975 Teachers' evaluations of sex-typed behavior in children: The role of teacher sex and school setting. *Dev. Psychol.* 11: 394–95

Fagot B I 1977 Consequences of moderate cross-gender behavior in pre-school children. *Child Dev.* 48(3): 902–07

French J, French P 1984 Sociolinguists and gender divisions: In: Acker S (ed.) 1984 *World Yearbook of Education 1983–84: Women and Education*. Kogan Page, London

Galton M, Simon B, Croll P J 1980 *Inside the Primary Classroom*. Routledge and Kegan Paul, London

Goldstein H 1987 Gender bias and test norms in educational selection. In: Arnot M, Weiner G(eds.) 1987

Gorman T, White J, Brooks G, Maclure M, Kispala A 1988 *Language Performance in Schools*. Review of APU Language Monitoring 1979–83 HMSO, London

Gould S J 1981 *The Mismeasure of Man*. W W Norton, New York

Griffin J 1972 Influence strategies: Theory and research a study of teacher behavior. Doctoral dissertation, University of Missouri, Columbia, Missouri

Jones V 1971 The Influence of teacher–student introversion, achievement and similarity on teacher–student dyadic classroom interactions. Doctoral dissertation University of Texas, Austin, Texas

Lees S 1987 The structure of sexual relations in school. In: Arnot M, Weiner G (eds.) 1987

Licht B G, Dweck C S 1983 Sex differences in achievement orientations: Consequences for academic clones and attainments. In: Marland M (ed.) 1983 *Sex Differentiation and Schooling*. Heinemann, London

Maccoby E M, Jacklin C N 1975 *The Psychology of Sex Differences*. Oxford University Press, London

Milner D 1983 *Children and Race: Ten Years On*. Ward Lock Educational, London

Nash S C 1979 Sex role as mediator of intellectual functioning. In: Wittig M A, Petersen A C (eds.) 1979 *Sex Related Differences in Cognitive Functioning: Developmental Issues*. Academic Press, Orlando, Florida

Nicholls J 1979 Development of perception of any attainment and causal attributions for success and failure in reading. *J. Educ. Psychol.* 71(1): 94–99

Phoenix A 1987 Theories of gender and black families. In: Weiner G, Arnot M (eds.) 1987 *Gender Under Scrutiny*. Hutchinson, London

Proctor C P 1984 Teacher expectations: A model for school improvement. *Elem. Sch. J.* 84(4): 469–81

Sarup M 1986 *The Politics of Multiracial Education*. Routledge, London

Scott-Hodgetts R 1986 Girls and mathematics: The negative implications of success. In: Burton L (ed.) 1986 *Girls into Maths Can Go*. Holt, Rinehart and Winston, London

Sikes J 1971 Differential behavior of male and female teachers with male and female students. Doctoral dissertation, University of Texas, Austin, Texas

Spender D 1980 *Man Made Language*. Routledge and Kegan Paul, London

Stanworth M 1983 *Gender and Schooling: A Study of Sexual Divisions in the Classroom*. Unwin and Hyman, London

Stobart G, Elwood J, Quinlan M 1992 Gender bias in examinations: How equal are the opportunities. *Br. J. Educ. Res.* 18(3): 261–76

Stone M 1981 *The Education the of Black Child in Britain: The Myth of Multiracial Education*. Fontana, London

Troyna B, Hatcher R 1992 *Racism in Children's Lives: A Study of Mainly-White Primary Schools*. Routledge, London

Weiner G 1994 *Feminisms in Education*. Open University Press, Buckingham

Wright C 1987 The relations between teachers and Afro-Caribbean pupils: Observing multicultural classrooms. In: Weiner G, Arnot M (eds.) 1987 *Gender Under Scrutiny*. Hutchinson, London

Grade Repeating

L. A. Shepard

When students are held in the same grade in school for an extra year rather than being promoted to the next grade with their age peers, the practice is called "grade repetition" or "grade retention." Although grade repeating is practiced as a corrective for academic failure, controlled studies have shown that repeating a grade decreases student achievement and increases the likelihood of dropping out of school. Policies and practices concerning grade repeating are discussed in light of the contradiction between popular beliefs and research evidence.

1. Statistics on Grade Repeaters

Countries differ dramatically in the percentage of students repeating grades each year. In developing countries such as Brazil, with an annual retention rate of 20 percent, some children may spend three or four years in the first grade (Davico 1990). Peru and Columbia have similarly high rates, while in Venezuela only 9 percent of elementary students repeat each year (UNESCO 1990). Among African nations the percentages of elementary (school) students repeating grades vary from approximately 30 percent in Cameroon, Chad, and Congo to 3 percent per year in Egypt. Some countries, such as Japan, Korea, Denmark, Norway, and Sweden have automatic promotion policies for first level education and thus report no repeaters; for Japan the automatic promotion policy applies to secondary education as well.

While annual repeater statistics are useful for comparative purposes, they are deceptive. These statistics do not give an accurate picture of what happens to a cohort of students over time. Except for students who repeat more than once, annual rates must be added to determine the total percentage of students who repeated at some time during their school career. For example, in theory a relatively low repeater rate of 9 percent per year would still build up to more than 50 percent by Grade 6. Cumulative effects are difficult to document, however, because of the close association between repeating and dropping out of school. In Brazil, Davico (1990) reported that 50 percent of children drop out or repeat by the second grade; 84 percent have been lost by Grade 8. In the United States, cumulative data show that 18 percent of students have repeated a grade by Grade 8. (National Centre for Education Statistics 1990). Based on increased annual retention rates during the 1980s, however, Shepard and Smith (1990) estimated that future cumulative rates of grade repeating in the United States might be higher than 30 percent.

In all countries where data is available, low-status and poor children are much more likely to repeat grades than are children from high socioeconomic backgrounds. In France, Levasseur and Seibel (1984) reported that only one-third of working-class children completed elementary school on schedule compared to an 84 percent rate for the children of professionals and executives. Similarly, Davico (1990) reported that grade failure mostly affected children from low-income families in Brazil and also found that teachers in schools with low repeater rates were better educated and more highly trained than teachers in schools with high repeater rates. According to a nationally representative survey of eighth graders in the United States (Hafner et al. 1990), American Indian, Hispanic, and African-American children were more likely to repeat a grade than were Asians or Whites. Furthermore, students whose parents never finished high school were three times as likely to repeat as students whose parents were college graduates.

2. Relation Between Grade Repeating and School Dropouts

As mentioned above, grade repeating is closely linked to dropping out of school. A 1984 UNESCO study used both repetition rates and dropout rates as indicators of educational "wastage." The Association of California Urban School Districts (1985) reported that in Los Angeles dropouts had been retained five times more often than graduates. In Chicago, Rice et al. (1987) documented a direct increase in dropout rates following the institution of a more stringent eighth-grade retention policy.

Although all studies show strong correlations between the two variables, the observed relationship might be due to poor achievement or to socioeconomic factors. Grissom and Shepard (1989) used causal modeling techniques in an attempt to examine the possible causal relationship between repeating and dropping out of school in three large United States' school systems. In each system repeating a grade contributed substantially to the risk of dropping out of school over and above the effects of socioeconomic status and prior achievement. For students who were equally low in achievement and other "at-risk" background characteristics, retained students were 20 to 30 percent more likely to drop out. In Austin, Texas, for example, African-American males with below average achievement had a 45 percent chance of dropping out of school. In contrast, African-American males with identical achievement scores who had repeated a year of school had a 75 percent chance of leaving school before graduation. A substantially increased risk for dropping out after repeating a grade was found even in a large affluent suburban school district with only a 4 percent annual drop-out rate.

3. Effects of Repeating on Academic Achievement and Personal Adjustment

Holmes (1989) provided the most complete review of controlled studies examining the effects of grade repetition on student achievement and personal adjustment. Meta-analytic techniques were used to aggregate the results from 63 research studies. In each study, students who repeated were compared in subsequent years to similar children who did not repeat. Taken together the results showed an average effect on academic achievement of −0.31. That is, in subsequent years, retained children were almost one-third of a standard deviation behind their matched counterparts on achievement measures. Contrary to the expectation that repeating a grade will improve academic performance, retained students actually did worse than similar students who did not repeat.

In an attempt to explain these findings, Holmes (1989) grouped studies by type of follow-up comparison. Studies in which the achievement of retained students in one grade was compared with their age-peers in the next higher grade showed the most negative effects, possibly because the nonretained or promoted students had been exposed to a more advanced curriculum. In contrast, studies using a same-grade comparison showed more positive effects for retention, particularly in the repeat year itself. For example, students who repeated third grade, did better their second year in third grade than their matched controls did their first time through. This positive effect disappeared after the first year, although the number of such studies is limited. Holmes' (1989) analysis may help explain the sharp contradiction between research results and popular beliefs about the benefits of retention. Retained students may show a relative advantage during the repeat year itself. Thus, educators are able to persist in their beliefs that retention is effective because they see these gains while at the same time being unaware of losses in subsequent years.

Twenty-seven of the studies analyzed by Holmes (1989) measured the effect of repeating grades on personal adjustment. The effect size (ES) was −0.21, meaning that retained students were behind nonretained students on measures of social, emotional, and behavioral adjustment by about one-fifth of a standard deviation. Based on 11 studies, retained students had essentially the same self-concept (ES = 0.06) as control students. Averaged over 10 studies, repeating had a negative effect on attitude toward school (ES = −0.18).

4. Policies and Practices Concerning Grade Repeating

National policies and practices on grade repeating appear to be influenced more by beliefs and traditions than by research evidence. Countries such as Japan, Korea, Denmark, Norway, and Sweden have traditionally followed automatic promotion policies with no apparent detriment to the quality of education in those nations. In countries that practice grade retention, however, increasing repeater rates follow from reform efforts aimed at raising educational standards (see Bruce 1988, Shepard and Smith 1989).

Educators and the lay public continue to believe that retention is an effective means to improve academic performance, despite compelling research evidence that repeating increases school dropouts and decreases academic skills. For example, Anderson-Levitt et al. (1991) have found that grade retention is practiced extensively in French elementary schools despite advisories from the Ministry of Education against retention. Although the huge numbers of repeaters (at one time affecting half of each age cohort) have been reduced since the early 1970s, retention in France is still an implicit form of tracking, undermining the goal of common schooling for all children. The Ministry promotes an individually paced model of reading development. However, according to Anderson-Levitt et al. (1991), teachers resist the idea that nonreaders should be promoted to second grade. Thus, teacher beliefs and traditional curriculum expectations circumvent research-based policy directives.

5. The Future of Grade Repeating

Given strongly held views in countries practicing grade repetition, change is not likely to occur easily. Policy reports developed in the states of California and Massachusetts are exemplary as potential agents of change, because they contain two types of information that seem to be critical in reforming retention practices. First, these reports summarize and disseminate the negative findings from research. Second, they offer practical alternatives for addressing the needs of low-achieving students. Alternative practices with greater chances for success than grade repeating include: developmentally appropriate instruction in the early grades, the Reading Recovery program and other intensive reading programs, multi-age grouping, extra help in the regular classroom, before and after school programs, and redesigned curricula emphasizing active learning and thinking rather than lock-step acquisition of skills (George 1991, Massachusetts Board of Education 1990).

References

Anderson-Levitt K M, Sirota R, Mazurier M 1991 Elementary education in France. *Elem. Sch. J.* 92(1): 79–95

Association of California Urban School Districts (ACUSD) 1985 *Dropouts from California's Urban School Districts: Who Are They? How do we Count Them? How can we Hold Them (or at Least Educate Them)?* ACUSD, Los Angeles, California

Bruce M G 1988 In Europe: Making the grade or marking time? *Phi Del. Kap.* 69(5): 383–84

Davico M I 1990 The repeat and drop-out problem: A study in Brazil on the role of the teacher. *Prospects* 20(1): 107–13

George C 1991 *Beyond Retention: A Study of Retention Rates, Practices, and Successful Alternatives in California.* California Department of Education, Sacramento, California

Grissom J B, Shepard L A 1989 Repeating and dropping out of school. In: Shepard L A, Smith M L (eds.) 1989

Hafner A, Ingels S, Schneider B, Stevenson D/National Center for Education Statistics 1990 *A Profile of the American Eighth Grader: NELS: 88 Student Descriptive Summary.* National Center for Education Statistics, Washington, DC

Holmes C T 1989 Grade level retention effects: A meta-analysis of research studies. In: Shepard L A, Smith M L (eds.) 1989

Levasseur J, Seibel C 1984 Réussite et échec scolaires. *Données Sociales* 5: 483–90

Massachusetts State Board of Education 1990 *Structuring Schools for Student Success: A Focus on Grade Retention.* Massachussetts Board of Education, Quincy, Massachusetts

Rice W K, Toles R E, Schulz E M, Harvey J T, Foster D L 1987 *A longitudinal investigation of effectiveness of increased promotion standards at eighth grade on high school graduation.* Paper presented at the annual meeting of the American Educational Research Association, Washington, DC

Shepard L A, Smith M L (eds.) 1989 *Flunking Grades: Research and Policies on Retention.* Falmer Press, London

Shepard L A, Smith M L 1990 Synthesis of research on grade retention. *Educ. Leadership* 47(8): 84–88

UNESCO 1984 Wastage in primary education from 1970 to 1980. *Prospects* 14(3): 347–67

UNESCO 1990 *Statistical Yearbook.* UNESCO, Paris

Student Diversity and Classroom Teaching

M. C. Wang

Advances in theory and research, particularly since the 1970s, have generated substantial conceptual changes in the understanding of the process of learning and increased recognition that certain student characteristics can be altered through schooling. Among the most important of these characteristics are family characteristics, such as parental expectation and family involvement (Comer 1986); cognition (or the processes of learning; de Bono 1976, Feuerstein 1980); intelligence (or the ability to learn; Husén and Tuijnman 1991); and student motivation (or the willingness to learn; Zimmerman 1986). The recognition of the alterability of these characteristics has led researchers to study ways of modifying the psychological processes and cognitive operations used by the individual learner, as well as modifying learning environments and instructional strategies to accommodate learner differences (Wang 1992). Findings from research, along with the practical wisdom culled from implementing innovative school programs, have significantly contributed to the current understanding of what constitutes effective practice and how the learning of diverse students can be enhanced in the same classroom.

Although research has identified numerous variables that are related to differences in student learning and achievement, the sheer number of these variables has posed a perplexing challenge to researchers, policymakers, and practitioners. To begin to address this challenge, these variables can be divided into two groups; those internal to students (e.g., ability and motivation) and those external to students (e.g., quality of instruction and task demands).

1. Models of School Learning

Carroll (1963) introduced educational researchers to the concept of a model of school learning. In his model, he put forth six constructs. Three of these constructs pertained to student differences (aptitude, ability to understand instruction, and perseverance), while the remaining three constructs applied to the classroom environment (clarity of instruction, task appropriateness, and opportunity to learn). These constructs became a point of departure for other models of school learning that were developed during the late 1960s and 1970s (Bennett 1978, Bloom 1976, Bruner 1966, Glaser 1976). Bloom's model specifically differentiated between two types of student characteristics: cognitive entry behaviors and affective entry characteristics.

In retrospect, all of these models recognized both types of entry characteristics. With respect to cognitive entry characteristics, for example, they included constructs such as aptitude, prior knowledge, and home background. With respect to affective entry characteristics, they included perseverance, self-concept, and attitudes toward school and specific subject matters. This acknowledgement of differences among students stood in contrast to more narrow psychological studies of influences on learning, which generally treated individual differences as a source of error, and focused instead on instructional treatment variables.

In addition to student variables, each of these models of school learning gave salience to constructs related to the classroom environment. These constructs varied in generality, some being as broad as "instructional events" or "clarity of instruction," and others as narrow as "use of cues" or "feedback and correctives." Although later models brought some refinement in the ways in which individual difference variables and instructional treatment variables were defined and the ways in which they were related to one another, the primary contributions of more recent models have been in extending the range of influences considered.

The evolution of models of school learning was further advanced with the introduction of models of adaptive instruction (Corno and Snow 1986, Glaser 1976, Wang 1992). School-based implementation of models of adaptive instruction was designed to help schools create classroom environments that maximized each student's opportunities for success in school. Particular attention was paid to new variables associated with instructional delivery systems, program design, and implementation. In particular, attention was given to those features that Glaser (1982) referred to as the "large practical variables," which included efficient allocation and use of teacher and student time, a practical classroom management system, systematic teacher feedback and reinforcement of student learning behavior and progress, instructional interactions based on the diagnosed learning needs of individual students, and flexible administrative and organizational patterns responsive to program implementation and staffing needs.

Another contribution to models of school learning came from researchers concerned with the identification and characterization of effective schools. Edmonds (1979) is most strongly associated with this identification of variables for exceptionally effective schools, especially for the urban poor. Significant contributions to effective school models were also made by Brookover (1979), Brookover and Lezotte (1979), and Rutter et al. (1979). Illustrations of the types of variables characterizing effective schools include degree of curriculum articulation and organization, school-wide staff development, parental involvement and support, school-wide recognition of academic success, maximized learning time, district support, clear goals and high expectations, orderly and disciplined school environment, and principal leadership characterized by attention to quality of instruction (Purkey and Smith 1983).

These various models of school learning have contributed greatly to the understanding of the relative contributions of different influences on student achievement and practical strategies for maximizing educational outcomes across a range of educational conditions and settings. The following section provides a synthesis of the research bases that undergird the design of these models of school learning. Although individual researchers and practitioners may focus their work on particular variables or constructs, the discussion in this section is intended to provide a synoptic view of the entire canopy of influences of learning.

2. The Knowledge Base of School Learning

Focusing on identifying variables related to processes of learning and student achievement, Wang et al. (1993) completed a knowledge base review. The data sources for this review were the consensus ratings from 61 educational research experts, results from 91 quantitative research syntheses, and findings in 179 handbook chapters and narrative reviews published since 1975. Thus, findings from this "meta-review" constitute a distillation of understandings and results from large numbers of primary research studies, quantitative research syntheses, and narrative reviews. They indicate a substantial agreement on the categories of variables that exert influence on student learning, as well as those that had little influence. Table 1 provides a summary list of factors that influence student learning and selected examples of each factor. The factors are placed into one of six major categories and 30 subcategories.

Of the six major categories (see Table 1), the highest ratings overall were assigned to "Program design variables," followed by "Out-of-school contextual variables." The category reflecting the quality of instruction, "Implementation, classroom instruction, and climate variables," ranked third in importance, closely followed by "Student variables." The last two categories, "School-level variables" and "State and district variables," received markedly lower ratings overall.

In the following section, the categories that received exceptionally high ratings are highlighted. The categories representing instruction as designed and instruction as delivered are discussed first. These are followed by out-of-school context and student characteristics.

2.1 Program Design Variables

This category includes instruction as designed and the physical arrangements for its delivery. Variables included in the program design category (Category 5 in Table 1) are organized into three subcategories. The first subcategory, "Demographic and marker variables," was rated the highest of the three. Furthermore, within this subcategory, the most highly rated variables are "size of instructional group (whole class,

Table 1
Variable categories of influences on learning with illustrative examples

Category/subcategory[a]	Illustrative variable

Category 1: State and district variables are associated with state- and district-level school governance and administration, including state curriculum and textbook policies, testing and graduation requirements, teacher licensure, specific provisions in teacher contracts, and some district-level administrative and fiscal variables.

District-Level demographics and marker variables	School district size
State-level policy variables	Teacher licensure requirements

Category 2: Out-of-school contextual variables are associated with the home and community contexts within which schools function. They include community demographics, peer culture, parental support and involvement, and the amount of time students spend out of school on activities such as television viewing, leisure reading, and homework.

Community variables	Socioeconomic level of community
Peer group variables	Level of peers' academic aspirations
Home environment and parental support variables	Parental involvement in ensuring completion of homework
Student use of out-of-school time variables	Student participation in clubs and extracurricular school activities

Category 3: School-level variables are associated with school-level demographics, culture, climate, policies, and practices. They include demographics of the student body, whether the school is public or private, and levels of funding for specific categorical programs; school-level decision-making variables; and specific school-level policies and practices, including policies on parental involvement in the school.

Demographic and marker variables	Size of school
Teacher-administrator decision-making variables	Principal actively concerned with instructional program
School culture variables (ethos conducive to teaching and learning)	School-wide emphasis on and recognition of academic achievement
School-wide policy and organization variables	Explicit school-wide discipline policy
Accessibility variables	Accessibility of educational program (overcoming architectural, communication, and environmental barriers)
Parental involvement variables	Parental involvement in improvement and operation of instructional programs

Category 4: Student variables are those associated with students, including demographics; academic history; and a variety of social, behavioral, motivational, cognitive, and affective characteristics.

Demographic and marker variables	Gender
Placement history variables	Prior grade retentions
Social and behavioral variables	Positive, nondisruptive behavior
Motivational and affective variables	Attitude toward subject matter instructed
Cognition variables	Level of specific academic knowledge in subject area instructed
Metacognition variables	Comprehension monitoring (plan, monitor effectiveness of attempted actions, monitor outcomes of actions)
Psychomotor variables	Psychomotor skills specific to area instructed

Category 5: Program design variables are associated with instruction as designed, and with the physical arrangements for its delivery. They include the instructional strategies specified by the curriculum and characteristics of instructional materials.

Demographic and marker variables	Size of instructional group (whole class, small group, one-on-one instruction)
Curriculum and instruction variables	Alignment among goals, contents, instruction, assignments, and evaluation
Curriculum design variables	Materials employ advance organizers

Category 6: Implementation, classroom instruction, and climate variables are associated with the implementation of the curriculum and the instructional program, including classroom routines and practices, characteristics of instruction as delivered, classroom management, monitoring of student progress, quality and quantity of instruction provided, student–teacher interactions, and classroom climate.

Classroom support variables	Establishing efficient classroom routines and communicating rules and procedures
Classroom instruction variables	Use of clear and organized direct instruction
Quantity of instruction variables	Time on task (amount of time students are actively engaged in learning)
Classroom assessment variables	Use of assessment as a frequent, integral component of instruction
Classroom management variables	Group alerting (teacher uses questioning/recitation strategies that maintain active participation by all students)
Student and teacher interactions: social variables	Student responds positively to questions from other students and from teacher
Student and teacher interactions: academic variables	Frequent calls for extended, substantive oral and written responses (not one-word answers)
Classroom climate variables	Cohesiveness (members of class are friends who share common interests and values and emphasize cooperative goals)

a Subcategories are listed below the description of each major category and are each illustrated with representative variables. For example, the first major category includes two subcategories, "District-level demographics and marker variables" and "State-level policy variables" small group, or one-on-one instruction)," "number of classroom aides," and "resources needed." Thus, the most important aspect of program design appears to be the intensity of educational services provided to each learner. More aides, smaller groups, or increased material resources are associated with significantly higher learning outcomes.

Ratings on the "Curriculum and instruction variables" suggest that the key to effective instructional design is the flexible and appropriate use of a variety of instructional strategies while maintaining an orderly classroom environment. The highest overall rating in this subcategory was for "use of classroom management techniques to control classroom disruptiveness." This variable was followed by "use of prescriptive instruction combined with aspects of informal or open education" and "presence of information in the curriculum on individual differences and commonalities," both of which explicitly relate to student diversity and individualization. Other highly rated variables referred to specific instructional strategies, including "use of mastery-learning techniques," "instructional cues, engagement, and corrective feedback," "use of cooperative learning strategies," and "use of diagnostic–prescriptive methods."

High ratings in the "Curriculum design variables" were given to the variables of "materials employ alternative modes of representation" and "degree of structure in curriculum accommodates needs of different learners," both of which reinforce the importance of offering a variety of instructional materials and approaches to accommodate individual differences. The importance of the organization of curriculum content is revealed by the two highest rated items in this subcategory: "materials employ learning hierarchies" and "material is presented in a cognitively efficient manner."

2.2 Implementation, Classroom Instruction, and Climate Variables

This category includes support of the curriculum and the instructional program; classroom routines; specific instructional, assessment, and classroom-management practices; quantity of instruction; academic and nonacademic student–teacher interaction; and classroom climate. It is by far the largest of the six major categories.

High ratings in the areas of implementation, classroom instruction, and climate point to the importance of maintaining an orderly classroom environment and providing clear, well-organized instruction appropriate to the needs of individual learners. In the overall ranking of all 30 subcategories, classroom management ranked second. Its most critical items were "group alerting (teacher uses questioning/recitation strategies that maintain active participation by all students)" and "learner accountability (teacher maintains student awareness of learning goals and expectations)." Smooth transitions from one instructional

activity to another, minimal disruptions, and teacher awareness of what is going on in the classroom at all times also received relatively high ratings.

Quantity of instruction was also highly rated. This subcategory includes time spent in direct instruction, especially direct instruction on basic skills; time spent on homework; and length of the school day and school year. The importance accorded to quantity of instruction is not surprising since it has appeared in many of the most widely cited models of school learning.

Student and teacher interactions were ranked highly, as were classroom climate variables. Taken together, the highly rated items in these two subcategories characterize a classroom in which teachers interact with students frequently for instructional purposes, and where students work with classmates, share common interests and values, and pursue cooperative goals. Students are actively engaged in learning and are involved in some classroom decisions. At the same time, the class is well-organized and well-planned, with a clear academic focus. Objectives of learning activities are specific and explicit, with the pacing of instruction appropriate for the majority.

High ratings were also given to the quality of the instruction provided to students, namely, the use of advanced organizers, the direction of students' attention to the content to be learned, the provision of clear and organized direct instruction, the systematic sequencing of lesson events, and the use of clear lesson transitions. Other highly rated variables included corrective feedback in case of student error, frequent academic questions, and accurate measurement of skills. Finally, the literature strongly supports the teaching of skills in the context of meaningful application, use of good examples and analogies, and teaching for meaningful understanding, together with explicit promotion of student self-monitoring of comprehension and gradual transfer of responsibility for learning from the teacher to the student.

2.3 Out-of-school Contextual Variables

This category includes variables associated with the home and community contexts within which schools function. Variables receiving high ratings under this category include peers' educational and occupational aspirations, parental involvement in ensuring completion of homework, parental participation in school conferences and related activities, and parental interest in students' schoolwork. The educational environment of the home (e.g., number of books and magazines) was also cited in numerous reference sources and received consistently high ratings. Student participation in clubs and extracurricular school activities and time spent on leisure reading were also moderately related to learning outcomes.

2.4 Student Variables

"Metacognition variables" was among the subcategories that received highest mean ratings. Highly rated variables in this subcategory include "comprehension monitoring (planning; monitoring effectiveness of attempted actions; testing, revising, and evaluating learning strategies)," "self-regulatory, self-control strategies (e.g., control of attention)," and "positive strategies to facilitate generalization of concepts." Other highly rated student variables include positive behavior and ability to make friends with peers, motivation for continual learning, and perseverance on learning tasks. These variables fall under the rubric of affective entry characteristics. Highly rated variables related to cognitive entry characteristics included general mental abilities, levels of basic skills sufficient to profit from instruction, and prior knowledge in the subject area instructed.

3. Implications for Improving Practice

Classroom teachers must respond to a multitude of influences interacting in kaleidoscopic patterns (Lockheed and Hanushek 1988, Purves 1989, Stevenson and Stigler 1992). While a large number of variables are moderately related to learning outcomes, few, if any, single variables are very strongly related to learning. Authors of original research studies and of reviews and syntheses are appropriately cautious in stating the importance of particular variables. Nonetheless, taken together, the extant research base suggests some powerful interactive effects on school learning.

Two sets of implications are particularly noteworthy. First, in contrast to the prevailing conception of the important influence of distal variables (notably, policy, demographic, and organizational), the extant research base suggests that these distal variables are relatively unimportant. One explanation of the limited impact of policy and organizational variables is that they are at least one step removed from the daily learning experiences of teachers and students. Simply implementing any one policy, such as the "extended school day," does not guarantee that students in a given classroom will receive instruction from a teacher who plans lessons with special attention to eliminating poor management practices and inefficient use of class time. Effective school policies require effective implementation by teachers at the classroom and student levels.

A second significant finding of the accumulated knowledge base on school learning is the consistent evidence of the impact of the home environment, classroom management, and metacognitive processes on student learning. There is an increasing research base that prescribes metacognitive processes and functions, such as comprehension monitoring, strategies to facilitate generalization of concepts, and self-regulatory and self-control strategies, and effective interventions, to teach metacognitive skills. Similarly, teachers must use a variety of instructional techniques, activities, and behaviors in their efforts to control classrooms and enhance learning. Examples include group alerting, learner accountability, smooth transitions, and teacher "with-it-ness." Finally, studies supporting the importance of the home environment have identified characteristics and behaviors of parents and extended family members that support student achievement. Parent behaviors such as attendance at school functions, interest in children's schoolwork, monitoring television viewing, engaging in conversations with children, and ensuring completion of homework and regular school attendance have positive effects on student achievement.

See also: Individualized Instruction

References

Bennett S N 1978 Recent research on teaching: A dream, a belief and a model. *Br. J. Educ. Psychol.* 48: 127–47
Bloom B S 1976 *Human Characteristics and School Learning.* McGraw-Hill, New York
Brookover W B (ed.) 1979 *School Social Systems and Student Achievement: Schools Can Make a Difference.* Praeger, New York
Brookover W B, Lezotte L W 1979 *Changes in School Characteristics Coincident with Changes in Student Achievement.* Michigan State University, Institute for Research on Teaching, East Lansing, Michigan
Bruner J S 1966 *Toward a Theory of Instruction.* Norton, New York
Carroll J B 1963 A model of school learning. *Teach. Coll. Rec.* 64: 723–33
Comer J P 1986 Parent participation in the schools. *Phi Del. Kap.* 67: 442–44
Corno L, Snow R E 1986 Adapting teaching to individual differences among learners. In: Wittrock M C (ed.) 1986 *Handbook of Research on Teaching*, 3rd edn. Macmillan Inc., New York
de Bono E 1976 *Teaching Thinking.* Temple Smith, London
Edmonds R 1979 Effective schools for the urban poor. *Educ. Leadership* 37(1): 15–27
Feuerstein R 1980 *Instrumental Enrichment: An Intervention Program for Cognitive Modifiability.* College Park Press, Baltimore, Maryland
Glaser R 1976 Components of a psychological theory of instruction: Toward a science of design. *Rev. Educ. Res.* 46: 1–24
Glaser R 1982 Instructional psychology: Past, present, and future. *Am. Psychol.* 37: 292–305
Husén T, Tuijnman A 1991 The contribution of formal schooling to the increase in intellectual capital. *Educ. Researcher* 20(7): 10–25
Lockheed M E, Hanushek E 1988 Improving educational efficiency in developing countries: What do we know? *Compare* 18(1): 21–38
Purkey S C, Smith M S 1983 Effective schools: A review. *Elementary Sch. J.* 83: 427–52
Purves A C (ed.) 1989 *International Comparisons and Educational Reform.* Association for Supervision and Curriculum Development, Cucamonga, California
Rutter M, Maughan B, Mortimore P, Ouston J, Smith A 1979 *Fifteen Thousand Hours: Secondary Schools and*

their Effects on Children. Harvard University Press, Cambridge, Massachusetts

Stevenson H W, Stigler J W 1992 *The Learning Gap.* Summit Books, New York

Wang M C 1992 *Adaptive Education Strategies: Building on Diversity.* Brookes Publishing, Baltimore, Maryland

Wang M C, Haertel G D, Walberg H J 1993 Toward a knowledge base for school learning. *Rev. Educ. Res.* 63(3): 249–94

Zimmerman B J (ed.) 1986 Discussions of role subprocesses in student self-regulated learning . *Contemp. Educ. Psychol.* 11(4)

(b) Classroom Environments

School Culture and Peer Groups

J. Hill

Age-grading is so central to the organization of large modern schools that disregarding it in school programs is often hailed as educational innovation. School culture is centered in the set of age-graded student cohorts defined by law and administrative practices, but includes the cultures of an array of peer groups that evolve informally out of relationships among students themselves. School culture also includes the professional culture of educators, and standards of local organizational and administrative practice. The ways that peer groups reinforce the official goals of an institution, or work at cross-purposes to them, have been a major focus of research in the anthropology of education for four decades.

1. Structure of Peer Groups

For more than a century anthropologists have been documenting variations in age-grading practices around the world. Some preindustrial societies have a formal system of age-sets that spans most or all of the human life-cycle (Steward 1977). (For examples that emphasize socialization see Mayer 1970.) To a limited extent, age-set systems resemble the student cohorts that pass through a modern school and continue as graduating classes of alumni. However, adult age-sets commonly perform major functions for the wider society. Modern graduating classes, by contrast, at most serve as support groups for their alma mater. In general, research on age-set systems has shown how they contribute to social order and cultural continuity.

In popular usage the term "peer group" refers to a cohort of persons close in age, most often teenagers or adolescents. In research on schools the term usually indicates student cliques, but not gangs. Research on gangs has tended to address issues in criminology more than issues in the understanding of school culture. Those who investigate peer groups in schools, on the other hand, have paid particular attention to cliques. Cliques form around pairs and triads of friends; these in turn may coalesce into larger groupings. In contrast to gangs, cliques more

often resemble constellations, with peripheral members loosely or ambiguously related to a central star or other core members. Age and gender are the primary criteria of membership, but social class and ethnicity are often important features of membership. Research has documented enormous variations, from one school to the next, in how clique groups are related to one another, in the features that define membership, in how exclusive memberships may be, and in clique histories, functions, and activities.

2. Peer Groups and Cultural Continuity

Others before him had described peer groups in modern schools, but Hollingshead's book, *Elmtown's Youth* (1949), brought the topic into the spotlight. At this time neither the academic program nor the administration did much to encourage students from poorer families to continue in school or to return once they had dropped out. Hollingshead found that student life in Elmtown High revolved around cliques and peer groups. Clothes fashions, participation in clubs and interschool sports, choices of courses and curricula, postgraduation aspirations: all these were shaped by a system of cliques that reflected social stratification in the local community. Peer groups, school board, and teachers all seemed to reinforce rather than modify unequal opportunities for social mobility.

By the 1960s researchers in the United States were taking the view that peer groups in school do not simply echo social strata in the community, but were youth centered. Coleman's (1961) study of 10 high schools found an adolescent world in the schools, in which students "constitute a small society" that has most of its interactions within itself and only "a few threads of connection with the outside adult society" (p.3). Perhaps what stirred most controversy was Coleman's claim that "separate subcultures can exist right under the very noses of adults," with languages, symbols, and even values of their own.

Coleman's study gave a scholarly cachet to 1960s American adult fears that the younger generation had veered off into a different cultural world, led by The

Beatles, Elvis, and other pied pipers of rock music. This adolescent world was labeled as "counter" culture and "peer dominated," and was seen as evidence of a serious structural break between generations.

Rohlen (1983) found almost the opposite in Japan in a study of five high schools. Adolescent society was not a radically separate world, nor did it have much effect upon high schools. It tended to flourish only in high schools that were not geared primarily for preparing students for college entrance examinations. Long school years and long hours of study at home left few opportunities for peer interaction. Indeed, Japanese parents and social critics complained that the "examination hell" was robbing students of the opportunity to enjoy being young.

3. Peer Groups and Culture Theory

The debate in the 1960s over different worlds and generation gaps was distorted by a prevailing concept of culture as monolithic. Researchers tended to see the school as an institution serving "a" community, which had one culture. This view was based on the assumption that an individual could effectively master and live by only one set of cultural rules at a time. To live in two cultures was thought to be improbable in theory and emotionally devastating in practice. If peer groups in the schools had a "separate" subculture then it must be *replacing* the cultural heritage of their parents.

This viewpoint also posited a continuum of individual acculturation, which involved great stress, as an individual shed a previous culture and acquired a new one. Research such as Polgar's (1960) study of Mesquakie Indian youths in Iowa challenged this cluster of assumptions. He found that boys living on the Mesquakie reservation while attending the regular public school in a nearby town learned both cultures concurrently and were able to participate effectively in different peer groups in school and on the reservation. They were not shunted into marginal roles in both societies, as predicted by theory.

Other scholars, notably Goodenough (1971), argued in favor of an analogy between culture and language, in which culture is comparable to a galaxy of dialects and language variants (the equivalent of subcultures and counter cultures) none of which is complete by itself. No individual person masters all of them, but any normal adult will be competent in several. Two persons can interact effectively, even though their origins differ radically, as long as they have in common at least one subculture—for example, as does international business, and as do Mesquakie and White students in an Iowa public school.

To approach culture as language entails viewing culture as a body of knowledge: the knowledge one must have in order to conduct oneself acceptably among the members of a group. Across social boundaries and from one group to the next this body of knowledge may vary dramatically. And since competence

can be brought to the level of mastery only through interaction with persons who already have mastered the system, competence can serve as a mark of social identity ("she behaves like a native"). The approach provides a theoretical rationale for understanding multiculturalism.

In order to capture this dynamic of culture as competence one has to examine it situation by situation. James Spradley pioneered this line of inquiry through his concept of "cultural scene" (Spradley and McCurdy 1972). He and his students documented the idea by collecting case studies of children's views in schools from kindergarten to junior high. However, their reports are mostly ethnosemantic accounts of the categories students use in order to make sense of the people, places, and activities around them in school. They do not address the problem of individual variability: the fact that even within the same small social unit, different persons using radically different categories may all be capable of performing competently.

To some scholars this rediscovery of individual cognitive variation suggests serious limits to the analogy between culture and language. This has drawn new attention to a venerable premise in anthropology: that culture is learned behavior. And this, in turn, is spurring fresh interest in the study of culture acquisition.

The aquisition of peer culture was studied on two college campuses by Holland and Eisenhart (1990), the study being based on the idea that culture content is organized in schema or models: a set of coherent, taken for granted ideas about the world that underlies the creation of meaning out of experience (Holland and Quinn 1987). Culture acquisition was investigated in 23 women students over several years in terms of the processes of identity formation and the development of expertise. The peer culture of romance centered on the idea that women's prestige on campus was gained through having romantic partners, an elaboration of the common cultural premise that attractiveness to the opposite sex is a desirable quality. Preoccupation with developing expertise in the culture of romance diverted many women's energies away from academic life and interrupted their pursuit of career goals and high-status occupations. Holland and Eisenhart (1990) thus linked acquisition of peer culture and women's career choices to the social reproduction of the gender hierarchy prevalent in the United States occupational structure.

4. Peer Groups versus Schools

In the Holland and Eisenhart study, involvement in peer groups led college women to reorder their priorities in directions that diverged from the official educational goals of the school. This "subversive" potential of peer groups has been a long-standing theme of research on the schooling of children from minority families. A good example can be seen in a study of the Oglala Sioux Reservation school (Wax et al. 1964).

In early elementary grades Sioux children in classrooms were eager and teacher-accommodating. By the upper-elementary grades they were "silent Indians," and nonparticipants in classroom instruction, effectively shutting out "Anglo" school culture fostered by foreign teachers, school authorities, and government agencies. As was also shown in a one-room school in a Kwakiutl village, the teacher became the enemy (Wolcott 1967). Anglo school staff and Oglala parents avoided one another. The classroom became a veritable "no man's land" where only the regard of peers held pupils in check. Verbal and often physical bullying by peers drove children to leave school. Indian parents had little inkling of how effectively the peer groups had sabotaged the academic process. Embittered teachers attributed the breakdown to the "uncivilized" condition of their charges.

McDermott (1974) described a similar situation in which failing in class becomes a peer group goal. Through a close analysis of communication breakdowns in a reading lesson due to differences in the teacher's and students' cultures of social interaction, McDermott shows how Black minority children learned *not* to read as one way to identify with and gain respect from their minority peers. Their achievement is school failure.

Wax and colleagues offered only a ray of hope: individual teachers could make a difference in the school achievement of Sioux children by harnessing peer groups to the education tasks. Other researchers are investigating this line of interest, under the rubric of "participant structures" (Philips 1972). For example, Erickson and Mohatt (1982) document the differences between two classroom situations, one of which is designed to operate in consonance with Indian modes of human interaction, thereby bridging the gap between school culture and Indian peer group culture. All these studies pivot on culture differences in the classroom to explain peer academic achievement and school failure.

Another line of reasoning underlies an array of studies carried out mostly in Europe and couched in the Marxist idiom of "social reproduction of inequality." Bourdieu (1972), perhaps the leading theorist of the social reproduction approach, offers the concept of "cultural capital" to explain why upper-class children are most likely to enter high-status occupations. For the most part, modern schools teach the skills, knowledge, and world-view of an upper-class heritage. Upper-class students are already equipped with a capital fund of this cultural heritage by the time they enter school. They are more easily able to "exchange" it in school for the credentials that provide access to privileged positions in adult society. Students from other classes have to "earn" their capital in school.

In *Learning to Labour*, Willis (1977) tried to break away from mechanistic social reproduction theory to answer why working-class children get working-

class jobs. "The Lads," the name used for their counter-school peer group by a set of nonacademic working-class boys in a male secondary school in the United Kingdom, saw the promise of social mobility for school conformity as a false promise and treated their school-conforming classmates with contempt. Mirroring the toughness, chauvinism, and roughness of industrial shop-floor culture, the Lads defined manual labor as masculine and physical, in forceful opposition to schoolwork, teachers, upper-class culture, women, and ethnic minorities. The counter-school peer culture of working-class boys grooms them for the "self-damnation" of taking subordinate roles.

5. Peer Groups and Multicultural Schools

Though downward mobility is a feature of any society with a system of open classes, it rarely inspires effort on the part of investigators. In studies such as that by Willis, social, through cultural, reproduction also offers a partial explanation of the "cooling-out process" in which failure in the eyes of society (or the school) is transmuted into personal success. But a perduring issue of upward mobility is ever more salient in a world of massive migrations and multicultural values. Why is it that, in some schools, some peer groups seem to help minority children to move up, while others do not?

Ogbu (1978) argues that much depends upon how a minority group's cultural model explains the group's circumstances. All minorities encounter discrimination and derogation but may interpret these differently. Voluntary migrants define their situation as temporary or due to foreignness, which is correctable through education. Groups brought into a society through slavery, conquest, or colonization come to regard all forms of acculturation, even conforming to school culture, as ploys to exclude them from a mainstream mobility system, because of their history of experiencing repeated social, political, and economic barriers and cultural and intellectual derogations. Gibson and Ogbu (1989) demonstrate the value of the approach in a recent collection of ten case studies done in six different societies. For example, peer groups of Blacks, working from the displacement model of acculturation, police "errant" minority members for any signs of "acting White" (see also Fordam and Ogbu 1986). Peer pressure within involuntary minorities imposes a painful dilemma by forcing the individual to choose between working toward academic success and a commitment to self-identity through the minority.

In contrast, among Mexicanos in central California, and Sikhs in the United Kingdom and the United States—all voluntary immigrants—peer group participation in school was found to be less intense than for other students. Sikh high school students experienced academic success while participating very little in the extracurricular programs of a school in the United States; however, peers in the Sikh community, backed by parents and relatives, actually intensified academic competition and conformity with the academic emphasis of school cultures: an example of "accommodation without assimilation" (Gibson and Ogbu 1989).

Ogbu and his colleagues argue culture difference is not the direct explanation of school problems experienced by minorities. Cultural and language differences may be present, but whether or not they affect the minority students' academic work in the classroom depends on how the minority's cultural model, taking effect through the culture of peer groups, organizes the minority student's interpretations.

6. Conclusion

There clearly have been phases in the studies of peer group culture. Through the changing definitions of problems, some progress has been made in the understanding of school culture and peer culture. Following the exposure in the 1950s of the parochialism of peer groups in their collusion in local stratification systems, peer group research addressed the problem of threats to intergenerational continuity in a world of change. That continuity, seen as a desirable state of affairs threatened by youth cultures, reinterpreted in the 1970s as social reproduction, then was viewed as a problem in itself. Much of the earlier research took a rather time-empty view of cultural and social differences. In contrast, Ogbu pays explicit and detailed attention to the history of a group's incorporation into the larger society.

Peer groups in schools are not temporary cells of adolescent life nor sore spots that will heal and go away. Peer groups and their cultures appear to be perduring means by which young people cope, in diverse ways and out of their own interests, with the huge, sprawling organizational networks in which current administrative theories of efficiency place them. Teachers are also caught up in efforts to survive, endure, act, and succeed in the same kinds of organization. Peer groups' linkages back to parents' views, origins, and circumstances have been of special interest. Yet teachers are usually seen only in terms of their reactions to the peer groups, rather than as caught in the same societal forces, that force them to group together to promote their own interests and pursue their own goals. Such studies of teachers exist, but not as a dynamic complement to equally detailed studies of peer group cultures. This research is clearly an important next step.

References

Bourdieu P 1972 *Esquisse d'une theorie de la pratique, précédé de trois études d'ethnologie kabyle*. Librairie Dros SA, Switzerland

Coleman J 1961 *The Adolescent Society: The Social Life of the Teenager and its Impact on Education*. Free Press, Glencoe, Illinois

Erickson F, Mohatt G 1982 Cultural organization of participant structures in two classrooms of Indian students. In: Spindler G 1982 *Doing The Ethnography of Schooling: Educational Anthropology in Action*. CBS College Publishing, New York

Fordam S, Ogbu J U 1986 Black students' school success: Coping with the "burden of 'acting white'." *Urban Review* 18(3): 176–206

Gibson M A, Ogbu J U 1989 *Minority Status and Schooling: A Comparative Study of Immigrant and Involuntary Minorities*. Garland Press, New York

Goodenough W 1971 *Culture, Language, and Society*. Addison-Wesley, Reading, Massachusetts

Holland D C, Eisenhart M 1990 *The Culture of Romance: Women, Resistance, and Gender Relations On Campus*. University of Chicago Press, Chicago, Illinois

Holland D C, Quinn N 1987 *Cultural Models In Language and Thought*. Cambridge University Press, Cambridge

Hollingshead A B 1949 *Elmstown's Youth*. John Wiley, New York

Mayer P (ed.) 1970 *Socialization: The Approach From Social Anthropology*. Tavistock, London

McDermott R 1974 Achieving school failure: An anthropological approach to illiteracy and social stratification. In: Spindler, G 1974 *Education and Cultural Process: Anthropological Approaches*. Holt, Rinehart and Winston, New York

Ogbu J U 1978 *Minority Education and Caste: The American System in Cross-cultural Perspective*. Academic Press, New York

Philips S U 1972 Participant structures and communicative competence: Warm Springs children in community and classroom. In: Cazden C, John V, Hymes D (eds.) 1972 *Functions of Language in the Classroom*. Teachers College Press, New York

Polgar S 1960 Biculturalism of Mesquakie teenage boys. *AA* 62: 217–35

Rohlen T 1983 *Japan's High Schools*. University of California Press, Berkeley, California

Spradley J P, McCurdy D W 1972 *The Cultural Experience: Ethnography in Complex Society*. Science Research Associates, Chicago, Illinois

Steward F H 1977 *Fundamentals of Age-Group Systems*. Academic Press, New York

Wax M L, Wax R H, Dumont R V 1964 *Formal Education In An American Indian Community: Peer Society and the Failure of Minority Education*. Waveland Press, Prospect Heights, Illinois

Willis P 1977 *Learning to Labour: How Working Class Kids Get Working Class Jobs*. Saxon House Teakfield Limited

Wolcott H F 1967 *A Kwakiutl Village and School*. Holt, Rinehart and Winston, New York

Further Reading

Corsaro W A 1988 Routines in the peer culture of American and Italian nursery school children. *Sociol. Educ.* 61: 1–14

Spindler G, Spindler L (eds.) 1987 *Interpretive Ethnography of Education: At Home and Abroad*. Erlbaum, Hillsdale, New Jersey

Trueba H T, Delgado-Gaiten C 1988 *School and Society: Learning Content Through Culture*. Praeger Press, New York

Peer Relations and Learning

W. Damon

Children's communication with their peers has qualities that differ from the qualities of adult–child communication. For example, peer dialogues are usually more equal than conversations between adult and child: children usually listen more respectfully to adults than to peers for information and guidance. Such differences have serious implications for learning. Educators have become aware of these differences and have begun to design classroom strategies that best exploit the learning opportunities provided by both peer and adult–child relations. This entry discusses contemporary methods for applying the special features of children's peer relations to their academic learning.

1. Special Features of Peer Communication

In his work on moral judgment, Piaget introduced the notion that children live within "two social worlds," one of unilateral adult–child commands, the other of mutual peer cooperation (Piaget 1932). Developmental psychologists have elaborated this distinction further (Youniss 1980, Hartup 1985). Whereas adult–child interactions reflect a fundamental asymmetry of power and knowledge, peers interact on an equal footing. This means that adults usually direct and structure the agenda in their conversations with children, whereas children negotiate and "co-construct" the agendas of their peer encounters.

The asymmetry of adult–child interactions creates a context for learning with many advantages: it provides the best available means of transmitting the culture's accumulated store of knowledge and a respect for the existing order of things (Youniss 1980). This unilateral respect, however, may lead to certain cognitive imbalances, such as an uncritical acceptance of the adult word and an overreliance on imitation in the attempt to acquire new skills. Peer relations, in contrast, encourage children to try out new ideas in a relatively supportive and uncritical environment. They create a context for sharing intimate thoughts, for engaging in close collaborative work, for questioning the known, and for attempting the unknown. In terms of their value for children's learning, peer relations offer a context for support and discovery but are not as useful as a forum for imparting basic information, formulas, or skills (Damon and Phelps 1989).

2. Three Types of Peer Learning

Although peer relations are generally more equal than adult–child relations, not all peer engagements are strictly alike. Peer relations themselves can be unequal to various extents. There are three main types of peer learning that have been introduced into classrooms by educational researchers. These have been called "peer tutoring," "cooperative learning," and "peer collaboration" (Damon and Phelps 1989). As in the contrast between adult–child and peer relations, the three distinct forms of peer learning offer different strengths and weaknesses for the educator.

2.1 Cooperative Learning

Cooperative learning, also called "small group learning" or "group work," has been introduced into many schools because the available methods are relatively easy for teachers to adopt. The techniques can be integrated into the normal school day without disruptions in the regular classroom routine. Some cooperative learning programs require as little as an hour or two a week of classroom time.

There are a variety of cooperative learning techniques now in use. All begin by dividing classrooms into small "teams" of no more than four or five children. These teams are generally heterogeneous with respect to students' abilities. The teacher presents a task to the team, and the team sets out to master it. All cooperative learning methods rely on team solidarity and the motivation that it engenders. The assumption is that students will want to perform well for their team and that they will work for the success of their fellow team members and the team as a whole.

Some widely adopted versions of cooperative learning are Aronson's "jigsaw teaching," Sharan's "group investigation," and Slavin's "student teams-achievement divisions" (Slavin 1978). In jigsaw teaching, each member of a student team becomes an expert on one aspect of a larger topic. After studying that aspect in depth, the expert reports back to the team on what he or she has found. The team as a whole is taught by each "specialist" member in turn. In Sharan's method, team members plan and assign themselves specialized roles and prepare detailed reports for each other's edification. Group discussion of the reports is encouraged. Slavin's method establishes competition between opposing teams. It encourages team members to share work and information with one another so that they will perform individually better than members of other teams on quizzes derived from the learning exercises.

Cooperative learning methods vary in the extent to which they encourage individual versus collective activity in the learning groups. In the jigsaw version, team members assume different roles while they are learning about the task. Only then do the team members share the results of their individual work with the rest of the team. In Slavin's version, the team works together to prepare for individual tests or performances that will be given later. Some versions, in contrast, encourage joint planning and discussion throughout the exercise.

Cooperative learning methods also vary in the extent to which they rely on competition between teams as a motivator. Many techniques extrinsically reward strong team performances in order to spur children's interest in the tasks. Rewards are usually allocated on the basis of scores on tests given after the exercise. The explicit message to the team is that they will jointly benefit by beating other teams only if they ensure that all team members master the task. Other cooperative learning approaches spurn this competitive component and rely on intrinsic motivation to engage the learning groups in the exercise.

2.2 Peer Tutoring

In this approach, a child trains another child in skills and subject matter that the first child has mastered. Because the first child has greater information or competence than the second child, the two do not begin the relationship with equal status: rather, the first child is considered an expert and the second child a relative novice. Moreover, the unequal status of the two children is often compounded by other factors as well. Most attempts at peer tutoring pair an older child with a younger child, or a bright child with an educationally disadvantaged one. Peer tutoring, in fact, is often called "cross-age" tutoring, since the tutor is usually two or more years older than the tutee.

Peer tutoring occupies an instructional ground somewhere between adult–child and true peer communication. Like adult–child instruction, peer tutoring is based upon a transmission-of-knowledge model. This model assumes that one party knows the answers and must communicate them to the other party. Knowledge is "passed down" from person to person in a linear fashion rather than co-constructed by persons who are both seeking answers. Unlike adult–child instruction, however, in peer tutoring the expert party is not

very far removed from the novice party in authority or knowledge; nor has the expert any special claims to teaching competence. Such differences affect the nature of discourse between tutor and tutee because they place the tutee in less of a passive role than does the adult–child instructional relation. Being closer in knowledge and status, the tutee in a peer relation feels freer to express opinions, ask questions, and risk untested solutions. The interaction between instructor and pupil is more balanced and more lively when the the tutor is a peer (Damon and Phelps 1989).

A theoretical grounding for peer tutoring can be found in L S Vygotsky's idea of the "zone of proximal development." Vygotsky wrote that problem-solving in collaboration with more capable peers could enable children to enter into new areas of potential (Vygotsky 1978). These new areas, which Vygotsky called the "leading edge" of children's intellectual growth, constitute the zone of proximal development; it is created when a child interacts with a more experienced mentor. Because the mentor guides the direction of the interaction in intellectually productive ways, the child's intellectual performance during the interaction surpasses anything that the child has been able to do outside of the interaction. In the course of such experiences, the child retains the ability to reproduce these jointly produced intellectual performances autonomously. When this happens, the achievement becomes part of the child's actual capabilities rather than merely a potential skill that can be realized only through interaction. In this sense, the insights and competencies become internalized. Vygotsky argues that it is not only information that is internalized, but also fundamental cognitive processes that are implicit in the communications. Accordingly, both parties in the communication stand to benefit. The tutee profits from the very acts of questioning, challenging, and providing feedback to the tutor. The tutor profits from the act of reformulating knowledge for transmittal to the tutee, from answering the tutee's questions, and from responding to the tutee's challenges. This is what is meant by the old axiom that one never really knows a subject until one tries to teach it.

When two children enter into a peer-tutoring relationship, they become exposed to new patterns of thought. This is because any peer dialogue is a cooperative, consensual, and nonauthoritarian exchange of ideas. As such, it relies on rationality for its maintenance and emulates several key features of critical thinking. In particular, beliefs must be justified and verified rather than merely asserted by force of mandate. This requires significant intellectual effort for both parties. It calls for skill in symbolically representing ideas as well as the ability to notice and resolve logical contradictions. These are central areas of cognitive competence, areas in which children at all levels and ages have room for improvement.

Of the three types of peer learning, it was peer tutoring that first made inroads into actual school settings. In the 1970s, a number of educators experimented with peer tutoring as an alternative form of instruction. Generally they found it to be effective in stimulating the educational progress of both tutor and tutee (Gartner et al. 1971).

From these and subsequent research programs, the following picture has emerged. Peer tutoring, when carried out over a substantial period of time with carefully trained and supervised tutors, is educationally valuable for its participants. It is also surprisingly cost-effective when compared with other instructional techniques. When done well, it can aid children's acquisition of both verbal and quantitative skills as well as substantive curriculum topics such as history, physics, and social studies. Finally, peer tutoring can also yield personal benefits for both tutor and tutee. Children's self-esteem, educational motivation, school adjustment, and altruistic inclinations all improve in the course of peer tutoring.

2.3 Peer Collaboration

In peer collaboration, a pair of novices work together to solve difficult tasks. This method differs from peer tutoring because the children begin at roughly the same levels of competence. It also differs from cooperative learning, because children work jointly on the same problem rather than individually on separate components of the problem. In actual practice, however, peer collaboration bears some resemblance to other types of peer learning. Even in peer collaboration, one child may assume the lead spontaneously; and the collaborators may separate for independent work.

Peer collaboration encourages children to communicate about strategies and solutions. It simulates the challenge of discovery learning, but places this challenge in a context of peer assistance and support. Like discovery learning, its promise lies in provoking deep conceptual insights and basic developmental shifts on the part of its participants. This is because it encourages experimentation with new and untested ideas and demands a critical reexamination of old assumptions. However, unlike discovery learning done alone, the child does not feel like an isolated incompetent. Rather, peer collaboration provides a sympathetic forum for the creative risk-taking that discovery learning can provoke. As the child works with a fellow novice, the insufficiencies in his or her own knowledge become less discouraging and the unknown becomes less forbidding.

As an educational intervention method, peer collaboration originally emerged from Piagetian studies in Europe and the United States. The studies focused on spatial and physical conversations, notions that had proven resistant to training through standard instructional techniques. Among the innovative experimental methods that developmentalists tried was asking children to work jointly with peers. The strategy of placing novices together on a difficult task and expecting them to come up with a productive approach initially seemed so odd that articles had such titles as "When two wrongs make a right" (Ames and Murray 1982). But peer collaboration proved to be the most consistently effective means of helping children acquire conversation and the basic reasoning skills underlying it.

The dominant rationale for the strategy of teaming novices together has been the Genevan construct of "sociocognitive conflict" (Doise and Mugny 1984). The idea is that social interactions between peers will lead to disagreements that present the participants with both a social and a cognitive conflict. Such conflicts lead children to a number of important realizations. First, they become aware that there are points of view other than their own. Second, they reexamine their own points of view and reassess their validity. Third, they learn that they must justify their own opinions and communicate them thoroughly if others are to accept them as valid.

In this way, children benefit both cognitively and socially from peer collaboration. The social benefits include their improved communication skills and their sharper sense of other persons' perspectives. The cognitive benefits derive from their forced reexamination of their own conceptions under the guidance of a peer's feedback. Piaget believed that these social and cognitive benefits were directly related in that improved social communication instigates progressive change. When people feel the need to explain and justify their beliefs to others, they realize that these beliefs must be rationalized as fully as possible. This sense of "social responsibility" in communication ultimately leads to improvements in the logical quality of one's reasoning. The Genevan explanation of peer collaboration, therefore, posits a clash of ideas that triggers a need to reexamine, rework, and justify one's understanding of the world.

Some questions have been raised about whether the notion of conflict alone is sufficient to account for the learning that follows from experiences of peer collaboration. There is increasing theoretical emphasis on the constructive or "coconstructive" aspects of peer collaboration. In this view, children learn through peer interaction because it introduces them to the possibilities of cooperative activity (Youniss 1980, Krappman 1992). In a truly cooperative effort, children devise plans together, share ideas, and mutually validate one another's initiatives. Not only is this a powerful procedure for generating new insights, it also yields solutions that are superior to those arrived at by an individual in isolation (Damon and Phelps 1989, Krappman 1992).

Unfortunately there have been very few studies that have attempted to identify the peer interaction processes leading to progressive change. This requires lengthy and complex videotape analyses of the sort not always available in experimental studies. The initial studies favor the co-construction process model over the sociocognitive conflict one.

In these initial studies, children who disagree with one another the most seem the least likely to progress, whereas children who accept one another's views and work positively with them are the most likely to change (Damon and Killen 1982, Damon and Phelps 1989). Constructive rather than conflictual interaction was clearly the key facilitator. Another analysis of children's peer interactions during task engagement found such interactions to be heavily loaded with "transactive" activity (Kruger and Tomasello 1986). Such activity is a constructive and compromising form of social discourse especially suited for joint exploration into unknown areas of thought.

Finally, a study of children's helping behavior with peers found that peer interactions indeed can provide a unique context for learning many important intellectual skills, provided that such interactions are well-balanced and mutual. The author concluded: "These collaborative efforts of peers, mostly friends, presented almost the only situations in which we found the capacities that the educational system promises to promote—exploration of different aspects of a problem, change of perspectives, experimentation with ideas, reconstruction of failed processes, analyses of mistakes, verification of the indubitable, search for criteria of good solutions—co-constructively developed and jointly applied" (Krappman 1992 p. 179).

Despite its promise, peer collaboration has been used less frequently in educational programs than have the other two forms of peer learning. This is probably because peer collaboration as a technique has its roots in experimental developmental psychology rather than in educational research. As yet, there are no systematic curricula designed around principles of peer collaboration. Still, some promising initial attempts have been made to apply techniques from developmental research on peer relations to actual educational settings (Damon and Phelps 1989, Krappman 1992).

3. Conclusion

During the 1970s and 1980s, educators have made increasing use of children's peer relations in the classroom. Because communication within a peer relation tends to be egalitarian, reciprocal, and lively, it offers a context of intellectual stimulation and social support for children's learning. Although peer learning cannot substitute for adult instruction, it can supplement it in unique ways.

Peer collaboration is perhaps the most promising method of promoting basic conceptual development in children, but there is still much to learn about its nature and its potential. In particular, under what inter-

actional conditions does peer collaboration flourish? To what extent does sociocognitive conflict describe these conditions? To what extent do ideas such as "co-construction" and "transaction" best describe them? What are the limits of peer collaboration in relation to other forms of peer learning, and what are its special strengths? How may peer collaboration be integrated with the other peer learning approaches?

References

Ames G, Murray F B 1982 When two wrongs make a right: Promoting cognitive change through social conflict. *Dev. Psychol.* 18(6): 894–97

Damon W, Killen M 1982 Peer interaction and the process of change in children's moral reasoning. *Merrill-Palmer Q.* 28(3): 347–67

Damon W, Phelps E 1989 Critical distinctions among three approaches to peer education. *Int. J. Educ. Res.* 13(1): 9–19

Doise W, Mugny G 1984 *The Social Development of the Intellect*. Pergamon Press, New York

Gartner A, Kohler W, Riessman F 1971 *Children Teaching Children: Learning by Teaching*. Harper & Row, New York

Hartup W W 1985 Relationships and their significance in cognitive development. In: Hinde R A, Perret-Clermont A, Stevenson-Hinde J (eds.) 1985 *Social Relationships and Cognitive Development*. Oxford University Press, Oxford

Krappman L 1992 On the social embedding of learning processes in the classroom. In: Oser F, Dick A, Patry J-L (eds.) 1992 *Effective and Responsible Teaching*. Jossey-Bass, San Francisco, California

Kruger A C, Tomasello M 1986 Transactive discussions with peers and adults. *Dev. Psychol.* 22(5): 681–85

Piaget J 1932 *The Moral Judgment of the Child*. Free Press, New York

Slavin R 1978 Student teams and comparison among equals: Effects on academic performance and student attitudes. *J. Educ. Psychol.* 70(4): 532–38

Vygotsky L S 1978 *Mind in Society: The Development of Higher Psychological Processes*. Harvard University Press, Cambridge, Massachusetts

Youniss J 1980 *Parents and Peers in Social Development: A Sullivan–Piaget Perspective*. University of Chicago Press, Chicago, Illinois

Further Reading

Damon W 1990 Social relations and children's thinking skills. In: Kuhn D (ed.) 1990 *Developmental Perspectives on Teaching and Learning Thinking Skills*. Karger, Basel

Perret-Clermont A-N 1980 *Social Interaction and Cognitive Development in Children*. Academic Press, New York

Learning Environments

A. Collins, J. G. Greeno, and L. B. Resnick

There has been a shift in perspective in educational psychology from teaching to learning. The change is subtle and reflects a move away from an information transmission view to a constructivist view of education. Because of the shift in perspective, this entry is called learning environments rather than teaching methods. Another shift in perspective involves recognizing that learning and work are not separate activities. In fact, learning takes place both in and out of school, and students' activity in school is a form of work. Resnick (1987) pointed out four contrasts between typical in-school and out-of-school learning: (a) individual cognition in school versus shared cognition outside; (b) pure mentation in school versus tool manipulation outside; (c) symbol manipulation in school versus contextualized reasoning outside; (d) generalized learning in school versus situation-specific competencies outside. The discussion of learning environments will consider those outside as well as within schools, keeping in mind the characteristics to which Resnick has called attention.

In looking broadly at different kinds of learning environments, there are three observable general functions that support different environments: (a) participating in discourse; (b) participating in activities; (c) presenting examples of work to be evaluated. Environments themselves may be divided into six kinds, two relevant to each general function:

(a) (i) communication environments, where learners participate in discourse by actively constructing goals, problems, meanings, information, and criteria of success;
   (ii) information transmission environments, where learners participate in discourse by receiving information;
(b) (i) problem-solving environments, where learners work on projects and problems;
   (ii) training environments, where learners practice exercises to improve specific skills and knowledge;
(c) (i) evaluative performance environments, where learners perform for an audience;
   (ii) recitation and testing environments, where learners demonstrate their ability to work problems or answer questions.

Most teaching and learning environments contain elements of all six types. The most effective learning environments combine the advantages of each type. Each of the following sections will discuss a particular type of environment.

1. Communication Environments

Constructivist views of education stress communication among students. In communication environments the goal is for people jointly to construct understandings of different ideas. Four kinds of communication environments can be distinguished, based on the following activities: discussion, argumentation, inquiry teaching, and brainstorming.

Discussion occurs when groups talk about some topic. In the context of school, discussions often take place concerning a text everyone has read or a video everyone has seen. Discussions are probably the most powerful medium for learning. Some discussions that are formally constituted, such as business meetings, convey information about social roles, provide occasions for individuals to report results of their work and to present proposals, and often result in shared commitments to action. Informal discussions by groups of friends are occasions for constructing shared attitudes, opinions, understandings, and norms of behavior.

As an example of how effective group discussions can be as learning environments, Lampert (1990) has shown how fifth-grade children can form a community of inquiry about important mathematical concepts. She engaged students in discussion of their conjectures and interpretations of each other's reasoning. Such techniques have been successful with even younger children and may underlie the success of Japanese mathematical education.

The Computer Supported Intentional Learning Environment (CSILE) developed by Scardamalia and Bereiter (1991) is a discussion environment where students communicate in writing over a computer network. They first formulate questions they want to investigate (e.g., "Why can humans speak when apes cannot?") and then each student in the group makes a conjecture about what they believe. Then they all begin to investigate the question, finding whatever relevant information they can from source materials and typing it into the system for others in the group to read. Through written discussions, they refine their theories for publication in the system. Other experimenters are exploring the potential for students at remote locations to learn through exchanges of electronic messages.

Argumentation is another important learning method. It has had limited use in school, even though it is pervasive in business, law, and academia. Argumentation involves making a case for a particular idea or decision, and counterarguments against possible alternatives. Debate teams foster argumentation in school settings, but debates are usually an extracurricular activity. Presentations of arguments are an integral part of activity in some discussion environments, including the Itakura method (Hatano and Inagaki 1991) and Lampert's (1990) conversational teaching. Being persuasive is an important skill. Schools may mistakenly undervalue argumentation as a learning experience.

Inquiry teaching is characterized by a teacher asking questions to help students construct a theory or design. The theory constructed may be one the teacher already had in mind, or it may be a novel theory. Inquiry teachers use systematic strategies for selecting cases (e.g., counterexamples) and for asking questions (Collins and Stevens 1983). The goal of inquiry teaching is to foster thinking and understanding by students.

Brainstorming is common in business and academia, but missing from school. The goal is for a group to generate ideas without trying to critique the ideas. Participants try to generate new ideas and to reformulate, extend, and synthesize other people's ideas. Brainstorming is a powerful learning environment that schools would do well to foster.

2. Information Transmission Environments

Traditional schooling stressed the transmission of knowledge and skills to students. These information transmission environments include reading and lectures as well as newer media formats such as broadcast radio and television, videotape, and film.

Reading is probably one of the two most common ways to learn through acquiring information (the other is television). Widespread schooling is built upon the book: printing changed the ways by which humans understand the world, because of the permanence and transportability of the printed word. It is probably the most effective way to become exposed to a wide variety of viewpoints, and has played a crucial role in movements of social change. At the same time, however, reading faces competition from the visual media, because of higher bandwidth and their wider scope.

Attending lectures differs from reading in that the sequence and pace are controlled by a speaker rather than the learner, and the information is spoken rather than written. Active interaction with a text includes rereading and searching for specific information. It is often possible to ask questions of a lecturer, although it is much more common in school for conversational interactions to be limited to the lecturer presenting questions to students to monitor their attention and understanding. Like reading, lecturing may ultimately be replaced by visual media.

Broadcast television and radio are the most passive of the information transmission media, but television has higher bandwidth than reading or lecturing. This allows it to capture significant aspects of the context of a situation, which can be critical to understanding. If a person is confused, however, it is not possible to ask questions (except to other viewers). It is not even possible to stop and resume study later unless an electronic record is made—a feature television shares with lectures. For this reason, it is much less likely to become an important learning environment than the next two media to be considered. Nevertheless, television shows such as Sesame Street and Cosmos have been major vehicles for learning around the world.

Videotape and film have the wide bandwidth of television, but also have the flexibility for stopping or replaying sections of the tape. They are under the learner's or teacher's control, and so can be scheduled whenever time allows. Stopping allows a group of viewers to mix discussion with viewing. Replaying allows the group to clarify misunderstandings, look for specific information, and call attention to items of information that support alternative interpretations of the material. Much of the world's collected knowledge will eventually be stored on film, so this is likely to be one of the most important learning environments of the future.

Interactive video, based on laserdisk technology, has the wide bandwidth of the visual media, together with the capability to access any piece of the video instantaneously. Two seminal uses of this technology are the Aspen video, with which a person can simulate a drive around the town of Aspen, Colorado, turning right or left at any cross street, and the Palenque video, with which one can walk through the Mayan ruin at Palenque in Mexico and ask for guidance at different points from an anthropologist. Interactive video is merging with intelligent tutoring system technology to provide even more powerful learning environments.

3. Problem-solving Environments

With the renewed emphasis on thinking in the curriculum, there has been a stress on creating different kinds of problem-solving environments in schools. There are several kinds of environments where problem-solving is the focus; namely, environments dedicated to problem-solving, apprenticeship and projects.

Problem-solving in school differs from problem-solving in other activities. Lave (1988) pointed out that school problems tend to be well-defined, have one correct answer, and a correct solution method. Problems that arise in life, which Lave called dilemmas, tend to be ill-defined, often unrecognized as problems, and have many possible solutions and solution methods. Schoenfeld (1985) identified many beliefs that students derive from school math problems: for example, that if the answer is not an integer, it is probably wrong; that all the problems at the end of a chapter use the methods introduced in the chapter; that if you cannot solve the problem in five minutes, you are not using the correct method, etc. Schoenfeld argued that most of these beliefs are counterproductive for problem-solving in life.

Apprenticeship occurs in work environments where apprentices are supervised by masters. In successful apprenticeship learning, masters teach by showing apprentices how to do a task (modeling), and then helping them as they try to do it on their own (coaching and fading). Lave and Wenger (1991) described four cases of apprenticeship and emphasized how productive apprenticeship depends on opportunities for the apprentice to participate legitimately, albeit peripherally, in work activities. Becoming a more central participant in a community of practice can provide a powerful motivation for learning, although what is learned in apprenticeship may not generalize easily to other contexts. Collins et al. (1989) characterized how the modeling, coaching, and fading paradigm of apprenticeship might be applied to learning the cognitive subjects of school in an approach they term "cognitive apprenticeship."

Projects are an attempt to bring research, design, and troubleshooting tasks from work environments into the school. For example, students in John Dewey's laboratory school in the early 1990s built a clubhouse for the school, where they learned planning, mathematical, and construction skills. As a research project in English and history, students in Mississippi interviewed people who had lived through the civil rights struggle in the state, and then produced and published a book based on the best of those oral histories. In Boston, fourth-graders each developed a computer program to teach third-graders about fractions (Harel 1991). In Rochester, New York, eighth-grade students carried out research by interviewing adults and finding source materials for a computer-based museum exhibit about the city. Project environments militate against the scope-and-sequence notion of curriculum because students typically need a wide variety of skills to carry out any project. The skills required to accomplish a project can be taught either before or during the project.

Simulation environments are an attempt to create situations that have significant features of authentic problem-solving. There have long been attempts to create simulated environments in schools. For example, in one Massachusetts school, students spend half of each day running a legislature, courts, businesses, and media. This serves as a context for learning the skills of citizenship, reading, writing, calculating, and thinking.

Video and computer technology have enhanced the ability to create simulation environments where students are learning skills in context. A novel use of video technology is the Jasper series developed by the Cognition and Technology Group (1990) at Vanderbilt University. In a series of six 15-minute videos, students are put into various problem-solving contexts: for example, deciding on a business plan for a school fair or a rescue plan for a wounded eagle. The problems reflect the complex problem-solving and planning that occur in real life.

There has been a proliferation of computer simulation environments for learning. For example, simulations let students control objects in a simulated Newtonian world without friction or gravity, or prices in a simulated economy. One series of simulations allows students to run a city, a planet, or an ant colony. Simulation allows students to gain knowledge and skills in contexts in which they could never participate naturally, to see features that are invisible in real environments (e.g., the center of mass, the inside of the human body), and to control variables that cannot be controlled in life.

4. Training Environments

People engage in training to develop skills they believe are valuable, either in themselves or as components of some other activity. In the traditional training environments—drill, rehearsal, and practice—there is an emphasis on skills and procedures rather than ideas, facts, concepts, and theories. Schooling has led to the invention of three kinds of training environments that focus on the skills of solving problems: programmed instruction, homework, and intelligent tutoring systems.

Drill involves repetitive training designed to achieve automaticity in a particular skill (Schneider and Shiffrin 1977). It is most commonly used in school to teach arithmetic and phonics, though Schneider has shown that it can be used to teach other skills, such as recognizing electrical circuits. Repetition helps master routine parts of performance, freeing capacity to concentrate on decision-making aspects of performance.

Rehearsal involves practicing scripted activities in preparation for a performance. While it teaches strategies for mounting a polished performance, the rehearsed activities may not be applicable beyond the performance, which limits the value of rehearsal as a general learning approach.

Practice emphasizes the conceptual and strategic as well as the routine, and can be carried out with or without a coach watching and guiding the practice. Practice is critical to gaining expertise, and successful techniques such as Reciprocal Teaching (Palincsar and Brown 1984) embody a strong practice component. Central to the whole notion of practice, however, is an ultimate performance. The major motivation for practice in school is to do well on tests, but many young people show growing aversion to tests.

Programmed instruction was developed by Skinner and reflects his emphasis on training and positive reinforcement. The tasks given are easy at first, so that students are likely to succeed and be reinforced for their success. There is an emphasis on repetition with variation to ensure practice, but more complex material is slowly introduced to ensure that students are dealing with new problems and tasks.

Homework has a dual purpose: it allows students to practice skills and procedures learned in school and to apply these skills in new contexts. Often homework is structured so that practice exercises come first, with transfer exercises later in order to foster problem-solving.

Intelligent tutoring systems are the latest attempt to create environments that combine training and problem-solving. For example, the geometry, algebra, and computer language tutors developed by Anderson and his colleagues (e.g., Anderson et al. 1985) start students with easy problems and slowly increase the complexity. Though the domain of intelligent tutoring systems may appear limited, they can be built on top of any simulation program (see above) to provide appropriate tasks and guidance for students. They are, however, expensive to build and it remains to be seen whether they will be cost effective.

5. Performance Environments

Learning takes place not just in practicing for performances, but also during performances themselves. Most performances can be distinguished from contests such as sporting events. Performances are high-stakes events where there is an audience, either live or present via a communication medium. Because the stakes are high, people are motivated to do well; performance, therefore, is the stimulus for most practice. To the degree teachers encourage performance, it is likely to provide a powerful motivation for students. The wide availability of recording technology makes performances easier to produce and to reflect upon. For example, students can now produce their own news broadcasts, musical performances, or plays, either on audiotape, videotape, or cable television, that are transmitted to other schools or to parents. Furthermore, they can play these back, reflect upon them, and edit them until they are polished. One of the best examples of the use of technology for recording performances has been in Arts Propel (Gardner 1991) with its cycle of performing, reflecting upon the performance in terms of a set of criteria, and then reperforming.

Contests differ from performances in that winning or losing provides an ultimate criterion for judging performance. Spelling bees, science fairs, debates, and music contests are school versions of contests, but athletic contests are much more common. Films and statistics are important ways to track performance during contests. As well as providing the basis for making important decisions with regard to future contests (who to start, where they should play), they help to guide practice. By designating certain characteristics to track, statistics provide important indicators of what is valued. Contests are highly motivating for most people, but their primary role in schooling is extracurricular.

6. Recitation and Testing Environments

Given the extracurricular nature of most performances and contests in school, it is not surprising that most students value extracurricular matters more than curricular matters. As substitutes for performances and contests, the curricular part of school has offered recitations and tests.

Recitations in their original form have almost died out in schools. The notion was that students would learn or memorize information that they were expected to recite in class, either in choral or solo form. For example, in the nineteenth century students in one class had to name all the bays along the eastern coast of the United States. The most common form of recitation today is for teachers to call on volunteers to answer questions to which the teacher knows the answer. This is a form of discourse that is peculiar to school. The learning that goes on in the course of recitations comes from listening to what others say or from being corrected by the teacher.

Testing is an attempt to bring a performance environment into the school, but it has taken on characteristics that other performance environments do not have; for example, tests are almost always written and rarely involve group performance. As a learning environment, testing is usually quite impoverished. Testing becomes more of a learning experience to the extent that tests are frequent, materials such as books and computers are available, tasks reflect the activities of people in the world, and feedback is given to students about how to perform the tasks given. But tests are mainly viewed as a means to find out what has been learned, rather than as learning experiences in themselves.

7. Conclusion

Participation in discourse, participation in activities, and presentation of work for evaluation are all essential to learning. Traditional schooling has emphasized reading and the lecture, problem-solving, drill and practice, homework, and recitation and testing as learning environments. In the shift from traditional learning environments to more constructivist learning environments, there has been a parallel shift to incorporate some of the characteristics of work environments, such as shared cognition, tool manipulation, and contextualized reasoning (Resnick 1987).

See also: Discussion; Homework; Simulations and Games; Teaching in Small Groups; Paradigms for Research on Teaching; Cooperative Learning

References

Anderson J R, Boyle C F, Reiser B J 1985 Intelligent tutoring systems. *Science* 228: 456–62

Cognition and Technology Group at Vanderbilt 1990 Anchored instruction and its relationship to situated cognition. *Educ. Researcher* 19(6): 2–10

Collins A, Brown J S, Newman S 1989 Cognitive apprenticeship: Teaching the crafts of reading, writing, and mathematics. In: Resnick L B (ed.) 1989 *Knowing, Learning, and Instruction: Essays in Honor of Robert Glaser*. Erlbaum, Hillsdale, New Jersey

Collins A, Stevens A L 1983 A cognitive theory of inquiry teaching. In: Reigeluth C M (ed.) 1983 *Instructional Design Theories and Models: An Overview of Their Current Status*. Erlbaum, Hillsdale, New Jersey

Gardner H 1991 Assessment in context: The alternative to standardized testing. In: Gifford B, O'Connor C (eds.) 1991 *Future Assessments: Changing Views of Aptitude, Achievement, and Instruction*. Kluwer, Boston, Massachusetts

Harel I 1991 *Children Designers: Interdisciplinary Constructions for Learning and Knowing Mathematics in a Computer-Rich School*. Ablex, Norwood, New Jersey

Hatano G, Inagake K 1991 Sharing cognition through collective comprehension activity. In: Resnick L, Levin J, Teasley S D (eds.) 1991 *Perspectives on Socially Shared Cognition*. American Psychological Association, Washington, DC

Lampert M 1990 When the problem is not the question and the solution is not the answer: Mathematical knowing and teaching. *Am. Educ. Res. J.* 27(1): 29–63

Lave J 1988 *Cognition in Practice: Mind, Mathematics, and Culture in Everyday Life*. Cambridge University Press, Cambridge, Massachusetts

Lave J, Wenger E 1991 *Situated Learning: Legitimate Peripheral Participation*. Cambridge University Press, Cambridge

Palincsar A S, Brown A L 1984 Reciprocal teaching of comprehension-fostering and monitoring activities. *Cognition and Instruction* 1(2): 117–75

Resnick L B 1987 The 1987 Presidential address: Learning in school and out. *Educ. Researcher* 16(9): 13–20

Scardamalia M, Bereiter C 1991 Higher levels of agency for children in knowledge building: A challenge for the design of new knowledge media. *Journal of the Learning Sciences* 1(1): 37–68

Schneider W, Shiffrin R M 1977 Controlled and automatic human information processing, I: Detection, search, and attention. *Psychol. Rev.* 84(1): 1–66

Schoenfeld A H 1985 *Mathematical Problem Solving*. Academic Press, New York

Classroom Environments

B. J. Fraser

The environment, climate, atmosphere, tone, ethos, or ambience of a classroom is believed to exert a powerful influence on student behavior, attitudes, and achievement. Although classroom environment is a somewhat subtle concept, remarkable progress has been made over the last quarter of the twentieth century in its conceptualization and assessment, which has led to an increased understanding of its determinants and effects.

1. An Historical Perspective on the Assessment of Classroom Environments

Murray (1938) introduced the term "alpha press" to describe the environment as assessed by a detached observer and "beta press" to describe the environment as perceived by those who inhabit it. Over the years, both observational instruments and questionnaires have been used to study the classroom environment.

Several structured observation schedules for coding classroom communication and events have been reviewed by Rosenshine and Stevens (1986) and Good and Brophy (1991). One of the most widely-known is Flander's Interaction Analysis System (FIAS) which records classroom behavior at three-second intervals using 10 categories (e.g., praising and encouraging, asking questions, student-initiated talk). Medley and

Mitzel constructed an omnibus instrument called OSCAR (Observation Schedule And Record) which includes 14 categories (e.g., pupil leadership activities, manifest teacher hostility, emotional climate, verbal emphasis, and social organization). Other systematic observation schemes are the Emmer Observation System, the Brophy–Good Dyadic Interaction System, and Blumenfeld and Miller's method of coding vocabulary (Good and Brophy 1991).

Since the 1970s, numerous questionnaires have been developed to assess student perceptions of their classroom environments (Fraser 1986; Fraser and Walberg 1991). Advantages claimed for questionnaires are that they can be more economical than classroom observation techniques; they are based on students' experiences over many lessons; they involve the pooled judgments of all students in a class; they can be more important than observed behaviors because they are the determinants of student behavior; and they have been found to account for more variance in student learning outcomes than have directly observed variables.

One of the most widely used questionnaires, the Learning Environment Inventory, was developed as part of the research and evaluation activities of Harvard Project Physics (Welch and Walberg 1972). About the same time, Moos began developing numerous social climate scales which ultimately resulted in the development of the well-known Classroom Environment Scale (Moos and Trickett 1987). Both of these questionnaires built upon the theoretical, conceptual, and measurement foundations laid by pioneers such as Lewin (1936), Murray (1938), and their followers (e.g., Stern 1970). Furthermore, research using these instruments was influenced by prior studies using structured observation instruments.

A more recent approach to studying educational environments involves the application of techniques of naturalistic inquiry, ethnography, and case study. In the early 1990s there is a growing acceptance of a combination of qualitative and quantitative methods (based on observation or student perceptions) in the study of classroom environment (Fraser and Tobin 1991).

2. A Summary of Questionnaires for Assessing Classroom Environments

Table 1 summarizes several questionnaires commonly used to assess student perceptions of classroom learning environment. Each questionnaire is suitable for convenient group administration, can be scored either by hand or computer, and has been shown to be reliable in extensive field trials. All questionnaires include multiple variables or scales. For example, the My Class Inventory contains five scales: cohesiveness, friction, satisfaction, difficulty, and competitiveness. A distinctive feature of most of these instruments is that, in addition to a form that measures perceptions of actual classroom environment, there is another form to measure perceptions of preferred classroom environment. The preferred forms are concerned with goals and value orientations and measure perceptions of the ideal classroom environment.

Table 1 includes the name of each scale contained in each instrument, the school level (elementary, secondary, or higher education) for which each instrument is suited, the number of items contained in each scale, and the classification of each scale according to Moos's (1974) scheme for classifying human environments. Moos's three basic dimensions are: Relationship (which identify the nature and intensity of personal relationships within the environment and assess the extent to which people are involved in the environment and support and help each other); Personal Development (which assess basic directions along which personal growth and self-enhancement tend to occur); and System Maintenance and System Change (which involve the extent to which the environment is orderly, clear in expectations, maintains control, and is responsive to change).

As mentioned above, the development of the Learning Environment Inventory (LEI) began in the late 1960s in conjunction with the evaluation and research on Harvard Project Physics (Fraser et al. 1982). The

LEI contains 105 statements (seven per scale) with response alternatives of "Strongly Disagree," "Disagree," "Agree," and "Strongly Agree." The scoring direction (or polarity) is reversed for some items. A typical item contained in the "Cohesiveness" scale is: "All students know each other very well."

The Classroom Environment Scale (CES) grew out of a comprehensive program of research involving perceptual measures of a variety of human environments including psychiatric hospitals, prisons, university residences, and work milieus (Moos 1974). Moos and Trickett's (1987) final version contains nine scales with 10 true–false items in each scale. Published materials include a test manual, a questionnaire, an answer sheet, and a transparent hand scoring key. A typical item in the CES is: "The teacher takes a personal interest in the students" (Teacher Support).

The Individualized Classroom Environment Questionnaire (ICEQ) differs from other classroom environment scales in that it assesses those dimensions which distinguish individualized classrooms from conventional ones. The final published version (Fraser 1990) contains 50 items with an equal number of items belonging to each of the five scales. Each item is responded to on a five-point scale with the alternatives of "Almost Never," "Seldom," "Sometimes," "Often," and "Very Often." A typical item is: "Different students use different books, equipment, and materials" (Differentiation). The published form consists of a handbook and test master sets from which unlimited numbers of copies of the questionnaires and response sheets may be made.

The LEI has been simplified to form the My Class Inventory (MCI) which is suitable for children in the 8–12 years age range (Fraser et al. 1982) and students in the junior high school, especially those who might experience reading difficulties with the LEI. The MCI differs from the LEI in four ways. First, in order to minimize fatigue among younger children, the MCI contains only five of the LEI's original 15 scales. Second, item wording has been simplified to enhance readability. Third, the LEI's four-point response format has been reduced to a two-point (Yes–No) response format. Fourth, students answer on the questionnaire itself instead of on a separate response sheet to avoid errors in transferring responses from one place to another. The final form contains 38 items. A typical item is: "Children are always fighting with each other" (Friction).

The College and University Classroom Environment Inventory (CUCEI) was developed for small classes (but not for lectures or laboratory classes) (Fraser and Treagust 1986) as a result of the fact that little work had been done in higher education classrooms parallel to the traditions of classroom environment research at the secondary and elementary school levels. The final form of the CUCEI contains seven-item scales. Each item has four responses ("Strongly Agree," "Agree," "Disagree," "Strongly Disagree") and polarity is reversed for approximately half the items. A typical item is: "Activities in this class are clearly and carefully planned" (Task Orientation).

An instrument specifically suited to assessing the environment of science laboratory classes at the senior high school or higher education levels was developed (Fraser et al. 1992) as a result of the critical importance and uniqueness of laboratory settings in science education. The Science Laboratory Environment Inventory (SLEI) has five scales and the response

alternatives for each item are "Almost Never," "Seldom," "Sometimes," "Often," and "Very Often." A typical item includes: "We know the results that we are supposed to get before we commence a laboratory activity" (Open-endedness). A noteworthy feature of the validation procedures employed is that the SLEI was field tested simultaneously in six countries (the US, Canada, England, Israel, Australia, and Nigeria).

In the Netherlands a learning environment questionnaire was developed to enable teacher educators to

Table 1
Overview of scales contained in seven classroom environment instruments (LEI, CES, ICEQ, MCI, CUCEI, SLEI, and QTI)

Instrument	Level	Items per scale	Relationship dimensions	Personal development dimensions	System maintenance and change dimensions
					Scale classified according to Moos's Scheme
Learning Environment Inventory (LEI)	secondary	7	cohesiveness friction favoritism cliqueness satisfaction apathy	speed difficulty competitiveness	diversity formality material environment goal direction disorganization democracy
Classroom Environment Scale (CES)	secondary	10	involvement affiliation teacher support	task orientation competition	order and organization rule clarity teacher control innovation
Individualised Classroom Environment Questionnaire (ICEQ)	secondary	10	personalization participation	independence investigation	differentiation
My class Inventory (MCI)	elementary	6–9	cohesiveness friction satisfaction	difficulty competitiveness	
College and University Classroom Environment Inventory (CUCEI)	higher education	7	personalization involvement student cohesiveness satisfaction	task orientation	innovation individualization
Science Laboratory Environment Inventory (SLEI)	upper secondary higher education	7	student cohesiveness	open-endedness integration	rule clarity material environment
Questionnaire on Teacher Interaction (QTI)	secondary elementary	8-10	helpful/friendly understanding dissatisfied admonishing		leadership student responsibility and freedom uncertain strict

give preservice and inservice teachers advice about the nature and quality of the interaction between teachers and students (Wubbels and Levy in press). Drawing upon a theoretical model of proximity (Cooperation–Opposition) and influence (Dominance–Submission), the Questionnaire of Teacher Interaction (QTI) was developed to assess eight scales: Leadership, Helpful/Friendly, Understanding, Student Responsibility and Freedom, Uncertain, Dissatisfied, Admonishing, and Strict Behavior. The QTI has 77 items altogether (approximately 10 per scale), and each item is responded to on a 5-point scale ranging from Never to Always. A typical item is "she or he gets angry" (Admonishing behavior). The validity and reliability of the QTI have been established for secondary school students in the Netherlands, the United States, and Australia (Wubbels and Levy in press).

3. Classroom Environment Research

The strongest tradition in classroom environment research in several countries has involved investigation of associations between students' cognitive and affective learning outcomes and their perceptions of their classroom environments (Fraser in press). Numerous studies have shown that student perceptions account for appreciable amounts of variance in learning outcomes often beyond that which can be attributed to student background characteristics. For example, better student achievement on a variety of outcome measures was found consistently in classes perceived as having greater cohesiveness and goal direction, and less disorganization and friction (Haertel et al. 1981)

Classroom environment measures were employed as dependent variables in curriculum evaluation studies, investigations of differences between student and teacher perceptions of classroom environment and studies involving other independent variables (e.g. different subject matters). The significance of curriculum evaluation studies is that classroom environment differed markedly between curricula, even when various achievement outcome measures showed negligible differences. Research involving teachers and students informs educators that teachers are likely to perceive the classroom environment more favorably than their students in the same classrooms. Research studies involving the use of classroom environment as a criterion variable have identified how the classroom environment varies with such factors as teacher personality, class size, grade level, subject matter, the nature of the school-level environment, and the type of school (see *Student Perceptions of Classrooms*).

4. Practical Uses of Classroom Environment Information

Knowledge of student perceptions can be employed as a basis for reflection upon, discussion of, and systematic attempts to improve classroom environments. For example, Fraser and Fisher's (1986) attempt to improve classroom environments made use of the CES with a class of 22 Grade 9 boys and girls of mixed ability studying science at a government school in Tasmania. The procedure incorporated five fundamental steps.

First, the actual and preferred forms of the CES were administered to all students in the class. Second, the teacher was provided with profiles representing the class means of students' actual and preferred environment scores. Third, the teacher engaged in private reflection and informal discussion about the profiles in order to provide a basis for a decision about whether an attempt would be made to change the environment in terms of some of the CES's dimensions. In fact, the teacher decided to introduce an intervention aimed at increasing the levels of teacher support and order and organization in the classroom. Fourth, the teacher used the intervention for approximately two months. For example, enhancing teacher support involved the teacher moving around the class more to mix with students, providing assistance to students and talking with them more than previously. Fifth, the actual form of the scales was readministered at the end of the intervention to see whether students were perceiving their classroom environment differently from before.

The results showed that some change in student perceptions occurred during the time of the intervention. Pretest–posttest differences were statistically significant only for teacher support, task orientation, and order and organization. These findings are noteworthy because two of the dimensions on which appreciable changes were recorded were those on which the teacher had attempted to promote change. Also, there appears to be a side effect in that the intervention could have resulted in the classroom becoming more task oriented than the students would have preferred. Overall, this case study suggests the potential usefulness of teachers employing classroom environment instruments to provide meaningful information about their classrooms and a tangible basis to guide improvements in classroom environments.

5. Future Research

Assessment involving students' perceptions of classrooms can involve either individual students' perceptions or the intersubjective perceptions of all students in the same class. This distinction in past classroom environment research has often been important when choosing an appropriate unit of statistical analysis (e.g., individual student scores or class mean scores; see Fraser 1986). The advances in multilevel analysis mean that more sophisticated techniques are available for analyzing the typical data (e.g., with students nested within classes) found in much research on classroom environments.

Although only limited progress has been made toward the desirable goal of combining quantitative and qualitative methods within the same study, the fruitfulness of this objective is illustrated in several studies (Tobin et al. 1990, Fraser and Tobin 1991). For example, in a study of higher-level cognitive learning, six researchers intensively studied the Grade 10 science classes of two teachers over a 10-week period (Tobin et al. 1990). Each lesson was observed by several researchers, interviewing of students and teachers took place on a daily basis, and students' written work was examined. The study also involved quantitative information from questionnaires assessing student perceptions of their classroom environments. An important finding was that students' perceptions of the environment within each classroom were consistent with the observers' field records of the patterns of learning activities and engagements in each classroom. For example, the high level of personalization perceived in one teacher's classroom matched the large proportion of time that she spent in small-group activities during which she constantly moved about the classroom interacting with students.

6. Conclusion

Positive classroom environments are generally assumed to be educationally desirable ends in their own right. Moreover, comprehensive evidence from past research establishes that classroom environments have a potent influence on how well students achieve a range of desired educational outcomes. Consequently, educators need not feel that they must choose between striving to achieve constructive classroom environments and attempting to enhance student achievement of cognitive and affective aims. Rather, constructive educational climates can be viewed both as means to valuable ends and as worthy ends in themselves.

See also: Class Size; Group Dynamics

References

Fraser B J 1986 *Classroom Environment*. Croom Helm, London

Fraser B J 1990 *Individualized Classroom Environment Questionnaire*. Australian Council for Educational Research, Melbourne

Fraser B J 1993 Classroom and school climate. In: Gabel D (ed.) 1993 *Handbook of Research on Science Teaching and Learning*. Macmillan, New York

Fraser B J, Anderson G J, Walberg H J 1982 *Assessment of Learning Environments: Manual for Learning Environment Inventory (LEI) and My Class Inventory (MCI)* (3rd version). Western Australian Institute of Technology, Perth

Fraser B J, Fisher D L 1986 Using short forms of classroom climate instruments to assess and improve classroom psychosocial environment. *J. Res. Sci. Teach.* 5: 387–413

Fraser B J, Treagust D F 1986 Validity and use of an instrument for assessing classroom psychosocial environment in higher education. *High. Educ.* 15: 37–57

Fraser B J, Tobin K 1991 Combining qualitative and quantitative methods in classroom environment research. In: Fraser B J, Walberg H J (eds.) 1991 *Educational Environments: Evaluation, Antecedents and Consequences*. Pergamon Press, Oxford

Fraser B J, Walberg H J (eds.) 1991 *Educational Environments: Evaluation, Antecedents and Consequences*. Pergamon Press, Oxford

Fraser B J, Giddings G J, McRobbie C J 1992 Science laboratory classroom environments at schools and universities: A cross-national study. Paper presented at the annual meeting of the National Association for Research in Science Teaching, Boston, Massachusetts

Good T L, Brophy J 1991 *Looking in Classrooms*, 5th edn. Harper Collins, New York

Haertel G D, Walberg H J, Haertel E H 1981 Sociopsychological environments and learning: A quantitative synthesis. *Br. Educ. Res. J.* 7: 27–36

Lewin K 1936 *Principles of Topological Psychology*. McGraw, New York

Moos R H 1974 *The Social Climate Scales: An Overview*. Consulting Psychologists Press, Palo Alto, California

Moos R H, Trickett E J 1987 *Classroom Environment Scale Manual*, 2nd. edn. Consulting Psychologists Press, Palo Alto, California

Murray H A 1938 *Explorations in Personality*. Oxford University Press, New York

Rosenshine B, Stevens R 1986 Teaching functions. In: Wittrock M C (ed.) 1986 *Handbook of Research on Teaching*, 3rd. edn. Macmillan, New York

Stern G G 1970 *People in Context: Measuring Person-Environment Congruence in Education and Industry*. Wiley, New York

Tobin K, Kahle J B, Fraser B J (eds.) 1990 *Windows into Science Classrooms: Problems Associated with Higher-Level Cognitive Learning*. Falmer Press, London

Welch W W, Walberg H J 1972 A national experiment in curriculum evaluation. *Am. Educ. Res. J.* 9: 373–83

Wubbels T, Levy J (eds.) in press. *Do You Know How You Look? Interpersonal Reationships in Education*. Falmer Press, London

Goal Structures

D. W. Johnson and R. T. Johnson

In every classroom, no matter what the subject area or age of students, teachers may structure lessons so that students: (a) work collaboratively in small groups ensuring that all members master the assigned material; (b) engage in a win–lose struggle to see who is best; (c) work independently on their own learning goals at their own pace and in their own space to achieve a preset standard of excellence. Knowing how and when to structure students' learning goals cooperatively, competitively, and individualistically are essential instructional skills all teachers need. Each way of structuring interdependence among students' learning goals has its place and an effective teacher will use all three appropriately. In order to discuss how cooperative, competitive, and individualistic goal structures may be used in an integrated way, it is first necessary to define what these concepts are, discuss the characteristics of each type of goal structure, and review the research on the relative effectiveness of the three goal structures.

Most instructional activities in classrooms are aimed at accomplishing goals and are conducted under a goal structure. A "learning goal" is a desired future state of demonstrated competence or mastery in the subject area being studied, such as conceptual understanding of mathematical processes, facility in the proper use of a language, or mastery in the procedures of inquiry. A "goal structure" specifies the type of social interdependence among students as they strive to accomplish their learning goals. It specifies the ways in which students will interact with one another and with the teacher during the instructional session.

1. Types of Social Interdependence

The way in which teachers structure interdependence among students' learning goals determines how students interact with one another which, in turn, largely determines the cognitive and affective outcomes of instruction. Each time teachers prepare for a lesson, they must make decisions about the goal structure they will use. Each goal structure has its place. All students should learn how to work collaboratively with others, compete for fun and enjoyment, and work autonomously. There is probably no aspect of teaching more important than the appropriate use of goal structures to determine social interdependence among students. To use them appropriately, educators must first understand what the goal structures are.

1.1 Cooperative Learning

"Cooperation" is individuals working together to maximize their own and each other's productivity and to accomplish shared goals. Thus, an individual seeks an outcome that is beneficial to himself or herself and to all other group members. In cooperative situations, individuals perceive that they can reach their goals only if the other group members also do so (Deutsch 1962, Johnson and Johnson 1991). Their goal attainments are positively correlated and, consequently, individuals discuss their work, assist one another to work hard, and encourage one another to work hard.

Teachers can structure lessons cooperatively so that students work together. Students are assigned to small groups and instructed to learn the assigned material, make sure that the other members of the group master the assignment, and make sure that all other members of the class master the assignment. Individual performance is checked regularly to ensure all students are learning. A criteria-referenced evaluation system is used. Students discuss material with one another, explain how to complete the work, help one another understand it, encourage one another to work hard, and provide academic assistance. Cooperative learning has been found to be effective with any school task. Cooperative learning groups may be used to teach specific content (formal cooperative learning groups), to ensure active cognitive processing of information during direct teaching (informal cooperative learning groups), and to provide students with long-term support and assistance for academic progress (cooperative base groups).

Many teachers believe that they are implementing cooperative learning when in fact they are missing its essence. In order for a lesson to be cooperative, five basic elements must be carefully structured (Johnson and Johnson 1991, Johnson et al. 1990). The first element of a cooperative lesson is positive interdependence. Students must believe that they are linked with others in such a way that one cannot succeed unless the other members of the group succeed (and vice versa). The second element is face-to-face, promotive interaction where students assist, encourage, and support one another's efforts to learn by orally explaining to others how to solve problems, discussing the nature of the concepts and strategies being learned, teaching their knowledge to others, and explaining the connections between present and past learning. The third element is individual accountability, where the performance of each individual student is assessed and the results given back to the group and the individual. It is important that group members know (a) who needs more assistance in completing the assignment and (b) that they cannot "hitch-hike" on the work of others. The fourth element is social skills. Groups cannot function effectively if students do not have and use the needed leadership, decision-making, trust-building, communication, and conflict-management skills. These skills have to be taught just as purposefully and precisely as academic skills. The fifth element is group processing. Groups process their functioning by answering two questions: (a) what is something each member did that was helpful for the group? and (b) what is something each member could do to make the group even better tomorrow? Such processing enables learning groups to focus on group maintenance, facilitates the learning of social skills, ensures that members receive feedback on their participation, and reminds students to practice the small-group skills required to work cooperatively.

1.2 Competitive Learning

In a competitive situation, students work against each other to achieve a goal that only one or a few can attain. Students are expected to work faster and more accurately than their peers. A competitive social situation is one in which the goals of the students are so linked that there is a negative correlation among their goal attainments; when one student achieves his or her goal, all others with whom he or she is competitively linked fail to achieve their goals (Deutsch 1962, Johnson and Johnson 1991). When lessons are structured competitively, students are given the goal of completing the assignments faster and more accurately than the other students in the class. Their performance on the assignments is ranked from highest to lowest in performance and grades are assigned to students on the basis of their relative standing. Thus, individuals seek an outcome that is personally beneficial but detrimental to all others in the situation. As a consequence, they either study hard to do better than their classmates or they take it easy because they do not believe they have a chance to win. They would be warned to work by themselves, without discussing the assignments with other students, and to seek help from the teacher if they needed it. Competition should probably only be used for tasks calling for drill or a review of facts.

For competition to exist, there must be perceived scarcity. "If I must defeat you in order to get what I want, then what I want is by definition scarce." Rewards are restricted so that only the few best or highest performers are acknowledged as being successful or are rewarded. Sometimes the scarcity is based on reality—for example, two hungry people may compete over one loaf of bread. It may also be artificially created. Students may compete for a limited number of A's but how many there are is an arbitrary decision made by the teacher and school. Schools create artificial shortages of A's in an attempt to motivate students through competition. Many competitions are based on such artificial shortages.

Competitions vary as to how many winners there will be. Only one baseball team can be the world champion. Not everyone who applies to a college may be admitted, but how many applicants "win" by being accepted varies from college to college. Competitions also vary as to the criteria for selecting a winner. In many cases, such as art contests, winning is based on subjective judgment. In other cases, such as track races, the winning is based on objective criteria. In either case, the criteria for success are uncertain in that what is needed for a win depends on the relative performance of the particular contestants. Competitions vary as to the interaction that takes place among participants. In a boxing match there is direct interaction between the two participants throughout the competition. In a track meet there is parallel interaction. Within college admissions, participants may never see each other. Whereas two javelin throwers take turns doing the same thing and do not interfere with each other, two chess players actively try to defeat each other. Finally, competitions require social comparisons. Competitive situations contain forced social comparisons in which participants are faced with information about their peers' performances and this comparative information is both salient and obtrusive. Competitors get the information on how they performed relative to others whether they want it or not.

1.3 Individualistic Learning

In an individualistic situation, students work by themselves to accomplish goals unrelated to and independent from the goals of others. Individual goals are assigned, individuals' efforts are evaluated on a fixed set of standards, and individuals are rewarded on the basis of their attainment of these standards. Students would be told to work by themselves, without disturbing their neighbors, and to seek assistance from the teacher. Whether an individual accomplishes his or her goal has no influence on whether others achieve their goals. Thus a person seeks an outcome that is personally beneficial, ignoring as irrelevant the goal achievement efforts of other participants in the situation. Individualistic learning is most appropriate when unitary, nondivisible, simple tasks needs to be completed, such as the learning of specific facts or the acquisition or the performance of simple skills. The directions for completing the learning task need to be clear and specific so that students do not need further clarification on how to proceed and how to evaluate their work. The learning goal must be perceived as important and achievable.

2. Importance of Instructional Use of Interdependence

There is a great deal of research comparing the impact of cooperative, competitive, and individualistic goal structures on a wide variety of instructional outcomes (Johnson and Johnson 1989a). These research studies began in the late 1800s and by the 1980s more than 550 experimental and 100 correlational studies had been conducted with different age subjects, in different subject areas, using different tasks, in different settings, and in a wide variety of countries in North and South America, Europe, Africa, Asia, and the Middle East (see Johnson and Johnson 1989a for a complete listing and review of these studies). As mentioned earlier, structuring situations cooperatively results in promotive interaction; structuring situations competitively results in oppositional interaction; and structuring situations individualistically results in no interaction among students. These interaction patterns affect numerous variables, which may be subsumed within the three broad and interrelated outcomes: achievement and productivity, quality of relationships among participants, and participants' psychological adjustment and social competence (Johnson and Johnson 1989a).

Working together to achieve a common goal produces higher achievement and greater productivity than does working alone. This finding is confirmed by so much research that it stands as one of the strongest principles of social and organizational psychology. Cooperative goal structures, furthermore, generally result in more higher-level reasoning, more frequent generation of new ideas and solutions (i.e., process gain), and greater transfer of what is learned within one situation to another (i.e., group to individual transfer) than does competitive or individualistic learning. The more conceptual the task, the more problem solving required; the more desirable higher-level reasoning and critical thinking, the more creativity required; and the greater the application required of what is being learned to the real world, the greater the superiority of cooperative over competitive and individualistic goal structures.

Individuals care more about each other and are more committed to each other's success and well-being when they work together to get the job done than when they compete to see who is best or work independently. This finding holds whether individuals are similar or different in terms of their intellectual ability, handicapping conditions, ethnic membership, social class, and gender. When individuals are in heterogeneous groups, cooperating on a task results in more realistic and positive views of others. As relationships become more positive, absenteeism and membership turnover decreases, while commitment to organizational goals, feelings of personal responsibility to the organization, and willingness to take on difficult tasks increase. In addition, motivation and persistence in working toward goal achievement, satisfaction and morale, willingness to endure pain and frustration on behalf of the organization, willingness to defend the organization against external criticism or attack, willingness to listen to and be influenced by colleagues, commitment to each other's professional growth and success, and productivity all increase.

Working cooperatively with peers and valuing cooperation results in greater psychological health and higher self-esteem than does competing with peers or working independently. Personal ego-strength, self-confidence, independence, and autonomy are all promoted by being involved in cooperative efforts with caring people committed to one another's success and well-being, and who respect one another as separate and unique individuals. When individuals work together to complete assignments, they interact (mastering social skills and competencies), they promote one another's success (gaining self-worth), and they form personal as well as professional relationships (creating the basis for healthy social development). Individual's psychological adjustment and health tend to increase when schools are dominated by cooperative efforts. The more individuals work cooperatively with others, the more they see themselves as worthwhile; and the greater their productivity, the greater their acceptance and support of others, and the more autonomous and independent they tend to be. Cooperative experiences are not a luxury; they are an absolute necessity for the healthy development of individuals who can function independently.

3. Using Interdependence Appropriately

In an ideal classroom, each goal structure has its place. This does not mean, however, that each will be used equally. The basic foundation of instruction, the underlying context on which all instruction rests, should be cooperation. Unless used within a context of cooperation, competitive and individualistic goal structures lose much of their effectiveness. Competition cannot exist if there is no underlying cooperation concerning rules and procedures. Most competitions have referees, umpires, judges, and teachers present to ensure that the basic cooperation over rules and procedures does not break down. Individualistic activities can be effectively used as part of a division of labor in which students master knowledge and skills that will later be used in cooperative activities. At the same time, it must be recognized that cooperative goal structures have the most widespread and powerful effects on instructional outcomes. Furthermore, although the cooperative goal structure is more complex to implement effectively than are competitive and individualistic goal structures, it should be the one most frequently used. Competitive and individualistic learning should be used to supplement and enrich the basic cooperation taking place among students. Finally, it is apparent that when the three goal structures are used appropriately and in an integrated way, they are far more powerful than is each one separately.

4. The Cooperative School

The research on goal structures applies as much to the school and the school district as it does to the classroom (Johnson and Johnson 1989b). Principals structure cooperation among teachers, and superintendents structure cooperation among administrators. Organizations are by their very nature cooperative, and competitive and individualistic structures must be used sparingly if schools are to remain effective. At its heart, cooperation is a basic change in organizational structure in which cooperative learning dominates the classroom, teacher support groups dominate the school, and administrator support groups dominate the school district.

5. Future Issues

The research on cooperative goal structures has moved into examining the specific dynamics within groups that mediate the relationships between cooperation and achievement, interpersonal attraction, and psychological health. There is evidence that in order for cooperation to be most effective, five components are essential: positive interdependence, promotive interaction, individual accountability, social skills, and group processing. Each of these components, however, needs further study. Different types of positive interdependence may have different effects on achievement, relationships, and psychological health. There has been very little study of the influence of group processing on the effectiveness of cooperation, few studies on the impact of various social skills on how effectively group members function, and little research on the impact of the goal structures on psychological adjustment and health. Finally, with the exception of a series of studies conducted by Johnson

and Johnson (1989a), there has been little research on the conditions under which competitive and individualistic learning outperform cooperation.

References

Deutsch M 1962 Cooperation and trust: Some theoretical notes. In: Jones M K (ed.) 1962 *Nebraska Symposium on Motivation*. University of Nebraska Press, Lincoln, Nebraska

Johnson D W, Johnson R 1989a *Cooperation and Competition: Theory and Research*. Interaction Book Company, Edina, Minnesota

Johnson D W, Johnson R 1989b *Leading the Cooperative School*. Interaction Book Company, Edina, Minnesota

Johnson D W, Johnson R 1991 *Learning Together and Alone: Cooperative, Competitive, and Individualistic Learning*, 3rd edn. Prentice-Hall, Englewood Cliffs, New Jersey

Johnson D W, Johnson R, Holubec E 1990 *Circles of Learning: Cooperation in the Classroom*, 3rd edn. Interaction Book Company, Edina, Minnesota

Further Reading

Deutsch M 1985 *Distributive Justice: A Social-Psychological Perspective*. Yale University Press, New Haven, Connecticut

Hertz-Lazarowitz R, Miller N (eds.) 1992 *Interaction in Cooperative Groups: The Theoretical Anatomy of Group Learning*. Plenum, New York

Kohn A 1986 *No Contest: The Case Against Competition*. Houghton Mifflin, Boston, Massachusetts

Sharan S (ed.) 1990 *Cooperative Learning: Research and Theory*. Praeger, New York

Slavin R 1983 *Cooperative Learning*. Longman, New York

Group Dynamics

J. P. Gall and M. D. Gall

A group can be defined as "two or more persons who are interacting with one another in such a manner that each person influences and is influenced by each other person" (Shaw 1981 p.8). As the definition implies, groups are dynamic. That is, a change in one group characteristic affects other characteristics. A change in a group's communication pattern, for example, can change its norms or cohesiveness.

An educational system comprises many groups, ranging from small cooperative learning groups in classrooms to large professional associations of educators. To understand and improve the functioning of these groups, educators need to know what researchers have learned about group dynamics. In this entry, theories and research findings about group dynamics

are reviewed and their applications to five important types of educational groups are discussed: (a) the entire school as a group; (b) school subsystems; (c) student social groups; (d) the class as a group; and (e) small groups within the class.

1. Essential Characteristics of Groups

The study of group dynamics came into prominence after the Second World War, as Lewin (1948) and others became interested in understanding how the behavior of individuals is influenced by the groups of which they are part. Their research led to the discovery of several important characteristics of groups and their dynamic interplay.

1.1 Group Development

Researchers who studied the same groups over time found that groups, like individuals, follow a development cycle. Often groups develop naturally, that is, without any action by external forces. For example, two same-age boys from the same neighborhood may become friends, with little or no parental intervention. Other groups are created solely for the purpose of achieving a specific goal. For example, a teacher may divide a class into small groups for the purpose of analyzing and writing a report on an assigned short story.

The interpersonal composition model of group development (Schutz 1958) posits three stages during which different interpersonal needs of group members are the focus of group activity and concern: inclusion, control, and affection. During the inclusion stage, members think about such questions as: "How will I fit in here? Who will accept me?" Once group membership has been achieved by most members, the group struggles with issues of control, namely the development of decision-making norms and sharing of responsibility. Following this stage, group members confront the emotional issues of interpersonal affection and closeness, asking such questions as "Who will like me?" and "Whom do I like?"

If a group is expected to deal with issues that are beyond the stage of development that it has reached, difficulties arise. Furthermore, unless a group receives help and direction to progress to later stages, it may remain fixated at an early stage of development, and thus never operate as a mature group. A group's goals, leadership, patterns of communication, norms, cohesiveness, and manner of expressing conflict vary depending upon its stage of development, and its success with the challenges of prior stages.

1.2 Group Goals

Researchers have theorized that what holds individuals together as a group is a shared goal. Unless an individual has a purpose that can be achieved by group membership, she or he is not likely to participate, or remain, in the group.

Goals can be specific or general. If the goal is specific, the group is likely to disband once the goal is achieved or fails to be achieved. Thus groups formed by a teacher for a specific purpose, such as a debate or class project, tend to be transitory. If the goal is general, the group may continue indefinitely because the goal is never achieved to everyone's satisfaction. Because of the fuzzy nature of many educational goals, groups such as school improvement committees may hold together over a period of years. These groups, however, must formulate more specific goals to keep individual members motivated and working together.

1.3 Group Leadership

Shaw (1981) defined leadership as an influence process which is directed toward goal achievement. A leader, then, is a member of a group who influences the group's progress toward a goal. A group can have one leader, or the influence process can be distributed across several members, each of whom may be a leader responsible for a different group goal or goal-oriented function.

In a pioneering study of leadership styles, Lewin et al. (1939) compared the behavior of boys in groups with a leader who expressed either an autocratic, democratic, or laissez-faire style of leadership. One of their findings relevant to education was that hostility, aggression, and scapegoating were far more frequently displayed by the boys when they were in groups with an autocratic leader than when they were in groups with a democratic leader.

Other research suggests that a group may benefit when two distinct types of leadership are present: task leadership, which focuses on achievement of the group's goal; and social-emotional leadership, which focuses on maintenance of positive relationships among members (Parsons and Bales 1955). Schmuck and Schmuck (1992a) argued that the social-emotional aspects of groups should be given as much attention and value as the task aspects, and that unless positive emotional relationships are fostered by the group leader, negative emotional relationships will emerge in the form of group conflict.

Another interesting line of research has compared the behavior of groups with a designated leader and the behavior of leaderless groups, in which leadership emerges from the group members in response to the task and social-emotional demands facing the group. In one such study (Carter et al. 1951), emergent leaders were found to behave in a more authoritarian manner than appointed leaders, especially in discussion tasks.

1.4 Communication

Group communication is the verbal and nonverbal dialogue that occurs among members of a group. A group usually develops a communication network, which is the arrangement of channels for dialogue among members. Communication networks vary in their degree of centrality. In a network with low centrality, communication can occur among any or all group members. High centrality means that communication must pass through a central person, such as a designated leader.

Researchers have compared the effects of different communication networks on the interpersonal processes and performance of small groups. In a classic laboratory study using physical restraints to represent communication barriers, Leavitt (1951) found that groups with centralized networks were initially more efficient in completing tasks requiring group communication, but had lower satisfaction than groups with decentralized networks.

Sommer (1967) adapted Leavitt's ideas to classroom settings by comparing communication patterns in classrooms in which students and the instructor sat in a circle (seminar-style seating) and classrooms in which the instructor faced rows of students (lecture-style seating). Sommer found that in the seminar arrangement, students directly facing the instructor participated more than students sitting to either side of the instructor. In the lecture arrangement, students in front participated more than students in the rear, and students in the center of each row participated more than students at the sides.

These findings suggest that students' ability to participate in the classroom communication network is influenced by their visibility to the teacher. Teachers typically dominate the classroom communication network (Sirotnik 1983). In a recent observational study of schools in small towns, Schmuck and Schmuck (1992b) found that three-fourths of the talk in most of the classrooms they observed was teacher talk, with most of it one-way communication from teacher to student and only an occasional student response to a teacher question.

1.5 Group Norms

Schmuck and Runkel (1985) defined norms as shared expectations, usually implicit, that help guide the psychological processes and the behaviors of group members. Norms are established only for aspects of group life that are important; they may apply more to some members than to others; they may be obeyed or disobeyed to a different extent by some or all members; and they may be publicly followed by some members but personally disbelieved. Groups may apply mild or extreme sanctions for violation of norms. For example, a girl who wears dresses to school while her classmates wear shorts or slacks may be the butt of increasingly pointed negative comments.

Because norms are implicit, they usually must be inferred from behavior or from members' statements. By contrast, rules and laws are formally encoded, typically in written form. In a classroom, for example, it is common to see a list of classroom rules, such as "Keep hands and feet to yourself." In many classrooms one can observe deviations from this rule and therefore infer that a different norm is operating, for example, that it is acceptable for a boy or girl to hold hands with or hug their "sweetheart," for girls to touch or hug other girls, and for boys to punch each other lightly on the arm or back.

1.6 Group Cohesiveness

Group cohesiveness is the extent to which the members of a group are attracted to each other. If cohesiveness is low, individual members will make attempts to increase the group's cohesiveness, through, for example, increased communication. If such attempts fail, the group may dissolve, as, for example, when a group of students stop calling or talking to a new student when it is discovered that he or she has very different beliefs or interests.

If a low-cohesive group is constrained from breaking up, interactions among group members may become restrained, infrequent, or openly hostile. For example, a teacher may unknowingly assign students who represent competing gangs or cliques to the same small group in class. Such a group is likely to be low in cohesiveness and thus not only ineffective in achieving group goals, but also likely to experience conflict. Conversely, assigning students who like each other to the same group increases the likelihood that they will have a productive learning experience.

1.7 Group Conflict

Group conflict is a situation in which incompatible activities occur, that is, when one activity blocks, interferes with, or otherwise makes another activity less likely or less effective. Schmuck and Schmuck (1992a) described three types of conflict that occur in schools: (a) prescribed conflict, which involves intentional competition based on standard rules, as in an athletic contest, game, or debate; (b) emergent conflict, characterized by unplanned battling over incompatible interests; and (c) destructive conflict, involving intentional efforts by each party to cause harm to the other parties involved in the conflict.

Schmuck and Schmuck found that emergent conflict is common both within and among classroom groups. For example, a teacher may seek to help a low-performing student by recommending less television time and less socializing. However, if the student is deeply concerned with peer acceptance and would like to spend even more time with friends, the teacher and student have an emergent conflict about goals. How the teacher responds to this type of conflict can determine whether it is resolved or escalates into destructive conflict.

As educators have become more aware of the causes and effects of conflict among groups in school, they have developed programs for conflict resolution. For example, Emerson (1990) studied a program in which elementary students served as peer conflict managers on the playground. He found that ongoing training for the peer conflict managers in role playing, communication skills, and problem-solving techniques was essential to the program's success.

2. Five Types of School-based Group

Principles of group dynamics operate in five types of school-based group. The first three types operate primarily outside the individual classroom: (a) the school as a group, (b) school subsystems, and (c) student social groups. The last two operate within the class: (d) the class as a group, and (e) small classroom groups.

2.1 The School as a Group

Lip service is often paid to the idea that the various members of a school—administrators, teachers, staff, students, and parents—are one big group, or "community." In practice, however, schools comprise various factions, subcultures, cliques, and individual personalities that often work separately from one another and toward different or competing goals. Furthermore, schools usually have well-established norms that keep individuals isolated from one another. Examples of such norms are that teachers will maintain quiet and routine in their classrooms by keeping students from interacting informally with each other; and that teachers' priority should be managing their often large workload rather than developing close collegial relationships with each other (Flinders 1988).

Another factor that keeps school members from being an effective total group is that much of the communication that occurs in schools is channeled through certain key roles, for example, the principal, the school secretary, or department heads. Thus, communication between most individuals in the teaching ranks and those holding administrative positions tends to be infrequent and characterized by impersonal dialogue or by superficially friendly "chat." During times of conflict, these communication channels may be entirely replaced by formal channels characterized by bargaining and litigation, as, for example, during a teacher strike.

The difficulty of forming a total school group is increased by the fact that each school year starts with a new "group." Each year some staff members are likely to move, die, or retire; similarly, students graduate, drop out, or move away.

Some educators have used the methods of organization development (OD) to solve the problems that keep many schools at a primitive level of group development and thus unable to operate as a working whole. The chief goal of OD is to help a school achieve the capacity to solve its own problems so that it can function effectively as a group to achieve the goals it has set for itself.

Schmuck and Runkel (1985) developed a theory of OD for schools and a validated technology for implementing it. The technology includes a variety of procedures for educators to use to diagnose their school's organizational health and to design appropriate organizational interventions so that the school becomes an effectively functioning work group.

In Europe, OD consultancy in education is most popular in countries with a history of democratic government, particularly the Netherlands and Scandinavia, where OD is often referred to as institutional development, or ID (Schmuck and Perry 1992). Major intellectual support for ID consultancy in Germany comes from the University of Dortmund (Philipp and Rolff 1990). Stratford (1987) has conducted pioneering OD work with school teachers in the United Kingdom.

2.2 School Subsystems as Groups

As the size of schools has grown, particularly in urban areas, educators have expressed concern about the difficulty of forming all its members into a cohesive group or learning community. One solution has been to develop smaller subsystems within a school. The premise is that because the subsystem has fewer members, it can form a more cohesive group than is possible in the total school. Movements to reorganize schools into smaller units, such as those to reduce class size, are based partly on the assumption that smaller group size, by increasing group cohesiveness, will promote greater student learning and self-esteem.

One type of school subsystem is referred to as a core, a concept which is increasingly common in United States middle schools. For example, a school of 600 students might be formed into four cores of 150 students each. The resources and curriculum for each core are fairly similar. Group norms are likely to develop in these subsystems. For example, one norm might be that people in the subsystem are to be treated differently from those outside of it. School staff may foster this norm by sponsoring competitive events among the cores, for example, student fund-raising activities, with the core raising the most funds receiving a special prize with which to enrich its curriculum. While engendering prescribed conflict among students in different cores, these activities can serve to increase group spirit and cohesiveness among the students in each core.

Another approach to developing school subsystems is to create alternative school programs. For example, a school might house both a traditional academic program and a parallel program based on an open school philosophy. While both programs are led by the same principal, a smaller number of teachers serves fewer students in each program. One can assume that there is more opportunity for face-to-face interaction among teachers and students in each of the smaller programs, and that such interaction will promote group development. Furthermore, the subsystems have defined different group goals, which may be more achievable because parents, and hopefully students, have been free to choose them.

There is not yet a body of research on the effectiveness of cores or alternative schools in fostering group cohesiveness and individual student achievement. However, forming such school subsystems appears to be a promising trend for improving school climate and student achievement, because they are based on sound principles of group dynamics.

2.3 Student Social Groups

Many of the groups to which students belong in school operate exclusively, or primarily, outside the classroom. These groups are of two types: natural groups, like gangs and cliques, that exist primarily for the purpose of companionship; and activity groups, like clubs and sports teams, that are designed to carry out a specific goal or activity. Some groups based on friendship or common activity develop among the adults in a school staff or among students in class. However, researchers have focused primarily on student social groups outside the classroom because of their visibility and their potential to affect learning outcomes.

The first type of student social group is natural or friendship groups that operate primarily outside of class. In their study of small schools, Schmuck and Schmuck (1992b) found that students viewed "being with friends" as the best thing about school. The primary goal of natural student groups is the social-emotional bonding of its members. Students who come from unstable families and who receive little help or encouragement from school staff often seek out gang membership as a means of belonging to a cohesive group (Huff 1990).

In highly cohesive groups, individuals tend to conform more closely to group norms (Shaw 1981). In the case of gangs, group norms usually require gang members to devalue academics and put little or no effort into schoolwork. For example, Vigil and Long (1990) described the subculture from which Mexican–American gang members are drawn in urban American cities: "like teenage subcultures throughout the United States, it has adopted characteristics that principally serve to render its participants distinct. Responsibilities beyond one's family and friends are not emphasized. Scholastic achievement is devalued..." (p.610). In this case, then, the price for membership in a cohesive group is adoption of norms contrary to those supporting success in the larger culture.

The second type of student social group is formed around a specific goal or activity, and students can elect to join the group if they meet eligibility requirements. Examples include clubs (e.g., language or computer clubs); sports teams (e.g., the university basketball team); music groups (e.g., the school band); support groups (e.g., groups for students with family members who are alcoholic); and societies (e.g., the National Honor Society). An individual seeks membership in such groups because he or she accepts the group's goal or wishes to engage in the activity that the group carries out.

Little is known about how membership in such activity groups affects student learning and satisfaction in school. However, it seems reasonable that educators should provide opportunities for such groups to form so that students can pursue extracurricular interests. Also, these groups are more likely to satisfy students' needs for inclusion, control, and affection than are classroom groups.

Students' contact with other students outside of class obviously affects their relationships inside the classroom. Teachers can better understand students' behavior in classroom groups, and can perhaps foster the development of such groups, if they have some knowledge of the natural and activity-based social groups to which their students belong.

2.4 The Class as a Group

Research findings support the instructional value of teachers creating a classroom that is high in "groupness," which is characterized by a climate of trust and activities among students and the teacher that allow mutual influence. For example, in an analysis of 116 junior high school science classrooms in Australia, Fraser and Fisher (1982) demonstrated sizable relationships between classroom climate and students' academic achievement. Measures of the degree to which students were encouraged to participate in classroom discussions, to assist each other and work together, to interact with the teacher in personal ways, and to be treated differently according to their skills and learning styles were all positively related to science achievement.

To develop class groupness, teachers first need to institute classroom management procedures that foster positive group dynamics. Charles (1992) describes numerous models of classroom management from which teachers can draw. One that appears particularly useful is a model in which teachers involve students in establishing class rules that are conducive to good learning, as well as sanctions for breaking the rules. The rules then operate as norms for student behavior, because they are written down and signed by all students to show that students understand the rules, agree to follow them, and will try to correct the underlying problem if any of the rules are broken.

Hertz-Lazarowitz (1992) provides a model for designing the physical arrangement, learning tasks, and teacher and student behavior within the classroom to foster movement from low to high levels of complexity. High complexity involves student academic and social behaviors that not only elicit a high level of thinking, but also a high level of interaction and mutual influence among class members.

Schmuck and Schmuck (1992a) describe numerous ice-breaker activities that help students in a classroom get to know each other, thus promoting development of class groupness. Competitive games also can be used for this purpose. For example, teachers might use a period to help students prepare for a test by giving an oral quiz. Each row of students is a team, and the team with the most correct answers receives a prize. The teacher can establish a rule that the first student to be called on must answer the item, but teammates can provide encouragement. This activity involves prescribed conflict, but if students are not evaluated it is fun and helps build group spirit.

Longer-term projects can be assigned to the entire class to promote groupness. For example, the class can select a dramatic play and then stage and perform it, with every student carrying out necessary tasks (e.g., designing sets, rehearsing for parts) individually or in small work teams.

Finally, interactive whole-class activities can be used. For example, Wilen (1990) describes procedures for engaging a class of 20 to 30 students in guided discussion, aimed at facilitating students' understanding and analysis of a topic; and reflective discussion, aimed at helping students think critically, engage in social interaction, and assume responsibility for their own learning outcomes.

2.5 Small Classroom Groups

The amount of time devoted to small group activity in traditional classrooms has been found to be minimal. For example, Sanford and Evertson (1983) found in a study of junior high schools that only 2 percent of the total time use in 52 mathematics classes and only 1 percent in 50 English classes involved small group instruction. In their observational study of small school districts, Schmuck and Schmuck (1992b) reported that they saw only five instances of cooperative learning groups in the sample of 50 classes.

The low frequency of small group work in classrooms is of concern to educators familiar with group dynamics because instructional methods that involve small groups are available and have been found to be effective. One of these methods is small group discussion, which is characterized by an open communication network that encourages student-to-student dialogue. Gall and Gall (1990) concluded from their review of research on the discussion method that it promotes mastery of subject-matter objectives (especially those involving higher-cognitive learning), problem-solving ability, moral development, attitude development and attitude change, and communication skills.

In an earlier review of research on discussion group processes, Gall and Gall (1976) found that group size is critical for an effective discussion, with five members being the optimal size to enhance participation and avoid deadlock. As group size increases beyond this number, the average number of remarks per member and the percentage of members who participate in a discussion decreases. Discussion groups that are small also have been found to be higher in cohesiveness, minimization of group conflict, and the probability of a leader emerging.

Members of small classroom groups can work together in different ways to achieve learning goals. McCarthey and McMahon (1992) described three categories of peer interaction involving learning to write: peer tutoring, cooperative learning, and peer collaboration. In peer tutoring, the primary goal of the group is for a student with better writing skills to assist another student. In cooperative learning, the goal is for each student to contribute individually to a joint group product, while giving each other help and encouragement. Since the 1980s a good deal of research has been conducted to demonstrate the benefit of cooperative learning and the necessary conditions for achieving them. Shlomo (1994) provides a comprehensive review. Finally, in peer collaboration, the goal is for students to work closely together in all stages of the writing process and produce a joint product that is "significantly different from a piece that either partner would have written alone" (p.28).

Small groups in classrooms need to have norms that are more or less clear and agreed upon by their members. Bridges (1990) identified four characteristics of a good discussion that provide a useful set of small group norms: (a) students talk to one another; (b) students listen to each other; (c) students are responsive in thought and word to what each other says; and (d) the exchange of dialogue is task centered.

If groups are composed of members who like each other, group cohesiveness will be high. A teacher can thus improve group functioning in class by knowing something about the social connections outside the classroom that students have with each other. For example, a close friendship pair of students may tend to relate only to each other and therefore ignore other group members. The teacher can improve cohesiveness of the entire small group by helping the members define group tasks and procedures that they find appealing and for which they have some ownership.

One reason that so little group activity occurs in most classrooms may be that group conflict inevitably arises when people interact. Schmuck and Schmuck (1992a) describe four types of conflict that can occur within a group. Goal conflict is disagreement over the goal itself. Procedural conflict is characterized by disagreement over the course of action that should be taken to reach a goal. Conceptual conflict is disagreement over ideas, information, theories, or opinions. Finally, interpersonal conflict is characterized by incongruity in personal styles and needs, and is perhaps the most difficult type of conflict to handle. Schmuck and Schmuck explain how the teacher can help students determine which type or types of conflict are occurring and use conflict resolution strategies to help students overcome them.

3. Conclusion

Principles of group dynamics are not commonly used to analyze and improve school and classroom processes, largely because the development of "groupness" has not been a priority at either the school or classroom level. There are signs that this situation is changing, (e.g., the growing interest in the United States in site-based school management and cooperative learning). If use of these methods continues, educators will be well advised to learn principles of group dynamics and apply them to improve the school and classroom experience of students.

References

Bridges D 1990. The character of discussion: A focus on students. In: Wilen W W (ed.) 1990 *Teaching and Learning through Discussion*. Charles C Thomas, Springfield, Illinois

Carter L, Haythorn W W, Shriver B, Lanzetta J 1951 The

behavior of leaders and other group members. *J. Abnorm. Soc. Psychol.* 46: 589–95

Charles C M 1992 *Building Classroom Discipline*, 4th edn. Longman, White Plains, New York

Emerson J M 1990 Conflict resolution for students: A study of problem solving and peer conflict management (Doctoral dissertation, University of Oregon)

Flinders D J 1988 Teacher isolation and the new reform. *Journal of Curriculum and Supervision* 4(1): 17–29

Fraser B, Fisher D 1982 Predicting students' outcomes from their perceptions of classroom psychosocial environment. *Am. Educ. Res. J.* 19(4): 498–518

Gall J P, Gall M D 1990 Outcomes of the discussion method. In: Wilen W W (ed.) 1990 *Teaching and Learning through Discussion*. Charles C Thomas, Springfield, Illinois

Gall M D, Gall J P 1976 The discussion method. In: Gage N L (ed.) 1976 *The Psychology of Teaching Methods*. National Society for the Study of Education, Chicago, Illinois

Hertz-Lazarowitz R 1992 Understanding interactive behaviors: Looking at six mirrors of the classroom. In: Hertz-Lazarowitz R, Miller N (eds.) 1992 *Interaction in Cooperative Groups*. Cambridge University Press, New York

Huff C R (ed.) 1990 *Gangs in America*. Sage, Newbury Park, California

Leavitt H J 1951 Some effects of certain communication patterns on group performance. *J. Abnorm. Soc. Psychol.* 46: 38–50

Lewin K 1948 *Resolving Social Conflicts*. Harper's, New York

Lewin K, Lippitt R, White R K 1939 Patterns of aggressive behavior in experimentally created "social climates." *J. Soc. Psychol.* 10: 271–99

McCarthey S J, McMahon S 1992 From convention to invention: Three approaches to peer interaction during writing. In: Hertz-Lazarowitz R, Miller N (eds.) 1992 *Interaction in Cooperative Groups*. Cambridge University Press, New York

Parsons T, Bales R 1955 *Family Socialization and Interaction Process*. Free Press, New York

Philipp E, Rolff H G 1990 *Schulgestaltung durch Organisationsentwicklung*. Verlag, Braunschweig

Sanford J P, Evertson C M 1983 Time use and activities in junior high classes. *J. Educ. Res.* 143–47

Schmuck R A, Perry E 1992 *Organization Development and Consultancy in Education*. UCEA Center on Organization Development in Schools, Eugene, Oregon

Schmuck R A, Runkel P J 1985 *The Handbook of Organization Development in Schools*, 3rd edn. Mayfield Press, Palo Alto, California

Schmuck R A, Schmuck P A 1992a *Group Processes in the Classroom*, 6th edn. William C Brown, Dubuque, Iowa

Schmuck R A, Schmuck P A 1992b *Small Districts Big Problems: Making School Everybody's House*. Corwin, Newbury Park, California

Schutz W 1958 FIRO: A Three Dimensional Theory of Interpersonal Behavior. Holt, Rinehart, & Winston, New York

Shaw M E 1981 *Group Dynamics: The Psychology of Small Group Behavior*, 3rd edn. McGraw-Hill, New York

Shlomo S (ed.) 1994 *Handbook of Cooperative Learning Methods*. Greenwood Press, Westport, Connecticut

Sirotnik K A 1983 What you see is what you get—consistency, persistency, and mediocrity in classrooms. *Harv. Educ. Rev.* 53(1): 16–31

Sommer R 1967 Classroom ecology. *Journal of Applied Behavioral Science* 3: 328–42

Stratford R 1987 Helping schools solve problems. *British Journal of Special Education* 14(3): 123–26

Vigil J D, Long J M 1990 Emic and etic perspectives on gang culture: The Chicano case. In: Huff C R (ed.) 1990

Wilen W W 1990 Forms and phases of discussion. In: Wilen W W (ed.) 1990 *Teaching and Learning through Discussion*. Charles C Thomas, Springfield, Illinois

(c) Paraprofessionals, Substitute Teachers, Parents, and Families

Technology and the Classroom Teacher

N. Hativa

The teacher has a key role in the introduction of technology into the classroom and in its successful adoption and application. This entry describes this role, the extent and patterns of the use of technology in the classroom, and factors that either promote or impede the successful integration of technology into the curriculum.

1. Teachers as Decision Makers in the Adoption and Use of Technology in the Classroom

During the twentieth century, there have been many attempts to penetrate schools with various technological innovations. Examples included the overhead projector, teaching machines, radio, 8 millimeter film, television, video-cassette recorders (VCRs), and computers. The majority of these technologies did not achieve widespread use in schools and did not survive the initial years of enthusiasm. The computer, on the other hand, has won widespread adoption and use, more than any of the other technologies.

Teachers are the most critical decision makers regarding the adoption and use of technology in schools. Concentrating on computers, teachers' decisions affect the type, frequency, and even the mere existence of computer experiences for students. Teachers also decide how to organize students' computer work socially: working individually, in pairs or in small groups, cooperatively or competitively. This social organization bears an important role in students' learning. Teachers' decisions regarding computer use in school are affected by their instructional style, flexibility in adapting to new teaching situations, attitudes toward computers, length of experience using computers in their own lessons, and their self-perception as computer users (Collis 1988).

2. Patterns of Teacher Use of Technology in the Classroom

A survey of teachers in 19 countries (China, India, Israel, Japan, New Zealand, and several countries in

Europe, examined the use of computers in education. As a result of this study, Pelgrum and Plomp (1991) identified two major applications of computers in schools worldwide. First, there is an emphasis on learning about computers, primarily on the acquisition of operational skills in handling computers or learning programming languages. Second, there is an emphasis on using computers as an aid in teaching and learning traditional school subjects. This latter application is often referred to as the "integration of computers into the curriculum or into classroom teaching" (Sheingold et al. 1987). In this regard, the integration of computers in a school is regarded as successful when the computers are used in a variety of subjects by a large proportion of students and teachers (Meister 1984).

2.1 Integrating Computers into Classroom Instruction

The successful integration of computers throughout the curriculum—either for the purpose of learning traditional subjects or for tool use—is a major school goal (Sheingold et al. 1987). Teachers implement this integration in many different ways depending on their personal characteristics, teaching styles and methods, subject matter, and class level (OTA 1988). Teachers use computers in quite a wide range of pedagogical approaches: to individualize instruction, encourage individual and group problem solving, provide drill and practice for promoting basic skills, provide peer work with social-science simulations, simulate laboratory experiments, and perform real laboratory experiments using computer-attached sensors. They also use the computer as a tool for improving the students' productivity in accomplishing academic tasks (e.g., using word processors for writing or incorporating database management for analyzing data for students' projects).

In schools in the United States teachers are increasingly seeing the computer as a tool for improving students' productivity but they continue to use it also as a method of improving students' basic skills in mathematics or language arts. The higher the school level, the more the computer is used as an academic tool (Becker 1990). In elementary schools, the most frequent computer applications are self-exploratory activities for students (often using LOGO), simulations, tutorials, drill-and-practice, and computer-based testing. A growing proportion of computer time is spent on instruction in keyboard techniques and in using word-processing programs. In lower secondary or middle schools computers are used most frequently for drill-and-practice and less frequently for self-exploratory activities. In upper secondary schools computers are used frequently as productivity tools or for teacher demonstration and exploration for the whole class (Becker 1990, Pelgrum and Plomp 1991).

A small proportion of teachers, identified as expert users of computers in schools (Sheingold and Hadley 1990), have been found to use a large software repertoire in multipurpose applications. They use tool-based computer environments to adapt and individualize tasks to students' needs and also operate small-group activity-based learning. They take multiple approaches to the use of computers in their classrooms for purposes as varied as demonstrating an idea in front of the class and individual student remediation. Most commonly, students make their own products with the computer.

2.2 Location and Number of Computers and their Use by Teachers

Whether computers are located in a computer laboratory or distributed among classrooms strongly affects teacher and student attitudes toward computer use, the type of computer use, students' access to computers, and the extent to which teachers integrate computers into ongoing subject matter learning experiences.

Whole-class concurrent individualized activities can take place only if the number of computers is at least the same as the number of students. Similarly, pair work with computers for the whole class is possible only if the number of computers is at least one half the number of students. For these two types of whole-class computer activities, the computers are usually located in a special laboratory, networked to a central source of software that manages students' learning, assigns them learning activities, tests them frequently, and records their advancement. In situations where there are not enough computers for the whole class to work on concurrently, classes are split up and one group of students perform other activities while the others are working at the computer.

Computers located in the classrooms are usually stand-alone stations (not networked) that require separate loading and printing facilities. The most common arrangement in this case is to have two students share one computer and work cooperatively on drill-and-practice, problem solving, or similar tasks. A single computer in a classroom can also be used by the teacher in a variety of ways at various occasions. It can be used as a learning station for individual students, or can be attached to a large CRT screen or to a projector

on a large screen for presenting interactive demonstrations, experimentations, problem solving, and new concepts to the whole class.

In lower secondary and middle schools computers are most frequently located in a laboratory while in upper secondary schools they are in the classrooms; in elementary schools both arrangements are found (Pelgrum and Plomp 1991). Locating computers in laboratory at the high school level causes several problems. Many teachers choose not to interrupt their preferred teaching routines in order to relocate student activity to a laboratory. In addition, many teachers feel uncomfortable about working in a laboratory because it is perceived as the "territory" of a subgroup of staff, typically the teachers of computer science, mathematics, or physical sciences. Consequently, the laboratory is underutilized by the majority of teachers and overutilized by that subgroup of staff (Collis 1988).

2.3 Computerized Learning Environments and Teacher Role and Behavior

The integration of computers into the curriculum requires teachers to identify software that is relevant to the curriculum and specific lessons and to provide feedback and suggestions to their students as they use computers. For each type of computer-based activity, teachers need to provide either explicit teaching or individualized support. Consider the following two examples of basic computer-based activities.

Software that manages individualized student work in a computer laboratory often prints out a computerized class report on request. This report has proved an extremely helpful tool for the teacher in adapting instruction to the individual learner in and outside the computer laboratory. Teachers use it for tailoring individualized seatwork, for forming homogeneous groups of students to work together on problems in-class, and for providing explanations to the whole class on topics identified by the report as problematic to many students (Hativa et al. 1990).

In computer-based environments where students learn in groups, the interactivity of the computer software and its management of the content presented to students frees the teacher to observe the groups in action and to concentrate on leading the students in their analysis and discussions (OTA 1988). The role of the teacher shifts from that of provider of content-specific information to facilitator of students' own information organization skills. Instruction techniques shift away from the direct delivery of information toward greater emphasis on shaping students' mastery of the information and promoting thinking skills such as finding relevant information, solving problems, asking questions, thinking critically, and communicating ideas (Sheingold et al. 1987).

Does the introduction of computers into classrooms affect the teacher's role, behavior and methods? Hativa et al.'s study (1990) reveals that increased experience with students' individualized computer-based practice led to substantial changes in teacher behavior and in teaching methods. The most substantial change observed was a switch from frontal teaching, found in a high proportion of teachers new to computerized work, to individualized or achievement-based grouping of students, found in a high proportion of teachers experienced in this work. Similarly, for most of the exemplary computer-using teachers identified by Sheingold and Hadley (1990), computers did make a real difference in their teaching and in their expectations of student performance. The teachers began to expect more of their students, present more complex material, conduct better individualization in learning, encourage students' independent work, and promote student-centered classes. These teachers acted more as coaches and facilitators than as information transmitters.

3. The Extent of Teachers' Use of Computers in Their Classes

In the United States the process of integrating computers into the curriculum has been relatively rapid. In a four-year period (1985–1989), the number of computer-using teachers doubled. In the early 1990s, 39 percent of all school teachers in the United States used computers in their classes. In other countries, the implementation of computers seems to be going much slower and to be at a much earlier stage. Outside the United States, computer applications in schools are still very limited. Learning about computers plays an important role, whereas the application of computers in existing subject areas frequently deals with drill and practice. Problem solving and simulation approaches, which are indicative of a more innovative approach to computer use in the classroom, are still rather scarce (Pelgrum and Plomp 1991).

However, the mere number of computer-using teachers can be misleading. The important issue is the effectiveness of computer use in achieving the goals of instruction. Research that has examined this issue shows a striking discrepancy between teacher-reported use and actual use of computers for instruction. Computers are being used only minimally and without apparent focus or educational rationales. Many teachers still lack clear vision of how to teach effectively with computer technology. Moreover, many teachers resist using computers for instruction and find subtle ways to circumvent pressure to integrate computers into their teaching that comes from school principals, superintendents, and computer coordinators. These teachers either use the microcomputers as an extension of what they have already been doing in the classroom, make token gestures regarding computer use, or avoid using computers altogether (Hativa 1991).

In contrast to teachers who avoid using computers effectively, there are teachers who are expert and enthusiastic users of computers and who do provide intellectually exciting educational experiences at all grade levels. Teachers of this type, referred to as "expert computer-using teachers," were identified by Sheingold and Hadley (1990) as constituting a broad cross-section of teachers from different regions and from different demographic and socioeconomic climates in the United States. They have their students use a wide variety of computer software in ways that are directly related to the teachers' major curricular goals.

In order to assess the actual impact of computers on school learning, the extent of effective computer use in schools and the proportion of expert computer-using teachers must be studied. Sheingold and Hadley's (1990) survey cannot provide this information because it has identified expert teachers only on the basis of their reputation. Becker (1992), using a probability sample of schools in the United States, found that expert computer-using teachers constitute only 5 percent of all computer-using teachers. In other words, 95 percent of computer-using teachers use the computer ineffectively to a certain degree. This surprisingly high proportion suggests that computer applications in schools are not yet very effective.

4. Obstacles to the Adoption and Use of Technology by Teachers

The evidence presented in the above section points to a lack of proper integration of computers into classroom teaching. However, this phenomenon has been observed with most attempts to penetrate schools with new technologies during the twentieth century. Bosco (1988) summarizes:

> Television, 8mm film, radio, teaching machines, and even the telephone, were all touted as technologies which would improve instruction in the schools. There was considerable effort to turn television into an educational tool, but this effort has had little effect. Teachers cited the inconvenience of broadcast schedules and lack of appropriate programming as the most common barriers to use of TV. One might think the solution to these problems would have been the VCR. Most schools have TVs and VCRs, both of which are less expensive than computers, and there is much excellent video software available. Yet, the resolution of the perceived barriers has not resulted in significantly expanded use of video technology. (1988 p. 1)

What then are the impediments to the adoption of computer technology by teachers? Several sources (Hativa 1991, OTA 1988, Pelgrum and Plomp 1991, Wiske et al. 1988) indicate the following obstacles:

(a) *Lack of teacher knowledge and inadequate training.* Teachers are not trained properly to operate hardware, choose appropriate software, or integrate software into classroom instruction.

(b) *Logistics obstacles.* Teachers do not know what software is available, find that available software is inappropriate for their classes, and struggle with a single disk when they really need multiple disks. For many teachers, having to schedule the computer laboratory in advance and make arrangements to relocate the class constitute a logistical burden.

(c) *Extra burden on teacher time and effort in lesson preparation and planning.* The teacher needs to choose the appropriate software, learn to work with it and with the computer, and plan a fallback lesson in case the computer malfunctions. In addition, it takes substantial planning to match software to the curriculum, and design separate activities for the students not using computers when there are not enough computers for a whole-class activity. Much computer software covers only one or a few instructional concepts; thus, the teacher needs to find the best way to incorporate sundry pieces of software into the overall curriculum.

(d) *Undesired changes in teacher role.* School reforms that attempted to foster student-centered classrooms have not taken root because the teacher-centered classroom has traditionally been accepted as the way to maintain order and to teach considerable instructional content to students. Since many computer applications produce changes in the traditional teacher role, they often fail to achieve widespread adoption. In addition, reducing the direct interaction between teacher and students as implied by many types of computer work reduces the likelihood of the psychological rewards that teachers experience with their teacher-centered instruction.

(e) *Difficulties in maintaining the traditional curriculum.* Teachers are reluctant to attempt innovative approaches when stringent curriculum requirements are reinforced by standardized tests. They feel accountable to uphold their professional responsibilities and to prepare their students to pass tests that constitute crucial gateways in their academic progress.

(f) *Fear.* The microcomputer produces strong anxiety among teachers. Teachers are afraid of the complex, technical nature of the microcomputer. Specifically, they fear that they are not able to use the hardware or software and that their students know more than they do about computers.

To conclude, the basic problem with the use of computer technology in schools is the attempt to incorporate it into the curriculum by adapting it to an existing infrastructure. Significant and innovative use of computers does not articulate well with the basic features of many classrooms. The effective use of computers requires social and organizational changes which take into consideration the fact that the classroom is an organizational entity with a well-established set of traditions and practices. This problem cannot be resolved by good hardware, software, and teacher training. Rather, only by direct confrontation with the elements in the classroom environment which create the logistical impediments to computer use can effective use of computers be increased.

5. Promoting the Successful Adoption of Technology in Schools

Despite the pessimism of the above section, several factors are related to the successful integration of computers into the curriculum and the classroom. Positive attitudes facilitate the adoption and use of technology by teachers. A crucial factor for teacher adoption of any innovation is having high satisfaction working with this innovation (Cuban 1984).

Positive attitudes toward integrating computers into teaching are formed as the result of the actual use of computers (Pelgrum and Plomp 1991). Sheingold and Hadley (1990) found that over time and with substantial experience—at least five to six years of teaching with computers—the exemplary computer-using teachers became increasingly comfortable and confident about using computers. Similarly, teacher satisfaction with computer-managed practice was found to be extraordinarily high for teachers who had used computers with their students for more than one year in comparison to teachers new to computer use (Hativa et al. 1990).

In addition to having substantial experience in teaching with computers, Sheingold and Hadley (1990) identified four additional conditions that must be met if teachers are to become exemplary school computer users. They are: (a) having high motivation for teaching; (b) receiving considerable support from their school and district in efforts for personal development as teachers; (c) being motivated by their students' using software tools for effective learning; and (d) having access in school to sufficient quantities of computers and to sophisticated technology (e.g., hard disk drives, laser printers, videodisc players). Similarly, Becker (1992) found that the likelihood of the development of exemplary teachers is enhanced in schools in which (a) social networks exist for fostering expert computer use; (b) there is sustained and widespread use of computers at the school for writing and publishing activities; (c) there is organized support for computer-using teachers in the form of staff development activities and a full-time computer coordinator role; and (d) the school leadership is concerned about equity of access to computers for all.

6. Conclusion and Needs for Future Research

The successful integration of computers into classroom teaching has been accomplished by only a very small proportion of computer-using teachers worldwide. The use of the computer for learning in school constitutes a logistical burden for many teachers. To increase the integration of technology into the classroom, the existing school infrastructure must be changed dramatically. Future research should examine the behavior of teachers using computers in different innovative school and learning environments.

References

Becker H J 1990 Computer use in United States schools: 1989. An initial report of US participation in the IEA Paper presented at the annual meeting of the American Educational Research Association, Boston, Massachusetts

Becker H J 1992 Exemplary vs. other computer-using teachers. Unpublished manuscript, Center for Social organization of Schools; John Hopkins University, Baltimore, Maryland

Bosco J J 1988 *Structural Impediments to Computer Integration in Schools in the US 5th International Conference on Technology and Education*, Vol. I. CEP Consultants Ltd, Edinburgh

Collis B 1988 Manipulating critical variables: A framework for improving the impact of computers in the school environment. Paper presented at the annual meeting of EURIT, Lausanne

Cuban L 1984 *How Teachers Taught. Constancy and Change in American Classrooms 1890–1980*. Longman, New York

Hativa N 1991 Teacher behavior and computer-based education. In: Husén T, Postlethwaite T N (eds.) 1991 *The International Encyclopedia of Education: Research and Studies*, Supplementary Vol. 2. Pergamon Press, Oxford

Hativa N, Shapira R, Navon D 1990 Computer-manager practice—effects on instructional methods and on teacher adoption. *Teach. Teach. Educ.* 6(1): 55–68

Meister G R 1984 *Successful Integration of Microcomputers in an Elementary School*. Program Report No. 84–A13, Institute for Research on Educational Finance and Goverance, Stanford University, Stanford, California

Pelgrum W J, Plomp T 1991 *The Use of Computers in Education Worldwide*. Pergamon Press, Oxford

Office of Technology Assessment (OTA) Staff 1988 *Power On! New Tools for Teaching and Learning*. Technonic Publishing Co, Lancaster, Pennsylvania

Sheingold K, Hadley M 1990 *Accomplished Teachers: Integrating Computers into Classroom Practice*. Center for Technology and Education, Bank Street College of Education, New York

Sheingold K, Martin M W, Endreweit M E 1987 Preparing urban teachers for the technological future. In: Pea R D, Sheingold K (eds.) 1987 *Mirrors of the Minds*. Ablex, Norwood, New Jersey

Wiske M S et al. 1988 *How Technology Affects Teaching*. Educational Technology Center, Education Development Center, Cambridge, Massachusetts

Availability and Use of Paraprofessionals

B. P. Reynolds

Available literature indicates that the use of paraprofessionals in education is widespread throughout the world. A general consensus is that the ultimate purpose of a paraprofessional program is to improve instruction. The belief that paraprofessionals should and do impact positively upon teachers and the quality of instruction provided to their students is prevalent. However, existing data on the qualifications, training, and use of paraprofessionals suggest that paraprofessionals spend the majority of their time engaged in direct instruction of students while at the same time having little in the way of qualifications or training to instruct these students. This entry discusses the availability, qualifications, training, and responsibilities of paraprofessionals and concludes with a discussion of recommendations for practice and research.

1. Definition and Availability of Paraprofessionals

The term "paraprofessional" is used to describe noncertified adults who help teachers. Otto (1964) used the term "paraprofessional" to refer to the noncertified member of a teaching team. This term was adopted by the International Reading Association in 1968. In 1967 the United States Department of Education defined "teacher aide," its term for paraprofessionals, as a person who assists a teacher in the performance of his or her professional or administrative duties. Whether called paraprofessional or teacher aide, the primary responsibility of this person is to provide support and assistance to teachers.

According to Miles (1964), 9 percent of the elementary and 18 percent of the secondary schools in the United States were using paraprofessionals in some manner during the 1960–61 school year. Lombardo (1981) reported 1.5 million paid paraprofessionals and 6 million unpaid paraprofessionals working in United States schools. Data provided by the United States Office of Educational Research or Improvement (USOERI) revealed that 46.7 percent (64,500) of the personnel employed in Chapter I classes were paraprofessionals (Birman et al. 1987).

2. Qualifications of Paraprofessionals

Two important qualifications of paraprofessionals are their level of education and their preparation for their jobs.

2.1 Educational Level

Numerous studies report that the average educational levels of paraprofessionals are well below the average level of the teachers they assist. Results of a survey of classroom assistants in the United Kingdom county of Essex (Bassett and Woolf 1988) reported that the majority of respondents (77.8 percent) had no professional qualifications. An Australian study by Foster and Stockley (1980), yielded similar results. Of the 118 ethnic aides in their study, 70.3 percent had completed secondary school only, 16.1 percent reported some type of postsecondary education, and 13.6 percent reported a university education.

In the United States, paraprofessionals are required to have at least a high school diploma. The data obtained during the most recent National Assessment of Chapter I, a federally funded program for economically disadvantaged, low-achieving students, indicated that among paraprofessionals who assisted Chapter I teachers, 71 percent held neither a college degree nor a teaching certificate and only 6 percent had earned a bachelor's degree. In a study of paraprofessionals serving remedial and compensatory programs in South Carolina, Reynolds (1990) found similar results. Of the 122 paraprofessionals surveyed, approximately 32 percent were high school graduates, 49 percent had completed some college, 12 percent were college graduates, and 6 percent reported attending graduate school. Earlier studies of educational backgrounds of paraprofessionals reported similar percentages (Shank and McElroy 1970, Brighton 1972, Evans 1980, Vasa et al. 1982).

In summary, the majority of paraprofessionals in Western countries possess a high school diploma. Only about one-sixth have received a college degree.

2.2 Job-related Training: Amount Received

Despite the successes reported by isolated training programs for aides, little evidence exists that job-related training is routinely provided to paraprofessionals. Reynolds (1990) found that approximately 90 percent of the paraprofessionals she surveyed had not received any training related to their responsibilities in serving remedial students. Vasa et al. (1982) conducted a survey of administrators, special education teachers, and special educations paraprofessionals and reported that 60 percent of the administrators, 82 percent of the teachers, and 81 percent of the paraprofessionals informed them that formal inservice training for the paraprofessionals was not provided.

Similarly, Foster and Stockley (1980) reported that only 11 percent of the paraprofessionals they surveyed had had training for their job prior to employment; however, approximately 50 percent did receive training after employment. Finally, Woolf and Bassett (1988) reported that 59 percent of the respondents had attended inservice training courses aimed particularly at their job; 37 percent stated that suitable inservice courses had not been available. In summary, less than one-half of the paraprofessionals receive training related to the job they are expected to perform. This figure may be as low as 10–20 percent.

2.3 Job-related Training: Effectiveness

Several studies of the implementation and follow-up evaluation of training programs for paraprofessionals report positive and significant gains in aide performance as a result of the training. Thus paraprofessionals can be trained, and well-trained paraprofessionals can better aid the instructional process. Examples of these studies include the Title I Great Cities Training Program (Monk 1980), the Columbus, Ohio Instructional Aide Program (Johnson 1986), the follow-up study of the Teacher Aide Program in Mississippi (Handley 1986), and the La Mesa-Spring Valley, California study (Renaud 1976).

3. Responsibilities of Paraprofessionals

This section discusses what paraprofessionals should and what they actually do.

Several lists of the activities that should be performed by paraprofessionals have been compiled (Shank and McElroy 1970, Brighton 1972, McManana 1972, Welty and Welty 1976, Clough and Clough 1978, Foster and Stockley 1980, Lombardo 1981, Womack 1987). One of the primary functions included on these lists is tutoring children. Other frequently mentioned duties involved working with small groups of students on teacher-made or teacher-selected materials, preparing or organizing for instruction, and performing housekeeping or clerical tasks.

Descriptions of what paraprofessionals could do and likely need to do seem logical and practical. But what is known about the activities and behaviors of paraprofessionals? Available studies report that paraprofessionals spend a large amount of time in direct instructional activities, often tutoring individual students or small groups of students. In fact, Green and Barnes (1988) have suggested that the role of paraprofessionals has gradually shifted toward more instructional responsibility.

Reynolds (1990) compared data regarding paraprofessional responsibilities collected from paraprofessionals using surveys with data collected by observing them in their schools and classrooms. Data from both sources indicated that in excess of 50 percent of paraprofessionals' time was spent working directly with students, either in small groups or in individual tutoring.

Paraprofessionals reported that their time was divided among the following activities: making presentations or giving explanations to large or small groups of students (12.8%); working with small groups of students on teacher-given assignments (25%); circulating around the classroom, helping those students who are in need of help (24.84%); correcting assignments and grading papers (13.7%); completing forms, photocopying, clerical tasks (12.6%); noninstructional supervision (3.6%); and other activities (7.9%).

Observers found slightly different allotments of time in some of these areas of responsibility: making presentations or giving explanations to large or small groups of students (2.1%); working with small groups of students on teacher-given assignments (32.8%); circulating around the classroom, helping those students who are in need of help (46%); correcting assignments and grading papers (3.8%); completing forms, photocopying, clerical tasks (8.4%); noninstructional supervision (1.4%); and other activities (2.6%). Two other areas of responsibility for paraprofessionals that were noted were observing the teaching of the supervising teacher (6.9%) and managing student behavior (4.1%).

Thomas (1987) surveyed 86 headteachers and 82 teachers in primary schools from one region in Oxfordshire in the United Kingdom to determine the amount, type, and organization of activity in these schools in which people other than the classroom teacher were involved. He found a wide range of involvement in curricular activity. Results indicated that roughly one-third of all parental assistance was involved with hearing students read. Just under two-thirds of the sessions of peripatetic teachers and welfare assistants were devoted to working with children with special needs, dividing their time fairly evenly between work with individuals and work with small groups.

Sangster (1989) reported the results of an evaluation of the Teacher Apprenticeship Program of North York, Ontario, Canada. Interviews with 17 of 19 apprentices revealed descriptions of their classroom responsibilities and activities. All apprentices reported working with small groups of students, 76 percent reported working with individual students, 76 percent reported participating in field trips, 72 percent reported performing clerical duties, 59 percent reported working with the whole class, and 47 percent reported generally

assisting and observing the mentor teacher. Slightly less than half of the apprentices reported assisting the mentor teacher in preparing the lessons. Only about one-sixth mentioned yard duty or taking over the class momentarily for the teacher.

Turner and Miles (1980) reported results of an evaluation of early education classes in Queensland, Australia. Through a survey, information was sought from teachers regarding the deployment of paraprofessionals and parent volunteers. Results revealed that very few paraprofessionals spent much time giving formal lessons; 93 percent spent one quarter or less of their time on this activity. There was a somewhat higher paraprofessional involvement in giving informal lessons; 32 percent spent more than one-quarter of their time in this activity. Twelve percent spent three-quarters of their time engaged in materials preparation and clerical or domestic duties, while 18 percent spent the same proportion of time in supervisory (monitoring) duties.

Parent volunteers' roles were slightly different. The activity that consumed most of their time was supervisory duties. Forty percent of the teachers reported that their parent volunteers spent three-quarters or more of their time supervising children. No parents were reported as spending nearly as much time on materials preparation and clerical or domestic duties, or in giving informal lessons.

Woolf and Bassett's (1988) survey of teaching assistants found that most spent 75 percent or more of their classroom time on educational activities, such as working with them on mathematics worksheets or hearing children read. Saterfiel and Handley's (1983) study of a Mississippi Teacher Aide Program revealed that approximately 85 percent of the paraprofessionals' time was spent in small group instruction. In a follow-up study Handley (1986) indicated that 74.4 percent of the paraprofessionals reported introducing new material to students in small groups, 61.2 percent reported working with individual students on a set schedule, 69.2 percent reported working with the entire class on reinforcing the teacher's instruction, and 54.9 percent reported working with small groups of children on the basic skills.

Vasa et al. (1982) surveyed special education paraprofessionals and observed that they reported spending the largest percentage of their time in providing direct instruction to individual students (34 percent) and to groups (29 percent). Chase and Mueller (1989) conducted a study of 62 first- and second-grade classrooms in Indiana. The most frequent activity for a paraprofessional was to work with a single child using a workbook/worksheet in a discussion/review activity (20% of the time).

In only one study did the findings indicate that paraprofessionals spent the majority of their time in duties outside the realm of direct instruction. Foster and Stockley (1980) supplied paraprofessionals in their study with a lengthy list of tasks a paraprofessional might do and asked them to indicate for each task whether they were performed often, sometimes, or never. The tasks most frequently carried out concerned the duplication of materials for teachers; distribution, collection, and filing of materials; typing and duplication of materials for the school office; preparation of class materials in ethnic languages for teachers, and preparation of notices to go home in ethnic languages. An interesting finding however, was that the task the paraprofessionals in the study most enjoyed was the one that involved direct assistance of students.

In summary, available studies indicate that paraprofessionals primarily function in an instructional capacity, typically working directly with small groups or individual students on specific instructional assignments. While some time is spent on clerical tasks, this time is far less than that spent interacting with students.

4. Recommendations for Research

On the basis of the studies cited above, several recommendations and implications for further study can be offered. First, additional studies of the ways in which paraprofessionals are used in classrooms should be conducted. In addition, studies of the effectiveness of paraprofessionals in their various roles should be made. Second, several studies of the results of training of paraprofessionals (Monk 1980, Handley 1986, Johnson 1986) reported moderate success. Additional studies of the effects of training of paraprofessionals on their effectiveness should be conducted. Furthermore, the effectiveness of training programs for paraprofessionals having different levels of education and prior work experience should be examined. In addition to contributing to the body of knowledge concerning training, these data could lend empirical support to a formulation of recommendations for minimum training requirements for prospective paraprofessionals. Finally, a need exists for systematic surveys of the training needs of paraprofessionals, both as recognized by themselves and by their supervisors.

5. Implications for Practice

Students, particularly those in remedial and special education programs, spend a large amount of time in individual or small group instructional settings assisted by paraprofessionals who are, for the most part, marginally qualified and minimally trained. Thus issues of the selection and preparation of paraprofessionals need to be addressed. Specifically, minimally acceptable qualifications should be established and monitored. The importance of matching the qualifications of paraprofessionals with job requirements should be emphasized.

Consideration should also be given to the provision of training for paraprofessionals, both prior to their employment and as part of their on-going development. Systems for continuously monitoring paraprofessional job performance should be developed and implemented. Finally, insufficient attention has been given to the preparation of teachers for the task of supervising and cooperating with paraprofessionals.

See also: Teachers as Professionals; Teacher Expertise; Teachers' Roles

References

Bassett S, Woolf M 1988 How classroom assistants respond. *British Journal of Special Education* 15(2): 62–64
Birman B et al. 1987 *The Current Operation of the Chapter 1 Program*. United States Office of Educational Research and Improvement. Washington, DC
Brighton H 1972 *Utilizing Teacher Aides in Differentiated Staffing*. Pendall, Midland, Michigan
Chase C I, Mueller D J 1989 *Teacher Aides: What Do They Really Do?* Indiana University Press, Bloomington, Indiana
Clough D B, Clough B M 1978 *Utilizing Teacher Aide in the Classroom*. Charles C. Thomas Publishers, Springfield, Illinois
Evans J 1980 *Responsibilities and Training Needs of Paraprofessionals: A Survey of Those Who Work with Young Handicapped Children*. Southwestern Educational Development Laboratory, Austin, Texas
Foster L, Stockley D 1980 *A Sociopolitical Study of the Concept and Role of Ethnic Teacher Aides in Victorian State Schools*. LaTrobe University, Bundoora, Australia
Green J E, Barnes D L 1988 Do your aides aid instruction? A tool for assessing the use of paraprofessionals as instructional assistants. *Teach. Educ.* 24(3): 3–9
Handley H M 1986 *A Process Evaluation of the Assistant Teacher Project during its Third Year of Operation*. Bureau of Educational Research and Evaluation, Mississippi State University, Mississippi
Johnson J 1986 *Adaptation of Curriculum, Instructional Methods, and Materials Component Instructional Aide Program: Final Evaluation Report*. Department of Evaluation Services, Columbus Public Schools, Columbus, Ohio
Lombardo V S 1981 *Paraprofessionals Working with Young Children: Infancy through Third Grade*. Charles C. Thomas Publishers, Springfield, Illinois
McManana J 1972 *An Effective Program for Teacher–aide Training*. Parker, West Nyack, New York
Miles M B 1964 The nature of the problem. In: Miles M (ed.) 1964 *Innovation in Education*. Teachers College Press, New York
Monk C C 1980 *Evaluation of the Great Cities Training Programs, 1979–80*. Michigan Department of Research and Evaluation, Detroit Public Schools, Detroit, Michigan
Otto H J, Sanders D C 1964 *Elementary School Administration and Organization*. Appleton-Century-Crofts, New York
Renaud A J 1976 *Paraprofessionals Math Guidebook: Selection, Inservice Workshop, and Evaluation Overview*. LaMesa Spring Valley School District, California

Reynolds B P 1990 A comparative study of the relationship of teacher aides' qualifications, performance responsibilities, and interactions with teachers to the effectiveness of selected remedial and compensatory programs in South Carolina. Unpublished doctoral dissertation, University of South Carolina, Columbia, South Carolina

Sangster S 1989 *Evaluation of the Impact of the Teacher Apprenticeship Program.* North York Board of Education, Willowdale, Ontario

Satterfiel T H, Handley H M 1983 An evaluation of placing teacher aides in elementary reading classrooms of Lee County, Mississippi. Paper presented at the Annual Meeting of the American Research Association, Montreal

Shank P C, McElroy W 1970 *The Paraprofessionals or Teacher Aides: Selection, Preparation, and Assignment.* Pendall, Midland, Michigan

Thomas G 1987 Extra people in the primary classroom. *Educ. Res.* 29(3): 173–81

Turner T, Miles J 1980 *An Evaluation of Early Education Classes in Queensland.* Queensland Department of Education, Brisbane

Vasa S F, Steckelberg A L, Roning L U 1982 *A State of the Art Assessment of Paraprofessional Use in Special Education in the State of Nebraska.* Department of Special Education, Nebraska University, Lincoln, Nebraska

Welty D A, Welty D R 1976 *The Teacher-aide in the Instructional Team.* McGraw-Hill, New York

Womack S T 1987 How to maximize the use of a teacher's aide. *Clearing House* 60: 331

Woolf M, Bassett S 1988 How classroom assistants respond. *British Journal of Special Education* 15(2): 62–64

Further Reading

Goodman G 1990 Utilizing the paraprofessional in the mainstream. *Supp. for Learn.* 5(4): 199–204

Hilleard F M 1988 The non-teaching assistant in the special school. *Wessex Studies in Special Educ.* 5: 52–61

Hulbert C M, Wolstenholme F, Kolvin I 1977 A teacher-aide program in action. *Special Education: Forward Trends.* 4(1): 27–31

Leleux S A 1989 Teacher assistant moderator. *Information Technology and Learning* 12(2): 42–43

Substitute Teachers

L. W. Anderson and C. Gardner

The use of substitute teachers when regular classroom teachers are absent varies widely from country to country. Only in those countries where more pressing educational needs such as adequate school facilities, reasonable class size, relevant instructional materials, and well-trained teachers have been addressed, does the provision of substitute teachers become a factor in classroom instruction. The purposes of this entry are to: (a) discuss the relationship between teacher absenteeism and substitute teachers, (b) describe the characteristics of substitute teachers, (c) explore the problems confronted by substitute teachers, and (d) examine the costs associated with the practice of employing substitute teachers.

1. Teacher Absenteeism and Substitute Teaching

Teachers are absent from work between seven and ten percent of the days schools are in session (Brace 1990, Trotter and Wragg 1990). The causes of teacher absenteeism are as varied as the schools in which they occur. In the United States, as teachers take advantage of contract provisions for personal and professional leave, substitute teachers are used more frequently (Deay and Bontempo 1986). In the United Kingdom substitute teachers are used to provide teaching services during inservice training for regular classroom teachers (Trotter and Wragg 1990). Latin American rural teachers are often absent to take reports or attend meetings at a distant central office, while Kenyan rural teachers may take a period of time off from teaching to work at a second job. In many developing countries, teacher absence is often determined by location of teacher residence, availability of reliable transportation, existence of roads, and status of local health conditions (Montero-Sieburth 1989, Roy 1980).

Like the causes of absenteeism, ways of covering teacher absences vary widely. In more developed countries where an approved list of substitutes is available, different administrative procedures for contacting substitutes when they are needed may be used. Teachers may be responsible for securing their own substitute, principals or their designées may make the contact, or a specified district or regional office employee may call substitute teachers for several schools. The size of the district or region is often a factor in determining the routine to be followed, with larger districts or regions likely to have a more formalized, centralized procedure (Koelling 1983).

In less developed countries, substitutes are not always available. The demand for teachers in these countries has exceeded the supply as universal primary education has been adopted (Hajjar 1983). Seventy students or more is a normal class size, and schools often operate two or more shifts (British Council

1985); therefore, staffing is a major problem and qualified substitute teachers are an unaffordable and unavailable luxury. When teachers are absent, students are supervised either by a close-by teacher with a large class of his or her own or an older student (Montero-Sieburth 1989).

2. Characteristics of Substitute Teachers

Many substitutes are certified teachers who for a variety of reasons are not currently full-time employees. They may have recently moved, are taking time out to raise families, are retired, or are just taking a career break. Most substitutes who are not certified teachers have some college training or a college degree. In some cases college students preparing for a career in teaching are called upon to substitute (Morris 1981). Also called on at times are librarians, counselors, or other classroom teachers who give up planning time or cancel classes (Meara 1983). Most substitute teachers are female with a wide range of teaching experience (from 1 to 30 years) (Trotter and Wragg 1990, Rose et al. 1987).

People substitute teach for a number of reasons. Trotter and Wragg (1990) found that flexibility in scheduling and remuneration were the two most frequently cited advantages of substitute teaching. There are demands on a person's time that preclude full-time employment (such as caring for children or elderly parents). Flexibility in scheduling allows these people to be employed on a part-time basis, choosing the days they work. Also, while substitute pay is not equivalent to what full-time teachers make, it usually averages from $25.00 to $50.00 daily; this daily rate is sufficient to attract a pool of part-time workers (Koelling 1983).

A reason that prospective teachers substitute teach is that preferential consideration is often given to substitute teachers when administrators are looking for full-time teachers (Rose et al. 1987). Retired teachers and other retired people substitute because it keeps them in touch with children and schools, while allowing them time to pursue their own interests.

3. Problems Associated with Substitute Teaching

Substitute teachers are often called at inconvenient hours to go to unknown locations, to work with people they do not know, to do a job for which they may or may not be prepared (Simmons 1991). Thus, despite the advantages discussed in the section above, it is not surprising that substitutes, when surveyed, mention disadvantages as well. Certain factors make the job of substitute teacher more stressful. Having no lesson plans or poor lesson plans left for them, teaching

outside their area of certification or expertise, and being given little or no information about the students regarding seating charts, classroom rules, and schedules are the major causes of apprehension in substitute teachers (Johnson 1988).

Trotter and Wragg (1990) found that substitutes listed lack of knowledge of the school, their colleagues, and particular children with difficulties as the greatest disadvantages in substitute teaching. These studies echo the findings of Deay and Bontempo (1986) who found that substitute teachers felt they most needed information about the following items in order of preference: (a) classroom plans and procedures, (b) school rules and regulations, (c) their professional role, (d) organizing and managing learning experiences, (e) discipline procedures, (f) knowledge of learner differences, and (g) knowledge of school programs. These issues reflect concern primarily with the immediate class situation and how to maintain order and the continuity of learning. Lack of advance information about these areas contributes to less than effective use of substitute teachers' time and makes their jobs more difficult.

Substitute teaching is often a marginally rewarding activity. Clifton and Rambaran (1987) found that substitutes often experience anxiety and do not feel satisfied, competent, or recognized as part of the education community. They see themselves as holding low status and prestige in the school and feel their efforts in classrooms often are unappreciated. Also, the substitute teachers in this study mentioned that they rarely received positive feedback in their work. They felt principals and other staff members saw them as one-day employees not worth much time and effort. Because they had no real authority over student progress, they occasionally felt that students did not see them as legitimate figures in the educational setting. All of these factors combined to create problems.

4. Costs Associated with Substitute Teaching

There are two types of costs associated with substitute teaching: financial and instructional. Of the two, financial costs are easier to estimate because specific amounts of money can be traced to the cost of teacher absenteeism and hiring substitute teachers. For example, a study conducted in Chicago, Illinois, by Meara (1983) examined costs over three years and found that approximately $54,000,000 a year was spent on all costs associated with teacher absence and substitute coverage (e.g., substitute pay, sick leave, and extra compensation for staff diverted from regular duties). This figure represented about 8.4 percent of the total annual amount budget for teacher salary expenditures.

The results of a study conducted in New York City supported the Chicago findings (Willerman and McGuire 1986). In this study approximately

$71,500,000 was found to be spent on substitute teacher costs, a figure which represented approximately 9 percent of total teacher salary expenditures. Thus, the costs of substitute teachers are a major administrative concern in days of upwardly spiralling school budgets.

Large as the financial costs are, the instructional costs may be even larger and are certainly more difficult to calculate. Classroom time is defined partly in terms of the activities that occur within it; thus student achievement is directly related to the way in which time is allocated and used in classrooms (Fisher and Berliner 1985). Schools are time-oriented; time should not be wasted through idleness, boredom, or passivity (Pronovost 1986).

One of the basic problems associated with substitute teaching, whether in a more developed country where trained substitutes are available or in a less developed country where older students are called on to monitor when a teacher is absent, is that it often leads to marginally functional activity on the part of students (Koelling 1983). Gaps in the continuity of learning occur when the regular classroom teacher is absent; often busywork assignments rather than meaningful learning activities are given to keep students occupied and quiet. Given that students on average may spend as much as 10 percent of their school time with someone other than the regular classroom teacher, sizable loss of meaningful student learning experiences can be inferred as instructional costs associated with substitute teaching.

5. The Future of Substitute Teaching

Three generalizations can be offered regarding the future of substitute teaching. First, as developing countries become better able to provide quality education services, the availability of a cadre of qualified substitute teachers to maintain meaningful student learning when teachers must be absent will become a more important instructional issue. Second, ways of integrating substitute teachers into the school community are likely to result in greater commitment on the part of substitute teachers and, ultimately, improved instructional opportunities for the students they encounter. Third, as costs of providing quality education services escalate, and as the demand for higher student achievement increases, better ways for substitute teachers to maintain continuity in learning when teachers are absent must be found. These may involve having specific staff development sessions for substitute teachers, developing a separate certification system for substitute teachers, developing a district

or regional pool of trained substitutes for a specific school or content area, and/or implementing policies and practices which provide more thorough advance information for substitute teachers when they are called into service.

See also: Teachers as Professionals

References

Brace D L 1990 Establishing a support system for substitute teachers. NASSP Bull. 74(526): 73–77
British Council—English Language and Literature Division 1985 *English Teaching Profile: Malawi*. British Council, London
Clifton R A, Rambaran R 1987 Substitute teaching: Survival in a marginal situation. *Urban Educ.* 22(3): 310–27
Deay A M, Bontempo B T 1986 Helping substitute teachers contribute to school effectiveness. *Clearing House* 59(8): 359–62
Fisher C W, Berliner D C 1985 *Perspectives on Instructional Time*. Longman, New York
Hajjar H 1983 *Intensive Training Courses on Microplanning and School Mapping Report*. (Omdurman: Democratic Republic of Sudan). International Institute for Educational Planning, Paris
Johnson J M 1988 Apprehensions of substitute teachers. *Clearing House* 62(2): 89–91
Koelling C H 1983 Substitute teachers—School policies and procedures in the north central region. *Education* 104(2): 155–71
Meara H 1983 *Class Coverage in the Chicago Public Schools: A Study of Teacher Absences and Substitute Coverage*. Chicago Panel on Public School Policy and Finance, Chicago, Illinois
Montero-Sieburth M 1989 *Classroom Management: Instructional Strategies and the Allocation of Learning Resources*, BRIDGES Research Report Series No. 4. Cambridge Institute for International Development, Harvard University, Cambridge, Massachusetts
Morris J E 1981 The use of student teachers as substitutes: A survey of practices and opinions. *Teacher Educ.* 17(2): 22–32
Pronovost G 1986 Introduction: Time in a sociological and historical perspective. *Int. Soc. Sci. J.* 107: 5–18
Rose T L, Beattie J R, White R 1987 *Current Practices and Procedures in the Use of Substitute Teachers*. Office of Special Education and Rehabilitative Services, Washington, DC
Roy A 1980 School and communities: An experience in rural India. *Int. Rev. Educ.* 26(3): 369–78
Simmons B J 1991 Planning to improve the quality of the substitute teacher program. NASSP Bull 75(531): 91–98
Trotter A, Wragg T 1990 A study of supply teachers. *Res. Papers Educ.* 5(3): 251–76
Willerman M, McGuire J 1986 Substitute effectiveness in a school for behaviour disordered students. *Planning Changing* 17(4): 233–38

School–Parent Relationships

M. A. Payne

It is widely agreed that good relationships between schools and their students' parents are desirable and important, for a variety of reasons. Research from many parts of the world repeatedly suggests that parents are more willing to play an active part in their children's education than many professional educators believe. However, few countries have clearly established policies and procedures for improving home–school collaboration, at either national or regional levels. As a result, the nature and scope of such collaboration tends to vary widely between and within school districts, depending on the types of initiative taken by local educational personnel and/or research groups. However, even within individual schools, relationships are typically much stronger with some parents than with others. For this and other reasons the potential negative as well as positive outcomes of schemes to enhance parental involvement must be recognized.

1. Nature and Scope of Relationships with Parents

Positive relations with parents serve many purposes. The nature of these relationships can vary widely. There are, however, some general trends in the types of relationships that are established.

1.1 Objectives

The primary objective of establishing and maintaining good relationships with parents is to promote the motivation and academic achievement of children in school. However, other important goals may be identified, such as providing support for parents, putting parents in touch with other community resources, bringing together parents whose children have similar special educational needs, and providing incentives for parents to upgrade their own academic skills or take other action to improve their quality of life (Brantlinger 1991, San Diego County Office of Education 1986). In communities in which existing curriculum materials are very limited, students and their families may be recruited to play a critical role in the development of resource materials for schools (Schiefelbein 1991).

1.2 Types of Relationships

Home–school interaction takes several forms to meet these various objectives. Some characteristically involve much higher levels of consultation with parents than others (Davies et al. 1992, Ramsay et al. 1990).

Schools may provide assistance to families in relation to their basic responsibilities for children's health, safety, supervision, discipline, and guidance. Schools may also inform parents about services available in the wider community. Parents may be regularly informed about school programs and events, and about their child's progress, via memos, telephone calls, newsletters, report cards, and special meetings. They may also be encouraged to provide or request specific information. Modern telecommunications technology can greatly enhance this aspect of home–school relations in terms of quantity of information exchanged and proportion of parents reached. An example is the Trans-Parent School model developed in Tennessee, in the United States, which uses computer-based automated telephone dialing systems and answering machines to handle daily teacher–parent messages (Bauch 1990). Discussion of children's needs and progress may also be conducted via established schemes of school conferences, home visiting, and Parent Teacher Associations.

Parents sometimes participate in activities to assist teachers, administrators, and children in classrooms and other areas of the school. They also help organize and attend student performances and school events. At home, parents monitor or assist their children in learning activities that can be coordinated with school-based instruction, and ensure that suitable conditions are provided for homework. Activities may be relatively informal, such as reading to children or visiting places of local interest. Some projects involve parents more formally, such as the Paired Reading technique in which parents act as tutors following clearly specified procedures (Topping 1986) or the "Portage" model which involves parents of special needs children in a systematic process of assessment and teaching (United Kingdom, Department of Education and Science 1990).

Parents' views are invited when decisions affecting their children are made. They help decide the content and emphasis of school programs. At the highest level of consultation they can be involved in both planning and evaluation of curricula and other aspects of school policy.

1.3 General Trends

Economic conditions, together with prevailing political and educational ideologies, determine general views regarding the desirability and feasibility of various types of home–school relationships. In most Western societies, relationships traditionally were limited to the one-way transfer of information and advice from teachers to parents. Extensive contact between schools and parents typically occurred only when problems arose regarding a child's school attendance, behavior, or performance. During the 1970s and 1980s, however, schools began to encourage parents to come beyond the school gate on a more regular basis. At first, visits were typically limited to formal discussions of children's progress or fairly unskilled supervisory assistance to teachers. Parents were then offered opportunities to play more constructive and responsible roles in classroom learning activities and to consult with their children's teachers on a more informal and friendly basis.

In the 1990s legislative changes in several countries increased parents' rights to be involved in educational decision-making—there were calls for parental "empowerment" at all levels of home–school relationships. The calls were based on the assumption that parents as well as teachers have strengths, are able to assess their own needs, and will make responsible choices when given the opportunity (Cochran and Dean 1991). Moreover, there was growing recognition of the influence of all family members, not just parents, on children's progress in school. For all these reasons many contemporary writers have preferred the term "school and family partnerships" to those of "parent involvement" or "home–school relationships" (Epstein 1992).

2. Factors Influencing the Quality of Relationships with Parents

Even when prevailing ideologies support and promote parental involvement, relationships between schools and a large proportion of their students' parents are often minimal. A general trend for parent involvement to decline dramatically after the early elementary grades has also been reported.

2.1 Common Barriers

Several barriers to good school and home partnerships have been identified. These barriers lie in the areas of communication, culture, and personal feelings.

Communication difficulties result from the scheduling of school meetings and events at times when many parents cannot attend; from unreliable or unsatisfactory communication routes between school and home; and from teachers' lack of communication skills. This last problem is particularly acute when teachers work with low-income families or parents whose home language is different from that of the school.

Recalling their own unhappy or unsuccessful school experiences, many parents often feel intimidated by school buildings, organizational structures, and personnel. They may doubt their ability to influence either their child's educational progress (especially at high school level), or school policy more generally to any significant extent.

Insensitivity to traditional customs, or to cultural differences in multicultural societies, may cause many parents to be unwilling or unable to interact with school personnel or participate in school-based activities.

Many teachers still doubt the wisdom of involving parents in certain partnership roles, fearing they may teach things incorrectly, put students under undue pressure at home, or impose undesirable or unworkable policies on schools. They may feel that their school's policy for increased interaction with parents puts unwarranted and stressful demands on their time.

2.2 Strategies for Improvement

None of the above barriers is insurmountable. Case studies of individual schools, reports of research projects, and papers delivered at national and regional conferences have identified a wide variety of developmental and remedial strategies. The following issues seem to be particularly critical.

Schools benefit from conducting periodic systematic assessment of the type, level, quantity, and quality of their home–school relations, in order to pinpoint gaps and weaknesses. The "Home–School Relations Planner" (San Diego County Office of Education 1986) is an example of an instrument devised for this purpose.

Strategies for making parents feel more welcome in schools are often needed. Examples of such strategies include the provision of attractive and friendly settings for meetings and consultations, introducing opportunities for unscheduled discussions with staff, training in interpersonal skills for receptionists, telephonists, and secretaries, and using teachers or others as interpreters and translators. In multicultural contexts it also requires a willingness to accept the validity of diverse traditions and to experiment with culturally appropriate procedures (e.g., Tripcony 1994).

Once in school parents must feel able to contribute freely to discussions and have confidence that their contributions will be valued. At the beginning of an ambitious project in New Zealand to increase parental participation in curriculum decision-making, Ramsay et al. (1990) observed that most attempts by schools to disseminate information or promote debate of important issues involved large parent–teacher meetings at which parents were either afraid, or given little opportunity, to speak. Alternative strategies, involving use of smaller groups, location of meetings on alternative sites in the community, and opportunities for parents to practice their contributions to collaborative decision-making in nonthreatening environments (often in the absence of teachers) met with considerable success in terms of increased parental confidence and increased staff willingness to listen.

Additional priorities arise when the objectives

include parent tutoring or teaching responsibilities. Schools need to identify systematic and detailed procedures to ensure that parents understand the relevance of what they are asked to do, are properly trained to perform tasks confidently, and obtain sufficient ongoing support.

Research clearly suggests that pre- and inservice training programs must pay much more attention to equipping teachers and administrators with both the knowledge of how good relationships with parents can enhance school effectiveness and the interpersonal skills to work with families. Teachers need more knowledge of family dynamics and the organization of schools and communities. They need to learn how to empathize with parents and recognize their strengths, make the most of parent–teacher conferences, and find creative ways to involve parents in school activities (Cochran and Dean 1991). If working with parents of children with special needs, they must also be more knowledgeable about legal issues, the nature of handicapping conditions, and services provided by agencies other than schools (Brantlinger 1991).

To promote parental involvement in school decision-making, administrators and teachers need skills to chair meetings, encourage dialogue, and relieve tensions. Since this level of collaboration requires a reworking of the delicate boundary that exists between professional prerogative and parental right, care will be needed to ensure that both parents and teachers feel "empowered" rather than "deskilled." Research suggests that a systematic process emphasizing interpersonal communication and policy-shaping skills for administrators, teachers, and parents helps each group to recognize the benefits of shared decision-making and provides an orderly mechanism for transferring tightly held power among groups (Cochran and Dean 1991, Ramsay et al. 1990). Additionally, carefully constructed inservice courses are needed which provide opportunities for analyzing successes and failures (Ramsay et al. 1990).

Schools that have low rates of parental involvement may find it difficult to initiate change by themselves. Opportunities should therefore be created for the staff of schools to meet, brainstorm, and share tested ideas. Alternatively, some projects have introduced outside personnel into schools over a more extended period to act as facilitators. In their New Zealand project, for example, Ramsay et al. (1990) imported experienced senior teachers into schools as "developers." In some cases developers merely legitimated what some teachers were already doing and empowered them to spread their practices more widely; in other cases they had the more substantial task of constructively challenging the existing school order.

2.3 Negative Outcomes

Despite widespread advocacy of the benefits of greater interaction between schools and families, possibilities for negative outcomes do exist. First, research clearly shows that almost all initiatives to date have been instigated by educators, with parental participation, at least at the initial stages, being very much on the teachers' terms. Expansion of programs in anything other than the spirit of genuine partnership therefore runs the risk of sustaining a "patronizing image of the professional expert benevolently guiding the ignorant parent" (Brantlinger 1991 p.257).

Second, there are potential dangers in expanding family support networks and using parents as teachers. An unintended consequence of increasing teachers' spheres of influence within the family can be the "deskilling" of parents by making too many suggestions as to how they might behave differently toward their children and reducing their input into decision-making regarding their child's education. Alternatively, parents who are encouraged to take on more formal responsibilities for their children's learning may end up feeling less, rather than more, competent. In the special needs situation in particular there is also the danger that overemphasis on the educative role of parents can interfere with nurturing or enjoying playful activities together (Brantlinger 1991).

Third, expansion of opportunities for home–school relationships, in the absence of sufficient effort to ensure participation of all parents, may serve to disadvantage further already disadvantaged families and groups. If the parents involved in the school process are not representative, then it may be likely that the knowledge and opinions valued by the dominant elite persist. Schools that on the surface appear to be happy, pleasant places with considerably enhanced learning may be such places because they conform to collaborative goals set by the power groups of the community (Ramsay et al. 1990).

3. Conclusion

Researchers and policymakers continue to struggle to identify key strategies for enhancing school effectiveness. The rapidly growing literature on relationships with parents attests to the critical contribution this factor is now thought to play in determining student achievement and attitudes to school. The 1990s have seen a marked upsurge of policymaker interest in this area (Palanki et al. 1992).

Nevertheless, establishment of successful programs of family–school collaboration remains to a great extent a function of the vision and dynamism of individual school principals and the willingness of teachers to accept additional responsibilities. However personally rewarding and mutually beneficial such efforts may be, greater coordination of policy and practice at local, regional, state, and national levels is essential to ensure, among other things:

(a) the provision of appropriate systematic and comprehensive pre- and inservice training programs for teachers and administrators;

(b) the establishment of guidelines for appointment of school staff to positions of responsibility for home–school liaison, the provision of additional staff to allow release of teachers for out-of-class consultation and support activities, and/or the employment of ancillary staff with particular skills (e.g., translators, community elders/ mediators); and

(c) the establishment of guidelines for provision of physical resources such as convenient and comfortable rooms in schools for parents attending meetings, and hospitality centers to facilitate parent–teacher consultations.

Issues of funding are, of course, critical. Discussing the situation in the United States, Palanki et al. (1992) noted that the potential for federal and state initiatives to be sustained and make a difference was endangered by changes in economic conditions and the inability of political leadership to agree about how to pay the bill to meet the needs that are increasingly being recognized.

For all these reasons, the need for further research is crucial. Innovative projects need to be carefully designed, implemented, and monitored, and existing practices carefully evaluated. Evaluation may be essentially objective, relating to specific outcome criteria such as levels of student absenteeism, student achievement, parental attendance at school meetings and events, or more subjective, including assessments of the views and opinions of the major participants.

In working with special needs children, for example, some professionals have estimated that parents need more services than parents themselves believe they require, and these professionals tend to assume that all forms of family outreach and intervention will prove worthwhile (Brantlinger 1991). Davies et al. (1992) noted on visits to schools that principals and staff generally assumed their outreach activities to be beneficial, but only rarely had them carefully documented and evaluated. Davies et al. also pointed to a lack of clarity and agreement about key definitions and concepts: words such as parent, family, involvement, community, collaboration, partnership, home visitors, family support, restructuring are used with very different meanings at the school level, as well as among researchers and policymakers.

Schools lack the time to pursue all possible strategies, and funding agencies do not have the money to finance them. Hence, it is critical that research informs policymakers and practitioners as to which strategies are most likely to yield the most positive outcomes, within the short and long term, within particular communities, and with particular partnership objectives in mind. It is also increasingly recognized that more

theoretical analysis of the deeper organizational issues implicated in collaborative ventures is crucial if projects are to avoid pitfalls deriving from institutional territoriality and the operation of "turf-maintaining incentives" (Crowson and Boyd 1993).

References

Bauch J P 1990 The TransParent school: A partnership for parent involvement. *Educational Horizons* 68: 187–89

Brantlinger E 1991 Home–school partnerships that benefit children with special needs. *Elem. Sch. J.* 91(3): 249–59

Cochran M, Dean C 1991 Home–school relations and the empowerment process. *Elem. Sch. J.* 91(3): 261–69

Crowson R L, Boyd W L 1993 Coordinated services for children: Designing arks for storms and seas unknown. *Am. J. Educ.* 101(2): 140–79

Davies D, Burch P, Johnson V R 1992 *A Portrait of Schools Reaching Out: Report of a Survey of Practices and Policies of Family-Community-School Collaboration.* Report No. 1, Center on Families, Communities, Schools and Children's Learning, Johns Hopkins University, Baltimore, Maryland

Epstein J L 1992 *School and Family Partnerships.* Report No. 6, Center on Families, Communities, Schools and Children's Learning, Johns Hopkins University, Baltimore, Maryland

Palanki A, Burch P, Davies D 1992 *Mapping the Policy Landscape: What Federal and State Governments are Doing to Promote Family-School-Community Partnerships.* Center on Families, Communities, Schools and Children's Learning, Johns Hopkins University, Baltimore, Maryland

Ramsay P et al. 1990 *"There's no going back": Collaborative decision-making in education.* Education Department, University of Waikato, Hamilton

San Diego County Office of Education 1986 *Strategies for Enhancing School Effectivenes: Focus on Home–School Relations.* San Diego County Office of Education, San Diego, California

Schiefelbein L 1991 *In Search of the School of the XXI Century: Is the Columbian Escuela Nueva the Right Pathfinder?* UNESCO/UNICEF, Santiago, Chile

Topping K 1986 *Parents as Educators.* Croom Helm, London

Tripcony P 1994 Completing the circle: Towards valued Aboriginal and Torres Strait Islander participation in schooling. In: Limerick B, Nielsen H (eds.) 1994 *School and Community Relations: Participation, Policy and Practice.* Harcourt Brace, Sydney

United Kingdom, Department of Education and Science 1990 *Portage Projects: A Survey of 13 Projects Funded by Education Support Grants, 1987–1989.* Her Majesty's Inspectorate, DES, London

Further Reading

Chavkin N E, Williams D L 1990 Working parents and schools: Implications for practice. *Education* 111(2): 242–48

Husén T et al. 1992 *Schooling in Modern European Society.* Pergamon Press, Oxford

Karas H 1985 *Parent Participation: Involving non-English*

Speaking Background (NESB) Parents in the Decision-Making Processes of Schools. Ministerial Advisory Committee on Multicultural and Migrant Education, Melbourne

Kellaghan T, Sloan K, Alvarez B, Bloom B S 1993 *Home Environments and School Learning*. Jossey-Bass, San Francisco, California

Krasnow J H 1990 *Improving Family–School Relationships: Teacher Research from the Schools Reaching Out Project*. Institute for Responsive Education, Boston, Massachusetts

McLeod F (ed.) 1989 *Parents and Schools: The Contemporary Challenge*. Falmer Press, Lewes

Montandon C 1991 *L'Ecole dans la vie des familles*. Report No. 32, Service de la Recherche Sociologique, Geneva

Munn P (ed.) 1993 *Parents and Schools: Customers, Managers or Partners?* Routledge, London

Payne M A, Hinds J O 1986 Parent–teacher relationship: Perspectives from a developing country. *Educ. Res.* 28(2): 117–25

Phi Delta Kappan 1991 72(5) (issue on parental involvement in schools)

Richardson B 1989 *Negotiating Your Child's Experience in the Public Schools: A Handbook for Black Parents*. The National Black Child Development Institute Inc., Washington, DC

Stacey M 1991 *Parents and Teachers Together*. Open University Press, Milton Keynes

Students and the Teaching–Learning Process

Introduction

L. W. Anderson

The teaching–learning process is often considered to be linear and unidirectional. Teachers teach; students learn. The entries in this section emphasize the student's role in learning and the impact of students on teachers and classroom teaching. The first six entries focus on what students bring to the classroom; their prior knowledge, cognitive styles, aspirations and expectations, motivation, and affective and emotional dispositions.

The next seven entries address the influence students have on teachers, the teaching-learning process, and their own learning. The topics of these entries include student roles in the classroom, student influences on teaching, student perceptions of classrooms, student cognitive processing and learning, attention in learning, academic learning time, and study habits and strategies.

In combination, these entries have two major implications for educators. First, teachers must understand their students in order to teach them well. In this regard, they may have to question some of the assumptions they make about their students. Second, instruction, in order to be effective, must be predicated on a view of students which differs greatly from the predominant view of the 1970s and 1980s. Students are not passive vessels into which knowledge is poured; rather, they are active participants in the learning process

1. Understanding Students

Quoting David Ausubel, Dochy suggests that the "most important single factor influencing learning is what the learner already knows. Ascertain this and teach him accordingly." Substantial empirical evidence supports this assertion (Dochy, Fraser). Unfortunately, this rather simple prescription is remarkably difficult to implement in practice. A major part of the difficulty stems from the complexity of "knowing." A further complication arises because

students differ widely on virtually all aspects of knowing.

1.1 The Complexity of Knowing

Knowing involves cognitive, affective, and conative elements (Saha). Cognitive knowing may be domain-specific or more generalized (e.g., metacognitive, strategic) (Dochy). It involves "knowing that" (declarative knowledge), "knowing how" (procedural knowledge), and "knowing when" (conditional knowledge) (Dochy, Winne and Butler).

Affective "knowing" includes aspirations, expectations, and ambitions (Saha) as well as the reasons students have for studying and learning (or failing to do so) (Lens). It also includes knowing about oneself and, based on that knowing, making appraisals of the likelihood of success on certain tasks and in certain situations (Boekarts). Finally, conative "knowing" translates cognitive and/or affective knowing into behavior or action (Saha).

While some "knowing" involves factual knowledge, much of what students know is subjective (Lens, Boekarts) or perceptual (Fraser). To complicate matters further, there are times when students do not know that they know something. This is referred to as "tacit knowledge" (Dochy).

1.2 Differences in Knowing

Students differ on every one of these many varieties of knowing. They differ in *what* they know, *how much* they know, and *how* they learn (Messick). They differ in *why* they study or attempt to learn. Some study to memorize the material; others to develop an understanding of it; still others to get good grades or marks (Lens, Messick).

Many but certainly not all of these differences can be attributed to at least some degree to differences in students' home environments (Fulgini and Stevenson). Parents differ in the extent to which they guide and control their children. They also differ in the amount of emotional support and control they provide for them. Finally, they differ as to how they explain their children's successes and failures.

These differences in the home environment impact on children in numerous ways. A strong parental belief in innate ability may undermine a student's motivation to study hard. When this happens, students with high ability learn they do not need to study, while students with low ability learn that studying will not benefit them a great deal (Fuligni and Stevenson). Similarly, parental influences on the type and amount of knowledge students bring to school, the amount of out-of-school assistance available to the students, and the degree to which children appreciate and value education have been identified.

The home environment effects certain characteristics or qualities of students more than others. For example, the home environment has been found to be more strongly related to expectations (that is, what students believe to be reasonable or possible) than to aspirations (that is, what students actually desire) (Saha). In addition, the impact of the home environment is quite different for children at different ages. There is some evidence, for example, that children do not differentiate effort from ability until approximately age 11 (Boekarts).

2. Students as Active, Inquiring Learners

As McCarthey and Peterson point out in their entry, much of the research on teaching and learning before the mid-1980s was based on descriptive data that indicated that students played a quite passive role in classrooms. Teachers initiated, students responded, and teachers evaluated. Since then a new role for students in classroom has emerged, based largely on shifts in thinking about how students learn and the factors that influence their learning. In their entry, Winne and Butler summarize this new view of the student succinctly.

The student is now an "active inquiring agent." *Active* means that the student is continuously involved in trying to make sense of the classroom environment and his or her place in it, as well as the task demands and the resources available to him or her to meet those demands. *Inquiring* implies that the student formulates tentative explanations to aid in this "sense making" and routinely tests them as instruction unfolds. Finally, the term *"agent"* suggests that the student does not merely observe and receive information; he or she also defines goals and seeks information to enable him or her to attain those goals. At some point, he or she may decide that the goal is unattainable or not worth the effort (Lens).

In this new conceptualization, then, students are believed to construct meaning based on what they bring to the classroom and what transpires therein. They do this by attending to certain things at the expense of others (Harischfeger), organizing the diverse elements of instruction (Mayer), and integrating these new experiences with their prior knowledge (Winne and Butler).

2.1 Implications for Students

This change in perspective is far more than semantic. It shifts the authority for knowing from the teacher to the student (McCarthey and Peterson). With this shift in authority come several responsibilities. Students must master what Winne and Butler term the "dynamics of learning from instruction." Winne and Butler use the acronym SMART to denote five strategies that must be mastered: Stimulating, Monitoring, Assembling, Rehearsing, and Translating. While Mayer suggests a slightly different set of strategies (i.e., summarization, text-structuring, and question-asking) and McCarthey and Peterson still another (i.e., summarizing, self-questioning, predicting, and clarifying), there is substantial overlap among them.

2.2 Implications for Teachers

The shift of authority for learning from teachers to students does not minimize the responsibility of teachers, it merely changes it. Teachers have different responsibilities, not fewer. Mayer hints at this changed responsibility when he states: "Students are expected to become professional learners, but they are rarely given any training in how to learn." Teachers must provide this training. Fortunately, there are several ways in which they can do so.

First, teachers can model learning strategies (McCarthey and Peterson). Rather than give an answer to a problem or question, they may ask aloud, "How could I find this answer for myself?" At the end of a class period in which a great deal of material was covered, the teacher may ask, "What are the most important things that I learned today?"

Second, teachers can help students activate their existing knowledge structures (Dochy). McCarthey and Peterson suggest a three stage process by which teachers can do this when the material to be learned is presented in a text. The first is activation of prior knowledge (typically through questioning). The second is consideration of the text (typically through reading, discussions, critiques, and the like). The third is making connections of the text to the activated prior knowledge. In each stage, the teacher's role can range from direct to indirect.

Third, teachers can become increasingly aware of the ways in which they "continually change their teaching practices in response to students' needs" (Marx and Collopy). This increased awareness can be used to minimize gender or ethnic bias in their transactions with students (Marx and Collopy), maximize academic learning time (Fisher), and increase the correspondence between students' perceptions of the classroom environment and the realities of the classroom (Fraser).

3. Summary

In 1976, Benjamin Bloom proffered a model of school learning that contained four constructs: cognitive entry behaviors, affective entry characteristics, quality of instruction, and student achievement (Bloom 1976) He hypothesized that a maximum of 50 percent of the variance in student achievement could be attributed to cognitive entry behaviors, while a maximum of 25 percent each could be attributed to affective entry characteristics and quality of instruction. Furthermore, Bloom defined quality of instruction in terms of its appropriateness given a student's cognitive entry behaviors and affective entry characteristics.

With changes in terminology, the entries in this section fit within Bloom's model. The authors of the first set of entries all emphasize the importance of cognitive entry behaviors and affective entry characteristics. The authors of the second set all argue that these entry behaviors and characteristics must be activated if the quality of instruction is to be optimized.

What these entries add to Bloom's model is a more complete conceptualization of these characteristics, coupled with a more dynamic and strategic definition of them. As a consequence, researchers are now in a better position to test and apply Bloom's model than they were in the 1970s. The information contained in the entries in this section should enable them to do so.

Reference

Bloom B S 1976 *Human Characteristics and School Learning*. McGraw-Hill, New York.

(a) Student Entry Characteristics: Cognitive and Affective

Home Environment and School Learning

A. J. Fuligni and H. W. Stevenson

Among the most important influences on children's academic achievement is their home environment. Until the 1970s, interest centered on determining the relation between school learning and demographic factors, such as gender, socioeconomic status, family size, and birth order. Although demographic factors have remained of interest, the major concern is no longer the description of correlates of school learning but the analysis of the *processes* whereby demographic and other variables exert their effects. When demographic factors are studied, they are likely to be those that are relevant to contemporary families, such as mothers' working status, fathers' presence in the home, and the time spent in different types of parent–child interaction. These changes in interest have led to research that encompasses a broader range of variables than was the case in the past.

1. Perspectives

The study of the effects of home environment on school learning, once almost the exclusive province of sociologists, has captured the attention of increasing numbers of developmental psychologists (see the review by Hess and Holloway 1984). By training and tradition, sociologists are interested in sociostructural variables. Psychologists are more likely to be interested in fine-grained analyses of behavior within the home environment. Both approaches are obviously important, and their combination is leading to a more detailed picture of the rich variety of ways in which the home environment can influence children's performance at school.

Contemporary sociologists such as Marjoribanks (1979) and Alexander and Entwisle (1988) have sought to bridge the gap between sociological and psychological approaches. Supplementing their work are analyses by psychologists of how environmental factors influence psychological processes, such as children's motivation, personality characteristics, attitudes, and beliefs, and how these in turn influence learning. The comprehensive nature of this research is illustrated in the collection of studies edited by Parke (1984).

The field has also benefited from the work of developmental psychologists who have highlighted the importance of the developmental status of the child. The home environment influences learning differentially according to the child's age. Variables affecting a 6- or 7-year old's learning do not necessarily operate in the same manner after the student has been in school for several more years. Moreover, the home environment may change markedly over this period. For example, parent–child interaction declines as children grow older. Parents may spend less than half the time in caretaking and interacting with children during the middle years of childhood than they did during the preschool years (Maccoby 1984). The meaning of other variables, such as paternal absence or parental level of education, may also differ according to the age of the child. By studying academic progress in conjunction with the rest of children's development, studies have yielded a better portrayal of the complex ways in which children may benefit or are impeded in their school learning by different types of home environments.

There has also been a growing interest in examining how home environments influence school learning in different cultures. This interest has its basis in both practical and theoretical concerns. The dramatic differences in academic achievement often found among children in different cultural groups has compelled researchers to look more closely at the environments in which these children live. Of more general theoretical concern is the interest in questions of whether the findings can be generalized across and within different cultural groups. The questions are of the following types: Does the amount of time spent assisting children at home with their schoolwork have an equally positive effect in cultures that place great value on education and in those where formal education is considered to be less important? Are variables that account for differences in achievement across cultures equally effective in explaining differences in achievement within cultures?

2. Changes in the Home Environment

The last half of the twentieth century has witnessed profound changes in family life throughout the world. Transitions from agrarian to industrialized economies, rapid advances in technology and automation, and breakdowns in traditional family structures have had ineradicable effects on the home life of families in both developing and industrialized societies. Stable, hierarchical organizations of family life have in many cultures given way to radical changes in the roles of parents and children. Traditional two-parent families have been replaced by single-parent households. Even in two-parent families, many mothers work full time and are unavailable during the day. The greater independence and at times estrangement of children from their parents is heightened in many societies by the high percentage of children who work in part-time jobs while attending school. As a consequence, factors outside the home come to play more important roles in children's lives. Peers often replace parents as the primary source of values and goals, and children's learning may depend more on their own social world than on what occurs at home.

These dramatic changes have required a new conceptualization of the home environment. Rather than considering the family as a firm structure in which roles are clearly defined and the direction of influence is predominantly from parents to children, the family is viewed as a dynamic system in which there is the potential for mutual influence among all participants. This view has added vitality to research on home influences, but there is only a vague understanding of how the complex interactions among family members influence the processes and outcomes of school learning.

3. Processes of Transmission

The influence of the home environment is transmitted to children in many different ways. These range from the effects of the objective, physical environment in which the child lives to the subjective, psychological environment created by parents through their child-rearing practices. Each of these will be explored in the following sections.

3.1 The Physical Environment

Little attention has been paid to the physical environment of the home as a contributor to school progress. Homes in industrialized countries are typically equipped with reasonable amounts of space, electricity, and other modern amenities. In contrast, homes in many developing countries lack even the most fundamental necessities, including adequate food and fresh water. It is hard to imagine how children living in these unhealthy environments can learn effectively at school. In many developing countries, the dramatic differences between the home environments of rural people, who lack nearly all modern conveniences, and those in the cities are accompanied by striking differences in what children are able to accomplish in school.

Even when economic conditions are not so dire, many parents in developing countries spend significant portions of their limited resources on tuition, books, and school uniforms. Their willingness to do this offers a much stronger indication to children of how their parents value education than is the case in more affluent societies where these expenditures place few limitations on other aspects of family life. Providing space for study imposes little sacrifice on families in industrialized societies, but places severe restrictions on the activities of other family members when the whole family must live in one or two rooms.

Children in economically sound families that do not allocate a quiet place in the home for studying or that fail to provide their children with desks or workbooks demonstrate their family's lack of support for education. Such conditions are less likely to occur in societies where strong emphasis is placed on education than in those where education is given a less central role in children's lives (Stevenson and Lee 1990).

3.2 The Child-rearing Climate

Explorations of the relation between the psychological climate within the family and children's development have a long tradition in research about children. One popular view is that of Baumrind (1973), who describes two important dimensions of family climates: (a) the degree of parental guidance and control; (b) the amount of emotional support and encouragement parents give to their children. A series of studies revealed small but consistent effects of child-rearing practices on children's academic performance during high school (Dornbusch et al. 1987, Steinberg et al. 1991). Students from "authoritative" households (those high in support and control) tended to have the highest grade-point averages. Their performance was better than that of students in either "authoritarian" households (those low in support and high in control) or in "permissive" households (those low in both support and control)

The relation between child-rearing and school performance is assumed to be mediated partly by the effects of child-rearing on other variables. For example, authoritative parenting is predictive of adolescents' self-reliance and feelings of autonomy. Thus, moderate amounts of parental control along with positive emotional support help to produce a sense of competence and confidence in children. These characteristics, in turn, are ones considered to be important for success in school.

Efforts have been made to ascertain whether the effects of authoritative parenting transcend cultural groups. Results from the Dornbusch et al. (1987) study of United States students suggest that the benefits are greatest for children from White households. Authoritative parenting was only slightly predictive of academic success among Hispanic-American adolescents, and not at all predictive among Asian- and African-American adolescents. Hess and Azuma (1991 p. 4) make a distinction between two modes of cultural transmission that influence the family climate: osmosis, where "nurturance, interdependence, and close physical proximity provide exposure to adult values and instill a readiness on the part of the child to imitate, accept, and internalize such values," and teaching, where "direct instruction, injunctions, frequent dialogue, and explanations are used." Japanese parents were much less willing than United States parents to assume the role of teacher. They tended to rely more strongly on modeling as the means of socialization, while parents in the United States depended upon a reward-based training strategy.

Children's success in school may depend, in part, on the extent to which mother–child interaction fits the cultural model and thereby matches the style of instruction in school. Hess and Azuma found, for example, that persistence in children, a highly admired trait among the Japanese, was significantly related to later academic achievement for Japanese children but not for children in the United States. In contrast, early independence, which is fostered in American culture, was a significant predictor for American, but not for Japanese children.

3.3 Parental Involvement

As children with increasingly diverse family backgrounds have begun to attend school, discord between the values and goals espoused by parents and by the schools has increased. For example, parents in many indigenous cultural groups appear to believe that a quiet child is preferable to a talkative one and may rely more closely on modeling and other nonverbal forms of instruction in teaching their children. Teachers at school, on the other hand, expect children to be able to express themselves verbally, and their teaching style relies heavily on verbal instruction. In attempting to reduce this discord between styles of teaching, efforts have been made to involve parents more closely in the activities of the school.

The degree of parental involvement varies widely. In some cases, teachers simply want to inform parents about their educational procedures and practices. In other cases, increased parental involvement means that parents are urged to become familiar with their children's daily assignments and progress. This may consist of attending parent–teacher meetings or of communicating daily with the teacher through the notebooks children carry back and forth between home and school. In still other cases, parents are expected to assume direct responsibility for establishing educational policies.

While the benefits of parental involvement in their children's education seem obvious, there has been little research to document the utility of the various forms this can take. Typical of the research that has been reported is the study of Stevenson and Baker (1987), who found that the extent to which parents were involved in school activities, such as parent–teacher organizations and parent–teacher conferences, was positively related to children's school performance. Involvement was greater among parents of younger children and among more highly educated mothers.

3.4 Cognitive Stimulation and Academic Assistance

More direct ways in which the home environment can influence school learning are through cognitive stimulation and assistance with schoolwork. Although in many societies these responsibilities lie with the mother, this is not always the case. In three-generation homes these tasks often become the province of grandparents; in other societies all members of the family, including siblings and other relatives, share these duties.

Despite the potential for cognitive stimulation that exists in all homes, some families do not provide their children with experiences that help assure their success in school. Efforts have been made to remedy these deficiencies by instructing parents about ways in which they can help their children, by talking with them, reading stories, providing toys, and playing games. In some programs, mothers also participate in groups that involve instruction and mutual support. Many of these home-based intervention programs have been found to improve children's later performance in school and, at times, to enhance their cognitive functioning (McCartney and Howley 1992). For example, simply having children read to their parents improves children's reading skills beyond what is achieved through ordinary instruction at school.

Parents' provision of out-of-home experiences, including taking children shopping, visiting zoos, museums, and libraries, can also stimulate cognitive development. These opportunities for informal learning about the everyday world increase the fund of general information available to the child—a factor that has frequently been found to be predictive of skill in such subjects as reading and language arts.

The influence of direct assistance by parents on children's schoolwork is little understood. It is generally agreed that parental involvement and interest are necessary ingredients for academic success, but the form they take varies widely. Most parents in industrialized societies are capable of offering direct help to their children during the early years of elementary school, but fewer are able to do this when their children are in the later grades. Because of this, the primary way in which this interest is expressed is through the supervision of homework and the creation of an environment conducive to study. The "education moms" in many societies are distinguished not by direct forms of teaching but by the intense interest in education they convey to their children and the support they give to their children's efforts to achieve.

The value of practicing what has been learned in school by doing homework is regarded differently in different cultural groups. This was one of the most extreme differences found by Stevenson et al. (1990) in their comparisons of White, Black, and Hispanic parents. When asked about the value of increasing the amount of homework for improving elementary schoolchildren's performance, 88 percent of Black mothers, 74 percent of Hispanic mothers, but only 46 percent of White mothers answered affirmatively. This occurred despite the fact that, according to estimates made by the children's teachers, homework assignments given the previous week to children enrolled in minority schools required twice as much time to complete as the assignments given to children enrolled in all-White schools.

3.5 Beliefs and Attitudes

More subtle in their influence are the beliefs and attitudes parents hold about ways in which the home environment can influence school learning. Several reviews (Goodnow and Collins 1990, Miller 1988) have documented how beliefs held by family members affect children's development and how these, in turn, are related to their success in school.

One focus has been on parental expectations and their satisfaction with their children's academic progress. In a study of Chinese and American children and their parents, Chen and Uttal (1988) sought to discover sources of Chinese children's high achievement. Mothers were asked what score they would expect their children to obtain on a test with a maximum score of 100 and an average score of 70. Chinese and American mothers were equally positive in their expectations, but when they were asked about the score with which they would be satisfied, American mothers reported a score lower than the expected score and Chinese mothers reported a score higher than the expected score. High standards are critical in establishing high levels of motivation for achievement; children cease to be motivated to work harder when they believe they are already meeting the standards set by their parents and teachers.

Parents also hold strong beliefs about the relative contribution of innate ability and effort to children's achievement. The importance of effort is acknowledged by parents in all cultures. What differs is the degree to which parents in different cultures believe innate abilities limit what children are capable of accomplishing. As part of their cross-cultural studies of students' achievement, Stevenson and Lee (1990) examined mothers' beliefs about the roles of ability and effort in Japan, Taiwan, and the United States. Japanese and Chinese mothers gave greater emphasis to effort than did American mothers. Conversely,

American mothers placed greater emphasis on the importance of innate abilities than the Japanese and Chinese mothers. A strong belief in innate ability undermines children's motivation to study hard. Parents, teachers, and children themselves believe that highly able children do not need to study hard to perform well and that intensive study is not especially productive for children with low levels of ability.

Beliefs and attitudes about ability and effort are also related to gender differences in academic achievement, especially in mathematics. Eccles (1983) is among those who have suggested that the gap in mathematics achievement between boys and girls in high school is due primarily to beliefs about their abilities and to the types of activities and classes in which they participate. Many parents believe that boys have innately superior abilities in mathematics. They believe that boys require less effort to do well in mathematics than do girls and they hold higher expectations for boys' performance. This is true even during the elementary school years, a period when boys and girls generally perform equally well. These beliefs about gender differences in mathematics ability exist in different cultures, even in such achievement-oriented countries as Japan and Taiwan (Lummis and Stevenson 1990).

4. Conclusion

The understanding of the relation of home environments to school learning is fragmentary and incomplete, despite its great practical importance to policymakers. Moreover, what is known comes primarily from studies undertaken in the West, which are often of little value to policymakers in other societies. There is great need for further expansion of research. Refinements in the meaning of categorical variables such as socioeconomic class have occurred. However, the means by which the economic and social status of families influence school learning is far from clear. The conceptualization of the home environment has expanded to include important factors such as belief systems and parent involvement, but research dealing with such topics needs to become more systematic and coherent.

Disentangling the direct and indirect ways in which factors within the home environment influence children's learning in school will be a slow process. Nevertheless, the increase in the number of cross-cultural and longitudinal studies, the greater interest in the interplay between children's developmental status and the characteristics of the home, and the trend toward studying variables that mediate between the home environment and school learning should gradually permit more comprehensive statements about this important topic.

References

Alexander K L, Entwisle D R 1988 Achievement in the first two years of school: Patterns and processes. *Monogr. Soc. Res. Child Dev.* 53(2): 1–157

Baumrind D 1973 The development of instrumental competence through socialization. In: Pick A D (ed.) 1973 *Minnesota Symposium on Child Psychology*, Vol. 7. University of Minnesota Press, Minneapolis, Minnesota

Chen C, Uttal D 1988 Cultural values, parents' beliefs, and children's achievement in the United States and China. *Hum. Dev.* 31(6): 351–58

Dornbusch S, Ritter P, Leiderman P, Roberts D, Fraleigh M 1987 The relation of parenting style to adolescent school performance. *Child Dev.* 58(5): 1244–57

Eccles J 1983 Expectancies, values, and academic behaviors. In: Spence J T (ed.) 1983 *Achievement and Achievement Motivation*. Freeman, San Francisco, California

Goodnow J, Collins W A (eds.) 1990 *Development According to Parents: The Nature, Sources, and Consequences of Parents' Ideas*. Erlbaum, Hove

Hess R D, Azuma H 1991 Cultural support for schooling: Contrasts between Japan and the United States. *Educ. Researcher* 20(9): 2–8

Hess R D, Holloway S D 1984 Family and school as educational institutions. In: Parke R D (ed.) 1984

Lummis M, Stevenson H 1990 Gender differences in beliefs and achievement: A cross-cultural study. *Dev. Psychol.* 26(2): 254–63

Maccoby E 1984 Middle childhood in the context of the family In: Collins W A (ed.) 1984 *Development During Middle Childhood: The Years from 6 to 12*. National Academy Press, Washington, DC

Marjoribanks K 1979 *Families and Their Learning Environments: An Empirical Analysis*. Routledge and Kegan Paul, London

McCartney K, Howley E 1992 Parents as instruments of intervention in home-based preschool programs. In: Okagaki L, Steinberg R J (eds.) 1992 *Directors of Development: Influences on the Development of Children's Thinking*. Erlbaum, Hillsdale, New Jersey

Miller S 1988 Parents' beliefs about their children's cognitive development. *Child Dev.* 59(2): 259–85

Parke R D (ed.) 1984 *Review of Child Development Research. Vol. 7: The Family*. University of Chicago Press, Chicago, Illinois

Steinberg L, Mounts N, Lamborn S, Dornbusch S 1991 Authoritative parenting and adolescent adjustment across varied ecological niches. *J. Res. Adol.* 1(1): 19–36

Stevenson D, Baker D 1987 The family–school relation and the child's school performance. *Child Dev.* 58(5): 1348–57

Stevenson H W, Chen C, Uttal D 1990 Beliefs and achievement: A study of Black, White, and Hispanic children. *Child Dev.* 61(2): 508–23

Stevenson H W, Lee S Y 1990 Contexts of achievement: A study of American, Chinese, and Japanese children. *Monogr. Soc. Res. Child Dev.* 55(1,2): 1–116

Further Reading

McAdoo H P, McAdoo J L (eds.) 1985 *Black Children: Social, Educational, and Parental Environments*. Sage, Beverly Hills, California

Mussen P H, Flavell J, Markman E (eds.) 1983 *Handbook of Child Psychology. Vol. 4: Socialization, Personality, and Social Development*. Wiley, New York

Rooparnine J L, Carter D B 1992 *Parent–Child Socialization in Diverse Cultures*. Ablex, Norwood, New Jersey

Stevenson H W, Stigler J W 1992 *The Learning Gap: Why our Schools are Failing and What We Can Learn from Japanese and Chinese Education*. Summit, New York

Prior Knowledge and Learning

F. J. R. C. Dochy

The work of Ausubel was certainly not the first to direct attention to the importance of prior knowledge. However, Ausubel highlighted an important moment in the development of instructional psychology. In his basic text *Educational Psychology: A Cognitive View* he unequivocally identified the crucial role of prior knowledge in learning: "If I had to reduce all of educational psychology to just one principle, I would say this: The most important single factor influencing learning is what the learner already knows. Ascertain this and teach him accordingly" (Ausubel 1968). This involves a tripartite assumption:

(a) that prior knowledge is a very important variable in educational psychology;

(b) that the degree (of content and organization) of prior knowledge of a student must be known or measurable for the achievement of optimal learning;

(c) that a learning situation is optimal to the degree to which it is in accord with the level of prior knowledge.

Also more recent investigations into human cognition (Alexander et al. 1992, Dochy and Alexander 1995) showed that prior knowledge is an important student variable in learning. The central finding of investigations of the past fifteen years is that a key to developing such an integrated and generative knowledge base is to build upon the learner's prior knowledge. "Indeed new learning is exceedingly difficult when prior informal as well as formal knowledge is not used as a spring-board for future learning. It has also become more and more obvious that in contrast to the traditional meas-ures of aptitude, the assessment of prior knowledge and skill is not only a much more precise predictor of learning, but provides in addition a more useful basis for instruction and guidance" (Glaser and De Corte 1992 p. 1).

After a definition of the concept "prior knowledge," the entry provides a summary of representative and well-known studies supporting the impact of prior knowledge on study results and processes. Some of the main theories that account for the facilitative effect of prior knowledge on learning are then reviewed. Final-ly, implications for instructional design and classroom teaching are highlighted and emergent issues for further research indicated.

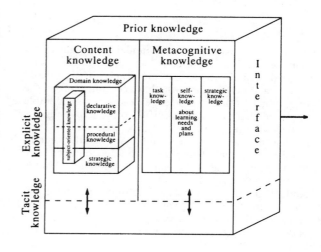

Figure 1
A map of prior knowledge
Source: Adapted from Dochy 1992

1. The Concept of Prior Knowledge

Definitions of the concept of prior knowledge, such as "what the learner knows in advance," are often too general and vague to be of much use. An exception to this is Bloom's (1982) concept "cognitive entry behaviors," used as a synonym for prior knowledge and defined as "those prerequisite types of knowledge, skills, and competencies which are essential to the learning of a particular new task or set of tasks" (p. 175). In the English-speaking world various terms are used interchangeably. "Prior knowledge" is widely used, but there are also terms such as "knowledge store," "prior knowledge state," "expertise," "expert knowledge," "preknowledge," and "personal knowl-edge," which are used as synonyms (Dochy and Alexander 1995). For the purposes of empirical re-search, prior knowledge is mostly defined as the whole of a person's actual knowledge that: (a) is available before a certain learning task, (b) is structured in schemata, (c) is declarative and procedural, (d) is partly explicit and partly tacit, (e) contains content knowledge and metacognitive knowledge, and (f) is dynamic in nature (see Fig. 1) and stored in the prior knowledge base (Dochy 1992). Research has shown that content knowledge, especially domain-specific knowledge, has most influence on learning (Alexander and Judy 1988, Weinert 1989a). In the past, most research on prior knowledge has focused on domain-specific knowledge.

Figure 1 portrays the previous definition by means of a conceptual map of prior knowledge as a snap-shot or "slice-out-of-time" representation. It should be noted that some basic assumptions about prior knowl-edge underlie this map, that is, forms of knowledge are fluid and dynamic and all forms of knowledge are interactive, which means that the presence or activa-

tion of one form of knowledge can influence any other form, directly or indirectly.

2. The Effect of Prior Knowledge on Learning Outcomes

In psychological models of educational performance, prior knowledge plays a major role (for an overview, see Haertel et al. 1983, Johanssen and Grabowski 1993). The effect of prior knowledge on learning outcomes has been shown in studies that attempt to ex-plain the variance in test scores, as well as in research that focuses on the construction of causal models.

2.1 Prior Knowledge and Variance in Post-test Scores

The fact that prior knowledge has been demonstrated to be a potentially important educational variable in the sense of contribution to post-test variance has been raised in several investigations (Tobias 1994). Knowl-edge measured prior to a course explained, on average, no less than 50 per-cent of the variance in the post-test scores. Comparable results were reported by Bloom (1982), who found correlations of 0.50 to 0.90 between pre-test and post-test scores. From these correlations, Bloom deduced the amount of explained variance. Investigations by Dochy (1992) in ecologically more valid settings (real-life classroom settings), using prior knowledge state tests, revealed that up to 42 percent of variance was explained by prior knowledge.

The results of these investigations into the effect of variables on study results indicates that prior knowl-edge explains between 30 and 60 percent (or more) of the variance in study results and that prior knowledge overrules all other variables.

2.2 Prior Knowledge and Research Using Causal Modeling Techniques

Attempts to explore causal models of educational achievement have resulted in "complex models," with a good overall fit and a multitude of significant structural coefficients, which stress once more the importance of prior knowledge. There is considerable evidence that "domain-specific" prior knowledge is usually the type of prior knowledge that affects the learning process and results. Above all, domain-specific prior knowledge should not be confused with the overall general ability called "intelligence." In the 1950s, it was still believed that more intelligent people could learn things that less intelligent people could not. A careful scrutiny of empirical findings casts doubt on this for various reasons. First, the correlation between intelligence and achievement is highly variable. Statistical meta-analyses have yielded overall coefficients that range between 0.34 and 0.51. Second, if one partials out the influence of prior knowledge, the correlation between intelligence and study result is drastically reduced to values ranging between 0.0 and 0.30 (Weinert 1989a).

Furthermore, the results from studies on metacognition show remarkable parallels with the results from intelligence studies that considered predictors of learning outcomes (r was between 0.07 and 0.20). Contrary to expectations, past research has shown that motivational variables and instructional characteristics contribute very little to the prediction of study performance.

The correlations between prior knowledge and performance remained significant even with intelligence scores partialed out. The conclusion may also be drawn that domain-specific knowledge can compensate for low intellectual ability, but high intellectual ability cannot compensate for low prior knowledge (Weinert 1989b Walker 1987).

The most important finding to emerge from causal models is the superior explanatory power of prior knowledge, the most significant path in the models. Overall, it may be concluded that the past is in fact the best predictor for the future. Differences in the knowledge base are the main source of intra-individual and interindividual differences in cognitive achievement, irrespective of chronological age or the specific domain of knowledge.

3. Effects of Prior Knowledge on the Learning Process

Effects of prior knowledge on the learning process, either positive or negative (support or hindrance), can be classified in three categories: (a) an overall facilitating effect of learning leading to better study results; (b) inherent qualities of prior knowledge (i.e., completeness, accessibility, amount, structure) influencing the facilitating effect (sometimes described as

independent effects); and (c) the effects of interaction between the first two types of effect.

3.1 Direct and Indirect Effects

The overall facilitating effect of prior knowledge is generally recognized as being the most important positive effect on learning. Some theories that give an explanation of this finding will be discussed later. Nevertheless, it should be borne in mind that not all facilitating effects are the "direct" results of prior knowledge. For the purpose of this review, a distinction can be made between:

(a) a direct effect of prior knowledge facilitating the learning process and leading to better study results;

(b) an indirect effect of prior knowledge, optimizing the clarity of study materials; and

(c) an indirect effect of prior knowledge, optimizing the use of instructional and learning time.

The different relationships can be illustrated when causal modeling is used to analyze the overall relational pattern of variables.

3.2 Inherent Qualities of Prior Knowledge Influencing the Facilitating Effect

The generally accepted facilitating effect of prior knowledge emerges from the implicit assumption that the subject has a high-quality knowledge base. In other words, the subject's prior knowledge state (PKS) has certain characteristics (i.e., qualities) as follows— it is reasonably complete and correct, of reasonable amount, of good accessibility and availability, and well-structured. Consequently, if the prior knowledge state is considered as the independent variable, and study results as a dependent variable, these qualities must be seen as intervening variables, causing interference (Fig. 2). When prior knowledge is used during

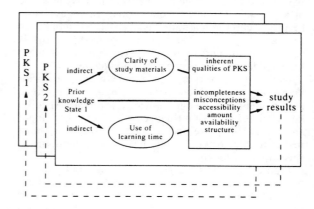

Figure 2
Interaction effects involving inherent quality effect and the facilitating effect

learning a study task, as shown in Fig. 2, the learning results are added to the original prior knowledge state (PKS 1) and designated "prior knowledge state 2" (PKS 2), which is used to start a second learning task.

Six inherent qualities of prior knowledge can be distinguished: incompleteness, misconceptions, accessibility, availability, amount, and structure. If these qualities differ from the assumed perception, the facilitating effect of prior knowledge (direct or indirect) will increase or decrease.

3.3 Interaction Effects Between Facilitating Effect and Inherent Qualities

Interaction effects occur between the inherent quality effects (IQE's) and the main facilitating effect (Fig. 2). For example, it was found that subjects from a high-knowledge group (with a high amount of relevant domain-specific knowledge) have several advantages over those with low knowledge when the other inherent qualities differ. Although the overall effect remained significant and dominant, high-knowledge students did not suffer so much from the effects caused by incompleteness and misconceptions in prior knowledge.

Such examples of interactions do suggest that there is a certain hierarchy in prior knowledge effects, in which effects with a higher classification overrule those with a lower classification. It seems obvious that the facilitating effect is at the top of this hierarchy, irrespective of whether the hierarchy is regarded as being based on the average occurrence or the average impact. There is, however, no evidence in past research to suggest a certain ranking in the lower levels.

4. Explaining the Effect of Prior Knowledge

In instructional psychology, many research attempts have been made to exclude the effect of prior knowledge as far as possible, for example by using nonsense syllables in experimental research situations. This was done in the hope—which has since been demonstrated as futile—that fundamental patterns in the learning process could thus be studied in isolation. When prior knowledge eventually did surface within this artificial and restricted framework, it was in a transfer experiment which investigated the influence of learning a series of syllable pairs on learning a second series.

However, a number of attempts have been made to manipulate prior knowledge actively or to apply it in the learning process. These attempts show that the activation of existing cognitive structures generally exerts a facilitating influence on the learning task. This empirically demonstrated phenomenon awaits a full explanation from more applied research. Among other things, it is unclear which cognitive process or processes are to be held responsible for this, and further research is necessary on how to use this facilitating effect in actual educational situations where increased return and improvement of quality are the objectives.

Nevertheless, a number of explanatory theories have been advanced, primarily on the basis of experimental research (see Dochy 1990). According to the restructuring theory, information is structured in a different way in the long-term memory (LTM). The accessibility theory states that prior knowledge increases the accessibility of knowledge and consequently reduces the load on the working memory so that more information per time unit can be processed. The selective attention hypothesis argues that attention is directed selectively at passages relevant to prior knowledge, which are subjected to a deeper level of processing. The retrieval-aid theory proclaims that prior knowledge and access to relevant cognitive structures increases retrieval. The elaboration theory states that the production of elaborations leads to multiple redundant retrieval paths in the cognitive representation.

The different theories are not necessarily mutually exclusive; they are primarily concerned with phases that follow one another during information processing. Accordingly, prior knowledge is said to influence each of these phases: the direction of attention, the encoding of information, its processing in working memory, storage in the long-term memory, and retrieval of information from long-term memory. The different theories or approaches recognize the positive influence of prior knowledge on the selection process from the knowledge base, the capacity of working memory, the elaborations carried out on new information, the storage of new information in long-term memory, and the retrieval of new information.

However, some remarks about the investigations discussed are in order. Some of the studies are characterized by a limited ecological validity. In other words, the experimental situation does not allow the generalization of the findings to real educational situations. This applies to the use of nonsense syllables and to experiments that use lists of words or one or two short sentences as the information that the student must learn. The activation of prior knowledge by short passages of text might also be given as an example here. Sometimes the information to be learnt deals with fictional subjects or non existent situations. Finally, the nature of the test (general questions or specific questions on the text, recognition or remembering, etc.) is seldom taken into account in the interpretation of the results.

5. Conclusion

The explanatory theories related to the effect of prior knowledge can mainly be situated at the knowledge-acquisition components level of information processing. This means that sifting out relevant new information, maximizing internal coherence of knowledge structures, and comparing knowledge structures are the processes where prior knowledge plays a major role. Most of the explanatory theories are strongly linked to the structure of prior knowledge. This implies that the different components of the prior knowledge should be taken into account and can be helpful in educational settings for diagnosis and as a basis for educational support. Further, the possibilities of using prior knowledge state tests (i.e., domain-specific tests measuring students' prior knowledge state) and knowledge profiles (i.e., plotting as a graph the raw or standardized test scores of a group or an individual on certain parameters) appear to be promising: they provide a rational basis for flexible learning, that is, for adaptation to different entry levels of students, for individualizing learning materials, and for providing individual support (see Dochy 1992, 1994).

It is clear that instruction is to be reconsidered on the basis of a new educational model of the learning process in which the overall assessment takes a central place and the students' prior knowledge state is the starting point (Glaser and De Corte 1992). According to this model (see Fig. 3), the students start by stating their learning goals. These relate to a certain part of the knowledge base (the content or the whole of a university course). After having taken a prior knowledge state test, the learning goals are reformulated (if necessary) and the students start with the appropriate learning tasks. During the learning process the students take progress tests regularly to check their progress, to determine the amount of guidance required, and to identify subsequent learning tasks (Frederiksen et al. 1990).

The trend in education to increase output and to raise student inflow creates new problems. The problem of pursuing two conflicting aims—a high output of student flow (minimum dropout) and more open access—can only be solved by taking the prior knowledge state of students into account. In this way, what appears to be a dilemma can be used to advantage.

In order to take the prior knowledge state of students fully into account, more research is required that allows flexible adaptations in the course materials to students' knowledge profiles, for example by using electronic learning systems. In the near future, research as well as educational practice, will have to focus on:

(a) refining the assessment procedures to grasp the full nature of a student's prior knowledge state;

(b) incorporating prior knowledge state tests as a recurrent feature in courses and curricula; and

(c) extending the feedback function of support provisions by making use of the information obtained by prior knowledge state tests and knowledge profiles.

See also: Cognitive Development Theories of Teaching

References

Alexander P A, Judy J E 1988 The interaction of domain-specific and strategic knowledge in academic performance. *Rev. Educ. Res.* 58: 375–404

Alexander P A, Kulikowich J A, Schulze S K 1992 How subject-matter knowledge affects recall and intertest. Paper presented at the XXV International Congress of Psychology, Brussels

Ausubel D P 1968 *Educational Psychology: A Cognitive View.* Holt, Rinehart and Winston, New York

Bloom B S 1982 *Human Characteristics and School Learning.* McGraw-Hill, New York

Dochy F J R C 1990 Instructional implications of recent research and empirically based theories on the effect of prior knowledge on learning. In: Pieters J M, Breuer K, Simons P R J (eds.) 1990 *Learning Environments* (Recent Research in Psychology Series) Springer-Verlag, Berlin

Dochy F J R C 1992 *Assessment of Prior Knowledge as a Determinant for Future Learning: The Use of Prior Knowledge State Tests and Knowledge Profiles.* Lemma, Utrecht and Jessica Kingsley, London

Dochy F J R C, Alexander PA 1995 Mapping prior knowledge: A framework for discussion among researchers. *Eur. J. Psychol. Educ.* 10(1)

Frederiksen N, Glaser R, Lesgold A, Shafro M G 1990 *Diagnostic Monitoring of Skill and Knowledge Acquisition.* LEA, Hillsdale, New Jersey

Glaser R, De Corte E 1992 Preface to the assessment of prior knowledge as a determinant for future learning. In: Dochy F J R C 1992 *Assessment of Prior Knowledge as a Determinant for Future Learning: The Use of Prior Knowledge State Tests and Knowledge Profiles.* Lemma, Utrecht and Jessica Kingsley, London

Haertel G D, Walberg H J, Weinstein T 1983 Psychological models of educational performance: A theoretical synthesis of constructs. *Rev. Educ. Res.* 53(1): 75–91

Johanssen D H, Grabowski B L 1993 *Handbook of Individual Differences Learning and Instruction.* LEA, Hillsdale, New Jersey

Tobias S 1994 Interest prior knowledge and learning. *Rev. Educ. Res.* 64(1) 37–54

Walker C H 1987 Relative importance of domain knowledge and overall attitude on acquisition of domain-related information. *Cognition and Instruction.* 4(1): 25–42

Weinert F 1989a The impact of schooling on cognitive

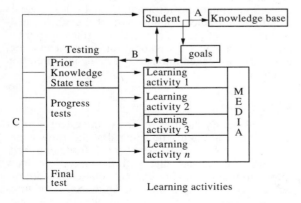

Figure 3

Components of the new model of the learning process

development: One hypothetical assumption, some empirical results, and many theoretical implications. EARLI News 8: 3–7

Weinert F (ed.) 1989b The relation between education and development. *Int. J. Educ. Res.* 13(8): 827–948

Further Reading

Alexander P A, Dochy F J R C 1994 Adults' views about knowing and believing. In: Garner R, Alexander P A (eds.) 1994 *Beliefs about Text and about Instruction with Text*. Lawrence Erlbaum Associates, Hillsdale, New Jersey

Alexander P A, Dochy F J R C in press Conceptions of knowlege and beliefs: A Euro–American comparison. *Educ. Psychol.*

Dochy F J R C 1994 Investigating one use of knowledge profiles in a flexible learning environment: Analysing students' prior knowledge states. In: Vosinadon S (ed.) 1994 *Psychological and Educational Foundations of Technology-based Learning Environments.* (NATO ASI Series F Special Program AET) Springer Veilag, Berlin

Praivat R S 1989 Promoting access to knowledge strategy and disposition in students: A research synthesis. *Rev. Educ. Res.* 59: 1–41

Schneider W 1985 Developmental trends in the metamemory memory behavior relationship: An integrative review. In: Fouest-Piessley D L, Mackinnon G E, Waller T G (eds.) 1985 *Cognition Metacognition and Human Performance* Vol 1. Academic Press, New York

Wagemans L J J M, Dochy F J R C 1991 Principles in the use of experimental learning as a source of prior knowledge *Distance Educ.* (12)85–108

Cognitive Styles and Learning

S. Messick

Cognitive styles are usually conceptualized as characteristic modes of perceiving, remembering, thinking, and problem-solving, reflective of information-processing regularities that develop in congenial ways around underlying personality trends. They are inferred from consistent individual differences in ways of organizing and processing information and experience.

Describing cognitive styles as self-consistent regularities implies that to some degree they are both integrative and pervasive. Yet they are pervasive not just in the sense of individual consistencies cutting across activities *within* broad domains such as thinking or interpersonal functioning, but often also in the sense of cutting *across* broad domains. As an instance, the cognitive style of field independence versus field dependence embraces personal/social and not merely cognitive consistencies: the field-independent person is characterized as analytical, self-referent, and impersonal in orientation, the field-dependent person as global, socially sensitive, and interpersonal in orientation (Witkin and Goodenough 1981).

1. Historical Roots

The idea that different individuals have contrasting personalities that differentially influence their modes of cognition and behavioral expression can be traced back to ancient classifications of temperament and physique. The idea is more closely linked to early twentieth-century European notions of type, as exemplified by Jung's conception of extroverted versus introverted types and thinking versus feeling types.

More recently, three major research traditions have contributed directly to work on cognitive styles. The first was differential psychology, especially the factor analysis of perceptual and intellective task performance as exemplified by the studies of Thurstone and Cattell, both of whom uncovered factorial dimensions similar to field-independence. Indeed, the first succinct formulation of the cognitive-style thesis was provided by Thurstone (1944 p. 6): "The attitudes which the subject adopts spontaneously in making the perceptual judgments in these experiments reflect in some way the parameters that characterize him as a person."

The second tradition was psychoanalytic ego psychology, wherein cognitive styles were viewed as organizing and regulating variables in ego adaptation to the environment (Gardner et al. 1959). Within this tradition, Thurstone's notion of "perceptual attitudes" was generalized first to "cognitive attitudes" and then to "cognitive controls," which are adaptive regulatory mechanisms for coping with cognitive environmental demands. The even more general term "cognitive style," which stresses organizing as well as controlling functions, was first used by Gardner (1953).

The third research tradition was the experimental psychology of cognition, with an emphasis on regularities in information-processing. Within cognitive psychology, the Gestalt movement's focus on issues of form in cognition was particularly influential because it led cognitive-style theorists such as Witkin to view individual consistencies in the manner or form of perceiving and thinking as critical psychological phenomena.

Over time, cognitive styles have been characterized

in a number of distinct but overlapping ways (Messick 1984). One way, as was seen, is to view cognitive styles as self-consistent characteristic modes of cognition. Another way views them as individual differences in structural properties of the cognitive system itself, such as degree of differentiation, of discrimination or articulation, and of hierarchic integration of cognitive units, which together comprise the style of cognitive complexity versus simplicity (Messick 1976). Another viewpoint conceives of styles as consistent intra-individual contrasts of abilities or of cognitive controls, as in converging versus diverging styles of thinking (Hudson 1968). Still other conceptions define cognitive styles as enduring preferences for different ways of conceptualizing and organizing the stimulus world; as preferred or habitual decision-making strategies; or, as differential preference (or facility) for processing different forms of information. As a final instance, cognitive styles are viewed as cognitive manifestations of underlying personality structures.

Since these various characterizations are overlapping rather than mutually exclusive, a core conceptualization is derived by playing down some features and emphasizing others in accord with empirical findings and theoretical rationales. This core conceptualization is best described by contrasting cognitive styles with intellective abilities and cognitive strategies so as to highlight their differential implications for learning.

2. Cognitive Styles versus Abilities and Strategies

In contrast with intellective abilities, which refer to the content and level of cognition (the questions of What? and How much?), cognitive styles refer to the manner or mode of cognition (the question of How?). Moreover, abilities are unipolar and value-directional (high amounts of ability are always preferable to low amounts and are uniformly more adaptive), while cognitive styles are typically bipolar and value-differentiated (each pole of a style dimension has different adaptive implications). Cognitive styles also differ from abilities in their breadth of coverage and pervasiveness of application. By and large, an ability is specific to a particular domain of content or function, such as verbal, numerical, or spatial ability or fluency and memory ability. A cognitive style, in contrast, cuts across domains of ability, personality, and interpersonal functioning.

In contrast with cognitive strategies, which refer to conscious decisions among alternative approaches as a function of task requirements and situational constraints, cognitive styles are spontaneously applied without conscious consideration or choice in a wide variety of situations having similar information-processing requirements. In comparison to styles, which tend to be stable and relatively pervasive across diverse areas, strategies are likely to be more amenable to change through instruction and training. Individuals may not only learn to use a variety of problem-solving and learning strategies that are consonant with their cognitive styles but, with effort, also learn to shift to less congenial strategies that are more effective for a particular task.

The bipolarity, pervasiveness, and value differentiation of cognitive styles are idealized properties of the core conceptualization. However, there is considerable variation in the extent to which these properties characterize particular cognitive styles in empirical research (Kogan 1983, Messick 1984). There is also controversy over whether some cognitive styles are value directional rather than value differentiated. In particular, although field-dependent persons may be interpersonally oriented as Witkin claimed, there is sparse evidence that such an orientation translates into interpersonal skill.

More generally, one might expect evidence of cross-situational generality and of value differentiation (i.e., optimal matches between styles and tasks) to be equivocal and complex. This follows because the critical match is not between the style and the task but between the style and the perception of the task and because task goals, and hence optimal strategies, vary both across people and for a given person over time. This raises the problem of the match between cognitive styles and learning tasks or contexts as well as the attendant need for stylistic flexibility in learning, which is addressed in Sect. 5.

3. Cognitive Styles and Information Processing

In addition to field independence versus field dependence and cognitive complexity versus simplicity, other cognitive styles having implications for learning include:

(a) reflection versus impulsivity, the tendency to evaluate alternative solution hypotheses versus the tendency to respond quickly with the first seemingly reasonable answer;

(b) focused scanning versus unfocused scanning or sharp-focus versus broad-focus scanning, a dimension of individual differences in the intensity and extensiveness of attention deployment;

(c) broad versus narrow categorizing, consistent preferences for broad inclusiveness as opposed to narrow exclusiveness in establishing the acceptable range for specified categories (also referred to as "category width" or "equivalence range");

(d) conceptualizing styles, individual consistencies in the utilization of particular kinds of stimulus properties and relationships as bases for forming concepts, such as the preferred use of thematic or functional relations among stimuli (thematic–relational conceptualizing) as opposed to the analysis of descriptive attributes (analytic–descriptive conceptualizing) or the inference of class membership (categorical–inferential conceptualizing);

(e) leveling versus sharpening, the tendency to minimize as opposed to exaggerate stimulus differences in memory and perception;

(f) converging versus diverging, an individual's relative reliance on convergent thinking (pointed toward logical conclusions and uniquely correct or conventionally best outcomes) as contrasted with divergent thinking (pointed toward variety, quantity, and originality of relevant output).

For further descriptions and references, see Kogan (1983) and Messick (1976, 1984). The two most widely studied cognitive styles, field independence versus field dependence and reflection versus impulsivity, continue to sustain vigorous research interest (Bertini et al. 1986, Globerson and Zelniker 1989, Wapner and Demick 1991).

These various cognitive styles can be distinguished from one another in a number of ways, but the most critical distinction relates styles to different phases of an input–output sequence of information-processing or problem-solving. For example, focused scanning versus unfocused scanning is implicated in information search, category width and conceptualizing styles in encoding, leveling versus sharpening in memory storage and retrieval, cognitive complexity versus simplicity in problem representation, field independence versus field dependence in problem-structuring and restructuring, converging versus diverging in hypothesis generation, and reflection versus impulsivity in strategy selection and decision-making. But such association is by no means one-to-one, because some cognitive styles appear to influence inforamtion-processing sequences at several points. As an instance, intensity and extensiveness of scanning affects information search of both external stimulus fields and internal fields of memory, meaning, and knowledge.

4. Learning Styles and Orientations Toward Instruction

Although acknowledged to be manifestations of cognitive styles and personality in learning and studying, a number of learning styles have been identified that are more closely tied to learning tasks than to underlying personality structures. (For references to research in this section, see Schmeck 1988.) In particular, three major learning styles or orientations

have been delineated in different research programs. In Entwistle's (1981) program, the three learning styles are labeled "meaning," "reproducing," and "achieving" orientations. They entail, respectively, a search for personal understanding, memorization, and whatever is required to attain high grades. Students with a meaning orientation are intrinsically motivated, those with a reproducing orientation are externally motivated by fear of failure, while those with an achieving style are extrinsically motivated by hope for success. Three similar dimensions isolated by Biggs (1987) are labeled "internalizing," "utilizing," and "achieving" approaches.

In related research by Pask (1976), two learning strategies and associated learning styles have been exhibited by students who were asked to learn principles and procedures well enough to teach them back to others. One strategy is labeled "holist"; consistency in its use indicates a style of comprehension learning. Comprehension learners adopt a global task approach, have a wide range of attention, rely on analogies and illustrations, and tend to construct an overall concept before filling in details. The contrasting learning strategy is labeled "serialist" and the associated style is operation learning. Operation learners adopt a linear task approach and focus attention on operational details and sequential procedures. Students who flexibly employ both strategies are called "versatile" learners.

Similar distinctions have been made by Marton (Marton and Säljö 1976), emphasizing a conclusion-oriented deep-processing approach to learning as opposed to a description-oriented shallow-processing approach. In conclusion-oriented learning, the student's intention is to understand the material and a deep-processing approach is adopted that relates arguments to evidence and ideas to personal experience. In description-oriented learning the student's intention is to memorize the material, and a shallow-processing approach is adopted focusing on discrete facts and disconnected information learned by rote.

In the terms used by Biggs (1987), Entwistle (1981), and Pask (1976), individuals with a meaning or internalizing orientation tend to adopt a deep-processing approach or a holist strategy, or both; students with a reproducing or utilizing orientation tend to adopt a shallow-processing approach or a serialist strategy, or both; and, those with an achieving orientation employ any approach that leads to high grades, deep-processing if understanding is rewarded or shallow-processing if reproduction is rewarded. Biggs demurs on the latter point, however, holding that achieving students develop a shallow approach even under conditions that should foster deep processing.

Although these learning styles clearly reflect stylistic consistencies in learning, Entwistle prefers the term orientation to refer to this style-like consistency. This usage serves to highlight his belief that stylistic consistencies in learning are heavily influenced by the student's perception of the situation, mediated by his or her motives.

5. *Optimal Learning and the Problem of the Match*

Accumulating research evidence indicates that at least some cognitive styles variously influence how students learn, how teachers teach, how students and teachers interact, and how educational and vocational choices are made. For example, teachers and students who are similar in cognitive style tend to view each other with greater mutual esteem than do those who are dissimilar. They also tend to communicate more effectively, as if they were on the same wavelength.

Cognitive styles might thus provide a basis for tailoring the mode of presentation as well as the nature and degree of substantive structure to stylistic characteristics of learners. Student style and instructional mode would be matched so as to develop, compensate for, or capitalize upon student style for the optimization of subject-matter learning. Contrariwise, depending on the educational goals, students might be deliberately confronted with instructional demands that are uncongenial to their cognitive styles so as to stimulate growth and flexibility.

There is thus a continuing tension over the relative value of matching educational treatments to learner characteristics as opposed to mismatching them. Although matching may be facilitative when the aim is to enhance immediate subject-matter achievement, mismatching may be needed when the aim is to promote flexibility and creative thinking. Such trade-offs are the essence of the problem of the match between learner styles on the one hand and the methods and materials of instruction as well as the conditions of learning on the other.

In this connection, because each direction of a cognitive style dimension has adaptive value under different circumstances, attention can be given to the possibility of effectively utilizing the positive features of both poles—as in Pask's (1976) "versatile" learners who combine comprehension and operation learning, in Hudson's (1968) "all-rounders" or intellectual "labiles" who combine converging and diverging, and in the "bicognitive" development of both field independence and field sensitivity espoused by Ramírez and Castañeda (1974). In this regard, Entwistle (1981) stressed the advantages of systematically alternating learning conditions that foster complementary modes of thought. This suggests that an important educational goal should be to develop and enhance flexibility in modes of thinking, thereby reducing to some extent the restrictiveness and preemptiveness of habitual or stylistic thought.

References

Bertini M, Pizzamiglio L, Wapner S 1986 *Field Dependence in Psychological Theory, Research, and Application*. Erlbaum, Hillsdale, New Jersey

Biggs J B 1987 *Student Approaches to Learning and Studying*. Australian Council for Educational Research, Hawthorn

Entwistle N 1981 *Styles of Learning and Teaching: An Integrated Outline of Educational Psychology for Students, Teachers, and Lecturers*. Wiley, New York

Gardner R W 1953 Cognitive styles in categorizing behavior. *J. Pers.* 22: 214–33

Gardner R W, Holzman P S, Klein G S, Linton H B, Spence D 1959 Cognitive control: A study of individual consistencies in cognitive behavior. *Psychol. Iss.* 1(4): 1–186

Globerson T, Zelniker T (eds.) 1989 *Cognitive Style and Cognitive Development*. Ablex, Norwood, New Jersey

Hudson L 1968 *Contrary Imaginations: A Psychological Study of the English Schoolboy*. Penguin, Harmondsworth

Kogan N 1983 Stylistic variation in childhood and adolescence: Creativity, metaphor, and cognitive style. In: Mussen P H, Flavell J H, Markman E M (eds.) 1983 *Handbook of Child Psychology. Vol. 3: Cognitive Development*. Wiley, New York

Marton F, Säljö R 1976 On qualitative differences in learning: I, Outcome and processes. *Br. J. Educ. Psychol.* 46(1): 4–11

Messick S 1976 Personality consistencies in cognition and creativity. In: Messick S (ed.) 1976 *Individuality in Learning: Implications of Cognitive Styles and Creativity for Human Development*. Jossey-Bass, San Francisco, California

Messick S 1984 The nature of cognitive styles: Problems and promise in educational practice. *Educ. Psychol.* 19(2): 59–74

Pask G 1976 Styles and strategies of learning. *Br. J. Educ. Psychol.* 46(2): 128–48

Ramírez M, Castañeda A 1974 *Cultural Democracy, Bicognitive Development, and Education*. Academic Press, New York

Schmeck R R (ed.) 1988 *Learning Strategies and Learning Styles*. Plenum, New York

Thurstone L L 1944 *A Factorial Study of Perception*. University of Chicago Press, Chicago, Illinois

Wapner S, Demick J 1991 *Field Dependence–Independence: Cognitive Style Across the Life Span*. Erlbaum, Hillsdale, New Jersey

Witkin H A, Goodenough D R 1981 *Cognitive Styles: Essence and Origins—Field Dependence and Field Independence*. International Universities Press, New York

Aspirations and Expectations of Students

L. J. Saha

The importance of social-psychological predispositions for behavior is widely recognized in the disciplines of psychology and sociology. These predispositions are generally treated under conceptual labels such as attitudes, values, or beliefs, and have been linked with a wide range of behaviors, such as child rearing, voting, and aspects of interpersonal behavior. One area which has been extensively studied is career ambitions and attainment.

Much research has been conducted on the educational and occupational ambitions of young people, and their influence on subsequent attainments. This body of research has included both the determinants of ambitions, and also work on the consequences of ambitions. The relationship between these career predispositions and attainments has become an important part of the study of school-to-work transitions, and in sociology, studies of education and occupational status attainment and the determinants of social mobility.

This entry focuses on a specific aspect of attitudes and behaviors, namely the career aspirations and expectations of secondary school students. The notion of career is taken to include both educational and occupational attainments. Since aspirations and expectations are related to attitudes, the entry first discusses attitudes, and the relationship between attitudes and behavior. The following sections then review the main issues and findings regarding the career aspirations and expectations of students, subsequent career attainments, and finally the policy implications arising from this research.

1. Attitudes and Behavior

1.1 Components of Attitudes

A major issue regarding attitudes is the extent to which they are related to subsequent behavior. In other words, is what people say they will do related to what they do? The empirical usefulness of the attitude construct and the measurement of attitudes is directly linked with their relationship to actual behavior. This is because attitudes are thought to consist of three components: the cognitive, the affective, and the conative. The cognitive component consists of the knowledge about the object of the attitude, or the properties attributed to the object. In addition to knowledge, attitudes also incorporate an affective component, that is, the extent to which the person likes or dislikes the object of the attitude. Finally, attitudes have a conative component which relates to intended behavior regarding an object.

1.2 Correspondence Between Attitudes and Behavior

There is no evidence to suggest that there should be a perfect correspondence between attitudes and behavior. The social-psychological literature documents correlations of between 0.30 and 0.60 for a wide range of attitudes and behaviors, with suggestions that in some circumstances the attitude–behavior link could be much lower (Oskamp 1991). In fact, McGuire (1985) argues that rarely do attitudes account for more than 10 percent of variation in behavior.

There are a number of reasons why attitudes may not correlate highly with behavior. The first is what writers call pseudoinconsistency, or the possibility that statements of intention and actual behavior have different situational thresholds. A second difficulty in evaluating the relationship between attitudes and behavior is the setting of what should be considered a high correlation between the two. In other words, according to what criteria does one determine whether a correlation of 0.30 is high or low, or that 10 percent of variance explained is an indication of the power of attitudes to explain actual behavior?

There are other explanations for inconsistencies between behavioral intentions and actual behavior. Fishbein and Ajzen (1975) list the following: (a) the instability of intentions over time, (b) other competing intentions, (c) the absence of ability or skills, (d) the unavailability of alternate behaviors, (e) perceptions of what is proper behavior, (f) expected consequences of behavior, (g) unexpected events which prevent one from carrying out the behavior, and (h) the lack of control over the behavior in question.

There are many reasons why the correlation between behavioral intentions and actual behavior is not perfect. Conversely, there is considerable evidence for intention–behavior similarity. This means that any intervention in changing attitudes will have some impact on actual behavior, or at least on the energy and effort expended in attempting to attain the object of the intentions.

2. Aspirations and Expectations as Attitudes

2.1 Aspirations and Expectations as Affective and Conative Components of Attitudes

Aspirations and expectations, as measured and analyzed in the social-psychological literature, are forms of attitude. This is especially the case with respect to educational and occupational aspirations and expectations. An educational or occupational aspiration or expectation designates a readiness to act toward the educational and occupational goals. However, aspiration can be defined as a reflection of what is thought to be socially desirable, while an expectation reflects what the person perceives as reasonable or likely as a goal, given the person's social position and understanding of the way that society operates.

2.2 Attitudes and Motivation

There are a number of similar concepts which are often related to attitudes. Ambition and motivation are two such concepts. Research on educational performance and attainments has often identified ambition and motivation as general social-psychological dimensions which explain a significant portion of the variation in educational behavior. Although ambition and motivation tend to be general concepts, they are usually operationalized in terms of some future objective or objectives which are seen as desirable by students. Most often these general notions specifically focus on educational and occupational goals which the students, at least at the time, claim to strive toward. Turner (1964) argued that the concept of ambition is related to the achievement motive, and defined it as "a desire to abandon one social position and attain another." He did not relate ambition or motivation to attitudes.

Most research into ambition and motivation variables has tended to use single indicators such as plans, aspirations, goals, expectations, and so on. Less attention has been directed toward the possibility of multiple dimensions of ambition or motivation which not only measure the desirability of objectives, but also include an assessment of the likelihood that those objectives might be achieved.

These dispositions have been seen as operative, though with continual readjustment and compromise, throughout one's social life. They are also particularly relevant for understanding the school and postschool behavior of young people. Research has shown that at relatively early ages children begin to form attitudes and values toward a wide range of objects, including the government, political parties, jobs, and sex roles. Although the knowledge upon which these dispositions are based may be naive, immature, and unstable, they nevertheless form the basis upon which future dispositional development takes place.

The difficulty with most research on these predispositions is the failure accurately to conceptualize and operationalize the concepts in question. Thus ambition, motives, aspirations, and expectations are used, sometimes interchangeably, in research into student predispositions to future actions and attainments. This has been the case with research into career aspirations and expectations among school students.

3. Aspirations and Expectations

3.1 Distinction Between Aspirations and Expectations

The distinction between aspirations and expectations does clarify the notion of career plans or ambitions. It has been argued that the class structure, reinforced by a school system which inculcates values and imparts knowledge to the advantage of the dominant class, "socializes" youth in such a way that educational and occupational choices coincide with a person's location in the class structure. What is less certain, however, is the mechanism whereby school students recognize, or have imposed on them, the structural limits to their career ambitions.

Han (1969) contended that career expectations are strongly affected by perceptions of restricted opportunity and that the difference between career wishes and career expectations reflects the "acceptance of the societal emphasis upon success and achievement," simultaneously with a recognition of the "class differential acceptance of these values" (p.681). Clearly, the distinction between aspirations and expectations is foreshadowed here.

Empirical support for the distinction between aspirations and expectations has been found in Canada, where Desoran (1977–78) concluded that occupational expectations were more strongly related to students' home background than aspirations, and that occupational aspirations tended to be higher in status than expectations. In Australia, research has found that children are socialized early both in the home and the school into recognizing the limits to their career aspirations, and the criteria which justify those limits— for example, innate intelligence, school success, and continued participation in the school system (Connell 1977, Russell and Smith 1979).

Saha (1982) based his analysis of aspirations and expectations on two questions: "If you had a completely free choice, what occupation would you choose?" and "Describe fully the occupation you expect to have during most of your working life." He found that male students had higher status occupational aspirations and expectations than females, and that the gap between aspirations and expectations is smaller for males. Furthermore, he found that occupational expectations were more predictable than occupational aspirations, which suggests that young people, in spite of having very high aspirations, do recognize the limits to what they can hope to achieve in their careers as adults. He concluded that the "realistic" expectations were more closely related to social characteristics such as socioeconomic status, sex, ethnicity, and type of school attended than were their occupational aspirations.

A related phenomenon was found in a study of career plans and expectations of final-year university students. Blau and Ferber (1991) analyzed the earnings expectations of male and female students and found that while both expected similar starting earnings, the males expected higher career earnings than the females. This difference remained even when the expected number of work years were controlled. In other words, the female students seemed to recognize limitations on their careers, or put differently, "they anticipate that they will do less well in terms of promotions" (p. 599). Furthermore, the authors show that expected lower earnings are not a factor which explains shorter expected careers.

Because of the distinction between aspirations and expectations, it is possible to understand further the conative dimension of attitudes, and the importance of social and structural variables on both attitudes and the attitude–behavior relationship. These external constraints on attitudes and behavior have been the center of continuing controversy, particularly since Fishbein and Ajzen (1975) suggested that the intention to perform an action is the best predictor of that action, and that the social and structural constraints, such as gender and social background, act directly on the formation of attitudes because of the impact of social norms.

Liska (1984) has disagreed with Fishbein and Ajzen, and has argued that the impact of background variables such as socioeconomic position and gender actually influence the resources available for realizing behavioral intentions, not the nature of the intentions themselves. This and other criticisms of the Fishbein/Ajzen model have led Liska and others to argue that the attitude–behavior model is more complex than the two authors contend, and must include the possibility of nonrecursive effects, such as behavior effects on attitudes. The findings of Carpenter and Fleishman (1987) in their study of secondary students' college plans and eventual college attendance supported Liska's argument: college attendance was affected by attitudes toward college, academic achievement, and parental encouragement, while the intentions were in turn affected by academic achievement, perceived academic ability, and perceived social norms.

3.2 Aspirations, Expectations, and Attainments

Like attitudes, the theoretical and empirical value of aspirations and expectations depends on the extent to which they are related to attainments.

Studies of either aspirations or expectations relating to educational or occupational attainment report correlations of a similar magnitude. There has been research on the effect of aspirations and expectations on educational and occupational attainment in Australia. In a small follow-up study of student educational and occupational aspirations, Poole (1982) found that 36 percent of those interviewed held the jobs they expected to have when they were 14 years old. Furthermore, Carpenter et al. (1980) found that the effect of Year 12 educational aspirations on eventual university enrollment was 0.48 for males and 0.42 for females. Their findings were consistent with the findings of comparable United States and Swedish studies and showed that "aspirations not only affect attainments but also act as key mediating variables in transmitting anterior factors into subsequent behaviours" (Carpenter et al. 1981). In a study of urban Australian youth from all capital cities, Saha (1985)

found that students' occupational aspirations (preferred occupations) exercised important independent effects (net of socioeconomic background and type of school attended) on both expected educational and occupational attainments. Carpenter and Fleishman (1987) found in an analysis of data from Queensland that the correlation between intentions and behavior was 0.62 for males and 0.50 for females.

In the case of aspirations and expectations, it is easier to make statements about what one aspires to, or expects, than it is to actually behave in such a way as to attain the objectives of those statements.

4. What Do Students Signify by their Aspirations and Expectations?

There is a wide range of interpretations about the meaning of student articulations of educational and occupational goals. Some argue that aspirations and expectations represent realistic assessments by young people as to what objectives are desirable and possible in society. In other words, these articulations reflect both the internalization of societal values, and the recognition of the processes (both in terms of advantages and obstacles) involved in realizing those goals.

Other researchers contend that aspirations and/or expectations reflect the values imbued by parents and can be interpreted as a form of family encouragement. Thus, apart from the realistic assessment of aspirations and expectations with respect to the "real world," one could regard them as surrogates for parental encouragement and a part of the "culture capital" passed on to young people in realizing eventual educational and occupational attainments.

Finally, there are those who reject the validity and reliability of aspirations and expectations and argue that they represent mere "flights of fancy." While it may be true that specific levels of education or specific occupations may be unrealistic, it remains true that the relationship between these "achievement motivations" and eventual attainments is too significant to be ignored in the study of educational performance and attainment, and of eventual career attainments.

5. Theoretical Perspectives Concerning Career Orientations

The subject of educational and occupational plans, either as aspirations, expectations, or both, has been studied extensively. The general concern of much of this research is the extent to which career orientations are linked with both educational and occupational attainments, and, given this link, the factors which determine these orientations. Research in industrial societies has shown that a variety of factors contribute to career orientations, the most important of which are the socioeconomic status background of the student, the peer group, and the school itself (Sewell and Hauser 1975, Kerckhoff 1976).

While social-psychological variables such as aspirations and expectations have been found to exert considerable influence on future occupational attainment (Otto and Haller 1979), there is less agreement about the origins and meanings of these variables, or the manner by which they influence attainment. Alexander and Cook (1979), for example, contend that career plans are, at most, a "rough sketch of some course of action." Nevertheless they also find that students who firmed up their career plans early in life had higher levels of educational and occupational achievement, which suggests that such plans are not necessarily unrealistic or fantasy based. Thus, they argue that career plans are not to be regarded solely as educational outcomes—that is, as consequences of educational experience and performance— but rather as intervening variables (along with school experience) between background factors and career attainment. This has been the conventional location of expressions of career plans in the Wisconsin status-attainment model of Sewell and his colleagues (Sewell and Hauser 1980).

There have been many theories about the formation of aspirations and expectations. It has been suggested that they represent the influence of family, peer group, and school socialization on the formation of occupational "role maps" (Musgrave 1967, Ford and Box 1967) or on the assessment of personal abilities (Blau et al. 1956, Portes et al. 1978). Others have contended that career plans are spontaneous and nonrational and the result of chance events (Jencks et al. 1972). Finally, some have suggested that they are the result of a rational matching of personality characteristics with educational and occupational demands (Holland 1973). However, no approach has been able to explain fully how young people may have a thorough knowledge of, and share, society's values about occupational status, and yet expect to attain only those occupations which are consistent with their background and gender.

6. Causal Variations in the Aspirations and Expectations of School Students

Educational performance and attainments are both the object and cause of aspirations, expectations, and later attainments. With regard to the first, the motivation with which young people approach study and other tasks related to schooling is clearly related to their school performance (grades) and eventual attainment.

Specific aspirations and expectations relate to educational objectives alone, while others relate to educational objectives only in an instrumental sense, that is, as a stepping-stone to other, more long-term objectives. Thus educational aspirations and expectations

may have meaning only in terms of career aspirations and expectations, such as for an occupation, wealth, or a particular life-style.

The ordering of aspirations and expectations with respect to educational and occupational attainments is important for research. In a causal model, the decision regarding the relative placing of these important variables can make a considerable difference both in analysis and in findings. Although it is quite likely that the actual relationship between variables is more complex than that which a linear causal model can analyze, decisions must be made about the ordering of these relationships. The ordering of the variables relates to the underlying theory which guides the research.

7. Future Directions for the Study of Aspirations and Expectations

In the end, the attitude–behavior controversy and the subsequent development of the model seem to support the distinction between aspirations and expectations. Thus, much of the inconsistency in findings might be due to a confusion, in conceptualization as well as in measurement, between aspirations, which refer to the valued norms of educational and occupational attainment, and expectations, which refer to the recognition (perceived or factual) of the social constraints which impede the attainment of aspirations. It is because of this difference that aspirations are generally higher than expectations, and why the gap between aspirations and expectations is greater for female students than male students, and possibly for other social groups as well.

It also explains why studies of aspirations, crudely defined and measured, often produce results which suggest that secondary and tertiary student aspirations far outstrip the capacity of countries to absorb them. This is especially the case in less developed countries where the gap between aspirations and prospective attainments appears the greatest (Saha 1992). Apart from the possible consequences of unfulfilled aspirations (Burris 1983, Post 1990), the problem is also due to poor measurement. Expectations more closely approximate a country's power to absorb students in those occupations which they expect to attain, rather than their aspirations, which are less constrained and more related to social and cultural desirability.

Researchers interested in the educational and occupational ambitions and life plans of students should give careful attention to the dimensions which they wish to measure. Inadvertent confusion of aspirations and expectations may result in inconsistencies which may appear to render the study of career behavioral intentions of little use in understanding career attitudes and behaviors, or in policy programs ranging from counseling to career planning. Clarification of career behavioral intentions as aspirations or expectations and the measurement of these accordingly, provide an additional direction for the development of models of attitude formation and behavioral attainments in educational and occupational careers.

References

Alexander K L, Cook M A 1979 The motivational relevance of educational plans: Questioning the conventional wisdom. *Soc. Psychol. Q.* 42(3): 202–13

Blau D M, Gustad J W, Jessor R, Parnes H S, Wilcox R C 1956 Occupational choice: A conceptual framework. *Industrial and Labor Relations Review* 9: 531–43

Blau F D, Ferber M A 1991 Career plans and expectations of young women and men: The earnings gap and labor force participation. *J. Hum. Resources* 26(4): 581–607

Burris V 1983 The social and political consequences of overeducation. *Am. Sociol. Rev.* 48(4): 454–66

Carpenter P G, Fleishman J A 1987 Linking intentions and behavior: Australian students' college plans and college attendance. *Am. Educ. Res. J.* 24(1): 79–105

Carpenter P G, Western J S, Foster W G 1980 Social background, aspirations and educational achievement among Queensland youth. In: Smith I D (ed.) 1980 *Youth, Schooling and Employment*. Australian Association for Research in Education, Melbourne

Carpenter P G, Western J S, Foster W G 1981 Origins, aspirations and attainments. In: Lawson M J, Linke R (eds.) 1981 *Inquiry and Action in Education*. Australian Association for Research in Education, Melbourne

Connell R W 1977 *Ruling Class, Ruling Culture*. Cambridge University Press, Cambridge

Desoran R A 1977/1978 Educational aspirations: Individual freedom or social justice? *Interchange* 8(3): 72–87

Fishbein M, Ajzen I 1975 *Belief, Attitude, Intention and Behavior: An Introduction to Theory and Research*. Addison-Wesley, Reading, Massachusetts

Ford J, Box S 1967 Sociological theory and occupational choice. *Sociol. Rev.* 15: 287–99

Han W S 1969 Two conflicting themes: Common values versus class differential values. *Am. Sociol. Rev.* 34(5): 679–90

Holland J L 1973 *Making Vocational Choices: A Theory of Careers*. Prentice Hall, Englewood Cliffs, New Jersey

Jencks C et al. 1972 *Inequality: A Reassessment of the Effect of Family and Schooling in America*. Basic Books, New York

Kerckhoff A C 1976 The status attainment process: Socialization or allocation? *Soc. Forces* 55(2): 368–81

Liska A E 1984 A critical examination of the causal structure of the Fishbein/Ajzen attitude–behavior model. *Soc. Psychol. Q.* 47(1): 61–74

McGuire W J 1985 Attitudes and attitude change. In: Lindsey G, Aronson E (eds.) 1985 *Handbook of Social Psychology: Vol. 2 Special Fields and Applications*, 3rd edn. Random House, New York

Musgrave P W 1967 Towards a sociological theory of occupational choice. *Sociol. Rev.* 15:33–46

Otto L B, Haller A O 1979 Evidence for a social psychological view of the status attainment process: Four studies compared. *Soc. Forces* 57 (3): 887–914

Poole M E 1982 *Youth: Expectations and Transitions*. Routledge and Kegan Paul, Melbourne

Portes A, McLeod S A, Parker R N 1978 Immigrant aspirations. *Sociol. Educ.* 51 (4): 241–60

Post D 1990 The social demand for education in Peru: Students' choices and state autonomy. *Sociol. Educ.* 63 (4): 258–71

Russell G, Smith J 1979 Girls can be doctors—can't they? Sex differences in career aspirations. *Australian Journal of Social Issues* 14 (2): 91–102

Saha L J 1982 Gender, school attainment and occupational plans: Determinants of aspirations and expectations among Australian urban school leavers. *The Australian Journal of Education* 26 (3): 247–65

Saha L J 1985 The legitimacy of early school leaving: Occupational orientations, vocational training plans, and educational attainment among urban Australian youth. *Sociol. Educ.* 58 (4): 228–40

Saha L J 1992 The effects of socio-economic development on student academic performance and life plans: A cross national analysis. *Int. J. Educ. Dev.* 12 (3): 191–204

Sewell W H, Hauser R M 1975 *Education, Occupation and Earnings: Achievement in the Early Career*. Academic Press, New York

Sewell W H, Hauser R M 1980 The Wisconsin longitudinal study of social and psychological factors in aspirations and achievements. In: Kerckhoff A C (ed.) 1980 *Research in Sociology of Education and Socialization: A Research Annual*, Vol. 1. JAI Press, Greenwich, Connecticut

Turner R H 1964 *The Social Context of Ambition*. Chandler, San Francisco, California

Further Reading

Ajzen I, Fishbein M 1980 *Understanding Attitudes and Predicting Social Behavior*. Prentice-Hall, Englewood Cliffs, New Jersey

Carpenter P G, Western J S 1989 *Starting a Career: The Early Attainments of Young People*. Australian Council for Educational Research, Hawthorn

Howell F M, Frese W 1982 *Making Life Plans: Race, Gender and Career Decisions*. University Press of America, Washington, DC

Motivation and Learning

W. Lens

Motivation is an important determinant of learning and its outcomes, as expressed in academic performances. It explains why some students enjoy school life and make the most of their school career, preparing them for a professional career and for life in general. It also explains why so-called demotivated students hate an important part of their daily life and why most of them underachieve, so harming themselves for the rest of their lives. Student motivation is a complex psychological process. There may be many personal and situational reasons why students are motivated or demotivated. This entry discusses the most important aspects of this complex situation and explicitly suggests different avenues that can be taken by teachers and parents to affect the motivation of their students and children.

1. Learning is Overdetermined

Learning and doing well in school are intentional, goal-oriented activities. As such, they are a function not only of cognitive skills and other abilities, but also of affective and motivational variables. Individual differences in the efficiency of learning processes and in their outcomes are explained by differences in abilities or capacities and in motivation. They result from an interaction between cognitive and motivational variables. Whether students learn or not, what they learn, how much time they devote to it, how efficient they are at it, and the level of proficiency they reach are all partly determined by how strongly they are motivated for their school work. The intentionality of school learning can be very complex. Students may have many and varied reasons for studying. They do it to develop their cognitive abilities; they want to know more. They do their best because they want to please the teachers and/or their parents, to be rewarded by them. They want to be successful and not to fail. They may even be highly motivated for their studies because they want to have a particular type of job or profession as adults. It is not unreasonable to assume that for most pupils and students school learning serves many purposes. Learning, then, is "overdetermined." It is instigated and sustained by different types of motivation.

In psychology there is no global theory of motivation that can explain all aspects of student motivation. Basic and more applied research has resulted in a series of more limited minitheories. Each of these theoretical approaches explains some aspect(s) or component(s) of the total motivation to learn and excel at school. This complexity or variety may be confusing for practitioners. They should consider the different theories as different glasses through which they can look at the same rich reality in the classroom or in the study. Each theory reveals different aspects of that reality and offers alternative ways to prevent or cure motivational problems. From such a practical perspective, it is important that educators—based on knowledge of individual students and their histories and family backgrounds—should be creative enough to borrow distinct elements from different theoretical approaches.

2. Motivation as a Psychological Process

Theories of human motivation can be roughly classified in two broad categories: content theories and process theories. Content theories view motivation as a more or less stable, inborn or acquired, personality characteristic (e.g., instincts, drives, needs, motives). They follow a more Aristotelian type of causal explanation: the movement (behavior is a kind of psychological movement) is attributed solely to characteristics of the moving object, in this case the acting individual, and not to the environment in which the movement takes place.

Process theories of motivation follow a Galilean type of explanation. The movement of objects is attributed to characteristics of the objects and of their environment. These theories consider motivation as a psychological process in which personality traits (e.g., needs, motives, abilities) interact with characteristics of the environment, as perceived by the individual (e.g., content and difficulty of the learning task, teachers and parents, the classroom environment). Lewin's conceptualization of behavior as resulting from the interaction between the individual personality and the perceived environment is extended to motivational processes. This implies that there are no students who will be very highly motivated for all types of subject matters or teachers, and that it is fruitless to attempt to create a learning environment in which all pupils will be optimally motivated (Atkinson 1978). Process theories suggest that both traits within the individual and situational circumstances should be taken into consideration in trying to understand, explain, and cure motivational problems and learning difficulties (Snow 1989, Snow and Swanson 1992).

3. Motivation: Explaining or Describing Behavior

Motivational theories intend to offer theoretical explanations for particular behavioral characteristics, such as the intentionality, initiation, persistence, degree of activity, and, for achievement tasks, the level of performance or efficiency. A motivational explanation requires a measure of motivation that is not based on the behavioral differences that need explanation. There is a considerable risk, certainly in daily practice, in failing to observe this rule. Parents and teachers alike often explain pupils' behavior by referring to motivational variables or processes as causes. However, the only empirical basis they have for talking about motivation are the behavioral characteristics themselves. In other words, they offer a pseudoexplanation and produce an unscientific circular argument. In such cases, motivation is not used as an explanatory concept but as a descriptive label. A teacher may, for example, observe that some students often arrive late for classes, do not do their homework, do not pay much attention to what the teacher says, that they try to disrupt the class and underperform in tests. The teacher may wonder why this should be the case, and arrive at the conclusion that they are not motivated for their studies. However, this inference does not explain the students' behavior; it only labels it. A causal explanation must prove that the students are demotivated and for what reasons, independently of the observed behavioral manifestations. Cause and effect should not be confused.

4. Motivation and Persistence in Study

Persistence in study or devoting much time to schoolwork is an important determinant of learning outcomes: practice makes perfect. Persistence is most often understood as being caused by a strong motivation to learn and to do well in school. Motivational psychology assumes a positive linear relationship between strength of motivation and persistence: the stronger the motivation to study, the more time spent studying. Schoolwork, however, should not be considered as an isolated, episodic activity, but as part of a continuous stream of behavior (Atkinson and Birch 1970). In other words, children are engaged in other activities both before and after they study. According to Atkinson and Birch's *The Dynamics of Action* (1970)—taken as a more general motivational theory—it is not only motivation that should be examined when attempting to explain persistence. The initiation and the persistence of learning activities are also dependent on the number and the strength of competing alternative motivational tendencies. Students who have a relatively strong motivation to study but who also have many and/or absorbing extracurricular interests may in fact spend less time learning (in class during lessons and at home in their study) than other students who are less motivated but who have fewer competing motivational interests. Motivational researchers and practitioners need to devote more attention to this important insight. The amount of time spent studying can be increased by enhancing the motivation to study and by decreasing the number and strength of competing motivational tendencies. Many students do not have enough time to learn because they have too many other interests.

Rollett (1987) introduced the concept of "effort-avoidance motivation" as an alternative explanation for low persistence or low "time on task." She distinguishes this type of negative motivation from low-achievement motivation and from high fear of failure or test anxiety. Rollett found that frustrating experiences during the first contacts with a particular domain may cause a domain-specific tendency to avoid effort. The goal of effort-avoiders becomes an exercise in convincing teachers and parents that they are no good as students. Rollett developed a questionnaire to measure effort-avoidance and a training program to help effort-avoiders.

The time spent on task and how efficiently it is used depend also on metamotivational skills such as volition or will. Volitional processes shield action intentions from hedonically or emotionally more tempting alternatives. They help ensure that such intentions are enacted (Halisch et al. 1987). Salomon and Globerson (1987) introduced the concept of mindfulness in learning contexts. Mindful learning requires sustained mental effort and concentration. Students can be distracted from the learning task by situational provocations and by covert cognitions. In general, it seems easier to control external distractions than internal cognitions that interfere with learning activities. The latter are dependent on rather stable personality traits. The less than optimal performances of failure-threatened or highly test-anxious students, for example, are mostly due to such interfering cognitions (when studying and taking tests). Success-oriented individuals are much less distracted by such task-irrelevant thoughts. The same difference can be found between action-oriented and state-oriented individuals (Kuhl 1986). Action-oriented individuals focus their attention on the actions that are necessary to reach an intended goal (e.g., learning or achievement goals). They persist longer in learning activities because they can more easily control internal and external difficulties and temptations. State-oriented individuals are more preoccupied with existing or desired internal or external states rather than with how to achieve or avoid those states. Such students are preoccupied with what they do not know or cannot yet do and with what they should be able to understand and master, rather than with how to bridge the gap between the two states. For them, it is more difficult to persist in a goal-oriented action. They are easily distracted.

5. Learning Goals and Performance Goals

Dweck (1989) makes a motivationally important distinction between two types of student goals: learning goals and performance goals. These correspond to the two main categories of activities that are expected from students in school: learning and performing. Most of the time students should be involved in learning activities. Their goal must then be to increase their knowledge and competencies, to understand more, and to master more complex issues. With such tasks individuals cannot fail but only improve or grow. Learning tasks offer teachers many opportunities to give positive feedback, enhancing the intrinsic motivation to learn (see Sect. 6) Consequently, there is no room for inhibitory test anxiety or fear of failure. Learning tasks arouse a task-orientation. Students are only occupied by the intellectual problem at hand, wanting to understand it and to find out how to solve it. They may well be attracted by challenging tasks.

Even the less intelligent students can improve their knowledge and problem-solving strategies. This gives them feelings of competence, which stimulate their intellectual curiosity.

At other times students have to take tests or exams. Such activities are organized in order to find out how much and how efficiently students have learned. The students' goal now becomes that of proving to themselves and to others (teachers, parents, friends, and peers) how good they are or that of concealing how bad they are. Performance tasks arouse an ego-orientation. The student is less occupied with the task than with how good or how bad he or she will look, and thus strives for success and tries to avoid failure. Performance tasks arouse achievement motivation and fear of failure (test anxiety). Failure-threatened students tend to be inhibited and defensive. Their main concern is to avoid a perception of incompetence (in their own eyes and in the eyes of important others). They avoid challenging tasks.

A potentially important problem for the intrinsic motivation to learn results from the fact that many students (and teachers) perceive learning tasks as performance tasks (Dweck 1989). They are self-oriented rather than task-oriented when they learn. Their goal is not to learn and improve their intellectual abilities, but to demonstrate to themselves and to others their high ability (or to conceal it). In a self-defensive reaction, many students therefore do not seek out challenging tasks or they invest little effort in tasks because the possible combination of high effort and low results would lead to the inference of low ability.

The perception of learning tasks as such or as performance tasks seems to be related to students' and teachers' implicit theory of intelligence (Dweck 1989). Students who conceive intelligence as a stable trait are inclined to show how much they possess. They turn learning tasks into achievement tasks. Such students and teachers believe that a person can have a high or low level of intelligence but also that intelligence cannot develop or grow. A more favorable implicit theory holds that intelligence is a cognitive ability that can be developed through exercise. Students who hold this theory are not afraid of challenging learning tasks. They want to learn, to enhance their intellectual abilities and knowledge. Learning tasks can only lead to growth, not to failure and the negative emotions that go with it. Such an attitude has a positive effect on the intrinsic motivation to learn.

6. Intrinsic Student Motivation

The total motivation to learn is a combination of intrinsic and extrinsic motivation. Children are *intrinsically* motivated when learning and performing at school are goals in themselves. They are *extrinsically* motivated when the activity is done for the sake of material or other rewards that are not intrinsically related to school learning. In this case, learning and performing well in tests and exams are instrumental activities to earn those rewards. Parents and teachers make much use of such rewards to motivate children. The behavioral effects of extrinsic rewards have been mainly studied in learning psychology (e.g., Skinnerian operant conditioning). Research on student motivation has been concerned predominantly with the different types of intrinsic motivation (Malone and Lepper 1987), even to the neglect of extrinsic motivation. (This has been much less so in research on work motivation.) Educational psychologists seem to assume that extrinsic motivation is far less important than intrinsic student motivation, but this is not the case. Most students—even those with a strong intrinsic motivation—are highly motivated by extrinsic rewards and goals.

6.1 Curiosity

Intellectual or epistemic curiosity is probably the most typical type of intrinsic motivation to learn. The desire to know and to understand intellectual problems is aroused by moderately discrepant, complex, and novel information. Familiar or simple information arouses only satiation and boredom. But learning tasks that are too complex or totally new instigate anxiety and withdrawal. A need for knowledge and information is very strong among young children, but seems to decrease with age. It is very low in many pupils from the end of primary school or the beginning of secondary education onward (about 12 years old), certainly for the type of intellectual problems and information offered in formal education. It is unclear as to what causes this decline in intrinsic curiosity. One potentially important explanation is the frequent use of extrinsic rewards in educational settings (see Sect. 7).

Teachers' own intrinsic interest in subjects and the way in which they present or introduce them have a strong effect on students' intellectual curiosity. From a motivational point of view, the common practice of punishing students for asocial or disruptive classroom behavior by giving them additional reading, writing, or mathematic assignments as home work is highly objectionable: it tells the students quite explicitly that such activities are not intrinsically interesting. By definition, a punishment is an unpleasant experience or activity.

6.2 Competence and Efficacy

The need for mastery, or at least competence and efficiency in solving challenging tasks is a second type of intrinsic motivation that is highly relevant for schoolwork. Perceptions and feelings of "self-efficacy" ("I am good at it"; "I can do it") are intrinsically motivating (Bandura 1986). People in general like to do things they are good at. (They usually also become good at things that they like to do.) Students are motivated and invest considerable effort when they expect that they can master a task. That is why challenging tasks can be more motivating. Tasks that are either too easy or too difficult do not arouse motivation. In such tasks, a person cannot expect to feel competent and efficient. Success in very easy tasks is not attributed to abilities or competence, but to the low degree of difficulty. When the task is too difficult a person does not expect to be successful. The probability of failure and hence the perception and feelings of incompetence are then very high. Students need positive feedback contingent upon good performance in order to feel competent (Weinert 1987). Success experiences require that the level of performance in the learning or achievement task is equal to or higher than the level of aspiration or the goal that was strived for, and that the outcome can be internally attributed to abilities and/or effort. Therefore, the use of an individual criterion (e.g., better than the previous performance) rather than a social criterion (e.g., other students' level of performance) in the evaluation of learning outcomes should be recommended. It permits more frequent positive feedback. With this type of criterion, a given learning or achievement task can be challenging for all students in a class, whatever the level of their cognitive abilities. Moreover, the less able students can experience growth in ability and knowledge, which will stimulate their feelings of competence and hence their intrinsic motivation. Students must learn to set realistic learning and achievement goals for themselves. Unrealistically high or low goals do not motivate.

This type of intrinsic motivation is closely related to the positive component of achievement motivation, namely, the motivation to strive for success (Atkinson 1983). Atkinson's theory of achievement motivation holds that success-oriented individuals are most motivated for achievement tasks with a medium degree of difficulty (probability of success around 0.5). For such tasks, the product of the probability of success (Ps) times the incentive value of success (1-Ps) is maximal.

Basic research on epistemic curiosity, on the need for competence or efficacy, and on achievement motivation suggests that these types of intrinsic motivation are strongly aroused in intellectually homogeneous classes. In such groups of students, teachers can set learning and achievement tasks that are optimally discrepant from what is already known and that are moderately difficult for all students. However, meta-analysis of research on the motivational and behavioral effects of homogeneous versus heterogeneous classes shows that this inference does not always hold, certainly not for low-ability groups (Slavin 1990). An alternative is to work, as often as possible, with individualized goals. This can easily be applied by parents when commenting upon their children's school results. Yet it is, of course, not easy for teachers to do so in large and very heterogeneous classes. Computer-

assisted learning can be very helpful in this regard, when students do not proceed to the next level until they have mastered tasks of the previous degree of difficulty. That means that they all receive the same amount of positive feedback (although not within the same period of time). With such programs the less able will be able to feel good about correctly solving intellectual problems. Such feelings motivate people. In many regular classes, students have to move on to more difficult tasks before they are able to handle the previous, less difficult ones.

6.3 Achievement Motivation and Test Anxiety

Traditional research on achievement motivation in educational settings has studied the positive motivation to strive for success and the negative, inhibitory tendency to avoid failure (test anxiety). Commentators have related preferences for achievement tasks of different degrees of difficulty and individual differences in persistence to individual differences in strength of achievement motivation or to the motivation to strive for success minus the motivation to avoid failure (Atkinson 1983). The resultant achievement motivation is only one component of the total task motivation, besides other sources of intrinsic and extrinsic motivation.

Important research on test anxiety has concentrated on the processes that can explain its negative effects on task performance. Research on the distinction between the cognitive (worry) and the emotional component (emotionality) of anxiety shows that the debilitating effects are mostly due to the worry aspect (interfering cognitions). Such process analyses have shown ways to treat test anxiety, to cope with it, and to avoid its negative consequences. This line of research however, has not taken into account individual differences in the need for achievement or in positive achievement motivation. Research indicates that combining measures of test anxiety and achievement motivation explains more variance than test anxiety (or the motive to achieve) by itself. Students with a high test anxiety and a low need for achievement differ from students with a high test anxiety and a high need for achievement. The latter group suffers less from their high anxiety and they perform better because their resultant achievement motivation is higher (Rand et al. 1991).

6.4 Control and Self-determination

Another type of intrinsic motivation has to do with perceptions of control and self-determination. Human beings want to control their environment and the outcomes of their actions. They want to be at the origin of what happens to them. Lack of control or choice causes demotivation. To feel like a pawn moved by external forces does not motivate (DeCharms 1984). Traditional learning environments in the classroom do not make much allowance for perceptions of control or self-determination; the teacher decides what the pupils have to do and when, and children have little choice. For many pupils this is in strong contrast with their experiences outside school, where they may enjoy considerable autonomy.

7. Attribution Theory

Students spontaneously try to explain their results, especially when a particular result was unexpected: "Why did I fail?" or "Why was I so successful in math?" They look for causes (causal attribution): "I failed because the test was much too difficult," or "I did well because I am very good in math." Such explanations are not always rational. They may be very biased in a self-defensive or self-enhancing way, attributing successes to themselves and failures to external factors. Educational research on Weiner's theory of causal attribution (Weiner 1986) has shown how students' causal explanations of successes and failures affect their emotional reactions to those outcomes, their expectations of future successes and failures, and their further motivation.

7.1 Causal Dimensions

Successes and failures can be explained by a broad variety of causal agents. Weiner developed a three-dimensional taxonomy. The first dimension concerns the locus of causality: internal versus external. The perceived or anticipated cause can be situated within the individual (e.g., abilities, effort) or in the external situation (e.g., luck, task difficulty, help from others). The second dimension concerns the temporal stability: stable versus unstable. Some causes are unstable. They may be present at one time and affect the outcome but absent the next time the same (type of) task has to be performed (e.g., luck, effort). Other causes are perceived as stable over time (e.g., abilities, task difficulty). The third dimension distinguishes controllable versus uncontrollable causes, but the question remains, controllable by whom? By me or by anyone? Weiner (1986 p.50) accepts "controllable by anyone" as the definition of controllability. Most other researchers, however, prefer to define it as "controllable by me." A student may think that a teacher's mood has an important effect on his or her marks; that the teacher can control his or her own mood, but that the student cannot control the teacher's mood. For Weiner, mood is then a controllable cause of good and bad marks.

From a motivational point of view, it is better to consider it as an uncontrollable cause. Controllable causes are only motivating when they can be controlled by the individual performers themselves. In 1978 Abramson et al. introduced a motivationally very relevant fourth dimension, the globality dimension. Causes can be more global or more specific. Global causes have an effect on success and failure in a broad variety of tasks, while specific causes only affect the outcome in a particular type of task. For example, general intelligence is a much more global cause of success and failure in intellectual tasks than is, say, the knowledge of a second language.

For the cognitive, emotional, and motivational consequences of causal attribution of successes and failures, it is not important to know if the perceived causes are objectively internal or external, stable or unstable, controllable or uncontrollable, and global or specific. What matters is how the individual perceives this.

7.2 Attributional Consequences

The affective reactions to success and failure depend on the type of outcome and on the locus dimension. Success arouses a positive affect, failure a negative affect. The emotions that are intrinsically related to success (pride) and failure (shame) require an internal causal attribution of success or failure. However, other emotional reactions are possible after an external causal attribution: success which is attributable to another's help may engender feelings of gratitude; failure attributable to someone else may lead to anger.

The stability or instability of the perceived causes affects future outcome expectancy. After an outcome (success or failure) is attributed to an unstable cause, it can be expected that the outcome in the next trial may be different from or be the same as in the previous trial. Causal attribution to a stable factor typically leads to the expectation that the outcome will be repeated and that its probability will increase: after attributing success to a stable cause, a person will expect to be successful again in the next trial and imagine that the subjective probability of success will be higher than in the previous trial. From a motivational point of view it is more optimal to attribute successes to internal, stable causes, and failures to external, unstable causes. It is always more motivating for a person if he or she can attribute outcome (success or failure) to causes under his or her control. Causal attribution theory provides a conceptual framework that can easily be used to change students' motivation via the cognitive processes of explaining success and failure.

8. Extrinsic Student Motivation

Extrinsic rewards and incentives are frequently used to increase student motivation. For students without any intrinsic interest, these are the only reasons for studying. Basic experimental research has shown that promised and salient extrinsic rewards that are exogenous to the nature of the learning and achievement task and that are given for activities for which there is already intrinsic motivation may undermine the intrinsic motivation to learn and perform well in school. They do so because they cause a shift in the locus of causality from internal to external. Students motivated only by intrinsic concerns perceive their interest in the subject matter to be the sole but important reason for studying it. When they then repeatedly receive extrinsic (material or immaterial) rewards, those rewards progressively become the perceived external reasons for learning. Thereafter the extrinsic rewards and not the intrinsic interest control the learning activities. The intrinsic interest disappears (Lepper and Greene 1978). For example, after experimental subjects received financial rewards for solving intrinsically interesting puzzles, they became less motivated to solve additional puzzles (without being paid) than subjects in a control condition who solved as many puzzles but who were not paid. Originally, subjects solved puzzles because it was fun to do so. When they then received extrinsic rewards, the rewards and not the fun become the reason or motive for doing it. It may be that the low level of intrinsic motivation among many high-school pupils is partly because of this undermining effect of the many extrinsic rewards they receive for doing their best at school and for obtaining high marks.

However, extrinsic rewards do not have this negative effect on intrinsic motivation when they are given in such a way that their controlling aspect is much less salient than their informative aspect. Extrinsic rewards can also be given in such a way that they tell students how good they are at the tasks for which the rewards are given. This can be done by making it very clear to the pupil that the quality or quantity of the reward follows from the skilled performance level and, in addition, by using rewards that are endogenous to the content or type of task that is rewarded. The rewards strengthen perceptions and feelings of competence, enhancing the intrinsic motivation (Deci and Ryan 1985). However, the ecological validity of this important empirical and theoretical work—started in the 1970s by Deci and his collaborators—needs more empirical research in real classroom settings.

Extrinsic incentives for learning may be immediate or delayed. Many students are motivated in their schoolwork by important goals they want to reach in the distant future. They are future-oriented. For them, a successful school career is highly instrumental for a successful career in life in general, and for a successful professional career in particular. The creation of a deep future time perspective by elaborating long, well-structured, and detailed behavioral plans and projects—composed of specific and challenging intermediate and final goals—can have a positive effect on early motivation (Lens 1987, Raynor and Entin 1982, Van Calster et al. 1987).

9. Conclusion

Research on student motivation reflects the complexity of this phenomenon as an interactional process with many aspects, each of which can be approached from different angles. This explains why there is no global theory of motivation for learning but several more partial approaches or "minitheories." It also explains why psychologists cannot offer a series of tailor-made solutions for the specific motivational problems of particular individual students in particular classrooms or learning environments.

However, the heterogeneity of the different approaches is less than it may seem at first sight. In almost all theoretical models, much motivational importance is given to individual cognitions or perceptions (e.g., the perception of competence and efficacy; the subjectively perceived probability of success or failure; the perceived locus, stability, and controllability of causes for success and failure). Therefore, it can be anticipated that the different theories will progressively converge around this common element, which may be labeled with Bandura's (1986) concept of "self efficacy." The motivational and behavioral effects of such cognitions are well-documented. More research is needed on their personal and situational determinants or antecedents. Such research is also a prerequisite for developing more practical training programs to prevent or cure motivational problems in learning situations.

Much research on motivation for learning has emphasized intrinsic motivation. Motivational research in educational psychology should devote more attention to the important role of extrinsic motivation for learning and to how it interacts with the different types of intrinsic motivation.

See also: Affect, Emotions, and Learning

References

Abramson L Y, Seligman M E P, Teasdale J D 1978 Learned helplessness in humans: Critique and reformulation. *J. Abnorm. Psychol.* 87: 49–74
Atkinson J W 1978 Motivational determinants of intellective performance and cumulative achievement. In: Atkinson J W, Raynor J O 1978 *Personality, Motivation and Achievement.* Hemisphere, Washington, DC
Atkinson J W 1983 *Personality, Motivation and Action.* Praeger, New York
Atkinson J W, Birch D 1970 *The Dynamics of Action.* Wiley, New York
Bandura A 1986 *Social Foundations of Thought and Action: A Social Cognitive Theory.* Prentice-Hall, Englewood Cliffs, New Jersey
DeCharms R 1984 Motivation enhancement in educational settings. In: Ames R E, Ames C (eds.) 1984
Deci E L, Ryan R M 1985 *Intrinsic Motivation and Self Determination in Human Behavior.* Plenum Press, New York
Dweck C S 1989 Motivation. In: Lesgold A, Glaser R (eds.) 1989 *Foundations for a Psychology of Education.* Erlbaum, Hillsdale, New Jersey
Halisch F, Kuhl J, Heckhausen H (eds.) 1987 *Motivation, Intention and Volition.* Springer-Verlag, Berlin

Kuhl J 1986 Motivation and information processing: A new look at decision making, dynamic change, and action control. In: Sorrentino R M, Higgins E T (eds.) 1986 *Handbook of Motivation and Cognition: Foundations of Social Bahavior*, Vol. 1. Wiley, New York

Lens W 1987 Future time perspective, motivation, and school performance. In: De Corte E, Lodewijks H, Parmentier R, Span P (eds.) 1987 *Learning and Instruction: European Research in an International Context*, Vol. 1. Leuven University Press, Leuven

Lepper M R, Greene D (eds.) 1978 *The Hidden Costs of Reward*. Erlbaum, Hillsdale, New Jersey

Malone T W, Lepper M R 1987 Making learning fun: A taxonomy of intrinsic motivations for learning. In: Snow R E, Farr M J (eds.) 1987 *Aptitude, Learning, and Instruction. 3: Conative and Affective Process Analyses*. Erlbaum, Hillsdale, New Jersey

Rand P, Lens W, Decock B 1991 Negative motivation is half the story: achievement motivation combines positive and negative motivation. *Scand. J. Educ. Res.* 35: 13–30

Raynor J O, Entin E E 1982 *Motivation, Career Striving, and Aging*. Hemisphere, Washington, DC

Rollett B A 1987 Effort avoidance and learning. In: De Corte E, Lodewijks H, Parmentier R, Span P (eds.) 1987 *Learning and Instruction: European Research in an International Context*, Vol. 1. Leuven University Press, Leuven

Salomon G, Globerson T 1987 Skill may not be enough: The role of mindfulness in learning and transfer. *Int. J. Educ. Res.* 11: 623–37

Slavin R E 1990 Achievement effects of ability grouping in secondary schools: A best-evidence synthesis. *Rev. Educ. Res.* 60: 471–99

Snow R E 1989 Cognitive-conative aptitude interactions in learning. In: Kanfer R, Ackerman P L, Cudeck R (eds.) 1989 *Abilities, Motivation, and Methodology*. Erlbaum, Hillsdale, New Jersey

Snow R E, Swanson J 1992 Instructional psychology: Aptitude, adaptation, and assessment. *Annu. Rev. Psychol.* 43: 583–626

Van Calster K, Lens W, Nuttin J 1987 Affective attitude toward the personal future: Impact on motivation in high school boys. *Am. J. Psychol.* 100: 1–13

Weiner B 1986 *An Attributional Theory of Motivation and Emotion*. Springer-Verlag, New York

Weinert F E 1987 Metacognition and motivation as determinants of effective learning and understanding. In: Weinert F E, Kluwe R H (eds.) 1987 *Metacognition, Motivation, and Understanding*. Erlbaum, Hillsdale, New Jersey

Further Reading

Ames R E, Ames C (eds.) 1984 *Research on Motivation in Education. Vol. 1: Student Motivation*. Academic Press, Orlando, Florida

Ames C, Ames R E (eds.) 1985 *Research on Motivation in Education. Vol. 2: The Classroom Milieu*. Academic Press, Orlando, Florida

Ames C, Ames R E (eds.) 1989 *Research on Motivation in Education. Vol. 3: Goals and Cognition*. Academic Press, Orlando, Florida

Covington M 1992 *Making the Grade: A Self-worth Perspective on Motivation and School Reform*. Cambridge University Press, Cambridge

Hastings N, Schwieso J (eds.) 1987 *New Directions in Educational Psychology. 2: Behaviour and Motivation in the Classroom*. Falmer Press, London

Stipek D J 1993 *Motivation to Learn: From Theory to Practice* (2nd edn.). Allyn, Bacon, W Lens, Massachusetts

Affect, Emotions, and Learning

M. Boekaerts

1. Introduction

It has become evident that effective teaching is not a question of putting information across to a group of students. It is more a question of initiating behavioral change in every student. Many authors have argued that past theories of learning and instruction have focused mainly on knowledge and skill acquisition, and have disregarded complicated but crucial aspects of human learning (e.g., the influence of affective variables on learning, learning in rich and authentic contexts). Indeed, it has become clear that students learn in dynamic social learning environments in which the various interactors continuously influence each other, thereby changing the learning situation itself as well as their own appraisal of the situation. Theories of learning that focus exclusively on information-processing theories cannot grasp this complexity. For this reason, empirical studies have been established to study the effect of affective variables on learning and performance. Such variables include beliefs about the self and about various school subjects, emotions, moods, and behavioral control mechanisms. Findings from these studies are slowly being incorporated in theories of learning and instruction. In this entry, the most important affective variables will be discussed and a model will be outlined to understand the relation between these constructs.

2. Emotions and Moods

At school, learning is embedded in an achievement context and is subject to social pressure and social comparisons. Hence, learning activities may activate specific concerns and a great variety of emotions. Emotions experienced in a classroom context can be categorized as positive (e.g., joy, excitement, pride) or negative (e.g., anxiety, anger, sadness) and as task-related or context-based. Curiously enough, much evidence is available on the effects of anxiety on learning, whereas little is known about the effect of other emotions such as anger, joy, or sadness on learning and performance. This lack of attention may be due to the fact that until the 1980s, clear theoretical frameworks were missing and measurement of emotions was complicated.

In the 1980s, several authors tried to parse emotional experiences into their separate components and they attributed a central role to the appraisal process. For example, Frijda (1986) argues that emotions are stored in memory along with declarative and procedural knowledge, and this information may be used as a gross discriminator to monitor upcoming and ongoing events in order to identify problematic and nonproblematic situations. Frijda explains that emotions are not present in a situation, but in the individual's appraisal of an event. In other words, events are made meaningful by linking them to internal representations that turn them into satisfiers (nonproblematic, benign–positive situations, associated with positive cognitions and emotions) or into annoyers (problematic, threatening situations that may cause damage, harm, or loss). This means that increased physiological arousal (e.g., increased muscle tension, rapid heartbeat, perspiration) will produce changes in readiness for action, but that the unique interpretation of the arousal, and the event that caused it, will determine the nature of the emotion and its effect on performance. Mandler's theory of mind and body (1984) has already been applied to mathematics learning by McLeod (1989). McLeod describes what happens when students' attempts at solving mathematics problems are interrupted or blocked.

2.1 Anxiety

Test anxiety research has extensively studied the subject's appraisals of achievement situations. A vast amount of evidence illustrates the detrimental effects of test anxiety on cognitive functioning (for a meta-analysis of the data, see Hembree 1988). It was demonstrated in many studies that: (a) anxiety attenuates or blocks task-relevant information processing, (b) grossly overlearned skills are not affected by anxiety, and (c) higher-order cognitive processes are impaired. These findings support the attention-deficit hypothesis of test anxiety, which postulates that anxiety competes with task-relevant information for processing capacity in working memory. This interpretation could also explain the finding that anxious students make use of inappropriate cognitive strategies for achievement. However, the literature is not very consistent here. What is clear is that anxiety acts for all students as a signal that loss of resources is unavoidable, unless something is done. Hence, feelings of increased arousal may occur in students with both high and low test anxiety, but differences occur both in the duration of the increased level of arousal, and in the way students interpret and label it.

2.2 Anger and Mood

In school, students may get angry for a variety of reasons, for example, when they are told off by the teacher, or when they are not allowed to finish an interesting task. Such situations may increase the level of physiological arousal in most students. Nevertheless, some students report only mild irritation while others indicate that they are furious. In an attempt to gain more insight into the types of situations that cause students to be angry in class, Boekaerts (1993) found that in primary and secondary school students, aged from 10 to 14, the situations that provoked most anger were those in which they believed that norms, rules, or rights were violated, and no acceptable excuses were available. However, in class it is not always possible to direct anger openly toward the source of provocation and pupils have to learn to suppress their anger in order to survive in a school context. Intense or frequent anger is often viewed as symptomatic of behavioral problems. Nevertheless, suppressing and controlling anger makes great demands on a person's processing capacity and may interfere with task performance. Moreover, research from health psychology indicates that keeping anger in the arousal system may be a serious health risk.

The effects of sadness, depression, joy, and happiness have not been studied extensively in a classroom context. Nevertheless, it may be assumed that increases in the level of arousal, labeled as sadness or joy, may evoke cognitions and feelings that compete with information-processing capacity. There is some evidence from mainstream psychology on the effect of positive and negative mood states on cognitive processing. Bower conducted many studies (see e.g., Bower 1981) which illustrate that situations that elicit a specific mood may affect the information-processing system. He reported that subjects who are in a positive mood state tend to recall positive experiences and focus on positive details in a text. They spend more time encoding information that matches their mood state, and remember later more positive things about a text. The reverse is true for negative mood states. He also described studies in which positive and negative mood states affect self-perceptions of competence, and influence problem-solving and decision-making processes. These studies allow for the inference that emotions and moods inform students that the environment in which they are working is *unproblematic* or *problematic*, and that they adapt their information processing accordingly.

3. Beliefs about the Self and about School Subjects

During their school career students develop a variety of beliefs about school, about learning and teaching, and about various subject-matter domains. These beliefs may be rather weak at first, but they may become quite strong and resistant to change. Beliefs about the self and about subject-matter domains may be regarded as the basis for motivation, and for the development of positive and negative attitudes. There is a vast literature dealing with students' beliefs about the self and their beliefs about school-related issues.

3.1 Beliefs about the Self

Beliefs about the self have been studied under different headings, including self-concept, self-efficacy, and causal attributions of success and failure. The self-concept can best be seen as a set of beliefs about the self. Important subsets of the self are conceptualizations of physical appearance and ability, emotional stability, social skills, and academic competence. Bandura (1982) argues that when a task is unfamiliar, or when individuals have reason to believe that their personal or social resources have altered in relation to a task, they make efficacy judgments. These self-conceptualizations are based on direct and vicarious experiences, on persuasion, and on self-attributions. The psychological literature offers ample evidence that individuals' beliefs about their competence and control in relation to a domain of knowledge play a major role in their performance. Students with high self-efficacy, reflected in high perceived personal control in a domain of study, score higher on tests of intelligence and on achievement tests, and they also earn better grades. The correlation between self-efficacy and achievement, which is moderately strong, is reciprocal in nature. A longitudinal study by Weinert et al. (1989) detailed that for mathematics this bidirectional relationship emerges in the middle of the sixth grade (age 11–12). Before that age, children's self-efficacy seems not to be consistently related to behavioral outcome, because children may misjudge self-efficacy due to incomplete information about what they need to learn, about their prerequisite skills, and about their ability to guide and monitor their own learning.

Beliefs about the self have also been studied in the context of attributions of success and failure. Weiner (1986) described three dimensions along which causal attributions can be classified: locus of control, stability, and controllability. For example, students who believe that they did poorly on a language test may ascribe their failure to the type of test being used (external, variable, uncontrollable) rather than to low ability (internal, stable, controllable) or lack of effort (internal, variable, controllable). At the start of elementary education children explain success and failure predominantly in terms of effort, or lack of

effort, and the second most commonly used factor is ability. Nicholls (1984) presented evidence that young children conceive of ability in a self-referenced manner as "learning through effort." Children do not clearly differentiate effort and ability until age 11. A more mature conception of ability involves a social comparison in which the effort/time required to reach a performance is taken into account. Adolescents conceive of ability as "capacity" relative to others. They determine their capacity within a domain of study by direct experiences, by comparing their performance and effort expenditure with that of their peers, and by the presence or absence of physiological symptoms. Unlike primary school students, adolescents realize that effort may compensate for low ability, thus masking true ability. This belief may lead to hiding effort and to effort avoidance.

3.2 Beliefs about Different School Subjects

Students may develop a variety of beliefs about different subject-matter domains. For example, they may see mathematics assignments as logic-based, important, and relevant, but nevertheless categorize them among the difficult school subjects, in which they have no intrinsic interests. By contrast, text comprehension may be viewed as common-sense based, important, easy to master, and intrinsically interesting. Beliefs about different school subjects have been studied under two main rubrics: attitudes and interests.

Attitudes are defined as relatively stable positive or negative feelings and cognitions about a subject area reflected in students' behavioral responses. Data on attitudes are traditionally collected by means of questionnaires, and they break down factor-analytically into different factors. McLeod (1989) argued that attitudes toward mathematics develop in two distinct ways. First, students may assign an attitude that has already been attached to a memory schema (e.g., geometry) to a new schema (e.g., algebra). Second, negative or positive attitudes may be based on a series of repeated emotional reactions to a set of mathematics tasks. In short, attitudes may be seen as quasi-automatic reactions to a subject-matter domain, and this property makes them resistant to change and difficult to measure.

Schiefele (1991) drew attention to the fact that people also develop specific relationships with different subject-matter domains, and that this relationship is reflected in their specific interest in that domain. He defines interest in a school subject as content-specific intrinsic motivational orientation, and argued that it should be distinguished from general motivational orientation and attitudes. He demonstrated that students who score high on interest want to become involved in a subject-matter domain for its own sake. For example, students who demonstrated interest in text comprehension not only recalled more information, but their cognitive strategies also reflected deep-level processing (i.e., they rehearse less, elaborate more, seek more

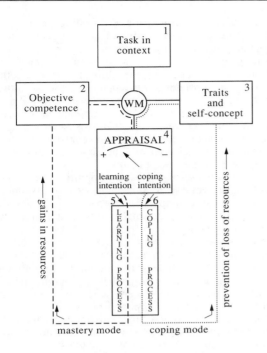

Figure 1
Heuristic model of the affective learning process

could be seen as a set of judgments about the task, combining beliefs about the self and beliefs about subject-matter domains. More concretely, students may judge how difficult the task is; how adequate their personal resources are to do the task; how much effort they will have to put in; the quality of the instructional and social context (including available instrumental and emotional support), and how attractive the task is and how eager they are to start. The net outcome of a dynamic appraisal may be expected or perceived gains in resources, expected or perceived losses in resources, or a null operation. When students do not perceive a discrepancy between the task demands and their resources to meet them, they do not expect losses in resources, and their well-being is not at stake; this is known as a null operation. By contrast, when students perceive a discrepancy between the task demands and their resources to meet them, it may elicit a threat (dominantly negative cognitions and emotions) or a challenge (dominantly positive cognitions and emotions).

Much more research is needed to explore the mechanisms whereby appraisals, concerns, interests, and emotions are linked to specific aspects of the learning process. However, it may be assumed that both null operations and challenge appraisals lead to a behavioral intention that starts or continues activity in the mastery mode (left pathway, Fig. 1). This learning-oriented pathway consists of components traditionally used to describe motivated learning. More specifically, a learning intention is formed and translated into actions (cognitive strategies and metacognitive skills) that guide the learning process and result in increased competence or perceived gains in resources. On the other hand, threat appraisals coincide with negative emotions and a decrease in well-being. Such appraisals lead to a coping intention that discontinues action in the mastery mode and starts activity in the well-being mode (right pathway, 6). When learners are on this non-learning-oriented route, their primary concern is to prevent loss in resources by using preferential coping techniques (problem-focused or emotion-focused coping) to maintain or restore well-being (see Boekaerts, in press a).

information, and engage more in critical thinking than students who display surface-level processing).

4. Appraisals, Effort, and Control Mechanisms

4.1 Appraisals

Drawing on the influential work of Lazarus and Folkman (1984) in stress research, Boekaerts (1991) describes appraisals as nonstop comparison processes between perceived task and situational demands on the one hand, and perceived personal and social resources to meet these demands on the other. She constructed a heuristic model in which appraisals are given a central position. As can be seen in Fig. 1, appraisals draw on three main sources of information. The first source of information is the perception of the task and the physical, social, and didactic context in which it is embedded (component 1). The second source of information is activated domain-specific knowledge and skills relevant to the task (component 2). The third source consists of personality traits, including a subset of the self-concept linked to emotions and attitudes (component 3). Information from these three sources is brought in working memory (WM) and used as a frame of reference to appraise learning situations, and one's own resources to deal with them. Hence, appraisals

4.2 Effort Expenditure

It has been explained that the differentiation of effort and ability as attributional concepts is essential in order to develop a realistic sense of efficacy. Helmke (1989) shed some light on the relation between self-efficacy and effort-expenditure. He reported an indirect relation between self-concept for mathematics and mathematics achievement. At the end of elementary education, students who score high on self-concept of mathematics ability invested qualitative effort which led to better grades. More specifically, these students expended mental effort during the instruction process in order to master the content of the lesson (e.g., attention, cognitive engagement, time-on-task, and school-related virtues such as diligence, circumspection, punctuality, and orderliness). By contrast, students who were low on self-efficacy invested quantitive effort, which was reflected in increasing preparation time for homework and exams. Quantitative effort led to increased anxiety and had a negative effect on mathematics achievement. Self-efficacy seems to create an optimal internal condition for the acquisition of new skills. Students who are self-efficacious believe that they have the necessary and sufficient skills to regulate their own learning process. This result can be linked to other findings, and it may be concluded that optimistic appraisals (Boekaerts 1992), content-specific interest (Schiefele 1991), high perceived task value (Pintrich and De Groot 1990), task orientation (Nicholls 1984), and high self-efficacy (Helmke 1989) should be seen as favorable learning conditions that prompt students to aim their effort at the learning task.

It is important to note, however, that students are not willing to invest effort when they perceive the learning conditions to be less than optimal. Otten and Boekaerts (1990) found that students from the first year of secondary education devoted an average of 3 hours to preparing for a history exam and only 10 minutes to preparing for a literature exam. Further analyses revealed that the students did not find history an attractive subject (attitude), but that they knew how to prepare for the history exam. By contrast, they enjoyed the literature lessons, but did not know how to prepare for the literature exam. When these students were asked to attribute their perceived results on the respective exams, many effort attributions were noted after the history exam, whereas few were observed after the literature exam. After the latter exam, perceived failure was attributed to low ability and to high level of task difficulty. These results seem to indicate that when students believe that effort will not result in mastery, they may refrain from putting in effort and settle for the belief that the subject matter is too difficult (stable, external attribution) or that their personal resources are inadequate (stable, internal attribution). These attributions may protect them from criticism in future, but they also trap them in a vicious circle. Indeed, students who refrain from putting in effort due to low self-efficacy loose their chances of enhancing self-efficacy, interest, and self-regulation.

4.3 Behavioral Control Mechanisms

A distinction between the terms discussed above, and terms coined in the framework of metacognition is needed. Most researchers agree that metacognition can be subdivided into two parts: knowledge of cognitions and regulation of cognitions. However, much conceptual confusion has arisen when data from effort management studies were integrated with data from studies on metacognition. In order to enhance conceptual clarity, Boekaerts (1992) proposed the term "cognitive strategies" to refer to processing activities that lead directly to learning results (e.g., recognition, recall, analyzing, structuring, elaborating), to reserve the term metacognitive skills for those processes that direct and steer the information-processing flow of the learning process (e.g., orienting, planning, monitoring, reflecting, repairing, evaluating), and to use the name "behavioral control mechanisms" for skills that exert control over behavior in general, and not just over the learning process. She distinguished between several behavioral control mechanisms, such as cognitive control, action control, emotion control, symptom control, and social control. The first three forms of control will be discussed below.

Cognitive control refers to cognitive processes involving affect (such as appraisals, beliefs about the self, or content-specific interests). As explained above, cognitive control that involves high intrinsic motivation and high self-efficacy, leads to behavioral intentions that start, or continue activity in the mastery mode, and affect the quantity and quality of effort expenditure. Nevertheless, it is important to note that in a learning context, many behavioral intentions are formed, some of them are enacted, while others fall short of the students' willpower or aspirations. Kuhl (1985) therefore argued that a distinction should be made between subjective control and actual attempts at control. He explained that in order to reach a particular goal, choice of that goal and persistence in striving for it is not enough. A certain amount of effort, or action control, is also necessary to maintain the behavioral intention and to protect it from competing action tendencies.

Kuhl pointed out that behavioral enactment of a learning intention is especially difficult in the presence of attractive behavioral alternatives, or when social pressure undermines a commitment. In such cases, students must actively direct their attention away from competing action tendencies and protect their learning intention. This active mode of control was labeled "action orientation" and contrasted with the passive mode of control, called "state orientation." Individuals who score high on state orientation are more engaged in exploring their emotional state than in exploring the task. A further distinction was made between students who lack action control in terms of: (a) an inability to initiate intended actions due to indecision, (b) an inability to continue intended actions due to lack of sustained interest, and (c) an inability to continue intended actions due to preoccupation with failure.

Boekaerts (1992) introduced the term "emotion control" to refer to the regulation of emotions. She explained that when well-being is distorted, students will change cognitive and behavioral efforts to restore their well-being. Attempts to regulate emotions may effectively relieve stress by changing the stressful transaction, but they may also temporarily calm down the student, thus only affecting the symptoms and not the underlying causes. Surprisingly little research is available concerning such fundamental issues as how students try to regulate their behavior during taxing or stressful learning situations. But, evidence is accummulating that successful forms of emotion control get the students off the well-being mode, and pave the path for reappraisal and activity in the mastery mode (see Boekaerts, in press b).

See also: Motivation and Learning

References

Bandura A 1982 Self-efficacy mechanisms in human agency. *Am. Psychol.* 37(2): 122–47

Boekaerts M 1991 Subjective competence, appraisals and self-assessment. *Learning and Instruction* 1(1): 1–17

Boekaerts M 1992 The adaptable learning process: Initiating and maintaining behavioural change. *Appl. Psychol.* 41(4): 375–97

Boekaerts M 1993 Being concerned with well-being and with learning. *Educ. Psychol.* 28(2): 149–67

Boekaerts M (in press a) The interface between intelligence and personality as determinants of classroom learning. In: Saklofske D H, Zeinder M (eds.) *Handbook of Personality and Intelligence.* Plenum Press, New York

Boekaerts M (in press b) Coping with stress in childhood and adolescence. In: Zeidner M, Endler N S (eds.) *Handbook of Coping.* John Wiley & Sons, New York

Bower G H 1981 Mood and memory. *Am. Psychol.* 36(2): 129–48

Frijda N H 1986 *The Emotions.* Cambridge University Press, Cambridge

Helmke A 1989 Affective student characteristics and cognitive development: Problems, pitfalls, perspectives. *Int. J. Educ. Res.* 13(8): 915–32

Hembree R 1988 Correlates, causes, effects and treatment of test anxiety. *Rev. Educ. Res.* 58(1): 47–77

Kuhl J 1985 Volitional mediators of cognition-behavior consistency: Self-regulatory processes and action versus state orientation. In: Kuhl J, Beckman J (eds.) 1985 *Action Control: From Cognition to Behavior.* Springer-Verlag, Berlin

Lazarus R S, Folkman S 1984 *Stress, Appraisal and Coping.* Springer, New York

Mandler G 1984 *Mind and Body: Psychology of Emotion and Stress.* Norton, New York

McLeod D B 1989 Information-processing theories and mathematics learning: The role of affect. *Int. J. Educ. Res.* 14(1): 13–29

Nicholls J G 1984 Achievement motivation: Conceptions of ability, subjective experience, task choice, and performance. *Psychol. Rev.* 91(3): 328–46

Otten R, Boekaerts M 1990 Schoolvakbeleving bij Geschiedenis, Nederlands en wiskunde bij leerlingen in de brugklas. In: Boekaerts M, De Corte E (eds.) 1990 *Onderwijsleerprocessen.* Instituut voor Toegepaste Sociale Wetenschappen, Nijmegen

Pintrich P R, De Groot E V 1990 Motivational and self-regulated learning components of classroom academic performance. *J. Educ. Psychol.* 82(1): 33–41

Schiefele U 1991 Interest, learning, and motivation. *Educ. Psychol.* 26(3/4): 299–323

Weiner B 1986 *An Attributional Theory of Motivation and Emotion.* Springer-Verlag, New York

Weinert F E, Schrader F W, Helmke A 1989 Quality of instruction and achievement outcomes. *Int. J. Educ. Res.* 13(8): 895–912

Further Reading

McLeod D B, Adams V M (eds.) 1989 *Affect and Mathematical Problem Solving: A New Perspective.* Springer-Verlag, New York

Pintrich P R, Marx R W, Boyle R A 1993 Beyond cold conceptual change: The role of motivation beliefs and classroom contextual factors in the process of conceptual change. *Rev. Ecuc. Res.* 63: 167–99

Schunk D H (ed.) 1990 Motivation and self-efficacy in education: Research and new directions. *J. Educ. Psychol.* 82(1): 3–91

(b)   Classroom Processes

Student Roles in Classrooms

S. J. McCarthey and P. L. Peterson

In the first edition of the *International Encyclopedia of Education*, student roles were conceptualized as behaviors characteristic of persons in a context (Tisher 1985). Researchers in the 1970s and early 1980s found that students in the typical classroom assumed a passive role, spending most of their time listening to the teacher (Goodlad 1984). Students talked no more than 30 percent of the time and this followed the teacher initiation–student response–teacher evaluation pattern (IRE) identified by Mehan (1979). Tisher (1985) suggested that classroom context influenced teachers' and students' observed behavior. For example, teachers in open classrooms asked more higher level cognitive questions than teachers in traditional classrooms. Thus, students in open classrooms received more opportunities to engage in higher level responding than those in traditional classrooms.

Since 1985, researchers have shifted away from a view of classroom roles and practices that focus only on teachers' and students' observed behavior, toward a view that also considers the understandings and perspectives of students and teachers within the social context of classrooms and schools. According to this view, roles are created by participants within a social situation such as a classroom. An understanding of student roles, then, involves understanding not only the observed roles of students in classrooms, but also teachers' and students' assumptions and beliefs about these roles.

1. A New Role for Students in Classrooms

During the late 1980s and continuing into the 1990s, curriculum development efforts in literacy and mathematics have focused on creating a more active role for students (Anderson et al. 1984, National Council of Teachers of Mathematics 1989). In order for students to assume such a role, however, changes in the traditional conceptions of knowledge, tasks, and discourse are needed.

Underlying the student's traditionally passive classroom role is a conception of knowledge that places the authority for knowing with the teacher. The teacher's role is to transmit knowledge to students who simply receive the knowledge transmitted. Underlying the new role for students is a conception of knowledge as an active construction of meaning by the learner, often in collaboration with peers.

Classroom tasks in traditional classrooms involve the use of basal texts in reading and mathematics and an endless array of worksheets that teach skills. Reformers recommend that teachers engage students in new kinds of tasks such as reading authentic children's literature, working on real problems, interpreting texts from a variety of perspectives, solving mathematics problems using a variety of strategies and tools, keeping journals that document learners' thinking, writing for real audiences about topics of students' own choice, and having students pose and solve mathematics problems for themselves.

Finally in traditional classrooms, teachers typically control the discourse. They ask convergent, factual questions for which they know the answers. Students respond by providing specific answers and generating few questions of their own (Mehan 1979). New discourse patterns in literacy instruction include teacher–student and peer conferences that provide students with their peers' perspectives and interpretations of their reading and writing (DiPardo and Freedman 1988). New discourse patterns in mathematics classrooms involve students in negotiating mathematical meaning, discussing and explaining their thinking and strategies for solving problems, justifying their answers, and creating and posing new mathematical problems for themselves (Lampert 1990).

1.1 Student Responses and Teacher Diagnosis

The active role of students has been conceived as involving more extended student responses than has been typical in traditional classrooms. Students have the opportunity to engage in authentic tasks involving reading, writing, solving mathematical problems, and using mathematical tools. While the teacher controls classroom discourse, students have opportunities to provide ideas. The role of the teacher is to construct knowledge, diagnose students' needs, and develop instruction accordingly, while attempting to make learning meaningful for students. The student's role is to acquire this knowledge in a meaningful way.

An example of such a program in literacy is Reading Recovery. Developed in New Zealand to help children having trouble learning to read, Reading Recovery is designed to serve the lowest achieving readers in first-grade classrooms (Clay 1982). Teachers provide daily 30-minute lessons to individual children during which they involve students in reading small books and in writing their own messages. The teachers respond to the students on a minute-to-minute basis according to the student's strengths, needs, and interests. The teacher introduces students to predictable books that they often reread to develop fluency. Additionally, the student has the opportunity to read a new book each day to become familiar with important ideas in stories. While the student is reading, the teacher watches and records substitutions, self-corrections, and omissions to aid in selecting materials for the next day. Students also compose a message each day with the aid of the teacher (Pinnell et al. 1990). Research conducted in New Zealand indicated that students at risk of failure made accelerated progress while enrolled in the Reading Recovery program (Clay 1985). Studies in Ohio showed that students who had participated in Reading Recovery scored significantly higher than comparison children and retained their gains at least two years after the intervention (Pinnell 1989).

Stevenson and Stigler (1992) have portrayed a similar approach to mathematics teaching in their vignettes of selected Japanese classrooms. They have argued that the success of mathematics teaching in Japanese classrooms is related to several important features of active student roles. Students work on real world problems and manipulate concrete objects to model problem solutions. Students discuss their solution strategies in a small or large group. Finally, the teacher diagnoses and remediates students' misconceptions during group discussion. The student's role is to manipulate objects and construct representations; the teacher's role is to assure that correct representations are produced. Class discussion emphasizes meaning, yet is teacher-controlled.

1.2 Learning Expert Strategies from Experts

Some educators have attempted to make students more autonomous, active learners using programs designed to teach strategies that researchers have identified as being employed successfully by experts. These programs are characterized by direct modeling of strategies by the teacher or a student with students gradually assuming more responsibility. Conceptions of knowledge often derive from social constructivist notions, suggesting the importance of teacher scaffolding instruction for the learner (Vygotsky 1978) or from cognitive scientists' ideas of identifying strategies of experts or those more knowledgeable than the student

and then teaching these strategies to novices (Romberg 1982). Again, these tasks are structured to promote a gradual internalization of problem-solving processes, emphasizing the learner's assuming metacognitive control (Baker and Brown 1984). Classroom discourse is often initiated by the teacher, but students gradually take over aspects of the dialogue and teach peers. Students assume an active role while receiving continued assistance from a person with greater expertise such as the teacher.

Palincsar and Brown (1989) developed what they term "reciprocal teaching" to increase both reading comprehension and the use of metacognitive strategies. Their premise is that students will come to internalize dialogue about text that is modeled by the teacher. The dialogue is structured around four strategies used by expert readers: summarizing, self-questioning, predicting, and clarifying. The teacher models these strategies and provides support as students gradually acquire the strategies to use independently in their reading, and students gradually take on more active roles in controlling the discourse. Reciprocal teaching has increased the reading comprehension of elementary- and junior-high students significantly; students were able to use the strategies independent of the teacher and to provide help to other students.

The Kamehameha Early Education Program (KEEP) has focused on altering discourse patterns during the reading of text to become more culturally congruent with the participation structures of native Hawaiians outside the classroom. Teachers use the experience–text–relationship (ETR) method that involves activating children's background experiences relevant to the text, close literal reading of the text, and the integration of information read with prior knowledge and experience. Teacher–student interactions are characterized by the talk story pattern in which students answer the teacher's questions without being called upon, building upon one another's answers. Studies suggest that a careful match between patterns of interaction and instructional goals can facilitate learning. The social organization of lessons permits students to show initiative and supports the transfer of control over text comprehension from teacher to student (Au and Kawakami 1986).

Cognitively Guided Instruction (CGI) is based on research on the development of young children's strategies for solving mathematics word problems (Carpenter and Moser 1982). The developers of CGI begin by sharing two research-based knowledge frameworks with teachers: (a) the framework of strategies that young children use in developing increasingly sophisticated approaches for solving mathematics word problems, and (b) the framework of problem types that children are able to solve. The assumption is that children construct knowledge by proceeding through a sequence of strategy development, and that the teacher's role is to facilitate the children's development of increasingly sophisticated problem-solving strategies.

In CGI classrooms, elementary mathematics teaching is characterized by a focus on solving word problems and other nonroutine problems; use of multiple strategies by students to solve problems, including counters and other mathematics tools; and listening to students explain and show their strategies and solutions for solving problems. Students in CGI classrooms tended to achieve higher on tests of mathematical problem-solving than students in traditional classrooms, and to recall their number facts with equal or greater facility (Peterson et al. 1989).

1.3 Collaborative Roles in Learning

In this conception of the active learner, students are seen as being actively involved in the negotiation of shared meaning with others in a learning community. Like Dewey (1916), these educators see communication as both the means of learning and the substance of what is learned. Communication is intertwined with the notion of community, developing what Dewey referred to as "participation in a common understanding." Teachers and students, then, are jointly responsible for learning.

In collaboration with others in their learning community, students choose the tasks and materials they use and communicate and collaborate with one another in order to develop new knowledge. Students' roles are dynamic and changing, depending on the text or problem in which they are engaged. As advocated by Freire (1986) in teaching Brazilian students, "the teacher is no longer merely the-one-who-teaches, but one who is himself taught in dialogue with the students" (p. 67).

Within this conception of the active learner, educators have developed student-led "book clubs" and "literature circles." Students use the book clubs for several purposes including sharing their written responses to a text, clarifying points of confusion, discussing main themes in a book, relating the text to other texts, identifying an author's purpose, critiquing an author's success, and relating the text to their personal experiences (Raphael et al. 1992). In literature circles, students have choices about which books to read before joining the circle. The types of discussion questions depend on readers' interests. These discussions take the form of reacting to the book, reading aloud favorite parts, and raising questions about parts they do not understand. Members of the circle often present the book to the rest of the class (Harste et al. 1984). Smagorinsky and Fly (1992) suggested that such student-led discussions can be very successful, especially when the teacher has made the interpretive process explicit at an earlier point in time.

Peer writing conferences or response groups consist of small groups of students who respond to each other's written texts. DiPardo and Freedman (1988) suggested a variety of purposes for these conferences depending on teachers' and students' goals, including responding to writing, thinking collaboratively, writing collaboratively, and editing written text. Groups provide a forum for discussing the writing process, generating ideas, understanding the functions of an audience, and providing support for engaging in writing. The assumption is that students benefit from talking together because the writer's knowledge becomes available in the discourse; the beginner's work is supported through questions, comments, and suggestions of others; beginning writers have opportunities to practice orally ways of using written language; and talking about text makes clear to writers the value of their work (Florio-Ruane 1988). Studies suggest that peer groups for writing collaboratively or responding to writing can positively influence students' writing (Dahl 1988). The nature of the discourse is an important element in determining the kinds of revisions that students make in their texts (Gere and Abbott 1985). Finally, the quality of the discourse influences the learning of individual students (Daiute 1985, Fitzgerald and Stamm 1990).

Lampert (1990) discussed approaches to mathematics teaching where learning mathematics involves the negotiation of shared meaning among students and the teacher within the mathematical community which exists in each classroom. Students assume authority for knowing mathematics and for explaining and justifying their mathematical thinking to others in their community. Students' ideas and knowledge become available for debate and discussion as part of the classroom discourse. New ways of thinking and mathematical ideas are developed and learned by all members of the community, and learning occurs on the part of the teacher as well as the students.

2. Making Sense of Classrooms

Three ways that educators have conceived of students as playing more active roles in the classroom have been described. These conceptions should result in rather different classroom scenarios; different from traditional classrooms and different from each other. But how will developers' conceptions impact on what actually happens in classrooms and how will the actors—teachers and students—actually construe their roles?

Although new curricula, tasks, and discourse structures that embody more active roles for learners have been designed, these new curricula, tasks, discourse structures, and roles will be transformed by the participants in their particular contexts (Bruce and Rubin 1993). The roles students actually play in each classroom will depend on how curricula, tasks, discourse, and role structures are created and recreated within classrooms. Influential factors include the beliefs of the participants and the culture of the classroom.

2.1 Teachers' and Students' Beliefs About Subject Matter

Nickerson (1992) reviewed studies that show how the

pupil's role in United Kingdom classrooms can vary dramatically according to the view of mathematics projected by the teacher. She contrasted pupil's roles as "accepting" versus "questioning" and suggested that pupils' participation in these different roles is related to the ideas they develop about mathematical knowledge. Similarly, Schoenfeld (1992) has shown how students' roles are intertwined with teachers' and students' existing beliefs about mathematical knowledge. Schoenfeld's analysis produced the following set of students' beliefs about the nature of mathematical knowledge.

(a) Mathematics problems have one and only one right answer.

(b) There is only one correct way to solve any mathematics problem, usually the rule the teacher has most recently demonstrated in class.

(c) Ordinary students cannot be expected to understand mathematics, they expect simply to memorize it and apply what they have learned mechanically and without understanding.

(d) Formal proof is irrelevant to processes of discovery or invention.

(e) Mathematics is a solitary activity, done by individuals in isolation.

(f) Students who have understood the mathematics they have studied will be able to solve any assigned problem in five minutes or less.

(g) The mathematics learned in school has little or nothing to do with the real world.

These beliefs have definite implications for students' roles. Students are expected to find the correct answer; to work alone; to memorize and apply procedures that are demonstrated by the teacher; to work quickly and efficiently; and to view their role as a "student" in school rather than as a lifelong "learner" in school and out.

Similarly, in the area of literacy, children and adults have a set of beliefs about text: what is, who created it, and how to evaluate it (Garner and Alexander in press). Once again these beliefs imply certain roles for students in the classroom.

2.2 Teachers' and Students' Beliefs About Teaching and Learning

The role of the student and what it means to be an active learner in the classroom also depend on the beliefs teachers and students have about learning and teaching. For example, among 20 teachers who were implementing Cognitively Guided Instruction (CGI) in their classrooms, Peterson et al. (1989) observed substantial differences among teachers related to their beliefs about the role of the student and the teacher.

Teachers who continued to see their roles as presenting knowledge rather than listening to students or facilitating children's construction of knowledge, implemented CGI by engaging in direct instruction and presenting the correct answer and correct mathematical strategy to be learned. Teachers who saw their roles as actively facilitating children's construction of knowledge created CGI classrooms where everyone listened to students' strategies for solving problems, tried to understand children's thinking, and encouraged the development of mathematical understanding.

In implementing new approaches to literacy learning, such as process writing and reciprocal teaching, teachers have "proceduralized" the substantive intervention and recreated the innovation within their existing conceptions of the learner, the teacher, and knowledge (Bruce and Rubin 1993). Florio-Ruane and Lensmire (1990), for example, found that teachers adopted and taught the steps of process writing, but did not alter their understandings of what it meant to be a good writer or the knowledge of authority relationships among teacher, student, and text.

2.3 The Culture of the Classroom and the School

The role of the student is one that is created solely within the context of the school. The role of the learner as conceived in school, however, is very different from the role of the learner in the contexts of work, family, and play where children and youth also learn (Resnick 1987). Outside of schools, children and youth often learn in authentic situations, such as apprenticeships (Collins et al. 1989) in which participants' work has real economic value and significance. What would happen if the role of learner were conceptualized within a community that is unbounded by school walls, but that encompasses the experiences of home and other learning contexts?

3. Transforming the Roles of Children and Youth as Learners in Schools and Out

Heath (in press) describes how effective organizations for inner-city youth in the United States differ from formal learning contexts in the ways in which learning and knowledge are conceived and the roles that youths play. She argues that formal learning contexts, such as schools, should change to encompass the following features.

(a) Effective youth organizations have open frank discussions and make learning possible primarily through demonstration, apprenticeship, extensive practice, and peer evaluation.

(b) Youth organizations place the control of knowledge within the group as team members committed to a central goal. Knowledge and skills blend together. The facts of a myth for a Ballet Folklorico dance go along with the skill inherent in specific dance routines.

(c) Learning is cumulative, multidirectional, and displayed through a variety of different kinds of symbols: verbal, kinesthetic, musical, and visual.

(d) Learning and thinking of the self as a learner for a set of purposes and goals of joint identification become synomous with one's life, just as knowing oneself as a member of a family unconsciously merges with an individual sense of identity (Heath in press).

Heath argues for changing schools to become more like effective youth organizations in order to create a "seamless life of thinking, development and learning." If such changes do come about, then in the next edition of the *International Encyclopedia of Education* this entry will be transformed and retitled to reflect the role of the student as merged within the multifaceted roles of young learners growing up in a global community.

See also: Teachers' Roles

References

Anderson R C, Hiebert E H, Scott J A, Wilkinson I A G 1984 *Becoming a Nation of Readers: The Report of the Commission on Reading.* The National Institute of Education, Washington, DC

Au K H, Kawakami A J 1986 The influence of the social organization of instruction on children's text comprehension ability: A Vygotskian perspective. In: Raphael T E (ed.) 1986 *The Contexts of School-based Literacy.* Random House, New York

Baker L, Brown A L 1984 Metacognitive skills and reading. In: Pearson (ed.) 1984 *Handbook of Reading Research,* Vol 1. Longman, New York

Bruce B B, Rubin A 1993 *Electronic Quills: A Situated Evaluation of Using Computers for Writing in Classrooms.* Erlbaum, Hillsdale, New Jersey

Carpenter T P, Moser J M 1982 The development of addition and subtraction problem-solving skills. In: Carpenter T P, Moser J M, Romberg T A (eds.) 1982 *Addition and Subtraction: A Cognitive Perspective.* Erlbaum, Hillsdale, New Jersey

Clay M M 1982 *Observing Young Readers.* Heinemann, Portsmouth, New Hampshire

Clay M M 1985 *The Early Detection of Reading Difficulties.* Heinemann, Portsmouth, New Hampshire

Collins A, Brown J S, Newman S E 1989 Cognitive apprenticeship: Teaching the crafts of reading, writing, and mathematics. In: Resnick L (ed.) 1989 *Knowing, Learning and Instruction: Essays in Honor of Robert Glaser.* Erlbaum, Hillsdale, New Jersey

Dahl K 1988 Peer conferences as social contexts for learning about revision. In: Readance J (ed.) 1988 *Dialogues in Literacy Research.* National Reading Conference, Chicago, Illinois

Daiute C 1985 Do writers talk to themselves? In: Freedman

S W (ed.) 1985 *The Acquisition of Written Language: Response and Revision.* Ablex, Norwood, New Jersey

Dewey J 1916 *Democracy and Education.* Macmillan, New York

DiPardo A, Freedman S W 1988 Peer response groups in the writing classroom: Theoretic foundations and new directions. *Rev. Educ. Res.* 58: 119–49

Fitzgerald J, Stamm C 1990 Effects of group conferences on first-grader's revisions of writing. *Written Communication* 7: 96–135

Florio-Ruane S 1988 How ethnographers of communication study writing in school. In: Readance J (ed.) 1988 *Dialogues in Literacy Research.* National Reading Conference, Chicago, Illinois

Florio-Ruane S, Lensmire T J 1990 Transforming future teachers' ideas about writing instruction *J. Curric. St.* 22: 277–89

Freire P 1986 *Pedagogy of the Oppressed.* Continuum Publishing, New York

Garner R, Alexander P (eds.) in press *Beliefs about Text and about Instruction with Text.* Erlbaum, Hillsdale, New Jersey

Gere A R, Abbott R D 1985 Talking about writing: The language of writing groups. *Research in the Teaching of English* 19: 362–85

Goodlad J I 1984 *A Place Called School.* McGraw-Hill, New York

Harste J C, Woodward V A, Burke C L 1984 *Language Stories and Literacy Lessons.* Heinemann, Portsmouth, New Hampshire

Heath S B in press Play for identity: Where the mind is everyday for inner-city youth. In: Mangieri J, Block C C (ed.) in press *Mindfulness: Increasing Thinking Abilities.* Harcourt, Brace, Jovanovich, New York

Lampert M 1990 When the problem is not the question and the solution is not the answer: Mathematical knowing and teaching. *Am. Educ. Res. J.* 27: 29–64

Mehan H 1979 *Learning Lessons.* Harvard University Press, Cambridge, Massachusetts

National Council of Teachers of Mathematics 1989 *Curriculum and Evaluation Standards for School Mathematics.* National Council of Teachers of Mathematics, Reston, Virginia

Nickerson M 1992 The culture of the mathematics classroom: An unknown quantity? In: Grouws D A (ed.) 1992 *Handbook of Research on Mathematics Teaching and Learning.* Macmillan, New York

Palincsar A S, Brown A L 1989 Classroom dialogues to promote self-regulated comprehension. In: Brophy J (ed.) 1989 *Advances in Research on Teaching,* Vol 1. JAI Press, Greenwich, Connecticut

Peterson P L, Carpenter T, Fennema E 1989 Teachers' knowledge of students' knowledge in mathematics problem solving: Correlational and case analyses. *J. Educ. Psychol.* 81: 558–69

Pinnell G S 1989 Reading Recovery: Helping at-risk children learn to read. *Elem. Sch. J.* 90 (2): 161–82

Pinnell G S, Fried M D, Estice R M 1990 Reading Recovery: Learning how to make a difference. *Read. Teach.* 43: 282–95

Raphael T E et al. 1992 Research directions: Literature and discussion in the reading program. *Lang. Arts* 69 (1): 54–61

Resnick L B 1987 Learning in school and out. *Educ. Researcher* 16 (9): 13–20

Romberg T 1982 An emerging paradigm for research on addition and subtraction skills. In: Carpenter T P, Moser J P, Romberg T A (eds.) 1982 *Addition and Subtraction: A Cognitive Perspective* Erlbaum, Hillsdale, New Jersey

Schoenfeld A 1992 Learning to think mathematically: Problem solving, metacognition, and sense making in mathematics. In: Grouws D A (ed.) 1993 *Handbook of Research on Mathematics Teaching and Learning*. Macmillan, New York

Smagorinsky P, Fly P K 1992 Patterns of discourse in small group discussions of literature. Paper presented at the Annual Meeting of the American Educational Research Association, San Francisco, California

Stevenson H, Stigler J 1992 *The Learning Gap*. Summit Books, New York

Tisher R P 1985 Student roles in the classroom. In: Husén T, Postlethwaite T N (eds.) 1985 *The International Encyclopedia of Education*, 1st edn. Pergamon Press, Oxford

Vygotsky L S 1978 *Mind in Society: The Development of Higher Psychological Processes*. Harvard University Press, Cambridge, Massachusetts

Student Influences on Teaching

R. W. Marx and R. M. B. Collopy

Teaching and learning in classrooms are complex, multiply determined phenomena. It is generally assumed that teachers, through their teaching, influence the learning of students. It is equally true, however, that students influence the ways in which they are taught. When in their classrooms, teachers may act or react on the basis of means–ends reasoning or "bounded rationality." That is, teachers adapt their methods of teaching (the means) to achieve certain goals (the ends) to differences among students. Similarly, teachers may teach students according to the expectations they have of them (see *Teachers' Expectations*).

The ways in which students influence teachers have been studied by many researchers using a variety of research methodologies. The results of these studies are presented and examined in this entry in terms of two guiding questions. First, what characteristics and behaviors of students influence teachers' classroom behavior and instructional practices? Second, what theoretical mechanisms account for teachers' differential behavior and practices?

1. Assumptions

There are two basic assumptions that guide this review. First, much of teaching is assumed to be a mindful enterprise. That is, teachers modify their actions toward different students based on some sort of means–ends reasoning. Second, teachers are assumed to be subject to influences other than those that are rational. Much theoretical and empirical work has examined the expectations of teachers, the ways in which these expectations are communicated to students, and the ways in which these expectations, once communicated, influence students. While the second assumption has been discussed widely (e.g., Rosenthal and Jacobson 1968), the first needs some elaboration.

Schools are institutions with particular social purposes (e.g., developing basic literacy and numeracy skills, cultivation of mind, socialization to cultural norms and practices, preparation for participation in the local and national economy). As the primary agents of this institution, teachers act in ways that are consistent with the attainment of some or all of these goals. This is not to say that all interactions between teachers and students are influenced by such a "bounded-rationality" conception, nor that such interactions actually optimize outcomes. Rather, it means that many of the interactions are influenced by such a conception.

Several instructional theories have been developed to examine how a bounded rationality of teaching might work in classrooms. One of the more elegant has been developed since the late 1960s by Snow (1988). The elegance in Snow's work lies in both its psychological sophistication and in its explicit reliance on how instruction can be adapted to individual differences in learners. Snow refers to these individual differences as "aptitudes," which are characteristics of the learner prior to instruction that influence the extent to which the instruction will be effective. Individual differences in characteristics such as sex, ethnicity, and prior achievement can serve as devices that teachers use to connect goals with instruction, learning, and, assessment.

2. Research on Students' Influence on Teaching

Studies of students' effects on teachers tend to focus on three characteristics of students: their sex, ethnicity, and prior level of educational achievement. Some studies have examined two, or in a small number of cases, all three of these characteristics. In a few studies, researchers have investigated interactions among these characteristics of students and the same characteristics of teachers (e.g., how the sex or ethnicity of the teacher interacts with sex or ethnicity of the students). Two lines of inquiry have been used in these studies: process–product and teacher expectancies. Much of the process–product research on classroom teaching has been based on a behavioral conception of classroom interaction. The goal of this research tradition is to identify those teacher behaviors and their antecedents that are associated with higher levels of student attainment. The research methodology is quantitative, relying on correlational and descriptive studies as well as subsequent field-based experiments to demonstrate the impact of particular teacher behaviors or clusters of behaviors on student learning. The second line of inquiry directly relevant to the ways in which students affect teaching is the research on teacher expectancies. Work along this line addresses more global or inferential dimensions of classroom action and relies on qualitative research methods such as ethnographies, case studies, and teacher narratives.

2.1 Process–Product Studies

An example of a process–product study based on a behavioral approach to studying students and teachers is that conducted by Nafpaktitis et al. (1985). These researchers were interested in teacher approval and disapproval of student behavior as a function of the students' on-task and off-task behavior. Their research methods included an interval time sampling observation procedure whereby 84 intermediate school teachers (Grades 6–9) and their students were observed for two or three 30-minute periods. Teacher approval and disapproval rates were calculated and correlated with rates of student off-task and on-task behavior. Nafpaktitis et al. found that teachers who tended to approve of off-task student behavior more often also had lower rates of on-task behavior. Similarly, teachers who tended to disapprove of off-task behavior had higher rates of student on-task behavior. Working in a similar tradition, Simpson and Erickson (1983) found that White teachers in the United States directed more verbal praise, nonverbal praises and verbal criticism toward first-grade males than toward first-grade females. However, they directed more nonverbal criticism to Black males than to any other sex–race grouping.

One of the problems with work in the genre of the Nafpaktitis et al. and the Simpson and Erickson studies is that the potential role of subject matter in conditioning the types of interactions between teachers and students and among students is ignored (Stodolsky 1988). Weber and Shake (1988), for example, examined teacher rejoinders (i.e., teachers' responses to students' answers) in the comprehension phase of reading instruction in second-grade classrooms. In the overwhelming majority of these rejoinders, teachers accepted students' answers as correct. Only about 6 percent of the rejoinders indicated that the students' answers were incorrect.

By and large, the finding that teachers tend to accept or approve of students' response has been replicated over a large number of studies, at least in United States classrooms. However, because students' understanding of these teacher responses interacts in many different ways with personal (e.g., beliefs about self as learner or what one considers valuable or worthwhile), social (e.g., norms for peer support), and situational (e.g., goal structures associated with grading practices) factors, it is difficult to make generalizable, theoretically robust predictions about student behavior based on such findings.

In a study of 36 fourth-grade mathematics classes in the United States, Fennema and Peterson (1986) found very complex interactions involving teachers' differential behavior toward boys and girls. The teachers' differential behavior also interacted with achievement differently for boys and girls, depending on whether the achievement was assessed by tasks that required higher or lower level thinking. As an example of the complexity of these findings, Fennema and Peterson stated that for lower level tasks, teachers' praise for girls' correct responses was positively related to test scores on these tasks. For boys, on the other hand, teacher praise following a correct answer to higher level tasks was associated with higher scores on high-level test items. This finding was one of several dozen complex interactions.

Undaunted by this complexity, Fennema and Peterson made a number of specific recommendations for specific teacher reaction to student responses depending on whether the goal is to increase higher or lower level achievement and if the student is a boy or a girl and if the task is higher or lower level. Over a dozen specific teacher responses were suggested.

2.2 Expectation Studies

Purely behavioral accounts of student and teacher interaction beg the question of the mechanisms that might mediate the effects of student characteristics and behaviors on the way teachers respond to students. Teaching decisions are not always based on rational decisions. They may stem from inappropriate or extraneous information such as stereotypical expectations for student behavior and performance. Such expectations may, in turn, lead to expectancy effects or self-fulfilling prophecies; that is, unwarranted differential treatment of students that reinforces or alters student outcomes. Since Rosenthal and Jacobson's (1968) study, a plethora of studies have examined the determinants and outcomes of teachers' differential expectations of students.

Studies indicate that teacher expectancies for student performance can be affected by a range of student characteristics including students' race, attractiveness, socioeconomic status, classroom conduct, and previous academic record (Dusek and Joseph 1983). Equivocal evidence has been found for expectancy effects based on several categories of student characteristics such as student gender, name stereotypes, and siblings' previous performance.

Differences in results may be attributed to several causes. First, teacher characteristics such as race and gender may influence expectancy effects (Irvine 1985). Teachers also differ on the importance they place on various student characteristics. In a study of 21 first-grade teachers, for example, Fedoruk and Norman (1991) found wide variance in the rankings teachers gave to 86 student descriptors as contributors to student success or failure. Furthermore, some teachers may be more susceptible to biasing information and expectancy effects than others (Babad and Inabr 1982). In addition, most studies of teacher expectancies have been experimental, not naturalistic. Because experimental studies neglect contextual elements, their validity has been questioned. They usually use nonteachers as participants, are not conducted with intact classrooms, and do not consider multiple, interactive determinants of teacher expectancies.

Students' behavior or performance may confirm teachers' original expectations because of expectancy effects, perceptual biases on the part of teachers, or because teachers tend to predict achievement accurately without influencing it (Jussim 1989). Some researchers have argued that teachers tend to be accurate predictors of student achievement and that differential treatment may reflect appropriate responses to needs of individual students. It may also reflect students' frequency of participation and quality of contributions to classroom discourse (e.g., it is more difficult to call on students who do not raise their hand). Research in Canada by Clifton and Bulcock (1987) has shown that expectations of students held by ninth-grade teachers are based more on judgments of intellectual ability and prior performance than ethnicity (in this case, Yiddish- and French-speaking adolescents). In addition, there is evidence that teachers tend to modify their expectations as their experience with individual students increases (Brophy 1983, Raudenbush 1984).

2.3 Qualitative Studies

Since the early 1980s, research on teachers and classrooms has expanded to include more detailed, qualitative studies, usually with smaller sample sizes than those used in process–product or expectation studies. These studies provide a rich understanding of teachers' beliefs and conceptions and how they influence the ways in which teachers modify their teaching in reaction to students. These studies also provide information about how social, institutional, and personal contexts influence the work of teachers.

In a simulation study of expert, novice, and postulant (subject matter experts who wish to teach, but who have not yet been prepared formally) teachers, Carter et al. (1987) have shown that the expert teachers differ with respect to their understanding of students and classrooms. They further explicate the role that this understanding plays in classroom decisions and subsequent classroom interaction. For example, while all three groups use categories to describe students

(e.g., discipline problems), expert teachers have a far richer understanding of the meaning that these categories have for their actions in the classroom. It is this more detailed understanding of teacher's beliefs, conceptions, and understandings that qualitative research methods uncover.

One of the findings from process–product and expectation studies is that teachers' judgments about students and their expectations for future performance are as likely to be based on realistic information from prior performance and classroom participation as they are to be based on bias and unfounded stereotype. This finding is supported by Barakett (1986) in her ethnography of English-speaking elementary school teachers in an inner-city school in Montreal, Canada. Barakett found that teachers' theories of students and instruction are to a large part based on teachers' experiences with students in their classrooms with respect to the type of activities and tasks that the teachers develop and use with these students. For example, the teachers in this school grouped children for learning using what, on the surface, might seem like conventional criteria (e.g., ability, motivation, family background). However, closer analysis suggested that classroom performance plays an even more powerful role than these conventional labels.

In a very different context, Abagi and Cleghorn (1990) found that rural and urban teachers in Kenya interpret and implement government policy about language of instruction in ways that are heavily influenced by their students' classroom performance. The policy for urban areas required that English be used as the language of instruction. The urban school teachers conformed to this policy. One of the rural schools in this study was situated geographically in the urban language policy jurisdiction. However, the students in this school largely spoke Kikuyu, not English, and the primary-grade teachers in this school used Kikuyu as the language of instruction, in violation of official policy. Clearly, in this as in many other instances in the literature, teachers modify their practices in conformance with their understanding of the students with whom they work more so than in reaction to official policy.

3. Conclusion

Early research on student effects on teaching and teachers was predicated on the search for behavioral regularities, that is, replicable statistical relationships between student and teacher behaviors. Since the early 1980s, researchers and theorists have recognized that an understanding of teachers and teaching requires an understanding of the minds of teachers and students. It is the beliefs, theories, and understandings of teachers that underlie whatever predictability that will be found between student and teacher behavior. Teachers' perceptions of students are filtered through their belief systems and mediate their behavior. Teachers continually change their teaching practice in response to students' needs and in reaction to the development of their own professional knowledge and expertise (Richardson 1991).

See also: Teachers' Beliefs and Belief Systems; Teachers' Expectations; Student Roles in Classrooms

References

Abagi J O, Cleghorn A 1990 Teacher attitudes towards the use of English, Kiswahili, and mother tongue in Kenyan primary classrooms. *Canadian and International Education* 19(1): 61–71

Babad E Y, Inabr J 1982 Pygmalion, Galatea, and the Golem: Investigations of biased and unbiased teachers. *J. Educ. Psychol.* 74(4): 459–74

Barakett J M 1986 Teachers' theories and methods in structuring routine activities in an inner city school. *Canadian J. Educ.* 11(2): 91–108

Brophy J E 1983 Research on the self-fulfilling prophesy and teacher expectations. *J. Educ. Psychol.* 75(5): 631–61

Carter K, Sabers D, Cushing K, Pinnegar S, Berliner D C 1987 Processing and using information about students: A study of expert, novice, and postulant teachers. *Teaching and Teacher Educ.* 3(2): 147–57

Clifton R A, Bulcock J W 1987 Ethnicity, teachers' expectations, and student performances in Ontario schools. *Canadian J. Educ.* 12(2): 294–315

Dusek J B, Joseph G 1983 The bases of teacher expectancies: A meta-analysis. *J. Educ. Psychol.* 75(3): 327–46

Fedoruk G M, Norman C A 1991 Kindergarten screening predictive inaccuracy: First-grade teacher variability *Excep. Child.* 57(3): 258–63

Fennema E, Peterson P L 1986 Teacher–student interactions and sex-related differences in learning mathematics. *Teaching and Teacher Educ.* 2(1): 19–42

Irvine J J 1985 Teacher communication patterns as related to the race and sex of the student. *J. Educ. Res.* 78(6): 338–45

Jussim L 1989 Teacher expectations: Self-fulfilling prophecies, perceptual biases, and accuracy. *J. Pers. Soc. Psychol.* 57(3): 469–80

Nafpaktitis M, Mayer G R, Butterworth T 1985 Natural rates of teacher approval and disapproval and their relation to student behavior in intermediate school classrooms. *J. Educ. Psych.* 77(3): 362–67

Raudenbush S W 1984 Magnitude of teacher expectancy effects on pupil IQ as a function of the credibility of expectancy induction: A synthesis of findings from eighteen experiments. *J. Educ. Psychol.* 76(1): 85–97

Richardson V 1991 Significant and worthwhile change in teaching practice. *Educ. Researcher* 19(7): 10–18

Rosenthal R, Jacobson L 1968 *Pygmalion in the Classroom: Teacher Expectation and Pupils' Intellectual Development.* Holt, Rinehart, and Winston, New York

Simpson A W, Erickson M T 1983 Teachers' verbal and nonverbal communication patterns as a function of teacher race, student gender, and student race. *Am. Educ. Res. J.* 20(2): 183–98

Snow R E 1988 Aptitude-treatment intervention as a framework for research on individual differences in learning. In: Ackerman P L, Sterberg R J, Glaser R (eds.) 1989 *Learning and Individual Differences.* Freeman, New York

Stodolsky S 1988 *The Subject Matters: Classroom Activity in Math and Social Studies.* University of Chicago Press, Chicago, Illinois

Weber R, Shake M C 1988 Teachers' rejoiners to students' responses in reading lessons. *J. Read. Behav.* 20(4): 285–99

Student Perceptions of Classrooms

B. J. Fraser

In contrast to earlier behaviorist views of students as passive recipients of information, late twentieth century theories of teaching and learning view students as being actively involved in their own learning and recognize the importance and relevance of student perceptions. Although this interest in students' perceptions is evident in the third edition of the *Handbook of Research on Teaching* (Wittrock 1986), it was largely absent from the first and second editions. Considerable research has provided insights into factors related to student perceptions as well as the associations between student perceptions and student outcomes.

The importance of students' perceptions is well supported by two lines of research. First, because research in numerous countries has revealed consistent differences between students' and teachers' perceptions (Fraser in press), a focus on students' rather than teachers' perceptions is likely to be more productive in attempts to improve and understand classroom learning. Second, student perceptions help to explain student outcomes beyond the effects of student abilities, instructional methods, and curricular materials (Fraser 1986, Schunk and Meece 1992). Because teacher behaviors can be considered relevant only when they are perceived as cues by students, student perceptions can be thought of as mediators between instruction and student outcomes.

Schunk and Meece (1992) edited a collection of studies of both students' self-perceptions (of their abilities, competence, interests, and goals) and their social perceptions (of teachers, peers, events, and situations). In addition to providing evidence supporting the validity of student perceptions, this collection of research studies shows that the student's perceptions not only affect his or her own behavior, but that perceptions themselves are influenced by student attributes and situational cues. For example, gender differences in student perceptions have been documented (Meece and Courtney 1992) and student perceptions of classroom climate have been related consistently to student outcomes when student aptitude differences were controlled (Fraser 1986, Haertel et al. 1981).

1. Measuring Student Perceptions of Classrooms

In the late 1960s, the Learning Environment Inventory was used as part of the research and evaluation activities of Harvard Project Physics (Welch and Walberg 1972). Around the same time, Moos began developing social climate scales for a wide variety of human environments, including the Classroom Environment Scale for use in school settings (Moos and Trickett 1987). Other instruments for assessing students' perceptions of classroom environment include the Individualized Classroom Environment Questionnaire, My Class Inventory, College and University Classroom Environment Inventory, Science Laboratory Environment Inventory, and Questionnaire on Teacher Interaction. Research involving the use of these instruments has been reviewed by Fraser (1986, in press) and Fraser and Walberg (1991) (see also *Classroom Environments*).

2. Factors Related to Student Perceptions

Fraser (1986) tabulated 39 studies in which students' perceptions of their classrooms were employed as dependent variables in (a) curriculum evaluation studies, (b) investigations of differences between student and teacher perceptions of actual and preferred environment, and (c) studies involving other independent variables. One promising but largely neglected use of students' perceptions is as process criteria in evaluating innovations and new curricula. A study involving an evaluation of the Australian Science Education Project (ASEP) revealed that, in comparison with a control group, students in ASEP classes perceived their classrooms as being more satisfying and individualized and having a better material environment (Fraser 1986). The significance of this evaluation, as well as Welch and Walberg's (1972) evaluation of Harvard Project Physics in the United States, is that student perceptions differentiated revealingly between curricula, even when various outcome measures showed negligible differences.

The fact that most instruments which assess perceptions have different forms for assessing actual and preferred conditions and forms for teachers and students permits investigation of differences between students' and teachers' perceptions, and differences between the actual situation and that preferred by students or teachers. Fisher and Fraser's (1983) research revealed that, first, students preferred a more positive classroom environment than they perceived as being actually present and, second, teachers perceived a more positive classroom environment than did their students in the same classrooms. These results replicate studies in school classrooms in the United States, Israel, and Australia (Fraser in press), as well as in other settings such as hospital wards and work milieus (e.g., Moos 1974).

In a study by Wubbels et al. (1992) in the Netherlands, the majority of teachers (70%) perceived the classroom environment more favorably than their students. However, the perceptions of another group of teachers (30%) were more negative than those of their students. Overall, this study suggested that teacher perceptions are shaped partly by their ideals about the learning environment (i.e., teachers' ideals can distort their perceptions of the actual learning environment). The discrepancy between teachers' and students' perceptions on average was larger for teachers who exhibited fewer behaviors that promoted student cognitive and affective outcomes than for teachers who exhibited more of those behaviors.

The third group of studies reviewed by Fraser (1986) shows that researchers in various countries have used students' perceptions as criterion variables in studies aimed at identifying how perceptions vary with such factors as teacher personality, class size, grade level, student gender, subject matter, the nature of the school-level environment, and the type of school. Studies into the transition from elementary to high school in the United States have revealed a deterioration in the perceived classroom environment when students move from generally smaller elementary schools to larger, departmentally organized lower secondary schools (Midgley et al. 1991). This decline could be attributable to less positive student relations with teachers and reduced student opportunities for decision-making in the classroom.

3. Associations Between Student Perceptions and Student Outcomes

A strong tradition in past research (Haertel et al. 1981) has shown that student perceptions of classroom environment account for appreciable amounts of variance in cognitive and affective learning outcomes, often beyond that attributable to background student characteristics. The practical implication from this research is that student outcomes might be improved by creating classroom environments found empirically to be conducive to learning.

Fraser (in press) has tabulated a set of 40 studies in which the effects of student perceptions of their classrooms on student outcomes were investigated in numerous countries. These studies involved a variety of cognitive and affective outcome measures, student perception instruments, and samples of students from a variety of grade levels.

The findings from prior research are highlighted in the results of a meta-analysis involving 734 correlations from 12 studies including 823 classes in eight subject areas containing 17,805 students in four nations (Haertel et al. 1981). Learning posttest scores and gains were found consistently and strongly to be associated with student perceptions of their classrooms, although correlations generally were higher in samples of older students and in studies employing collectivities such as classes and schools (in contrast to individual students) as the units of statistical analysis. In particular, higher achievement on a variety of measures was found in classes perceived by students as having greater cohesiveness, satisfaction, and goal direction, and less disorganization and friction. In a study of science laboratory classes in Nigeria, Israel, the United Kingdom, Canada, the United States, and Australia, students' perceptions were more positive in settings in which integration between theory and laboratory classes was perceived to be greater (Fraser et al. 1992).

Fraser and Fisher (1983) used a person–environment interaction framework in exploring whether or not student outcomes depend, not only on student perceptions of the actual classroom environment, but also on the match between students' preferences and the actual environment. Overall, the findings suggest that similarity between actual and preferred environment could be as important as the actual environment in predicting student achievement of important affective and cognitive aims.

4. Current Trends and Desirable Future Directions

While speculations on numerous trends and directions can be offered, three topics are treated briefly in this section. They are school psychology, constructivist learning environments, and personal forms of scales.

4.1 School Psychology

Given the school psychologist's changing role, the work on student perceptions of classrooms provides a good example of an area that furnishes a number of ideas, techniques, and research findings that could be valuable in school psychology. Traditionally, school psychologists have tended to concentrate heavily and sometimes exclusively on their roles in assessing and

enhancing academic achievement and other valued learning outcomes. Understanding student perceptions of classrooms enables school psychologists to become sensitized to subtle but important aspects of classroom life. Burden and Fraser (in press) report some ways in which students' perceptions were used in the United Kingdom in helping teachers change their classroom interactive styles, and in using discrepancies between students' perceptions of actual and preferred environment as an effective basis to guide improvements in their classrooms.

4.2 Constructivist Learning Environments

Traditionally, teachers have conceived their roles to be concerned with revealing or transmitting the logical structures of their knowledge, and directing students through rational inquiry toward discovering the predetermined universal truths expressed in the form of laws, principles, rules, and algorithms. Developments in history, philosophy, and sociology have provided educators with a better understanding of the nature of knowledge development. At the level of the individual learner, there has been a realization that meaningful learning is a cognitive process of making sense, or purposeful problem-solving, of the experiential world of the individual in relation to the totality of the individual's already constructed knowledge. This sense-making process involves active negotiation and consensus building. Because a new learning environment instrument is needed to assist researchers to assess the degree to which a particular classroom's environment is perceived by students to be consistent with a constructivist epistemology, and in order to assist teachers to reflect on their epistemological assumptions and reshape their teaching practice, the Constructivist Learning Environment Survey (CLES) was developed. The CLES includes four scales: autonomy, prior knowledge, collaboration, and reflection (Taylor and Fraser 1991).

4.3 Personal Forms of Student Perception Scales

There is potentially a major problem with nearly all existing classroom environment instruments when used to identify differences between subgroups within a classroom (e.g., boys and girls) or in the construction of case studies of individual students. The problem is that items are worded in such a way that they elicit an individual student's perceptions of the class as a whole, as distinct from that student's perceptions of his or her own role within the classroom. For example, items in the traditional class form of classroom environment instruments might seek students' opinions about whether "the work of the class is difficult" or whether "the teacher is friendly toward the class." In contrast, a personal form of the same items would seek opinions about whether "I find the work of the class difficult" or whether "the teacher is friendly toward me."

A vivid example of the way in which certain subgroups of students within a class perceived different subenvironments because of the teacher's differential treatment of them is provided by a study of "target" students (i.e., pupils who monopolized the verbal interaction during whole-class activities) (see Fraser in press). It was found that target students perceived significantly greater levels of involvement and rule clarity than did nontarget students. Furthermore, these perceptions were consistent with classroom observations that the teachers directed more questions at target students and allowed them (and not other students) to call out answers without being asked. Similarly, Tobin et al.'s (1990) case studies of individual students revealed that meaningful differences in perceptions existed between certain students, and that those differences were consistent with the teacher's expectations of and attitudes toward individuals. The findings of these two studies highlight the need for a new generation of student perception instruments which are more capable of detecting the differences in perceptions between individuals or subgroups within the class.

Fraser et al. (1992) developed and validated parallel class and personal forms of both an actual and preferred version of the Science Laboratory Environment Inventory (SLEI), and reported three uses of the new personal form. First, students' perceptions on the class form were found to be systematically more favorable than their scores on the personal form, perhaps suggesting that students have a more detached view of the classroom as it applies to the class as a whole. Second, as hypothesized, gender differences in perceptions were somewhat larger on the personal form than on the class form. Third, although a study of associations between students' outcomes and their perceptions of the science laboratory revealed that the magnitudes of associations were comparable for class and personal forms, commonality analyses showed that each form accounted for appreciable amounts of outcome variance which was independent of that explained by the other form. This finding serves to justify the decision to evolve separate class and personal forms.

5. Conclusion

Outcome measures alone cannot provide a complete picture of the educational process, so student perceptions of classrooms also should be used to provide information about subtle but important aspects of classroom life. However, because teachers and students have systematically different perceptions of the learning environments of the same classrooms (the "rose-colored glasses" phenomenon), student feedback about classrooms is important in teacher education, staff development, and school improvement efforts.

See also: Classroom Environments; Classroom Assessment

References

Burden R, Fraser B J in press Use of classroom environment assessments in school psychology: A British perspective. *Psychol. Sch.*

Fisher D L, Fraser B J 1983 A comparison of actual and preferred classroom environment as perceived by science teachers and students. *J. Res. Sci. Teach.* 20(1): 55–61

Fraser B J 1986 *Classroom Environment*. Croom Helm, London

Fraser B J in press Classroom and school climate. In: Gabel D (ed.) in press *Handbook of Research on Science Teaching and Learning*. National Association for Research in Science Teaching, Washington, DC

Fraser B J, Fisher D L 1983 Student achievement as a function of person–environment fit: A regression surface analysis. *Br. J. Educ. Psychol.* 53(1): 89–99

Fraser B J, Walberg H J (eds.) 1991 *Educational Environments: Evaluation, Antecedents and Consequences*. Pergamon Press, Oxford

Fraser B J, Giddings G J, McRobbie C J 1992 Assessment of the psychological environment of university science laboratory classrooms: A cross-national study. *Higher Ed.* 24: 431–51

Haertel G D, Walberg H J, Haertel E H 1981 Sociopsychological environments and learning: A quantitative synthesis. *Br. Educ. Res. J.* 7(1): 27–36

Meece J L, Courtney D P 1992 Gender differences in students' perceptions: Consequences for achievement-related choices. In: Schunk D H, Meece J L (eds.) 1992

Midgley C, Eccles J S, Feldlaufer H 1991 Classroom environment and the transition to junior high school. In: Fraser B J, Walberg H J (eds.) 1991

Moos R H 1974 *The Social Climate Scales: An Overview*. Consulting Psychologists Press, Palo Alto, California

Moos R H, Trickett E J 1987 *Classroom Environment Scale Manual*, 2nd. edn. Consulting Psychologists Press, Palo Alto, California

Schunk D H, Meece J L (eds.) 1992 *Student Perceptions in the Classroom*. Erlbaum, Hillsdale, New Jersey

Taylor P C, Fraser B J 1991 Development of an instrument for assessing constructivist learning environments. Paper presented at the annual meeting of the American Educational Research Association, Chicago, Illinois

Tobin K, Kahle J B, Fraser B J (eds.) 1990 *Windows into Science Classrooms: Problems Associated with Higher-level Cognitive Learning*. Falmer Press, London

Welch W W, Walberg H J 1972 A national experiment in curriculum evaluation. *Am. Educ. Res. J.* 9(3): 373–83

Wittrock M C 1986 Students' thought processes. In: Wittrock M C (ed.) 1986 *Handbook of Research on Teaching*, 3rd. edn. Macmillan, New York

Wubbels T, Brekelmans M, Hooymayers H P 1992 Do teacher ideals distort the self-reports of their interpersonal behavior? *Teaching and Teacher Education* 8(1): 47–58

Further Reading

Raudenbush S, Bryk A S 1986 A hierarchical model of studying school effects. *Sociol. Educ.* 59(1): 1–17

Student Cognitive Processes

P. H. Winne and D. L. Butler

In the mid-twentieth century conceptions about learning and about how instructional events help students learn underwent a transition. A new view of learning—that the learner adapts to events as they unfold in an instructional environment—replaced one that saw the learner's behavior as controlled by instructional stimuluses (Anderson and Gates 1950). Research into this adaptive process aimed to discover principles for designing instructional environments that could specify "the experiences which most effectively implant in the individual a disposition to learn . . . the ways in which a body of knowledge should be structured so that it can be most readily grasped by the learner . . . the most effective sequences in which to present the materials to be learned . . . the nature and pacing of rewards and punishments in the process of learning and teaching" (Bruner 1964 pp. 307–08). A rapprochement between psychology and instructional research was underway that would sweep up the field of educational psychology within the larger cognitive revolution (Glaser 1982). As research accumulated over the next 40 years, perspectives on learning, instruction, and the learner would evolve significantly.

The view of learning that came to guide theory and research characterizes the learner as an active inquiring agent. Classifying the learner as "active" implies that he or she is continuously involved in cognition about self and environment. Elements interacting in cognition are the learner's mental structures of knowledge and the learner's current perceptions of events, people, and objects in the environment, which are developed in terms of the student's existing knowledge. Thus this conception emphasizes the intrinsic and central role of the learner's prior knowledge as a background for interpreting instruction and as a resource with which to construct new achievements in school subjects.

Characterizing the learner as "inquiring" emphasizes the central role played by hypothesis-framing and testing as the student takes part in the instructional environment. Theoretically, the student creates provisional models and theories about matters at hand; for example, how to participate in a discovery lesson, how to explain why some heavy objects float, how to gain acceptance by peers, and how to achieve personal satisfaction. Means for inquiring into phenomena, models of systems, and theories are themselves learned and can become objects of inquiry.

Finally, acknowledging the learner as an "agent" recognizes that the student does not merely observe surroundings and receive information available therein. Beyond observational and receptive qualities, the student also steps forward to define goals and to seek specific information from peers, a text, or the teacher. Thus, the learner shapes and takes actions in the instructional environment. These acts, mental and physical, elicit information which the student seeks for the purpose of guiding subsequent thinking and acting. In this way, students co-create events that comprise instructional tasks and generate their own learning-from-instruction.

1. A Framework Describing Cognition and Instruction

Many models have been proposed to characterize forms of cognition and the kinds of information that are cognitively manipulated as learners participate in instruction. Literature that predates this entry is summarized in Winne (1985, 1991a, 1991b) and Wittrock (1986). Figure 1 presents a model which describes a learner's cognitive participation in instruction. It involves three broad classes of variables: characteristics of the learner, characteristics of the instructional tasks, and events that transpire as the learner interacts with instructional tasks. Other contemporary models of instructional cognition differ primarily in the variables they assign to these different classes. Variables in Fig. 1 are representative of those in other models and, obviously, are not exhaustive.

Figure 1 should not be interpreted as suggesting that values for variables or relationships among variables are static. Over time, variables are reciprocally determined and interact. That is, changes in a variable in one class can affect other variables within that same class, and may influence variables in other classes as well. In turn, the affected variable(s) may induce changes in other variables, including the one focused on initially. In this reciprocally determined system, identifying a single "cause" is difficult because choosing the slice in time within which to observe change is arbitrary. For instance, consider the case of a section heading within a textbook chapter. At the time the student is reading the chapter, it seems that the heading (a characteristic of the task environment) induces the student to retrieve (an event transpiring when the learner interacts with the text) some particular prior knowledge (a characteristic of the student). Earlier, however, when the textbook author was writing the chapter, the decision to insert the heading (a characteristic of the task environment) was probably based on a prediction about the prior knowledge that an average reader would possess (a characteristic of the student), and on the author's understanding about how inducing students to retrieve that prior knowledge might help

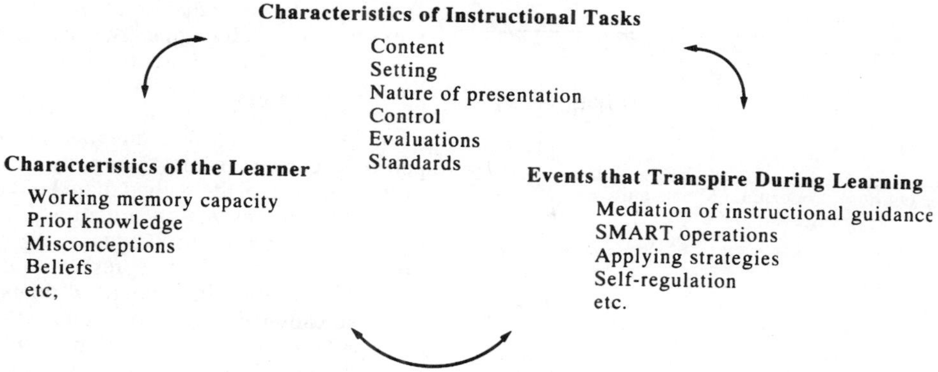

Characteristics of Instructional Tasks

Content
Setting
Nature of presentation
Control
Evaluations
Standards

Characteristics of the Learner

Working memory capacity
Prior knowledge
Misconceptions
Beliefs
etc,

Events that Transpire During Learning

Mediation of instructional guidance
SMART operations
Applying strategies
Self-regulation
etc.

Figure 1
Contextual model of instructional information processing

them to construct an understanding of information in the chapter (an event transpiring when the learner interacts with the text). At this earlier time, then, the character of learners' prior knowledge affected the task environment by causing the author to include the heading in the text.

2. Characteristics of the Learner

Characteristics of the learner provide resources for and set limits on how a student reciprocally interprets and shapes instructional tasks. In information-processing models there are two main divisions of these characteristics: (a) features of the cognitive system that processes information; (b) kinds of knowledge (information) represented in the student's mind, both as products of information processing and as vehicles for processing information.

2.1 The Information-processing System

The mind is a biological and physical system and, hence, its functioning is influenced in part by its physical architecture (Newell 1990). While learning is partly a function of characteristics of human biological systems, those characteristics rarely have a direct, observable impact on learning in a classroom or in self-study situations. Two exceptions are notable, however.

Working memory, the metaphorical mental location where information is processed, has a limited channel capacity or span. This capacity is a joint function of the brain's neurophysiological properties and characteristics of the information being processed. Approximately 5 ± 2 information-processing events, such as maintaining conceptual knowledge in memory or performing a routine based on procedural knowl-

edge, can be carried out simultaneously. The more structured knowledge is—chunked or schematized, in the case of conceptual knowledge; composed and automated, in the case of procedural knowledge—the greater the apparent capacity of working memory. This explains how experts can appear to have huge capacity relative to novices when the fact is that experts use highly structured or automated forms of information in approximately the same "mental volume" in which a novice processes considerably less "dense" information. In general, the interaction of properties of working memory and of information's structure jointly influence information processing during learning from instruction.

The second area where physical properties of the mind clearly influence information processing in instruction arises in cases of learners with a typical neurological conditions (e.g., specific learning disabilities).

2.2 Knowledge

Terms for and theories about knowledge are legion (Alexander et al. 1991). Figure 2 revises Alexander et al.'s model by distinguishing two forms for representing knowledge—declarative and procedural; two levels of awareness about knowledge—tacit and explicit; and three kinds of information in knowledge—conceptual, metacognitive, and sociocultural.

Declarative knowledge is descriptive information, or "knowledge that." It remains static until changed by learning. Hosts of terms describe organizations in which declarative knowledge is organized or stored in memory. Some of the more common are analogy, chunk, concept, frame, image, metaphor, proposition, and schema.

Procedural knowledge is rules, often called condition–action rules or if–then rules, because only

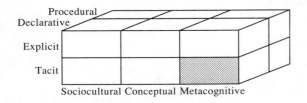

Figure 2
Facets of knowledge

if particular conditions are satisfied is this knowledge invoked. One type of procedural knowledge classifies situations based on their properties. It is typically referred to as conditional knowledge because it defines when, where, and why declarative knowledge or a rule is relevant. Conditional knowledge plays a central role in students' use of cognitive strategies. A second type of procedural knowledge, referred to simply as a rule, acts on information to transform knowledge, such as translating information into a visual image. Procedural knowledge underlies the processes that students perform, such as organizing materials and the surrounding environment in preparation for studying. The certainty of the output obtained by applying procedural knowledge can vary. Thus algorithms, which yield reliable outcomes, are distinguished from heuristics, which are predictive but do not assure a determinate result. Sets of rules, in which the conditions of some are satisfied by the output of other rules' actions, are called production systems.

Tacit knowledge (Polanyi 1966) is knowledge the learner possesses which influences cognitive processing but of which the learner is not really aware. It is proposed to exist because, so far, it has not been possible to account fully for information processing and achievements in terms of explicit, reportable forms of knowledge. Iran-Nejad (1990) hypothesized the existence of cognitively local and relatively independent units of procedure-like knowledge that students accumulate through experience. These units are "dynamic," that is, they process information automatically and in parallel with processing that occurs in working memory, but lie "outside" working memory itself. Such dynamic components of knowledge may constitute tacit knowledge and, because of their independence from working memory, explain the apparent impenetrability of tacit knowledge.

Explicit knowledge is knowledge a learner can consciously inspect, including tacit knowledge that converts to explicit form by becoming an "object of thought" (Prawat 1989). Alexander et al. (1991) distinguish two kinds of explicit knowledge, conceptual and metacognitive knowledge, each of which is further divided.

Conceptual knowledge, according to Alexander et al. has two major divisions. The first, content knowledge, is information a student has about his or her physical, social, and mental world. It can be used informally or, especially in the context of schooling, it can be formalized into domains of study such as spelling, science, music, gymnastics, and art. Discourse knowledge, the second main kind of conceptual knowledge, represents information about common forms and functions of language, as well as other symbol systems used to represent and convey conceptual knowledge. In formalized domains of study, discourse knowledge may be unique to the domain and undergird procedures for developing new knowledge in that domain. In science, for instance, a mixture of text structures, mathematical formalisms, and graphic symbol systems are found in academic textbooks. These same discourse structures are used generatively by scientists as tools to extend knowledge of their domain.

As described above, students' extant or prior content knowledge has a powerful influence on information processing and resulting achievements (Perkins and Simmons 1988). Misconceptions may block accurate perceptions of information presented in instruction. Also, students can have difficulty translating and integrating information presented in different discourse systems, such as words and mathematical expressions (Dee Lucas and Larkin 1991), because they lack knowledge about how the two systems correspond. With instruction about what such structures are and how they can be used as schemata for building and monitoring comprehension benefits are observed in recall, problem solving, and transfer (Cook and Mayer 1988, Fuson and Willis 1989).

Metacognitive knowledge is the knowledge that provides the means by which learners actively inquire about knowledge. It is a second-order construct that represents reflections on or knowledge about knowledge, and the procedures by which a student regulates cognition and action. Since metacognition is effortful, conscious cognition, the cells in Fig. 2 where metacognitive and tacit knowledge intersect are shaded to indicate that the model's factors are not fully independent. Alexander et al. (1991) differentiate four interrelated facets of metacognitive knowledge: task knowledge, self-knowledge, strategy knowledge, and goals and plans.

Task knowledge is information a student perceives about the circumstances in which a task is situated and about features of the task itself. It is a composite of the student's prior knowledge about tasks similar to the one now being addressed, plus information provided by the teacher, peers, or directions on assignments. Typical aspects of task knowledge include the number and clarity of criteria by which progress and final products of the task will be evaluated, time allocated for the task, resources that can be acquired to assist with work on the task, whether the student or someone else controls the processes by which the task can develop, and the timing and nature of feedback about performance. These kinds of information create elements of a stable backdrop for performance and, in the case of accessible resources and feedback, new and updated information about how to work on the task and how that work is progressing relative to criteria.

Students may have misconceptions about tasks that interfere with achieving the goals of instruction. For example, Anderson et al. (1991) observed that low-achieving first-grade students often approached seatwork tasks in reading with the understanding that they were to "get the work done" rather than understand information in the task, and develop strategies for accomplishing tasks such as those assigned. In this instance, the students' views of criteria by which the tasks' processes and products would be evaluated were antithetical to developing conceptual knowledge from reading and enhancing procedural knowledge for reading with comprehension.

Self-knowledge consists of a student's idiosyncratic motivational orientations to topics and instructional tasks, plus the student's characteristic beliefs about learning. This knowledge has a fundamental impact on the goals and plans a learner adopts. Winne (1991b) described four constituents of motivational orientation. Incentives are the values—positive, neutral, and negative—that a student perceives to be associated with goals to be accomplished in a specific task. Efficacy judgments are the student's beliefs about skills, abilities, and power to achieve those goals in relation to resources and constraints in the task environment. Outcomes are the results the student predicts will follow from engaging with the task by applying knowledge and skills considered in making the efficacy judgment. Attributions identify reasons, such as a person's ability or the difficulty of a task, that explain why work on the task yields the predicted (or realized) outcomes. All four kinds of motivational knowledge combine in a descriptive profile of the task's utility relative to other approaches to this task or to other tasks.

Strategy knowledge is knowledge about how to process information in tasks to promote comprehension, learning, remembering, and transfer. More specifically, strategy knowledge consists of cognitive procedures that students can use to construct and refine conceptual knowledge, and to develop and elaborate strategy knowledge itself. Four main categories of cognitive strategies, each subclassified at two levels of tasks, basic and complex, can be identified (Weinstein and Mayer 1986). Rehearsal strategies, such as mentally repeating information or copying text, enhance remembering. Elaboration strategies, such as developing mnemonics or assembling new material with prior knowledge using analogies, construct links for encoding knowledge. Organizing strategies—for instance, developing categories or translating and extending newly presented information as spatial maps—promote the assembly of new information into chunks and schemata. Monitoring strategies identify shortcomings in performance and point toward repairs that improve it.

To use strategy knowledge productively, students need to blend several kinds of knowledge. First, they require conceptual knowledge about the subject that is the focus of the task, plus conceptual knowledge about the strategy. The latter includes knowledge of the parts or steps that comprise the strategy (declarative component), knowledge about how to perform those steps (procedural component), and knowledge about which strategies are appropriate given present circumstances surrounding particular tasks (conditional component). Finally, they need metacognitive knowledge about the task, themselves as learners, the implementation of strategies in the context of tasks, and the probable impact of each strategy on performance.

Goals and plans are mental constructions that students, as active inquiring agents, create. Goals are multifaceted representations of states to be achieved that inherently fuse affects (information that represents feelings and emotions) with the various kinds of knowledge previously discussed. Plans are mental structures that range from small, focused, one-step rules to grand and encompassing orchestrations of events. Plans give shape to a student's information processing, constituting how the student addresses instructional tasks. Metaphorically, goals are the "reason qua motive" for engaging in a task, and plans provide instrumental knowledge on which the student calls to realize goals.

Sociocultural knowledge is the accumulated collection of attitudes and beliefs that a student has acquired as a result of experiences in a social and cultural milieu. In relation to instruction, it is about the forms, content, and functions of instruction that have developed from students' previous participation in a variety of instructional tasks. Sociocultural knowledge typically resides at the tacit level; it can, however, be addressed directly, thus becoming explicit. As tacit knowledge, however, sociocultural knowledge can influence information processing without students being aware of it.

A study by Ortony et al. (1985), for example, indicated that Afro–American children who engaged often in a turn-taking verbal riposte called "playing the dozens" are in a stronger position to understand figurative language in literary tasks. More generally, students' differential experiences involving social and cultural conventions influence their abilities to recognize narrators' or speakers' use of literary devices and characters' departures from social conventions that emphasize unusual events (Beach and Hynds 1991). These differences in tacit sociocultural knowledge thus affect what students can glean from tasks and how they judge accomplishments in tasks.

3. Instructional Tasks and Student Cognition

Instructing students is an intentional act in which an instructor strives to improve the cognitive resources that students need to perform tasks. If instruction is effective, students develop more knowledge than they would develop if they were left entirely on their own. That is, the instructor presumes that, by managing students' encounters with curricular information and by guiding them in cognitively processing the subject matter, educational objectives can be achieved more effectively than if they were left to their own devices. Thus, from the point of view of an instructor, instruction consists of (a) deliberately arranging (b) features of the instructional environment (c) to guide (d) the student's modification of aptitudes (e) for performing (f) specified tasks that reflect instructional objectives. From the student's point of view, participating in instruction has three main facets: mediating instruction, learning, and demonstrating achievements.

Corresponding to elements (b) and (c) of instruction, the student perceives features of the instructional environment and decides whether and how to make use of them. The match between students' perceptions and the instructor's guidance is a first step toward instructional effectiveness. For example, an author may mark sections of a text by headings, or a teacher may use transition statements to close segments of a lesson and introduce upcoming content or activity structures. These kinds of information or mediating instruction are features of the environment by which the instructor is attempting to improve what the student might learn from a text.

For the instructor's intentions to be realized, the student must perceive these communications as a particular kind of information, namely, information about what is to be learned and the means for learning it. Moreover, the student must elect to apply particular cognitive processes to that information so that prior knowledge becomes integrated with new subject matter that will be presented in the next moments. In addressing this task, the student determines whether and how to participate in instructional events as the instructor created them.

Corresponding to part (d) of instruction is the student's processing of information—or learning—available in the instructional environment in concert with prior knowledge. To learn from the text or the lesson, the student must construct temporary structures of knowledge in working memory, such as a hypothesis about schemata useful for understanding information that will be presented next in the text or in an upcoming segment of the lesson. Then, as new information comes available, the student must integrate it with prior knowledge to modify and extend it. The dynamic events comprising students' engagements in information processing form the topics of Sect. 5.

Corresponding to parts (e) and (f) of instruction is the student's job of demonstrating learning by attempting to perform tasks that reflect instructional objectives. For example, having read a text or engaged in a lesson's activities, the student might be invited to discuss issues raised, solve problems posed by the teacher, or design an activity that requires applying information recently presented.

4. Task Characteristics

Because features of tasks are relatively much easier to manipulate and control than are characteristics of students, thousands of research articles have described thousands of experiments in which task characteristics have been investigated as independent variables. To organize this immense variety, five facets of tasks can be identified: conditions under which the task is performed; operations that carry out the task; products that result from operations; evaluations that feed back information about products; standards by which achievement is gauged (Winne 1991b).

Winne and Marx (1989) suggest that there are three conditions under which classroom tasks are performed. These include the content to be learned (declarative and procedural knowledge), the setting (resources available, social features, time allocation), and the nature of the presentation (the medium, goals, and performance cues). Students confronted with academic tasks develop a tentative model representing their interpretation of these conditions, and these perceptions mediate the students' development of goals, plans, and cognitive processing in response to those conditions.

Task conditions interact with the student's information processing to determine the "cognitive load" of a task. Cognitive load can be thought of as a ratio of the demands placed on the student's information-processing system relative to its capacity. Optimum load is a value less, but not greatly less, than 1. A combination of variables, such as rate of presentation, permanence of information display, and the meaningfulness, amount, and complexity of information, operationally define the cognitive load of a task. As noted in Sect. 2.1, there is a relation between information-processing capacity and the degree of organization or automaticity of a student's prior knowledge.

Another important facet of a task is the location of control of the operations needed to carry out the task. Models of instruction vary from discovery environments, in which the student controls most of the task operations, to strongly didactic environments, in which the instructor controls instructional events. When control is vested with the student, cognitive load increases, because the student must regulate most of the information processing. Under most conditions, when learners are granted control, they often exit tasks before they fully achieve knowledge of the subject.

5. Dynamics of Learning from Instruction

This section examines the dynamic interplay among variables and classes of variables in Fig. 1. It is divided into two parts: learning operations and the promotion of self-regulation.

5.1 Learning Operations

Winne (1991a) has described five primitive cognitive operations in which students engage while completing tasks: *s*timulating, *m*onitoring, *a*ssembling, *r*ehearsing, and *t*ranslating. In combination, they form the SMART operations. Stimulating transfers information from long-term memory into working memory, making it "the object of thought". Monitoring matches or compares features of items which are active in working memory. Assembling forms new relations between items of information. Rehearsing maintains information in working memory and can transfer it into long-term memory. Finally, translating recodes information.

Typically, these SMART operations are combined in a learning task to create three main kinds of strategies (Zimmerman 1989). Behavioral strategies lead to choices about overt behavior for pursuing a task. For example, a student might seek feedback by looking up answers after working problems in a text. Environmental strategies are those where the learner modifies conditions of a task to make them more favorable. For instance, a learner might move closer to the teacher to receive more attention. Finally, covert strategies are sequences of cognitions by which a learner guides learning. For example, a learner might mentally summarize a section in a text to improve comprehension.

Although highly automated strategies are tacit, as when an expert engages in tasks that do not challenge expertise, deliberate use of strategies is associated with greater gains in achievement when learners address new material or engage in transfer tasks. Thus, while education aims to help students acquire a large repertoire of automatic–tacit strategies, effective learners also must consciously regulate learning in response to challenging instructional tasks. Such learners are called self-regulated (Paris and Byrnes 1989, Zimmerman 1989) or self-instructive (Wang and Palincsar 1989).

In models of self-regulated learning, students first interpret a task's conditions. Next, perceptions about the values of a task's goals (incentives), judgments of competence and control over learning (efficacy judgments), and beliefs about the roles of effort and ability in learning (attributions) mediate between the student's understanding of task demands and the goals he or she adopts for learning. For example, in the face of low expectation for success, a student may choose task avoidance. In contrast, if a task's goals have high incentive and the student is moderately confident that success can be achieved with effort, setting a goal to understand is probable.

Based on the goals they adopt, self-regulated learners then develop a plan for action, grounded in prior knowledge. A central feature of this plan is obtaining feedback by monitoring intermediate products against goals. Incrementally, the learner modifies knowledge, motivational beliefs, goals, and strategies in response to that feedback. Thus, interaction with the task evolves "strategically" based on dynamic engagements involving the learner, the task and the events that transpire during learning.

Rumelhart and Norman (1978) describe three mechanisms by which new learning is acquired and integrated with prior knowledge in this process. Accretion involves monitoring new information in terms of an existing general schema and encoding the new material as a particular instantiation of that general structure. Tuning is undertaken when new information does not correspond to an existing schema and the student reorganizes elements of prior knowledge to accommodate the new information. For example, a child who has overgeneralized the concept "dog" to include all furry, four-legged animals tunes a schema to differentiate cats from dogs. Finally, restructuring is necessary when no schema adequately encompasses new information or when existing schemata are inadequate for making sense of new knowledge. Here, students construct entirely new knowledge structures by assembling existing knowledge or by inducing a new schema.

Perkins and Simmons (1988) described three classes of misconceptions that parallel Rumelhart and Norman's learning mechanisms. Naive misconceptions are characteristic of insufficient background knowledge. These misconceptions can be remedied by accretion. Ritual misconceptions arise when students have formalized knowledge but can not apply it easily or transfer it. Tuning schemata, for example, by developing analogies, can remedy this problem. Finally, Gordian misconceptions are those where complex formalized knowledge is faulty. Repairing these misconceptions requires the entire conceptual frame to be restructured, producing a personal paradigm shift.

5.2 Promoting Self-regulated Learning

To assist students in developing self-regulated learning, explicit instruction about cognitive strategies should be integrated with subject matter. In this format, subject matter knowledge grows in parallel with declarative and procedural knowledge about strategies, and with conditional knowledge that can guide choices about when to apply particular strategies under specific conditions. To promote transfer and students' independent use of strategies following instruction, metacognitive strategies can be taught that can guide students in planning how to approach tasks and in monitoring progress (Wang and Palincsar 1989). Teaching students positive motivational beliefs, such as refocusing attributions toward effortful use of strategies (Borkowski et al. 1988), is another critical element in promoting self-regulation (Paris and Byrnes 1989).

An assumption underlying students' independent use of strategies is that they consciously and reflectively choose strategies. Salomon and Perkins (1989) highlighted the importance of consciously chosen strategies in their distinction between two kinds transfer. "Low-road transfer" can be promoted by repeated experiences that involve using knowledge in a variety of contexts. It results in automatic transfer across the range of task conditions the student has experienced. "High-road transfer," in contrast, requires the student deliberately to abstract principles about applying strategies. Promoting such reflection in instruction invites the student to decontextualize principles, extending their range of application beyond past experiences. In this analysis, the process of approaching high-road transfer equates to independent use of cognitive strategies.

6. Conclusion

By viewing the student as an active, inquiring agent who constructs knowledge, rather than a mere receiver of information, theories of information processing have come to emphasize the role of a student's prior knowledge and of processes that create achievements through the student's participation in instruction. To realize these theories, researchers have devised and tested systems that characterize prior knowledge and that describe information-handling processes. Modern theories also view instruction as an interaction between features in a teaching environment and each student's prior knowledge, rather than as a unidirectional effect of instruction on students. The student's mediation of instructional events and self-regulation of approaches to learning are recognized as potent factors that influence the development of achievements. An important advance has been a gain in knowledge about ways of guiding students in mediating instruction and in regulating information processes that build knowledge. Continued research in these areas promises gains in theoretical and practical understandings about how instruction can be optimized for effectiveness relative to each student's individual differences.

See also: Information Processing Theories of Teaching; Cognitive Styles and Learning

References

Alexander P A, Schallert D L, Hare V C 1991 Coming to terms: How researchers in learning and literacy talk about knowledge. *Rev. Educ. Res.* 61(3): 315–43
Anderson G L, Gates A I 1950 The general nature of learning. In: Henry N B (ed.) 1990 *Learning and Instruction*, 49th Yearbook of the National Society for the Study of Education, Pt 1. University of Chicago Press, Chicago, Illinois
Beach R, Hynds S 1991 Research on response to literature. In: Barr R, Kamil M L et al. (eds.) 1991 *Handbook of Reading Research*, Vol. 2. Longman, New York
Borkowski J G, Wehing R S, Carr M 1988 Effects of attributional retraining on strategy-based reading comprehension in learning-disabled students. *J. Educ. Psychol.* 80: 46–53
Bruner J S 1964 Some theorems on instruction illustrated with reference to mathematics. In: Hilgard E R (ed.) 1964 *Theories of Learning and Instruction*, 63rd Yearbook of the National Society for the Study of Education, Pt 1. University of Chicago Press, Chicago, Illinois
Cook L K, Mayer R E 1988 Teaching readers about the structure of scientific text. *J. Educ. Psychol.* 80(4): 448–56
Dee Lucas D, Larkin J H 1991 Equations in scientific proofs: Effects on comprehension. *Am. Educ. Res. J.* 28(3): 661–82
Fuson K C, Willis G B 1989 Second graders' use of schematic drawings in solving addition and subtraction word problems. *J. Educ. Psychol.* 81(4): 514–20
Glaser R 1982 Instructional psychology: Past, present, and future. *Am. Psychol.* 37: 292–305
Iran-Nejad A 1990 Active and dynamic self-regulation of learning processes. *Rev. Educ. Res.* 60(4): 573–602
Newell A 1990 *Unified Theories of Cognition.* Harvard University Press, Cambridge, Massachusetts
Ortony A, Turner T, Larson-Shapiro N 1985 Cultural and instructional influences on figurative language comprehension by inner-city children. *Research in the Teaching of English.* 19(1): 25–36
Paris S G, Byrnes J P 1989 The constructivist approach to self-regulation in classrooms. In: Zimmerman B J, Schunk D H (eds.) 1989 *Self-regulated Learning and Academic Achievement.* Springer-Verlag, Berlin
Perkins D N, Simmons R 1988 Patterns of misunderstanding: An integrative model for science, math, and programming. *Rev. Educ. Res.* 58: 303–26
Polanyi M 1966 *The Tacit Dimension.* Anchor Press, Garden City, New York
Prawat R S 1989 Promoting access to knowledge, strategy, and disposition in students: A research synthesis. *Rev. Educ. Res.* 59: 1–41
Rumelhart D E, Norman D A 1978 Accretion, tuning, and restructuring: Three modes of learning. In: Cotton J W, Klatzky R (eds.) 1978 *Semantic Factors in Cognition.* Erlbaum, Hillsdale, New Jersey
Salomon G, Perkins D N 1989 Rocky roads to transfer: Rethinking mechanisms of a neglected phenomenon. *Educ. Psychol.* 24: 11–142
Wang M C, Palincsar A S 1989 Teaching students to assume an active role in their learning. In: Reynolds M C (ed.) 1989 *Knowledge Base for the Beginning Teacher.* Pergamon Press, Oxford
Weinstein C E, Mayer R E 1986 The teaching of learning strategies. In: Wittrock M C (ed.) 1986 *Handbook of Research on Teaching*, 3rd edn. Macmillan Inc., New York
Winne P H 1985 Cognitive processing in the classroom. In: Husén T, Postlethwaite T N (eds.) 1985 *The International Encyclopedia of Education* 1st edn. Pergamon Press, Oxford

Winne P H 1991a Instructional psychology and a model of teaching. In: Short R H, Stewin L L, McCann S J (eds.) 1991 *Educational Psychology: Canadian Perspectives*. Copp Clark Pittman, Toronto

Winne P H 1991b Motivation and teaching. In: Waxman H, Walberg H A (eds.) 1991 *Effective Teaching: Current Research*. McCutchan, Berkeley, California

Winne P H, Marx R W 1989 A cognitive–processing analysis of motivation within classroom tasks. In: Ames C, Ames R (eds.) 1989 *Research on Motivation in Education: Goals and Cognitions*. Academic Press, San Diego, California

Wittrock M C 1986 Students' thought processes. In: Wittrock M C (ed.) 1986 *Handbook of Research on Teaching*, 3rd edn. Macmillan Inc., New York

Zimmerman B J 1989 A social cognitive view of self-regulated academic learning. *J. Educ. Psychol.* 81: 329–39

Attention in Learning

A. Harnischfeger

"Attention" is a term used daily by teachers:

> Everyone knows what attention is. It is the taking possession by the mind, in clear and vivid form, of one out of what seem several simultaneously possible objects or trains of thought. Focalization, concentration, of consciousness are of its essence. It implies withdrawal from some things in order to deal effectively with others. . . . (James 1890 pp. 403–04).

1. Background

Psychologists of the nineteenth century were well aware of the importance of attention in choosing and directing perception and learning. Yet for most of the twentieth century, attention was of little interest to the predominant schools of research, Gestalt and behaviorism. Gestalt psychologists, mostly focusing on perception, had no need of a concept like attention, because they assumed isomorphism between the environmental stimuli and their cortical representations. Behaviorists, although quite interested in learning, focused on stimulus–response research with quite simple learning tasks, mainly involving memorization. They disregarded internal psychological processes, as they assumed that behavioral changes occurred as a consequence of learners' relatively passive responses to environmental stimuli. The only active behavior required of the learner for subsequent reinforcement was an overt response.

In contrast, the new field of cognitive science that evolved from neuropsychology and cognitive psychology from the early 1970s onward realized that the learner's internal cognitive activity is of central importance in learning and that learner-selected stimuli are sometimes perceived in ways not intended by the experiment (anticipated by Underwood 1963 as functional versus nominal stimulus). This selection of stimuli is referred to as "attention."

During the late 1980s, the role of motivation in attentional processes was addressed. Even volition, a concept abandoned by motivational psychology in the 1930s, was rediscovered as relevant for focus and intensity of attention (Heckhausen 1988).

2. Conceptual Models

Neurophysiological studies indicate that attentional processes occur in many areas of the brain, but certain areas appear to be of special importance: attended sensory information is processed in the parietal lobe; the hypocampus seems to play a role in short-term attention; and the frontal lobes play a central role in attentionally directed behavior. However, little is known about how complex attentional processes, such as those required in reading, are linked to underlying neural functions (Friedman et al. 1986).

Attention may involve selection of stimuli either entering the sensory system or coming from memory. Conceptual models of attention assume that selection of stimuli occurs either at entry into the sensory system or in a central system of information analysis. Selection is required, because stimuli seek access to the same information-processing structures, creating a bottleneck effect (structural interference model) or because stimuli compete over limited attentional resources (resource-competition model). The prevailing assumption in cognitive science is to conceive of attention as a resource capacity (Kahneman 1973, Posner 1978). It is also assumed that individuals differ in attentional capacity and that attention can be insufficient as a consequence of resource limitation—that is, low attentional capacity or low allocation of capacity to a specific activity, or as a consequence of data-limitation such as insufficient relevant task information.

The powerful role that attention plays as an input and processing selector in short-term or working memory has been emphasized in a model that locates attention in a central executive system controlling the "visuospatial" and the phonological systems

(Baddeley 1986). Whether such a central system should be conceived of as a unitary general processor or as multiple subprocessors with distinct capabilities is disputed (Barber 1989). This conception has implications for the number and kinds of tasks that can be attended to simultaneously.

Two components of attention have been identified: (a) involuntary, phasic attention, also called "arousal" or "orienting response" (Sokolov 1990), which is primarily a short-term response to stimuli; and (b) voluntary, tonic attention, which requires greater activity of the attending individual and tends to be of longer duration. Cognitive and instructional psychology are primarily concerned with voluntary attention, especially of a sustained nature, but arousal plays a role in activating sustained attention.

In the late 1980s models of attention were linked with concepts of motivation and ability. For example, Kanfer and Ackerman (1989) defined all individual differences in ability as differences in attentional resources. They identified three ways in which motivation affects attention: thus, motivation (a) directs behavior and controls (b) intensity and (c) persistence of effort. More attentional resources are required for more difficult tasks, and sustained attentional effort is necessary for complex skill acquisition. Motivational and volitional forces support such long-term attentional resource allocation.

3. Measurement

Although the models of attention are specified in psychological terms, neuroscience has aided in defining and measuring attention through recording of electrical brain waves, cerebral blood flow, and heart rate. Psychological measurements of attention have employed observation of individuals and recall by an individual. In classroom settings, observation of learners by the teacher or observers, who rate attentiveness by means of a rating scale, is a widely used procedure. Eye contact is considered a strong indicator of attention. The other widely used procedure is recall of attentional processes by an individual through questions or stimuli intended to facilitate self-observation. Such measures are only gross indicators of attention, with inaccuracies resulting from feigning and lack of sensitivity due to differences in intensity of attention.

4. Empirical Research in Teaching–Learning Settings

Empirical research on attention outside the laboratory, that is, in instructional settings, has focused heavily on the teaching and learning of reading and on children with learning disabilities and attention deficits.

Much research has focused on comparison of sustained voluntary attention and short-term voluntary and involuntary attention, especially as these vary between normal learners and learning-disabled, mentally retarded, and hyperkinetic learners. No differences in short-term response were found between the groups, but mentally retarded learners and learners with learning disabilities, behavior and hyperkinetic problems were found to have a lower sustained voluntary attention span, generally referred to as "attention deficit" or "distractability." However, these differences in attention were more pronounced in school learning than in nonacademic out-of-school settings. Sustained attention was also found to be task-specific. This points to the importance that motivation and volition play in learning.

Empirical research in reading has indicated that working memory capacity is an important aspect in the development of reading skills. Selecting relevant information seems to be more difficult for younger readers and for poor readers, as was also shown in studies where visual or phonological distractors such as words between the lines were used. Readers with better recall and comprehension seemed to employ more effective "selective attention strategies." Wittrock (1986) reported that text comprehension can be increased by directing the reader's attention with orienting stimuli such as questions inserted into text. Questions inserted before a related text facilitate verbatim learning, indicating that they help focus attention on relevant details. Questions at the end of a text require recall and reprocessing in working memory and tend to direct attention more broadly. Prior statement of learning objectives seems to focus attention on relevant information. Poor readers benefit more from such guidance than good readers.

How much attention a certain task requires or how fast information can be processed is also dependent on individuals' relevant prior knowledge and skills. Task demands and familiarity with the task are important determinants of speed of task completion. With increasing practice tasks require fewer attentional resources. They become increasingly "resource-insensitive." Research on automaticity in cognitive processes also indicates that well-practiced tasks require fewer attentional resources (i.e., less working memory) than new ones, thus making it possible to attend to multiple tasks simultaneously (Beech 1989). Self-regulation of attentional processes, including self-efficacy, was found to be an important aspect of attentional effort and consequently of school achievement (Bandura 1988, Zimmerman and Schunk 1989).

5. Implications of Findings for Teaching and Learning

Varied cognitive teaching strategies that enhance sustained voluntary attention have been developed.

The most commonly employed approach to increasing involuntary attention or arousal is through instructional materials that are appealing to the learner. Illustrations and layout may create interest, and so initiate attention.

A widely used strategy to increase attention, following the behaviorist tradition, is to reward attentional behavior. Many studies of behavior modification report positive results. Other strategies attempt to increase attention through restricting the amount of stimuli presented. Task-irrelevant information and distracting sensory stimuli are minimized. Often this stimulus reduction is combined with a focus on structuring the learning task clearly.

While the above strategies conceive of the learner as passive, cognitive strategies focusing on the learner as active teach self-help in building selective attentional strategies and sustained voluntary attention. The most widely used selective attention strategy is perhaps speed reading. Strategies building sustained voluntary attention use predominantly self-verbalization, often a variation of "stop, look, and listen."

In general, cognitive strategies have been more successful in increasing sustained voluntary attention in classroom settings than approaches that assume a passive learner. Research on active learning, motivation, cognitive strategies for stimuli selection, and self-control has produced effective tools for classroom teaching and learning.

6. Possible Directions for Research

Research on attentional processes has gained importance in cognitive science. Significant advances have been made in model-building and basic research. Research applicable to school learning has not yet absorbed these advances. Although some relevant and potent findings have reached the classroom, attentional processes need to be studied in actual classroom settings on the basis of recent conceptual models of attention. Further, most of applied research has focused on learning-disabled learners. Outside the area of reading, the study of typical learners has hardly advanced beyond observation of time on task and time off task.

Research on attention also needs to be integrated into more broadly defined conceptual models of teaching and learning (Wittrock 1991) and school learning (Harnischfeger and Wiley 1977, 1985). This would allow the study of attention within the framework of important aspects of instruction and the study of heterogeneous groups of learners who differ in ability, prior knowledge, learning style, and motivation. Cognitive psychology has been moving strongly in the direction of reconceptualizing ability and relating it to motivation and working memory processes, assigning attention a central role.

References

Baddeley A 1986 *Working Memory*. Clarendon Press, Oxford

Bandura A 1988 Self-regulation of motivation and action through goal systems. In: Hamilton V, Bower G H, Frijda N H (eds.) 1988 *Cognitive Perspectives on Emotion and Motivation*. Kluwer, Dordrecht

Barber P J 1989 Executing two tasks at once. In: Colley A M, Beech J R (eds.) 1989 *Acquisition and Performance of Cognitive Skills*. Wiley, New York

Beech J R 1989 The componential approach to learning reading skills. In: Colley A M, Beech J R (eds.) 1989 *Acquisition and Performance of Cognitive Skills*. Wiley, New York

Friedman S L, Klivington K A, Peterson R W (eds.) 1986 *The Brain, Cognition, and Education*. Academic Press, San Diego, California

Harnischfeger A, Wiley D E 1977 Kernkonzepte des Schullernens. *Zeitschrift für Entwicklungspsychologie und Pädagogische Psychologie* 9: 207–28 (1978 Conceptual issues in models of school learning. *J. Curric. Studies* 10 (3): 215–31)

Harnischfeger A, Wiley D E 1985 Origins of active learning time. In: Fisher C W, Berliner D C (eds.) 1985 *Perspectives on Instructional Time*. Longman, New York

Heckhausen H 1988 *Motivation und Handeln*. Springer-Verlag, Berlin (1991 *Motivation and Action*. Springer-Verlag, Berlin)

James W 1890 *The Principles of Psychology*, Vol. 1. Dover, New York

Kahneman D 1973 *Attention and Effort*. Prentice-Hall, Englewood Cliffs, New Jersey

Kanfer R, Ackerman P L 1989 Dynamics of skill acquisition: Building a bridge between intelligence and motivation. In: Sternberg R J (ed.) 1989 *Advances in the Psychology of Human Intelligence*. Erlbaum, Hillsdale, New Jersey

Posner M I 1978 *Chronometric Explorations of Mind*. Erlbaum, Hillsdale, New Jersey

Sokolov E N 1990 The orienting response and future directions of its development. *Pavlov J. Biol. Sci.* 25(3): 142–50

Underwood B J 1963 Stimulus selection in verbal learning. In: Cofer C N, Musgrave B S (eds.) 1963 *Verbal Behavior and Learning: Problems and Processes*. McGraw-Hill, New York

Wittrock M C 1986 Education and recent research on attention and knowledge acquisition. In: Friedman S L, Klivington K A, Peterson R W (eds.) 1986 *The Brain, Cognition, and Education*. Academic Press, San Diego, California

Wittrock M C 1991 Generative teaching of comprehension. *Elem. Sch. J.* 92: 169–84

Zimmerman B J, Schunk D H (eds.) 1989 *Self-regulated Learning and Academic Achievement: Theory, Research, and Practice*. Springer-Verlag, New York

Academic Learning Time

C. W. Fisher

Academic learning time is a psychological construct intended to capture learning as it occurs in the context of day-to-day activities undertaken by students during classroom instruction. The term is also identified with a model of classroom learning in which the influences of classroom instructional processes and environment (including teaching functions and behaviors) on student achievement are mediated by academic learning time. While it is sometimes difficult to separate the construct from the model, for present purposes the former is emphasized over the latter.

Academic learning time emerged in the mid-1970s as a potential solution to problems encountered in attempts to model, and empirically verify, mechanisms through which classroom teachers facilitate knowledge acquisition among their students. Many of the teaching actions being studied at that time, especially those performed when teachers interacted with students, fluctuated relatively rapidly. That is, teachers changed questioning strategies, grouping for instruction, or task requirements from lesson to lesson and often within a single lesson. However, student learning traditionally had been assessed by paper and pencil tests that were somewhat sensitive to substantial changes in knowledge occurring over semesters or years, but were notably insensitive to minute by minute or daily changes. Even if this were not the case, the intrusiveness of repeated administrations of paper and pencil tests rendered this approach impracticable. Any attempt to quantify relationships among narrowly defined, rapidly changing teaching behaviors and broadly defined, slowly changing achievement test scores appeared problematic.

An even greater problem was inherent in attempting to relate teaching actions directly to achievement test scores. Since students learn through their own actions, whether overt or covert, then if teaching actions are to affect student learning, they must first mediate students' actions and thoughts during (and after) the instructional events. To understand relationships between day-to-day teaching actions and student learning it is necessary to have some representation of students' thoughts and actions that is, at least approximately, coextensive in time with the teaching event. Attempts to relate teaching actions directly to student achievement test scores leave student action and thought unrepresented and, therefore, the mechanisms of teaching effects inaccessible. Academic learning time, advanced as an index of learning as it occurs, was intended to address these and other issues in research on classroom teaching and learning.

1. Definition

Academic learning time is defined as the amount of time that a student spends engaged in an academic task that he or she can perform with high success (Fisher et al. 1980). On a given schoolday, a particular amount of time is set aside for, or allocated to, a curricular area. This allocation, in United States schools, is made primarily by classroom teachers within guidelines set by district and state educational agencies. For students, the amount of time allocated to a content area constitutes an upper limit on the amount of academic learning time in that content area for that schoolday. For a variety of reasons, a given student will be engaged in the academic task at hand for a portion of the allocated time and, of the engaged time, only a portion will be spent on tasks that the student can complete successfully. It is this latter portion of instructional time, when the student is engaged in tasks at a high rate of success, that is referred to as academic learning time. The more time a student spends in these conditions, the more academic learning time is accumulated, and the more the student learns.

Academic learning time can be thought of as the product of allocated time, student engagement rate, and student success rate on academic tasks. In most United States schools, time allocations tend to vary between classes, but with the exception of variations due to student absences from school, allocations tend to be similar for students in the same class. Engagement rates and success rates on academic tasks vary considerably from student to student within a class and the class distributions of these rates also vary considerably from class to class. As a result, academic learning time, being the product of these three factors, shows remarkable variability both within and between classes.

Academic learning time, as outlined above, is a generic concept in the sense that it is not dependent on subject matter considerations. However, in most cases, educators are interested in learning in some particular domain, say mathematics, and relating this learning to teaching actions during classroom mathematics instruction, measures of outcomes in mathematics (i.e., achievement test scores or performance measures), or both. Academic learning time in mathematics would be a function of time allocated to mathematics, engagement rate during mathematics tasks, and success rate on those tasks. If one were interested in a very specific learning domain, say addition of two-digit numbers, then academic learning time on addition of two-digit numbers could be obtained by restricting the time allocation, engagement, and success rate components accordingly.

As academic learning time in a specified domain is accumulated day after day and week after week, differences among students on this measure of classroom learning are reflected in student achievement test scores in that domain. Since academic learning time has been restricted to classroom instruction, achievement in subject matter areas on which students spent substantial amounts of time in informal education or other out-of-school learning environments would be expected to have relatively weak relationships with time-based measures of classroom learning.

2. Related Concepts

The development and application of time variables, that is, the use of duration of events or conditions to characterize aspects of learning and learning environments, built directly on the seminal work of John Carroll (1963, 1985). While there were earlier applications of time variables to educational issues (e.g., Morrison 1926), most modern interest can be traced to Carroll's model of school learning. In this model, originally developed in the context of foreign language learning and later applied to a wide variety of learning settings, Carroll proposed five constructs, of which three were expressed as durations of time.

Two of these variables, opportunity to learn and perseverance, have been used directly or modified in some way by a considerable number of researchers. Opportunity to learn was originally defined as the amount of time allowed for learning a task (Carroll 1963) and seems equivalent to allocated time as used here. Opportunity to learn and allocated time are differentiated from a similar concept, content covered, by the latter's specific, as opposed to general, focus on the subject matter dealt with during instruction.

Perseverance or the amount of time the learner is willing to engage actively in learning appears to be similar to engaged time, active learning time, and time-on-task (see Anderson 1984, Berliner 1990, Carroll 1985, Harnischfeger and Wiley 1985 for more detailed discussions of these and other time variables). Time-on-task, a term frequently used by educators, is sometimes confused with academic learning time. Academic learning time differs from time-on-task and its aliases in that academic learning time includes only that part of time-on-task which is spent on tasks the learner can perform at a high rate of success. In other words, academic learning time is a subset of time-on-task.

Time-on-task, by connotation more than denotation, leaves the task unspecified. In educational practice there seems to be a tendency to accord more importance to the quantity of time and to diminish the importance of the quality of the task or tasks on which the time was spent. It is all too easy, though erroneous,

to assume either that all learning tasks are of equal quality, or that task quality is somehow subordinate to simple duration.

Inclusion of success rate as a component in the definition of academic learning time was intended to incorporate at least one index, though a crude one, of task quality (Marliave and Filby 1985). Adding the success rate component increased the complexity of the overall concept and amounted to a departure from the elegance, if not the spirit, of the Carroll model. Carroll maintained that what was important was not simply the amount of time spent but the amount of time spent in appropriate circumstances. By including success rate in the definition of academic learning time, a deliberate attempt was made to capture some aspect of task quality. In the process, academic learning time incorporated and confounded aspects of what in the Carroll model had been represented separately as quality of instruction and the learner's ability to understand instruction.

Success rate, reflecting both teacher decisions about which tasks to pursue and the learner's understanding of the instructional tasks, was intended to index task appropriateness for that learner. Hence, different students would have different success rates on the same task or set of tasks. As a result, academic learning time combined, in one concept, aspects of quality of teaching, learner characteristics, and curriculum. Combining three of the four commonplaces of schooling in this manner was considered a liability by many (Harnischfeger and Wiley 1985). However, it maintained the spirit of Carroll's model, though this was not a consideration at the time, by providing a rough estimate of "time actually spent" (the numerator in Carroll's deceptively simple and elegant equation). In formulating academic learning time in this way, the intention was to create a dynamic index of learning itself, an index which could be, on the one hand, related to narrowly defined teaching actions, and on the other, "integrated" over time, so to speak, to approximate traditional measures of achievement. Though the research team that developed academic learning time conceptualized the construct as a unified entity, they tried to have their cake and eat it too, in that, in empirical work, the various components were typically measured and entered into analyses separately (Fisher et al. 1978). (Due to various measurement problems, academic learning time was not assessed directly as a single variable. Components of the construct were measured directly.)

There is a second aspect of success rate as a component of academic learning time that bears elaboration. Success rate was partitioned into three broadly defined categories. High success characterized situations where students had a good grasp of the task and made only occasional errors. Low success described situations where students did not understand the task and made correct responses at about the chance level. Medium success, reflecting partial understanding of the task, included situations between low and high success. The definition of academic learning time suggests that more time spent on tasks with high success represents more learning. However, this does not necessarily imply that all of a learner's time be spent on tasks with high success. If a learner works only on tasks that are so easy (for that student) that he or she is not challenged by new material, then little learning is likely to occur. Generally, some balance between high and medium success tasks produces the most learning, while low success tasks are detrimental to learning.

This issue of balance in the distribution of tasks is not obvious from a cursory examination of the academic learning time concept, yet it is critically important since the balance is likely to be different depending upon the students, subject matter, and context in which the instruction occurs. The balancing of more and less challenging tasks can also be thought of in terms of curriculum pacing or providing appropriate amounts of independent practice on a task before introducing one or more novel tasks.

3. Research

A variety of procedures has been used for measuring the components of academic learning time. Typically, allocated time has been estimated using teacher logs, one-time survey items, or direct observation. Measurements of engagement rates have relied primarily on direct observation while indexes of success rates have been derived from direct observation and scoring of student responses on paper and pencil curriculum materials. Measures of allocated time are, in general, easier to obtain and are characterized by somewhat higher reliabilities than either engagement or success rates. The latter two variables are particularly difficult to assess during portions of classroom lessons when students make few overt responses.

By the early 1990s, several dozen studies, mostly conducted in the process–product framework with an increasing number in the case study and descriptive traditions, have presented data on allocated and engaged times. A small subset of these studies has included data on success rates. The vast majority of these studies have been conducted in the United States and therefore reflect American elementary and secondary education practices. The general findings that are outlined below are summarized from a variety of journal articles, chapters, and books (see, e.g., Anderson 1984, Fisher and Berliner 1985, Wittrock 1986).

3.1 Distributional Aspects of the Components of Academic Learning Time

Descriptive studies have yielded information on the components of academic learning time, most often in elementary classrooms. Perhaps the most striking results are the sizes of variations found between

classes on allocated time for practically all subject matter areas and, both between and within classes, on engagement and success rates. It is apparently not unusual to find time allocations to a school subject matter area that differ by a factor of three or more for students at the same grade level.

Elementary school students are typically engaged in school tasks about three-fourths of the time with class averages sometimes exceeding 0.90 as well as dipping below 0.50. Variation in engagement rates within classes is usually somewhat greater. In a number of studies, engagement rates have been shown to vary from one organizational arrangement to another within the same class. For example, engagement rates in teacher-led groups are consistently higher than those in independent work groups.

Even general statements about success rates, or error rates as they are more commonly called, must be very tenuous indeed because there seems to be surprisingly little data from ordinary classroom instruction and when there are data, differences in measurement procedures and classroom contexts make comparisons less than straightforward. From the original studies of academic learning time examining basic skills instruction in elementary schools in California, the proportion of time on high success tasks to medium success tasks was approximately one to one.

3.2 Academic Learning Time and Achievement

Since learning occurs over time and since zero time results in no learning, logic maintains that the correlation between time spent trying to learn and achievement in a given domain will be nonnegative. This logical relationship notwithstanding, a considerable number of researchers from several countries have studied the connection between measures of student achievement and allocated time, engaged time, or some variant of these entities. Using a variety of correlational analyses, measures of opportunity to learn and measures of time spent trying to learn have shown positive relationships with student achievement. The consistency of this finding over a wide variety of settings and subject matters has been the inevitable conclusion of a number of sizable reviews giving the finding widespread credence.

For academic learning time per se, its relationship with student achievement was estimated by the research group who developed the construct in the context of basic skills learning in elementary schools in California. Generally speaking, the components of academic learning time, taken together, accounted uniquely for approximately 10 percent of the variation in scores on paper and pencil achievement tests. This estimate represents the contribution of academic learning time after accounting for entering achievement scores but without attempting to make adjustments for errors of measurement. The apparent size and robustness of the relationship between academic learning time (and, generally speaking, other estimates of instructional time) and student achievement is unusual. Within this research framework, few, if any, single measures of classroom instructional phenomena, other than entering achievement level, have shown as much promise.

3.3 Academic Learning Time and Teaching Process Variables

While academic learning time is influenced by a number of different sources, its relationships with teaching process variables have received by far the most attention. In general, student engagement rates have been shown to vary with the amount of substantive interaction between teachers and students. For example, academic monitoring and academic feedback seem to have consistently positive associations with student engagement. Relationships between student success rates and both preactive and interactive teaching process variables have been examined in a number of studies; however, the findings have been somewhat inconsistent.

4. Future Research

Much of the earlier work on academic learning time and many other time-based constructs was done in the context of direct instruction and other pedagogies that rely primarily on "telling" as a metaphor for the teacher–student relationship in classroom learning. As educators in many countries begin to broaden their views on pedagogy, especially to include models based on constructivist principles, some may lose interest in time-based constructs. However, to the extent that students learn what they do in classrooms, academic learning time continues to be a useful construct.

One of its distinctive features, student success rate, was an attempt to include classroom task characteristics directly in studies of classroom learning. While this facet of academic learning time pointed in a useful direction and studies of mediated learning have made substantial progress in this area, educators need more and better understandings of classroom tasks. Ways must be found to conceptualize both the cognitive and social aspects of learning as it occurs in the context of classroom tasks. Doyle's (1983) conceptualization of academic work continues to offer insights in this arena and studies of classroom tasks and task structures (e.g., Fisher and Hiebert 1990, Mergendoller 1988, Stodolsky 1988) shed some light on the conditions in which students and teachers pursue classroom learning. At this point, the mainstream of research on classroom teaching and learning focuses on conceptualizations of, and relationships among, the thoughts and actions of students and teachers. In suggesting a broader and deeper consideration of classroom tasks, the point is to balance this focus with information on the social and cognitive tasks that students and teachers engage in and the contexts in which these thoughts, actions, and tasks are embedded.

See also: Time, Allocated and Instructional

References

Anderson L W (ed.) 1984 *Time and School Learning*. St. Martin's Press, New York

Berliner D C 1990 What's all the fuss about instructional time? In: Ben-Peretz M, Bromme R (eds.) 1990 *The Nature of Time in Schools*. Teachers College Press, New York

Carroll J B 1963 A model of school learning. *Teach. Coll. Rec.* 64:723–33

Carroll J B 1985 The model of school learning: Progress of an idea. In: Fisher C, Berliner D (eds.) 1985

Doyle W 1983 Academic work. *Rev. Educ. Res.* 53:159–99

Fisher C et al. 1978 *Teaching Behaviors, Academic Learning Time, and Student Achievement: Final Report of Phase III-B, Beginning Teacher Evaluation Study*. Far West Laboratory for Educational Research and Development, San Francisco, California

Fisher C et al. 1980 Teaching behaviors, academic learning time, and student achievement: An overview. In Denham C, Lieberman A (eds.) 1980 *Time to Learn*. National Institute of Education, Washington, DC

Fisher C W, Berliner D C 1985 *Perspectives on Instructional Time*. Longman, New York

Fisher C, Hiebert E 1990 Characteristics of tasks in two approaches to literacy instruction. *Elem. Sch. J.* 91:1–13

Harnischfeger A, Wiley D 1985 Origins of active learning time. In: Fisher C, Berliner D (eds.) 1985

Marliave R, Filby N N 1985 Success rate: A measure of task appropriateness. In: Fisher C, Berliner D (eds.) 1985

Mergendoller J (ed.) 1988 Schoolwork and academic tasks. *Elem. Sch. J.* 88 (special issue)

Morrison H C 1926 *The Practice of Teaching in the Secondary School*. University of Chicago Press, Chicago, Illinois

Stodolsky S S 1988 *The Subject Matters*. University of Chicago Press, Chicago, Illinois

Wittrock M C (ed.) 1986 *Handbook of Research on Teaching*, 3rd edn. Macmillan, New York

Further Reading

Bennett N, Desforges C, Cockburn A, Wilkinson B 1984 *The Quality of Pupil Learning Experiences*. Erlbaum, London

Ben-Peretz M, Bromme R (eds.) 1990 *The Nature of Time in Schools*. Teachers College Press, New York

Study Habits and Strategies

R. E. Mayer

Study habits and strategies refer to activities carried out by a learner during the learning process for the purpose of improving learning. This definition has three components, concerning the what, when, and why of study habits and strategies, respectively. First, study habits and strategies are behaviors that the learner produces. Second, they occur at the time of learning. Third, they are intended as aids to learning. This definition also corresponds to a definition of learning strategies (Mayer 1987, Weinstein and Mayer 1986) (see *Learning Strategies: Teaching and Assessing*). Examples of study strategies for reading a textbook lesson include underlining key terms, creating an outline, and taking elaborative notes.

For students—including children in elementary schools, youngsters in secondary schools, and adults in colleges or training programs—learning from teachers and books becomes a dominant activity in their lives. They are expected to become professional learners, but they are rarely given any training in how to learn (Mayer 1992, Norman 1980, Weinstein and Mayer 1986). In spite of their importance, study habits and strategies often remain part of the hidden curriculum (i.e., material that is not heavily taught but that students are expected to learn). Successful students somehow acquire study strategies even though "strategy instruction has not been incorporated into the curriculum on a large scale" (Presley 1990 p. 7). In contrast, some learning disabilities can be described as cognitive processing deficits (Swanson and Keogh 1990).

1. Cognitive Processes and Outcomes During Learning

The basis for a theory of study strategies comes from the information-processing approach to human learning (Mayer 1984, 1987, Sternberg 1985). Figure 1 summarizes aspects of an information-processing model that are most relevant to a discussion of study strategies. The model highlights three memory stores represented as boxes—namely sensory memory, short-term memory, and long-term memory—and three cognitive learning processes represented by arrows—namely, selecting, organizing, and integrating.

The arrow from sensory memory (SM) to short-term memory (STM) refers to the process of selecting relevant information, such as paying attention to the important principles stated in textbook lesson. Mayer (1984, 1987) describes this process as focusing attention whereas Sternberg (1985) describes it as selective

encoding. The arrow from STM back to itself refers to the process of organizing the incoming information, such as noting that one event is the cause of another event. Mayer (1984, 1987) calls this cognitive activity building internal connections while Sternberg (1985) calls it selective combination. Finally the arrow from long-term memory (LTM) to STM refers to the process of integrating incoming information with existing relevant knowledge from LTM, such as relating a lesson on radar to one's existing knowledge about a ball bouncing off a wall. Mayer (1984, 1987) refers to this cognitive activity as building external connections and Sternberg (1985) calls it selective comparison.

The information-processing model in Fig. 1 suggests four possible learning outcomes. First, if the learner fails to select relevant information, no learning will occur. Consequently, the student will perform poorly both on retention tests, which cover the presented material, and transfer tests, which require applying the material in new situations. Second, if the learner pays attention to the material but does not work on organizing it, then nonmeaningful learning will occur. In this case, the student would be expected to perform well on retention tests, but poorly on transfer tests. Third, partially meaningful learning occurs when the learner selects and organizes relevant incoming information but fails to integrate it with existing knowledge. This learner would perform well on retention and on certain types of transfer tests. Fourth, when all three learning processes are engaged, the learner builds a meaningful learning outcome that supports good retention and transfer performance.

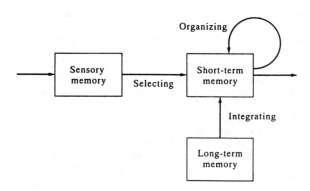

Figure 1
An information-processing model of cognitive processes in learning

2. Guiding Cognitive Processes During Learning

Study habits and strategies are intended to elicit and guide one's cognitive processes during learning. A self-directed learner possesses appropriate study strategies and uses them at the appropriate times and places during learning. Knowing when to use or modify use of a study strategy is a kind of metacognitive skill (see *Learning Strategies: Teaching and Assessing*).

When the learner's goal is solely good retention performance, then study strategies that promote the selecting process are important. When the learner's goal is good transfer performance (as well as good retention performance), then study strategies should be used that engage selecting, organizing, and integrating processes.

Study strategies can be categorized in terms of the cognitive processes they affect; strategies to promote selecting, organizing, and/or integrating. Underlining and verbatim copying of selected words in a textbook lesson are examples of a study strategy aimed primarily at the selection of relevant information. These kinds of activities are most likely to guide the learner's attention toward the material that is copied or underlined. Outlining the material in a textbook is an example of a study strategy which affects both selecting relevant information and organizing it into a coherent structure. Writing a description in one's own words of how the material relates to something else, may elicit all three of the major learning processes. By encouraging the learner to go beyond the information presented, elaboration strategies cause learners to use their existing knowledge in long-term memory to make sense out of the incoming material.

Pressley and his colleagues (Pressley 1990) have suggested several study strategies that could become part of the curriculum. They include summarization strategies, text-structuring strategies, and question-asking strategies. Summarization strategies involve writing or stating the content of a passage or lecture in condensed form. Since summarization strategies can be expected to activate the cognitive processes of selecting relevant information, they should improve students' retention performance. Research supports this expectation. For example, students who were asked to write a single sentence to summarize a paragraph retained more of the information than students who simply read the paragraph (Doctorow et al. 1978). Similarly, elementary-school students who were taught how to write a single-sentence summary of a paragraph were subsequently better able to retain the main ideas from paragraphs they read than were untrained students (Rinehart et al. 1986).

In some cases, summarization strategies that emphasize outlining of the material can encourage learners both to select and organize relevant information, resulting in good performance on retention and on some types of transfer tests. For example, Barnett et al. (1981) asked some students to listen to an 1800-word lecture on the history of roads whereas other students were asked to identify and outline the main ideas as they listened. The students who outlined recalled more than twice as much of the information as those students who listened only. Similarly, seventh-grade students who were taught how to write hierarchical outlines for social studies lessons outperformed untrained peers on recalling key information and answering questions about social studies passages they had read (Taylor and Beach 1984). Other forms of outlining instruction that have improved student learning include network training (Dansereau et al. 1979) and concept mapping (Novak and Gowin 1984).

Text-structuring strategies involve selecting pieces of information from a passage that fit within a general structure. For example, the structure of a story may include a main character, a place, a time, one or more major events, and a final outcome. When elementary school children who were poor readers were taught to find these kinds of elements in stories that they read, their retention test performance improved toward the level of good readers (Idol and Croll 1987, Short and Ryan 1987). In contrast to narrative prose, expository prose can be organized in several ways: generalization (i.e., a main idea followed by supporting pieces of information); enumeration (i.e., a list of facts all related to the same topic); sequence (i.e., a series of steps in a process); classification (i.e., a set of categories and subcategories); or comparison (i.e., a description of similarities and differences between two or more things along several different dimensions). Cook and Mayer (1988) taught junior college students how to recognize and outline paragraphs from their textbooks based on these kinds of text structures. On a post-test involving new expository passages, trained students remembered more of the relevant information and solved more transfer problems than untrained students.

Question-generation strategies occur when a reader creates questions based on text material. When the learner generates transfer questions that require integration and extension of the material in the passage, he or she is encouraged to engage in selecting, organizing, and integrating processes which result in superior retention and transfer performance. For example, Davey and McBride (1986) taught elementary-school students how to generate transfer questions for expository texts. On subsequent tests trained students performed better than untrained students on remembering and comprehending text passages. In another study, King (1990) taught college students how to generate transfer questions based on a lecture that they had just heard. Again, trained students who were asked to generate questions performed better on a post-test involving retention and transfer questions than untrained students who were simply asked to discuss the lecture.

3. Future Research on Study Habits and Strategies

Research on study habits and strategies has made clear that successful learners do more than read (or listen to) every word in a lesson; when necessary, they also engage in what Wittrock and his colleagues (Doctorow et al. 1978) have called "generative processes" (i.e., active strategies aimed at improving learning). Research on cognitive strategy instruction also suggests that many study strategies are domain-specific; that is, they can be used mainly for studying a single kind of material such as mathematics, science, or literature (Pressley 1990). For example, strategies for how to represent algebra story problems as diagrams (Lewis 1989) are useful for learning to solve story problems, but not for learning to solve problems in history or computer programming. Future research is needed to determine the specific study strategies used by skilled learners in each subject-matter field and to devise methods for teaching these strategies to unskilled learners who have failed to learn them otherwise. These strategies are likely to include more effective methods for note-taking as well as for studying with peers.

See also: Learning Strategies: Teaching and Assessing

References

Barnett J E, DiVesta F J, Rogozinski J T 1981 What is learned in note taking? *J Educ. Psychol.* 73: 181–92
Cook L K, Mayer R E 1988 Teaching readers about the structure of scientific text. *J. Educ. Psychol.* 80: 448–56
Dansereau D F et al. 1979 Development and evaluation of an effective learning strategy program. *J. Educ. Psychol.* 71: 64–73
Davey B, McBride S 1986 The effects of question generation training on reading comprehension. *J. Educ. Psychol.* 78: 256–62
Doctorow M, Wittrock M C, Marks C 1978 Generative processes in reading comprehension. *J. Educ. Psychol.* 70: 109–18
King A 1990 Enhancing peer interaction and learning in the classroom through reciprocal questioning. *Am. Educ. Res. J.* 27: 664–87
Idol L, Croll V J 1987 Story-mapping training as a means of improving reading comprehension. *Learning Disability Quarterly* 10: 214–29
Lewis A B 1989 Training students to represent arithmetic word problems. *J. Educ. Psychol.* 81: 521–31
Mayer R E 1984 Aids to text comprehension. *Educ. Psychol.* 19: 30–42
Mayer R E 1987 *Educational Psychology: A Cognitive Approach.* Harper Collins, New York
Mayer R E 1992 Guiding students' cognitive processing of scientific information. In: Pressley M, Harris K, Guthrie J (eds.) 1992 *Promoting Academic Competence and Literary in Schools* Academic Press, Orlando, Florida
Norman D A 1980 Cognitive engineering and education. In: Tuma D T, Reif F (eds.) 1980 *Problem Solving and Education.* Erlbaum, Hillsdale, New Jersey
Novak J D, Gowin D B 1984 *Learning to Learn.* Cambridge University Press, Cambridge
Pressley M 1990 *Cognitive Strategy Instruction That Really Improves Children's Academic Performance,* Brookline Books, Cambridge, Massachusetts
Rinehart S C, Stahl S A, Erickson L G 1986 Some effects of summarization training on reading and studying. *Read. Res. Q.* 21: 422–28
Short E J, Ryan E B 1987 Metacognitive differences between skilled and less skilled readers: Remediating deficits through story grammar and attribution training. *J. Educ. Psychol.* 76: 225–35
Sternberg R J 1985 *Beyond IQ: A Triarchic Theory of Human Intelligence.* Cambridge University Press, Cambridge
Swanson H L, Keogh B (eds.) 1990 *Learning Disabilities: Theoretical and Research Issues.* Erlbaum, Hillsdale, New Jersey
Taylor B M, Beach R W 1984 The effects of text structure instruction on middle-grade students' comprehension and production of expository text. *Read. Res. Q.* 19: 134–46
Weinstein C E, Mayer R E 1986 The teaching of learning strategies. In: Wittrock W C (ed.) 1986 *Handbook of Research on Teaching,* 3rd edn. Macmillan, New York

Teaching for Specific Objectives

Introduction

L. W. Anderson

The importance of adapting teaching to differences among students has long been recognized (see the entry by Anderson in Part A Section III). A more recent realization is the need to adapt teaching to what students are being taught; that is, to their learning objectives. Teachers know at least intuitively that teaching problem-solving is quite different from teaching rote memorization. Similarly, teaching critical reading is different from teaching written composition. Oftentimes, however, this knowledge is not acted upon.

The entries in this section focus on 10 major learning objectives. They are: memory, comprehension, written composition, motor skills, concept learning, problem-solving, critical reading, learning strategies, creativity, and metacognitive strategies.

This section is divided into four subsections The first addresses major differences among these objectives. The second focuses on different ways of teaching them. The third section emphasizes common elements of these objectives. The final section contains a brief summary.

1. Differences Among Learning Objectives

The first four entries address fairly traditional objectives of schooling: memory, comprehension, written composition, and motor skills. With the possible exception of motor skills, these objectives roughly correspond with the "three R's" or, using more modern terminology, the basic skills.

The next two objectives, concept learning and problem-solving, emphasize a deeper understanding of the material being taught. A concept is a class or a category that permits students to make sense of the tremendous amount of information and vast array of experiences they encounter (Tennyson). Furthermore, interrelationships among concepts provide the conceptual framework or schemata that students develop as a result of their education, which help them make sense

of future information and experiences (Schnotz and Ballstaedt). Similarly, problem-solving requires that students apply what they have learned to a variety of settings and situations, some of which are quite similar to those that the students were taught while others are quite different (Mayer).

The final four entries address somewhat non-traditional, but quite promising, learning objectives. Critical reading emphasizes the student's "personal response to literature" (Luke and Walton). Luke and Walton argue that texts are not neutral receptacles for information. Rather, the authors of texts do in fact shape students' "portrayals of the world" (Luke and Walton).

Learning strategies pertain to how students learn what they learn or reorganize what they already know. Learning strategies include memorization strategies, time management, note-taking, listening, preparing for and taking tests, and dealing with academic stress (Weinstein and Meyer).

Creativity refers to innovative or adaptive thinking and behavior that produces ideas, inventions, or objects which are accepted by experts as being of scientific, aesthetic, social, or technological value (Feldhusen). In simpler terms, creativity produces *novel* and *appropriate* solutions to open-ended tasks (Feldhusen).

Finally, metacognitive strategies permit students to monitor and regulate their own thinking and learning (Simons). Thus, metacognitive strategies empower students to learn for themselves.

2. Differences in Teaching Methods and Strategies

With 10 different learning objectives, 45 comparisons are possible (memory with comprehension, memory with concept learning, comprehension with concept learning, and so on). Rather than present a listing of the comparisons, three comparisons will be used for illustrative purposes.

2.1 Teaching Comprehension and Teaching Critical Reading

Comprehension refers to undertanding the meaning of a text as it was intended by the author or the teacher. In contrast, critical reading implies that the reader will make sense of the text on the basis of his or her understanding of the world in which he or she lives.

Because of these different purposes, the methods used for teaching comprehension and critical reading are quite different. Teaching comprehension involves the activation of prior knowledge and the triggering of comprehension activities (through the use of inquiry-oriented teaching and/or adjunct questions) (Schnotz and Ballstaedt). In contrast, teaching critical reading requires that students read multiple texts with conflicting discourse. The teacher uses these texts to generate differences, recognize conflicts, and engage in debate (Luke and Walton).

2.2 Teaching Memorization and Facilitating Concept Learning

Memorization implies that students are able to recall or recognize what they were taught in virtually the same manner as they were taught it. Concept learning, on the other hand, requires that students form classes or categories of information or experiences or correctly assign particular information or specific experiences to appropriate classes or categories. Because of these differences, different approaches to teaching are appropriate.

Teaching memorization involves the use of rehearsal, elaboration, imagery, mnemonics, and retrieval strategies (Pressley and Van Meter). All of these aids have been found to produce greater memory. In contrast, effective concept teaching requires a two-stage process. The teacher begins by teaching the concept label, the concept definition, identifying and explaining the best example, adding expository examples, and concluding with worked examples. Next, opportunities for practice, including self-directed experiences, are provided (Tennyson).

2.3 Teaching Problem-solving and Creativity

The primary difference between problem-solving and creativity lies in the initial approach made by the student. In problem-solving, the emphasis throughout the process is convergent (Mayer). That is, students are looking for *an* answer or solution or *the* answer or solution. The initial phase of creativity, on the other hand, is divergent. That is, students begin by looking for *all* possible answers or solutions. Subsequently, students look for those answers or solutions that are both "novel and appropriate" (Feldhusen).

Once again, different teaching strategies are needed. When teaching problem-solving, teachers would do well to focus on (a) teaching component skills rather than a general problem-solving ability, and (b)

domain-specific rather than context-free settings (Mayer). In contrast, creativity is "enhanced or nurtured," rather than directly taught (Feldhausen). That is, teachers should create conditions that promote motivation, use instructional materials that require creativity, and find ways of actively involving students in their learning.

3. Common Elements of Teaching Methods and Strategies

The focus thus far has been on differences in teaching strategies and approaches. Interestingly, however, the entries in this section contain a set of commonalities that cut across the various objectives. Two of the most important commonalities are described briefly.

3.1 Relating New Learning to Prior Knowledge

The role of prior knowledge in learning is explicitly discussed by Pressley and Van Meter (in terms of memory), Freedman (in terms of written composition), Tennyson (in terms of concept learning), Luke and Walton (in terms of critical reading), Schnotz and Ballstaedt (in terms of comprehension), and Simons (in terms of metacognitive strategies). The importance of prior knowledge is consistent with the widely accepted view that students actively construct what they learn and what they ultimately know. They interpret new learning experiences within the context of what they already know. They are not vessels into which teachers pour knowledge.

This view of learners and learning has several implications for teachers and teaching. First, how students learn is as important as what they learn. Students may need to be taught memorization strategies (Pressley and Van Meter), approaches to time management (Weinstein and Meyer), and ways to monitor their learning progress and make adjustments as necessary (e.g.,"how am I doing?" "what, if anything, do I need to do differently?") (Schnotz and Ballstaedt).

Second, teachers must help students make connections between new learning and prior knowledge. The process of making these connections is known as "scaffolding" (Van der Sanden, Simons). Some students make these connections almost automatically. Others require considerable assistance from the teacher.

Third, learning takes time. With respect to memorization, Pressley reminds us that virtually all memory enhancement strategies require considerable practice. Similarly, Freedman points out that writing "involves thinking through ideas, drafting, and redrafting." She adds that "most people never fully master any kind of writing." Finally, metacognitive strategies require that responsibility for learning be shifted gradually to the students themselves (Simons).

This "gradual shift" likely will take place over months and, more likely, years.

3.2 Activity Involving Students in Learning

The importance of active involvement of students in learning is emphasized by Pressley and Van Meter (in terms of memorization), Van der Sanden (in terms of motor skills), Mayer (in terms of problem-solving), Weinstein and Meyer (in terms of learning strategies), Feldhusen (in terms of creativity), and Simons (in terms of metacognitive strategies). The nature of this active involvement may differ somewhat depending on the objective being taught.

The most obvious illustration of the necessity of actively involving students lies in the area of motor skills. In this regard, Van de Sanden reminds readers that if students are to become efficient, consistent, and fluid in these skills, sufficient practice coupled by appropriate, specific feedback is necessary. At the other end of the spectrum, Mayer suggests that teachers working on problem-solving should engage students in generating ideas, formulating questions, and restating problems.

What is the role of teachers when the focus in teaching turns to the learners themselves? Teachers have multiple roles to assume. They need to provide tasks and materials that encourage or require active student involvement (Pressley and Van Meter, Luke and Walton, Feldhusen). They need to provide or arrange for support and feedback that maintain involvement and ultimately lead to success (Freedman, Mayer, Van der Sanden). They may need to assist students in developing strategies that produce effective and efficient learning (Pressley and Van Meter, Simons, and Weinstein and Meyer).

4. Summary

Teaching different objectives requires that teachers rely on a general set of teaching strategies, while at the same time using methods that are somewhat unique to the objective being taught. The authors of the entries in this section tend to agree that the learner is central to learning. Thus, teachers need to involve them actively in their own learning and help them make connections between what they are learning and what they already know.

At the same time, however, each author emphasizes techniques that tend to produce successful learning of a specific type of objective. Just as differences among students have been well-documented, so have differences among learning objectives. The major task confronting teachers, then, is to find ways of bridging the gap between what students already know and what they are expected to learn. The techniques included in these entries are intended to help teachers do so.

Memory: Teaching and Assessing

M. Pressley and P. Van Meter

Students are required to remember great amounts of material in school. Sometimes the demand is explicit, resulting in students intentionally attempting to memorize material; at other times memory is incidental, as when students remember information in text that was read for some other purpose or recall information related to a science or mathematics problem that was solved as part of school work. In general, two factors are cited most frequently as affecting memory of new material: whether the new information is consistent with or can be related to prior knowledge, and how the new information is processed (e.g., whether and which cognitive strategies are applied to the material). Information that is consistent with or can be related to prior knowledge is more easily remembered than information that is not consistent with or relatable to prior knowledge. With respect to information processing, both encoding processes (i.e., activities during study) and retrieval processes (i.e., activities during testing) are known to be critical determinants of how information is organized in long-term memory and how much of it is remembered.

In short, "what the head knows … has an enormous effect on what the head learns and remembers" (Flavell 1985 p. 213). Whether a person uses the strategies that they possess and coordinates the use of these strategies with other knowledge, however, depends on a third factor, metacognitive competence. Metacognitive competence refers to the awareness of when, where, and how to use and adapt (i.e., self-regulate) strategies and various types of knowledge (see *Metacognitive Strategies: Teaching and Assessing*).

A critical issue with respect to memory is whether assessments of it are sensitive to all that has been learned. The amount and type of information detected as "remembered" varies with the type of test administered and the degree to which this test stimulates processing compatible with the processing that occurred during study. For example, the amount remembered is likely to be higher if tests stimulate retrieval processes that complement the student's encoding processes while studying. Although most memory tests have focused on the memory product (i.e., what can be remembered), there has been increasing emphasis in the 1970s and 1980s, on measuring the processes that produce remembered information.

The scientific study of memory is an extremely technical field with more than a century of tradition, dating back to Ebbinghaus's classical work in late nineteenth-century Germany. The art of memory enhancement through strategies and the relating of new knowledge to prior knowledge is much older, with important memorization techniques known to have been used by the ancient Greeks (Yates 1966). The study of memory continues to be prominent with experimental and cognitive psychologists, and interventions to enhance memory of educationally relevant content are regularly reported in mainstream educational psychology journals. Although it is impossible to provide anything approaching an exhaustive discussion of a field with such a long history, what follows is a brief discussion of some of the most prominent educationally relevant issues in contemporary memory research.

1. Incidental Versus Intentional Memory

Incidental learning is said to occur when students are not aware that material being covered will be tested for memory. When they are aware of an upcoming memory test, learning is said to be intentional. Even preschoolers are more likely to exert effort and attempt to use memory strategies to remember material when learning is intentional rather than incidental (Baker-Ward, et al. 1984). Other things being equal, intentional memory usually exceeds incidental memory. Simply informing students of an upcoming memory test will usually improve memory by increasing cognitive activities that enhance memory.

2. Role of Prior Knowledge in Determining Memory

Memory is often affected by the relationship between incoming information and information already stored in long-term memory (i.e., prior knowledge). If, for example, children have learned about the culture of Indonesia, and are then exposed to a new story about Indonesia, memory of the new story will be affected by what had been learned previously about Indonesia. The encoding of the new story sometimes may be distorted to be consistent with prior knowledge (Brown et al. 1977). Students are more likely to be able to learn material which is related to prior knowledge than material not related to prior knowledge. For example, music students learn sentences about music easily; baseball fans are able to rapidly encode information about baseball. Only music students who are baseball

fans have an easy time encoding both types of content (Kuhara-Kojima and Hatano 1991).

One of the most important findings is that even preschoolers rely on well-organized prior knowledge to facilitate their encoding and retrieval of information. For example, preschoolers use their knowledge of birthday parties and eating at fast-food restaurants to remember stories about these events. It has been found that their recall often includes information consistent with prior knowledge that was not included in the to-be-learned stories (Hudson and Nelson 1983).

Whether and how well material is encoded and retrieved depends much more on the compatibility of the material with prior knowledge than on other characteristics of the learners, such as intelligence. For example, highly intelligent children with little soccer knowledge remember less about a soccer story than less intelligent students who are extremely knowledgeable about the game (Schneider et al. 1989).

3. Role of Strategic Processing in Determining Memory

During the 1970s and 1980s, Jenkins (1974) and Flavell (1985) advanced the position that what is remembered is determined by what the learner does while studying. Thus, if given a list of words and instructed to count the number of consonants in each word, a learner will later be unable to recall the words, but will remember if words with five consonants occurred with greater frequency on the list than words with three or seven consonants. In contrast, a person asked to construct an image depicting the referent of each noun on the list (e.g., an image of a cat if "cat" is on the list) will remember many of the specific words later but would probably have difficulty deciding the relative frequencies of words on the list with three, five or seven consonants.

The contention that the specific cognitive processing carried out by a person determines what they remember has inspired two lines of research. The first is work related to determining the processes people use as they attempt to learn material. The second is research to determine whether children and adults can be taught to use more efficient strategies than they inherently do. Studies addressing the former question have produced documentation showing that a variety of memory strategies are more likely to be used naturally with increasing age and education during the childhood and adolescent years (Schneider and Pressley 1989 Chap. 3). Even so, adolescents and adults often fail to use efficient memory strategies, although they are quite capable of carrying out such procedures when taught how to do so (Pressley et al. 1983).

What is a strategy? A strategy is composed of "cognitive operations over and above the processes that are natural consequences of carrying out the task, ranging from one such operation to a sequence of interdependent operations. Strategies achieve cognitive purposes (e.g., comprehending, memorizing) and are potentially conscious and controllable activities" (Pressley et al. 1985 p. 4). Thus, a person can read a book once, carrying out the processes that are a natural consequence of reading, or they can supplement such reading with specific strategies to remember what is being read. An important point to make here is that for younger students such memory-enhancing strategies during reading seem to increase with development, although many adults benefit from explicit instruction in use of the strategies cited below as well as other strategies during reading (Pressley et al. 1992).

Although many variations exist, relatively few different types of encoding strategies have been studied systematically by researchers. (For reviews, see Pressley et al. 1982, Pressley et al. 1989b.)

3.1 Rehearsal Strategies

When given lists of information to learn, 10-year olds are more likely to repeat the listed material over and over than are 5-year olds. Rehearsal is a common strategy among older children and adults for learning materials that can be listed easily.

3.2 Organization and Reorganization Strategies

When to-be-remembered material contains semantic elements which can be related to prior knowledge, a reorganization strategy can increase the ease of encoding. For example, if a learner is presented with a list of items in random order, but which can be categorized as vehicles, furniture, toys, and foods, reorganization into these categories can enhance learning.

3.3 Elaboration Strategies

The learner can often elaborate to-be-learned material by relating this new information to what is already known. If given a long list of paired associates such as needle–balloon, table–chair, and dog–hamburger, memory for the pairings can be improved by thinking about meaningful relationships between the paired items. For example, the learner could think, "A needle can pop a balloon," "The chairs go under the table," and "Dogs love to eat hamburger."

New facts also can be learned through elaborative processes. Canadian students presented with a great deal of information about one of their provinces (e.g., there are more union members in British Columbia than in any other province) were able to remember the information by asking themselves why the facts are sensible based on their prior knowledge (e.g., Why does it make sense that there are a lot of unions in British Columbia? Well, there certainly are a lot of strikes, and there are a large number of longshoremen serving the west coast fishing and shipping industries). Adults often fail to make such linkages to their prior knowledge unless explicitly instructed to use elaboration strategies to learn to-be-acquired information (Pressley et al. 1992).

3.4 Prior Knowledge Activation Strategies

When people activate knowledge related to to-be-learned content before processing it, their memory of the material is affected. Thus, if asked to activate prior knowledge about burglaries before reading a description of a house, memory of information in the passage relevant to burglary is encoded more effectively. If prompted to activate information relevant to home buying before reading, information pertinent to the purchase of the house is more likely to be remembered from the description (Anderson et al. 1977).

3.5 Imagery

Since Paivio's (1971) seminal work on dual coding theory, it has been recognized that constructing both visual (i.e., imagery) and verbal encodings of to-be-learned material facilitates learning and memory. This effect has been observed with both laboratory tasks (such as list learning) and more ecologically valid tasks (such as learning from connected text).

3.6 Summarization

Attempting to identify the main idea of meaningful material increases memory of the main points of such content. This strategy may occur naturally or be prompted by teacher directions.

3.7 Transformational Mnemonics

There are a variety of memory "tricks" for learning various types of materials. Thus, when remembering a list of items in order, the English learner can use words that rhyme with one, two, three, and so on to facilitate memory. For example, the learner can imagine the first list item in an interaction with a bun, the second in interaction with a shoe, the third with a tree. Then, at recall the learner can retrieve the poem "One is a bun, two is a shoe, three is a tree" along with the images of the bun, shoe, and tree. This retrieval permits the recall of the first three list items. A second transformational mnemonic is the keyword mnemonic, which has been studied extensively since the late 1970s. Keyword mnemonics are useful for learning vocabulary. So to learn the meaning of an unfamiliar vocabulary item (e.g., malachite is a green mineral), the learner thinks of a familiar word or phrase that sounds like the new word (e.g., Mel's kite). The learner then constructs an image containing the referent for this "keyword" and elements of the meaning of malachite. Mel can be seen flying a green kite, with the tail of the kite made of pieces of green ore. (See Levin for many other examples of keyword mnemonic applications.)

3.8 Retrieval Strategies

In addition to encoding strategies, memory can also be affected by the strategies employed at retrieval.

Thus, a person who has read a description of a house remembers it differently if cued at testing to think back to the passage from the perspective of a burglar than if cued at testing to recall from the perspective of a home buyer (Anderson and Pichert 1978). Sometimes children encode information in the form of images but "forget" at testing to think back to the images they created. Their memory for this information can be greatly improved by explicit instruction to retrieve and use the images created at encoding (Pressley and Levin 1980). In general, the use of various retrieval strategies increases with development during the elementary-school years (Kobasigawa 1977).

3.9 Learning Memory Strategies

Children and adults can be taught to use memory strategies. Although execution of strategies is at first slow and deliberate, with practice, strategies can be executed with much less effort than required during this initial acquisition. In other words, with practice, strategy execution becomes automatic (Anderson 1983). Such automatization is essential if strategies are to be used to mediate complex tasks which require coordinated application of a number of strategies. When these strategies are used in combination with other prior knowledge, the result is effective learning of new content.

4. Coordination of Strategies and Other Knowledge

Any complex memory task, for example, remembering the content of a history chapter on the colonization of Africa, requires that a variety of strategies be used in conjunction with prior knowledge activation. How much such learning involves the use of strategies and how much the activation of prior knowledge depends in part on the extent of development of each capacity.

A student with extensive knowledge about African colonization would be able to use that background to quickly understand and relate the new material in the chapter to prior knowledge. As suggested earlier, however, the student might need to be prompted to use his or her prior knowledge as completely as possible (e.g., by cuing of elaboration strategies). Explicit, extensive use of other strategies might be unnecessary for this student. For another student, who lacked knowledge of the colonization of Africa, memory of the material included in the chapter might be much more dependent on use of strategies such as imagery, summarization, and reorganization.

Although there are theorists who continue to argue that memory and memory enhancement are comprehensible in terms of either strategies or knowledge, the prevalent view is that memory, at its best, inevitably involves both strategies and prior knowledge. These two processes must be orchestrated and combined in complementary ways (Baron 1985, Brown et al. 1983, Pressley et al. 1989a).

5. Metacognition and Self-regulation

Although students can execute many strategies when given explicit instructions to do so, they typically fail to continue to use these strategies once the cues have been removed. These failures can take the form of both maintenance (i.e., use of the strategy on similar tasks) and transfer (i.e., generalization to new tasks) failures. Thus, having taught a student to use a strategy in no way assures continued use of the strategy in either similar or new contexts.

Many theorists and researchers believe that durable use of strategies will be achieved only when students are provided with considerable practice on diverse tasks in diverse settings. This type of practice allows the students to develop understanding about when and where to use the strategies taught as well as how to adapt these strategies to new situations. Good strategy users have extensive and detailed metacognitive knowledge (stored in long-term memory) about the appropriate use of their strategies. Unfortunately, however, many adults do not have detailed metacognitive understanding about the strategies they have acquired, understanding that could be used to guide the effective application of strategies (Dixon and Hertzog 1988).

Critical though such long-term understanding is for the regulation of strategies and other knowledge as part of skilled comprehension and memorization, other types of metacognition also are critical. Awareness of whether what is being studied is actually being learned (termed self-monitoring) can be a critical determinant of strategy use. Awareness that current efforts are not leading to learning should motivate attempts to use different strategies. Substantial data suggest, however, that neither children nor adults are always accurate in monitoring the effectiveness of their current strategies or other cognitive processes (for reviews, see Ghatala 1986, Pressley and Ghatala 1990).

In short, at a theoretical level it is easy to make a case for the criticality of both long- and short-term metacognition in regulating strategies and cognition in general. That gaps in metacognitive knowledge and difficulties in monitoring are common is consistent with the frequent observation that adult learning and cognition often is anything but effectively strategic (Pressley et al. 1992).

6. Assessment of Memory

The traditional way that memory has been measured is to provide a learner with a memory task and subsequently administer a memory test on the content presented during the task. For example, there have been many laboratory studies in which learners have been presented lists of words (e.g., dog, peach, radio, car, lamp, ... stone, book). A recall test for such a list would require that the learner remember the items on the list. A serial recall test would require the items to be remembered in order. A recognition test would involve presentation of another list of items, and learners would be required to recognize items from the first list (e.g., Was "cat" on the list? Was "car?" How about "rock?" Was "peach?").

In general, the more demanding the memory test, the more completely the learner must encode the information during study in order to do well on the test. That is, a serial recall test requires more complete encoding of information than a simple recall test. Recognition generally requires less encoding than recall, although there are exceptions, for example, when distracters on the recognition test are very similar to items on the original study list.

The specific items that are remembered and how they are remembered can often reveal the way in which the information was processed. Thus, if words on a list are presented in a random order but recall occurs in a categorical fashion (e.g., all of the foods recalled together, all of the vehicles recalled together), the inference can be made that reorganization occurred. It is often not clear, however, whether the reorganization took place at encoding or at retrieval (Lange 1978). If semantic associates of original list items are reported as occurring on a recognition test (e.g., "rock" is reported as occurring on a list that actually contained "stone"), there is evidence that coding of study list items stimulated "spreading activation" in the memory system. That is, reading "stone" activated the associated knowledge, "rock," in the long-term knowledge base (Anderson 1983).

Many have argued that using test performance data to make inferences about study processes is relying on indirect measures of processing. More direct measures of processing have been developed and validated in the 1970s and 1980s. If learners are given a list of items to study, the length of time spent on each item can be measured and study strategies can be inferred from the pattern of study times (Belmont et al. 1978). For example, if there is a short pause after the first item on the list, a slightly longer pause after the second, a longer pause still after the third, and so on, the inference can be made that the learner is cumulatively rehearsing the items on the list as they are presented (e.g., saying "dog" after presentation of "dog," saying "dog, peach" after presentation of "peach," saying "dog, peach, radio" after "radio"). Verbal protocol analysis (Ericsson and Simon 1983) is another method now being used to examine processing during study. With this method of measurement, the learner is asked to think aloud, verbally reporting what he or she is doing while studying to-be-learned material.

In summary, several methods are now available for determining the memory processes used by a learner. These methods range from more indirect measures, such as analyses of memory test performance data, to more direct measures, such as time analysis and verbal protocols. The most compelling evidence that the processing involved during a memory task is understood is when the results of several measures converge to support a process interpretation, for example, when the memory test performance (e.g., categorizable items on a list are remembered together) and verbal protocol analyses (e.g., reports of sorting list items into categories during study) coincide. These various methods of testing have permitted insights about the processing of many different types of material, from laboratory lists to connected text.

7. Conclusion

The various topics in this entry are interrelated. Active use of strategies and attempts to relate new material to prior knowledge are more common when a memory task directs intentional learning than when the need to learn is unclear (i.e., memory is incidental). The role of prior knowledge and strategies in memory have only become apparent because of substantial increases in the sophistication of memory assessment, with the procedures for the analysis of test performances and study patterns expanding greatly since the early 1970s. There has been progressively less reliance on indirect measures (i.e., analyses of what was remembered) as psychologists have refined more direct measures (e.g., protocol analyses, pause-time analyses).

What both the indirect and direct analyses have revealed is that memory, at its very best, involves sophisticated articulation of a repertoire of strategies and diverse prior knowledge. Additionally, sophisticated learners are aware of when the use of particular strategies is appropriate. These learners also monitor accurately when strategies and prior knowledge currently in use are permitting effective memorization of new content.

Unfortunately, with increasing sophistication of memory processing assessment, deficiencies in memory processing have also become more apparent. Fully effective, self-regulated use of memory strategies and prior knowledge to enhance the memorization of important new content is rare. More positively, however, many memory strategies can be taught to children and adults. There is growing understanding of the extensive, long-term instruction and practice required for learners to automatize strategies and use them appropriately.

See also: Learning Strategies: Teaching and Assessing

References

Anderson J R 1983 *The Architecture of Cognition*. Harvard University Press, Cambridge, Massachusetts
Anderson R C, Reynolds R E, Schallert D L, Goetz E T 1977 Frameworks for comprehending discourse. *Am. Educ. Res. J.* 14(4): 367–82
Anderson R C, Pichert J W 1978 Recall of previously

unrecallable information following a shift in perspective. *J. Verbal Learn. Verbal Behav.* 17(1): 1–12

Baker-Ward L, Ornstein P A, Holden D J 1984 The expression of memorization in early childhood. *Journal of Experimental Child Psychology* 37(3): 555–75

Baron J 1985 *Rationality and Intelligence.* Cambridge University Press, Cambridge

Belmont J M, Butterfield E C, Borkowski J G 1978 Training retarded people to generalize memorization methods across tasks. In: Gruneberg M M, Morris P E, Sykes R M (eds.) 1978 *Practical Aspects of Memory.* Academic Press, London

Brown A L, Smiley S S, Day J D, Townsend M A R, Lawton S C 1977 Intrusion of a thematic idea in children's comprehension and retention of stories. *Child Dev.* 48: 1454–66

Brown A L, Bransford J D, Ferrara R A, Campione J C 1983 Learning, remembering, and understanding. In: Flavell J H, Markman E M (eds.) 1983 *Handbook of Child Psychology. Vol 1: Cognitive Development.* Wiley, New York

Dixon R A, Hertzog C 1988 A functional approach to memory and metamemory development in adulthood. In: Weinert F E, Perlmutter M (eds.) 1988

Ericsson K A, Simon H A 1983 *Verbal Protocol Analysis.* MIT Press, Cambridge, Massachusetts

Flavell J H 1985 *Cognitive Development.* Prentice-Hall, Englewood Cliffs, New Jersey

Ghatala E S 1986 Strategy-monitoring training enables young learners to select effective strategies. *Educ. Psychol.* 21: 43–54

Hudson J, Nelson K 1983 Effects of script structure on children's story recall. *Dev. Psychol.* 19(4): 625–35

Jenkins J J 1974 Remember that old theory of memory? Well, forget it! *Am. Psychol.* 29(11): 785–95

Kobasigawa A 1977 Retrieval strategies in the development of memory. In: Kail R V, Hagen J W (eds.) 1977

Kuhara-Kojima K, Hatano G 1991 Contribution of content knowledge and learning ability to the learning of facts. *J. Educ. Psychol.* 83(2): 253–63

Lange G 1978 Organization-related processes in children's recall. In: Ornstein P A (ed.) 1978 *Memory Development in Children.* Erlbaum and Associates, Hillsdale, New Jersey

Levin J R 1983 Pictorial strategies for school learning: Practical illustrations. In: Pressley M, Levin J R (eds.) 1983

Cognitive Strategy Research: Educational Applications. Springer-Verlag, New York

Paivio A U 1971 *Imagery and Verbal Processes.* Holt, Rinehart, and Winston, New York

Pressley M, Levin J R 1980 The development of mental imagery retrieval. *Child Dev.* 51(2): 558–60

Pressley M, Heisel B E, McCormick C G, Nakamura G V 1982 Memory strategy instruction with children. In: Brainerd C J, Pressley M (eds.) 1982 *Verbal Processes in Children: Progress in Cognitive Development Research,* Vol 2. Springer-Verlag, New York

Pressley M, Levin J R, Bryant S L 1983 Memory strategy instruction during adolescence: When is explicit instruction needed? In: Pressley M, Levin J R (eds.) 1983 *Cognitive Strategy Research: Psychological Foundations.* Springer-Verlag, New York

Pressley M, Forrest-Pressley D L, Elliott-Faust D J, Miller G E 1985 Children's use of cognitive strategies, how to teach strategies, and what to do if they can't be taught. In: Pressley M, Brainerd C J (eds.) 1985 *Cognitive Learning and Memory in Children.* Springer-Verlag, New York

Pressley M, Borkowski J G, Schneider W 1989a Good information processing: What it is and what education can do to promote it. *Int. J. Educ. Res.* 13: 668–78

Pressley M, Johnson C J, Symons S, McGoldrick J A, Kurita J A 1989b Strategies that improve children's memory and comprehension of text. *Elem. Sch. J.* 90(1): 3–32

Pressley M, Ghatala E S 1990 Self-regulated learning: Monitoring learning from text. *Educ. Psychol.* 25: 19–34

Pressley M, El-Dinary P B, Brown R 1992 Skilled and not-so-skilled reading: Good information processing and not-so-good information processing. In: Pressley M, Harris K R, Guthrie J T (eds.) 1992 *Promoting Academic Competence and Literacy: Cognitive Research and Instructional Innovation.* Academic Press, San Diego, California

Schneider W, Körkel J, Weinert F E 1989 Domain-specific knowledge and memory performance: A comparison of high- and low-aptitude children. *J. Educ. Psychol.* 81(3): 306–12

Schneider W, Pressley M 1989 *Memory Development Between 2 and 20.* Springer-Verlag, New York

Yates F A 1966 *The Art of Memory.* Routledge and Kegan Paul, London

Comprehension: Teaching and Assessing

W. Schnotz and S.-P. Ballstaedt

This entry is about comprehension as a central aspect of meaningful learning in the context of teaching. First, basic characteristics of human comprehension are described. Comprehension is considered as a mental construction process. Based on these considerations, possibilities for educational guidance of these construction processes through teaching are discussed. Then, methods for testing and evaluating certain aspects of comprehension are described. Finally, perspectives for further research activities are pointed out.

1. Components of Human Comprehension

Understanding human comprehension requires an understanding of the major components of comprehension. Five primary components are addressed in this section.

1.1 Effort after Meaning

A central task of education is to help people orientate themselves in a complex real and symbolic world and understand its various phenomena. Comprehension can be considered as the most demanding human mental activity since it can encompass perception, memory, thinking, and problem solving. Humans principally assume that information about the world is understandable. Bartlett (1932) has called this basic anthropological attitude an "effort after meaning." Within interpersonal communication a distinction can be made between comprehension on the content level and comprehension on the communication level. One can understand the conveyed information about the content and one can understand the intention of the message.

1.2 Mental Construction

Findings from hermeneutics, psycholinguistics, cognitive psychology, and artificial intelligence since the early 1980s gave rise to a constructive theory of comprehension (Bransford 1979, Hörmann 1978). The theory's basic assumption holds that comprehension is an active and goal-oriented construction of coherent mental representations based on newly acquired information and prior knowledge. In most cases, comprehension of verbal information has served as a paradigm for the analysis of comprehension. Other forms of comprehension as, for example, comprehension of situations or social behavior have received only little attention.

1.3 Interaction Between External and Internal Influences

Comprehension is not a single act. It results from a complex interaction between different levels of information processing influenced by external and internal conditions (Engelkamp 1984). On the one hand, comprehension activities are usually triggered by external information which provides the material for mental constructions. Teaching can influence these mental construction processes by presenting certain verbal or pictorial information in an appropriate learning environment. On the other hand, comprehension is being controlled by internal conditions, especially prior knowledge, aims, interests, and expectations. In order to comprehend then, a student must assimilate the new information into pre-existing cognitive structures and/or accomodate these structures according to the new information. Trying to make new information as meaningful as possible by forming coherence with already existing knowledge can sometimes lead to misunderstandings (as when a learner comprehends the presented information in his or her own way but misinterprets the teacher's meaning). The integration of old and new information into a coherent whole requires knowledge-based inferences and can be controlled by metacognitive processes.

1.4 Open-ended Processes

Comprehension is principally an open-ended process. Neisser (1976) has developed a comprehension cycle to explain comprehension. New information enlarges prior knowledge which influences subsequent processing, leading again to a knowledge modification, and so on. Depending on the number of processing cycles, comprehension can be deeper or more superficial. An individual can break off further comprehension efforts for practical reasons. Nevertheless, already understood material can be put into a new context and then be comprehended again in a new way or at a deeper level.

1.5 Context Dependency

Information is always embedded in a context which influences its meaning (Bransford 1979). Actions, for example, are embedded in social situations, words are embedded in sentences and these again are embedded in texts, and so on. The respective context serves to avoid ambiguity and misunderstandings. The context dependency of comprehension is a central issue in situated learning and cognitive apprenticeship.

2. Teaching for Comprehension

Teaching can only lead to comprehension by stimulating an individual to engage in certain mental construction processes. On the one hand, the learner needs sufficient guidance to interrelate new information into prior knowledge. On the other hand, mental construction processes require a certain degree of individual freedom which should not be unnecessarily limited. A balance has to be found between necessary instructional guidance and the required cognitive independence of the learner.

2.1 Activation of Prior Knowledge

In meaningful learning an individual is expected not only to pick up information about isolated facts but to assemble pieces of knowledge to coherent higher order structures. Coherence formation requires the activation of prior knowledge. According to the theory of cognitive subsumption by Ausubel (1968), a teacher should activate clear, stable, and distinct concepts which allow anchoring of the new information in the learner's knowledge structure. This activation, using advance organizers, provides a general framework which can then be further elaborated through progressive differentiation. A similar notion can be found in the elaboration theory of instruction (Reigeluth 1983). According to this theory, prior knowledge is activated through a preceding epitome which provides a conceptual framework for the integration of new information. Such an epitome contains a few simple central concepts and interconnects them using semantic relations. The subject matter is then described first in a crude, general way. Subsequently, more detailed descriptions follow step by step.

Activation of prior knowledge can also be achieved by the use of examples. On the one hand, examples can help to illustrate general statements and to make instructions more lively by personally affecting the learner. On the other hand, learners often consider an example in isolation without recognizing its relationship to the more general content (Marton and Wenestram 1978). Examples often have a stronger influence on comprehension than explicitly conveyed general information. A frequent recommendation, therefore, is to start with typical examples and then gradually to reduce typicality.

2.2 Triggering of Comprehension Activities

There frequently exists a gap between what learners can do and what they actually do. Many students think that comprehension is a passive reception of knowledge from a teacher or textbook rather than a generative constructive process. Therefore, the question arises how to stimulate learners to engage in the appropriate comprehension activities. Instead of simply presenting ready-made knowledge structures with the help of advance organizers or epitomes, teachers can use genetic or inquiry-oriented teaching. Here, the learner is being stimulated to discover essential coherence relations on his or her own. The teacher requires students to structure problem situations independently, to infer global interrelations from presented examples, to generate hypotheses and to test them (Wagenschein 1989). Epistemic motivation is stimulated through inducing cognitive conflicts (Berlyne 1960). In these less structured learning situations, however, the correlation between general intelligence of the learner and learning outcome usually becomes higher than in highly structured learning environments.

Comprehension activities can also be triggered by adjunct aids like the explication of educational objectives or adjunct questions. A teacher can make educational objectives explicit through providing information about tasks which will have to be solved later on. On the one hand, such information gives learners an orientation basis for directing their processing. On the other hand, however, there is the danger of learners being too selective with regard to the conveyed information. They might then only concentrate on seemingly goal-relevant contents and neglect the other information with the consequence that higher order relations are not recognized.

Well-suited adjunct questions can stimulate reflection or deeper-level processing, evoke cognitive conflicts, or demand an application of what has been understood. Rothkopf (1970) has used the term "mathemagenic activities" for such deeper processing initiated by adjunct questions. In order to support coherence formation, such questions should aim especially at establishing higher order relations. Questions can either precede each instructional section and therefore enhance mainly intentional learning of question-relevant contents, or can follow each instructional section. Then they initiate, on the one hand, intentional learning through recapitulation of the conveyed content, and on the other, incidental learning through generating a specific cognitive orientation. The learner comes to expect similar questions in the following instructional sections and organizes his or her processing activities accordingly (Rickards and Denner 1978).

The application of such adjunct aids has to be well-measured and matched with the cognitive-processing capacity of the learner. Too many educational objectives and adjunct questions can be quite confusing instead of being supportive for the learner. The efficiency of such aids seems to follow a u-inverse function. In the case of very favorable conditions (for example, good individual learning prerequisites, well-structured teaching materials, and sufficient learning time), studies often show no effect since such aids are actually not needed. Under very unfavorable conditions there is again no effect since the aids cannot be utilized appropriately. However, a supportive effect with regard to comprehension and learning can be expected in case of average processing conditions (Hartley and Davies 1976).

2.3 Metacognitive Control and Self-regulation

Comprehension as a mental construction is a goal-directed process. Learners are capable of adapting their cognitive processing to context conditions and expected demands. In order to achieve flexible and adaptive cognitive processing, metacognitive strategies concerning comprehension monitoring and control of one's own processing are necessary. Flavell (1979) has emphasized the importance of metacognitive knowledge (i.e., knowledge about human cognition) for monitoring and controlling one's own processing. However, the role of this metacognitive knowledge is being disputed; even experts often have difficulties in verbalizing their metacognitive self-regulation. Furthermore, existing metacognitive knowledge is often not used.

The regulation of cognitive processing is usually automatized. Only in the case of comprehension problems which cannot be solved with automated procedures is cognitive processing consciously controlled through metacognitive knowledge (Brown et al. 1986). However, learners frequently have inadequate standards for evaluating their comprehension. They often do not realize that they do not really understand. They establish coherence only at the local level and not at the global level or they ignore inconsistencies but are nevertheless under the asumption that they understand well. Glenberg et al. (1982) have called this the "illusion of knowing."

2.4 Strategy Training

Various methods exist aimed at preventing learners from superficial comprehension by teaching them certain processing strategies (Mandl and Friedrich 1992). Some of these strategy training programs, for example, instruct the learner to emphasize central information through self-questioning and to connect this information with other information. Learners can also be supported in independently summarizing what they have understood with the help of certain techniques, such as mapping procedures. Using mapping procedures, the learner graphically depicts the superordinate structure of the learning content. The results are two-dimensional maps which represent the basic structure of a subject area in the form of a diagram and which can be considered as graphical summaries (Anderson 1979). These procedures require the learner to go beyond local coherence and to direct his or her attention also to the higher-order global relations. The techniques usually require many hours of intensive training until they can be mastered and used relatively efficiently. Other strategy training programs emphasize time-planning, concentration management, self-perception, motivational–affective factors, individual learning styles, and social–psychological aspects of learning in groups (e.g., McKeachie et al. 1985, Weinstein 1988).

Studies on the effectiveness of strategy training programs frequently show positive effects with inexperienced learners whereas experienced learners often either profit little or show a decline in comprehension and learning performance. Experienced learners usually follow certain habits in their processing which are relatively resistant to change. If a training program is to have positive effects on learning it must first dismantle these old learning habits before it can establish a new regulatory system. Furthermore, the learner has to concentrate during strategy training on the subject matter and, simultaneously, on the learning techniques to be acquired. Due to this division of attention the cognitive capacity available for the subject matter itself is reduced, which can result in temporarily impaired learning performance. Strategy training programs are probably most efficient when they aim at global coherence formation with less experienced learners.

Newly acquired strategies are often dropped under the pressure of a specific learning situation. The learner then returns to his or her usual processing style. This finding suggests the need to engage in indirect promotion of strategies. The learner is placed in a learning situation and given certain tasks which stimulate the desired processing activities. Such indirect training makes the acquisition of strategies a by-product of subject matter learning. Strategies should not just be practiced. Rather, learners should be convinced of their usefulness in order to increase their willingness to apply them. Furthermore, strategy application depends on motivational transfer, attributional beliefs, and on the learner's self-concept (Borkowski et al. 1988). Comprehension strategies need to be supplemented through socioemotional coping strategies in order to help less efficient learners overcome the negative emotions associated with learning (Lehtinen 1992).

2.5 Situatedness

Context dependency of comprehension implies that the cognitive processes are embedded into situations of everyday life. Therefore, the social aspect of comprehension must be considered. This view has been emphasized by Palincsar and Brown (1984) in what they have called "reciprocal teaching" which supports comprehension activities by embedding them into a social context. Teachers and learners alternately conduct dialogues on instructional text-sections and summarize, make predictions, ask questions, and clarify where necessary. This interaction provides many possibilities to uncover misunderstandings on the part of the individual learner.

The context dependency of comprehension is especially emphasized in the situated learning approach. According to this view, comprehension is best supported in authentic situations with meaningful goal-oriented activities which provide the possibility for a cognitive apprenticeship. The teacher shows the learners, for example, a specific action (modeling) and conveys an orientation base for its execution (scaffolding). The learners then carry out the action themselves while the teacher observes and supports them (coaching). The more the learners become able to master the task, the less help they receive (fading out). Comprehension is viewed here as a process of enculturation whereby the learner adopts knowledge, abilities, and beliefs of social groups (Collins et al. 1989).

3. Testing for Comprehension

Comprehension cannot be measured directly. It is only possible to measure performances which require comprehension as a prerequisite. These indicators can be measured during comprehension (on-line) or after comprehension (off-line). The methods used for testing comprehension only address aspects of these complex comprehension processes (Anderson 1972, Ballstaedt and Mandl 1988).

3.1 Questions

Answering questions is probably the oldest and the most versatile method for testing comprehension (Graesser and Black 1985). Such questions require not only the retrieval of facts, but also additional processing which goes beyond the previously presented information. There is a distinction between open questions which allow answers to be constructed and closed questions which allow only a choice among various possible answers. Multiple-choice questions have proved very efficient in testing. Several variants of such questions are distinguished depending on how many possible answers are being provided and how many of them are correct. The difficulty of constructing multiple-choice questions lies in finding optional answers which require higher order cognitive processing to check their correctness.

3.2 Free Recall

The free recall of a previously learned content using one's own words is also a common method for testing comprehension. The corresponding evaluation can take into account both the quantity and the quality of the response, especially the coherence of recall. The basic assumption that comprehension allows correct reproduction assumes that the learner has created a conceptual representation of the presented information which he or she can then verbalize if required. Different learners will, of course, produce different sequences of the content, use different words, and generate different sentences. This creativity is considered as proof of the integration into prior knowledge. The connection between comprehension and remembering, however, is sometimes rather weak. There are contents which learners understand and then forget and there are contents which they do not understand but can nevertheless remember.

3.3 Summarizing

The task of summarizing the most important elements from a large amount of information is especially well-suited for written testing. Here as well, the quantity and quality of the summary can be of interest; the most important information has to be included and the summary has to be coherent. Summaries are quite valid indicators for comprehension since their mental construction requires higher order coherence formation processes. The reduction processes involved in summarizing have been analyzed in detail and a list of macro-operations such as deletion, selection, integration, and generalization has been produced (van Dijk 1980).

3.4 Thinking Aloud

This method requires the verbalization of ongoing cognitive processes while solving a task. Recording and transcribing a protocol are necessary to preserve the material for further evaluation. Thinking aloud is only possible in a single learner situation. Furthermore, it requires that systematic quantitative and qualitative evaluation criteria be developed according to the respective goals of the analysis. The method usually costs a great deal of time, but it allows on-line insight into the actual development of comprehension or misunderstanding (Graesser 1981).

The protocols provide qualitatively rich and distinctive material which reflects various comprehension processes: knowledge activation, inferences, establishment of coherence, and metacognition. Nevertheless, thinking aloud brings only the tip of the iceberg of all the processes of comprehension into view.

Much more is going on in the head of a learner than he or she can verbalize. Furthermore, the central assumption that ongoing mental processes can be verbally expressed without distortions has repeatedly been doubted. The objection is that the unusual task of continually verbalizing actually interferes with the comprehension processes.

3.5 Cloze Procedures

The standard form of a cloze procedure consists in a text presented to the subject in which one word out of five is missing. The learner has to fill in the missing words. The percentage of correctly filled blanks is used as the measure of comprehension. There are numerous variants (e.g., only one out of five content words can be deleted, or the learner is presented with the fragment of a text or sentence which he or she has to complete appropriately). Cloze procedures can also be applied for visual tests of comprehension, when empty spaces have to be correctly filled within a picture or a graph. There is disagreement about what kind of comprehension processes are being measured with cloze procedures. Some researchers doubt that comprehension is being measured at all. The question remains to what extent guessing plays a role since due to pre-existing content and linguistic knowledge a number of empty spaces can be filled without any comprehension of the passage.

3.6 Structure Displays

These testing procedures can be viewed as a variant of the mind-mapping technique. Subsequent to a comprehension process the learner externalizes his or her knowledge through writing concept words on cards and connecting them with a set of given content relations. The procedure has been standardized, but it can easily be modified for various aims (Scheele 1992). Unfortunately, no theory-based set of relations has been developed. The possibilities of quantitative and qualitative criteria of formal and content-related analyses are manifold. Measures for the internal coherence and differentiatedness of the knowledge can be calculated. The concepts can also be categorized using content analysis. Structure displays exhibit coherence relations and can be used for knowledge diagnosis. If the prior knowledge about a certain topic is displayed before learning, then the new conceptual interrelations acquired during teaching can be identified.

3.7 Application

In many cases the application of what has been understood in performing a certain behavior is the most valid method for testing comprehension. Examples of this method include conducting an experiment, using an apparatus, and similar activities. The quality of such a performance can be judged by the number of mistakes, the required amount of time, or other appropriate criteria. The use of video-recording allows repeated observation, also with slow motion. Since this procedure requires individual sessions and since the evaluation is costly in terms of time, practical application as a test for comprehension is accordingly rare. In addition, successful performance can sometimes occur on the basis of procedural knowledge rather than conceptual knowledge. In this case, the person being tested acts correctly although he or she did not grasp the meaning of that action. Therefore, tasks have to be constructed so that they are only solvable with the comprehension of the entire content.

4. Future Perspectives

Further research on teaching and testing for comprehension should analyze more deeply the interaction between cognitive, motivational, emotional, and social aspects of understanding. Furthermore, research should not be restricted to language comprehension, since nonverbal comprehension processes also play an important role in education.

In order to promote comprehension processes, a deeper analysis of the interplay between cognitive and metacognitive processes in the self-regulation of comprehension seems to be promising. Related to this analysis is the question of how direct training of comprehension and learning strategies and indirect support of such strategies should be combined. Another important problem is the optimal combination of the cognitively oriented strategies and the motivationlly oriented supportive strategies for specific learner groups.

The provision of indirect support for comprehension strategies is closely related to the situated learning approach to teaching comprehension since in both cases teaching is tied to authentic social and pragmatic contexts. Formal objective tests for comprehension play a limited role in these approaches since comprehension is constantly being evaluated in the social context (communicative validation). The complexity of the field requires multidisciplinary research from the perspectives of cognitive psychology, psycholinguistics, educational psychology, and instructional design.

References

Anderson R C 1972 How to construct achievement tests to assess comprehension. *Rev. Educ. Res.* 42(2): 145–70

Anderson T H 1979 Study skills and learning strategies. In: O'Neil H F, Spielberger D (eds.) 1979 *Cognitive and Affective Learning Strategies*. Academic Press, New York

Ausubel D P 1968 *Educational Psychology: A Cognitive View*. Holt, Rinehart and Winston, New York

Ballstaedt S-P, Mandl H 1988 The assessment of comprehensibility. In: Ammon U, Dittmar N, Mattheier K J (eds.) 1988 *Sociolinguistics. An International Handbook of the Science of Language and Society*. Walter de Gruyter, Berlin

Bartlett F C 1932 *Remembering. A Study in Experimental and Social Psychology*. Cambridge University Press, Cambridge

Berlyne D E 1960 *Conflict, Arousal, and Curiosity*. McGraw-Hill, New York

Borkowski J G, Weyhing R S, Carr M 1988 Effects of attributional retraining on strategy-based reading comprehension in learning-disabled students. *J. Educ. Psychol.* 80(1): 46–53

Bransford J O 1979 *Human Cognition: Learning, Understanding, and Remembering*. Wadsworth, Belmont, California

Brown A L, Armbruster B B, Baker L 1986 The role of metacognition in reading and studying. In: Orasanu J (ed.) 1986 *Reading Comprehension. From Research to Practice*. Erlbaum, Hillsdale, New Jersey

Collins A, Brown J S, Newman S E 1989 Cognitive apprenticeship: Teaching the crafts of reading, writing, and mathematics. In: Resnick L B (ed.) 1989 *Knowing, Learning, and Instruction*. Erlbaum, Hillsdale, New Jersey

Engelkamp J 1984 Verstehen als Informationsverarbeitung. In: Engelkamp J (ed.) 1984 *Psychologische Aspekte des Verstehens*. Springer, Berlin

Flavell J H 1979 Metacognition and cognitive monitoring: A new area of cognitive-developmental inquiry. *Am. Psychol.* 34(10): 906–11

Glenberg A M, Wilkinson A C, Epstein W 1982 The illusion of knowing: Failure in the self-assessment of comprehension. *Memory and Cognit.* 10(6): 597–602

Graesser A C 1981 *Prose Comprehension Beyond the Word*. Springer, New York

Graesser A C, Black J B (eds.) 1985 *The Psychology of Questions*. Erlbaum, Hillsdale, New Jersey

Hartley J, Davies I K 1976 Preinstructional strategies: The role of pretests, behavioral objectives, overviews and advance organizers. *Rev. Educ. Res.* 46: 239–65

Hörmann H 1978 *Meinen und Verstehen. Grundzuge einer psychologischen Semantik*. Suhrkamp, Frankfurt

Lehtinen E 1992 Lern- und Bewältigungsstrategien im Unterricht. In: Mandl H, Friedrich H F (eds.) 1992

Mandl H, Friedrich H F (eds.) 1992 *Lern- und Denkstrategien*. Hogrefe, Göttingen

Marton F, Wenestram C G 1978 Qualitative differences in understanding and retention of the main points in some texts based on the principle-example structure. In: Gruneberg M M, Morris P E, Sykes R N (eds.) 1978 *Practical Aspects of Memory*. Academic Press, London

McKeachie W J, Pintrich P R, Lin Y G 1985 Learning to learn. In: d'Ydewalle G (ed.) 1985 *Cognition, Information Processing, and Motivation*. North-Holland, Amsterdam

Neisser U 1976 *Cognition and Reality. Principles and Implications of Cognitive Psychology*. Freeman, San Francisco, California

Palincsar A M, Brown A L 1984 Reciprocal teaching of comprehension-fostering and comprehension-monitoring activities. *Cognition and Instruction* 1(2): 117–75

Reigeluth C M (ed.) 1983 *Instructional-design Theories and Models: An Overview of Their Current Status*. Erlbaum, Hillsdale, New Jersey

Rickards J P, Denner P R 1978 Inserted questions as aids to reading text. *Instr. Sci.* 7(3): 313–46

Rothkopf E Z 1970 The concept of mathemagenic activities. *Rev. Educ. Res.* 40(3): 325-36

Scheele B (ed.) 1992 *Struktur-Lege-Verfahren als Dialog-Konsens- Methodik*. Aschendorff, Munster
van Dijk T A 1980 *Macrostructures*. Erlbaum, Hillsdale, New Jersey

Wagenschein M 1989 *Verstehen lehren*. Beltz, Weinheim
Weinstein C E 1988 Assessment and training of student learning strategies. In: Schmeck R R (ed.) 1988 *Learning Strategies and Learning Styles*. Plenum Press, New York

Written Composition: Teaching and Assessing

S. W. Freedman

Written composition includes all aspects of writing, from children's earliest efforts to form letters and words, to older students' and adults' increasingly complex and extended pieces for varied audiences (e.g., teachers, self, peers, community members, employers) and for varied purposes (e.g., to display knowledge, to entertain, to learn subject matter across the curriculum, to conduct business). Schools generally are expected to teach and assess multiple aspects of writing although precise values associated with writing and therefore the emphases given to different aspects of writing will vary from one country to another.

In all cases, writing is one aspect of language learning; it relates to talking, listening, and reading. The acquisition of language in general and writing in particular follows a developmental process that educators need to understand and support across time. At any given moment, writers engage in an extended problem-solving process that educators also need to understand and encourage. In setting up instructional environments that facilitate development across time and writers' processes at a given moment, teachers need to work with their students. Together, they must structure writing activities that engage students in writing and motivate them to want to write. Teachers also must arrange for their students to receive helpful feedback as they write.

1. Learning to Write as an Aspect of Learning Language

Writing is learned best when it is taught alongside reading, speaking, and listening; for like them, writing is part of language learning. If literacy is not considered in its full language context, problems that surface in writing are often misunderstood as "literacy problems" when, in fact, they have little to do with literacy per se. For example, garbled writing may be rooted in garbled ideas, not in difficulties with print communication.

Like speaking, writing is a form of language production. Since speech is learned first and does not have to be transcribed, writers sometimes find it helpful to delay transcription and to develop and refine their ideas for writing first by talking, sometimes even by talking to themselves. In fact, very young writers can get started putting their thoughts into print by dictating and thereby bypassing the transcribing process entirely. In classrooms, students gain much by discussing their writing with their teachers in the course of one-on-one conferences, with their friends, in small groups, or during class discussions. As Moffett and Wagner (1992) explain, "Monologue, the basic act of writing, is born of dialogue" (p. 26).

Just as reading and writing develop best when connected to speaking and listening, it is also important to connect reading and writing. In early literacy acquisition, writing often helps students break the print code, and see how sounds and letters relate, thus stimulating progress in both reading and writing. Reading is invariably tied to writing as students read their own writing, for to write well, one must learn to be a careful and sensitive reader of one's own writing. Through reading, writers gain a sense of the sounds and rhythms of written language. Activities that tightly intertwine reading and writing, allowing the skills to build on one another, include dialogue journals between teacher and students or other writing exchanges between students. In these activities readers write and writers read, with writers often modeling their writing on what they have just read. For additional practical suggestions for integrating writing, reading, speaking, and listening inside classrooms, see Britton (1989) and Moffett and Wagner (1992).

2. Writing Development

Young children's writing develops and matures across time, but not all children develop on the same schedule nor do all learn the same way. Children learn to write by building on what they already know about language. They come into school with varied kinds of experiences of and knowledge about language. It is crucial for teachers to understand their knowledge and experiences in order to help them build from what they know.

In the primary grades, for example, stories are usually a staple of children's early exposure to both reading and writing (see Dyson and Freedman 1991). Storytelling is ubiquitous in human culture, and children generally come to school with quite specific ideas about how stories are structured and how they function. However, stories function differently in different cultures and have different forms. Especially in multicultural settings, children may enter school with varied out-of-school experiences with stories (Heath 1983).

During early literacy acquisition teachers need to know how to help children build on the narrative knowledge they bring to school, especially when that knowledge differs from the kind of narratives in school reading books or the kind of narratives children are expected to produce in writing. Since development depends on building on past knowledge, it is critical for teachers to know what their students do know, not just what they do not yet know.

When youngsters are learning to write in a second language, the developmental process becomes more complex. For these writers, it is important for teachers to have specific knowledge about what the writers know about writing in their first language and how they might build on native-language literacy skills (Valdés 1992).

Given that writers approach learning to write with varied but meaningful language experiences, it is difficult to make blanket statements about how writing develops. Furthermore, writing is too complex an enterprise to admit sequences of development. In the first place, most people never fully master any kind of writing. Even professional novelists feel that they could write better narratives, and they know that some of their efforts are more successful than others. Similarly, some business letters require very complex rhetorical moves, and experienced professionals often fail to persuade their readers to accept their ideas. However, many people do reach a point where they can spell most words they need, where they can form complete, if not always elegant, sentences, and where they can write what for them are routine pieces with relative ease.

Whereas the whole of writing is too complex to make statements about development, knowledge about how certain strands develop does exist (Dyson 1987). For example, for languages with alphabetic writing systems, children learn very early that letters and sounds correspond and that letters can be grouped to make words. When children first begin combining sounds with letters, they use "invented spelling." These invented spellings are patterned and provide important clues about children's understandings of sound–symbol relationships. As their ability to compose develops, children gradually come to use conventional spellings.

No particular discourse form is inherently more difficult to acquire than any other; however, within each form there are levels of complexity. That is, stories are not necessarily easier to write than arguments, but young children write much simpler stories and arguments than do older children. Developmentally, writers gradually learn to generalize from their personal experiences, to incorporate into their writing what they read as well as what they experience first-hand, to control increasingly complex and longer sentences, to develop their ideas at some length, and to engage in increasingly more extended decision-making processes.

3. The Processes of Writing

Writing involves thinking through ideas, drafting, and redrafting, with writers moving back and forth among these three aspects of composing as they solve the problems posed by their evolving piece (Hayes and Flower 1980). When students become engaged in this kind of expanded problem-solving process, writing becomes a powerful tool for helping them grapple with complex ideas. Researchers have found that "writing process instruction" goes awry when teachers bypass the complicated problem-solving that is at the heart of an expanded writing process, in favor of relatively rigid sets of procedures for all students to follow (e.g., plan on Monday, draft on Tuesday, revise on Wednesday, edit on Thursday) (see Dyson and Freedman 1991). Such rigid procedures are counter to what is known about the fluid ways in which writers write. Instead of thinking about the process as a set of steps to be followed (plan, draft, revise), it is more productive for teachers to think about the kind of support writers need to engage in this complex problem-solving process.

Studies of the specific nature of this problem-solving process reveal that, even given the same topic, different writers solve different problems. Just as writers develop in different ways, they also compose differently. Although the process may vary from student to student, variation is not idiosyncratic; rather it is patterned. Teachers need to identify the diverse patterns in their classrooms.

4. Teaching Writing

At least two major issues face teachers attempting to set up classrooms to support the teaching and learning of writing. First, they must consider how to get their students to write on topics that are interesting to them, to which they feel in some way connected, and from which they are able to learn. Second, as students write, teachers will need to arrange the kind of support and feedback that will allow them to produce their best work and that will carry over to future writing.

4.1 Setting Up Classrooms

A major difficulty in addressing the first issue is that much writing in school has been restricted in audience and purpose; students write mostly for a teacher or examiner audience and mainly for a grade (Britton et al. 1975). This restricted "school writing" fails to interest many students who write merely to complete a school task, not because they are intellectually or emotionally engaged.

A number of activities can expand the audiences and functions for student writing and can help to engage students. For example, Heath and Mangiola (1991) arranged for 10-year olds who were experiencing difficulty in school to tutor 6-year olds who were just learning to read and write with the goal of interesting the older students in literacy learning. One group of tutors wrote a book for the parents of the 6-year olds explaining how the parents could assist them in their efforts.

In another setting community college students who were not native English speakers studied the languages of their communities and thought explicitly about the varieties of language use and the appropriateness of using particular varieties in particular contexts. Their studies of language in action became the base for their own literacy curriculum. Freedman (1994) describes an audience exchange between inner-city secondary students in the United States and the United Kingdom which involved the students in producing extended pieces for one another—autobiographies, books about their schools and communities, guide books for visiting teenagers, and teenage magazines. Levin et al. (1985) set up a news service on computer networks involving students from around the world.

Even though they were theoretically sound, in no case did these activities in and of themselves create involved and motivated students; rather, what brought the activities to life were the ways they were enacted in particular classrooms. Generally, when these activities were successful, writing was integrated with other language processes; students tackled extended pieces of writing as they engaged in meaningful projects; they were given sufficient time to write; they were involved in planning the writing they did; and they received help as they composed.

The increasing availability of the computer is also beginning to affect the possibilities for interesting students in writing in school. In addition to the international networks that Levin and his colleagues describe, hypermedia programs allow new forms of composition that mix art, sound, and print. Desktop publishing makes school newspapers and other inhouse professional publications possible. Finally, computers can encourage more decentralized classrooms that lead to individualization and collaboration as students write together in class and share computer resources (Greenleaf 1994).

Writing can also be a useful tool to help students learn the content of mathematics, science, social studies, or other subject areas. Writing is particularly useful for helping students understand complex ideas, but not for helping them learn facts (Langer and Applebee 1987). In addition, when students write about new concepts, teachers get feedback on what their students do and do not understand.

4.2 Providing Feedback to Writers

The second issue to be addressed in classrooms that support the teaching and learning of writing is the kind of feedback writers receive as they write. In addition to being genuinely interested in their writing, writers need to grapple with pieces of writing or aspects of a piece of writing that are too challenging for them to manage alone but that they can manage with the help of others. They then are working within what Vygotsky (1978) calls their "zone of proximal development," that developmental area when the learner cannot perform a task alone but can do so with the assistance of a more expert helper. Assuming that writers are working within this zone, it is time to examine the nature of the assistance the more expert helper provides.

The most effective assistance, from the point of view of expert teachers in both the United States and the United Kingdom, is individualized, oral response from the teacher during the writing process (Freedman 1994). Generally, these responses let writers know whether they are communicating what they intended to communicate in the way they intended. Teachers find it difficult, especially when class size is large, to talk to each student about every piece that he or she writes. However, some have demonstrated ways to provide this important kind of response for their students (Freedman 1987, Sperling 1990). Another kind of response during the writing process comes from peers who are often organized by teachers into peer response groups. These groups are most useful when students are generating ideas; they are less reliable for providing feedback on drafts of text (see DiPardo and Freedman 1988).

The traditional form of feedback, the comments teachers write on student papers after a piece of writing is completed, is the least helpful kind of response. These comments normally accompany a grade on the writing. Many a teacher has reported the sinking feeling that comes when a student looks at the grade and tosses a fully annotated piece of writing in the trash can, without even reading the teachers' comments. Analyses of teachers' comments have shown that they often function more to justify the grade than to teach the student (Sommers 1980). Furthermore, when students do read the teachers' comments, they often misinterpret them (Sperling and Freedman 1987).

Other issues have surfaced about the substance of the help that teachers give. There is some debate about how explicit the teaching of writing needs to be, especially when speakers of foreign languages and speakers of nonstandard dialects are learning to write in formal standard varieties of written language. Generally, the recommended time to push for formal correctness is toward the end of the writing process, with fluency most valued during draft writing. However, Delpit (1988) argues that a stress on fluency early in the process often comes at the expense of formal correctness for many speakers of Black English vernacular. Regardless of how this issue is resolved, study after study has shown that having students complete skill exercises in grammar books or workbooks does not help them use correct forms when they write; rather, correctness is best taught by giving students feedback on what they actually write, in the context of their writing (Elley et al. 1979).

5. Assessing Writing

Given the complexity of learning to write, it is no surprise that it is difficult to assess students' writing. The writing portfolio, consisting of a number of varied samples of student writing selected to represent the student's best efforts, provides the most valid data for evaluating an individual's writing abilities and development across time. Portfolios have been used in national assessments (e.g., the General Certificate of Secondary Education in the United Kingdom); in state and school district assessments (e.g., Vermont's Writing Assessment Program, 1990–91); and in local school assessments that track student progress (e.g., *The Primary Language Record* 1988, Wolf 1989). Constructing portfolios can support good instruction as teachers work together with students to compile the portfolio and as students assess their own progress.

Different approaches have been devised for evaluating portfolios. The GCSE method assigns a single letter grade to the entire portfolio. The Vermont method provides a number of analytic scores, some of them for individual pieces. The PLR uses more descriptive methods, where standardized scores are not required. Unfortunately, there is a tendency to move away from this kind of pedagogically useful assessment approach because it is time-consuming and expensive.

Other approaches to large-scale assessment include collecting and scoring samples of student writing on assigned topics in timed conditions. Examples include the National Assessment of Educational Progress (Applebee et al. 1990) in the United States and the International Education Association Writing Assessment Study in England and Wales (see Gubb et al. 1987). These tests measure a narrow aspect of students' skills as writers and are generally used to assess groups of students for the purpose of informing policy decisions, not for making judgments about individuals.

6. Emergent Trends

In the teaching and assessment of written language there has been much activity in recent years, resulting both in advances in research and changes in practice. This progress will need to continue at a rapid rate.

The "global village" is linked by ever-increasing and more immediate communication capacities; writing plays a central role in this global communication (as scripts for satellite television broadcasts; as messages sent over electronic networks; as the text of faxed notes, letters, and other documents; and as much of what runs businesses behind the scenes). As the twenty-first century approaches, writing is taking on ever-widening functions worldwide. Future research will need to examine these changing functions and will have to consider how global schools can best prepare the children of tomorrow to meet global needs.

References

Applebee A et al. 1990 *The Writing Report Card, 1984–88: Findings from the Nation's Report Card*. Educational Testing Service, Princeton, New Jersey

Britton J 1989 Writing and reading in the classroom. In: Dyson A H (ed.) 1989 *Collaboration Through Writing and Reading: Exploring Possibilities*. National Council of Teachers of English, Urbana, Illinois

Britton J, Burgess T, Martin N, McLeod A, Rosen H 1975 *The Development of Writing Abilities: 11–18*. Macmillan Education Ltd, London

Delpit L 1988 The silenced dialogue: Power and pedagogy in educating other people's children. *Harv. Educ. Rev.* 58: 280–98

DiPardo A, Freedman S W 1988 Peer response groups in the writing classroom: Theoretic foundations and new directions. *Rev. Educ. Res.* 58(2): 119–49

Dyson A H 1987 Individual differences in beginning composing: An orchestral vision of learning to compose. *Written Communication* 4: 411–42

Dyson A H, Freedman S W 1991 Writing. In: Jensen J, Flood J, Lapp D, Squire J (eds.) 1991 *Measures for Research and Teaching the English Language Arts*. Macmillan Inc., New York

Elley W B, Barham I H, Lamb H, Wyllie M 1979 *The Role of Grammar in a Secondary School Curriculum*. New Zealand Council for Educational Research, Wellington

Freedman S W 1987 *Response to Student Writing*. National Council of Teachers of English, Urbana, Illinois

Freedman S W 1994 *Exchanging writing, exchanging cultures: Lessons in School Reform from the United States and Great Britain*. Harvard University Press, Cambridge, Massachusetts

Greenleaf C 1994 Technological indeterminancy: The role of classroom writing practices and pedagogy in shaping student use of the computer. *Written communications* 11: 85–130

Gubb J, Gorman T, Price E 1987 *The Study of Written Composition in England and Wales*. NFER–NELSON, Windsor

Hayes J R, Flower L S 1980 Identifying the organization of writing processes. In: Gregg L W, Steinberg E R (eds.) 1980 *Cognitive Processes in Writing*. Erlbaum, Hillsdale, New Jersey

Heath S B 1983 *Ways with Words*. Cambridge University Press, Cambridge

Heath S B, Mangiola L 1991 *Children of Promise: Literate Activity in Linguistically and Culturally Diverse*

Classrooms. National Education Association, Center for the Study of Writing, American Educational Research Association, Washington, DC

Langer J, Applebee A 1987 *How Writing Shapes Thinking.* National Council of Teachers of English, Urbana, Illinois

Levin J, Reil M, Rowe R, Boruta M 1985 Muktuk meets jacuzzi: Computer networks and elementary school writers. In: Freedman S W (ed.) 1985 *The Acquisition of Written Language.* Ablex, Norwood, New Jersey

Moffett J, Wagner B J 1992 *Student-Centered Language Arts, K 12,* 4th edn. Boynton/Cook Heinemann, Portsmouth, New Hampshire

ILEA 1988 *The Primary Language Record: Handbook for Teachers.* ILEA Centre for Language in Primary Education, London

Sommers N I 1980 Revision strategies of student writers and experienced adult writers. *College Composition and Communication* 31(4): 378–87

Sperling M 1990 I want to talk to each of you: Collaboration and the teacher-student writing conference. *Research in the Teaching of English* 24(3): 279–321

Sperling M, Freedman S W 1987 A good girl writes like a good girl: Written response to student writing. *Written Communication* 4(4): 343–69

Valdés G 1992 Bilingual minorities and language issues in writing: Toward professionwide response to a new challenge. *Written Communication* 9(1): 85–136

Vermont's Writing Assessment Program, Pilot Year 1990–1991. The Vermont Department of Education, Vermont

Vygotsky L S 1978 *Mind in Society: The Development of Higher Psychological Processes.* Harvard University Press, Cambridge, Massachusetts

Wolf D P 1989 Portfolio assessment: Sampling student work. *Educ. Leadership* 46(7): 4–10

Further Reading

Daiute C 1985 *Writing and Computers.* Addison-Wesley, Reading, Massachusetts

Hillocks G Jr 1986 *Research on Written Composition: New Directions for Teaching.* ERIC Clearinghouse on Reading and Communication Skills, Urbana, Illinois

Motor Skills: Learning and Instruction

J. M. M. Van der Sanden

The term "motor skills" refers to an individual's acquired ability to make accurate, efficient, smooth, and coordinated bodily movements in order to achieve some goal. Bodily movement implies the use, spatio-temporal coordination and control of various muscles and joints. The goal to be achieved may have to do with: (a) moving, balancing, and controlling (certain parts of) the body, as in walking, certain sports, dance (body-related movements); or (b) manipulating objects and tools, as in handwriting, operating equipment and machines, playing musical instruments, and driving a car (object-related movements).

1. Motor Skills Research: Scope and History

Learning motor skills has long been regarded as a matter of merely watching some expert performing skilled movements and then trying to imitate this skilled behavior in a process of trial and error. Medieval and postmedieval on-the-job apprenticeship systems for job-training are clearly based on this approach. When traditional craftsmanship in a predominantly rural society was replaced by large-scale industrial production systems, it became necessary to select and train large numbers of industrial personnel. Scientific research programs were judged necessary to furnish a knowledge base for selection and training. Frederick Winslow Taylor's time-and-motion studies

of employees performing work tasks, produced in the early twentieth century, are a well-known example of the so-called "scientific management" approach. This approach required industrial workers to be capable of maximum performance on rather restricted skills, which, in line with prevailing thinking, were seen as stimulus–response chains. Thus, training focused on automatization of limited skills, thereby maximizing speed and minimizing errors.

The Second World War had a major influence on motor skills research. The sudden need for all kinds of military personnel raised difficult problems of selection and training. These problems gave rise to new research programs in the United States and United Kingdom. The main issues in these projects shifted from selection and individual differences in psychomotor abilities to training procedures emphasizing retention and transfer of motor skills. The move away from the behaviorist perspective on learning and instruction allowed cognitive theories to influence motor skills research. Attention was given to the role of motor programs, schemata, and cognitive processes in performing and controlling motor activities.

2. Analysis and Categorization of Motor Skills

Skillful motor behavior is characterized by a focus on the goal, accuracy, and speed; it is not just effective, but also efficient—irrelevant information is ignored, a minimum amount of energy is spent, future situations and problems are anticipated, errors are avoided as far as possible and, if they do occur, are rapidly detected and corrected. Skillful movements are characterized by a remarkable smoothness, indicating optimum coordination between different parts of the body. All of these characteristics hold up under varying conditions: this makes for consistency and adaptability.

All motor skills involve bodily movements, but there are wide differences in these movements. To come to grips with this diversity, several researchers and theorists have tried to analyze and classify motor skills. Fleishman (1975) described four different approaches for classifying (psychomotor) tasks: the behavior description approach, the behavior requirements approach, the ability requirements approach, and the task characteristics approach.

The behavior description approach is characterized by the recording and classification of behavior that can be observed when somebody performs a certain task.

The behavior requirements approach involves the making of an inventory of the cognitive operations that are required to perform a certain (type of) task successfully. Romiszowski's "expanded skill cycle" (see Romiszowski 1981) is an example of this approach. Romiszowski assumed that performing a skilled activity involves a cycle of four stages: (a) perceive relevant stimuli, (b) recall necessary prerequisites, (c) plan necessary actions, and (d) perform actions. Each stage requires three specific cognitive operations. In the planning stage, for instance, these operations are analysis, synthesis, and evaluation. Together these operations make up a list of 12 factors that are, to a greater or lesser extent, required for successful task performance. An important distinction is made between reproductive and productive skills. Reproductive skills are characterized by the application of procedures and algorithms and require little or no conscious planning operations. Productive skills are characterized by the application of principles and strategies and require conscious planning operations.

The ability requirements approach tries to find the relatively stable psychomotor abilities that are necessary for effective performance on a certain (type of) task. Fleishman's (1975) factor-analytic work is an example of this approach. He distinguished 11 psychomotor abilities that could account for the performance differences of some 200 different (merely laboratory) psychomotor tasks. Among these abilities are control precision, multilimb coordination, manual dexterity, finger dexterity, arm–hand steadiness, and reaction time.

The task characteristics approach looks for task and task-situation characteristics that serve as conditioning features for effective task performance. A number of task characteristics have been described in the literature. Perhaps the most important distinction is that between open and closed tasks, which is based on the predictability of the task environment. Closed tasks occur in a predictable environment and can be planned in advance (e.g., writing a letter). Open tasks occur in an unpredictable environment and cannot be fully planned in advance (e.g., playing football). In between are tasks that occur in a semipredictable environment (e.g., driving a car).

3. Learning and Control of Motor Skills

Psychomotor skills differ greatly with regard to the task requirements, task and task-environment characteristics, and psychomotor abilities involved. In spite of this diversity, the learning of many (reproductive) motor skills appears to proceed from a predominantly cognitive phase through an associative phase to an autonomous phase (Fitts and Posner, 1967). In the cognitive phase the emphasis is placed on the cognitive activities involved in acquiring knowledge of the skill to be learned, the goals to be reached, and the steps and procedures to be followed. Performance is jerky and inconsistent; responses are executed step by step, each step requiring conscious application of knowledge. Information necessary for initiating and controlling the task performance is supplied almost exclusively by the eyes. Learning curves are steep in this phase. In the associative phase there is a more gradual performance improvement. Movements are becoming more fluid, integrated, consistent, and regular, and error rates decrease. Information from nonvisual channels increasingly plays a regulatory role. In the autonomous phase it can be observed that conscious cognitive control of movements is no longer necessary. Performance has become efficient and consistent. Attention can be given to things other than the movements per se.

Fitts and Posner's (1969) description of the three phases in learning motor skills is generally recognized as a valid picture of the normal course that the learning of reproductive motor skills takes. When it comes to an explanation of the cognitive processes and structures involved, however, there is much less agreement. This situation is evidenced by a number of different theoretical positions. Some major points of disagreement concern the role of feedback and motor programs in the learning and control of skilled movements.

In closed-loop theories (e.g., Adams 1971) it is assumed that motor behavior is controlled by feedback mechanisms. When performing motor actions, proprioceptive feedback becomes available from internal sensory receptors in muscles and joints and from the vestibular apparatus. In addition, there is external feedback from the auditory and visual channels. This information is compared with some internal representation of the desired state to be reached. When discrepancies of a certain magnitude and direction are detected, corrective actions are undertaken subsequently so that the desired state is reached or maintained. Closed-loop theories are particularly suited to explaining relatively slow or continuous motor behavior, such as in tracking tasks (e.g., driving a car). They encounter difficulties, however, when explaining rapid (ballistic) movements, which once initiated cannot be adjusted. Open-loop theories assume that movements are produced and controlled by central commands from motor programs, which do their work without error-detecting and error-correcting mechanisms. Schmidt's schema theory (Schmidt 1975) is a special kind of open-loop theory that postulates schemata instead of programs. A schema is a generalized motor program pertaining to a certain class of motor actions. The schema concept offers a solution for two kinds of problems, which are inherent to the motor program notion: (a) the storage problem: if it is necessary to have a motor program for every conceivable motor action, it seems impossible to store all these programs; (b) the novelty problem: if a motor program is needed for movements to occur it would be impossible for somebody to make new movements.

There is another problem to which neither open-loop nor closed-loop theories can offer acceptable solutions; the so-called "degrees-of-freedom" problem. The elements of the motor system involved in producing movements (muscles, joints, motor units) together have a considerable number of degrees of freedom. Theories of motor control must account for the way all the elements of the motor system are regulated. Turvey (1977) stated that simultaneous control of all the individual elements involved in performing motor acts is an impossible task for the central nervous system. Therefore he postulated so-called "coordinative structures": in other words, relatively autonomous functional combinations of muscles which are tuned to environmental stimulus configurations. In this approach, perception and action systems are seen as functionally inseparable. Coordinative action structures are tuned to and directly influenced by perceptual states instead of being controlled by calculating, homunculus-like central brain structures. Because of the strong emphasis on man-environment interactions and the tendency to use natural research settings this approach is sometimes referred to as "ecological viewpoint."

4. Instruction and Training of Motor Skills

An issue that continues to provoke debate among researchers and teachers is the question of when to apply discovery and when to apply expository instructional methods. The emphasis in instructional psychology on problem-solving, metacognition, and self-regulated learning has given a new turn to this discussion. Many metacognitive theorists support the notion of expository and direct instruction in strategies for self-regulated discovery learning.

Proponents of Russian activity theory advocate an expository approach to the teaching of motor skills. They emphasize the formation of complete and coherent movement schemata before executing motor activities.

For the training of reproductive skills, Romiszowski (1981) proposed predominantly expository methods, consisting of modeling, massed or distributed practice on increasingly complex tasks, and feedback on results. For the training of productive skills, however, (guided) discovery methods should be added to the expository modeling of basic skills. This is considered important because productive skills require not only procedural knowledge, but also conditional knowledge and planning skills.

According to Anderson (1987), skill learning implies the transformation of declarative into procedural knowledge. Jelsma (1989) has argued that the speed of proceduralization (i.e, automatization) should depend on prevailing transfer conditions. Fast automatization is desirable for skills that are identical in different task situations (near transfer). The process of automatization should be slowed down, however, for skills that vary over task situations (far transfer).

As a consequence of technological developments and changes in the organization of work and production processes (e.g., total quality management) transfer, problem-solving, and autonomous learning are becoming increasingly important in many jobs. Dissatisfaction with traditional trainer-centered training methods led to the development of new trainee-centered methods. In German industry, for instance, the *Leittext* method has been developed. In this autonomous learning and the transfer of productive motor and cognitive skills are fostered by a six-step heuristic, requiring active and constructive, instead of passive and reproductive, learning activities from the trainee.

New theoretical perspectives in instructional psychology, such as functional context training, cognitive apprenticeship, and constructivism, though primarily adressed to the cognitive domain, are of great promise for the field of motor skills. They can provide new insights and tools for designing on-the-job training and informal learning situations. These situations should be designed in such ways that maximum advantage is taken from interactions of trainees with expert performers engaged in authentic and functional job activities. As was pointed out by Collins et al. (1989), modeling, coaching, scaffolding, articulation, reflection, and exploration should be the key instruments in these authentic learning environments.

References

Adams J A 1971 A closed loop theory of motor learning. *Journal of Motor Behavior* 3(2): 111–49
Anderson J R 1987 Skill acquisition: Compilation of weak-method problem situations. *Psychol. Rev.* 94: 192–210
Collins A, Brown J S, Newman S E 1989 Cognitive apprenticeship: Teaching the crafts of reading, writing and mathematics. In: Resnick L B (ed.) 1989 *Knowing, Learning and Instruction: Essays in Honor of Robert Glaser*. Erlbaum, Hillsdale, New Jersey

Fitts P M, Posner M I 1969 *Human Performance.* Brooks/Cole, Belmont, California

Fleishman E A 1975 Toward a taxonomy of human performance. *Am. Psychol.* 30(12): 1127–49

Jelsma O 1989 *Instructional Control of Transfer.* Twente University, Enschede

Romiszowski A J 1981 *Designing Instructional Systems: Decision Making in Course Planning and Curriculum Design.* Kogan Page, London

Schmidt R A 1975 A schema theory of discrete motor skill learning. *Psychol. Rev.* 82(4): 225–60

Turvey M T 1977 Preliminaries to a theory of action with reference to vision. In: Shaw R, Bransford J (eds.) 1977 *Perceiving, Acting and Knowing: Toward an Ecological Psychology.* Erlbaum, Hillsdale, New Jersey

Further Reading

Schmidt R A 1982 *Motor Control and Learning: A Behavioral Emphasis.* Human Kinetics Publishers, Champaign, Illinois

Singer R N 1980 *Motor Learning and Human Performance: An Application to Motor Skills and Movement Behaviors,* 3rd edn. Macmillan Inc., New York

Concept Learning: Teaching and Assessing

R. D. Tennyson

Concepts represent the fundamental elements of all content areas. In formal content situations, concepts are classes of objects, symbols, and events that are grouped together in some fashion by shared characteristics. An important purpose of education is to provide a learning environment in which students can both readily learn new concepts and improve the use of acquired concepts. The purpose of this entry is to present the instructional design guidelines for the preparation of instruction to improve concept learning and employment.

1. Overview of Design Guidelines

The learning of concepts involves three basic cognitive behaviors: (a) understanding the characteristics of a given concept and the association of that concept within a content area; (b) applying a given concept; and (c) knowing when, where, and why to employ a given concept. These cognitive behaviors are best learned when acquired within meaningful contexts. That is, teaching of concepts is more than a mere presentation of information. Where possible, the instruction should draw upon students' existing knowledge to put the concepts into a context that has meaning and employment potential. For example, historical (i.e., event) concepts are meaningful when viewed within the context or culture of the current environment. When designing concept lessons, the rule of thumb is to include learning objectives that integrate behaviors of content acquisition with improving and extending cognitive strategies for employment (e.g., recall, problem-solving, creativity).

Like the learning of concepts, instructional design as it applies to concepts involves three main activities: (a) the identification of the goals and objectives of the learning environment; (b) the analysis and sequence of the concepts to be learned; and (c) the development of the instruction, which includes selecting the appropriate instructional strategies and means of delivery (e.g., lecture, print materials, electronic). Given the scope of this entry, the design process of selecting the delivery system will not be addressed.

2. Preparing Goals and Objectives

Goals are broad statements that reflect the overall educational outcomes usually associated with a curricular area. Goals can be classified as either statements dealing with acquisition of concepts or the improvement in cognitive strategies for employment of concepts. From these two broad categories, objectives can be directly referenced that specify the type of behavior to be learned and improved. Because behaviors vary according to the complexity of outcomes, objectives are usually labeled to reflect the type of behavior desired. The labeling scheme selected for this entry is influenced by contemporary educational goals associated with improving higher-order cognitive skills and strategies. By directly linking the goals and objectives of the learning environment, it is also possible directly to link the objectives to instructional prescriptions.

In Table 1, an instructional design (ID) model is presented that shows the direct integration of cognitive learning theory with prescribed instructional strategies. In addition to the direct linkages between the various memory systems and instructional strategies, the model includes direct reference to formal classroom instructional time. The times presented in the model focus on goals dealing with acquiring and employing knowledge. The suggested times should be manipulated by the individual curricular situation based upon focus of the goals. The major components of the ID model are: memory systems, learning

Table 1
The Instructional Design (ID) model[a]

Model components	Educational goals				
	Acquisition of knowledge			Employment of knowledge	
Memory systems	Declarative knowledge	Procedural knowledge	Contextual knowledge	Cognitive complexity	Cognitive constructivism
Learning objectives	Verbal information	Intellectual skills	Contextual skills	Cognitive strategies	Creative processes
Instructional times	10%	20%	25%	30%	15%
Instructional prescriptions	Expository strategies	Practice strategies	Problem-oriented strategies	Complex–dynamic strategies	Self-directed experiences

a Tennyson 1992

objectives, instructional time, and instructional pre-scriptions.

2.1 Memory Systems

The proposed ID model is directly associated with cognitive theories of learning. Because the goals of the ID model include both the acquisition and the employment of knowledge, the memory systems reference the long-term memory subsystems of storage and retrieval. The storage system is composed of three basic forms of knowledge:

(a) declarative knowledge, knowing *that* about the information;

(b) procedural knowledge, knowing *how* to use information; and,

(c) contextual knowledge, knowing *when*, *where*, and *why* to use given concepts and associated cognitive skills.

The retrieval system is composed of cognitive strategies associated with the processes of recall, problem-solving, and creativity.

2.2 Learning Objectives

The purpose of learning objectives is to elaborate further the curricular goals of knowledge acquisition and employment. Objectives are important in the planning of concept teaching because they provide the means of both allocating instructional time and identifying specific instructional strategies. Five learning objectives can be identified: verbal information, intellectual skills, contextual skills, cognitive strategies, and creative processes.

Verbal information deals with the learner acquiring

an awareness and understanding of the concepts within a specified domain of information (i.e., declarative knowledge).

Intellectual skills involve the learner acquiring the skill to use correctly the concepts of a specified domain of information (i.e., procedural knowledge).

Contextual skills focus on the learner's acquisition of a knowledge base's organization and accessibility (i.e., contextual knowledge). The organization of a knowledge base refers to the modular structure of the information, whereas the accessibility refers to the complex cognitive skills that provide the means necessary to employ the knowledge base in the service of recall, problem-solving, and creativity. Contextual knowledge includes the criteria, values, feelings, and appropriateness of a given content domain's modular structure. For example, simply knowing how to classify examples or knowing how to use a concept does not imply that the learner knows when, where, and why to employ specific concepts.

Cognitive strategies deal with both the improvement and development of cognitive strategies and the extension of such strategies to domain-specific cognitive skills. Thus, this learning objective deals with two important issues in education. The first is the elaboration of cognitive strategies that will arm the students with increased domain-specific contextual knowledge (i.e., cognitive skills). The second is the development of the cognitive abilities of differentiation and integration. These abilities provide the cognitive tools to employ and improve the knowledge base effectively; therefore, they are integral to any educational goals seeking to improve higher-order cognition.

Creative processes deal with the most elusive goal of education: the development and improvement of creative abilities. Creativity is a twofold ability: (a) constructing knowledge to solve a problem from the external environment, and (b) constructing the problem as well as the knowledge to solve the problem. Integral to the construction of both the problem and knowledge are the criteria by which consistent judgment can be made. There are two sets of criteria. The first consists of criteria that are known and which can be applied with a high level of consistency. In contrast are those criteria that are developed concurrently with the problem and/or knowledge, and are consistently applied across a high level of productivity. Students should be informed of the criteria in the former and, in the latter, of the necessity to develop criteria.

2.3 Instructional Time

A key factor in implementing the cognitive goals of knowledge acquisition and employment is the allocation of learning time to defined objectives. For example, Tennyson and Rasch (1988) suggest that if improvements in problem-solving and creativity are to occur, there needs to be a significant change in how instructional time is allocated. They recommend that the conventional instructional time allocation for learning be altered so that, instead of 70 percent of instruction being aimed at the declarative and procedural knowledge levels of learning, 70 percent should be devoted to learning situations that involve acquisition of contextual knowledge and development of cognitive strategies.

Using Tennyson and Rasch's recommended figures on instructional time allocation, learning time can be divided into the two main subsystems of long-term memory: storage and retrieval. Within the guidelines illustrated in Table 1, time is assigned according to the cognitive objectives defined in the section above. In the storage system, learning time is allocated among the three memory systems making up a knowledge base as follows: declarative knowledge 10 percent, procedure knowledge 20 percent, and contextual knowledge 25 percent.

Contextual knowledge learning time should be about equal to the other two knowledge forms because of the necessity to both organize a knowledge base and develop accessibility to it once organized. The value of a knowledge base is primarily in the functionality of its organization and accessibility. Without a sufficient base of contextual knowledge, the opportunity for employment, future elaborations, and extension of the knowledge base is severely limited.

For knowledge acquisition goals, the focus of learning time allocation is on contextual knowledge, and away from the usual practice of heavy emphasis on amount of information. Declarative and procedural knowledge acquisition is believed to be an interactive process that is improved when employing the knowledge base in the service of higher-order thinking situations (i.e., those involving problem-solving and creativity). Time allocated for declarative and procedural knowledge focuses on establishing an initial base of necessary conceptual knowledge that can be

used within a context of a problem situation. That is, learning time should include the opportunity for the learner to gain experience in employing the learned concepts.

The learning times presented in Table 1 do not imply a linear sequence of knowledge acquisition going from declarative to contextual. Rather, they represent total amounts in an iterative learning environment where learners are continuously acquiring each form of knowledge. For example, students may engage in contextual knowledge acquisition prior to declarative knowledge acquisition if they currently have sufficient background knowledge (i.e., a discovery method of instruction as contrasted to a structured method) (see *Discovery Learning and Teaching*).

3. Concept Analysis

An important component of instructional design is the analysis of the concepts to be learned. There are two basic types of analysis: (a) a content (task) analysis that focuses on defining the critical characteristics of the concepts and the relationship of those characteristics according to superordinate and subordinate organizations; and (b) a contextual analysis that focuses on the memory or knowledge base organization of the concepts. The first analytic method identifies the external structure of the concepts (either a taxonomy or hierarchy) but does so independently of how it might actually be stored in human memory. However, research in cognitive psychology on human memory suggests that the internal organization of concepts in a knowledge base is based more on employment needs than by attribute characteristics or taxonomic/hierarchical connections (Fodor 1983). That is, the utility of the knowledge base is attributed to its situational organization, not necessarily the amount of information. The implication of knowledge base organization is the need for a contextual analysis of the concepts better to understand their possible internal organization (Garner 1990). Better organization in memory may also imply better accessibility within the knowledge base for such higher order cognitive activities as problem-solving and creativity (Harré 1984).

To understand the nature of knowledge base organization, cognitive psychologists analyze problem complexity and the way individuals try to solve given problems (Klahr et al. 1987). By analyzing problems, it is possible to identify the concepts employed; and, by analyzing the solutions, it is possible to identify the associations of those concepts within given problem situations. The implication for concept teaching is that the sequence of concepts for instruction should be based in part on internal situational associations as well as external structures (Bereiter 1990). The assumption is that because external structures are independent of employment needs, an analysis of possible internal associations would improve the initial organization of the new concepts, resulting in better employment.

A second analytical method, contextual analysis, is proposed when the goals of the curriculum include employment and improvement of cognitive skills and strategies, such as problem-solving, decision-making, and trouble-shooting. Contextual analysis includes five basic steps:

(a) Define the context for the employment of the concepts to be learned. A context is a meaningful application of the concepts. For example, a simulation, a game, a role-playing situation, or a case study provides an instructional vehicle for presenting a meaningful context.

(b) Define the complex problems (problems requiring more than one concept for solution) associated with the context. This step follows a knowledge engineering approach where problems associated with a given context are identified.

(c) For each problem, identify concepts employed for the solution or decision-making.

(d) Identify possible clusters of concepts employed in the solution of the various problems. That is, within a context certain concepts may be employed for a certain set of problems while other concepts may be employed in other sets.

(e) Sequence the clusters according to increasing complexity. For example, the first cluster may involve only two concepts while more complex clusters may have additional concepts. Analyzing problems within a context and then identifying the concepts and their employment organization (i.e., cluster) provides a means for sequencing the instruction to improve higher order cognition. In other words, the sequence of the instruction is based on the objective of improving employment of knowledge in addition to improvement in acquisition.

4. Instructional Prescriptions

This section describes instructional strategies found through empirical research to improve concept learning. Selection of the various strategies is based upon the learning objectives and the prerequisite knowledge of the students. For students with minimal prerequisite knowledge, an instructional program would probably utilize all of the strategies to insure adequate declarative and procedural knowledge. However, for students with a good knowledge base within the targeted curriculum area, an instructional program would emphasize more of the discovery type of instruction.

4.1 Expository Strategies

The category of expository strategies represents those instructional variables designed to provide an environment for learning of declarative knowledge (see Table 1). The basic instructional variables provide a context for the concepts to be learned. That is, advance organizers are used to provide a meaningful context for the concepts as well as a mental framework of the given domain's abstract structure. In addition to providing a context for the information, meaning can be further enhanced by adapting the context to individual student background knowledge.

The context establishes not only the initial organization of the domain, but also introduces both the "why" of the theoretical nature of the concepts and the "when and where" of the criterion nature of the domain's standards, values, and appropriateness (Bereiter and Scardamalia 1989). Personalizing the context to student background knowledge improves understanding of the information by connecting, within working memory, knowledge that is easily retrieved. Thus, the new knowledge becomes directly connected or associated with existing knowledge.

Following the contextual introduction of the concepts, five additional expository instructional variables are used to present the concepts in forms that extend existing knowledge and that aid in establishing new knowledge. These are as follows:

(a) *Label*. Although a simple variable, it is often necessary to elaborate on a label's origin so that the student is not just trying to memorize a nonsense word.

(b) *Definition*. The purpose of a definition is to connect the new concepts with existing knowledge in long-term memory; otherwise the definition may convey no meaning. That is, the student should already know the critical attributes of the concept. To improve understanding of the new concepts further, definitions may, in addition to presentation of the critical attributes (i.e., prerequisite knowledge), include information linked to the student's background or personal knowledge.

(c) *Best example*. To help students establish initial prototypes or abstractions of a domain's concepts, expository examples that are clear representations should be provided first.

(d) *Expository examples*. Additional examples should provide increasingly divergent representations of the concepts, perhaps also in alternative contexts.

(e) *Worked examples*. This variable provides an expository environment in which the examples are presented to the student in statement forms that elaborate application. The purpose is to help the student in becoming aware of the application (i.e., intellectual skill) of the concept within the given context(s). For example, to learn a mathematical operation, the student can be presented with the steps of the process in an expository problem while concurrently being presented with explanations for each step. In this way, the student may more clearly understand the procedures of the mathematical operation without developing possible misconceptions or overgeneralizations.

4.2 Practice Strategies

The category of practice strategies contains a rich variety of variables and conditions which can be designed into numerous teaching methods to improve learning of procedural knowledge. The term "practice" is used because the objective is for the student to learn how to use procedural knowledge correctly; therefore, it requires constant interaction between student learning (e.g., problem-solving) and instructional system monitoring. Practice strategies should attempt to create an environment in which (a) the student learns to apply procedural knowledge to previously unencountered concepts, while (b) the instructional system carefully monitors the student's performance so as both to prevent and correct possible misconceptions of procedural knowledge.

The basic instructional variable in this strategy is the presentation of problems that have not been previously encountered. Other variables include means for evaluation of learner responses (e.g., pattern recognition), advice (or coaching), elaboration of basic information (e.g., text density), format of information, number of problems, use of expository information, error analysis, and lastly, refreshment and remediation of prerequisite information.

4.3 Problem-oriented Strategies

Problem-oriented strategies involve problem-oriented techniques (e.g., simulations). Simulations improve the organization and accessibility of concepts within a knowledge base by presenting problems that require students to search through their memory to locate and retrieve the appropriate knowledge to propose a solution. Within this context, a simulation is a problem rather than an expository demonstration of some situation or phenomenon (Breuer and Kummer 1990).

Basically, problem-oriented strategies focus on the students trying to use their declarative and procedural knowledge in solving domain-specific contextual problems. Problem-oriented simulations present problem situations that require the student to (a) analyze the problem, (b) work out a conceptualization of the problem, (c) define specific goals for coping with the problem, and (d) propose a solution or decision. Unlike problems in the practice strategies that focus on acquiring procedural knowledge, problem-oriented simulations present situations that require employment of the domain's declarative and procedural knowledge. Thus, the student is in a problem-solving situation that requires establishing cognitive skills (i.e., contextual knowledge) among the concepts of specific domains of information.

4.4 Complex-dynamic Problem Strategies

Complex-dynamic strategies require students to employ their knowledge in the generation of solutions to complex, dynamic problems. Such learning processes are expected to improve the cognitive abilities of students (i.e., differentiation and integration; see Table 1). Five basic features should be considered in the design of instruction for improving cognitive complexity:

(a) The context is meaningful and of interest to the student.

(b) The context permits the student to construct concepts through his or her own cognitive efforts and employ this knowledge in proposing solutions and making decisions.

(c) The context provides a responsive, changing environment in which the student can receive feedback relevant to his or her evolving cognitive skills and strategies.

(d) The context permits the student to move from knowledge employment and improvement to knowledge acquisition, back to knowledge employment, and so on. It is this movement from one process (employment) to another (acquisition), from the employment of discrepant information to the combination of concepts in cognitive strategies that helps overcome boredom and creates interest.

(e) The context measures the degree of cognitive strategy employment independently from the knowledge acquisition.

Complex-dynamic simulations within such domains as politics and economics have been developed. Each simulation starts from a complex scenario that allows individual information searches and decision-making processes. The simulations are responsive as they reflect the decision-making processes of students by changing the status of the variables and conditions that represent the situation. The simulations are open-ended, as all decisions entered bring about a different and usually new status of the depicted situation, which can be "improved" or "optimized" by the student again. The simulation features create steady involvement of students and the repeated need for movement between knowledge and cognitive strategies. Additionally, the need for cognitive activity is supported by organizing the learning and thinking processes within cooperative learning groups. These groups provide opportunities for explanation, argumentation, justification, and adaptation.

4.5 Self-directed Experiences

An important goal of education is the development of learners who can be responsible for not only employing their existing knowledge but for the creating of new knowledge. The purpose of this instructional strategy category is to provide an environment in which students have instructional opportunities to improve their abilities to construct new knowledge.

For the most part, this process of cognitive constructivism can be improved by instruction that is self-directed. That requires a learning environment that is rich in resources and time for the student to seek out answers to both predefined and self-defined problems. Although cognitive constructivism may occur under unplanned environments, planned instructional environments can help create spheres of domain focus. For example, if the area of interest is social studies, the environment may include resources that would benefit creation of knowledge in that area as opposed to domains in the physical sciences.

Several programs of research in writing have shown improvements in basic writing skills as well as creativity through the use of computer-based word-processing systems (Reed 1992). In less planned environments, such as computer-based interactive games, there are findings that individuals construct the necessary concepts to continue improving their performances. For example, computer-based programs provide rich facilities that are under control of the student and, with intelligent systems, allow students to query the system.

A mixed initiative learning environment simulates the interaction between a domain expert and a novice learner. Thus, the student can artificially alter the time necessary to create new knowledge. Interest in virtual reality techniques is especially high in this area because of the total landscape of the artificial environment. Students may have the opportunity to explore just about any avenue of the domain without constraints that may be inherent in the real environment.

5. Concept Evaluation

Evaluation of concepts should take place within four stages of student assessment, ranging from preinstruction (for the purpose of evaluating entry behavior) to postcurriculum (for the purpose of evaluating educational goals). Thus, teachers should view evaluation as an integral component of classroom instruction.

5.1 Pre-instruction Evaluation

Before teaching concepts to students, the teacher should evaluate student entry knowledge. Where possible, the ideal evaluation plan would include assessing two types of knowledge: prior knowledge and prerequisite knowledge. A pretest that measures prior knowledge would identify what concepts to teach and whether any remediation for misconceptions is necessary. A pretest that measures prerequisite knowledge would identify the amount of remedial instruction required before formal instruction of the concepts to be learned begins. Additionally, preinstructional evaluation of aptitude and general achievement would help teachers to establish appropriate levels of difficulty.

5.2 During-instruction Evaluation

A major concern in concept teaching is the amount of instruction required for mastery (i.e., successful employment of learned concepts). Assessment of learning during instruction will help in determining the amount of instruction needed. Methods of evaluation should focus on products that make it possible to assess progress and effort. This type of evaluation can be integrated with the instructional prescriptions for problem-oriented and complex–dynamic strategies.

5.3 Post-instruction Evaluation

In most cases, students should not be required to take a posttest unless the teacher can assume mastery of concept employment. Students and the teacher should be well aware of progress and effort such that post-instruction measures truly evaluate the student at his or her highest level of achievement. Testing methods for learning objectives include final products and criterion-referenced objective tests. Norm-referenced tests may be useful for evaluation of curricular goals (e.g., school district outcome-based goals).

5.4 Postcurriculum Evaluation

Student success in schools is often measured by performance on standardized tests that evaluate students across curricular settings. In such testing individual student knowledge is compared to a large population; rarely does this information identify specific concept knowledge. Rather, postcurriculum evaluation informs the students of their relative level of general achievement in reference to their peers.

6. Conclusion

Teaching and evaluation of concepts can be enhanced when viewed within an integrated instructional program, that is, an instructional program planned to provide both acquisition and employment of concepts. Concepts are valuable when the learner can employ them in future situations. The instructional design (ID) model for concept teaching and evaluation described in this entry meets the educational goals of acquisition and employment. The guidelines presented are flexible and can be manipulated by teachers in reference to their given environment. As such, the guidelines are tools to be controlled by the teacher and, for the most part, improved with experience in their use.

References

Bereiter C 1990 Aspects of an educational learning theory. *Rev. Educ. Res.* 60: 603–24

Bereiter C, Scardamalia M 1989 Intentional learning as a goal of instruction. In: Resnick L B (ed.) 1989 *Knowing, Learning, and Instruction: Essays in Honor of Robert Glaser*. Erlbaum, Hillsdale, New Jersey

Breuer K, Kummer R 1990 Cognitive effects from process learning with computer-based simulations. *Comput. Hum. Behav.* 6: 69–81

Fodor J A 1983 *The Modular Theory of Mind: An Essay on Faculty Development*. Bradford Books, Lexington, Massachusetts

Garner R 1990 When children and adults do not use learning strategies: Toward a theory of settings. *Rev. Educ. Res.* 60: 517–29

Harré R 1984 *Personal Being: A Theory for Individual Psychology*. Harvard University Press, Cambridge, Massachusetts

Klahr D, Langley P, Neches R (eds.) 1987 *Production System Models of Learning Development*. MIT Press, Cambridge, Massachusetts

Reed W M 1992 The effects of computer-based writing tasks and mode of discourse on the performance and attitudes of writers of varying abilities. *Comput. Hum. Behav.* 8: 97–120

Tennyson R D 1992 An educational learning theory for instructional design. *Educ. Technol.* 32(1): 36–41

Tennyson R D, Rasch M 1988 Linking cognitive learning theory to instructional prescriptions. *Instr. Sci.* 17: 369–85

Further Reading

Alexander P A, Judy J E 1988 The interaction of domain-specific and strategic knowledge in academic performance. *Rev. Educ. Res.* 58: 375–404

Merrill M D, Tennyson R D, Posey L 1992 *Teaching Concepts: An Instructional Design Guide*, 2nd edn. Educational Technology, Englewood Cliffs, New Jersey

Tennyson R D 1990a Cognitive learning theory linked to instructional theory. *J. Struct. Learn.* 10: 249–58

Tennyson R D 1990b Computer-based enhancements for the improvements of learning. In: Dijkstra S, van Hout Wolters B H A M, van der Sijde P C (eds.) 1990 *Research on Instruction: Design and Effects*. Educational Technology, Englewood Cliffs, New Jersey

Wertsch J (ed.) 1985 *Culture, Communication, and Cognition: Vygotskian Perspectives*. Cambridge University Press, Cambridge, Massachusetts

Problem-solving: Teaching and Assessing

R. E. Mayer

Teaching and testing for problem-solving have become central issues in education. As Charles and Silver (1989) state: "The topics of teaching and evaluating problem solving are high interest topics for teachers, teacher educators, curriculum developers, and administrators . . . . Since 1980, many educators . . . have come to accept the important role problem solving can play in the curriculum" (p.5). National and international assessments of educational progress also have contributed to the interest in evaluating and improving students' ability to solve problems.

1. Teachable Aspects of Problem-solving

The term "problem-solving" has several definitions and has been embedded in a variety of theoretical frameworks. Understanding research on problem-solving is enhanced by viewing modern research within a historical context.

1.1 Definition of Teachable Problem-solving

Teaching of problem-solving can be defined in several different ways. Taking a narrow view, the goal of teaching for problem-solving is to improve students' performance on retention tests that contain routine problems (i.e., problems identical or very similar to those which the students encountered during instruction). For example, drill and practice on solving two-column subtraction problems such as "$56 - 43 =$ ___" may improve students' performance on solving similar problems such as "$67 - 52 =$ ___."

Taking a broader view, the goal of teaching for problem-solving is to improve students' performance on transfer tests containing non-routine problems (i.e., problems they have not solved previously). For example, conceptually based instruction that helps a student develop an understanding of place value may enable the student to transfer what he or she has learned about two-column subtraction problems, such as "$56 - 43 =$ ___," to solving three-column subtraction problems, such as "$567 - 423 =$ ___." This broader view, which could be called "teaching for transfer," is more consistent with the definition of problem-solving than is the narrower view, which could be called "teaching for retention." For this reason, teaching problem-solving is most appropriately defined as teaching students to be able to solve problems they have never solved before.

1.2 Theoretical Framework for Teachable Problem-solving

Mayer (1989, 1992) has summarized three major issues in the design of an effective program for teaching problem-solving: what to teach, how to teach, and where to teach. First, problem solving can be taught as a single, monolithic ability that can be strengthened through training and exercise (e.g., mathematical problem-solving skill or language skill), or as a collection of smaller, component skills that can be specifically taught (e.g., how to represent problems, how to devise solution plans, or how to monitor one's comprehension). Second, problem-solving can be taught by emphasizing the product of problem-solving (namely, getting the right answer), or by emphasizing the process of problem-solving (that is, the method or steps that one goes through to arrive at an answer). Third, problem-solving can be taught in a general, domain-free context in hopes of promoting transfer across many domains or within the context of specific subject domains such as mathematics, science, social studies, or writing, with the expectation that students are generally able to apply a problem-solving strategy only within a particular domain. Although a review of successful and unsuccessful (or undocumented) problem-solving programs does not provide definitive resolutions of these issues, the research suggests that problem-solving is most effectively taught when the focus is on teaching component skills rather than a single general ability, on process rather than product, and on domain-specific rather than context-free settings (Mayer 1989, 1992).

1.3 History of Teachable Problem-solving

A persistent concern of educators has been how to teach problem-solving to students (Chipman et al. 1985, Mayer 1989). In the early eighteenth century, Latin schools were established to provide students with proper "habits of mind" (Rippa 1980); in the 1980s and early 1990s, scholars have developed more modest thinking skills programs. Unfortunately, however, for many of the problem-solving courses, researchers have not been able to produce convincing evidence that attempts to improve problem-solving in one domain transfers well to different domains (Mayer 1987). Overall, attempts to teach transferable problem-solving skills have a disappointing history in educational psychology, leading Mayer (1987) to decry "the elusive search for teachable aspects of problem solving" (p.327). At the same time, however, a review of problem-solving programs sheds light on the characteristics of effective problem-solving instruction.

The first major attempt to teach problem-solving skills to students in school was the Latin School movement (Rippa 1980). The motivating principle of Latin schools was the doctrine of formal discipline, the idea that the study of subjects such as Latin and geometry would improve students' mental discipline and hence improve their thinking in general. Although this remained the prevailing theory through the early part of the twentieth century, research studies conducted by Thorndike and his colleagues (Thorndike and Woodworth 1901) failed to find empirical support for the idea that learning Latin had a positive effect on learning and problem-solving in other domains. Based on these findings, Thorndike proposed the theory of identical elements, the idea that transfer of learning occurs only when specific components that were parts of previously learned material are also parts of new learning (Singley and Anderson 1989).

During the 1930s and 1940s, educators initiated creativity programs in industry (Crawford 1954, Osborn 1963). As early as 1931, Crawford (1954) established a course to teach creative thinking within an industrial setting, including techniques to help designers create new ideas for improving products. Shortly thereafter Osborn (1963) helped to generate creativity courses that emphasized brainstorming, a procedure in which a group tries to generate as many ideas as possible without criticizing any ideas. Unfortunately, there is little scientific data concerning the effectiveness of these kinds of programs (Bouchard 1971, Weisberg 1986), and the preponderance of laboratory-based research studies calls into question the effectiveness of techniques such as brainstorming (Taylor et al. 1958, Weisskopf-Joelson and Eliseo 1961).

During the 1950s, problem-solving programs began to appear in colleges and universities. For example, Bloom and Broder (1950) taught college students how to solve examination problems by having them describe the thought process they used to solve problems from particular domains (e.g., economics), listen to an expert describe his or her process for the same problem, and then compare the two descriptions. The results indicated that the program was successful in improving students' examination performance. In this case the instruction meets the three criteria for successful programs by focusing on component skills, emphasizing process, and teaching within a subject domain.

During the 1960s, problem-solving programs were developed for primary and secondary school students. The Productive Thinking Program (Covington et al. 1974), for example, taught elementary school children skills such as generating ideas, formulating questions, and restating a problem, by asking them to read a series of cartoon-like booklets that presented mystery stories. Students were given a chance to model the thinking process of several characters in the booklets, such as two children and an uncle, who described their thinking processes in trying to solve the mysteries. Evaluation studies have demonstrated that the program improves students' performance on solving problems like those in the booklets but there is less evidence that problem-solving is improved in other domains (Mansfield et al. 1978). Again, this program meets the three criteria of successful programs: a focus on component skills such as "generating hypotheses," a focus on modeling the thinking processes of others, and a focus on improving problem-solving within a limited domain.

Since the 1970s, a variety of programs have been developed for use in schools. They include CORT (DeBono 1985), Instrumental Enrichment (Feuerstein et al. 1985), and Odyssey (Chance 1986). The CORT program teaches specific skills such as how to establish objectives or how to evaluate an idea by describing the skill and giving students guided practice in using the skill on specific problems. Although the program is widely used in schools around the world, including the United Kingdom where it was developed, there is "no adequate evidence . . . and thus no support for the effectiveness of the program" (Polson and Jeffries 1985 p.445). Instrumental Enrichment is a multiyear program, developed in Israel, aimed at entering students who school administrators might label as mentally retarded or slow learners. Through interaction with an instructor, students learn how to solve a variety of problems that might be found on tests of nonverbal intelligence, including spatial and numerical problems. Although the program requires a major time commitment, evaluation studies reveal that the training has positive effects on students' spatial, mathematical, and nonverbal reasoning.

Finally, Odyssey is an elementary-level program, developed in Venezuela, aimed at teaching specific skills such as inducing a pattern. Through interaction with peers and instructors, as well as working on their own, students learn to solve a series of problems such as determining what would come next in a series of geometric shapes. After a year of training, students performed much better than nontrained students on solving problems like those given during instruction, but only slightly better on solving problems that were unlike the instructed problems. The pattern that emerges from research on thinking skills programs is that it is possible to teach component skills, using process-based methods, within a specific domain.

2. Testable Aspects of Problem-solving

Testing for problem-solving refers either to evaluating the degree to which a person can successfully solve problems or describing the process that a person uses to solve problems. An example of the testing-as-response-evaluation approach is a multiple choice test item in which the student is given an arithmetic story problem and asked to select the correct answer. In general, this approach to testing focuses on the product of problem-solving, on using short items that each require a single response, and on asking questions that

do not require a great amount of transfer. An example of the testing-as-process-description approach is a performance test in which a student is given laboratory equipment such as beakers, scales, and eye droppers, and is asked to determine which of three paper towels holds more water (Baxter et al. 1992). In general, this approach focuses on the process of problem-solving, involves realistic problems that require more than a single response, and requires the problem-solver to generate novel solutions (Wiggins 1989).

Three issues in testing for problem-solving concern what to test, how to test, and where to test. First, tests can focus on tabulating the number of correct and incorrect responses or on the cognitive processes and strategies that the problem-solver uses. If the focus is on the product of problem-solving, then the test items call for a final answer. In contrast, if the focus is on the process of problem-solving, then the test items may assess processes such as how the problem-solver represents the problem, plans a solution, and monitors progress toward solving the problem. Second, concerning how to test, tests can present a series of short items measuring separate skills in isolation or can require the problem-solver to engage in higher-level problem-solving on a realistic task in which various skills must be integrated. Third, the issue of where to test concerns whether to rely on routine problems like those presented during instruction or on nonroutine problems that require the problem-solver to invent a novel solution. Although problem-solving tests traditionally have focused on scoring the number of correct responses to short problems that are routine, more recent trends involve describing people's cognitive processes on realistic problems that are nonroutine (Baxter et al. 1992, Frederiksen and Collins 1989).

In general, useful tests of problem-solving are valid, reliable, and objective. Validity means that the test measures what it is intended to measure, so that a test of mathematical problem-solving should not consist entirely of recalling memorized history facts, for example. Performance testing may improve validity by using realistic tasks, whereas traditional, multiple-choice tests may lack validity if they evaluate individual skills in isolation. For this reason, a performance test can be seen as an example of what has been called authentic assessment. Furthermore, the creation of tasks that can change in response to the test taker's actions, such as a hands-on situation or an interactive videodisk system, allow for a performance test to be viewed as an example of dynamic assessment (Campione and Brown 1987, Feuerstein 1979). Reliability means that the test results are consistent; that is, a person will achieve approximately the same score on each administration of the test. Because performance-based tests allow for many alternative methods of solution, they may not be as reliable as traditional methods of tests. This drawback can be partially mitigated by using several different kinds of problems. Objectivity means that different scorers or raters would produce the same result. Although multiple-choice tests are highly objective, well-defined coding procedures can allow performance-based tests to achieve acceptable levels of objectivity.

3. Conclusion

The teaching of problem-solving, which requires an understanding of "what is taught," is intricately tied to testing problem-solving, which requires a specification of "what is learned." If the goal of problem-solving instruction is to improve the cognitive processing of students when they are confronted with a novel problem, then the goal of problem-solving assessment is to describe the cognitive processes they use in their problem-solving. Nickerson (1989) noted that "the need for tests that do a better job of assessing thinking is widely recognized" (p.4). Future developments in the teaching and testing of problem-solving are required to satisfy this educational need. These developments include the design and use of teacher-made tests for higher-order thinking as well as the inclusion of higher-order thinking in large-scale standardized testing programs (Linn 1991) and the use of tests to diagnose problem-solving processing deficiencies that can be remediated (Bejar 1984, Brown and Burton 1978).

References

Baxter G P, Shavelson R J, Goldman S R, Pine J 1992 Evaluation of procedure-based scoring for hands-on science assessment. *J. Educ. Meas.* 29: 1–17
Bejar I I 1984 Educational diagnostic assessment. *J. Educ. Meas.* 21(2): 175–89
Bloom B S, Broder L J 1950 *Problem-solving Processes of College Students: An Exploratory Investigation.* University of Chicago Press, Chicago, Illinois
Bouchard T J 1971 What ever happened to brainstorming? *J. Creat. Behav.* 5(3): 182–89
Brown J A, Burton R R 1978 Diagnostic models for procedural bugs in basic mathematical skills. *Cognit. Sci.* 2(2): 155–92
Campione J C, Brown A L 1987 Linking dynamic assessment with school achievement. In: Lidz C S (ed.) 1987 *Dynamic Assessment: An Interactional Approach to Evaluation Learning Potential.* Guilford, New York
Chance P 1986 *Thinking in the Classroom: A Survey of Programs.* Teachers College Press, New York
Charles R I, Silver E A (eds.) 1989 *The Teaching and Assessing of Mathematical Problem Solving.* Erlbaum, Lawrence, Hillsdale, New Jersey
Chipman S F, Segal J W, Glaser R (ed.) 1985 *Thinking and Learning Skills. Vol. 2: Research and Open Questions.* Erlbaum, Hillsdale, New Jersey
Covington M V, Crutchfield R S, Davies L B, Olton

R M 1974 *The Productive Thinking Program.* Merrill, Columbus, Ohio
Crawford R P 1954 *The Techniques of Creative Thinking.* Hawthorn, New York
DeBono E 1985 The CoRT thinking program. In: Segal J W, Chipman S F, Glaser R (eds.) 1985 *Thinking and Learning Skills. Vol. 1: Relating Instruction to Research.* Erlbaum, Hillsdale, New Jersey
Feuerstein R 1979 *The Dynamic Assessment of Retarded Performers: The Learning Potential Assessment Device, Theory, Instruments, and Techniques.* University Park Press, Baltimore, Maryland
Feuerstein R, Jensen M, Hoffman M B, Rand Y 1985 Instrumental enrichment, an intervention program for structural cognitive modifiability: Theory and practice. In: Segal J W, Chipman S F, Glaser R (eds.) 1985 *Thinking and Learning Skills. Vol. 1: Relating Instruction to Research.* Erlbaum, Hillsdale, New Jersey
Frederiksen J R, Collins A 1989 A systems approach to educational testing. *Educ. Res.* 18(9): 27–32
Linn R L 1991 Dimensions of thinking: Implications for testing. In: Idol L, Jones B F (eds.) 1991 *Educational Values and Cognitive Instruction: Implications for Reform.* Erlbaum, Hillsdale, New Jersey
Mansfield R S, Busse T V, Krepelka E J 1978 The effectiveness of creativity training. *Rev. Educ. Res.* 48(4): 517–36
Mayer R E 1987 The elusive search for teachable aspects of problem solving. In: Glover J A, Ronning R R (eds.) 1987 *Historical Foundations of Educational Psychology.* Plenum, New York
Mayer R E 1989 Teaching for thinking: Research on the teachability of thinking skills. In: Cohen I S (ed.) 1989 *The G. Stanley Hall Lecture Series*, Vol. 9. American Psychological Association, Washington, DC
Mayer R E 1992 *Thinking, Problem Solving, Cognition*, 2nd edn. Freeman, New York
Nickerson R S 1989 New directions in educational assessment. *Educ. Researcher* 18(9): 3–7
Osborn A E 1963 *Applied Imagination.* Scribners, New York
Polson P, Jeffries R 1985 Instruction in general problem solving: An analysis of four approaches. In: Segal J W, Chipman S F, Glaser R (eds.) 1985 *Thinking and Learning Skills. Vol. 1: Relating Instruction to Research.* Erlbaum, Hillsdale, New Jersey
Rippa S A 1980 *Education in a Free Society: An American History.* Longman, New York
Singley M K, Anderson J R 1989 *The Transfer of Cognitive Skill.* Harvard University Press, Cambridge, Massachusetts
Taylor D T, Berry P C, Block C H 1958 Does group participation when using brainstorming facilitate or inhibit creative thinking? *Admin. Sci. Q.* 3(1): 23–47
Thorndike E L, Woodworth R S 1901 The influence of improvement in one mental function upon efficiency of other functions. *Psychol. Rev.* 8: 247–61
Weisberg R W 1986 *Creativity: Genius and Other Myths.* Freeman, New York
Weisskopf-Joelson E, Eliseo T S 1961 An experimental study of the effectiveness of brainstorming. *J. Appl. Psychol.* 45: 45–49
Wiggins G 1989 A true test: Toward more authentic and equitable assessment. *Phi Del. Kap.* 70(9): 703–13

Critical Reading: Teaching and Assessing

A. Luke and C. Walton

In conventional literature and reading instruction, critical reading has been defined in terms of personal response to literature, and in terms of the comprehension of disciplinary, nonfiction texts. However, reading has been redefined as part of a critical social literacy which entails the analysis and evaluation of textual ideologies and cultural messages, and an understanding of the linguistic and discursive techniques with which texts represent social reality, relations, and identity. This entry discusses conventional approaches and contrasts these with contemporary "critical pedagogy" and "discourse analytic" approaches to critical reading, noting future directions and unresolved issues in teaching and assessment.

1. Conventional Approaches to Critical Reading

The use of the term "critical" as a descriptor for modern curriculum and instruction has a controversial history. John Dewey and other early twentieth-century progressive educators used the term to signal the need for teaching social analysis to enable student participation in industrial development and social transformation. Of course, the degree to which state educational systems encourage and discourage student criticism of the distribution of power and wealth varies according to historical and political conditions. In this light, it should not be surprising that socially critical approaches to curriculum remain a matter of ongoing debate: they range from the encouragement of students to engage in explicit criticism of cultural, economic, and political structures, to more neutral approaches which affiliate reading with individuals' "thinking skills" and the weighing of information.

What has come to count as critical reading in United States, United Kingdom, Australian, Canadian, and New Zealand education has followed broad trends in the fields of secondary school English language and literature study, and elementary school reading and language arts instruction. Consequently, many extant approaches to critical reading have been directed by educational applications of, respectively, literary criticism and theory, and psychological theories of reading.

Since the early 1960s, secondary English teaching has been influenced by approaches to literary study which emphasize the value and variability of reader affective response to texts. In the United States and United Kingdom this movement has drawn strongly from antiformalist literary theories forwarded by Louise Rosenblatt, Stanley Fish, David Bleich, and others, and from the progressive educational aim of the development of individual identity and expression. Targeting traditional and classicist approaches to literature study, many approaches to teacher education and curriculum development emphasize exploration of personal response through literature (see Willinsky 1989). Within such models, critical reading is conceptualized according to Romantic literary criteria of "experience" and "understanding," as against more traditional emphases on literary appreciation and the reproduction of classical genres. This approach to secondary literature study has correlatives in holistic, child-centered approaches to early reading and writing, which also conceive of literacy in terms of "meaning making" and individual growth.

Drawing from sociological and poststructuralist theories of texts and subjectivity, critiques of these models make several key points. First, the search for student creativity in response to literature does not adequately consider how student response in the form of speech and writing is constructed and assessed in power relations in the classroom and, indeed, the larger culture (Gilbert 1989). Furthermore, like their classicist predecessors, these approaches tend to begin from a veneration of literature, such that the resultant classroom practices are unlikely to encourage questioning of why a specific text or genre should be studied in the first place, or of the value of personal response as an appropriate or effective way of dealing with text and identity.

A further critique of the personal response model arises from those advocates of psychologically based reading instruction, who argue that its stress on literature neglects students' needs to use nonfiction texts for the retrieval and analysis of disciplinary knowledge. Such critiques are the basis of calls for direct instruction in "content-area" reading comprehension across secondary schools. However, on closer inspection, concepts of critical literacy in reading psychology are theoretically and practically limited. Where it is mentioned, critical reading is taken to refer to "higher order skills" with text, such as the capacity to make semantic predictions, to infer and construct alternative outcomes and authorial intents, or to spot propaganda and bias. In the *Handbook of Reading Research* "critical reading" warrants only two comments. Baker and Brown (1984) define critical reading in terms which complement a neutral, information-processing model of reading. Thus, critical reading involves "not only imposing sense on the material in the way the author intended, but also going beyond the information given and critically evaluating it" (p. 356). They further observe that in most United States reading programs instruction in critical reading is developmentally delayed, and often given little more than token attention in comparison to, for example, the teaching of decoding or recall skills.

These limitations of conventional reading instruction are not simply a matter of instructional emphasis and timing, however. Research in the psychology and pedagogy of reading has a long history of shunting normative social and cultural issues to the sidelines of instruction, as subordinate to the acquisition of cognate skills, whether described as "basic," "functional," or "higher order" text-processing strategies. Over a century-long history, "basal" reading curricula have followed "technocratic" approaches that view teaching and learning as scientific procedures and processes best divorced from issues of values and ideology (Luke 1988). These key theoretical and practical omissions are continuing characteristics of cognitive and psycholinguistic approaches to reading.

Schema theories of reading, for example, recognize the relationship between structured, culture-specific background knowledge that readers bring to texts and the knowledge demands of text. However, such models stop short of recognizing how knowledges and texts can be ideological, that is, how particular knowledge structures operate in the interests of social configurations of power (Freebody et al. 1991). In this way, psychological versions of reading tend to privatize and individuate social and cultural knowledge. Where comprehension and critique are defined as matters of the personal deployment of individualized knowledge resources, a socially critical model of reading is not possible.

The two conventional approaches to reading described here remain areas of curriculum development and reform. In fact, educational systems in many developing countries have turned toward personal growth and psychologically based reading curricula to deal with the problems of mass literacy education. Although they draw upon radically different disciplinary theories and educational philosophies, these approaches construct reading along similar lines: as affective and cognitive processes internal to the student reader. What is omitted from both reader response and psychological approaches is recognition of two key aspects of reading and texts. First, reading is not a private act but a social practice, not a matter of individual choice or proclivity but of learning the reading practices of an interpretive community. Second, texts are not timeless aesthetic objects or neutral receptacles for information. Rather they are important sites for the cross-generational reproduction of discourse and ideology, identity and power within these same communities.

2. Reading and Critical Pedagogy

Reading and writing are transitive verbs; that is, texts are always about something in the world. Reading, accordingly, always entails an engagement with problems and values of the social world. This insight is at the heart of Brazilian educator Paulo Freire's critique of traditional literacy education. Freire (1970) argues that schooling tends to be based on a "banking" model of education, where students are cast as passive, empty vessels, to be filled with knowledge and skills deemed appropriate by teachers. In this transmission model of education, the very texts and genres for reading and writing are imposed by external educational authorities and, typically, disconnected from students' lives, experiences, and immediate problems. Freire argues that in both First and Third World education systems, these approaches lead to failure, alienation and, even where successful, disempowered forms of literacy characterized by political disenfranchisement and passivity.

For Freire, literacy has the potential for "doubling" the world, for naming and renaming its human agents, structures, and elements. Critical reading is a means for holding that world up for analytic scrutiny, analysis, and social action. What Freire proposes is a "critical pedagogy" which centers on teaching students to "read the word and the world." Reading is a means of achieving "critical consciousness," an understanding of the forces and ideologies that shape one's life; writing is a means for clarification, articulation, and liberation of the oppressed's voice, position, interests, and possibilities for action (Freire and Macedo 1987).

Since the initial applications of Freire's literacy pedagogy in countries like Brazil, Peru, and Mozambique in the 1960s and 1970s, critical pedagogies have been applied in a range of United States and British educational settings, including adult literacy programs, migrant and English as a Second Language instruction, and early literacy programs. A central feature of the model is that beginning reading instruction should occur simultaneously with beginning writing, specifically the writing of those key words which "name" the everyday experience and problems of the learners. The resultant texts, in the form of life descriptions, observations, recounts, and personal narratives, become the texts for learning to read critically, for making connections between biography and larger social structures and issues.

Freire's model is thus openly ideological and political. As against skills approaches to reading which stress functional skills and, implicitly, an acquiescence to extant institutions which require those skills, he puts forward a pedagogy which aims to "identify, understand, and act to transform, social relationships and practices in which power is structured unequally" (Lankshear and Lawler 1987 p. 74). At the heart of the Freirian model, then, is an emphasis on the politics of identity.

Several criticisms have been raised about theoretical and practical aspects of critical pedagogy. Freirian pedagogy begins from the assumption of a unified, androgynous subject based on common experience. It furthermore grounds its teaching in the truth, authenticity, and accessibility of repressed "voice." This position contrasts with the feminist proposition that woman's identity is socially constructed and multiple; not fixed or unified, but rather the object of fluid and continually changing discourses (Luke and Gore 1992). A related concern regards the centrality and neutrality of the teacher/leader in critical pedagogy and the danger that she or he will simply supplant dominant ideologies with equally manipulative and patriarchal substitutes. Finally, the instructional emphasis on "voice" risks obscuring the profound differences between specialized techniques, genres, and practices of spoken language, on the one hand, and written language, on the other.

Many of these critiques are based on developments in poststructuralist and feminist educational theories, which share an undertaking that identity, everyday social relations, and understandings of social and material reality are constructed in and by categories of discourse. It is this insight into the constitutive role of discourse, texts, and textuality which is the basis of those approaches which redefine reading in terms of critical language awareness and discourse analysis.

3. Critical Reading and Discourse Analysis

While there is a recognition of the constitutive role of discourse in these versions of critical pedagogy, there are significant gaps in their explanatory and practical approaches to language, discourse, and text. Critical pedagogy retains an instructional emphasis on expression and negotiation of the marginal and oppressed "self." It stops short of calling for direct instruction and explicit knowledge of specialized written genres and textual techniques. Relatedly, it presupposes that critical and powerful competence with these genres and techniques can evolve from a pedagogy which is centered on "voice."

Written texts are not neutral, transparent windows on the realities of the social and natural world. Nor are they simply vehicles or vessels of ideologies and values, dominant or otherwise. Rather they are refractive; that is, they actively construct and represent the world. To read critically, then, requires awareness of and facility with techniques by which texts and discourses construct and position human subjects and social reality. Models of critical reading as discourse critique have set out to engage students in the practices of critiquing reading, writing, and speaking practices, such that the political power and knowledge relations expressed and represented by texts and discourses are foregrounded (Baker and Luke 1991). Instruction based on text and discourse analysis aims to give students insights into how texts work, and more specifically, how texts situate and manipulate readers. In so doing, its purpose is to engage readers directly and actively in the politics of discourse in contemporary cultures, to open institutional sites and possibilities for alternative readings and writings.

The theoretical parameters for a discourse-analytic approach to reading are drawn from poststructuralist discourse theory, functional linguistics, and neo-Marxist cultural studies. Kress (1985) outlines how texts construct "subject positions" and "reading positions." That is, texts both represent and construct "subjects" in the social and natural world, and they position and construct a model reader. The lexical, syntactic, and semantic devices of texts thus portray a "possible world," and they position the reader to read or interpret that possible world in particular ways. Accordingly, a discourse analytic approach to critical reading would include, for instance, an understanding of how words and grammatical structures shape portrayals of the world, human agency, cause and effect, and so forth. It would also point out many of the linguistic techniques that texts use to define and manipulate readers (e.g., imperatives, pronominalization).

Fairclough (1989) views the "critical language awareness" yielded by this kind of text analysis as a prerequisite for student readers to see how social power operates through everyday language practices, to contest texts, and to develop powerful competences with a broad range of texts and discourses. In contrast with the aforementioned models, then, a discourse-analytic approach does not aim for effective "comprehension," the valorization of the "power" of literature, the liberation of "voice" or, for that matter, the development of esoteric skills of "deconstruction." Rather, it sets out to teach critical reading as "an understanding of how texts are public artifacts available to critique, contestation, and dispute" (Freebody et al. 1991 p. 453).

In a related development, Gee (1990) defines critical literacy in terms of discourse critique. Discourses are built up from systematic and related sets of statements and texts. They comprise fields of knowledge which may be disciplinary (e.g., physics, sociology), institutional (e.g., governmental, workplace), and community-based (e.g., street or family talk). When deployed in contexts and texts, discourses are tied up with culture- and subculture-specific ways of behaving, knowing, valuing, and acting. Gee argues that both community and academic, dominant and subordinate discourses have limited, finite capacities for self-criticism, and that it is difficult to critique a discourse from within itself. In part this is because participation in a discourse and its interpretive community requires that one operate within given first principles and definitions.

Gee (1990) defines critical literacy in terms of having access to multiple discourses: "we can only talk about a literacy being 'liberating' ('powerful') if it can be used as a 'meta-language' . . . for the critique of other literacies and the way they constitute us as persons and situate us in society" (p. 153). According to this definition, critical reading entails far more than just the development of a set of analytic techniques or the embrace of particular perspectives or ideologies. It requires access to and facility with multiple discourses in order to read, critique, second-guess, and reconstruct other discourses, particularly those of dominant cultural groups and texts which tend to be taken as "truths" beyond criticism.

Classroom frameworks and practices developed for discourse-analytic approaches to critical reading include the reading of multiple texts and conflicting discourses against each other within single lessons, the encouragement of alternative readings and writings which attempt to bring community and familiar discourses to bear on those represented in texts, and the foregrounding of the histories and cultural contexts of texts and discourses under study. This instructional agenda begins from several guiding principles. First, the emphasis on juxtaposing texts and discourses to be "read against each other" (Freebody et al. 1991) aims to generate difference, conflict, and debate— focal points for teaching critical reading. Second, these classroom debates can be informed by teaching which makes explicit and foregrounds how texts work ideologically.

4. Conclusion

The question of what will count as critical reading in literate cultures cannot be addressed solely by reference to literary descriptions of the features and virtues of literature, psychological descriptions of mental processes, or linguistic descriptions of texts. How nations, communities, and school systems decide to shape the social practices of reading are normative cultural and sociological decisions, decisions tied up with how power and knowledge are to be distributed in print cultures (Luke 1994). Western late-capitalist cultures center on semiotic exchange, where signs, symbols, and discourse have become the principle modes of economic exchange and value. Reading is clearly essential for participation in the lived realities of everyday life, childhood, work, and leisure, but to become a functional reader may, quite ironically, make one more susceptible to the discourses and texts of a consumer culture which at every turn builds and defines readers' identities, actions, and their very senses of "reality." That is, possession of rudimentary decoding, pragmatic, and semantic skills to construct and use meaning from text may appear empowering, but in fact may open one to multiple channels of misinformation and exploitation (Freebody and Luke 1990).

In this kind of literate environment, conventional reader response and comprehension teaching may fall short of meeting the necessities of social participation and citizenship. Critical reading would need to entail an explicit understanding of both how texts are ideological, and how reading is a potential avenue toward constructing and remaking the social and natural worlds. Classroom instruction can be reshaped to enable students to read and write "differently,"

to see, discuss, and counter the techniques that texts use to position and construct their very identities and relations.

There have been significant developments toward implementing discourse-analytic frameworks for teaching critical reading in Australia and the United Kingdom, particularly in alternative approaches to literature study and "critical language awareness." However a range of questions about contexts and procedures for teaching critical reading requires continued investigation and innovation. A central issue is the viability of nonneutral, openly ideological approaches in educational systems run by conservative governments and local school authorities. In such contexts, as is evidenced in both the United States and United Kingdom, a critical reading curriculum which stresses social analysis and ideology critique may have to be lodged within progressive, personal growth models (e.g., Edelsky 1991) and curricula that stress explicit knowledge of language systems (e.g., Carter 1990).

Such attempts lead back to questions about the centrality and sequencing of critique in the programs. Conventional reading programs, both humanist and skills-based, tend to delay developmentally the introduction of critical textual analysis, assuming that basic reading and writing skills are required before students can engage with larger value and ideology systems in texts. There is, however, empirical evidence of the capacity for children at very early ages to engage with and talk about critical reading of narratives (Davies 1987, Gee 1990). If indeed children's senses of the functions, uses, and potentials for reading as a social, community, and intellectual practice are being shaped in preschool literacy activities, then there would seem to be both theoretical and practical grounds for teaching critical approaches to rewriting and contesting texts at all stages of reading instruction, especially in initial training.

A final unresolved issue concerns assessment. Reading assessment has largely been constrained by psychological theorizations of reading, and attendant models for standardized testing. That is, what has come to count as reading in both classroom and more formal assessment environments has been driven by what has been measurable by extant testing devices. With the demand for accountability in schooling, this typically leads to situations where curriculum and instruction are driven by what is visibly testable. As shown here, what is psychologically testable excludes critical, ideological, and discourse-analytic approaches to reading. Furthermore, where assessed within conventional approaches, success or failure at achieving critical reading has been evaluated in terms of student writing in response to literature (e.g., essays, journals, and literary response pieces), and via standardized tests of reading comprehension.

Since the early 1980s, there has been an expanded effort to develop reading assessments that are qualitative, descriptive, and sensitive to student and contextual variables. These include culture-appropriate practices and tasks, face-to-face task assessments in early childhood, case study approaches for adult literacy programs, and classroom observation techniques (e.g., Lytle and Schultz 1990). However, appropriate and credible means for assessing critical reading have yet to be developed. These methods would require tasks sensitive to the emergent definitions, contexts, and purposes of critical reading. For instance, the effectiveness of Freirian or discourse-analytic approaches by definition cannot be assessed by conventional pencil and paper psychometric devices. Assessment of these curricula might require evidence, for example, that the student had developed an articulated social analysis and attendant action plan, or that students were able to deconstruct ideological textual devices. All assessment of reading is premised on theoretically driven observation of student talk and writing. Consequently, the redefinitions of critical reading examined here of necessity will require the development of alternative, innovative approaches to assessment.

References

Baker C D, Luke A (eds.) 1991 *Towards a Critical Sociology of Reading Pedagogy.* John Benjamins, Amsterdam

Baker L, Brown A L 1984 Metacognitive skills and reading. In: Pearson P D (ed.) 1984 *Handbook of Reading Research.* Longman, New York

Carter R (ed.) 1990 *Knowledge about Language and the Curriculum.* Hodder and Stoughton, London

Davies B 1987 *Frogs and Snails and Feminist Tales.* Allen and Unwin, Sydney

Edelsky C 1991 *With Literacy and Justice for All: Rethinking the Social in Language and Education.* Falmer Press, London

Fairclough N 1989 *Language and Power.* Longman, London

Freebody P, Luke A 1990 Literacies programs: Debate and demands in cultural contexts. *Prospect: J. Aust.* TESOL. *5(3): 7–16*

Freebody P, Luke A, Gilbert P H 1991 Reading positions and practices in the classroom. *Curric. Inq.* 21: 435–58

Freire P 1970 *Pedagogy of the Oppressed.* Seabury Press, New York

Freire P, Macedo D 1987 *Literacy: Reading the Word and the World.* Bergin and Garvey, South Hadley, Massachusetts

Gee J P 1990 *Social Linguistics and Literacies: Ideology in Discourses.* Falmer Press, London

Gilbert P H 1989 *Writing, Schooling and Deconstruction: From Voice to Text in the Classroom.* Routledge and Kegan Paul, London

Kress G 1985 *Linguistic Processes in Sociocultural Practice.* Oxford University Press, Oxford

Lankshear C, Lawler M 1987 *Literacy, Schooling and Revolution.* Falmer Press, London

Luke A 1988 *Literacy, Textbooks and Ideology: Postwar Literacy Instruction and the Mythology of Dick and Jane.* Falmer Press, London

Luke A 1994 *The Social Construction of Literacy in the Classroom.* Macmillan, Melbourne

Luke C, Gore J (eds.) 1992 *Feminisms and Critical Pedagogy.* Routledge, New York

Lytle S L, Schultz K 1990 Assessing literacy learning with adults: An ideological approach. In: Beach R, Hynds S (eds.) 1990 *Developing Discourse Practices in Adolescence and Adulthood.* Ablex, Norwood, New Jersey

Willinsky J 1990 *The New Literacy: Redefining Reading and Writing in the Schools.* Routledge, New York

Further Reading

Baker C D, Freebody P 1989 *Children's First Schoolbooks: Introductions to the Culture of Literacy.* Basil Blackwell, Oxford

Johnston P 1984 Assessment in reading. In: Pearson P D (ed.) 1984 *Handbook of Reading Research.* Longman, New York

Shannon P 1989 *Broken Promises: Reading Instruction in Twentieth-Century America.* Bergin and Garvey, Granby, Massachusetts.

Learning Strategies: Teaching and Assessing

C. E. Weinstein and D. K. Meyer

Learning strategies can include thoughts, emotions, and behaviors that facilitate the acquisition of knowledge and skills, or the reorganization of one's knowledge base. These strategies are taught and assessed in order to help students become more strategic learners; that is, learners who are willing and able to take significant responsibility for their learning.

Two primary methods are used in teaching strategic learning. The adjunct approach involves creating some adjunct or addition to a course or the general curriculum. These adjuncts can range from a seminar or workshop focusing on a specific strategy to semester- or year-long courses focusing on a broad range of strategies and skills. The metacurriculum approach involves integrating learning strategies instruction into regular content instruction. This approach can focus on strategies specific to the content covered in the course, a broad range of strategies, or a combination of the two.

Assessments of strategic learning primarily involve using self-report methods as diagnostic screening devices to identify students' strengths and weaknesses in a variety of areas related to academic success. These assessments can be used to help students become more aware of their current state of academic self-regulation. They also can contribute to the creation of interventions or programs designed to enhance students' strategic learning. This entry focuses on issues and methods in the teaching and testing of learning strategies.

1. The Importance of Becoming a Strategic Learner

Education involves more than increasing content knowledge and skills. Students also must learn how to manage their learning. Strategic learners want to and know how to take responsibility for optimizing their learning in both academic and nonacademic contexts (Biggs 1987, Entwistle 1992, Pintrich 1991, Weinstein and Van Mater Stone 1993, Zimmerman and Schunk 1989). Strategic learning has tremendous implications for lifelong learning in a rapidly changing, increasingly technological world.

2. What Are the Characteristics of a Strategic Learner?

What does it mean to be an expert strategic learner? First, strategic learners have at least five different knowledge bases they call upon and integrate to help meet educational or performance goals. They are: knowledge about themselves as learners; knowledge about different types of academic tasks; knowledge about strategies and tactics for acquiring, integrating, and applying new learning; prior content knowledge; and knowledge of both present and future contexts in which the knowledge could be useful. However, knowledge alone is not sufficient for expertise. Expert learners also must know how to integrate and use their knowledge and skills to meet their learning goals and how to monitor their progress so they can adjust what they are doing if a problem occurs.

In addition to knowing what to learn and how to learn, students also must want to learn. Effective learning requires the integration of skill and will components. Motivation and positive affect for learning interact with and result from many factors. These factors include goal setting, goal analysis, and goal using; efficacy expectations; outcome attributions; interest; valuing; instrumentality; and utility value.

Finally, strategic learners have the metacognitive awareness and control strategies needed to integrate, orchestrate, and manage their studying and learning. This self-regulation involves a number of interacting activities, which dynamically impact each other. These activities include: creating a plan to reach a goal; selecting the specific strategies or tactics to use to achieve the goal; implementing the methods selected to carry out the plan; monitoring progress on both a formative and a summative basis; modifying the plan, the methods, or even the original goal, if necessary; and evaluating what was done to decide if this would be a good way to go about meeting similar goals in the future. Evaluating this entire process helps students build a repertoire of effective strategies that can be used in the future when similar situations arise.

3. Teaching Learning Strategies

Instruction designed to enhance students' strategic learning takes a variety of forms. Generally, these forms fall into two categories, adjunct instruction and the metacurriculum.

3.1 Adjunct Instruction

Adjunct instruction involves freestanding interventions that can last from an hour to a year. The shorter forms, such as one-hour seminars on textbook reading strategies, usually focus on a specific strategy or related set of strategies. Often these programs are sponsored by learning assistance centers, an administrative unit responsible for student affairs, or taught as supplementary programs through academic departments or units.

A second type of adjunct intervention involves offering strategy instruction as part of the formal instruction in a content course. Usually this instruction is provided in special supplementary or laboratory sessions focusing on strategic learning and studying, or as part of the method called supplemental instruction. For example, many introductory-level college mathematics courses in the United States offer special sessions focusing on how to study and learn mathematics.

The third type of adjunct instruction is the most extensive. It involves long-term interventions designed to help students become more strategic learners in a variety of areas. Often these interventions take the form of a semester- or year-long course, possibly for academic credit. A case study describing a semester-long intervention is described in Sect. 3.2.

3.2 A Case Study: A Course to Teach Strategic Learning

A semester-long course in strategic learning is taught in the Department of Educational Psychology at the University of Texas at Austin. It is a three-credit course, taken for a grade, which meets on a Monday–Wednesday–Friday schedule for one hour each day. The skill, will, and self-regulation components described at the beginning of this entry are addressed in the course.

3.2.1 Student population. A variety of students register for this course, including students predicted at entry to be vulnerable to academic failure, students who experience academic difficulties after entry, and students who simply want to improve their grades. Students meet in classes of 25.

3.2.2 Instructors. The class is taught by graduate students who receive advanced training either through prior experience with similar courses or by auditing the course the semester before they teach it. All new instructors are assigned to a mentor. Weekly meetings are held with all instructors to consider the next week's curriculum, review and critique the past week's classes, and discuss any problems.

3.2.3 Curriculum. The content focuses on all three components of strategic learning: skill, will, and self-regulation. The first three days of the course are used for introductions and pretesting. The pretest data help both instructors and students to identify students' strengths and weaknesses. The measures are used for diagnostic purposes and help create a baseline against which to measure future growth and achievement. (The specific measures used will be described in Sect. 3.2.4.)

The first week is devoted to presenting a model of strategic learning. The metaphor used describes students as managers of their learning. The knowledge, metacognitive, motivation, and executive control components of strategic learning are introduced. The students are told that they will learn how to generate management and implementation plans for common academic tasks such as taking notes in a lecture or from a book, listening in class, completing projects, giving presentations, preparing for and taking examinations, and completing semester projects.

As a part of this process, it is explained that strategic learners are goal directed and use strategies in pursuit of their studying and learning goals. To help them get started, the next topic is setting, using, and analyzing goals. The discussion about establishing and using goals leads into other topics related to motivation and positive affect toward learning. For example, efficacy expectations, valuing, attributions, and utility value are all discussed as components of motivation that are under the students' control.

After a few weeks a semester-long project is introduced. For this project students are asked to choose another class they are taking and select a goal for one of the tasks assigned in the class. The goals usually include things like getting a certain grade on a test, paper, or laboratory project. After setting the goal, the students develop, implement, and monitor a plan for reaching their goal. The purpose of the project is to encourage students to integrate the topics covered already in the course, and topics to be presented. Several class periods are devoted to helping students devise, use, and revise their plans.

Throughout the course all topics are related back to the model of strategic learning. Thus, students

are given a schema they can use to make sense of new information and which they can refine as their understanding deepens. Specific topics covered in the second half of the course include: knowledge acquisition strategies; the relationship between understanding and long-term memory; pre-, during-, and post-reading strategies; time management and dealing with procrastination; attention and concentration; note taking; listening skills; preparing for and taking tests; and dealing with academic stress.

The final week of the class is devoted to assessment so that students can see where they have improved. Students also receive feedback about areas they might want to continue working on through the university's learning skills center or other special help programs in some of the individual colleges.

3.2.4 Assessment. The specific measures used depend on research needs or course development needs being addressed in any given semester. However, a measure of strategic learning and a reading comprehension measure are always used. The measure of strategic learning is the Learning and Study Strategies Inventory (LASSI) (Weinstein et al. 1987). The LASSI is a 77-item diagnostic/prescriptive self-report measure of strategic learning that focuses on thoughts and behaviors that can be changed and enhanced through educational interventions.

Reading comprehension is assessed using the Nelson-Denny Reading Comprehension Test, Forms E and F (Brown et al. 1981). Half of the students are chosen at random to receive one form at pretest and the parallel form at posttest. National norms are available for each college level (e.g., freshman, sophomore).

3.2.5 Course evaluation. A variety of means are used to evaluate the course, including course instructor surveys, students' performance in the course (e.g., class tests, selected homework assignments, the semester-long project), students' performance in other classes in the semesters following the course, and changes in the pretest measures at posttesting. Both the instructors and the course receive high ratings from most students.

On the average, students who register for the course have grade-point-averages (GPAs) that are one-half grade point (on a 4-point scale) below other students at the same college level. In the semester after taking the course their GPAs are indistinguishable from other students at their level. Furthermore, this change is maintained over the succeeding semesters. In fact, for freshmen and sophomores, their improvement increases over time. Significant changes are also found for students' scores on the LASSI and Nelson-Denny Reading Comprehension Test, and for measures of self-concept and metacognitive awareness.

3.3 The Metacurriculum

Delivering content without instruction in how to learn the material is like giving someone a state-of-the-art personal computing system without any instructions on how to assemble and use it. Effective instruction includes assuming responsibility for helping students learn how to learn the course material (Entwistle and Tait 1992, Svinicki 1991, Weinstein and Meyer 1991). Just as strategic learners take responsibility for their learning, good teachers provide many opportunities for students to develop and assume this role. When the instruction of learning strategies is integrated with the regular curriculum of a course, then strategy instruction becomes the "metacurriculum."

The metacurriculum includes strategy instruction for all facets of strategic learning: skill, will, and control. For example, teachers may demonstrate learning strategies for understanding and remembering the content. They also can help students develop motivational strategies for initiating, maintaining, and intensifying interest in and self-efficacy for the course content. They may teach abstract concepts by asking students to apply them to situations in their lives.

Teachers can help students set personal goals for the course. In addition, they may require students to monitor their goals and reflect on their degree of success. They also can help students take control of their learning strategies by providing them with organizational tools for planning their course study and assessing their progress.

Teaching students how to learn the course material is a critical aspect of transferring responsibility to the learner because this process involves teaching the skills necessary for assuming responsibility. As Wang and Peverly (1986) argued, if good students are defined as motivated, active, planful, and resourceful, then they should be taught the skills for assuming these roles. In addition, teaching learning strategies as an integrated part of a course allows for course-specific and domain-specific strategies to be applied in meaningful ways. Many of the learning skills students acquire as part of a course also may be transferred to other courses and work situations. (See Entwistle and Tait 1992 for a collection of examples of implementing a metacurriculum approach.)

Finally, the benefits for students of being provided with strategy support while they are learning course topics also extends to teachers. Teachers become more aware of how students learn and of the effectiveness of specific learning strategies for their particular courses.

3.4 A Case Study: The Metacurriculum in a Finance Class

Professor Keane teaches an introductory course in finance. In addition to teaching her students about the various governmental economic regulations and agencies, she also teaches them how to learn the course material. Professor Keane begins her metacurriculum by being very explicit about her goals for the course. After her introduction to the course, she requires that each student (there are 70 students on the course) submit a one-page description of how the course

can help them achieve their academic and professional goals.

Professor Keane consistently addresses possible motivational strategies for maintaining interest in the course. She challenges students to present interesting applications of the course topics (e.g., newspaper or magazine articles, cartoons) that can help the class enjoy learning the material. During lectures, Professor Keane makes a point of asking students how they see the current topic helping them in their chosen career (context knowledge).

She also elicits student volunteers to explain basic concepts or review previous topics to check prior knowledge before beginning a new topic (content knowledge). At the same time, she is explicit in asking the entire class to reflect on how much of this information they knew already, and where they might go for extra background information. In addition, students are asked to reflect on why they did not know the information (self-knowledge). For example, were they confused about the topic, were they behind in course readings, or were they disinterested in the class and had been daydreaming?

Professor Keane's lectures are integrated with instruction on how to make sense of content (strategy knowledge). For example, a difficult set of government regulations is reviewed by providing students with meaningful ways to memorize the regulations. Professor Keane is explicit about what information students should highlight in their notes, or suggests note-taking strategies such as, "You might want to number the regulations in your handout for reference in your notes."

Finally, Professor Keane shares her organizational plans for the course with the class so that they can plan the best way to study for examinations, use the textbook and ancillary readings, and pursue their course project. One midterm assignment that she requires is that each student obtains the business card of the person they must interview for their final class project. After collecting all the cards, she asks, "So how has this assignment helped you with your project?" Many students talk about how it helped them avoid procrastinating, or that getting an interview was not as easy as they first thought and they are glad they did not wait until the end of the semester. The session always ends with a discussion of how this experience can be used to help them be more effective in future assignments.

4. Assessment of Learning Strategies

Assessment of students' learning strategies can take a number of forms, most of which involve some type of self-report (Garner 1988). Because it is impossible to observe cognitive processes directly, multiple assessments are often used to obtain converging evidence of students' strategy use.

4.1 Methods Used to Assess Learning Strategies

Three major methods are used to help externalize cognitive and metacognitive strategies: think-aloud procedures, interviews, and strategy-use inventories. Think-aloud procedures require students to describe what they are thinking or doing while completing an actual task. Their verbalizations are concurrent with the activity, which is only interrupted long enough for the verbal report. Students' verbal reports are elicited by instructions or probes that vary in generality (Garner 1988). For example, the students may be asked to "Say everything that you think or do while you complete this reading assignment."

Interviews are used to elicit retrospective reports about what students have thought or done with respect to a recent task or at some time in the past. These reports focus on the cognitive and metacognitive activities that have been completed. This method is also sometimes used to obtain data about hypothetical or prototypical situations that the student has not experienced directly. Interviews are more structured than think-aloud procedures in that at least some questions or probes are planned in advance. Other materials, such as the student's notes or a videotape of the learning situation can be used to stimulate recall (Garner 1988).

Strategy-use inventories are similar to interviews in that they ask students to respond to past, hypothetical, or prototypical situations. They differ, however, in that they are usually administered in written form. An advantage of the written format of strategy-use inventories is that they can be administered individually or to groups of students.

All three forms of assessment should be administered with caution. Students should not report strategies they cannot demonstrate; students should report strategies they would use, not those they think they *should* use; and students should be encouraged to report strategies they might think too obvious or unimportant to mention (Garner et al. 1983). The most important way of authenticating self-report is to gather multiple sources (Ericsson and Simon 1984), especially combining a self-report with a product such as student lecture notes, an examination, or written assignment (Garner 1988).

4.2 A Sample Strategy-use Inventory: The Learning and Study Strategies Inventory (LASSI)

The LASSI is a diagnostic assessment that is used to help students (and their teachers) identify their strengths and weaknesses in 10 different areas related to the skill, will, and self-regulation components of strategic learning. It has been used in about 1,500 post secondary institutions in the United States in a variety of ways, including as a pretest or pretest/posttest measure in learning strategies courses. The LASSI provides standardized scores (percentile score equivalents) and national norms for each of the following

10 scales: Attitude, Motivation, Time Management, Anxiety, Concentration, Information Processing, Selecting Main Ideas, Study Aids, Self Testing, and Test Strategies.

The Attitude Scale contains items addressing students' attitude toward and interest in college, and their general motivation for succeeding in school (sample item: I feel confused and undecided as to what my educational goals should be). The Motivation Scale addresses students' diligence, self-discipline, and willingness to work hard at academic tasks (sample item: When work is difficult I either give up or study only the easy parts). Time Management Scale items address students' use of time management principles and methods to help them organize and control their time (sample item: I only study when there is the pressure of a test). Anxiety Scale items address the degree to which students worry about school and their performance (sample item: Worrying about doing poorly interferes with my concentration on tests). The Concentration Scale items address students' ability to direct their attention to academic tasks, including study activities (sample item: I find that during lectures I think of other things and don't really listen to what is being said). Items on the Information Processing Scale address how well students can use imaginal and verbal elaboration, organization strategies, and reasoning skills to help build bridges between what they already know and what they are trying to learn and remember (sample item: I translate what I am studying into my own words). The Selecting Main Ideas Scale items measure students' skills at selecting important information to concentrate on for further study (sample item: Often when studying I seem to get lost in details and can't see the forest for the trees). Items on the Study Aids Scale measure students' ability to use or create study aids that support and increase meaningful learning (sample item: I use special helps, such as italics and headings, that are in my textbooks). The Self Testing Scale items address comprehension monitoring methods such as reviewing and practicing (sample item: I stop periodically while reading and mentally go over or review what was said). Items on the last scale, Test Strategies, address students' use of test preparation and test-taking strategies (sample item: I have difficulty adapting my studying to different types of courses).

An example of an inventory designed to measure strategic learning as well as approaches to studying can be found in Entwistle's (1992) monograph on student learning.

5. Conclusion

Strategic learners can take responsibility for their learning and they know how to help themselves reach their learning goals. Given the importance of strategic learning for success in education and for meeting lifelong learning goals, it is important for every student to learn how to learn effectively and efficiently. It is also the responsibility of teachers to help their students become more strategic learners.

References

Biggs J B 1987 *Student Approaches to Learning and Study.* Australian Council for Educational Research, Melbourne

Brown J I, Bennett J M, Hanna G 1981 *Nelson-Denny Reading Test, Forms E and F.* Riverside Publishing, Chicago, Illinois

Entwistle N J 1992 Student learning and study strategies. In: Clark B R, Neave G (eds.) 1992 *The Encyclopedia of Higher Education.* Pergamon Press, Oxford

Entwistle N J, Tait H 1992 Promoting effective study skills. In: Cryer P (ed.) 1992 *Learning Actively on One's Own.* CVCP Universities' Staff Development and Training Unit, Sheffield

Ericsson K A, Simon H A 1984 *Protocol Analysis: Verbal Reports as Data.* MIT Press, Cambridge, Massachusetts

Garner R 1988 Verbal-report data on cognitive and metacognitive strategies. In: Weinstein C E, Goetz E T, Alexander P A (eds.) 1988 *Learning and Study Strategies: Issues in Assessment, Instruction, and Evaluation.* Academic Press, San Diego, California

Garner R, Wagoner S, Smith T 1983 Externalizing question-answering strategies of good and poor comprehenders. *Read. Res. Q.* 18(4): 439–47

Pintrich P R (ed.) 1991 Special issue: Current issues and new directions in motivational theory and research. *Educ. Psychol.* 26(3 and 4)

Svinicki M D 1991 Practical implications of cognitive theories. In: Menges R J, Svinicki M D (eds.) 1991 *College Teaching: From Theory to Practice. New Directions for Teaching and Learning.* Jossey-Bass, San Francisco, California

Wang M C, Peverly S T 1986 The self-instructive process in classroom learning contexts. *Contemp. Educ. Psychol.* 11(4): 370–404

Weinstein C E, Palmer D R, Schulte A C 1987 *LASSI: Learning and Study Strategies Inventory.* H and H Publishing, Clearwater, Florida

Weinstein C E, Meyer D K 1991 Cognitive learning strategies and college teaching. In: Menges R J, Svinicki M D (eds.) 1991 *College Teaching: From Theory to Practice. New Directions for Teaching and Learning* (45). Jossey-Bass, San Francisco, California

Weinstein C E, Van Mater Stone G 1993 *Broadening Our Conception of General Education: The Self-regulated Learner,* New Directions Series. Jossey-Bass, San Francisco, California

Zimmerman B J, Schunk D H 1989 *Self-regulated Learning and Academic Achievement: Theory, Research, and Practice.* Springer-Verlag, New York

Creativity: Teaching and Assessing

J. F. Feldhusen

People of all ages are constantly confronted by problems and situations that require decisions and provide them with opportunities to improve the human condition and enable them to understand phenomena in their lives. Every day they must act or behave in new or different ways because they are unable to solve the problems or resolve the situations using their current repertoire of knowledge and skills. Thus, these problems and situations require creativity, that is, innovative or adaptive thinking and behavior.

Creative thinking can be taught, enhanced, or nurtured. It is a complex cognitive activity that includes the development and effective use of a large knowledge base, critical thinking skills, decision-making skills, and metacognitive control processes. This entry will focus on (a) definitions, models, and theories of creativity; (b) methods of assessing creativity; and (c) ways of teaching or developing creative ability.

While often contrasted with intelligence, creativity rarely is restricted to cognitive or intellectual functioning or behavior as is intelligence. Rather, researchers and theorists are apt to include as part of their definition of creativity, personality and a host of motivational factors, cognitive processes (perhaps the heart of the matter), press, climate, environmental or zeitgeist conditions, chance factors, and even products or the result of creative functioning Feldhusen (1993).

It is possible that creative, inventive, or innovative thinking and behavior can only be understood in the context of specific disciplines. Creative functioning in science may be unique and totally different psychologically from creativity in political science, jurisprudence, or art. Much of the research on creativity has been conducted in specific domains with little effort expended on seeking generalities across domains. There is also a broad tendency in the field of creativity research to seek insights about the process of creativity by studying people at the upper end of creative functioning (for example, leaders or eminent individuals in various fields).

1 Definitions, Conceptions, Models, and Theories

Vernon (1989) suggested that there is a consensus that creativity means a "person's capacity to produce new or original ideas, insights, restructurings, inventions, or artistic objects, which are accepted by experts as being of scientific, aesthetic, social, or technological value" (p.94). Getzels (1975), on the other hand, claimed that "there is no universally agreed upon definition of creativity" (p.327). Rather, according to Getzels, conceptions of creativity tend to be product-oriented, process-oriented, or based on subjective experiences.

Torrance (1979) offered a definition which he proposed would be useful in understanding, predicting, and developing creative behavior. Torrance believed that creativity consists of a set of abilities, skills, and motivations; furthermore, it is inextricably linked to dealing with problems. In this latter regard, "no creative thinking . . . is likely to occur until there is a recognition or awareness of a problem . . . , there is some definition of the problem, and commitment to deal with it" (p. 13).

One of the major leaders in creativity research and theory development, Amabile (1987), offered one of the simplest and most straightforward definitions: "A product or response is creative if it is a novel and appropriate solution to an open-ended task" (p. 227). This definition, she argues, meets criteria of novelty, correctness or value, and nonalgorithmic or heuristic quality. Elsewhere she says that "a product or response is creative to the extent that appropriate observers independently agree it is creative" (p. 231).

Treffinger et al. (1990) proposed a comprehensive theoretical model of productive thinking (see Fig. 1). This model seeks mainly to account for creativity as a set of cognitive processes contributing to a broader process of productive thinking or problem-solving. As a foundation for productive thinking, it posits a knowledge base which in turn consists of information and skills, motivations and dispositions, and management or metacognitive systems. The intermediate "tool" skills in productive thinking are specific creative (or divergent) thinking abilities and critical thinking skills. Finally, there are the complex methods of problem-solving and decision-making.

As can be seen from the definitions and accompanying model, creativity is an extremely complex phenomenon. It manifests itself chiefly as a set of processes within individuals. Within the individual, creative or adaptive behavior is a complex of cognitive skills and abilities, personality factors, and motivations as well as styles, strategies, and metacognitive skills. However, it also can be studied by focusing on the environmental context or press surrounding creative individuals as well as the impact their products, ideas, and performances have on the world around them. Creativity can perhaps be best understood when one realizes that its manifestation in different domains such as the sciences, arts, humanities, and business depends on quite different interactions among the elements or factors delineated as the creative process.

2. Assessing Creativity

Given the complexity of the models and conceptions of creativity which involve environmental press, processes, and products, the assessment of creativity is equally complex. Thus, a single test instrument or battery is likely to be inappropriate. As a consequence, most efforts to assess creativity have used a variety of instruments which, in combination, have focused on individuals and on their cognitive abilities, personality characteristics, motivations, or background experiences.

Hocevar and Bachelor (1989), for example, offered a "Taxonomy and a Critique of Measurements Used in the Study of Creativity." They proposed eight categories of creativity assessment: (a) tests of divergent thinking, (b) attitude and interest inventories, (c) personality inventories, (d) biographical inventories, (e) ratings by teachers, peers, and supervisors, (f) judgments of products, (g) eminence, and (h) self-reported creative activities and achievements. They also presented examples of major instruments for each category.

Hocevar and Bachelor carried out an elaborate analysis of creativity measurements using several subtests from the Torrance Tests of Creative Thinking and from the Wallach and Kogan (1965) creativity battery in a path model using confirmatory factor analysis. Writing was the outcome variable. They concluded that verbal fluency subtests of both the Torrance Tests of Creative Thinking and the Wallach–Kogan battery were sufficiently valid and reliable.

2.1 Evaluation of Products

Amabile (1990), has been singularly successful in having subjects create products and using "expert" judges to rate their creativity. Amabile reported quite high and satisfactory levels of agreement among judges.

O'Quin and Besemer (1989) have developed the Creative Product Semantic Scale (CPSS), which was based on the Creative Product Analysis Matrix (CPAM) originally proposed by Besemer and Treffinger (1981). The CPSS consists of 71 bipolar adjectives divided into 11 subscales, each measuring one aspect of the CPAM. While some positive evidence of reliability and validity was reported, the authors suggest that more research is needed to understand more completely the nature of creativity as evidenced in subjects' products.

2.2 Self-report Measures

Kirton (1987) has addressed the problem of creativity assessment very successfully by differentiating two bipolar styles of psychological functioning: innovators and adaptors. According to Kirton, "adaption is the characteristic behavior of individuals who, when confronted with a problem, turn to the conventional rules, practices, and perceptions of the group to which they belong" (p. 294). In contrast, "innovation is the characteristic behavior of individuals who, when confronted with a problem, attempt to reorganize or restructure the problem, and to approach it in a new light" (p. 294). Kirton has developed a sound theoretical underpinning for the adaptor–innovator conception as well as an excellent instrument for assessing the construct.

Another widely used scale for creativity assessment is the Group Inventory for Finding Creative Talent (GIFT). The scale is offered at three sets of grade levels, K–2, 3–4, and 5–6, and consists of 32, 34, and 33 items respectively. Students respond "yes" or "no" to self-description and biographical items such as "I like to paint pictures" and "I ask a lot of questions." Additional instruments have also been developed for higher grade levels, GIFFI-I, Group Inventory for Finding Interests, Grades 6–9, and GIFFI-II, for Grades 9–12 and college students. Davis and Rimm (1989) reported that reliabilities and validity coefficients from a number of studies in seven countries were very high and support the use of the instruments as measures of creative ability.

2.3 Assessment of the Environment

Amabile and Gryskiewicz (1989) reported on their development of the Creative Environment Scales, Work Environment Inventory (WEI). The WEI focuses on factors or conditions in the work environment that are most likely to affect creative ideation. They conclude that work so far shows the WEI to be a reliable and valid instrument.

2.4 Assessment Batteries

Milgram (1990) has developed series of tests for use in her own research program. The first is a standardized ideational fluency measure with "lenient solution standards" meaning that all responses are considered solutions. The second test includes clearly defined verbal and nonverbal problems, and calls for solutions that are both unusual and of high quality as well as being true solutions to the problems. The third test is a self-report biographical questionnaire assessing both creative performances and leisure activities. Milgram reported that the tests have demonstrated sufficient validity and reliability in research settings.

The Structure of Intellect (SOI) tests (Meeker et al. 1985) grew out of the research and theoretical formulations of Guilford (1967), and became popular as measures of creative or divergent thinking. Serious questions were raised, however, by several researchers about the tests and the factor analyses underlying the theoretical framework for the SOI. Clarizio and Mehrens (1985) reviewed research on the SOI tests as well as the evidence available in publications related to the tests and concluded that there are major psychometric weaknesses in SOI tests which seriously limit their usefulness.

2.5 Measures of Creativity and Creative Achievement

Do tests used to assess creativity predict or link real-life creative achievements? A major criticism of creativity tests is that they do not. Torrance (1975), however, argued that a number of studies using the Torrance Tests of Creative Thinking clearly demonstrated predictive validity for creative achievement over long periods of time. Among the criteria were creativity of occupation, creativity of writing, and reported creative achievements.

2.6 Lists and Reviews of Instruments

Several lists and reviews of creativity tests have been prepared to guide practitioners and researchers in selecting instruments to measure creativity, its correlates, and its components. Hocevar and Bachelor (1989) offer a fairly comprehensive listing and evaluation of the most promising instruments. Other reviews and listings include those of Petrosko (1978), Kaltsounis and Honeywell (1980), and the Educational Testing Service (1987).

3. Teaching Creativity

Can people be taught to be more creative, to do better creative thinking, to invent or design more creative products, to write more creatively, or to perform more creatively? If the answer is yes, how can they best be taught? What is the substance or curriculum of our teaching efforts, and how or with what teaching methods can creative thinking be taught most effectively?

3.1 Models for Teaching Creativity

Perhaps the best cues to guide the developers of creativity training programs derive from theories or models of creativity or creative thinking processes. For example, Speedie et al. (1973) reviewed the theoretical and research literature on creativity and problem-solving. Based on this review and a factor analysis of a large database of children's creativity and problem-solving test scores, they concluded that 11 skills or strategies are the key components of problem-solving and creative thinking:

(a) sensing that a problem exists;

(b) formulating questions to clarify the problem;

(c) determining causes of the problem;

(d) identifying relevant aspects of the problem;

(e) judging if more information is needed to solve the problem;

(f) determining the specific problem;

(g) clarifying the goal or desired solution;

C. The complex methods

Problem–solving	Decision–making
Understanding the problem	Identify the objective
Identifying broad goals or objectives	Describe the setting, context, and obstacles
Describing an opportunity, concern, or challenge	Gather relevant information
Gathering and sorting relevant data	Specify and analyze alternative actions
Defining a specific problem	Delineate possible outcomes
Generating ideas	Estimate payoffs or satisfaction for each outcome
Planning for action	Choose best action
Evaluating promising solutions	Develop implementation plan
Building acceptance and creating a plan	
Monitoring implementation and feedback	

B. The "tool" skills

Creative thinking	Critical thinking
Fluency	Delineate a cognitive task or problem
Flexibility	Understand and interpret information
Originality	Judge accuracy and relevance of information
Elaboration and Synthesis	Identify assumptions and biases
Curiosity	Detect fallacies and biases
Openness to many ideas, paradoxes,	Derive and evaluate inductive conclusions
dealing with complexity, tension, and ambiguities	Reason deductively and judge validity of
Risk-taking	conclusions
Imagination and humour	Apply strategies to compare, contrast, refine,
Finding "essences" and constructive resolution	and/or strengthen ideas or arguments

A. The foundations

Knowledge base (expertise, not just mechanical)		Motivation and dispositions	Management or metacognitive systems
Content	Strategies and intellectual skills	Characteristics / Style / Attitudes / Self-confidence / Self-esteem / Persistence and focused energy / Strong personal commitment / Freedom from blocks / Supportive context	Goal-setting / Possible strategies / Choose/apply strategies / Feedback / Monitoring or "self-checking" evaluations

Figure 1
Organization and structure of productive thinking

(h) redefining or creating a new use for a familiar object or concept;

(i) seeing implications of a possible action;

(j) selecting the best or most unusual solution among several possible solutions; and

(k) sensing what follows problem solutions.

Houtz and Feldhusen (1976) developed a training program to teach these skills to fourth-grade children and found that significant gains in their creativity were made after six weeks of training.

Urban (1990) reviewed literature from research on creativity and theory development and proposed a model of creativity that could serve as a comprehensive guide to creativity training. The model embraces cognitive and noncognitive components and delineates six major areas of ability or process: (a) a general knowledge base; (b) a domain-specific knowledge base; (c) divergent thinking abilities; (d) task commitment; (e) motives; and (f) tolerance for ambiguity.

479

From this model, guides to cognitive and noncognitive components of creative thinking can be derived.

3.2 Programs for Enhancing Creativity

Creative problem-solving is one of the most widely promulgated models for teaching creativity Torrance (1993). Isaksen and Treffinger (1985) published a comprehensive set of training materials. Their work builds upon the model and materials for creative problem-solving developed by Parnes. Parnes (1975) reviewed the history of and research on creativity and concluded that it is eminently teachable, and the skills generalized to usefulness in real-life situations. More recently Parnes (1987) reviewed the research on the teaching of creativity, especially via the creative problem-solving model, and again concluded that the results are virtually all positive.

Perhaps the most widely known creativity training system is deBono's CORT program (1976). This program consists of a set of training materials for use by teachers and students in the classroom. Lateral thinking or seeking alternatives is a major goal of the program. The lessons can be used across a wide age range (8–17), but are probably most effective in the 10–12 age range. The lessons can be used in any subject matter for periods of about 35 minutes at a time with children in groups of four to six. The program has been widely disseminated and used throughout the world, has been researched very little, but has come to be accepted – even acclaimed – as a major success in teaching thinking.

The Purdue Creative Thinking Program (Feldhusen 1983) is a set of 36 units of instruction on the skills and personal factors of creativity. Each program is built around historical figures: statespeople, scientists, inventors, pioneers, or famous sport figures. Their lives and their creativity are used as models and vehicles for discussions on creative thinking. Much research supports the effectiveness of the program in developing creative thinking skills and motivation.

3.3 Reviews of the Effectiveness of Teaching Creativity

Torrance (1987), a lifelong researcher and developer of creativity training programs, conducted an extensive review of materials, programs, and research on the teaching of creativity. In all, 142 studies were examined. In addition to concluding that there is ample evidence that creativity can be taught, Torrance reported that the successful programs stress both cognitive skills and personality factors, provide good motivating conditions, and involve students actively in the creative thinking process.

Feldhusen and Clinkenbeard (1986) reviewed instructional materials designed to teach creativity, focusing both on the quality of the materials and on evidence of their instructional effectiveness. They found a great deal of published material that had been neither subjected to any evaluation or research nor built upon a theoretical model of creativity, creative thinking, or creative process. Nevertheless, they did find a basic core of good programs of material such as the Productive Thinking Program (Covington et al. 1972), the Purdue Creative Thinking Program (Feldhusen 1983), and Imagination Express (Davis and DiPelo 1973) which have been built on a theoretical model of creativity and found to be instructionally effective.

Finally, Rose and Lin (1984) used meta-analysis to evaluate creativity research. They concluded that most creativity training programs have a positive effect on verbal fluency and originality but little impact on figural creativity.

4. Conclusion and Future Directions

Creative thinking and creative problem-solving are teachable aspects of human cognition and behavior. The goals of such teaching are both cognitive and noncognitive. A number of aspects of personality, motivation, styles, metacognition, and attitudes are involved in creativity.

There should be great emphasis on learning creativity in domain or subject matter contexts and on helping students see the potential use of creativity in real-life situations. Developing creativity should be viewed as a long-range process leading to adult creative achievement and self-fulfillment.

References

Amabile T M 1987 The motivation to be creative. In: Isaksen S C (ed.) 1987 *Frontiers of Creativity Research*. Bearly Buffalo, New York

Amabile T M 1990 Within you, without you: The social psychology of creativity, and beyond. In: Runco M A, Albert R S (eds.) 1990 *Theories of Creativity*. Sage, Newbury Park, California

Amabile T M, Gryskiewicz N D 1989 The creativity environment scales: Work environment inventory. *Creat. Res. J.* 2(4): 231–53

Besemer S P, Treffinger D J 1981 Analysis of creative products: Review and synthesis. *J. Creat. Behav.* 15(3): 158–78

Clarizio H F, Mehrens W A 1985 Psychometric limitations of Guilford's Structure-of-Intellect model for identification and programming of the gifted. *Gift. Child Q.* 29(3): 113–20

Covington M V, Crutchfield R S, Olton R M, Davies L 1972 *Productive Thinking Program*. Brazelton, Berkeley, California

Davis G A, DiPelo G 1973 *Imagination Express: Saturday Subway Ride*. DOK, Buffalo, New York

Davis G A, Rimm S B 1989 *Education of the Gifted and Talented*, 2nd edn. Prentice-Hall, Englewood Cliffs, New Jersey

deBono E 1976 CORT VI, Teacher's Handbook, Thinking Action. Pergamon Press, New York

Educational Testing Service 1987 *Annotated Bibliography of Tests: Creativity and Divergent Thinking*. Educational Testing Service, Princeton, New Jersey

Feldhusen J F 1983 The Purdue Creative Thinking Program. In: Sato I S (ed.) 1983 *Creativity Research and Educational Planning*. Leadership Training Institute for the Gifted and Talented, Los Angeles, California

Feldhusen J F 1993 A conception of creative thinking and creative training. In: Isaksen S G, Murdoch M C, Firestein R L, Treffinger D S (eds.) 1993 *Nurturing and Developing Creativity: The Emergence of a Discipline*. Ablex Publishing Corporation, Norwood, New Jersey

Feldhusen J F, Clinkenbeard P M 1986 Creativity instructional material: A review of research. *J. Creat. Behav.* 20(3): 153–82

Getzels J W 1975 Creativity: Prospects and issues. In: Taylor I A, Getzels J W (eds.) 1975 *Perspectives in Creativity*. Aldine, Chicago, Illinois

Guilford J P 1967 *The Nature of Human Intelligence*. McGraw-Hill, New York

Hocevar D, Bachelor P 1989 A taxonomy and critique of measurements used in the study of creativity. In: Glover J A, Ronning R R, Reynolds C R (eds.) 1989 *Handbook of Creativity. Assessment, Research, and Theories*. Plenum Press, New York

Houtz J C, Feldhusen J F 1976 The modification of fourth graders' problem solving abilities. *J. Psychol.* 93(2): 229–37

Isaksen S, Treffinger D J 1985 *Creative Problem Solving: The Basic Course*. Bearly, Buffalo, New York

Kaltsounis B, Honeywell L 1980 Additional instruments useful in studying creative behavior and creative talent. Part 4: Non-commercially available instruments. *J. Creat. Behav.* 14(1): 56–67

Kirton M J 1987 Adaptors and innovators: Cognitive styles and personality. In: Isaksen S G (ed.) 1987 *Frontiers of Creativity Research*. Bearly, Buffalo, New York

Meeker M, Meeker R, Roid G 1985 *Structure-of-Intellect Learning Abilities Test (SOI-LA)*. Western Psychological Services, Los Angeles, California

Milgram R M 1990 Creativity: An idea whose time has come and gone? In: Runco M A, Albert R S (eds.) 1990 *Theories of Creativity*. Sage, Newbury Park, California

O'Quin K, Besemer S P 1989 The development, reliability, and validity of the revised creative product semantic scale. *Creat. Res. J.* 2(4): 267–78

Parnes S J 1975 AHA! In: Taylor I A, Getzels J W (eds.) 1975 *Perspectives in Creativity*. Aldine, Chicago, Illinois

Parnes S J 1987 The creative studies project. In: Isaksen S G (ed.) 1987 *Frontiers of Creativity Research*. Bearly, Buffalo, New York

Petrosko J 1978 Measuring creativity in elementary school: The current state of the art. *J. Creat. Behav.* 12(2): 109–19

Rose L H, Lin H T 1984 A meta-analysis of long-term creativity training programs. *J. Creat. Behav.* 18(1): 11–22

Speedie S M, Houtz J C, Ringenbach S, Feldhusen J F 1973 Abilities measured by the Purdue Elementary Problem Solving Inventory. *Psychol. Rep.* 33(3): 959–63

Torrance E P 1975 Creativity research in education: Still alive. In: Taylor I A, Getzels J W (eds.) 1975 *Perspectives in Creativity*. Aldine, Chicago, Illinois

Torrance E P 1979 *The Search for Satori and Creativity*. Creative Education Foundation, Buffalo, New York

Torrance E P 1987 Teaching for creativity. In: Isaksen S G (ed.) 1987 *Frontiers of Creativity Research*. Bearly, Buffalo, New York

Torrance E P 1993 Experience in developing technology for creative education. In: Isaksen S G, Murdoch M C, Firestein R L, Treffinger D S (eds.) *Understanding and Recognizing Creativity: The Emergence of a Discipline*. Ablex Publishing Corporation, Norwood, New Jersey

Treffinger D J, Feldhusen J F, Isaksen S G 1990 Organization and structure of productive thinking. *Creat. Learn. Today* 4(2): 6–8

Urban K K 1990 Recent trends in creativity research and theory in Western Europe. *Eur. J. High Abil.* 1: 93–113

Vernon P E 1989 The nature–nurture problem in creativity. In: Glover J A, Ronning R R, Reynolds C R (eds.) 1989 *Handbook of Creativity*. Plenum Press, New York

Wallach M, Kogan N 1965 *Modes of Thinking In Young Children*. Rinehart and Winston, New York

Metacognitive Strategies: Teaching and Assessing

P. R.-J. Simons

Metacognition is primarily concerned with those human reasoning processes that are necessary to solve problems for which no completely developed or automated procedures are available. Both knowledge of these processes and their control or regulation are typically subsumed in the concept of metacognition. This entry addresses a series of six questions related to teaching and assessing metacognition. These questions are:

(a)   What aspects of metacognition should be taught?

(b)   Who is likely to benefit from metacognitive instruction?

(c)   What are the basic principles of metacognitive instruction?

(d)   What is an appropriate amount of time for metacognitive instruction?

(e)   What tasks should be used to teach metacognition?

(f)   Where should metacognition be taught?

The answers to these questions are based primarily on the results of a series of related research studies (De Jong 1987, De Jong and Simons 1988, Simons and De Jong in press; Simons 1989, Simons and Lodewijks 1987, Vermunt and Van Rijswijk 1988). Additional research studies are cited in support of answers to some of the questions. Several methodological issues are then discussed and a series of guidelines for future studies of metacognitive instruction is offered.

1. What Aspects of Metacognition Should Be Taught?

The selection of content to include in metacognitive instruction is not an easy task. Appropriate content can be chosen by examining the differences in metacognition of groups of students: high performing and low performing. Ideally, a diagnosis of the kinds of metacognitive processes not used by low-performing students would be made to corroborate this initial evidence obtained from the comparison.

A second source of content is the information contained in the theoretical and empirical literature. From this literature, three kinds of strategies and skills emerge: awareness of relevant regulatory processes, the possession of regulatory skills, and the availability and use of processing skills. These strategies and skills can form the basis for metacognitive instructional programs.

2. Who Is Likely to Benefit from Metacognitive Instruction?

Teaching students skills and strategies they already possess is not likely to be very effective, but if students lack some basic cognitive skills and affective dispositions, the success of metacognitive instruction also may be impaired. Students who lack essential reading skills, for example, can hardly be expected to benefit from instruction aimed at the improvement of study skills or self-regulatory reading skills. Similarly, students who do not believe that it is possible to regulate their own learning or who dislike the strategies being taught to them are not likely to benefit from metacognitive instruction.

Ideal students, then, are those who lack metacognitive skills and strategies, but who are not deficient in other respects. As a consequence, some diagnosis of the students' knowledge and emotional base seems necessary to the success of metacognitive instruction.

3. The Basic Principles of Metacognitive Instruction

Several principles can be derived from current research on metacognitive teaching and learning. Among the most important are the following:

(a) Learning activities and processes, rather than learning outcomes, must be emphasized (Process Principle).

(b) Learning is "thematized" and students are helped to become aware of their learning strategies, self-regulation skills, and the relationship of these strategies and skills to learning goals (Reflectivity Principle).

(c) The interaction of cognitive, metacognitive, and affective components of learning is central (Affectivity Principle).

(d) Students must be made constantly aware of the use and function of knowledge and skills (Functionality Principle).

(e) Teachers and students should strive for transfer and generalization, without expecting either to occur without practice in context (Transfer Principle).

(f) Learning strategies and self-regulation skills need to be practiced regularly, with sufficient time provided and with practice occurring in appropriate contexts (Context Principle).

(g) Students should be taught how they can regulate, diagnose, and revise their own learning (Self-Diagnosis Principle).

(h) Instruction should be designed in such a way that there is an optimal balance between the quality and quantity of learning activity (Activity Principle).

(i) The responsibility for learning should be shifted gradually to the students (Scaffolding Principle).

(j) Especially with younger students, relationships with parents and other adults should be emphasized so that initial attempts at self-regulated learning can be supervised (Supervision Principle).

(k) Cooperation and discussion among students is necessary (Cooperation Principle).

(l) Higher cognitive learning goals which require deeper cognitive processing should be emphasized (Goal Principle).

(m) New subject matter is learned as it becomes anchored to existing knowledge and preconceptions (Preconception Principle).

(n) Instruction should be tailored to the current conceptions of students (Learning Conception Principle).

Not all programs need to include all principles. At the same time, however, programs which adhere to more of these principles are likely to be more effective.

4. Time Needed for Metacognitive Instruction

In general, too little time is allocated to metacognitive instruction in most programs. This assertion does not mean that short training programs cannot have effects. In a study with adult students learning a foreign language vocabulary, impressive results were attained within one hour (Simons and De Jong in press). At the same time, however, short programs generally are not effective with younger children, less able students, and learning-disabled students. Longer programs are more likely to be effective than shorter ones, although research on the optimal length of instructional programs for teaching metacognition is clearly needed.

5. Tasks Needed to Teach Metacognition

The tasks used to teach metacognition should be ecologically valid. That is, they should resemble those tasks that students frequently encounter in and outside of school. If possible, the tasks should be those that students are expected to master in school and on which their performance is systematically monitored and evaluated. Tasks not meeting these criteria are often seen as irrelevant to students.

In addition, tasks assigned to students should be of appropriate difficulty. If the tasks are too easy, students can rely on routine, automatic procedures, and there is no need for regulatory processes. Overly difficult tasks are also problematic. For example, when high and low performing students were given a very difficult task, low performing students stopped working on the task, while high performing students kept trying to accomplish the task despite the fact that their efforts were ineffective, inefficient, and not improving (Simons and Liew-On 1991).

Finally, tasks assigned to students should be similar to those they are likely to be assigned in the "real world." While dissimilar tasks are appropriate from an experimental research perspective to examine issues of transfer and generalizability, it must be realized that the likelihood of transferring learning from tasks used in instruction to very dissimilar tasks is extremely small for most students (Salomon and Perkins 1989).

6. The "Where" of Teaching Metacognition

Since tasks used to teach metacognition should be as ecologically valid as possible, the most appropriate placement of these tasks is in the school curriculum. This embedding of metacognitive instruction in schools is not without its problems, however. Embedding often confuses students. Instead of only having to study and solve problems, students are asked to regulate the processes involved in studying and solving problems.

Prawatt (1991) has offered a resolution to this dilemma. He proposed that "immersion" approaches be developed. In immersion approaches the regulation skills are activated by the teacher without much attention from students. As a consequence, they initially are not viewed by the students as competing requirements. Only after they have been practiced by students and shown to be beneficial to them do they receive attention in the classroom.

7. Methodological Issues in Research on Metacognition

There are several methodological issues that need to be resolved in order to gain a substantially greater understanding of metacognition during the decade of the 1990s. They fall into three categories: experimental design, fidelity of implementation, and assessment of the effects of metacognition.

7.1 Experimental Design

One important question is the composition of a proper control group. Since only students who lack certain strategies and skills should receive instruction, the best control group consists of students who also lack the strategies and skills being taught, but who are not selected for treatment. Of course, random assignment to groups is essential in this case.

When random assignment is not possible, high achieving students who already possess the skills can be used as a "control group." Although these students do not comprise a control group in the traditional sense, they are better than no control group at all. The goal of metacognitive instruction is to give poorer students the strategies and skills used regularly by better students. In this regard, successful metacognitive instruction should be expected to reduce or remove the initial differences between poorer students who are provided with metacognitive instruction and better students left unaided.

7.2 Fidelity of Implementation

A second methodological issue concerns whether the metacognitive instruction envisioned by the designer of the instructional program actually occurs in the form intended in the experimental classrooms and does not occur in the control classrooms. There have been many instances in which intended interventions were distorted completely. In other cases students in control groups have been given the treatment, despite requests by researchers not to do so. Finally, students themselves can also distort interventions by failing to engage in or complete assigned work or failing to use materials or instructional aids offered to them.

7.3 Assessment of Metacognition

A third methodological problem occurs in the area of assessing the effects of metacognitive instruction.

Most often, the goals of metacognitive instruction are stated in process terms. That is, instruction is expected to change the ways in which students process information (e.g., summarize information, monitor their acquisition of information). Only indirectly is this instruction expected to influence student learning outcomes. Process measures are not always easy to design, efficient to use, or effective in terms of their technical qualities (e.g., validity, reliability). Nonetheless, the availability and use of adequate assessment techniques are the keys to understanding metacognition and improving metacognitive instruction.

8. Guidelines for Future Studies of Metacognitive Instruction

Based on the foregoing discussion, a set of guidelines pertaining to the design of studies attempting to increase or improve metacognition can be offered.

(a) Develop an instructional program which has the greatest likelihood of producing the desired results, and examine the effectiveness of the components of the program after its implementation by systematically dismantling it.

(b) Derive the content of the instructional program by looking at studies of the differences between high and low performers, experts and novices, and writings in a variety of theoretical frameworks.

(c) Develop an instructional program which includes at least the following goals or objectives: metacognitive awareness, regulatory skills, learning skills, and affective–motivation skills.

(d) In evaluating the effectiveness of the program, use students who lack the strategies and skills which are included as program goals or objectives. This will quite likely require some diagnosis of the current metacognitive levels of students.

(e) Extend the length of the program to ensure that the students have a reasonable chance of acquiring the metacognitive strategies and skills being taught.

(f) Evaluate the effectiveness of the program both during the program and after its completion.

(g) Incorporate into the program tasks that are ecologically valid and are of appropriate and varied levels of difficulty.

(h) Use effectiveness measures that estimate immediate achievement, "near transfer" of learning, and "far transfer" of learning. "Near transfer" can be facilitated by contextualizing the instruction; "far transfer" can be enhanced by decontextualizing the strategies and skills. Make sure that the learning process, rather than or in addition to learning products or outcomes are monitored.

(i) Embed instruction and immerse students in metacognitive learning in real school settings.

(j) Use control groups that either are composed of similar students (who are randomly assigned to treatment or control groups) or high performing students who serve as benchmarks for program success.

(k) Monitor the program to ensure that it is being implemented as intended; also, monitor the control group to check on the strategies and skills, if any, that they are being taught.

9. Conclusion

Understanding and being able to regulate what and how human beings think is central to teachers' ability to improve substantially how they teach their students. Providing students with metacognitive strategies and skills enables them to negotiate and meet the demands of a wide variety of educational settings and situations. While some students appear to use such strategies and skills almost naturally, most students can be taught to acquire and use them if the principles of effective metacognitive instruction are followed.

References

De Jong F P C M 1987 Differences in the self-regulation processes between successful and less successful students and the prediction of learning performances in the case of comprehension and learning of text. In: Simons P R J, Beukhof G(eds.) 1987 *Regulation of Learning*. svo-Selecta, The Hague

De Jong F P C M, Simons P R J 1988 Self-regulation in text processing. *European Journal of Psychology of Education* 3(2): 177–90

Prawatt R 1991 The immersion approach to learning to think. *Educ. Researcher*

Salomon G, Perkins D N 1989 Rocky roads to transfer: Rethinking mechanisms of a neglected phenomenon. *Educ. Psychol.* 24(2): 113–42

Simons P R J 1989 Modifying the regulation processes of learning: Two exploratory training studies. *Canadian Journal of Educational Communication* 18(1): 29–48

Simons P R J, Lodewijks J G L C 1987 Regulatory cognitions during learning from text. In: De Corte E, Lodewijks H, Parmentier R, Span P (eds.) 1987 *Learning and Instruction: European Research in an International Context*, Vol. 1. Leuven University Press/Pergamon Press, Oxford

Simons P R J, Liew-On M 1991 Breadth of orientation: Individual differences and training. In: Carretero M, Pozo M, Pope M, Simons P R J(eds.) 1991 *Research on Learning and Instruction*. Pergamon Press, Oxford

Simons P R J, De Jong F P C M in press Self-regulation and computer-aided learning. *Appl. Psychol.*

Vermunt J D H M, Van Rijswijk F 1988 Analysis and development of students' skill in self-regulated learning. *High. Educ.* 17(6): 647–82

Further Reading

Bereiter C, Scardamalia M 1989 Intentional learning as a goal of instruction. In: Resnick L B(ed.) 1989 *Knowing, Learning, and Instruction: Essays in Honor of Robert Glaser*. Erlbaum, Hillsdale, New Jersey

Collins A, Brown J S, Newman S E 1989 Cognitive apprenticeship: Teaching the crafts of reading, writing, and mathematics. In: Resnick L B (ed.) 1989 *Knowing, Learning, and Instruction: Essays in Honor of Robert Glaser*. Erlbaum, Hillsdale, New Jersey

Flavell J H 1979 Metacognition and cognitive monitoring: A new area of cognitive-developmental inquiry. *Am. Psychol.* 34: 906–11

Palincsar A S, Brown A L 1989 Instruction for self-regulated learning. In: Resnick L B, Klopfer L E (eds.) 1989 *Toward the Thinking Curriculum: Current Cognitive Research*. Association for Supervision and Curriculum, Arlington, Virginia

The Study of Teaching

Introduction

L. W. Anderson

Much of the information contained in this volume was derived from the systematic study of teachers and teaching. Quite clearly, the authors of the entries added their own interpretations to the available information. Nonetheless, the basis for the vast majority of the entries was research evidence. In fact, many authors were quick to point out the lack of evidence in certain situations and cases. The six entries in this section focus on the ways in which teachers and teaching are studied, on the meaning derived from the results of these studies, and on the applications of these results to the improvement of teaching practice.

1. Methods Used to Study Teachers and Teaching

To gather information about teachers and teaching, researchers use a variety of methods. Among the most frequently used methods are paper-and-pencil tests, observations, interviews, and questionnaires. Medley and Shannon suggest that researchers use different methods for different purposes. To assess what they call teacher competence (that is, what teachers *know*), researchers tend to rely on paper-and-pencil tests and, increasingly, interviews. In contrast, to assess teacher performance (that is, what teachers *do*), researchers rely primarily on classroom observation. Finally, to assess teacher effectiveness (that is, the *influence* teachers have on their students), researchers may use tests, observations, or questionnaires.

When assessing teacher effectiveness, however, the focus is primarily on the students, not the teachers. For example, tests can be administered to students before and after instruction to determine how much they learned from their teachers or as the result of a particular teaching strategy or technique. Similarly, questionnaires can be administered to students to determine how effective they believed the teacher or teaching to be (Marsh).

Galton's entry focuses on classroom observation. Approaches to classroom observation differ in two respects. The first is whether the categories used to

record the observation are determined a priori or post hoc. Approaches that specify the categories in advance are referred to as structured observational systems. Those in which the categories are derived from the observation are termed narratives.

A second difference in approaches to classroom observation concerns the level of inference permitted or required by the observer. Low-inference systems contain "unambiguous criteria for assigning events to categories" (Galton). In contrast, high-inference systems permit greater observer judgment in determining the category to which an event is assigned. Furthermore, high-inference systems may require observers to evaluate an event on a scale of, say, one to five within an assigned category. Examples of such scales include teacher clarity (where 1 = vague and 5 = clear) and teacher enthusiasm (where 1 = little and 5 = much). These systems are referred to as rating scales.

Marsh's entry examines the role of students in assessing teacher performance and effectiveness. He argues that teaching effectiveness is a multidimensional phenomenon and further suggests nine dimensions that can be incorporated into a questionnaire administered to students. They are: learning/value, instructor enthusiasm, organization/clarity, group interaction, individual rapport, breadth of coverage, examinations/grading, assignments/readings, and workload/difficulty. Students rate teachers and their teaching on each of these factors, typically on a five-point scale.

2. Interpreting the Results of Studies of Teachers and Teaching

Contrary to some people's opinion, data collected from systematic studies of teachers and teaching do not "speak for themselves." Someone, preferably an individual possessing both substantive and methodological knowledge and skill, must interpret the data. Interpretation is necessary both for individual studies and for collections of studies conducted on similar problems, questions, or topics.

Sound interpretation of the results of individual studies almost always involves some type of comparison. In discussing the results of classroom observation studies, Galton discusses the role of sequences of events in interpreting specific events with the sequences. For example, a teacher question following a statement made by a student is quite different from a teacher question initiating a dialogue or discussion. Understanding the sequence of events permits researchers to make the necessary different interpretations of the two questions. Without this understanding, researchers might conclude simply that two questions were asked.

In his first entry, Dunkin summarizes a set of international studies of teachers and teaching. He suggests that comparisons across countries can help educators in two ways. First, they permit a greater understanding of the present educational system of a country. Second, they may suggest changes that can be made to improve the current operation of the system.

Problems of interpretation increase exponentially when multiple studies of a single problem, question, or topic are involved. Different studies tend to be conducted differently and, thus, produce slightly or substantially different results. In his second entry, Dunkin addresses the question of how best to make sense of results from different studies on the same problem, topic, or question. He suggests that there are different methods of summarizing or synthesizing a series of research studies (e.g., vote counting, combined significance tests, effect size estimates). Furthermore, he warns that different methods may produce very different results.

3. Translating Research into Practice

Studies of teachers and teaching tend to be directed toward one of two purposes. First, they may be attempts to increase our understanding of teachers and teaching. Second, they may be attempts to produce better teachers and more effective teaching. It should be pointed out that these are quite different purposes.

Understanding comes primarily from the relationship of theory and research. That is, researchers either use or build theories that enable them to make sense of the data they have collected. In contrast, the application of research to improved practice requires a more instrumental view of research.

Weinert suggests that this instrumental view has led to a large gap between research and practice. The magnitude of this gap can be attributed to both researchers and practitioners. Researchers tend to issue general statements that are difficult for practitioners to implement. Similarly, practitioners tend to rely more on historical data (e.g., traditional practices) than on current research evidence in informing their practice. To close this gap, Weinert suggests that research results or findings be viewed as *one* source of background knowledge for practitioners. In other words, researchers should be more interested in informing practitioners than in influencing practice.

4. Conclusion

The authors of the entries in this section suggest that the systematic study of teachers and teaching is critical if the quality of education that students receive is to be understood and ultimately improved. If research is to be linked to improved practice, however, several matters must be attended to. First, valid and reliable data on important characteristics of teachers and components of teaching must be collected. Second, the data must be interpreted properly, both in terms of what they mean (theoretical) and how they relate to effective teachers and teaching (instrumental). Third, the data must be integrated or synthesized across a set or series of studies addressing similar characteristics or components, initially looking for common findings and ultimately resolving contradictory ones. Finally, ways must be found to translate research effectively into practice. If these matters are not attended to, the future will be one of operating within traditional constraints and moving forward on the basis of expert opinion rather than data and evidence.

Teacher Evaluation

D. M. Medley and D. M. Shannon

Teacher evaluation is a two-step process. The first step is to obtain information about each teacher who is to be evaluated. The second step is to use that information to form an evaluative judgment about the teacher. Although there is some question about how information about teachers should be used in evaluating them,

there is no question that the validity of an evaluation depends on the accuracy and relevance of the information upon which it is based. This entry deals with the first step only. Procedures presently used to obtain information are described and ways of improving their accuracy and relevance are discussed.

1. Types of Information

Ideally, all evaluations of teachers should be based on information about teacher effectiveness. However, because direct information about teacher effectiveness is not always available when decisions must be made, many teacher evaluations are based on information about teacher competence or teacher performance.

Information about teacher performance is not available until the teacher can be observed on the job. Decisions about preservice teacher education students and candidates for teaching certificates or licenses must therefore be based on information about their competence obtained in artificial or "test" situations.

Most decisions about practicing teachers (i.e., decisions about hiring, firing, tenure, and promotion) must be made and implemented without information about teachers' effects on students. Evaluations of teachers meant to inform such decisions must therefore be based on information about teacher performance.

Underlying the use of information about competency and performance to evaluate teachers are two assumptions. The first is that the effectiveness of a teacher depends on how well the teacher performs on the job. The second is that how well a teacher performs on the job depends on how competent the teacher is. If these assumptions are valid, it seems reasonable also to assume that evaluations based on information about teacher competence and performance contain information about teacher effectiveness.

2. Evaluating Teacher Competence

Evaluations based on information about teacher competence may be and are used for two main purposes. One is to monitor the progress of students enrolled in preservice teacher education programs and programs designed to increase teacher competence. Most of the information is obtained with paper and pencil examinations designed to measure knowledge.

In many parts of the world, government agencies exist whose function it is to prevent incompetent teachers from practicing in their jurisdictions. They therefore require all teachers to present evidence of competence before they are given certificates or licenses to teach. While some agencies accept graduation from a preservice program as evidence of competence, an increasing number require the candidate to pass one or more examinations specially constructed for the purpose, called teacher competency tests. Most teacher competency tests are paper and pencil tests very similar to the examinations used in teacher preparation programs.

2.1 Teacher Competency Tests

A typical teacher competency test is designed to measure knowledge of two kinds: content knowledge and professional knowledge. The content knowledge tested usually includes both knowledge of the specific subject matter the teacher is expected to teach and general knowledge of the kind that any educated adult is expected to possess. The importance of knowledge of the subject matter to be taught is generally taken for granted. The importance of general knowledge reflects the fact that most teachers serve as role models as well as instructors. For some children, the teacher may be the first educated adult they get a chance to observe closely.

Professional knowledge consists of knowledge about the kinds of teacher behavior believed or known to be effective in helping students progress toward important educational goals. While most of it comes from the accumulated experience of the profession, some comes from systematic research in disciplines on which teaching is based and some from what is known as process–product research, that is, research intended to discover relationships between teacher behavior and student learning (see Brophy and Good 1986). In the early 1990s, some findings of research intended to discover relationships between students' classroom activities and student learning started to appear (see Berliner 1990). However, there is much less agreement about the importance of professional knowledge than of content knowledge.

2.2 Validity of Teacher Competency Tests

There is only one teacher competency test in the United States that has been used long enough and often enough to generate a useful amount of information about the validity of scores on such tests, the National Teacher Examinations (NTE) (Educational Testing Service 1940–1976). Because of the care taken to ensure that the content of these tests represented the best current wisdom of the profession, the content validity of these examinations was at least as high as that of any similar test.

Some 50 studies of the predictive validity of the so-called Common Examinations of the NTE have been conducted. In these studies scores on the Weighted Common Examinations (WCE) were correlated with measures of teacher performance and measures of teacher effectiveness. A review of these studies revealed no evidence that the correlation either between WCE scores and ratings of teacher performance or between WCE scores and measures of teacher effectiveness was greater than zero (see Quirk et al. 1973).

These findings provide no empirical support for the assumption that scores on this or any other teacher competency test contain information about teacher effectiveness. They also raise serious questions about the validity of current teacher competency tests for making decisions about prospective teachers.

2.3 Improving Teacher Competency Tests

One way to account for these findings is to make a distinction between academic knowledge, that is,

489

knowledge useful in performing well on paper and pencil tests, and functional knowledge, that is, knowledge useful in performing well in the classroom. The fact that the NTE has high content validity (i.e., its content includes most of the things that educators believe to be important to teachers) can be taken as evidence that the test measures academic knowledge. The fact that it has low predictive validity (i.e., possession of this knowledge is unrelated to classroom performance) can be taken as evidence that it does not measure functional knowledge.

The implications of this distinction for the direction that future efforts to improve teacher competency tests should take are clear. Changes in test content are unlikely to increase either the content or predictive validity of the tests. However, modifications in what the tests require students to do with existing content might increase the predictive validity. Current tests include items that require prospective teachers to apply their knowledge to teaching problems. But the skills used to answer such items correctly are of no use when the prospective teacher is trying to apply the same knowledge to similar problems when they are encountered in the classroom.

It is clearly time to abandon the printed test booklet filled with multiple-choice items, and replace it with something else. A likely place to find a replacement is among the new modes, sequences, and formats made available by innovative technological tools such as personal computers, videotape and videodisc recorders, and the like.

One alternative to teacher certification based on competency test scores is performance-based teacher certification. All teaching candidates are allowed to teach from one to three years without having demonstrated competence. During this time their performance is rated one or more times; if the ratings are satisfactory, the teacher receives a certificate or a license to teach.

There are two disadvantages to this approach. One is its cost, which is very high. The other is that its adoption defeats the purpose of certification by permitting incompetent teachers to teach for up to three years before they are barred from the classroom.

2.4 Issues in Evaluating Teacher Competency

Some fundamental questions have been raised about the usefulness of the professional knowledge that teacher competency tests are designed to measure. Some question whether there is anything to know; others assume that there is, but question whether the amount of this knowledge that is known is great enough to make a difference. In other words, would a teacher who knew all that teacher educators can teach him or her be any more effective than one who possessed none of it?

The answer to this question depends on whether teaching should be regarded as one of the so-called learned professions. The nature of such a profession is that its practitioners help others deal with a category of difficult human problems by applying to them a specialized body of knowledge which is incomplete (i.e., which does not contain solutions to all problems in that category). If teaching is a profession, then its members are obligated to know and use whatever there is to know, however inadequate it may be.

A second question that has been raised concerns the nature of a teacher's professional knowledge. The question hinges on whether the competencies necessary for effective teaching of different subjects and grades, and even of different topics in the same subject or grade, may be so different that no valid common examination can be constructed. Instead, many different instruments must be developed for evaluating competence to teach different subjects and topics. A project to develop a national teacher assessment program using such multiple instruments is under way (see Haertel 1991).

These assumptions may be appropriate for the project described, since its focus is on teacher excellence, but they are inappropriate for present uses of competency tests which focus on entry-level competence. It is widely agreed that excellence can only be acquired from extensive experience, and may well be highly specific to the content taught. The survival skills beginning teachers need, however, which must be acquired before they have any experience, may have little to do with the specific content they are to teach.

3. Evaluating Teacher Performance

Teacher performance has been evaluated in one way or another as long as there have been teachers to evaluate. It has been evaluated by the teachers' employers, by the parents of their pupils, and by the pupils themselves. And rarely has the validity of any of these evaluations been questioned.

Almost anyone who watches a teacher for a few minutes forms a definite impression of how "good" the teacher is; and for most of the history of education, teachers were evaluated in just this way. In many schools supervisors still observe and evaluate teachers on the basis of global impressions formed in much the same way. Growing concern about the competence of some supervisors to make valid evaluations in this fashion has led to the adoption of the multifactor teacher rating scale.

3.1 Teacher Rating Scales

A multifactor teacher rating scale is an instrument used by evaluators while observing teachers. The instrument specifies the number and duration of the observations to be made and defines the aspects of the performance that are to be observed and judged. It also provides a numerical or graphic scale on which the evaluator's judgment, or rating, of each factor or item is recorded. Raters are instructed to rate each item on its own merits and without regard to ratings on other items.

The overall evaluation of the teacher is obtained later by combining the separate ratings into a composite description. Sometimes teachers' profiles on individual items are used to diagnose teacher difficulties and plan corrective action.

3.2 Validity of Teacher Ratings

The influence of the evaluator's expertise on the validity of evaluations made with a rating scale should be reduced or eliminated because the aspects of teacher performance to be evaluated are predetermined. Validity is further enhanced if the items to be rated reflect aspects of performance known or believed to be related to teacher effectiveness.

Just as the content validity of a test depends on the items it contains, so does the content validity of a rating scale. Thus, the items on a valid teacher competency test should correspond to the items on a valid teacher rating scale. Much wisdom and effort has gone into the construction of rating scales to ensure that the items incorporate the best available knowledge and current beliefs about effective teacher performance; the best of them can be said to have high content validity (for examples, see Kowalski 1978). As was the case with teacher competency tests, however, content validity of rating scales does not guarantee their validity as predictors of teacher effectiveness.

It is therefore important to establish the predictive validity of each rating scale empirically; that is, by testing whether the ratings correlate with direct measures of teacher effectiveness. The number of studies of this kind that have been reported is surprisingly small, and the findings of the few that have been reported have been consistently negative. There is no empirical evidence that correlations between supervisors' ratings of teacher performance and direct measures of teacher effectiveness differ from zero. Thus, they apparently do not contain the information about teacher effectiveness they are assumed to contain (see Medley and Coker 1987).

One likely reason for these findings is the strong tendency for ratings on individual items to be distorted by the rater's overall impression of the teacher, a distortion known as the halo effect (see Cooper 1981). The halo effect manifests itself in unduly high correlations between ratings of the same teacher by the same rater on different items. It is not unusual to find that different items on a teacher rating scale correlate extremely highly. The key to valid ratings lies in the reduction or elimination of the halo effect so that the ratings depend on the item content they purport to measure.

3.3 Improving Ratings

The most practical way to increase the validity of teacher ratings is to take steps to decrease the influence of halo on the ratings. Halo is most likely to distort ratings when no behavior relevant to an item to be rated is observed. In such cases the rating must be based either on behavior irrelevant to the item or on the rater's overall impression of the teacher, neither of which yields a valid rating.

The risk of this occurring depends first of all on the item itself. The rating scale used should include behaviors that may be expected to occur frequently enough to make it likely that the rater will see them in the classroom of each teacher who is to be rated. The duration and frequency of periods of observation should be sufficient to provide ample opportunity for behaviors relevant to every item on the scale to occur, and raters should undergo enough training, practice, and retraining so that they will see and recognize relevant behaviors when they occur.

3.4 Issues in Performance Evaluation

A more drastic step that has been proposed is to abandon teacher rating scales entirely, and replace them with "low-inference observation schedules." A low-inference observation schedule consists of a list of observable items of behavior. When an item of behavior occurs, it is recorded by the observer. There is no explicit indication of the factors on which the evaluation is based or which item is relevant to which factor. Scores on the factors are obtained by applying objective scoring keys to the record (see Medley et al. 1984).

Instruments of this type have less face validity and are more costly to develop than rating scales, and are considered less sensitive to the complexities of classroom behavior. However, scores on them have been shown to be much less susceptible to the effects of halo than ratings. Also, unlike teacher ratings, they have been shown to predict teacher effectiveness in research studies (see Brophy and Good 1986).

4. Evaluating Teacher Effectiveness

Evaluations of teachers based on measures of students' gains on achievement tests of educational goals have great appeal to the lay public as a basis for decisions about teachers regarding hiring, firing, tenure, and promotion. Methods for deriving information about teacher effectiveness from their students' scores on achievement tests are available, but educators are reluctant to use these methods for reasons which will be examined later in this section.

4.1 Measuring Teacher Effectiveness

Before teacher effectiveness can be evaluated it must be clearly defined. The definition must specify in measurable terms both the outcomes to be achieved and the kind of student with whom they are to be achieved. The outcomes may be specified in measurable terms by selecting a valid test of achievement of those outcomes. The test chosen should be administered to the students in a class taught by each teacher who is to be evaluated at the end of a school term. Scores on this test will be referred to as posttest scores.

The type of student to be affected by the teacher may be defined by specifying one or more measurable student characteristics. The most important of these is student ability, defined for this purpose by students' scores on an achievement test administered at the beginning of the term (pretest scores). This test should be equivalent to the posttest, or as nearly so as possible. Other student characteristics such as sex, ethnic origin, and attitude toward school may also be used.

Pretest and posttest scores of students in each class are used to set up a within-class regression equation for predicting future posttest scores from pretest scores in each class. When the specified pretest score (or set of scores) is entered into this equation, an estimate of the posttest score the student(s) would be expected to get in that class is obtained. Since the equations are different in different classes, the expected outcomes will also be different in different classes.

The expected posttest scores in each class estimate how much students should learn in that class in light of their pretest scores. Differences in these expectations in different classes are partly due to differences in teacher effectiveness and partly due to differences in the classes.

Among the class characteristics most likely to affect the amount a student learns are the mean ability and the range of abilities of the students in the class. The mean and standard deviation of pretest scores in the class serve as convenient measures of these factors. The effect of these two factors is dealt with by setting up a between-class regression equation in the group of teachers for predicting expected posttest scores from class characteristics. When the characteristics of a class are entered into this equation, a second estimate of the defined student's expected posttest score in that class is obtained.

When the estimated posttest score obtained from the between-class equation in a class is subtracted from the one obtained from its within-class equation, the difference may be interpreted as a measure of the effectiveness of the teacher of that class. How accurate the estimate is depends on how many of the class characteristics that affect student learning have been identified and eliminated.

4.2 Validity Problems

The fact that the achievement test used to measure student achievement by the process just described is valid is no guarantee that measures of teacher effectiveness based on that test will also be valid. On the contrary, using students' scores for such a purpose will almost certainly destroy the validity of the test.

Suppose, for example, that a school administrator notices that scores on the reading test administered annually as part of the school's testing program have been going down, and announces a campaign to improve the teaching of reading in the school. Henceforth all reading teachers will be evaluated on the basis of their students' performance on the test, and extra supervisory assistance will be given to teachers whose students' scores are below par. The intention, of course, is to improve the teaching of reading.

If past experience is any guide, at that point the primary goal of most if not all of the reading teachers in the school will change from teaching students to be better readers to teaching them to get better scores on the reading test. Instead of improving, the quality of the teaching of reading in the school will begin to decline. The administrator will not know this, because the action he or she has taken has destroyed the validity of the reading test. Instead of declining (as they would if they measured reading achievement), scores will begin to rise. Under these conditions the test measures how effective teachers are in raising students' test scores, not how effective they are in teaching them to read.

4.3 Using Measures of Teacher Effectiveness

Valid measures of teacher effectiveness can be derived from students' achievement test scores if and only if they are used for other purposes than the evaluation of individual teachers. Perhaps the most important use that can be made of such measures is to monitor and, if necessary, help increase the validity of the rating scales that are actually used to evaluate teachers.

If a school routinely administers a battery of achievement tests to its students for other purposes, as many do, the data needed to do this are available at little or no extra cost. Simple correlation coefficients between ratings of teachers and measures of their effectiveness derived from the test data will clearly indicate whether more effective teachers tend to get higher ratings than less effective ones, as they should. If they do not, correlations between ratings on individual items and the same measures of teacher effectiveness can be used to identify items that are not working so that they can be revised or replaced. It should not be necessary to point out the importance of protecting the anonymity of the teachers when this is done.

5. Conclusion

There is no consensus either about how teachers should be evaluated or about the uses to which the evaluations should be put. The main objectives of this entry have been to describe the procedures most educators use to obtain information about teachers on which to base their evaluations and to offer suggestions for strengthening these procedures.

All but the most primitive procedures for evaluating teachers assume the existence of a body of professional knowledge, knowledge of ways of teaching that maximize teachers' effectiveness in helping students achieve defined educational goals. Competence to teach is defined in terms of possession of two kinds of knowledge, knowledge of subject matter and professional knowledge, and training programs are developed to help students become competent in this sense. Prospective teachers are required to demonstrate minimum competence before they are recognized as teachers. The main instruments used to collect information to be used in evaluating teacher competence are paper-and-pencil tests of knowledge called teacher competency tests.

Once teachers are deemed competent, decisions about their employment are based on evaluations of their ability to use their knowledge on the job. The principal tools used to obtain information about teacher performance are observation instruments called teacher rating scales. Finally, teacher effectiveness is estimated by collecting data about the teacher's influence on the progress a specified kind of student makes toward a defined educational goal. Procedures for collecting data on teacher effectiveness are most appropriate for verifying and adding to the content knowledge base that is used for evaluating teacher competence and teacher performance.

See also: Characteristics of Prospective Teachers

References

Berliner D C 1990 What's all the fuss about instructional time? In: Ben-Peritz M, Bromme R (eds.) 1990 *The Nature of Time in Schools: Theoretical Concepts, Practitioner Perceptions.* Teachers College Press, New York

Brophy J E, Good T L 1986 Teacher behavior and student achievement. In: Wittrock M C (ed.) 1986 *Handbook of Research on Teaching*, 3rd edn. Macmillan, New York

Cooper W H 1981 Ubiquitous halo. *Psych. Bull.* 90(2): 218–44

Educational Testing Service 1940–1976 *The National Teacher Examinations.* Educational Testing Service, Princeton, New Jersey

Haertel E H 1991 New forms of teacher assessment. *Rev. Res. Educ.* 17: 3–29

Kowalski J P 1978 *Evaluating Teacher Performance.* Educational Research Service, Arlington, Virginia

Medley D M, Coker H 1987 How valid are principals' judgments of teacher effectiveness? *Phi Del. Kap.* 69(2): 138–40

Medley D M, Coker H, Soar R S 1984 *Measurement-based Evaluation of Teacher Performance: An Empirical Approach.* Longman, New York

Quirk T J, Witten B J, Weinberg S F 1973 Review of studies of the concurrent and predictive validity of the National Teacher Examinations. *Rev. Educ. Res.* 43: 89–113

Further Reading

Bell L (ed.) 1988 *Appraising Teachers in Schools: A Practical Guide.* Routledge, London

Gorth W P, Chernoff M L 1985 *Testing for Teacher Certification.* Lawrence Erlbaum Associates, Hillsdale, New Jersey

Millman J, Darling-Hammond L 1990 *The New Handbook of Teacher Evaluation: Assessing Elementary and Secondary School Teachers.* Sage Publications, Newbury Park, California

Mitchell J V, Wise S L, Plake B S 1990 *Assessment of Teaching: Purposes, Practices, and Implications for the Profession.* Lawrence Erlbaum Associates, Hillsdale, New Jersey

Poster C, Poster D, Benington M 1991 *Teacher Appraisal: A Guide to Training.* Routledge, London

Smith D C (ed.) 1983 *Essential Knowledge for Beginning Educators.* ERIC Clearinghouse on Teacher Education, Washington, DC

Wragg E C 1987 *Teacher Appraisal: A Practical Guide.* Macmillan Education, Basingstoke

Student Evaluation of Teaching

H. W. Marsh

Students' evaluations of teaching effectiveness (SETs) are commonly collected in United States and Canadian universities, are widely endorsed by teachers, students, and administrators, and have stimulated thousands of studies. Considered here are the purposes for collecting SETs, SET dimensions, issues of reliability, validity and generalizability, potential biases in SETs, and the use of SETs for improving teaching effectiveness. (For earlier reviews see Marsh 1987, Marsh and Dunkin 1992.)

1. Purposes for Collecting SETs

Various SETs are collected to provide: (a) diagnostic feedback to faculty for the improvement of teaching; (b) a measure of teaching effectiveness for personnel decisions; (c) information for students for the selection of courses and instructors; (d) an outcome or a process description for research on teaching. The first purpose is nearly universal, but the next three are not. At many universities, systematic student input is required before faculty are even considered for promotion; at others the inclusion of SETs is optional or not encouraged at all. The results of SETs are sold to students in some university bookstores as an aid to the selection of courses or instructors, whereas at other universities the results are considered to be strictly confidential. Surprisingly, SET research has not been systematically incorporated into broader studies of teaching and learning (see Marsh and Dunkin 1992).

2. Dimensions of SETs

Because effective teaching is a multidimensional construct (e.g., a teacher may be organized but lack enthusiasm), it is not surprising that SETs are also multidimensional (Marsh 1987, Marsh and Dunkin 1992). Information from SETs depends upon the content of the items. Poorly worded or inappropriate items will not provide useful information. If a survey instrument contains an ill-defined mix of items and SETs are summarized by an average of these items, then there is no basis for knowing what is being measured. Careful attention should be given to the components of teaching effectiveness that are to be measured.

Marsh and Dunkin (1992) noted three overlapping approaches to constructing and evaluating multidimensional SET instruments: (a) empirical approaches such as factor analysis and multitrait–multimethod analysis; (b) logical analyses of the content of effective teaching and the purposes the ratings are intended to serve, supplemented by reviews of previous research and feedback from students and instructors; and (c) a theory of teaching and learning. In practice, most instruments are based on the first two approaches—particularly the second. The literature on SETs contains examples of instruments that have a well-defined factor structure, such as the four instruments presented by Marsh (1987). Factor analyses have identified the factors that each of these instruments is intended to measure, demonstrating that SETs do measure distinct components of teaching effectiveness. The systematic approach used in developing these instruments, and the similarity of the factors they measure, support their construct validity.

The strongest support for the multidimensionality of SETs comes from research based on the nine-factor SEEQ (Students' Evaluations of Educational Quality) instrument (Marsh 1987). The SEEQ factors are: learning/value; instructor enthusiasm; organization/clarity; group interaction; individual rapport; breadth of coverage; examinations/grading; assignments/readings; and workload/difficulty. Developers of the SEEQ relied on four sources of information. First, a large item pool was obtained from a literature review, forms in current usage, and interviews with faculty and students about what they saw as effective teaching. Second, students and faculty were asked to rate the importance of items. Third, faculty were asked to judge the potential usefulness of the items as a basis for feedback. Finally, open-ended student comments were examined to determine if important aspects had been excluded. These criteria, along with psychometric properties, were used to select items and revise subsequent versions, thus supporting the content validity of SEEQ responses. (The SEEQ scales are summarized in Table 1.) Marsh and Dunkin (1992) also demonstrated that the content of SEEQ factors is consistent with general principles of teaching and learning.

Factor analytic support for the SEEQ scales is particularly strong. Marsh and Hocevar (1991b), starting with an archive of 50,000 sets of class-average ratings (reflecting responses to 1 million SEEQ surveys), defined 21 groups of classes that differed in terms of course level (undergraduate/graduate), instructor rank (teaching assistant/regular faculty), and academic discipline. The nine *a priori* SEEQ factors were identifiable in each of 21 separate factor analyses. The average correlation between factor scores based on each separate analysis and factor scores based on the total sample was over 0.99. In other research, instructors evaluated their own teaching effectiveness on the same SEEQ form as completed by their students; factor analyses of their self-evaluations also identified the nine SEEQ factors (see Marsh 1987 p. 295). Six studies conducted in Australia, New Zealand, Spain, and Papua New Guinea (see Marsh and Dunkin 1992) provided support for the applicability of SEEQ factors outside the North American context in which they were developed.

Feldman (1976) logically derived the components of effective teaching by categorizing the characteristics of the superior teacher from the student's point of view. He reviewed research that either asked students to specify these characteristics or inferred them on the basis of correlations with global SETs. In a content analysis of factors identified in well-defined multidimensional SET instruments, Marsh (1987) demonstrated that Feldman's categories tended to be more narrowly defined constructs than the empirical factors. Whereas SEEQ provided a more comprehensive coverage of Feldman's categories than other SET instruments considered, most SEEQ factors represented more than one of Feldman's categories (e.g., Feldman's categories "stimulation of interest" and "enthusiasm" were both included in the SEEQ "instructor enthusiasm" factor).

In summary, the debate about which specific components of teaching effectiveness can and should be measured has not been resolved. At the same time, however, there seems to be consistency in those components that are identified in responses to the most carefully designed instruments such as SEEQ. Such instruments, apparently, are applicable to a wide variety of educational settings.

3. Reliability, Stability, and Generalizability

Careful design is an important element of a sound, useful instrument for measuring SETs. The reliability,

Table 1
Categories of effective teaching[a]

Feldman's categories	SEEQ factors
1) Stimulation of interest	Instructor enthusiasm
2) Enthusiasm	Instructor enthusiasm
3) Subject knowledge	Breadth of coverage
4) Intellectual expansiveness	Breadth of coverage
5) Preparation and organization	Organization/clarity
6) Clarity and understandableness	Organization/clarity
7) Elocutionary skills	None
8) Sensitivity to class progress	None
9) Clarity of objectives	Organization/clarity
10) Value of course materials	Assignments/readings
11) Supplementary materials	Assignments/readings
12) Perceived outcome/impact	Learning/value
13) Fairness, impartiality	Examinations/grading
14) Classroom management	None
15) Feedback to students	Examinations/grading
16) Class discussion	Group interaction
17) Intellectual challenge	Learning/value
18) Respect for students	Individual rapport
19) Availability/helpfulness	Individual rapport
20) Difficulty/workload	Workload/difficulty

a Adapted From Feldman (1976) and the Students' Evaluations of Educational Quality (SEEQ) and endeavor factors most closely related to each category

stability, and generalizability of the responses made to the instrument by students also form a critical element.

3.1 Reliability

The reliability of SETs is most appropriately determined from studies that assess the error caused by lack of agreement among different students enrolled in the same course (see Gilmore et al. 1978 for further discussion). The correlation between responses made by any two students in the same class (i.e., the single rater reliability) is typically in the 0.20s. However, the reliability of the class-average response depends upon the number of students rating the class: 0.95 for 50 students, 0.90 for 25 students, 0.74 for 10 students, and 0.60 for five students. Given a sufficient number of students, then, the reliability of class-average SETs compares favorably with that of the most objective tests (Marsh 1987).

3.2 Stability

Cross-sectional studies typically report that SETs are negatively related to age and years of teaching experience (Feldman 1983). This effect may vary somewhat with the particular SETs dimension and there is some suggestion that SETs may increase slightly during the first few years of teaching. Cross-sectional studies, however, provide a poor basis for inferring how ratings of the same person will change over time. In a longitudinal study, Marsh and Hocevar (1991a) examined

changes in ratings of a diverse sample of 195 teachers who had been evaluated continuously over a 13-year period. They found that the mean ratings for this sample showed almost no systematic changes in any of the SEEQ factors. This result held for teachers with little, intermediate, or substantial amounts of teaching experience.

3.3 Generalizability

Some critics have suggested that students cannot recognize effective teaching until they have been called upon to apply what they have learned in further coursework or after graduation. However, cross-sectional studies show good agreement between responses by current students and alumni (see Marsh 1987, Centra 1979). For example, in a longitudinal study (Marsh 1987) ratings in 100 classes correlated 0.83 with ratings by the same students when they again evaluated the same classes retrospectively several years later.

Researchers have also asked how highly correlated SETs are in different courses taught by the same instructor or in the same course taught by different teachers. The results demonstrate that the results of SETs are primarily due to the instructor who teaches a class and not the particular class being taught. For example, Marsh (1987) reported that for the overall instructor rating, the correlation between ratings of different instructors teaching the same course was virtually zero (−0.05), while correlations for the same instructor in different courses (0.61) and in two different offerings of the same course (0.72) were much larger. These results support the validity of SETs as a measure of teacher effectiveness, but not as a measure of course effectiveness independent of the teacher.

Gilmore et al. (1978), applying generalizability theory to SETs, suggested that ratings for a given instructor should be averaged across different courses to enhance generalizability. If it is likely that an instructor will teach many different classes during his or her subsequent career, then tenure decisions should be based upon as many different courses as possible—Gilmore et al. suggest at least five. These recommendations require that a longitudinal archive of SETs is maintained for personnel decisions. These data would provide the basis for more generalizable summaries, the assessment of changes over time, and the determination of which particular courses are best taught by a specific instructor. It is indeed unfortunate that some universities systematically collect SETs but then fail to keep a longitudinal archive of the results.

3.4 Generalizability of Profiles

Marsh and Bailey (1993) used profile analysis to demonstrate that each teacher has a characteristic profile on the nine SEEQ scores (e.g., consistently high on organization and consistently low on enthusiasm). For each teacher who had been evaluated continuously over a 13-year period a characteristic profile of SEEQ scores was determined by averaging across all his or her ratings. Each instructor's characteristic profile was distinct from the profiles of other instructors, generalized across course offerings over the 13-year period, and generalized across undergraduate- and graduate-level courses. This support for the existence of instructor-specific profiles has important implications for the use of SETs as feedback and for the relation of SETs to other criteria such as student learning. The results also provide further support for the multidimensionality of SETs and their generalizability.

4. Validity

Once the development of the instrument and the reliability of the responses have been examined, attention must turn next to the validity of the responses. There are several ways of investigating and estimating validity.

4.1 The Construct Validation Approach

SETs, as one measure of teaching effectiveness, are difficult to validate since no single criterion of effective teaching is sufficient. Historically, researchers have emphasized a narrow, criterion-related approach to validity in which student learning is the only criterion of effective teaching. This limited framework, however, inhibits a better understanding of what is being measured by SETs, what can be inferred from SETs, and how findings from diverse studies can be understood within a common framework. Instead, Marsh (1987) advocated a construct validation approach in which SETs are posited to be positively related to a wide variety of other indicators of effective teaching. In this approach, specific rating factors are hypothesized to be most highly correlated with variables to which they are most logically and theoretically related. Within this framework, evidence for the long-term stability of SETs, the generalizability of ratings of the same instructor in different courses, and the agreement in ratings of current students and alumni can be interpreted as support for the validity of SETs.

Whereas the most widely accepted criterion of effective teaching is student learning, other criteria include changes in student behaviors, instructor self-evaluations, ratings by colleagues and administrators, the frequency of occurrence of specific behaviors observed by trained observers, and the effects of experimental manipulations. A construct validity approach to the study of SETs now appears to be widely accepted (e.g., Cashin 1988, Howard et al. 1985). A difficulty in this approach is obtaining criterion measures that are reliably measured and validly reflect effective teaching. Generally, criterion measures that lack reliability or validity should not be used as indicators of effective teaching for research, policy formation, feedback to faculty, or personnel decisions.

4.2 The Multisection Validity Study

Student learning inferred from standardized examinations typically cannot be compared across different courses. In the multisection validity paradigm, such a comparison may be possible. An ideal study within this paradigm should include the following characteristics: (a) there should be many sections within a large multisection course; (b) students should be randomly assigned to sections so as to minimize initial differences between sections; (c) there should be pretest measures that correlate substantially with final course performance to serve as covariates;(d) each section should be taught completely by a separate instructor; (e) each section should have the same course outline, textbooks, course objectives, and final examination; (f) the final examination should be constructed to reflect common objectives and, if there is a subjective component, it should be graded by an external person; (g) students in each section should evaluate teaching effectiveness on a standardized evaluation instrument, preferably before they know their final course grade and without knowing how performances in their section compare with those of students in other sections; and (h) section-average SETs should be related to section-average examination performance, after controlling for pretest measures.

Despite methodological problems (Abrami et al. 1990, Marsh and Dunkin 1992), meta-analyses of multisection validity research have supported the validity of the SETs by demonstrating that the sections that evaluate the teaching as most effective near the end of the course are also the sections that perform best on standardized final examinations. Cohen (1987), in his summary of 41 "well-designed" studies, reported that the mean correlations between achievement and different SET components were structure (0.55), interaction (0.52), skill (0.50), overall course (0.49), overall instructor (0.45), learning (0.39), rapport (0.32), evaluation (0.30), feedback (0.28), interest/motivation (0.15), and difficulty (−0.04), in which all but the last two were statistically significant. Feldman (1989b) extended this research by demonstrating that many of Cohen's broad categories were made up of more specific components of SETs that are differentially related to student achievement. Thus, for example, Cohen's broad "skill" category was represented by three dimensions in Feldman's analysis that correlated with achievement 0.34 (instructor subject knowledge), 0.56 (clarity and intelligibility), and 0.30 (sensitivity to class level and progress). Cohen (1987) also reported that correlations were higher when specific SET components were measured with multi-item scales instead of single items.

4.3 Multiple Evaluators

Teaching effectiveness can be evaluated by current students, former students, the instructor himself or herself, colleagues, administrators, or trained external observers. Instructors can be asked to evaluate themselves in a wide variety of educational settings, even using the same instrument used by their students to provide tests of convergent and divergent validity. Despite the apparent appeal of instructor self-evaluation as a criterion of effective teaching, it has had limited application. Feldman's (1989b) meta-analysis of correlations between SETs and self-evaluations, based on only 19 studies, reported a mean correlation of 0.29 for overall ratings and mean correlations ranging from 0.15 to 0.42 for specific SET components. Marsh apparently conducted the only two studies in which large numbers of instructors (81 and 329) were asked to evaluate their own teaching on the same multifaceted evaluation instrument that was completed by students (see Marsh 1987 p. 295). In both studies: (a) separate factor analyses of SETs and self-evaluations identified the same SEEQ factors (see Table 1); (b) student–teacher agreement on every dimension was significant (median correlations of 0.49 and 0.45) and typically larger than agreement on overall teaching effectiveness (correlations of 0.32); (c) mean differences between student and faculty responses were small and unsystematic; and (d) multitrait–multimethod analyses provided support for both convergent and discriminant validity of the ratings.

Colleague and administrator ratings not based upon classroom visitation have been sometimes substantially correlated with SETs, but it is likely that peer ratings are based on information from students (Marsh 1987, Marsh and Dunkin 1992). In contrast, colleague and administrator ratings based on classroom visitation do not appear to be very reliable (i.e., ratings by different peers do not even agree with each other) or to correlate substantially with SETs or with any other indicator of effective teaching (see Marsh 1987, Centra 1979). While these findings neither support nor refute the validity of SETs, they suggest that the colleague and administrator ratings based on classroom visitation are not valid indicators of teacher effectiveness (see also Murray 1980).

Murray (1980) concluded that SETs outcomes "can be accurately predicted from external observer reports of specific classroom teaching behaviors" (p. 31). For example, Cranton and Hillgartner (1981) examined relationships between SETs and specific teaching behaviors observed on videotaped lectures in a naturalistic setting. They found that (a) SETs reports on effectiveness of discussion were higher "when professors praised student behavior, asked questions and clarified or elaborated student responses"; and that (b) SETs outcomes on organization were higher "when instructors spent time structuring classes and explaining relationships" (p. 73).

In one of the most ambitious observation studies, Murray (1983) trained observers to estimate the frequency of occurrence of specific teaching behaviors of 54 university instructors who had previously obtained high, medium, or low SETs in other classes. A total of 18 to 24 sets of observer reports were collected for each instructor. The median of single-rater reliabilities (i.e., the correlation between two sets of observational reports) was 0.32, but the median reliability for the average response across the 18–24 reports for each instructor was 0.77. Factor analysis of the observations revealed nine factors, and their content resembled factors in SETs described earlier (e.g., clarity, enthusiasm, interaction, rapport, organization). The observations significantly differentiated among the three criterion groups of instructors.

Unfortunately, Murray only considered SETs on an overall instructor rating item, and these were based upon ratings from a previous course rather than the one that was observed. Hence, multitrait–multimethod analyses could not be used to determine if specific observational factors were most highly correlated with matching student-rating factors. The findings did show, however, that instructors who are rated differently by students do exhibit systematically different observable teaching behaviors.

Howard et al. (1985) compared multiple indicators of teaching effectiveness for 43 teachers who were each evaluated in one course by current students in the course (mean N = 34 per class), former students who had previously taken the same course or one selected by the instructor as being similar (minimum N = 5), one colleague who was knowledgeable of the course content and who attended two class sessions, and eight advanced graduate students specifically trained in judging teaching effectiveness who attended two class sessions. They concluded that "former-students and student ratings evidence substantially greater validity coefficients of teaching effectiveness than do self-report, colleague and trained observer ratings" (p. 195). Whereas self-evaluations were modestly correlated with current SETs (0.34) and former SETs (0.31), colleague and observer ratings were not significantly correlated with each other, current SETs, or self-evaluations (see also Feldman 1989a and the discussion of his review by Marsh and Dunkin 1992).

4.4 Other Criteria

A limited amount of research has related SETs to experimentally manipulated teaching situations. Studies of teacher clarity and teacher expressiveness (see reviews by Marsh 1987, Marsh and Dunkin 1992) demonstrated the important potential of this approach. Both of these variables are amenable to experimental and correlational designs, can be reliably judged by students and by external observers, are judged to be important components of teaching effectiveness by students and by teachers, and are related to student achievement in naturalistic and experimental studies. In experimental settings, scripted lessons which differ on these variables are videotaped and randomly assigned groups of subjects view different lectures, evaluate teaching effectiveness, and complete achievement tests. Manipulations of these variables are significantly related to SETs; specifically, they are more strongly related to matching SETs dimensions than to nonmatching SETs dimensions. These results support the inclusion of clarity and expressiveness on SETs instruments, demonstrate that SETs are sensitive to natural and experimentally manipulated differences in these variables, and support the construct validity of the multidimensional SETs.

Teaching and research are typically seen as the most important products of university faculty. Marsh (1987) contrasted opposing theoretical perspectives positing that indicators of the two activities should be positively correlated, negatively correlated, or uncorrelated. Research (see Centra 1983, Feldman 1987, Marsh 1987) suggests that there is a zero to low-positive correlation between measures of research productivity and SETs or other indicators of effective teaching, although correlations may be somewhat higher for student-rating dimensions that are most logically related to research effectiveness. While these findings seem neither to support nor refute the validity of SETs, they do demonstrate that measures of research productivity cannot be used to infer teaching effectiveness or vice versa.

Marsh (1987) also discusses the validity of SETs in relation to student motivation, affective criteria, subsequent coursework selection, student study strategies, and the quality of student learning. More generally, he argued that it is imperative to expand substantially the range of validity criteria used in SETs research (see also Marsh and Dunkin 1992).

4.5 Implications of Validity Research

Because effective teaching is a hypothetical construct for which there is no adequate single indicator, the validity of SETs or of any other measure of effective teaching must be demonstrated through a construct validation approach. SETs are significantly and consistently related to the ratings of former students, student achievement in multisection validity studies, faculty self-evaluations of their own teaching effectiveness, and, perhaps, the observations of trained observers on specific processes such as teacher clarity. In contrast, colleague and administrator ratings based on classroom visitation, and research productivity are not systematically related to SETs or other indicators of effective teaching, calling into question colleague and administrator ratings as measures of effective teaching.

5. Potential Biases in Students' Evaluations

To the extent that SETs are biased, it is important to understand the nature of the biases and how they can be controlled. However, the voluminous study of potential biases to SETs is frequently atheoretical,

methodologically flawed, and not based on a well-articulated definition of what constitutes a bias. Marsh (1987) reviewed several large-scale studies of the multivariate relationship between a comprehensive set of background characteristics and SETs. Depending upon the content of the SET items, between 5 and 25 percent of the variance in SETs could be explained by the background characteristics, perhaps the academic discipline, and perhaps the institution(s) where the study was conducted (see also Centra 1979).

In two comprehensive multivariate studies (see Marsh 1987), a set of 16 background characteristics explained about 13 percent of the variance in the set of SEEQ dimensions. However, the amount of variance explained varied from more than 20 percent in the overall course rating and the learning value dimension, to about 2 percent of the organization and individual rapport dimensions. Four background variables were most important and could account for most of the explained variance. They were higher prior subject interest, higher expected grades, higher levels of workload/difficulty, and a higher percentage of students taking the course for general interest only. Path analyses demonstrated that prior subject interest had the strongest impact on SETs, and that this variable also accounted for about one-third of the relationship between expected grades and SETs.

Even these relatively modest relations, however, apparently do not reflect biases. The workload/difficulty relation is in the opposite direction to that predicted by a bias. Prior subject interest primarily influences ratings of learning/value and overall course ratings; a similar pattern of relations was found with instructor self-evaluations of their own teaching effectiveness. Part of the expected grade relation is apparently spurious and is eliminated when prior subject interest is controlled. Furthermore, part of this relation apparently reflects a positive relation between student learning and SETs (see Marsh 1987, Marsh and Dunkin 1992).

Support for a bias hypothesis, as with the study of validity, must be based on a construct approach such as that proposed by Marsh and Dunkin (1992). If a particular background variable has a similar influence on multiple indicators of teaching effectiveness, then that background variable may reflect a valid influence on teaching effectiveness. Similarly, if the pattern of relations between a particular background variable and the multiple dimensions of SETs match *a priori* predictions, then the results may support the construct validity of the SETs instead of a bias.

For example, the SEEQ factors most logically related to class size are group interaction and individual rapport. Empirical results indicate that class size is moderately correlated with these two SEEQ factors and nearly uncorrelated with other SEEQ factors. A similar pattern is observed in instructor self-evaluations. These results suggest that class size actually does affect group interaction and individual rapport in a manner that is accurately reflected in SETs and instructor self-evaluations. Whereas a comprehensive review of potential biases is beyond the scope of this entry, perhaps the best summary of this area is McKeachie's (1979) conclusion that a wide variety of variables that could potentially influence SETs apparently has little effect.

6. *Utility of Student Ratings*

Using a series of related logical arguments, Braskamp et al. (1985), Marsh (1987), Marsh and Dunkin (1992), Murray (1987), and many others have argued that the introduction of a broad institutionally based, carefully planned program of SETs is likely to lead to the improvement of teaching. In support of his argument, Murray's (1987) summary of surveys from seven universities indicated that about two-thirds of faculty staff said that SETs were useful and about 80 percent indicated that SETs led to improved teaching.

None of these observations, however, provides an empirical demonstration of improvement of teaching effectiveness resulting from SETs. In most studies of the effects of feedback from SETs, teachers have been randomly assigned to experimental (feedback) or one or more control groups; SETs have been collected during the term; ratings of the feedback teachers have been returned to instructors as quickly as possible; and the various groups have been compared at the end of the term according to a second administration of SETs and sometimes on other variables as well. In his classic meta-analysis, Cohen (1980) found that instructors who received midterm feedback were subsequently rated about one-third of a standard deviation higher than controls on the total rating (an overall rating item or the average of multiple items), and even larger differences were observed for ratings of instructor skill, attitude toward subject, and feedback to students. Studies that augmented feedback with consultation produced substantially larger differences, but other methodological variations had little effect (see also L'Hommedieu et al. 1990).

The most robust finding from the feedback research reviewed here is that consultation augments the effects of written summaries of SETs, but insufficient attention has been given to determine the type of consultative feedback that is most effective.

Marsh and Roche (1993) evaluated a feedback/consultation intervention developed by Wilson (1986) and compared the effects of midterm and end-of-term feedback. Teachers completed self-evaluation surveys and were evaluated by students at the middle of semester 1 and at the end of semesters 1 and 2. Three randomly assigned groups received the feedback/consultation intervention at midterm of semester 1, at the end of semester 1, or received no intervention (control). Intervention teachers "targeted" specific SEEQ dimensions (e.g., Organization, Enthusiasm, Group Interaction) that became the focus of his/her individually struc-

tured intervention based on teaching improvement strategies developed for each dimension. The ratings for all groups improved over time, but ratings for end-of-term feedback was more effective than the midterm feedback. For the intervention groups, targeted dimensions improved more than nontargeted dimensions. The study further demonstrated that SET feedback coupled with consultation is an effective means to improve teaching effectiveness and provided a useful procedure for providing feedback/consultation. The specificity of the intervention effects to the targeted dimensions also provided further support for the multidimensionality of the SETs.

7. *Research in Primary and Secondary Classrooms*

This entry is based almost exclusively on research at tertiary level. Despite the voluminous research on teacher effectiveness at the primary and secondary levels, there is a dearth of appropriate SETs research—with a few notable exceptions. Whereas it is tempting to conclude that secondary and particularly primary students apparently lack the sophistication to evaluate teaching effectiveness appropriately, the results from several research programs suggest that this conclusion is false.

Aubrecht et al. (1986) specifically patterned their research on Marsh's university research to determine whether the findings generalized to the high school level. High school teachers and their students completed the commercially available high school version of the IDEA instrument. Factor analyses of both sets of responses revealed similar factor structures and MTMM analyses provided support for convergent and discriminant validity. Aubrecht et al. (1986) concluded that these results "provide support for the validity of high school student ratings of instruction" (p. 223) and predicted that SETs will find a place in high school merit pay systems and professional development activities as they have at university level.

Similarly, Fox et al. (1983) sought to test the generalizability of university findings to the elementary school level. For two consecutive years, 53 sixth-grade teachers were evaluated by their students and observed by different trained observers on multiple occasions. The class-average SETs were stable over the two years (r=0.68) and significantly related to each of the three observation scales (organized, stimulating, understanding) in each year of the study (with correlations ranging from 0.38 to 0.68). Noting the need for further research, Fox et al (1983) concluded that the SETs by sixth-grade students "appear to be reliable, valid, useful measures of teacher behavior" (p. 21) (see also Peck et al 1978).

There is clearly need for more research about SETs at the primary and secondary levels, but research programs summarized here suggest that results based on responses by university students may generalize to responses by younger students. Although not the focus of this entry, a provocative question is: why is there so much relevant SETs research at the tertiary level and so little at the primary and secondary levels?

8. Overview and Implications

Research described in this entry demonstrates that SETs are multidimensional, reliable, and stable, primarily a function of the instructor who teaches a course rather than the course that is taught, relatively valid against a variety of indicators of effective teaching, relatively unaffected by a variety of potential biases, and seen to be useful by faculty, students, and administrators. Researchers should adopt a construct validation approach in which the following points are recognized: that effective teaching and SETs designed to reflect teaching effectiveness are multidimensional; that no single criterion of effective teaching is sufficient; and that tentative interpretations of relations with validity criteria and with potential biases should be evaluated critically in different contexts and in relation to multiple criteria of effective teaching. In contrast to SETs, however, there are few other indicators of teaching effectiveness whose use is systematically supported by research findings. As Cashin noted (1988), "student ratings tend to be statistically reliable, valid, and relatively free from bias, probably more so than any other data used for faculty evaluation" (p. 5).

See also: Teacher Evaluation

References

Abrami P C, Cohen P A, d'Apollonia S 1990 Validity of student ratings of instruction: What we know and what we do not. *J. Educ. Psychol.* 82(2): 219–31
Aubrecht J D, Hanna G S, Hoyt D P 1986 A comparison of high school student ratings of teaching effectiveness with teacher self-ratings: Factor analytic and multitrait-multimethod analyses. *Educational and Psychological Measurement* 46(1): 223–31
Braskamp L A, Brandenburg D C, Ory J C 1985 *Evaluating Teaching Effectiveness: A Practical Guide.* Sage, Beverly Hills, California
Cashin W E 1988 Student ratings of teaching: A summary of research. IDEA paper No. 20, Kansas State University, Division of Continuing Education, Manhattan, Kansas ERIC Document Reproduction Service No. ED 302 567
Centra J A 1979 *Determining Faculty Effectiveness.* Jossey-Bass, San Francisco, California
Centra J A 1983 Research productivity and teaching effectiveness. *Res. Higher Educ.* 18(4): 379–89
Cohen P A 1980 Effectiveness of student-rating feedback for improving college instruction: A meta-analysis of findings. *Res. Higher Educ.* 13: 321–41
Cohen P A 1987 A critical analysis and reanalysis of the multisection validity meta-analysis. Paper presented at the 1987 Annual Meeting of the American Educational

Research Association, Washington, DC (ERIC Document Reproduction Service No. ED 283 876)
Cranton P A, Hillgarten W 1981 The relationships between student ratings and instructor behavior: Implications for improving teaching. *Can. J. Higher Ed.* 9(1): 73–81
Feldman K A 1976 The superior college teacher from the student's view. *Res. Higher Educ.* 5(3): 243–88
Feldman K A 1983 The seniority and instructional experience of college teachers as related to the evaluations they receive from their students. *Res. Higher Educ.* 18: 3–124
Feldman K A 1987 Research productivity and scholarly accomplishment of college teachers as related to their instructional effectiveness: A review and exploration. *Res. Higher Educ.* 26: 227–98
Feldman K A 1989a Instructional effectiveness of college teachers as judged by teachers themselves, current and former students, colleagues, administrators, and external (neutral) observers. *Res. Higher Educ.* 30(2): 137–94
Feldman K A 1989b Association between student ratings of specific instructional dimensions and student achievement: Refining and extending the synthesis of data from multisection validity studies. *Res. Higher Educ.* 30(6): 583–645
Fox R, Peck R F, Blattstein A, Blattstein D 1983 Student evaluation of teacher as a measure of teacher behavior and teacher impact on students. *J. Educ. Res.* 77(1): 16–21
Gillmore G M, Kane M T, Naccarato R W 1978 The generalizability of student ratings of instruction: Estimates of teacher and course components. *J. Educ. Meas.* 15(1): 1–13
Howard G S, Conway C G, Maxwell S E 1985 Construct validity of measures of college teaching effectiveness. *J. Educ. Psychol.* 77(2): 187–96
L'Hommedieu R, Menges R J, Brinko K T 1990 Methodological explanations for the modest effects of feedback. *J. Educ. Psychol.* 82(2): 232–41
Marsh H W 1987 Students' evaluations of university teaching: Research findings, methodological issues, and directions for future research. *International Journal of Educational Research* 11(3): 253–388
Marsh H W, Bailey M 1993 Multidimensionality of students' evaluations of teaching effectiveness: A profile analysis. *J. Higher Educ* 64(1): 1–18
Marsh H W, Dunkin M J 1992 Students' evaluations of university teaching: A multidimensional perspective. In: Smart J (ed.) 1992 *Higher Education: Handbook of Theory and Research.* Agathon, New York
Marsh H W, Hocevar D 1991a Students' evaluations of teaching effectiveness: The stability of mean ratings of the same teachers over a thirteen-year period. *Teaching and Teacher Education* 7(4): 303–14
Marsh H W, Hocevar D 1991b The multidimensionality of students' evaluations of teaching effectiveness: The generality of factor structures across academic discipline, instructor level, and course level. *Teaching and Teacher Education* 7(1): 9–18
Marsh H W, Roche L 1993 The use of students' evaluations and an individually structured intervention to enhance university teaching effectiveness. *Am. Educ. Res. J.* 30: 217–51
McKeachie W J 1979 Student ratings of faculty: A reprise. *Academe* 65(6): 384–97
Murray H G 1980 *Evaluating University Teaching: A Re-*

view of Research. Ontario Confederation of University Faculty Associations, Toronto

Murray H G 1983 Low inference classroom teaching behaviors and student ratings of college teaching effectiveness. *J. Educ. Psychol.* 71(1): 856–65

Murray H G 1987 Impact of student instructions ratings on quality of teaching in higher education. Paper presented at the 1987 Annual Meeting of the American Educational Research Association, Washington, DC. ERIC Document

Reproduction Service No. ED 284 495

Peck R F, Olsson N G, Green J L The consistency of individual teaching behavior. Paper presented at the 1978 Annual Meeting of the American Educational Research Association, Toronto. ERIC Document Reproduction Service No. ED 189 058

Wilson R C 1986 Improving faculty teaching: Effective use of student evaluations and consultants. *J. Higher Educ.* 57: 196–211

Classroom Observation

M. Galton

Structured observation, as used to monitor classroom events, requires an observer to assign such events to previously defined categories. These events may be recorded by mechanical means (e.g., film, audiotape, or videotape) and subsequently coded, or the observer can simultaneously record and code the events while present in the classroom. The three stages of the process therefore involve: (a) the recording of events in a systematic manner as they happen, (b) the coding of these events into prespecified categories, and (c) subsequent analysis of the events to give descriptions of teacher–pupil interaction.

Structured observation is also referred to as systematic observation or more particularly as interaction analysis, although the latter term is more typically applied to observation systems derived from the Flanders Interaction Analysis Category System (FIAC). According to Flanders (1964), interaction analysis is a "specialised research procedure that provides information about only a few of the many aspects of teaching and which analyses the content-free characteristics of verbal communication" (p. 198). Since, structured observation techniques have also been used to monitor nonverbal behaviors, Flanders's definition of the methodology is now seen to be too restrictive.

1. The Origins of Structured Observation

The origin of these observational techniques arose, in part, from the creation of the Committee of Child Development by the American National Research Council at the beginning of the 1920s. This committee sponsored research into teaching methods in nursery schools and kindergartens. Researchers found it necessary to observe these infants and record their behavior "as it happened." Initially, observers prepared diaries or narrative logs of the activities observed, but the sheer volume of descriptive material collected made the task a very arduous one. Olson (1929) introduced the notion of time sampling, whereby certain catego-

ries of behaviors were recorded at specified fixed intervals of time. An essential distinction used to classify behaviors by workers in the child development movement was that between direct teaching, where pupils were told what to do, and indirect teaching, where pupils were consulted and decisions reached by means of discussion and consensus.

By the early 1970s, an anthology of United States observation systems listed 92 instruments (Simon and Boyer 1970), the majority of which were derived from FIAC (Rosenshine and Furst 1973). The Flanders system has been widely criticized, however, for its limited applicability in that it was originally designed for relatively static classrooms where teachers stood in front of pupils who were arranged before them in rows while working on the same subject matter (Hamilton and Delamont 1974). With the increase of "open" or informal approaches to classroom organization, a greater variety of observational methods have been developed. In the 1980s, for example, a review of United Kingdom observation studies (Galton 1979) identified only two systems derived from FIAC. Most of this research had been carried out at the primary stage of schooling where informal approaches are more likely to be found. More recent discussion of the different methodologies can be found in Croll (1986) and Anderson and Burns (1989).

2. Characteristics of Structured Observation

Structured observation involves low-inference measurement (Rosenshine 1970) which requires the development of unambiguous criteria for assigning the various events into categories. Provided that the criteria are sufficiently explicit to be shared by different people, then different observers should arrive at identical descriptions of the same events. Thus an important requirement of a successful systematic observation system is high interobserver agreement.

Although the choice of categories and the definition

of the criteria may be highly subjective, reflecting the values of those who construct the system, the technique itself is objective in the sense that the criteria used to describe classroom life are clearly defined. Thus, when the system is used correctly it is unaffected by the personal biases of individual observers. This is in sharp contrast to ethnographic methods where the researcher, although sometimes claiming to take a total view of the classroom before gradually focusing on the more meaningful features (Hamilton and Delamont 1974), in practice can only offer a partial view because the criteria governing the selection are rarely available for consideration by others.

While Anderson and Burns (1989) contrast a number of approaches based upon different theoretical perspectives, most modern observation schedules are, in practice, combinations of category and sign systems (Croll 1986). The selection of behaviors for use in a sign system is dependent upon those which are thought to be most useful for the particular research purpose. In classroom research, such variables are usually selected because they are thought to be related to learning outcomes or to systematic differences between teachers and their pupils.

3. Data Collection

Galton (1987) lists a number of ways in which a permanent record of classroom events can be obtained, thereby enabling an observer to conduct a subsequent analysis under less pressurized circumstances than those that exist under conditions of live recording. The two most frequently used approaches involve tape and video recorders. There are advantages and disadvantages to such methods.

The availability of relatively cheap hand-held video recorders has increased the popularity of using this method to record classroom events. The method's main advantage is that it supplies permanent visual and sound records which can be played and replayed and then edited. Thus the likelihood of observer agreement during subsequent analysis is increased. Set against this advantage is the highly selective representation of the camera which does not inform the viewer of what is going on in other parts of the classroom. For example, a category such as *target pupil is interested in another pupil's work* would be difficult to code using a video recorder, since the viewer would be uncertain whether the pupil was looking elsewhere in the classroom at what was happening between the teacher and another pupil or whether the pupil was totally distracted.

In an attempt to overcome such difficulties two cameras are sometimes used, one focused on the teacher or pupil and the other using a wide-angle lens to provide a general view of the classroom. Such arrangements, however, can be potential sources of distraction for both pupils and teachers so that what is gained in reliability may be lost in validity.

Another method of producing visual cues is to use stop-frame photography with synchronized sound (Adleman and Walker 1974). The flexibility of such a system has been greatly increased by the use of radio microphones which allow the teacher to move freely around the classroom and reduce the problem of background noise (Bennett 1985). However, the process of transcribing the permanent record from a recording can be very tedious and time-consuming.

It is estimated that to transcribe one hour of audiotape takes nearly a week of an efficient typist's time. Research involving a large number of teachers will, therefore, tend to favor direct observation methods because of the costs of transcribing and processing the data. More importantly, when an observer records events "as they happen," the presence of the observer in the classroom over a period of time has the advantage of enabling him or her to appreciate the shared understanding which exists between pupils and teacher so that certain behaviors can more easily be interpreted. This understanding is particularly important when the investigation concerns aspects of teacher–pupil relationships where private jokes (see Adleman and Walker 1975) are a common feature.

The general view is that it is preferable, at least in the early stages of an investigation, to make use of permanent records only when the focus of interest is in the children's language. Detailed descriptions of the methodology involved in such studies are provided by Edwards and Westgate (1987).

4. Training Observers

According to Flanders (1967), one of the main problems of training observers in the use of systematic observation is "converting men into machines" (p. 158). The usual training technique is to concentrate on a few categories at a time using a teach–test and feedback–reteach cycle. Details of the process are given by Jasman (1980).

Anderson and Burns (1989) provide a number of suggestions for a comprehensive training program. They draw attention, in particular, to the advantage of systematic observation in not requiring highly qualified, experienced observers because the training tends to be more rigorous. The method is, therefore, eminently suitable when employing teachers, who often have greater credibility with colleagues in school.

Usually audiotape and videotape recordings are used to introduce the observer to the problems of classifying particular categories and at the end of a training session another tape can be used to test if the observers can achieve acceptable levels of agreement. It is important to provide simple examples initially, with the guarantee that most observers will obtain total mastery, since observers who fail to identify behaviors correctly during training can often develop hostile reactions to the observation instrument. It is also useful to provide observers with experience of coding under classroom conditions as soon as possible. As stated earlier, it is often difficult to identify the context in which a behavior takes place on videotape which in turn means that the decision about the use of a particular category is not as clear-cut as the trainer might wish.

Once the initial training has been completed, it is important to build into any observation study refresher periods in which the observers go over the categories and check their reliability. These periods protect against what is termed "observer drift," which occurs when observers, who have come to accept criteria which do not conform to their own view of a particular behavior, gradually modify the category definitions over time to fit their own view.

5. Reliability and Validity

Most studies use only observer agreement as a test of reliability. The simplest measure of agreement is the percentage of occasions on which a pair of observers agree. However, this does not allow for the fact that two observers who were coding categories at random would still code the same categories on certain occasions by chance. The Scott (1955) coefficient corrects for this chance effect and is a more rigorous test of reliability. A weakness of this method, however, is that it does not permit study of observer agreement in research using a number of teachers. Medley and Mitzel (1963) offer several designs, based upon analysis of variance, in which each teacher is visited on one occasion by two observers, with the pairing of observers organized so that different observers are paired on each visit. Such a design also allows the teacher stability coefficient to be estimated.

Croll (1986) argues that *absolute agreement*, where the individual coding decisions of the observer are correlated, is preferable to *marginal agreement*, where only the total frequency of each category is compared irrespective of how an observer arrived at this total. Some systems, however, notably those which use broad sampling procedures, prevent any calculation of absolute agreement in the manner recommended by Croll. Croll (1986) also warns against including within a reliability coefficient a number of categories which are described as part of a single variable, but which are not mutually exclusive. If multiple categories can be coded simultaneously, they should be treated as separate variables with separate coefficients (Harrop 1979).

If an observation instrument is to be used by researchers other than those who developed the instrument, then the question of interinvestigator agreement arises, since each group may achieve high levels of observer agreement but interpret the categories differently (Rosenshine and Furst 1973). Anderson and Burns (1989) argue that in certain cases objectivity, expressed as observer agreement, is less important than the question of objectivity viewed as a measure of observer detachment. In some cases differences between observers mask real differences in interpretation and need to be investigated. However, in most cases of structured observation, differences between observers are regarded as error. Some developers of observation systems provide videotape examples already coded so that new users can check their degree of agreement with the developers on a trial tape (Eggleston et al. 1975).

Many researchers concern themselves only with the face validity of the observation instrument, assuming that the definition of the categories is so clear-cut that validity may be assumed providing observer agreement is high. The more complex the observation instrument, however, the less advisable it is to take this face validity for granted. In this case a number of alternative procedures can be employed.

When cluster analysis is used to create a typology of teaching styles or pupil types, observers can be asked to write descriptive accounts (mini case studies) of the teachers and the appropriate pupils. These accounts can then be cross-referenced with the descriptions derived from the clusters. Such descriptions can also be fed back to the observed teachers who can be asked to identify their own particular style or recognize particular types of pupils present in their classrooms.

Where two different observation systems exist having a similar focus, they can be used in the same classroom to compare and contrast results. While this type of cross-validation is recommended by Rosenshine and Furst (1973), only a few studies have attempted this task. In the ORACLE study, however, both the teacher and the pupils were observed using two instruments and the asymmetry of classroom behavior from both the teachers' and pupils' perspective was contrasted (Galton et al. 1980). The same study also made it possible to compare and contrast the "real curriculum" as perceived through both the teachers' and the pupils' activity.

Anderson and Burns (1989) argue that in some contexts, notably the study of different subject matter, it may be more important to investigate the inconsistencies across classrooms rather than seeking to submerge or eliminate these differences. They argue that inconsistencies across occasions are more problematic than inconsistencies across classrooms because of the limited amount of data collected.

Anderson and Burns (1989) conclude that one of the most important tests of validity is the reception of the evidence by teachers. In this regard Anderson and Burns (1984) quote claims that teachers often remarked, after the presentation of the research findings, "You've been in my classrooms." Similar responses have been found in United Kingdom classrooms with respect to reports of research from the ORACLE and PRISMS studies (Galton et al. 1980, Galton and Patrick 1989).

503

6. Coding and Analysis

In any observation system, discrete analytic units must be used in order to code the behaviors. The simplest division is based on some form of time sampling, where the time unit may vary from three seconds, as used by Flanders, to five minutes as used in Medley and Mitzel's (1958) OSCAR schedule. Every system has its own ground rules which differentiate between the beginning and the end of successive time units and which deal with the problem of behaviors which overlap from one unit to the next. It is important to choose time units so that observed behaviors do not regularly overlap into the next unit since, when this happens, it is found that the degree of agreement between observers decreases rapidly. Observer agreement is also improved when a steady rhythm of recording can be maintained.

Various methods exist for recording behavior and these are discussed in some detail by Croll (1986). These include event sampling (which records a particular event whenever it occurs), instantaneous time sampling (where only events occurring at a particular pretimed interval are recorded), scanning (where the number of individuals within a class who are engaged in a particular activity is recorded at pre-timed intervals), and continuous recording (where an ongoing record is made and the exact time in which a change in activity takes place noted). Finally, there exists a little-used method, one–zero time sampling, where only the first occurrence of a particular event within a given time interval is recorded.

With time sampling methods the extent to which the sample of behavior recorded is representative of the total behavior that occurred during a lesson is clearly dependent on the length of the interval between recordings. If the period is too short, the observers are likely to make mistakes; if the time interval is too long, they may record the behavior accurately but underestimate its overall frequency.

Consequently, when difficult and complex decisions have to be made by the observer, some researchers have preferred to use one–zero time sampling procedure, where the observer records the behavior only once as it occurs within a given time unit. If the time interval is short, then one–zero time sampling approximates to continuous recording of a classroom activity. With longer time intervals—for example, five minute units as used by Eggleston et al. (1975)—only the minimum frequency of occurrence is recorded. Such data, therefore, cannot be used to estimate the overall occurrence of individual categories within the classroom.

Criticisms of one–zero time sampling by Croll (1986) and Dunkerton (1981) are essentially correct in arguing that such systems are unsatisfactory in describing general aspects of classroom behavior. However, in cases where behaviors which discriminate among teachers are very infrequent, as for example in science lessons where it was rare to find teachers encouraging pupils to hypothesize (Eggleston et al. 1975), the method has some advantages in that it discriminates among teachers while, at the same time, allowing the observer sufficient time to recognize and code these infrequent complex interactions.

Critics of this type of coding system have been distracted from its prime purpose because such schedules still retain a number of frequently used categories. The presence of such categories is, however, irrelevant to the purpose for which the schedule is designed. Commonly occurring categories are included primarily to aid reliability, since observers who are not able to code continuously tend to become anxious, with the result that their concentration and reliability decreases. Such systems do, however, have very limited application. They are only preferable in cases where the complexity and variety of behaviors within the observation system require that the observer be given time to reach decisions in more difficult coding areas.

The simplest approaches to analysis operate at a descriptive level and are concerned with an estimation of either the frequency of occurrence of different events or the proportions of time taken up by different activities. The latter analysis is usually the product of time sampling systems.

More sophisticated schedules can be developed which allow the exact moment in time when a particular event occurs to be determined. Time sampling systems, provided the interval is very short, can also be used to determine the sequence of events taking place, since the observer is, in effect, recording a change of category rather than sampling a behavior within a defined period.

Recording a new behavior every time a different category is used employs the use of what are termed "naturalistic units." Here the problem for the researcher is to define a set of rules which will identify the unit of classroom transaction which can be coded under a particular category. Smith and Meux (1962) defined these natural units as "episodes" and "monologues," where an episode involved more than one speaker and a monologue identified a solo performance. The ground rules for identifying the nature of the transaction, however, make it difficult, if not impossible, for an observer to use such a system live in a classroom. For this reason, naturalistic units are most frequently used for the analysis of transcribed recordings. Observers can play and replay recordings until general agreement is obtained on the classification of each transaction.

When naturalistic units are used, the total number of episodes represents the total recorded behavior, since one tally only is made for each episode. In such a case, some record of the sequence of events can be obtained, but the most usual practice is to count the number of recorded tallies for each category and to divide this number by the total number of analytic units observed. With naturalistic units, this ratio closely represents the proportion of the total behavior occurring in a particular category. With longer time units, when a point–time sampling procedure is used, the ratio of the sum of tallies in a particular category compared to the total number of tallies recorded can again be interpreted as a proportion of total behavior.

One–zero time sampling methods in which frequently occurring events may only be coded once during a time unit can give no absolute value for the frequency of the particular behavior. Instead, an estimate of the minimum frequency of occurrence is obtained by dividing the total number of tallies obtained for a category by the total number of observation units.

The simplest analytic approach is that of Flanders (1964). Using a 10×10 matrix, the position of each subsequent event can be coded relative to the preceding interaction. Attempts to extend these procedures beyond the two category model have not been successful. For this reason Croll (1986) suggests the use of developmental profiles.

Anderson and Burns (1989) raise a number of important issues involved in the analysis of quantifiable data such as those obtained from structured observation, specifically the procedures for data aggregation and data reduction and the methods used to establish relationships between different variables. Croll (1986) also discusses a number of multivariate analyses which can be used to interpret observational data, including the use of multiple regression and the analysis of covariance in conducting analysis of the relationships between the observation processes and classroom products such as standardized tests.

With transcribed accounts of lessons, either from videotape or audiotape, greater attention can be paid to the sequential character of exchanges between teacher and pupils. Once suitable units of transcript have been identified, then different patterns in the sequence of these units can be observed. Unfortunately, researchers have tended to use different units for this analysis. The "episode" developed by Smith and Meux (1962) became the "incident" in Nuthall and Lawrence's (1965) study, while others have defined "pedagogical moves" (Bellack et al. 1966). Comparison between different studies is therefore difficult and although it is attractive to believe that effective teaching will eventually be explained in terms of sequential behavior rather than simple frequency units, there has been little progress in this direction since the early 1970s.

7. General Conclusions

In spite of these difficulties, there remains a continued interest in the collection of systematic observational data. Reviews of research on teaching in the United States list a large number of studies which have been carried out since the publication of Rosenshine's review (Rosenshine and Furst 1973). According to Brophy and Good (1986), there is now firm evidence about the most effective teaching strategies for improving pupil performance when measured on standardized tests of reading, language, and mathematical computation. Similar evidence has emerged from studies in the United Kingdom (Galton 1989), although Rosenshine warns that the more complex the intellectual activity the less likely are these direct instructional procedures to be effective. Subsequently (e.g., Galton and Patrick 1990), observational research has concentrated less on teaching behaviors and has instead examined aspects of the curriculum, supporting the view of Anderson and Burns (1989) that the instructional task, particularly the nature of its subject matter, largely determines the frequency and type of teacher–student interaction.

For the future, research is likely to concentrate on two major areas. The first of these concerns itself with models of teacher development. A large amount of research in the 1990s has concentrated on establishing differences between novice and expert teachers (Berliner 1992). However, little information exists about the intervening stages of development. As a consequence, the design and use of structured observation systems which will discriminate between these different stages is likely to assume greater importance. Second, the political attention given to reward systems for teachers based upon related performance criteria means that structured observation systems will increasingly play a part in both systems of appraisal and in school inspection to the neglect of more important issues concerning pupil learning strategies.

References

Adelman C, Walker R 1974 Stop-frame cinematography with synchronized sound: A technique for recording in school classrooms. *Journal of the Society of Motion and Picture and Television Engineering* 83: 189–91

Adelman C, Walker R 1975 *A Guide to Classroom Observation*. Routledge, London

Anderson L, Burns R 1989 *Research in Classrooms*. Pergamon Press, Oxford

Bellack A A, Hyman R T, Smith F L, Kliebard H M 1966 *The Language of the Classroom*. Teachers College Press, Columbia University, New York

Bennett N 1985 Interaction and achievement in classroom groups. In: Bennett N, Deforges C (eds.) 1985 *Recent Advances in Classroom Research* monograph No 2, *British Journal of Educational Psychology*. Scottish Academic Press, Edinburgh

Berliner D 1992 Some characteristics of experts in the pedagogical domain. In: Oser F, Dick A, Patry J (eds.) 1992 *Effective and Responsible Teaching: The New Synthesis*. Jossey-Bass, San Francisco, California

Brophy J, Good T 1986 Teacher behaviour and student achievement. In: Wittrock M (ed.) 1986 *Handbook of Research on Teaching*, 3rd edn. Macmillan, New York

Croll P 1986 *Systematic Classroom Observation*. Falmer Press, London

Dunkerton J 1981 Should classroom observation be quantitative? *Educ. Res.* 23: 144–51

Edwards T, Westgate D 1987 *Investigating Classroom Talk.* Falmer Press, London

Eggleston J F, Galton M J, Jones M E 1975 *A Science Teaching Observation Schedule.* Macmillan, London

Flanders N A 1964 Some relationships among teacher influence, pupil attitudes and achievement. In: Biddle B J, Ellena W J (eds.) 1964 *Contemporary Research on Teacher Effectiveness.* Holt, Rinehart, and Winston, New York

Flanders N A 1967 Problems of observer training and reliability. In: Amidon E J, Hough J E (eds.) 1967 *Interaction Analysis: Theory, Research and Applications.* Addison-Wesley, Reading, Massachusetts

Galton M 1979 Systematic classroom observation: British research *Educ. Res.* 21: 109–15

Galton M 1987 An ORACLE chronicle: A decade of classroom research. *Teaching and Teacher Education* 3(4): 229–312

Galton M 1989 *Teaching in the Primary School.* David Fulton, London

Galton M, Patrick H (eds.) 1990 *Curriculum Provision in the Small Primary School.* Routledge, London

Galton M, Simon B, Croll P 1980 *Inside the Primary Classroom.* Routledge and Kegan Paul, London

Hamilton D, Delamont S 1974 Classroom research: A cautionary tale. *Res. Educ.* 11: 1–15

Harrop L 1990 Unreliability of classroom observation. *Educ. Res.* 21(3): 207–11

Jasman A 1980 Training observers in the use of system-atic observation techniques. In: Galton M, Simon B, Croll P 1980

Medley D M, Mitzel H E 1958 A technique for measuring classroom behavior. *J. Educ. Psychol.* 49: 86–93

Medley D M, Mitzel H E 1963 Measuring classroom behavior by systematic observation. In: Gage N L (ed.) 1963 *Handbook of Research on Research on Teaching: A Project of the American Educational Research Association.* Rand McNally, Chicago, Illinois

Nuthall G A, Lawrence P J 1965 *Thinking in the Classroom: The Development of a Method of Analysis.* New Zealand Council for Educational Research, Wellington

Olson W C 1929 *The Measurement of Nervous Habits in Normal Children.* University of Minnesota Press, Minneapolis, Minnesota

Rosenshine B 1970 Evaluation of classroom instruction. *Rev. Educ. Res.* 40: 279–300

Rosenshine B, Furst N 1973 The use of direct observation to study teaching. In: Travers R M W (ed.) 1973 *Second Handbook of Research on Teaching: A Project of the American Educational Research Association.* Rand McNally, Chicago, Illinois

Scott W A 1955 Reliability of content analysis: The case of nominal coding. *Public Opinion Questionnaire* 19: 321–25

Simon A, Boyer E G (eds.) 1974 *Mirrors for Behavior: An Anthology of Classroom Observation Instruments.* Research for Better Schools, Philadelphia, Pennsylvania

Smith B O, Meux M 1962 *A Study of the Logic of Teaching.* Bureau of Educational Research, University of Illinois, Urbana, Illinois

Comparative and International Studies of Teaching and Teacher Education

M. J. Dunkin

Comparative and international research on teaching examines similarities and differences in behavior among teachers from different systems of education from different countries. It also investigates whether influences upon teaching vary from one system or country to another and whether the effects of teaching behaviors and practices also vary from system to system and country to country.

Dunkin (1989) described the different types of research that contribute information of the above types and reviewed relevant research that had been reported up to that time. Most of the studies he discussed had been conducted under the auspices of the International Association for the Evaluation of Educational Achievement (IEA). Since then a new generation of IEA studies has been completed and two of them have had their reports published—*The IEA Study of Mathematics* (Robitaille and Garden 1989, Travers and Westbury 1989) and *The IEA Classroom Environment Study* (Anderson et al. 1989). This entry focuses upon those studies.

1. The Second IEA Study of Mathematics

Although this study was essentially of mathematics curricula, it also involved some teacher and teaching variables. The two reports cited above contain material obtained from a total of 20 participating systems of schooling as follows—Belgium (Flemish system), Belgium (French), Canada (British Columbia), Canada (Ontario), England and Wales, Finland, France, Hong Kong, Hungary, Israel, Japan, Luxembourg, the Netherlands, New Zealand, Nigeria, Scotland, Swaziland, Sweden, Thailand, and the United States of America. Two target populations of students were defined, Population A and Population B.

Population A consists of all students in the grade in which the modal number of students has attained the age of 13.0–13.11 years by the middle of the school year. Population B consists of all students who are in the normally accepted terminal grade of the secondary school system, and who are studying mathematics as a substantial part (approximately 5 hours per week) of their academic program (Travers and Westbury 1989 p. 11).

Data for the study were gathered between 1980 and 1982 and included the following teacher variables: age, gender, experience, teaching loads (hours per week), education and qualifications (especially in mathematics, mathematics pedagogy, and general pedagogy), degree of specialization, and teaching practices involving the use of resources, teaching activities, allocation of time, and differentiation of instruction, and teachers' perceptions of opportunity to learn mathematics content included in the achievement tests.

Some of the findings for these variables were as follows. The proportion of male teachers ranged for Population A from 20 percent in Hungary to 90 percent in the Netherlands. In Canada (Ontario), Hong Kong, New Zealand, and Scotland, male teachers outnumbered female teachers by between 10 percent and 50 percent, while in Canada (British Columbia), Japan, Luxembourg, the Netherlands, Nigeria, and Sweden, male teachers predominated to a great extent. In three systems—Hungary, Israel, and Thailand— more than 50 percent of the teachers were female. For Population B the balance ranged from 40 percent male in Hungary to 96 percent. In the 15 systems which participated in the study of this population the trend was toward greater proportions of male teachers at this upper level. Robitaille and Garden (1989) commented on these findings as follows: "With such marked gender differences in the composition of the mathematics teaching force in some systems, there is rich ground for investigation of the societal pressures which lead to this situation and of the consequences for mathematics education" (p. 42).

The least experienced Population A teachers came from Swaziland and Thailand, both of which averaged 7 years, and the most experienced came from Japan, averaging 17 years. For Population B the least experienced teachers were from Hong Kong on 9 years and the most experienced from Sweden on 18 years. Teaching loads were measured in terms of number of contact hours per week. These ranged on average from 13 in Belgium (French) to 22 hours in the Netherlands for Population A, and from 14 hours in Japan, Sweden, and Thailand to 21 hours in British Columbia and Scotland for Population B.

In 8 systems more than 10 percent of Population A teachers had not studied any mathematics at postsecondary level and in 6 systems 25 percent of teachers or more had undertaken no study of mathematics pedagogy at postsecondary level. An analysis of the mathematics preparation for Population B teachers produced similar results. In France, Canada (Ontario), Sweden, Hong Kong, and Swaziland large proportions (26%–47%) of Population A teachers had experienced formal training in general pedagogy, while in Sweden, Finland, and Hong Kong over 40 percent had had no such training at the level of

Population B. Mathematics teachers of Population A students in Nigeria, Scotland, Japan, Thailand, and Belgium (French) were specialists in between 70 and 96 percent of the cases, while almost none of them were in Canada (Ontario) and Sweden. Specialism at the Population B level was almost exclusively the case in Japan, Scotland, and Thailand but was not common in Sweden, Finland, and Hong Kong.

As regards the study of teaching practices, it was found that the most commonly used resource was the textbook which was used at least "often" by teachers in all systems for Population A. Individualized materials, visual materials, and published tests received very little use in almost all systems. Resource usage was similar for Population B. For population A, in Belgium (Flemish system) teachers spent a median period of 270 minutes in a typical week on preparation and grading. This ranged down to 60 minutes in Scotland. When marking and grading were expressed in terms of time per student, the greatest time was found in both Belgian systems, Thailand, and France, and the least in New Zealand, Scotland, Finland, Japan, and Sweden. Both preparation time and grading time were higher for Population B students.

Werry (1989) reported the findings for in-class teacher activities as follows:

> In every system and at both levels, most of the time is spent explaining new content, that is, in expository teaching or lecturing. This is especially true for Population B classes. In most systems, between 5 percent and 10 percent of the time in the four categories in Population A classes, on average, is spent on administrative matters, with slightly less in Population B classes. A similar amount of time is spent in maintaining order for Population A, but very little with Population B students . . .
>
> . . . It can be concluded . . . that expository, lecturing styles of teaching are relatively prominent in Belgium (Flemish), Hong Kong, and the United States, but rarer in England and Wales, Israel, Scotland, and Sweden. (p. 56)

The last two teaching activities studied were teachers' allocation of class time and differentiation of instruction. Teachers estimated that in a typical week tests and examinations took up 10 to 15 percent of students' time for both populations in most systems. Highest percentages were reported in France, Luxembourg, the Netherlands, Nigeria, Israel, and the United States, and least in England and Wales, Scotland, and Sweden. Small group work was not common at either level, with the greatest use of it being made with Population B in England and Wales, Israel, and Thailand. Seatwork and listening–discussion groups together accounted for over 70 percent of classroom time for both populations. More than 75 percent of the teachers at both levels claimed that they never or rarely used differentiated tasks for particular groups of students. The highest percentage of usage was in Swaziland and Nigeria, while the lowest was in Luxembourg, Hungary, and France for population A. In general, less use was made of differentiation in

Population B where the most common users were Hungary, New Zealand, and Thailand, and those making least use were Finland and Scotland.

Teachers from Hungary and Swaziland reported mean percentages of content coverage across the various subject domains of more than 80 percent for Population A classes. All the others reported mean coverage of between 61 and 80 percent, with the exception of Luxembourg and Sweden, where the mean reported coverage was between 41 and 60 percent. For population B classes, variations in teachers' perceptions of coverage of the items of the achievement tests varied greatly among the systems for the different subject domains. While teachers in all systems reported more than 80 percent coverage in algebra there was great variation, for example, in probability and statistics, for which coverage ranged from 40 percent or less in Hungary to over 80 percent in Finland, Japan, and New Zealand. Unfortunately, the main findings regarding teaching processes from the second IEA study of mathematics were not available at the time of writing this entry.

2. The IEA Study of Classroom Environments

The main report on this study is by Anderson et al. (1989), which presented findings from the following participating systems: Australia, Canada (Ontario/English system), Canada (Ontario/French), Canada (Quebec), Hungary, Israel, the Republic of Korea, the Netherlands, Nigeria, and Thailand. Essentially, this was a classroom observational study involving the 15 constructs shown in expected relationship with each other in Fig. 1, which depicts the "core model" of the study. Table 1 lists the specific variables for which data were obtained and analyzed. Table 2 provides an overview of the execution of the research, where it is shown that the grade level of the classes studied ranged

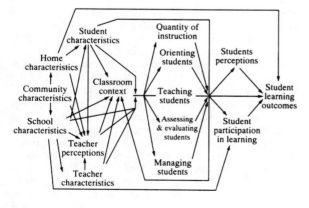

Figure 1
The core model of the classroom environment study
Source: Anderson et al. 1989 p. 23

from 5 to 8; the subject matter was mathematics in 7 of the systems but physics, science, and history formed the focal points in 3 systems. Sample sizes of schools, classes, and students varied greatly. Most of the data collection occurred from 1981 through to 1983. Teachers' characteristics were summarized as follows:

> The participating countries . . . differed in the predominant sex of the teachers, and their age and years of experience. Within most countries, however, differences among the teachers in age and years of experience also were notable. The vast majority of teachers included in the study were certified at the elementary school level. Those certified at the secondary school level were exceptions (even for the teachers of seventh and eighth grade students).
>
> Teachers in the various countries also differed in their subject matter training, the number of hours per week spent teaching the subject matter, and the number of additional subjects taught. Fairly large within-country differences in subject matter training also existed. The vast majority of teachers in all countries taught a total of 11 to 30 hours per week. (Anderson et al. 1989 p. 70)

The major findings of the Classroom Environment Study were summarized in two groupings. The first of these were categorized as "descriptive findings," and the second as "associations and influences." Teachers' perceptions of autonomy in decisions about assignments, organization of classrooms, and use of tests, that is, within-classroom matters, were greater than their perceptions of autonomy in determining the curriculum and in holding meetings with parents, that is, outside-classroom matters. Perceptions of autonomy also varied from system to system. Teachers made great use of textbooks but infrequent use of audio-visual and programmed materials. Across the systems, teachers made little use of small group instruction but most use of whole class instruction. Homework assignments were used mainly to identify learning deficiencies and formal tests to assign grades. Less frequent use was made of projects and written reports for those purposes.

Opportunity to learn the content included on the final test varied greatly within systems. Across the systems, teachers were very active in their classrooms, spending most of their time interacting with their students. Communications in the classroom were mostly from teachers to students, with student communications mainly comprised of brief responses to teachers' questions. Apart from Hungary, lectures, seatwork, and management occupied from 50 to 80 percent of all observed activities.

Among the associations and influences reported were the following: differences in specific teaching behaviors observed were unrelated to differences in students' final achievement. Such behaviors were more consistently related to students' academic engagement than to their final achievement. Teachers in larger classes spent less time than other teachers in explaining, structuring, and directing, and more time in classroom management. Teachers who rated their

Table 1
Constructs and variables used in the IEA Classroom Environment Study

Construct/Variables	Construct/Variables
Community characteristics	Oral practice drill
School location	Reading at seats
School characteristics	Written seatwork
Type of school (TYPESC)	Laboratory work
Grade level organization	Direction of verbal interactions
Size of school	Explanation
Time allocated to subject (per year)	Explanation using materials
Teacher characteristics	Demonstration
Sex (SEXT)	Use of examples
Age (AGET)	Structuring cues
Years of experience (YRS)	Directives
Certification	Student questions
Subject area training	Student contributions
Subject contact hours (per week)	Social interactions
Number of additional subjects taught	Silence (absence of verbal interactions)
Total contact hours (per week)	Frequency of extra help
Home characteristics	Number receiving extra help
Father's education	Timing of extra help
Mother's education	Format of extra help
Father's occupation	Type of extra help
Language used in home	Assessing and Evaluating students
Student characteristics	Questioning student
Sex (SEXS)	Questioning group
Age (AGES)	Asks recall questions
Pretest (PRETEST)	Asks higher order questions
Aspirations (ASPIRATION)	Asks opinion questions
Attitude toward school (ATTSCH)	Asks effectiveness questions
Attitude toward subject (PREATTSUBJ)	Amount of questioning
Classroom context	Waits for student(s) response
Typical use of grouping	Student short response
Observed use of grouping	Student recitation
Use of types of materials	Student extended response
Student access to books outside school	Student doesn't answer
Lesson emphasis	Positive acknowledgement
Lesson objective	Says answer wrong
Class size	Repeats answer
Number of adults per classroom	Redirects question
Student attendance	Gives answer
Teacher perceptions	Probes
Teacher autonomy	Probes to student
Relative class ability level	Probes to group
Percent of students needing remediation	Tests for grading purposes
Quantity of instruction	Diagnostic testing
Amount of homework	Managing students
Time for homework	Management and routine administration
Opportunity to learn	Procedural interactions
Allocated time	Transitional interactions
Instructional time	Disciplinary actions
Orienting students	Uninvolved teacher
Specifying objectives	Student perceptions
Reviewing content	Task orientation (TASK)
Teaching students	Structure of lesson (STRUCTURE)
Teacher interacting	Teacher feedback (FEEDBACK)
Teacher monitoring	Student participation
Monitoring individual seatwork	Percent of students engaged in learning (ENGPCT)
Monitoring group work	Student outcomes
Lecture	Student achievement (POSTTEST)
Discourse discussion	Attitude toward subject (POSTATTSUBJ)

Source: Adapted from Anderson et al 1989 pp. 40–43

Table 2
Overview of the execution of the Classroom Environment Study[a]

Country	Grade level	Subject matter	No. of schools	No. of classes	No. of students	Study length (months)	No. of observations
Australia	5	Maths	39	75	1,963	3	8–10
Canada Ontario/English	8	Maths	18	27	751	7	8
Canada Ontario/French	8	Maths	14	18	420	6	8
Canada Quebec	7–8	Maths	9	30	749	6	10
Hungary	5	Physics	40	40	1,180	—	5
Israel	6	History	11	22	671	4	1–5
Korea (ROK)	5	Science	15	45	2,400	2	8
Netherlands	8	Maths	17	50	1,125	7	8
Nigeria	8	Maths	35	35	1,416	—	4
Thailand	5	Maths	77	87	2,572	9	6

Source: Anderson et al. 1989 p. 48

a The number of classes shown in this table represent those classes in which at least one observation was conducted. As a result of various editing procedures and the application of missing data rules, the numbers of classes (and hence the numbers of students) included in each analysis are typically lower than those shown in this table. Finally, in Hungary and Nigeria the study length was not provided by the NRCs.

classes as having lower ability spent more time asking the students questions and probing to assess and evaluate them. More experienced teachers spent less time on classroom management. The amount of time students spent engaged in learning was positively related to posttest achievement adjusted for pretest achievement. Student learning was directly affected by the quantity of instruction they received in the form of content coverage and/or homework.

The space constraints of this entry do not permit the presentation of between-country comparisons. Perhaps more important are the implications the authors of the report drew from the findings. These were as follows:

(a) The constraints under which teachers operate impose a sameness on their behavior which makes it difficult for research to test whether variations in teaching affect student learning.

(b) Teachers tend to be occasionally inconsistent, with the result that within-teacher differences are greater than between-teacher differences, again making it difficult for studies such as this present review to identify associations with student learning.

(c) Larger, composite units of teacher behavior which overcome the problem of unreliability of smaller units and result in stronger associations with student learning were identified.

(d) Because student variables, such as their prior knowledge, their perceptions of classrooms and teachers, and their classroom behavior were more closely related to outcome variables than were teacher or teaching variables, classroom research should focus more on students than on teachers.

(e) Studies of teaching should be designed so that classrooms contain students of similar degrees of prior knowledge or ability, variables are conceptually sound and reliably measured, experimental rather than correlational designs are used, differences in opportunity to learn are minimized, and observational instruments are suited to the purposes of the research and the nature of the data required.

(f) Variations in classroom time spent in different subjects—in teacher preparation to teach them and in behaviors exhibited during the teaching of different subjects—suggest that the structure of the subject matter has a strong influence upon classroom teaching.

(g) As teacher classroom behavior appeared to account for only small proportions of the variation in student learning, teacher education should emphasize teacher conceptualizing, theorizing, and decision-making as well as teaching behavior.

3. Conclusion

Anderson and Postlethwaite (1989) reviewed what they described as three generations of IEA studies and arrived at five major generalizations which they thought had emerged about teachers and teaching:

Generalization 1: Greater teacher experience and subject matter knowledge are associated with greater skills in classroom management and higher levels of student achievement. Two main implications were seen to arise from this generalization. The first was that needs for in-service training in such matters as classroom management and instructional strategies are likely to vary for teachers of different levels of experience so that individualization of this training might need to be provided. The second implication was that more attention should be given to teachers' subject-matter knowledge.

Generalization 2: Students who have greater opportunities to learn the knowledge and skills included on the achievement tests are likely to have higher levels of achievement. Two main implications were also seen to arise from this generalization. The first was that differences in opportunity to learn might conceal differences in the effectiveness of teachers and their teaching practices when they are studied in research. The second was that students' opportunity to learn and issues associated with it warrant careful consideration in relation to educational goals, achievement tests, and instruction so that the proper alignments might result.

Generalization 3: The greater amount of time spent on teaching and learning, the greater the achievement of students. This generalization was not seen to warrant simplistic interpretations such as that adding more instructional time in amounts of minutes per day or hours per year would significantly increase achievement. Rather the implications seemed to be more for the careful study of pacing and homework in relation to achievement.

Generalization 4: Differences in the behaviors that teachers exhibit in their classrooms are unrelated to differences in student achievement. Again, two main implications were drawn from this generalization. First, the study of relationships between differences in teacher behavior and differences in student behavior might be more rewarding than the study of the corresponding relationships involving teacher behavior and student achievement. Second, exclusively behaviorist views of teaching are misleading and counterproductive.

Generalization 5: Students' perceptions of what transpires in the classroom are more valid than those of trained observers (and perhaps those of teachers). The implications of this generalization were seen to

be that teachers need to monitor students constantly, to provide feedback on their progress, and to assist them in making adjustments where required, and that "teachers should be less egocentric and more sensitive to impact they have (or fail to have) on their students" (Anderson and Postlethwaite 1989 p. 85).

These generalizations yielded by the IEA studies might seem to some observers to be simplistic. Anderson and Postlethwaite (1989 p. 85) responded to such criticism in the following terms:

> We suggest that the strength of the findings of the IEA studies resides not in their insights, but in their grounding in the everyday experiences of school administrators and teachers . . . We contend that the knowledge provided by the IEA studies does, in fact, "ring true." The extent to which the "commonsense" knowledge provided by these studies becomes "commonplace" remains the responsibility of practitioners.

See also: Characteristics of Teacher Educators

References

Anderson L W, Postlethwaite T N 1989 What IEA studies say about teachers and teaching. In: Purves A C (ed.) 1989 *International Comparisons and Educational Reform.* Association for Supervision and Curriculum Development, Washington, DC

Anderson L W, Ryan D W, Shapiro B J (eds.) 1989 *The IEA Classroom Environment Study.* Pergamon Press, Oxford

Dunkin M J 1989 Teaching: Comparative studies. In: Husén T, Postlethwaite T N (eds.) 1989 *The International Encyclopedia of Education,* Supplementary Vol. 1. Pergamon Press, Oxford

Robitaille D F, Garden R A (eds.) 1989 *The IEA Study of Mathematics II: Contexts and Outcomes of School Mathematics.* Pergamon Press, Oxford

Travers K J, Westbury I (eds.) 1989 *The IEA Study of Mathematics I: Analysis of Mathematics Curricula.* Pergamon Press, Oxford.

Werry B 1989 The teachers of mathematics. In: Robitaille D F, Garden R A 1989

Further Reading

Anderson L W, Burns R 1990 *Research in Classrooms: The Study of Teachers, Teaching, and Instruction.* Pergamon Press, Oxford

Houston R (ed.) 1990 *Handbook of Research on Teacher Education.* Macmillan, New York

Wittrock M C (ed.) 1986 *Handbook of Research on Teaching,* 3rd edn. Macmillan, New York

Synthesizing Research on Teaching

M. J. Dunkin

Hundreds of studies of teaching are completed each year. Programs of international conferences abound with papers reporting research on teaching. Dozens of scholarly journals publish articles about research on teaching. Several entire handbooks containing thousands of pages have been devoted exclusively to research on teaching. What does all this research amount to? How do people charged with responsibility for making wise decisions about educational practice glean the best guidance from this great mass of research? How do researchers themselves reach conclusions about what has or has not been established about teaching by the mountain of research that has been reported during the twentieth century? These are the questions which those who attempt to synthesize research on teaching address. During the 1970s, 1980s, and 1990s the synthesis of research on teaching has itself become an important and controversial topic of research. Several different approaches are to be found in the literature, each with its own advocates, critics, strengths, and shortcomings.

1. The Importance of Synthesizing Research on Teaching

The findings of research on any one topic, whether in the "hard" physical sciences or the "soft" social sciences, almost always vary from one study to another. Sometimes results are obtained that support a given hypothesis, while on other occasions the results do not support it. Sometimes the support is strong while at other times it is weak. Sometimes the results of one study actually contradict the findings of another. The reasons for these variations are many.

The social or cultural context in which research is conducted may play a part in the results obtained. For example, in some cultures it is regarded as impolite for children to ask questions of adults such as teachers. It might be expected therefore that research would find that students ask questions in classrooms of that culture much less frequently than in another culture where the etiquette regarding questioning does not exist.

Results of testing a hypothesis or answering a question depend on conceptual and methodological variations in research. For example, teachers often ask rhetorical questions in the classroom. Researchers inquiring into the relationship between teacher questioning and student learning have the problem of deciding whether to count such questions. Their results will depend in part on the decision they make.

The researcher who wants to establish the state of the art in research on teacher questions or on any other aspect of teaching has to be aware of these types of variations and develop procedures for dealing with them in coming to general conclusions. Similarly, educational practitioners seeking guidance from research need to know how to take into account such influences on research results. Erroneous conclusions about the accumulated evidence of a body of research can have disastrous consequences when action based on those conclusions is taken. On the other hand, real progress in the form of significantly improved professional practice can be the consequence of appropriate conclusions emerging from the synthesis of research.

Giaconia and Hedges (1987) claimed that there are three aims of research syntheses, as follows: "(a) to summarize findings across studies; (b) to assess the consistency of findings across studies; and (c) to resolve contradictory findings across studies" (p. 124). Furthermore, they suggested that the "careful execution" of research syntheses is important for two main reasons:

> First, research on teaching effectiveness, as a field of inquiry that purports to have a scientific basis, has as one of its aims the cumulation of knowledge. As such, the field should maintain the same degree of rigor in the methods used to synthesize research studies (cumulate knowledge about a topic) that are required in executing the primary research studies that are to be synthesized. Second, the practical uses made of research syntheses suggest the importance of maintaining high standards in their execution . . . Thus valid ways of combining the evidence across the research studies and resolving the often conflicting findings are important in helping public policy makers arrive at the correct conclusions about the true effects of a treatment or the true degree of relationship between variables. (p. 124)

2. Methods of Research Synthesis

Giaconia and Hedges (1987) described four methods of research synthesis: narrative approaches, vote counting methods, combined significance test methods, and effect magnitude methods. To these must be added qualitative research syntheses discussed by Walberg (1986).

2.1 Narrative Approaches

Narrative approaches "consist of a verbal description of the research studies and particular topic, usually chronologically arranged, in terms of what the investigators of each study did and the results they found" (Giaconia and Hedges 1987 p. 128). Walberg (1986) referred to narrative syntheses as "reviews" as distinct from "research syntheses" since they seldom quantitatively analyze studies. Rather, they usually summarize and evaluate them one at a time. McGaw (1985) referred to narrative integration as "the traditional process" which he saw as "essentially intuitive" and lacking in specification of methods. He cited a case in which different reviewers used the same studies to support contradictory conclusions. To McGaw, the most difficult problem for the narrative approach is coping with the volume of relevant literature, leading often to selectivity on the basis of usually unspecified criteria of methodological quality. In spite of these shortcomings, Giaconia and Hedges saw the following advantages in narrative approaches: (a) "a richness of detail about study characteristics . . . that methods that rely heavily on the reported results" cannot provide; (b) a chronological arrangement of studies indicating evolution of aspects of knowledge about the topic; and (c) the ability to synthesize two or more different areas of research that may have an indirect relationship with each other.

Biddle and Anderson (1986) saw traditional reviews as providing the following advantages for the reader:

> a convenient source of references, a conceptual orientation to the field, a discussion of methodological strengths and weaknesses found in published studies, a summary of major findings and conundrums in the data, suggestions for building explanatory theory, and an invitation to explore primary sources for additional information . . . They may . . . help the neophyte to orient himself or herself to the field and warn readers of weaknesses in the research conducted to date." (p. 235)

However, there are deficiencies in narrative approaches, as Jackson (1980) found when he analyzed 87 review articles and found that few of them specified their procedures for identifying studies. Similar observations were made by Waxman and Walberg (1982) who analyzed 19 reviews of process—product research on teaching.

2.2 Vote Counting Methods

Vote counting methods, sometimes called "box-score" methods, "involve categorizing studies on the basis of the direction and statistical significance of the reported results" (p. 129). According to Light and Smith (1971), in vote counting methods:

> all studies which have data on a dependent variable and a specific independent variable of interest are examined. Three possible outcomes are defined. The relationship between the independent variable and the dependent variable is either significantly positive, significantly negative, or there is no significant relationship in either direction. The number of studies falling into each of these three categories is then simply tallied. If a plurality of studies falls into any one of these three categories, with fewer falling into the other two, the modal category is declared the winner. This modal categorization is then assumed to give the best estimate of the direction of the true relationship between the independent and dependent variable. (p. 433)

Giaconia and Hedges (1987) report that vote counting methods arose from the sheer number of studies conducted on particular topics. They saw advantages in speed and replicability of these methods but argued that they were weak in terms of reliability, and unable to indicate the size of treatment effects, resolve contradictory results, or assess the degree of consistency of findings. To McGaw (1985), vote counting methods give so much weight to results that are greatly influenced by sample size that "trivial findings from large studies will be counted as revealing an effect simply because they achieve statistical significance" (p. 3322). Furthermore, common interpretations of frequency counts could be misleading. On this point, Giaconia and Hedges conclude, "for sample sizes and effect magnitude that are typical of research on teaching effectiveness, as the number of studies to be combined increases, the probability that vote counting methods will detect a true treatment effect approaches zero!" (p. 131).

2.3 Combined Significance Test Models

Combined significance test models "involve combining either the probabilities (*p*-values) or common test of significance statistics . . . across several studies addressing the same research question and assessing the statistical significance of this overall value" (Giaconia and Hedges 1987 p. 132). These methods are described in detail by Rosenthal (1978), and include such procedures as adding logs, *p*'s, *t*'s, *Z*'s, and weighted *Z*'s, as well as testing mean *p* and mean *Z*. Combined significance test methods alleviate problems of small sample sizes in primary studies by pooling numbers of cases across studies, thereby increasing the likelihood that true treatment effects will be discovered. Giaconia and Hedges (1987) illustrated three of the methods. They also acknowledged that this approach conceals inconsistencies in findings across studies and does not indicate the magnitude of treatment effects or degree of relationships between variables.

2.4 Meta-analysis or Effect Magnitude Methods

The term "meta-analysis" was first used by Glass (1976) to refer to syntheses of research that use quantitative and statistical approaches. Since then the term has been applied chiefly to methods that involve the calculation of effect magnitude, which Giaconia and Hedges (1987) define as "a standardized numerical index of the strength of the treatment effect or degree of relationship between variables that can be derived for individual studies or independent findings within studies" (p. 133). These indexes can then be combined across studies to produce an overall index of treatment effect or degree of relationship. The indices most commonly used are correlation coefficients and standardized mean differences (effect sizes).

The population values of these indexes have the advantage of being independent of sample size and of the variance of any particular test used to measure the dependent variable. Cohen (1969) offered the following guidelines for assessing the magnitude of the effect represented by the population value of the correlation coefficient:

small effect: 0.1
moderate effect   0.3
large effect: 0.5

and for effect size:

small effect: 0.2
moderate effect: 0.5
large effect: 0.8

Giaconia and Hedges (1987) explained the usefulness of these indices in estimating effect magnitudes in single studies, summarizing results, and resolving contradictory findings across studies. While it would appear that these approaches offer advantages not available in others, they are not without their critics. For example, Biddle and Anderson (1986) pointed to six potential problems in meta-analysis which they summarized as follows:

> Meta-analysis appears attractive if one is focused narrowly on findings and strength of evidence, if one assumes simple relationships among terms, concepts, and methods, if one is uninterested in deviant cases, if one is not particularly worried about theory, and—above all—if one wants to make simple knowledge claims from research. Once one begins to question these assumptions, meta-analysis becomes less appealing. (p. 236)

One of the most assiduous critics of meta-analysis is Slavin (1984) who wrote:

> Meta-analysis imparts, in my judgement, a certain patina of science that somehow makes many readers forget that the meta-analysis is no better than the studies that went into it, and focuses readers on a few unqualified main effects, when often the effects cannot really be understood without considering interactions and conditioning variables submerged in the meta-analytic procedure. (p. 12)

McGaw (1985) drew attention to the problem of the conceptual homogeneity of independent variables used in meta-analyses by observing that "blind aggregation of studies is certainly not justified in any review but it is appropriate to count 'apples' and 'oranges' together as long as the concern is with 'fruit'" (p. 3323). Giaconia and Hedges (1987) argued that many of the criticisms leveled at meta-analysis are equally applicable to other approaches.

2.5 Qualitative Research Syntheses

Miles and Huberman (1984) argued that qualitative researchers needed to develop shared, explicit methods for synthesizing findings. Walberg (1986) observed that some qualitative researchers attempted to generalize on the basis of multiple case studies but cited Green (1982) as the only researcher he knew who had proposed and used an explicit approach to the synthesis of case studies research on teaching. After a brief description of the approach, Walberg commented that Green

reported "many insightful and useful observations that appear generalizable across a variety of contexts and investigations" (p. 216).

3. Syntheses of Research on Teaching

Concerted attempts to synthesize the findings of research on teaching using other than narrative approaches probably began with Rosenshine's (1971) work using a vote-counting approach. It was soon followed by other attempts and by the early 1990s dozens had been reported and several books had been published on methods of synthesizing research.

3.1 Comparisons of Different Approaches to Synthesis

One of the most interesting stories in the development of methods of synthesizing research on teaching concerns a body of research on the relationship between teacher indirectness and pupil achievement. Dunkin and Biddle (1974) used a combination of a narrative and a vote-counting procedure in their attempt to synthesize the findings of 29 studies reporting findings on this relationship. Twenty of those studies reported findings regarding linear relationships obtained in correlational field studies. Dunkin and Biddle found that the majority (15) of the 20 studies found no significant relationship, while 10 found a significant positive relationship (five of the studies found both, as a result of using two different measures of indirectness). Gage (1978) used a combined significance test procedure to synthesize the results of 19 of the above studies. He found that, across the studies, there was a statistically significant relationship ($p<0.001$) between the two variables. Glass et al. (1977) conducted a meta-analysis with the same 19 studies and found that for Grades kindergarten to 6 the combined effect was small ($r=0.16$) but that for Grades 7 to 12 the effect was moderate ($r=0.30$). This story indicates that the procedures used to synthesize research findings influence the outcomes of that synthesis. To Giaconia and Hedges (1987) it seemed that Glass's meta-analysis was the most informative of the three approaches because it provided an index of the magnitude of the effect, as well as a finding relating the context of the studies to that effect.

A second application of alternative methods to the same body of research concerned the relationship between cognitive levels of teachers' questions and pupil achievement. First, Winne (1979) combined a narrative approach with a vote counting approach and applied them to 18 experiments. He found that 15 percent of the results were in favor of higher order questions, 25 percent favored fact questions, and 60 percent favored neither. Accordingly, Winne was unable to reach a "sturdy conclusion" about the relationship. Two years later Redfield and Rousseau (1981) reported the results of their meta-analysis of 13 of the original 18 studies and obtained an effect size of 0.73 indicating a moderate to large effect in favor of higher order questions.

A third example of the application of different methods in synthesizing research on teaching involved the effects of open classroom methods upon pupil learning. The syntheses were those by Horwitz (1979), Peterson (1979), and Hedges et al. (1981). Horwitz used vote-counting procedures to summarize the findings of approximately 200 studies, most of which compared open education programs with traditional education programs. He concluded that there were no significant differences between the two methods for academic achievement, self-concept, anxiety and adjustment, and locus of control outcomes, but that in relation to attitude to school, creativity, independence and conformity, curiosity, and cooperation, results favored open education methods.

Peterson (1979) conducted a meta-analysis of 45 of the studies analyzed by Horwitz. She did not include doctoral dissertations or studies that did not allow the calculation of effect sizes that were included in Horwitz's study. Peterson found that for most student outcomes effect sizes were so small as to indicate little or no advantage for either method. For mathematics, reading, and composite achievement they were in favor of traditional methods but were only about 0.1 in size. Similarly effect sizes approaching zero were found for locus of control and anxiety. A very slight advantage of open education methods in the form of effect sizes averaging between 0.1 and 0.2 was found for creativity, attitude to school, and curiosity. Larger effect sizes, averaging between 0.33 and 0.5, were found in favor of open education for independence and attitude to teacher.

Finally, Hedges et al. (1981) used methods of meta-analysis that were refinements of those used by Peterson (1979) and added about 90 doctoral dissertations to the latter's sample. For student adjustment, attitude to school, curiosity, and general mental ability, Hedges et al. found that average effect sizes were about 0.2 and were all in favor of open education. For cooperativeness, creativity, and independence, average effect sizes were between 0.25 and 0.33 and were also in favor of open education. For language, mathematics, and reading achievement, although results favored traditional education, average effect sizes were close to zero.

Giaconia (1987) summarized the results of these three attempts at synthesis as follows:

> First, in general, open education is somewhat more effective than traditional education for nonachievement measures. Traditional education is only slightly more effective than open education for the traditional academic achievement measures. For many student outcomes, there are near zero differences between open and traditional education. Second, these general conclusions . . . must be tempered by the fact that the variability of the effects of open education programs is often quite high. (p. 250)

3.2 Syntheses of Syntheses of Research on Teaching

Books by Brophy (1989, 1991) and by Waxman and Walberg (1991) contain numerous examples of syntheses of research on teaching. In addition, Ball (1991) synthesized research on teaching mathematics with a focus on teachers' subject-matter knowledge, while Smith and Neale (1991) reported on the accumulation of evidence about teachers' subject-matter knowledge in primary science teaching. Indeed, the stage has been reached at which the number of syntheses of initial research on teaching are so numerous that syntheses of those syntheses are becoming common. Giaconia's (1987) work is a good example and there are others. Possibly the most comprehensive is the work by Anderson and Burns (1989).

In the final chapter of their book, Anderson and Burns (1989) described their procedures for "reviewing the research reviews." Faced with the dramatic increase in the volume of research on teaching that had occurred during the 1970s and 1980s, Anderson and Burns decided that they would rely on the syntheses of the research that had been conducted in seven earlier works in order to produce generalizations about teachers, teaching, and instruction. As a result of their efforts, Anderson and Burns derived four generalizations about teachers, four about teaching, and five about instruction. Examples of the generalizations in each set are as follows:

> "There is no universal definition of an excellent, good, or effective teacher" (p. 343);
> "Teacher characteristics do not impact directly on student achievement" (p. 345);
> "Teachers progress through a fairly predictable set of qualitatively distinct stages as they move from novice to expert status" (p. 345);
> "Teachers assume a very central, directive, and active role in their classrooms" (p. 346);
> "Differences in individual teaching behaviors are not reliably associated with differences in student achievement" (p. 348);
> "Considering teaching from a functional, rather than behavioral, point of view is more likely to result in a greater understanding of teaching in general and effective teaching in particular" (p. 350);
> "The subject matter being taught impacts on some, if not all, of the other components of instruction" (p. 351);
> "While lecture, recitation, and seatwork predominate in classrooms, there is little if any evidence that changes in format would result in higher levels of student achievement" (p. 352); and,
> "Instructional time, content coverage, and pacing are associated with higher levels of student achievement" (p. 353).

4. Conclusion

It is possibly a matter of considerable disappointment that after many decades of research on teaching so few generalizations may be gleaned. Anderson and Burns (1989) described their list as "fairly conservative" (p.

354) and it is certain that others would not share their conservatism. Wang and Walberg (1991), for example, surveyed the opinions of over 1,000 educationists and arrived at a list of approximately 40 instructional and teaching variables that they considered to be "highly important," while Walberg (1986) described his "selective summary of a decade of educational research" as having arrived at "impressive" results (p. 224). It seems clear, on the basis of such disagreements among experts as to the generalizations that syntheses of research on teaching permit that the procedures employed in such syntheses and in syntheses of syntheses continue to deserve much attention from scholars.

See also: Comparative and International Studies of Teaching and Teacher Education; Behavioristic Theories of Teaching; Social Psychological Theories of Teaching

References

Anderson L W, Burns R B 1989 *Research in Classrooms: The Study of Teachers, Teaching, and Instruction.* Pergamon Press, Oxford
Ball D L 1991 Research on teaching mathematics: Making subject-matter knowledge part of the equation. In: Brophy J (ed.) 1991
Biddle B J, Anderson D S 1986 Theory, methods, knowledge, and research on teaching. In: Wittrock M (ed.) 1986 *Handbook of Research on Teaching*, 3rd edn. Macmillan, New York
Brophy J 1989 *Advances in Research on Teaching: A Research Annual*, Vol. 1. JAI Press, Greenwich, Connecticut
Brophy J 1991 *Advances in Research on Teaching: A Research Annual*, Vol. 2. JAI Press, Greenwich, Connecticut
Cohen J 1969 *Statistical Power Analysis for the Behavioral Sciences.* Academic Press, New York
Dunkin M J, Biddle B J 1974 *The Study of Teaching.* Holt, Rinehart, and Winston, New York
Gage N L 1978 *The Scientific Basis of the Art of Teaching.* Teachers College Press, New York
Giaconia R M 1987 Open versus formal methods. In: Dunkin M (ed.) 1987 *The International Encyclopedia of Teaching and Teacher Education: Research and Studies.* Pergamon Press, Oxford
Giaconia R M, Hedges L V 1987 Synthesizing research evidence. In: Dunkin M (ed.) 1987 *The International Encyclopedia of Teaching and Teacher Education: Research and Studies.* Pergamon Press, Oxford
Glass G V 1976 Primary, secondary and meta-analysis of research. *Educ. Researcher* 5(10): 3–8
Glass G V et al. 1977 Teacher "indirectness" and pupil achievement: An integration of findings. Unpublished manuscript, University of Colorado, Boulder, Colorado
Green J L 1982 *Research on Teaching as a Linguistic Process: The State of the Art.* University of Delaware, Newark, Delaware
Hedges L V, Giaconia R M, Gage N L 1981 *Meta-analysis of the Effects of Open and Traditional Instruction.* Final Report, Stanford Program on Teaching Effectiveness, Meta-analysis Project, Vol. 2, Stanford, California

Horwitz R A 1979 Psychological effects of the "open classroom." *Rev. Educ. Res.* 49(1): 71–86
Jackson G B 1980 Methods of integrative reviews. *Rev. Educ. Res.* 50(3): 438–60
Light R J, Smith P V 1971 Accumulating evidence: Procedures for resolving contradictions among different studies. *Harv. Educ. Rev.* 41(4): 429–72
McGaw B 1985 Meta-analysis. In: Husén T, Postlethwaite T N (eds.) 1985 *The International Encyclopedia of Education: Research and Studies*, 1st edn. Pergamon Press, Oxford
Miles M B, Huberman A M 1984 Drawing valid meaning from qualitative data: Toward a shared craft. *Educ. Researcher* 13(5): 20–30
Peterson P L 1979 Direct instruction reconsidered. In: Peterson P L, Walberg H J (eds.) 1979 *Research on Teaching: Concepts, Findings, and Implications.* McCutchan, Berkeley, California
Redfield D L, Rousseau E W 1981 A meta-analysis of experimental research on teacher questioning behavior. *Rev. Educ. Res.* 51(2): 237–45
Rosenshine B 1971 *Teaching Behaviors and Student Achievement.* National Foundation for Educational Research, Slough
Rosenthal R 1978 Combining results of independent studies. *Psych. Bull.* 85(1): 185–93
Slavin R E 1984 Meta-analysis in education: How has it been used? *Educ. Res.* 13(8): 6–15
Smith D C, Neale D C 1991 The construction of subject-matter knowledge in primary science teaching. In: Brophy J 1991
Walberg H J 1986 Syntheses of research on teaching. In: Wittrock M (ed.) 1986 *Handbook of Research on Teaching*, 3rd edn. Macmillan, New York
Wang M C, Walberg H J 1991 Teaching and educational effectiveness: Research synthesis and consensus from the field. In: Waxman H C, Walberg H J (eds.) 1991
Waxman H C, Walberg H J 1982 The relation of teaching and learning. *Contemp. Educ. Rev.* 20: 103–20
Waxman H C, Walberg H J (eds.) 1991 *Effective Teaching: Current Research.* McCutchan Publishing, Berkeley, California
Winne P H 1979 Experiments relating teachers' use of higher cognitive questions to student achievement. *Rev. Educ. Res.* 49(1): 13–49

Further Reading

Cooper H 1982 Scientific guidelines for conducting integrative research reviews. *Rev. Educ. Res.* 52(2): 291–302
Cooper H 1984 *The Integrative Research Review: A Systematic Approach.* Sage Publications, Beverly Hills, California
Hedges L V, Olkin I O 1985 *Statistical Methods for Meta-analysis.* Academic Press, Orlando, Florida
Hunter J E, Schmidt F L 1989 *Methods of Meta-analysis: Correcting Error and Bias in Research Findings.* Sage Publications, Newbury Park, California
Light R J, Pillemer D B 1984 *Summing Up: The Science of Reviewing Research.* Harvard University Press, Cambridge, Massachusetts

Translating Research into Practice

F. E. Weinert

After 100 years of systematic research in the fields of education and educational psychology, there is, in the 1990s, still no agreement about whether, how, or under what conditions research can improve educational practice. Although research and educational practice each have changed substantially since the beginning of the twentieth century, the question of how science can actually contribute to the solution of real educational problems continues to be controversial.

Because there are no general rules or strategies for translating research into practice, the first part of this entry focuses briefly on some of the basic problems concerning the relation between theory and practice in education. Next, six different approaches that attempt in various ways to make research findings relevant to education, particularly in schools, are discussed. These approaches concern: (a) using theoretical knowledge to improve technology for teaching and learning; (b) facilitating teacher expertise as a practical application of research on teaching; (c) using studies on classroom learning to provide the scientific basis for ability grouping, mastery learning, and adaptive teaching; (d) using research on cognitive development and learning as a source of scientific information about how to train student's learning competencies and self-instructional skills; (e) using educational research to design, implement, and evaluate new models of schooling and instruction; and (f) using research findings as a source of background knowledge for practitioners. Suggestions for how research can be made more relevant to educators and for ways in which educational practice can be more research-based are proposed on the basis of these different approaches.

1. The Gap Between Research and Educational Practice

Most research in education and educational psychology is conducted with the explicit or implicit goal of directly or indirectly improving educational practice. As Anderson and Burns (1985) stated, "the primary purpose of classroom research is to help educators to improve the conditions of learning and the quality of learning of increasingly large numbers of students" (p. ix). The kinds of necessary research, the required theoretical insights, and the ways that scientific findings should be translated into practice to attain this goal are issues that have not yet been resolved.

When empirical and experimental research on educational phenomena began, there was a widespread vision, conviction, and expectation that it would generate a scientifically informed basis for educational practice. In 1893, for example, Rein (1893) stated that "there is only one way in teaching that corresponds to nature; to follow carefully the laws of the human mind and to arrange everything according to these laws. The attainment of adequate instructional procedures follows from knowledge of and insight into these laws" (p.107).

When these ambitious hopes did not seem to be realized, there was substantial disappointment among both scientists and practitioners. It was not clear how teachers could use such very general and vague recommendations as those, for example, based on a synopsis of classical learning theories by Thorpe and Schmuller (1954). They concluded that instruction was especially effective when learners were motivated; when task demands matched learners' aptitudes; when learners received sufficient opportunities to relate elements of the learning task to the learning goal; when learners could use external criteria to judge their progress; and when the learning process occurred under conditions that facilitated adaptation to the total situation. Although these conclusions are probably valid, it is not surprising that such nonspecific psychological statements and such obvious educational recommendations led the educational community to the cynical conclusion that learning theorists were perhaps the only ones who could derive personal benefit from learning theory.

Dissatisfaction was not limited to problems in finding practical applications for learning theory. The results from research on teaching also seemed unproductive in providing educators with practical guidance. This can be seen, for example, in Bloom's (1966) resigned summary of the state of research: "large class, small class, TV instruction, audiovisual methods, lecture, discussion, demonstration, team teaching, programmed instruction, authoritarian and nonauthoritarian instructional procedures, etc. all appear to be equally effective methods in helping the student learn more information or simple skills" (p. 217).

The limited applicability of educational science for educational practice has resulted in several metatheoretical debates that have contributed only a little to improving the research situation or to solving practical problems. Some examples of the debated issues are:

(a) Is the gap between scientific and practical work the result of a production deficit in research, a reception deficit in the practitioners, or deficits in translating theoretical knowledge into practical suggestions? This debate has led at least to the insight that scientists and practitioners have different ways of perceiving the world, prefer to define their problems in different ways, and thus speak different "languages."

(b) How relevant is basic, as opposed to applied research, for education? This debate is especially unproductive, both theoretically and practically. On the one hand, it is difficult to differentiate pure or basic research from applied research; on the other hand, it has become clear that findings from both research prototypes have specific advantages and disadvantages with respect to their practical applications.

(c) Is it more appropriate to use quantitative or qualitative methods in educational research? This debate has almost become a religious war for many, even though the theory of science convincingly teaches that both approaches are necessary and complementary components of any system of research in the social sciences.

2. Theory and Research

These metatheoretical debates and the many concrete attempts to derive practical applications from research findings have led to a variety of different proposals for solving the research–practice problem. Two positions are especially characteristic of these proposals: the first is that theory should take precedence; the second is that empirical work should take precedence.

The first characteristic position, that theory should be preeminent, can be captured by a quotation from Mook (1983), who, in agreement with many other scientists, recalled the truth of the classical adage that nothing is more useful than a good theory.

> Ultimately, what makes research findings of interest is that they help us in understanding everyday life. That understanding, however, comes from theory or analysis of the mechanisms; it is not a matter of generalizing the findings themselves. . . . The validity of those generalizations is tested by their success and predictions and has nothing to do with their naturalness, representativeness or even non-creativity of the investigations on which they rest. (p.386)

Examples of the ways in which theoretical models have aided in the solution of practical problems include the use of attribution theory to provide a better understanding of students' intuitive explanations for their success and failure; the use of findings from the expert–novice research paradigm to estimate the relative importance of general abilities and domain specific knowledge in the solution of demanding tasks; and the use of theories of prejudice in the analysis of social conflicts.

The second characteristic position, focused on empirical research, is invoked in instances where there are competing theories, where context conditions determine psychological processes, or where descriptive or causal models must be transposed into prescriptive statements. Sequential research strategies are proposed to solve such problems. One example is the description of "six steps on the road from pure learning research to technological research and development in the classroom" suggested by Hilgard (1964): step 1—research on learning with no regard for its educational relevance; step 2—pure research on learning with content that is similar to school subject matter; step 3—research on learning that is relevant to education because the subjects are students, the material learned is school subject matter, and/or the learning conditions are similar to classroom situations; step 4—research on learning and instruction in special laboratory classrooms; step 5—use of experimentally tested learning and teaching strategies in normal classrooms; step 6—developmental work related to advocacy and adoption, for a wider use of the research based educational strategies (p.405–11).

These and similar sequential research strategies are followed in many research and development centers around the world. The differences among the programs are, however, too large to allow conclusions about the success of such a strategy. In principle, the possibilities and limits of this approach also depend on the basic relation between educational research and educational practice. Good educational practice is not simply applied science, nor does it consist in the correct use of findings from applied research. Science can at best only provide an important and useful, but always limited, theoretical basis for the planning, analysis, control, support, reflection, and better understanding of educational practice.

The limits of scientific prediction and explanation of educational outcomes are expressed in the conclusions reached by Haertel et al. (1983) based on a comparison of different psychological models of educational performance. They concluded that:

> Classroom learning is the multiplicative, diminishing-returns function of four essential factors—student ability and motivation and quality and quantity of instruction—and possibly four supplementary or supportive factors—the social-psychological environment of the classroom, education-stimulating conditions in the home and peer group, and exposure to mass media. Each of the essential factors appears to be necessary but insufficient by itself for classroom learning; that is all four of these factors appear required at least at minimum levels for classroom learning to take place. It also appears that the essential factors may substitute, compensate, or trade-off for one another in diminishing rates of return. (p.75f)

3. Models for Bridging the Gap between Research and Educational Practice

There is no general rule that specifies correct, expedient, or appropriate ways to use scientific findings to solve the practical problems of education. More importantly, there can in principle be no such rule. There are, however, various approaches available that show how research can be used in different ways and the strategies that can be used to translate research into practice.

3.1 From Learning Theories to Teaching Technologies

Educational technology consists of systems of rules, tools, and activities designed to bring students to the point where they can achieve specific learning goals systematically, effectively, and economically. Even more, Glaser and Cooley (1973) perceive technology "as a vehicle for making available to schools what psychologists have learned about learning" (p.855). Such standardized technologies should of course be derived from explicit and tested scientific theory. Although not a necessary component of educational technology, technical devices are frequently used with the purpose of minimizing the negative consequences of fluctuation in attention to errors or mistakes, whether by students or teachers.

The first researcher who, from theoretical grounds, wanted to replace normal instruction in the classroom with almost revolutionary mechanical teaching techniques was Skinner (1954). In the early 1950s Skinner argued that the behaviorist models of learning and conditioning and the psychological laws specifying how to shape behavior through contingent reinforcement of desired reactions were the scientific prerequisites for successful and effective instruction. It was his belief that these principles could not be used in classroom teaching because teachers were not able to present the material to be learned in sufficiently elementary components and were not able to provide the requisite number of reinforcements in the necessary contiguity to learners' behavior, verbal or nonverbal. Thus, he recommended programmed instruction and the use of teaching machines.

Beyond Skinner's initial attempts, the development of educational technologies made dramatic progress in the 1970s and 1980s. Computer-assisted instruction, integrated learning systems, intelligent tutoring systems, instructional media, and intelligent learning environments are some of the key concepts referring to the development, study, and use of modern technical aids for improving educational practice (for a review see Niemiec and Walberg 1992, Scott et al. 1992)

In particular, modern computer technology offers a variety of possibilities for the technical design of controlled, but flexible, adaptive, and intelligently guided, instructional systems and learning processes. The prerequisites for these systems are general learning theories and domain-specific models of knowledge acquisition that allow the following:

(a) analysis of the learning goal in terms of competent performance (specification of the learning task);

(b) description of the initial state of the learner (specification of individual differences in relevant skills and knowledge);

(c) determination of the methods that effectively lead to knowledge acquisition (specification of instructional methods); and

(d) assessment of the effects of these instructional methods (specification and measurement of learning progress).

Although there is no disagreement that educational technologies provide an up-to-date tool for education as well as an excellent opportunity for employing research results in a practical way, the level of these technologies is quite different in developing and developed countries. It is also clear that although such technologies are one way to improve educational practice, they are not the only way.

3.2 Research on Teaching and the Acquisition of Teacher Expertise

A large part of educational research is directed toward investigating educational productivity, teacher effectiveness, and the relation between instructional quality and learning outcomes. Although the empirical findings are very impressive, they are also quite diverse and are not stable across different studies. In a synthesis of the effects of instructional variables on learning, the following rank ordering of noncontent related factors was found (with decreasing effect strength): reinforcement, accelerated learning programs, cues and feedback, cooperation programs, personalized instruction, adaptive instruction, tutoring, and higher order questions (Fraser et al. 1987).

If one considers that the effects of single instructional variables can be masked or mediated by combined, compensatory, and interactive effects from other teaching, student and context variables (Weinert et al. 1989), it becomes apparent that training single teaching skills cannot be a practical implication of these research results.

It seems considerably more effective to provide a combined training program for teachers that uses the results from research on teaching (Tillema and Veenman 1987). The paradigm of the expert teacher provides an interesting theoretical perspective for the practical application of such research findings. Prompted by work in cognitive psychology, this paradigm investigates how experienced and successful teachers differ from inexperienced and/or unsuccessful teachers in their knowledge about education and in their teaching activities (Berliner 1992). The research results from this paradigm have already been applied in the design of teacher training.

This paradigm allows the integration of two research traditions that have been portrayed as alternative approaches (Stolurow 1965): "Model the master teacher or master the teaching model?" (see also Weinert et al. 1992). In the expert teacher paradigm, it is possible to directly and systematically relate research on teaching and learning in the classroom to teacher training. Such training should not be directed toward producing a uniform type of "expert teacher," but should explicitly assume that there are interindividual differences in the teacher competencies to be trained (Anderson and Burns 1985).

3.3 Studies of Classroom Learning

In contrast to the subject pools used in most experimental investigations of learning, the classroom is best described as a group of students with very different learning prerequisites who are to be instructed at the same time in the same place. Massive interindividual differences in cognitive abilities, knowledge, skills, motivation, interests, attitudes, and study habits affect both students' learning behavior and their learning achievements. The relevant research concerning these factors is very extensive. It has led to a large number of psychological theories about how personality states and traits are relevant to learning, and has contributed to the development of measurement models and instruments for diagnosing individual differences in learning prerequisites and learning outcomes.

Carroll (1963) provided an important contribution to the practical application of this psychological research with his "model of school learning." Described simply, Carroll proceeded from the assumption that, given equivalent learning time, students with different aptitudes would diverge in their learning performance: that is, some students would not attain the required performance goal. To avoid this outcome, each learner must be allowed the learning time he or she needs to attain a specific learning goal.

This model has had a strong influence on subsequent research; in many respects it has been further specified, broadened, and extended, and it has also been used for a variety of different practical applications (see Anderson 1984). For example, the following concepts and procedures can be traced to Carroll's original model: time on task (the time during which a student is actually involved in a learning task); the personalized system of instruction; individually prescribed instruction; mastery learning; and, largely independent of Carroll's model of school learning, the aptitude–treatment interaction (ATI) research program (Snow 1989). All these approaches have been concerned with the question of whether and to what extent undesired effects of individual student aptitude differences on learning outcomes can be reduced by variations in instruction.

Research on the dependence of school achievement on aptitude differences and instructional conditions has led to several important practical applications. Three of these are grouping students for learning, mastery learning, and adaptive teaching.

The educational benefits of grouping students for learning are controversial and seem to depend on the effects of a variety of factors. Furthermore, these benefits are both student- and criterion-specific (Slavin 1990). A successful practical application of ATI research has not been made.

Mastery learning is the attempt to ensure that as many students in a class as possible (90–95%) meet a required learning criterion (90–95% correct items in a criterion test). This goal is achieved by a limited increase in learning time (about 20%) and optimal instructional use of the learning time. Although what one can actually expect from mastery learning in normal school instruction is somewhat controversial (Slavin 1987, Kulik et al. 1990), there is no doubt that it is a fruitful model that allows productive research and practical applications.

Adaptive teaching is based on many ideas from Carroll's model of school learning and ATI research. Adaptive teaching

> involves both learner adaptation *to* the environmental conditions presented and teacher adaptation *of* the environmental conditions to the learners' present state, to effect changes in that state. The teacher's goal, in other words, is to make environmental variations 'nurtured' rather than merely 'natural' for each learner of concern. (Corno and Snow 1986 p.607)

"Adaptive teaching" is thus an omnibus term covering a large number of different standardized and informal procedures for adapting teaching in variable, flexible, and dynamic ways to students' individual differences, so that optimal learning conditions can be provided for each student.

3.4 Fostering Students' Learning Competencies and Self-instructional Skills

In the above characterization of adaptive teaching it was noted that the optimization of individual learning requires not only that instruction be compatible with the cognitive and motivational demands of the student, but also that students' learning competencies and learning motivation be explicitly fostered. There is considerable research in cognitive psychology, developmental psychology, and educational psychology that addresses how to promote competencies and motivation. At the forefront are investigations on transfer of training, learning to think, the promotion of metacognitive skills, and the development of self-instructional skills.

Much of the theoretically oriented research also includes suggestions for applying the findings. Relevant support programs have been tried for elementary, secondary, and university students. Although these programs have demonstrated that intellectual skills and thinking performance cannot be arbitrarily trained, they have also convincingly shown that the training of metacognitive competencies and self-instructional skills can result in lasting improvements (Blagg 1991). When such programs have realistic goals, are provided over an extensive time frame, and, if possible, are directed toward the acquisition of domain specific knowledge, all students can profit.

3.5 The Use of Research Findings for New Models of Schooling

Research can be used not only to improve existing educational institutions, school organizations, and instructional conditions, but also to plan new models for schooling. Such an approach to change is needed when it is unclear whether an educational goal can be reached by gradual and piecemeal changes in current activities. Both theoretical discussion and practical experiences are available for using research findings in this way (Salisbury 1993). Such change requires consideration of the factors that must be considered in planning a new educational system, the strategies that should be employed, the problems that must be addressed, and the implementation tasks that must be performed.

3.6 Research as a Source of Background Knowledge for Practitioners

The practical application of research consists of more than the instrumental use of research findings. In addition, science and research have an educational function; that is, they provide individuals with knowledge about themselves and the world, and allow individuals to act rationally.

Because people think, decide, and act primarily on the basis of their available knowledge (whether it is correct or incorrect, complete or incomplete, objective or biased), it is important and necessary for those involved in the educational process (politicians, administrators, principals, teachers, parents, students, and researchers) to be able to change or replace their personal beliefs, intuitive knowledge, prejudices, and suppositions with reliable and valid information. Such a replacement is not only a prerequisite for reflective, responsible, and effective individual action, but also a condition for rational communication and discourse among educational practitioners. Although it is not possible to measure the effectiveness of this function of research, it nonetheless seems plausible and important to translate as many research results as possible into the language of the practitioner.

4. Conclusion

The relation between research and practice is complex and difficult. As a consequence, there is no simple, uniform solution to the problem of translating scientific results into practical suggestions. Nonetheless, some general conclusions can be drawn.

First, many different types of research are applicable to educational practice. The value of a scientific study for educational practice is not in any way directly related to the extent to which it mirrors typical features of an applied educational setting.

Second, research results can be used in educational practice in different ways. Six typical examples have been noted: the development of educational technologies, teacher training, the optimization of instruction, fostering students' learning competencies, the design of new models of schooling, and the use of scientific information as background knowledge for practitioners.

Third, these different strategies for applying research results are not mutually exclusive. Rather, it is desirable to combine several variants to improve the practical situation.

Finally, exploring the processes by which theoretical knowledge can be transformed into practical action must itself be an important domain of educational research.

References

Anderson L W (ed.) 1984 *Time and School Learning*. Croom Helm, London
Anderson L W, Burns R B 1985 *Research in Classrooms*. Pergamon Press, Oxford
Berliner D C 1992 The nature of expertise in teaching. In: Oser F K, Dick A, Patry J L (eds.) 1992 *Effective and Responsible Teaching*. Jossey-Bass, San Francisco, California
Blagg N 1991 *Can We Teach Intelligence?* Erlbaum, Hillsdale, New Jersey
Bloom B S 1966 Twenty-five years of educational research. *Am. Educ. Res. J.* 3(3): 211–21
Carroll J B 1963 A model of school learning. *Teach. Coll. Rec.* 64: 723–33
Corno L, Snow R E 1986 Adapting teaching to individual differences among learners. In Wittrock M C (ed.) 1986 *Handbook of Research on Teaching*, 3rd edn. MacMillan Inc., New York
Fraser B J, Walberg H J, Welch W W, Hattie J A 1987 Synthesis of educational productivity research. *Int. J. Educ. Res.* 11: 145–252
Glaser R, Cooley W 1973 Instrumentation for teaching and instructional management. In: Travers R M W (ed.) 1973 *Second Handbook of Research in Teaching*. Rand McNally, Chicago, Illinois
Haertel G D, Walberg H J, Weinstein T 1983 Psychological models of educational performance: A theoretical synthesis of constructs. *Rev. Educ. Res.* 53(1): 75–91
Hilgard E R 1964 A perspective on the relationship between learning theory and educational practice. In: Hilgard E R (ed.) 1964 *Theories of Learning and Instruction*. The National Society for the Study of Education, Chicago, Illinois
Kulik C L C, Kulik J A, Bangert–Drowns R L 1990 Effectiveness of mastery learning programs: A meta-analysis. *Rev. Educ. Res.* 60: 265–99
Mook D A 1983 In defense of external invalidity. *Am. Psychol.* 38(4): 379–87
Niemiec R P, Walberg H J 1992 The effect of computers on learning. *Int. J. Educ. Res.* 17(1): 99–108
Rein W 1893 *Pädagogik im Grundriß*, 2nd edn. Göschen, Stuttgart
Salisbury D F 1993 Designing and implementing new models of schooling. *Int. J. Educ. Res.* 19(2): 99–195

Scott R, Cole M, Engel M 1992 Computers and education: A cultural constructivist perspective. In: Grant G (ed.) 1992 *Rev. Res. Educ.* 18: 191–251

Skinner B F 1954 The science of learning and the art of teaching. *Harv. Educ. Rev.* 24(2): 86–97

Slavin R E 1987 Mastery learning reconsidered. *Rev. Educ. Res.* 57(2): 175–213

Slavin R E 1990 Achievement effects of ability grouping in secondary schools: A best-evidence synthesis. *Rev. Educ. Res.* 60(3): 471–99

Snow R E 1989 Aptitude–treatment interaction as a framework for research on individual differences in learning. In: Ackerman P L, Sternberg R J, Glaser R (eds.) 1989 *Learning and Individual Differences.* Freeman, New York

Stolurow L M 1965 Model the master teacher or master the teaching model? In: Krumbholtz J D (ed.) 1965 *Learning and the Educational Process.* Rand McNally, Chicago, Illinois

Thorpe L P, Schmuller A M 1954 *Contemporary Theories of Learning.* Wiley, New York

Tillema H H, Veenman S A M (eds.) 1987 Development in training methods for teacher education. *Int. J. Educ. Res.* 2(5): 517–600

Weinert F E, Helmke A, Schrader F W 1992 Research on the model teacher and the teaching model. In: Oser F K, Dick A, Patry J L (eds.) 1992 *Effective and Responsible Teaching—The New Synthesis.* Jossey-Bass, San Francisco, California

Weinert F E, Schrader F W, Helmke A 1989 Quality of instruction and achievement outcomes. *Int. J. Educ. Res.* 13(8): 895–914

Further Reading

Bloom B S 1976 *Human Characteristics and School Learning.* McGraw-Hill, New York

Glaser R 1977 *Adaptive Education: Individual Diversity and Learning.* Holt, Rinehart, and Winston, New York

Snow R E, Federico P A, Montague W E (eds.) 1980 *Aptitude, Learning, and Instruction,* Vols. 1, 2. Erlbaum, Hillsdale, New Jersey

PART B
Teacher Education

SECTION I
Concepts and Issues in Teacher Education

Introduction

L. W. Anderson

Concepts and issues form the building blocks for understanding and ultimately improving the quality of teacher education. Concepts are categories that are formed to give meaning to experiences. A person's concept of "friend," for example, will depend on their experiences both direct and vicarious, with other people. Likewise, our concept of evaluation depends on experiences with the form and substance of evaluation.

An issue is a "question that implies at least two or more answers with good reasons available to support [each one of] them" (Raths). A consideration of issues makes it possible to think about possibilities critically and, as a result, to make decisions that result in improved understanding and practice in a given discipline or field.

The authors of the entries in this section spend considerable time clarifying key concepts and identifying major issues. The first three entries pertain to students and teachers; the next five are concerned with organization and curriculum; and the final two deal with accreditation and certification. In this introduction, a few of the key concepts and major issues included in these entries are highlighted.

1. Students and Teachers

Adult development and gender issues are central to understanding the relationships among prospective teachers, practicing teachers, and teacher educators.

1.1 Adult Development

Adult development is an important concept in teacher education for at least two reasons. The first is fairly obvious. It is known that adults move through a sequence of qualitatively distinct, hierarchically integrated stages of thought and development (Oja). Thus, for initial teacher education programs to be successful, the designers of these programs must take into consideration the predominant stage of development of young adults.

A second reason for the importance of adult development in teacher education is somewhat less obvious, but perhaps more important. In any given school, there are likely to be found teachers at all stages of development. As a consequence, some are likely to be more concrete in their thinking, while others are able to engage in more abstract thought. Similarly, some are likely to be more rigid, while others, more flexible (Oja). As a consequence, one of the keys to the success of continuing teacher education is likely to be the ability of the program designer or deliverer to adapt to these differences among teachers.

1.2 Gender Issues in Teacher Education

The vast majority of prospective teachers are females who were raised in lower to middle class homes (Neururer). In contrast, the vast majority of teacher educators are males in their late 40s or early 50s who have spent the previous 15 years on average at their institutions (Ducharme). Furthermore, the majority of the administrators of the schools in which these prospective teachers will work are male. Ducharme suggests that these conditions "relay a direct message to prospective and practicing female teachers: you can teach, but those who prepare you to teach and those who administer the schools in which you will teach are likely to be male." These gender differences also exist in teacher preparation institutions. Female faculty members tend to have lower faculty ranks, be given more responsibility for supervising field experiences, and spend less time on scholarship. The predominance of female teachers also influences the perceptions of teaching held by prospective teachers. They expect easy access to a teaching position, light work, and a discontinuous work life. They also express the opinion that their academic preparation is irrelevant, an opinion that reinforces the relatively low status in which teachers are held and decreases the likelihood of the emergence of a true teaching profession (Neururer).

2. Organization and Curriculum

Curriculum development in teacher education is increasingly dependent on the identification of a knowledge base of teaching. In order to deliver the curriculum effectively and efficiently, issues of governance and evaluation of teacher education must be addressed.

2.1 The Knowledge Base of Teaching

Prospective teachers and critics alike have raised serious questions about the curriculum of teacher education. As was mentioned in the previous section, prospective teachers tend to view their academic preparation as irrelevant. They are particularly harsh on educational foundation courses. They see these courses as having marginal value and being composed of "haphazard collections of themes and topics" (Ben-Peretz). Galluzo extends this criticism to teacher education in general. He writes:

> All too often teacher education is a collection of courses which offer no consistent image of what it means to teach, nor what it means to learn to teach. This allows students to proceed through their programs confirming what they already believed teaching to be and rejecting or ignoring those concepts and practices which are inconsistent with their preconceived notions of teaching.

In response to these criticisms, teacher educators have begun to approach curriculum development from the perspective of building a knowledge base. According to Galluzo, this knowledge base includes a "set of beliefs, a body of supportive literature, and a set of clearly articulated expectations for students."

At the present time this knowledge base consists of four major areas: general education, content knowledge, pedagogical knowledge, and pedagogical content knowledge (Gimmestad and Hall, Ben-Peretz). While the first three of these areas are fairly traditional, pedagogical content knowledge is a rather new concept. Coined in the mid-1980s by Lee Shulman, pedagogical content knowledge includes:

> knowledge of typical misconceptions that students will have when learning a particular concept . . . knowledge of and the ability to draw upon powerful analogies, illustrations, examples, explanations, and demonstrations that will make sense to specific students . . . [and] knowledge of the background of experiences and culture that learners bring to the classroom and the frames of reference they bring to the learning of specific subject-matter concepts and principles. (Gimmestad and Hall)

The identification of an appropriate knowledge base for teachers will undoubtedly result in rethinking and restructuring current course offerings. If made properly, these changes will minimize what Ben-Peretz refers to as the null curriculum (i.e., content that should be included but is not). Examples include ethics, the biological roots of human behavior, and professional dispositions.

2.2 Issues in the Governance and Evaluation of Teacher Education

There appears to be a definite lack of a knowledge base when it comes to matters of the governance and evaluation of teacher education. Galluzo labels program evaluation as teacher education's "orphan," arguing that it is "one of the more poorly practiced aspects of the field." He continues: "the application of educational evaluation models to teacher education lacks the rich history one would expect to find in an area where the literature is almost 50 years old."

Gideonse issues a remarkably similar statement in the context of governance. He writes:

> Given the centrality of teachers to national education systems, it is surprising that so little scholarly literature exists on the governance of teacher education. . . . While expertise on these matters does exist, it has not been generated by members of the scholarly community. Rather, expertise resides in the experience of the practitioners of policy; that is, those who have lived through or have been affected by its processes and products. . . . The absence of a substantial literature . . . means each new generation must discover these matters anew.

In the light of the absence of a knowledge base, both Galluzo and Gideonse raise a number of issues that must be addressed by teacher educators and policymakers in both of these areas. The major issues are as follows:

(a) What are the appropriate qualifications for entry into teacher education programs and the appropriate exit requirements for leaving them successfully?

(b) What is the proper length and type of preparation for prospective teachers intending to teach at varying school levels (e.g., primary, secondary)?

(c) What are the continuing education expectations for practicing teachers?

(d) What is the proper balance between political and professional authority in the governance of teacher education?

(e) What is the proper relative weight to be given to national, regional and local interests in governance matters?

(f) What criterion variables (e.g., knowledge, teaching skill, affective dispositions, perceptions of preparation) should be used in teacher evaluation?

(g) How can the institutional-specific nature of program evaluation be overcome so that the beginnings of a knowledge base can be established?

(h) What is the relative importance of formative and summative evaluation in teacher education?

(i) To what extent is teacher education perceived as a field of inquiry?

3. Accreditation and Certification

Conceptual confusion appears to be rampant in these two areas. Additionally, several issues confront those working in these areas.

3.1 Criteria and Standards

Raths suggests that educators and policymakers tend to confuse these two concepts. He then proceeds to offer carefully worded definitions of each.

> It is often helpful to think of criterion as a name of a variable that is subject to review. A criterion is a basis for comparison, and is usually named in accordance with the upper end of a continuum of values that the variable might take (e.g., "clarity" or "accuracy"). Alternatively, the variable name itself implies a higher and lower end of its own scale (e.g., "faculty productivity," or "quality of students.") A standard, on the other hand, is not a range, but a setting within a range that is taken as desirable, minimal, or honorific.

The problem with teacher education accreditation, according to Raths, is that it typically is carried out with well-specified criteria, but "with no standards or with only vague notions of standards." He concludes: "Interestingly, the making of judgments with criteria but without standards is seen as the essence of professional practice."

3.2 Licensure and Certification

A similar confusion exists with licensure and certification. Some educators and policymakers in fact treat them as synonymous. As Scannell and Scannell point out, however, they are not. Licensure is quality control exercised by a governmental authority (i.e., state, region, nation). Certification, on the other hand, is "quality control exercised by peer review."

In most true professions, licensure precedes certification. That is, a person receives a license to practice after an initial period of preparation. Subsequently, after some time in practice coupled with the development of expertise in that practice, a person applies for certification. Notice the use of the phrase "applies for" in the previous sentence. This phrase is important for two reasons. First, certification most often is voluntary, while licensure is required. Second, not all who apply for certification meet the standards for certification.

In terms of teacher education, the distinction between licensure and certification is important and

useful. Initial teacher education programs should lead to licensure, while continuing teacher education programs should focus on certification. Furthermore, certification permits the recognition of different ranks of status among practicing teachers. Such recognition may help keep our "brightest and best" teachers in the classroom.

3.3 Issues

The authors of the entries on accreditation and certification raise a series of issues. Among the most important are the following:

(a) Who should control teacher certification?

(b) What is the proper balance of content, theory, and clinical practice?

(c) What requirements should be established for continuing professional development?

(d) To what extent should accreditation emphasize inputs versus outputs?

(e) How specific should accreditation criteria be?

(f) How high should accreditation standards be set?

4. Conclusion

As a set, the entries in this section attempt to reduce conceptual confusion and raise critical issues that must be addressed by teacher educators. Conceptual clarity is essential if there are to be meaningful conversations and discussions about teacher education. Without conceptual clarity, the study of teacher education is difficult and substantial improvements will be virtually impossible.

The presence of so many critical issues says a great deal about the state of the field of teacher education. There are more questions than answers. Furthermore, in some respects, there are no generic answers to the questions. Rather, the answers are culturally specific. At the same time, however, another reason for a lack of answers must be recognized; namely, a lack of significant, systematic research and careful study. The author of virtually every entry in this section makes this point. The critical issues raised by these authors amount to a useful starting place for a carefully planned research program in the field.

(a) Students and Teachers

Characteristics of Prospective Teachers

J. Neururer

The future of educational systems throughout the world depends to a large extent on the number and quality of prospective teachers. Who are these prospective teachers? How many are there and do their numbers meet the expected future demand for teachers? What do we know about prospective teachers in terms of academic ability and affective characteristics? What changes in the characteristics of prospective teachers need to be made to ensure their effectiveness in the classroom? These questions will be addressed in this entry.

1. Number of Prospective Teachers

Prospective teachers include those in traditional teacher education programs, those who have graduated from traditional teacher education programs but who are not currently teaching, degree recipients who did not major in education fields but who meet the requirements for licensure or certification in teaching, and those who are interested in becoming teachers but who lack the official prerequisites for entry into teaching. While there may be a tendency to limit any conception of the current teaching pool to those in traditional teacher education programs and those who have graduated from such programs, it must be pointed out that more than 30 percent of the teachers hired during the mid-1980s in the United States majored in fields other than education (Stern and Chandler 1987). Furthermore, the teaching pool includes those who have "stopped out" of teaching for some period of time, but who intend to return to teaching in the future.

Thanks to their variety, it is difficult to obtain an accurate figure for the number of prospective teachers, let alone describe them. In this regard, Murnane and his colleagues (1991) stated that it is impossible to provide a truly accurate impression of the corps of prospective teachers in the United States as there are no national data on trends in the number of prospective teachers or the characteristics of new licensees. This lack of valid and complete data also exists in other countries, particularly in those undergoing modernization or social upheaval (Leavitt 1991).

To complicate matters further, there is an important difference between prospective and beginning teachers. Not all of those who are licensed to teach seek or obtain employment in schools. In the People's Republic of China, for example, almost 60 percent of those who completed teacher training programs were unwilling to enter the teaching force in 1989 (Chang and Paine 1992). Similarly, in the United States, the Carnegie Foundation for the Advancement of Teaching (CFAT) reported that only 60 percent of all holders of a bachelor's degree who gained licensure or certification for teaching in 1980 were actually teaching in the early 1980s (CFAT 1986, 1987).

Problems of decreased teacher supply and increased teacher demand are worldwide. Between 1990 and 2000, United States schools will require more than 2 million new teachers (Murnane et al. 1991) and less than 65 percent of this demand will be met by new teacher graduates (CFAT 1986, 1987). The Arab Gulf States, Australia, China, Egypt, Malawi, and the Commonwealth of Independent States all cite the recruitment into and retention of academically able individuals in teaching as a critical issue (Leavitt 1992). In the former Soviet Union, low pay and poor living conditions have dissuaded many from choosing a teaching career (Leavitt 1991). In order to meet teacher shortages in Spain, the ministry of education mandated an elimination of any admission requirements for teacher education (Benejam and Espinet 1992).

2. Portrait of a Prospective Teacher

Although it is difficult to delineate clearly the prospective teaching population, a well-known portrait of the teacher, particularly in the United States, has emerged. Virtually every descriptive study conducted in the United States notes the propensity of the teaching population to be White, lower to middle class, and female (McDiarmid 1990, Ross and Smith

1992, Zimpher 1989). Women outnumber men by more than four to one, with a higher percentage of women at the elementary level than at the secondary and postsecondary levels. This profile also applies to prospective teachers, at least those enrolled in teacher education programs (Brookhart and Freeman 1992).

It should be noted that most of these reviews have been subjected to harsh criticism. Lanier and Little (1986), for example, argued that the data are often inadequately analyzed and synthesized, thus perpetuating stereotypes, misinformation, and misunderstandings. Brookhart and Freeman (1992) questioned the design of the research suggesting that researchers tend to lack a theoretical framework to guide their interpretations, rely on a single method of data collection and/or on a sample from a single institution, and make an "inadequate distinction among subpopulations" (p. 53).

3. Cognitive Characteristics of Prospective Teachers

Spurred on by criticism of the United States educational system, numerous studies of the academic abilities of prospective teachers have been conducted (Vance and Schlecty 1982). The results of these studies are similar. Prospective teachers were over represented among the lowest scorers on standardized aptitude tests, and underrepresented among the highest scorers. Only four fields recorded lower scores than intended education majors. Furthermore, the gap between the mean scores of prospective teachers and those of all other fields combined widened from approximately 60 to 80 points from the mid-1970s to the mid-1980s (CFAT 1986).

Similar results have been obtained in other countries. In Nigeria, for example, disproportionate numbers of undergraduates in education come the lowest 10 percent of university students; 50 percent of those who applied for admission to education had been rejected from their favored programs of study (Avoseh 1992).

These findings have led to the conclusion that to improve the quality of education more academically able prospective teachers must be recruited. This conclusion has not been without its critics, however. As Darling-Hammond (1990) pointed out:

Test scores are not clear evidence of quality or lack of quality. What we mean by teacher quality should be more influenced by what teacher candidates learn after they enter college than by the entrance examination scores they presented at matriculation. (pp. 272–73)

Furthermore, the desire to enlist students with the highest grade average and test scores can be questioned on several grounds. First, a "positive relationship between a single attribute, academic ability, and quality teaching has not been forthcoming" (Otis-

Wilborn et al. 1988 p. 108). Second, despite the vociferous criticism leveled at the teaching field, a consensus has yet to emerge as to the vital academic, personal, and professional qualifications of prospective teachers, particularly in light of the number of new teachers needed (Darling-Hammond 1990).

4. Affective Characteristics of Prospective Teachers

Like the data on academic ability, the available data on affective characteristics of prospective teachers are disappointing. As Lanier and Little (1986) pointed out:

The research evidence suggests that both prospective and practicing teachers maintain low expectations for the professional knowledge aspects of their education. The desire for serious and continued learning for improvement purposes is also understandably low in light of growing declines in extrinsic and intrinsic rewards for the occupation of teaching itself. (p. 542)

Furthermore, the belief that teaching is a low-status profession may hurt the self-esteem of prospective teachers (Murnane et al. 1991).

At the same time, however, prospective teachers have a stronger orientation to human welfare than their college peers and place greater emphasis on personal relationships. They also "place less emphasis on economic success and what is seen by other groups as efficient or practical" (Coulter 1987 p. 591). Overall, the students majoring in education "have values that differ from those in other fields and, in fact, seem to be somewhat more traditional in their outlook" (CFAT 1986 p. 29).

Brookhart and Freeman (1992) reviewed 44 studies of beginning education students and offered the following synthesis. Candidates for teaching are motivated by a concern for others, possess confidence in their teaching abilities, express greater concern for mastering content than for managing interpersonal relationships, perceive the nurturing aspects of teaching as more important than academic requirements, and interpret the teaching act as one of dispensing information.

Finally, whereas professionals in other fields expect difficult access, hard work, a continuous work history, and enter with a keen appreciation for their academic preparation, preservice teachers express attitudes about teaching that reflect the contrary. They expect easy access, light work, and a discontinuous work life. They also express the opinion that their academic preparation is irrelevant (Lanier and Little 1986).

Research on affective characteristics of prospective teachers has been criticized for its reliance on descriptive studies, many of which are narrowly bounded and framed, and for the lack of attention to socialization issues. For example, folk wisdom dictates that a relationship exists between attitudes of prospective teachers and their teaching effectiveness. However, early research "revealed little evidence of relationships of any strength, consistency, or consequence between student teacher effectiveness and their values, attitudes, or interests" (Coulter 1987 p. 593). Levis (1987) also noted the "limited usefulness of knowledge gained from such research" (p. 587). In the early 1990s researchers called for a different type of research to explore this possible relationship in greater depth. This research would be field-based and qualitative and would include detailed interviews and observations (Brookhart and Freeman 1992).

5. Changing the Characteristics of Prospective Teachers

Most preservice teachers complete their teacher preparation programs without an examination of their deepest values and beliefs, even on such vital issues as pedagogy, teacher roles and responsibilities, curriculum, and the cultural diversity of students (McDiarmid 1990). In addition to examining these issues, changes in the values, attitudes, and beliefs of prospective teachers as they relate to these issues may be necessary.

Concerning the cultural diversity of students, for example, Larke et al. (1990) asserted that teacher attitudes regarding minority students shape educational outcomes. Thus, understanding and reshaping stereotypical attitudes are imperative. However, little research on attitude change has been conducted in the context of preservice teaching. Multicultural education efforts to change attitudes has not been assessed empirically (Grottkau and Nickolai-Mays 1989). In at least some instances little change is expected because the efforts lack strength and direction (Ross and Smith 1992).

As the demographics of the student population change, examining and, when necessary, altering teachers' views on racial minorities become critically important. In the United States, for example, approximately 40 percent of all children enrolled in public schools will be members of minority ethnic groups by the year 2000 (Graham 1987). This figure is substantially higher in the largest cities of the United States. In the 15 largest cities, between 70 and 96 percent of children will be members of minority groups, while less than 5 percent of the teachers of these children will represent minority groups (Ross and Smith 1992).

Particularly troubling in this regard is the finding that prospective teachers prefer to work in a school environment that mirrors their own experiences, thus maintaining their cultural insularity (Ross and Smith 1992, Zimpher 1989). Only 20 percent of prospective teachers in one United States study indicated a preference to work with students from diverse racial and cultural backgrounds (Larke 1990). This problem is compounded by a shrinking number of minority teachers (Murnane et al. 1991), the constantly changing realities of a pluralistic society (Grottkau and Nickolai-Mays 1989), and the lack of awareness of cultural differences that will serve as obstacles to the academic success of minority students (Larke 1990).

6. Conclusion

Information about prospective teachers is limited. Because of the various categories of prospective teachers, the number of prospective teachers in the United States population is uncertain. What is known about prospective teachers is not necessarily flattering. Prospective teachers tend to have lower academic ability than their contemporaries pursuing other professional careers. They also tend to subscribe to more traditional values than their peers. They generally regard the job of teaching as relatively easy and have confidence in their teaching abilities. They are motivated more by humanistic interests than economic concerns. Perhaps because of these other perceptions, they tend to view the academic side of their teacher preparation as difficult and irrelevant.

During the 1980s, serious attention was paid for the first time to answering a variety of questions concerning the characteristics of prospective teachers. The future will determine if the right questions have been asked.

See also: Teacher Recruitment and Induction; Professional Socialization of Teachers

References

Avoseh O 1992 Nigeria. In: Leavitt H B (ed.) 1992
Benejam P, Espinet M 1992 Spain. In: Leavitt H B (ed.) 1992
Brookhart S M, Freeman D J 1992 Characteristics of entering teacher candidates. *Rev. Educ. Res.* 62(1): 37–60
Carnegie Foundation for the Advancement of Teaching (CFAT) 1986 Future teachers: Will there be enough good ones? *Change* 18(5): 27–30
Carnegie Foundation for the Advancement of Teaching (CFAT) 1987 Prospective teachers: Career choices. *Change* 19(2): 31–35
Chang M C, Paine L 1992 China. In: Leavitt H B (ed.) 1992
Coulter F 1987 Affective characteristics of student teachers. In: Dunkin M J (ed.) 1987 *International Encyclopedia of Teaching and Teacher Education.* Pergamon Press, Oxford
Darling-Hammond L 1990 Teachers and teaching: Signs of a changing profession. In: Houston N R (ed.) 1990 *Handbook of Research on Teacher Education.* Macmillan Inc., New York
Graham P A 1987 Black teachers: A drastically scarce resource. *Phi Del. Kap.* 69(8): 598–605
Grottkau B J, Nickolai-Mays S 1989 An empirical analysis of a multi-cultural education paradigm for preservice teachers. *Educ. Res. Q.* 13(4): 27–33
Lanier J E, Little J W 1986 Research on teacher education: Studying the students of teaching. In: Wittrock M C (ed.) 1986 *Handbook of Research on Teaching,* 3rd edn. Macmillan Inc., New York
Larke P J 1990 Cultural diversity awareness inventory: Assessing the sensitivity of preservice teachers. *Action in Teacher Education* 12(3): 23–30

Larke P J, Wiseman D, Bradley C 1990 The minority mentorship project: Changing attitudes of preservice teachers for diverse classrooms. *Action in Teacher Education* 12(3): 5–11

Leavitt H B 1991 Worldwide issues and problems in teacher education. *J. Teach. Educ.* 42(5): 323–31

Leavitt H B (ed.) 1992 *Issues and Problems in Teacher Education: An International Handbook.* Greenwood, New York

Levis D S 1987 Teachers' personality. In: Dunkin M J (ed.) 1987 *International Encyclopedia of Teaching and Teacher Education.* Pergamon Press, Oxford

McDiarmid G W 1990 Challenging prospective teachers' beliefs during early field experience: A quixotic undertaking? *J. Teach. Educ.* 41(3): 12–20

Murnane R J, Singer J D, Willett J B, Kemple J J, Olsen R J 1991 *Who will Teach? Policies that Matter.* Harvard University Press, Cambridge, Massachusetts

Otis-Wilborn A K, Marshall J D, Sears J T 1988 Commitment: A reflection of the quality of preservice teachers. *Peabody Journal of Education* 65(2): 107–29

Ross D D, Smith W 1992 Understanding preservice teachers' perspectives on diversity. *J. Teach. Educ.* 43(2): 94–103

Stern J P, Chandler M O (eds.) 1987 *The Condition of Education: A Statistical Report.* United States Department of Education, Center for Education Statistics, Washington, DC

Vance V S, Schlechty P S 1982 The distribution of academic ability in the teaching force: Policy implications. *Phi Del. Kap.* 64(1): 22–27

Zimpher N C 1989 The RATE Project: A profile of teacher education students. *J. Teach. Educ.* 40(6): 27–30

Characteristics of Teacher Educators

E. R. Ducharme

The body of research on teacher educators is meager. As Lanier and Little (1986) have written:

> research on teaching teachers stands in stark contrast to research on teaching youngsters . . . . Teachers of teachers—what they are like, what they do, what they think—are systematically overlooked in studies of teacher education. (p. 528)

That same year, Ducharme (1986) conducted a review of research literature in the field. He was able to locate only seven references to teacher educators, most of which focused on education faculty in general. Based on his review, Ducharme concluded that teacher educators knew very little about themselves and, furthermore, that the term "teacher educator" was ill-defined.

While teacher educators have been largely absent from reputable research literature, traditionally they have not been ignored by the literature of hyperbole, innuendo, and quasi-research. Kramer's (1991) polemic, *Ed School Follies*, followed the line of argument earlier expounded in Koerner's (1963) *The Miseducation of American Teachers.* Even Clark (1987) in his scholarly work *The Academic Life: Small Worlds, Different Worlds* relied on anecdotal barbs to make his points about education faculty.

In the late 1980s, however, things began to change. A series of books and reports appeared which systematically examined teacher education and teacher educators. Books by Warren (1989), Clifford and Guthrie (1988), Goodlad et al. (1990), and Wisniewski and Ducharme (1989) included lengthy sections on teacher educators. Howey and Zimpher's (1990) chapter "Professors and Deans of Education" in the *Handbook of Research on Teacher Education* reviewed studies of teacher educators; their *Profiles of Pre-service Education: Inquiries into the Nature of Programs* (1989) includes insightful sections on teacher educators and their work. *Phi Delta Kappan*, the *Journal of Teacher Education*, and other journals have either run feature issues on teacher educators or have published articles on the topic. The RATE committee of the American Association of Colleges for Teacher Education (AACTE) has annually published monographs based on annual surveys of education faculty and cooperating teachers. By the end of the first five years of surveys, over 12,000 faculty and more than 200 cooperating teachers had completed questionnaires.

1. Demographics of Teacher Educators

The AACTE studies from 1987 to 1991, the Ducharme and Agne data (1982, 1989) and the Howey et al. data (1978) are the major sources of information about teacher education faculty in the United States. Based on these data, a composite teacher educator can be described. This teacher educator is a White male in his late forties or early fifties, tenured at either the full or associate professor level. He acquired a doctorate while studying part-time and has been at his current place of employment for over 15 years, during which time he has published six or seven articles in refereed publications. He taught for a minimum of three years in the lower schools prior to his employment in higher education.

This composite teacher educator is from either a middle or lower middle class background. Scholars have contended that teacher educators, inasmuch as they generally come from the ranks of teachers, reflect the social class origins of teachers. Mattingly

(1975), Powell (1980), Lanier and Little (1986), and Ducharme and Agne (1989) agree on this point: all suggest that the lower and lower middle social-class origins affect professional lives in higher education. Lanier and Little (1986), by way of summary, observed that:

A disproportionately large number of faculty teaching teachers most directly have come from lower middle-class backgrounds. It is very likely that they obtain conformist orientations and utilitarian views of knowledge from their experiences at home, educational opportunities in school, and restrictive conditions of work as teachers before coming to higher education. (p. 535)

Lanier and Little's observation that teacher educators likely have "utilitarian views of knowledge" is provocative; if accurate, it may account for the high comfort level many teacher educators have historically had with such utilitarian, mechanistic movements as Competency Based Teacher Education.

This hypothetical faculty member fails, of course, to reflect the variation among teacher educators. For example, in-depth analyses of the data indicate that recently hired, generally younger faculty entered higher education faculty ranks earlier in their careers than did their older teacher education colleagues. Based on their early productivity, it can be predicted that they are likely to publish more in their careers than have the older faculty; they anticipate moving at least once in the future. They are somewhat more likely to be female, but less likely to be non-White.

These demographic data raise provocative issues for analysis and further study. For example, the teaching ranks in United States elementary schools remain largely female, while those who teach them are predominantly male. The hordes of female graduates of these programs take positions in elementary schools, the majority of which have male principals. Surely these conditions relay a direct message to prospective and practicing female teachers: you can teach, but those who prepare you to teach and those who administer the schools in which you will teach are likely to be male. A "plantation mentality" may prevail as a consequence of these conditions, irrespective of good intentions. Teacher education faculty—both male and female—would do well to provide prospective teachers with better models, to confront a sometimes sexist professional world and a curriculum and set of experiences that will enlighten and empower them to live and teach effectively in that world.

Female teacher educators perform more field work than do males. They are more likely to supervise students in early field experiences and in student teaching than are their male counterparts. They are also likely to have more advisees, and spend more time in advising and in committee work, even while reporting that they spend about the same number of hours per week doing their own work. Significantly, they report spending less time on scholarly and research activities (AACTE, 1989, 1990).

Female teacher educators also hold lower faculty ranks than do males. In the 1989 AACTE survey, for example, women comprised 28 percent of the teacher education professoriate. However, only 12 percent of the faculty at the rank of full professor were female (AACTE 1990).

The reasons for these conditions are unknown. Various explanations occur, and while all of them might explain part of the matter, no single explanation suffices. Among the explanations are their later entry into the ranks of higher education; interrupted careers to bear and raise children; lower scholarly output; inappropriate assignment or acceptance of duties with heavy emphasis on "nurturing" tasks; prejudice and bias, and a lack of a female counterpart to the "old-boy" network (including mentoring while in doctoral work). These explanations are likely to be interrelated. For example, lower scholarly productivity may be a function of an interrupted career pattern, inappropriate assignments, lack of mentoring, or all three.

The demographics on race contain an even more pernicious message. With the exception of faculty in historically Black colleges, there are virtually no Black or other minority faculty in teacher education. Year after year in the AACTE studies, regardless of the area of teacher education under study (elementary education, secondary education, educational foundations), the percentage of minority faculty never rises above 10 percent.

Teacher education units may take some solace from the fact that this is the condition in higher education generally, but this would be an unjustifiably complacent attitude. The increasingly strident voices of those administering accreditation of teacher education are calling for faculty and student diversity. Teacher education must face this issue and move toward some new manifestation of diversity if it is to be an effective force in the preparation of educators for the twenty-first century.

2. Research and Scholarship of Teacher Educators

There is a lack of clarity about the degree and kind of research and scholarship in which teacher educators engage. Judge (1982) contended that research is the major driving force in the large private and state flagship universities. The AACTE studies show clear differences in scholarly productivity among faculty at institutions catering for bachelors only and those providing master's and doctoral degrees, with faculty scholarly productivity growing as the level of institutional complexity increases. Critics such as Koerner (1963) and Kramer (1991) contended that what *is* published by teacher education scholars is of little merit in any event. While Ducharme and Agne (1982) suggested that research and scholarly productivity of education faculty is at about the level of higher education faculty generally (a view consistent with the successive AACTE reports), there is little from which sound, empirically based conclusions about education faculty scholarship can be drawn.

There is, however, a widely held belief that education faculty may be less *interested* in research and scholarship than are faculty in other disciplines—indeed, someone spending time on a higher education campus might draw a similar conclusion for many of the education faculty. What is the reason for this? Ducharme (1986) and Lanier and Little (1986), among others, have speculated that the years spent in the lower schools with their low priority for active scholarship and high priority for long hours of work may contribute to some individual teacher educators' low scholarly productivity. For some, old workplace habits may be too ingrained for them to change behaviors to meet the loosely applied but rigidly held scholarly standards of higher education. Ducharme (1993) found that the 34 teacher education faculty whom he interviewed were, in the main, highly productive, despite differing views of the value of such work among the different generations represented in his interviewees and despite their attending a variety of types of institutions.

Faculty scholarship is uneven among institutions and individuals. Ducharme and Agne (1982) concluded that faculty have an average of slightly more than five refereed publications during their lifetime. This conclusion has also been supported by the AACTE studies. In RATE V, for example, the average number of lifetime publications for faculty in refereed journals was 5.4 and in nonrefereed journals was 4.7 (AACTE 1992). Focusing only on the average may be misleading, however. Some faculty members have as many as 26 refereed publications; others have none.

The AACTE data also suggest that younger faculty are publishing at a pace that indicates that they will surpass their older colleagues. Schuttenberg et al. (1985) have argued that younger education faculty value scholarship more highly than more mature faculty and also believe their potential for scholarship to be higher. Ducharme and Agne (1989) have contended that new faculty increasingly come with a predisposition toward becoming scholars. The rise in scholarly orientation among incoming faculty raises a new question. Will the increased emphasis on and interest in research and scholarship distance teacher educators from the field of practitioners (with whom many of them have historically worked, thus forming a bridge between theory and practice)?

It is clear from every indicator of faculty productivity that not all faculty publish extensively, nor do they want to do so. Likewise, faculty do not teach or provide professional service on an equal basis. It is important that units contain faculty who produce exemplary scholarship, teach well, and provide effective service. Such a constellation of faculty might well be the rallying cry for units in the late 1990s and early twenty-first century.

3. Working Conditions of Teacher Educators

Demographics and working conditions are in some ways inextricably related. That is, who people are and where they come from often condition what they do. Nonetheless, there are some unique conditions of teacher education faculty life that merit discussion.

Teacher educators spend considerable time in primary and secondary schools. Nash (1993) observed that the nature of the work of teacher educators is such that they are in frequent conflict with both the field of practice and their own institutional values. Ducharme (1986) stated this point in the following way: "Professors of education are caught between the traditional scholarship and research norms of higher education and the professional and technical demands of practitioners" (p. 1). While some emphases may change, it seems likely that the split responsibilities and lack of understandings of role will endure.

Faculty who specialize in elementary school teaching methods reported that they spent an average of more than 28 hours per month in the schools (AACTE 1989). What faculty do while in the schools cannot be divined precisely, but the AACTE data suggest that they likely divide their time among the following activities: observing student teachers, meeting with supervisors, conducting pre- and postconferences with student teachers, or—more unlikely—providing inservice or workshop activities for teachers, or conducting research in the schools. The faculty reported that they spend 6.8 hours per month in student teaching supervision and 1.6 hours per month in research activities.

As teacher educators assess their roles and responsibilities, they might consider the amount of time they spend in school settings and determine how that time might be better coordinated and used more effectively. Key questions such as the following can be used to guide this examination. Is that time well spent? Can the time and the faculty be better organized? What are the research questions implied in this condition?

Teacher education faculty spend more time in schools among teachers and children than do any other group of higher education faculty. This condition makes sense in terms of their students and their responsibilities, but it may also partially explain the low esteem in which they are held. The banal axiom that the closer a professional works to children the less esteem he or she gathers may well apply. Preschool staffs, Head Start teachers, day care center employees, elementary school teachers—all are held in low regard by various elements of the greater society. Why, then, should those who prepare them expect to be accorded much esteem from the highly structured and hierarchical world of higher education?

4. Summary and Conclusion

Teacher education has come a long way from Allison's (1989) depiction of the itinerant early professors of education in Tennessee; these were individuals whose hard work, practical know-how and entrepreneurship were not matched by their academic integrity. There is a body of literature, as Wisniewski and Ducharme (1989) pointed out, that suggests that teacher education faculty have achieved status on university campuses. For some, their presence on campuses is vital for the income their programs generate; for others, for the service they provide; for still others, for the inquiry into teaching and learning they conduct.

But while the process of teaching is ageless, the profession of teacher educator is relatively young. Studies are beginning to show the value of teacher education in the preparation of teachers. Evertson et al. (1985), Ashton and Crocker (1987), and Ferguson and Womack (1993) have built a case for the proposition that professional teacher preparation makes a difference in the lives of teachers and, perhaps more importantly, in the lives of their students. Despite the remarkable advances made by these and other researchers, much more study is needed. The hope for teacher educators is that they can retain their reputation for being caring individuals while continuing to develop meaningful and effective ways of preparing teachers. In a world that appears increasingly to lean to the empirical while yearning for the spiritual, teacher education has the potential to satisfy both aspirations.

See also: Inservice Teacher Education

References

Allison C 1989 Early professors of education: Three case studies. In: Wisniewski R, Ducharme E R (eds.) 1989
American Association of Colleges for Teacher Education (AACTE) 1988 RATE I: Teaching Teachers: Facts and Figures. AACTE, Washington, DC
AACTE 1989 RATE II: Teaching Teachers: Facts and Figures. AACTE, Washington, DC
AACTE 1990 RATE III: Teaching Teachers: Facts and Figures. AACTE, Washington, DC
AACTE 1991 RATE IV: Teaching Teachers: Facts and Figures. AACTE, Washington, DC
AACTE 1992 RATE V: Teaching Teachers: Facts and Figures. AACTE, Washington, DC
Ashton P, Crocker L 1987 Systematic study of planned variations: The essential focus of teacher education reform. *J. Teach. Educ.* 38(3): 2–8
Clark B 1987 *The Academic Life: Small Worlds, Different Worlds.* Carnegie Foundation for the Advancement of Teaching, Princeton, New Jersey
Clifford G, Guthrie J W 1988 *Ed School: A Brief for Profes-*
sional Education. University of Chicago Press, Chicago, Illinois
Ducharme E R 1986 *Teacher Educators: What Do We Know?* ERIC Digest 15. ERIC Clearing-house on Teacher Education, Washington, DC
Ducharme E R, Agne R 1982 The education professorate: A research-based perspective. *J. Teach. Educ.* 33(6): 30–36
Ducharme E R, Agne R 1989 Professors of education: Uneasy residents of academe. In: Wisniewski R, Ducharme E R (eds.) 1989
Ducharme E R 1993 *The Lives of Teacher Educators.* Teachers College Press, New York
Evertson C, Hawley W, Zlotnik M 1985 Making a difference in educational quality through teacher education. *J. Teach. Educ.* 36(3): 2–12
Ferguson P, Womack S 1993 The impact of subject matter and education coursework on teaching performance. *J. Teach. Educ.*
Goodlad J, Soder R, Sirotnik K (eds.) 1990 *Places Where Teachers are Taught.* Jossey-Bass, San Francisco, California
Howey K, Yarger S, Joyce B 1978 *Improving Teacher Education.* Association of Teacher Educators, Washington, DC
Howey K, Zimpher N 1989 *Profiles of Pre-service Education: Inquiry into the Nature of Programs.* State University of New York, Albany, New York
Howey K, Zimpher N 1990 Professors and deans of education. In: Houston W R (ed.) 1990 *Handbook of Research on Teacher Education.* Macmillan Inc., New York
Judge H 1982 *American Graduate Schools of Education: A View from Abroad.* The Ford Foundation, New York
Koerner J 1963 *The Miseducation of American Teachers.* Houghton Mifflin, Boston, Massachusetts
Kramer R 1991 *Ed School Follies: The Miseducation of America's Teachers.* Free Press, New York
Lanier J, Little J 1986 Research on teacher education. In: Wittrock M C (ed.) 1986 *Handbook of Research on Teaching,* 3rd edn. Macmillan Inc., New York
Mattingly P H 1975 *The Classless Profession: American Schoolmen in the Nineteenth Century.* New York University Press, New York
Nash R J 1993 Rita Kramer's follies: The misrepresentation of America's teacher educators. *J. Teach. Educ.*
Powell A 1980 *The Uncertain Profession: Harvard and the Search for Educational Authority.* Harvard University Press, Cambridge, Massachusetts
Schuttenberg E, Patterson L, Sutton R 1985 Self-perceptions of productivity of education faculty: Life phase and gender differences. Paper presented at the annual meeting of the American Educational Research Association (AERA), Chicago, Illinois (ERIC Document Reproduction Service No. ED 257 807)
Warren D (ed.) 1989 *American Teachers: Histories of a Profession at Work.* Macmillan Inc., New York
Wisniewski R, Ducharme E R (eds.) 1989 *The Professors of Teaching: An Inquiry.* State University of New York, Albany, New York

Further Reading

Ducharme M K, Ducharme E R 1993 School-based teacher education in the United States: An uneven evolution. *Australian Journal of Teacher Education* 18(2): 15–22

Adult Development and Teacher Education

S. N. Oja

Age theories suggest a pattern of tasks that confront adults throughout their life cycles. Beginning teachers in their 20s may be concerned with initial commitments to teaching, living arrangements, and relationships. In subsequent life-cycle periods such as their 40s, teachers may question their priorities and values as they realize that time is finite and success and achievement have limitations. At each age-related transition, a person's developmental task is to create a better fit between the life structure he or she has defined and the reality of life's challenges.

The concept of structure building and structure changing (Levinson 1986) is particularly important to a conception of life periods in adulthood. A number of extensive reviews of life-age and life-cycle theories were completed in the 1980s by researchers such as Chickering, Havighurst, Neugarten, and Hagestad. These researchers discussed sociological changes (political, technological, economic, and demographic), age norms, the social clock, and on- and off-time crises that can result in life-cycle changes which may have a significant impact upon the functioning of the individual.

1. Teachers' Professional Life Cycles and their Careers

A variety of researchers have used age-related life-cycle literature to understand better the phases of a teacher's career. Since space in this entry does not permit a detailed review of these studies, readers are referred to the literature review by Burden (1990); A few studies are mentioned in this section to give the reader a general picture of the research in this area.

Huberman's (1989) life-cycle research with Swiss teachers used collaborative autobiography to analyze teacher career paths and attitudes toward teaching. His work raised issues about the disjointed nature of teachers' development which can result in either rigid or flexible endpoints.

Fessler and Christensen (1992) provided descriptions of the complex environmental factors which may influence a teacher's career and the major characteristics of each career cycle: induction, competency building, enthusiasm and growth, career frustration, stability, wind-down, and exit. Their work discussed growth needs as well as the incentives and support systems for each phase in a teacher's career cycle.

Vonk and Schras (1987) focused on professional development during the first 4 years of teaching in the Netherlands, and Burden (1990) presented an extensive review of research on preservice teachers

and inservice teacher development, mostly in the United States. This research produced suggestions for effective ways to educate new teachers and to train experienced teachers as mentors.

2. Stages of Teacher Development

Cognitive–developmental stages are not defined by age; teachers at the same age are frequently at different stages of development. Stage theorists have focused on underlying patterns of thought and problem-solving which play a central role in determining an individual's approach to the world. The stages are structural in nature, qualitatively different from one another, hierarchically integrated, and emerge—according to these theories—in an unvaried sequence or progression. The sequence of development progresses from simpler to more complex and differentiated modes of thought and functioning. Levine (1988) has reviewed stage theories in teacher development.

3. Moral/Ethical Development

A number of researchers have used a Kohlbergian perspective, referred to as a "morality of justice," to determine teacher stage and level of moral judgment. There are two ways of collecting data—a moral judgment interview based on dilemma situations, or an objective questionnaire called the Defining Issues Test (DIT). Six stages of development have been identified, ranging from preconventional through conventional to postconventional thinking.

Johnson (1989) found a positive relation between moral reasoning levels and teachers' understanding of individualized instruction. She also summarized a number of previous studies that led to the conclusion that moral developmental levels are related to teachers' understanding of curriculum, student–teacher roles, management issues, rules, and teaching practices. Thomas and Rest (1987) investigated moral sensitivity in 30 student teachers and found that moral judgment was related to teaching performance, though the magnitude was not large.

Yeazell and Johnson (1988) investigated levels of moral judgment of faculty and students in a teacher education program. They found that the faculty were able to recognize principled postconventional moral judgments while none of the three student groups (undergraduate beginning teacher education students, student teachers, or graduate students) exhibited similar abilities. They were surprised that the three different student groups did not differ from each other in their moral judgment scores, even though they represented different educational levels and many of the graduate students were full-time teachers. As a result of their findings, Yeazell and Johnson called for increasing attention to the important teaching competency called "moral sensitivity."

Finally, in a study of 27 teachers in Perth, Australia, MacCallum (1991) found that teachers' moral judgments were related to various aspects of discipline. Thus, the importance of challenging teachers to address the moral issues inherent in the teaching/learning environment was confirmed.

3.1 Moral Reasoning and the School Environment

The influence of the school as a workplace on the moral development of teachers is an important topic of research. For example, Oser and Zutavern (1987) described an inservice program in which teachers analyzed the extent to which they created a "just community" for their students. In the process, they deepened their understanding of moral and social theories, the school atmosphere, democratic decision-making, and transformation procedures with respect to the authority of teachers and principals. Similarly, Miserandino (1989) discussed a successful case study of a teacher workshop which was designed as part of a staff development program and focused on the moral development of teachers in one school. Teachers were provided with a work environment that demanded choice, autonomy, dialogue, reflection, and teachers' close collaboration with the principal and the students.

3.2 Women's Moral/Ethical Development

Researchers investigating women's development have identified a pattern referred to as a "morality of response and care" (Gilligan 1988). This pattern consists of three developmental levels and two transitional phases in a spiraling evolution of care and responsibility to oneself and others. Gilligan et al.'s research challenged the dominant developmental models that equated maturity with separation, independence, and self-sufficiency. Through the lens of Gilligan's theory, a primary focus on attachments and relationships can be understood, validated, and added as another important perspective of the moral/ethical domain.

3.3 Moral Perspectives on Justice and Care

The research on the two moral perspectives of care and justice suggested that women and men do raise both justice and care concerns in describing moral conflicts, but they tend to focus their attention on either justice or care, elaborating one set of concerns and minimally representing the other. This tendency to focus on one perspective means that loss of the other perspective is a liability that both men and women share.

Gilligan (1988) suggested that adult moral maturity can be defined by the ability to see in at least two ways and to speak in at least two languages, the voice of justice and the voice of care. Lyons (1990) used the care and response perspective to explore the nature and meaning of the moral dilemmas teachers encounter in their work as they respond to and interpret the tasks of learning and teaching. Through analyses of teacher narratives, she revealed how the teachers' perspectives toward knowledge and their views of themselves and their students as knowers enter into their work and can at times be part of their continuing adult development. The work of Gilligan and Lyons has been followed by teachers and researchers who continue to focus on the themes of connection and separation in the paradoxical struggle to become autonomous within the context of relationships (see, e.g., Witherell and Noddings 1991).

4. Ego Development

Ego development theory may have strong potential for explaining observed differences between teachers and administrators. A growing number of researchers have used Loevinger's (1976) model of ego development in investigating teacher development. Ego development includes moral and personality development, cognitive complexity, and interpersonal style. Ego development, especially at the preconventional and conventional ego stages, can be measured by a well-researched test, the Washington University Sentence Completion Test (SCT), using Loevinger's self-training manuals. The postconventional stages of adult development and an additional transitional stage are defined more clearly and scored more adequately using methods reported by Cook-Greuter (1990).

Teachers at different stages respond to and need different environments. In a study of 58 Canadian teachers, Cummings and Murray (1989) found that views on issues such as teacher role and sources of knowledge differed significantly by ego level.

Richardson and Thompson (1982) surveyed 70 principals and 308 teachers using the SCT to measure each principal's ego development level and the teachers' perceptions of each principal's reliance on different power bases. The SCT scores of these principals clustered at conventional levels: the conformist, self-aware, and conscientious ego stages. With this restricted sample, the results showed no statistically significant differences in the patterns of power base used by the principals according to levels of ego development. Studies of this type will be important for the future; however, an extended sample which includes principals scoring at postconventional stages will be necessary.

Kegan and Lahey (1984) illustrated how teachers and principals operating at different stages of ego development have conflicting perceptions regarding leadership and authority in a school. At a time when administrators and teachers are being urged to work much more collaboratively in strategic planning and restructuring for the twenty-first century, educators need to consider the impact of ego development on their work.

5. Cognitive, Intellectual, and Epistemological Development.

Piaget (1972) postulated continuing cognitive development through adulthood in two ways. Initially, there is a transition from concrete operations into the stage of formal abstract thought, evidenced by the ability to reason, to view a situation from a variety of perspectives, and to use alternative problem-solving solutions. Later, a stabilization of formal abstract thought occurs, evidenced by increasing application of abstract thinking processes to progressively more complex issues in religion, politics, management, and interpersonal relationships. Subsequent investigations supported the finding that cognitive development was not completed in adolescence; research among adults suggested that even when abstract thinking levels have been attained, they may not be retained across the life span.

Significant cognitive development can take place during adulthood. Thus, any inservice program which assumes that adults have attained abstract operations in all aspects of their thinking is likely to encounter problems. Efforts need to be made to aid teachers in the transition from concrete to abstract modes of thought in new areas of teaching and learning. In some contexts an appropriate educational goal would be to foster development beyond abstract operations to a stage of problem-posing and to foster cognitive development of a different sort, such as dialectical thought.

5.1 Teachers' Conceptual Levels

Research in conceptual development (for a review, see Miller 1981) is particularly applicable to teacher education. Stages of conceptual level are defined by degree of abstractness as well as by degree of interpersonal maturity. Hunt's (1971) work provided a key empirical and theoretical bridge connecting developmental concepts to classroom teaching. Key concepts from Hunt's work were developmental match and constructive mismatch as ways for educators to plan for growth of teachers in ways that would be appropriately challenging and continuously supportive.

This research suggested that teachers at higher stages are more flexible, more tolerant of stress, and more adaptive to changing circumstances than teachers at lower stages. These higher stage teachers are more able to function in highly student-centered environments where their role is to utilize the learner's frame of reference and to encourage students to question and hypothesize. Furthermore, teachers at higher stages are able to assume multiple perspectives, utilize a wide variety of coping behaviors, employ a broader repertoire of teaching models, and consequently be more effective with a wide range of learning styles and needs of students.

Subsequent researchers found that teachers at higher levels of development were also more effective in supervisory interactions with preservice teachers (see review by Burden 1990).

Perry's (1981) longitudinal research provided vivid descriptions of the emotional turmoil connected with intellectual growth. Perry identified four main positions and five transitions of intellectual growth from dualism through multiplicity, from relativism to commitment. As a person progresses through these intellectual positions in response to new experiences and learning, personal identity is affirmed. Perry's account of intellectual development is helpful in understanding the growth of reflective judgment, reasoning in action, and the teacher's ability to be a reflective practitioner. Significant new work in teacher reflective thinking was evident in Simmons et al. (1989).

5.2 Women's Intellectual/Epistemological Development

Another approach to the study of intellectual development is that of Belenky et al. (1986). Analyzing interview data from 135 women, these researchers identified five different epistemological positions that represent women's experience of themselves as knowers. The positions are silence, received knowledge, subjective knowledge, procedural knowledge, and constructed knowledge. In the fifth position of constructed knowledge, speaking and listening are used equally in active dialogue with others, in situations in which knowledge is constructed by persons who experience themselves as equals. This work highlights the gender-related aspects of women's educational experience.

One of the most important findings is the evidence of two subcategories at the procedural level: separate and connected knowing. The separate way of knowing functioned under standard rules and conventions of rational thought, much like that described in Perry's model, and focused on principles and critical thinking procedures. In the connected way of knowing, knowledge and reason were gained through personal experience and relationships. Women at all levels preferred connected rather than separate modes of learning, a finding which has significant applications to teaching. Connected knowing describes an educational environment in which individuals value personal individual experience; nurture each other's thoughts to maturity; construct truth through consensus rather than conflict; bridge private and shared experience; accord respect to each others' unique perspectives; and base authority on cooperation, not subordination.

6. Staff Development and Collaborative Problem-solving

Oja's research with her colleagues (for a summary, see Oja 1991) consisted of four staff development programs whose goals were increased ego maturity, moral reasoning, conceptual complexity, and interpersonal functioning as a means to improve teacher effectiveness. This work suggested that collaborative action research could create a school-based problem-solving environment which stimulated postconventional stages of adult development. These researchers noted that teachers who were developing toward postconventional stages preferred the conditions of the action research team in contrast to the more permanent context of the school environment. The action research team context was nonhierarchial and self-managed; it had norms of collegiality and experimentation; power was diffused among the team; teachers developed their own tasks and flexibly undertook a variety of roles and responsibilities; the setting allowed reflective thinking and cognitive expansion; decision-making was participatory and collaboratively shared. A subsequent study found that teachers and administrators who self-selected to be involved in collaborative supervision and who sustained their involvement in the program over a period of years were at the postconventional stages. The collaborative supervisory teams in the action research program had both challenged and supported postconventional stage educators.

7. Conclusion

The research summarized in this entry, drawn from a larger body of research on adult development and teacher education, suggests that adults at different developmental stages exhibit different attitudes toward teaching and learning, attitudes toward decision-making and change, perceptions of group organization and process, and perceptions of leadership, supervision, and evaluation. This knowledge base can be used to understand how teachers change throughout their careers. It also can be used to promote teacher development with the proper use of supervision and a series of appropriate staff development programs.

See also: Teacher Development

References

Belenky M F, Clinchy B M, Goldberger N, Tarule J 1986 *Women's Ways of Knowing: The Development of Self, Voice, and Mind.* Basic Books, New York

Burden P R 1990 Teacher Development. In: Houston W R (ed.) 1990 *Handbook of Research on Teacher Education.* Macmillan, New York

Cook-Greuter S 1990 Maps for living: Ego-development theory from symbiosis to conscious universal embeddedness. In: Commons M M et al. (eds.) 1990 *Adult Development*, Vol. 2. Praeger, New York

Cummings A L, Murray H G 1989 Ego development and its relation to teacher education. *Teaching and Teacher Education* 5(1): 21–32

Fessler R, Christensen J C (eds.) 1992 *The Teacher Career Cycle: Understanding and Guiding the Professional Development of Teachers.* Allyn and Bacon, Boston, Massachusetts

Gilligan C 1988 *A Contribution of Women's Thinking to Psychological Theory and Education Mapping the Moral Domain.* Harvard University Press, Boston, Massachusetts

Huberman M 1989 *Vie Des Enseignants: Evolution et Bilan d'une Profession.* Delachaux et Niestle, Paris/Neuchâtel

Hunt D E 1971 *Matching Models in Education: The Co-ordination of Teaching Methods with Student Characteristics.* Ontario Institute for Studies in Education, Toronto

Johnston M 1989 Moral reasoning and teachers' understanding of individualized instruction *Journal of Moral Education* 18(1): 45–59

Kegan R, Lahey L L 1984 Adult leadership and adult development: A constructivist view. In: Kellerman B (ed.) 1984 *Leadership: Multidisciplinary Perspectives.* Prentice-Hall, Englewood Cliffs, New Jersey

Levine S 1988 *Promoting Adult Growth in Schools: The Promise of Professional Development.* Allyn and Bacon, Boston, Massachusetts

Levinson D J 1986 A Conception of adult development. *Am. Psychol.* 41(1): 3–13

Loevinger J 1976 *Ego Development: Conceptions and Theories.* Jossey-Bass, San Francisco, California

Lyons N 1990 Dilemmas of knowing: Ethical and epistemological dimensions of teachers' work and development. *Harv. Educ. Rev.* 60(2): 159–80

MacCallum J A 1991 Teacher reasoning and moral judgment in the context of student discipline situations. Paper presented at the Annual Meeting of the American Educational Research Association, Chicago

Miller A 1981 Conceptual matching models and interactional research in education. *Rev. Educ. Res.* 51(1): 33–84

Miserandino A 1989 *Supervision for Growth: A Practitioner's Perspective.* Paper presented at the Annual Meeting of the American Educational Research Association, San Francisco

Oja S N 1991 Teacher and supervisor development: A report of four studies from 1978 to 1988 In: Campos B P (ed.) 1991 *Psychological Intervention and Human Development.* Instituto de Consulta Psicologica, Formacao e Desenvolvimento, Porto

Oser F, Zutavern M 1987 *Berufsethos von Lehrer/innen.* Pädagogisches Institut, Universität Fribourg, Fribourg

Perry W G 1981 Cognitive and ethical growth: The making of meaning. In: Chickering A W (ed.) 1981 *The Modern American College.* Jossey-Bass, San Francisco, California

Piaget J 1972 Intellectual evolution from adolescence to adulthood. *Hum. Dev.* 15(1): 1–12

Richardson R, Thompson B 1982 Ego development and power base reliance of school principals. Paper presented at the Annual Meeting of the American Educational

Research Association, New York

Simmons J M et al. 1989 Exploring the structure of reflective pedagogical thinking in novice and expert teachers: The birth of a developmental taxonomy. Paper presented at the annual meeting of the American Educational Research Association, San Francisco

Thomas S J, Rest J 1987 Moral sensitivity and judgment in the development and performance of student teachers. *Moral Education Forum* 12(3): 15–20

Vonk J H C, Schras G A 1987 From beginning to experienced teacher: A study of the professional development of teachers during their first four years of service. *European Journal of Teacher Education* 10(1): 95–110

Witherell C, Noddings N (eds.) 1991 *Stories Lives Tell: Narrative and Dialogue in Education*. Teachers College Press, New York

Yeazell M I, Johnson S F 1988 Levels of moral judgment of faculty and students in a teacher education program: A micro study of an institution. *Teach. Educ. Q.* 15(1): 61–70

Further Reading

Holly M L, McLoughlin C S (eds.) 1989 *Perspectives on Teacher Professional Development*. Falmer Press, London

Huberman M (ed.) 1989 Research on teachers' professional lives. *Int. J. Educ. Res.* 13(4): 341–466

Loucks-Horsely S et al. 1987 *Continuing to Learn: A Guidebook for Teacher Development*. The Regional Laboratory for Educational Improvement of the Northeast and Islands, and the National Staff Development Council, Andover, Maryland

Oja S N, Smulyan L 1989 *Collaborative Action Research: A Developmental Approach*. Falmer Press, Basingstoke

(b)   Organization and Curriculum

Planning Teacher Education

S. Shah

The purpose of this entry is to examine the current status of planning in teacher education throughout the world and to discuss the need for planning in teacher education. Planning in teacher education is becoming more significant and its scope is increasing. These changes reflect an increasing awareness of the connection between education and national development, and the complexity of the teaching–learning process.

1. Nature and Significance of Planning in Teacher Education

While planning in education has long been important, planning in teacher education has only recently begun to receive the same level of attention. With the emphasis in the poorer countries on educating all children, there has been more concern about the sufficiency of the teaching force—both in terms of numbers and quality. While traditional planning models have been used to project the numbers of available and needed teachers, newer models are required to plan teacher education programs that produce teachers capable of functioning effectively in the ever increasing complexity of classrooms and schools. In this regard, Windham (1992) has asserted that teachers must pay greater attention to the full range of intellectual, ethical, and technical needs of students and society. No longer can teachers be viewed simply as "transmitters of information."

Both the emphasis on planning in teacher education and the type of planning being done vary enormously from country to country. In some countries, particularly industrialized ones, teacher education is governed by ongoing policies which have been developed over decades, perhaps centuries. In these countries, tradition often takes precedence over formal planning. In contrast, the preparation of five year plans is a key feature in many poorer countries. In these countries, a great deal of attention is focused on planning models and practices. In the main, however, planning in many countries has been haphazard and usually short term (Dove 1986).

Since the 1980s there has been an increased concern for careful and comprehensive planning in teacher education. Much of this concern can be attributed to a variety of reform efforts in various countries (e.g., Department of Education and Science 1985, Ministry of Education, Kenya 1988, Chung-it et al.1985). While these reform efforts have resulted in a major upheaval for certain educational groups (e.g., teachers), they signify the need to address fundamental questions about the value of education to society, the purposes of education, and the most effective and efficient ways in which these purposes can be achieved.

2. Models for Planning Teacher Education

Planning models have been developed by several educators and researchers. Some of these models are quite linear, moving from a readiness to accept innovation to the actual implementation of the change process (Verspoor and Lewo 1986). Most of these models emphasize externally generated or imposed changes.

Other models portray planning as a cyclical process involving changes in the interpretative frameworks of teachers (Avalos 1993). These models tend to be most appropriate when the emphasis is on the teacher as the primary agent of educational change.

Models used in national planning are often based on what Carron (1986) terms the techno-rational framework. The base for these models tends to be statistical in nature. The models have been quite useful in estimating the availability of and/or need for teachers, such as science teachers and female teachers (Dove 1986).

3. The Process of Planning in Teacher Education

Several elements of the planning process are crucial to its overall success. Among the most important are the analysis of the educational and social context, the analysis of programmatic alternatives, and the involvement of major stakeholders in the process.

3.1 Analysis of the Educational and Social Contexts

Teacher education needs to be understood within the total context of the purpose of education, the rationale for the type and level of teachers needed, and the system for monitoring, reviewing, and updating the programs. Ishumi (1986) has suggested that the primary emphasis in planning has been quantitative rather than qualitative. That is, concerns for numbers of teachers have generally been more important to educational planners than the knowledge, skills, attitudes, and values these teachers possess. Qualitative aspects of planning can only be addressed by a careful analysis of the demographic, structural, and cultural contexts within which teacher education programs and teachers are expected to function (Haddad 1985).

3.2 Analysis of Programmatic Alternatives

Planning effective teacher education programs requires that alternative programs and options within programs are carefully examined. In this way, the likelihood of selecting or developing programs that are most appropriate to particular settings and situations is enhanced. While knowledge of alternatives may be derived from experiences within other countries, an intensive analysis of the alternatives and their appropriateness within a specific country must be conducted.

Research is an integral part of choosing among alternatives. During the planning process many questions are raised which can only be answered by gathering relevant data. The importance of considering empirical evidence can be shown in the studies commissioned in response to the Swann Report in Great Britain (Department of Education and Science 1985). In this report a case was made for multiethnic education even in schools where there was little evidence of cultural diversity.

3.3 Involvement of Stakeholders in the Planning Process

In the planning of teacher education, several key stakeholders can be identified. Among the most prevalent are teacher educators, teachers, prospective teachers, employers, and government representatives. Not all of these stakeholders are involved in planning, however.

Ross (1990), for example, noted that members of the teaching profession were eliminated from discussions of the gradual adjustment of professional education courses to accommodate the changing needs of practising teachers in Great Britain. As a result, the accumulated experience of these professionals was not considered in the planning process. Ross warns of the dangers that can arise when centralized decisions are imposed on all teachers. In contrast, he suggests that involvement helps teachers understand the rationale behind a program which, in turn, motivates them to support it and increases the feeling of ownership.

Prospective teachers are another group often excluded from the planning process. Their involvement is also important for at least two reasons (Dove 1986). First, a recent thrust in higher education in many countries is to view students as independent learners. As a result, their involvement in the planning and decision-making process is quite important. Second, in order to plan a teacher education program that focuses on helping teachers to be more than "transmitters of information," a greater understanding of the current knowledge, concerns, and problems of prospective teachers is vital (Dove 1986).

Teacher education programs are likely to be more effective if those who ultimately will employ their graduates are included in the planning process. Depending on the country, these employers may be government officials, school administrators, or members of some other group. Regardless of who the employer is, involving the employer increases the probability that a good match is made between the demands of the employer and the capabilities of prospective teachers to meet these demands.

In summary, then, a planning process which includes opportunities for major stakeholders to express their views and concerns is more likely to yield teacher education programs that are widely accepted and supported. Without acceptance and support, the chances that such programs will be successful are very small.

4. Planning the Objectives and Content of Teacher Education

Dove (1986) has identified four principles for the selection of the objectives and content of teacher education programs. They are: (a) policy goals and aims; (b) characteristics and needs of prospective teachers; (c) the roles expected of teachers; and (d) the findings gleaned from evaluation and research studies.

4.1 Goals, Aims, and Objectives

Many plans are very ambitious, with resources being wasted when the goals and objectives of such programs have not been fully realized. The consideration of both long-term and short-term goals and objectives has the advantage of monitoring progress while at the same time putting into place the structures that may be essential for meaningful and long-lasting changes to occur.

Haddad (1985) has emphasized that an objective should be clear, specific, and, whenever feasible, measurable. Many plans have suffered from vaguely stated objectives; that is, objectives lacking in specificity and performance expectations.

4.2 Characteristics and Needs of Prospective Teachers

Do prospective teachers need specialization in a subject area, a more holistic approach to knowledge, or some combination? Quite different plans are likely to be developed depending on the answer to this question. To what extent do prospective teachers need to understand the need to go beyond academic learning and attend to issues such as the equality of race, gender, and cultures (Shah 1989)? To what extent should the emphasis of teacher education be on personal development, the imparting of subject matter, or, again, some combination? All of these questions must be addressed in response to the characteristics and needs of prospective teachers.

4.3 Teacher Roles

Not only do teacher education plans need to reflect the current status of prospective teachers, they also must reflect the future roles these teachers will assume in schools and classrooms. As was mentioned earlier, as the role of the teacher shifts from "giver of knowledge" to "facilitator of learning," changes in teacher education programs are needed. These changes will only occur when adequate, appropriate, and workable plans for change have been developed.

4.4 Research and Evaluation

Planned, ongoing research and evaluation coupled with a systematic review of the results is an important element in the design and implementation of effective teacher education programs. Research and evaluation studies should be included in the initial planning of these programs, not added on in order to comply with some external requirement.

5. Planning the Delivery of Teacher Education

In addition to planning the objectives and content of teacher education, the delivery of teacher education also must be carefully planned. This type of planning focuses on at least four separate issues: sequence and linkages, delivery methods, educating teacher educators, and partnerships between schools and teacher preparation institutions.

5.1 Sequence and Linkages

The order in which prospective teachers are expected to complete their courses and the proper sequence of formal coursework and field experiences must be planned (Dove 1986). Questions such as "Should foundations courses precede methods courses?" and "Should prospective teachers enrol in courses in their academic discipline and education concurrently or sequentially?" need to be addressed.

Linkages between teacher preparation institutions and schools must be established and maintained if the field experiences are to be maximally beneficial to prospective teachers. Oftentimes planning ceases when the linkages have been established. The development of some mechanism for maintaining proper

relationships and making modifications as needed should also be a part of planning.

5.2 Delivery Methods

Traditional delivery methods include lectures, discussions, demonstrations, and tutoring. Shaeffer (1993) has described a series of alternative delivery methods that may be useful in teacher education. Examples include cooperative learning and reflective self-instruction. Shaeffer is quick to point that none of these alternatives is a panacea. Much research is needed on the teaching practices associated with these alternative delivery methods as well as what goals and objectives are best served by each.

5.3 Educating Teacher Educators

One of the possible barriers to the use of alternative delivery methods, such as those mentioned above, is the lack of training received by teacher educators themselves. Verspoor and Lewo (1986) discuss specific projects in which those responsible for implementing the project were not adequately trained or prepared.

Many of the alternative delivery methods require new understandings and ways of thinking on the part of both teacher educators and teachers. Furthermore, these methods typically require that teachers and teacher educators assume new roles. Teacher educators, then, must be sufficiently flexible and confident to deviate from their traditional roles and practices.

5.4 Partnerships Between Schools and Teacher Preparation Institutions

Such partnerships are becoming fairly widespread in many countries. These partnerships are based on two major assumptions or beliefs. The first is the belief that teacher preparation programs are likely to be inappropriate if teacher educators are not in touch with the reality of schools and classrooms. The second is the recognition that the traditional organizational hierarchy that places teacher preparation institutions above the schools has been a major obstacle in moving toward the design and implementation of effective, efficient teacher education programs.

The creation and operation of true partnerships places great demands on educational planners and planning. Specifically, these partnerships require joint planning of the curriculum, joint assessment and evaluation of prospective teachers, open exchanges of ideas, research, and practices, and, perhaps, exchanges of faculty of the teacher preparation institutions and school teachers.

6. Conclusion

Teacher education is a complex, multifaceted activity. In the mid-1990s, countries have been adopting different approaches to teacher education, with planning, research, and evaluation of these approaches often done in a piecemeal fashion. As the roles of teachers increase in importance in schools, teacher education will be forced to change as well. Planning is at the heart of any formal change. Without careful, systematic planning, innovative teacher education programs are likely to be implemented haphazardly and to be short-lived.

References

Avalos B 1993 Teacher training in developing countries. In: Farrell J, Oliviera J (eds.) 1993 *Teachers in Developing Countries: Improving Effectiveness and Managing Costs.* World Bank, Washington, DC

Carron G 1984 Educational planning: past approaches and new prospects. In: Hetland A, Ishumi A (eds.) 1984 *Educational Planning in Developing Countries.* Almquist and Wiksell, Stockholm

Chung-it Y, Moo-Sub K, Il-Hwan C, Jae-Dong K 1985 *Korean Education 2000.* Korean Educational Development Institute, Seoul

Department of Education and Science 1985 *Education for All.* Her Majesty's Stationery Office, London

Dove L A 1986 *Teachers and Teacher Education in Developing Countries* Croom Helm, London

Haddad W D 1985 *Teacher Training: A Review of World Bank Experience.* World Bank, Washington, DC

Ishumi A 1984 Educational planning: Its meaning and its relevancy in developing countries. In: Hetland A, Ishumi A (eds.) *Educational Planning in Developing Countries.* Almquist and Wiksell, Stockholm

Ministry of Education, Kenya 1988 *Sessional Paper no. 6 on Education and Manpower Training for the Next Decade and Beyond.* Report of the Presidential Working Party on Education and Manpower Training for the Next Decade and Beyond. Ministry of Education, Nairobi

Ross A 1990 The Council for Teacher Education: A general teaching council for England and Wales. In: Graves N (ed.) 1990 *Initial Teacher Education: Policies and Progress.* Kogan Page, London

Shaeffer S 1993 Participatory approaches to teacher training. In: Farrell J, Oliviera J (eds.) 1993 *Teachers in Developing Countries: Improving Effectiveness and Managing Cost.* World Bank, Washington, DC

Shah S 1989 Effective permeation of race and gender issues in teacher education courses. *Gender and Education* 1(3): 221–36

Verspoor A, Lewo J 1986 *Improving Teaching: A Key to Successful Educational Change: Lessons from World Bank Experiences.* Occasional Paper no. 38, World Bank, Washington, DC

Windham D M 1992 *Education for All: The Requirements.* UNESCO, Paris

Further Reading

Cees J H M 1983 *Primary Teacher Education in Egypt.* Centre for the Study of Education in Developing Countries, CESO, The Hague

Goodings R, Byran M, McPartland M (eds.) 1982 *Changing Priorities in Teacher Education.* Croom Helm, London

Thomas E, Sharma M, Khanna A, Jatoi H 1993 *Policy and Practice in Initial Teacher Training.* Commonwealth Secretariat, London

Curriculum of Teacher Education Programs

M. Ben-Peretz

The curriculum of preservice teacher education programs across different countries and cultures may vary in important aspects, such as institutional context, content areas, time allocations, and the forms of practical experiences for students. In spite of this variability, however, most programs share some common curricular features.

The curriculum of teacher education programs is generally based on four components: subject-matter studies (whether taught concurrently or consecutively with other studies), foundation of education studies, professional studies (such as method courses), and the practicum (supervised practice). In this entry each of these components is treated separately. Curricular concepts, such as the hidden curriculum (Martin 1976) and the "null curriculum" (Flinders et al. 1986), are presented and curricular issues and some future directions are discussed.

1. Institutional Context

Programs may be housed in special institutions for teacher education, which may or may not be connected to a university system. Examples are the special institutions for training primary teachers in the United Kingdom, India, or Israel (McNamara 1990, Govinda and Buch 1990, Ben-Peretz 1990, Tisher and Wideen 1990). Programs in such institutions are mostly characterized by a "concurrent" curricular mode; namely, the simultaneous study of subject areas and professional subjects.

In many cases, programs for the education of secondary teachers are university-based and are likely to reflect a "consecutive" curricular mode; namely, candidates study professional courses and participate in the practicum after they have completed their subject courses and received a university degree. Examples are programs in the United Kingdom (McNamara 1990), the Netherlands (Kieviet 1990), Germany (Klinzig 1990), and Japan (Sato and Ushiwata 1990). In Japan in 1986, 28 percent of university graduates earned teacher certificates (Sato and Ushiwata 1990).

Teacher education programs may also be situated in schools. Several such programs have been established in the United Kingdom (MacLennan and Seadon 1988). Indeed, from the 1980s onward there has been a movement toward the increased provision of such courses. The reasoning behind this movement is that teacher education must start from classroom practice so that educational theory is then considered in its proper professional context.

2. Subject-matter Studies

The teaching of subjects during the training of secondary teachers is often in the hands of the various disciplinary departments of a university (Loewenberg-Ball and McDiarmid 1990, Houston et al. 1990). On the other hand, elementary teachers tend to take a range of courses in a variety of disciplines in liberal arts departments. In most programs, the professional training in colleges does not concern itself to a large degree with the subject-matter knowledge that prospective teachers need in order to teach. Edmundson (1990), discussing a Study of the Education of Educators (SEE) in 29 institutions, states that "not one institution in our study has substantial coordination and integration across general and professional studies" (p. 718).

In rare cases the curriculum integrates subject-matter studies with professional studies such as courses on teaching methods. An example of such integration is provided by the teacher education programs of the Kibbutz movement in Israel. In these programs, subject domains are taught in a college of education with concurrent emphasis on educational and instructional issues. These programs may be more appropriate for the preparation of teachers because they tend to focus on pedagogical content knowledge, and not solely on the substantive knowledge of a discipline (Shulman 1987). Such programs reflect an orientation toward specific, rather than generic, aspects of learning to teach.

Loewenberg-Ball and McDiarmid (1990) claim that until the mid-1980s it was taken for granted that the teaching of subjects to trainee teachers was adequate and appropriate. Since the mid-1980s, however, questions have been raised concerning the adequacy of such preparation. Kennedy (1991), for example, argued that "majoring in an academic subject in college does not guarantee that teachers will have the kind of subject matter knowledge they need for teaching" (p. 14). Treatment of subject matter in a way that relates it to pedagogic issues may yield more valid and useful knowledge for prospective teachers. An emphasis on knowledge about an academic discipline

and the development of positive dispositions toward the subject studied have been considered by some writers to be essential components of teacher education curricula (Loewenberg-Ball and McDiarmid 1990, Kennedy 1991).

3. Foundation of Education Studies

The nature of educational foundation studies in the curriculum of teacher education is a matter of some dispute among teacher educators. Sirotnik (1990) included history, philosophy, and sociology of education, as well as the study of contemporary issues and educational policy. Borman (1990) cited a study in which 20 different "foundation of education" courses offered in public and private institutions across the United States were examined. Multicultural education, philosophy of education, and history of education were the most frequently listed courses. Borman concluded that during the 1980s educational foundations as a field became more involved with educational equity issues. This emphasis contrasts with the earlier apolitical, more strictly disciplinary, and academically focused foundation studies.

Sirotnik (1990) claimed that students have perceived foundation courses as irrelevant and marginal and warned of the possibility of a serious erosion of foundational studies in teacher education programs. Similarly, Edmundson (1990) reported that foundation courses are usually an early element of programs and consist of haphazard collections of themes and topics. In reviewing studies undertaken in Japan, Sato and Ushiwata (1990) found that foundation studies, even though viewed as promoting professional development, were characteristically vague in their approach.

A proposed remedy to this situation is the integration of foundation studies with practical experience throughout the curriculum of teacher education (Sirotnik 1990). Borman (1990) argued for the need to strengthen the role of educational foundations in teacher education and claimed that "by developing normative, interpretive, and critical perspectives on the teaching and learning process and on institutional patterns and societal practices more generally, foundations scholars and teachers can and do play an important role in teacher education" (p. 401). It is apparent that educators in the 1990s have suggested curricular approaches that emphasize the construction of a dialectical relationship between theory and practice, placing theory in its concrete, real-life context.

4. Professional Studies

Professional studies may include methods courses, curriculum courses, and courses based on knowledge generated through research on teaching. The common prevailing view concerning the professional content of teacher education perceives it to be a component of preparation for which institutions of teacher education are specifically responsible. The skills and knowledge taught in these courses are supposed to have a direct bearing on professional practice.

Tom and Valli (1990) examined the professional knowledge base of teacher education from the point of view of contrasting epistemologies—positivistic, interpretive, and critical—and clarified the knowledge–practice relationship implied by each. For instance, in the positivistic epistemology, generalizations and rules specify a direct link between knowledge and practice using a "logistic" approach. The movement of competency-based teacher education (CBTE) exemplifies such an approach. Interpretive scholarship, on the other hand, may reveal and clarify unknown aspects of teaching. "Revealing the underlying complexities of teaching is generative in the sense that these revealed complexities can suggest novel means for teachers to achieve practical ends" (Tom and Valli 1990 p. 386). Finally, critically oriented teacher educators strive to examine inequalities in education and society and to encourage a commitment to social values and to emancipatory actions.

Methods courses that focus on rules of conduct for teachers may often lack an interpretive and critically oriented knowledge base, which draws on case studies and on learning from cases. A case literature in teacher education is developing, providing resources for more interpretive frames of relating theory to practice in professional studies (see *Case Methods in Teacher Education*).

Two of the major categories suggested by Shulman (1987) as constituting the professional knowledge base of teaching, are pedagogical content knowledge and curriculum knowledge. Curriculum studies in teacher education programs serve to develop this knowledge base. The aim of such studies is to provide teachers with the knowledge and skills needed in order to implement and use available curricular materials and to participate in school-based curriculum development. There has been a growing demand for inclusion of curriculum studies as specific courses in teacher education (Ben-Peretz 1984, Goodman 1986). In this regard, Silberstein (1991) distinguished between generic curriculum courses, applicable to any subject taught in school, and curriculum courses oriented toward subject matter.

5. The Practicum

In many countries, the practicum is the most favorably viewed component of teacher education. Tisher (1990), focusing on teacher education in Australia, claimed "school experience to be an extremely important, practical, satisfying component of pre-service education! The trainees say they gain a lot from it; that it is the most realistic aspect of their courses, helps reduce their anxiety about teaching, fosters their practical teaching skills ... they feel it should be increased" (p. 75). The literature from Germany has viewed the practicum as a necessary and valuable, though also doubtful, component of teacher education programs (Klinzig 1990). Supervised practice is a central part of the German *Studienseminar*, a mandatory, postgraduate component of the teacher education process, focusing on induction into school life.

The time devoted to practice teaching varies greatly between institutions although there is a growing tendency to increase field-based experiences. An interesting view of the practicum was expressed by White (1989) who saw it as a "rite of passage" which allows neophytes to acquire cultural knowledge about teaching. One of the major strengths of the practicum is its focus on specialized teaching activities, thus counteracting one of the criticisms of teacher education programs; namely, their concentration on general aspects of schooling and lower regard for specialized activities (Lortie 1975).

Distinctions have been made between four different levels of the practicum (Furlong et al. 1988). Level (a) is direct practice; i.e., teaching experiences in schools. Level (b) is indirect practice; i.e., training conducted in classes or workshops in teacher education institutions. Level (c) is practical principles; i.e., the study of principles of practice. Finally, level (d) is disciplinary theory, the study of practice and its principles in the light of research and theory. The authors claimed that traditional teacher education programs engage students in levels (b), (c), and (d), before introducing them into direct practice. However, more school-based teacher education programs have been evolving (MacLennan and Seadon 1988).

Though the practicum tends to be highly valued by student teachers and practitioners, questions concerning the value of learning from these experiences have been raised (Feiman-Nemser and Buchman 1983). Edmundson (1990) claimed that student teaching experiences do not provide students with opportunities for reflective inquiry. Tom (1987) argued that teacher education curricula should replace pedagogical knowledge with pedagogical questions, using the reality of teaching as their starting point and addressing both moral and craft elements of teaching. Tom states that "as compared to topically organized knowledge, practice-based study tends to be a more potent form of learning for novice teachers" (p. 16). In a similar vein, Pearce and Pickard (1987) warned that "the practicality of practical studies cannot be rooted in a particular predetermined content. No checklist of skills or body of theory can correlate with the complexity of what it is to be a teacher, because what teachers do is necessarily bound up with what teachers are" (p. 42).

An example of an innovative teacher education program that reflects an approach to teacher education rooted in a personal practical knowledge perspective was described by Clandinin et al. (1992). In this program a collaborative group of 28 student teachers, 6 university teachers, and 28 school teachers worked together. Through sharing and responding to each other's stories, a new opportunity for teacher education was created. Dialogue journals, response groups, and renegotiated assignments were planned collaboratively and became central components of the curriculum of this alternative teacher-education program.

6. The Hidden Curriculum and the Null Curriculum

A discussion of the curriculum of teacher education programs is incomplete without reference to the hidden curriculum. Ginsburg and Clift (1990) conceptualized the hidden curriculum of teacher education as the messages transmitted to students through the institutional context, as well as the structure and processes of the programs themselves. They claimed that these messages relate to several themes. First, teaching is a low-status profession and teachers as a professional group lack power. Their field experiences expose student teachers to the low professional status of teaching. Their coursework communicates the message that college teachers hold power only over students and are "subordinated to administration, university professors and politicians" (Parsons and Beauchamp 1985 p. 55). The perception of teachers' lack of power is further reinforced by the notion that curriculum decision-making is not a central component of teachers' professional role (Ginsburg and Clift 1990).

Second, the hidden curriculum of teacher education tends to communicate a fragmented view of knowledge, both in coursework and in field experiences. Moreover, knowledge is "given" and unproblematic. These views of knowledge are likely to become quite problematic as teachers gain experience.

Teacher education programs can also be characterized by their "null curriculum"; that is, what is not included in the curriculum (Flinders et al. 1986). Examples include the ethics of teaching and the biological roots of human behavior. The development of professional dispositions (e.g. the disposition to suspend judgment about children, the consideration of alternative interpretations of situations) is not commonly included as a goal of teacher education programs (Katz and Raths 1985). Uncovering the null curriculum of teacher education programs may have far-reaching implications for the development of programs.

7. Issues and Possible Directions

Several questions can be posed to highlight some of the basic curriculum issues confronting teacher educators. First, should the curriculum focus on generic or on specific aspects of the knowledge of teaching?

The curriculum may aim at introducing students to generic aspects of teaching, such the use of varied instructional strategies. Conversely, the curriculum may attempt to provide students with methods that can be used to teach specific subject matters in a variety of educational settings.

Second, what is the proper relationship between theory and practice? Theory may be seen as guiding practice through a process of translation and application. In contrast, theory may be seen as being derived from practice. That is, practice is itself a fluid and changeable theory in action (McKeon 1952).

Third, what is the role of the innovative curriculum in teacher education? Innovation can impact on the choice of content to be included in the curriculum, on the institutional context of teacher education programs, and on the structure of courses included in a program. For example, rather than have separate courses in educational foundations, it may be possible to have "reflective seminars in which students could discuss critically their daily experiences in schools and relate them to their foundational studies" (Sirotnik 1990 p. 716).

It is important to note that reform movements such as the Holmes Group (1986) and the Carnegie Forum on Education and the Economy (1987) have proposed that preservice teacher education should be extended and made more academically demanding. At the same time, however, students are being called on to play a more active role in planning and directing their programs and the educational experiences they encounter within them.

Further approaches to teaching might have considerable impact on the curriculum of teacher education programs. First, the construction of teaching from the perspectives of teachers themselves. Brown and McIntyre (1993) argue for the exploration of the "professional craft knowledge" of teachers by beginning teachers, as well as in staff development courses. These exploration efforts might lead to the articulation of the relatively routine aspects of what teachers do well in their classrooms. Such knowledge is potentially generalizable, and so can be shared. This sharing process is especially important in view of current moves towards more school-based forms of preservice teacher education. According to Brown and McIntyre (1993), the main purpose of student teachers gaining access to the professional craft knowledge of experienced teachers would be to learn the nature of the craft they were trying to master, and not to "initiate wholesale the individual experienced teachers with whom they happen to work" (p. 113). Brown and McIntyre claim that the craft aspects of teaching are not a set of standardized teaching behaviours, but rather teacher's work is to be viewed as an individually expressive process with certain generalizable features.

Another exciting new approach to teacher education is based on the notions of teacher collegiality, and the perceived importance of teachers' communities.

Talbert and McLaughlin (1994) argue that professionalism evolves within active learning communities of teachers. Their study supports the thesis that teacher professionalism depends on the extent and character of teacher communities embedded in multiple local contexts of teaching: subject area departments, schools, and districts. Collegial settings foster higher levels of shared standards for curriculum and instruction, a stronger service ethic in relations with students, and a deeper commitment to the teaching profession. To foster communities among teachers Westheimer and Kahne (1993) propose an experience-based model of teacher education, that gives student-teachers a positive community experience, and provides them with experience-based pedagogical and curricular tools.

See also: Case Methods in Teacher Education

References

Ben-Peretz M 1984 Curriculum theory and practice in teacher education programs. In: Katz L G, Raths J D (eds.) 1984 *Advances in Teacher Education*, Vol. 1. Ablesc, Norwood, New Jersey

Ben-Peretz M 1990 Research on teacher education in Israel: Topics, methods and findings. In: Tisher R P, Wideen M F (eds.) 1990

Borman K M 1990 Foundations of Education in Teacher Education. In: Houston W R, Haberman M, Sikula G (eds.). 1990

Brown S, McIntyre D 1993 *Making Sense of Teaching*. Open University Press, Buckingham

Carnegie Forum on Education and the Economy (Task Force on Teaching as a Profession) 1987 *A Nation Prepared: Teachers for the Twenty-first Century*. Carnegie Commission on the Improvement of Teaching, New York

Clandinin D G, Davis A, Hogan P, Kennan B 1992 *Learning to Teach, Teaching to Learn: Stories of Collaboration in Teacher Education*. Teachers College Press, New York

Edmundson P G 1990 A normative look at the curriculum in teacher education. *Phi Del. Kap.* 71(9): 717–22

Feiman-Nemser S, Buchman M 1983 Pitfalls of experience in teacher education. In: Tamir P, Hofstein A, Ben-Peretz M (eds.) 1983 *Preservice and Inservice Education of Science Teachers*. Balaban International Science Services, Philadelphia, Pennsylvania

Flinders D G, Noddings N, Thornton S J 1986 The null curriculum: Its theoretical basis and practical implications. *Curric. Inq.* 16(1): 33–42

Furlong V T, Hirst P H, Pocklington K, Miles S 1988 *Initial Teacher Training and the Role of Schools*. Open University Press, Milton Keynes

Ginsburg M B, Clift R T 1990 The hidden curriculum of preservice teacher education. In: Houston W R, Habberman M, Sikula G (eds.) 1990

Goodman J 1986 Teaching preservice teachers a critical approach to curriculum design: A descriptive account. *Curric. Inq.* 16(2): 179–201

Govinda R, Buch M B 1990 Indian research in teacher education: A review. In: Tisher R P, Wideen M F (eds.) 1990

Holmes Group 1986 *Tomorrow's Teachers*. Holmes Group, East Lansing, Michigan

Houston W R, Haberman M, Sikula G (eds.) 1990 *Handbook of Research on Teacher Education*. Macmillan Inc., New York

Katz L G, Raths J D 1985 Dispositions as goals for teacher education. *Teaching and Teacher Educ.* 1(4): 301–07

Kennedy M M 1991 Some surprising findings in how teachers learn to teach. *Educ. Leadership* 49(3): 14–17

Kieviet F K 1990 A decade of research on teacher education in the Netherlands. In: Tisher R P, Wideen M F (eds.) 1990

Klinzig H G 1990 Research on teacher education in West Germany. In: Tisher R P, Wideen M F (eds.) 1990

Loewenberg-Ball D L, McDiarmid G W 1990 The subject matter preparation of teachers. In: Houston W R, Haberman M, Sikula G (eds.) 1990 *Handbook of Research on Teacher Education*. Macmillan Inc., New York

Lortie D 1975 *Schoolteacher: A Sociological Study*. Chicago University Press, Chicago, Illinois

MacLennan S, Seadon T 1988 What price school based work? Reflections on a school sited PGCE method course. *Camb. J. Educ.* 18(3): 387–403

Martin J R 1976 What should we do with a hidden curriculum when we find one? *Curric. Inq.*, 6(2): 135–51

McKeon R 1952 Philosophy and action. *Ethics* 62(2): 79–100

McNamara D 1990 Research on teacher training in a changing society: The case of Britain in the late 1980s. In: Tisher R P, Wideen M F (eds.) 1990

Parsons G, Beauchamp L 1985 The hidden curriculum of student teacher evaluation. ERIC Document Reproduction Service ED 261983, Washington, DC

Pearce G, Pickard A 1987 Being a teacher: towards an epistemology of practical studies. In: Smyth G (ed.) 1987 *Educating Teachers: Changing the Nature of Pedagogical Knowledge*. Falmer Press, London

Sato A, Ushiwata G 1990 Research on teacher education in Japan. In: Tisher R P, Wideen M F (eds.) 1990

Shulman L S 1987 Knowledge and teaching: Foundations of the new reform. *Harv. Educ. Rev.* 57(1): 1–22

Silberstein M 1991 Curriculum studies in teacher education. In: Lewy A (ed.) 1991 *International Encyclopedia of Curriculum*. McGraw-Hill, London

Sirotnik K E 1990 On the eroding foundations of teacher education. *Phi Del. Kap.* 71(9): 710–16

Talbert J A, McLaghlin M W 1994 Teacher professionalism in local school contexts. *Am. J. Educ.* 102: 123–53

Tisher R P 1990 One and a half decades of research on teacher education in Australia. In: Tisher R P, Wideen M F (eds.) 1990

Tisher R P, Wideen M F (eds.) 1990 *Research in Teacher Education: International Perspectives*. Falmer Press, London

Tom A R 1987 Replacing pedagogical knowledge with pedagogical questions. In: Smyth M (ed.) 1987 *Educating Teachers: Changing the Nature of Pedagogical Knowledge*. Falmer Press, London

Tom A R, Valli L 1990 Professional knowledge for teachers. In: Houston W R, Haberman M, Sikula G (eds.) 1990

Westeimer J, Kahne J 1993 Building school communities: An experienced-based model. *Phi Del. Kap.* (December): 324–28

White J W 1989 Student teaching as a rite of passage. *Anthropol. Educ. Q.* 20(3): 177–95

Structure of Teacher Education Programs

M. J. Gimmestad and G. E. Hall

The structure of programs for the initial preparation of teachers is examined in this entry from several perspectives: (a) the nature of the institutional setting in which the program is offered, (b) the length and sequence of the program, and (c) the structure of the knowledge and skills included in the program. A brief examination of each perspective follows, along with a discussion of the relationship of initial teacher education to induction into the profession and ongoing inservice education.

1. Structure of Settings for Initial Teacher Preparation

Although there is variation in the design and structure of preparation programs nearly all are found within institutions of postsecondary education. Types of institutions of higher education offering programs range from those that exist for the sole purpose of preparing teachers to large universities in which teacher education may be just a small part of the overall instruction, research, and service mission.

1.1 Teachers' Colleges

Professional schools are a relatively new phenomenon in the history of higher education. Until the nineteenth century most professions consisted of individuals who were considered generally well-educated, either by virtue of having had a university education (baccalaureate) or as a result of private tutoring, and who had served a period of apprenticeship under an established practitioner of the profession. However, as a profession, teaching fell short even of this standard; it was regarded simply as the transmission of information and values. Consequently, there was an expectation that if one "possessed" the knowledge, then one could transmit it to others with little or no formal preparation in teaching. Teachers for primary grades could have as little as 8 years of schooling. During the twentieth century the number of years of formal education required for teachers has steadily increased. In the 1990s, in nearly all countries, 3 to 4 years of college/university preparation is the standard.

The history of teacher education in the United Kingdom provides a common example. Until the late nineteenth century, teachers in the primary schools were basically required to be of good character and to have mastered the content they were to teach only at the level of mastery of the grade level they were to teach. Preparation of teachers for the secondary schools was nonexistent. Universal education of the citizenry at the secondary level did not exist. Only the small portion of the populace destined to become well-educated had the privilege of a secondary education, and secondary teachers were selected from among those who had studied an academic discipline at the university level (Thomas 1990).

In the late 1800s, specialized institutions for the preparation of teachers began in the United Kingdom and the United States with the founding of "seminaries" or "normal schools." These were single-purpose institutions only serving students preparing to become teachers, and usually offering programs which extended two years beyond the completion of a secondary school program. In the United States the movement to require secondary teachers to undergo pedagogical training was accompanied by extension of the two-year programs for elementary teachers in normal schools to full four-year programs leading to the baccalaureate degree. Normal schools also offered degrees for secondary teachers, usually with an academic major in "secondary education," which included concentrated study in an academic discipline.

The expansion to four-year degrees required extensive growth in the curricular offerings in the liberal arts and sciences in order to provide sufficient breadth and depth. With the move to four-year status, the "normal schools" became "teachers' colleges," both in name and in purpose. Similar institutions, called Colleges of Advanced Education, were established in Australia in the mid-1900s.

Few institutions of higher education at the close of the twentieth century include the term "teachers' college" in the institutional title. Most institutions which began as "normal schools" subsequently became "teachers' colleges," then "state colleges" (offering liberal arts degrees and a limited range of professional programs) and many today include the term "university" in their title. The distinguishing characteristics of these institutions, regardless of title, are that they have maintained a clear primary purpose of preparing teachers, the range of other baccalaureate programs is limited, and they offer few, if any, graduate programs (usually only master's degrees in education.) With few exceptions, these institutions primarily serve a state or regional student population. The commitment to teacher education exemplified by these institutions is reflected in the principles of the Renaissance Group (1990), including a commitment to campus-wide involvement in teacher education.

1.2 Liberal Arts Colleges

The liberal arts colleges are smaller institutions that provide education at the baccalaureate level with a primary focus on in-depth studies within an academic discipline and a well-rounded "general education" in the liberal arts and sciences. Offering teacher education programs is a relatively new objective for many liberal arts colleges. The majority of liberal arts colleges are private, rather than publicly supported, and the majority of these private colleges are supported by, or affiliated with, one or more religious organizations.

The liberal arts colleges have limited historical links to the professions—primarily restricted to providing baccalaureate study, which is seen as preparatory to entry to the ministry and to the medical professions. As professional programs have been added these have been cast in the context of the general goals of the liberal arts institution. Students undertaking a teacher education or a nursing curriculum have often been expected to complete coursework in these areas as electives within an overall program with the same graduation requirements as those for students not in professional programs.

Liberal arts colleges tend to share the following characteristics. Professional programs have a lower priority within them than liberal arts programs, as the allocation of institutional resources reflects. Graduate program offerings have been limited, if they have existed at all, but the situation is changing in this respect as financial conditions have led many liberal arts colleges to develop focused master's degree programs to serve a local area adult student population. The colleges are relatively small (20–50 teacher graduates per year) and attract primarily a state and regional student population (exceptions would be the few best known liberal arts colleges, which serve a national and international student population). Finally, teacher education programs in these institutions are usually administered by a Department of Education, whose faculty members teach the courses in pedagogy and supervise field experiences.

1.3 Comprehensive Colleges and Universities

There exists a large number of colleges and universities which either were created as multipurpose institutions or evolved as such from single-purpose institutions. For those institutions within this group which offer only the baccalaureate degree, the primary factor which distinguishes them from teachers' colleges and liberal arts colleges is the fact that they award a significant portion of their degrees in two or more professional or occupational disciplines such as engineering, business administration, nursing, and education. Within these institutions, however, teacher education typically does not hold any special priority.

Included within this group are institutions which offer graduate programs through the master's degree. In the United States approximately 60 percent of these institutions are public institutions and 40 percent are private. Characteristics of these institutions include a heavy commitment to instruction and service and less emphasis on research, some degree of role confusion

and ambivalence as to future aspirations of the institution (particularly in relationship to growth in breadth of program offerings and addition of graduate programs), and a separate college or school of education as an administrative unit on par with schools or colleges of arts and sciences, business, and engineering.

1.4 Research and Doctorate-granting Universities

The final type of higher education institution in which teacher education programs are found is the university which offers doctoral programs. In the United States these institutions are further categorized by the Carnegie Foundation for the Advancement of Teaching into two subtypes. "Research Universities" offer a full range of programs up to and including the doctorate, award at least 50 doctorates annually, give a high priority to research, and receive significant federal grant funds to support research. "Doctorate-Granting Universities" also offer a full range of programs through to the doctorate, usually award fewer doctorates annually in fewer program areas, place less emphasis on research as an institutional priority, and have limited federal grant funding in support of research.

In both types of doctorate-granting institutions the teacher education program is typically located in a separate school or college of education. Programmatic relationships between the school or college of education and other schools or colleges in the university tend to focus more on relationships based on doctoral programs and faculty research than on the basic teacher preparation program. In the United States approximately 100 of these institutions are members of and have endorsed the principles of the Holmes Group (1986) or the Renaissance Group (1990).

2. Structure of Programs: Time and Organization

The number of countries in which teacher preparation begins in upper secondary school is diminishing rapidly. The worldwide trend is toward requiring a minimum of a bachelor's degree for programs to prepare teachers. Ghani (1990) summarized data gathered in the mid-1980s on teacher preparation in developing countries in four regions of the world. He found the total number of years of education (primary/elementary, secondary, postsecondary) for primary/elementary teachers in 24 countries to range from 8 in Nigeria, to 16 in Sri Lanka. For secondary teachers in these 24 countries the total years of education ranged from 14 in Nepal and Afghanistan, to 18 in Malaysia (for "upper-level secondary"). Ghani reported a trend toward requiring more general education as well as more extensive professional/pedagogical training.

Distinctions between the amount and nature of educational preparation for primary teachers and secondary teachers are also disappearing. An example of this is the increase from 2 years to 4 years in professional preparation required for elementary teachers in Taiwan, a change that was implemented in 1988. In several states in the United States an additional year of postbaccalaureate study is required. In fact, some institutions of higher education have chosen to offer their teacher education programs only at the postbaccalaureate level. Consequently, worldwide there are a number of arrangements whereby the teacher candidate engages in preparation for the profession.

2.1 Four-year Programs

The majority of teacher preparation programs are conducted within the context of a four-year program leading to a baccalaureate degree. The exceptions are of two types: those programs designed intentionally to take 5 years, and those programs to which requirements have been added, either within the pedagogical component of the program or in academic major disciplines, with the result that it has become impossible for students to complete the program in 4 years.

Four-year programs may be further described in three types of program organization.

(a) *Continuous four-year programs.* In these programs the student is admitted to the professional education program at the beginning of college studies, with the professional or pedagogical component of the baccalaureate studies beginning in the first year and continuing through to the completion of the degree program.

(b) *"One-plus-three" programs.* These programs require students to complete 1 year of college work in general studies and/or the academic major prior to formal admission to the professional teacher education program. In these programs professional or pedagogical studies typically begin in the second year of college and continue through to the completion of the baccalaureate program.

(c) *"Two-plus-two" programs.* The third design for four-year programs is the "two-plus-two" design, in which students are admitted after the completion of 2 years of college study. During the first 2 years they are generally expected to have completed general education or "core" studies as well as significant work on a major in an academic discipline. This third type of program design is found most frequently in institutions with strong links to junior (or community) colleges that offer the first 2 years of college study.

2.2 Five-year Programs

A small number of institutions of higher education offer programs of study for prospective teachers which are intentionally designed to take five full academic years to complete. These programs also vary as to

point of entry, in the same manner as the four-year programs. Some institutions grant a baccalaureate degree at the completion of the five-year program; some grant a baccalaureate degree at the completion of the first 4 years (when requirements for a liberal arts degree have been met) and grant a master's degree upon completion of the fifth year.

2.3 Fifth-year Programs

An increasing number of institutions have developed teacher preparation programs which are conducted entirely at the postbaccalaureate degree level. These programs require that students hold a baccalaureate degree with a major in the liberal arts or sciences for admission. All professional coursework and field experiences are offered within the context of a master's degree program. During the 1960s and early 1970s a number of Master of Arts in Teaching programs were developed in order to qualify persons who had already completed a liberal arts degree.

The Carnegie Forum on Education and the Economy recommended, in the report of its Task Force on Teaching as a Profession (1986), that all teacher education become a graduate-level enterprise, built upon substantive study in the arts and sciences at the undergraduate level. The graduate degree, to be offered by graduate schools of education, would emphasize systematic study of teaching and clinical experiences. The Holmes Group (1986), a consortium of schools of education in American research universities, has also adopted this position. A number of American universities offer master's degree programs of this kind.

3. Structure of Learning in Teacher Education Programs

Teacher education programs are organized and structured according to a sequence of courses and the balancing of on-campus and in-school experiences. Another basis for structuring teacher education programs uses learning as the framework. The different components of knowledge and skills that teachers need become the basis for organizing the program. This approach establishes program structure on an established knowledge base.

In the United States, the National Council for Accreditation of Teacher Education (1992) has outlined parameters for a knowledge base. The first of its standards for accreditation of programs states that "professional education programs are based on essential knowledge, established and current research findings, and sound professional practice" (p. 47). Judgments about accrediting a teacher education program are based on the degree to which faculty have developed, and students have an understanding of, this knowledge base.

Galluzzo and Pankratz (1990) have described five attributes of a knowledge base: (a) a collectively held and systematically reinforced set of beliefs that guides program development and instruction; (b) a focus on organizing those beliefs in a manner that reflects the ultimate purpose of the program; (c) explicit descriptions of the knowledge, skills, and dispositions that a program graduate should possess; (d) a set of source documents that describe the essential knowledge that a program graduate needs; and (e) a model or a series of models that show how the various elements form an integrated program.

In the past, major distinctions existed between the knowledge that future teachers needed to acquire in regard to subject matter and pedagogy. In fact, these two domains of knowledge were formerly presented by higher education faculty housed in separate schools or departments. The future teacher had the implicit responsibility of synthesizing and integrating knowledge learned about subject matter from one group of faculty members with knowledge learned about pedagogy from a different faculty. This dichotomy is dissolving in the 1990s and there is a new appreciation of the importance of integration of learnings from different fields. Four general domains of knowledge are now being addressed in the preparation of teachers.

3.1 General Education

There is a body of knowledge and skills that all college graduates should possess as educated citizens. These expectations are true for all students across the campus, regardless of academic major or professional aspirations. This domain includes the ability to communicate in written and oral language, basic computational and mathematical skill, the uses of technology, and general knowledge of history, literature, the arts, and the sciences.

3.2 Content Knowledge

Teachers need to have an in-depth knowledge of the subject matter they will be teaching. The depth of knowledge expected will vary by the level of teaching that is anticipated. For example, preschool through fifth grade (elementary school) teachers should have basic subject-matter knowledge across a number of fields, since they will be expected to teach a wide array of topics. In contrast, grades 6–8 (middle-school) teachers are expected to have in-depth knowledge in two subject fields, since they will most likely be part of an interdisciplinary team and be teaching in two subject areas. Grades 9–12 (high school) teachers are expected to have extensive knowledge of a subject matter in one area, which will be their primary teaching assignment. However, knowledge of subject matter alone is not sufficient preparation to become an effective teacher.

3.3 Pedagogical Knowledge

Knowing how to teach is another critical domain for successful teaching. Future teachers need to develop an array of knowledge and skills related to the act of teaching. Many of these tend to be independent from the subject matter and level being taught. Pedagogical knowledge includes such areas as learning theories, strategies for assessing student learning, classroom management, use of technology in teaching, and multicultural issues in education.

3.4 Pedagogical Content Knowledge

Perhaps the most important of these four domains and certainly the most complex is that of pedagogical content knowledge (PCK). Shulman (1986) proposed the concept of PCK as a result of studies of novice and expert teachers. PCK represents more than a simple combination of general knowledge, content knowledge, and pedagogical knowledge. While it is an amalgam of these, it is also a representation of additional knowledge and skills that expert teachers possess.

Included in PCK is knowledge of typical misconceptions that students will have when learning a particular concept. PCK entails having knowledge of and the ability to draw upon powerful analogies, illustrations, examples, explanations, and demonstrations that will make sense to specific students. It also includes knowledge of the background of experiences and culture that learners bring to the classroom and the frames of reference they bring to the learning of specific subject-matter concepts and principles. The concept of pedagogical content knowledge has become an organizing force in the redesign of teacher education programs (Cochran 1991).

4. Relationships Among Preservice, Induction, and Inservice

Since the mid-1980s there has been a rapid growth in induction programs designed to provide special training, support, and evaluation for beginning teachers. All of these aspects of professional development of a teacher may be described in a continuum of shared involvement between higher education and the schools. Both are involved throughout the career of a teacher, with the institution of higher education having the greatest involvement in the earliest stages of formal teacher preparation, less involvement as the teacher moves through induction, and still less as the teacher undergoes inservice education throughout his or her career. Conversely, although they are involved throughout all stages, the level of involvement and responsibility of the schools in the professional education and development of teachers follows an inverted path to that of institutions of higher education. Formal partnerships between colleges or universities and schools have resulted in this shared responsibility becoming more systematic, effective, and efficient.

See also: Curriculum of Teacher Education Programs; Governance of Teacher Education; Characteristics of Teacher Educators

References

Carnegie Forum on Education and Economy Task Force on Teaching as a Profession 1986 *A Nation Prepared: Teachers for the 21st Century.* Carnegie Forum on Education and the Economy, New York

Cochran K F, King R A, DeRuiter J A 1991 Pedagogical content knowledge: A tentative model for teacher preparation. Paper presented at the annual meeting of the American Educational Research Association, Chicago. ERIC Document Reproduction Service No. ED 340 683, Washington, DC

Galluzzo G R, Pankratz R S 1990 Five attributes of a teacher education program knowledge base. *J. Teach. Educ.* 41(4): 7–14

Ghani Z 1990 Pre-service teacher education in developing countries. In: Rust V D, Dalin P (eds.) 1990 *Teachers and Teaching in the Developing World.* Garland, New York

National Council for the Accreditation of Teacher Education 1992 *Standards, Procedures, and Policies for the Accreditation of Professional Education Units.* NCATE, Washington, DC

Shulman L S 1986 Those who understand: Knowledge growth in teaching. *Educ. Researcher* 15(2): 4–14

The Holmes Group 1986 *Tomorrow's Teachers: A Report of the Holmes Group,* The Holmes Group Michigan State University, East Lansing, Michigan

The Renaissance Group 1990 *Teachers for a New World: A Statement of Principles of the Renaissance Group.* The Renaissance Group, College of Education, University of Northern Iowa, Cedar Falls, Iowa

Thomas J B (ed.) 1990 *British Universities and Teacher Education: A Century of Change.* Falmer Press, London

Further Reading

Collins K A 1989 The development of teacher education in Japan 1868–1980s. *Teaching and Teacher Education* 5: 217–28

Goodlad J L, Soder R, Sirotnik K A (eds.) 1990 *Teachers for Our Nation's Schools.* Jossey-Bass, San Francisco, California

Houston W R (ed.) 1990 *Handbook of Research on Teacher Education.* Macmillan, New York

Howsam R B, Corrigan D C, Denemark G W 1985 *Educating a Profession.* American Association of Colleges for Teacher Education, Washington, DC

Kerr S T 1991 Beyond dogma: Teacher education in the USSR. *J. Teach. Educ.* 42(5): 332–49

Leavitt H B (ed.) 1992 *Issues and Problems in Teacher Education: An International Handbook.* Greenwood, Westport, Connecticut

National Institute for Educational Research (NIER) 1989 *Teacher Training in Japan. NIER Occasional Paper 03/89.* NIER, Tokyo (ERIC Document Reproduction Service No. ED 313 360)

Reynolds M (ed.) 1989 *Knowledge Base for the Beginning Teacher.* American Association of Colleges for Teacher Education, Washington, DC

Smith B O 1980 *Design for a School of Pedagogy.* US Office of Education (ERIC Document Reproduction Service No. ED 193 215)

Stewart D K 1991 Teacher education in countries around the world: Studies in the ERIC data base. *J. Teach. Educ.* 42(5): 350–56

Voorbach J T, Prick L G M 1989 *Teacher Education 5: Research and Developments on Teacher Education in the Netherlands.* SVO, The Hague

Evaluation of Teacher Education Programs

G. R. Galluzzo

The effect that a teacher education program has on the knowledge, skills, and dispositions of its graduates is a constant source of inquiry at teacher preparation institutions. The practice in the field, however, is not advanced. This entry describes the application of educational evaluation methods to the preparation of teachers.

1. Background Literature

Almost 90 percent of teacher education institutions in the United States collect program evaluation data (Adams and Craig 1983), and for the majority the reason is one of external accountability. Such evaluations are based on quite diverse philosophical underpinnings. Medley (1977), using the behaviorist process–

product paradigm, defined program evaluation as "the extent that the training experiences produce the competencies defined as objectives of the training program" (p. 69). In contrast, Stufflebeam (1982) stated that evaluation is "the process of delineating, obtaining, and applying descriptive and judgmental information about the worth or merit of some program's goals, design, implementation, and impact in order to promote improvements, serve needs for accountability, and foster understandings" (p. 138). What is common to the philosophies of these two definitions is that for program evaluation to be meaningful it must address the needs of the local audiences, and must be focused on obtaining data for making judgments about the degree to which the program meets its stated goals.

2. Evaluation Models

The initial impetus for the growth of program evaluation can be traced to the increasing number of social programs. To begin with there were few guidelines as to what constituted acceptable evaluation. Thus, evaluators typically applied research methods to social settings. As the need for reliable information that could be used to demonstrate the worth and merit of a program increased, project planners needed methods which were both flexible (to be applied in natural setting) and systematic. As a result, models of evaluation were developed, which incorporated research methods from various disciplines.

Popham (1975), for example, described an objectives-based model in which the judgment about a program is determined by the extent to which the program meets its stated objectives. Stake (1967), on the other hand, designed the more comprehensive "countenance" model which borrowed from qualitative research methods. This model was composed of antecedents (that is, those conditions which existed when the program was begun); transactions (that is, those events which transpired during the program); and outcomes (that is, those intended and unintended results of the program). Stufflebeam et al. (1971) developed an evaluation model with four dimensions: contexts, (the conditions under which the program began); inputs (the resources and commitments necessary to operate the program); processes (the events which occurred during the operation of the program); and products (the results or outcomes of the program).

3. Applications to Teacher Education

Galluzzo and Craig (1990) labeled program evaluation teacher education's "orphan," as it is one of the more poorly practiced aspects of the field. The application of educational evaluation models to teacher education lacks the rich history one would expect to find in an area where the literature is almost 50 years old. In a seminal analysis of teacher education program evaluation Troyer and Pace (1944) documented the evaluation efforts at a variety of institutions. They examined the methods used to evaluate the contributions of various program components (including general education, professional education, and student teaching), and conducted a more general analysis using follow-up studies. While their contribution may be considered dated, remarkably the impression is that practice at the end of the twentieth century is only slightly more sophisticated.

The most visible model for program evaluation in teacher education was developed by Sandefur (1970) who outlined in his monograph the necessary features of an evaluation model for teacher education. Like Popham (1975) Sandefur viewed the evaluation of a program as measuring the degree to which students can demonstrate the competencies which serve as the outcomes of the program. Included in his model are assessments of teaching skill, classroom personality, and students' perceptions of teacher preparation.

More recent models have challenged Sandefur's competency-based, quantitative approach to evaluation. Borrowing from the research methods of anthropology, de Voss and Hawk (1983) developed a model based more on documentation than on assessment. In their model, students and faculty are not data points; rather, they are informants who characterize the processes and the outcomes of the program.

Some approaches use both documentation and assessment. Zimpher and Loadman (1986), for example, described a large-scale documentation and assessment system that included data on students when they began the program, throughout the program, upon completion, and in follow-up.

Nelli and Nutter (1984) applied Stake's "countenance model" to teacher education. Throughout their application, they suggested building evaluation around the questions that a program faculty would want to ask in each of the antecedents, transactions, and outcomes phases of the evaluation.

More recently, Rickards and Diez (1992) described an essentially outcomes-based program evaluation effort for teacher education, but the nature of the outcomes, many of which are nonbehavioral, challenged conventional notions of such programs. Their model included a mix of quantitative and qualitative data on each student.

There has been one debate that challenges the utility of evaluation in teacher education. In 1981 Katz et al. raised the question of whether what is learned from program evaluation studies justifies the resources expended. Following a review of 26 follow-up studies, Katz et al. identified major threats to the validity of the investigations, including sampling, the validity of the conclusions, and the evaluation method. They concluded that the methodological shortcomings were sufficiently great to call into question the worth of the findings. In response, Adams et al. (1981) claimed that the review methods used had been more appropriate for research studies than for evaluation studies, and thus Katz et al. had drawn erroneous conclusions.

4. Impediments to Quality Evaluation

Many weaknesses beset program evaluators beside those singled out by Katz et al. They include the identification of criterion variables and independent variables, as well as issues concerning the design of the evaluation.

4.1 Criterion Variables

Criterion variables fall into four broad categories: (a) knowledge, (b) teaching skill, (c) affective dimensions, and (d) perceptions of preparation. Teacher knowledge can be divided into three areas: general knowledge, subject-matter knowledge, and professional knowledge. Galluzzo (1983) followed 19 preservice teachers from their point of entry into professional education as freshmen through to their graduation in order to assess the growth in their knowledge over the four years of professional preparation. At the beginning of the freshman year, the students were administered the National Teachers Examination; each spring thereafter, they were measured with alternative forms of the same test. The results indicated no significant differences in their general knowledge but, in contrast, there were significant and positive differences in scores on the test of professional knowledge.

Later interpretations of teacher knowledge have regarded it as beyond simple measurement on a paper-and-pencil test. Shulman (1986) contended that teacher knowledge is the application of knowledge to simulated teaching settings, and thus focused on the way teachers use knowledge, not only the knowledge they possess.

Teaching skills typically evaluated using performance assessments include, among many others, the teacher's use of higher order questioning, the use of praise, and the ability to stop misbehavior in a timely and accurate manner. Many instruments to measure teaching skills have been developed based on the teacher effectiveness research (Borich 1977, Cooper 1983).

There is a great deal of debate surrounding the direct observation of teaching. Compelling arguments exist concerning the timing of the observation, the teacher's expectation for the lesson, and the teacher's expectation for the students. Context greatly influences classroom processes, and yet it is rare for direct observations to consider the role that context plays in what is being observed.

There is a persistent belief that attitudes toward teaching or children influence how teachers teach. It follows, then, that programs in teacher education should have certain expectations for the attitudes held by beginning teachers and that the program should help foster appropriate attitudes. The measurement of teachers' attitudes occupies a great deal of the literature, but has not been highly conclusive. Either the instruments lack validity or it is difficult to trace the resultant scores to the effects of the program. Perhaps the most promising work in this area is that contributed by Katz and Raths (1986). According to Katz and Raths, a disposition is a cognitive orientation which is operationalized as the tendency on the part of the teacher to act in a consistent manner. The concept of dispositions introduces a more powerful interpretation to the important and confusing area of affective criterion variables.

Perceptions of programs typically refer to how satisfied teachers are with their preparation. Perceptions are usually gained through mailed questionnaires, and

the resultant data usually define program effectiveness. Lindsay (1985) has outlined a set of procedures for conducting useful surveys of graduates, but unfortunately, many researchers do not follow them. Thus, while satisfaction is the most frequently measured criterion, it is also the least validly and reliably measured.

4.2 Independent Variables

This next area of weakness is somewhat more obscure in the literature, but is nonetheless potent. The critical question is whether the teacher education program should really be expected to affect students in substantial ways. Galluzzo and Pankratz (1990) argued that a teacher education program must be grounded in a knowledge base that includes a set of beliefs, a body of supportive literature, and a set of clearly articulated expectations for students. All too often teacher education is a collection of courses which offer no consistent image of what it means to teach, nor what it means to learn to teach. This allows students to proceed through their programs confirming what they already believed teaching to be and rejecting or ignoring those concepts and practices which are inconsistent with their preconceived notions of teaching.

4.3 Design Problems

Teacher educators must organize a systematic strategy for collecting data that can be used to conduct meaningful evaluation of the program. Program evaluation efforts in teacher education are typically institution-specific studies designed to inform the local setting and the findings are rarely generalizable to other institutions. Given these limitations, it is incumbent on the faculty members who teach in the program to be clear as to their purposes, processes, and outcomes.

5. Model Efforts to Evaluate Teacher Education Programs

Over time, researchers have attempted to conduct evaluations that are useful for meeting accountability concerns, for improving programs, and for contributing to the body of literature. This section summarizes some of the more promising of these efforts.

Hummel and Strom (1987) used a survey to study the relationship between the graduates' perceptions of their preparation and the number of years the graduates had been teaching. Graduates with less teaching experience viewed their preparation more positively than did graduates with more teaching experience. Specifically, graduates with two or more years of experience were significantly less positive in their perceptions than were those who had taught for only one year.

Another cross-sectional study was conducted by Kochmann (1993) to study the effect of time in teaching on graduates' perceptions of their programs. Teachers with one to six years of teaching were surveyed (n=634) to examine whether the amount of time teachers have been teaching affects their evaluation of their programs. The results suggest that, in the main, time was not a factor. There were few significant differences across the years. However, the survey did uncover the effects of changes in the program over time. Specifically, teachers with one or two years of teaching experience rated their preparation in teaching for thinking and problem-solving significantly higher than did teachers with three to six years. This difference located the point in time when the program faculty changed the curriculum to include instruction in thinking and problem-solving.

Pigge (1978) also surveyed recent graduates. He reported a high correlation between teachers' perceived need for a particular competency and their proficiency at it. He also found the teachers reporting that "high need" competencies were developed in the workplace and not during the teacher education program. Unfortunately, teachers also reported that "low need" competencies in teaching were developed in the teacher education program.

Gideonse (1988) asked his colleagues to list the names of students who had great potential as teachers and then interviewed the resulting 43 nominees. The interview method allowed the researcher to gather the rich and anecdotal data that is so often lost in a mailed survey. Gideonse was able to quote students to make his points, and the categories of strengths and weaknesses were created jointly by the interviewees and the researcher.

A highly useful volume is the summary of an international conference on the preparation of science teachers held in Jerusalem (Tamir 1985) which contains several papers from researchers in many countries, outlining problems in the preparation of science teachers. These papers focused both on the content of science and science curriculum materials. Generalizations emerged on the role of science in society, the role of science education, and the role of the science teacher.

Perhaps the most comprehensive study is that conducted by Furlong et al. (1988) in the United Kingdom. Included in the design were direct observations; interviews with students, professors, and mentors; survey questionnaires; and anecdotal record-keeping. The subjects were 75 students enrolled in four programs. Although the focus of the study was on learning to teach, there was an emphasis on becoming a thoughtful, analytic, and reflective teacher. The work of Furlong et al. is an excellent example of what can be accomplished with available resources.

Because of the institution-specific nature of program evaluation efforts it is difficult to make generalizations, nonetheless, a few notable themes emerge. Internationally, there is difficulty in linking theory to practice. Students report that programs are effective in teaching the preactive skills of teaching (e.g., planning, materials development, materials selection) and less effective in teaching the interactive skills

of teaching (e.g., alternate instructional strategies, classroom management and discipline, and lesson development). Research appears to be most necessary on the effects of teacher education programs on these interactive skills. Little is known about why students rate their preparation programs as less effective in these areas.

6. Conclusion

In this entry, the application of educational evaluation processes to teacher education has been outlined briefly. Concerns for program evaluation increase when concerns for accountability increase. At the same time, however, it is important to recognize that program evaluation can serve multiple purposes besides accountability, namely, in improving programs, fostering an understanding of the programs, and contributing to the body of literature on teacher education and program evaluation. The future of practice in this area is dependent on the degree of importance accorded to researchers' conceptions of teacher education as a field of inquiry. Internationally, there is still a great deal to learn about the extent to which teacher education affects teachers' knowledge, behavior, dispositions, and perceptions, and how to measure these effects.

References

Adams R, Craig J 1983 A status report of teacher education program evaluation. *J. Teach. Educ.* 34(2): 33–37
Adams R, Craig J, Hord S, Hall G 1981 Program evaluation and program development in teacher education: A response to Katz et al. 1981 *J. Teach. Educ.* 32(5): 21–24
Borich G 1977 *The Appraisal of Teaching: Concepts and Processes.* Addison-Wesley, Reading, Massachusetts
Cooper J 1983 Basic elements in teacher education program evaluation: Implications for future research and development. In: Howey K R, Gardner W E (eds.) 1983 *The Education of Teachers: A Look Ahead.* Longman, New York
de Voss G, Hawk D 1983 Follow-up models in teacher education. *Educ. Eval. Policy Anal.* 5(2): 163–71
Furlong V, Hirst P, Pocklington K, Miles S 1988 *Initial Teacher Training and the Role of the School.* Open University Press, Milton Keynes
Galluzzo G 1983 An evaluation of a teacher education program. Paper presented at the annual meeting of the American Educational Research Association, New Orleans. ERIC Document No. ED 229 373
Galluzzo G, Craig J 1990 Evaluation of preservice teacher education programs. In: Houston W (ed.) *Handbook of Research on Teacher Education: A Project of the Association of Teacher Educators.* Macmillan, New York
Galluzzo G, Pankratz R 1990 The five essential attributes of a teacher education program knowledge base. *J. Teach. Educ.* 41(4): 7–14
Gideonse H 1988 Follow-up study of a selected sample of elementary and secondary education graduates. Unpublished manuscript. University of Cincinnati, Cincinnati, Ohio
Hummell T, Strom S 1987 The relationship between teaching

experience and satisfaction with teacher preparation: A summary of three surveys. *J. Teach. Educ.* 38(5): 28–36

Katz L G, Raths J D 1986 Dispositions as goals for teacher education. *Teaching and Teacher Education*, 1(4): 301–307

Katz L, Raths J D, Mohanty C, Kurachi A, and Irving J 1981 Follow-up studies: Are they worth the trouble? *J. Teach. Educ.* 32(2): 18–24

Kochmann B J 1993 *An Evaluation of the Elementary/Middle School Program at the University of Northern Colorado.* University of Northern Colorado, Greeley, Colorado

Lindsay M 1985 Procedures for follow-up studies of teacher education graduates. *J. Teach. Educ.* 35(2): 29–33

Medley D M 1977 *Teacher Competence and Teacher Effectiveness: A Review of Process–Product Research.* American Association of Colleges for Teacher Education, Washington, DC (ERIC Document Reproduction Service No. ED 143 629)

Nelli E, Nutter N 1984 *A Model for Evaluating Teacher Education Programs.* National Institute of Education, Washington, DC

Pigge F 1978 Teacher competencies: Need, proficiency, and where proficiency was developed. *J. Teach. Educ.* 29(4): 70–6

Popham W J 1975 *Educational Evaluation.* Prentice-Hall, Englewood Cliffs, New Jersey

Rickards W, Diez M 1992 Integrating multiple internal and external data sources in the institutional evaluation of teacher education. Paper presented at the American Educational Research Association, San Francisco, California

Sandefur J T 1970 *An Illustrated Model for the Evaluation of Teacher Education Graduates.* American Association of Colleges for Teacher Education, Washington, DC

Shulman L 1986 Those who understand: Knowledge growth in teaching. *Educ. Researcher*, 15(2), 4–14

Stake R 1967 The countenance of educational evaluation *Teach. Coll. Rec.* 68(7): 523–40

Stufflebeam D 1982 Explorations in the evaluation of teacher education. In: Hord S, Savage T, Bethel L (eds.) 1982 *Toward Usable Strategies for Teacher Education Program Evaluation.* University of Texas R & D Center for Teacher Education, Austin, Texas

Stufflebeam D, Foley W, Gephart W, Guba E, Hammond R, Merriman H, Provus M 1971 *Educational Evaluation and Decision-making.* Peacock, Itasca, Illinois

Tamir P 1985 *Preservice and Inservice Education of Science Teachers.* ERIC Document Reproduction Service No. ED 258 839

Troyer M, Pace C R 1944 *Evaluation in Teacher Education.* American Council on Education, Washington, DC

Zimpher N, Loadman W 1986 *A Documentation and Assessment System for Student and Program Development.* American Association of Colleges for Teacher Education, Washington, DC

Governance of Teacher Education

H. D. Gideonse

Nations establish policies to recruit and prepare teachers and maintain and enhance their skills because the heart of any nation's educational system is to be found in the quality of its teachers. The governance of teacher education embraces the *structures* of government agencies and teacher preparation institutions responsible for addressing such policy matters. It embraces also the *processes* employed by those structures in arriving at policy (e.g., sources of initiative, advisory input, opportunities for review, accountability schemes). Finally, governance includes the *functions* of teacher education policy (e.g., establishing entrance qualifications, levels of preparation, nature of the preparation program, exit standards).

Given the centrality of teachers to national education systems, it is surprising that so little scholarly literature exists on the governance of teacher education. Most of what exists either focuses on Western or developed countries or is found in the literature coming from the same sources. Educational systems are always deeply rooted in their cultures. Given the increasing complexity, diversity, and vigor of cultural expression in the world, as the astounding developments in the early 1990s in Central and Eastern Europe

and Asia attest, conceptualizing across cultural and national boundaries can be extremely risky. In considering the governance of teacher education, therefore, the potential for bias exists not only as to the meaning of specifics addressed in the literature but also as regards the very frames established for understanding the issues of governance in the first place.

While expertise on these matters does exist, it has not been generated by members of the scholarly community. Rather, expertise resides in the experiences of the practitioners of policy; that is, those who have lived through or have been affected by its processes and products. Practitioners of policy do not frequently write of their experiences, but they are often deeply knowledgeable. Mindful of the particular perspectives their roles and positions may have afforded them, individuals who have served in or who currently occupy positions in teacher education policy can be important sources of valuable information and insight into the structure, processes, and functions of the governance of teacher education. The absence of a substantial literature, however, means each new generation must discover these matters anew.

A final caveat, taking something of the form of a

conundrum, deserves mention. The very concept of governance implies a degree of purposiveness and rationality that is often belied by reality. Scholars of governance warn of the rationalistic fallacy—the belief that orderly argument, well-marshalled data, and careful logic will determine policy (see Clark and McNergney 1990; Hawley 1990). The reality is much less neat and much more political.

1. Governance Structures: Policy

Any conceptual framework for analyzing the governance of teacher education should begin with those structures that develop policies affecting teacher education. The term "policy" embraces decisions about rules, criteria, incentives, priorities, and resources. The term "Structure" refers to the institutional forms, including their interrelationships, with formal responsibility for making such decisions.

Throughout the world, national ministries of education are the most common structural arrangement for determining policy and for governing teacher education. These ministries are sometimes devoted exclusively to education (e.g., in China, Cuba, Finland, Italy, Jamaica, Spain, Turkey, and Uganda). Sometimes, however, the education portfolio is combined with others, as in Bolivia (Ministry of Education and Culture), Japan (Ministry of Education, Science, and Culture), Norway (Ministry of Education, Research and Church Affairs), or the Philippines (Ministry of Education, Culture, and Sports). In yet other instances, the governance responsibility is bifurcated. An example is Bolivia where urban teacher education is governed by the Ministry of Education and Culture and rural teacher education by the Ministry of Rural Affairs.

Nations that are federal in structure (e.g., Australia, Brazil, Canada, Germany, Switzerland, or the United States) have vested responsibility for education in the ministries of education (or their equivalent) at the province or state level. However, for economic as well as for policy reasons, the role of the federal counterpart to the provincial or state authorities is becoming increasingly more vigorous worldwide.

A second source of governance authority over teacher education is legislative or parliamentary. Instances of legislative action directly impacting teacher education are found in the 1988 Education Act for England and Wales, Norway's 1973 Act concerning teacher education, and Italy's 1973 Act on the legal status of teachers. Policies handled in some nations by executive decision within a ministry may instead be proposed to a parliament and determined legislatively, or initiated within the legislative body; on adoption, these policies establish the ministry's administrative responsibilities.

A third structural form is where the teaching profession itself is granted authority to make important governance decisions. Typically, these structures are known as "professional standards boards," or "professional standards and practices boards." In the United States, for example, such boards exist in the states of Oregon, California, Nevada, and Minnesota; and in Canada, in British Columbia. In Scotland, the board is called the General Teaching Council.

The mechanisms that exist rarely exercise comprehensive governance responsibilities affecting teacher education. For example, they typically cannot make major resource commitments to teacher education. Rather, their policy actions impact on entrance qualifications to teacher education, specifications for preparation programs, and exit standards for candidates including, possibly, the definition and implementation of professional licensure examinations. Where the board also has responsibility for standards of practice, it will have important obligations for defining and enforcing expectations about how teachers and other licensed education personnel perform their duties. One of the most vigorous of such bodies is the California Commission on Teacher Credentialing (Mastain and Brott 1992).

Many countries approach the governance of teacher education by formally specifying advisory bodies to their ministry of education. Although authority for making decisions is retained by the administrative entity to whom the body is advisory, such structures provide formal means for injecting ideas into policy processes and for subjecting policy proposals to review prior to implementation. The Teacher Training Council (Denmark), the Federal Council of Education (Germany), the National Council for Teacher Education (Finland), the National Education Committee (Nepal), the National Council for Teacher Education (Norway, and also India), and the National Council for Education (Zambia) are examples of advisory bodies.

A fifth form of governance structure can be labeled "voluntary." One form of such an organization is the private foundation; from time to time these support systematic innovation in teacher education. Examples of this, both in the United States and especially in developing nations, may be seen in the work of the Ford, Carnegie, and Exxon Foundations. In the United States, the accreditation function for teacher education units has been undertaken at national level by a voluntary association, the National Council for Accreditation of Teacher Education (NCATE). The governing board of NCATE is weighted in four equal parts representative of teachers, teacher educators, policy bodies responsible for education, and so-called "specialty groups", such as learned societies and organizations representing various teaching specializations. A voluntary organization of a somewhat different, supranational sort, is the Organization for Economic Cooperation and Development (OECD). Through the mechanism of country reviews as well as through its subsidiary Centre for Educational Research and Innovation, OECD has had an impact on policy development in member countries.

A final structural device is the temporary commission or task force. Sometimes established by government, sometimes not, commissions and task forces can give high-level attention for a specified period of time to an issue or issues. This work culminates in a set of recommendations for established structures to consider. The Plowden Commission in the United Kingdom, the 1983 Commission on Educational Excellence in the United States, or the Congress of Education and Instruction organized every five years in Romania are examples.

2. Governance Structures: Teacher Education Programs

Within the policy literature, distinctions are made between policy formation (governance) and policy implementation (administration). Despite the locus of governance responsibility for teacher education policy in government agencies or professional associations, in most countries throughout the world real autonomy exists for the colleges and universities responsible for the initial preparation of teachers. While important policy guidelines may be established by ministerial, parliamentary, or professional bodies, teacher preparation programs often have a fair amount of latitude within which to operate. Thus, understanding the governance of teacher education programs is of considerable importance.

The governance of higher education institutions is a domain of interest in its own right, not without its own complexities and contradictions. While traditions of collegial faculty governance are strong, the collegial governance of the teacher education unit can be deeply affected by the collegial governance of the larger or superior governance unit at the college or university level. Administrative officers within the college or university can wield great power. In addition, formal and informal advisory bodies may exist, affording avenues for students, practitioners, alumni, and others to affect programs. Finally, collaboration between teacher education programs having clinical and/or field components, and schools and school authorities, places special constraints on the governance of programs.

3. Functions of Governance for Teacher Education

A handful of core functions engage the bulk of governance attention in teacher education. Entrance qualifications, levels of preparation, length of training, nature of the preparation program, and exit requirements are principal among these.

Entrance qualifications are governed in a variety of ways. Completion of specified levels of schooling is one approach. In Austria, for example, the secondary school certificate (*Matura*) is required in order to enter the teacher-training colleges. Achieving a pass score on one or more examinations may be required for entry into or continuation in a program. In some jurisdictions in the United States, for example, pass scores on specified basic skills tests may be a requirement.

The level of preparation is often differentiated as to the type of licensure sought. It is not uncommon to have nursery school, kindergarten, and elementary school licensure accomplished through a secondary school (e.g., in Bulgaria, China, Cuba, Ecuador, Egypt, and Libya). In contrast, secondary licensure almost universally requires preparation at the university level. Where resources permit, there has been a slow but steady trend throughout the world toward moving all licensure programs to the college or university level.

One of the most visible governance functions in teacher education is the specification of the elements of the training program itself. This governance function is undertaken in several ways. Where ministries of education operate the training colleges (as in Algeria, Cuba, Malawi, the Netherlands, Norway, and Saudi Arabia, for example), they exercise direct control over the teacher preparation curriculum. In other countries, licensure standards are defined by the appropriate authority, and preparing institutions develop curricula to meet those standards. A program-approval process is then employed where the institutions proposing to certify teachers in terms of the licensure standards are examined by the agency to determine whether the programs are consistent with the standards as defined (most jurisdictions in the United States follow this procedure, for example). In the United Kingdom, a subsidiary agency, the Council for Accreditation of Teacher Education, has been established to undertake the program examination.

Governance authorities also establish exit requirements, which are sometimes defined in terms of preparation-program completion. Requirements may also be defined in terms of completion of an internship or other successful teaching experience following, or instead of, a preparation program (e.g., as in New Zealand, and in alternative certification programs in the United States). These requirements may also take the form of a pass mark on a specified examination, which may be designed and administered by the ministry (e.g., in, Algeria, Austria, Egypt, France, Germany, the Philippines, and Turkey), or may be devised by another agency to which the ministry has given sanction (e.g., the privately developed National Teacher Examination used by a number of states in the United States).

The governance of teacher education can include the specification and provision of incentives for individuals to undertake preservice teacher preparation. These may take the form of subsidized enrollment at teacher preparation institutions, or scholarships, or fellowships (e.g., as in Australia, Germany, Norway, New Zealand, or Saudi Arabia), or forgivable loans to attend preparation programs in instructional areas of special needs (e.g., science, languages, or specified handicapping conditions).

Governance has also included indirect or partial provision of teacher education programs. As noted above, direct provision is where a ministry operates teacher preparation programs as part of its overall responsibility. Indirect provision occurs when resources are made available to preparing institutions, either preservice or inservice, to help subsidize the type of program the ministry has defined as being desirable.

Finally, governance includes the specification of continuing education requirements. Such requirements may be directed to induction programs or to continuing education needs which may, in turn, be defined either locally or centrally. They may also take the form of additional educational qualifications necessary for securing a permanent license. At least one system, that of Japan, seems to place even greater emphasis on continuing professional education than on preservice preparation.

4. Governance Processes

Education is an intensely political function for any society, but it is also, at least in the eyes of its principal actors, a professional endeavor. This dual character, awareness of which is increasing worldwide, has made advisory input into political governance processes critically important. Claims for advisory access may come from a wide range of stakeholders: teachers' and parents' organizations, preparation faculty (both professional and academic), preparation program administrators, employers of teachers, and many others.

Opportunities for policy review prior to promulgation is another process consideration. Authorities may not always wish or be able to provide such opportunities. Reviews of this kind may create delays, not only for the review process itself but also as a consequence of having to address questions that may be raised. Prepromulgation review increases the likelihood that all relevant considerations will be examined before decisions are taken.

Two kinds of accountability processes can be identified. The first is policy accountability, a subsidiary question of structure. Administrative authority is responsible to the legislature in a parliamentary system, to the elected executive in presidential systems, and essentially to itself in nondemocratic systems. For legislatively derived policy, accountability is ultimately to those who elect the legislative body. For professional standards and practices boards, accountability is to the appointing bodies and, ultimately, to the authority responsible for authorizing the board structure.

The second kind of accountability is performance accountability. For teacher education, especially, the dictum that the operations *are* the policy is well-remembered. Economic considerations, intentions that exceed a nation's current capacity, or mutually incompatible policy provisions may affect performance (for instance, in Malta teachers have received formal designation as professionals equal to other professionals but remain severely constrained by administrative control—see Farrugia 1992). Incapacity, disagreements over policy, or recalcitrance respecting policy may also figure in the discrepancy between policy intentions and actual performance. Sanctions in such instances may range from denial of individual licenses to loss of appropriations, program approval, or employment.

5. Issues in Governing Teacher Education

This final section briefly illustrates three categories of issues and topics that need to be considered in the course of governing teacher education. They are: substantive topics, governance topics, and meta-questions of governance.

5.1 Substantive Topics

The substantive topics are numerous. Questions concerning entry and exit qualifications of candidates, length and level of preparation, character of program, incentives to encourage candidacy, types and requirements of full licensure, and continuing education expectations remain to be answered.

Special circumstances frame the governance of teacher preparation in particular national contexts. Belgium's complex cultural mix has generated a policy structure with five education ministers. Bolivia's mountainous geography and isolated rural populations create special problems for teacher education. Rapid democratization of schooling in, say, Algeria and the People's Republic of China (plus the sheer size of China's 8.7 million teaching force) challenges aspirations to maintain or enhance standards.

Teacher education in Botswana confronts rural migrations to urban areas and a school curriculum ill-suited to the immediate needs of the population. Compensation arrangements compromise the ability of many Latin American countries to convene university faculty for purposes of program conceptualization. Indonesia, the world's fifth most populous country, is culturally extremely diverse and spans an archipelago embracing 13,000 islands.

Nations associated with former colonial empires must address the superimposition of European forms on indigenous cultures (e.g., Bolivia, Nicaragua, Nigeria, and Ghana). South Africa's system of four separate school systems for Blacks, Whites, Coloureds, and Asians will almost certainly undergo new challenges as a result of the dismantling of apartheid.

5.2 Governance Issues

A second set of issues focuses on governance itself. Examples include the balance between political and professional authorities in governance; the method of representing various professional specialties in teaching; the necessity for governance; and the relative weight to be given to national, regional, and local interests.

5.3 Meta-questions of Governance

Fundamental considerations of the nature of teaching, the role of the teacher in the facilitating the learning of others, and the part that expertise plays in carrying out a teacher's responsibilities also impact on the governance of teacher education. So too does the critically important "chicken-and-egg" question—how the desired new kinds of teachers can be prepared and placed if schools themselves are not transformed first.

Teaching, for example, may be conceived as the transmission of knowledge and skills or as the process of helping children reconstruct that knowledge for themselves. The teacher may be thought of as an authority, or as speaking on behalf of authority, or as a facilitator for developing the independent authority of the learner. High-quality teaching may be viewed as more a commitment to values and effective adult models and less a question of technical facility in the arts and crafts of curriculum, instruction, evaluation, and managing student behavior. Finally, when current schools and the conditions of practice in them are perceived to be antithetical to better models of teaching that might be advanced, the governance of teacher education may well become inseparable from the governance of new kinds of schools embracing state-of-the-art practice.

References

Clark D L, McNergney R F 1990 Governance in teacher education. In: Houston W R, Haberman M, Sikula J (eds.) 1990 *Handbook of Research on Teacher Education.* Macmillan, New York

Farrugia C J 1992 Authority and control in the Maltese educational system. *Int. Rev. Educ.* 38(2): 155–72

Hawley W D 1990 Systematic analysis, public policy-making, and teacher education. In: Houston W R, Haberman M, Sikula J (eds.) 1990 *Handbook of Research on Teacher Education.* Macmillan, New York

Mastain R, Brott R 1992 The California Commission on Teacher Credentialing: Seeking the ingredients for change. In: Gideonse H D (ed.) 1992

Further Reading

Ashton P T (ed.) 1991 Theme: Comparative teacher education. *J. Teach. Educ.* 42(5): 322–78

Churukian G A, Kissock C (eds.) 1991 Teacher education: Perspectives from abroad. *Action Tchr. Educ.* 13(3): 1–64

Gideonse H D (ed.) 1992 *Teacher Education Policy: Narratives, Stories, and Cases.* State University of New York Press, Albany, New York

Gumbert E B (ed.) 1990 *Fit to Teach: Teacher Education in International Perspective.* Georgia State University, Atlanta, Georgia

Leavitt H B 1992 *Issues and Problems in Teacher Education: An International Handbook.* Greenwood Press, Westport, Connecticut

Rust V D, Dalin P (eds.) 1990 *Teachers and Teaching in the Developing World.* Garland, New York

Tisher R P, Wideen M F (eds.) 1990 *Research in Teacher Education: International Perspectives.* Falmer Press, London

Vos A J, Brits V M 1990 *Comparative Education and National Education Systems.* Butterworths, Durban

(c)   Accreditation and Certification

Teacher Education Accreditation and Standards

J. Raths

Teacher education accreditation is the process by which an agency or organization evaluates and recognizes a program of study as meeting certain predetermined qualifications or standards (Selden 1976). Accreditation is usually a high-stakes procedure, whose main purpose is to assure the public that a program and its graduates are worthy of respect.

Accreditation can be applied at either of two levels: the institution as a whole, or specialized programs within an institution. As Larson (1983) noted, "the quality of programs within an institution is invariably uneven, and low quality programs may benefit from the lofty reputation of its institution" (p. 323). Thus, there is a need to accredit programs as well as institutions, especially when the graduates of programs are likely to impact on the health, safety, or welfare of the public.

This entry describes practices in teacher education accreditation in a number of countries. The criteria used in accreditation are outlined and some of the unresolved and most enduring issues that characterize the accreditation process are discussed.

1. Practices in Teacher Education Accreditation

This section summarizes selected attributes of the accreditation processes of particular nations and/or provinces.

1.1 Australia

Accreditation is carried out indirectly in Australia. The requirements of teacher registration (licensure) in each state set the guidelines for teaching programs. All institutions are required to produce graduates who can be registered to teach. This relationship is ensured by the threat of legal action by a candidate if, upon completion of the course, licensure is denied.

The requirements of registration are set by registration boards which have representatives of employers and teacher unions. Teacher colleges in Australia, termed "tertiary institutions," were once accredited by

state authority, but with the amalgamation of teacher colleges into universities in the 1970s, accreditation is no longer required. However, some programs engage in informal peer reviews. (This description includes information provided by Northfield 1992, and Peacock 1992.)

1.2 Botswana

In Botswana there is no formal process for accrediting teacher education institutions. The University of Botswana and the ministry of education, jointly, are the final arbiters of standards in teacher education, since they approve all proposals submitted by boards of affiliation, a group of individuals appointed to liaise between teacher education institutions and the University. External examiners play a prominent role in the maintenance of standards in the teacher education programs. (This description includes information provided by Mogami 1992.)

1.3 Canada

Education in Canada is seen as a provincial and not a federal concern. Thus each province is responsible for approving its teacher education programs.

In British Columbia the principal accreditor is the Council of Teachers of the British Columbia College of Teachers. The Council has 20 members, 15 of whom are elected on a zonal basis by the full College membership. The Council makes use of surveys of teachers who have recently obtained licenses through the institutions, self-studies by the Faculty of Education, an external team visit, and forums of representatives of groups interested in teacher education.

In Saskatchewan the Board of Teacher Education and Certification (BTEC) has as its mandate the task of reviewing teacher education programs and making recommendations to the University of Saskatchewan about them. The Board has never met this mandate, but has diverted its attention to setting and implementing criteria for granting teaching licenses in Saskatchewan.

As is the case with most Canadian provinces, in

Alberta the principal accreditor of teacher education is the provincial government itself, through the offices of the Ministry of Education. Once a teacher education program has been granted approval, there is no further review process relating to accreditation. Closing down a program in teacher education would reflect a financial exigency, rather than a negative assessment of program quality. (This description includes information provided by Blakey and Jamieson 1992, Housego 1992, Laferrière 1992, Robinson 1992, and Smart 1992.)

1.4 England and Wales

The Council for the Accreditation of Teacher Education (CATE) has sole responsibility for recommending to the Secretary of State for Education and Science the programs leading to Qualified Teacher Status that should be approved. Members of the Council are nominated by the Secretary of State. The Council establishes the criteria used in the program approval process, acting on the advice of a number of stakeholders in the process—groups of training institutions represented on local committees, the National Curriculum Council, and Her Majesty's Inspectorate of Schools (proposed to be abolished). The percentage of programs approved is not widely known, but it is estimated that in the final analysis all institutions that volunteer to become approved receive approval. (This description includes information provided by Brown 1992, Calderhead 1992, Chambers et al. 1992, Gammage 1992, and Gibson 1992.)

1.5 Scotland

The professional scrutiny and accreditation of all courses of initial teacher education in Scotland are the responsibility of the General Teaching Council for Scotland (GTCS). The GTCS is a statutory body, established by the Teaching Council (Scotland) Act of 1965.

The Council is empowered to appoint and dispatch visitors to review the general content and arrangement of courses of instruction offered by the colleges of education. The visitors subsequently report their findings to the Council. If the Council, as a result of the visitors report, deems that a change should be made in a college's courses, it will make a recommendation to the college's governing body. If the recommendation is not accepted, after negotiations the nonfeasance is reported to the Secretary of State. (This description includes information provided by Sutherland 1992.)

1.6 United States

In the United States a distinction is made between entitlement programs and accredited programs. Entitlement programs are those that are reviewed and approved by various arms of the state government. These approval bodies include a state department of education, or an autonomous body, sometimes referred to as the State Teacher Quality Control Board. The term "entitlement" means that graduates from the program are "entitled" to a license. Only approved programs can guarantee licenses to their graduates. Graduates of "unapproved programs" have the possibility of submitting transcripts to the state for a review by an office of the department of education. However, the latter process is time-consuming and not without risk.

Accreditation is quite different. The Council on Postsecondary Accreditation (COPA) is commissioned by the federal government to regulate all the country's accrediting bodies. In effect, COPA accredits accrediting agencies. In teacher education, COPA has recognized the National Council for the Accreditation of Teacher Education (NCATE) as the sole agency for the purpose of carrying out national accreditation of college and university units for the preparation of teachers and other professional school personnel (see United States, National Council for Accreditation of Teacher Education 1992 pp. 2–3).

NCATE is funded by contributions from the American Association of Colleges of Teacher Education, the National Education Association, and a large number of associated groups with vested interests in quality teacher education, such as the National Council of Teachers of Mathematics, the National Council of Teachers of English, and 19 other agencies with similar missions. Similarly, NCATE is governed by the education profession, both the practicing and preparation areas, and others who have a stake in the outcomes of professional education programs.

Having national accreditation status has dubious value. It does confer prestige on an institution, and the attainment of accreditation is cited in catalogs and recruiting brochures. At the same time, there is little evidence to suggest that schools, when hiring teachers, pay much attention to the accreditation status of the programs from which applicants for teaching jobs have graduated.

2. Criteria of Accreditation

One of the problems in understanding the evaluation process, of which accreditation is but one example, is that policymakers and practitioners seem to confuse the terms "criterion" and "standard" (see Cavell 1979 pp. 11–14). It is often helpful to think of "criterion" as a name of a variable that is subject to review. A criterion is a basis for comparison, and is usually named in accordance with the upper end of a continuum of values that the variable might take (e.g., "clarity" or "accuracy"). Alternatively, the variable name itself implies a higher and a lower end of its own scale (e.g., "faculty productivity," or "quality of students").

A standard, on the other hand, is not a range, but a setting within a range that is taken as desirable, minimal, or honorific (see Lipman 1992 pp. 3–4). Quite often, accreditation is carried out with well-specified criteria, but with no standards or with only vague notions of standards. Interestingly, the making of judgments with criteria but without standards is seen as the essence of professional practice. If, indeed, both criteria and standards were well-specified, then ordinary citizens could make accreditation decisions. For example, within a family of criteria associated with quality of the faculty, if one of the standards was that 90 percent of the faculty should have earned a doctorate, then almost anyone could survey the faculty roster to determine if this criterion were fairly met. However, issues of quality and excellence are not so easily defined or assessed. Faculty quality involves complex issues of productivity, commitment to the profession, ethical behavior, and much more besides—all defying the specification of widely held and publicly accepted standards. In matters such as these, judges serving as accreditors apply criteria without explicit standards, which has given cause for concern in some quarters. In the overview provided by this entry, the criteria used in selected nations and/or provinces can be examined.

2.1 Australia

Because of the indirect nature of accreditation in Australia, no national set of criteria for accreditation of programs exists. The licensure requirements in each state function as guidelines for each teacher education institution. A National Project on the Quality of Teaching and Learning has been undertaken in Australia with a view to producing criteria for teacher education programs (Northfield 1992).

2.2 Botswana

Proposals for new programs are reviewed by the University of Botswana and the Ministry of Education in three areas: (a) admission regulations; (b) syllabuses, courses, and assessment policies; (c) academic staffing and teaching organization policy and criteria (Mogami 1992).

2.3 Canada

In British Columbia, where the Council of Teachers of the College of Teachers approves teacher education programs, precise formulations of criteria do not exist (Smart 1992). Evidently the data collected, as described in the previous section, are analyzed holistically. In Quebec, the focus of program review is on content topics of programs, not the quality of the student body or the characteristics of the management system (Laferrière 1992). In Alberta, examples of criteria used to approve programs (ones that are quite difficult to pass) include length of practicum, program components, staff qualifications, library resources, and community support (Blakey and Jamieson 1992).

2.4 England and Wales

The major categories in England and Wales under which accreditation criteria are classified are: (a) cooperation between institutions, local authorities, and schools; (b) students' school experience and teaching practice; (c) phase and age range; (d) subject studies and subject application to pupils' learning; (e) curriculum studies in primary courses; (f) educational and professional studies; (g) selection and admission to initial teacher training.

Illustrative criteria under each category include the following: (a) institutions should ensure that experienced teachers from schools are involved in the selection of prospective teachers; (b) there should be practical classroom experience during the first term of a course; (c) secondary courses should cover the age ranges 11–16 or 11–18; (d) subject studies work should develop in prospective teachers an understanding of the underlying principles of their specialist subject or subjects; (e) courses for primary phase prospective teachers should prepare them so that they can teach and assess the core subjects of the National Curriculum to the attainment targets appropriate to the age range for which they are being trained; (f) on completion of their course, prospective teachers should be able to teach controversial issues in a balanced way; (g) no candidate should be admitted for a course without a personal or group interview (United Kingdom, Department of Education and Science 1989).

2.5 Scotland

The major criteria employed in Scotland for the accreditation of teacher education can be outlined in the following questions. Does a course demonstrate coherent balance and progression? Are professional studies taught in an integrated way? Are there clear links between college and school elements of the course? Are a variety of teaching methods employed? Are a variety of assessment methods employed? Are schools and colleges involved in a partnership in training and assessment? Do adequate student selection procedures exist, involving consideration of references and interviews as well as entry qualifications? Are serving teachers involved in the selection process? Do teaching staff in colleges possess "recent, relevant and successful" experience of teaching in schools? Are special education needs adequately catered for? Are cross-curricular issues—gender equality, European awareness, antiracist education—clearly addressed? Does the college have a structured system of course evaluation (Sutherland 1992)?

2.6 United States

The National Council for the Accreditation of Teacher Education (NCATE) makes use of 17 criteria organized into five categories: knowledge bases for professional education; relationship to the world of practice; students; faculty; and governance and resources. Examples of criteria within each category include: (a) the unit ensures that education students attain a high level of academic competence and understanding in the area in which they plan to teach or work; (b) the unit makes certain that clinical and field-based experiences in the professional education curriculum are designed to prepare students to work effectively in specific education roles; (c) the unit's admission procedures encourage the recruitment of quality candidates and that those quality candidates represent culturally diverse populations; (d) the unit ensures that faculty in professional education are qualified to perform their assignments and also reflect cultural diversity; (e) the governance system for the professional education unit ensures that all professional education programs are organized, unified, and coordinated to allow the fulfillment of its mission.

3. Issues in Accreditation

An issue is a question that implies at least two or more answers with good reasons available to support them. The following is a summary of key issues in accreditation, with an attempt to address at least two sides of each question.

Accreditation focuses a great deal on inputs such as finances, library quality, and involvement of the practicing profession. Why is there concentration on such criteria if a program's graduates are skilled and capable? Ought the focus to be upon the outputs of the program? The counterargument is that the input–output view trivializes professional education. There are no widely accepted criteria for assessing program graduates. Instead, the public must rely on the cumulative judgments of professional faculty to assess the degree to which teacher candidates will eventually work effectively in the classroom.

How specifically should the criteria used to award accreditation status be stated? If they are too specific, the criteria are likely to miss the essence of quality that should be the focus of the process. On the other hand, if the criteria are vague and ambiguous, the accreditation process can be an uncertain affair, subject to the whims and prejudices of accreditors.

How high should accreditation standards be set? The issue can best be framed by an analogy. A state may license a restaurant to sell food to the public. The state interest is not to attest to the savoriness of the offerings or the nutritive value they represent. To the contrary, the state merely asserts that it would be unlikely for a customer to come away from the restaurant with ptomaine poisoning. On the other hand, private (or professional) associations, such as the Michelin Guide or the American Automobile Association, give ratings that have connotations of quality.

Is there a need for a similar two-tier process in teacher education accreditation—the first to identify those institutions that graduate safe, reliable, and effective teachers; the second to identify programs of exceptional quality, from which students graduate who demonstrate superior performance? It seems unlikely that one system can perform both functions.

Nevertheless, the two tracks might serve mutual but complementary interests.

If all teacher education programs within a province or a nation are approved or accredited using the same procedures or standards, teacher education is likely to become standardized, with a professionally correct way of going about the process. Some level of homogeneity might constitute an improvement in a number of countries, if it raises the performance of the weaker programs. However, once an optimal level of standardization is reached, there is a need to stimulate variation, innovation, and experimentation. How can these values be protected realistically in any accreditation system or process?

In most settings, the accreditation process is enormously costly, in both time and fiscal resources. Efforts to streamline the process have led to superficial inspections and surface-level evaluations. There is a need to find ways in which accreditation processes can be streamlined without sacrificing the credibility of the guarantees they are meant to deliver.

One of the main difficulties of accreditation is the perception that its principal goal is to stimulate "program improvement." This confusion lies in mixing formative and summative evaluation functions. Formative evaluation is a process that prompts faculty to improve their programs. Summative evaluation, as its name implies, renders a judgment about the quality of the programs.

The central focus of accreditation is summative; given the costs of the process there are concerns about whether even a positive result leading to accreditation is of sufficient worth to justify the expense. It is unlikely that accreditation efforts can be both summative and formative, but this issue is debated.

To what extent should accreditors be specialists in teacher education or trained in making evaluative judgments? Is it proper for classroom teachers as accreditors to visit a graduate program in English education to judge whether or not the program has merit? There is some notion is the argument that engaging teachers in the process is a healthy and wholesome activity, likely to advance their professional consciences. On the other hand, some teacher educators are wary of a "know-nothing" mentality that is manifest in some practitioners in many professions—the belief that an apprentice form of professional training is all that is needed. Engaging teachers promises to bring apprenticeship views to the fore, and in some instances where in the process teachers actually hold sway, they may become controlling.

4. Conclusion

The purpose and the ethics of undergoing teacher education accreditation were summarized well by Gideonse (1992 p. B3).

> Professional accreditation is not primarily a hurdle, successful leaping of which leads to a reward. Its worth and

meaning cannot be judged by simple comparison to the efforts expended. . . . Accreditation is a *contribution* institutions make, a *service* they render, first to the profession of which they are a part and then second to the welfare of society.

See also: Inservice Teacher Education; Teacher Certification and Standards; Structure of Teacher Education Programs

References

Blakey J, Jamieson S 1992 (Personal correspondence.) Faculty of Education, University of Alberta, Edmonton

Brown G 1992 (Personal correspondence.) School of Education, University of East Anglia, Norwich

Calderhead J 1992 (Personal correspondence.) School of Education, Bath

Cavell S 1979 *The Claim of Reason: Wittgenstein, Skepticism, Morality, and Tragedy.* Clarendon Press, Oxford

Chambers P, Barrett I, Hassall D 1992 (Personal correspondence.) Bradford and Ilkley Community College, Bradford

Gammage P 1992 (Personal correspondence.) School of Education, University of Nottingham. Nottingham

Gibson M R 1992 (Personal correspondence.) Faculty of Education, Kingston Polytechnic, Kingston on Thames

Gideonse H 1992 Letter to the editor. *Chron. Higher Educ.* 15 April 1992: B3

Housego B E J 1992 (Personal correspondence.) Faculty of Education, University of British Columbia, Vancouver

Laferrière T 1992 (Personal correspondence.) Doyenne de la Faculté des sciences de l'éducation, Université Laval, Quebec

Larson C W 1983 Trends in the regulation of professions. In: Young K E, Chambers C M, Kells H R (eds.) 1983 *Understanding Accreditation.* Jossey-Bass, San Francisco, California

Lipman M 1992 Criteria and judgment in critical thinking. *Inquiry* 9(4): 3–4

Mogami H S 1992 (Personal correspondence.) Ministry of Education, Gaborone

Northfield J R 1992 (Personal correspondence.) Faculty of Education, Monash University, Melbourne

Peacock D 1992 (Personal correspondence.) National Project on the Quality of Teaching and Learning, Canberra

Robinson S 1992 (Personal correspondence.) College of Education, University of Saskatchewan, Saskatoon

Selden W K 1976 *Accreditation and the Public Interest.* Council on Postsecondary Accreditation, Washington, DC

Smart W D 1992 (Personal correspondence.) British Columbia College of Teachers, Vancouver

Sutherland D I M 1992 (Personal correspondence.) General Teaching Council, Edinburgh

United Kingdom, Department of Education and Science 1989 *Initial Teacher Training: Approval of Courses*, Circular No. 24/89. Department of Education and Science, London

United States, National Council for Accreditation of Teacher Education 1992 *Standards, Procedures, and Policies for the Accreditation of Professional Education Units.* NCATE

Further Reading

Bowman J 1990 *Issues in Teacher Education.* British Columbia College of Teachers, Vancouver

Chambers J, Chambers P 1984 Teacher educators and teachers: In: Alexander J, Craft M, Lynch J (eds.) 1984 *Change in Teacher Education.* Holt, Rinehart and Winston, New York

Gilroy P 1992 The political rape of initial teacher education in England and Wales: A JET rebuttal. *J. Educ. for Teacher* 18(1): 5–23

Gosden P H J H 1989 Teaching quality and the accreditation of initial teacher training courses. In: McClelland V A, Varma V P (eds.) 1989 *Advances in Teacher Education.* Routledge, London

Graves N J (ed.) 1990 *Initial Teacher Education: Policies and Progress.* Kogan Page/Institute of Education, University of London, London

Taylor W 1983 The crisis of confidence in teacher education: An international perspective: *Oxford Rev. Educ.* 9(1): 39–49

Teacher Certification and Standards

M. M. Scannell and D. P. Scannell

What qualifications does a person need to become a teacher? The answer to this question lies at the heart of teacher licensure and certification decisions. In fact, there are multiple answers, depending on the country and the time period in which it is asked.

Some countries require different levels of education (e.g., 2 or 3 years vs. 4 years) or types of education (e.g., teacher training institutes vs. universities) for primary school and secondary school teachers; other countries require essentially the same level and type for all teachers. Similarly, some countries require

prospective teachers to pass licensure or certification examinations before being licensed or certified, while others do not (Holmes 1983, Kurian 1988, Farrell 1989).

Licensure and certification standards also depend on the relationship of teacher supply and demand. Tarvin and Faraj (1990) have stated this relationship quite succinctly: "In periods of rapid expansion of student population, low standards of qualifications have been accepted in hiring teachers" (p. 92). They illustrate this generalization with examples from China, Nepal, Sri

Lanka, and Pakistan. Lockheed and Verspoor (1990) provided specific data to highlight the magnitude of this problem. In separate studies, 54 percent of primary school teachers in Zimbabwe and fewer than 10 percent of primary school teachers in Haiti were classified as qualified. In Kano State in Nigeria only 9 percent of the primary teachers held formal teacher certification.

When licensure and certification standards are lowered, status is decreased. As Lockheed and Verspoor (1990) have asserted, "in countries experiencing rapid expansion of their educational systems, underqualified applicants are recruited to meet the growing demand for teachers; this further lowers the public perception of the occupation's prestige" (p. 64).

Issues concerning teacher licensure and certification, then, are quite different in developing and industrialized countries. In many developing countries, the problem is how to attract prospective teachers and educate them to meet minimal standards. In the words of Altbach (1987), "In the Third World, there is concern that a sufficient number of teachers be provided and that these teachers have appropriate training" (p. 326). In many industrialized countries, on the other hand, the problem is inherent in the standards themselves. The major questions in these countries are as follows. What licensure and certification standards should be established? Who should establish them? What evidence is needed to determine whether the standards have been achieved?

In light of the previous discussion, this entry focuses primarily on industrialized countries, with most of the examples taken from the United States. At the same time, however, the concepts and ideas presented and discussed are applicable to virtually all countries. For, as Altbach has written:

> Concern about the teaching profession is worldwide. Many countries have realized that teachers are at the center of the educational process and that without good teachers, all other innovations are doomed to failure . . . There is also widespread dissatisfaction with the current situation of schooling in many nations—and teachers have come in for their share of criticism. (Altbach 1987 p. 326)

1. Certification, Credentialing, and Licensure

In the first edition of *The International Encyclopedia of Education* Zimpher (1985) noted that the terms "certification," "credentialing," and "licensure" are frequently used interchangeably in the field of education. In this entry, "licensure" will refer to quality control excercised by states, while "certification" will refer to quality control exercised by peer review.

There are two primary reasons for these definitions. First, they are consistent with the use of the terms in most professions and occupations requiring state authorization to practice. In these fields, the term "licensure" is used to indicate that the state has authorized an individual to practice. In contrast, the term "certification" indicates peer approbation, usually provided at the conclusion of some specified minimal period of practice, after completion of a course of study to achieve some specialty, and/or after success on an examination covering the speciality. If teaching were to use terms consistent with the practice of other fields, communication with those in the recognized professions and the general public would be enhanced.

Second, in 1987 the National Board for Professional Teaching Standards (NBPTS) was created in the United States. "The mission of the NBPTS is to establish high and rigorous standards for what accomplished teachers should know and be able to do, to develop and operate a national voluntary system to assess and certify teachers who meet these standards, and to advance related education reforms for the purpose of improving student learning in American schools" (NBPTS 1991 p. 1). With the advent of this form of professional certification, clarity of communication will be improved if the term "license" is used to signify a state authorization to practice in the public schools, and the term "certification" restricted to denoting professional recognition of accomplished practice.

2. The Policy Context for Certification and Licensure

In a 1990 review of literature on "Roles and Authority of States in Policies for Teachers and Teaching," Scannell noted that since the 1960s there have been three major shifts in the locus of educational decision-making in the United States. These shifts have had an impact on the standards and processes for licensure of teachers.

Timar and Kirp (1988) credited the 1954 Supreme Court decision in Brown v. Board of Education for causing the movement of much decision-making in education from the local level to national and state levels. In contrast to many other developed countries, the United States has a tradition of local decision-making with final authority vested at the state level. Thus, the Brown v. Board of Education decision resulted in states moving some delegated authority from local districts to the state level; it also caused the federal government to become involved because of the need to monitor desegregation efforts and by virtue of increased federal spending for education. The publication in 1983 of *A Nation at Risk* (National Commission on Excellence in Education 1984) caused a second shift in the locus of decision-making by advocating a reduced federal role, insisting that schooling is essentially a state and local matter. The third shift, according to Darling-Hammond (1988), occurred in 1986 when a second wave of reform reports in the United States advocated a change from centralized, highly regulated decisions by state policymakers to control at the local level by professionals. It might also be contended that the third shift has evolved into a fourth—one in which decision-making is done by local schools and teachers within a renewed emphasis on nationalization. This context includes national education goals, national curriculum standards, national assessment programs for teachers, and teacher education programs.

3. Processes Associated with Certification and Licensure

The purpose of licensing is to protect the public. Licensing is a method of quality control at the level of the individual applicant for admission to the field of teaching. As was noted by Zimpher (1985), legal authority for licensure in the United States is at the state level, but in many other countries authority for certification is vested in national ministries or national councils. In the United States the process for awarding licenses has been administered by State Departments of Education (SDEs). Standards, and to some extent processes, have been established by State Boards of Education, sometimes with the assistance of advisory boards of teachers, administrators, and teacher educators. These standards are usually enacted by state legislatures and, therefore, can be changed only through legislative action. (Some states have autonomous standards boards that recommend standards and processes for certification and teacher education program approval directly to the state board of education or the state legislature. Autonomous boards are discussed at greater length later in this entry, but these boards are an exception to the prevailing policies.) The processes used for awarding a license to teach can be ordered into five categories: (a) the approved program approach, (b) transcript analysis or credit count, (c) testing, (d) alternative certification, and (e) regional certificates.

3.1 The Approved Program Approach

Since the 1980s the system most widely used by SDEs to award licenses has been based on the graduation of candidates from "approved programs." This process is quite similar to accreditation (see *Teacher Education Accreditation and Standards*). Institutions undertake a self-study and, using a specified format, prepare reports. Visiting teams of educators are appointed by the SDE, which visit the institutions to verify the institution's reports and prepare their own report. Final decisions are made by the State Board of Education, a lay-body either elected directly or appointed by the state governor. After this process has been completed, graduates of the approved programs have usually been automatically granted a license.

3.2 Transcript Analysis

A second approach is called "transcript analysis" or "credit count." This procedure is used to provide

an avenue to licensure for people graduating from institutions that do not have approved programs and for individuals who have earned course credits from a number of institutions. The process involves an assessment of a candidate's transcript(s) to ascertain whether the aspiring teacher has taken courses that are likely to have included the knowledge and skills implied by the state's standards and to ascertain whether the credits earned in the teaching field meet the state's requirements, in terms of both number of credits and the content of courses taken.

3.3 Testing

The use of testing as part of the licensure process has increased dramatically in the United States since the publication of *A Nation at Risk* in 1984. Some states have contracted for the development of tests for this purpose, but typically states have used commercially available tests. Among these, the National Teacher's Examination (NTE) published by the Educational Testing Service (ETS) has been most widely used.

The areas covered in teacher testing include basic skills, general education, pedagogy, and teaching field content. In many states basic skill testing is done near the midpoint of the baccalaureate program and adequate scores are required for admission to teacher education programs. The other components of the test are normally administered after graduation. In many states the standards for the award of a license are stated as "graduation from an approved program and successful completion of the licensure tests."

3.4 Alternative Certification

As states have increased the formal standards for access to a teaching credential, they also have created permissive policies for emergency licenses and alternative certification (Scannell 1988). Darling-Hammond and Berry (1988) observed, "Ironically, even as states have increased their influence over teacher preparation programs, they have created or expanded loopholes allowing more candidates to avoid these same requirements" (p. 9). In 1991, 30 states had some form of alternative certification program not driven by teacher shortages.

Although alternative certification programs vary across states, a common pattern is to use test scores to establish a baseline for acceptance of college graduates into the program, provide candidates with some exposure to pedagogy in an intensive, short summer workshop, and provide a temporary permit for the candidate to teach for one year. During this time an experienced teacher is to serve in a mentoring capacity, the candidates meet periodically for seminars, and often additional coursework in pedagogy is required within a specified period of time.

3.5 Regional Certification

A relatively novel approach to credentialing is a regional "certificate" developed by states in the

567

northeastern part of the United States. Teachers credentialed in one of the participating states can apply for a regional credential which authorizes the person to teach in any of the states (Newton et al. 1989). The regional certificate can be thought of as a form of reciprocity among the participating states, one that facilitates movement of teachers within the region. More traditional forms of reciprocity are based on agreements among states that have similar accreditation standards and a large number of states will credential out-of-state applicants who have graduated from accredited institutions.

4. Issues and Trends

Several initiatives have been undertaken to raise the status of the teaching occupation, which by some definitions has not achieved the characteristics of a true profession. One of these, noted earlier, is the NBPTS which expects to award its first certificates recognizing accomplished teaching in 1994. During subsequent years additional fields will be brought on-line until all fields are operational. Although the NBPTS has engendered significant financial and moral support, it also has its critics.

Eligibility requirements for NBPTS applicants include graduation from a regionally accredited institution and three years of teaching experience. Critics who support the Board's goal of professionalizing teaching cite the eligibility requirements as inadequate, noting that other professions require graduation from an institution that holds specialized accreditation. In addition, applicants to the NBPTS process do not have to hold the state license to teach; in some parts of the United States, a license is not required to teach in private schools. The counter arguments to the criticisms are that the significant proportion of private school teachers should not be excluded and that if the standards are rigorous, candidates will have to develop high skill levels through either formal education or effective self-directed study.

It is important to note again that the NBPTS does not grant licenses: this authority is vested in state governments. Even so, it is having an impact on state licensing requirements and processes. An organization has been established by the Council of Chief State School Officers to create recommendations for state licensure requirements that are appropriate for beginning teachers and that reflect the standards the NBPTS will use for recognizing accomplished teaching. The Interstate New Teacher Assessment and Support Consortium (INTASC) has the direct involvement of 17 states, both major teacher unions and several major educational organizations. An additional 22 states have expressed interest in participation and will facilitate public review of the draft standards.

Two major advantages will be achieved if INTASC is successful. First, there will be widespread agreement on what a beginning teacher needs to know and should be able to do, and thus there will be common standards in most of the states. Second, an articulation between standards for novices and accomplished teachers will contribute to a better integration of initial, or basic, teacher education programs with continuing professional development programs.

Zimpher (1985) cited as a recent trend the issue of who would control the licensure and certification process—the traditional state board comprised of lay people or professional standards and practices boards (PSPBs) comprised of educators? At that time three states had delegated responsibility for the process to autonomous PSPBs—California, Oregon, and Minnesota. The question needs to be cited again as a trend and issue.

In 1989 Scannell et al. noted that the original group of three states had been increased to four but that 44 additional states had advisory PSPBs. Since 1989 several additional states have converted advisory boards into autonomous boards to bring the number to nine (AACTE 1990), and teacher unions continue to work for the creation of additional autonomous boards. Within the major efforts to professionalize teaching, it seems likely that additional autonomous boards will be created.

4.1 Testing Teachers

As was noted earlier, one of the first and most widespread reactions following the publication of *A Nation at Risk* was an increase in teacher testing. Testing was introduced as a requirement for entry into teacher education programs and as a final hurdle to qualify for the initial license. Support for these policies came more from outside than inside the educational establishment. Those who support the practice asserted that testing would weed out the incompetents and at the same time restore public confidence in teachers. The opposition formed ranks around two major issues, questions of validity and the differential effect of testing on ethnic and racial groups.

Most teacher tests have been paper-and-pencil multiple-choice tests. Publishers and users of these tests have conducted studies to establish curricular and occupational validity. Even so, major questions remain about whether the tests can adequately assess the personal qualities needed for effective teaching and the ability to use the knowledge of pedagogy effectively.

The concern about differential failure rates centers on the assertion that minorities and people for whom English is a second language do not perform well on written, multiple-choice tests. To this concern is added the observation that the minority presence in the teaching work force, once over 12 percent, is falling rapidly toward 5 percent, at the same time as the percentage of minority students in public schools is increasing rapidly. These concerns have led to the development of a variety of assessment practices to determine the competence of both beginning and experienced teachers. A key component in both the NBPTS and INTASC efforts is the use of multiple assessment strategies. Included are portfolios that encompass: peer assessments; examples of teacher artifacts and student work; videotapes of classroom performance; and assessment center activities including structured interviews, inbasket exercises, simulations, and written tests.

4.2 Required Coursework

An increasingly important issue in the credentialing of teachers is the distribution of coursework to be required for the initial license. The trend in the early 1990s in the teacher education curriculum in the United States is toward undergraduate majors in an arts or science field followed by a year of pedagogy and clinical experiences. In addition, the content of the teaching field is being modified in response to new standards being created by professional groups. The field furthest advanced is mathematics, although science, English, social studies, and other fields are engaged in the creation of national "frameworks." It seems likely that majors based on new standards in academic fields will continue to expand as the norm for preservice teacher preparation.

Related to the issue noted above is a question of whether a separate license is needed for the middle grades. Sparked by the publication of *Turning Points* (Carnegie Council on Adolescent Development 1989), considerable energy has been invested in developing a unique middle school curriculum and teacher preparation consistent with the program. The past practice of allowing elementary and secondary teachers also to qualify for the middle grades seems virtually certain to be discontinued. As a result, new standards for middle-level teacher education will be developed and implemented.

5. The Future of Teacher Licensure and Certification

There are five major questions that will guide the setting of standards and processes for licensure and certification in the immediate future. The questions are likely to be applicable throughout the world.

First, who will control licensure? The issue here is whether professionally dominated, autonomous boards will be given the opportunity to serve roles commonly assigned to other professional fields.

Second, what will be the balance among content, theory, and clinical practice required for the initial license? Subject-matter baccalaureate majors followed by a period of pedagogy and clinical practice seem to be the trend. This includes increased time spent in clinical experiences and the addition of an internship year.

Third, how will established standards be assessed?

Performance assessment seems likely to become more prevalent, at least in the short run. However, there will remain an issue of whether other forms of competency assessment will continue to supplement graduation from an approved program or perhaps replace program approval entirely.

Fourth, how will requirements for continuing professional development relate to standards for initial licensure and how will accomplished practice be assessed? It seems likely that the future will see a rational continuum of expectations from those for novice teachers to those for peer approbation of accomplished practice. If NBPTS and INTASC are successful, major advancement toward professional status for teaching will be achieved.

Fifth, will policymakers continue to support "back-door entry" into teaching or will policies support the movement toward the professionalization of teaching? Teacher shortages provided the motivation for creating emergency and alternative routes to licensure. Teacher education critics expanded the alternative routes to attract career changers on the assumption that knowledge of an academic field was adequate for successful teaching.

Several of these questions (especially the second, fourth, and fifth ones) create a tension between policymakers and educators. How these questions are resolved will have a major impact on the future of teaching as a profession and as a career.

See also: Curriculum of Teacher Education Programs; Teacher Evaluation

References

American Association of Colleges for Teacher Education 1991 *Teacher Education Policy in the States: A 50-State Survey of Legislative and Administrative Actions.* AACTE, Washington, DC
Altbach P G 1987 Teaching: International concerns. *Teach. Coll. Rec.* 88(3): 326–29
Carnegie Council on Adolescent Development 1989 *Turning Points.* Carnegie Council on Adolescent Development, Washington, DC
Council of Chief State School Officers 1992 *Model Standards for Beginning Teacher Licensing and Development: A Resource for State Dialogue.* Interstate New Teacher Assessment and Support Consortium, Washington, DC
Darling-Hammond L 1988 Policy and professionalism In: Lieberman A (ed.) 1988 *Building a Professional Culture in Schools.* Teachers College Press, New York
Darling-Hammond L, Berry B 1988 *The Evolution of Teacher Policy.* Rand Corporation, Washington, DC
Education Testing Service 1992 *The Praxis Series: Professional Assessments for Beginning Teachers.* Education Testing Service Princeton, New Jersey
Farrell J P 1989 International lessons for school effectiveness: The view from the developing world. In: Holmes M, Leithwood K A, Mussella D F (eds.) 1989 *Educational Policy for Effective Schools.* OISE Press, Toronto

Holmes B (ed.) 1983 *International Handbook of Education Systems. Vol. 1: Europe and Canada*. Wiley, Chichester

Kurian G T (ed.) 1988 *World Education Encyclopedia*. Facts on File, New York

Lockheed M E, Verspoor A M 1990 *Improving Primary Education in Developing Countries: A Review of Policy Options*. World Bank, Washington, DC

National Board for Professional Teaching Standards 1991 *Toward High and Rigorous Standards for the Teaching Profession*, 3rd edn. National Board for Professional Teaching Standards, Detroit, Michigan

National Commission on Excellence in Education 1984 *A Nation at Risk: The Imperative for Educational Reform*. United States Department of Education, Washington, DC

Newton A et al. 1989 *Implementation of a Northeast Regional Credential for Educators in New England and New York*. Regional Laboratories, Andover, Massachusetts

Scannell D P, Andersen D G, Gideonse H D 1989 *Who Sets the Standards?* Association of Colleges and Schools of Education in State Universities and Land-Grant Colleges and Affiliated Private Universities, Las Vegas, Nevada

Scannell M M 1988 Factors influencing state policies restricting entry to teaching. (Doctoral dissertation, George Washington University)

Tarvin W L, Faraj A H 1990 The quest for qualified teachers in developing countries of south and southeast Asia. *Int. Rev. Educ.* 36(1): 89–101

Timar T B, Kirp D L 1988 *Managing Educational Excellence*. Falmer Press, New York

Zimpher N L 1985 Certification and licensing of teachers. In: Husén T, Postlethwaite T N (eds.) 1985 *The International Encylopedia of Education*, 1st edn. Pergamon Press, Oxford

Further Reading

McDonnell L M, Elmore R F 1987 Getting the job done: Alternative policy instruments. *Educ. Eval. Policy Anal.* 9(2): 133–52

Scannell M M 1990 *Roles and Authority of States in Policies for Teachers and Teaching*. American Association of Colleges for Teacher Education, Washington, DC

Generic Initial Teacher Education

Introduction

L. W. Anderson

The education that teachers receive before being licensed to teach is referred to as initial teacher education. Throughout the world initial teacher education generally takes place in postsecondary institutions (e.g., colleges, universities). The typical initial teacher education program includes two major components: formal coursework and field experiences. The ultimate field experience is generally referred to as student teaching or practice teaching. The six entries in this section focus on these two components of initial teacher education.

1. Formal Coursework

Formal cousework comprises the vast majority of the credits earned in initial teacher education programs in most countries. Prospective teachers attend regularly scheduled classes and learn about their academic discipline, foundations of education, and curriculum and instruction.

For prospective secondary school teachers, the academic discipline is the subject area they intend to teach. Mathematics teachers, for example, must complete courses in mathematics, while history teachers must complete courses in history. For prospective primary and elementary school teachers, the academic discipline is a wide range of general knowledge and ways of knowing coupled with an extensive body of knowledge of the children they will be teaching. The primary purpose of courses in the academic discipline is to ensure that prospective teachers have a good grounding in the subject area or areas they intend to teach.

Educational foundations consist of courses in history, philosophy, psychology, and sociology as these disciplines apply to education. The inclusion of educational foundations courses in initial teacher education programs is based on the premise that teachers should know and appreciate past events, develop a philosophy that guides their actions, understand how their students learn (or fail to learn), and be cognizant of the social institutions that interact with and influence what happens in schools.

Courses in curriculum and instruction focus on the aims of education, the structure of knowledge, means by which the knowledge to be learned can be sequenced and integrated, ways of assessing learning, and methods or strategies that can be used to transmit knowledge and facilitate learning. The purpose of these courses is to help prospective teachers build a bridge between what children already know and what they are expected to learn, help students cross this metaphorical bridge, and determine when they have, in fact, crossed it.

2. The Delivery of Formal Coursework

While the categories of formal coursework have changed little since the late nineteenth century, changes have occurred in the methods used to teach these courses, particularly those in the area of curriculum and instruction. Three of the entries in this section discuss these changes.

Increasingly, courses included in initial teacher education programs tend to follow the traditional lecture-laboratory approach used in the teaching of science. Furthermore, the "lecture" portion is being supplemented or supplanted by the use of case methods in teaching (McAninch). Cases detail events encountered by experienced teachers or problems confronted by them. As a consequence, case analysis permits prospective teachers to learn from the experiences of others. What they, in fact, learn depends to a large extent on the nature of the cases themselves. They may learn the underlying theory, elements of the teaching craft, or how teachers deal with broader social issues. What is important to note is that these prospective teachers do not learn (i.e., memorize) the cases; rather, they learn *from* them.

The laboratory portion of formal coursework may

include games and simulations, role playing, microteaching, peer teaching, and the observation and analysis of demonstrations (either live or via videotape) (Metcalf). Laboratory experiences differ from real life or field experiences primarily in terms of the degree of complexity and the amount of control exerted by the instructor. Simply stated, laboratory experiences are less complex and permit the instructor a greater degree of control.

Microteaching is a special case of laboratory experiences (Metcalf). Unlike games, simulations and role playing, microteaching involves actual teaching. Microteaching differs from classroom teaching in three respects (MacLeod). First, the number of students being taught is typically smaller (e.g., 5 to 10). Second, the length of the lesson is typically shorter (e.g., 20 to 30 minutes). Third, the focus of each microteaching lesson is typically on a single teaching skill.

The role of the course instructor in laboratory experiences is generally agreed upon (MacLeod). First, the teaching skill or other "target outcome" must be introduced. This introduction can occur via videotape or be incorporated in a written case. Second, the prospective teacher must have an opportunity to practice what has been demonstrated or read about. This practice should be recorded, again either in writing or on audiotape or videotape. Third, some type of feedback or critique is needed. This feedback or critique may be provided by the course instructor, the prospective teacher, or both. Finally, the prospective teacher should have the opportunity to reteach the lesson using the teaching skill under consideration, with subsequent feedback or critique provided as necessary and appropriate.

3. Field Experiences

Field experiences constitute the second major component of initial teacher education. Field experiences may include visits to schools, discussions with teachers, classroom observations, and actual teaching. Student or practice teaching is arguably the ultimate field experience. Two of the entries in the sections are concerned with field experiences. Morine-Dershimer and Leighfield examine student teaching. Cooper describes the role of supervision in field experiences.

As Morine-Dershimer and Leighfield state, "student teaching and field experiences are the major vehicles for providing practical experience in any teacher education program. This is the program area, therefore, where the traditional conflict between theory and practice is felt most strongly." This conflict is particularly acute when universities (rather than teachers' colleges or normal schools) are responsible for teacher preparation and when student teaching is seen as an apprenticeship (rather than a laboratory experience). The distinction between apprenticeship and laboratory experiences is especially important in this regard (Cooper).

If student teaching is an apprenticeship experience, the expectation is that student teachers are to copy or mimic their cooperating or "mentor" teacher. If, on the other hand, student teaching is a laboratory experience, the expectation is that student teachers are to try out different ways of teaching, reflect on the outcomes of the various teachniques, and make modifications accordingly. As an apprenticeship experience, formal theory may be of questionable value. As a laboratory experience, on the other hand, theory is useful if not essential in framing issues about teaching and facilitating decision-making.

When engaged in field experiences, prospective teachers generally have two supervisors. The first is a member of the university or college faculty. The second is the teacher in the school in which the prospective teacher is placed. The presence of multiple supervisors has led to several problems both for the supervisors and the prospective teachers (Cooper). Many of these problems typically result from the lack of coordination between the supervisors in terms of their relative responsibilities for observing, providing feedback, and assigning grades.

4. Professional Development Schools

As the reader of the entries in this section will note, those involved in initial teacher education have more questions than answers. Among the most important questions that require answers at the present time are the following. How can theory and practice be combined to produce better teachers? What is the proper balance between coursework and field experiences? How can coursework be used to prepare students for field experiences? What is the proper "mix" of the academic disciplines, educational foundations, and curriculum and instruction in teacher preparation? How can the relation among college and university supervisors, cooperating teachers, and prospective teachers be enhanced for the betterment of all? In an attempt to find answers to these questions, teacher educators in the United States have begun to develop professional development schools (PDSs).

Stallings, Knight, and Wiseman define a professional development school in the following manner: "APDS [is] a site where practicing teachers and administrators are brought together with university faculty in partnerships that improve teaching and learning on the part of their respective students and thus unite theory and practice." Cooper defines a PDS as the educational equivalent of a teaching hospital. The site is typically a "regular elementary, middle, or high school that works in partnership with a university."

Professional development schools have great promise, but are likely to experience grave difficulties.

The promise stems from the possibility of a truly collaborative, concerted effort to improve dramatically the quality of initial teacher education. The problems stem from the simple magnitude of the task. As Gherke (cited in Stallings, Knight, and Wiseman) has emphasized: "We are looking at changing no less than the personality of an occupation and the character of two well-established institutions."

5. Conclusion

Coursework is perceived by prospective teachers as less satisfying and less valuable than field experiences (Cooper). Within formal coursework, however, laboratory experiences are seen by prospective teachers as more satisfying and more valuable than lectures and discussions (Metcalf). Case methods have the

potential of increasing the perceived value of formal coursework, but the research on these methods is sparse (McAninch).

Interestingly, teacher educators do not necessarily share the students' viewpoints (Cooper). They question whether field experiences are sufficiently grounded in theory so as to permit prospective teachers to solve problems and make appropriate decisions when left on their own.

Unfortunately, there is little empirical evidence to resolve this apparent conflict. MacLeod suggests that the effectiveness of microteaching is "more often assumed than tested." Similarly, Metcalf states that teacher educators have "emphasized development and innovation to the neglect of evaluation." As mentioned earlier, one is left with more questions than answers after reading the entries in this section. Fortunately, they appear to be the correct questions to be asking at this time.

Microteaching in Teacher Education

G. MacLeod

The term "microteaching" is used to describe a cluster of teacher education techniques which allow teachers, especially beginning teachers, to acquire, practice, or refine teaching skills in a setting of reduced complexity. The term itself and the approaches underlying it were formulated at Stanford University in the United States in the early 1960s. The aim was to provide for more effective teacher education than the process of "theoretical discussion followed by trial by fire" (Bush 1968.)

In one of the early descriptions, microteaching was depicted as a "scaled-down encounter in class size and class time" (Allen et al. 1965 p. 1). Later, Allen and Ryan (1969) suggested that the basis of microteaching was to be found in five essential propositions, namely: (a) microteaching is real teaching, in which (b) the complexities of normal classroom teaching are reduced, in which (c) there is a focus on training for the accomplishment of specific tasks, which (d) allows for the increased control of practice, and which (e) greatly expands the normal knowledge-of-results or feedback dimension.

Although later writers have offered a variety of different descriptions and definitions of microteaching, it is clear that the early Stanford models and descriptions provided the basis for the development of microteaching around the world. As Batten (1979) put it, differences in program descriptions "merely reflected different purposes and resources of the user, and overall the format developed at Stanford

for the microteaching experience was followed elsewhere" (p. 8).

1. The Essence of Microteaching

A typical microteaching encounter begins with a preparation phase in which the teaching skill to be practiced is introduced, perhaps through videotaped models. This introduction is followed by a practice or "teach" phase in which students are given an opportunity to undertake their own practice of the modeled skill. Next, a feedback or "critique" phase takes place in which a videotape replay of the "teach" session is viewed and discussed by student and supervisor. This phase might be followed by a "reteach" phase in which the student repractices the skill in light of initial feedback and then reviews the second performance.

While many variations of this approach have occurred, what remains constant is the opportunity to practice teaching in an environment reduced in complexity through a decrease in class size and lesson length and through focus on only one aspect or skill of teaching at any one time. Although these scaling-down factors are the defining characteristics of microteaching, microteaching also offers the opportunity to scale-up or increase the intensity both of the precision of the preparation for the teaching encounter and of the opportunity for trainees to gain detailed feedback on the effects of their teaching. Microteaching not only gives teacher educators an excellent chance of gaining greater control of their students' learning-to-teach experiences, but also, by its very controllability, it provides opportunities for researchers into teaching and teacher education to explore systematically the effects and effectiveness of different educative techniques. The very nature of microteaching, with its distinct phases and components, means that controlled experimentation can readily occur.

As a result, microteaching enjoyed immense popularity both as a teacher education technique and as a focus of research interest in the 1970s. Use of the approach became rapidly widespread in teacher education institutions throughout the United States (Jones 1979) and major research or development programs were identifiable within the United States (Allen and Ryan 1969), in Australia (Turney et al. 1973), and in the United Kingdom (Brown 1975).

2. Research on Microteaching

Shortly after its development, microteaching became the focus of intense research interest. Figure 1, which charts the citation incidence of the keyword "microteaching" in the ERIC database, gives an indication not only of the sudden explosion of research interest in microteaching but also of the almost equally dramatic decline in research and publication on the topic.

Much of the eearly work on microteaching was concerned with experimental studies on the components of microteaching while later efforts concentrated more on the overall effects of microteaching, on the transfer of skills performance from a microteaching setting to the classroom, and on developing or exploring some of the concepts or models underlying microteaching. This entry follows a similar pattern in that it first provides summaries of research on the preparation, practice, and feedback components of microteaching. This discussion is followed by an outline of conceptual models underlying microteaching and a brief discussion of the overall outcomes of microteaching.

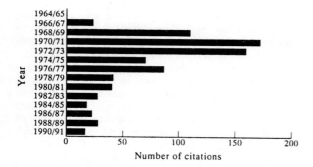

Figure 1
Citations of the keyword "microteaching" in the ERIC database 1964–91

2.1 Research on the Preparation Phase

Reviews of research on the preparation phase have been provided by MacLeod (1985) and Pegg (1985). In general, much of this work has focused on modeling and has been guided by Bandura's work on social learning theory (Bandura 1977), especially the work demonstrating that film-mediated models could be as effective as live models (Bandura et al. 1963).

One of the early interests was the relative efficacy of positive and negative models. Studies by Koran et al. (1972) and Gilmore (1977) showed that the use of positive models was more effective than the use of negative models, although it was demonstrated that negative models were also useful aids to skill acquisition. MacLeod (1985) pointed to difficulties of interpretation of these outcomes in the light of possible differences in the information value of the positive and negative models provided to the subjects.

Researchers who have compared the effects of symbolic (written materials) and perceptual media (film or videotape) have demonstrated a slight favoring of perceptual over symbolic modeling (Phillips 1973). This difference has been attributed to the greater motivational or attention-drawing value of perceptual models. As Bandura (1977) put it, people "rarely have to be compelled to watch television, whereas oral or written reports of the same activities would not hold their attention for long" (p. 40). Perhaps more significant than the intended experimental comparisons of these studies was the clear demonstration that modeling, no matter what the medium, was a powerful facilitator of skill acquisition.

Research on focus in modeling indicated that where cueing, coding, or labeling of the modeled activities was provided, the effectiveness of the modeling treatment was greater (Allen and McDonald 1967). This effect was particularly strong when focus was provided through some form of discrimination training whereby trainees learned to code and label appropriate and inappropriate behaviors (Wagner 1973). Studies by MacLeod et al. (1977) and Pegg (1985) suggested that modeling with discrimination training may be sufficient for at least some skill acquisition. Pegg's study further revealed that a modeling/discrimination treatment may be at least as favorably received by trainees as the practice/feedback component of microteaching.

2.2 Research on the Practice Phase

Practice of skills in microteaching has been so readily assumed to be necessary that there are very few direct studies of its efficacy. In the initial Stanford programs, practice of skills was seen as a central part of the process. In an intriguing follow-up of work on discrimination training and modeling, Pegg (1985) compared the effects of discrimination training including modeling with the effects of skill practice on the acquisition of two teaching skills, variation and higher order questioning. These two skills were selected by

Pegg to reflect differences on a posited dimension of "behavioral–cognitive" so that this dimension might be used in an explanatory way if the obtained results of the experimental comparison required it. On higher order questioning there were no performance differences between the groups; on variation, students who had undertaken the discrimination training significantly outperformed those who had undertaken skill practice. Pegg concluded that "practice was not an essential requirement for skill acquisition, at least for the two skills used in his study" (p. 227).

More commonly, questions about practice in microteaching have been concerned with the role of the reteach component in microteaching. Several studies (e.g., Wragg 1971) indicated that the benefits of the reteach were perhaps less than had been supposed. The surveys of microteaching usage cited above indicated that most institutions did not see the value of the reteach session in microteaching and only a minority of microteaching programs were making use of it at the time of the surveys.

2.3 Research on the Feedback Phase

Research on feedback in microteaching has tended to focus on experimental comparisons of different modes of mechanical feedback, such as videotape or audiotape, or different modes of supervisory feedback, but with little recent development of the field being apparent. Griffiths (1974) reviewed a series of studies that compared audiotape with videotape feedback. On the basis of the mixed and sometimes complex results of these studies, Griffiths concluded that "videotape feedback is not necessarily more effective than audiotape feedback the contribution of mechanical feedback within microteaching is . . . than some writers admit" (p. 6). Some 10 years later, in his review of feedback in microteaching, Levis (1985) drew a similar conclusion and suggested that it "has more often been assumed than tested" (p. 3356) that videotape feedback is more effective than other forms of feedback. Levis further suggested that the work he reviewed on feedback in microteaching demonstrated the importance of powerful modeling procedures as a determinant of student skill performance.

Studies of supervisory feedback in microteaching have also been disappointing in that they reveal very little about the effectiveness of different approaches, except that the outcomes are complex and probably represent an interaction of a variety of factors (Claus 1969). Typical of the inconclusive research of this kind was an experimental study of the effects of four supervisory treatments on the acquisition of the skill (Griffiths et al. 1977). With one minor exception, no skill-related differences were found among the groups assigned to the four treatments. Instead, subjects in each of the groups asserted that what they wanted was that which had *not* been provided to them in the carefully controlled experimental treatments. "If the supervision was direct, they wanted more opportunity to discuss their own perceptions, but if the supervision was directed, they wanted to know more about how the *supervisor* had perceived the lesson; if the supervision had concentrated upon their strengths, they wanted to have advice on how they could *improve* their use of the skill, but if the supervision had concentrated on suggesting alternatives, they wanted to be told what they were *doing well* already" (MacLeod and McIntyre 1977 p. 256).

3. Models Underlying Microteaching

Questions about the overall effectiveness and contribution of microteaching depend upon the aims of particular microteaching programs. Those aims are themselves dependent upon the models of participant learning underlying the program. From the literature on microteaching, four distinct but sometimes overlapping models may be discerned: pragmatism, behavior modification, social skills, and the cognitive model.

First, there was the apparent "easy pragmatism" of the early programs. Microteaching was seen within a general training paradigm; concepts from psychology, such as modeling and reinforcement, were freely borrowed, and the emphasis was upon "what worked." In the words of Allen and Ryan, "the decisions as to what skills should be developed ... were not made in light of any set of rules about what good teaching consists of or what teachers need to know, but resulted from the discussions and debates of the microteaching staff" (Allen and Ryan 1969 p. 14). Thus, the criteria for success were skill acquisition and measures of general teaching effectiveness. The task for research on microteaching was to discover the optimal combinations of the components of microteaching for effective skill acquisition.

Behavior modification as a model for microteaching has been espoused strongly by McDonald, one of the original researchers at Stanford. Teaching skills are simply sets of behaviors which may be acquired through the application of classical, well-established behavior modification procedures. Other than research of a very simple practical kind, "there is very little else about microteaching as a methodological device that is worth studying" (McDonald 1973 p. 73). However, few microteaching programs have operated according to behavior-modification principles, leading McDonald to write that "many users of microteaching did not see the relevance of behavior modification procedures" (p. 72). Furthermore, McDonald contended that the "most undesirable consequence of the promotion of microteaching was that the role of behavior modification . . . was obscured" (p. 73).

The social skills training model of Argyle (1969) has been applied in a microteaching context by Brown (1975). Teaching skills, like other social skills, are seen as analogous to perceptual and motor skills, so that the focuses of Brown's training program related to the selection of aims, the selective perception of relevant cures, motor response (or practice), and feedback and correction. McIntyre (1983) suggested that Argyle's model has not been fully utilized by researchers on microteaching and that, in particular, the cognitive processes involved in the coordination and organization of skilled performance have been neglected. Thus, although the model has been used as a means of conceptualizing the skills involved in microteaching, it has had little applicability to the design of programs planned to facilitate acquisition of these skills.

A cognitive model for microteaching, emphasizing participants' thinking about their teaching, was proposed by MacLeod and McIntyre (1977). This model was based on inferences drawn from the results of research on microteaching and suggested that microteaching should be viewed as a procedure facilitating long-term changes in student teachers' thinking about teaching rather than short-term changes in their teaching behavior. Attention was drawn to the importance of students' conceptual structures when they entered a microteaching program, to the apparent stability of these structures, and to the effects upon these structures of academic discipline or teaching-subject background. This cognitive model was set within a framework of an analysis of classroom life which drew attention to the heavy information-processing demands imposed by the complexity of classroom environments and the cognitive strategies that teachers use to cope with that complexity. The cognitive model assumes that teaching skills should be reconceptualized as "ways of thinking" rather than as "ways of behaving," and that the effectiveness of microteaching should be assessed in terms of whether it provides "for the development and induction of functional and adaptive cognitive structures" (MacLeod and McIntyre 1977 p. 26). Pegg's (1985) study of the effects of practice on skill acquisition was carried out within the framework of this cognitive model and in general produced results supportive of the model.

4. Outcomes of Microteaching

Like many educational programs, the effectiveness of microteaching is judged in terms of both behavioral and affective outcomes. In this section, attitudinal outcomes are discussed, followed by a discussion of performance outcomes.

4.1 Attitudinal Outcomes of Microteaching

Perhaps the most consistently reported outcome of research on microteaching is that participants find it a valuable and enjoyable activity (Gregory 1986), with favorable assessments being reported from both preservice and inservice participants. Among teacher educators, attitudes toward microteaching have been mixed. Although many immediately accepted and implemented the innovation, others questioned the assumptions implicit in the practice of microteaching. In particular, doubt was cast upon whether the complex and dynamic art of teaching could readily be dissected into component parts or skills.

4.2 Performance Outcomes of Microteaching

A meta-analysis by Butcher (1981) provided a clear demonstration that microteaching produces short-term change in teaching behavior. What is much less clear is whether microteaching produces long-term behavioral change or the transfer of teaching skills to classroom settings. MacLeod (1981) carried out a detailed review of five experimental studies that attempted to assess the effectiveness of microteaching through use of skill acquisition as a criterion and two experimental studies that attempted to assess the effectiveness of microteaching through use of a pupil performance criterion. He concluded that the results of these studies did little to alleviate ignorance of the effects of microteaching and that it was difficult to conceive of any satisfactory test of the effectiveness of microteaching that made use of student performance criteria. In general, the results of these studies lent support to McIntyre's (1980) "commonsense generalization patterns of teaching are commonly successful in attaining the goals towards which they are most commonly directed" (p. 6).

5. Conclusion

Despite some 30 years of research effort, there are few definitive conclusions that can be drawn about the effectiveness of microteaching other than that the participants tend to have favorable attitudes to the experience. It is clear that microteaching enjoyed almost faddish popularity after its introduction and that this produced a plethora of studies on it; however, only a few useful generalizations could be drawn from the results of the studies. Similarly, it is also very clear that there has been no recent sustained research program that has attempted to draw both on these generalizations and the lessons learned in the execution of the early research.

Simple verdicts on the effects of microteaching are unlikely to be reached. Microteaching, like any other teaching method, is complex: complex in terms of the variety of components it uses, the aims it attempts to achieve, and the conceptual models that underlie these aims. It is evident that much of the early experimental research was sterile, providing only a situation-specific evaluation of particular and local sets of training components rather than a testing of coherent and generalizable theory about learning to teach, its form and function. Nonetheless, microteaching did represent a major breakthrough in thinking about teacher education and its advent clearly sparked a major research enterprise which contributed substantially to teacher education thinking and practice.

See also: Onservice Teacher Education

References

Allen D W et al. 1965 *Microteaching: A Description*. School of Education, Stanford University, Stanford, California

Allen D W, McDonald F J 1967 *Training Effects of Feedback and Modeling Procedures on Teaching Performance*. Stanford Center for Research and Development in Teaching, Stanford University, Stanford, California

Allen D W, Ryan K 1969 *Microteaching*. Addison-Wesley, Reading, Massachusetts

Argyle M 1969 *Social Interaction*. Methuen, London

Bandura A 1977 *Social Learning Theory*. Prentice-Hall, Englewood Cliffs, New Jersey

Bandura A, Ross D, Ross S 1963 Imitation of film-mediated aggressive models. *J. Abnorm. Soc. Psychol.* 66(1): 3–11

Batten H D 1979 Factors influencing the effectiveness of microteaching in a teacher education programme Doctoral dissertation, University of Stirling, Stirling

Brown G A 1975 *Microteaching: A Programme of Teaching Skills*. Methuen, London

Bush R N (ed.) 1968 *Microteaching: A description*. Stanford University, Stanford, California (mimeo)

Butcher P M 1981 An experimental investigation of the effectiveness of a value claim strategy unit for use in teacher education. Master's dissertation, Macquarie University, Sydney

Claus K E 1969 Effects of modeling and feedback treatments on the development of teachers' questioning skills. Technical report No 6, Stanford Center for Research and Development in Teaching, Stanford University, Stanford, California. ERIC Document Reproduction Service No. ED 033 081, Washington, DC

Gilmore S 1977 The effects of positive and negative models on student teachers' questioning behaviours. In: McIntyre D I, MacLeod G R, Griffiths R (eds.) 1977 *Investigations of Microteaching*. Croom Helm, London

Gregory I 1986 Third World–First World: Time for another look at microteaching. *Journal of Education for Teaching* 12(3): 173–88

Griffiths R 1974 The contribution of feedback to microteaching technique. Paper presented at the APLET/NPLC Conference, Reading

Griffiths R, MacLeod G R, McIntyre D I 1977 Effects of supervisory strategies in microteaching on students' attitudes and skill acquisition. In: McIntyre D I, MacLeod G R, Griffiths R (eds.) 1977 *Investigations of Microteaching*. Croom Helm, London

Jones P E 1979 A survey of microteaching in secondary teacher education programs of NCATE accredited colleges and universities. Paper presented at the AERA Conference, San Francisco, California. ERIC Document Reproduction Service No. ED 173 336, Washington, DC

Koran J J, Koran M L, McDonald F J 1972 Effects of different sources of positive and negative information on observational learning of a teaching skill. *J. Educ. Psychol.* 63(5): 405–10

Levis D S 1985 Feedback in microteaching. In: Husén T, Postlethwaite T N (eds.) 1985 *The International Encyclopedia of Education*, 1st edn. Pergamon Press, Oxford

MacLeod G R 1981 Experimental studies of the outcomes of microteaching. *South Pac. J. Teach. Educ.* 9(1): 31–42

MacLeod G R 1985 Microteaching: Modelling. In: Husén T, Postlethwaite T N (eds.) 1985 *The International Encyclopedia of Education*, 1st edn. Pergamon Press, Oxford

MacLeod G R, Griffiths R, McIntyre D I 1977 The effects of differential training and of teaching subject on microteaching skills performance. In: McIntyre D I, MacLeod G R, Griffiths R (eds.) 1977 *Investigations of Microteaching*. Croom Helm, London

MacLeod G R, McIntyre D I 1977 Towards a model for microteaching. In: McIntyre D I, MacLeod G R, Griffiths R (eds.) 1977 *Investigations of Microteaching*. Croom Helm, London

McDonald F J 1973 Behavior modification in teacher education. In: Thoresen C E (ed.) 1973 *Behavior Modification in Education*. University of Chicago Press, Chicago, Illinois

McIntyre D I 1980 The contribution of research to quality in teacher education. *South Pacif. J. Teach. Educ.* 4(1/2): 4–19

McIntyre D I 1983 Social skills training for teaching: A cognitive perspective. In: Ellis R, Whittington D (eds.) 1983 *New Directions in Social Skills Training*. Croom Helm, London

Pegg J E 1985 The effect of practice on the acquisition of teaching skills. Doctoral dissertation, University of New England, Armidale, New England

Phillips W E 1973 Effects of a videotaped modeling procedure on verbal questioning practices of secondary social studies student teachers. Final report, Fairmont State College, Fairmont, West Virginia. ERIC Document Reproduction Service No. ED 079 967, Washington, DC

Turney C, Clift J C, Dunkin M, Traill R 1973 *Microteaching: Research, Theory and Practice*. Sydney University Press, Sydney

Wagner A C 1973 Changing teaching behavior: A comparison of microteaching and cognitive discrimination training. *J. Educ. Psychol.* 64(3): 299–305

Wragg E C 1971 The influence of feedback on teachers' performance. *Educ. Res.* 13(3): 217–21

Laboratory Experiences in Teacher Education

K. K. Metcalf

A laboratory experience in teacher education is a direct or simulated activity that allows observation, application, study, and analysis of educational events or phenomena in a controlled, usually simplified setting. Laboratory experiences can be of varying degrees of reality, control, and complexity. However, the element of control of one or more variables in the environment is requisite. Thus, although field-based experiences such as student teaching are often considered to be laboratory-like, they seldom afford sufficient control of the environment to qualify as such. As suggested by Broudy (1964), using a natural classroom as a laboratory is analogous to learning chemistry by using a petroleum complex as a laboratory.

1. Available Forms of Laboratory Experience

A number of laboratory experiences are available for use in teacher preparation. The following materials and activities have been suggested as laboratory experiences in teacher education:

(a) audio and video recordings of regular or simulated educational phenomena;

(b) books or other written materials which provide detailed descriptions of educational events or phenomena;

(c) case studies;

(d) counseling arrangements;

(e) demonstrations (live or recorded);

(f) extensive clinical discussions of critical events;

(g) games;

(h) microteaching;

(i) minicourses;

(j) mirror teaching;

(k) peer teaching;

(l) protocols;

(m) reflective teaching;

(n) role playing;

(o) simulators;

(p) simulations (computer and nontechnological); and

(q) transcriptions of classroom or educational events.

2. Extent of Use

The most commonly used laboratory experience is microteaching, a technique which was developed at Stanford University in the 1960s. According to McIntyre (1991), 91 percent of teacher education institutions reported using microteaching. Demonstrations were the next most commonly used laboratory experience (84 percent). No other laboratory experience was reported to be used by more than 40 percent of responding institutions. Thus, although an array of experiences exist which can be used to allow students of teaching to experiment and analyze educational events, it appears that few of these experiences are included in teacher preparation.

McLeod (1987), Cruickshank and Metcalf (1990) and others have indicated that use of laboratory experiences in teacher education has declined since the late 1970s. Berliner (1985) and Evertson (1990) noted that this decline is associated with a concurrent trend toward extensive field-based experiences, in spite of evidence indicating that field experiences are often unsuccessful in developing desirable professional attitudes, behavior, or ways of thinking.

3. Research on Laboratory Experience

Research on the effects of laboratory experiences in teacher education was pronounced in the late 1960s and early 1970s, but has diminished substantially since then. Most studies compared the effects of particular laboratory experiences (e.g., microteaching) to didactic classroom instruction rather than to other forms of laboratory experience or to field experiences. Furthermore, available reviews of research synthesize only studies of a single type of laboratory experience. Although useful, these studies do not provide information as to the broader or more general effects or effectiveness of laboratory experiences in teacher education.

3.1 Effects

Across studies of microteaching, minicourses, simulations, protocols, role playing, case method, recordings, reflective teaching, and other laboratory methods, three consistent findings emerge.

First, participants believe laboratory experiences to be positive, enjoyable, and professionally beneficial. This is the single most consistently reported finding in research of laboratory experiences. Students generally believe laboratory activities to be more beneficial than any other dimension of their preparation except student teaching (Cruickshank 1985, Gilliom 1969,

Rentel 1974). Further, inservice and preservice teachers appear equally to value laboratory experiences, and, it must be noted, often believe the experience to be beneficial in spite of research findings to the contrary.

Second, laboratory experiences produce desirable results when outcomes are evaluated in laboratory settings. Microteaching, minicourses, protocol materials, media-based simulations and simulators, reflective teaching, and recordings consistently have been found to develop teachers' instructional behavior, reflective and analytical abilities, understanding of educational concepts, as well as their attitudes toward teaching and learning.

Relatedly, some intensive laboratory experiences appear to affect a variety of desirable outcomes. For example, microteaching, developed for and primarily intended to promote skill development, is also found to promote teachers' ability to reflect on teaching and their understanding of desirable instructional principles (Winitsky and Arends 1991). Reflective teaching, a guided form of peer teaching and analysis, has been found to promote improved self-confidence, greater analytical ability, and improved student teaching performance (Cruickshank and Metcalf 1990). Thus, laboratory experiences may promote positive and concurrent changes in teachers' affect, behavior, and understanding. To the extent that this carryover effect occurs, laboratory experiences are more efficient than is generally supposed.

Third, and in spite of the above, research on the extent to which participants transfer learning from on-campus settings to natural classroom settings is sparse and has generally been viewed as inconsistent. For example, Goldwaite (1968), Young and Young (1969), and Jensen and Young (1972) report significant differences in student teaching behavior between those teachers who had participated in microteaching and those who had not. However, Copeland (1977), Copeland and Doyle (1973), Kallenbach and Gall (1969) and others report no significant differences. Similar inconsistencies are found in research on minicourses (Borg 1975), protocols (Cruickshank and Haefele 1987), and simulations (Copeland 1982). Thus, many researchers have concluded that laboratory experiences are neither effective nor efficient.

Closer examination of the individual studies does not bear this out (Metcalf 1994). When research into the effects of laboratory experience on natural classroom practice is examined by differentiating studies of preservice teachers from those of inservice teachers, the findings are much more consistent. Generally, on-campus laboratory experiences consistently result in significant and desirable changes in the natural classroom behavior of *inservice* teachers, and are often associated with improved student performance (Gage 1989). In contrast, on-campus laboratory experiences only inconsistently produce significant change in the natural classroom behavior of *preservice* teachers.

Copeland (1982) hypothesizes that inservice teachers who participate in laboratory experiences are afforded opportunities to assimilate their use of the behaviors in their own classrooms, whereas preservice teachers are not. Further, while inservice teachers are applying the desirable behaviors in their classrooms, their learners are becoming attuned to the teachers' new behavior. In contrast, student teachers who participate in on-campus "laboratories separate from their student teaching assignment have no opportunity to shape the system into which they will move to engage in student teaching. The likelihood of their future use of the target skills is not enhanced by unintentional pupil training" (Copeland 1982 p. 1011).

3.2 Factors Influencing the Effectiveness of Laboratory Experiences

When viewed across studies of individual forms of laboratory experience, research provides insight into several components and characteristics which appear to impact the efficacy of laboratory experiences.

3.2.1 Integration. At the broadest level, laboratory experiences are most effective when integrated into a broader, organized pattern of instruction. Laboratory experiences are best viewed not as ends in themselves, but rather as ways of "anchoring" and enhancing didactic or field experiences. Laboratory experiences used in conjunction with didactic instruction to achieve desired outcomes or objectives produce more consistent and more desirable effects than either laboratory experiences or didactic instruction alone. Further, it appears that both didactic instruction and laboratory activities are improved when explicitly and directly interrelated.

3.2.2 Multidimensionality. Research which has examined the effects of combining multiple forms of laboratory experience is minimal. However, available research suggests that the effectiveness of laboratory experiences is enhanced when several diverse experiences are provided in an organized series of laboratory situations. A varied but structured series of experiences which includes videotaped role playing or teaching with guided discussion, peer and self-analysis, qualitative feedback, and some controlled experience with learners of school age is likely to promote a broader range of desirable outcomes, to develop participant learning which is more resilient to forgetting, and to make transfer of learned abilities from laboratory settings to natural classrooms more likely.

3.2.3 Focus on conceptual understanding. A growing body of literature reinforces the importance of conceptually-based or conceptually-oriented dimensions of laboratory experiences (Gliessman and Pugh 1987, 1991). According to these investigators, laboratory experiences are more effective when they emphasize participant conceptual understanding of the desired outcomes primarily through the use of filmed, videotaped, or audiotaped examples or models. Gliessman and Pugh (1987, 1991) believe this component to be the single most important factor in the efficacy of laboratory training.

Other studies lend support to the importance of conceptual development aspects of laboratory experiences. For example, protocols and minicourses tend to emphasize understanding of desirable behavior or concepts and thus have been found to be successful in producing desirable results, both in understanding and behavior (Cruickshank and Haefele 1987). Similarly, Troyer (1988) found that reflective teaching was made significantly more effective when participants received instruction regarding the reflective process prior to the laboratory experience.

3.2.4 Participant knowledge of "target outcomes." Not unrelated to conceptual dimensions of laboratory training are findings which indicate that laboratory experiences are more effective when participants are given a clear and thorough understanding of the intended outcomes of the experience. Participants respond more positively to laboratory experiences when they are first made aware of the objectives of the experience, the importance of the behaviors or outcomes of the experience (i.e., their rationale), the critical factors that constitute proficient and timely application or use of the outcomes, and criteria and methods by which they can monitor their own performance.

3.2.5 Practice. Laboratory experiences in teacher education are characterized by the opportunities they afford participants to apply or "try out" professional behavior or ways of thinking in controlled or simplified settings. Practice or rehearsal has long been assumed to be a critical factor in the success of laboratory experiences. However, research indicates that extensive, repetitive practice appears to produce only slight or nonsignificant improvement in desirable outcomes. Based upon a meta-analysis of research on laboratory training, Gliessman and Pugh (1991) concluded that the "number of practice sessions was unassociated with level of skill acquisition" (p. 10). It would seem that practice components are most appropriately used to provide opportunities for application and analysis rather than rehearsal. As such, the focus of practice should be on furthering participants' awareness and understanding of the critical aspects of their performance by allowing controlled application, feedback, and guided reflection, rather than on developing habits of performance.

3.2.6 Feedback. A critical factor in the effectiveness of laboratory experiences—which is related to practice—is the provision of frequent qualitative feedback to participants. Experiences which do not focus participants' attention on the desired objectives or provide feedback regarding participants' performance are seldom successful. Feedback based upon guided, critical analysis by self, peers, or instructors appears to be equally effective in promoting desirable outcomes, although feedback provided by the instructor is viewed most positively by participants. Feedback is most useful when it: (a) is directed toward outcomes or objectives of which the participant has been made aware, (b) is focused on only a few critical aspects of performance, and (c) offers specific information which enhances the participant's understanding and can be used to improve future performance. It should be noted that effective feedback through self-analysis requires that the participant has a clear understanding of the desired performance criteria and can accurately apply a directive, systematic approach to the analysis.

3.3 Transfer to Natural Settings

As indicated above, research indicates that a variety of laboratory experiences in teacher education are effective in developing desired ways of thinking, behavior, and affect in those laboratory settings. However, particularly in the case of preservice teachers, this learning often fails to transfer to natural classrooms. Investigations of the integration or interrelation of laboratory and natural classroom experiences are lacking. Nonetheless, when transfer to natural classroom practice is the goal, it is important that guided laboratory experience includes work with school-aged pupils (Gliessman and Pugh 1991, Metcalf 1994). Whether this experience with school-age pupils should occur in the laboratory or in natural classrooms, how much of this experience is necessary, and when this experience should occur is unclear. What is known suggests that practice with school-age learners need not be extensive; furthermore, a series of laboratory experiences need not culminate in natural classroom practice. Rather, limited, guided, and controlled experiences with school-age learners which are preceded and followed by simulated, purely laboratory experiences may be most successful (Gilliom 1971, Gliessman and Pugh 1991).

4. Interim Conclusions

Drawing on the findings above, several broad conclusions appear reasonable regarding the effects of laboratory experiences in teacher education.

First, laboratory experiences including microteaching, minicourses, media-based simulations, reflective teaching, protocols, role playing, videotape recordings, and case method can produce significant and desirable changes in teachers' affect, behavior, understanding, and ways of thinking. Controlled laboratory experiences appear to be equally effective in producing desired outcomes with inservice and preservice teachers when assessed in laboratory settings. When assessed in natural classroom settings, laboratory experiences are more effective with inservice than preservice teachers.

Second, and related to the above, transfer of developed abilities or attributes from laboratory to natural classroom settings is problematic in the preparation of preservice teachers. However, when limited, controlled experiences with school-age pupils are included in on-campus laboratory experiences, transfer to natural classrooms is more likely to occur. Furthermore, although laboratory and field experiences have seldom been directly interrelated in teacher education, it appears that laboratory experiences may be most effective when experience with school-age pupils in natural settings occurs within a broader series of controlled, laboratory activities.

Third, while newer forms of laboratory experience, such as case method and computer simulation, appear to hold promise, evidence of their effects or transfer is to date insufficient. Proponents of these laboratory experiences press for their inclusion in teacher education programs despite this evidence. While there is evidence that computer simulations and case methods produce desirable change in preservice teachers' behavior and their ways of thinking in on-campus settings, there is no evidence that these changes influence their behavior, affect, or cognition during natural classroom teaching.

Fourth, and relatedly, efforts to produce laboratory experiences have often emphasized development and innovation to the neglect of evaluation. Developers of laboratory experiences seem mostly to disregard the body of research which could inform their work. The substantial collective body of research on microteaching, minicourses, media-based simulators, protocols, and, to a lesser extent, reflective teaching seems not to be considered by those who develop or implement computer simulations or case methods.

Fifth, renewed interest in providing "anchored" instruction for teacher education students often disregards or rejects earlier forms of laboratory experience, such as microteaching or videotape demonstration, on the grounds that they are no longer appropriate for contemporary outcomes (e.g., the development of reflective or analytic ability). In fact, research suggests that many of these experiences can affect a variety of desirable and contemporary results.

5. Future Implications

5.1 Implications for Practice

Laboratory experiences in teacher education should draw from and include a variety of experiences which are selected on the basis of the intended outcomes, not instructor familiarity with the technique. Thus, microteaching, although commonly used and a powerful tool, should not be used in isolation or without consideration of the intended outcomes. In addition, laboratory experiences must be integrated into and interrelated with didactic or classroom instruction and should include controlled experiences with school-

age learners. Finally, laboratory experiences promoted since the late 1980s (e.g., computer and interactive video simulations, case method), which have limited research support and which do not include systematic, controlled experiences with school-age pupils, should be used with caution.

5.2 Implications for Research and Development

Trends prevalent in the 1990s may make laboratory experiences a desirable alternative to extended and extensive field experiences. Among these trends are: (a) increasing evidence of the potentially negative effects of extended field experiences, (b) increasing difficulty in identifying and maintaining desirable field placements, and (c) growing demands for the professional preparation of teachers to include experiences with diverse student populations, often not easily available. However, although cumulative research would seem to indicate that laboratory experiences can be effective in the professional preparation of teachers, much remains to be discovered about the most effective and efficient ways in which they can be used.

There has been a particularly disquieting tendency for proponents of both field-based and laboratory experiences to overlook the results of research from each area that can inform and improve practice. Certainly, field-based experiences could be enhanced by considering and integrating the aspects of laboratory experience found to optimize effectiveness: guided application of "target" behaviors or concepts, analysis of behavior and effectiveness, and feedback. Similarly, laboratory experiences, which are highly effective in promoting desirable change but often do not transfer to natural classroom practice, should integrate what is known about effective field experiences.

5.2.1 Broad issues and problems.
Existing research on laboratory experiences has most often focused on the effects of a single or particular form of laboratory experience, usually compared with "traditional" or didactic classroom instruction. Future studies of laboratory experiences must examine the value and use of laboratories and laboratory experiences within the broader scope of teacher preparation. For example, the following research questions are representative:

(a) How do the effects of particular laboratory experiences compare with one another rather than with didactic or field-based instruction?

(b) How can laboratory experiences best be integrated systematically into a program of teacher preparation?

(c) What is the most efficacious balance between laboratory, field, and didactic forms of instruction in developing proficient professional educators?

(d) What forms of laboratory experience are most likely to result in particular cognitive, affective, or behavioral outcomes?

(e) In what ways do various forms of laboratory experience interact, and how can these interactions be optimized. For example, what might be the result of integrating case study, computer simulation, and microteaching with analysis into a single, organized series of experiences?

(f) How can the interaction between on-campus laboratory experiences and field-based experiences be used to reduce the negative dimensions and maximize the positive attributes of each?

5.2.2 Specific issues and questions. If, in fact, some laboratory experiences (i.e., microteaching and reflective teaching) affect multiple desirable outcomes in laboratory settings, how best can these broad outcomes be transferred to natural classrooms?

How extensively can any one laboratory method be used before its effects are diminished? For example, what is the optimal number of videotaped teaching episodes with analysis and feedback?

Guided experience with school-age pupils seems critical to the transfer of laboratory-learned attributes to natural classroom use. How much of this type of experience is necessary and where in the laboratory sequence is it best placed?

6. Conclusion

Cumulative research indicates that laboratory experiences can be a powerful tool in the preparation or improvement of preservice and inservice teachers. At the same time, however, laboratory experiences alone, like extensive field-based experience, are unlikely to maximize desired outcomes in behavioral, affective, or cognitive domains. Thus, research of laboratory experiences, when viewed in the light of research on field-based experiences, seems to suggest that teacher preparation which emphasizes controlled laboratory experiences with peers and school-age pupils, integrated with complementary, guided field-based experiences may be most likely to produce desired outcomes.

See also: Microteaching in Teacher Education; Case Methods in Teacher Education; Curriculum of Teacher Education Programs

References

Berliner D C 1985 Laboratory settings and the study of teacher education. *J. Teach. Educ.* 36(6): 2–8

Borg W 1975 Protocol materials as related to teacher performance and pupil achievement. *J. Educ. Res.* 69(1): 23–30

Broudy H S 1964 Laboratory, clinical, and internship experiences in the professional preparation of teachers. Address given at the conference of the National Association of Laboratory School Administrators, Chicago, Illinois

Copeland W D 1977 Some factors related to student teacher classroom performance following microteaching training. *Am. Educ. Res. J.* 14(2): 147–57

Copeland W D 1982 Laboratory experiences in teacher education. In: Mitzel H (ed.) 1982 *Encyclopedia of Educational Research*, Vol. 2. Free Press, New York

Copeland W D, Doyle W 1973 Laboratory skill training and student teacher classroom performance. *J. Exp. Educ.* 42(1): 16–21

Cruickshank D R 1985 Uses and benefits of reflective teaching. *Phi Del. Kap.* 66(10): 704–06

Cruickshank D R, Haefele D 1987 Teacher preparation via protocol materials. *Int. J. Educ. Res.* 11(5): 543–54

Cruickshank D R, Metcalf K K 1990 Training within teacher preparation. In: Houston W R (ed.) 1990 *The Handbook of Research on Teacher Education*. Macmillan, New York

Evertson C M 1990 Bridging knowledge and action through clinical experiences. In: Dill D et al. (eds.) 1990 *What Teachers Need to Know: The Knowledge, Skills, and Values Essential to Good Teaching*. Jossey-Bass, San Francisco, California

Gage N L 1989 Process-product research on teaching: A review of criticisms. *Elem. Sch. J.* 89(3): 253–300

Gilliom M 1969 Microteaching in the methods course: Bridging the confrontation gap. *Soc. Educ.* 33: 165–83

Gliessman D H, Pugh R C 1987 Conceptual instruction and intervention as methods of acquiring teaching skills. *Int. J. Educ. Res.* 11(5): 555–63

Gliessman D H, Pugh R C 1991 Cognitive learning and the acquisition of teaching skills. Paper presented at the annual meeting of the Mid-Western Educational Research Association, Chicago, Illinois

Goldwaite D 1968 A study of microteaching in the preservice education of science teachers. Doctoral dissertation, Ohio State University, Columbus, Ohio

Jensen L C, Young J I 1972 Effect of televised simulated instruction on subsequent teaching. *J. Educ. Psychol.* 63(4): 368–73

Kallenbach W W, Gall M D 1969 Microteaching versus conventional methods in training elementary intern teachers. *J. Educ. Res.* 63(4): 136–41

McIntyre D J 1991 The utilization of laboratory experiences in undergraduate teacher education programs. Paper presented at the annual meeting of the Association of Teacher Educators, New Orleans, Louisiana

McLeod G R 1987 Microteaching: Modelling. In: Dunkin M (ed.) 1987 *The International Encyclopedia of Teaching and Teacher Education*. Pergamon Press, Oxford

Metcalf K 1994 Laboratory experiences in teacher education: A meta-analytic review of research. Working paper, Indiana University, Bloomington, Indiana

Rentel V 1974 A protocol materials evaluation: The language of children. *J. Teach. Educ.* 25(4): 323–29

Troyer M 1988 The effects of reflective teaching and a supplemental theoretical component on preservice teachers' reflectivity in analyzing classroom teaching situations. Doctoral dissertation, Ohio State University, Columbus, Ohio

Winitsky N, Arends R 1991 Translating research into practice: The effects of various forms of training and clinical experience on preservice students' knowledge, skill, and reflectiveness. *J. Teach. Educ.* 42(1): 52–65

Young D, Young D 1969 The effectiveness of individually prescribed microteaching modules on an intern's subsequent classroom performance. Paper presented at the annual meeting of the American Educational Research Association

Case Methods in Teacher Education

A. R. McAninch

Case methods can be defined as "the methods of pedagogy employed in conjunction with teaching cases" (Shulman 1992 p. 19). It is useful to distinguish between case methods, a form of pedagogy, and case study methods, a form of qualitative research. A good case study may at times be useful for pedagogical purposes, whereas case studies are generally not written with that aim in mind. This entry includes discussions of the following topics: the context for research on case methods; case methods in law and business; a heuristic of case methods in teacher education; and finally, some issues for future research.

1. The Context for Research on Case Methods

Since the mid-1980s, research on how cases can contribute to the teacher education curriculum has burgeoned. In the United States, the growing interest in case methods can be partly attributed to Shulman's (1986) seminal conceptualization of the knowledge base of teaching. Shulman asserted that cases have an important role to play in the education of teachers, and that case knowledge is a key component of the knowledge base of teaching. Interest in case methods since the mid-1980s can also be traced to the pressure exerted by politicians to professionalize teaching. For example, the Carnegie Forum on Education and the Economy (1986) recommended that the case method be introduced into teacher education programs. Thus, some teacher educators have studied the preparation of professionals in more prestigious fields, such as law, medicine, and business, and concluded that the apparently efficacious methods of preparing these practitioners also has a role to play in teacher education. As Sykes and Bird (1992) noted, "proponents of case teaching for teacher education frequently argue by analogy to case teaching in other fields of professional education" (p. 458).

Finally, since the mid-1980s, some teacher educators have turned away from science and the university as a source of knowledge for teaching and have looked instead to the practical setting. In rejecting the "applied science" conception of teaching, for example, proponents of craft knowledge argue that teaching is so highly contextual that knowledge for teaching is found in the situated knowledge of teachers. As Carter (1990) wrote:

> New ways of talking about the knowledge of teaching have emerged, many of which have signaled a need to rethink the conduct of teacher education and to explore richer ways of representing what experienced teachers know about classrooms and what new teachers need to know to function successfully in such inherently complex environments. (p. 109)

The study of cases is held to accord with this new view of teacher knowledge, which gives emphasis to the complexity of the practice setting, to reflection on experience, and to teacher wisdom. For these and other reasons, "the case idea" (Sykes and Bird 1992) has caught the imagination of many teacher educators.

This is not to say that using case methods in teacher preparation programs is a new idea. Case collection and study formed a part of teacher education programs at New Jersey State Teacher's College at Montclair during the 1920s (Sperle 1933). Merseth (1991) reported that the faculty of the Harvard Graduate School of Education briefly considered—but ultimately rejected—such a method for its programs in the 1920s. Furthermore, casebooks for use in both preservice and inservice programs have been published throughout the twentieth century (McAninch 1991). Indeed, it is interesting to speculate as to why case methods became a mainstay in the preparation of a whole range of professionals from lawyers to social workers, but not teachers. Before proceeding to a discussion of case methods in teacher education, it is useful to survey briefly the case methods in law and business, the two fields which have received the most attention from teacher educators interested in developing a case method for their own field (Kleinfeld 1992, Merseth 1992).

2. Case Methods in Law and Business

It is useful to study case methods in fields other than teacher education in order to underscore the idea that case methods, and what constitutes a case, vary. There is an array of case methods across professional disciplines, and even within disciplines. In addition, the literature that has emerged in other professions indicates some of the theoretical issues associated with case teaching.

2.1 The Case Method in Law

The case method in legal education is associated with Harvard Law School and its first dean, Christopher Columbus Langdell, who was appointed in 1870 (Stevens 1983, Thorne 1973). Langdell argued that decided opinions of the courts formed the basic data for rendering the study of the law scientific and therefore worthy of university status. The earliest casebooks were collections of appellate court cases, offered without commentary or materials. Further, he maintained that the curriculum should consist entirely of the study of cases, which reinforced the Common Law view that judges pronounce the law. Finally, Langdell asserted that students should be taught by the Socratic method, so that they could induce the skein of legal precedent themselves, rather than merely be told what the law said through didactic methods.

Early in the twentieth century, when adherence to Common Law fell from favor, Langdell's successors rhetorically shifted the rationale of the case method to teaching students the process of legal reasoning. Yet, as Stevens noted, Langdell's case method remains virtually intact to this day:

> Throughout the hierarchy of law schools, from the most famous national ones to the most locally-oriented, it is the analysis of the appellate decisions through case classes which takes pride of place. The skills developed in today's students tend to be substantially the same as those inculcated in the students of the 1870s largely because the structure of legal education has remained unchanged. Law teaching, no matter how differently the case method is used, is still predominantly a matter of a single professor dissecting innumerable cases before a class consisting of large numbers of students. (Stevens cited in Thorne 1973 p. 107)

This model of the case method and legal education in general have been attacked on various grounds. Some critics, for example, argue that the legal case method develops technical skills at the expense of fostering a concern for the moral consequences of any given outcome (Stevens 1983).

2.2 The Case Method in Business

The use of cases in business education originated at Harvard Business School in the early part of the twentieth century. Unlike the field of law, however, where cases are generated by the practice itself, business cases had to be formulated for the curriculum. A business case is generally a written account of a business problem that demands action on the part of an executive or group of executives. In 1920, the Harvard Business School allocated funds specifically for the purpose of case development and a group of graduates was employed to go out into the field to collect and write-up "real" business problems. Later, case writing became an activity of business school faculty.

The literature on the case method in business education suggests a much more eclectic approach than is in law. Dooley and Skinner (1977) found nearly endless variations of case use in business classes. Van Woerden (1988) listed a variety of case formats, including in-baskets and simulations.

Unlike the case method in law, the emphasis in business is on group process and discussion for the purpose of developing problem-solving and decision-making skills (Christensen and Hansen 1987). Because the aim of this method is the development of executive judgment, business cases are generally open-ended

and allow for more than one credible solution. The role of the professor is that of discussion leader, rather than Socratic questioner. In comparing these two models of case methods, Shulman (1992) characterized one of the key distinctions:

> Where legal case methods typically ask students to discern underlying principles, business cases are more likely to press students to examine the likely consequences of each action they propose. Legal cases focus student attention on judgments and reasons; business cases focus on actions and consequences. (p. 29)

One final point must be made before moving to an examination of case methods in teacher education. For all the rhetoric attesting to the efficacy of case methods in law, business, and other fields, there is a dearth of research which supports the conclusion that they are more effective in meeting instructional goals than other discussion methods or didactics (Shulman 1992).

3. A Heuristic of Case Methods in Teacher Education

Extending the work of Merseth (1991), research on case methods can be usefully organized into categories representing various conceptual orientations of teacher education programs. The classification scheme used here is advanced by Feiman-Nemser (1990), who divided programs into five categories or orientations: (a) academic, (b) practical, (c) technological, (d) personal, and (e) critical/social. She asserted that each orientation "has a focus or thesis that highlights certain aspects of teaching, learning, and learning to teach; directs attention to a central goal of teacher preparation; and manifests itself in particular practices" (p. 221).

3.1 The Academic Orientation

The academic orientation "is primarily concerned with the transmission of knowledge and the development of understanding ... the academic orientation emphasizes the teacher's role as intellectual leader, scholar, and subject-matter specialist" (Feiman-Nemser 1990 p. 221). This conception is exemplified by the work of Shulman (1986, 1992) and Broudy (1990).

Shulman's (1986) essay on the knowledge base of teaching is an excellent starting point for a review of literature on case methods in teacher education. His paper remains one of the most important theoretical contributions in this area. According to Shulman, not only are there different types of content knowledge, but also different forms of knowledge, one of which is case knowledge. Case knowledge stands in contrast to knowledge represented in propositional form. Shulman defined case knowledge as "knowledge of specific, well-documented, and richly described events. Whereas cases themselves are reports of events or sequences of events, the knowledge they represent is what makes them cases" (p. 11). Cases represent theoretical knowledge: thus, cases and theory are inextricably linked.

> To call something a case is to make a theoretical claim—to argue that it is a "case of something," or to argue that it is an instance of a larger class. A red rash on the face is not a case of something until the observer has invoked theoretical knowledge of disease. (Shulman 1986 p. 11)

Thus, Shulman argued, there can be no case knowledge without theoretical knowledge. Furthermore, he pointed out that "generalizability does not inhere in the case, but in the conceptual apparatus of the explicator. An event can be described; a case must be explicated, interpreted, argued, dissected, and reassembled" (p. 12). Shulman thus called for the development of cases in teacher education which would illuminate this relationship between the concrete and the theoretical.

There are three types of cases: prototypes, precedents, and parables. Prototype cases exemplify and illustrate the theoretical propositions. Precedents provide guidelines or models to follow. Parables serve to communicate a moral or value, which Shulman regarded as particularly useful in teacher socialization.

A single case may serve more than one function, as in the following example.

> A teacher was confronted with repeated incidents of students coming to class without pencils. Rather than either supplying them with replacements (thus making it possible for them to keep up with their work, although running the risk of reinforcing their poor habits), or forcing them to sit through the lesson without benefit of participation, the following strategy was reported. The teacher kept a box of very short pencil stubs in his desk. Whenever a student approached who had forgotten to bring a pencil, the teacher produced the shortest stub available and lent it to the student, who was then expected to use it in completing all of that day's work. (Shulman 1986 p. 12)

Shulman noted that this case serves as both a precedent for managing classroom problems and a prototype for the principle of avoiding accidentally reinforcing inappropriate behavior.

Also in the academic tradition, Broudy (1990) argued that the development of a case literature can help teacher educators develop a "consensus of the learned" regarding the key concepts and "canonical literatures" of the field, a consensus he considered woefully lacking in teacher education. A consensus, Broudy contended, is more likely to emerge around a set of problems than a set of taxonomies or theories. For that reason, he maintained that the identification of "paradigmatic problems"—problems that are so generic and important that virtually all teachers will be familiar with them—was a vital element in the professionalization of teaching.

At the University of Illinois, a case method project developed by Broudy and his colleagues has sought to identify standard problems from teacher surveys and their portrayal on videotape. A final component of the project has been the collection of a body of scholarly literature to accompany each case (Broudy 1990).

3.2 The Practical Orientation

The practical orientation, according to Feiman-Nemser (1990),

> focuses attention on the elements of craft, technique, and artistry that skillful practitioners reveal in their work. It also recognizes that teachers deal with unique situations and that their work is ambiguous and uncertain ... the practical orientation endorses the primacy of experience as a source of knowledge about teaching. (p. 222)

Teacher educators working within this tradition have generally proposed two different types of case methods. Kleinfeld (1992) and Merseth (1991, 1992) have argued that teaching is in some important ways analogous to the field of business, and maintained that the business case method is the appropriate model for the field. Teaching, like the business world, is an "ill-structured domain" (Merseth 1991), a view also reflected in the casebook developed by Silverman et al. (1992). In contrast, Carter (1990, 1992) argued for the importance of learning how experienced teachers understand the complexity of classrooms and helping others acquire those understandings through cases (see also Silberstein and Tamir 1991).

Kleinfeld (1992) reported her work at the University of Alaska at Fairbanks in developing cases for a problem-based fifth-year teacher education program entitled "Teachers for Alaska." She listed five objectives of case teaching: (a) to provide students with vicarious experience, (b) to show students how an expert teacher constructs educational problems, (c) to model an expert teacher's process of inquiry, (d) to rehearse and broaden the students' repertoire of teaching strategies, and (e) to develop the habit of reflection.

Merseth (1991, 1992), working within the context of the business model, has developed cases written especially for pedagogical purposes. In one case, entitled "It ain't fair!," a novice teacher attempted to use a cooperative learning methodology in a multiracial, urban school setting. In the case discussion, participants analyzed the situation and suggest plans of action. The instructor focused the discussion on answers to two major questions: "Why would you do that? What are the implications of your proposed actions?" Thus, Merseth aimed at helping teacher candidates think through alternative courses of action and their consequences.

The casebook by Silverman et al. (1992) also embraced the business case method model and emphasized student problem-solving and analysis in preparation for the "real world of teaching" (p. xv). Each case describes a dilemma facing a classroom teacher. The authors wrote that the aim of the text is "to encourage student generated analysis rather than teacher-manufactured solutions" (p. xv). Thus, the cases, which dealt with topics such as classroom management and effective teaching, were open-ended and intended to promote the development of possible action plans.

Finally, Carter (1990, 1992) focused on the value cases may have in communicating expert teachers' knowledge and comprehension of classrooms to novices. The cases she developed, all dealing with classroom management, were comprised of three parts: (a) general description of the management structure of a teacher's classroom based on observations, (b) an account of the teacher's reaction to unforeseen managerial problems, and (c) a metaphor suggested by Carter to capture the way in which the teacher seemed to think about management. In the cases describing more successful classroom managers, for example, she found the metaphors "pathfinder" and "pacesetter" useful, while she described less successful managers' actions using metaphors such as "arbiter of adult conscience" or "defender of a territory" (Carter 1990 p. 110). A portion of her case discussions is devoted to analyzing how apt the metaphor is as an attribution to the teacher described in the case.

3.3 The Technological Orientation

The technological orientation in teacher education aims to prepare teachers who can carry out teaching tasks proficiently. Teachers are expected to acquire principles and practices derived from the scientific study of teaching (Feiman-Nemser 1990). Advocates of the case method who work within this tradition focus on the opportunities cases provide to practice a model of rational decision-making or the application of theoretical or scientific principles to instances. Like the teacher educators working within the practical tradition, those working within this tradition, frequently emphasize decision-making and analysis. Unlike the practical orientation, however, the technological conception stresses a specific decision-making procedure which yields effective decision-making. In short, university-generated knowledge takes pride of place. A casebook which reflects this perspective is that produced by Greenwood and Parkay (1989). Also within this tradition, Gliessman (1984) and others (see Sykes and Bird 1992 for a review) used videotape cases to facilitate teachers' acquisition of skills and behaviors derived from research on teaching.

Greenwood and Parkay posed the question "Why do so many teachers not learn to use research-based theory and research in their decision-making activities?" (1989 p. 7.). They asserted that teachers lack a procedure for doing so and suggested a six-step process for incorporating research into decision-making. The first four steps involve examining the situation, collecting and interpreting data, searching for alternatives, and making a decision on the basis of the inquiry. The last two steps consist of reviewing the earlier steps and evaluating the course of action chosen. Research enters into the decision-making process, as each of these steps is to be carried out in light of a single theoretical perspective. In other words, the analysis is to proceed consistently from a Skinnerian perspective or a Piagetian view throughout the inquiry. In this way, the teacher candidate rehearses the rational decision-making procedure for addressing future teaching problems.

Gliessman (1984) used videotape and film protocols to portray teacher skills and behavior derived from empirical research on teaching, and coupled the protocols with instruction aimed at acquisition of the skills portrayed in the film. The skills are treated as concepts to be attained by the teachers. The use of the videotapes facilitated the acquisition of these concepts, a key factor in changing teacher performance.

3.4 The Personal Orientation

According to Feiman-Nemser (1990), the personal orientation stresses the personal growth and development of teacher candidates: "Learning to teach is construed as a process of learning to understand, develop, and use oneself effectively" (p. 225). The personal orientation "places the teacher-learner at the center of the educational process" (Merseth 1991). As in the practical orientation, teacher experience is highly valued here, but a person's own experience and their reflection on it is seen as central.

Approximately 50 cases are contained in *The Mentor Teacher Casebook* (Shulman and Colbert 1987), which was written by mentor teachers working in the Los Angeles Unified School District (LAUSD). The cases are intended to be first a guide to understanding that will help other mentor teachers learn about some important issues related to mentoring. Second, the cases might serve as a guide to action. The idea that the cases can serve as precedents suggests that this orientation is based on the legal case method model, rather than the business case method which underlies much of the work done in the practical orientation. Shulman and Colbert (1987) were quick to point out that the cases are not meant to be prescriptive or open-ended, nor do they beg a response from the reader. Rather, they are cases that enable mentors to see how other mentors confront situations similar to their own.

The cases included in *The Mentor Teacher Casebook* are generally relatively brief descriptions of a conflict or problem. Some of the narratives are followed by a brief reaction of an other mentor teacher. Shulman et al. (1990) reported that, in debriefing over their finished work, many of the mentor teachers commented that their casebook had a tremendous ego-building effect and that the experience was valuable for its positive affective outcomes for the mentors.

Richert (1991) argued that two program structures found in professional education programs in other fields help foster reflection. One is the provision of opportunities for students to interact and collaborate among themselves and with faculty. The second is the use of artifacts, such as records, charts, or blueprints. Richert claimed that a case methodology "combines the artifactual and social elements ... . The artifactual component is the case itself, which is typically a description of an actual teaching situation" (pp. 135–36). The social element occurs during the case discussion. Richert wrote that case discussions are particularly empowering: "Working together, contemplating the dilemmas of practice and building on each other's ideas, are at the core of the method" (p. 144).

3.5 The Critical/Social Orientation

The critical/social orientation, which has its roots in social reconstructionism, "combines a progressive social vision with a radical critique of schooling" (Feiman-Nemser 1990 p. 226). To date, teacher educators working within this tradition have generally expressed little interest in case methods. While not espousing either a particular rationale or proposal for the use of cases, or a particular theory of teacher education, the texts developed by Soltis and his colleagues (see, e.g., Feinberg and Soltis (1992), can be usefully included under this heading. These texts, designed for social foundations courses, contain teaching cases that address broad social issues and topics that critical theorists see as fundamental to the study of education: ideology, hidden curriculum, power, gender, race, class, and so on.

Feinberg and Soltis's (1992) text consists of seven chapters which review theories of the relationship between school and society. The final chapter of the book contains approximately 20 cases which describe incidents related to the theoretical content in the previous six chapters. For example, in one case entitled "College or Workforce?" a Hispanic parent complained to a high school principal about the over representation of Hispanic students in the school's vocational track. The principal confronted the guidance counselor, who defended her advising practices. This case raises issues related to class, race, and equal educational opportunity in schooling, among others. Thus, these texts contain useful case materials for teacher educators working within the critical tradition.

4. Issues for Research

While teaching with cases is a promising pedagogy for teacher education, it is not without its disadvantages. Much of the literature on case methods in teacher education and in other fields cites the inefficiency of this type of teaching. Case methods are slow, and cases are "episodic, discontinuous, hard to structure and organize into larger wholes in the minds of students" (Shulman 1992 p. 27). In addition, teaching by the case method is a difficult form of discussion and places an extra demand on teacher educators who may already be overburdened. Finally, the enthusiasm for case methods in teacher education is more a matter of conjecture and faith than of evidence. One important direction for future research is to assess empirically the contribution teaching with cases can make compared to other instructional methodologies.

This brief review of the research on case methods gives some indication of the various directions of inquiry and harks back to Broudy's point about diversity in teacher education. Can case methods, or any form of pedagogy, make a lasting contribution to the field before prior questions are answered regarding the aims and purposes of teacher education? As Broudy wrote, "Delightful and interesting as this diversity may be, it makes a shambles of the claim of teacher education to a consensus of the learned" (1990 pp. 450–51). Questions fundamental to the development of case methods that can have a transformative impact on teacher education, such as what constitutes a case, what are the aims and purposes of case teaching, and what is a successful case, all seem to hinge on greater agreement than teacher education enjoys regarding its aims and purposes in the early 1990s. Whether, as Broudy hopes, the identification of standard problems leads to greater consensus remains to be seen.

See also: Curriculum of Teacher Education Programs

References

Broudy H 1990 Case studies—why and how. *Teach. Coll. Rec.* 91(3): 449–59
Carnegie Forum on Education and the Economy/Branscomb L 1986 *A Nation Prepared: Teachers for the 21st Century.* Carnegie Forum, New York
Carter K 1990 Meaning and metaphor: Case knowledge in teaching. *Theory Pract.* 29(2): 109–15
Carter K 1992 Toward a cognitive conception of classroom management: A case of teacher comprehension. In: Shulman J H (ed.) 1992 *Case Methods in Teacher Education.* Teachers College Press, New York
Christensen C R, Hansen A J 1987 *Teaching and the Case Method: Text, Cases, and Readings.* Harvard Business School, Boston, Massachusetts
Dooley A R, Skinner W 1977 Casing case method methods *Academy of Management Review* 2(2): 277–89
Feiman-Nemser S 1990 Teacher preparation: Structural and conceptual alternatives. In: Houston W R, Haberman M, Sikula J (eds.) 1990, *Handbook of Research on Teacher Education.* Macmillan, New York
Feinberg W, Soltis J F 1992 *School and Society*, 2nd edn. Teachers College Press, New York
Gliessman D 1984 Changing teaching performance. In: Katz L G, Raths J D (eds.) 1984 *Advances in Teacher Education*, Vol 1. Ablex, Norwood, New Jersey
Greenwood G E, Parkay F W 1989 *Case Studies for Teacher Decision Making.* Random House, New York
Husén T, Postlethwaite T N (eds.) 1985 *The International Encyclopedia of Education* 1st edn. Pergamon Press, Oxford
Kleinfeld J 1992 Learning to think like a teacher: The study

of cases. In: Shulman J H (ed.) 1992 *Case Methods in Teacher Education*. Teachers College Press, New York

McAninch A R 1991 Casebooks for teacher education: The latest fad or lasting contribution? *J. Curric. St.* 23(4): 345–55

Merseth K 1991 The early history of case-based instruction: Insights for teacher education today. *J. Teach. Educ.* 42(4): 243–49

Merseth K 1992 Cases for decision-making in teacher education. In: Shulman J H (ed.) 1992 *Case Methods in Teacher Education*. Teachers College Press, New York

Richert A E 1991 Case methods and teacher education: Using cases to teach teacher reflection. In: Tabachnick B R, Zeichner K M (eds.) 1991 *Issues and Practices in Inquiry-Oriented Teacher Education*. Falmer, London

Shulman J H, Colbert J A(eds.) 1987 *The Mentor Teacher Casebook*. ERIC Clearinghouse on Educational Management, University of Oregon, Eugene, Oregon

Shulman J H, Colbert J A, Kemper D, Dmytriw L 1990 Case writing as a site for collaboration. *Teach. Educ. Q.* 17(1): 63–78

Shulman L S 1986 Those who understand: Knowledge growth in teaching. *Educ. Researcher* 15(2): 4–14

Shulman L S 1992 Toward a pedagogy of cases. In: Shulman J H (ed.) 1992 *Case Methods in Teacher Education*.

Teachers College Press, New York

Silberstein M, Tamir P 1991 The expert case study model: An alternative approach to the development of teacher education modules. *J. Educ. Teach.* 17(2): 165–79

Silverman R, Welty W M, Lyon S 1992 *Case Studies for Teacher Problem Solving*. McGraw-Hill, New York

Sperle D H 1933 *The Case Method Technique in Professional Training*. Teachers College, Columbia University, New York

Stevens R 1983 *Law School: Legal Education in America fro the 1850s to the 1980s*. University of North Carolina Press, Chapel Hill, North Carolina

Sykes G, Bird T 1992 Teacher education and the case idea. In: Grant G (ed.) 1992 *Review of Research in Education, 18*. American Educational Research Association, Washington, DC

Thorne B 1973 Professional education in law. In: Hughes E C, Thorne B, DeBaggis A M, Gurin A, Williams D, 1973 *Education for the Professions of Medicine, Law, Theology, and Social Welfare*. McGraw-Hill, New York

Van Woerden W M 1988 Interaction as a key factor in the teaching-learning process of the case-method. In: Klein H E 1988 *Case Method Research and Case Method Application: An International Forum*. World Association for Case Method Research and Case Method Application, Needham, Massachusetts

Student Teaching and Field Experiences

G. Morine-Dershimer and K. Leighfield

Classroom experience is critical to the development of skill as a teacher, but there are disagreements about the appropriate weight to be given to practical experience relative to theoretical principles of teaching and learning. This entry provides a general introduction to the problem, reports on variations in teacher education programs in the provision of classroom experience, reviews research-based criticisms of the effects of such experience and the roles played by those who supervise the experience, identifies recommendations for change, and indicates some directions for future research.

1. Introduction

The general purpose of early field experiences and student teaching is to provide prospective teachers with classroom practice in a supportive environment, enabling them gradually to assume the range of responsibilities associated with full-time professional practice. Early field experiences typically begin with structured observations in classrooms, and may proceed to tutoring individual pupils and eventually include teaching isolated lessons to small groups of

pupils. Placement within a classroom is usually of short duration (a few hours distributed over a few weeks). Student teaching typically involves more extended practice (e.g., full days for 1–6 weeks) in one setting and often culminates with the prospective teacher planning and teaching all lessons for several days.

Student teaching and field experiences are the major vehicles for providing practical experience in any teacher education program. This is the program area, therefore, where the traditional conflict between theory and practice is felt most strongly. Leavitt (1991) notes that program content is one of eight worldwide issues in teacher education, and says that the problem derives from the fact that teacher education must answer to both the university and the school. University pressures are for more subject-matter content and more research-based pedagogical content. School system pressures are for more practice-oriented courses and more practical experience in classrooms. The amount of time devoted to student teaching and field experiences in any teacher education program is determined by which of these two pressures is stronger in the given setting. There is clear variation among programs, both between and within countries.

2. Types of Variation

Student teaching and field experiences vary in the point in the program where initial placement occurs, the number and variety of placements for a given student, the duration of individual placements, the total hours in all placements, the frequency of supervision by college/university personnel, and the degree of responsibility for evaluation accorded the cooperating teacher in whose classroom a student teacher is placed.

2.1 Variation Between Countries

An examination of three universities in three different countries reveals some of the variations that exist.

University of Western Ontario, Canada. The one-year post-baccalaureate teacher preparation program in operation at the University of Western Ontario involves most students in a total of ten weeks of practice teaching in three periods (October, February, and April) at three different sites. The placements are split to provide practice in a student's two areas of certification. Supervision and evaluation are shared between university supervisors and teachers (called "associate teachers" here, and "clinical instructors" or "cooperating teachers" in other programs) in classrooms where students are placed. However, the university supervisor may see a student teacher only once in the entire year, as each supervises many students who are dispersed over a wide geographical area. Associate teachers therefore shoulder the bulk of the supervisory responsibility.

Yokohama National University, Japan. The undergraduate teacher preparation program at Yokohama National University in Japan engages students in education courses during the last two years of college. An early field experience in the junior year is one week long, involving two days of observation and two days of lectures and discussions led by university professors, school administrators, and school teachers. Student teaching in the senior year lasts four weeks. Students observe their own class and other classes at the same level. They gradually increase the number of lessons taught and must teach from one to three full days of classes. In the final week they prepare one particularly detailed lesson plan, and a college professor observes that lesson. All other evaluation is done by the "mentor" teacher (called "cooperating teacher" elsewhere in this entry). All mentor teachers are selected by their school principals.

University of New Hampshire, United States. The five-year preparation program at the University of New Hampshire, in the United States, culminates in a year-long teaching apprenticeship. Cooperating teachers noted for their excellence are carefully chosen by the university and provided with additional training. Some participate as instructors in weekly student seminars. Student teachers are placed in schools in clusters, contributing to a close working relationship between the university and the schools. University supervisors often offer informal consultation and assistance to the cluster schools.

2.2 Variation within Countries

Ben-Peretz and Rumney (1991) describe sharp variations between universities and teacher education colleges in Israel. Universities prepare teachers for junior and senior high schools, stress theoretical subjects, and require only 14–40 total practicum hours during a two-year preparation program. Teacher education colleges, in contrast, require 80–150 hours of observation and teaching for prospective elementary and secondary teachers in each of three to four years of study.

The Research About Teacher Education (RATE) study in the United States reports on data from 90 teacher education institutions organized by level of degree offered (bachelor's, master's, or doctorate) (AACTE 1990). Time spent in student teaching and field experiences across these institutions varies from 0 to 400 hours, with secondary education candidates spending less time than elementary or special education candidates. The average times for all students are 75–100 hours in early field experiences and 12 weeks at 40 hours per week in student teaching. Half the institutions surveyed have no stated requirements to become an associate/cooperating teacher and rewards for this contribution are minimal, averaging US$113 per teacher. College supervisors are primarily graduate students and assistant professors. Cooperating teachers surveyed consider student teachers well-prepared, but college supervisors are less enthusiastic. Similar differences are noted in perceptions of teacher education faculty at institutions offering only bachelor's degrees (i.e., they think student teachers are well-prepared) compared to those offering doctorates (i.e., they think student teachers are less well-prepared).

3. Criticisms of Approaches

Criticisms of typical approaches to student teaching and field experiences abound, with most reflecting the tension between theory and practice.

3.1 Criticism of what is Learned

Joyce (1988) cites studies indicating that the general effects of field experience are poorer attitudes toward pupils, suspicion of innovative teaching methods, and negative views of educational research and theory. Furthermore, teacher candidates tend to imitate the attitudes and behavior of their cooperating teachers, resulting in a limitation of the variety of teaching strategies practiced, rather than development of an expanded repertoire.

Feiman-Nemser and Buchmann (1987) concur that

experience is not necessarily the best proving ground for prospective teachers. They argue that effective student teaching must differentiate between appropriate and inappropriate lessons of experience, and they present case studies which demonstrate that experiential learning can be misdirected despite the best intentions. They note that cooperating teachers may not take their responsibilities as teacher educators seriously and should have special preparation for this new role.

Kagan (1992) reports on a review of 40 qualitative learning-to-teach studies, and identifies five components of professional growth associated with classroom experiences of prospective and beginning teachers. These are: increased awareness of their knowledge and beliefs about pupils and classrooms; reconstruction of idealized and inaccurate images of pupils and of self-as-teacher; shifts in attention from self, to instructional issues, and then to pupil learning; development of standardized routines for management and instruction; and development of problem-solving skills that are multidimensional and context-specific. Kagan concludes that student teaching would be more beneficial if teacher education programs presented more information about classroom routines, encouraged students to explore images of self-as-teacher, provided for extended interaction with pupils in early field experiences, and placed students with cooperating teachers holding beliefs different from their own, to promote cognitive dissonance.

Grossman and Richert (1988) have observed and interviewed student teachers to identify their perceptions of the comparative contributions of coursework and fieldwork to their knowledge of teaching. They report that fieldwork is cited as a source of knowledge slightly more frequently than coursework. Coursework is seen as providing conceptions of subject matter, theoretical principles of learning/instruction/management, and "images of the possible." Fieldwork is seen as providing practical survival skills, knowledge of pupil interests and difficulties with subject matter, and additional learning about specific topics within the subject content.

Other studies have used questionnaires to examine prospective teachers' feelings of readiness to teach successfully, termed "self-efficacy." Canadian students responding just prior to each of three student teaching experiences, distributed over time, exhibited high ratings of self-efficacy in October, before any actual classroom experience, and these positive feelings grew progressively stronger with each classroom placement (Housego 1990). The greatest changes over time were in perceptions of skills in classroom management and instructional planning. Areas of least change included questioning skills, motivating individual learners, and assessment of pupil learning.

A study conducted in the United States (Weinstein 1990) has examined feelings of self-efficacy associated with early field experiences. Weinstein asked students to predict their own effectiveness as student teachers and first-year teachers compared to other students in their teacher education program. Prior to their field experience the large majority of students saw themselves as well above average in ability to teach. After the field experience their optimism declined somewhat, but an "unrealistic optimism" (p. 280) still remained. A matter of particular concern to Weinstein was that interpersonal relations were regarded as a more important reason for personal success than the academic dimensions of teaching.

Weinstein recommended use of alternative materials in college classes (videotaped teaching sessions and written cases depicting critical classroom events) to promote more astute observation and thoughtful reflection on teaching and learning. She also supported the use of field placements that prompt students to re-examine their beliefs by confronting them with the differing beliefs of a successful cooperating teacher.

Another United States study (Ellwein et al. 1990) used semistructured interviews during which student teachers were asked to describe one successful and one unsuccessful lesson and explain why the lessons were successful or unsuccessful. Successful lessons were defined on the bases of pupil interest and participation, effective implementation (challenge to pupils, relevance to pupil experience), and use of unique materials or activities. Unsuccessful lessons were defined on the bases of pupil reactions (lack of interest or engagement) and problems with behavior management, lesson organization, or clarity of goals. A large majority of the student teachers showed a willingness to be self-critical, acknowledging their own contribution to lack of success in the unsuccessful lessons; yet they were not sophisticated in their use of self-criticism, probably because their teaching situations only nominally encouraged such activity.

3.2 Criticism of Supervisory Roles

Questions about what is learned during student teaching and field experiences lead inevitably to questions about the roles of college supervisors and cooperating teachers in providing feedback to prospective teachers. Christensen (1988) analyzed feedback of university supervisors in the United States and compared patterns to results of a similar study of cooperating teachers' feedback. Discussions between student teachers and college supervisors involved predominantly evaluative comments about the lesson from both participants. This contrasts with patterns observed in discussions between student teachers and cooperating teachers, which predominantly involved simple reviews of events and student teaching activities. Cooperating teachers were described as dominant and directive in the interviews, telling student teachers what to do and how to do it, apparently assuming that what works in their own situation will be appropriate for other situations, regardless of classroom context. College supervisors, on the other hand, encouraged student teachers to think, and modeled problem-solving and decision-making approaches to classroom problems.

Ben-Peretz and Rumney (1991) report other differences between cooperating teachers and university supervisors in Israel. In discussions between student teachers and cooperating teachers, evaluative comments by cooperating teachers dominated the conversation. Suggestions about alternative procedures were rare or nonexistent, as were any references to educational theory by cooperating teachers. University supervisors' meetings with the same student teachers dealt with alternative instructional methods and educational theory. Student teachers were less passive in meetings with university supervisors.

Koerner (1992) provides some possible explanations for the conferencing behavior of cooperating teachers, based on journals they kept on their experiences in these discussions. These teachers reported that student teachers interrupted classroom instruction, displaced the teacher from the central role in the classroom, disrupted and replaced carefully established classroom routines, and shifted the cooperating teachers' time and energy from instruction of their pupils to instruction of the student teacher. A more positive effect is the breaking of teachers' isolation by providing the opportunity to discuss classroom experiences with another adult. However, teachers felt that the "university ideas" student teachers brought with them were not relevant to their classrooms.

4. Some Trends and Recommendations for Change

Several types of change are proposed to address the problems associated with student teaching and field experiences revealed by research.

4.1 Changes in Duration of Experience

Despite the clear controversy about the value of what is typically learned in student teaching and field experiences, trends in many nations involve some increase in the time that prospective teachers spend in field settings. In some cases this increase is mandated by governmental policy changes. For example, a 1991 regulation by the Ministry of Education in Japan increased the minimum student teaching time required for secondary education candidates from two weeks to four. In 1986, the National Council for the Accreditation of Teacher Education (NCATE), a nongovernmental agency in the United States, issued new guidelines which mandated an increase in student teaching time from eight to ten weeks.

4.2 Changes in Field Settings

Teacher educators, who are aware that quality is at least as important as quantity, have initiated more collaborative arrangements between schools and universities for the provision of field experiences. The Holmes Group, an association of 100 research universities in the United States with teacher preparation programs, has issued a call for the establishment of "professional development schools" (PDSs) (Holmes Group 1990). A PDS is envisioned as an institution formed by a partnership between schools and universities that can provide clinical experiences for the development of prospective teachers, as well as opportunities for the continued professional development of experienced teachers. A PDS is also a site for research and development activities conducted collaboratively by teachers and university professors. A number of universities have collaborated with schools to establish such sites, but the movement is still young and it is too early to tell how successful this innovation will be.

This movement is not limited to the United States. The University of Western Ontario in Canada is working to establish Teacher Education Centres (TECs). Each TEC would involve a small number of schools with several student teachers in each school. All supervision of student teachers would be handled by the associate (cooperating) teachers; university faculty would provide liaison between the school and university. The TECs are expected to provide sites for observation, demonstration, practice, research, and evaluation.

In Spain, a 1986 order published in the *Generalitat Official Bulletin* discussed the possibility of setting up Classified Practice Centers (CPCS), and noted the conditions that would make such schools qualified to take on prospective teachers as trainees. These CPCS are experimental and limited in number. Professors at the University of Barcelona have developed a model to guide the provision of practical experience for students in their program (Fernández et al. 1988). This model specifies essential qualifications for the teacher-tutor (cooperating teacher), including both theoretical and practical knowledge of teaching and training in group dynamics. The student teaching experience is envisioned as a period of cooperative problem-solving, involving the student teacher, the teacher-tutor, and the college tutor (supervisor) working together. The planners acknowledge two major difficulties in implementing this model. First, there are problems inherent in negotiating permission for the college tutor to enter the school classroom to observe teaching practice. Second, the attitudes of some college lecturers interfere with the establishment of cooperative relationships with schools.

4.3 Changes in Preparation for Classroom Experience

Most criticisms of traditional approaches to student teaching and field experiences, as well as many recommendations for improvement in the effectiveness of these experiences, focus directly on the field setting. In the continuing debate about theory versus practice, advocates of learning from practice propose increases in the length of time spent in the field setting and the enhancement of the role and status of the cooperating teacher. Advocates of learning from theory propose changes in the nature of overall professional development in the field setting by involving experienced teachers in classroom-based research and development.

Some alternative recommendations for improvement focus on changes in preparatory experiences provided in college courses. These recommendations stem from assumptions that locate the problem not in the field setting, but in the preconceptions that prospective teachers bring to their teacher education programs. Advocates of these alternative approaches discuss the need for conceptual change, requiring prospective teachers to confront their limited conceptions of teaching and learning and replace them with more inclusive concepts.

Describing these preconceptions as "world images," Wubbels (1992) suggests that the logical or technical language of teacher education courses is not suited to change. A more appropriate language is that of imagery or metaphor. Exploration of alternative metaphors for the teacher (e.g., entertainer, ship's captain, lion tamer) may encourage prospective teachers to consider new perspectives and raise questions about the types of classroom they want to create. The use of aphorisms, like "when the teacher stops teaching, the students start learning" might help teachers realize that effective teaching involves more than clear explanations. Wubbels also recommends the use of visual images through photographs and video, and encouraging students to choose between illusory alternatives, for example authoritarian and *laissez-faire* classroom settings.

4.4 Changes in Type of Field Experience

In response to increases in rates of poverty, crime, substance abuse, teenage pregnancy, and homelessness, United States schools serving pupils who are "at risk" have begun to provide a broader array of services to children and their families (Levin 1994). Most projects are operated in collaboration with community service agencies, and many are funded by private foundation grants. They provide comprehensive services, such as assistance with problems including medical, dental, mental health, social welfare, housing, employment, and parent and adult education. Services may be provided at the school site, or case managers working at the school may help families access services provided in the community.

School-linked comprehensive services programs require cooperation and teamwork by the education and human service professionals who work with children and their families. Such collaborative roles are new to teachers as well as to service professionals, and they require preparation in order to perform effectively.

A limited number of teacher preparation institutions in the United States have begun to establish early field experiences that place prospective teachers in schools or community agencies where school-linked comprehensive services are being provided to children and families. In these settings, preservice teachers work in teams with human service professionals, and learn directly about the types of non-academic problems affecting the lives of at-risk pupils. Seminars running concurrently with the field placements afford the opportunity for students to analyze and interpret their experiences. In some cases these seminars provide "interprofessional preparation" in that they are attended by students preparing to work in various human service professions, as well as by prospective teachers. These seminars encourage the development of cooperative problem solving techniques that are needed by teachers working in schools which operate under a comprehensive services model.

These types of early field experiences are relatively new for prospective teachers, and where they are available they tend to be voluntary rather than required. While this appears to be a promising approach to preparing teachers to work in inner-city schools, evaluation of program outcomes is very limited to date.

5. Future Research

Most research in the area has tended to focus on perceptions and beliefs of prospective teachers, cooperating teachers, and college supervisors, with limited attention to observations of interaction among them. Furthermore, minimal reference has been made to academic or social outcomes for the pupils instructed by student teachers. These types of data should be included in future studies, particularly in those that evaluate new approaches such as professional development schools and interprofessional preparation of teachers.

References

American Association of Colleges for Teacher Education 1990 RATE 4, Teaching Teachers: Facts and Figures. (Research About Teacher Education Project). AACTE, Washington, DC

Ben-Peretz M, Rumney S 1991 Professional thinking in guided practice. *Teaching and Teacher Education* 7 (5/6): 517–30

Christensen P A 1988 The nature of feedback student teachers receive in post-observation conferences with the university supervisor: A comparison with O'Neal's study of cooperating teacher feedback. *Teaching and Teacher Education* 4(3): 275–86

Ellwein M C, Graue M E, Comfort R E 1990 Talking about instruction: Student teachers' reflections on success and failure in the classroom. *J. Teach. Educ.* 41(5): 3–14

Feiman-Nemser S, Buchmann M 1987 When is student teaching teacher education? *Teaching and Teacher Education* 3(4): 255–73

Fernández M, González R, Subirats A 1988 The tutor's role in teaching practice in initial teacher training. *European Journal of Teacher Education* 11(2/3): 123–30

Grossman P L, Richert A E 1988 Unacknowledged growth: A re-examination of the effects of teacher education. *Teaching and Teacher Education* 4(1): 53–62

Holmes Group 1990 *Tomorrow's Schools: Principles for the Design of Professional Development Schools*. The Holmes Group, East Lansing, Michigan

Housego B E J 1990 Student teachers' feelings of preparedness to teach. *Can. J. Educ.* 15(1): 37–56

Joyce B R 1988 Training research and preservice teacher education: A reconsideration. *J. Teach. Educ.* 39(5): 32–36

Kagan D M 1992 Professional growth among preservice and beginning teachers. *Rev. Educ. Res.* 62: 129–79

Koerner M E 1992 The cooperating teacher: An ambivalent participant in student teaching. *J. Teach. Educ.* 43: 46–56

Leavitt H B 1991 Worldwide issues and problems in teacher education. *J. Teach. Educ.* 42(5): 323–31

Levin R A 1994 *Greater than the Sum: Professionals in a Comprehensive Services Model*. Monograph No. 17. ERIC Clearninghouse on Teacher Education, Washington DC

Weinstein C S 1990 Prospective elementary teachers' beliefs about teaching: Implications for teacher education. *Teaching and Teacher Education* 6(3): 279–90

Wubbels T 1992 Taking account of student teachers' preconceptions. *Teaching and Teacher Education* 8(2): 137–49

Further Reading

Calderhead J 1991 The nature and growth of knowledge in student teaching. *Teaching and Teacher Education* 7(5/6): 531–35

Griffin G 1986 Issues in student teaching: A review. In: Raths J, Katz L (eds.) 1986 *Advances in Teacher Education*, Vol. 2. Ablex Publishing, Norwood, New Jersey

Guyton E, McIntyre D J 1990 Student teaching and school experiences. In: Houston W R (ed.) 1990 *Handbook of Research on Teacher Education*. Macmillan, New York

Supervision in Teacher Education

J. M. Cooper

Supervision in teacher education programs occurs mainly during field experiences and, particularly, during student teaching. Supervision of teacher education students is conducted primarily by a college or university supervisor and a cooperating teacher, the teacher in whose classroom the teacher education student is working. This entry examines the purposes of supervision and the roles of these two major actors in the supervision process. It also identifies problems and issues related to the supervision of teacher education students, reviews major research findings and conceptual models for conducting supervision, and presents emergent trends and issues.

1. Purposes of Supervision

The major purpose of supervision is to help the teacher education student become a competent teacher. Through a variety of field experiences in elementary or secondary classrooms, including student teaching, teacher education students attempt to implement what they have learned in their teacher education courses as well as gaining practical experience in teaching and managing a classroom. Although teacher education students consistently describe their student teaching as the most valuable element in their preparation for teaching, many researchers criticize student teaching as being atheoretical, lacking a standard structure, and being overly dependent on an outmoded apprenticeship model. During student teaching both the cooperating teacher and the university supervisor supervise and guide the student teacher's development.

Unfortunately, the goals of supervision are too often not agreed upon, unarticulated, or lack congruence with the rest of the teacher education program. The student teaching experience, where most supervision occurs, seems to have two contrasting major conceptualizations, perhaps best articulated by Dewey (1904). One conception is that of apprenticeship, where university supervisors and cooperating teachers assist students in gaining techniques and feelings of self-confidence that will help them survive more comfortably within existing school situations, without questioning the status quo. A number of researchers conclude that this apprenticeship model predominates in teacher education. The other conception is more akin to a laboratory experience where the student teacher receives supervisory assistance in developing habits of personal inquiry and reflection about teaching and the contexts in which it occurs. In this conception, student teachers are taught and encouraged to consider a range of possibilities beyond the existing school situation.

Depending on which of these two conceptualizations is held by the university supervisor and cooperating teacher, their expectations for themselves and the student teacher will differ remarkably. One study that examined 122 cooperating teachers and 25 university supervisors (Cleary 1988) found that cooperating teachers exhibited significantly more conventional thinking than university supervisors and stifled student teachers' inclinations to function as agents of change. In other words, they were more inclined toward the apprenticeship model than the laboratory model.

2. The Role of Cooperating Teachers and University Supervisors

Both cooperating teachers and university supervisors are important to the success of the student teaching experience. However, as might be expected, they play somewhat different roles.

2.1 Cooperating Teachers

Cooperating teachers are expected to be exemplary practitioners of teaching so that student teachers can observe and emulate good practice. In addition, cooperating teachers' perceptions of their roles as supervisors include helping student teachers develop competence in classroom management, lesson planning, and lesson delivery (O'Neal 1983).

Grimmett and Ratzlaff (1986) compared studies from the United States and Canada regarding expectations about the role of cooperating teachers as held by student teachers, university supervisors, and cooperating teachers. In both countries, cooperating teachers were expected to hold conferences with their student teachers and to provide instruction on skills of presentation and classroom management. The same researchers found that cooperating teachers were generally unprepared for the task of student teaching supervision. Boothroyd (1979) found similar results in England.

Zimpher et al. (1980) reported that many cooperating teachers were not interested in observing student teachers. They perceived student teachers as aides who could help lessen their workload. Thus, being an effective classroom teacher does not ensure that an individual will be an effective cooperating teacher.

Evidence from a number of studies suggests that training cooperating teachers for their roles is effective and is a policy supported by the teachers themselves. For example, in a study at a Canadian university, Twa (1984) found that, as a result of training, cooperating teachers valued their clinical-supervision expertise, improved their supervisory skills, felt more comfortable as supervisors, and were more eager to accept student teachers. By common assent, the skills that are needed by cooperating teachers include the ability to observe well, to provide constructive criticism to guide student teachers in their practices, and to provide encouragement and support.

What are the incentives for teachers to become cooperating teachers? Guyton (1987) found that teachers wanted to work with student teachers because they believed student teaching to be important, felt they had something to offer and had a professional responsibility to prepare new teachers, thought they would gain new ideas, believed they would enhance their pupils' performance by having two adults working in the classroom, thought they would enjoy sharing ideas and working with another adult and thereby revitalize themselves as teachers. Others have identified money, recognition of the cooperating teacher's role, special status, and the opportunity to take tuition-free university courses as incentives. Although money may be a motivation for some, cooperating teachers are poorly compensated by universities for their services. Honoraria for supervising a student teacher in the United States in the early 1990s typically ranged from US\$25 to US\$500, with the average approximately US\$100 or less.

Although the processes for the selection of cooperating teachers vary, colleges and universities typically have little control over the settings in which they place student teachers and in the selection and qualifications of the cooperating teachers in those settings. Schools, rather than universities, assign cooperating teachers and often make the assignments on the basis of who volunteers, whose turn it is, or for other political or administrative reasons. As a consequence, quality control is often a problem.

2.2 University Supervisors

In many ways the role of the university supervisor overlaps that of the cooperating teacher. Both are expected to observe, provide feedback, and encourage and support the student teacher's development as a professional. Although some studies show that university supervisors have as much or more influence with student teachers in comparison with cooperating teachers (Boschee et al. 1978), many more studies indicate that cooperating teachers have the major influence on student teachers (Koehler 1984, Yee 1969, Zimpher et al. 1980). In a survey of 500 randomly selected student teachers in England and Wales, for example, almost 75 percent reported that their cooperating teachers were of greater help than their university supervisors (Yates 1982). This finding is hardly surprising, since the cooperating teacher works in close contact with the student teacher for 300 hours or more during the student teaching practice or practicum, while the university supervisor is unlikely to spend more than 10 to 20 hours with the student teacher.

At many universities the supervision of student teachers has low status and is often assigned to junior faculty, graduate students, or tenured faculty members who are not regarded as having a useful function in other areas. Student teachers and cooperating teachers generally perceive few differences in the supervisory effectiveness of university faculty and graduate students, and between those who had had significant teaching experiences and those who had not (Lamb and Montague 1982).

Supervisors typically visit student teachers once a

week or every other week, spending 30–90 minutes with each student. Full-time university supervisors may be assigned as few as 12, or as many as 36 student teachers. Heavy assignments are common and often reduce the time a supervisor can spend working intensively with the student teacher. Consequently, many university supervisors are unable to provide substantial observation, data collection, and feedback for the student teacher. Their role is often reduced to one of liaison and moral support (Koehler 1984).

3. Problems of Supervision

Communication among the members of the student teaching triad (student teacher, cooperating teacher, and university supervisor) is often reported to be a problem. Areas of difficulty include uncertain role expectations, university–school communications, and interpersonal interactions. Yee (1969) observed that groups consisting of three members are inherently unstable since there is a strong tendency for two members of such groups to bond together and isolate the third member. Since the cooperating teacher and the student teacher work together for long periods of time each day, whereas the university supervisor is only periodically a member of the group, the supervisor is most likely to become the isolated member of the group. Stones and Morris (1972) also reported considerable research evidence of conflicting values among student teachers, cooperating teachers, and supervisors.

Inadequate training and lack of time also create difficulties for cooperating teachers and supervisors. One study in the United States reported that most schools, colleges, and departments of education have fewer than 20 percent of their cooperating teachers trained in supervision (Johnson and Yates 1982), even though, as mentioned, considerable evidence exists that shows the training of cooperating teachers for their roles to be effective and that cooperating teachers support the idea of special training for themselves. Lack of time and funding seem to be the major impediments in supporting these training programs.

Evaluation of student teachers is another problem area. Gatekeeping, or determining entrance to the profession, is one of the major functions of the student teaching experience. In most programs, assigning the final grades for student teaching is the responsibility of the university supervisor, but the cooperating teacher often has a say. The possibility of disagreements occurring is quite real, particularly if poor communication has existed.

For the university supervisor, having the dual responsibilities of helper and evaluator often creates problems in developing a close, trusting relationship with the student teacher. The evaluation function of supervision may lead some student teachers to attempt to project a positive image of themselves to the supervisor, rather than admitting a weakness or problem area. Differences in opinions between the supervisor and the cooperating teacher regarding the performance of the student teacher is another potential area of tension.

4. Models of Supervision

Several models of supervision have been proposed. These differ in terms of the theoretical underpinnings and the extent of their application.

4.1 Contrasting Approaches

Most of the models of supervision have been developed with, and applied to, the supervision of experienced teachers. These include clinical supervision (Goldhammer 1969, Cogan 1973), counseling supervision (Mosher and Purpel 1972), and developmental supervision (Glickman 1985). Little research exists about supervisory practice in teacher education based on the application of these models. In a review of research on university supervision of student teaching, Zimpher (1987) identified three contrasting supervisory approaches that have been studied in preservice teacher education: Siedentop's use of an applied behavioral approach; Gitlin's model of horizontal supervision; and Copeland's studies of directive and nondirective supervision.

Siedentop's research program was designed to develop a model of supervision based on behavior analysis that could impact student teacher behavior. The model enables supervisors and others: (a) to agree on a set of teacher behaviors or competencies; (b) to design a reliable and valid system for observing the behaviors; (c) to observe significant student teacher behavior change as a result of the observation/feedback intervention; and (d) to ensure continuation of the behavior change through regular feedback and follow-up.

In Gitlin's horizontal supervision, supervisors and student teachers together established and defined goals. Lessons focusing on the goals were observed and comparisons were made of the student teachers' practice compared with the intent. Case studies of this model in action demonstrated that its use led to more reflective and self-evaluative prospective teachers, who viewed teaching holistically rather than as a set of technical skills.

Copeland conducted a series of studies comparing directive supervision (offering the teacher immediate and useful advice for overcoming instructional problems) and nondirective supervision (asking questions to solicit the teacher's opinions and suggestions, reflecting the teacher's ideas, and offering information only as the teacher requested it). Copeland discovered that student teachers preferred the directive approach early in the internship but progressed toward a preference for the nondirective approach by the end of the teaching experience. He concluded that the university supervisor and the cooperating teacher might well initiate conferences and feedback more directly early in student teaching, but move toward a more nondirective approach as the student teacher gained the ability to be more self-analytic toward teaching.

Copeland's findings are consistent with Glickman's (1985) theory of developmental supervision, in which the supervisor uses a directive, collaborative, or nondirective orientation to supervision depending on the teacher's ability and willingness to assume responsibility for improvement. Copeland's results may help to explain how such contrasting approaches as Siedentop's and Gitlin's can each be viewed as effective. That is, they show, depending on the student teacher's maturity and ability to be self-analytical, that both highly prescriptive and reflective approaches to supervision can work. This suggests, however, that the supervisor and cooperating teacher need to assess the student teacher's capabilities and to modify their supervisory approaches as the student teacher develops greater reflective abilities.

4.2 Theoretical Paradigms

May and Zimpher (1986) examined the theoretical underpinnings of different approaches to supervision and concluded that most seem to be rooted in three major world views or paradigms: (a) positivism; (b) phenomenology; (c) critical theory. The positivist's perspective in supervisory practice shows itself as behavioristic, technical, or rationalistic. A supervisor with a positivistic view would tend to diagnose problems during observation, prescribe effective courses of action with reinforcement, and evaluate to see if the objectives were mastered. Siedentop's model of supervision reflects a positivistic perspective.

The phenomenological view of supervisory practice reflects humanistic concerns. Supervisors who work from this perspective care about student teachers' values, their views of the classroom, and their feelings. Such supervisors see their role as helping student teachers develop their own teaching styles, based on their own values and attitudes. Knowledge and teaching are highly individualized and personal. The supervisor's role is more that of counselor than trainer and ranges in style from nondirective to collaborative.

The critical theorist supervisor wants to help to create a better world and addresses the question of "what ought to be." Values of justice, equality, and happiness guide the critical theorist supervisor's work with student teachers. Such supervisors work to help prospective teachers assume a greater role in shaping educational environments that exemplify these core values. They believe that teaching is a reflective, moral, and ethical action. Gitlin's model of horizontal supervision exemplifies a critical theory perspective.

May and Zimpher (1986) concluded that supervisory practice in teacher education programs has been eclectic, rather than rooted in any one theoretical position. Moreover, the array of labels and models of supervision has often confused and masked the underlying belief systems that guided particular supervisory approaches.

Sergiovanni (1982) urged the development of a theory of supervisory practice concerned with three major questions, each of which can be addressed in the three paradigms of thinking described above: What is going on in this classroom? What ought to be going on? And what do these events, activities, and aspirations mean? He goes on to say:

> Establishing what is requires the development of accurate descriptions and explanations of the real world of teaching. Establishing what ought to be requires that one give attention to stated values and attempt to discover those more implicit in teacher and teaching. Establishing what events mean requires a closer study of classroom life and its events in pursuit of understanding. Establishing meaning requires that supervisors cultivate the art of interpretation (p. 68).

Effective supervisors, then, need to be able to answer each of these questions regardless of which of the three paradigms the supervisor embraces.

4.3 Alternative Approaches

Dissatisfaction with traditional types of student teaching supervision has resulted in various proposals to remedy the problems. At one extreme are proposals to abolish the role of the university supervisor, based on empirical evidence that cooperating teachers are more influential and university supervisors add little of value. Such proposals would simply shift issues of evaluation to the cooperating teacher and enhance the apprenticeship model of learning to teach, a model that has many critics.

A more promising alternative is that proposed by Emans (1983), who reviewed the professional literature on student teaching and supervisory practices and concluded that the roles of university supervisor and cooperating teacher should be redesigned. He proposed changing the functions of university supervisors so that they would have less direct responsibility for the supervision of student teachers and would instead work with school personnel, particularly cooperating teachers, on curriculum development and the improvement of teaching. The university supervisors would become the major agent for bringing about change in schools and in teacher education. They would continue to provide the liaison teacher education between university and schools and would still be available for troubleshooting. Their main influence, however, would be on the cooperating teacher and, indirectly, on the school environment.

Emans likened this redefined supervisor's role to that of the agricultural agent in colleges of agriculture, who works to see that the latest research and best practice are accessible to the farmer (i.e., the teacher). Under this model, the cooperating teacher would receive much greater training and assume more responsibility for the supervision of the student teacher, but would receive ongoing support from the university supervisor. Barriers to the implementation of this proposal might include (a) school personnel, who might feel threatened by having university faculty members so intimately involved in their operations; (b) university faculty members, who might be reluctant to engage in school change; and (c) universities, which might be reluctant to commit resources to the improvement of schools.

5. *Emergent Trends and Issues*

Although dissatisfaction with the dominant supervisory patterns in teacher education permeates the professional literature, these patterns have proven remarkably resilient. The existence of the student teaching triad, the dominant influence of the cooperating teacher on the student teacher, the relatively infrequent visits by the university supervisor, inadequate training for cooperating teachers, the atheoretical nature of the student teaching experience, and reliance on the apprenticeship model seem to be in little danger of extinction. Many examples exist of instances where the negative effects of these patterns have been counteracted through training or new models. However, on the whole, they have not succeeded in replacing these long-standing dominant patterns.

Why is this the case? There are several plausible explanations. First, teacher education is an underfunded enterprise in higher education: training and adequately compensating cooperating teachers, and lowering student teacher to university supervisor ratios, require money that all too often is unavailable. Second, the supervision of student teachers is a low-status activity for university faculty members who consequently expend little time and effort on the endeavor. Reward structures within higher education would have to be changed for faculty members to spend more time in schools. Third, the atheoretical nature of student teaching and its dependence on the apprenticeship model is often a reflection of the teacher education program. Where teacher education programs have coherence or a thematic orientation (e.g., teacher as a reflective practitioner), the student teaching experience is more likely to exhibit that theme and provide a common understanding of the experiences and outcomes expected of student teaching.

One emerging trend in the United States that has the the potential to address some of the problems related to supervision in teacher education is the concept of "professional development schools." These schools would be the educational analogue of a teaching hospital, where best practice, induction for new professionals, and inquiry into educational problems and issues pertinent to that school would all exist. Creating

such sites where university faculty, teacher trainees, and teachers and administrators in the school work together to achieve these three goals would go a long way toward providing a context in which research on learning, teaching, and supervision could flourish.

See also: Structure of Teacher Education Programs; Governance of Teacher Education

References

Boothroyd W 1979 Teaching practice supervision: A research report. *British Journal of Teacher Education* 5(3): 243–50

Boschee F, Prescott D R, Hein D D 1978 Do cooperating teachers influence the educational philosophy of student teachers? *J. Teach. Educ.* 29(2): 57–61

Cleary M J 1988 Thinking styles of supervisors and implications for student teaching. *Teacher Educator* 24(1): 16–23

Cogan M L 1973 *Clinical Supervision.* Houghton Mifflin, Boston, Massachusetts

Dewey J 1904 The relation of theory to practice in education. In: McMurray C A (ed.) 1904 *The Third Yearbook of the National Society for the Scientific Study of Education.* Public School Publishing, Bloomington, Illinois

Emans R 1983 Implementing the knowledge base: Redesigning the function of cooperating teachers and college supervisors. *J. Teach. Educ.* 34(3): 14–18

Glickman C D 1985 *Supervision of Instruction, a Developmental Approach.* Allyn and Bacon, Newton, Massachusetts

Goldhammer R 1969 *Clinical Supervision: Special Methods for the Supervision of Teachers.* Holt, Rinehart and Winston, New York

Grimmett P P, Ratzlaff H C 1986 Expectations for the cooperating teacher role. *J. Teach. Educ.* 37(6): 41–50

Guyton E 1987 Working with student teachers: Incentives, problems, and advantages. *The Professional Educator* 10(1): 21–28

Johnson J, Yates J 1982 A national survey of student teaching programs. ERIC Document Reproduction Service No. ED 232 963, Washington, DC

Koehler V R 1984 The instructional supervision of student teachers. ERIC Document Reproduction Service No. ED 271 430, Washington, DC

Lamb C E, Montague E J 1982 Variables pertaining to the perceived effectiveness of university student teaching supervisors. ERIC Document Reproduction Service No. ED 212 613, Washington, DC

May W T, Zimpher N L 1986 An examination of three theoretical perspectives on supervision: Perceptions of preservice field supervision. *Journal of Curriculum and Supervision* 1(2): 83–99

Mosher R L, Purpel D E 1972 *Supervision: The Reluctant Profession.* Houghton Mifflin, Boston, Massachusetts

O'Neal S 1983 An analysis of student teaching cooperating teacher conferences as related to the self-concept, flexibility, and teaching concerns of each participant. ERIC Document Reproduction Service No. ED 234 030, Washington, DC

Sergiovanni T J 1982 Toward a theory of supervisory practice: Integrating scientific, clinical, and artistic views. In:

Sergiovanni T J (ed.) 1982 *Supervision of Teaching*. Association for Supervision and Curriculum Development, Alexandria, Virginia

Stones E, Morris S 1972 *Teaching Practice: Problems and Perspectives: A Reappraisal of the Practical Element in Teaching Preparation*. Methuen, London

Twa J 1984 Teacher associate perceptions of the effectiveness of the clinical supervision workshop. ERIC Document Reproduction Service No. ED 269 855, Washington, DC

Yates J W 1982 Student teaching: Results of a recent survey. *Educ. Res.* 24: 212–15

Yee A 1969 Do cooperating teachers influence the attitudes of student teachers? *J. Educ. Psychol.* 60(4): 327–32

Zimpher N 1987 Current trends in research on university supervision of student teaching. In: Haberman M, Backus J M (eds.) 1987 *Advances in Teacher Education*, Vol. 3. Ablex, Norwood, New Jersey

Zimpher N L, deVoss G, Nott D 1980 A closer look at university student teacher supervision. *J. Teach. Educ.* 31(4): 11–15

Further Reading

Boydell D 1986 Issues in teaching practice supervision research: A review of the literature. *Teaching and Teacher Education* 2(2): 115–25

Goodman J 1988 University culture and the problem of reforming field experiences in teacher education. *J. Teach. Educ.* 39(5): 45–51

Stones E 1987 Teaching practice supervision: Bridge between theory and practice. *European Journal of Teacher Education* 10(1): 67–79

Turney C et al. 1982 *The Practicum in Teacher Education: Research, Practice, and Supervision*. Sydney University Press, Sydney

Laboratory and Professional Development Schools

J. A. Stallings, S. L. Knight, and D. L. Wiseman

There has been interest in the professional development of teachers since the establishment of the first teacher preparation institutions in seventeenth-century Europe. In the United States, schools participating with universities and colleges in providing opportunities for professional development in teacher education have been given various labels over time: model schools, practice schools, training schools, clinical schools, laboratory schools, portal schools, professional practice schools, and professional development schools. Although notable differences in the organization, scope, and emphasis of these schools have emerged, all share the common feature of providing professional development experiences for preservice and/or inservice teachers in school settings. In particular, the themes of demonstration and practice have consistently dominated the thinking of teacher educators.

This entry describes and compares the evolution, functions, and issues associated with two of the predominant professional practice school movements in the twentieth century: laboratory schools and professional development schools. It begins by tracing the history of the laboratory school movement, which started at the turn of the century. The difficulties with laboratory schools that ultimately led to their decline in the mid-twentieth century are then summarized. Next, the development of professional development schools is described and examples of successful schools are provided. Differences between the laboratory school movement and the later professional development school movement are highlighted. The entry concludes with a discussion of the status of and prospects for the professional development school movement.

1. Laboratory Schools

In the late 1800s, during a period of concern about the purposes and functions of United States public schools, the Committee of Ten convened school and university educators to discuss ways of improving education (Clark 1988). In this atmosphere of school reform, John Dewey established his laboratory school at the University of Chicago in 1896. Influenced by the scientific movement in education, Dewey envisioned a teaching laboratory to test pedagogical theory and to add to the knowledge base about teaching (Dewey 1896). Located on or near a college campus, such laboratory schools were designed to focus on research activities directed at improving teaching and the experiences of students studying to be teachers (Stallings and Kowalski 1990). Dewey's laboratory school, primarily experimental in nature, was followed by a series of experimental schools at Teachers College, Columbia University, the University of Missouri, and at Ohio State University (Turney 1987). These schools served as models for laboratory schools, which were developed in conjunction with numerous teacher preparation programs across the country.

By 1926 the concept of the laboratory school had been adopted as a standard by the American Association of Colleges of Teacher Education. Despite the fact that Dewey had not intended his school to become heavily involved in actual teacher training, the primary functions of most of the subsequent laboratory schools soon involved demonstration and practice. Dewey's primary focus on experimentation was expanded to encompass six common functions: the education of children; the development of innovative practices; preparation of new teachers; research; inservice training; and dissemination of innovations. During the 1930s laboratory schools refined the techniques of preservice participation in teaching activities and inservice demonstration programs (Turney 1987).

While many laboratory schools implemented high-quality education for future teachers and school-children, the focus on experimentation and research waned as they responded to the need to prepare greater numbers of teachers (Stallings and Kowalski 1990, Turney 1987). In addition, although the expanded functions of laboratory schools could be considered complementary, limited resources required prioritization of activities. Since faculty incentives, resources, and teaching loads were seldom modified in laboratory schools to encourage research, other functions soon took precedence. As a result, laboratory schools ultimately contributed very little to the development of theory in teacher education (Kowalski et al. 1988). Without the element of research, laboratory schools were hard-pressed to convince detractors that their functions could not be performed better in public school settings at considerably less expense (Turney 1987).

By the 1950s, serious criticism of laboratory schools emerged. The increase in numbers of teacher education students required the use of public schools unconnected with the campus for practical experiences. Critics of laboratory schools cited their atypical student populations and isolated contexts as major weaknesses for teacher preparation, especially when compared with experience opportunities in public schools. In general, pressures created by lack of funds, excessive teacher preparation demands leading to over-use of facilities, lack of autonomy and clearly delineated purpose, frequent turnover of teachers and administrators, inadequate representation of diverse students and societal cultures, and problems associated with financing the collaborative arrangements led to the decline of laboratory schools at the end of the 1960s (Turney 1987). In the United States the number of laboratory schools dwindled from a peak of 212 schools in the mid-1960s to 95 in 1988 (Stallings and Kowalski 1990).

2. Portal Schools

The decline of laboratory schools did not reduce the desirability of collaborative arrangements between schools and teacher preparation institutions to improve the quality of education for all participants. The laboratory schools of the first half of the twentieth century encouraged the evolution of several other types of school–university partnerships for teacher education. These included model schools, practice schools, training schools, and demonstration schools. While the names varied and goals were stated with a slightly different focus, they were similar to the laboratory schools in many respects.

One derivative of school–university partnerships, portal schools, evolved out of the reform efforts of the 1970s which focused on improving the quality of education at all levels. Portal schools were to serve as "a point of entry for promising new curricula and practices" (Chambers and Olmstead 1971 p. 2). Proponents of portal schools hoped that the public school system, which was presumed to suffer from a lack of relevance to the real world as experienced by school-age and teacher education students, would be transformed through the collaborative efforts of university- and school-based educators. The unified educational focus was designed to build the self-renewal process into the school system. A recurrent theme centered on the teacher as an agent of change and required the type of teacher education experiences in schools that would prepare teachers for this role (Joyce 1972).

Portal schools remedied many of the weaknesses attributed to laboratory schools. Since they were regular schools, their pupils were representative of the pupils that teachers would likely encounter. While the specific characteristics of portal schools differed in response to specific contexts, all exhibited organizational frameworks that included an advisory council made up of representatives from several groups (e.g., teachers, unions, preservice teachers, administration, community, university); firm support from the top administrators in universities and schools; adequate planning time; and formal agreements specifying governance, purposes, and plans (Lutonsky 1972).

Portal schools were not without problems, however. As with laboratory schools, research and evaluation were neglected. As a consequence, little evidence existed to support claims of effectiveness. This lack of evidence may possibly have contributed to funding problems and their subsequent decline; portal systems were virtually nonexistent by the 1980s (Stallings and Kowalski 1990).

3. Professional Development Schools

In the United States public clamor for reform, similar to that of the 1970s, reemerged in the 1980s. Falling test scores of public school students, increased school dropout rates, lack of attention to issues associated with rapidly growing classroom diversity, questions about teacher quality and preparedness, and a generally low regard for education encouraged a proliferation of reports calling for improvement of schools and teachers (see, e.g., Sikula 1990). Much of the criticism of teacher preparation targeted the perception that universities were failing to involve future teachers in relevant experiences that would prepare them for today's classrooms. The need for improvement both of the preparation of teachers and of educational experiences across the whole range of compulsory schooling from kindergarten through Grade 12 (referred to as the "K–12 curriculum") resulted in renewed interest in the formation of partnerships between universities and public schools to improve the nature of schooling at all levels (Carnegie Task Force on Teaching as a Profession 1986, Holmes Group 1986).

The Carnegie Task Force and the Holmes Group introduced the concept of school–university partnerships as a solution to educational ills. In reports published separately, the two groups encouraged creation of school–university partnerships to focus on the development of high-quality educational experiences for preservice and inservice teachers, administrators, and public school students. The Carnegie Task Force proposed clinical schools located in outstanding public schools to link faculties in elementary and secondary schools, colleges of education, and colleges of arts and sciences in order to provide the best possible learning environment for both inservice and preservice teacher education. As conceptualized, clinical schools are very similar to teaching hospitals. Students of teaching undergo a two-year course of graduate study with the first year spent in coursework and internship and the second year in supervised residency in the clinical school.

Another term used to describe a concept similar to the clinical school is professional practice school. Professional practice schools are public schools that are structured, staffed, and supported to attain three goals: student achievement, teacher induction, and support of research directed at the continuous improvement of educational practice. Professional practice schools, like clinical schools, involve the collaboration of universities and public schools and perform functions similar to those of medical teaching hospitals (Levine 1990). Both envision teacher education as a graduate-level function, incorporate a residency under the supervision of outstanding practicing teachers, and support research as a function of the school.

The Holmes Group added a new institutional label, the professional development school (PDS), to the list of school–university partnerships. Their study, *Tomorrow's Schools* (1986), much like the Carnegie report, described a PDS as a site where practicing teachers and administrators are brought together with university faculty in partnerships that improve teaching and learning on the part of their respective students and thus unite theory and practice. Although this study initially supported the concept of teacher education as a graduate-level function, the model was later modified to be used at undergraduate level as well. According to the 1986 report by the Holmes Group, a PDS can be defined as

a regular elementary, middle, or high school that works in partnership with a university to develop and demonstrate:

- fine learning programs for diverse students, and
- practical, thought-provoking preparation for novice teachers, and
- new understandings and professional responsibilities for experienced educators, and
- research projects that add to all educators' knowledge about how to make schools more productive.

Although the Holmes Group popularized the term and concept of a PDS, an earlier description of school reform by the American Federation of Teachers (AFT) (Levine 1990) also set out many of the ideas associated with PDSs. However, the AFT publication was not widely distributed among teacher educators (Gehrke 1991); as a result, this document did not have the impact it might have had.

Even earlier, based on his studies of the nature and quality of experiences of teachers and students in public schools, Goodlad (1984) advocated the notion of educating teachers in situations where innovative practices and research would be combined with the preparation and continuing education of expert practitioners. He supported the Holmes Group and Carnegie concepts, but felt that their goals could best be accomplished at undergraduate level (Goodlad 1991). Clinical settings for teacher education would serve as places where prospective teachers learned the best in research and practice. Consequently, in 1986 he established 12 pilot sites throughout the United States that were charged with establishing school–university partnerships to focus on teacher education (Sirotnik and Goodlad 1988, Goodlad 1994).

3.1 Organization and Activities

While few models exist that suggest what a PDS should look like (Winitzky et al. 1992), there are common features in descriptions of PDSs. Establishment of a PDS usually involves school and university constituencies who establish a common vision, set goals, determine ways to achieve the goals, and agree on research and evaluation to accompany the partnership efforts (Stallings et al. 1995). Often the formation process is initiated by universities, although there are several examples in which schools or school districts have taken the first steps. Most of the partnerships exhibit shared school–university governance structures, information dissemination processes, problem-solving mechanisms, and external funding sources (Clark 1991).

Activities associated with PDS are wide-ranging in diversity and scope. The focus of a PDS may be the K–12 curriculum, preservice teacher education, inservice teacher education, or a combination of all three. A PDS provides the vehicle for schools and universities to restructure inservice and/or preservice education, K–12 curriculum, school and university course delivery, and research and evaluation of curricular projects or PDS activities as a whole.

A most recent thrust of PDSs includes community comprehensive integrated services and interdisciplinary training programs for educators, health and human resources, and community professionals (Corrigan 1994). As part of the effort to bring about an interdisciplinary approach to the professional preparation of future teachers, schools serve as the center of training efforts for education, health and human services professionals. This movement recognizes the importance of including the family as well as professionals who work with children and families. Such programs tend to be family-centered, neighborhood-based, multidisciplinary, and make an effort to consider the cultural diversity that is represented in schools and neighborhoods (Rodriquez 1990).

It is unusual for a PDS to be concerned equally with all aspects of restructuring (Clark 1991). For example, a very involved PDS may target inservice teacher development, preservice internships, and action research, while another PDS may focus solely on one aspect of restructuring, such as the joint development and delivery of preservice methods courses. An examination of directories of school–university partnerships (Wilbur et al. 1987, 1988) revealed the existence of PDSs that reflect two different overall emphases: professional development for inservice teachers, and professional development for preservice and induction teachers. Professional development schools that focus primarily on providing first-year teachers with supervision by outstanding senior teachers in an inner-city setting are often referred to as "induction schools" (Wise et al. 1987).

3.2 Recurrent Themes

Despite the diversity of activities and focuses, several recurrent themes can be identified in the current PDS movement. First, considerable emphasis is given to the necessity for dual restructuring. A basic assumption of the PDS is that both schools and universities will change the way they function. In fact, as Gehrke (1991) wrote, "We are looking at changing no less than the personality of an occupation and the character of two well-established institutions" (p. 48).

A second theme involves the nature of the relationship between schools and universities. Past partnerships have been plagued by perceptions of inequality in the status of teachers and professors and by tensions created by the knowledge orientation of professors and the practice orientation of teachers. An assumption underlying the PDS movement is that the foundation of the partnership is based on parity, with each entity working together to satisfy mutual self interests (Callan 1990).

Finally while PDSs reflect a diversity of emphases and activities, they all share common goals. Each exemplifies a partnership that attempts to unite teachers, administrators, and college faculties in restructuring the preparation and induction of teachers into the teaching profession, improving the teachers'

workplace, and increasing the quality of education for students.

3.3 Research

Research and evaluation should focus on partnership processes as careful consideration of reforms in specific contexts will most likely reveal predominate issues and promising patterns (Cuban 1990). Research and evaluation activities can provide a context in which successful components and patterns in school–university collaboration are identified. As PDSs continue to evolve and mature, the initial research being conducted in or about these settings has been primarily descriptive and qualitative. Descriptions of topics related to partnerships include the creation of a professional development school (Darling-Hammond 1994, Murray 1993), role changes of school and university faculty (Harris 1991, Lampert 1992, Stoddart 1993), school–university programmatic changes (Teitel 1992, Whitford 1994), and challenges associated with collaborative activities (Dixon and Ishler 1992, Knight, Wiseman and Smith 1992, Rushcamp and Roehler 1992, Winitzky, Stoddart and O'Keefe 1992, Zimpher 1990). National research efforts are beginning to emerge in the area of school-linked comprehensive services. In the fall of 1994, a national conference was sponsored by Office of Educational Research Initiatives, American Educational Research Association, and American Association of Classroom Teacher Educators to determine a research agenda related to this expanded view of collaborative models (Stallings 1994).

While research initiatives are still sparse, the nature of collaborative inquiry in professional development schools is evolving from initial efforts and being defined in ways that may be characterized differently than research conducted in traditional university settings. The need to monitor change and collect information that can be immediately applied to PDS classrooms has led researchers to question basic fundamental beliefs about educational inquiry, methodological procedures, and the role of formal research (Cochran-Smith and Lytle 1993, Richardson 1994). Issues of ownership and control in partnership research are part of the change that occurs when collaborative efforts between schools and universities evolve (Hunkins, Wiseman and Williams in press). Research designed for PDS encourages teachers and university faculty in collaborative ventures to collect and analyze data related to classrooms and schools that have an immediate impact on practice (Noffke 1992).

4. Comparison of Laboratory Schools and Professional Development Schools

There are several differences between former conceptualizations and implementations of school–university partnerships and the PDS concept. One of the criticisms of the laboratory school movement was that schools located on university campuses were isolated and did not reflect the reality of the classroom. The cost of developing and maintaining the schools proved to be greater than the results justified. Current PDS models, rather than building new institutions, develop existing partnerships with schools. By choosing sites carefully or by using multiple sites, they can obtain a representative mix of students from different cultures and socioeconomic levels and avoid the impression of elitism sometimes inferred from the university-based laboratory schools. This configuration also allows the necessary energy and resources to focus on the tasks of communication, consensus building, curriculum development, reallocation of funds, and role development, all of which are crucial to restructuring efforts (Winitzky et al. 1992).

In many of the earlier partnerships, development was mandated or came from sources other than the school-based professionals. Often, university-based professionals or superintendents and deans decided on the nature of activities and structures to be implemented in the school (Winitzky et al. 1992). The current PDS movement emphasizes the development of school-based teachers who are capable of restructuring schools to meet the challenges of the twenty-first century and changing traditional teaching roles. However, teacher leadership in this area requires concurrent changes in teacher preparation and in the teacher workplace. For this reason, the notion of dual restructuring of the places where teachers work and where they are educated has become a predominant theme. Furthermore, collaboration of teachers, administrators, and teacher educators will be needed to facilitate concurrent, consistent restructuring of both institutions. PDS structures encourage links between faculty and administrators who support changes shaped by practitioners who have relevant roles in restructuring (Rushcamp and Roehler 1992).

Simultaneous restructuring of schools and universities is beginning to change the way that teachers are prepared: however, the systemic impact remains to be seen. Major professional organizations are encouraging research that documents the effects upon school and university faculties. The difficulties encountered by laboratory schools in the past (particularly the excessive demands that were placed on schools, resulting often in conflicting activities, lack of prioritization of functions, lack of research and evaluation, staffing difficulties, and funding problems) may also plague the current PDS movement.

Another characteristic that is more pronounced than in past partnerships involves the networks and support systems associated with the PDS movement (Gehrke 1991). Local, state, and national networks that combine the energy and efforts of several PDS efforts have existed for several years and continue to increase the number of schools and activities associated with the partnerships. In conjunction with PDS goals and network establishment, efforts are also being made to bring a wider variety of participants into the collaborative process. Business, government, industry, social agencies, and parental groups are participating in the collaborative efforts. In the United States funding agencies such as the Ford Foundation, Southwestern Bell, the Danforth Foundation, and E24on have made grants to school–university partnerships (Center for Educational Renewal 1992). In addition, faculty from arts and sciences departments have participated in the partnerships in several instances. For five years, the Carnegie-funded "Project 30," developed collaboratively by a dean of education and a dean of liberal arts, has directly encouraged arts and science involvement with education in school reform efforts.

The support rendered by networks, however, provides little assurance that professional development schools will fare any better than the portal schools of the past. Portal schools were given considerable support from the Council of Great City Schools, the Teacher Corps, and the American Federation of Teachers in the 1970s. Teacher Corps even provided some federal funding for Portal School network activities (Stallings and Kowalski 1990). In spite of this support, the movement lasted only a few years. Perhaps the expanded support base for PDS, consisting of business, government, private foundation, and university representatives, will make a difference.

5. *The Future of Professional Development Schools*

The current genre of professional development schools has been emerging since the late 1980s and tests of longevity, generalizability, or empirical scrutiny are just beginning to emerge. The movement has been described as the beginning of a paradigm shift in teacher preparation which fundamentally alters the power and role relationships in teacher education (Darling-Hammond 1993, Zeichner 1992). However, the future success or failure of the effort is still difficult to predict. Nevertheless, nearly a century of history of similar models provides some indication of the likely strengths and weaknesses of PDSs. Several themes emerge from the scrutiny of past attempts.

Support for school–university collaboration in teacher education has remained consistent. While periods of intense school reform coincide with the rise and decline of these movements (e.g., the laboratory school appeared during the reform movement at the turn of the century and lost status during the reform movement of the 1950s), interest in and the need for PDSs have not waned. In general, the PDS provides opportunities for demonstration, experimentation, and practice that are necessary for preservice and inservice teachers. The success or failure of particular models revolves around issues of context, organization, priorities, focus, and funding which are linked to exigencies of time and place.

In some measure, the inability to address and resolve issues of context, prioritization, organization, and focus is rooted in the controversy about research and evaluation which has emerged with every variation of the model. In general, research and evaluation, although invariably cited as goals of new school–university models, have been abandoned or relegated to a position of low priority. Several reasons for this neglect have been suggested, including the tension created between universities and schools by the research and practice paradox (Goodlad 1991), the inhibiting interference of research in the dimensions of demonstration and practice, or the inability of partnerships to obtain enough resources, time, and staff to engage in research as well as teacher preparation. Even the laboratory school movement, which Dewey initiated expressly for research and experimentation about teaching, was unsuccessful in maintaining a research focus.

Consequently, a century of the existence of PDSs has contributed little to teaching theory, despite the seeming opportunity such schools provide to address questions rooted in actual practice. While this may not be a problem for schools focused primarily on issues of practice, colleges of education reside in academic communities devoted to the production of knowledge. If research is not a priority of professional development schools, why involve colleges of education? The most recent genre of PDS, with its emphasis on dual restructuring, will necessarily confront the research issue when it focuses on the renewal of colleges or schools of education.

While the lack of research has been problematic, since it affects the commitment and involvement of universities, the absence of systematic evaluation of the processes and products of various models has been critical. Decisions and choices about school sites, goals, activities, and organizational features must be made by the initiators of professional development schools with little knowledge of the impact of different variations on teachers, students, or institutions. The vagaries of funding, often linked to the failure of innovations, may actually be attributed to a reluctance to invest in entities whose effects are unknown.

See also: Laboratory Experiences in Teacher Education

References

Callan P M 1990 *An Interview with John Goodlad*. Education Commission of the States, Denver, Colorado

Carnegie Task Force on Teaching as a Profession 1986 *A Nation Prepared: Teachers for the 21st Century*. Carnegie Forum on Education and the Economy, New York

Center for Educational Renewal 1992 *Center Correspondent*. Center for Educational Renewal, University of Washington, Seattle, Washington

Chambers M, Olmstead B 1971 Teacher corps and portal schools. *Portal Schools* 1(1): 2–8

Clark R W 1988 School–university relationships: An interpretive review. In: Sirotnik K A, Goodlad J I (eds.) 1988 *School–university Partnerships in Action: Concepts, Cases, and Concerns*. Teachers College Press, New York

Clark R W 1991 School–university partnerships in action. *Metropolitan Universities: An International Forum* 2(1): 33–41

Cochran-Smith M, Lytle S 1993 *Inside Outside: Teacher Research and Knowledge*. Teachers College Press, New York

Corrigan D 1994 Future directions of partnerships in education: Schools, universities and human service systems. In: O'Hair M J, Odel S J 1994 *Partnerships in Education*. Harcourt Brace, Fort Worth, Texas

Cuban L 1990 Reforming again, again, and again. *Educ. Researcher* 19(1): 3–13

Darling-Hammond L 1994 *Professional Development Schools: Schools for Developing a Profession*. Teachers College Press, New York

Darling-Hammond L 1993 Reframing the school reform agenda: Developing capacity for school transformation. *Phi Del. Kap.* 74(10): 753–61

Dixon P N, Ishler R E 1992 Professional Development Schools: Stages in collaboration. *J. Teach. Educ.* 43(1): 28–34

Dewey J 1896 The university school. *University Record* 5: 417–42

Gehrke N 1991 Simultaneous improvement of schooling and the education of teachers: Creating a collaborative consciousness. *Metropolitan Universities: An International Forum* 2(1): 43–50

Goodlad J I 1984 *A Place called School*. New York: McGraw-Hill, New York

Goodlad J I 1994 *Educational Renewal*. Jossey Bass, San Francisco, California

Harris R C 1991 Educational renewal: Not by remote control—Work of a university professor in a partner school. *Metropolitan Universities* 2(1): 61–71

Holmes Group 1986 *Tomorrow's Teachers*. Holmes Group, East Lansing, Michigan, Missouri

Holmes Group 1990 *Tomorrow's Schools: Principals for the Design of Professional Development Schools*. Holmes Group, East Lansing, Michigan, Missouri

Hunkins F, Wiseman D L, Williams R in press The partner school: Centers of inquiry. In: Osguthorpe R, Cutler B (eds.) in press *School-University Partnerships*. Ablex, Norward, New Jersey

Joyce B 1972 The teacher-innovator: A program for preparing educators. In: Joyce B, Weil M (eds.) 1972 *Perspectives for Reform in Teacher Education*. Prentice-Hall, Englewood Cliffs, New Jersey

Knight S L, Wiseman D L, Smith C W 1992 The reflectivity-activity dilemma in school-university partnerships. *J. Teach. Educ.* 43(3): 269–77

Kowalski T, Glover J, Krug D 1988 The role of the laboratory school in providing a research base for teacher education. *Contemp. Educ.* 60(1): 19–22

Lampert M 1992 Looking at restructuring from within a restructured role. *Phi. Del. Kap.* 72(9): 670–74

Levine M (ed.) 1990 *Professional Practice Schools: Building a Model*, Vol. 2. American Federation of Teachers, Washington, DC (ERIC Document Reproduction Service

No. ED324299)

Lutonsky L 1972 Toward a definition of portal schools. *Portal Schools* 1(3): 1–19

Murray F 1993 "All or none" criteria for professional development schools. *Educ. Policy* 7(1): 61–73

Noffke S E 1992 Action research and the work of teachers. In: Clift R, Evertson C M (eds.) 1992 *Focal Points: Qualitative Inquiries into Teaching and Teacher Education.* Teacher Education Monograph No. 12, pp. 1–21. ERIC Clearinghouse on Teacher Education, Washington, DC

Richardson V 1994 Conducting research on practice. *Educ. Researcher* 23(5): 5–10

Rodriquez G 1990 Preparation and professional development programs for early childhood educators: Emerging needs for the next decade. Paper presented at the Conference on Preparation and Professional Development Programs for Early Childhood Educators: Emerging Needs for the Next Decade, New York

Rushcamp S, Roehler L R 1992 Characteristics supporting change in a professional development school. *J. Teach. Educ.* 43(1): 19–27

Sikula J 1990 National commission reports of the 1980s. In: Houston W R (ed.) 1990 *Handbook of Research on Teacher Education* Macmillan Inc., New York

Sirotnik K, Goodlad J 1988 *School–university Partnerships in Action: Concepts, Cases, and Concerns* Teachers College Press, New York

Stallings J A 1994 Personal communication, May 5

Stallings J A, Kowalski T 1990 Research on professional development schools. In: Houston W R (ed.) 1990 *Handbook of Research on Teacher Education* Macmillan, Inc., New York

Stallings J A, Wiseman D L, Knight S K 1995 Professional development schools: A new generation of school–university partnerships. In: Petrie H G 1995 *Professionalization, Partnership and Power: Building*

Professional Development Schools. State University of New York Press, New York

Stoddart T 1993 The professional development school: Building bridges between cultures. In: Altback P G, Petrie H G, Shujaa M J, Weiss L (eds.) 1993 *Professional Development Schools.* Corwin Press, Newbury Park, California

Teitel L 1992 The impact of professional development school partnerships on the preparation of teachers. *Teaching Education* 4(2): 77–86

Turney C 1987 Laboratory schools. In: Dunkin M (ed.) 1987 *International Encyclopedia of Teaching and Teacher Education.* Pergamon, Press, Oxford

Whitford B L 1994 Permission, persistence, and resistance: Linking high school restructuring with teacher education reform. In: Darling-Hammond L (ed.) 1994 *Professional Development Schools: Schools for Developing a Profession.* Teachers College Press, New York

Wilbur F, Lambert L, Young M 1987 *National Directory of Schools Partnerships: Current Models and Practices.* American Association for Higher Education, Washington, DC

Wilbur F, Lambert L, Young M 1988 *School–college Partnerships: A Look at the Major National Models.* National Association of Secondary School Principals, Reston, Virginia

Winitzky N, Stoddart T, O'Keefe P 1992 Great expectations: Emergent professional development schools. *J. Teach. Educ.* 43(1): 3–18

Wise A et al. 1987 *Effective Teacher Selection: From Recruitment to Retention* (R-3462-NIE/CSTP). Rand Corporation, Santa Monica, California

Zeichner K 1992 Rethinking the practicum in the professional development school partnership. *J. Teach. Educ.* 43(4): 296–307

Zimpher N L 1990 Creating professional development school sites. *Theory Pract.* 29(1): 42–49

SECTION III
Continuing Teacher Education

Introduction

L. W. Anderson

As was mentioned in the first section of this volume, teachers pass through a fairly predictable set of stages as they progress from novice to expert (Berliner). As a consequence, inservice teacher education, regardless of its quality, can produce at best a very good novice teacher. The movement from "advance beginner" through "competence" and "proficiency" and ultimately to the development of "expertise" depends on the experiences that teachers have *after* leaving their initial teacher preparation.

Once they have completed their preparation program and have achieved licensure, teachers can look forward to moving through several phases as they make the transition from student to teacher. The major phases are recruitment, employment, induction, and socialization. The movement from one phase to the next can be aided by inservice or onservice educational opportunities or inhibited by the lack thereof.

The entries in this section address all of these topics. Since the major differences among them pertain to the *purpose* for the activity (recruitment, employment, induction, and socialization) and the *form* the activity takes (inservice, onservice), this introduction includes two major subsections: purpose and form.

1. Purpose

Before teachers can teach, they must be recruited and employed. As Bolam points out, the importance of recruitment depends on the nature of the educational system in a particular country. More centralized systems operate within the framework of a national unit plan. Within these plans, recruitment is unnecessary. In order to be employed, teachers must submit their qualifications for teaching and indicate their desire to teach to some national body (e.g., a ministry of education). Once a teacher is approved, he or she is assigned to a particular school based on the needs and requests of local education authorities (LEAs).

In more decentralized systems, in contrast, LEAs have much more authority in recruiting and employing teachers. They typically develop job descriptions and advertise. They then select their teachers from a pool of qualified applicants. In either system, whether a teacher is employed depends not only on the qualifications of the teachers but the needs and social context of the particular school (Watson and Hatton).

Once teachers are employed, it is important that they are helped to make successful transitions from their previous position (e.g., student) or job (e.g., teacher at another school) to their new one. The process is referred to as induction. As defined by Bolam, induction is the process of support and training for a successful first year of teaching. The term "first year" may apply either to the first year of teaching in general or the first year of teaching in a new school.

What do "first year" teachers say they need? They need some time away from regular teaching responsibilities in order to acclimatize to their new jobs. They need school-based support, most often in the form of mentors. They need planned, systematic school-based activities. These activities include discussions, observations, and periodic feedback. They need planned, systematic out-of-school or external activities. Such activities are usually associated with new ideas and possibilities. Finally, these teachers need the explicit and active support of their administrators.

It is not surprising that these are the components of effective teacher induction programs. Of these components, teachers are most receptive to opportunities to meet with other new teachers and the provision of extra time to plan, think, and reflect on their teaching.

Once teachers are employed and inducted, they need to be socialized. Socialization is the "process of change by which [they] become members of the teaching profession and then take on progressively more mature roles, usually of higher status, within the profession" (Lacey). In many respects, socialization is the "glue" that holds teachers together. Socialization permits teachers to gloss over variations and disagreements and to focus on those issues and concerns that teachers share as members of the teaching profession. In fact, without proper socialization, the existence of the teaching profession is problematic if not impossible.

On the one hand, then, socialization is necessary. But, it may be a necessary evil. There are two problems associated with socialization. First, socialization errs on the side of the institution rather than the individual. That is, teachers may feel a conflict between their own needs and desires and those of the school and/or school district in which they are employed. For first year teachers, part of this conflict stems from their transition from students to teachers. College students are idealistic and somewhat radical. When they become teachers, they need to become more realistic and practical (Lacey).

Second, and related to the first, socialization favors the status quo. As the term implies, socialization is based on the current social structure, a structure in which tradition is important. As a consequence, socialization often makes innovation and change quite difficult (Lacey).

2. Form

The two major forms in which activities are provided to practicing teachers are inservice and onservice. They differ primarily in the location at which the activities are provided and the availability of the activities to teachers. Onservice activities are offered at the school site or a nearby site such as a community education center (Gardner). In contrast, inservice activities typically occur away from the school site (Eraut). Inservice activities are scheduled and periodic (e.g., short courses, workshops), while onservice activities are available to teachers on an ongoing basis (e.g., teacher centers, peer observation, opportunities for consultation). Both share a common purpose, however; namely, to help teachers "improve their

professional knowledge, skills, and attitudes in order that they can educate children more effectively" (Eraut).

Regardless of whether continuing teacher education is inservice or onservice, substantial support is needed. Eraut identifies three areas in which such support is important: (a) support for the change process in general; (b) training of administrators and trainers; and (c) direct training of teachers. The provision of this support is dependent on time and money.

Time is important for two reasons. First, change takes time. Second, teachers need time to engage in professional development activities. Eraut criticizes much inservice teacher education on the basis of its "insufficient length and breadth."

Cost factors also must be considered. Teacher centers require materials and staff. Inservice activities are often conducted by outside consultants who often need to be paid. If teachers are relieved from teaching for a day or two each term to observe colleagues, substitute teachers must be paid. If they are relieved from teaching one or more classes to engage in peer coaching, additional teachers will need to be employed.

Conclusion

The entries in this section all deal with the education of teachers after they have completed an initial teacher education program. Unlike initial teacher education, which is carefully planned and regulated, continuing teacher education tends to be rather haphazard both in planning and regulation. Furthermore, the costs of initial teacher education tend to be much larger than those for continuing teacher education.

Nonetheless, continuing teacher education holds the key to teacher growth and development as well as long-term, sustained improvement of schools. All of the authors of the entries in this section suggest ways in which continuing teacher education can be improved for the betterment of all.

Teacher Placement and School Staffing

A. J. Watson and N. G. Hatton

Teacher placement refers to the activity of locating a teacher in a particular school within an educational system. School staffing refers to broader issues involved in managing teacher placement. Staffing must not only enable teachers to go where they are needed, but must also provide the conditions and support necessary to keep them there long enough to be effective. Thus, while placement focuses on the individual

teacher, staffing focuses on the administrative policies and practices of a school or, more frequently, a system.

Both placement and staffing have a bearing on the quality and equality of educational provision. While the issues related to placement and staffing are complex, demanding, and problematic in all countries, research in the area is seriously lacking. As a consequence, this entry relies primarily on general descriptions of current practices and alternatives. It is divided into three major sections: (a) methods of teacher placement in schools; (b) problems of staffing related to those methods; and (c) concerns with staffing for effective teaching.

1. Methods of Placement

Two staffing questions preliminary to the actual placement of teachers must be answered. First, how many teachers should be allocated to a particular school? Second, what kinds of teachers should they be?

1.1 Number and Kinds of Teachers for a School

The determination of the number of teachers for a school (the teacher–pupil ratio) is inevitably a decision of the funding body for the school. This statement holds true even in highly decentralized systems such as that of Switzerland where the cantons (under which local boards of education operate with a high level of independence) set a formula for funding based on the number of pupils and the kind of school. In systems with locally managed schools (e.g., "grant maintained" schools in the United Kingdom or, "schools of the future" in Victoria, Australia), the school council has scope to determine staff numbers, but in practice is limited by the funding formula.

With regard to the kinds of teachers employed (e.g., specialist staff), systems generally allow some local initiative within the limits of the staffing formula. In a centralized system such as that of Germany, while specialists may be allocated locally, there are also some central initiatives for which schools receive additional staff. One recent example in Brandenburg has been the central funding of support teachers to assist the integration of children with disabilities into the mainstream of education. While systems may vary in determining the *number* of teachers for a school and the *kinds* of teachers they will be, much greater differences between systems arise when the question is asked, which teacher should be employed in a particular school?

1.2 Teacher Placement

The methods adopted in different countries for the placement of teachers are as varied as the history, cultural attitudes, and political policies which guide their formulation. At some risk of oversimplification, they may be represented along a continuum from central to local control, although comparison of the extent of central or local authority must be qualified, *inter alia*, by the size of the system. To give some sense of how systems differ, approaches to teacher placement in five countries will be described: Germany, Canada, Switzerland, United Kingdom, and Australia.

The German education system, in which the state employs teachers and appoints them through the regional administration and district school inspectors, is centralized and hierarchical in nature. The local school or community has no authority in the placement of teachers. A similar pattern seems to operate across all German states, including the five in the former German Democratic Republic which have adopted the West German system since reunification (see Lehmann 1994). In Bavaria, for example, new graduates apply to the state, are ranked (with equal weight being given to academic marks and practicum results), and subsequently allocated to schools that need teachers.

In Canada, both central and local influences operate. Staffing is a responsibility of the district boards which have a range of from 2 to approximately 40 schools in their care. School principals notify the district office of their specific staffing needs and new teachers apply for a job to the district office. In most districts, the principal is included in the interviewing committee and is very influential in determining who is placed at his or her school.

In Switzerland, where local autonomy has deep historical and cultural roots and is very jealously guarded, there is no federal system of education. Rather, there are 26 cantonal systems, some of which serve a very small population; Uri, for example, has 35,000 inhabitants and about 7,000 children in schools (see Organisation for Economic Co-operation and Development 1991). For staffing and other educational management decisions most cantons delegate authority to elected community educational boards on which teachers have a consultative voice. Each board may have many schools under its care. A vacancy is advertised in the cantonal gazette and new teachers apply to the board, which appoints a subcommittee to select candidates on the basis of their academic and practicum reports, their performance in demonstration lessons, and their responses in an interview. Although there are likely to be teacher representatives on the subcommittee, they are usually not from the school with the vacancy. School staffing in Switzerland, while determined in the local community, is not as devolved as it has become in the United Kingdom.

In England and Wales (and in Scotland by 1997, as a result of the 1988 Education Reform Act), the school's governing body (which includes parents and teachers) has responsibility for all staffing. In practice the governors delegate the task of interviewing and choosing to a subcommittee which usually includes the principal.

In Australia, where education is a state responsibility, all administrative decisions including staffing were highly centralized until around 1990. Since then, however, as part of an attempt to improve the quality of schooling, a major devolution has taken place in most states. Different states now approach teacher placement in different ways, representing the entire range from central to local control. Queensland, for example, with some 550,000 children enrolled in primary and secondary schools, retains a highly centralized approach whereby all staff appointments are made by the Department of Education to which new teachers must apply for work. In contrast, New South Wales, with just over 1 million children, has devolved authority for the choice of the principal and senior staff to the local school council. However, a government suggestion that other staff be chosen locally met with stiff opposition from the teachers' union and parent groups.

2. Problems in School Staffing

Staffing problems related to three issues will be discussed in this section. They are: difficult-to-staff locations; fluctuations in teacher supply and demand; and staff turnover.

2.1 Difficult-to-staff Locations

Strong teacher preference to work in some geographical areas but not others creates locations that are difficult to staff. Such areas are likely to be found where there are distinct subpopulations, such as recent immigrants, indigenous people, the poor, or isolated rural dwellers. While it is likely that most countries with such groups of people have difficult-to-staff locations, little research has been conducted to identify and study their educational experiences. Nevertheless, some evidence for their existence does exist. In the United Kingdom, for instance, many overseas teachers have been recruited in recent years by private agencies for inner-London schools to teach immigrant and poor sectors of the population, because insufficient English graduates have been prepared to teach there. The difficult-to-staff places in the United States have been identified as central districts of big cities (Darling-Hammond 1990), while in Canada most occur in remote, rural locations (Canadian Education Association 1992). In Australia, such locations have been identified on the growing fringes of large urban populations and in distant rural areas (Hatton et al. 1991).

At a time when there is no teacher shortage, this phenomenon may not be noticed. However, the study of longitudinal teacher movements and of teacher locational preferences for short- and long-term appointments is likely to reveal a strong persistent movement away from schools in less favored areas to those in more favored ones (Hatton et al. 1991).

As a consequence, children in less favored areas are taught by the least experienced teachers who stay for the minimum time. Thus, systems with central staffing methods which grant priority of location to those with the longest service could seriously disadvantage children in difficult-to-staff locations unless there are

compensatory provisions to overcome this staffing pattern.

The problems of difficult-to-staff locations, however, become most acute when there is a teacher shortage and excessive teacher turnover. These issues will be considered in the next two sections.

2.2 Fluctuations in Teacher Supply and Demand

Sudden shifts between shortage and surplus have become a characteristic of the teacher labor market in much of the developed world. Economic upturn, bringing with it attractive opportunities for work in other industries, a rise in teacher resignations, and a surge in the school population can quickly turn today's surplus into tomorrow's shortage. The fluctuations of teacher supply and demand are a good test of staffing policy. A policy which works well during surplus may be less adequate when the cycle turns.

2.2.1 Teacher surplus. When there is a surplus of teachers a critical task for staffing policy is to enable schools to get the best teachers. The question is: does the policy allow selection of those teachers who are the strongest in terms of each particular school's needs? Local matching is desirable because teacher roles are increasingly complex and specific to a school and its existing staff, especially in countries with diverse populations. If the demands of the job are to be met, specialization and team work are called for. For this reason, a local selection process that includes input from existing staff and community members, as operates in "grant maintained" schools of the United Kingdom or in the "locally governed" schools of New Zealand, would be more likely to make a suitable match.

Whether selection is central or local, however, it is possible to use merit as its basis and so select the best in general terms. Some centralized staffing systems, such as Germany's, use academic work and practice teaching to select staff on merit. However, a country's staffing policy does not always allow this to happen. In New South Wales, until the 1990s, all new teachers were employed in the chronological order in which they applied for a job without any reference to quality. When it was recognized that private schools were engaging the best and most creative teachers, the employing authority began to interview final-year students and the best were given priority for appointment as "targeted graduates." Likewise, in British Columbia, Canada, which had a surplus of teachers in the mid-1990s, new graduates, even the best, were not given any priority but had to form a queue behind those teachers returning from leaves of absence and those who had acted as substitutes.

During a surplus of teachers, unless a mechanism is found to employ the most promising new graduates, the system will suffer an adverse long-term cohort effect of this loss of teaching talent as they find employment elsewhere. A time of surplus is an opportunity to strengthen the quality of the teaching service. The issue is whether the staffing method grants enough freedom to achieve this purpose.

2.2.2 Teacher shortage. A staffing policy receives its most critical test during a shortage. In this regard, two questions can be raised. Can schools be staffed without compromising professional standards? Can they be staffed without major disadvantage to schools in difficult-to-staff locations?

With respect to the compromise of standards, a widespread teacher shortage has the capacity to undermine the quality of education in several ways. Systems or schools, glad to hire any teachers, are not as discriminating about the quality of staff they engage. Class sizes may be increased, teachers may be required to teach outside their area of competence, and/or classes in some subjects may be cancelled. The effect that has greatest relevance to staffing policy is that unqualified or ill-qualified teachers may be hired.

A general shortage requires central system-wide measures. A local staffing method is clearly unable to take effective action. Furthermore, systems with centralized staffing are likely to be more quickly sensitive to the problem and better able to provide a coordinated response. The range of strategies used to boost teacher supply include attracting more students into teacher education courses by scholarships (which, however, may take too long), salary increases, recruitment from other states or systems, and enticing those who have left teaching for a time to return (e.g., mothers). None of these need imply a compromise of professional standards.

On the other hand, the lowering of entry requirements by providing short course certification or on-the-job training is very likely to compromise standards. As an example of an emergency entry response to teacher shortage in the United States, Darling-Hammond (1989) reported that 46 states offered "emergency teaching certificates" and 23 had created alternative modes of preparation which enable a recruit to begin teaching after a course of four to six weeks. If there is a knowledge base for teaching and a range of pedagogical skills that teachers should possess, such emergency certification cannot but lower professional standards. Darling-Hammond, with biting irony, comments (1989 p.3): "If one disallows any criterion of quality, qualified teachers are not difficult to find." This seems more likely to occur when local staffing is coupled with the absence of a strong centralized professional or union body to resist central government inclinations to implement solutions to urgent staffing problems at the cost of professional standards.

Shortage affects different systems in different ways. In systems where staffing decisions were devolved to the school's governing body, as in the United Kingdom, New Zealand, and Victoria, Australia, there is little scope for effective local action to address shortage without additional budget allowance or the acceptance of emergency certification. The problem is made worse if the school happens to be in an area difficult to staff. Devolution in these three countries happened to be introduced at a time of teacher surplus. There is some reason to fear that policy changes in the United Kingdom have mostly consolidated inequalities of educational opportunity (Halpin and Troyna 1994). A shortage of teachers will provide the acid test of devolved staffing methods.

In Switzerland, where teacher salaries are amongst the highest in the world and teaching conditions are very favorable (there are 17–25 students in a primary school class), teacher shortage does not provide a major problem. However, a report on Swiss education (Organisation for Economic Co-operation and Development 1991) points to staffing difficulties in some cantons resulting from obstacles to teacher mobility such as the lack of recognition of qualifications across cantons. In this example, a country faces difficulty in providing equal educational opportunity for all its citizens because it has no national policy of education (Gretler 1994).

With respect to the effect of shortage on difficult-to-staff schools, it is clear that shortage does not make its impact across a system in a random way. When there are fewer teachers than there are jobs, teacher preference for some locations above others means that the difficult-to-staff places are more likely to miss out. Indeed, it is a common phenomenon that even when there is an overall surplus of teachers in a system there can be a shortage of teachers for some locations or subject disciplines. Furthermore, simply preparing more teachers may not solve the problem. They may not be inclined to go to the places where they are most needed.

To remedy a selective shortage, it is first necessary to discover the basis of teacher preference for some locations and refusal of others and to devise strategies guided by that knowledge. The difficulty of getting new teachers to accept rural appointments in New South Wales led to a study which illustrates the issues involved (Watson et al. 1987). Final semester students who were surveyed indicated that the most important reasons for refusal to accept a rural appointment were fear of the unknown and isolation from family and friends. Another highly significant reason was an expectation that the climate and setting would be harsh and unfavorable. Measures proposed to address the problems included provision of more effective information about rural teaching, opportunity for more students to do their teacher education in a rural university or to do a rural practicum, and a range of incentives. It was concluded that financial incentives, though necessary for some locations, would neither address the principal cause of the reluctance to go, namely, fear of the unknown, nor help teachers with a city background prepare to be effective rural teachers.

2.2.3 Staff turnover. While a moderate level of staff turnover is desirable in a school to allow the introduction of new ideas and to permit unsuitable staff to move on, a high rate of staff turnover is quite harmful. The stagnation which may result from too little turnover is a common problem in times of teacher surplus, while the instability stemming from excessive turnover is most likely in times of shortage. A staffing system is put to a good test by its capacity to manage turnover.

With respect to maintaining a moderate level of turnover, many systems, even when staff are inefficient or unsuitable, have little scope to require a formal staff review and find it nearly impossible to terminate employment. For example, in Germany, where staff are civil servants (*Beamte*) with secure tenure and status controlled by federal law, and in Switzerland (Zürich), where they are elected by vote of the local community every six years and very rarely disapproved, it is virtually impossible to remove or move a teacher. The use of renewable contracts for senior leadership positions in New South Wales and for principals in British Columbia makes it easier to remove or replace staff, but employing all teachers on contract is difficult to implement, meeting with understandable opposition from teachers who see security of tenure as a compensation for salaries lower than those of their peers with the same length of training in other occupations. Limiting the period for which a teacher is allowed to stay in one school, say to 7 or 10 years, has proved difficult to implement. For example, it was recently tried in South Australia but discontinued. Requiring a 7- (or 10- year) appraisal and review before teachers can continue at a school may prove more workable.

Sustained high staff turnover has adverse effects upon schooling at several levels. It results in excessive transfer costs to the system, longer settling-in time for the school, greater difficulty maintaining staff cohesion, and weaker ties with the community. These factors are likely to have a harmful impact on student learning. Evidence suggests that there is a negative relationship of teacher turnover to pupil achievement (Walberg 1974).

These adverse effects are heightened by related factors. Most schools with high turnover are difficult to staff and the least experienced teachers, lowest in the staffing pecking order, are the most likely to be sent there, as experienced teachers transfer to more congenial schools. Furthermore, children in such places are more likely to be from disadvantaged backgrounds, requiring the most expert teaching. The result is a disproportionate number of beginning teachers being asked to teach some of the most demanding students but with few experienced teachers to advise them. While the greater stability induced by teacher surplus

may ameliorate this problem, it can be very harmful during a shortage.

3. Staffing for Good Teaching

There are two basic approaches to solving problems of staffing. One is the "deficit model," the other, the "challenge model" (Ankhara-Dove 1982). Each operates from a different set of assumptions and proposes a different set of practical recommendations. The deficit model assumes that teachers are reluctant to go to areas perceived to be difficult and uses compulsory minimum terms of appointment and incentives of various kinds to compensate for the deficits of the posting. In contrast, the challenge approach assumes teachers can gain intrinsic motivation from working in difficult locations if they adjust well, find the job satisfying, and can make career progress in that place. Although in practice a system is likely to use aspects of both models, the deficit approach is usually a response to some urgent need and often implies short-term expediency, while the challenge approach requires longer-term planning and emphasis upon qualitative implications of staffing decisions, not just the quantitative concern to fill all vacancies.

3.1 The Deficit Approach

The strengths and limitations of staffing incentives need to be understood. Higher salaries can increase the number of applicants seeking to enter teaching and the length of time teachers will stay in the profession (Murnane 1994). Incentives will also increase teacher willingness to accept and remain in difficult appointments; for example, priority of transfer for next appointment, lump sum on completion of term (Hatton et al. 1991). However, incentives are not very effective for improving the quality of teaching. Though the numbers of students interested in enrolling in teacher education have increased when there are teacher salary increases, the quality of applicants is likely to be unchanged (Murnane 1994). Furthermore, competitive aspects of incentives, which pit individual against individual, or, to a lesser extent, individual against a fixed standard, undermine commitment to the job. This, together with related evidence, led Firestone and Pennell (1993) to conclude that measures other than incentives be used to foster good teaching.

3.2 The Challenge Approach

While compulsory postings and incentives may in some measure be necessary for the difficult-to-staff locations, the need for them can be reduced by establishing programs specifically designed to prepare teachers for such places. The programs will be more effective if students enrolled in them can be recruited from among the subpopulation groups situated in areas which are hard to staff (Darling-Hammond 1990). If the teacher education of these recruits can take the form of a university off-campus extension program, such as occurs in British Columbia, Canada, or an on-campus special focus program, as occurs in New South Wales, they are more likely to teach voluntarily where they are most needed and to be well-informed and soundly equipped for that location. Furthermore, such teachers are likely to stay longer, further their careers there, and, as a consequence, help to overcome problems associated with high turnover.

Good teaching requires persistence in such unglamorous and routine tasks as lesson planning and preparation, careful marking, and detailed record keeping. A deep sense of work satisfaction and a strong commitment are needed to nourish the will to sustain the long-term effort needed.

A strong body of evidence suggests that the central source of satisfaction for teachers is the relationships associated with the job—with fellow staff, with students, and perhaps with parents and the community (Chapman et al. 1993, Firestone and Pennell 1993, Watson et al. 1991). An impersonal central staffing process is less likely to provide a suitable match with staff and community than a process that includes local staff and community representatives. Satisfaction, however, is subtle, rather subjective, and may not be readily amenable to efforts aimed at its improvement. Adjustment, though related to it, is more objective and may be a more productive focus for efforts to raise satisfaction. Once staff have been selected and placed, the adequacy of the induction (see *Teacher Recruitment and Induction*), the usability of resources, the quality and availability of inservice education (see *Inservice Teacher Education*), and the support of fellow staff, are all important for good adjustment and satisfaction (Watson et al. 1991).

However, increased career satisfaction may not in itself lead to improved teaching. It may produce complacency when there is a need to improve instructional practices (Chapman et al. 1993). Commitment and the stimulus to improve are also required. Commitment, which is voluntary attachment to a purpose or person that produces effort beyond the call of duty, seems to be a deeper and more abiding source of motivation than satisfaction, though nourished by it. Firestone and Pennell (1993) present evidence that commitment in teaching is best nurtured by increasing teacher participation in decision-making (at school and district levels), encouraging collaboration between staff (e.g., scheduling time for work-group meetings and planning), and increasing feedback on teaching from mentors and senior staff. It is this last source in particular that provides the stimulus for improvement.

4. Conclusion

Many systems have devolved staff decision-making to a local body, in the plausible belief that better teacher fit will help promote satisfaction and commitment and

so lead to better teaching. Teacher placement should also be concerned to provide equality of opportunity in difficult-to-staff locations. The critical test is whether the staffing system can allow local participation and at the same time provide high-quality education for all students, not just those in schools attractive to teachers.

References

Ankhara-Dove L A 1982 The development and training of teachers for remote rural schools in less developed countries. *Int. Rev. Educ.* 28: 3–27

Canadian Education Association 1992 *Teacher Recruitment and Retention: How Canadian School Boards Attract Teachers: A Report.* Canadian Education Association, Toronto

Chapman D W, Snyder C W, Burchfield S A 1993 Teacher incentives in the third world. *Teaching and Teacher Education* 9: 301–16

Darling-Hammond L 1989 Teacher supply, demand, and standards. *Educ. Policy* 3(1): 1–17

Darling-Hammond L 1990 Teachers and teaching: Signs of a changing profession. In: Houston W R (ed.) 1990 *Handbook of Research on Teacher Education.* Macmillan, New York

Firestone W A, Pennell J R 1993 Teacher commitment, working conditions and differential incentive policies. *Rev. Educ. Res.* 63: 489-526

Gretler A 1994 Switzerland: System of education. In: Husén T, Postlethwaite T N (eds.) 1994 *The International Encyclopedia of Education*, 2nd edn. Pergamon, Oxford

Halpin D, Troyna B 1994 Lessons in school reform from Great Britain? The politics of education policy borrowing. Paper prepared for the symposium "Lessons in school reform from Great Britain?: The politics of educational policy appropriation and transfer". Annual meeting of the American Education Research Association, New Orleans, Louisiana, 6 April 1994

Hatton N G, Watson A J, Squires D S, Soliman I K 1991 School staffing and the quality of education: Teacher stability and mobility. *Teaching and Teacher Education* 7: 279–93

Lehmann R H 1994 Germany: System of education. In: Husén T, Postlethwaite T N (eds.) 1994 *The International Encyclopedia of Education*, 2nd edn. Pergamon, Oxford

Murnane R J 1994 Supply of teachers. In: Husén T, Postlethwaite T N (eds.) 1994 *The International Encyclopedia of Education*, 2nd edn. Pergamon, Oxford

Organisation for Economic Co-operation and Development 1991 *Reviews of National Policies for Education: Switzerland.* OECD, Paris

Walberg H 1974 *Evaluating Educational Performance.* McCutchan, Berkeley, California

Watson A J, Hatton N G, Squires D S, Grundy S 1987 Graduating teachers and their attitudes towards rural appointments. *South Pac. J. Teach. Educ.* 15: 1–17

Watson A J, Hatton N G, Squires D S, Soliman I K 1991 School staffing and the quality of education: Teacher adjustment and satisfaction. *Teaching and Teacher Education* 7: 63–77

Teacher Recruitment and Induction

R. Bolam

There is widespread agreement that the achievement of successful schooling is crucially dependent on the quality of the teaching force. This quality, in turn, is significantly influenced by the effectiveness of the processes of recruiting and inducting beginning teachers. This entry focuses on these two processes, outlining the factors that affect their formulation, implementation, and effectiveness, including those in the broader policy context. It does not deal directly with such related matters as the supply and demand for teachers, teacher accreditation, the characteristics of beginning teachers, or the induction of experienced teachers who have changed schools.

1. Recruitment

Teacher recruitment policies of all governments are affected by basic factors such as their economic policies (specifically, the amount of money they allocate to education), increases or decreases in birthrates, and teacher supply and demand. These policies are also influenced by country-specific factors. Normally, for example, strategic decisions about the numbers to be recruited into initial teacher education and the qualifications needed to be a teacher are made nationally within the context of each government's policy for teacher supply. Thus, teachers are usually required to be college graduates, but this is not always true in developing countries. In Pakistan, for instance, only 9 percent of primary school teachers held a bachelor's degree in 1989. Similarly, although the majority of teachers are usually female, especially in the primary school sector, in Islamic countries qualifications are not the essential ingredient since a common aim is to recruit more women to teach girls. In some African countries, recruitment and selection decisions may be influenced by tribal allegiances, in India, caste is important; and in several countries, political and union affiliations may be considered.

The status of teachers in the eyes of society at large and, more concretely, their salaries and career prospects, must also be taken into account. Teachers are often civil servants with severely restricted "professional" autonomy. Indeed, the very concept of the "professional," about which so much is written in English-speaking countries, has no apparent equivalent in many other languages. Hence, teaching is much more likely to be regarded as just another occupation in non-English-speaking countries.

The nature of the career structure also varies a great deal among countries. In the United Kingdom the head teacher of a school may earn over four times

the salary of a beginning teacher and the intervening career ladder offers substantial salary incentives at each stage. In Spain, by contrast, headteachers are elected by their colleagues, receive only a nominal salary increase, and there are no salary incentives, nor any significant career ladder, for teachers. Women have relatively poor career prospects in teaching and are significantly underrepresented in senior positions. Nevertheless, they continue to constitute the majority of teachers in most countries.

In those countries such as Germany, Ireland, Belgium, and Japan, where there was an overall surplus of teachers in the 1980s and 1990s, teacher unemployment, linked to a highly competitive entry process, has been the main issue in recruitment policy. In other countries there has been an overall shortage. However, the notion of a shortage is problematic. A shortage may occur for demographic or economic reasons, because of inaccurate forecasting and planning, or because of related policy decisions. The indisputable shortage that exists in developing countries is due quite simply to the fact that there is an insufficient number of qualified people.

In countries such as the United Kingdom, the numbers entering teacher training are strictly controlled on the basis of national demographic projections. In others, such as Italy, effectively no initial training for secondary teachers existed until relatively recently. In some countries, such as Greece, there is a pool of unemployed, qualified teachers. However, this is not true in those countries, particularly in the Third World, in which a teaching qualification is sought primarily as a means to a better paid job in industry or commerce. Virtually all countries have shortages in highly marketable subjects such as science, mathematics, and computing, but even here there are exceptions. Again in Greece, there has been an oversupply of physics teachers in the late 1980s and early 1990s. Shortages in particular student age-ranges or geographic regions are also common, but the reasons are often country-specific. The nature and scope of these shortages are partly contingent on related policy decisions; for example, those on teacher–student ratios and class size, which affect the number of teachers to be recruited.

1.1 Teacher Recruitment and Teaching Quality

Most governments aim to improve the quality of their teaching force via teacher recruitment. Once again, their approaches vary. For instance, in most European countries candidates for higher education and teacher training must pass a rigorous academic examination at age 18 and, as a result, the national debate about quality is focused on subject knowledge and teaching skills rather than on basic academic competence. By contrast, many states and some school districts in the United States have introduced their own entry testing procedures to try to ensure that prospective teachers have a satisfactory level of competence in basic literacy and numeracy skills. In Europe, each member state of the European Community is now able to recruit teachers from the other states, thanks to mutual recognition of national teacher training qualifications. This in itself is a powerful new factor in promoting teacher recruitment and teaching quality throughout Europe.

1.2 Approaches to Teacher Recruitment

In centralized systems of education, including those in developing countries, teachers are usually recruited by a national unit within the framework of a national plan and then deployed by national, state, or regional administrators. The individual teacher and school have little say in the decision. Thus, new teachers are recruited to the total teaching force and may then be allocated to a school in a remote part of the country. Redeployment and promotion decisions are frequently taken in the same manner.

In systems that are relatively decentralized, such as those of the United States and the United Kingdom, on the other hand, such decisions are taken at the local or school level. Specific vacancies are advertised locally or nationally and the successful candidates are appointed after passing through a selection process conducted by the local education authority or by the governing body of the individual school. Hence, both new and experienced teachers have optimum choice over where they can apply to teach, while schools and local authorities can decide whom to select.

In general, several recruitment methods are being tried out by national and local authorities. They include the following. First, flexible entry routes and preparatory access courses are used to help candidates who are underqualified on normal criteria. Second, new forms of initial training and teacher licensing are being introduced. Third, courses for qualified candidates from other fields, for teachers wishing to switch subjects or types of school, and for married women "returners" are being converted and updated. Fourth, qualified teachers from other countries are being recruited. Fifth, specific incentives such as higher salaries, job sharing, creche facilities, and inexpensive housing are being offered to increase recruitment in shortage areas. The relative effectiveness of these various methods is unclear and, in any case, most of the available research is highly context-bound.

2. Induction

The term "induction" refers to the process of support and training that is increasingly being seen as necessary for a successful first year of teaching. Policymakers tend to be more interested in induction

when there are recruitment problems, regarding it as a means of improving retention rates by encouraging a greater proportion of beginning teachers to stay on beyond the first year. Professionals tend to be interested in it as a bridging period between initial and inservice training and, hence, as the foundation of continuing professional development.

The first year of teaching has been the focus of considerable research and development since the 1960s, although principally in only a few countries (e.g., the United Kingdom, the United States, Australia, New Zealand, Canada, and Hong Kong). In other developed countries, interest in induction into teaching varies. In Germany, for example, the final two years of initial training have for many years incorporated what is, in effect, an induction period. Similarly, in the Netherlands, induction has been the subject of much research. In developing countries, induction is far less important than the improvement of initial teacher training.

The first year of teaching has several strands to it. The term "beginning teacher" is commonly used in North America, and to a lesser extent elsewhere, to refer to teachers who have completed their initial training, have received some form of professional accreditation, are employed by a school district, and are in their first year of service, with a more or less normal teaching work load. The first year is often coterminous with a period of probation during which the provisional licensure acquired by the teacher during or at the end of initial training is subject to ratification.

2.1 Principal Components of Induction Programs

By the end of the 1970s informed professional opinion and published research in the United States, United Kingdom, and Australia were, broadly speaking, in agreement regarding the principal components of a successful induction program. They are as follows: (a) additional release time, that is, time away from teaching for the beginning teacher; (b) school-based support from a colleague acting as a mentor or professional tutor, who also receives some additional release time plus training; (c) planned and systematic school-based activities, including discussion groups, classroom observation and support; (d) planned and systematic externally based activities organized by the local education authority (LEA) and university staff; and (e) the explicit and active support of school principals and other administrators. During the 1980s induction increasingly came to be considered within the broader context of staff development; since schools only recruit beginning teachers periodically, staff development is the most cost-effective way of managing the organization and staffing of the school's induction scheme.

There was, and probably still is, less operational agreement about the fundamental aims of induction. Where it is coterminous with probation, the two tend, in practice, to become conflated and confused. This situation is related to a more basic dilemma, namely, should the aim be to induct new teachers into the knowledge, skills, and values promoted by the national system, the employing LEA, the particular school, or the wider profession? The understandable response from program organizers is that a balance must be struck between all four. However, in practice, they are usually influenced by the program's funding body (i.e., the Government, the LEA, or the school) and consequently it is the fourth aim which tends to be underplayed or even omitted. Thus, few induction programs follow the approach adopted by many initial training institutions in aiming to equip new teachers to make informed, independent, professional judgments about a range of curricular and pedagogical issues or about the worthwhileness of the current policies and practices of their national or local system or school.

This "fact of life" is hardly surprising, not only from the perspective of *realpolitik*, but also because the evidence is clear that new teachers are overwhelmingly concerned with the practical problems with which they have to deal in their classrooms, departments, and schools. This concern of new teachers can be attributed largely to the "reality shock" they encounter when they move from their relatively sheltered position in initial training to a situation where they are accountable for all aspects of their professional work. Specifically they are responsible for the learning of groups of students who are frequently uncooperative or even actively hostile, while simultaneously undergoing what may be radical change in their personal lives. Small wonder that the first year of teaching is often experienced and portrayed as traumatic. Unlike most other beginning professionals, teachers work in relative isolation, behind the classroom door.

2.2 Induction Programs, Relevance, and Mentoring

Beginning teachers judge the effectiveness of induction programs primarily in terms of their practical relevance to their own current problems. They tend to be skeptical about external courses which emphasize administrative and legal information or are overly theoretical. They do value the opportunity to meet with other new teachers in "neutral" settings, such as a university, where they may be relieved to discover that their problems are not peculiar to them, and where they are able to discuss them with sympathetic peers and supportive, more experienced group leaders. Above all, they value time to plan, to mark students' work, and to think. Thus, a reduced teaching load coupled with the provision of practical help given by colleagues whom they respect and who have the skills and time to help them, are needed.

It is partly for this reason that there has been much greater emphasis since the early 1980s on mentoring. The importance of support teachers was evident much earlier, for example in the British professional tutor role. During the 1980s, however, the mentor concept was developed, partly in the light of industrial models, in relation to initial training and principal training

as well as induction. While definitions vary, mentors are experienced school colleagues who are responsible for helping beginning teachers. This help may be given directly or indirectly. Mentors may provide information, conduct orientations, observe classrooms and give feedback on what they saw and heard, engage in discussion groups, provide liaison with other staff, the LEA, and the university, and, sometimes, perform assessments and evaluations. Although this list would probably attract general agreement, there are many program-specific approaches to mentoring. They include, for example, the degree of emphasis on subject knowledge (and, hence, on whether or not the mentor should have expertise in the same subject or age-range specialism as the inductee) and pedagogical expertise. Many of the skills needed by mentors (for instance, those associated with classroom observation, clinical supervision, reflective practice, and coaching) are familiar in other contexts but they do require careful adaptation to mentoring.

3. Emerging Trends, Issues, and Research

Many trends are, of necessity, specific to particular countries. In England and Wales, for example, the abolition of the probationary year, the introduction of a national teacher appraisal scheme, the introduction of school-controlled and school-based initial training, and the possible introduction of a General Teaching Council, all have significant implications for both recruitment and induction. More generally, several countries are introducing forms of restructuring that will have direct consequences for recruitment and induction, again as illustrated by experience in England and Wales. Under the system of school-based management that is now well-established there, school governors, advised by parent and community representatives, are responsible for staff appointments and for both the overall school and staff-training budgets.

The risk of a parochial and inward-looking recruitment policy being adopted in this situation is evident. Moreover, given the limited budgets available, there are strong pressures for governors to appoint less costly beginning teachers, often on short-term contracts, in preference to experienced but more expensive teachers. Governors are also likely to be reluctant to spend money from the training budget on induction training and support unless it is earmarked for that purpose within the funding formula. The logical next step in this system of school self-management, especially since it is associated with the promotion of competition between schools within a regulated market approach, is the introduction of site-level pay bargaining together with performance-related pay linked to appraisal. The implications of such developments for recruitment and induction will be considerable.

While these policy-related issues will require careful monitoring, there are several technical matters that also should be studied. Recruitment and retention are underresearched topics, partly because they are so context-bound within particular national systems. Nevertheless, it would be instructive to see which selection methods, including the interview, were effective and under what circumstances; to do the same for innovative recruitment strategies, such as the articled and licensed teacher schemes in the United Kingdom; and to study the implications of these methods and strategies for other national systems.

Several theoretical perspectives can be used profitably to study induction, including those arising from work on teacher socialization, adult learning, teacher cognition, teacher effectiveness, and teacher biographies. There is a need for further research on the roles and training needs of mentors; the role of competence-based methods in induction; the implications of the distinctive features of curriculum subjects for induction; and the relationship of induction to staff development and human resource development.

However, the most fundamental research priority arises from an issue of policy. Although the research evidence is sometimes less than robust and must always be interpreted in relation to the national context within which it was produced, the messages about the value of induction, the main components of an effective induction scheme, and, to a lesser extent, the impact of induction on retention rates, are consistently positive. It comes as some surprise, then, that so few induction programs have become established. In the United States, for example, Conant's (1963) report advocated systematic induction and six years later the National Association of Secondary School Principals (Hunt 1969) produced a set of practical guidelines which were, in their essentials, indistinguishable from those still being advocated in the early 1990s. Similarly, in England and Wales, following the recommendations of the influential James Report on the need for systematic induction (United Kingdom, Department of Education and Science 1972), a series of government-funded research and development activities resulted, by 1978, in national agreement on the nature, scope, and practical details of successful teacher induction. At the same time, however, several subsequent studies by the national inspectorate reported that induction support is patchy and sometimes nonexistent.

In both countries, induction has moved up and down the policy agenda since the 1960s, apparently depending on the perceived scale and political significance of the teacher recruitment and retention problem. A major task for policy researchers, therefore, should be to study two issues. First, how can better use be made of existing technical knowledge about the design and implementation of effective induction schemes? Second, what kind of policy and structural changes are needed for such schemes to become firmly institutionalized in a national inservice teacher education system? Only when these issues are resolved will

educators be in a position to establish whether or not induction can make a consistent and positive impact on teacher recruitment and retention.

References

Conant J B 1963 *The Education of American Teachers*. McGraw-Hill, New York

Hunt D W 1969 *Project on the Induction of Beginning Teachers*, Booklets 1–3. National Association of Secondary School Principals, Reston, Virginia

United Kingdom, Department of Education and Science 1972 *Teacher Education and Training* (James Report). HMSO, London

Further Reading

Ashton P T (ed.) 1992 Editorial—Special issue: Induction and mentoring. *J. Teach. Educ.* 43(3): 162

Bolam R 1987 Induction of beginning teachers. In: Dunkin M J (ed.) 1987 *International Encyclopedia of Teaching and Teacher Education*. Pergamon Press, Oxford

Calderhead J, Lambert J 1992 *The Induction of Newly Appointed Teachers*. General Teaching Council, London

Cooke B L, Pang K C 1987 Experiences and needs of trained and untrained beginning teachers in Hong Kong: A pilot study. *Educ. Res. J.* 2: 18–27

Earley P 1992 *Beyond Initial Teacher Training: Induction and the Role of the LEA*. National Foundation for Educational Research (NFER), Slough

Education, Science and Arts Committee 1990 Second Report: The Supply of Teachers for the 1990s, Vol. 1. HMSO, London

Huling-Austin L, Odell S J, Ishler M, Kay R S, Edelfelt R A 1989 *Assisting the Beginning Teacher*. Association of Teacher Educators, Reston, Virginia

Instance D 1990 *The Teacher Today: Tasks, Conditions, Policies*. Organisation for Economic Co-operation and Development, Paris

Le Métais J 1990 *The Impact on the Education Service of Teacher Mobility*. National Foundation for Educational Research, Slough

Little J W, Nelson L (eds.) *Mentor Teacher: A Leader's Guide to Mentor Training*. Far West Laboratory for Educational Research and Development, San Francisco, California

Maclean R 1992 *Teachers' Careers and Promotional Patterns: A Sociological Analysis*. Falmer, London

Oldroyd D, Hall V 1991 *Managing Staff Development: A Handbook for Secondary Schools*. Chapman, London

Tickle L 1994 *The Induction of New Teachers: Reflective Professional Practice*. Cassell, London

United Kingdom Department of Education and Science 1988 *The New Teacher in School*. HMSO, London

Veenman S 1984 Perceived problems of beginning teachers. *Rev. Educ. Res.* 54(2): 143–78

Wise A E, Darling-Hammond L, Berry B 1987 *Effective Teacher Selection: From Recruitment to Retention*. Rand Corporation, Santa Monica, California

Zeichner K, Gore T 1990 Teacher socialization. In: Houston W R, Howsam R, Sikula J (eds.), 1990 *Handbook of Research on Teacher Education*. Macmillan, New York

Professional Socialization of Teachers

C. Lacey

The term "professional socialization of teachers" refers to the process of change by which individuals become members of the teaching profession and then take on progressively more mature roles, usually of higher status, within the profession. It is clear from this description that the particular characteristics of this process depend on the nature and structure of the teaching profession. Hence, the radical changes that affected the education systems of many countries in the 1980s will be seen to have had a clear effect on the professional socialization of teachers.

The term does not refer to a single period of transformation from student to teacher. Rather, it is a progressive, continuous process with options and choices and sometimes with recognizably different career channels. Nevertheless, there are important similarities in this process which make the study of professional socialization of teachers a rewarding field for researchers. Furthermore, the field is also of great interest to an audience of administrators and teachers whose consciousness of international issues and comparisons is constantly on the increase.

This entry is organized into four major sections: definition, descriptions of research models, research findings, and recent educational changes and international comparisons. The account is enriched by weaving in a number of the themes which illustrate conflicts of ideology and purpose. These themes permeate the subject matter of each section, and relate to contemporary social issues and likely future crises. For example, the question arises as to whether teachers should be more like functionaries of the state, namely bureaucrats who merely carry out the designs and purposes of those who control the state, or whether, as professionals, they should be predominantly educators and visionaries in their own right, whose common purpose is guided and modified by their personal philosophy and individual appraisal of the priorities of education for an increasingly uncertain future. This dilemma underlies many of the contemporary conflicts and disputes within education. The different directions in which this contest is moving has produced contrasting outcomes in many countries, both developed and developing.

1. The Definition of Professional Socialization

In an early classical study of medical students, Merton et al. (1957) produced an important definition of socialization: "The process by which people selectively acquire the values and attitudes, the interests, skills and knowledge—in short the culture—current in

groups to which they are, or seek to become a member" (p. 287). The process of professional socialization into teaching therefore amounts to far more than just learning to teach. By including values, attitudes, and interests, Merton indicates that becoming a teacher involves more than the simple acquisition of academic knowledge and the skills necessary to conduct lessons.

Despite the undoubted strength and usefulness of Merton's definition, it falls short of modern practice in a number of respects. There is a strong suggestion in the definition that teaching is a single culture, an agreement about the basic values and practices within the profession; in technical terms, a "central value system." Researchers who have adhered to this view have usually also adopted a "functionalist" model of society and their research can often be described as central tendency analysis.

The major weakness of this viewpoint is that it glosses over the variations and disagreements that almost inevitably arise in any profession, but are particularly marked in teaching. Merton's definition refers to selective acquisition of values, but does not give the process much emphasis. Nor does the definition give prominence to the interactive, conflictual, and situational elements in this process of acquisition and practice. All of these elements have been stressed in later studies of the professional socialization of teachers and therefore need to be examined carefully. In fact, substantial and fundamental conflicts do exist; individuals are active in choosing and selecting from this variety of values and practices; and these individuals are often careful about to whom and in what situation they reveal their views and practices.

2. Early Research Models in the Study of Professional Socialization

As mentioned above, early studies of professional socialization were almost entirely based on functionalist models of society and used relatively crude central tendency methods of analysis. The basic assumptions underlying functionalist views of society are best expressed in the analogy of society as an organism. Parts of society are seen as functioning parts of the whole, carrying out essential tasks in harmony with the main purpose of society. In practical terms, adherence to this model implies that experienced and responsible members of society or members of the profession can recognize "good practice" or "good teachers." This assumption of a widely held and recognizable consensus lay at the root of a research tradition established in the 1950s and 1960s which "arose from a practical

616

interest in finding better methods for selecting persons who would make 'good' teachers and in improving the training and assessment of students and practitioners" (Morrison and McIntyre 1969 p. 13).

This research tradition failed because of its theoretical and methodological weakness. It embodied a philosophy of education and a view of professional socialization that was subjected to increasing critical scrutiny in the 1970s. In addition, it failed in a practical sense to predict the best new teachers and improve the quality of training (Morrison and McIntyre 1969).

Nevertheless, this research tradition is always capable of resuscitation and rebirth. Since the 1980s governments have shown a growing tendency to intervene in reshaping education systems. They have also funded and shaped research into education to supply answers to their major concerns, which may be categorized broadly as making teachers more "efficient" and education more relevant to the needs of industry and production. These pressures have had the effect of regenerating functionalist approaches to research.

The transition from student to professional person has often been characterized as dramatic and abrupt. In Western societies the obvious change in dress from casual or eccentric student styles to the neat relatively formal dress required in schools is easily recognized and often regarded as signifying a more profound transformation of the person to accepting more socially conservative values and practices. Early studies of teacher socialization stressed the relative lack of power of initiates to the profession and gave prominence to the differences between the idealistic and radical opinions of students and the realistic and practical orientations they developed as they became teachers. Teaching appeared to produce an even more dramatic transformation than most professions because the conservative influence of senior colleagues was coupled with the chastening experience of unruly classes for those who failed to adopt authoritarian classroom discipline. Functionalist theories coupled with predominantly central tendency questionnaire designs conspired to legitimate and substantiate these findings.

3. Developments in Adult Socialization

Two publications in the early 1960s paved the way for substantial advances in the study of adult socialization. Becker et al. (1961) undertook a detailed participant observation study of medical students. Earlier socialization research had usually been based on questionnaire studies, designed to allow comparisons to be made over time or with some expected outcome. Becker et al. were more concerned with detailed observation of social processes and identifying a set of concepts that accurately portrayed their understanding of a complex process. They established a tradition of research within the study of professional socialization

and a set of usefully applied concepts (e.g., culture, latent culture, perspective, and commitment) that could be used in the study of the professional socialization of teachers.

Wrong's (1961) contribution was very different. His seminal essay points to the oversocialized conceptualization of "man" (sic). He portrayed culture as a violation of human nature and as a consequence described socialization as an imperfect or partial process in which essential elements of individuals can, through choice, stay outside. His conceptualization represents an important modification of early functional theories of socialization in which individuals are assumed to conform or fail because of inability or deviance.

These two contributions represented an important stimulus to later research and although Becker et al. still emphasized the power of the socializing institution (through the concept of situational adjustment, in which individuals transform themselves "into the kind of person the situation demands"), the basis for a deeper, more complex understanding of professional socialization had been established.

4. Modern Research Tradition and its Findings

The modern research tradition in professional socialization can be characterized as bringing together a wider range of research methodologies and a richer framework of concepts and theory, including less determinant notions of culture. It has also broadened the scope of relevant factors to be included in major studies. Earlier studies focused on:

(a) the quality of the training or learning experience;

(b) the stresses experienced in the classroom as students or young teachers struggle with the problems of classroom control, pupil learning difficulties, and a heavy workload;

(c) the influence of important "others" (e.g., tutors, fellow students or teachers, head teachers).

The modern tradition has included these factors, often obtaining deeper insights into these processes and their significance through the use of participant observation as well as questionnaire and interview techniques. This tradition has also given greater emphasis to other factors that have enabled new theoretical insights and concepts to be developed. For example:

(a) the process of selection by which students choose training courses or schools in which to start their careers;

(b) the importance of personal agendas, relating to individuals' purposes in teaching, their ideas

617

about career and their values as well as the contribution that individuals make to building institutions and cultures;

(c) the external influences of government or markets that shape the institutions in which teachers teach, and enlarge or constrict their choices in the various areas of teaching.

4.1 Modification of Early Models of Professional Socialization of Teachers

As noted above, the functionalist social theory and questionnaire methodologies established a picture of teacher socialization as a reversion to the conservative practices of the classroom that new teachers experienced as pupils and that they reexperienced as relatively powerless neophyte teachers. This analysis depended on seeing teaching as a relatively monolithic culture heavily constrained by agreements on what constituted "good practice" and classroom situations that were able to deliver substantial punishment to new teachers who failed to conform: the "reality shock."

During the 1960s and 1970s changes took place within education that made these assumptions less valid. Educational provision expanded in almost all industrial and developing countries. Large numbers of pupils experienced levels of education unknown to their parents' generation. Educators searched for new pedagogies and new subject matter to cater to the new cohorts of pupils, and education entered a phase of flux and experimentation.

Some studies failed to take serious account of these changes. Shipman (1967) felt able to explain student "progressivism" as "impressional management" that withered away as soon as the college situation no longer existed and the reality of the staffroom and classroom became relevant. Similarly, Hanson and Herrington (1976) summarized their conclusions from their study of probationary teachers as follows: "... the only way apparently open to the probationers was to conform to the conventional wisdom and recipe knowledge of those around them, and this was largely an accumulation of the indigenous traditions and folkways of (the) staffroom" (p. 61).

The modern tradition has not totally negated these findings nor shown that they do not exist. Rather, it has demonstrated their partial nature and their exclusion of many competing processes. The modern picture of professional socialization emerges from the literature as being closer to a struggle in which individuals confront institutions and make their purposes felt. While this struggle often occurs on an individual basis, it can also arise from group action. The results of these studies reveal the complexity of the interactive process in which individuals may change while at the same time maintaining some stable and unchanging element in their practice and purpose. The studies also demonstrate a link between adult socialization and social change through microchanges produced within institutions.

4.2 Process of Selection and Anticipatory Socialization

Professions are frequently differentiated on the basis of status. Prestigious training institutions are able to attract high-flying individuals from social elites who will go on to obtain prominent positions within their professions and therefore ensure the reputation and high standing of the training institution with the next generation of aspirants. Where competition for entry is fierce this hierarchy of institutions, usually backed by real advantages in career and income, can have a marked socializing effect. It is necessary for individuals to prepare themselves quite carefully to become the kind of person that the professional norms demand. This process of preparation, often termed "anticipatory socialization," is most marked in the older, better paid professions. It is less marked in teaching and it is important to understand the reasons for this.

In all modern societies teaching is a large, relatively open profession. It is difficult for it to become or remain socially exclusive. Most children obtain detailed insights into teaching by attending school. It is therefore the obvious profession for aspiring working class or low caste children to enter. Thus, teaching acts as a channel for social mobility in many societies. It is also a profession with a "caring" as well as a "technical" role. Teaching has traditionally attracted a high proportion of women. While it is possible to demonstrate that in most countries women are discriminated against in terms of promotion and senior posts, it is often the case that teaching represents a relatively good career for women. The reverse is the case for men, where the availability of careers in the older, usually more lucrative, professions of medicine, law, and engineering means that teaching represents only one among many alternative careers. While this pattern is changing slowly, particularly in the rich industrialized countries, it remains a general phenomenon.

Teaching is a divided profession in other respects. It is differentiated according to subject discipline, the qualifications and training that the professionals bring to the classroom, the status of the schools in which they teach, the professional associations and unions that represent the profession, and disagreements over the aims, purposes, and philosophy of education. Some of these divisions are particularly important for the process of professional socialization.

Disputes over the aims and purposes of education have always existed. Education prepares young people for entry into society. As differences of opinion have emerged about the nature of society, so their effect has been felt in education and the training of teachers. One recurring dispute concerns a difference of opinion about the very nature of knowledge. Is knowledge easily defined within subject boundaries, authoritatively laid down within the curriculum, and properly passed on as a series of skills and facts? Or is knowledge less easily defined, subject to individual interpretation, and best "discovered" by the learner who is assisted by the teacher? In the United Kingdom in the 1960s and 1970s, these and other similar questions gave rise to recognizably different approaches to the training of teachers. Some university courses became recognizably innovative; others remained relatively traditional. In turn these differences were registered by students, who were able to choose a course that suited their philosophy.

In a study of five university departments of education in the United Kingdom, Lacey et al. (1973) were able to demonstrate this process at work. The five courses in the study had been selected along a traditional–innovatory course dimension derived from course descriptions. The reasons for students choosing their courses were examined and coded according to whether they took the educational content or organization of the courses into account.

The results suggested that students clearly used their knowledge of the way in which the courses were taught to obtain the kind of socializing experience they desired. As a consequence, they influenced the student membership in each course and hence attended a course in the company of students who were more like themselves than would have been the case on other courses. This aspect of student choice is often neglected in studies of socialization.

4.3 Social Strategies

The use of participant observation and intensive interviewing within studies of professionalization gave rise to a wealth of data, much of which could not be explained by existing theories or described using existing concepts. In particular, the complex behavior of individuals observed in seminars or classrooms often could not be reconciled with the descriptive statistics derived from questionnaires. In addition, case studies of individuals showed that action in one situation apparently contradicted action in another. It was not until the individual's purpose in and definition of the situation were taken into account that the actions were capable of interpretation.

The concept of social strategy, developed by Blumer (1969) within interactionist theory, was adopted by a large number of researchers (Lacey 1977, Woods 1977, Hargreaves 1977, 1980). This concept suggests that individuals are purposeful beings, choosing between different courses of action which offer (apparent) solutions to the problems they face. Lacey (1977) developed the concept of situational adjustment into three broad strategies that incorporate the innovatory aspect of human action as well as the conforming aspects stressed by functionalists. They are: (a) internalized adjustment, (b) strategic compliance, and (c) strategic redefinition.

In the internalized adjustment strategy, the individual complies with the constraints and believes that the constraints of the situation are for the best.

Strategic compliance is the strategy where the individual complies with the authority figure's definition of the situation and the constraints on his or her action but retains private reservations about them. This latter strategy is exemplified by the student teacher who, in a written response, explained,

> Although I disagreed with my teacher-tutor, the only way to cope was to concur with her when she was present i.e., discipline of children, approach to timetable, artwork, and importance of art and the story in the curriculum. (Lacey 1977 p. 93)

Strategic redefinition is a strategy in which the individual engages in innovating within situations and, in some measure, actually changes the situation. Strategic redefinition strategies were pursued by individuals who did not possess the formal power to change situations but who nevertheless did succeed in changing them. They achieved this in most cases by causing or enabling those with formal power (tutors or head teachers) to change their interpretation of what was appropriate in any given situation.

Cooper (1990) and Zeichner and Tabachnick (1985) explored the strategies employed by student teachers and new teachers in pursuit of innovatory teaching techniques during practice teaching and early employment. Detailed case studies of a small number of teachers were made. The results suggested that individuals were able to pursue innovatory teaching methods despite substantial difficulty in doing so. Cooper found that when trying to implement investigations within mathematics teaching the main problem was the student teachers' own inexperience with a new and complex methodology. Zeichner and Tabachnick found that, within the closed system of the classroom, teachers had substantial freedoms and were able to maintain subsystems that conflicted with the expectations of the main school.

5. Educational Change and International Comparisons

Since the mid-1970s the economic expansion that followed the Second World War has been interrupted by a series of recessions. The optimistic support of educational expansion, accompanied by measures designed to produce greater equality of opportunity, has given way to criticism. Education has sometimes been made the scapegoat for economic failure. Throughout the world, education has been put under pressure to serve the economic needs of society rather than the educational needs of children. While such pressure has been similar in both rich and poor countries, the outcomes have been surprisingly different.

The education systems of the poor, predominantly agricultural countries, have been characterized by very few resources, including a lack of adequately trained teachers who are restricted to didactic, recitative methods of teaching. Teachers' freedom is often strictly circumscribed by bureaucracy, with little autonomy accorded them in shaping the curriculum. Teachers are usually at the bottom of a formidable hierarchy of political and administrative control and have little choice where and whom they teach. This system has been shown to alienate both teachers and pupils and is largely held responsible for the low levels of literacy and educational achievement in many poor countries.

After the World Conference on Education for All was held in Jomtien, Thailand in 1990, a new consensus emerged. The emphasis was now placed heavily on primary education and a drive for literacy and basic numeracy in poor rural and urban areas was instigated. Changes in educational policy, supported by donor organizations, have produced changes in teacher training and professional socialization. In India and Indonesia, for example, large-scale state-wide projects have been set up to provide inservice training for teachers. This training introduces child-centered techniques, group work, discussion, working with materials, and similar activities. The professional socialization of teachers has moved toward the model of teaching developed in the Western industrialized countries in the 1960s and 1970s and could represent a radical change if it proves to be successful.

In contrast, the critique of education in industrialized countries has occasionally centered on the very teaching methods being adopted in these new projects. The United Kingdom government has been most radical in this respect and has attempted to introduce market mechanisms as a source of competition and control. Schools are expected to publish examination results (including results of new tests introduced by the government), the curriculum has been centralized, and the proportion of the nation's resources allocated to schools reduced. The effects on the professional socialization of teachers will be most marked as teachers and schools compete in a market for pupils and resources. The change from a bureaucratic–professional milieu in which educational and social issues were highlighted to a market–competitive milieu in which a premium is placed on examination results

and pupil numbers represents one of the most radical experiments ever undertaken in education. It will have important, and as yet unknown, effects on the patterns of teacher socialization. Now that the mechanisms and processes of adult socialization are better understood, much material for discussion and dispute is set to emerge from this field of study in the 1990s.

References

Becker H S, Geer B, Hughes E 1961 *Boys in White: Student Culture in Medical School*. University of Chicago Press, Chicago, Illinois

Blumer H 1969 *Symbolic Interactionism: Perspective and Method*. Prentice-Hall, Englewood Cliffs, New Jersey

Cooper B 1990 PGCE students and investigational approaches in secondary maths. *Research Papers in Education* 5(2): 127–51

Hanson D, Herrington M 1976 *From College to Classroom: The Probationary Year*. Routledge and Kegan Paul, London

Hargreaves A 1977 Progressivism and pupil autonomy. *Sociol. Rev.* 25(3): 585–621

Hargreaves A 1980 Synthesis and the study of strategies: A project for the sociological imagination. In: Woods P (ed.) *Pupil Strategies*. Croom Helm, London

Lacey C 1977 *The Socialization of Teachers*. Methuen, London

Lacey C, Horton M, Hoad P 1973 *Tutorial Schools Research Project: Teacher Socialization, the Post Grad Training Year*, Social Science Research Council, London

Merton R K, Reader G G, Kendall P L (eds.) 1957 *The Student Physician: Introductory Studies in the Sociology of Medical Education*. Harvard University Press, Cambridge, Massachusetts

Morrison A, McIntyre D 1969 *Teachers and Teaching*. Penguin, Harmondsworth.

Shipman M D 1967 Theory and practice in the education of teachers. *Educ. Res.* 9(3): 208–12

Woods P E 1977 Teaching for survival. In: Woods P E, Hammersley M (eds.) 1977 *School Experience*. Croom Helm, London

Wrong D H 1961 The oversocialized conception of man in modern sociology. *Am. Sociol. Rev.* 26(2): 183–93

Zeichner K M, Tabachnick B R 1985 The development of teacher perspectives: Social strategies and institutional control in the socialization of beginning teachers. *Journal of Education for Teaching* 11(1): 1–25

Inservice Teacher Education

M. Eraut

The abbreviation INSET is widely used to refer to the inservice education and training of teachers. Two types of definition are in common use: official and functional. The official definition comprises all activities supported by INSET budgets. In practice, this

can mislead even the officials who use it, because the budget rarely accounts for the total cost. The teaching may be conducted by teacher educators, inspectors, or teachers whose salaries are paid by other budgets. Thus, financial arrangements often reflect the somewhat marginal role allocated to INSET by educational planners and policymakers. Greenland (1983) divides INSET into the following four categories:

(a) INSET for unqualified teachers (mainly certification courses);

(b) INSET to upgrade teachers;

(c) INSET to prepare for new roles, such as principal or teacher educator;

(d) Curriculum-related INSET (mainly courses linked to planned curriculum change or ad hoc refresher courses).

Where there are large numbers of unqualified teachers, both full-time and part-time provision can be found. In China, for example, there is a network of dedicated inservice colleges and a national television channel transmitting programs for part-time students. Several African countries combine full-time provision with part-time correspondence courses supplemented by visits and residential summer schools. Other countries, however, employ very few unqualified teachers; thus, their definition of INSET often excludes them.

The most widely used functional definition of INSET is that developed by an Organisation for Economic Co-operation and Development (OECD) project which characterized INSET as:

> those education and training activities engaged in by primary and secondary school teachers and principals, following their initial professional certification, and intended mainly or exclusively to improve their professional knowledge, skills, and attitudes in order that they can educate children more effectively. (Bolam 1982 p. 3)

This definition includes activities which are not courses and which are not officially funded, but still requires that INSET is the main intention. However, teachers also learn a great deal from participation in activities such as curriculum development which would not be classified under INSET. Participation in these activities will be accommodated under the heading "staff development," which is defined in this entry as that dimension of school life which concerns the professional learning of staff.

1. Orientations toward INSET

Underpinning much of the debate about INSET are three distinct yet complementary rationales. Human resources development (HRD) is concerned with (a) ensuring an adequate supply of appropriately trained and prepared people for all positions in the system; and (b) maximizing the potential of all current personnel. HRD is a form of investment in human capital, which seeks to enhance people's experience and develop their ex-

pertise to meet future demands. Since such demands are not wholly predictable, HRD focuses on enhancing people's general capability, resourcefulness, flexibility, and capacity to change.

The management of planned change (MPC) has been given by far the greatest attention in the education literature. MPC is generally associated with top-down or center–periphery strategies, although the "top" may be either central or local government, or even the principal of a school. Chin (1967) made an important distinction between three centralist approaches: empirical–rational, normative–reeducative, and power–coercive—although the term "political–administrative" (CERI/OECD 1973) is perhaps more appropriate for the third. These distinctions are important because they affect both the power relationships and the perceived purpose of any accompanying INSET.

The third rationale is based on self-development by schools and teachers supported by various kinds of external funding, advice, and learning opportunities. The arguments in favor of it are threefold. First, schools and teachers will be more committed to changes they have initiated and planned themselves. Second, that change will be institutionalized, "real" change, rather than token change. Third, needs and priorities are best decided at local level, because it is only there that people have sufficiently detailed knowledge of situations and circumstances.

In practice, strategies tend to be mixed. Effective self-development at the school or district level requires expertise in needs assessment and the management of change that is still very scarce. Hence, an appropriate HRD program is often required to make it work. Once a school or district has identified a need for change, it may be able to develop its own response unaided. More often, however, a search for relevant ideas, practices, and materials is required. Support systems for schools can play an important role in aiding such a search, by fostering social interaction among schools, districts, and higher education.

Introducing schools to new ideas and approaches is an important purpose of INSET. However, this introduction is often conducted within the rationale of a district or university which adopts a somewhat patronizing, normative–reeducative approach to change rather than having the school gather intelligence about ideas, materials, and practices which it may want to use. Moreover, INSET of this kind is rarely well-designed for the purpose. School representatives are not well-briefed for their intelligence-gathering role, and are given very little scope to pursue it systematically. Independent assessment of products by school representatives is rare, and those few occasions are dominated by the uncritical accounts of the products' proponents. It is usually only in the higher education context that more critical approaches are encouraged.

The political–administrative approach to change involves either mandated change or sponsored change. Mandated change arises when new policies are introduced, and INSET is needed to guide and support the implementation. Sponsored change occurs when government provides special funding or advice to facilitate particular changes. In some contexts this is simply a mechanism for enabling schools to adopt unusually expensive or complex innovations or to support a local trial of a new idea. In others, sponsorship is perceived as coming very close to a mandate, and schools believe that refusal will jeopardize their relationship with their district.

A further dimension is added when one considers the role of individual decision makers. Attendance at voluntary INSET and the adoption of approved innovations are means by which teachers can attract the attention of district officials and possible support for their further education or promotion. Career progress can also be an important explanatory factor for a district official's own behavior. Thus, in practice, there is a continuum of central influence between mandated change at one extreme and support for independent school-based change at the other.

Both centralized and decentralized approaches to change are dependent on effective INSET; furthermore, many combinations of centralized and decentralized strategies are possible. However, competition between the two approaches will always be uneven. Griffin (1987) points out that mandated change is rarely accompanied by sufficient additional resources, so the system has to redirect resources to meet the new requirements. "The implementation (of mandated change) pulls away energy, time and other resources, often well beyond the expected level of effort that might be allocated to a competing staff development program" (p. 22). Hence there are clear limits to the amount of mandated change a school system can handle without rendering impotent attempts to develop school-based staff development programs. Since research on the implementation of mandated change suggests that schools need internal staff development programs in order to develop the capability to implement and institutionalize change properly, the issue of the right balance between external and internal initiatives is crucial (Steadman et al. 1992).

2. The Identification and Prioritization of INSET Needs

The prevailing view that INSET planning should be based on assessment of need poses more questions than it provides answers. Whose needs are to be assessed? Those of a particular group of pupils, an individual teacher, a department within a school, the school itself, the district, or even the nation? Moreover, who will be making the assessment? One clear finding of research is that, if INSET participants do not recognize a need as having sufficient priority for them, activities aimed at meeting that need will be judged irrelevant. Yet it would be undemocratic if teachers

were to be regarded as the sole definers of INSET needs without considering the views of other members of society. This suggests two possible strategies for INSET managers: (a) considerable effort is devoted before or during INSET to convincing participants of the importance of certain needs, or (b) the needs assessment process is decentralized so that schools and teachers define their own needs, with some safeguard to ensure that views of other groups are taken into account.

Devolution of the needs assessment process, however, is no guarantee that it will be properly conducted. Logically, to define a need implies: (a) some view of the current situation, and (b) aspirations for, or expectations of, a future situation that is different. The quality of the needs assessment will depend on both these factors. For example, a person's view of the current situation will comprise:

(a) Information about context, conditions, processes, activities, intentions and outcomes;

(b) Standards, values and criteria by which these are judged; and

(c) Frameworks and perspectives which determine how it is interpreted and understood (Eraut 1989a).

Such a view may be constructed from existing perceptions with little further inquiry or reflection. On the other hand, there may be considerable effort to go beyond first thoughts by collecting new information, becoming more aware of other perspectives and interpretations, and reflecting more on this evidence and underpinning educational values. This process would itself be a process of staff development.

Similarly, thinking about the future must necessarily involve the following:

(a) Some awareness of alternatives to current policy and practice,

(b) Some assessment of the feasibility of these options, and

(c) Some evaluation of the desirability of options and their anticipated outcomes (Eraut 1989a).

Once again, such thinking is enhanced by INSET, particularly by the kind of intelligence gathering mentioned above. The dangers are that awareness of alternatives will remain rather superficial and that significant changes will be prematurely dismissed as impractical without serious study.

2.1 School Self-review

Bollen and Hopkins (1987) argue that school self-review is a necessary but not sufficient condition for school improvement, and that developing schools' capability for self-review should be a priority for HRD programs. However, this argument does not prevent schools without such capability from formulating school INSET plans in a more pragmatic, though probably less effective, way. Ongoing monitoring by teachers and awareness of innovations and practice elsewhere are capable of generating more needs than many schools are able to fulfill. Schools in the United Kingdom are becoming accustomed to producing development plans for their governors and for internal planning of change. They also are required to produce INSET plans in order to get government funds to support their INSET programs. These plans play an important role in determining and coordinating INSET activities at a time when there is an exceptionally high level of externally mandated change.

2.2 Individual Teacher Needs

School INSET plans also have to take into account individual needs, which in the United Kingdom are identified through school-based systems of teacher appraisal. The central purpose of such appraisal is professional development, and targets are jointly agreed and/or reviewed on each occasion (Bradley 1991). These targets may relate to classroom strategies, wider school roles, or career development. Part of the "bargain" is the provision of support, including if necessary the use of some of the school's own INSET funds.

It is important that this support is not just short-term and instrumental in nature. Teachers also need encouragement to participate in external professional meetings in order to widen their horizons, stimulate their thinking, and prevent the school from becoming too insular. On the whole, the privacy of an appraisal interview appears to offer a better context for the expression of need than a more public school self-review; however, more evidence is needed to confirm this hypothesis. Whatever the system, the crucial research question still remains to be answered: under what conditions and circumstances will teachers diagnose their own learning needs, engage in the collection of evidence to deepen that diagnosis, or agree with a diagnosis made by another person?

3. The Development of Professional Knowledge and Learning

One of the more critical developments in educational research during the 1980s and early 1990s has been an attempt to characterize the nature of teachers' professional knowledge and to study how it gets used (Eraut 1995). As a result, the problems facing the INSET designer can now be better understood. For any practical situation there is a large amount of potentially relevant theoretical knowledge which can contribute to its understanding; however, its relevance may not become apparent until it has become part of each teacher's conceptual framework. In other words, theory acquires relevance through use, and use involves thought and discussion in periods of time set aside for that purpose.

On the other hand, practical knowledge is partly tacit in nature, and is not easily articulated or explained. Some INSET goals cannot be achieved by words alone, as teachers have to experience and do things for themselves. The concomitant problem is that what teachers do is unlikely to be fully understood and only partly under their critical control. Thus, if INSET is to develop new and valid practice, it will have to combine the use of theoretical and practical knowledge in some kind of dialogical relationship, involving close linkage between off-the-job reflection and ongoing classroom experience. The models of professional learning discussed below have all been developed as responses to these problems.

3.1 Joyce and Showers' Approach to Skill Development

Joyce and Showers' (1988) approach was designed to expand teachers' repertoires by teaching them new teaching techniques such as inquiry teaching, higher order questioning, or groupwork. Although they identify five essential components of their model, the model's most distinctive feature is a substantial period of off-the-job practical training (not dissimilar to that used in microteaching) followed by transfer into the normal classroom supported by coaching. The contribution to learning of each component is clearly explained.

(a) An exploration of theory through discussions, readings, and lectures is necessary for understanding the rationale. "Study of theory facilitates skill acquisition by increasing one's discrimination of the demonstrations, by providing a mental image to guide practice and clarify feedback, and by promoting the attainment of executive control" (p. 68).

(b) The demonstration or modeling of skills through video, or live in the training setting. There are advantages in interweaving the theory and demonstration components, as each facilitates the understanding of the other.

(c) Practice under simulated conditions, teaching either a group of peers or small groups of children. For a technique of medium complexity, this practice requires 20 to 25 trials over a period of 8 to 10 weeks in a setting which approximates the normal workplace.

(d) Feedback can be provided by peers under guidance, once the model has been understood. Audio or video recording is desirable, and feedback should be as soon as possible after practice.

(e) Coaching provides continuing support during the

difficult process of transferring acquired skills into the normal classroom setting.

Joyce and Showers refer to their final goal as not just the use of new skills in the classroom, but the acquisition of "executive control," which is defined as "the consistent and appropriate use of new skills and strategies for classroom instruction" (1988 p. 68). They expect flexibility in multiple situations, not the delivery of a blueprint. Coaching must be attached to a proper training program and should remain under its overall guidance even when most of it is provided by peers. Thus the transfer of training, supported by coaching, is seen as the experimental component of a period of continuous study. Interaction between theory and practice takes place throughout the program.

3.2 Reflective Models

While Joyce and Showers' model can be seen as a method of introducing into schools techniques and approaches whose credibility derives from research, reflective models aim to build on teachers' own experience by increasing their capacity to learn from it. They are a deliberate attempt to counteract the "dailiness" of teaching by encouraging teachers to attend to different features and seek new information about the flow of classroom events, then put aside time to reflect upon it and discuss it with others. As Schutz (1967) has noted, an "act of attention" is required to distinguish an "experience" from the flow of life in order that it can be reflected upon. Furthermore, a reflective glance may penetrate more or less deeply depending on its purpose and how much is taken for granted. Reflective models, therefore, are highly dependent on teachers' willingness to attend, to reflect, and to take greater control over their practice.

Reflective models have received considerable impetus from research into teachers' thinking which has presented an increasingly sophisticated account of teachers' professional knowledge, much of which has been found to be tacit and intuitive. Classroom behavior is characterized by routines interspersed with rapid intuitive decisions which require instant interpretations of the developing situation and almost immediate responses. The appropriateness of such decisions can only be considered during reflection after the event, if there is the time and the will to do it. The argument as to why teachers should engage in reflection is essentially moral, and is derived from teachers' responsibility for the progress and well-being of the students in their classes. This argument is underpinned by a particular view of teachers' professionalism and accountability. Thus, Eraut (1995) argues that being a professional teacher implies:

(a) A moral commitment to serve the interests of students by reflecting on their well-being and their

progress and deciding how best it can be fostered or promoted.

(b) A professional obligation to review periodically the nature and effectiveness of one's practice in order to improve the quality of one's management, pedagogy, and decision-making.

(c) A professional obligation to continue to develop one's practical knowledge both by personal reflection and through interaction with others.

Although there is considerable debate about how these goals can best be promoted, it is possible to describe the range of practices which have been tried in terms of their experiential and reflective components. The experiences to be reflected upon may be based, on either (1) normal occurrences in a teacher's own classroom, possibly enhanced by the collection of more information than usual (e.g., recordings, children's views, observations by a colleague, analysis of children's work); or (2) changes or experiments and their effects. The reflection which follows may include (3) a discussion of the above, possibly aided by questions or issues previously agreed; and/or, (4) action-planning for some modified practice or experiment. Finally, the whole process may be supported by, (5) readings to illuminate (or divert?) the discussion; and/or, (6) an internal or external consultant as a facilitator and/or resource person.

According to the context, the combination of (1) and (3) has been described as mutual observation, peer-assisted review, self-evaluation, or even needs assessment. The sequence (1),(2),(4),(2),(3) is often described as "action research," although Elliott (1991) raises the question of whether the starting point should not be (2) rather than (1). In this, he refers to two rather different accounts of how teachers might reflectively develop their practices:

(a) The teacher undertakes research into a practical problem and on this basis changes some aspect of his or her teaching. The development of understanding precedes the decision to change teaching strategies. In other words, reflection initiates action.

(b) The teacher changes some aspect of his or her teaching in response to a practical problem and then self-monitors its effectiveness in resolving it. Through the evaluation the teacher's initial understanding of the problem is modified and changed. The decision to adopt a change strategy therefore precedes the development of understanding. Action initiates reflection (Elliott 1991 p. 23)

Elliott adds that the first account may constitute "a projection of academic bias into the study of teachers' thinking," while the second "may reflect the natural logic of practical thinking more accurately" (1991 p. 23). Another interpretation might be that the first account is more typical of a deliberately created action research group or project (Stuart 1991), the second of ongoing reflective practice by individual teachers who have developed a strong self-monitoring capability.

Research on reflective models gives little guidance on the relative effectiveness of these different approaches, but consistently draws attention to the enabling or disabling effect of school management and ethos. The main personal barriers to participation appear to be the commitment of time and the loss of self-esteem which accompanies initial confrontation with new evidence from one's own classroom. Appropriate support can help overcome these problems, where the teacher accepts the underpinning view of teacher professionalism.

Eraut (1989b) has argued that while reflection at the level of self-monitoring is an ongoing professional obligation, reflection at the level of self-review ought to be treated more as a periodic activity. It is unrealistic to expect major changes in classroom practice to arise from waves of innovation, inadequately resourced for INSET support, or an accumulation of small adjustments triggered by school-based staff development and an appraisal system. Continual disturbance may actually lower the quality of teaching by reducing teachers' sense of efficacy and allowing too little time for any specific change to take root. The question arises as to whether it would not be better to build periods of self-renewal into the professional life cycle of teachers, so that every 5–10 years they engage with a few colleagues in a period of reflection and action research with proper support. Such a strategy would make sense to teachers, establish such interludes as a normal part of professional life, and focus support structures more effectively on teacher development.

3.3 Project-based Models

Project-based models originated within advanced courses provided by higher education. These are best placed within the HRD approach to inservice education, since most participants are preparing to take up more senior positions at school or district level, or posts in teacher education. The types of projects used in such courses range from research into classroom events or institutional problems, through evaluations of courses, materials or policies, to design or development work. Relevant theory and research is required, and the quality of analysis is what a university would expect.

The primary goal is to develop the students' capacity to work independently and collaboratively as reflective professionals, a goal which is supported not only by their own project experience but by accompanying discussion, comparison, and contrast with accounts in the literature and the work of their fellow-students. A secondary goal is to make a positive contribution to students' own institutions, which helps to sustain their support for the course. Some far-seeing schools see it as a cheap form of consultancy! While some universities place projects at the end of courses, others construct courses around a series of projects, which are informed by and fed into ongoing seminar discussions.

Project-work of this kind is chosen by teachers and combines a high degree of authenticity with a more rigorous analysis than is commonly found in schools. Not only does it prepare people for leadership roles but it improves the general quality of professional work (Vulliamy and Webb 1991). Experience of supporting such projects also improves the knowledge-base of the university, leading to better consultancy services and improved teaching and research.

3.4 Professional Development Opportunities

At the beginning of this entry, it was noted that professional learning can occur during many activities not primarily intended for that purpose. Much more use can be made of these professional development opportunities (PDOs) if they are recognized in advance and consciously used for learning purposes. In order to do so, there is a need for:

(a) prior recognition of a professional development need, perhaps as a result of appraisal;

(b) agreement that engaging in a particular activity will provide a learning opportunity relevant to that need; and

(c) planning for an experiential learning cycle of setting targets, providing support, self-evaluation, and feedback from others.

Thus personal PDOs are jointly created by a teacher and a support person, either by selecting some of the teacher's normal professional tasks for special attention or by choosing some special learning activity to assist in the achievement of agreed learning goals. Examples of the former might be conducting an unusually thorough review of the progress of a particular student causing concern, or giving special attention to preparing for the teaching of a new topic. Targets would include both professional quality reports on the task (important for confidence and sustaining a sense of professionalism) and learning goals (with potential for transfer to other cases and situations). Examples of the latter might include studying practice in another classroom (or even another school), shadowing another member of staff prior to taking on some new responsibility, or chairing a school committee. In all such cases, there is a clear learning focus agreed at the beginning; advice and support are provided as appropriate (not only by the designated support person, who may negotiate for additional help); and self-evaluation of what has been achieved and what has been learned is followed by constructive feedback from others.

While PDOs may be weak on the theoretical side, they are highly motivating and relevant for the teacher. Moreover, they are less difficult to initiate than the other models discussed earlier. Although they have been discussed in terms of purely school-based activity, they are equally applicable to the professional development of educational personnel outside schools. Such activities can also be incorporated into INSET courses, to which they bring a wealth of fresh experience to stimulate discussion. Eraut (1988), for example, discusses their use on management courses to change the attitudes and perceptions of those who apparently know all. Similarly, Day (1990) describes how reflective models can be built into INSET courses of 10 to 30 days duration.

4. Conditions for Effective INSET and Staff Development

Fullan (1987) identifies four factors as crucial for successful staff development:

(a) redefining staff development as a process of learning,

(b) the role of leadership at the school level,

(c) organizational culture at the school level, and

(d) the role of external agencies especially at the local or regional level.

To understand the significance of these factors it is useful to distinguish between three facets of INSET/staff development:

(a) its management (that is, decisions about what to do, for what purpose and with what support; the provision of support; and the evaluation of INSET programmes and policies);

(b) its design and conduct; and

(c) its ongoing interaction with the life of schools and the behavior and intentions of individual teachers.

All those involved need to have some understanding of each of these factors if the process of professional learning is to be understood, the purposes of programs are to be agreed, and the culture of the school is going to have a positive rather than negative influence on development.

Other entries in this encyclopedia focus on issues such as the role of the principal, school improvement, and the effective school. All emphasize the importance of leadership and organizational culture in school development. INSET/staff development is an integral part of that development. However, rather than regarding effective leadership and a positive organizational culture as preconditions for successful INSET/staff development, it is perhaps more constructive to ask how INSET/staff development can help to create the necessary leadership and culture. There is a strong argument that, while the role of principal will always be the most

important, the function of leadership should be quite widely distributed for a school to be effectively run. Thus management development programs should be an important component of INSET planning. In addition, the staff development role is important at every level of management. The person best placed to support a teacher's development is usually the senior teacher in his or her subject or grade-level group. Many schools have also evolved roles such as mentor, professional tutor, appraiser, or INSET coordinator whose *raison d'être* is staff development. All these people need training to strengthen their roles.

At a practical level, schools have to create time for INSET and staff development, while still preserving continuity of teaching (Hewton and Jolley 1991). In many countries staff development days are set aside for this purpose, though schools do not always have the expertise to make good use of them (Ekholm 1988). However, time is still needed for functional groups to meet in school and teachers to attend courses and meetings outside school. The former can be timetabled and teachers can be replaced when away; both require careful advance planning by a capable and committed principal.

5. Role of External Agencies

Very strong evidence exists to show that substantial external support is needed for all three INSET orientations (Fullan 1991, Louis et al. 1985, Tangyong et al. 1989). Three strategies can be distinguished:

(a) Support for the change process in general, as opposed to specific innovations. This includes (i) INSET directed at building up schools' capacity for managing change (both internally and externally initiated); and (ii) ongoing management consultancy on school-based review and development, including staff development.

(b) Training school-based trainers and supporting them through a specific program of change. This includes (i) INSET for teachers designated as school-based trainers and (ii) follow-up support with their own internal programs.

(c) Direct training of teachers for a specific program of change. This includes (i) externally provided INSET for all teachers concerned in the change, and (ii) follow-up support in their classrooms.

Each strategy has been described in terms of both an INSET component and a follow-up component. Evidence is now overwhelming that follow-up is essential for effective implementation (Huberman and Miles 1984, Bradley 1991). Since proper follow-up is highly dependent on the schools themselves, as well as external agencies, strategies (b) and (c) above will be wasted if schools lack the capacity to manage the process of change. Hence strategy (a) has to be given first priority. Strategy (c) is extremely expensive, but can provide a useful means of developing practical experience and expertise prior to switching to strategy (b).

Although strategy (b), involving the training of trainers, tends to be favored, it is rarely employed effectively. The main mistakes are:

(a) limited school capacity for change, resulting from insufficient attention to strategy (a) above;

(b) failure to train the trainers as change-agents and INSET providers, as well as classroom implementers;

(c) failure to provide continuing support for trainers throughout the implementation phase; and

(d) the provision of training of insufficient length and breadth.

Significant benefits have also been noted from training pairs of trainers from each school rather than individuals. Not only can they assist and encourage each other, but there is also a safeguard against staff mobility and illness.

6. Conclusion

The capacity of school districts to implement any of the above strategies must be called into question. Often innovations fail because district staff lack expertise in INSET/staff development and the management of change. INSET leaders may lack sufficient practical experience of the innovations they are promoting (Noor Azmi 1991). The level of investment per teacher in most INSET programs is too low to make significant changes in classroom practice a likely outcome for the majority of participants.

Some countries control INSET at national level, which can make communication with schools very difficult. However, it does offer the opportunity to mount a coherent INSET program. The proliferation of uncoordinated initiatives has been a major weakness of INSET planning in multilevel governments and has often undercut schools' attempts to manage the process of change properly. Hence, Blackburn and Moisan (1987) suggest that INSET is best organized through a system of local, regional, and national networks, which can foster social interaction, build INSET teams, and coordinate INSET efforts. Many countries are beginning to address a wide range of problems as increasing recognition is paid to the role of INSET in improving the quality of education. It remains to be seen whether, during a period of economic stringency, the funding will match the rhetoric.

See also: Onservice Teacher Education; Curriculum of

Teacher Education Programs; Structure of Teacher Education Programs

References

Blackburn V, Moisan C 1987 *The In-service Training of Teachers in the Twelve Member States of the European Community.* Presses Interuniversitaires Européenes, Maastricht

Bolam R 1982 *In-service Education and Training of Teachers: A Condition of Educational Change.* Final Report of CERI Project on INSET. OECD, Paris

Bollen R, Hopkins D (eds.) 1987 *School Based Review: Towards a Praxis.* International School Improvement Project, OECD, Paris

Bradley H 1991 *Staff Development.* Falmer Press, London

Chin R 1967 General strategies for affecting change in human systems. In: Morphet E, Ryan C (eds.) 1967 *Designing Education for the Future.* Citation Press, New York

CERI/OECD 1973 *Case Studies of Educational Innovation IV: Strategies for Innovation in Education.* CERI/OECD, Paris

Day C 1990 In-service as consultancy: *The Evaluation of a Management Programme for Primary School Curriculum Leaders.* In: Aubrey C (ed.) 1990 *Consultancy in the United Kingdom.* Falmer Press, London

Ekholm M 1988 *In-service Teacher Education and School Development: Overview and Soliloquy* Swedish National Board of Education, Stockholm

Elliott J 1991 *Action Research for Educational Change.* Open University Press, Milton Keynes

Eraut M 1988 Learning about management—The role of the management course. In: Day C, Poster C (eds.) 1988 *Partnership in Educational Management.* Routledge, London

Eraut M 1989a Review of research on in-service education: In: Wilson J (ed.) 1989 *The Effectiveness of In-Service Education and Training of Teachers and School Leaders.* Swets and Zeitlinger, Amsterdam

Eraut M 1989b Teacher appraisal and/or teacher development: Friends or foes? In: Simons H, Elliot J (eds.) 1989 *Rethinking Appraisal and Assessment.* Open University Press, Milton Keynes

Eraut M 1995 Developing professional knowledge within a client-centred orientation. In: Guskey T, Huberman M (eds.) 1995 *New Paradigms and Practices in Professional Development.* Teachers College Press, New York

Fullan M 1987 Implementing the implementation plan. In: Wideen M F, Andrews I (eds.) 1987 *Staff Development for School Improvement.* Falmer Press, New York

Fullan M G 1991 *The New Meaning of Educational Change,* 2nd edn. Cassells, London

Greenland J (ed.) 1983 *The In-Service Training of Primary School Teachers in English-Speaking Africa: A Report.* Macmillan, London

Griffin G A 1987 The School in society and social organization of the school: implications for staff development. In: Wideen M F, Andrew I (eds.) 1987 *Staff Development for School Improvement.* Falmer Press, New York

Hewton E, Jolley M 1991 *Making Time for Staff Development.* Occasional Paper 14, University of Sussex Education Area, Brighton

Huberman M, Miles M 1984 *Innovation Up Close: How School Improvement Works.* Plenum Press, New York

Joyce B, Showers B 1988 *Student Achievement through Staff Development*. Longman, New York

Louis K S, Van Velzen W G, Loucks S, Crandall D 1985 External support systems for school improvement. In: Van Velzen W G et al. (eds.) 1985 *Making School Improvement Work*. International School Improvement Project, OECD, Paris

Noor Azmi I 1991 Inservice training in Malaysia for the new primary curriculum (KBSR). In: Lewin K M, Stuart J S (eds.) 1991 *Educational Innovation in Developing Countries: Case-Studies of Changemakers*. Macmillan, Basingstoke

Schutz A 1967 *The Phenomenology of the Social World*. Northwestern University Press, Evanston, Illinois

Steadman S, Eraut M, Fielding M, Horton A 1992 INSET effectiveness. Report to the Department of Education and Science, London

Stuart J S 1991 Classroom action research in Africa: A Lesotho case study of curriculum and professional development. In: Lewin K M, Stuart J S (eds.) 1991 *Educational Innovation in Developing Countries: Case-Studies of Changemakers*. Macmillan, Basingstoke

Tangyong A F, Wahgudi R, Hawes H 1989 *Quality through Support for Teachers: A Case-Study from Indonesia*. University of London Institute of Education, London

Vulliamy G, Webb R 1991 Teacher research and educational change: An empirical study. *Br. Educ. Res. J.* 17(3): 219–36

Onservice Teacher Education

R. Gardner

The training, retraining, and updating of practicing teachers are widely recognized as essential factors in the development of teacher quality. Teacher quality is a major, perhaps the major, factor contributing to improved learning outcomes of students. It is both vital and appropriate that the education and training of practicing teachers should receive increasing attention.

1. Definitions of Teacher Training

The most common distinction adopted in discussions of the education and training of teachers is that between the provision made before teachers begin teaching (preservice) and that which takes place after they are employed as teachers (inservice). However, this distinction is too simple. While preservice training is often equated with initial training, the term does not apply when teachers are employed without training and must obtain qualifications on the job. Similarly, while in general all postappointment training has been called inservice and the use of the acronym INSET (for Inservice Education and Training) has become commonplace, this term also covers a range of provision.

A different distinction is necessary because of the wide variety of practice that exists throughout the world. In this regard, inservice and onservice are suggested as two broad categories of practice.

1.1 Inservice and Onservice Training

The spectrum of postappointment training can be represented by a continuum. At one end is a form of training that takes place wholly away from the school, possibly in some specifically designed training environment. At the other end of the continuum are practices where all the training takes place in the schools in which the teachers normally work. We might call the one end "inservice" (INSET) and the other, "onservice" (ONSET). (See Fig. 1). Between the two poles of the continuum might be a series of practices that provide training to greater or lesser degrees in or out of school.

Edelfelt (1985) has adopted a different approach and has associated "onservice training" with unqualified teachers and "inservice training" with qualified teachers. This distinction has not been adopted in this entry, although it recognized that the difference in teachers' backgrounds will have important effects on how training is arranged and received.

1.2 A Philosophy for Postappointment Training and Retraining

The basic tenet of inservice and onservice training is that teachers need continual renewal of their knowledge and their capabilities to provide appropriate learning strategies for their students. Commitment to the ongoing training of teachers is evident from the universal practice of providing opportunities for teachers to meet and receive such training. This commitment may be small in many education systems—indeed, it may be one of the first areas of an educational budget to be cut during periods of austerity. Nonetheless, nearly all education systems do attempt to provide for the continuing professional stimulation of teachers during their careers. The frequency, duration, and value of the training may be open for discussion, but the availability and organization of training continue to receive attention from educational planners, managers, and teachers.

The mechanism for the provision of postappointment training is as important as the training itself.

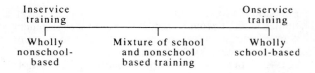

Figure 1
Continuum from insevice to onservice training

The practice of providing short courses (perhaps 1–2 hours) at long intervals has given way to the recognition that the frequency of professional contact is of the greatest importance. The emergence of local places for teachers to meet has been a signal development since the late 1970s. The teachers center, which may be part of an overall network linking teachers across a state, has been widely recognized as having great potential for influencing professional practice. The need for teachers to meet to exchange ideas and work together to define and solve common problems has been accepted, and the value of peer interaction among teachers has been stressed as a means to instill confidence to bring about change in classroom practices. Countries such as Kenya, with its teachers center and subcenters, and Tanzania, with its community education centers, provide just two examples where locally based resource facilities intended to support teacher development have received support not only from the central authorities but also from teachers at large.

2. Three Case Studies

Three case studies, from Indonesia, India, and Pakistan, are useful in examining the value of onservice training. While the first two have many similarities, the third provides an important contrast.

2.1 The Active Learning through Professional Support Project (ALPS)

As a result of the 1973 increase in oil prices, Indonesia was able to undertake a massive program of expansion of primary education. It swiftly provided near-universal access to primary education. While Indonesia was highly successful in quantitative terms, considerable concern was expressed about the qualitative aspects of primary education. An in-depth study conducted in 1976 showed that there was significant underachievement in primary schools. The study examined factors that might explain this problem and identified the teacher as being the most consistent factor affecting school quality. It was decided to establish a program to improve quality. The resulting project became known as the Cianjur Project after the district in which it was located.

The Cianjur Project took as its starting point the proposition that it is possible to identify specific aspects of teacher behavior that might be modified in order to bring about improvements in classroom practice. Preparing realistic teaching plans, encouraging children's investigations, encouraging children's talk and interaction, marking books and providing feedback, and keeping appropriate records were some of the aspects of teacher behavior targeted for change. It was also realized that in order to bring about these changes, which represented a step forward in the learning process from Indonesia's traditional didactic mode, teachers would need support. Such support had to be directed at the teacher and be provided where it was needed most, namely in the classroom and school, and not in a college environment some distance from the school.

Some direct training was provided for teachers at an induction course organized in local schools, but this component was kept to a minimum, largely because of cost. One main part of the support for teachers was provided through the reexamination of the roles of head teachers and the local inspectors, both of which had been seen as almost solely administrative. Head teachers and inspectors were encouraged to adopt more professionally oriented stances, which in turn raised important questions about the ability of these categories of staff to support innovations in practice. Neither the headteachers nor the inspectors resisted the innovations, but for each category problems arose. For the headteachers, the new approach required a reorientation of thinking for them and their staffs to the interventions that they could or should make in the classroom. For the inspectors, it demanded a restructuring of their schedules to permit them to spend more time in schools with teachers to help them bring about the required changes.

It was recognized by all involved that opportunities to meet were needed to discuss problems as well as ways of moving forward. A series of "clubs" were established, one for each category of staff. The schools were divided into groups and the teachers from the schools within each group met on a regular basis. Similarly, the head teachers and inspectors met separately, normally on a monthly basis.

After the start of the Cianjur Project in 1980, the introduction of activity-based learning spread to other provinces in Indonesia. By 1990, 7 out of 27 provinces had become involved. While the model for the provision of support remained basically the same (i.e., induction courses in a school, school groups, teacher clubs, heads and inspector clubs and teachers centers, and provision of a meeting place with some resources), there have been wide variations in the ways in which the detailed arrangements are organized. In particular, attendance at the teachers clubs varies considerably. Tangyong et al. (1990) recorded that in Cianjur teachers attended clubs four to six times a year. However, in other areas the teachers attended monthly (as in South Sulawesi), or even weekly (Lampung). These variations in the application of

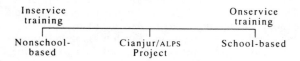

Figure 2
Cianjur/ALPS project on the training continuum

the model arose from the process of decision-making about implementation, where the emphasis was upon the selection of priorities for support by local officials at the provincial level.

In the Cianjur Project, which in 1987 became known as the Active Learning through Professional Support (ALPS) project, the emphasis has been upon small groups of teachers meeting frequently to help each other. These meetings have taken place in school, during school time, and dealt with issues identified by the group members as important. In some areas these are essentially staff meetings at an individual school, the staff of which are, by regulation, expected to meet on Saturday mornings. These staff meetings were intended for minor school administrative issues, but their purpose has been revised to provide opportunities for discussion of professional concerns and the agreement of action to be taken in the ensuing period.

ALPS as a project was reviewed by Tangyong et al. (1990). The spread of the model led to the adoption of active learning as a national policy for education. Experiential learning was then included in the new national curriculum (1994), with textbooks prepared to complement this approach to learning in the primary school. With the implementation of Indonesia's nine-year Basic Education cycle, active learning will spread to higher classes and eventually will be common practice for classes 1–9 (6–15 years of age) throughout Indonesia.

The position of the Cianjur/ALPS Project on the inservice–onservice continuum is shown in Fig. 2. The conduct of courses in a school did require teachers to be absent from classes and for some of them to leave their school to attend meetings elsewhere. The same applied to attendance at the teachers clubs. However, the brevity of these absences from the classroom might suggest that the meetings were more directly based on school problems and realities than on conventional inservice courses, which may offer a set program for professional orientation that is not directed fully at immediate and local interests. As a consequence, the ALPS Project might be positioned slightly to the right of the center on the continuum to reflect the school-based nature of the professional development that takes place.

2.2 The Andhra Pradesh Primary Education Project (APPEP)

The second project is the Andhra Pradesh Primary

Education Project (APPEP) in India. This project, funded by the United Kingdom Overseas Development Administration, has many features similar to those of ALPS (also funded by the Administration). APPEP started in 1985 with a large pilot project involving 328 schools and 794 teachers in 11 (out of 23) districts of Andhra Pradesh, one of the poorest states of India. Originally the districts were selected to represent different climate zones in Andhra Pradesh and the locations for training activities were chosen to provide for the poorest areas. The pilot project (now called Phase I) was essentially a building program with a training element. Again, the intention of the training program was to bring about changes in teaching styles toward a more activity-oriented and investigative approach to learning in the primary school. An evaluative study in 1987 showed a satisfactory implementation of the basic ideas of APPEP. Full-scale state-wide dissemination of APPEP to 175,000 teachers in 50,000 schools commenced in 1989 with a five-year program in each district.

There are some important differences between ALPS and APPEP. Although the basic educational philosophy, with its emphasis on "hands-on" experience, was common to both, differences in the structure of the training were obvious. In the case of ALPS, the provision of courses for induction was dependent upon the local supply of funds to support the program. In the case of APPEP, however, funds were provided through bilateral aid for an agreed-upon program of training. This program provided for not only the induction of teachers but also the preparation of tutors able to conduct the training of the teachers.

In order to reach all teachers in the period allotted and to include all new appointees, a highly coordinated program was needed, directed by a project headquarters. There was no room for local initiative and action in the training program. Teachers (and local inspectors) were sent to the District Institute of Education and Training (DIET) (previously the government teacher training institutes, which had been upgraded in 1986 under the National Policy on Education) or to local centers. These courses all took place during the school year. In some areas the schools were closed for a period while all teachers attended courses.

Another common feature of ALPS and APPEP was teachers' meetings. Under APPEP the teachers clubs of ALPS were called "teacher centers." All teachers in a group of schools were expected to attend a compulsory meeting at the center on the third Saturday of the month. On that day the schools were closed and children were free. In some cases groups of children were taken to the centers to participate in demonstration lessons, a regular feature of programs at the centers.

One feature that was different in APPEP was the role of the head teachers and the local inspectors. With an average teacher–school ratio of 3.5:1, and with many schools having only two teachers, the system was severely understaffed. There were many schools

Figure 3
APPEP project on the training continuum

without a formally appointed head teacher. In these schools one of the staff acted in a senior coordinating capacity. Elsewhere heads were usually also full-time class teachers and hence had little opportunity or will to attempt to bring about the large-scale changes demanded by APPEP. Most of the local inspectors were too absorbed in administration to be able to undertake professional development. Nonetheless, they all agreed that such engagement should be part of their contribution to the overall improvement of the quality of primary education in Andhra Pradesh. With the absence of support from head teachers and inspectors, progress in the adoption of the project's principles was dependent upon: (a) the quality of the induction course provided, and (b) the extent to which the teacher center meetings were attended.

In combining elements of inservice and onservice training, APPEP was a large and ambitious project. However, in placing APPEP on the continuum, it might be appropriate to locate it more toward the inservice end and to the left of ALPS. In APPEP the whole of the training and, for most teachers, the attendance at teacher center meetings required teachers to leave their schools for shorter or longer periods of time. Like the ALPS teachers, teachers in the APPEP project who showed particular interest and ability were encouraged to assume leadership roles in the centers. These teachers emerged spontaneously. Their activities were confined to leading meetings of teachers, and as such they made a valuable contribution to the success of a vital part of the project. It would have been better if these teachers had been given sufficient assistance to enable them to provide more direct help to their fellow teachers on a more regular basis. Administrative structures did not permit the creation of posts equivalent to the Advisory Teacher in the United Kingdom's system, where teachers have the opportunity to interact on a one-to-one basis with a colleague who could assist with the development of improved strategies. The World Bank in creating a project (Primary Education Quality Improvement Project—PEQIP) parallel to ALPS in Indonesia attempted to create posts of field tutors, but difficulties arose over the status, role, and functions of such posts as well as over the qualifications of those who might have filled them.

2.3 Field-based Teacher Development Program (FBTD)

The third project is of a different character and

conforms more easily to all the criteria established for onservice provision (see Fig. 4). The Field-based Teacher Development (FBTD) program in the northern areas of Pakistan was initiated in 1984 to provide training for unqualified teachers (Bude 1991). Large numbers of unqualified teachers were working in primary schools in this part of Pakistan. The small capacity of the only government elementary teacher-training college, at Gilgit, did not permit a rapid increase in the supply of qualified teachers. At a time of increasing enrollments in primary schools, there was a need for a new approach to initial training. Through the joint initiative of the government of Pakistan and the Aga Khan Foundation, FBTD was introduced.

FBTD tried to improve the quality of primary education by (a) providing on-the-job training in specially designated courses for untrained primary teachers; (b) providing general inservice courses of two weeks' duration, open to every primary school teacher in the area.

The on-the-job training took place in middle or high schools under the supervision of qualified and experienced "master trainers." The primary section of a middle or high school was turned into a center, the qualified teachers were transferred to the centers, and the centers took in unqualified teachers for training. The maximum number of trainees was limited to ten. Two untrained teachers were put in charge of each class, one teaching and the other observing in turn.

The trainees were supervised by a master trainer and an assistant master trainer, who were selected for their outstanding teaching capabilities. They received a short period of training before joining a center and then guided the trainees in the conduct of the classes. They observed the trainees, made careful notes on their performance, and from time to time demonstrated better teaching techniques. At the end of the school day the master trainers and the trainees met to review the day's work and plan for the next day. In addition, time was spent on those subjects the trainees had to pass to obtain the primary teacher's certificate (e.g., school administration, child development, arts and crafts). Some additional help was also provided for the trainees with the content of primary-school subjects.

The government teacher-training college at Gilgit also prepared manuals in the five main primary school subjects for use by the trainees in preparing their lessons. Inservice courses of two weeks were conducted

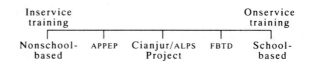

Figure 4
FBTD project on the training continuum

twice yearly for 120 primary school teachers. Trainees took part along with other teachers.

In reviewing the progress of the FBTD program Bude (1991) noted that over 4 years 320 teachers had been trained, 88 percent receiving the primary teacher's certificate on their first or second attempt. The FBTD used different schools throughout the period, with 27 schools participating in the training of the trainees. Only two Aga Khan Foundation and three government schools were used twice. By using different schools every year, FBTD was spread throughout the northern area.

3. Conclusion

These three examples of postappointment training for primary teachers represent different patterns of organization. FBTD is similar to arrangements for teachers in the Sudan, where in the mid-1970s the Omdurman Teachers' College provided coordinated in-college and in-school programs for professional development. The emphasis in the FBTD on the provision of direct support in schools took advantage of the possibilities of drawing upon the services of qualified staff near at hand. The use of a master trainer was a feature that depended on their ready availability, a situation that could be exploited in the northern areas of Pakistan.

In both the Indonesian and Andhra Pradesh studies there was little opportunity to draw upon other more senior staff. Schemes had to be developed that relied entirely on available expertise and facilities within the primary school system. Hence, in these cases there was less reliance on outside support. Rather, there was a tendency to look for what could be provided through mutual support, with teachers, head teachers, and local inspectors having a role to play. Essentially in ALPS and APPEP the mainspring of development was at ground level, with teachers taking the leading role. Through their frequent meetings and the exchange of ideas, a climate for professional growth was created which stimulated innovative approaches to teaching. For the most part, this stimulus was provided in the schools and formed the basis of the onservice training provided.

Onservice training seeks to encourage professional development and change without removing teachers from the everyday realities of the classroom. The conduct of training in schools, with teachers and their problems forming the main focus of programs, means that the daily demands of the school are not forgotten as ideas for classroom practices are investigated. This constant reminder of the possibilities and limitations of classroom change may have a retarding impact on the introduction of new practices as teachers carefully examine the implications of what is being requested of them. On the other hand, the detailed revision of possible ideas against a framework of school and classroom does ensure that ideas, once examined and accepted, have a better-than-average chance of being accepted and introduced into practice. Perhaps future developments will include a lessening of the reliance on courses—short or long—at a college or center where teachers are taken from the classroom, and a greater acceptance of school-based training. If so, then perhaps onservice training may be seen to be more cost-effective and more likely to lead to professional development and growth.

See also: Inservice Teacher Education; Supervision in Teacher Education

References

Bude U 1991 *Improving Primary School Teaching.* Deutsche stiftung für Internationale Entwicklung (DSE), Bonn
Edelfelt R 1985 *An Analysis of Policy Needs for In-service Education in Indonesia.* The International Learning Co-op (IMTEC), Oslo
Tangyong A F et al. 1990 *Quality through Support for Teachers: A Case Study from Indonesia.* Office of the Educational and Cultural Research and Development, Ministry of Education and Culture, Jakarta/DICE, Institute of Education, London

Further Reading

Bell L, Day C 1991 *Managing the Professional Development of Teachers.* Open University Press, Buckingham
Hopkins D, Wideen M 1984 *Alternative Perspectives on School Improvement.* Falmer, Philadelphia, Pennsylvania
Joyce B, Showers B 1980 Improving inservice training: The messages of research. *Educ. Leadership* 37: 379–85
McMahon A, Bolam R 1984 *A Handbook for LEAs.* Chapman, London

List of Contributors

Contributors are listed in alphabetical order together with their affiliations. Titles of articles which they have authored follow in alphabetical order, along with the respective page numbers. Where articles are co-authored, this has been indicated by an asterisk preceding the article title.

AIRASIAN, P. W. (Boston College, Chestnut Hill, Massachusetts, USA)
Classroom Assessment 290–94

ANDERSON, L. M. (Michigan State University, East Lansing, Michigan, USA)
Assignment and Supervision of Seatwork 264–68

ANDERSON, L. W. (University of South Carolina, Columbia, South Carolina, USA)
Individualized Instruction 155–61; **Instructional Pacing* 212–14; *Introduction (Part A, Section I)* 3–5; *Introduction (Part A, Section II)* 89–91; *Introduction (Part A, Section III)* 137–38; *Introduction (Part A, Section IV)* 185–87; *Introduction (Part A, Section V)* 305–07; *Introduction (Part A, Section VI)* 375–77; *Introduction (Part A, Section VII)* 437–39; *Introduction (Part A, Section VIII)* 487–88; *Introduction (Part B, Section I)* 525–27; *Introduction (Part B, Section II)* 571–73; *Introduction (Part B, Section III)* 605–06; **Substitute Teachers* 367–69; *Time, Allocated and Instructional* 204–07

ARTERO-BONAME, M. T. (University of Guam, Mangilao, Guam, USA)
*Questioning 242–48

BALLSTAEDT, S.-P. (University of Jena, Jena, Germany)
*Comprehension: Teaching and Assessing 444–50

BARR, R. (National College of Education, Evanston, Illinois, USA)
Grouping Students in the Classroom 192–96

BEN-PERETZ, M. (University of Haifa, Haifa, Israel)
Curriculum of Teacher Education Programs 543–47

BERLINER, D. C. (Arizona State University, Tempe, Arizona, USA)
Teacher Expertise 46–52

BIDDLE, B. J. (University of Missouri, Columbia, Missouri, USA)
Teachers' Roles 61–67

BLOCK, J. H. (University of California, Santa Barbara, California, USA)
*Teachers' Beliefs and Belief Systems 25–28

BOEKAERTS, M. (University of Leiden, Leiden, The Netherlands)
Affect, Emotions, and Learning 402–07

BOLAM, R. (University College, Swansea, UK)
Teacher Recruitment and Induction 612–15

BORICH, G. (University of Texas, Austin, Texas, USA)
*Grading and Evaluating Students 299–303

BURNS, R. B. (University of California, Riverside, California, USA)
Paradigms for Research on Teaching 91–96

BUTLER, D. L. (University of British Columbia, Vancouver, British Columbia, Canada)
*Student Cognitive Processes 420–27

CAIRNS, L. (Monash University, Gippsland, Victoria, Australia)
Analysis and Modification of Behavior 227–31

CALDERHEAD, J. (University of Bath, Bath, UK)
Teachers as Clinicians 9–11

COHEN, S. A. (University of San Francisco, San Francisco, California, USA)
Instructional Alignment 200–04

COLLINS, A. (Northwestern University, Evanston, Illinois, USA)
*Learning Environments 340–44

COLLOPY, R. M. B. (University of Michigan, Ann Arbor, Michigan, USA)
*Student Influences on Teaching 413–16

COMBER, L. C. (Kenilworth, Warwickshire, UK)
*Demonstrating 238–42

COOPER, J. M. (University of Virginia, Charlottesville, Virginia, USA)
Supervision in Teacher Education 593–98

CRUICKSHANK, D. R. (Ohio State University, Columbus, Ohio, USA)
*Explaining 232–38

CUDWORTH, A. L. (Nottingham Trent University, Nottingham, UK)
Simulations and Games 260–64

DAMON, W. (Brown University, Providence, Rhode Island, USA)
Peer Relations and Learning 336–39

DELAMONT, S. (University of Wales, Cardiff, UK)
Teachers as Artists 6–8

DILLON, J. T. (University of California, Riverside, California, USA)
Discussion 251–55

DOCHY, F. J. R. C. (University of Heerlen, Heerlen, The Netherlands)
Prior Knowledge and Learning 382–87

DUCHARME, E. R. (Drake University, Des Moines, Iowa, USA)
Characteristics of Teacher Educators 531–34

DUNKIN, M. J. (University of New South Wales, Oatley, New South Wales, Australia)
Comparative and International Studies of Teaching and Teacher Education 506–11; *Synthesizing Research on Teaching* 512–16

EMMER, E. T. (University of Texas, Austin, Texas, USA)
Teacher Managerial Behaviors 219–23

ERAUT, M. (University of Sussex, Brighton, UK)
Inservice Teacher Education 620–28

EVERTSON, C. M. (Vanderbilt University, Nashville, Tennessee, USA)
Classroom Rules and Routines 215–19

FELDHUSEN, J. F. (Purdue University, West Lafayette, Indiana, USA)
Creativity: Teaching and Assessing 476–81

FINN, J. D. (State University of New York, Buffalo, New York, USA)
*Class Size 310–15

FISHER, C. W. (University of Northern Colorado, Greeley, Colorado, USA)
Academic Learning Time 430–33

FRASER, B. J. (Curtin University of Technology, Perth, Western Australia, Australia)
Classroom Environments 344–48; *Student Perceptions of Classrooms* 416–19

FREEDMAN, S. W. (University of California, Berkeley, California, USA)
Written Composition: Teaching and Assessing 450–54

FULIGNI, A. J. (University of Michigan, Ann Arbor, Michigan, USA)
*Home Environment and School Learning 378–82

GALL, J. P. (University of Oregon, Eugene, Oregon, USA)
*Group Dynamics 352–58

GALL, M. D. (University of Oregon, Eugene, Oregon, USA)
*Group Dynamics 352–58; **Questioning* 242–48

GALLUZZO, G. R. (University of Northern Colorado, Greeley, Colorado, USA)
Evaluation of Teacher Education Programs 552–56

GALTON, M. (University of Leicester, Leicester, UK)
Classroom Observation 501–06

GARDNER, C. (University of South Carolina, Columbia, South Carolina, USA)
*Substitute Teachers 367–69

GARDNER, R. (University of London, London, UK)
Onservice Teacher Education 628–32

GIDEONSE, H. D. (University of Cincinnati, Cincinnati, Ohio, USA)
Governance of Teacher Education 556–60

GIMMESTAD, M. J. (University of Northern Colorado, Greeley, Colorado, USA)
*Structure of Teacher Education Programs 548–52

GINSBURG, M. B. (University of Pittsburgh, Pittsburgh, Pennsylvania, USA)
*Political Work of Teachers 67–72

GLASER, R. (University of Pittsburgh, Pittsburgh, Pennsylvania, USA)
*Assessment in the Service of Learning 279–82

GLATTHORN, A. (East Carolina University, Greenville, North Carolina, USA)
Teacher Development 41–46

GOOD, T. L. (University of Arizona, Tucson, Arizona, USA)
Teachers' Expectations 29–35

GREENO, J. G. (Stanford University, Stanford, California, USA)
Learning Environments 340–44

GROSSMAN, P. L. (University of Washington, Seattle, Washington, USA)
Teachers' Knowledge 20–24

GUSKEY, T. R. (University of Kentucky, Lexington, Kentucky, USA)
Mastery Learning 161–67

HALL, G. E. (University of Northern Colorado, Greeley, Colorado, USA)
Structure of Teacher Education Programs 548–52

HARGREAVES, A. (Ontario Institute for Studies in Education, Toronto, Ontario, Canada)
Realities of Teaching 80–87

HARNISCHFEGER, A. (Northwestern University, Evanston, Illinois, USA)
Attention in Learning 427–29

HATIVA, N. (Tel Aviv University, Tel Aviv, Israel)
Technology and the Classroom Teacher 359–63

HATTON, N. G. (University of Sydney, Sydney, New South Wales, Australia)
Teacher Placement and School Staffing 606–11

HAZEL, E. (University of Technology, Sydney, New South Wales, Australia)
Science Laboratory Instruction 171–74

HAZELIP, K. (University of California, Santa Barbara, California, USA)
Teachers' Beliefs and Belief Systems 25–28

HECKMAN, P. E. (University of Arizona, Tucson, Arizona, USA)
Age Grouping of Students 315–18

HELMKE, A. (University of Landau, Landau, Germany)
Diagnosing Students' Needs 286–90; *Diagnostic–Prescriptive Teaching* 174–78

HENDRICKS-LEE, M. S. (University of Cincinnati, Cincinnati, Ohio, USA)
Teacher Planning 188–92

HILL, J. (University of Illinois, Champaign, Illinois, USA)
School Culture and Peer Groups 332–36

HOLLINGSWORTH, S. (Michigan State University, East Lansing, Michigan, USA)
Teachers as Researchers 16–19

HOYLE, E. (University of Bristol, Bristol, UK)
Social Status of Teaching 58–61; *Teachers as Professionals* 11–15

JOHNSON, D. W. (University of Minnesota, Minneapolis, Minnesota, USA)
Goal Structures 349–52; *Social Psychological Theories of Teaching* 112–17

JOHNSON, R. T. (University of Minnesota, Minneapolis, Minnesota, USA)
Goal Structures 349–52; *Social Psychological Theories of Teaching* 112–17

KAMAT, S. G. (University of Pittsburgh, Pittsburgh, Pennsylvania, USA)
Political Work of Teachers 67–72

KEEVES, J. P. (The Flinders University of South Australia, Bedford Park, South Australia, Australia)
Demonstrating 238–42

KNIGHT, S. L. (University of Houston, Houston, Texas, USA)
Laboratory and Professional Development Schools 598–604

KRATOCHWILL, T. R. (University of Wisconsin-Madison, Madison, Wisconsin, USA)
Reinforcement 224–27

KUBISZYN, T. (University of Texas, Austin, Texas, USA)
Grading and Evaluating Students 299–303

LACEY, C. (University of Sussex, Brighton, UK)
Professional Socialization of Teachers 616–20

LAMBERT, N. M. (University of California, Berkeley, California, USA)
Seating Arrangements 196–200

LANE, S. (University of Pittsburgh, Pittsburgh, Pennsylvania, USA)
Assessment in the Service of Learning 279–82

LEIGHFIELD, K. (University of Virginia, Charlottesville, Virginia, USA)
Student Teaching and Field Experiences 588–93

LENS, W. (University of Leuven, Leuven, Belgium)
Motivation and Learning 395–402

LINACRE, J. M. (University of Chicago, Chicago, Illinois, USA)
Individualized Testing in the Classroom 295–99

LUKE, A. (James Cook University of North Queensland, Townsville, Queensland, Australia)
Critical Reading: Teaching and Assessing 467–71

MCANINCH, A. R. (Knox College, Galesburg, Illinois, USA)
Case Methods in Teacher Education 583–88

MCCARTHEY, S. J. (University of Texas, Austin, Texas, USA)
Student Roles in Classrooms 408–13

MACLEOD, G. (University of New England, Lismore, New South Wales, Australia)
Microteaching in Teacher Education 573–77

MARLAND, P. W. (University of Southern Queensland / Toowamba, Queensland, Australia)
Implicit Theories of Teaching 131–36

MARSH, H. W. (University of Western Sydney, Macarthur, New South Wales, Australia)
Student Evaluation of Teaching 493–501

MARX, R. W. (University of Michigan, Ann Arbor, Michigan, USA)
Student Influences on Teaching 413–16

MAYER, R. E. (University of California, Santa Barbara, California, USA)
Feedback 249–50; *Problem-solving: Teaching and Assessing* 463–66; *Study Habits and Strategies* 434–36

MEDLEY, D. M. (University of Virginia, Charlottesville, Virginia, USA)
Teacher Evaluation 488–93

MEDWAY, F. J. (University of South Carolina, Columbia, South Carolina, USA)
Tutoring 271–74

MEISTER, C. (University of Illinois, Champaign, Illinois, USA)
Direct Instruction 143–49

MESSICK, S. (Educational Testing Service, Princeton, New Jersey, USA)
Cognitive Styles and Learning 387–90

METCALF, K. K. (Indiana University, Bloomington, Indiana, USA)
Explaining 232–38; *Laboratory Experiences in Teacher Education* 578–82

MEYER, D. K. (University of Texas, Austin, Texas, USA)
Learning Strategies: Teaching and Assessing 471–76

MORINE-DERSHIMER, G. (University of Virginia, Charlottesville, Virginia, USA)
Student Teaching and Field Experiences 588–93

MURNANE, R. J. (Harvard University, Cambridge, Massachusetts, USA)
Supply of Teachers 72–76

NEURURER, J. (University of South Carolina, Columbia, South Carolina, USA)
Characteristics of Prospective Teachers 528–31

NUTHALL, G. (University of Canterbury, Christchurch, New Zealand)
Heuristic Models of Teaching 122–27

OAKES, J. (University of California, Los Angeles, California, USA)
Age Grouping of Students 315–18

OJA, S. N. (University of New Hampshire, Durham, New Hampshire, USA)
Adult Development and Teacher Education 535–39

OSER, F. K. (University of Fribourg, Fribourg, Switzerland)
Teacher Responsibility 35–41

PASCHAL, R. A. (Northern Illinois University, De Kalb, Illinois, USA)
Homework 268–71

PATRY, J.-L. (University of Fribourg, Fribourg, Switzerland)
Teacher Responsibility 35–41

PAYNE, M. A. (University of Waikato, Hamilton, New Zealand)
School–Parent Relationships 370–74

PETERSON, P. L. (Michigan State University, East Lansing, Michigan, USA)
Student Roles in Classrooms 408–13

PRESSLEY, M. (University of Maryland, College Park, Maryland, USA)
Memory: Teaching and Assessing 439–44

RATHS, J. (University of Delaware, Newark, Delaware, USA)
Teacher Education Accreditation and Standards 561–65

RESNICK, L. B. (University of Pittsburgh, Pittsburgh, Pennsylvania, USA)
Learning Environments 340–44

REYNOLDS, B. P. (University of South Carolina, Columbia, South Carolina, USA)
Availability and Use of Paraprofessionals 363–67

ROSENSHINE, B. (University of Illinois, Champaign, Illinois, USA)
Direct Instruction 143–49

SAHA, L. J. (Australian National University, Canberra, ACT, Australia)
Aspirations and Expectations of Students 391–95

SCANNELL, D. P. (University of South Carolina, Columbia, South Carolina, USA)
Teacher Certification and Standards 565–70

SCANNELL, M. M. (South Carolina Commission on Higher Education, Columbia, South Carolina, USA)
Teacher Certification and Standards 565–70

SCHNOTZ, W. (University of Jena, Jena, Germany)
Comprehension: Teaching and Assessing 444–50

SCHRADER, F.-W. (University of Landau, Landau, Germany)
Diagnostic–Prescriptive Teaching 174–78

SCHWAB, R. L. (Drake University, Des Moines, Iowa, USA)
Teacher Stress and Burnout 52–57

SHAH, S. (University of Hertfordshire, Hatfield, UK)
Planning Teacher Education 540–43

SHANNON, D. M. (Auburn University, Auburn, Alabama, USA)
Teacher Evaluation 488–93

SHARAN, S. (Tel Aviv University, Tel Aviv, Israel)
Teaching in Small Groups 255–59

SHEPARD, L. A. (University of Colorado, Boulder, Colorado, USA)
Grade Repeating 324–26

SIMONS, P. R.-J. (University of Nijmegen, Nijmegen, The Netherlands)
Metacognitive Strategies: Teaching and Assessing 481–85

SLADECZEK, I. E. (University of Wisconsin-Madison, Madison, Wisconsin, USA)
Reinforcement 224–27

SLAVIN, R. E. (Johns Hopkins University, Baltimore, Maryland, USA)
Cooperative Learning 139–43

SMITH, H. A. (Queen's University, Kingston, Ontario, Canada)
Nonverbal Teacher Behavior 274–78

SNOW, R. E. (Stanford University, Stanford, California, USA)
Aptitude–Treatment Interaction Model of Teaching 127–31

SPRINTHALL, N. A. (North Carolina State University, Raleigh, North Carolina, USA)
Cognitive Developmental Theories of Teaching 101–06

STALLINGS, J. A. (Texas A&M University, College Station, Texas, USA)
Laboratory and Professional Development Schools 598–604

STEVENSON, H. W. (University of Michigan, Ann Arbor, Michigan, USA)
Home Environment and School Learning 378–82

SULZER-AZAROFF, B. (University of Massachusetts, Amherst, Massachusetts, USA)
Behavioristic Theories of Teaching 96–101

TAMIR, P. (Hebrew University, Jerusalem, Israel)
Discovery Learning and Teaching 149–55

TENNYSON, R. D. (University of Minnesota, Minneapolis, Minnesota, USA)
Concept Learning: Teaching and Assessing 457–63

THIBADEAU, G. (Indiana University of Pennsylvania, Indiana, Pennsylvania, USA)
Open Education 167–71

TORPER, U. (University of Lund, Lund, Sweden)
Frame Factors 308–10

TORREY, P. (University of South Carolina, Columbia, South Carolina, USA)
Instructional Pacing 212–14

VAN DER SANDEN, J. M. M. (Tilburg University, Tilburg, The Netherlands)
Motor Skills: Learning and Instruction 454–57

VAN METER, P. (University of Maryland, College Park, Maryland, USA)
Memory: Teaching and Assessing 439–44

VILLAR, L. M. (University of Seville, Seville, Spain)
Reflective Teaching 178–83

VOELKL, K. E. (State University of New York, Buffalo, New York, USA)
Class Size 310–15

WALBERG, H. J. (University of Illinois at Chicago, Chicago, Illinois, USA)
Homework 268–71

WALTON, C. (Northern Territory University, Darwin, Northern Territory, Australia)
Critical Reading: Teaching and Assessing 467–71

WANG, M. C. (Temple University, Philadelphia, Pennsylvania, USA)
Student Diversity and Classroom Teaching 326–31

WATSON, A. J. (University of New South Wales, Kensington, Australia)
Teacher Placement and School Staffing 606–11

WEILER, K. A. (Tufts University, Medford, Massachusetts, USA)
Women and the Professionalization of Teaching 76–80

WEINER, G. (South Bank University, London, UK)
Gender and Racial Differences Among Students 319–23

WEINERT, F. E. (Max Planck Institute for Psychological Research, Munich, Germany)
Translating Research into Practice 517–22

WEINSTEIN, C. E. (University of Texas, Austin, Texas, USA)
Learning Strategies: Teaching and Assessing 471–76

WINNE, P. H. (Simon Fraser University, Burnaby, British Columbia, Canada)
Information Processing Theories of Teaching 107–12; *Student Cognitive Processes* 420–27

WISEMAN, D. L. (Texas A&M University, College Station, Texas, USA)
Laboratory and Professional Development Schools 598–604

WRAGG, E. C. (Exeter University, Exeter, UK)
Lesson Structure 207–11

YINGER, R. J. (University of Cincinnati, Cincinnati, Ohio, USA)
Teacher Planning 188–92

YOUNG, R. (University of Sydney, Sydney, New South Wales, Australia)
Linguistic and Sociolinguistic Theories of Teaching 117–22

ZAHORIK, J. A. (University of Wisconsin, Milwaukee, Wisconsin, USA)
Evaluating 283–86

Name Index

The Name Index has been compiled so that the reader can proceed directly to the page where an author's work is cited, or to the reference itself in the bibliography. For each name, the page numbers for the bibliographic section are given first, followed by the page number(s) in parentheses where that reference is cited in text. Where a name is referred to only in text, and not in the bibliography, the page number appears only in parentheses.

The accuracy of the spelling of authors' names has been affected by the use of different initials by some authors, or a different spelling of their name in different papers or review articles (sometimes this may arise from a transliteration process), and by those journals which give only one initial to each author.

Abagi J O, 416 (415)
Abbott R D, 412 (410)
Abelard P, (252)
Abraham H, 155 (151, 152)
Abrami P C, 500 (496)
Abramson L Y, 401 (400)
Abt C C, 263 (261, 262)
Achilles C M, 315 (313)
Acker S, 86 (83, 84)
Ackerman P L, 429 (428)
Acosta J M, 191 (189)
Adams A, 45 (44)
Adams D M, 263 (260, 261)
Adams J A, 251 (250), 456 (455)
Adams R, 555 (552, 553)
Adams R J, 299 (298)
Adams R S, 66 (66)
Adams R W, 199 (198)
Adams V M, 407
Adelman C, 505 (502)
Adger C R, 199 (197)
Aggarwal Y P, 199 (198)
Agne R, 534 (531, 532, 533)
Ahlbrand W, 121 (119)
Aiken W M, 106 (105)
Aikenhead G S, 174 (172)
Airasian P W, 294 (291, 292, 293)
Aitkin M, 210 (209)
Ajzen I, 28 (25), 395 (391, 393)
Alberto P A, 101
Alderson J C, 299
Alexander K L, 195 (193, 195), 382 (378), 395 (394)
Alexander P A, 111 (108), 386, 386 (382, 383, 383), 412 (411), 426 (421, 422, 423), 463
Alleman J, 267 (264, 265), 294 (292)
Alleman-Brooks J, 267 (264, 266)
Allen D W, 577 (573, 574, 575)
Allen J D, 223 (223)
Allen V L, 131 (127), 273 (272, 273)
Alley R, 67 (61, 65)
Allington R, 195 (194, 195)
Allison C, 534 (534)
Allport G, 143 (142)
Alpert B, 247 (243)
Altbach P G, 569 (566)
Althof W, 40 (38, 39)

Alvermann D E, 254 (252)
Amabile T M, 480 (477, 478)
Ames C, 28 (25)
Ames G, 339 (338)
Ames R, 28 (25)
Andersen D G, 570 (568)
Anderson C W, 195 (195), 267 (265)
Anderson D S, 516 (513, 514)
Anderson G J, 348 (345)
Anderson G L, 426 (420)
Anderson J R, 343 (343), 443 (442, 443), 456 (456), 464 (464)
Anderson L M, 218 (215, 216), 267 (264, 266)
Anderson L W, 15 (11, 14), 160 (156, 158), 166 (162), 178 (177), 206 (205, 206), 214 (213), 285 (285), 294 (290), 315 (311), 433 (431, 432), 505 (501, 502, 503, 505), 511 (506, 508, 510, 511), 516 (515), 521 (517, 520)
Anderson M B, 56 (55)
Anderson R C, 412 (408), 443 (441, 442), 449 (447)
Anderson R E, 207 (205)
Anderson R H, 318 (316)
Anderson T H, 237 (234), 449 (447)
Anderson V, 111 (110)
Anderson-Levitt K M, 326 (325)
Andrae J, 170 (167, 168)
Ankenmann R, 282 (281)
Ankhara-Dove L A, 75 (72, 74), 611 (610)
Anthony H, 285 (285)
Anyon J, 28 (26)
Apple M W, 15 (14), 71 (67, 69). 79 (77), 86 (81)
Applebee A, 453–54 (452, 453)
Arends R, 582 (579)
Arfwedson G, 309 (309)
Argyle M, 577 (575)
Aries P, 318 (315)
Arlin M, 214 (212), 223 (222)
Armbruster B B, 237 (234), 449 (446)
Arnot M, 79, 323 (320)
Aronowitz S, 121 (119)
Aronson E, 57 (55), 143 (141, 142), (336)
Arredondo D E, 166 (164, 166)
Arter J A, 178 (174, 175)
Åsén G, 310 (309)
Ashby E, 101 (99)

Ashcroft L, 204 (202)
Ashton D, 18 (17)
Ashton P T, 86 (80, 83, 86), 534 (534), 560
Atkinson E P, 174 (172)
Atkinson J W, 116 (114), 401 (396, 397, 399)
Atkinson P A, 8 (8), 121
Au K H, 247 (245), 267 (267), 412 (409)
Aubrecht J D, 500 (499)
Aussiker A, 218 (215), 223 (222)
Austin G A, 251 (250)
Ausubel D P, 155, 285 (284), 386 (382), 449 (445)
Avalos B, 543 (540)
Avoseh O, 530 (529)
Axtell R E, 278
Azuma H, 382 (380)

Babad E Y, 416 (415)
Bachelor P, 481 (477, 478)
Bacon F, (151), (252)
Baddeley A, 429 (428)
Bagunywa A, 71 (68)
Bailey M, 500 (495)
Baird J R, 174 (173, 174)
Baker C D, 471 (469)
Baker D, 382 (380)
Baker E L, 191 (188), 282 (280, 281)
Baker F B, 299
Baker L, 412 (409), 449 (446), 471 (467)
Baker-Ward L, 444 (440)
Bales R, 358 (353)
Ball D L, 24 (21), 267 (265), 516 (515)
Ballstaedt S-P, 449 (447)
Bandura A, 116 (115), 401 (398, 401), 407 (404), 429 (428), 577 (574)
Bangert-Drowns R L, 160 (159), 167 (161, 165, 166), 318 (317), 521 (520)
Bank B J, 66 (65)
Bantock G H, 211 (209)
Bany M A, 231 (227)
Barakett J M, 416 (415)
Barba R, 247 (244)
Barber L, 8
Barber P J, 429 (428)
Barham I H, 453 (453)
Barker R G, 96 (94), 318 (317)
Barker-Lunn J C, 195 (194)

Barnes D L, 143 (139), 366 (365)
Barnett J E, 436 (435)
Baron J, 444 (442)
Baron R, 34 (30)
Barr A, 96 (93)
Barr K B, 231 (230)
Barr R, 195–96 (192, 193, 194, 195), 214 (213)
Barrett B, 106 (103)
Barrett I, 565 (562)
Barro S M, 75 (72)
Barshis D, 167 (165)
Bar-Tal D, 117
Barth R S, 170 (167, 168)
Bartlett F C, 449 (445)
Barton R F, 263 (260)
Bassett G W, 61 (60)
Bassett S, 366–67 (364, 365)
Bassok M, 131 (130)
Bates G C, 174 (172)
Batten H D, 577 (573)
Battistich V, 41 (40)
Bauch J P, 373 (370)
Baumann J F, 148 (144)
Baumrind D, 382 (379)
Baxter G P, 466 (465)
Baxter M B, 170 (168, 169)
Beach R W, 426 (423), 436 (435)
Bean T W, 148 (145)
Beattie J R, 369 (368)
Beauchamp L, 547 (546)
Becker F D, 199 (198)
Becker H J, 363 (360, 361, 362)
Becker H S, 620 (617)
Becker J, 323 (321, 322)
Becker R M, 148 (146)
Becker W C, 101 (100), 148 (146), 231 (230)
Beckerman T M, 214 (213)
Bee J, 199 (198)
Beech J R, 429 (428)
Beecher C, (77)
Bejar I I, 466 (466)
Belenky M, 79 (78)
Belenky M F, 18 (18), 538 (537)
Bell A, (272)
Bell K E, 101 (100)
Bell L, 493, 632
Bell S R, 299 (298)
Bellack A A, 106 (102), 237 (236, 237), 309 (308), 505 (505)
Belmont J M, 444 (443)
Benally A, 248 (244)
Benejam P, 530 (528)
Benington M, 493
Bennett J M, 476 (473)
Bennett N, 170 (167, 168), 267 (264, 266), 285 (283), 433, 505 (502)
Bennett S N, 199 (198), 210–11 (209), 330 (326)
Ben-Peretz M, 24 (21), 207, 433, 547 (543, 545), 592 (589, 591)
Bents M, 52 (48)
Bents R, 52 (48)
Bereiter C, 344 (340), 463 (459, 460), 485
Berends M, 196 (193, 194)
Bergem T, 40 (35, 39)

Bergstrom B A, 299 (296)
Berkowitz M W, 106 (104)
Berliner D C, 24 (21), 52 (48, 49, 50, 51), 207, 223 (220), 369 (369), 416 (415), 433 (431), 493 (489), 505 (505), 521 (519), 582 (578)
Berlyne D E, 116 (114), 449 (446)
Bernagozzi T, 226 (225)
Bernbaum G, 61 (59)
Bernstein B, 121 (118, 119), 309 (309)
Berry B, 569 (567)
Berry P C, 466 (464)
Bertini M, 390 (389)
Berube M, 71 (70, 71)
Besemer S P, 480–81 (477)
Bessant B, 15 (13)
Betz M, 61 (60)
Beyerbach B A, 11 (11)
Biddle B J, 66 (62, 63, 65, 66), 96 (93), 516 (513, 514)
Biddle J, 238 (236)
Biddulph F, 126 (125)
Biggs J B, 390 (389), 476 (472)
Bijou S W, 227
Biklen S K, 79 (78, 79)
Billingsley B, 285 (285)
Birch D, 401 (397)
Bird T, 588 (583, 586)
Birman B, 366 (364)
Bixby J, 126 (126)
Bjorklund D F, 199 (197)
Black A, 200 (199)
Black J B, 449 (447)
Blackburn V, 627 (627)
Blagg N, 521 (520)
Blakey J, 565 (562, 563)
Blaney N T, 143 (141, 142)
Blase J, 56 (55), 71 (68)
Blattstein A, 500 (499)
Blattstein D, 500 (499)
Blau D M, 395 (392)
Blau F D, 395 (394)
Bledstein B, 79 (76)
Bleich D, (467)
Bliss J, 174 (172)
Block C H, 466 (464)
Block J H, 160 (159), 166 (162, 164, 166)
Bloom B J, 273 (272)
Bloom B S, 28 (27, 28), 160 (159), 166 (161, 162, 164, 166), 203 (203), 247 (243), 330 (326), 377 (377), 386 (383), 466 (464), 521–22 (517)
Bloome D, 218 (217)
Blum A, 71 (68, 69, 70, 71)
Blumenfeld, (344)
Blumenfeld P C, 267 (264, 265)
Blumer H, 620 (619)
Blundell D, 199 (198)
Bobbitt S A, 75
Boekaerts M, 407 (403, 405, 406)
Boersma F J, 323 (319)
Bolam R, 627 (621), 632
Boles K, 18 (17), 79
Bollen R, 627 (622)
Bolster A, 96 (94)

Bolvin J O, 214 (212)
Bontempo B T, 369 (367, 368)
Boocock S S, 263 (260)
Book C, 86 (81)
Boothroyd W, 597 (594)
Borg W R, 247 (246, 247), 582 (579)
Borich G, 303 (300, 302), 555 (554)
Boris R B, 203 (203)
Borko H, 52 (47, 50), 148 (146), 191–92 (189, 190)
Borkowski J G, 126 (123), 426 (426), 444 (442, 443), 449 (447)
Borman K M, 547 (544)
Boruta M, 454 (452)
Boschee F, 597 (594)
Bosco J J, 363 (361)
Bossert S T, 196 (193), 219
Botkin M, 35 (31)
Bouchard T J, 466 (464)
Boud D J, 174 (171, 172)
Bourdieu P, 335 (334)
Bower G H, 251 (250), 407 (403)
Bowers C A, 223
Bowman J, 565
Box S, 395 (394)
Boyd W L, 373 (373)
Boydell D, 598
Boyer E G, 506 (501)
Boyle C F, 343 (343)
Brace D L, 369 (367)
Braden J, 227 (225)
Bradley C, 531 (530)
Bradley H, 627 (623, 626)
Brah A, 323 (320)
Brandenburg D C, 500 (499)
Bransford J D, 111 (110), 444 (442)
Bransford J O, 449 (445)
Brantlinger E, 373 (370, 372, 373)
Braskamp L, 117 (116)
Braskamp L A, 500 (499)
Brattesani K, 34 (31)
Braverman H, 15 (11, 13)
Brekelmans M, 419 (417)
Brennan J, 323 (321)
Breuer K, 463 (461)
Brewster M E, 126 (124)
Bridges D, 211 (208), 255 (251, 252, 253), 357 (357)
Briggs L J, 111 (108)
Brighton H, 366 (364)
Brinko K T, 500 (499)
Brits V M, 560
Britton J, 143 (139), 453 (450, 452)
Britzman D P, 24 (22)
Broadfoot P, 15 (14), 45 (42)
Broady D, 309 (309)
Broder L J, 466 (464)
Broeckmans J, 191 (189)
Bromme R, 11 (10), 207, 433
Brookhart S M, 530 (529, 530)
Brookover W B, 330 (327)
Brooks B D, 101 (99)
Brooks D M, 52 (49), 278 (275, 277)
Brooks G, 323 (319)
Brophy J E, 11 (9), 24 (21, 22), 34 (29, 30,

31), 148 (144), 178 (177), 223, 247–48 (244, 246), 267–8 (264, 265), 285 (283, 284), 294 (292), 323 (321, 322), 348 (344), 416 (415), 493 (489, 491), 505 (505), 516 (515)

Brott R, 560 (557)

Broudy H S, 582 (578), 587 (584, 585, 587)

Brown A L, 111 (108), 126 (122, 123), 148 (145, 146), 282 (280), 286 (285), 344 (342), 412 (409), 444 (440, 442), 449 (446, 447), 466 (465), 471 (467), 485

Brown G A, 565 (562), 577 (574, 575)

Brown J, 285 (285)

Brown J A, 466 (466)

Brown J I, 476 (473)

Brown J S, 126 (123, 126), 148 (145), 251 (250), 267 (265, 266), 344 (342), 412 (411), 449 (447), 456 (456), 485

Brown R, 444 (441, 442)

Brown S, 11 (10), 136 (135), 547 (546)

Brubaker N L, 267 (264, 266)

Bruce B B, 412 (410, 411)

Bruce M G, 326 (325)

Brudner H J, 214 (212)

Bruner J S, 18 (17), 24 (22), (122), 154 (149, 153), 251 (250), 330 (326), 426 (420)

Bryan W L, 52 (47)

Bryant S L, 444 (440)

Bryk A S, 419

Buch M B, 547 (543)

Buchmann M, 547 (545), 592 (589)

Bude U, 632 (631, 632)

Bulcock J W, 416 (415)

Bull B L, 15 (11, 15), 40 (36)

Bullough R, 52 (47), 294 (290)

Bunderson C V, 290 (289)

Burbules N L, 15 (15)

Burch P, 373 (370, 372, 373)

Burchfield S A, 611 (611)

Burden P R, 45 (41), 538 (535, 537)

Burden R, 419 (418)

Burgess T, 453 (452)

Burk F, (155)

Burke C L, 412 (410)

Burke R J, 56 (55)

Burns R B, 160 (157, 159), 166 (162), 204 (201), 505 (501, 502, 503, 505), 511, 516 (515), 521 (517, 520)

Burris V, 395 (394)

Burstall C, 294 (293)

Burton R R, 251 (250), 466 (466)

Bush R N, 577 (573)

Busse T V, 466 (465)

Buswinka H F, 191 (190)

Butcher P M, 577 (576)

Butterfield E C, 444 (443)

Butterworth T, 416 (414)

Byrne B M, 56 (54)

Byrnes J P, 426 (425, 426)

Cabezon E, 166 (165)

Cadinale L, 247 (244)

Cahen L S, 214 (213)

Cai J, 282 (281)

Calderhead J, 11 (11), 24, 136 (133), 294 (290), 565 (562)

Calderhead T, 15 (11, 13)

Calhoun J F, 56 (55)

Callan P M, 603 (601)

Callewaert S, 309–10 (309)

Cambone J, 223 (223)

Campione J C, 444 (442)

Campione J C, 126 (122, 123), 148 (146), 282 (280), 466 (465)

Canieso-Doronila M L, 71 (68)

Canter L, 231 (227)

Canter M, 231 (227)

Caplan R D, 56 (54)

Carini P, 18 (16)

Carlsen W S, 24 (21), 34 (34), 247–48 (242, 243, 245)

Carlson D, 71 (67)

Carmeli M, 274 (272)

Carnahan R S, 191 (189)

Carnine D W, 101 (100), 148 (146)

Carpenter P G, 395 (393)

Carpenter T C, 290 (289), 412 (410, 411)

Carpenter T P, 24 (21), 412 (409)

Carr M, 290 (289), 426 (426), 449 (447)

Carr W, 182 (182)

Carrascosa J, 126 (122)

Carroll J B, 330 (326), 433 (431), 521 (520)

Carron G, 543 (540)

Carta J J, 274 (272)

Carter D B, 382

Carter K, 24 (20, 21), 52 (49, 50, 51), 136, 223 (221), 416 (415), 587 (583, 585, 586)

Carter L, 357 (352, 353)

Carter R, 471 (470)

Cashin W E, 500 (496, 500)

Cason H, 251 (250)

Castañeda A, 390 (390)

Cataldo M F, 101 (98)

Catania A C, 101 (97)

Cattell R B, (387)

Cavell S, 565 (562)

Cazden C, 121 (118, 121), 126 (123), 191 (190)

Centra J A, 500 (495, 497, 498)

Chalmers-Neubauer I, 255 (252)

Chambers J, 565

Chambers M, 603 (599)

Chambers P, 565 (562)

Champagne A B, 174 (173)

Chan K S, 166 (165)

Chance P, 466 (465)

Chandler M O, 531 (528)

Chang M C, 530 (528)

Chao C-I, 112 (108)

Chapman D W, 57 (55), 611 (611)

Chapman J W, 323 (319)

Charles C M, 178 (175), 231 (230), 358 (356)

Charles R I, 466 (463)

Chase C I, 366 (365)

Chase W G, 52 (49)

Chaudron C, 248 (246)

Chen C, 382 (381)

Chernoff M L, 493

Chi M T H, 52 (48, 50, 51), 154 (153),

282 (279)

Chickering A W, (535)

Chin R, 627 (621)

Chipman S F, 466 (464)

Christensen C R, 587 (584)

Christensen J C, 538 (535)

Christensen P A, 592 (590)

Christenson S L, 178 (176, 177)

Chung-it Y, 543 (540)

Churukian G A, 560

Clandinin D G, 547 (545)

Clandinin D J, 18 (16), 24 (22, 23), 136 (134)

Clarizio H F, 480 (478)

Clark B, 534 (531)

Clark C, 96 (95)

Clark C M, 11 (10), 24 (21), 28 (25), 45 (44), 136 (134), 178 (176), 191 (189), 290 (286), 294 (290, 291, 292)

Clark D L, 560 (557)

Clark J L, 248 (243)

Clark R W, 603 (598, 600, 601)

Clark S M, 171 (169)

Claus K E, 577 (575)

Clay M M, 412 (409)

Cleary M J, 597 (593)

Cleghorn A, 416 (415)

Clement, 251 (250)

Clements B S, 219, 223 (220)

Clifford G, 534 (531)

Clift J C, 577 (574)

Clift P, 323 (320)

Clift R T, 11 (10, 11), 547 (546)

Clifton R A, 369 (368), 416 (415)

Clinchy B M, 18 (18), 79 (78), 538 (537)

Clinkenbeard P M, 481 (480)

Clough B M, 366 (364)

Clough D B, 366 (364)

Cobb P, 248 (244)

Cochran K F, 552 (551)

Cochran M, 373 (372)

Cochran-Smith M, 603 (601)

Cockburn A, 267 (264, 266), 433

Cogan M L, 597 (595)

Cohen E G, 196 (193), 223 (223), 259 (257, 258)

Cohen J, 516 (513)

Cohen L, 299 (296)

Cohen P A, 101 (100), 274 (272), 500 (496, 499)

Cohen S A, 204 (201, 202, 203)

Cohen S B, 238 (235)

Cohn M M, 136

Coker H, 493 (491)

Coladarci T, 290 (288)

Colarusso R P, 178 (174)

Colbert J A, 588 (586)

Cole M, 318 (318), 522 (519)

Coleman J, 335 (332)

Collins A, 126 (123, 126), 148 (145), 267 (265, 266), 282 (280, 281), 285 (285), 344 (341, 342), 412 (411), 449 (447), 456 (456), 466 (465), 485

Collins C, 126 (126)

Collins K A, 552

Collins W A, 106 (105), 382 (381)

Collis B, 363 (359, 360)
Colman J E, 8 (6)
Combs R, 34 (32)
Comeaux M A, 52 (50, 51)
Comenius, (167)
Comenius J A, (161)
Comer J P, 330 (326)
Comfort R E, 592 (590)
Conant J B, 615 (615)
Conley S, 45 (45)
Connell R W, 8 (7), 71 (67, 68, 69, 71),
    79, 323 (319), 395 (392)
Connell W F, 323 (319)
Connelly M F, 24 (22, 23)
Conner J, 255 (252)
Conners D A, 200
Conway C G, 500 (496, 497)
Cook L K, 426 (422), 436 (435)
Cook M A, 195 (193, 195), 290 (288),
    395 (394)
Cook-Greuter S, 538 (536)
Cooley W W, 214 (212), 521 (519)
Cooper B, 620 (619)
Cooper H M, 28 (26), 34 (29, 30, 31), 206
    (206), 271, 516
Cooper J, 555 (554)
Cooper L, 143 (142)
Cooper P, 323 (319)
Cooper W H, 493 (491)
Copeland W D, 582 (579), (595)
Coppedge F L, 226 (225)
Corcoran T B, 46 (43)
Corey S, 18 (16)
Corno L, 130 (128, 129), 160 (155, 157,
    158, 159, 160), 178 (175, 176), 290 (288),
    330 (327), 521 (520)
Corrigan D C, 552, 603 (601)
Corsaro W A, 335
Coulter F, 530 (529, 530)
Counts F A, 61 (58)
Courtney D P, 419 (417)
Covington M V, 466 (464), 480 (480)
Cox J, 214 (212, 213)
Coxon A P M, 61 (58)
Craig J, 555 (552, 553)
Crandall D, 628 (626)
Crane S, 56 (54)
Cranton P A, 500 (497)
Craven R G, 226 (225)
Crawford G, 214 (213)
Crawford R P, 466 (464)
Creemers B P M, 191 (190)
Crehan E, 86 (86)
Creton H A, 218–19 (218)
Crocker L, 534 (534)
Croll P J, 323 (321), 505–06 (501, 502,
    503, 504, 505)
Croll V J, 436 (435)
Cronbach L J, 96 (94, 95), 130 (127, 129,
    130), 154 (150)
Cronbach R J, 178 (175, 176)
Crowell R, 204
Crowson R L, 373 (373)
Cruickshank D R, 238 (236), 582 (578,
    579, 580)

Crutchfield R S, 466 (464), 480 (480)
Csikszentmihalyi M, 271 (270)
Cuban L, 86 (83), 138, 160 (159), 251
    (250), 363 (362), 603 (601)
Culbertson S A, 227 (224)
Cummings A L, 538 (536)
Cummings W K, 196 (192)
Cushing K S, 52 (49, 50, 51), 416 (415)
Cusick P, 28 (26, 27)

Dagher Z R, 238 (233)
Dahl K, 412 (410)
Dahlberg G, 309 (309)
Dahllöf U, 309–10 (308)
Daiute C, 412 (410), 454
Dalin P, 560
Daly J A, 199 (197)
Damon W, 40 (36, 39), 339 (336, 337,
    338, 339)
Dance K A, 130 (127)
Daniel N, 214 (212, 213)
Dansereau D F, 436 (435)
Dantonio M, 248 (242)
d'Apollonia S, 500 (496)
Darling-Hammond L, 46 (44), 259 (259),
    493, 530 (529), 569 (566, 567), 603 (601,
    602), 611 (608, 609, 610)
Darwin C R, (274)
Davey B, 436 (435)
Davico M I, 326 (324)
Davies A, 18 (16)
Davies B, 471 (470)
Davies D E, 226 (225), 373 (370, 372, 373)
Davies I K, 449 (446)
Davies L B, 466 (464), 480 (480)
Davis A, 547 (545)
Davis G A, 480 (478, 480)
Davis M, 278 (274)
Day C, 627 (626), 632
Day J D, 444 (440)
De Corte E, 386 (382, 386)
De Groot E V, 407 (406)
De Jong F P C M, 484–85 (482, 483)
De Lyon H, 71 (69, 70, 71)
de Voss G, 555 (553)
Dean C, 373 (372)
Deane E M, 148 (145)
Deay A M, 369 (367, 368)
DeBono E, 330 (326), 466 (465), 480 (480)
Debus R L, 226 (225)
DeCharms R, 116 (115), 401 (399)
Deci E L, 401 (401)
Decock B, 402 (399)
Decroly O, (155)
Dee Lucas D, 426 (422)
deGroot A D, 52 (49)
Deitz S M, 226 (224)
Delamont S, 8 (8), 506 (501, 502)
Delgado-Gaiten C, 336
Deliyanni-Kouimtzi K, 323 (320)
Delpit L, 18 (17), 453 (453)
Delucchi K, 41 (40)
Demick J, 390 (389)
Denemark G W, 552

Denner P R, 449 (446)
Deno S L, 178 (176)
Denscombe M, 223 (220)
Densmore K, 15 (15), 79 (77)
DePaulo B M, 274 (272)
Derber S, 248 (245)
Dermody M, 148 (145)
Derr T F, 227 (225)
DeRuiter J A, 552 (551)
Desforges C, 267 (264, 266), 285 (283), 433
Deshler D D, 126 (124, 126)
Desoran R A, 395 (392)
Deutsch M, 116 (113, 114), 352 (349, 350)
deVoss G, 598 (594)
DeVries D L, 143 (140, 142)
Dewe P, 56 (53, 54)
Dewey J, 106 (102, 103, 105), 126 (122)
    (139), (151), (167), 182 (179), (209), (252),
    259 (255), (316), (342), 412 (410), (467),
    597 (593), 603 (598)
Dick A, 40 (38, 40)
Diez M, 556 (553)
Dillard J A, 191 (190)
Dillon D R, 254 (252)
Dillon J T, 8 (6), 248 (242, 244), 255 (251,
    252, 253)
Dilworth M E, 46 (42)
Dinh Te H, 278 (276)
DiPardo A, 412 (408, 410), 453 (452)
DiPelo G, 480 (480)
DiVesta F J, 436 (435)
Dixon P N, 603 (601)
Dixon R A, 444 (442)
Dmytriw L, 588 (586)
Dochy F J R C, 386 (383, 385, 386)
Doctorow M, 436 (435, 436)
Doise W, 339 (338)
Dole J A, 111 (110, 111)
Dolton P, 75 (74)
Doneau S J, 248 (242)
Dooley A R, 587 (584)
Doran R L, 204 (202)
Dornbusch S, 382 (379)
Dove L A, 71 (67, 69, 70), 543 (540, 541, 542)
Dowden D E, 248 (247)
Dowdeswell W H, 174 (172)
Doyle W, 28 (26), 34 (32), 96 (93, 94, 95),
    170 (168), 218 (215, 217, 218), 223 (220,
    221, 222), 267 (264, 265, 266), 285 (283),
    433 (433), 582 (579)
Dreeben R, 28 (26), 196 (192, 193, 194,
    195), 214 (213)
Dreikurs R, 231 (227)
Dreyfus A, 255 (253)
Dreyfus H L, 52 (47)
Dreyfus S E, 52 (47)
Driver R, 154 (149, 152, 153)
Du Rietz L, 309 (309)
Dubreucq-Choprix F L, 160 (155, 157)
Ducharme E R, 534 (531, 532, 533, 534)
Duckworth E, 106 (103)
Duffy G G, 111 (110, 111), 238 (236, 237),
    267 (264, 266)
Dumont R V, 335 (334)
Dunbar S B, 282 (280, 281)

Dunkerton J, 505 (504)
Dunkin J, 66 (63)
Dunkin M J, 66 (66), 96 (93), 238 (236), 267 (264), 500 (493, 494, 496, 497, 498, 499), 511 (506), 516 (514), 577 (574)
Dunn J G, 174 (171, 172)
Dunn K J, 160 (157)
Dunn R S, 160 (157)
Durkin D, 206 (205)
Dusek J B, 416 (414)
Dweck C S, 323 (321), 401 (397, 398)
Dworkin A G, 56 (53)
Dyke W E, 166 (165)
Dykman B J, 199 (197)
Dykstra R, 148 (145)
Dyson A H, 453 (451)

Easley J A, 174 (172, 173)
Eason G, 315 (313)
Easton J Q, 167 (165)
Eccles J S, 34 (32), 382 (381), 419 (417)
Ecob R, 160 (156, 157), 207 (205, 206), 214 (212)
Eddinger S S, 248 (243)
Edelfelt R, 632 (628)
Edelsky C, 471 (470)
Edmonds J, 149 (145)
Edmonds R, 330 (327)
Edmundson P G, 547 (544, 545)
Edwards A D, 121 (118)
Edwards C H, 148 (146)
Edwards J, 174 (172)
Edwards T, 506 (502)
Eggleston J F, 506 (503, 504)
Ehly S W, 274
Eisenberg T, 274 (272)
Eisenhart M, 52 (47), 335 (333)
Eisner E W, 8 (6, 8), 191 (188)
Ekholm M, 627 (626)
Ekman P, (274)
Elbaz F, 24 (22, 23), 28 (26, 27), 294 (290, 291)
Elbing E, 199 (197)
El-Dinary P B, 126 (126), 444 (441, 442)
Elgood C, 263 (260)
Elias J W, 170 (169)
Elias P, 148 (144)
Elias S F, 170 (169)
Eliseo T S, 466 (464)
Elkin V B, 274 (271)
Elkjaer B, 323 (320)
Elley W B, 453 (453)
Ellgring J H, 199 (197)
Elliott J, 18 (16, 18), 182 (179), 627 (624)
Elliott-Faust D J, 444 (441)
Ellis H C, 204 (202)
Ellwein M C, 592 (590)
Elmore R F, 570
Elwood J, 323 (319, 321)
Emans R, 597 (596)
Emerson H, 34 (32)
Emerson J M, 358 (354)
Emmer E T, 218–19 (215, 216), 223 (220, 221, 222)

Endler N S, 130 (127)
Endreweit M E, 363 (359, 360)
Engel M, 522 (519)
Engelkamp J, 449 (445)
Englemann S, 101 (100), (146)
Englert C, 285 (285)
Englund T, 309 (309)
Ennis R H, 238 (233)
Entin E E, 402 (401)
Entwisle D R, 382 (378)
Entwistle N J, 390 (389, 390), 476 (472, 474, 475)
Epstein C, 79 (76)
Epstein J L, 373 (371)
Epstein W, 449 (446)
Eraut M, 627–28 (622, 623, 624, 625, 626)
Erickson B, 255 (253)
Erickson F, 218 (217), 335 (334)
Erickson L G, 436 (435)
Erickson M T, 416 (414)
Ericsson K A, 444 (443), 476 (475)
Erikson E, 40 (39), 116 (115)
Eshel Y, 170 (169)
Espinet M, 530 (528)
Estice R M, 412 (409)
Etaugh C, 323 (320)
Etzioni A, 79 (76, 77)
Evangelou D, 318 (317, 318)
Evans J, 366 (364)
Evertson C M, 207 (206), 218–19 (215, 216), 223 (220, 221), 358 (357), 534 (534), 582 (578)
Evertson D, (502)
Exendine L, 226 (225)

Fagot B I, 323 (320)
Fahey P A, 204 (202)
Fairclough N, 471 (469)
Fairhurst M A, 238 (232, 234, 235)
Fajardo D E, 101 (98)
Faraj A H, 570 (565)
Farber B A, 56 (54, 55)
Farber I, 56 (53)
Farnish A M, 143 (140)
Farr M, 52 (48, 50, 51)
Farrell J P, 569 (565)
Farrugia C J, 560 (559)
Fasching J, 255 (253)
Feather N, 116 (114)
Fecho B, 18 (17)
Federico P A, 522
Fedoruk G M, 416 (415)
Feeley F M, 71 (68, 69, 70, 71)
Feiman S, 46
Feiman-Nemser S, 294 (290, 291), 547 (545), 587 (584, 585, 586, 587), 592 (589)
Feinberg W, 587 (587)
Feinman-Nemser S, 28 (26)
Feldhusen J F, 481 (476, 477, 478, 479, 480)
Feldlaufer H, 34 (32), 419 (417)
Feldman K A, 500 (494, 495, 496, 497, 498)
Feldman R S, 101 (98), 117, 278 (274)
Fend H, 290 (289)
Fennema E, 24 (21), 290 (289), 412 (410,

411), 416 (414)
Fensham P, 174 (172)
Fenstermacher G D, 24 (23), 294 (294)
Fenwick J E, 214 (212)
Ferber M A, 395 (394)
Ferguson P, 534 (534)
Ferguson R F, 75 (74)
Ferguson T, 255 (252)
Fernández M, 593 (591)
Ferrara R A, 444 (442)
Ferster C B, 204 (200), 227 (224)
Fessler R, 538 (535)
Feuerstein R, 106 (103), 290 (287), 330 (326), 466 (465)
Fielding L, 111 (110)
Fielding M, 628 (622)
Filby N N, 214 (213), 433 (431)
Finn J D, 315 (313)
Firestone W A, 611 (610, 611)
Fish S, (467)
Fishbein J E, 101 (99)
Fishbein M, 28 (25), 395 (391, 393)
Fisher C W, 160 (156, 157), 171 (168), 207, 369 (369), 433 (430, 431, 432, 433)
Fisher D L, 348 (347), 358 (356), 419 (417, 418)
Fisher G, 238 (237)
Fitts P M, 457 (455)
Fitzgerald J, 315 (313), 412 (410)
Flanagan J C, 106 (102), 214 (212)
Flanders N A, 211 (210), 506 (501, 502, 505)
Flavell J H, 382, 444 (439, 440), 449 (446), 485
Fleer M, 127
Fleishman E A, 457 (455)
Fleishman J A, 395 (393)
Fletcher J D, 160 (155, 159)
Flinders D G, 547 (543, 546)
Flinders D J, 223, 358 (355)
Floden R E, 28 (26, 27), 46, 294 (290, 291)
Flood R, 206 (205)
Florio-Ruane S, 412 (410, 411)
Floud J, 61 (60)
Flower L S, 453 (451)
Floyd C, 318 (316)
Fly P K, 413 (410)
Fodor J A, 463 (459)
Fogelman K, 207 (206)
Foley W, 556 (553)
Folkman S, 407 (405)
Ford J, 395 (394)
Forman S G, 101, 335 (334)
Forrest-Pressley D L, 444 (441)
Foshay A W, 28 (27)
Foster D L, 326 (324)
Foster L, 366 (364, 365)
Foster W G, 395 (393)
Foucault M, (119)
Fowler H S, 155 (154)
Fox R, 500 (499)
Fraleigh M, 382 (379)
Francis E, 255 (252)
Fraser B, 285 (284), 358 (356)
Fraser B J, 348 (344, 345, 346, 347, 348), 419 (416, 417, 418, 419), 521 (519)

Frasson C, 274 (273)
Frederick W C, 271 (269)
Frederiksen J R, 282 (280, 281), 466 (465)
Frederiksen N, 111 (108), 290 (288), 386 (386)
Fredrick W C, 207 (205, 206)
Freebody P, 471 (468, 469, 470)
Freedman S W, 18 (17), 79 (78), 412 (408, 410), 453–54 (451, 452)
Freeman D J, 34 (33), 86 (81), 530 (529, 530)
Freiber H J, 182 (182)
Freire P, 106 (102, 103, 104, 105), 412 (410), 471 (468)
French J R Jr., 56 (54), 323 (321)
French P, 323 (321)
Frese W, 395
Fresko B, 274 (272)
Freudenberger H J, 56 (53)
Fried M D, 412 (409)
Friedler Y, 174 (172, 173)
Friedman I A, 56, 56 (54)
Friedman S L, 429 (427)
Friedrich H F, 449 (447)
Friedson E, 15
Friesen D, 56 (53)
Frijda N H, 407 (403)
Froebel F, (167), (209)
Fuchs D, 160 (159), 178 (176)
Fuchs L S, 160 (159), 178 (176)
Fullan M G, 46 (43, 45), 86 (82, 84, 85), 627 (626)
Fuller B, 207 (205)
Fuller F F, 40 (39)
Funder D C, 290 (288)
Furnham A, 56 (54)
Furst N F, 238 (237), 506 (501, 503, 505)
Furth H, 106 (104)
Fuson K C, 426 (422)

Gable R K, 56 (55)
Gage N L, 8 (6, 7), 11 (9), 24 (22), 96 (92, 93, 94, 95, 96), 136 (134), 516 (514, 515), 582 (579)
Gagné R M, 111 (108), 154 (149)
Gall J P, 248 (244), 358 (357)
Gall M D, 247–248 (242, 243, 244, 245, 246), 358 (357), 582 (579)
Gallagher J, 285 (285)
Gallagher P A, 223 (222)
Galluzzo G R, 552 (550), 555 (553, 554)
Galton M J, 323 (321), , 506 (501, 502, 503, 504, 505)
Gammage P, 565 (562)
Gamoran A, 196 (192, 193, 194, 195), 248 (243), 286 (284)
Garden R A, 511 (506, 507)
Gardner H, 126 (126), 344 (343)
Gardner M, 127
Gardner R W, 390 (387)
Garfinkel A, 238 (233)
Garland J, 61 (60)
Garner R, 412 (411), 463 (459), 476 (474, 475)

Gartner A, 274 (272), 339 (338)
Garwood S F, 200 (198)
Garza T J, 199 (198)
Gastright J F, 214 (213)
Gates A I, 426 (420)
Gauthier G, 274 (273)
Gee J P, 471 (469, 470)
Geer B, 61 (61), 620 (617)
Gehrke N, 603 (600, 601, 602)
Geller E S, 227 (226)
Gennari P, 161 (157, 158, 159)
George C, 326 (325)
Gephart W, 556 (553)
Gere A R, 412 (410)
Gershon R C, 299 (296)
Gersten R, 148 (146)
Getzels J W, 199 (199), 481 (477)
Ghani Z, 552 (549)
Ghatala E S, 444 (442)
Giaconia R M, 170 (168, 169), 516 (512, 513, 514, 515)
Gibb C, 227 (225)
Gibbs G I, 263 (260, 261)
Gibson M A, 335 (334, 335)
Gibson M R, 565 (562)
Gick M L, 204 (202)
Giddings G J, 348 (346), 419 (418, 419)
Gideonse H D, 555 (555), 560, 565 (564), 570 (568)
Gilbert P H, 471 (467, 468, 469, 470)
Gill W M, 170 (169, 170), 199 (199)
Gilligan C, 40 (36), 79 (78), 86 (81), 538 (536)
Gilliom M, 582 (578, 580)
Gillmore G M, 500 (495)
Gilmore S, 577 (574)
Gil-Perez D, 126 (122)
Gilroy P, 565
Ginsberg H, 106 (103)
Ginsburg M B, 71 (67, 69, 70, 71), 547 (546)
Giroux H, 71 (67), 121 (119)
Gitlin A D, (595)
Givon H, 268 (267)
Glaser R, 52 (48, 49, 50, 51), 130–31 (128, 129, 130), 267 (265, 266, 267), 282 (279, 280, 281), 330 (326, 327), 386 (382, 386), 426 (420), 466 (464), 521–22 (519)
Glass G V, 315 (310, 312, 313), 516 (513, 514)
Glasser W, 28 (27), (222), 231 (227)
Glatthorn A A, 46 (42, 43, 44, 45)
Glaubman R, 170 (168, 169, 170)
Glazer M, 79 (76)
Glenberg A M, 449 (446)
Glenn J, 126 (126)
Glickman C D, 45–46 (41, 44), 597 (595, 596)
Gliessman D H, 248 (247), 582 (579, 580), 587 (586)
Globerson T, 268 (267), 390 (389), 402 (397)
Glover J, 603 (599)
Glynn A, 200 (197)
Glynn T, 223 (222)
Gmelch W, 56 (52)
Goetz E T, 443 (441)
Goldberger N R, 18 (18), 79 (78), 538 (537)

Goldhammer R, 597 (595)
Goldin L, 34 (32, 33)
Goldman S R, 466 (465)
Goldminz E, 155 (149, 153)
Goldstein H, 323 (321)
Goldstein Z, 56 (53)
Goldwaite D, 582 (579)
González R, 593 (591)
Good T L, 24 (21, 22), 34 (29, 30, 31, 32), 148 (144), 178 (177), 214 (213), 223, 247 (246), 248 (244), 285 (283, 284), 323 (321, 322), 348 (344), 493 (489, 491), 505 (505)
Goodenough D R, 390 (387)
Goodenough W, 335 (333)
Goodlad J I, 56 (54), 106 (102), 318 (316), 412 (408), 534 (531), 603, 604 (600)
Goodlad J L, 552
Goodlad J T, 255 (252)
Goodman G, 367
Goodman J, 547 (545), 598
Goodnow J J, 251 (250), 382 (381)
Gore J M, 182–83 (182), 471 (469)
Gorman T, 323 (319), 453 (453)
Gorth W P, 493
Gosden P H J H, 565
Gould S J, 323 (321)
Govinda R, 547 (543)
Gowin D B, 436 (435)
Grabowski B L, 386 (383)
Grace G, 72 (67, 68, 69, 70, 71)
Graesser A C, 449 (447, 448)
Graham K, 121 (119, 120)
Graham P A, 530 (530)
Graham S, 116 (115)
Grajia M L, 148 (145)
Granheim M, 310
Graue M E, 592 (590)
Graves N J, 259 (257), 565
Graves T, 259 (257)
Green J E, 366 (365)
Green J L, 121–22 (119, 120), 218–19 (217), 501 (499), 516 (514)
Greenblat C, 263 (260)
Greene D, 251 (250), 402 (401)
Greenglass E R, 56 (55)
Greenland J, 627 (621)
Greenleaf C, 453 (452)
Greeno J, 52 (49)
Greenwood C R, 101 (99), 274 (272)
Greenwood G E, 587 (586)
Gregory I, 577 (576)
Gretler A, 611 (609)
Griffey D C, 52 (49)
Griffin G A, 627 (622)
Griffin J, 323 (320)
Griffin P, 318 (318)
Griffith C R, 199 (198)
Griffiths R, 577 (574, 575)
Grimmett P P, 86 (86), 182 (181), 597 (594)
Grissmer D W, 75 (74, 75)
Grissom J B, 326 (324)
Gross N, 66 (61, 66)
Grossman P L, 24, 136 (135), 593 (590)
Grottkau B J, 530 (530)
Grouws D A, 214 (213)

Grumet M, 79 (78)
Grundy S, 611 (609)
Grunwald B, 231 (227)
Gryskiewicz N D, 480 (478)
Guba E, 556 (553)
Gubb J, 453 (453)
Gudmundsdottir S, 24 (21, 22), 136 (135)
Guilford J P, 481 (478)
Gumbert E B, 560
Gump P, 96 (94)
Gunstone R F, 174 (173)
Gunz H, 263 (263)
Guskey T R, 160 (159), 166–67 (161, 162, 163, 165, 166)
Gustad J W, 395 (392)
Gustafsson C, 310 (309)
Gustafsson J E, 131 (130)
Guthke J, 290 (287)
Guthrie J T, 127
Guthrie J W, 534 (531)
Gutierrez R, 318 (317)
Guyton E, 597 (594)

Haberman M, 547 (544)
Habermas J, 183 (180)
Haddad W D, 543 (541)
Hadley M, 363 (360, 361, 362)
Haefele D, 582 (579, 580)
Haertel E H, 348 (347), 419 (417, 418), 493 (490)
Haertel G D, 331 (327), 348 (347), 386 (383), 419 (417, 418), 521 (518)
Hafner A, 75, 326 (324)
Hagger H, 11 (10)
Hajjar H, 369 (367)
Haley-Oliphant A, 191 (190)
Halisch F, 401 (397)
Halkitis P N, 299 (296)
Hall E T, 278
Hall G, 555 (553)
Hall R V, 227 (224), 274 (272)
Hall V C, 112 (110)
Haller A O, 395 (394)
Haller E J, 196 (194)
Hallinan M T, 196 (193, 194, 195)
Halmos P, 15
Halpin D, 611 (609)
Hamaker C, 111 (110), 248 (244)
Hamilton D, 506 (501, 502)
Hamilton S F, 196 (192)
Hammond K M, 24 (21), 191 (190), 219 (215, 216, 218)
Hammond R, 556 (553)
Han W S, 395 (392)
Handley H M, 366–67 (364, 365, 366)
Hanna G S, 476 (473), 500 (499)
Hanninen G, 52 (51)
Hansen A J, 587 (584)
Hanson D, 620 (618)
Hanson E, 15 (14)
Hanushek E A, 75 (73), 315 (310, 312, 314), 330 (330)
Harbison R W, 75 (73)
Harding S, 18 (17)

Hare V C, 111 (108), 426 (421, 422, 423)
Harel I, 344 (342)
Harel K, 34 (32)
Hargreaves A, 46 (43), 86 (80, 84, 85), 620 (619)
Hargreaves D H, 8 (7), 86 (81, 82), 219 (215, 216, 217)
Haring T G, 227 (225)
Harker J O, 218 (217)
Harnischfeger A, 429 (429), 433 (431)
Haroutunian-Gordon S, 255 (252)
Harper G F, 248 (246)
Harré R, 463 (459)
Harris D, 154 (149, 150, 154)
Harris F C, 263 (261)
Harris J, 282 (282)
Harris K R, 127
Harris L J, 207 (205)
Harris N D C, 174 (172)
Harris R C, 603 (601)
Harrison J, 170 (168, 169, 170)
Harrop L, 506 (503)
Harste J C, 412 (410)
Hart M M S, 148 (145)
Harter N, 52 (47)
Hartley J, 449 (446)
Hartley W, 143 (142)
Hartman, 318 (317, 318)
Hartup W W, 339 (336)
Harvey J T, 326 (324)
Hashweh M Z, 24 (21)
Haskell T, 80
Hassall D, 565 (562)
Hatano G, 344 (341, 444 (440)
Hatcher R, 323 (322)
Hativa N, 363 (360, 361, 362)
Hattie J A, 285 (284), 521 (519)
Hatton N G, 611 (608, 609, 610, 611)
Hauser R M, 395 (394)
Havinghurst R J, 40 (39), 61 (60), (535)
Hawes H, 628 (626)
Hawk D, 555 (553)
Hawke J, 52 (49)
Hawkins A, 52 (49, 50)
Hawley W D, 534 (534), 560 (557)
Hayes J R, 453 (451)
Haythorn W W, 357 (352, 353)
Heath S B, 412 (411, 412), 453 (451, 452)
Heckhausen H, 131 (130), 401 (397), 429 (427)
Hedges L V, 170 (168, 169), 516 (512, 513, 514, 515)
Hegarty E H, 174 (172, 173)
Hegarty P, 170 (167, 168)
Hegarty-Hazel E, 174 (171, 172, 173)
Heibert E H, 167 (166)
Heid H, 40 (36)
Heider F, 116 (115)
Heimlich E P, 278 (277)
Hein D D, 597 (594)
Heisel B E, 444 (441)
Helmke A, 178 (177), 290 (287, 288, 289, 290), 407 (404, 405, 406), 522 (519, 520)
Hembree R, 407 (403)
Hendrix J, 255 (253)

Henson K T, 155
Herbart JF, (161)
Herman R, 170 (168)
Heron T E, 227 (224)
Herrington M, 620 (618)
Herrmann B A, 238 (236, 237)
Hertz-Lazarowitz R, 259 (256, 258), 352, 358 (356)
Hertzog C, 444 (442)
Hesketh J, 210 (209)
Hess R D, 382 (378, 380)
Hester S K, 219 (215, 216, 217)
Hewton E, 627 (626)
Hickson D J, 15 (12)
Hidi S, 111 (110)
Hiebert B, 56 (53)
Hiebert E H, 412 (408), 433 (433)
Higginbotham-Wheat N, 214 (213)
Hilgard E R, 521 (518)
Hilleard F M, 367
Hiller J, 238 (237)
Hillgarten W, 500 (497)
Hillocks G Jr, 454
Hirst P, 555 (555)
Hirst P H, 547 (545)
Hoad P, 620 (619)
Hocevar D, 481 (477, 478), 500 (494, 495)
Hocking K, 19 (16)
Hodge R W, 61 (58)
Hoetker J, 121 (119)
Hoffman M B, 466 (465)
Hoffman N, 79 (77)
Hofmeister A, 101 (100)
Hogan P, 18 (16), 547 (545)
Hoge R D, 290 (288)
Holden D J, 444 (440)
Holland D C, 335 (333)
Holland J L, 395 (394)
Hollingshead A B, 335 (332)
Hollingsworth S, 18 (18)
Hollingworth S, 136 (133)
Holloway S D, 382 (378)
Holly M L, 539
Holmes B, 570 (565)
Holmes C T, 326 (325)
Holt J, 263 (262)
Holubec E, 117 (113), 352 (349)
Holvast A, 219 (218)
Holyoak K J, 204 (202)
Holzman P S, 390 (387)
Honeywell L, 481 (478)
Hooymayers H P, 218 (218), 419 (417)
Hopkins D, 19 (16), 627 (622), 632
Hopmann S, 24 (22)
Hord S, 555 (553)
Hörmann H, 449 (445)
Horton A, 628 (622)
Horton M, 620 (619)
Horwitz R A, 170 (167), 516 (515)
Housego B E J, 565 (562), 593 (590)
Houser J E, 251 (250)
Housner L D, 52 (49)
Houston R, 511
Houston W R, 11 (10), 547 (544), 552
Houtz J C, 481 (478, 479)

Hovell M F, 101 (96, 99)
Howard G S, 500 (496, 497)
Howe L W, 41 (39)
Howell F M, 395
Howey K, 534 (531)
Howley E, 382 (380)
Howsam R B, 552
Hoyle E, 15 (12, 14), 61 (61), 86 (84)
Hoyles C, 255 (253)
Hoyt D P, 500 (499)
Hsu T-C, 299 (295)
Huberman A M, 516 (514)
Huberman M, 46 (42), 86 (82), 538–39 (535), 627 (626)
Hubert J A, 56 (55)
Hudgins B B, 238 (232, 235)
Hudson J, 444 (440)
Hudson L, 75 (75), 390 (388, 390)
Huff C R, 358 (356)
Hughes E, 620 (617)
Hughes J A, 136 (134)
Hughes P, 46
Hughes V, 323 (320)
Hulbert C M, 367
Hull R, 264
Hummell T, 555 (554)
Hunt D, (41), 106 (104, 105)
Hunt D E, 160 (155, 157), 538 (537)
Hunt D W, 615 (615)
Hunt J, 116 (114)
Hunt S, 101 (99)
Hunter J E, 516
Hunter M, 148 (144)
Husén T, 204 (201), 315 (310), 330 (326), 587
Hutchins T T, 248 (247)
Hyman J S, 204 (201, 202, 203)
Hyman R T, 106 (102), 237 (236, 237), 309 (308), 505 (505)
Hynds S, 426 (423)

Ibrahim M A, 207 (206)
Idol L, 436 (435)
Il-Hwan C, 543 (540)
Inabr J, 416 (415)
Inagake K, 344 (341)
Ingels S, 326 (324)
Inouye D K, 290 (289)
Iran-Nejad A, 426 (422)
Irvine J J, 416 (415)
Irvine J W, 274 (272)
Irving J, 556 (553)
Isaacs M, 200 (198)
Isaksen S G, 481 (477, 480)
Ishii S, 278 (275)
Ishler R E, 603 (601)
Ishumi A, 543 (541)
Iwanicki E F, 56–57 (53, 54, 55)
Iwata B, 227 (226)

Jacklin C N, 323 (319, 321)
Jackson B, 196 (192)
Jackson D, 227 (224)

Jackson G B, 516 (513)
Jackson J, 18 (17), 79
Jackson P W, 8 (6), 15 (13), 116 (112), 294 (290, 292)
Jackson S E, 56–57 (54, 55)
Jacobson L, 34 (29), 117 (113), 416 (413, 414)
Jacobson W J, 204 (202)
Jae-Dong K, 543 (540)
Jäger R S, 290 (289)
James W, 8 (6), 106 (102, 105), 429 (427)
Jamieson S, 565 (562, 563)
Jamous H, 8 (7)
Janke R, 143 (142)
Jansen J, 72 (67, 68, 70)
Janssen S, 40 (39)
Jarausch K, 72 (68, 69, 70, 71)
Jasman A, 506 (502)
Jeffries R, 466 (465)
Jelsma O, 457 (456)
Jencks C, 395 (394)
Jenkins J J, 444 (440)
Jenkins J R, 178 (174, 175)
Jenkins S, 56 (55)
Jensen L C, 582 (579)
Jensen M, 466 (465)
Jenson W R, 101
Jessor R, 395 (392)
Johanssen D H, 386 (383)
John P D, 11 (11)
Johnson C J, 444 (441)
Johnson D W, 101 (99), 116–17 (113, 114), 143 (141, 142), 259 (258), 352 (349, 350, 351, 352)
Johnson J M, 366 (364, 366), 369 (368), 597 (595)
Johnson K R, 101 (100)
Johnson L V, 231 (227)
Johnson R T, 101 (99), 116–17 (113, 114), 143 (141, 142), 259 (258), 352 (349, 350, 351, 352)
Johnson S F, 136, 539 (535, 536)
Johnson S M, 46 (43), 75 (72)
Johnson V R, 373 (370, 373)
Johnston J M, 101 (98)
Johnston M, 538 (535)
Jolley M, 627 (626)
Jonas H, 40 (35)
Jones C L, 61 (58)
Jones D, 52 (47)
Jones E, 34 (29)
Jones K, 263 (260)
Jones L S, 223
Jones L V, 106 (102)
Jones M E, 506 (503, 504)
Jones M G, 199 (198)
Jones N, 223 (221)
Jones P E, 577 (574)
Jones R E, 19 (16)
Jones V F, 223, 323 (322)
Joseph G, 416 (414)
Joyce B R, 106 (104), 111 (107, 109), 534 (531), 593 (589), 603 (599), 628 (623, 624), 632
Judge H, 534 (532)

Judy J E, 386 (383), 463
Jung C G, (387)
Jungck S, 86 (81)
Jussim L, 34 (29, 30, 31), 416 (415)
Juster F T, 271 (269)

Kaess W, 238 (237)
Kafry D, 57 (55)
Kagan D M, 11, 136, 182 (180), 593 (590)
Kahle J B, 348 (348), 419 (419)
Kahn R L, 56 (54)
Kahne J, 547 (547)
Kahneman D, 429 (427)
Kallenbach W W, 582 (579)
Kallós D, 310 (309)
Kaltsounis B, 481 (478)
Kaminsky J, 204 (202, 203)
Kane M T, 500 (495)
Kanfer R, 429 (428)
Kansanen P, 211 (208)
Kariya T, 196 (192)
Karlin L, 242 (240)
Karweit N, 143 (142), 214 (213)
Katz L G, 318 (317, 318), 547 (546), 556 (553, 554)
Kaufmann I, 200 (197)
Kawakami A J, 412 (409)
Kazdin A E, 101, 227 (226)
Keats D M, 66 (65)
Keats J A, 66 (65)
Kegan R, 40 (39), 106 (105), 538 (536)
Keith T Z, 271
Keller F S, 101 (100), (158), 274 (273)
Kelley M L, 247 (246)
Kelly G, 72 (68, 69, 70, 71), 80
Kelsall H M, 66 (65)
Kelsall R K, 66 (65)
Kemmis S, 19 (17), 182 (182)
Kemper D, 588 (586)
Kemple J J, 75 (73, 74), 531 (528, 529, 530)
Kendall P L, 620 (616)
Kennan B, 547 (545)
Kennard B, 18 (16)
Kennedy C H, 227 (225)
Kennedy J, 238 (236)
Kennedy M M, 148 (146), 547 (544)
Keogh B, 436 (434)
Kerchner C T, 5 (3)
Kerckhoff A C, 196 (192), 395 (394)
Kerr M M, 223 (220)
Kerry T, 211 (209)
Kershaw J A, 76
Key M R, 278 (274)
Kieslar E R, 155
Kieviet F K, 547 (544)
Killen M, 339 (339)
Kim H, 167 (165)
King A, 286 (285), 436 (435)
King R A, 552 (551)
Kirby S N, 75 (74, 75)
Kirp D L, 570 (566)
Kirschenbaum H, 41 (39)
Kirton M J, 481 (477, 478)
Kispala A, 323 (319)

Kissock C, 560
Klahr D, 463 (459)
Klausmeier H J, 214 (212), 318 (317)
Kleiman A B, 248 (243)
Klein G S, 390 (387)
Klein Z, 170 (169)
Kleinfeld J, 278, 587 (583, 585)
Kliebard H M, 106 (102), 237 (236, 237), 309 (308), 505 (505)
Kline F M, 126 (124, 126)
Klinzing H G, 248 (242, 245, 246, 247), 547 (544, 545)
Klinzing-Eurich G, 248 (242, 245, 246)
Klitgaard R E, 75 (72, 74)
Klivington K A, 429 (427)
Klopfer L E, 174 (171, 172)
Knight S K, 604 (600)
Knight S L, 603 (601)
Knowles E S, 200 (198)
Knowles J, 86 (82)
Kobasigawa A, 444 (442)
Kochmann B J, 556 (554)
Koczor M L, 204 (202)
Koehler V R, 597 (594, 595)
Koelling C H, 369 (367, 368, 369)
Koerner J, 534 (531, 532)
Koerner M E, 593 (591)
Kogan N, 390 (388, 389), 481 (477)
Kohlberg L, 40 (36, 38, 39), 106 (102, 103, 104, 105), 121 (118)
Kohler M C, 274 (272)
Kohler W, 339 (338)
Kohn A, 352
Kolb D A, 263
Kolvin I, 367
Koniarski C, 101 (99)
Koran J J, 577 (574)
Koran M L, 577 (574)
Körkel J, 444 (440)
Korthagen F, 182 (182)
Koskinen P S, 274 (273)
Kottkamp R B, 136, 182 (182)
Kounin J S, 211 (209), 223 (222), 231 (227)
Kowalski J P, 493 (491)
Kowalski T, 603–04 (598, 599, 602)
Krabbe M A, 52 (49)
Kramer R, 534 (531, 532)
Krams M, 101 (99)
Krappman L, 339 (338, 339)
Kraska K, 131 (130)
Kratochwill T R, 227 (224)
Kremer-Hayon L, 56 (53)
Krepelka E J, 466 (465)
Kress G, 471 (469)
Krug D, 603 (599)
Kruger A C, 339 (339)
Krupp J, 86 (82)
Kubiszyn T, 303 (300, 302)
Kuhara-Kojima K, 444 (440)
Kuhl J, 131 (130), 401–02 (397), 407 (406)
Kuhn D, 126 (125)
Kuhn T S, 96 (91, 92, 93, 95, 96), (151)
Kulik C C, 160 (156), 167 (161, 165, 166), 274 (272), 318 (317)
Kulik C E, 160 (159)

Kulik C-L C, 101 (100), 521 (520)
Kulik J A, 101 (100), 160 (155, 156, 157, 158, 159), 167 (161, 165, 166), 178 (175), 274 (272), 318 (317), 521 (520)
Kulikowich J A, 386 (382)
Kummer R, 463 (461)
Kurachi A, 556 (553)
Kurian G T, 570 (565)
Kurita J A, 444 (441)
Kurt-Schai R, 40 (39)
Kurtz B E, 290 (289)
Kyriacou C, 56 (54)

Laan S, 282 (282)
Lacey C, 8 (7), 620 (619)
Laferrière T, 565 (562, 563)
Lahey L L, 538 (536)
Laird S, 79 (78)
Lakatos I, 96 (95)
Lalik R V, 182 (181)
Lam Y Y, 200 (198)
Lamb C E, 597 (594)
Lamb H, 453 (453)
Lambert L, 604 (601)
Lambert N M, 200 (199)
Lamborn S, 382 (379)
Lampert M, 19 (16), 24 (22), 191 (190), 267 (265, 266), 344 (340, 341), 412 (408, 410), 603 (601)
Lancaster J, (272)
Lane S, 282 (281)
Langdell C C, (583, 584)
Lange G, 444 (443)
Langeheine R, 167 (165)
Langer J, 454 (452)
Langer P, 247 (246)
Langford G, 15 (15)
Langley P, 463 (459)
Lanier J, 534 (531, 532, 533)
Lanier J E, 28 (26), 530 (529)
Lankshear C, 471 (468)
Lanzetta J, 357 (352, 353)
Lapco A, 227 (225)
Larke P J, 530–31 (530)
Larkin J H, 148 (145), 426 (422)
Larsen S C 1980, 274
Larson C W, 565 (561)
Larson M S, 15 (13), 61 (59), 79 (76)
Larson R, 271 (270)
Larson S, 86 (84)
Larson-Shapiro N, 426 (423)
Lasker B, 255 (252)
Lauglo J, 72 (70)
Lave J, 318 (317, 318), 344 (341, 342)
Lawler M, 471 (468)
Lawn M, 15 (13), 72 (67, 68, 69, 70, 71)
Lawrence P J, 238 (236), 506 (505)
Lawry J R, 160 (155, 157)
Lawson S, 15 (151, 152)
Lawton S C, 444 (440)
Layng T V J, 101 (100)
Layton D, 174 (171, 174)
Lazarus R S, 407 (405)
Leavey M B, 143 (140, 142)

Leavitt H B, 531 (528), 560, 593 (588)
Leavitt H J, 358 (353)
Lederman N G, 126 (125, 126)
Lee S Y, 382 (379, 381)
Lees S, 323 (320, 322)
Leggatt T, 15
Lehmann R H, 611 (607)
Lehtinen E, 449 (447)
Leiderman P, 382 (379)
Leinhardt G, 24 (20, 21), 52 (49), 136, 191 (190), 211 (208), 214 (212, 213), 219 (215, 216, 218)
Leithwood K A, 46 (41, 43)
Leleux S A, 367
Lemke J L, 122
Lens W, 402 (399, 401)
Lensmire T J, 412 (411)
Leone C M, 207 (205), 271 (269, 270)
Lepper M R, 251 (250), 402 (398, 401)
Lesgold A, 52 (48), 386 (386)
Levasseur J, 326 (324)
Levin H M, 315 (312, 314)
Levin J R, 444 (440, 441, 442), 454 (452)
Levin R A, 593 (592)
Levine D U, 61 (60), 167 (162), 204 (201)
Levine D W, 200 (198)
Levine M, 603 (600)
Levine S, 538 (535)
Levinson D J, 538 (535)
Levis D S, 531 (530), 577 (575)
Levy J, 348 (347)
Lewin K, 19 (16), 117 (113), 348 (345), 358 (352, 353), (396)
Lewis A B, 436 (436)
Lewis D, 160 (156, 157), 207 (205, 206), 214 (212)
Lewis M, 131 (127)
Lewo J, 543 (542)
Lewy A, 204 (201)
Lezotte L W, 330 (327)
L'Hommedieu R, 500 (499)
Licht B G, 323 (321)
Lieberman A, 46 (44)
Lieberman R, 255 (253)
Liebig, (171)
Liew-On M, 484 (483)
Light R J, 516 (513)
Lightfoot S L, 8 (8)
Lin H T, 481 (480)
Lin Y G, 449 (447)
Lindsay M, 556 (554)
Lindvall C M, 214 (212)
Linn M C, 148 (145)
Linn R L, 282 (280, 281), 466 (466)
Linton H B, 390 (387)
Linton R, (62)
Lipman M, 565 (562)
Lippitt R, (272), 358 (353)
Liska A E, 395 (393)
Lissitz R W, 294 (293)
Liston D P, 183
Little J W, 28 (26), 46 (41, 43), 86 (86), 530 (529), 534 (531, 532, 533)
Liu M, 282 (281)
Livingston C, 52 (50), 191 (190)

Livingston S A, 263 (260, 261, 262)
Llorens M, 227 (225)
Lloyd J W, 178 (175)
Loadman W, 556 (553)
Lochhead J, 251 (250)
Lockheed M E, 315 (311), 330 (330), 570 (566)
Lodewijks J G L C, 484 (482)
Loevinger J, 538 (536)
Loewenberg-Ball D L, 547 (544)
Lohman D F, 131 (130), 282 (279)
Lombardo V S, 366 (364)
Long J M, 358 (356)
Lortie D C, 15, 28 (26), 66 (64), 79 (77), 86 (81), 294 (290, 291), 547 (545)
Loucks S, 539, 628 (626)
Louden W, 86 (80, 81, 82)
Louis K S, 46 (43), 628 (626)
Lourde A, 19 (18)
Loveless D, 204 (202)
Loveluck C, 263 (263)
Luke A, 471 (468, 469, 470)
Luke C, 471 (469)
Lummis M, 382 (381)
Lund D, 227 (224)
Lundgren U P, 11 (10), 211 (208), 214 (212), 238 (237), 309–10 (308, 309)
Lunz M E, 299 (296)
Lutonsky L, 604 (599)
Lutz F W, 56 (55)
Lynch R H, 248 (244)
Lyon S, 588 (585)
Lyons N, 538 (536)
Lysakowski R, 204 (202)
Lytle S L, 471 (471), 603 (601)

McAdoo H P, 382
McAdoo J L, 382
McAlpine A, 11 (10)
McAninch A R, 588 (583)
McBride S, 436 (435)
MacCallum J A, 538 (536)
McCarthey S J, 358 (357)
McCartney K, 382 (380)
McCarty T L, 248 (244)
McClelland D, 117 (114)
McCloskey O S A, 136
Maccoby E M, 323 (319, 321), 382 (378)
McCormick C G, 444 (441)
McCurdy D W, 335 (333)
McCutcheon G, 11 (10), 136 (132, 133)
McDaniel E, 248 (245)
McDermott R, 335 (334)
McDiarmid G W, 267 (265), 531 (528, 530), 547 (544)
McDonald F J, 148 (144), 577 (574, 575)
McDonald P J, 200 (198)
MacDonald R E, 238 (233, 234, 235)
McDonnell L M, 570
McEachern A W, 66 (61, 66)
Macedo D, 471 (468)
McElroy W, 367 (364)
McGaw B, 516 (513, 514)
McGeevor P, 323 (321)

McGoldrick J A, 444 (441)
McGuire J, 369 (368)
McGuire W J, 395 (391)
McIntosh P, 19 (18)
McIntyre D I, 11 (10), 136 (135), 547 (546), 577 (574, 575, 576), 620 (617)
McIntyre D J, 582 (578)
McIntyre T, 56 (55)
McKeachie W J, 449 (447), 500 (499)
McKean R N, 76, 148 (146)
McKenzie G R, 248 (245, 246)
McKeon R, 547 (546)
McKernan J, 19 (16)
McKibbin M, 106 (104)
Mackie M, 67 (61, 65)
MacKinnon A M, 182 (181)
McKnight C C, 315 (311)
McLaghlin M W 1994, 547 (547)
McLaughlin H J, 40 (36)
McLaughlin M W, 46 (43), 86 (85), 170 (169)
McLaughlin T F, 200 (197), 226 (225)
MacLennan S, 547 (544, 545)
McLeod A, 453 (452)
McLeod D B, 407 (403, 404)
MacLeod G R, 577 (574, 575, 576), 582 (578)
McLeod M A, 191 (189)
McLeod S A, 395 (394)
McLoughlin C S, 539
Maclure M, 323 (319)
McMahon A, 632
McMahon S, 358 (357)
McManana J, 366 (364)
Macmillan R, 86 (85)
McNamara D, 547 (543, 544)
McNamara T P, 111 (110)
McNergney R F, 560 (557)
McRobbie C J, 348 (346), 419 (418, 419)
McTaggert R, 19 (17)
Madden N A, 143 (140, 142)
Maddirala J, 56 (55)
Madsen C H, 231 (230)
Maehr M, 117 (116)
Mager R F, 101 (96, 98), 191 (188)
Magnusson D, 130–31 (127)
Magone M, 282 (281)
Maheady L, 248 (246)
Maher C A, 101
Malanowski J, 56 (55)
Mallette B, 248 (246)
Malone T W, 402 (398)
Mandl H, 449 (447)
Mandler G, 407 (403)
Mangiola L, 453 (452)
Mann H, (77)
Mansfield R S, 466 (465)
Manski C F, 75 (74)
Marchman V A, 267 (264)
Marjoribanks K, 382 (378)
Mark A J, 278 (277)
Market R W, 214 (212)
Markle S, 101
Markman E, 382
Marks C, 436 (435, 436)
Markus H, 34 (29)

Marland P, 136 (135)
Marland S P, 161 (155)
Marliave R, 433 (431)
Marsh D D, 40 (39)
Marsh H W, 226 (225), 500 (493, 494, 495, 496, 497, 498, 499)
Marshall H H, 34–35 (31), 136, 170 (167)
Marshall J D, 531 (529)
Martin J R, 79 (78), 547 (543)
Martin M W, 363 (359, 360)
Martin N, 453 (452)
Marton F, 390 (389), 449 (446)
Marx R, 96 (95)
Marx R W, 112 (107), 191 (189), 427 (424)
Maslach C, 56 (53)
Mason D, 34 (32)
Mason J M, 196 (192), 247 (245)
Mason W S, 66 (61, 66)
Masschelein J, 122
Mastain R, 560 (557)
Masters G, 299 (296)
Mattingly P H, 534 (531)
Maughan B, 330 (327)
Maurer R E, 223 (222)
Maxwell S E, 500 (496, 497)
May W T, 597 (596)
Mayer G R, 101 (97, 99), 231, 416 (414)
Mayer P, 335 (332)
Mayer R E, 111 (110), 251 (249, 250), 426 (422, 423), 436 (434, 435), 466 (464)
Mazurier M, 326 (325)
Mead G H, (62)
Meara H, 369 (368)
Medawar P B, (151)
Medlex, (344)
Medley D M, 493 (491), 506 (503, 504), 556 (552)
Medway F J, 274 (271, 272, 273)
Meece J L, 419 (416, 417)
Meeker M, 481 (478)
Meeker R, 481 (478)
Mehan H, 191 (190), 412 (408)
Mehrens W A, 204 (202, 203), 480 (478)
Meister C, 286 (283, 285)
Meister G R, 363 (359)
Mellor F J, 219 (215, 216, 217)
Melosh B, 79 (76)
Menges R J, 500 (499)
Mercer N, 121 (118)
Mergendoller J R, 267–68 (264, 265), 433 (433)
Merrill M D, 463
Merriman H, 556 (553)
Merseth K K, 11 (10), 588 (583, 584, 585, 586)
Mertens T, 255 (253)
Merton R K, 620 (616)
Messick S, 282 (281), 390 (388, 389)
Metcalf K K, 238 (236), 582 (578, 579)
Metcalf L E, 238 (234)
Metge J, 126 (122)
Metz M, 87 (85)
Meux M O, 238 (236), 506 (504, 505)
Mevarech Z R, 167 (164, 165)
Meyer D K, 476 (474)

Meyers P, 72 (70)
Micceri T, 248 (242)
Middleton S, 80
Midgley C, 34 (32), 419 (417)
Miel A, 259 (255)
Migniuolo F W, 71 (69, 70, 71)
Miles J, 367 (365)
Miles M B, 117 (113), 366 (363), 516 (514), 627 (626)
Miles S, 547 (545), 555 (555)
Milgram R M, 481 (478)
Milheim W D, 214 (212)
Mill J S, (151), (252)
Millen, (344)
Miller G E, 444 (441)
Miller A, 106 (104), 538 (537)
Miller D L, 111 (110)
Miller G E, 126 (124)
Miller J A, 274 (273)
Miller L, 46 (44)
Miller N, 352
Miller S, 382 (381)
Millman J, 46 (44), 493
Milner D, 323 (320)
Minhas R, 323 (320)
Mintz S L, 192
Miracle A W, 196 (193)
Miserandino A, 538 (536)
Mislevy R J, 282 (282)
Mitchell D E, 5 (3)
Mitchell J V, 493
Mitman A L, 267 (264)
Mitzel, (344)
Mitzel H E, 96 (93), 506 (503, 504)
Moffett J, 454 (450)
Mogami H S, 565 (561, 563)
Mohanty C, 556 (553)
Mohatt G, 335 (334)
Moisan C, 627 (627)
Monk C C, 366 (364, 366)
Monk D H, 207 (206)
Montague E J, 597 (594)
Montague W E, 522
Montero-Sieburth M, 369 (367, 368)
Montessori M, (146), (209), (316)
Mook D A, 521 (518)
Moore D W, 200 (197)
Moos R H, 348 (345), 419 (417)
Moo-Sub K, 543 (540)
Morero J, (62)
Morgan N, 248 (242)
Morine-Dershimer G, 11 (9), 191 (189)
Morris I, 8 (6)
Morris J E, 369 (368)
Morris S, 598 (595)
Morrison A, 620 (617)
Morrison H C, 433 (431)
Mortimer R G, 242 (240)
Mortimore P, 160 (156, 157), 207 (205, 206), 214 (212), 330 (327)
Moser J M, 412 (409)
Mosher R L, 597 (595)
Mossenson L, 282 (282)
Mounts N, 382 (379)
Mueller D J, 366 (365)

Mugny G, 339 (338)
Mulopo M M, 155 (154)
Munby H, 24 (22), 136 (132, 134)
Murnane R J, 75–76 (73, 74), 531 (528, 529, 530), 611 (610)
Murphy J, 259 (259)
Murphy S B, 182 (181)
Murray F B, 339 (338), 604 (601)
Murray H A, 348 (344, 345)
Murray H G, 500–01 (497, 499), 538 (536)
Musella R, 171 (168)
Musgrave P W, 395 (394)
Mussen P H, 382
Muthukrishna N, 126 (123)

Naccarato R W, 500 (495)
Nafpaktitis M, 416 (414)
Nakamura G V, 444 (441)
Nash R J, 40 (35, 36, 39), 534 (533)
Nash S C, 323 (320)
Navon D, 363 (360, 362)
Neale D C, 24 (21), 516 (515)
Neches R, 463 (459)
Neef N A, 227 (226)
Neidermeyer F C, 204 (200, 201)
Neill S, 278 (275)
Neisser U, 449 (445)
Nelli E, 556 (553)
Nelson C M, 223 (220)
Nelson K R, 52 (50, 51), 444 (440)
Nespor J, 8
Neufeld R W J, 87 (81), 130 (127)
Neugarten B L, (535)
Newell A, 52 (49), 426 (421)
Newman D, 318 (318)
Newman J D, 19 (18)
Newman R, 34 (32, 33)
Newman S E, 126 (123, 126), 148 (145), 267 (265, 266), 285 (285), 344 (342), 412 (411), 449 (447), 456 (456), 485
Newton A, 570 (568)
Nias J, 87 (81, 82, 84)
Nicholls J G, 148 (146, 148), 323 (321), 407 (404, 406)
Nickerson M, 412 (410)
Nickerson R S, 106 (102), 466 (466)
Nickolai-Mays S, 530 (530)
Niemiec R P, 521 (519)
Niles J A, 182 (181)
Nilsson B, 309 (309)
Ninomiya A, 56 (54)
Nisbett R E, 251 (250)
Nitko A J, 178 (176), 290 (288), 299 (295)
Noble G, 61 (59)
Noddings N, 79 (78), 539 (536), 547 (543, 546)
Noffke S E, 604 (601)
Nolen L L, 204 (203)
Noor Azmi I, 628 (627)
Norman C A, 416 (415)
Norman D A, 426 (425), 436 (434)
North B, 299
Northfield J R, 565 (561, 563)
Nott D, 598 (594)

Novak J D, 174 (173, 174), 436 (435)
Nuthall G A, 238 (236), 248 (246), 506 (505)
Nutter N, 556 (553)
Nuttin J, 402 (401)
Nwagwu N, 72 (69, 70, 71)
Nystrand M, 248 (243)
Nystrom M, 286 (284)

Oakes J, 28 (26), 87 (85), 160 (156), 196 (192, 193, 194, 195)
O'Brien D G, 254 (252)
Odden A, 315 (314)
Ogborn J M, 174 (171, 172, 173)
Ogbu J U, 335 (334, 335)
Oishi S, 143 (142)
Oja S N, 19 (16), 538–39 (538)
Okato T, 56 (54)
O'Keefe P, 604 (600, 602)
Olds D, 200 (198)
Oliveros A, 72 (69)
Olkin I O, 516
Olmstead B, 603 (599)
Olsen J B, 290 (289)
Olsen R J, 75–76 (73, 74), 531 (528, 529, 530)
Olson W C, 506 (501)
Olsson N G, 501 (499)
Olton R M, 466 (464), 480 (480)
O'Neal E C, 200 (198)
O'Neal S, 597 (594)
Opper S, 106 (103)
O'Quin K, 481 (477)
Ornstein P A, 444 (440)
Ortony A, 426 (423)
Ory J C, 500 (499)
Osborn A E, 466 (464)
Osborn J, 267 (264)
Osborn M, 15 (14), 45 (42)
Osborne A, 136 (135)
Osbourne R, 126 (125)
Oser F, 40 (35, 36, 37, 38, 39, 40), 106 (104, 105), 538 (536)
Otis-Wilborn A K, 531 (529)
Otten R, 407 (406)
Otto H J, 366 (363)
Otto L B, 395 (394)
Ouston J, 330 (327)
Owings J, 75
Oxley B, 199 (198)
Oyserman D, 34 (29)
Ozga J, 15 (13), 72 (67, 68, 69, 71)

Pace C R, 556 (553)
Packer M J, 267 (264)
Pagano J, 79 (78)
Page R N, 196 (192, 193, 194, 195)
Paine L, 530 (528)
Paivio A U, 444 (441)
Palanki A, 373 (372, 373)
Palincsar A M, 286 (285), 449 (447)
Palincsar A S, 111 (108), 126 (123), 148 (145), 248 (245), 282 (280), 344 (342), 412 (409), 426 (425), 485
Palmer D R, 476 (473)

Pankratz R S, 552 (550), 555 (554)
Paolitto D P, 274 (272)
Paradise L V, 248 (242)
Paris S G, 426 (425, 426)
Parkay F W, 587 (586)
Parke R D, 382 (378, 379)
Parker R N, 395 (394)
Parnes H S, 395 (392)
Parnes S J, 481 (480)
Parsons G, 547 (546)
Parsons T, 67 (65), 358 (353)
Paschal R, 271 (268, 269)
Pask G, 390 (389, 390)
Paterson R K, 255 (252)
Patrick H, 506 (503, 505)
Patry J-L, 40 (38, 39, 40)
Patterson L, 534 (533)
Pavan B N, 46 (44), 318 (317)
Payne M A, 56 (54)
Peacock D, 565 (561)
Pearce G, 547 (545)
Pearl A, 238 (235)
Pearson P D, 111 (110, 111)
Peck R F, 500–01 (499)
Pedro E, 310 (309)
Pegg J E, 577 (574, 576)
Pelgrum W J, 363 (359, 360, 361, 362)
Peloille B, 8 (7)
Penn D M, 40 (39)
Pennell J R, 611 (610, 611)
Pennypacker H, 101 (98)
Pepper F, 231 (227)
Perkin H, 15 (12)
Perkins D N, 426 (422, 425, 426), 484 (483)
Perret-Clermont A-N, 339
Perrott C, 122
Perry E, 358 (355)
Perry W G, 263 (262), 538 (537)
Pervin L A, 131 (127)
Pestalozzi J H, (161), (167)
Peter L J, 264
Peters T, 40 (40)
Petersen P, (316)
Peterson D W, 274 (273)
Peterson J, 34 (32)
Peterson P L, 11, 24 (21), 28 (25), 52 (50, 51), 96 (95), 136 (134), 178 (176), 191 (189), 290 (286, 289), 294 (290, 291, 292), 412 (410, 411), 416 (414), 516 (515)
Peterson R W, 429 (427)
Petrosko J, 481 (478)
Pettersson S, 310 (309)
Peverly S T, 476 (474)
Phelps E, 339 (336, 337, 338, 339)
Philipp E, 358 (355)
Philips S U, 278 (276), 335 (334)
Phillipps R W, 204 (201)
Phillips W E, 577 (574)
Phoenix A, 323 (320)
Piaget J, 40 (39), 106 (102, 103, 104, 105), 117 (114), 121 (118), (122), (167), 339 (336), 538 (537)
Pichert J W, 443 (442)
Pickard A, 547 (545)
Pigge F, 556 (555)

Pigott T D, 167 (161, 165, 166)
Pillemer D B, 516
Pine J, 466 (465)
Pines A, 57 (55)
Pinnegar P, 52 (49)
Pinnegar S, 136, 416 (415)
Pinnell G S, 412 (409)
Pintrich P R, 407 (406), 449 (447), 476 (472)
Pitcher G D, 223
Pizzamiglio L, 390 (389)
Plake B S, 493
Plato, (122), (252)
Plomp T, 363 (359, 360, 361, 362)
Pocklington K, 547 (545), 555 (555)
Poland S, 223
Polanyi M, 426 (422)
Polgar S, 335 (333)
Pollard A, 182 (182)
Polson P, 466 (465)
Polya G, 52 (48)
Poole M E, 395 (393)
Popham J W, 191 (188)
Popham W J, 556 (553)
Popkewitz T L, 160 (158)
Popp M, 200 (198)
Popper K, (151)
Porter A, 34 (33), 207 (205)
Portes A, 395 (394)
Posch P, 19 (17)
Posey L, 463
Posner M I, 429 (427), 457 (455)
Post D, 395 (394)
Poster C, 493
Poster D, 493
Postlethwaite T N, 204 (201), 206 (205), 271 (268), 315 (310, 311), 511 (510, 511), 587
Powell A, 534 (532)
Power C, 174 (172)
Power C N, 174 (173), 238 (237)
Pratt D, 318 (315, 317)
Prawat R S, 426 (422)
Prawatt R, 484 (483)
Prescott D R, 597 (594)
Pressley M, 126–27 (123, 126), 148 (145), 251 (250), 436 (434, 435, 436), 444 (440, 441, 442)
Price E, 453 (453)
Prick L G M, 552
Proctor C P, 323 (320)
Prokop C M, 56 (53)
Pronovost G, 369 (369)
Provenzo E F, 136
Provus M M, 318 (317), 556 (553)
Pugach M C, 11 (10)
Pugh R C, 248 (247), 582 (579, 580)
Purkey S C, 330 (327)
Puro P, 218 (217)
Purpel D E, 597 (595)
Purves A C, 204 (201), 330 (330)
Putnam R T, 11 (10), 24 (21)

Quicke J C, 274 (272)
Quinlan M, 323 (319, 321)

Quinn N, 335 (333)
Quinn R P, 56 (54)
Quintilian, (272)
Quirk T J, 493 (489)

Rackliffe G, 238 (236, 237)
Radley G W, 263 (262)
Rambaran R, 369 (368)
Ramírez M, 390 (390)
Ramsay P, 373 (370, 371, 372)
Rand P, 402 (399)
Rand Y, 466 (465)
Randall P E, 227 (225)
Rankin E F Jr., 66 (65)
Ransom K, 248 (245)
Raphael T, 285 (285)
Raphael T E, 248 (247), 412 (410)
Rasch M, 463 (459)
Rathbone C J, 170 (167)
Raths J D, 547 (546), 556 (553, 554)
Ratzlaff H C, 597 (594)
Raudenbush S W, 416 (415), 419
Raviv A, 200 (199)
Raynor J O, 402 (401)
Readence J E, 148 (145)
Reader G G, 620 (616)
Reckase M D, 299 (295)
Reder L M, 112 (110)
Redfield D L, 516 (514)
Reed W M, 463 (462)
Reese E P, 101 (99)
Reid M, 8 (8)
Reif F, 148 (145)
Reigeluth C M, 112 (107, 108), 449 (445)
Reil M, 454 (452)
Rein W, 521 (517)
Reis H T, 199 (197)
Reisel E, 200 (199)
Reiser B J, 343 (343)
Reissman F, 274 (272)
Renaud A J, 366 (364)
Renner J, 106 (103), 155 (151, 152)
Rentel V, 582 (579)
Resnick D, 303 (302)
Resnick L B, 148 (147), 286 (284), 303 (302), 344 (340, 343), 412 (411)
Rest J, 106 (103, 105), 539 (535)
Reynolds A J, 207 (206)
Reynolds B P, 367 (364, 365)
Reynolds M, 552
Reynolds R E, 443 (441)
Rhody T, 248 (242, 243, 245)
Rice J M, 148 (144)
Rice W K, 326 (324)
Richards M H, 207 (205), 271 (269, 270)
Richardson R, 538 (536)
Richardson V, 416 (416), 604 (601)
Richert A E, 24 (20), 588 (586), 593 (590)
Rickards J P, 449 (446)
Rickards W, 556 (553)
Riessman F, 339 (338)
Rimé B, 278 (274)
Rimm S B, 480 (478)
Rinehart S C, 436 (435)

Ringenbach S, 481 (478)
Rippa S A, 466 (464)
Risley T R, 101 (98)
Rist R, 196 (193, 194)
Ritchie S M, 136 (132)
Ritter P, 382 (379)
Rivlin L G, 200
Roberts D, 382 (379)
Robinson G E, 315 (311, 313)
Robinson J T, 174 (172), 264
Robinson S, 565 (562)
Robitaille D F, 511 (506, 507)
Robson M, 11 (11), 136
Roche L, 500 (499)
Rodgers-Jenkinson F, 57 (55)
Rodriquez G, 604 (601)
Roeder M, 211 (208)
Roehler L R, 111 (110, 111), 238 (236, 237), 604 (602)
Rogers C R, 170 (168)
Rogers D, 40 (37, 39)
Rogers K W, 323 (319)
Rogers T, 248 (243)
Rogoff B, 318 (317, 318)
Rogozinski J T, 436 (435)
Rohlen T, 335 (333)
Rohrkemper M M, 11 (9)
Roid G, 481 (478)
Rolff H G, 358 (355)
Rollett B A, 402 (397)
Romberg T, 413 (409)
Romiszowski A J, 457 (455, 456)
Roning L U, 367 (364, 365)
Rooparnine J L, 382
Rose L H, 481 (480)
Rose T L, 369 (368)
Rosemberg F K, 227 (225)
Rosen H, 453 (452)
Rosenbaum J E, 196 (192, 194, 195)
Rosenblatt L, (467)
Rosencranz H A, 66 (65, 66)
Rosenfeld D, 143 (142)
Rosenfield P, 200 (199)
Rosenholtz S J, 28 (26), 46 (43), 87 (80, 86), 318 (318)
Rosenshine B V, 11 (9), 112 (108), 149 (144, 145), 187 (185), 238 (237), 242 (240), 248 (243, 245, 246, 247), 286 (283, 284, 285), 348 (344), 506 (501, 503, 505), 516 (514)
Rosenthal A, 72 (69)
Rosenthal R A, 34–35 (29, 31), 56 (54), 117 (113), 416 (413, 414), 516 (513)
Ross A, 543 (541)
Ross D D, 531 (528, 530), 577 (574)
Ross P A, 227 (225)
Ross S, 577 (574)
Rossi P, 61 (58)
Rossmiller R A, 318 (317)
Rothenberg J, 170 (170)
Rothkopf E Z, 449 (446)
Rothrock D, 160 (155)
Rousseau E W, 516 (514)
Rousseau J-J, (149), (167)
Rowan B, 196 (193)

Rowe R, 454 (452)
Roy A, 369 (367)
Rubin A, 412 (410, 411)
Rubin D, 35 (31)
Rubin L J, 8 (6, 7)
Rumelhart D E, 426 (425)
Rumney S, 592 (589, 591)
Runkel P J, 358 (354, 355)
Rushcamp S, 604 (602)
Russell B, 136 (132)
Russell G, 395 (392)
Russell T, 136 (132, 134)
Rust V D, 560
Rutter M, 330 (327)
Rutter R A, 46 (43)
Ryan D W, 160 (156), 178 (177), 206 (205, 206), 214 (213), 315 (311), 511 (506, 508)
Ryan E B, 436 (435)
Ryan K, 577 (573, 574, 575)
Ryan R M, 401 (401)

Sørensen A B, 196 (193, 194, 195)
Sabers D, 52 (49, 50, 51), 416 (415)
Sacca K, 248 (246)
Saha L J, 395 (392, 393, 394)
Saigh P A, 101 (99)
Saily M, 318 (317)
Salisbury D F, 521 (521)
Säljö R, 390 (389)
Salomon G, 40 (38), 268 (267), 402 (397), 426 (426), 484 (483)
Salvia J, 178 (175)
Salzberg C L, 101 (100)
Sammons P, 160 (156, 157), 207 (205, 206), 214 (212)
Samson G E, 248 (242)
Sandefur J T, 556 (553)
Sandelbach N B, 191 (189)
Sanders D C, 366 (363)
Sanders D P, 136 (132, 133)
Sanford J P, 207 (206), 223 (220), 358 (357)
Sangster S, 367 (365)
Sarason S B, 28 (25), 87 (83, 85), 259 (255, 259)
Sarros J C, 56 (53)
Sarup M, 323 (319)
Sato A, 547 (544)
Satterfiel T H, 367 (365)
Saur R, 200 (198)
Saxe L, 117
Saxton J, 248 (242)
Scannell D P, 570 (568)
Scannell M M, 570 (567)
Scardamalia M, 344 (340), 463 (460), 485
Schafer W D, 294 (293)
Schallert D L, 111 (108), 426 (421, 422, 423), 443 (441)
Schaps E, 41 (40)
Schecter S R, 19 (17)
Scheele B, 450 (448)
Scheu J A, 267 (267)
Schiefelbein L, 373 (370)
Schiefele U, 407 (404, 406)
Schild E O, 263 (260)

Schlechty P S, 531 (529)
Schmalt H D, 131 (130)
Schmeck R R, 390 (389)
Schmidt F L, 516
Schmidt R A, 457 (456)
Schmidt R E, 200 (197)
Schmuck P A, 259 (257), 358 (353, 354, 356, 357)
Schmuck R A, 259 (257), 358 (353, 354, 355, 356, 357)
Schmuller A M, 522 (517)
Schneider B, 326 (324)
Schneider K, 131 (130)
Schneider W, 131 (130), 344 (342), 444 (440, 442)
Schoenfeld A H, 344 (341), 413 (411)
Schon D, 52 (48)
Schon D A, 11 (10), 182 (179, 182), 294 (290)
Schoonman W, 299
Schrader F-W, 178 (177), 290 (287, 288, 290), 407 (404), 522 (519, 520)
Schras G A, 539 (535)
Schroeter D, 34 (32)
Schubert N A, 170 (168, 169)
Schuder T, 126 (126)
Schuler R A, 56–57 (54, 55)
Schulte A C, 476 (473)
Schultz K, 471 (471)
Schulz E M, 326 (324)
Schulze K G, 238 (235)
Schulze S K, 386 (382)
Schumaker J B, 101 (96, 99), 126 (124, 126)
Schunk D H, 407, 419 (416), 429 (428), 476 (472)
Schuttenberg E, 534 (533)
Schutz A, 628 (624)
Schutz W, 358 (353)
Schwab J J, 19 (16), 155 (150, 151, 152)
Schwab R L, 56–57 (53, 54, 55)
Schwartz F, 196 (193, 195)
Scott J A, 412 (408)
Scott J R, 274 (271)
Scott R, 522 (519)
Scott W A, 61 (60), 506 (503)
Scott-Hodgetts R, 323 (321)
Seadon T, 547 (544, 545)
Sears J T, 531 (529)
Sebeok T A, 278
Sederberg C H, 171 (169)
Segal J W, 466 (464)
Seibel C, 326 (324)
Selander S, 310 (309)
Selden W K, 565 (561)
Self J A, 112 (111)
Seligman M E P, 401 (400)
Selim M A, 155 (154)
Selman R L, 41 (39, 40)
Selmes I P, 267 (265, 266)
Seregny S, 72 (70)
Sergiovanni T J, 597 (596)
Sewell W H, 395 (394)
Seyle H, 57 (52, 53)
Shachar C, 143 (139, 142)
Shachar H, 259 (258)

Shaeffer S, 543 (542)
Shafro M G, 386 (386)
Shah S, 543 (542)
Shake M C, 416 (414)
Shank P C, 367 (364)
Shanker A, 15 (13)
Shanner W M, 214 (212)
Shapira R, 363 (360, 362)
Shapiro B J, 160 (156), 178 (177), 206
   (205, 206), 214 (213), 315 (311), 511
   (506, 508)
Shapiro E S, 178 (174, 175, 176, 177),
   227 (225)
Shapson S M, 315 (313)
Sharan S, 143 (139, 141, 142), 259 (255,
   256, 257, 258), (336), 352
Sharan S (ed.), 259 (257, 258)
Sharan Y, 143 (141), 259 (255, 257)
Sharp L, 35 (31)
Sharpe T, 52 (49, 50)
Sharpley A M, 274 (272)
Sharpley C F, 274 (272)
Shaunnessey M, 214 (213)
Shavelson R J, 11 (9), 178 (174, 177), 191
   (189), 290 (287), 466 (465)
Shavit Y, 196 (192)
Shaw M E, 358 (352, 353, 356)
Sheingold K, 363 (359, 360, 361, 362)
Sheldrake P, 8 (8)
Shepard L A, 326 (324, 325)
Sherman J A, 101 (96, 99)
Shiang C P, 248 (245)
Shiffrin R M, 344 (342)
Shimron J S, 160 (157), 214 (213)
Shinn M R, 223 (220)
Shipman M D, 620 (618)
Shlomo S, 358 (357)
Short A H, 263 (261, 262)
Short E J, 436 (435)
Showers B, 111 (107, 109), 628 (623,
   624), 632
Shrigley R L, 155 (154)
Shriver B, 357 (352, 353)
Shuell T, 52 (47)
Shulman J H, 24, 588 (586)
Shulman L S, 24 (20, 21, 23), 96 (92, 93,
   95), 136 (135), 155 (149, 150, 152, 153),
   286 (284), 547 (544, 545), 552 (551), 556
   (554), 588 (583, 584, 585, 587)
Shultz J, 218 (217)
Siedentop D, (595)
Sigel I, 286 (284)
Sikes J, 143 (141, 142), 323 (321)
Sikula G, 547 (544)
Sikula J, 604 (599)
Silberman C E, 171
Silberstein M, 547 (545), 588 (585)
Silver E A, 282 (281), 466 (463)
Silverman R, 588 (585)
Simmons B J, 369 (368)
Simmons J M, 539 (537)
Simmons R, 426 (422, 425)
Simon A B, 41 (39), 506 (501)
Simon B, 323 (321), 506 (503)
Simon H A, 52 (49), 444 (443), 476 (475)

Simons H, 19 (17)
Simons P R J, 484–85 (482, 483)
Simpson A W, 416 (414)
Simpson C, 318 (318)
Sinclair K E, 323 (319)
Singer J D, 75 (73, 74), 531 (528, 529, 530)
Singer R N, 457
Singh J, 101 (98)
Singh M, 199 (198)
Singh N N, 101 (98)
Singley M K, 466 (464)
Sirota R, 326 (325)
Sirotnik K A, 248 (242, 243, 245), 358
   (354), 534 (531), 552, 604 (600)
Sirotnik K E, 547 (544, 546)
Skinner B F, 101 (97, 99), 204 (200),
   227 (224), 231 (227), 251 (249), (398),
   522 (519)
Skinner W, 587 (584)
Slater M, 79 (76)
Slavin R E, 143 (139, 140, 141, 142), 161
   (156, 159), 167 (165), 196 (193, 195), 223
   (221), 238 (235), 315 (312, 314), 318
   (317), 339 (336), 352, 402 (399), 516
   (514), 522 (520)
Slavings R, 34 (32)
Sloane H N, 101
Sluckin A, 318 (317)
Smagorinsky P, 413 (410)
Smart W D, 565 (562, 563)
Smiley S S, 444 (440)
Smith A, 330 (327)
Smith B O, 238 (235, 236), 506 (504,
   505), 552
Smith C W, 603 (601)
Smith D, 79 (78), 183, 218 (217)
Smith D A, 24 (20, 21)
Smith D C, 24 (21), 493, 516 (515)
Smith E L, 191 (189)
Smith F L, 106 (102), 237 (236, 237), 309
   (308), 505 (505)
Smith G P, 75 (74)
Smith H, 19 (16)
Smith H A, 278 (275)
Smith J, 255 (253), 395 (392)
Smith M L, 315 (310, 312, 313), 326
   (324, 325)
Smith M S, 330 (327)
Smith P V, 516 (513)
Smith T, 476 (475)
Smith W, 531 (528, 530)
Smulyan L, 19 (16), 539
Smylie M A, 218 (216)
Smyth J, 46 (44), 182 (181)
Smythe W J, 207 (205)
Snapp M, 143 (141)
Snoek J K, 56 (54)
Snow R E, (50), 96 (95), 112 (107), 130–31
   (127, 128, 129, 130), 160–61 (155, 157,
   158, 159, 160), 178 (175, 176), 282 (279),
   290 (288), 330 (327), 402 (396), 416
   (413), 521–22 (520)
Snyder C W, 611 (611)
Soar R S, 493 (491)
Sockett H, 19 (17)

Soder R, 534 (531), 552
Sokolov E N, 429 (428)
Soled S W, 167 (164)
Soliman I K, 611 (608, 610, 611)
Solomon D, 41 (40)
Soltis J F, 587 (587)
Sommer R, 199–200 (198), 358 (353)
Sommers N I, 454 (452)
Spaull A D, 15 (13)
Speed T J, 263 (261)
Speedie S M, 481 (478)
Spence D, 390 (387)
Spender D, 323 (319)
Sperle D H, 588 (583)
Sperling M, 454 (452)
Spindler G, 336
Spindler L, 336
Spradley J P, 335 (333)
Sprinthall N A, 46 (42), 106 (102, 105),
   274 (271)
Sprinthall R C, 106 (102)
Squires D S, 204 (201), 611 (608, 609,
   610, 611)
Stafford F P, 271 (269)
Stahl S A, 436 (435)
Stake R E, 174 (172, 173), 556 (553)
Stallings J A, 604 (598, 599, 600, 601, 602)
Stamm C, 412 (410)
Stanworth M, 323 (322)
Steadman S, 628 (622)
Steckelberg A L, 367 (364, 365)
Steigler J, 28 (26)
Stein P, 52 (50, 51)
Steinberg L, 382 (379)
Stenhouse L, 19 (16)
Stephan C, 143 (141)
Stephan S, 143 (142)
Stern G G, 348 (345)
Stern J P, 531 (528)
Stern P, 178 (174, 177), 290 (287)
Sternberg R J, 131 (130), 436 (434)
Stevens A L, 344 (341)
Stevens D, 285 (285)
Stevens R, 149 (144), 187 (185), 242 (240),
   348 (344), 588 (583, 584)
Stevens R J, 143 (140)
Stevenson D, 326 (324), 382 (380)
Stevenson H W, 28 (26), 207 (205, 206),
   214 (213), 268 (265, 266), 331 (330), 382
   (379, 381), 413 (409)
Steward F H, 335 (332)
Stewart J P, 200 (197)
Stewart L, 323 (319)
Stiegelbauer S, 86 (82, 85)
Stigler J E, 196 (193), 413 (409)
Stigler J W, 207 (205, 206), 214 (213), 268
   (265, 266), 331 (330), 382
Stipek D J, 28 (25), 290 (288)
Stires L K, 200 (198)
Stobart G, 323 (319, 321)
Stockley D, 366 (364, 365)
Stoddart T, 87 (82), 604, 604 (600, 601, 602)
Stodolsky S S, 46 (44), 214 (212, 213), 255
   (252), 294 (292), 416 (414), 433 (433)
Stoll C S, 263 (260, 261, 262)

Stoll L, 160 (156, 157), 207 (205, 206), 214 (212)
Stolurow L M, 522 (519)
Stone C, 282 (281)
Stone M H, 299 (296, 323 (320)
Stoner G, 223 (220)
Stones E, 598 (595)
Stover G, 204 (202)
Stratford R, 358 (355)
Strauss H, 170 (170)
Strike K A, 41 (35)
Strom S, 555 (554)
Stroobant R E, 323 (319)
Strykowski B, 248 (242)
Stuart J S, 628 (624)
Stufflebeam D, 556 (552, 553)
Style E, 19 (18)
Subirats A, 593 (591)
Suchman J R, (151)
Suite A, 199 (197)
Sullivan E V, 160 (157)
Sultana R, 72 (68, 71)
Sulzbacher S I, 251 (250)
Sulzer-Azaroff B, 101 (97, 98, 99), 231
Suter L, 75 (72)
Sutherland D I M, 565 (562, 563)
Sutton R, 534 (533)
Svinicki M D, 476 (474)
Swanson H L, 436 (434)
Swanson J, 131 (130), 402 (396)
Swarthout D, 267 (264, 265)
Swift L F, 238 (234)
Sykes G, 15 (13), 182 (181), 588 (583, 586)
Symons S, 444 (441)

Tabachnick B R, 160 (158), 183 (181), 620 (619)
Tait H, 476 (474)
Talbert J A, 547 (547)
Talbert J E, 46 (43)
Tamir M, 155 (149, 150, 152, 153), 174 (172, 173), 556 (555), 588 (585)
Tangyong A F, 628 (626), 632 (629, 630)
Tann S, 182 (182)
Tannatt L M, 290 (288)
Tanner D K, 267 (267)
Tansey P J, 263 (260)
Tarule J M, 18 (18), 79 (78), 538 (537)
Tarvin W L, 570 (565)
Taylor B M, 286 (285), 436 (435)
Taylor D T, 466 (464)
Taylor F W, (454)
Taylor J L, 263 (261)
Taylor M, 154 (149, 150, 154)
Taylor P C, 419 (416, 418)
Taylor P H, 191 (188)
Taylor S C, 126 (125, 126)
Taylor W, 565
Teasdale J D, 401 (400)
Teitel L, 604 (601)
Tennyson R D, 463 (459)
Thatcher D C, 264
Thelen H, 259 (255)
Theodorou E, 218 (217)

Thibadeau G, 171 (167)
Thies-Sprinthall L T, 46 (42), 106 (105)
Thirkell B, 200 (197)
Thomas D R, 231 (230)
Thomas G, 367 (365)
Thomas J B, 552 (548)
Thomas M W, 15 (12)
Thomas R M, 28 (25)
Thomas S C, 171 (167)
Thomas S J, 539 (535)
Thompson B, 538 (536)
Thompson J, 214 (213)
Thorndike E L, 251 (249), 466 (464)
Thorne B, 588 (583, 584)
Thornton S J, 547 (543, 546)
Thorpe L P, 522 (517)
Thucydides, (252)
Thurstone L L, 390 (387)
Tillema H H, 522 (519)
Timar T B, 570 (566)
Tisher R P, 238 (236), 413 (408), 547 (543, 545), 560
Tissot P, 204
Tobias S, 386 (383)
Tobin K G, 136 (132, 134), 248 (246), 348 (345, 348), 419 (419)
Toles R E, 326 (324)
Tom A R, 547 (545)
Tom D Y H, 28 (26), 34 (30)
Tomasello M, 339 (339)
Tomic W, 161 (159)
Tomich E, 66 (66)
Tomlinson T M, 315 (311, 314)
Topping K, 373 (370)
Torper U, 310 (309)
Torrence E P, 242 (241), 481 (477, 478, 480)
Townsend M A R, 444 (440)
Trabasso T R, 251 (250)
Traill R, 577 (574)
Traub R, 171 (168)
Travers K J, 511 (506)
Travers R M W, 8 (6)
Treagust D F, 348 (345)
Treffinger D J, 480–81 (477, 480)
Treiman D J, 61 (58, 59)
Trickett E J, 348 (345), 419 (417)
Tripcony P, 373 (371)
Trotter A, 369 (367, 368)
Troutman A C, 101
Trowbridge M H, 251 (250)
Troyer M, 556 (553), 582 (580)
Troyna B, 323 (322), 611 (609)
Trueba H T, 336
Trumbull D J, 8 (7)
Tsugawa T, 19 (18)
Tuijnman A, 330 (326)
Tullgren R, 52 (49)
Turner F J, (234)
Turner R H, 395 (392)
Turner T, 367 (365), 426 (423)
Turney C, 577 (574), 598, 604 (598, 599)
Turvey M T, 457 (456)
Twa J, 598 (594)
Twyman J P, 66 (66)
Tyler R W, 19 (16), 106 (102), 191 (188)

Umar A M, 101 (99)
Underwood B J, 429 (427)
Urban K K, 481 (479)
Ushiwata G, 547 (544)
Uttal D, 382 (381)

Valdés G, 454 (451)
Vale C D, 299 (295)
Vallance E, 191 (189)
Valli L, 547 (545)
Van Calster K, 402 (401)
Van Der Sijde P C, 161 (159)
van Dijk T A, 450 (448)
Van Manen M, 183 (180)
Van Mater Stone G, 476 (472)
Van Patten J, 112 (108)
Van Rijswijk F, 485 (482)
Van Velzen W G, 628 (626)
Van Woerden W M, 588 (584)
Vance V S, 531 (529)
Vasa S F, 367 (364, 365)
Veenman S A M, 106 (104), 522 (519)
Vermunt J D H M, 485 (482)
Vernon P E, 481 (476)
Verspoor A M, 315 (311), 543 (542), 570 (566)
Vigil J D, 358 (356)
Villar L M, 183
Vonk J H C, 539 (535)
Voorbach J T, 552
Vos A J, 560
Vulliamy G, 628 (625)
Vygotsky L S, 35 (31), 106 (102, 103, 104), 121 (117, 118), 126 (123), 282 (280), 286 (285), 339 (337), 413 (409), 454 (452)

Wade B, 170 (167, 168)
Wagenschein M, 450 (446)
Wager W W, 111 (108)
Wagner A C, 577 (574)
Wagner B J, 454 (450)
Wagoner S, 476 (475)
Wahgudi R, 628 (626)
Walberg H J, 106 (103), 167 (165, 166), 171 (167), 178 (177), 204 (202), 207 (205, 206), 248 (242), 271 (268, 269, 270), 285–86 (284), 331 (327), 348 (344, 345, 347), 386 (383), 419 (417, 418), 516 (512, 513, 514, 515, 516), 521 (518, 519), 611 (610)
Walczyk J J, 112 (110)
Walford R, 263 (261)
Walker C H, 386 (384)
Walker H M, 223 (220)
Walker L, 106 (103)
Walker R, 505 (502)
Wallace S, 248 (244)
Wallach M, 481 (477)
Wallat C, 122, 219 (217)
Waller W, 8 (7), 28 (26), 61 (61), 67 (65)
Wang M C, 161 (157, 158, 159), 331 (326, 327), 426 (425), 476 (474), 516 (516)

Wang N, 282 (281)
Wansart W, 285 (285)
Wapner S, 390 (389)
Warren D, 72 (69, 70, 71), 534 (531)
Washburne C W, 161 (155)
Washington K, 34 (32)
Wasik B H, 101 (99)
Waterman R, 40 (40)
Watson A J, 611 (608, 609, 610, 611)
Watson M, 41 (40)
Wax M L, 335 (334)
Wax R H, 335 (334)
Waxman H C, 161 (157, 158, 159), 182 (182), 516 (513, 515)
Weade R, 121 (119, 120)
Webb J, 40 (37, 39)
Webb R, 86 (80, 83, 86), 628 (625)
Weber L, 171
Weber R, 416 (414)
Wehing R S, 426 (426)
Wehlage G, 160 (158)
Weidman C, 24 (21), 219 (215, 216, 218)
Weil M, 111 (107, 109)
Weiler K, 72 (67, 68, 70), 79
Weinberg S F, 493 (489)
Weiner B, 117 (115), 402 (400), 407 (404)
Weiner G, 19 (18), 323 (320, 323)
Weinert F E, 131 (130), 290 (287), 386–87 (383, 384), 402 (399), 407 (404), 444 (440), 522 (519, 520)
Weinstein C E, 426 (423), 436 (434), 450 (447), 476 (472, 473, 474)
Weinstein C S, 200, 593 (590)
Weinstein R, 34–35 (31, 33)
Weinstein T, 248 (242), 271 (268, 269), 386 (383), 521 (518)
Weisberg R W, 466 (464)
Weiss D J, 299 (295)
Weiss J, 171 (168)
Weisskopf-Joelson E, 466 (464)
Weistein C S, 200 (197)
Welch W W, 174 (172), 285 (284), 348 (344), 419 (417), 521 (519)
Wellington J J, 155 (149, 150, 154)
Welsh W W, 207 (205)
Welty D A, 367 (364)
Welty D R, 367 (364)
Welty W M, 588 (585)
Wenestram C G, 449 (446)
Wenger E, 344 (342)
Wennås O, 309 (309)
Werry B, 511 (507)
Wertsch J, 191 (190), 463
Wesselman R, 238 (236)
West R P, 101 (100)
Westbury I, 511 (506)
Westeimer J, 547 (547)
Westerhof K, 191 (190)
Western J S, 395 (393)
Westgate D, 506 (502)
Weyhing R S, 449 (447)
Wheldall K, 200 (198), 223 (222)
Whipple G M, 161 (155)
White G, 72 (70)
White J W, 323 (319), 547 (545)

White R, 369 (368)
White R K, 358 (353)
White R T, 126 (123, 124)
Whiteside T, 61 (59)
Whitford B L, 604 (601)
Whiting B B, 318 (317)
Whiting J W M, 318 (317)
Wideen M F, 547 (543), 560, 632
Wideman C, 191 (190)
Wiersma W, 161 (158)
Wiggins G, 466 (465)
Wigginton E, 19 (16)
Wilbur F, 604 (601)
Wilcox R C, 395 (392)
Wilczenski F L, 101 (98)
Wilderson F, 143 (142)
Wildman T, 148 (146), 285 (285)
Wilen W W, 255 (252), 358 (356)
Wiley D E, 271 (268), 315 (311), 429 (429), 433 (431)
Wilkinson A C, 449 (446)
Wilkinson B, 267 (264, 266), 433
Wilkinson I A G, 412 (408)
Willerman M, 369 (368)
Willett J B, 75 (73, 74), 531 (528, 529, 530)
Williams R, 196 (192)
Willinsky J, 471 (467)
Willis G B, 426 (422)
Willis P, 335 (334)
Wilson R C, 501 (499)
Wilson R M, 274 (273)
Wilson S M, 24 (20, 21)
Wimpelberg K, 255 (252)
Windham D M, 543 (540)
Wineburg S S, 24 (21), 278 (275)
Winitzky N, 582 (579), 604 (600, 602)
Winne P H, 96 (95), 112 (107, 108, 111), 426–27 (420, 423, 424, 425), 516 (514)
Winter R, 19 (18)
Wiratchai N, 196 (193, 194)
Wise A, 604 (601)
Wise S L, 493
Wiseman D L, 531 (530), 603–04 (600, 601)
Wishnick T K, 204 (202)
Wiske M S, 363 (361)
Wisniewski R, 534 (531, 534)
Witherell C, 539 (536)
Witkin H A, 390 (387)
Witt J C, 274 (273)
Wittebols J H, 315 (311, 313)
Witten B J, 493 (489)
Wittgenstein I, 310 (308)
Wittrock M C, 126 (122, 124, 125), 155 (149, 150), 294 (290), 419 (416), 427 (420), 429 (428, 429), 433 (432), 436 (435, 436), 511
Wivatchai N, 214 (213)
Wixson K K, 248 (244)
Wolcott H F, 8 (8), 335 (334)
Wolf D P, 126 (126), 454 (453)
Wolfe D M, 56 (54)
Wolfgang A, 278
Wolstenholme F, 367
Womack S T, 367 (364), 534 (534)
Wong B Y L, 248 (245)
Wonnacott C A, 248 (247)

Wood P, 56 (55)
Wood T, 248 (244)
Woodley K K, 149 (145)
Woods P E, 87 (82), 620 (619)
Woodward J, 148 (146)
Woodward V A, 412 (410)
Woodworth R S, 466 (464)
Woolf M, 366–67 (364, 365)
Woolfolk A E, 278 (275, 277)
Word E, 315 (313)
Worrall N, 200 (197)
Worsham M E, 219, 223 (220)
Wragg E C, 211 (208, 209, 210), 493, 577 (575)
Wragg T, 369 (367, 368)
Wright B D, 299 (296, 298)
Wright C J, 248 (246), 323 (321)
Wright E N, 315 (313)
Wright H F, (94), 318 (317)
Wright H F, 67 (61, 65)
Wrong D H, 620 (617)
Wubbels T, 218–19 (218), 348 (347), 419 (417), 593 (592)
Wulf K M, 200 (198)
Wyllie M, 453 (453)

Yackel E, 248 (244)
Yao T, 299 (295)
Yarger S, 534 (531)
Yates F A, 444 (440)
Yates J W, 597–98 (594, 595)
Yeazell M I, 539 (535, 536)
Yee A, 598 (594, 595)
Yelon S, 204 (201)
Yinger R J, 11 (9, 10), 191 (189, 190)
Young D, 582 (579)
Young J I, 582 (579)
Young K R, 101
Young M, 604 (601)
Young R E, 101 (100), 121 (121)
Youniss J, 339 (336, 338)
Ysseldyke J E, 178 (175, 176, 177)

Zahn K G, 214 (213)
Zahorik J A, 191 (188, 189), 286 (284)
Zeichner K M, 19 (18), 183 (181), 604 (602), 620 (619)
Zeigler H, 72 (67, 68, 70, 71)
Zellermayer M, 268 (267)
Zelniker T, 390 (389)
Zeman B R, 199 (197)
Ziedler D L, 126 (125, 126)
Ziegler S, 143 (142)
Zimmerman B J, 331 (326), 427 (425), 429 (428), 476 (472)
Zimpher N C, 531 (529, 530), 534 (531), 556 (553), 598 (595)
Zimpher N L, 570 (566, 567, 568), 597–98 (594, 596), 604 (601)
Zlotnik M, 534 (534)
Zuckerman J V, 242 (240)
Zutavern M, 538 (536)

Subject Index

The Subject Index has been compiled as a guide to the reader who is interested in locating all the references to a particular subject area within the Encyclopedia. Entries may have up to three levels of heading. Where the page numbers appear in bold italic type, this indicates a substantive discussion of the topic. Every effort has been made to index as comprehensively as possible and to standardize the terms used in the index. However, given the diverse nature of the field and the varied use of terms throughout the international community, synonyms and foreign language terms have been included with appropriate cross-references, As a further aid to the reader, cross-references have also been given to terms of related interest.

Ability
  computer assisted testing
    algorithm for 296
  conceptions of 404
  and energy expenditure 404, 405
    parent attitudes 381
  estimation of
    and computer assisted testing 295
  individual differences 428
  and performance
    in instructional alignment 203
  vs. cognitive style 388
  See also Academic ability; Aptitude;
    Cognitive ability
Ability grouping *192–96*
  academic achievement 195
  classroom research 193
  criticisms of
    de facto segregation 195
    learning theories 195
  and curriculum
    educational objectives 194
  educational experience 193
  flexible progression 194
  instructional effectiveness 156
  interpersonal relationship 195
  learning theories 192
  social influences 193
  student attitudes 195
Absenteeism *See* Attendance; Employee
  absenteeism
Academic ability
  teachers' beliefs 26
Academic achievement
  and ability grouping 195
  and attendance 206
  and class size 305
  classroom environment
    and group unity 356
  compared with energy expenditure 301
  cooperative learning
    teamwork 139
  and examinations 138
  factors affecting
    research 520
  and faculty mobility 610
  and family environment 306, *378–82*

homework 205
influences 177
and learning motivation 396
and learning processes
  research 327
and open plan schools
  research synthesis 515
and parent child relationship 379
and questioning techniques
  problems 242
  research synthesis 514
  sex differences 321
and teacher expectation of students 29
teacher guidance 188
and teacher indirectness
  research synthesis 514
of teachers 60
teachers' beliefs 25
and time factors (learning) 205
and time on task 206
Academic aptitude
  evaluation
    and student needs 287
  individualized instruction 157
    instructional effectiveness 157
Academic education
  teacher commitment to 81
Academic failure
  grade repetition *324–26*
Academic learning time *430–33*
  academic achievement 432
  applications 430
  fundamental concepts of 430
  success rate 431
  task analysis 433
  teacher student relationship 433
  See also Time on task
Accountability
  and governance
    of teacher education 559
Accreditation (teacher education
    institutions) *561–65*
  Australia 561, 563
  Botswana 561, 563
  Canada 561, 563
  criteria 562, 564
  England and Wales 562, 563

formative evaluation 564
input output analysis 564
issues 564
Scotland 562, 563
standardization 564
summative evaluation 564
United States 562, 563
Acculturation
  and peer groups 333
  relationship with social mobility 334
Achievement
  and improvement
    grading 301
  See also Academic achievement; High
    achievement; Low achievement
Achievement gains
  and grading 301
Achievement need
  Atkinson's theory 399
  and test anxiety 399
  theory of 114
    application 115
Achievement tests
  matrix sampling 281
  and questioning techniques 243
  and student needs
    diagnosis of 287
  See also Criterion referenced
    tests; Mastery tests; Nor
    mreferenced tests
Acting
  and teaching 6
Action learning *See* Experiential learning
Action research
  inservice teacher education 624
Activism
  teachers 67
Activity learning *See* Experiential
  learning
Adaptive instruction *See* Adaptive
  teaching
Adaptive Learning Environments
    Model (ALEM)
  instructional effectiveness 159
Adaptive teaching
  characteristics of 520
  and learning theories 327

Adaptive testing
  in the classroom 295
Administrator teacher relationship
  See Teacher administrato
    rrelationship
Administrators
  sex differences 525
Adult development
  teacher education 525, *535–39*
Adults
  socialization
    participant observation 617
Advisory committees
  on governance of teacher education
    557
Affective behavior
  effect on learning *402–07*
  heuristic model 405
Age grade placement *315–18*
  cross cultural studies 332
  historical background 315
  and school organization 332
Algorithms
  for computer assisted testing 296
  PROX 296
Allocated time *See* Time management
Allocation of resources *See* Resource
  allocation
Alternative programs *See* Nontraditional
  education
Alternative schools *See* Nontraditional
  education
Alternative teacher certification 567, 569
  issues and trends 568
  regional 567
Ambition *See* Aspiration
American Association of Colleges for
  Teacher Education (AACTE)
  study of teacher educators 531
Anger
  effect on performance 403
Anxiety
  and aptitude treatment interaction 130
  effect on learning 403
  and eye contact
    in classrooms 276
  See also Test anxiety
Aptitude
  grading according to 300
  See also Academic aptitude
Aptitude treatment interaction (ATI)
  and cognitive development 103
  definitions of 127
    statistical 128
    substantive 127
  diagnostic teaching 175
  evaluation 129
  future research 130
  instructional effectiveness 176
  and instructional systems
    examples 129
  methodology 128
  model
    teaching *127–31*
  research

problems 128, 129
Argumentation *See* Persuasive discourse
Arousal patterns
  effect on learning 403
Artists
  teachers as *6–8*
Aspiration
  causal variations 394
  compared with expectation 392
  and educational attainment 393
  future research 394
  student interpretation of 393
  of students *391–95*
  See also Occupational aspiration;
    Parent aspiration
Assessment
  criterion-referenced *See* Criterion-
    referenced tests
  and learning *279–82*
  performance
    grading 302
    teacher education 554
  See also Measurement; Testing
Assignments
  completion of
    social contexts 265
    and teacher assistance 266
  criticisms of 264
  future trends 267
  issues 265
  supervision of *264–68*
  types of 264
  and understanding 265
  See also Homework; Seatwork
Associative learning
  and memory 441
At risk persons
  and field experience programs 592
Attendance
  and academic achievement 206
  See also Teacher attendance
Attention *427–29*
  and ability
    individual differences 428
  in cognitive science 427
  conceptual models 427
  definition 427
  empirical educational research
    428
  future research trends 429
  involuntary arousal 428
  measurement 428
  and motivation 427, 428
  and neurophysiology 427
  role in short term memory 427
  selective strategies 427, 428, 429
  voluntary 428
Attention control
  self efficacy
    and academic achievement 428
Attention deficit disorders 428
Attitudes
  components of 391
    affective 391
    cognitive 391

conative 391, 393
  correspondence with behavior 391, 393
  and motivation 392
Attribution theory
  in education 115
  and learning motivation 399
Australia
  faculty mobility 610
  school staffing
    problems 608
  teacher education
    accreditation 561, 563
  teacher placement
    methods 607
  teacher student ratio 607
Australian Science Education Project
  (ASEP) 417
Authority structure *See* Power structure
Autism
  reinforcement 225
Autodidaxy *See* Independent study
Autonomous learning *See* Independent
  study

Beginning teacher induction *612–15*
  process 605
Beginning teachers
  needs 605
  probationary period
    conformity 618
  teacher education programs *548–52*
  teacher orientation 613
Behavior
  functional analysis of 226
  nonverbal
    in classrooms *274–78*
  and role theory
    in schools 112
Behavior chaining 97
Behavior change
  and behavioral theories
    of teaching 97
Behavior modification
  and classroom techniques 186
  contingency management
    negative reinforcement 229
    positive reinforcement 229
    punishment 229
    response cost 229
    social reinforcement 229
    timeout 229
    token reinforcement 229
  criticisms of 230
  diminishing behavior 98
  to increase attention 429
  planning of 228
  program evaluation 230
  research
    theory practice relationship 226
  schedules of reinforcement 230
  self control
    and learning 406
  teacher role 228
Behavior problems

modification 228
teacher response 222
intervention 222
reality therapy 222
See also Attention deficit disorders
Behavior theories
chaining 97
diminishing behavior 98
and learning theories 519
maintenance 98
principles 90
shaping 97
stimulus control 97
of teaching *96–101*
transfer 98
See also Attribution theory;
Mediation theory
Behavioral instruction
individualized 100
programs 99
group management 99
peer teaching 99
precision teaching 100
programmed instruction 99
social skills training 99
token economies 99
Behavioral objectives 397
cognitive strategies 458
contextual skills 458
creative processes 458
and educational objectives 98
intellectual skills 458
and teaching methods 437
time factors (learning) 459
verbal information 458
Behavioral science research
and educational research 97
prediction 226
Behaviorism
feedback
in learning and instruction 249
teacher attitudes toward 227
Behaviorist psychology *See* Behaviorism
Beliefs
evaluation 25
influence on learning 404
sex differences 381
Black stereotypes
socialization 320
Black students
and teacher education 74
Body language
in classrooms
cultural differences 276
research 275
Botswana
teacher education
accreditation 561, 563
Brainstorming 341
and problem solving 464
British Columbia
faculty mobility 610
teacher selection
methods 608
Broadcast television

and learning 341
Burnout
human services 53
psychological patterns 53
See also Teacher burnout
Business
case methods 584

Canada
elementary school teachers
studies 84
school staffing
problems 608
student teaching
field experience programs 589
teacher education
accreditation 561, 563
teacher placement
methods 607
teacher student relationship
research 415
Capitalism
and hidden curriculum 68
Career choice
factors affecting
teaching 74
Career development
teachers
factors affecting 82
Career planning
theoretical perspectives 393
Caring
feminist ethics of 78
moral development 536
Carnegie Forum on Education
teacher education curriculum 546
Carnegie Task Force 600
Case studies
in preservice teacher education 571
Causal attributions *See* Attribution theory
Centre for Educational Research and
Innovation (CERI)
teacher education 557
Centroid method of factor analysis *See*
Factor analysis
Character *See* Personality
Child care *See* Child rearing
Child development
attitudes and motivation 392
and family environment 378
See also Piagetian theory
Child parent relationship *See* Parent
child relationship
Child rearing
family environment 379
Child role
transformation of
factors 411
Chronemics *See* Time management
Class activities
knowledge acquisition 283
and teacher behavior 283
teacher student relationship 220
thinking tasks 283

and teacher behavior 284
types of 283
Class organization
group dynamics 356
planning of 221
managerial behavior 221
rules 186
seating arrangement 185, *196–200*
and teacher knowledge 21
teacher role
small group instruction 219
and teaching methods 185
Class size
and academic achievement 305, 310
research 312, 313
cost effectiveness
production function approach 312
ecological approach
research problems 311
measurement techniques 310
research 311
comparative analysis 311
Project STAR 313
and teacher shortage 609
theoretical debates 137
See also Small classes
Classroom communication
international studies
comparative analysis 508
language patterns 119
educational effectiveness 120
student role 120
teacher student relationship 119
research 120, 217
routines
systems approach 218
rules
context effect 217
and small group instruction 257
social control 119
Classroom design
flexible facilities
teacher attitudes toward 168
open education
student development 168
teaching methods 168
and personal space 275
for small group instruction 257
student development 197
See also Class organization; Seating
arrangement
Classroom environment *344–48*
and computer uses in education 360
co-operation
and cognitive development 280
cultural differences
and peer influence 333
evaluation
alpha press 344
beta press 344
evaluation methods *344–48*
higher education 345
questionnaires 344
science laboratories 346
factors affecting 305, 306

group unity
and academic achievement 356
improvement
Classroom Environment Scale 347
interaction
cognitive processes 190
and learning factors 329
and learning theories 327
and nonverbal communication 277
and outcomes of education
studies 417
paradigm of 93
questionnaires
Classroom Environment Scale 344
Learning Environment Inventory
344
My Class Inventory 345
teacher student relationship 346
research
affective objectives 347
cognitive objectives 347
and student attitudes 347, 348, 417
and student behavior 408
and teacher behavior 408
teacher role 219
teachers
political attitudes 67
Classroom Environment Scale (CES)
345, 417
Classroom management *See* Classroom
techniques
Classroom observation techniques 345,
501–06
audiotape recordings
interaction process analysis 505
cluster analysis
validity 503
coding
time sampling 504
data collection
electronic equipment 502
electronic equipment
criticism of 502
Flanders Interaction Analysis
System 344
interaction 501
international studies
comparative analysis 508
micro vs. macro aspects 283
naturalistic observation 502
Observation Schedule and Record 344
and small group instruction 258
structured observation 501
characteristics of 501
history of 501
and student evaluations of teacher
effectiveness 497
for teacher evaluation 487
teacher role
naturalistic observation 292
videotape recordings
interaction process analysis 505
See also Student behavior
Classroom organization
frame factors 305

Classroom research
categories of 89
instructional effectiveness 505
interaction process analysis 504
lesson structure ***207–11***
observation instruments
validity 503
observers
training of 502
reliability
testing for 503
routines 216
rules 216
teacher development 505
teacher evaluation 505
Classroom tasks *See* Class activities
Classroom techniques
discipline
and educational change 138
factors ***305–07***
group dynamics 356
for individual testing ***295–99***
and learning factors 327, 329
and lesson structure 209
preparation and planning 185
routines 215
rules 215, 216
and teacher knowledge 21
types of 22
See also Discipline; Reinforcement
Classrooms
behavior standards 354
nonverbal behavior in ***274–78***
student attitudes to ***416–19***
student role in ***408–13***
traditional
tasks in 408
Clinical supervision (of teachers)
teacher improvement 44
Cloze procedure
Sentence Completion Test (SCT) 536
Coaching *See* Tutoring
Coaching for tests *See* Test coaching
Cognitive ability
constructs
and aptitude treatment interaction
130
See also Thinking skills
Cognitive anthropology *See* Ethnography
Cognitive development
acceleration of 103
adult development
teachers 537
cognitive apprenticeship model 342
concept formation 107
instructional design model 457
and learning 102
measurement techniques
academic learning time 430
memory systems 458
methods
characteristics of 105
parent student relationship
helping relationship 380
Piagetian theory

psycholinguistics 118
problems 105
teacher role 38, 118
theories of
revision 103
and teaching ***101–06***
Vygotsky's zone of proximal
development
and dynamic assessment 280
See also Intellectual development
Cognitive knowledge *See* Cognitive
structures
Cognitive measurement ***279–82***
test validity
evaluation criteria 281
Cognitive processes
cognitive control 406
comprehension
effort after meaning 445
direct instruction 145
guiding of
and study habits 435
and heuristics 123, 124
information processing approach
and study habits 434
instruction ***107–12***
and instructional tasks 424
and knowledge
theories of 421
and learning ***420–27***
and memory
research 440
metacognition 446
reading comprehension 110
and student characteristics 421
and task analysis 424
See also Creative thinking; Learning
processes; Memory;
Metacognition; Problem solving
Cognitive psychology
feedback
in learning and instruction 249
and heuristics 122
implications for testing 279
and psychometrics ***279–82***
Cognitive restructuring
in long term memory 385
Cognitive skills *See* Thinking skills
Cognitive structures
activation of 376
constructivist 152
evaluation of
pre-instructional 462
and learning processes 375
and teacher behavior 284
Cognitive style
attention control
individual differences 388
classification 388
cognitive psychology
Gestalt psychology 387
concept formation 388
concepts of 387
historical development 387
conceptual tempo 388, 389

convergent thinking 389
core conceptualization 388
field dependence independence
    387, 389
and individual psychology 387
information processing approach
    388, 389
in learning *387–90*
and memory 440
perception
    discrimination learning 389
and psychoanalysis
    ego development 387
and teaching methods 390
vs. ability 388
vs. learning strategies 388
Cognitive theory *See* Epistemology
Cognitively Guided Instruction (CGI)
and student role 409, 411
Collaboration *See* Co-operation
Collaborative demonstration *See*
    Demonstrations (educational)
    co-operation
College programs
    problem solving 464
Colleges
professional autonomy
    and governance of teacher
        education 558
Colleges of education *See* Schools of
    education
Collegiality
contrived
    and teacher cultures 86
and teacher education curriculum 546
teacher improvement 45
Commitment
teachers
    career-continuance 82
    professional 81
    vocational 81
Communication
demonstrations (educational) 238
and learning 340
Community characteristics
and learning factors 327, 329
Community school relationship *See*
    School community relationship
Comparative area studies
in educational research
    advantages 488
Competence
perceptions of
    and self esteem theory 115
and self motivation 399
of teachers 47
Competency-based teacher education 489
curriculum 545
Competition
and performance
    learning 343
performance factors 350
and social interdependence theory 113
Complementary education *See* Literacy
    education

Comprehension
constructive theory 445
context effort 445
educational objectives
    teacher guidance 446
influences
    cognitive processes 445
learning processes 445
social context
    reciprocal teaching 447
    situated learning 447
teaching methods 438, *444–50*
    adjunct questions 446
    advance organizers 445
    educational effectiveness 446
    elaboration theory 445
    examples 446
    inquiry-oriented teaching 446
testing of
    application 448
    cloze procedure 448
    free recall 448
    questioning techniques 447
    structure displays 448
    summarizing 448
    thinking aloud 448
Comprehensive colleges
teacher education programs 549
Computer adaptive testing *See* Computer
    assisted testing
Computer assisted instruction (CAI)
cognitive development 110
programmed tutoring
    explanation in 235
writing (composition) 452
Computer assisted testing
algorithms for 296
in the classroom *295–99*
computer software for 295
for diagnosis 298
feedback of results 296
and mastery tests 297
speeding up item presentation 297
and student development 298
and test anxiety 297
test items
    construction of 295
Computer-based instruction *See*
    Computer assisted instruction
    (CAI)
Computer games 262
    See also Real time games
Computer programs *See* Computer
    software
Computer simulation 262
laboratory training
    teacher education 581
and learning 342
Computer software
for computer assisted testing 295
teacher use of 360
Computer technology *See* Computers
Computer tutoring systems *See*
    Programmed tutoring
Computer uses in education

and assignments 267
barriers to 361
behavioral instruction 100
and classroom environment 360
in classroom instruction 359
extent of
    in classrooms 361
future research 363
and learning theories 519
promotion of 362
and questioning techniques 245
studies 359
and teacher role 359
tutoring 273
Computers
per student 360
in schools
    location of 360
Concept formation *457–63*
behavioral objectives 457
complex-dynamic strategies 461
and educational objectives 104
educational strategies 460
evaluation of
    during instruction 462
    postinstructional 462
expository strategies
    instructional variables 460
practice strategies
    instructional variables 461
problem-oriented strategies 461
self-directed experiences 462
    computer assisted instruction 462
teachers 133
Concept teaching *457–63*
behavioral objectives 458
explanation *232–38*
methods 438
and student experience 437
Concepts
learning capability
    teachers 104
Conceptual knowledge *See* Declarative
    knowledge
Conceptual tempo 388, 389
Conferences
writing
    and student role 410
Confidence *See* Self esteem
Conflict
management of
    procedures for 114
Conflict resolution
playground programs 354
Conflict theory
in education 114
Conformity
in schools
    and social mobility 334
Construct validity
and aptitude treatment interaction 127
and student evaluations of teacher
    effectiveness 496
Constructivism
and educational environment 418

learning and *340–44*
and teaching methods 284
Constructivist Learning Environment
    Survey (CLES) 418
Content analysis
    periodicals
        and teachers as artists 7
    and student evaluations of educational
        quality 494
Context effect
    and questioning techniques 243, 244
Contingency management
    feedback in 250
Continuing education
    for teachers *605–06*
Continuing professional education
        See Professional continuin g
    education
Control *See* Locus of control
Control groups
    composition of
        and metacognition research 483
Conventional instruction
    vs. small group instruction 258
Cooperating teachers 589
    attitudes to student teachers 594
    incentives 594
    results of feedback 590
    selection 594
    teacher education for 594, 595
    and teacher supervision 594
Co-operation
    and small group instruction 257
    and social interdependence theory 113
    and teacher cultures 85
Cooperative learning *139–43*, 357
    academic achievement 141
        teamwork 139
    and behavioral instruction 99
    group investigation 337
    individual development
        self concept 351
    instructional effectiveness 351
    integrated activities
        jigsaw method 141, 336
        reading 140
        writing (composition) 140
    interpersonal relationship 349, 351
    mastery learning 163
    and peer relationship 336, 338
    performance factors
        instructional effectiveness 351
    and questioning techniques 246
    self-esteem 142
    socioeconomic status 142
    student teams achievement divisions
        337
    teamwork 139
    use of competition 337
Cooperative planning
    teacher improvement 45
Coordination (psychomotor) *See*
        Psychomotor skills
Coping
    self control

and learning 406
    strategies for
        teachers 83
Corporate training *See* Industrial training
Correspondence argument *See* Hidden
    curriculum
CoRT thinking program 465
    and creativity training 480
Council for the Accreditation of Teacher
    Education (England and Wales)
    558, 562
Council for the International Evaluation
    of Educational Achievement *See*
    International Association for
    the Evaluation of Educational
    Achievement (IEA)
Council on Postsecondary Accreditation
    (US) 562
Course content
    and teacher knowledge 20
Course evaluation
    and learning strategies
        teaching of 473
    See also Curriculum evaluation
Course selection (students)
    sex differences 320
Creative thinking
    cognitive style
        and teaching methods 390
    Purdue Creative Thinking Program 480
    teaching of
        in industry 464
    See also Productive thinking
Creativity *476–81*
    concept of 437
    context 477
    definitions of 476
    environmental influences
        evaluation of 478
    evaluation of 477
    fundamental concepts of 476
    and teachers as artists 7
    teaching of 478
        evaluation 480
        methods 438
        problem solving 480
Creativity research
    limitations 476
Creativity tests
    assessment batteries
        evaluation of 478
    and creative achievement
        relationship between 478
    evaluation of 477
    self-report measures
        evaluation of 477
Creativity training
    CoRT program 480
    model for 479
    Purdue Creative Thinking Program 480
Criterion referenced tests 177
    grading 300
    and instructional alignment 200
    See also Achievement tests;
        Mastery tests

Critical pedagogy *See* Pedagogy, critical
    approach
Critical reading *467–71*
    discourse analysis 469
        classroom techniques 470
    evaluation of 470
    fundamental concepts 467
    and learning strategies 437
    place in curriculum 470
    psychological model
        cognitive processes 468
    reader response model
        psychological criticism of 467
        sociological criticism of 467
    secondary school curriculum
        reader response model 467
    as social analysis 467
    sociological perspective 468, 470
    teaching methods 438
Critical theory
    instruction 120
    language 121
    learning 120
    and teacher supervision 596
Cross age teaching
    Bell–Lancaster system 272
    historical background 272
    tutoring 272
Cultural capital
    and occupational aspiration 393
    and peer influence 334
Cultural context
    and teacher education planning 541
Cultural pluralism
    and communicative competence
        (language) 333
Cultural transmission
    and family environment 379
    See also Socialization
Culture
    as language
        and peer groups 333
Curiosity
    and self motivation 399
Curriculum
    and computers
        integration of 359
    and instructional alignment 201
    and item banks 298
    learning strategies
        teaching of 473
    and metacognition
        instruction 483
    and politics of education 67
    preservice teacher education 571
    racial bias 320
    sex bias in 320
    See also Hidden curriculum
Curriculum change *See* Curriculum
        development
Curriculum design
    and learning factors 329
    student role in
        and small group instruction 257
    teacher role in

and small group instruction 257
Curriculum development
    action research 16
    classroom techniques
        discipline 221
    discovery learning 149
    process model 16
    and teacher attitudes 81
    in teacher education 526
    and teacher expectation of students 33
    and teacher knowledge 21
    and teacher militancy 68
    teacher role 17
        first-order research 16
        second-order research 16
Curriculum evaluation
    and achievement tests 287
    See also Program evaluation
Curriculum improvement *See* Curriculum
    development
Curriculum materials *See* Instructional
    materials
Curriculum reform *See* Curriculum
    development

Data interpretation
    in educational research 487
Decision making
    teachers 292
        and educational technology 359
Declarative knowledge 421
    measurement of 279
Defining Issues Test (DIT) 535
Delivery systems
    in preservice teacher education 571
    in teacher education 542
Demonstrations (educational) *238–42*
    communication 238
    co-operation
        computer assisted instruction 241
        evaluation 241
        teaching skills 241
    evaluation 242
    learning processes 239
    mathematics instruction 240
    physical education 240
    program development 239
    roles 239
    science instruction 240
    teacher education 578
    teacher student relationship 239
    technological advancement 239
Denmark
    teacher salaries 72
Departments of education *See* Schools
    of education
Descriptive knowledge *See* Declarative
    knowledge
Deskilling *See* Skill obsolescence
Developed nations
    teacher certification 566
    teacher education
        planning 540
    teachers

work environment 72
Developing nations
    on service teacher education *628–32*
    teacher certification 566
    teacher education
        planning 540
    teachers
        work environment 72
Developmental tasks
    adult development
        teachers 535
Diagnostic teaching *9–11*, *174–78*
    aptitude treatment interaction 175
    beliefs about
        criticism of 175
    decision making 175
    individualized instruction 175
    special education 175
    and student needs *286–90*
        relevance 286
    summative evaluation 176
Diagnostic tests 176, 177
    and student needs 288
Dialogs (language)
    and questioning techniques 244
Difficulty level
    academic learning time 432
Direct instruction *143–49*
    cognitive development 147
    cognitive processes 145
        academic achievement 145
        reading comprehension 145
    criticism of 146
    fundamental concepts of 146, 147
    teacher effectiveness 144
    See also Programmed tutoring
Disadvantaged
    and nonverbal communication 277
Disadvantaged schools
    and teacher shortage 609
Disadvantaged youth
    and school staffing 608
Discipline *215–19*, *219–23*
    behavior modification *227–31*
    in classrooms
        and educational change 138
    positive reinforcement 225
    teacher role 220
Disciplines (intellectual) *See* Intellectual
    disciplines
Discourse analysis
    function of 469
Discourse participation
    and learning experience 340
Discovery learning *149–55*
    academic achievement 153
    and aptitude treatment interaction 129
    criticisms of 150
    deduction 151
    discussion (teaching technique) 152
    induction 151
    instructional effectiveness 153
        science curriculum 154
    intellectual development 149
    learner controlled instruction 151

learning motivation 149
    retention (psychology) 149
Discussion
    group dynamics 252
    history of 252
    prerequisites 253
    school environment 254
    social environment 254
    See also Interpersonal communication
Discussion (teaching technique) *251–55*
    in classrooms 408
    cognitive processes 253
    educational effectiveness
        criticism of 254
    history of 252
    and questioning techniques 244
    statistical analysis 252
    student characteristics 253
    student development 254
    teacher attitudes 254
    teacher characteristics 253
    teacher role 253
Discussion groups
    and learning 340
    small group instruction 357
Distal variables *See* Frame factors
Distance education
    communications satellites
        evaluation 268
DISTAR
    academic achievement
        at risk persons 146
Document analysis *See* Content analysis
Domain mastery tests *See* Mastery tests
Drills (practice)
    feedback in 250, 541
    and learning 342
Dropouts
    and grade repetition 324

Early school leavers *See* Dropouts
Earnings differentials
    teachers vs. other occupations 73
Economics
    of teacher supply and demand *72–76*
Education
    social nature of 112
    social psychology of 116
Educational administration
    and faculty mobility 610
    and learning factors 330
    role of
        in teacher education planning 541
    and teacher placement 607
    See also School administration
Educational assessment
    and prior learning 386
Educational change
    barriers to 138
    educational researchers
        teachers as 18
    frame factors 309
    international comparisons 619
    practicalities of 80

and research findings 521
teacher education
    planning 540
and teacher socialization
    developed nations 620
    developing nations 619
teachers' beliefs 25, 27
See also Educational reform
Educational computing *See* Computer
    uses in education
Educational environment
and computers 360
and social status
    of teachers 60
and teacher expertise 49
See also Classroom environment;
    Learning environment
Educational experience
influences
    classroom research 193
Educational facilities improvement
teachers
    professional development 45
Educational finance
substitute teachers 368
See also Resource allocation
Educational games
behavioral objectives 262
skill analysis 261
Educational improvement
class size
    cost effectiveness 312
teacher role
    structural critique 17
    women faculty 18
Educational inequality *See* Equal
    education
Educational innovation
and small group instruction 259
and student attitudes
    research 417
and teacher attitudes
    age differences 82
See also Educational reform
Educational level *See* Academic
    achievement
Educational management *See*
    Educational administration
Educational materials *See* Instructional
    materials
Educational objectives
and behavioral objectives 98
and cognitive processes 423
and computer uses in education
    effectiveness of 361
influences
    frame factor theory 308
    tradition 309
and learning strategies 473
and moral development 104
and student needs 286
and study habits 435
and teacher education 541, 618
teaching
    and cognitive development

approach 102
and teaching methods 185, 437
See also Outcomes of education
Educational opportunities
access to education
    and testing 280
international studies
    comparative analysis 511
Educational philosophy *See* Philosophy
    of education
Educational policy
and learning factors 330
and teacher education programs 541
and teacher placement 606
and teacher supply and demand 608
Educational practices
and research
    translation of *517–22*
Educational psychology
and prior learning 382
and theory practice relationship 517
Educational quality
and accreditation of teacher
    education 564
and characteristics of preservice
    teachers *528–31*
and governance of teacher education
    556–60
and grade repetition 325
and learning factors 329
and teacher certification *565–70*
and teacher recruitment 612
Educational reform
and teacher responsibility 81
and teaching
    realities of 80
See also Educational change;
    Educational innovation
Educational research
applications 521
approaches 517
assignments 264
and behavioral science research 97
criticisms of 517
findings
    and models of schooling 521
interpretation of data 487
learning processes
    and student characteristics 326
nonverbal communication 275
pedagogical content knowledge 135
and practice
    gap between 517
    historical background 517
    translation into *517–22*
professional development schools 601
and questioning techniques 242
teacher characteristics 3
and teacher education planning 541
and teacher education programs 542
teacher expectation of students 29
and teacher expertise 519
and teacher knowledge 20
    effects on 23
teachers and teaching *487–88*

teaching
    imagery 134
    metaphors 134
    paradigms for *91–96*
    synthesizing *512–16*
teaching methods
    instructional effectiveness 160
theory practice relationship
    future trends 488
trend analysis 121
variables
    classroom environment 347
Educational researchers
beliefs of
    educational change 28
    students 27
teachers as
    Boston Women Teachers' Group 17
    curriculum development 16
    educational change 17, 18
    feminism 18
    professional development 17
    social change 17, 18
    theory practice relationship *16–19*
Educational Resources Information
    Center (ERIC) (US)
    questioning techniques
    research reports 242
Educational strategies
frame factors
    piloting 309
    steering group 309
and instructional programs *137–38*
learning processes 349
mastery learning
    formative evaluation 162
small classes 314
Educational technology
adoption of
    barriers to 361
development of 519
and learning
    theories of 519
and teacher role *359–63*
teacher use of
    patterns 359
See also Instructional systems
Educational television
barriers to use of 361
Educational testing
objectives 284
Educational Testing Service (ETS) (US)
National Teachers Examination 567
Educational theories
influences 133
operant model 227
teacher attitudes toward 13
teachers *131–36*
    participatory research 133
    relevance (education) 132
    research 134
    vs. reflective teaching 138
See also Frame factor theory;
    Philosophy of education
Educational trends

futures (of society)
  teacher burnout 56
  teacher development 45
Effect size
  research synthesis
    methods 513
  in teacher expectation of students 31
Effective schools research
  and learning theories 327
  See also School effectiveness
Effective teaching *See* Teacher
    effectiveness
Effort *See* Energy expenditure
Ego development
  Sentence Completion Test 536
  teachers 536
Elementary school curriculum
  problem solving programs 464
Elementary school teachers
  use of explanation 235
Emotional experience
  effect on learning 402
Emotional problems
  effect on learning 403
Employee absenteeism
  teachers *367–69*
    causes 367
    developing nations 367
    resource allocation 367
Employment
  See also Work
Employment opportunities
  in teaching
    females 73
    minority groups 73
Encoding (psychology)
  and memorization
    strategies 441
Energy expenditure
  compared with academic achievement
    301
  in learning processes 405
England and Wales
  teacher education
    accreditation 558, 562, 563
  teacher placement
    methods 607
  See also National Curriculum
English (second language)
  teaching
    as art 6
Enrichment
  teaching methods
    mastery learning 163
Enterprise *See* Business
Environmental influences
  and behavioral theories 98
Epistemology
  feminist theories 78
  information processing in 421
  social theories 17
  theoretical framework 420
Equal education
  and aptitude treatment interaction 128
  and heuristics 122

Equity (impartiality) *See* Justice
Error correction
  teaching methods
    mastery learning 163
Esteem *See* Prestige
Ethics
  of care
    and teaching 81
  fundamental concepts of 36
Ethnic groups
  educational strategies
    small classes 314
  See also Minority groups
Ethnography
  research
    paradigm 94
Evaluation
  of creativity *476–81*
  of teachers 487
Evaluative thinking
  and emotional response
    effect on learning process 403, 405
Examinations
  in instructional programs
    and academic achievement 138
Expectation
  causal variations 394
  compared with aspiration 392
  and educational attainment 393
  future research 394
  interpersonal
    theory of 113
  research 29
  student interpretation of 393
  by students *391–95*
Expenditures
  academic achievement
    class size 312
Experiential learning
  games 260
  programs
    studies 105
  simulation 260
Experimental design *See* Research design
Experimental pedagogy *See* Educational
    research
Expertise
  development of
    stages 47
  measurement of
    and test construction 279
  and psychological studies 47
Explanation
  concept teaching *232–38*
  evaluation criteria 234
  functions of 232
  given by students
    evaluation criteria 234
  research methods 236
    Columbia University Instrument 236
    Hermann's Pupil Awareness Rating
      Form 237
    Illinois Instrument 236
    Rating Teacher Explanation
      Instrument 237

    types of 232
Explanatory learning *See* Discovery
    learning
Expository writing
  organization of
    and study skills 435
Extended teacher education programs 550
Extension education
  and teacher recruitment 610
Extrinsic motivation *See* Incentives
Eye contact
  in classrooms 276
    cultural differences 276

Facial expressions
  research 274
  See also Body language; Smiling
Factor analysis
  and student evaluations of educational
    quality 494
Faculty mobility
  and academic achievement 610
  management of 610
Faculty workload
  and educational change 138
Family
  employed women 379
  See also One parent family
Family characteristics
  and learning factors 327, 329
Family environment
  and academic achievement 306,
    378–82
    cultural differences 378
    changes in 379
    and child rearing 379
    influence on learning in school
      378–82
    age variables 378
    developmental psychology
      perspective 378
    and learning factors 330
    and learning processes 375
    physical environment 379
    developing nations 379
Family school relationship 371
  and field experience programs 592
  and professional development
    schools 601
  and teacher attitudes 306
Fear
  of technology
    teachers 362
Federal regulation
  and governance of teacher education
    557
Feedback *249–51*
  in behavioral modification 249
  in classrooms
    and teacher student relationship 283
  and computer assisted testing 296
  definition of 249
  educational uses 249
  in instruction

behaviorist views 249
cognitive psychology views 249
in learning 249
behaviorist views 249
cognitive psychology views 249
in skill development 249
and student reaction 284
teaching methods
mastery learning 163
Female psychology
feminist theories 78
Females
intellectual development 537
moral development 536
teaching
professionalization of *76–80*
Feminism
analysis of teaching as work 78
critique of professionalization 76, 78
educational research 18
ethics of caring 78
and hidden curriculum 68
philosophy of education 78
teacher education 17
theories on epistemology of females 78
theories on female psychology 78
Field dependence independence 387, 389
Field experience programs
changes in types of 592
effects on student teachers 589
and laboratory experience compared
571
in preservice teacher education 572
supervision 572
vs. formal coursework 573
student teaching *588–93*
Films
and learning 341
Finance *See* Educational finance
Firm-based training *See* On the job
training
Flexible progression
and tests of prior learning 386
Flexible scheduling 213
Formal coursework
delivery systems 571
in preservice teacher education 571
vs. field experience programs 573
Formative evaluation
feedback
remedial instruction 162
individualized instruction 162
mastery learning 162
student motivation 162
teaching methods 163
Foundations of education *See* Philosophy
of education
Frame factor theory *308–10*
curriculum theory 309
Frame factors
concept of 305
France
grade repetition 324, 325
Frankfurt School *See* Critical theory
Functionalism

and occupational prestige 59
and teacher socialization 616

Games *260–64*
evaluation 262
fundamental concepts of 261
intercultural communication 262
objectives of 261
rewards 261
rules of 261
student attitudes toward 262
student development 262
student role
decision making 261
time factors (learning) 263
See also Computer games; Educational
games; Real time games
Gaze *See* Eye contact
Gender (sex) *See* Sex
Gender differences (sex) *See* Sex
differences
General Teaching Council for
Scotland 562
Generalizability theory
and student evaluations of teacher
effectiveness 495
Geographic regions
effects on teacher supply and
demand 74
Germany
educational research
questioning techniques 245
faculty mobility 610
teacher characteristics 607
teacher placement
methods 607
Germany, Federal Republic of (FRG)
(former)
educational research
questioning techniques 247
Gestures (nonverbal communication)
See Body language
Gifted
and teacher expertise 51
Girls *See* Females
Goal structures *See* Learning strategies,
behavioral objectives
Governance
and learning factors 327
in teacher education 526
See also Federal regulation
Grade levels *See* Instructional program
divisions
Grade point average (GPA)
and learning strategies
teaching of 473
Grade repetition *324–26*
and dropouts 324
effect on academic achievement 325
effect on adjustment 325
effect on dropout rates 324
and frame factors 306
France 324, 325
and low achievement 324

policies and practices 325
and socioeconomic status 324
United States 325
Grade repetition rate
comparative studies 324
Grades (program divisions) *See*
Instructional program divisions
Grading
with aptitudes 300
comparison of achievement with
effort 301
criterion referenced tests 300
disadvantages 300
equating achievement with
improvement 301
established standards
comparison with 300
norm referenced tests 299
disadvantages 299
with other students 299
performance assessment 302
symbols used 302
checklists 302
letters 302
numerical 302
pass–fail 302
trends 302
United States *299–303*
Greek civilization
and teaching style 122
Group activities
and cooperative learning 141
Group behavior
behavior standards 354
and behavioral instruction 99
Group discussion
classes (groups of students) *251–55*
student characteristics 253
student participation 354
Group dynamics *352–58*
definition of 352
discussion 252
and role theory 113
small group instruction 357
Group instruction
mastery learning 163
See also Small group instruction
Group Investigation (GI) method
and small group instruction 255, 258
stages 255
Group processes *See* Group dynamics
Group unity 354
Grouping (instructional purposes) 161,
192–96
and academic achievement
research 520
comparative analysis 192
streaming 192
intergroup relations 142
mainstreaming 142
mixed-age grouping 317
multigraded classes 316
nontraditional education 195
organization 193
pacing

teacher role 212
student placement
    teacher expectations of students 193
teacher student relationship
    learner controlled instruction 194
    teacher expectations of students 195
teachers
    managerial behavior of 219
United States
    track system 193
See also Ability grouping; Age
    grade placement; Heterogeneous
    grouping; Nongraded
    instructional grouping
Groups
    characteristics of 352
    communication 353
    composition of
        and teacher effectiveness 137
    conflict in 354
        classrooms 357
    development of 353
        interpersonal composition model
        353
    leadership 353
    objectives 353

Haptics *See* Touching behavior
Harvard Business School
    case methods 584
Hawaii
    reading instruction
        methods 409
Headteachers *See* Principals
Helping relationship
    and learning 339
Heterogeneous grouping 195
    educational improvement 318
    educational objectives 318
Heuristic models
    purpose of 89
Heuristics
    historical development 122
    models
        of teaching *122–27*
Hidden curriculum
    feminist approaches 68
    and political power 68
    and racial relations 68
    teacher education 546
High achievement
    learning strategies
        group instruction 162
    and teacher behavior 31
    and teacher expectation of students 30
High school students
    and tutoring 272
History
    psychological explanation of events
        234
Holistic approach
    to teacher education planning 541
    to teaching 80
Holistic evaluation

and teacher expertise 48
Holland *See* Netherlands, The
Holmes Group 600
    professional development schools 591
    teacher education curriculum 546
Home environment *See* Family
    environment
Home schooling 268
Homework *268–71*
    academic achievement 205, 270
    educational policy 270
    evaluation 268
    High School Homework Helpers
        Program (US) 272
    learning processes 269
        feedback 269
    parent role
        academic achievement 270
    and parent student relationship 380
    and skill development 343
    student motivation 270
    teacher role
        teacher aides 270
    time factors (learning)
        student motivation 270
    time on task
        comparative analysis 268
Homogeneous grouping
    academic achievement 192
    See also Ability grouping
Households *See* Family
Human posture
    teachers 276
Hypothesis testing
    and research methodology 512

Ideology
    professionalism and power 76, 78
Imagery
    and memorization 441
Imperialism
    teachers
        and curriculum development 68
Impulsiveness *See* Conceptual tempo
Incentives
    learning motivation 399
        and delay of gratification 401
    See also Rewards
Independent study
    and assignments 267
    and heuristics 124
    learning strategies 425
    promotion of
        and cognitive processes 425
    skills
        motivation 520
India
    on service teacher education 630
    teacher education
        Andhra Pradesh Primary Education
        Project 630
Individual autonomy *See* Personal
    autonomy
Individual differences

and teacher student relationship 413
teaching methods
    mastery learning 162
See also Sex differences
Individual testing
    in the classroom *295–99*
Individualism
    and teacher cultures 85
Individualized Classroom Environment
    Questionnaire (ICEQ) 345
Individualized education programs 155
Individualized instruction *155–61*
    Adaptive Learning Environments
        Model 158
    and aptitude treatment interaction
        127, 129
    and behavioral instruction 100
    and computers 360
    cooperative learning 140
    decision making 176
    diagnostic teaching *174–78*
    educational trends
        futures (of society) 159
    history of 155
    Individually Guided Education 158
    mastery learning 158, 161
    outcomes of education 193
    pacing
        instructional effectiveness 157
    Personalized System of Instruction
        (PSI) 158
    tutoring 273
    and tutoring 271
    See also Diagnostic teaching; Flexible
        progression
Indonesia
    on service teacher education 629
    teacher education
        Active Learning through
        Professional Support 629
Industrial training
    creative thinking 464
    See also Job training; On the job
        training
Industrializing countries *See* Developing
    nations
Informal assessment
    decision making 177
    instructional effectiveness 177
    teacher effectiveness 177
Information processing
    in epistemology 421
    theories 90
Information technology
    and classroom techniques 185
Initial teacher education *See* Preservice
    teacher education
Inquiry
    discussion (teaching technique) 152
    principles 90
    teaching method 341
Inservice teacher education *620–28*
    compared with on service teacher
        education 628
    costs 620

effectiveness 626
external support agencies 626
human resource development 621
laboratory training 579
management of planned change 621
needs assessment 622
  individual teachers 623
  schools 622
and onservice teacher education
  compared 605
Organisation for Economic Cooperation and Developmen
  tdefinition 621
outcomes of 605
professional development 623, 625
  project-based models 625
  skill development 623
reflective model 624
relationship with preservice teacher
  education 551
relationship with teacher orientation
  551
self-development by schools and
  teachers 621
support for
  factors affecting 606
for unqualified teachers 621
INSET *See* Inservice teacher education
Institutional characteristics
and learning factors 327
Institutional development *See*
  Organizational development
Instruction
classroom
  dimensions of 256
cognitive participation in
  variables 420
cognitive processes *107–12*
and computers
  integration of 359
concept formation *178–83*
critical theory 120
explicit teaching model 108
  sequencing 108
feedback in *249–51*
formative evaluation of
  criticism of 292
frame factors
  structuralist view 308
inquiry-oriented instruction model 109
linguistic theory *117–22*
planning of
  educational resources 291
  student characteristics 291
programs
  prescriptions vs. guidelines 138
  and strategies *137–38*
sequential approach
  the Learning Cycle 151
  and questioning techniques 245
  science laboratories 151
sociolinguistics *117–22*
summative evaluation of 292
  educational planning 293
  influences 293
and teacher knowledge 21

teacher led 144
  criticism of 147
and teaching compared 89
text comprehension 110
theoretical framework 420
Instructional alignment
and transfer of training 202, 203
Instructional design
content analysis 459
contextual analysis 460
and learning factors 327
and student needs 286
Instructional effectiveness
and assignments 264
and cognitive development 107
and cognitive processes 424
evaluation methods
  paper and pencil tests 293
factors affecting 517
instructional alignment *200–04*
  curriculum alignment 201
  philosophical approaches 203
  research 202
  stimulus control 200
  studies 202
  testing implications 203
See also Teacher effectiveness
Instructional materials
attention arousing 429
DISTAR 146
evaluation
  teacher role 292
international studies
  comparative analysis 507
See also Textbooks
Instructional methods *See* Teaching
  methods
Instructional processes *See* Teaching
  methods
Instructional program divisions
and questioning techniques 245
small classes
  academic achievement 314
See also Age grade placement
Instructional systems
and aptitude treatment interaction
  examples 129
international studies
  comparative analysis 507
Instructional technology *See* Educational
  technology
Instructional television *See* Educational
  television
Instructional time *See* Time on task
Instrumental Enrichment Program 465
Integrated activities
Computer Supported Intentional
  Learning Environment (CSILE) 340
Integrative analysis *See* Meta analysis
Intellectual development
adult development
  teachers 537
females 537
Intellectual disciplines
beliefs about

effect on learning 404
interests 404
knowledge of
  and teacher expectation of
  students 33
levels
  and questioning techniques 245
Intelligence
attitudes to
  and learning motivation 398
and prior learning 384
See also Cognitive ability
Intelligent tutoring systems *See*
  Computer assisted instruction
  (CAI) programmed tutoring
Intention
and behavior 391, 393
Intentional learning
and motivation 396
Interaction
uses of 127
See also Aptitude treatment
  interaction; Group dynamics
Interaction process analysis
time sampling
  criticisms of 504
  naturalistic units 504
uses of 505
Interactionism
and teacher socialization 618, 619
  internalized adjustment 619
  strategic compliance 619
  strategic redefinition 619
Interactive video
and learning 341
Intercultural education *See* Multicultural
  education
International Association for the
  Evaluation of Educational
  Achievement (IEA)
Classroom Environment Study
  research on teaching 508
First Mathematics Study 201
Second Mathematics Study (SIMS)
  research on teaching 506
International studies
mathematics achievement 265
Interpersonal communication
discussion 251
Interpersonal competence
training for
  and behavioral instruction 99
Interpretive skills
and teacher expertise 50
Interstate New Teacher Assessment and
  Support Consortium 568
Intervention
and learning strategies
  teaching of 472
programs
  and teacher expectation of
  students 33
Intervention *See* Behavior modification
Interviews
and learning strategies

and learning strategies
   evaluation 475
See also Questioning techniques
Intrinsic motivation *See* Self motivation
Invalidity *See* Validity
Israel
   kibbutzim
     teacher education curriculum 544
   problem solving
     teaching of 465
Italy
   nonverbal communication
     touching behavior 275
Item banks
   calibration of 298
   computer assisted testing 295
   and curriculum 298
Item response theory (IRT)
   and computer assisted testing 295
   and test theory 282
Item writing techniques
   student evaluations of teacher
     effectiveness 494

Japan
   mathematics education
     and student role 409
   nonverbal communication
     touching behavior 275
   student teaching
     field experience programs 589
Java *See* Indonesia
Job analysis
   indeterminacy 7
   teaching 7
   See also Task analysis
Job satisfaction
   and school staffing 611
Job training
   psychomotor skill development
     454–57
   See also On the job training
Journals *See* Periodicals
Justice
   moral development 536

Kamehameha Early Education Program
   (KEEP) (Hawaii) 409
Keller Plan *See* Individualized
   instruction, Personalized System
   of Instruction (PSI)
Kenya
   teacher student relationship
     research 415
Kibbutzim
   teacher education curriculum 544
Kinesics *See* Body language
Knowledge
   conceptual 422
   conditional 421
   content 422
   discourse 422

domain specific
   and prior learning 383
   and teacher expertise 49
explicit 422
and learning strategies 472
metacognitive 422
sociocultural 423
strategy 423
tacit 422
task 422
teachers
   requirements 60
theories of
   and cognitive processes 421
transfer of
   and social psychology 112
See also Declarative knowledge;
   Procedural knowledge
Knowledge acquisition
   and teacher behavior 283
Knowledge level
   prior learning *382–87*
Knowledge structures *See* Cognitive
   structures
Kohlberg's Moral Judgment Scales 103
Korea, Republic of
   teacher salaries 72

Labor market
   and teachers *72–76*
   See also Teacher supply and demand
Labor market training *See* Job training
Laboratories
   computers in 360
Laboratory schools
   teacher education *598–604*
     compared with professional
       development schools 601
     criticism of 599
     Dewey's influence 598
     history 598
Laboratory training
   student teacher attitudes 578
   teacher education *578–82*
     case studies 581
     computer simulation 581
     concept formation 579
     evaluation research 578
     factors influencing effectiveness 579
     feedback 580
     implications for practice 581
     participant observation 580
     research trends 581
     student teaching 580
     and transfer of training 579, 581
     types of 578
Language
   critical theory 121
Language acquisition
   writing (composition) 450
Language attitudes
   racial differences
     dialects 319
   sexism in language 319

Language development *See* Language
   acquisition
Language of instruction
   English
     and teacher student relationship 415
Latent trait theory *See* Item response
   theory (IRT)
Latin schools movement
   and problem solving 464
Leadership
   groups 353
Leadership styles
   and group dynamics 353
Learner characteristics *See* Student
   characteristics
Learner controlled instruction
   and aptitude treatment interaction 129
   discovery learning 151
   inquiry 151
Learning
   acquisition
     and knowledge 425
   classroom
     studies of 520
   cognitive developmental 102
   and cognitive processes *420–27*
   cognitive style in *387–90*
   collaborative roles in 410
   and constructivism *340–44*
   critical theory 120
   effect of affective behavior on *402–07*
   factors affecting 327, 518
   models of 377
   orientations
     and learning strategies 389
   and peer relationship *336–39*
   receptive language
     explanation 235
   time factors in *See* Time factors
     (learning)
   traditional approaches 102
   See also Cognitive processes; Prior
     learning
Learning activities
   and learning motivation 397
   participation in 341
Learning by doing *See* Experiential
   learning
Learning environment *340–44*
   communication 340
   Computer Supported Intentional
     Learning Environment (CSILE) 340
   performance 343
   problem solving 341
   and teaching methods *340–44*
   training 342
   See also Educational environment
Learning Environment Inventory (LEI)
   345, 417
Learning to learn *See* Learning strategies
Learning materials *See* Instructional
   materials
Learning motivation *395–402*
   and academic achievement 396
   attention control 397

effort avoidance 397
goal orientation 397
incentives 399
individual power 397
self motivation 399
student role in 306
and test anxiety 397
See also Self motivation; Student
  motivation
Learning objectives *See* Behavioral
  objectives
Learning outcomes *See* Outcomes of
  education
Learning potential *See* Aptitude
Learning processes
  and academic achievement
    research 327
  and aptitude treatment interaction 127
  cognitive development 109
  discovery processes 149, 152
  dynamics of
    variables 425
  effect of prior learning on *382–87*
  evaluative thinking
    and emotional response 405
  feedback in *249–51*
  guidance 150
  induction 149
  inquiry 152
  measurement of 443
  measurement techniques
    academic learning time 431
  and memory
    research 440
  metacognition 107
  misconceptions 425
  research
    historical background 420
  schemata (cognition) 108
  sex differences 321
  and student characteristics
    research 326
  student participation in 439
  student role in *375–77*
  and study habits 434
  and teacher behavior 284
Learning rate *See* Time factors (learning),
  conceptual tempo
Learning resources *See* Educational
  resources
Learning strategies
  and aptitude treatment interaction 130
  behavioral objectives *349–52*
    intergroup relations 349
  cognitive mapping 447
  cognitive processes 423
  competition 350
  conclusion-oriented 389
  cooperative learning 349
  deep approach 265
  description-oriented 389
  educational objectives 350
  evaluation 472
    methods 474
  expert

and student role 409
group instruction
  high achievers 162
holistic approach
  comprehension learning 389
individualized instruction 350
mastery learning *161–67*
and memory
  research 440
and metacognition 482
models of 473
promotion of 447
reciprocal teaching
  and student role 409
research 139
serialist approach
  operation learning 389
SMART operations 425
and student responsibility 376
and students 472
  characteristics 472
  teacher understanding of 104
surface approach 265
and teacher responsibility 376
teaching of *471–76*
  adjunct instruction 472
  case study 474
  course evaluation 473
  courses in 472
  measurement 473
  metacurriculum 473
  types of 471
testing of *471–76*
  training programs 446
    educational effectiveness 447
  types of 437, 471
  See also Study skills
Learning and Study Strategies Inventory
  (LASSI) 473, 475
Learning style *See* Cognitive style
Learning theories
  ability grouping 192
  accessibility theory 385
  and cognitive restructuring 385
  and educational technology 519
  elaboration theory 385
  information processing model 385
  linguistic theory *117–22*
    interaction 119
    sociocultural patterns 118
    structuralist 118
  models
    of school learning 326, 520
  psycholinguistics 118
  relationship 117
  retrieval aid theory 385
  selective attention theory 385
  sociolinguistics *117–22*
  and student attitudes 416
  and student characteristics 420
  See also Piagetian theory
Learning time *See* Time on task
Learning by using *See* On the job
  training
Lecture method 341

Legal education (professions)
  case methods 583
Legislation
  and governance of teacher education
    557
Lesson
  concept of 207
Lesson plans 208
  and teacher effectiveness 305
  and teacher knowledge 21
Lesson structure *207–11*
  context 209
  factors influencing 207
  future research 210
  interaction process analysis 210
  learning activities 209
  and nongraded instructional grouping
    208, 209
  pacing 209
  and small group instruction 208
  student attitudes research 210
  student role 208
  teacher role 208
  teaching methods 208
Liberal arts
  colleges
    teacher education programs 548
Life events
  teachers
    influences on 82
Linguistic theory
  research 90
Literacy education
  Freirian critique 468
    critical pedagogy 468
  reciprocal teaching 411
  and student reaction 409
Literacy skills *See* Literacy
Literature
  circles
    student role in 410
Local education authorities (LEAs) (UK)
  and teacher recruitment 605
Locus of control
  teacher burnout 55
Logical thinking
  and heuristics 125
Logistic models *See* Rasch measurement
  models
Long term memory (LTM)
  and cognitive processes 434
  cognitive restructuring in 385
  and prior learning 440
Longitudinal studies
  teacher expectation of students 32
Low achievement
  and grade repetition 324
  minority group children
    and peer influence 334
  peer influence 334
  and teacher behavior 31
  and teacher expectation of students 30
    Good's passivity model 31
  See also Academic failure
Low income groups

educational strategies
small classes 314

Magazines *See* Periodicals
Master teachers 77
as artists 6
Mastery learning *161–67*
and academic achievement 161
research 520
evaluative thinking
and emotional response 405
group instruction 163
individual differences 159
instructional effectiveness 159
Mastery tests
and computer assisted testing 297
Mathematics achievement
international studies 265
Mathematics education
and heuristics 123
and student role 409
and teacher expectation of students 32
Mathematics instruction
demonstrations (educational) 240
explanation in 236
and student role 410
Measurement objectives
and instruction 284
Mediation theory
paradigm of 93
Medieval history
and teaching style 122
Memorization
encoding strategies
elaboration 441
imagery 441
learning memory 442
prior knowledge activities 441
rehearsal 441
reorganization 441
retrieval 441
summarization 441
transformational mnemonics 441
learning strategies 438
and prior learning
factors 439
teaching methods 438
Memory
evaluation of 442
incidental vs. intentional 440
measurement of 442
and prior learning
role of 440
scientific study of
historical background 440
sensory (SM)
and cognitive processes 434
strategic processing
coordination 442
role of 440
teaching and testing for *439–44*
tests
types of 439, 442
See also Long term memory (LTM);

Recall (psychology); Recognition
(psychology); Short term
memory (STM)
Mentors
teacher education 586
Meta analysis
criticisms of 514
and questioning techniques 247
and student evaluations of teacher
effectiveness 496
See also Research synthesis
Metacognition 406
and cognitive processes 422
definition of 481
instruction
choice of students for 482
content 482
curriculum issues 483
evaluation of 483
future research 484
guidelines 484
principles 483
tasks for 483
time factors 483
and learning factors 329, 330
and reciprocal teaching 409
research 520
design 483
implementation problems 483
methodological issues 483
studies 482
strategies 437, 439
and self-regulation 442
teaching and assessing *481–85*
Metamemory *See* Metacognition
Microteaching
discrimination training 574
evaluation studies 579
feedback 575
modeling (psychology) 574
models
behavior modification 575
cognitive 576
pragmatism 575
social skills 575
practice 574
in preservice teacher education 572
program evaluation
attitudes 576
behavior change 576
research on 574
teacher education *573–77*, 578
Middle schools
cores
United States 355
Militancy *See* Activism
Ministries of education *See* State
departments of education
Minority group students
academic achievement
and peer influence 334
and social mobility 334
Minority groups
employment opportunities
teaching 73

involuntary
peer influence 334
small classes
academic achievement 314
test score decline
administrative change 311
social change 311
voluntary 334
See also Ethnic groups
Mnemonics
and memorization 441
Models
and teacher knowledge 22
and teaching methods 285
underlying assumptions 90
use of term 89
See also Paradigms
Moods
effect on learning 402, 403
Moral development
Defining Issues Test (DIT) 535
educational objectives 104
females 536
in schools 104
Moral values
and teaching 81
value judgment
teachers 535
Motivation
and academic persistence 397
and attention 427, 428
and attitudes 392
behavior theories 396
content theories 396
and learning strategies 472
teaching of 474
process theories 396
psychological patterns in 396
See also Learning motivation; Self
motivation; Student motivation;
Teacher motivation
Motor skills *See* Psychomotor skills
Movement education
behaviorist approach 454
cognitive approach 454, 455
ecological approach 456
psychomotor skills *454–57*
Multicultural education
and peer groups in schools 334
Multiculturalism *See* Cultural pluralism
Multiple choice tests
and problem solving 465
Multivariate analysis
and student evaluations of teacher
effectiveness 498
My Class Inventory (MCI) 345

National Board for Professional Teaching
Standards (NBPTS) (US) 566, 568
National Council for the Accreditation
of Teacher Education (NCATE)
(US) 550, 557, 562, 563
National Curriculum (UK)
demands of 81

National Teacher Examinations (NTE) (US)
  content validity
    academic knowledge 490
  predictive validity
    functional knowledge 490
Negative reinforcement 224
Nelson–Denny Reading Comprehension
  Test 473
Netherlands, The
  classroom environment
    attitudes to 417
  teacher salaries 72
New South Wales
  beginning teachers
    staffing problems 609
  faculty mobility 610
  teacher selection
    methods 608
New technology *See* Technological
  advancement
New Zealand
  literacy education
    Reading Recovery 409
Nongraded instructional grouping *192–
  96* , 316, 325
  ability grouping 316
  and academic achievement 317
  individualized instruction
    Individually Guided Education 317
  open education 317
  student development 317
Nontraditional education
  grouping (instructional purposes) 195
  open education
    and group unity 355
  See also Home schooling
Nonverbal communication
  in classrooms 186, *274–78*
    future research 278
    types of 275
  educational research 275
  influences 277
  studies
    historical background 274
Norm referenced tests 177
  grading 299
  and instructional alignment 203
  See also Achievement tests
Norms
  school
    and role theory 113

Objective referenced tests *See* Criterion
  referenced tests
Objectives
  and teaching methods *437–39*
Occupational aspiration
  and expectation 392
  sex differences 392
  social psychological approaches
    391–95
Occupational training *See* Job training
Occupations
  teaching in hierarchy of professions 76

Odyssey (Venezuela)
  problem solving program 465
On the job training
  teacher education *628–32*
On service teacher education *628–32*
  case studies 629
  compared with in service teacher
    education 628
  India 630
  Indonesia 629
  Pakistan 631
  See also Inservice teacher education
One parent family 379
Onservice teacher education
  and inservice teacher education
    compared 606
Open classroom teaching (OCT) *See* Open
  plan schools
Open education *167–71*
  academic achievement 169
  characteristics of 137
  comparative analysis 168
  concepts of 167
  decline of 170
  evaluation of 170
  history of 167
  Israel
    program development 169
    teacher characteristics 169
  outcomes of education
    student development 169
  program attitudes 168
  program design 168
  student attitudes 170
  student behavior 169, 170
  teacher attitudes toward 169
    student development 169
  teacher characteristics 168
  teacher motivation 169
  teacher role 168
  teaching methods
    teacher student relationship 168
Open learning *See* Open education
Open plan schools
  and academic achievement
    research synthesis 515
  See also Classroom design
Open schools *See* Open education
Open University (OU) (UK)
  and distance education 268
Opportunities
  learning
    and instructional alignment 201
Organizational development
  school restructuring 355
Originality *See* Creativity
Outcomes of education
  and aptitude treatment interaction 128
  cognitive
    information processing model 434
  and instructional alignment *200–04*
  and predictive measurement 518
  and student attitudes
    studies 417
Outlining (discourse)

  and study skills 435

Pacing
  academic achievement 213
  educational effectiveness 214
  instruction *212–14*
    comparative analysis 213
  learner-controlled instruction 212
  learning theories 213
  rate of 213
  teacher role 212
    decision making 213
    grouping (instructional purposes)
    212
Pakistan
  on service teacher education 631
  teacher education
    Field Based Teacher development
    Program 631
  teacher supply and demand 74
Paradigms
  concept of 91
    research 92
    schematic representation 92
    uses 96
  definitions of 93, 94, 95
  Kuhn's thesis 91
  for research
    on teaching *91–96*
  of teaching
    classification 95
    classroom ecology 93
    criterion of effectiveness 93
    extended process–product 94
    intact teaching styles 94
    machine 93
    mediating process 93
    overview 89
    process–product 93
    teacher cognition and decision
    making 95
    teaching process 93
  use of term 89
  See also Models
Paralinguistics
  in classrooms 277
Paraprofessional school personnel
  363–67
  educational attainment 364
  educational effectiveness 363
  job training 364
    educational effectiveness 364
  noninstructional responsibility 365
  occupational information
    comparative analysis 364
    evaluation 365
  parent role 365
  remedial programs 366
  research proposals 366
  special education 366
  statistical analysis 363
  teacher aides 363
Paraprofessionals
  effects on classroom environment 306

Parent aspiration 381
Parent attitudes
    developing nations 379
    influence on learning 381
    and learning processes 376
Parent child relationship
    and academic achievement 379
Parent influence
    on academic achievement *378–82*
Parent participation
    cultural differences 380
    in decision making 371
        school policy 370
    and learning factors 329
Parent rights
    and history of parent school
        relationship 371
Parent role
    as paraprofessional school personnel
        365
Parent school relationship *370–74*
    academic achievement 372
    administrative problems 372
    communication problems 371
        cultural differences 371
    educational experience of parents 371
    educational policy 372
        funding 373
    evaluation of 371, 373
    history of
        parent rights 371
    interpersonal communication
        participative decision making 372
    objectives 370
    problems in 372
    public relations 371
    student attitudes 372
    teacher attitudes 371
    teacher influence 64
    teacher orientation 372
    See also School community
        relationship
Parent student relationship
    helping relationship
        and cognitive development 380
Parent teacher conferences
    parent participation
        and academic achievement 380
Parent teacher co-operation 380
Parenting skills
    and socialization
        via modeling (psychology) 380
Parents as teachers 365, 372
    and academic achievement 380
    problems 372
    school activities 370
Participant observation
    and teacher socialization 617
Participation
    in classrooms
        and questioning techniques 245
    See also Student participation
Participative decision making
    and teacher effectiveness 611
Pattern recognition

and teacher expertise 50, 51
Pedagogy
    critical approach
        criticisms of 468
    See also Instruction
Peer co-operation
    cooperative learning 357
Peer groups
    and cultural continuity 332
    and culture theory 333
    and learning motivation 306
    and multicultural education 334
    in schools
        ethnography *332–36*
        participant structures 334
    and social stratification 332
    structure
        anthropology 332
    use of term 332
    vs. schools 333
Peer influence
    and learning in school 379
Peer relationship
    constructive aspects 338
    and cooperative learning 336, 338
    and discovery learning 338
    helping relationship
        and learning 339
    interpersonal communication 336
    and learning *336–39*
    and sociocognitive conflict 338
Peer teaching 337
    behavioral instruction 99
    critical thinking in 337
    evaluation research 338
    han 270
    tutoring 272
    and Vygotsky's zone of proximal
        development 337
Performance
    automaticity
        and prior learning 428
    as learning experience 343
    and learning motivation 343
    See also Expertise
Performance objectives *See* Behavioral
        objectives
Performance tests
    and problem solving 465
    reliability 281
    See also Standardized
Performing arts *See* Theater arts
Periodicals
    content analysis
        and teachers as artists 7
Persistence
    in children
        Japan 380
Person–environment interaction 127
Personal autonomy
    in children
        United States 380
Personal narratives
    and teacher expertise 51
    and teacher knowledge 23

Personal space
    classrooms
        cultural differences 275
    and nonverbal communication 275
Personality traits
    cognitive style 387
Personalized instruction *See*
        Individualized instruction
Perspective taking
    explanation 234
    programs
        studies 105
Persuasive discourse
    and learning 340
        conversational teaching 340
        Itakura method 340
Phenomenology
    and teacher supervision 596
Philosophy of education
    feminist 78
Physical attractiveness
    and nonverbal communication 277
Physical characteristics
    and nonverbal communication 277
Physical education
    demonstrations (educational)
        educational technology 240
Physical plant *See* Educational facilities
Piagetian theory
    cognitive development 118
        and learning 102, 103
    and controversy theory 114
    and heuristics 122
Planned activity check (PLA-check) 98
Planning
    educational effectiveness 188, 189
    interaction
        comparative analysis 191
        holistic approach 190
    models of 188
    teacher attitudes
        educational objectives 188
        objectives 189
    teacher education *540–43*
    teacher education programs 541
    teacher role *188–92*
        context effect 189
        psychological evaluation 189
        research methodology 188
        teacher student relationship 189
    teachers
        cognitive processes 10
        participatory research 189
Platonism
    and teaching style 122
Playground programs
    conflict resolution 354
Political power
    of teachers *67–72*
Politics 67
    and teachers 4
Politics of education
    in schools 67, 68
    and teachers *67–72*
Portal schools

teacher education 599, 602
Positive reinforcement 224
    discipline 225
    teacher response 225
Positivism
    and teacher supervision 596
Posttest scores *See* Pretests–posttests
Posture *See* Human posture
Poverty areas
    and school staffing 608
Power structure
    and sex differences
        hidden curriculum 68
    teachers and *67–72*
Practicum supervision
    student teaching *593–98*
Precision teaching
    and behavioral instruction 100
Predictive measurement
    and outcomes of education 518
Preschool children
    and prior learning 440
Prescriptive knowledge *See* Procedural
    knowledge
Prescriptive teaching *See* Diagnostic
    teaching
Preservice teacher education *571–73*
    curriculum *543–47*
    incentives 558
    laboratory training 579
    programs 571
    relationship with inservice teacher
        education 551
    relationship with teacher orientation
        551
Preservice teachers
    attitude change 530
        multicultural education 530
    attitudes 529
    characteristics of *528–31*
    cognitive ability 529
    emotional development 529
    values 529
Prestige
    concept of 58
    occupational
        concept of 58
    of teaching 58
Pretests–posttests
    and instructional alignment 202
Principal components analysis *See* Factor
    analysis
Principals
    ego development 536
Prior knowledge *See* Prior learning
Prior learning *382–87*
    and academic achievement
        causal models 384
    and aptitude treatment interaction 130
    assessment of 383
    and cognitive structures 383, 385
    concept of 383
    effect on learning processes 384
    and heuristics 124
    and learning strategies

teaching of 474
    and memorization 439, 441
        strategies 442
    and outcomes of education 383
    role of 438
        and memory 440
    and variance in pretest–posttest
        scores 383
Private schools
    teacher certification 568
Problem solving
    cognitive processes
        creative development 478
    instruction
        feedback 250
    learning environments 341
    and teacher expertise 50, 51
    and teaching methods 437, 438
    teaching of
        definitions of 463
        history 464
        programs 465
        theoretical framework 464
    teaching and testing for *463–66*
    testable aspects of 465
    tests
        future trends 466
        reliability 465
        validity 465
    See also Creative thinking
Procedural knowledge 421
    females
        intellectual development 537
    See also Expertise
Process–product research
    paradigm of 93
    and teacher behavior 283, 284
Productive thinking
    explanation and 235
    model of 477
Productive Thinking Program 464
Professional autonomy
    and governance of teacher education
        557
    international studies
        comparative analysis 508
    and power structure 69
Professional continuing education
    teacher education 559
Professional development
    teacher role 132
Professional development schools
    definition of 572, 600
    future of 602
    history of 599
    Holmes Group 591
    organization and activities 600
    research 601
    teacher education 572, *598–604*
        United States 597
    themes 601
Professional occupations
    criteria
        functionalist theory 12
        teaching 12

fundamental concepts 13
    social science research
        sociology 12
    social theories
        criticism of 12
Professional recognition
    ideology
        and power structure 69
    teaching 4
Professional standards and practices
        boards
    and teacher unions 568
Professionalization
    feminist critique of 76, 78
    and sex discrimination 76
    of teaching
        and females *76–80*
Profile analysis
    of student evaluations of teacher
        effectiveness 495
Profiles
    prior learning in 386
Program evaluation
    teacher education *552–56*
Programmed instruction
    and behavioral instruction 99
    feedback in 249
    and learning 342
    See also Programmed tutoring
Programmed tutoring
    feedback in 250
    and skill development 343
Propositional knowledge *See* Declarative
        knowledge
Protocol analysis
    verbal 443
Proxemics *See* Personal space
Psychological characteristics
    teachers 4
Psychological evaluation
    and learning processes *279–82*
Psychological patterns
    affective behavior
        and learning *402–07*
Psychological studies
    and expertise 47
    and learning 520
Psychology
    ecological
        paradigm 94
Psychometrics
    and cognitive psychology *279–82*
Psychomotor skills
    analysis and categorization 454
    discovery learning
        and direct instruction 456
    imitation 454
    instruction and training 456
    learning and control 455
    movement education *454–57*
    patterned responses 454
    perceptual motor coordination *454–57*
    retention and transfer 454
    scope and history of research 454
    skill development

ability requirements approach 455
automatization 456
behavior description approach 455
behavior requirements approach 455
degrees of freedom problem 456
developmental stages 455
feedback 455
learner controlled instruction 456
schema theory 456
task characteristics approach 455
teaching methods 439
Public agencies
and governance of teacher education
558
Punishment 224
Pygmalion effect *See* Self fulfilling
prophecies

Qualitative research
and research synthesis 514
and teacher student relationship 415
Questioning techniques *242–48*
and academic achievement
problems 242
research synthesis 514
contextual factors 244
implications 247
and research methodology 512
and small group instruction 257
and student reaction
assistance 246
and study skills 435
and teacher behavior 284
training students in 247
training teachers in 247
types of questions
clear 246
discussion 243
higher cognitive 242
lower cognitive 242
recitation 243
test-relevant 244
wait time 246
See also Interviews

Racial bias
educational improvement 323
Racial differences *319–23*
educational theories 319
and frame factors 305
students
self concept 320
Racial relations
and hidden curriculum 68
and teacher associations 69
Radio
and learning 341
Rasch measurement models
and computer assisted testing 295, 296
Rating scales
content validity 491
teacher effectiveness 491

improvement 491
predictive validity 491
halo effect 491
Reading
learning by 341
See also Critical reading; Reading
aloud to others; Remedial reading;
Speed reading;
Reading aloud to others
parent audience 380
Reading comprehension
and attention control 428
and teacher explanation 236
tests
Nelson–Denny test 473
Reading material selection
sex differences 319
Reading Recovery program (US)
dyslexia 325
research
New Zealand 409
Reading skills
selective attention strategies 428
and short term memory 428
Reading writing relationship
learning processes 450
Real time games 263
FLEXIGAME 263
Project Proteus 263
Reasoning skills *See* Thinking skills
Recall (psychology)
retrieval aid theory
and prior learning 385
tests
and memory 442
Reciprocal teaching 108
and practice 342
Recitation
and learning 343
Recognition (psychology)
tests
and memory 442
Reflective teaching *178–83*
cognitive development
educational strategies 179, 182
cognitive processes 178, 180
problem solving 179
cognitive structures 181
creative thinking 179
critical thinking 180
evaluation of 179
teaching skills 179
inservice teacher education 624
interaction
educational outcomes 180
limited extent of 181
model
field experience programs 180
research methodology 179
teacher attitudes
wholeheartedness 179
teacher characteristics 179
open-mindedness 179
teacher education
evaluation 579

teacher responsibility
ethics 179
teaching skills 182
vs. educational theories 138
Regression (statistics)
and aptitude treatment interaction 129
Rehearsal
and learning 342
Reinforcement *224–27*, 249
autism 225
behavior problems
parent participation 225
and behavioral theories
of teaching 96, 97
concept of 186
contracting 230
differential
and stimulus control 97
generalized reinforcers 224
learning 200
primary (unlearned) reinforcers 224
schedules of 224
secondary (learned) reinforcers 224
self management 230
student problems 225
and student reaction 283
tangible reinforcers 224
Reliability
problem solving tests 465
of student evaluations of teacher
effectiveness 495
Remedial instruction
teaching methods
mastery learning 163
Remedial programs
paraprofessional school personnel 366
Remedial reading
Reading Recovery program (US) 325
Remediation *See* Remedial instruction
Repetition rate *See* Grade repetition rate
Report cards
daily
and behavioral theories 99
Research
empirical
precedence of 518
See also Action research; Educational
research
Research design
metacognition 483
Research methodology
sequential 518
for studies of teachers and teaching 487
See also Scientific methodology
Research practice relationship *See*
Theory practice relationship
Research projects
and learning 342
Research synthesis
methods 512
combined significance test models
513
effect size 513
narrative 512
qualitative 514

vote counting 513
objectives 512
on teaching *512–16*
comparative studies 514
syntheses of 515
See also Meta analysis
Resource allocation
substitute teachers 367
Response contingent testing *See*
Adaptive testing
Responsibility
moral issues 36
Retention (in grade) *See* Grade repetition
Retention (psychology)
and study skills 435
Revolution
teacher participation 70
Rewards
as incentives 250
See also Incentives
Role conflict
in schools 113
teachers 66
Role perception
teachers
role conflict 65
Role taking *See* Perspective taking
Role theory
and social organizations
educational 112
Rote learning
criticisms of 102
historical background 102
Routines *215–19*
and classroom environment 217
formal 216
fundamental concepts of 215
informal 216
instructional effectiveness 215
research into 216
objectives of 216
research methodology 217
Rules *215–19*
categories of 216
and classroom environment 217
formal 216
fundamental concepts of 215
informal 216
instructional effectiveness
research into 216
research methodology 217
Rural schools
staffing problems 609

Salaries
and career choice
teaching 74
See also Teacher salaries
Scholastic aptitude *See* Academic
aptitude
School administration
and learning factors 327
See also School-based management
School attendance *See* Attendance

School-based management
recruitment and orientation 614
and teacher shortage 609
See also School restructuring
School business management *See* School
administration
School characteristics *See* Institutional
characteristics
School community relationship
communications 370
and field experience programs 592
and professional development
schools 601
School culture
and social psychology 115
and student role 411
School demography
and learning factors 327
School district autonomy
and teacher placement 607
School dropouts *See* Dropouts
School effectiveness
and role theory 113
See also Effective schools; Effective
schools research
School environment *See* Classroom
environment; Educational
environment
School failure *See* Academic failure;
Low achievement
School finance *See* Educational finance
School improvement *See* Educational
facilities improvement
School management *See* School
administration
School organization
co-operation 351
ethnography *332–36*
and teacher effectiveness 305
teachers
personal autonomy 14
School parent relationship *See* Parent
school relationship
School principals *See* Principals
School psychologists
and student attitudes
to classrooms 418
School responsibility
noninstructional 370
School restructuring
organizational development 355
See also School-based management
School role
noninstructional responsibility 370
and teacher student relationship 413
School site management *See* School-
based management
School staffing
levels 607
problems 608
challenge approach 610
deficit approach 610
and teacher effectiveness 610
and teacher placement *606–11*
and teacher shortage 609

and teacher surplus 608
use of term 606
School subjects *See* Intellectual
disciplines
School to work transition *See* Education
work relationship
Schools
behavior standards 355
group dynamics 354
as mass education systems 83
organization of
racial bias 320
politics of education 67, 68
power structure
professional autonomy 64
subsystems as groups 355
and teacher education institutions
partnerships 542
and teacher education programs 542
and teachers
effectiveness factors *305–07*
Schools of education
teacher education programs 548
Science *See* Sciences
Science education
and heuristics 125
and paradigms
concept of 91
Science instruction
demonstrations (educational) 240
teacher effectiveness 241
laboratories *171–74*
cognitive processes 173
educational objectives 171
inquiry 172, 173
learning processes 172
student behavior 173
teacher behavior 173
teaching methods 171
technical skills 172
Science Laboratory Environment
Inventory (SLEI) 419
Science laboratory instruction *See*
Science instruction, laboratories
Science teachers
use of explanation 233
Sciences
disciplinary
development of 91
Scientific methodology
cognitive processes 151
discovery learning 153
Scoring
partial credit analysis 282
Scotland
General Teaching Council 557
teacher education
accreditation 562, 563
Seating arrangement *196–200*
academic achievement 198
in class organization 185
instructional effectiveness 196
interpersonal relationship 197
language enrichment 197
student attitudes 199

memorization 197
student behavior 198
  behavior modification 198, 199
student motivation 198
teacher attitudes 199
teacher expectations of students 199
teacher role
  educational objectives 199
teacher student relationship 197
Seatwork
  assignment and supervision of *264–68*
  and cognitive processes 423
  definitions of 264
  future trends 267
  perspectives 264
Secondary school students
  in part time employment 379
Secondary school teachers
  contexts 85
  preservice teacher education 571
Self concept
  attribution theory
    success and failure 404
  and cognitive processes 423
  effect on performance 404
  and learning processes 375
  performance
    and learning motivation 398
  students
    research 416
  teacher burnout 55
  and teacher knowledge 22
  teachers 3
    adult development 536
Self confidence *See* Self esteem
Self control
  and learning 406
  learning strategies 472
Self determination
  and self motivation 399
  See also Personal autonomy
Self directed learning *See* Independent
  study
Self efficacy
  and academic achievement 404
  attention control
    and academic achievement 428
  and self motivation 399, 401
Self esteem
  theory
    in education 115
Self evaluation (individuals)
  cognitive measurement 280
  and learning strategies 472
  and metacognition 442
Self fulfilling prophecies
  and teacher expectation of students 29
    Brophy–Good model 30
Self instruction *See* Independent study
Self knowledge *See* Self concept
Self motivation
  and computer assisted instruction 399
  and homogeneous grouping 399
  and learning motivation 399
Self paced instruction *See* Individualized

instruction, pacing
Self perception *See* Self concept
Self regulated learning *See* Independent
  study
Self regulation *See* Self control
Self-verbalization *See* Verbalization
Seminars
  in field experience programs 592
Semiotics
  and nonverbal communication 274
Sentence completion tests *See* Cloze
  procedure
Sex bias
  educational improvement 323
Sex differences *319–23*
  and academic achievement 321
  course selection (students) 320
  in education
    fundamental concepts of 319
  educational theories 319
  and frame factors 305
  learning processes 321
  reading material selection 319
  students
    self concept 319
  teacher associations
    and power structure 70
  and teacher behavior 414
    in questioning techniques 244
  and teacher education 525
  teaching
    prestige of 60
  writing (composition) 319
Sex discrimination
  in schools 320
Sex stereotypes
  socialization 320
Sexism *See* Sex bias
Sexual harassment
  in schools 320
Sexual identity
  and peer influence 333
Short term memory (STM)
  and accessibility theory 385
  and cognitive processes 434
  processes 421
  role of attention in 427
Significance *See* Statistical significance
Silence
  in classrooms 277
Simulation *260–64*
  advantages and disadvantages 261
  evaluation 262
  formative evaluation 261
  fundamental concepts of 260
  as interaction 260
  intercultural communication 262
  and learning 342
  planning of
    teacher role 260
  student development 262
  teacher role 260
  See also Computer simulation
Single parent family *See* One
  parent family

Skill development
  and expertise 47
  and learning 342
Skill obsolescence
  of teachers
    and teacher-proof curriculum 77
Small classes *310–15*
  academic achievement 310, 313
    instructional program divisions 314
  educational strategies 314
  evaluation *310–15*
  and group unity 355
  minority groups
    academic achievement 314
  outcomes of education 313, 314
  problems 310
    cost effectiveness 314
  teacher attitudes 313
  teacher behavior 313
  teacher morale 310
  teacher student relationship 310
Small group instruction *139–43, 255–59*
  behavior standards 357
  and classroom communication 257
  classroom design for 257
  and curriculum design 257
  effective
    requirements for 258
  group dynamics 357
  group unity 357
  and teacher administrator relationship
    258
  teacher control function 256
  teacher role
    observers 258
  teaching methods
    teamwork 140
  vs. conventional instruction 258
  vs. large group instruction 256
  See also Group Investigation (GI)
    method
Smiling
  and student behavior 276
  and teacher behavior 276
Social change
  educational researchers
    teachers as 18
  teacher role 70
Social characteristics
  of teaching 59
Social class
  teacher background 59
Social competence *See* Interpersonal
  competence
Social constructivism *See* Constructivism
Social learning *See* Socialization
Social movements *See* Activism
Social organizations
  educational
    and role theory 112
Social psychology
  aspiration
    and educational and occupational
    attainment *391–95*
  of education 116

and school culture 115
theories
achievement motivation 114
attribution 115
conflict 114
distributive justice 114
interdependence 113
self esteem 115
of teaching *112–17*
uses of 116
Social reproduction
and peer influence 334
Social sciences
textbooks
explanation in 234
Social skills *See* Interpersonal
competence
Social status
of teaching *58–61*
Socialization
of beginning teachers 605
black stereotypes 320
cooperative learning 139
and course selection (students) 619
definitions of 616
peer groups
and individual variability 333
professional development of teachers
616–20
sex stereotypes 320
social class
and aspiration 392
of teachers 80
See also Cultural transmission
Software *See* Computer software
Spain
teacher education
Classified Practice Centers 591
Special education
diagnostic teaching 175
outcomes of education
and aptitude treatment interaction
129
paraprofessional school personnel 366
Specialization
and school staffing 608
Speed reading
selective attention strategies 429
Staff development
action research 538
collaborative problem solving 538
inservice teacher education 622, 626
Standard International Occupational
Prestige Scale (SIOPS) 58
Standardized tests
and student needs 287
Standards
and teacher certification *565–70*
See also Professional standards
State boards of education
teacher certification
standards 567
State departments of education
and governance of teacher education
557

teacher certification 567
State government
teachers
professional autonomy 14
Statistical models
for teacher education planning 540
Statistical significance
test models
and research synthesis 513
Status
concept of 58
occupational
concept of 58
Stimuli
control
and reinforcement 97
Strategic learning *See* Learning strategies
Streaming *See* Ability grouping
Stress (psychological)
fundamental concepts of 52
See also Anxiety
Stress management
social support groups 55
teachers 55
Stress variables
burnout 55
teacher burnout 55
teachers 53
research and development 55
role ambiguity 54
role conflict 54
school organization 54
social influences 54
student attitudes 54
and teaching 84
Structuralism
and occupational prestige 59
Student achievement *See* Academic
achievement
Student aptitude *See* Academic aptitude
Student assignments *See* Assignments
Student attitudes
and assignments 266
to classrooms *416–19*
factors 417
future research 418
measurement of 417
personal 418
trends 418
computer uses in education
factors 360
intellectual disciplines
content of 410
to learning
and student role 411
managerial behavior 223
and outcomes of education
studies 417
research 416
sex differences
secondary school students 322
to teacher behavior
differential 31
Student behavior
analysis of *227–31*

body language 276
and classroom environment 408
classroom techniques
discipline 230
evaluation methods 293
modification of *227–31*
and self concept 416
sex differences
elementary school students 321
and teacher expectation of students
30, 415
teacher guidance 221
teacher response 219
and teacher student relationship
research 414
Student characteristics
affective entry 326
and aptitude treatment interaction 127
cognitive entry 326
and cognitive processes 421
emotions
teacher perceptions of 289
individual differences
individualized instruction 156
and learning factors 327, 329
and learning processes 375
and learning theories 420
naturalistic observation 291
noncognitive
data sources for 289
and questioning techniques 244
racial differences *319–23*
sex differences *319–23*
and student needs 286
teacher evaluation of 290, 291
and student needs 288
and teacher expectation of students 414
and teacher student relationship 413
and teaching *326–31*
Student development
and computer assisted testing 298
Student differences *See* Student
characteristics
Student engaged time *See* Time on task
Student evaluation
and computer assisted testing 298
data interpretation
teacher role 293
diagnostic teaching 177
ethics 294
formative 176
standardized tests 293
standards
types of 287
and student needs 287
and teacher behavior *283–86*
trends 285
types of 284
and teacher effectiveness
studies 283
and teacher role 288
teacher role 186, *290–94*
decision making 291
Student evaluation of teacher
performance *493–501*

international studies
  comparative analysis 511
  See also Student evaluations of teacher
    effectiveness (SETs)
Student evaluations of educational
    quality (SEEQ)
  content validity 494
  factors of 494
Student evaluations of teacher
    effectiveness (SETs) *493–501*
  bias in 498
  dimensions of 494
  generalizability of 495
  measurement of 494
  multiple evaluators 496
  profile analysis of 495
  purposes of 493
  reliability of 495
  research
    implications 500
    primary and secondary schools 499
  research studies 497
  stability of 495
  studies 499
  utilization 499
  validity
    construct 496
    multisection 496
    research implications 498
  See also Student evaluation of teacher
    performance
Student experience
  and concept teaching 437
  and learning processes 375
  and memorization 439
Student motivation
  individualized instruction 157
  teacher judgments of 289
  teachers' beliefs 25
Student needs
  diagnosis of *286–90*
    and achievement tests 287
    alternative approaches 288
    methods 287
    trends 289
  and student characteristics
    teacher evaluation of 288
Student outcomes *See* Outcomes of
    education
Student participation
  influences
    on teaching *413–16*
  and learning processes 376, 439
Student perceptions *See* Student attitudes
Student placement
  testing problems 176
Student progress *See* Academic
    achievement
Student promotion
  policies of automatic 324, 325
Student reaction
  to educational objectives
    and behavioral theories 98
    and feedback 284
    and nonverbal communication 277

and questioning techniques 246
  assistance 246
  and reinforcement 283
  and teacher behavior
    risks 32
  and teacher diagnosis 408
  and teacher expertise 50
Student responsibility
  and assignments 266
  and learning strategies 376, 473
Student role
  changes in 376
  in classrooms *408–13*
    change in 408
    factors 410
  in learning processes *375–77*
  in small group instruction 257
  in teacher evaluation 487
  transformation of
    factors 411
Student school relationship
  and learning motivation 306
Student subcultures
  group unity 356
Student teacher attitudes
  laboratory training 578
Student teacher evaluation 595
Student teacher supervisors
  cooperating teachers 594
  criticism of role 590
  university supervisors 594, 596
Student teachers
  attrition rate 74
  educational theories
    relevance (education) 132
  instructional innovations 619
  preconceptions 592
  required characteristics of 541
  role of
    in teacher education planning 541
  self-efficacy 590
  and teachers
    mismatch problems 105
Student teaching
  as apprenticeship 572
  field experience programs *588–93*
    Canada 589
    comparative analysis 589
    criticisms of 589
    international comparisons 589
    Japan 589
    time factors 589, 591
    trends and recommendations 591
    United States 589
  practicum supervision *593–98*
  practicums 545
  and professional development 590
  supervision
    apprenticeship model 593, 596
    laboratory model 593
  theory practice relationship *588–93*
Students
  aspirations *391–95*
  expectations *391–95*
  interpersonal relationship

racial bias 322
peer influence
  sexuality 322
social groups 355
  clubs 355, 356
  friendship 355
socialization
  teacher influence 26
Study habits
  and cognitive processes 434
    guiding of 435
  definitions of 434
  future research 436
  and study skills *434–36*
Study skills
  future research 436
  and metacognition 482
  and study habits *434–36*
  summarization strategies 435
  types of 435
Study strategies *See* Study skills
Subcultures
  youth 332
  See also Student subcultures
Subject disciplines *See* Intellectual
    disciplines
Substitute teachers *367–69*
  educational finance 368
  educational trends
    futures (of society) 369
  effects on classroom environment 306
  incentives 368
  instructional effectiveness 369
  job satisfaction
    problems 368
  quality of working life 368
    problems 368
  stress variables 368
  teacher background 368
Sudan
  teacher education 632
Summative evaluation
  and student needs 287
Supply of teachers *See* Teacher supply
    and demand
Swann Report 1985 (UK)
  multicultural education 541
Sweden
  teacher salaries 72
Switzerland
  faculty mobility 610
  teacher placement
    methods 607
  teacher shortage
    strategies 609
  teacher student ratio 607

Tactual behavior *See* Touching behavior
Tailored testing *See* Adaptive testing
Tape recordings
  and learning 343
Task analysis
  and cognitive processes 422, 424
  See also Job analysis

Teacher administrator relationship 69
  group dynamics 355
  and small group instruction 258
Teacher aides
  academic achievement 314
  occupational information
    comparative analysis 365
Teacher associations
  political influences 69
  and power structure
    sex differences 70
  and racial relations 69
  and teacher militancy 69
Teacher attendance
  employee absenteeism *367–69*
Teacher attitudes *25–28*
  beginning teachers
    evaluation 554
  to classrooms 417
  computer uses in education
    factors 360
  to computers
    anxiety 362
    positive 362
  and curriculum development 81
  and educational change 80
  and educational innovation
    age differences 82
  and family school relationship 306
  graduates 554
  intellectual disciplines
    content of 410
  to learning
    and student role 411
  managerial behavior 223
  political influences 68
  and school staffing
    geographical factors 608
  students
    moral issues 39
  and teacher knowledge 4
  and teacher placement
    choice factors 609
  and teacher student relationship 415
  to teaching 4
  tutoring 273
  value judgement 39
Teacher autonomy *See* Professional
  autonomy
Teacher background
  social class 59
  teachers' beliefs 132
Teacher behavior
  and academic achievement
    comparative analysis 508, 511
  body language 276
  and class activities 283
    thinking tasks 284
  and classroom environment 408
  decision making 37
  differential
    student attitudes to 31
  educational environment
    and computers 360
  of expert teachers 48

functional analysis 63
and knowledge acquisition 283
modification
  and teacher expertise 49
and power structure
  United States 68
and questioning techniques 243
reactive 219
research methodology
  classroom observation techniques 63
  questionnaires 63
  self evaluation 181
and sex differences 320
  in questioning techniques 244
small classes
  academic achievement 312
and small groups 255
and student evaluation *283–86*
  trends 285
and student evaluations of teacher
    effectiveness 497
teacher background 131
and teacher expectation of students 30
and teacher student relationship
  research 414
teachers' beliefs about 131
and teaching experience 47
Teacher burnout *52–57*
  characteristics of 4
  psychological patterns 53
  research and development 55
Teacher centers
  professional continuing education 629
Teacher certification
  developed nations 566
  developing nations 566
  future of 569
  and governance of teacher education
    558
  issues 527
  job performance 490
  policy context
    United States 566
  processes 567
    testing 567, 568
    transcript analysis/credit count 567
    validated programs 567
  and standards *565–70*
  teacher education curriculum 569
  use of terms 566
Teacher characteristics 80, *3–5*
  and coping strategies 83
  exemplary
    computer users 362
  expectation 65
  generalized
    research syntheses 515
  international studies
    comparative analysis 508
  prospective teachers 541
  psychological 4
  and questioning techniques 245
  and school staffing 607
  and teacher expectation of students 415
  and teacher expertise 47, 50

and teacher student relationship 413
Teacher competency tests
  content knowledge 489
  improvement 490
  National Teacher Examinations (US)
    content validity 489
    predictive validity 489
  professional knowledge 489
  teacher effectiveness 489
  technological advancement 490
Teacher cultures
  content of 85
  forms of 85
    balkanization 85
    collaborative 85
    contrived collegiality 86
    individualism 85
Teacher developed materials
  achievement tests 288
Teacher direction
  concept of 137
Teacher education
  accreditation *561–65*
    and certification compared 527
  adult development *535–39*
  and Black students 74
  case methods *583–88*
    academic orientation 584
    context for research 583
    critical/social orientation 587
    definition of 583
    expert novice research 586
    heuristics 584
    personal orientation 586
    practical orientation 585
    research issues 587
    technological orientation 586
  Classified Practice Centers
    Spain 591
  and cognitive development 104
  concepts and issues *525–27*
  conceptual development research 537
  continuing *605–06*
  costs 73
  coursework
    student teachers attitudes 590
  critical thinking 180
  curriculum
    criticisms 526
  curriculum development
    knowledge base approach 526
  definitions of 628
  evaluation models 553
    competency-based 553
    countenance 553
    documentation and assessment 553
    objectives-based 553
    outcomes-based 553
    Stufflebeam's 553
  evaluation of 526
  evaluation studies 554
  feminism 17
  foundations of education courses 544
  governance *556–60*
    administrative organization 558

admission criteria 558
  curriculum 558
  functions 558
  issues in 559
  level of preparation 558
  policy formation 557
  processes 559
governance in 526
and heuristics
  problems 126
history
  United Kingdom 548
institutions 543, 548
  and school partnerships 542
  and school relationship 542
international studies
  comparative analysis *506–11*
laboratory schools *598–604*
laboratory training *578–82*
licensure and certification compared
  527
masters degrees 550
mathematics
  comparative analysis 507
mentors 586
microteaching *573–77*
on the job training *628–32*
performance assessment 554
planning *540–43*
  delivery systems 542
  future trends 542
  models for 540
  objectives 541
  processes 540
  stakeholders in 541
professional development schools
  572, *598–604*
Research About Teacher Education
  (US) 589
self evaluation 180
simulated environment *578–82*
supervision *593–98*
Teacher Education Project (UK)
  lesson structure and student
    ability 208
  and teacher expertise 519
  teaching skills
    teacher attitudes 180
  theory practice relationship 544, 546
  See also Competency-based teacher
    education; Inservice teache
    reducation; On service teacher
    education; Preservice teacher
    education; Reflective teaching;
    Student teaching
Teacher education curriculum *543–47*,
  550
  Carnegie Forum on Education 546
  and collegiality 546
  consecutive mode 543
  content knowledge 551
  and educational innovation 546
  general education 551
  hidden curriculum 546
  Holmes Group 546

integrated 180
intellectual disciplines 544
issues and directions 546
kibbutzim 544
methods courses 544
null 546
pedagogical content knowledge 551
pedagogy 551
practicums 545
and teaching experience 546
Teacher education programs
  content 588
  developing nations 549
  evaluation 542, *552–56*
    and accountability 552
    criterion variables 553
    independent variables 554
    methods 554
    problems with 553
  field experience
    cognitive development 180
    student teachers' attitudes 590
    trends 592
  four year 550
  graduate study 550
  objectives 541
  parent school relationship
    interpersonal communication 372
  planning 541
  provision 559
  sequencing factors 542
  special needs students 372
  structure of *548–52*
  time and organization 549
Teacher educator education
  and teacher education programs 542
Teacher educators
  characteristics of *531–34*
  demography 531
  females 532
  minority groups 532
  reflective teaching
    educational objectives 181
  research and scholarship of 532
  role of 542
  sex differences 525
  and social class 531
  student teacher supervisors 533
  and teacher accreditation 564
  work environment 533
Teacher effectiveness
  and cognitive development approach
    104
  and commitment 611
  components of 494
  and composition of groups 137
  and computer uses in education 361
  direct instruction 144
  and educational change
    barriers 138
  and educational reform 80
  evaluation 490
    academic achievement 491
  evaluation criteria 491
    student characteristics 492

and eye contact 276
measurement of 487
measurement techniques 492
  pretests–posttests 492
paradigm of 93
planning
  performance factors 190
pretests–posttests
  test validity 492
process–product model 144
requirements for 187 , 611
and school staffing 610
student evaluation of 493
  studies 283
and teacher attitudes
  preservice teachers 529
and teacher knowledge 21
  research 21
and teacher student relationship 375
and teacher supply and demand 73
use of explanation 235
Teacher evaluation *488–93*
  and aptitude treatment interaction 127
  competency-based teacher education
    489
  criteria 489
  faculty development
    criteria 563
  improvement 490
  job performance 489
  judgment accuracy approach 288
    research 288
  low-inference observation schedules
    491
  methods 487
  problems 490
  rating scales 490
  Rating Teacher Explanation
    Instrument 237
  student improvement
    test validity 492
  teacher improvement 44
  and teacher selection 608
  See also Student evaluation of
    teacher performance; Teacher
    effectiveness
Teacher expectations of students *29–35*
  academic achievement 113
  definitions of 29
  differential
    and teacher behavior 30
  effects
    types of 29
  future research 34
  importance of 31
  increasing
    effects of 32
  induced 29
  influences 291
  intervention programs 33
    findings 33
  and low achievement
    Good's passivity model 31
  natural 29
  racial bias 320

research 29, 413, 414
  directions 33
  types of 29
secondary school students
  sex bias 322
and self fulfilling prophecies 29
  Brophy–Good model 30
sex bias 320
and student needs 288
and teacher knowledge 4
variations over time 32
Teacher experience *See* Teaching
    experience
Teacher expertise *46–52*
  and automaticity 49
  and computers 361
  context factors 48
  descriptive propositions 48
  and educational environment 49
  and educational research 519
  and flexibility 50
  and pattern recognition 50, 51
  and problem solving 50, 51
  stages
    advanced beginner 47
    competent 47
    expert 48
    novice 47
    proficient 48
  studies 48, 51
  and teacher expectation of students 33
  vs. teaching experience 46
  See also Teacher knowledge
Teacher guidance
  Socratic Method 152
  testing 162
Teacher improvement *41–46*
  clinical supervision (of teachers) 44
  collegiality 45
  cooperative planning 45
  self actualization 44
  teacher evaluation 44
Teacher indirectness
  and academic achievement
    research synthesis 514
Teacher induction *See* Teacher
    orientation
Teacher influence
  educational change *16–19*
  social change *16–19*
  students
    socialization 26
Teacher knowledge *20–24*
  of content 20
  domains 20
    integration of 22
  dynamic nature of 22
  evaluation of 487
  future research 23
  and instruction 21
  level
    teacher student relationship 489
  research 20
  and self concept 22
  and teacher attitudes 4

types of 4, 20
  and classroom techniques 22
  narrative 23
  paradigmatic 22
  See also Teacher expertise
Teacher militancy
  and curriculum development 68
  United Kingdom 68
Teacher morale
  and burnout 53
  See also Teacher burnout; Teachers,
    occupational stress
Teacher motivation
  and burnout 53
  influences
    professional development 42
  See also Teacher burnout; Teachers,
    occupational stress
Teacher orientation
  beginning teacher induction *612–15*
  mentors 614
  and national policies 615
  preservice and inservice teacher
    education 551
  process 605
  program content 613
  relevance (educational) 614
  trends
    issues and research 614
Teacher parent co-operation *See* Parent
    teacher co-operation
Teacher participation
  in revolution 70
Teacher performance *See* Teacher
    effectiveness
Teacher persistence
  factors affecting 82
Teacher placement
  comparative area studies 607
  methods 607
  and school staffing *606–11*
  use of term 606
Teacher preparation *See* Teacher
    education
Teacher qualifications *565–70*
  and social class 60
Teacher quality *See* Teacher
    effectiveness
Teacher recruitment *612–15*
  approaches to 613
  and career structure 612
  incentives 610
  policy context 612
  problems in 528
  significance of 605
  and social class 60
  strategies 609
  and teacher effectiveness 612
  and teacher shortage 612
  trends
    issues and research 614
Teacher response
  positive reinforcement 284
  and questioning techniques 246
  and teacher behavior 284

Teacher responsibility *35–41*
  conflict resolution
    moral issues 38
  and educational reform 81
  and learning strategies 376
  moral values 35, 39
  research
    theory practice relationship 35
  self concept of 4
  teacher effectiveness 40
  and teaching experience 47
Teacher role *35–41*, *61–67*
  and acting 6
  behavior 62
  changes in 540
    and computer uses in education 362
  in class organization 186
  in classrooms 408
  cognitive development 118
  computers
    and educational environment 360
  decision making
    classroom environment 290
  development of 45
  educational technology *359–63*
    adoption of 359
  evaluation 13
  expectation 64, 65
    research methodology 64
    role conflict 65
    teacher behavior 66
  fundamental concepts of 62
    behavior 62
    expectation 62
    social status 62
  and heuristics 125
  and intensification 84
  in learning processes 439
  planning *188–92*
    research methodology 188
  in preservice teacher education 572
  and professionalization 84
  research problems 62
  and small groups 255
  social structure
    evaluation methods 63
  and student evaluation 288
  in teacher education planning 541
  and teacher education programs 542
Teacher salaries 64, 72
  school staffing 610
  vs. other occupations 73
Teacher selection
  and anticipatory socialization 618
  central vs. local 608
Teacher shortage
  and school staffing policy 609
  and teacher recruitment 612
Teacher stereotypes 65, 528
Teacher student ratio
  determination of 607
Teacher student relationship
  and assignments 266
  classroom design
    seating arrangement 198

commitment 81
communication
    for small group instruction 257
expectation studies 414, 415
feedback
    in classrooms 283
and learning factors 327
and learning strategies 474
and lesson structure 210
mismatch problems 105
process–product studies 414, 415
qualitative studies 415
racial bias 321
sex bias 321
    in secondary schools 322
sex differences 321
    elementary schools 321
and social status 61
and status
    problems 85
student characteristics 309
systems approach 218
in teacher education 525
and teacher effectiveness 375
and teaching methods 413
tutoring 273
Teacher supervision *593–98*
alternative approaches 596
applied behavioral approach 595
counseling 595
directive and nondirective 595
models 595
problems of 595
purposes 593
theoretical paradigms 596
trends and issues 597
Teacher supply and demand *72–76*
attrition rate 74
demographic effects on 75
determinants of 72
females 73
as a function of geographic regions 74
and inservice teacher education 621
minority groups 73
number of preservice teachers 528
and school staffing
    problems 608
and teacher certification 565
and teacher education planning 541
and teacher effectiveness 73
Teacher trainers *See* Teacher educators
Teacher training *See* Teacher education
Teacher turnover *See* Faculty mobility
Teacher unions *See* Unions
Teachers
academic achievement of 60
affective behavior
    research 223
as *animateurs* 70
as artists 3, *6–8*
    and creativity 7
    research 6
    types of 7
    use of metaphor 6
beliefs of *25–28*

academic ability 26
academic achievement 25
educational change 27
educational research 27, 135
    research 25
    student motivation 25
and teacher attitudes 82
values education 26
See also Teacher attitudes
career development 41, 42, 535
factors affecting 82
as clinicians 3
cognitive ability
    planning 190
cognitive development 41
    developmental stages 535
cognitive processes 10
    curriculum agenda 10
    curriculum script 10
    decision making *9–11*
    interactive teaching 10
    reflection-in-action 10
    teacher education 10
cognitive structures
    evaluation 13
    research utilization 11
commitment 81
community involvement
    political influences 70
as cultivators
    use of metaphor 7
decision making
    educational history 9
    ethics 36
    policy-capturing studies 9
    research methodology 9
    stimulated recall studies 9
developmental stages 41
educational theories *131–36*
    external pressures on 138
impact of students on *375–77*
individual development
    teacher education 586
international studies
    sex differences 507
life events of
    influences 82
lives
    research 83
managerial behavior of *219–23*
    academic tasks 221
    influences 219
    preventive strategies 220
    procedures 220
    reactive strategies 220
    research 223
    routines 220
moral development 535
    influence of school environment 536
occupational stress *52–57*
perceptions of 3
personal autonomy
    and role in state 616
    school organization 14
political attitudes *67–72*

political influences *67–72*
and politics of education *67–72*
prestige 64
professional autonomy 64
    bureaucratic constraints *11–15*
    and lesson structure 207
    organizational climate 14
    state government 14
professional continuing education
    628–32
professional development 14,
    41–46, 535
    educational facilities improvement
        45
    environment 43
    futures (of society) 45
    individual characteristics 41
    instructional leadership 43
    and market forces 620
    participant observation 617
    peer influence 43
    school attitudes 43
    school policy 43
    social influences 43
    socialization *616–20*
    teaching methods 43
professional knowledge 489
    evaluation 490
as professional personnel 3
    and political power 67, 69
professional recognition
    and power structure 69
as researchers 3
    teacher education 586
reserve pool of
    source of supply 75
retraining *628–32*
schemata
    educational research 135
and schools
    effectiveness factors *305–07*
sex differences 525
social status 63
socialization
    and attitude changes 617
    and values 616
socio-political view of 4
staff development 41
studies of *487–88*
unqualified
    and inservice teacher education 621
work environment 72
Teachers' colleges *See* Schools of
    education
Teaching
as an activity
    factors 60
aptitude treatment interaction model
    of *127–31*
art or science 6
attitudes to
    and social status 61
behavioral theories of *96–101*
    characteristics 97
    field of study 96

future research 100
principles 97
trends 100
career choice
factors affecting 74
classroom
and student characteristics *326–31*
cognitive development approach
framework 102
and students 103
and teachers 103
theories *101–06*
contexts
contemporary 84
continuing 83
of diversity 84
coping strategies 83
females
caring role 618
heuristic models of *122–27*
characteristics 125
direct strategy 124
generative 124
historical development 122
interactive 124, 125
logical argument 125
modern 123
reciprocal 123
self-instructional strategy 124
transactional strategy 123
humanistic theories of *101–06*
indeterminacy of 7
and instruction compared 89
interactive
and cognitive development
approach 102
international studies
comparative analysis *506–11*
job analysis 7
metaphors 132
as moral enterprise 81
occupational prestige of
and sex differences 60
studies 58
paradigms for research on *91–96*
as performing art 6
professional recognition 4, *11–15*
professional values
client centeredness 14
professionalization of
and females *76–80*
realities of *80–87*
research
lessons for 8
research synthesis *512–16*
importance of 512
in small groups *255–59*
social characteristics of 59
social functions of 59
and social mobility 618
social status *58–61*
evaluation 13
student evaluation of *493–501*
student influences on *413–16*
assumptions 413

research 413
studies of *487–88*
technology of
and behavioral theories 98
theories and models of *89–91*
theories of
social psychological *112–17*
traditional approaches 102
as women's work 77
Teaching (process) *See* Instruction
Teaching experience
and expertise 47, 49
general characteristics 3
international studies
comparative analysis 507, 511
progression 4
and teacher education curriculum 546
and teacher knowledge 23
vs. teacher expertise 46
Teaching load
and computer uses in education 362
research 84
Teaching machines
and learning theories 519
paradigm of 93
and programmed instruction 99
Teaching materials *See* Instructional
materials
Teaching methods
academic achievement
academic learning time 430
and class organization 185
cognitive processes 145, 424
collaborative dialog 244
common elements in 438
conversations 243
differences in 437
discussion *251–55*
explanation *232–38*
improvement of
implications 330
instructional sequencing 151
international studies
comparative analysis 507
and learning environments *340–44*
and learning factors 327, 329
and models 285
and objectives *437–39*
overview 186
paradigm of 93
and questioning techniques 243
questioning techniques
and teacher behavior 284
research
developments 94
and student needs 287
and teacher knowledge 21
research 21
and teaching skills *185–87*
tutoring *271–74*
See also Direct instruction; Reflective
teaching
Teaching models
pedagogical content knowledge 135
Teaching practices *See* Teaching methods

Teaching skills
improvisation 190
requirements 60
and teacher effectiveness
measurement 73
and teaching methods *185–87*
Teaching styles
and body language 275
of expert teachers 48
expert vs. novice 49
intact
paradigm of 94
and lesson structure 209
Teamwork
cooperative learning 139
Technological advancement
demonstrations (educational) 239
and psychomotor skill development
456
Technology
and teacher role *359–63*
Temperament *See* Personality
Test administration *See* Testing
Test anxiety
and achievement need 399
attention-deficit hypothesis 403
and computer assisted testing 297
effect on cognitive processes 403
Test bias
and achievement tests 288
Test coaching
and instructional alignment 201
Test construction
items
and computer assisted testing 295
racial bias 321
sex bias 321
Test items
intentional vs. incidental 244
and problem solving 465
validity of
in computer assisted testing 296
See also Item writing techniques
Test taking anxiety *See* Test anxiety
Test theory
implications of cognitive measurement
for 281
standard 279
Test use
grouping (instructional purposes) 161
learning problems
remedial instruction 162
Test validity
achievement tests 287
differential item functioning 281
See also Construct validity
Testing
of cognitive processes 283
and cognitive psychology *279–82*
feedback
error correction 162
implications of instructional alignment
for 203
and instructional effectiveness
instructional alignment *200–04*

as a learning experience 343
memory *439–44*
problem solving *463–66*
See also Adaptive testing; Assessment;
    Computer assisted testing;
    Educational testing; Individual
    testing; Tests
Tests
conventional instruction
    behavioral objectives 279
prior learning in 386
See also Achievement tests; Testing
Tests of significance *See* Statistical
    significance
Text structure
and study skills 435
Textbooks 291
Theater arts
teaching as 6
Theories
and models compared 89
precedence of 518
of teaching *89–91*
underlying assumptions 90
See also Hypothesis testing
Theory practice relationship
education *517–22*
    issues 517
    models 518
    and research findings 521
    proposals 518
    teachers and teaching 488
Thinking *See* Cognitive processes
Thinking aloud protocols *See* Protocol
    analysis
Thinking skills
and heuristics 125
Third World *See* Developing nations
Time factors (learning) *204–07*, 329
academic achievement 205, 432
behavioral objectives 459
Carroll's model 431
conceptual tempo
    individualized instruction 157
knowledge acquisition 459
memory systems
    storage 459
opportunity to learn 431
research methodology 432
substitute teachers 369
and teaching methods 185
United States 430
Time management
classroom techniques
    comparative analysis 507, 511
in classrooms 277
schools *204–07*
    comparative analysis 204
    homework 205
    literacy 205
    mathematical concepts 205
    policy formation 206
    time on task 206
Time on task 431
and academic achievement 206

comparative analysis 268
elementary school students 432
and learning motivation 397
schools *204–07*
    comparative analysis 206
See also Academic learning time;
    Time management
Token economy
behavioral instruction 99
Touching behavior
and nonverbal communication 275
Trace line *See* Item response theory (IRT)
Track system (education)
and academic achievement 195
flexible progression 194
Trade unions *See* Unions
Traditional instruction *See* Conventional
    instruction
Training
occupational *See* Job training
See also Industrial training; Job
    training
Transfer of training
and instructional alignment 202, 203
and problem solving 463
Tutoring *271–74*
adolescents 272
benefits of 272
of children 271
course 273
definition of 271
emergency 273
evaluation
    studies 272
future trends 273
guidelines 273
high school
    types of 273
Personalized System of Instruction 273
research 273
resources 273
structured 273
uses of 271
young adults 272
See also Programmed tutoring
Tutors
characteristics of 271
types of 271

Understanding
and assignments 265
and heuristics 124
Unions
and professional standards and
    practices boards 568
teachers
    and power structure 69
United Kingdom (UK)
school staffing
    problems 608
teacher education
    planning 541
teacher shortage
    strategies 609

teacher student ratio 607
United States (US)
academic achievement
    national surveys 102
classroom environment
    attitudes to 417
computer uses in education 359
educational research
    questioning techniques 242
grade repetition 325
learning strategies
    teaching of 472
peer teaching 272
programs 99
school staffing
    problems 608
student teaching
    field experience programs 589
teacher certification
    and standards *565–70*
teacher education
    accreditation 562, 563
teacher shortage
    strategies 609
Units of study
lesson structure *207–11*
Universal education *See* Equal education
Universities
and public schools
    Carnegie Task Force 600
    Holmes Group 600
    teacher education 599, 601, 602
    and student evaluations of teacher
        effectiveness 498
teacher education
    doctoral programs 549
    and field experience programs 591
    programs 549

Validity
problem solving tests 465
See also Construct validity; Test
Values education
teachers' beliefs 26
Venezuela
problem solving
    teaching of 465
Verbal communication
and learning strategies
    evaluation 475
Verbalization
cognitive processes
    and heuristics 124
Videotape recorders
barriers to use of 361
Videotape recordings
and learning 341
Vietnam
nonverbal communication
    in classrooms 276
    smiling 276
Vocations *See* Occupations
Voluntary agencies
on governance of teacher education